June 10–14, 2013
Eugene, Oregon, USA

Association for
Computing Machinery

Advancing Computing as a Science & Profession

ICS'13

Proceedings of the 2013 ACM
International Conference on Supercomputing

Sponsored by:

ACM SIGARCH

Supported by:

Microsoft Research, ARM, Microsoft, EGI, NVIDIA, IBM, Intel, Hewlett Packard, CRAY, ParaTools, Data Direct Networks, and University of Oregon

Association for Computing Machinery

Advancing Computing as a Science & Profession

The Association for Computing Machinery
2 Penn Plaza, Suite 701
New York, New York 10121-0701

Notice to Past Authors of ACM-Published Articles
ACM intends to create a complete electronic archive of all articles and/or other material previously published by ACM. If you have written a work that has been previously published by ACM in any journal or conference proceedings prior to 1978, or any SIG Newsletter at any time, and you do NOT want this work to appear in the ACM Digital Library, please inform permissions@acm.org, stating the title of the work, the author(s), and where and when published.

ISBN: 978-1-4503-2130-3

Additional copies may be ordered prepaid from:

ACM Order Department
PO Box 30777
New York, NY 10087-0777, USA

Phone: 1-800-342-6626 (USA and Canada)
+1-212-626-0500 (Global)
Fax: +1-212-944-1318
E-mail: acmhelp@acm.org
Hours of Operation: 8:30 am – 4:30 pm ET

ACM Order Number: 415131

FSC www.fsc.org MIX Paper from responsible sources FSC® C102081

Printed in the USA

General Chair's Welcome

Welcome to the *27th ACM International Conference on Supercomputing (ICS)*, the oldest and longest running conference on high-performance computing. ICS is well known as the premier technical forum where researchers present their latest results and share with colleagues their perspectives on the state-of-the-art in the field in a focused, intimate environment. *ICS 2013* continues this strong tradition with an exceptional technical program, thought-provoking keynote addresses, interesting workshops and tutorials, and opportunities for student participation. The conference rotates between the United States and international locations in Europe and Japan. This year ICS is taking place in beautiful Eugene, Oregon, the "Emerald City" of the Willamette Valley and the home of the University of Oregon. It is my pleasure to serve as the General Chair for *ICS 2013* and I hope that you will find the meeting to be a rich and rewarding experience.

The success of *ICS 2013* is the result of an outstanding team of people. I want to thank the Organizing Committee who brought important skills, positive energy, and good humor throughout the endeavor. The hard work of the Program co-Chairs, Samuel Midkiff and Mario Nemirovsky, delivered an excellent technical program and I sincerely appreciate their leadership and contribution. Many thanks to the Program Committee for their dedicated reviewing efforts. Stewardship of the Workshops and Tutorials was in the capable hands of Co-Chairs Shirley Moore and Richard Vuduc, and the Posters and ACM Student Research Competition organization was led by Co-Chairs Hank Childs and Boyana Norris. These important components provide breadth to the *ICS 2013* technical offerings and I want to thank the Co-Chairs for their valuable assistance. *ICS 2013* would not be possible without competent attention to logistical details. The "behind the scenes" efforts of Darren Kerbyson (Financial Chair), Sameer Shende (Local Arrangements Chair), Matt Sottile (Registration Chair), Kevin Huck (Web Chair), Todd Gamblin (Submission Chair), and Jeff Hammond (Publication Chair) kept our planning on track and any crisis under control. Thank you. I also want to acknowledge Karen Karavanic for her leadership as the Student Travel Grants Chair, where she managed and allocated important financial support for student participation. I am further grateful to Pete Beckman for helping to bring corporate support to ICS in his role as Industry Chair. Finally, a special thanks to Alex Veidenbaum, Chair of the ICS Executive Committee, for his confidence in me, guidance, and thoughtful oversight.

The ACM provided invaluable support to *ICS 2013* throughout the process. In particular, I want to thank Ashely Cozzi for her help in conference logistics and finances, and Adrienne Griscti who coordinated ICS publication with ACM-Sheridan Proceedings Service and Lisa Tolles.

Finally, the continued sponsorship of ACM SIGARCH for ICS contributes significantly to the viability of the conference as a leading venue for high-performance computing research. The generous financial contributions of our corporate supporters from ARM, Cray, Electrical Geodesics, Inc., HP, IBM, Intel, Microsoft, NVIDIA, and ParaTools, Inc. recognize the value of the ICS mission and will translate directly to a positive *ICS 2013* experience for everyone.

I hope that *ICS 2013* provides a stimulating and productive meeting where you can engage technically and socially with other researchers, colleagues, and friends from around the world.

Allen D. Malony
ICS 2013 General Chair
University of Oregon, USA

Table of Contents

Session 6: Communication and Heterogeneous Systems

Session 7: Architecture 1

Session 8: Algorithms

Session 9: Architecture 2

Session 10: Irregular Algorithms

Session 11: Memory

Session 12: Keynote Address

Session 13: Runtime Techniques

Session 14: Order in the House

Session 15: GPUs

Session 16: Posters

ICS 2013 Organization

General Chair: Allen D. Malony *(University of Oregon, USA)*

Program Chairs: Mario Nemirovsky *(Barcelona Supercomputing Center, Spain)*
Sam Midkiff *(Purdue University, USA)*

Workshops / Tutorials Chairs: Shirley Moore *(University of Texas, El Paso, USA)*
Rich Vuduc *(Georgia Institute of Technology, USA)*

Finance Chair: Darren Kerbyson *(Pacific Northwest National Laboratory, USA)*

Local Arrangements Chair: Sameer Shende *(University of Oregon, USA)*

Publicity Chairs: Bob Lucas *(Information Sciences Institute / USC, USA)*
Paul H.J. Kelly *(Imperial College London, UK)*
Kazuki Joe *(Nara Women's University, Japan)*

Registration Chair: Matt Sottile *(Galois, USA)*

Student Travel Grants Chair: Karen Karavanic *(Portland State University, USA)*

Publication Chair: Jeff Hammond *(Argonne National Laboratory, USA)*

Submission Chair: Todd Gamblin *(Lawrence Livermore National Laboratory, USA)*

Poster / ACM SRC Chairs: Boyana Norris *(Argonne National Laboratory, USA)*
Hank Childs *(University of Oregon, USA)*

Industrial Chair: Pete Beckman *(Argonne National Laboratory, USA)*

Web Chair: Kevin Huck *(University of Oregon, USA)*

Program Committee: Nancy Amato *(Texas A&M, USA)*
Dan Banks *(Cisco, USA)*
Taisuke Boku *(University of Tsukuba, Japan)*
Ali R. Butt *(Virginia Institute of Technology, USA)*
Jose Castanos *(IBM Research, USA)*
Nikos Chrisochoides *(Old Dominion University, USA)*
Adrian Cristal *(Barcelona Supercomputer Center, Spain)*
James Dehnert *(Google, USA)*
Rudolf Eigenmann *(Purdue University, USA)*
Yoav Etsion *(Technion, Israel)*
Kyle Gallivan *(Florida State University USA)*
Stratis Gallopoulos *(University of Patras, Greece)*
Georgi N. Gaydadjiev *(Chalmers University, Sweden)*

Program Committee (continued):

Filippo Gioachin *(HP Labs, Singapore)*
Ananth Grama *(Purdue University, USA)*
Canturk Isci *(IBM Research, USA)*
Yutaka Ishikawa *(University of Tokyo, Japan)*
Omer Khan *(University of Connecticut, USA)*
Keiji Kimura *(University of Tokyo, Japan)*
Jaejin Lee *(Seoul National University, Taiwan)*
Wei Li *(Intel, USA)*
Zhiyuan Li *(Purdue University, USA)*
Michael Mascagni *(Florida State University, USA)*
Bilha Mendelson *(IBM Research, Israel)*
Jose Moreira *(IBM Research, USA)*
Walid Najjar *(University of California, Riverside, USA)*
Toshio Nakatani *(IBM Research, Japan)*
Nacho Navarro *(Universitat Politecnica de Catalunya, Spain)*
Alex Nicolau *(University of California, Irvine, USA)*
Yale Patt *(University of Texas, USA)*
Miquel Pericas *(Tokyo Institute of Technology, Japan)*
Enoch Peserico *(University of Padova, Italy)*
Dmitry Ponomarev *(Binghampton University (SUNY), USA)*
Geppino Pucci *(University of Padova, Italy)*
Philip C. Roth *(Oak Ridge National Laboratory, USA)*
P. Sadayappan *(Ohio State University, USA)*
Toshinori Sato *(Fukuoka University, Japan)*
Lutz Schubert *(University of Stuttgart, Germany)*
Henk Sips *(Delft University of Technology, The Netherlands)*
Guri Sohi *(University of Wisconsin, USA)*
Rajeev Thakur *(Argonne National Laboratory, USA)*
Sasa Tomic *(Barcelona Supercomputer Center, Spain)*
Dan Tsafrir *(Technion, Israel)*
Theo Ungerer *(University of Augsburg, Germany)*
Eric Van Hensbergen *(ARM, UK)*
Robert Van Engelen *(Florida State University, USA)*
Harry Wijshoff *(Leiden University, The Netherlands)*
Wayne Yamamoto *(Imagination Technologies, USA)*
Lixin Zhang *(Institute of Computing Technology, China)*

Steering Committee: Eduard Ayguade *(Universitat Politecnica de Catalunya, Spain)*
Utpal Banerjee *(University of California at Irvine, USA)*
Bronis R. de Supinski *(Lawrence Livermore National Laboratory, USA)*
Kyle Gallivan (*Florida State University, USA)*
Jim Goodman *(University of Auckland, New Zealand)*
Mike Gschwind *(IBM Research, USA)*
David K. Lowenthal *(University of Arizona, USA)*
Sally A. McKee *(Chalmers University of Technology, Sweden)*
Avi Mendelson *(Microsoft, Israel)*
Jose Moreira *(IBM Research, USA)*
Alex Nicolau *(University of California at Irvine, USA)*
Constantine Polychronopoulos *(U. Illinois, Urbana-Champaign, USA)*
Valentina Salapura *(IBM Research, USA)*
John Sopka *(EMC, USA)*
Mateo Valero *(Universitat Politecnica de Catalunya, Spain)*
Alex Veidenbaum *(University of California at Irvine, USA (Chair))*
Harry Wijshoff *(Leiden University, The Netherlands)*

ICS 2013 Sponsor & Supporters

Sponsor:

Supporters Platinum:

Supporters Gold:

Supporters Silver:

Supporter Bronze:

Business Meets Supercomputing

Keynote Talk

Bob Blainey
IBM Canada
Toronto, Ontario
blainey@ca.ibm.com

ABSTRACT

Organizations of all size, whether in business or government are recognizing the strategic role of data and the huge challenge they have to derive value from it. Consumer businesses want to better understand and engage with their customers. Logistics companies want to better optimize their operations. Governments want to find ways to deliver services more effectively and to reduce costs. We see the same patterns repeat across multiple industries. Conventional data management and data mining techniques are breaking down because of the huge volumes of data that need to be processed, because of the variety of ways that data is collected and stored and because of the need to make decisions quickly and on the most current information. The convergence of these trends is creating new opportunities for innovation in algorithms, programming models and computer architecture. In this talk, I will offer a perspective on the emerging field of business analytics on big data and explore connections with the world of high performance computing.

Categories and Subject Descriptors

E.0 [**Data**]: General

Keywords

business analytics

Short Biography

Bob is an IBM Fellow and the technical architect of the Hardware Acceleration Laboratory in IBM's Software Group. Bob has been with IBM for over 20 years, with a consistent focus on deep optimization of software for IBM systems. He spent many years working on program transformations for parallelism and for high performance on systems such as IBM Power and System z. More recently, Bob has had a focus on re-imagining the relationship between software and hardware in the post-scaling world, which includes optimization of IBM systems and software in the short term and the creation of new system structures in the longer term using disruptive technologies.

ICS'13, June 10–14, 2013, Eugene, Oregon, USA.
ACM 978-1-4503-2130-3/13/06.

Abstractions to Separate Concerns in Semi-Regular Grids

Andrew Stone
Colorado State University
Computer Science Department
1873 Campus Delivery
Fort Collins, CO 80523
stonea@cs.colostate.edu

Michelle Mills Strout
Colorado State University
Computer Science Department
1873 Campus Delivery
Fort Collins, CO 80523
mstrout@cs.colostate.edu

ABSTRACT

In various applications including atmospheric and ocean simulation programs, stencil computations occur on semi-regular grids where subdomains of the grid are regular (e.g., can be stored in an array) but boundaries between sub-domains connect in an irregular fashion. Implementations of stencils on semi-regular grids often have grid topology details tangled with stencil computation code. This tangling of details makes updating stencil code difficult as it requires the programmer to have full knowledge of the current grid topology. Existing libraries and tools for separating the concerns of stencil computations from grid connectivity have not dealt with semi-regular grids and instead have focused on purely regular grids with possible periodicity or purely irregular grids. In this paper we introduce programming abstractions for the class of semi-regular grids and describe a prototype Fortran 90+ library called GridLib that implements these abstractions. Implementing these abstractions requires solving issues involving nodes in the grid with a non-standard number of neighbors and determining the communication schedule given an orthogonal specification of the grid decomposition. We present solutions to these issues that work within the context of grids used in atmospheric and ocean simulations. We also show that to maintain the performance while still providing this separation of concerns, it is necessary for a source-to-source translator to perform inlining between user code and the GridLib run-time library code. We present performance results for a stencil computation extracted from the Parallel Ocean Program.

Categories and Subject Descriptors

D.1.3 [**Programming Techniques**]: Concurrent Programming—*Parallel programming*; D.2.2 [**Software Engineering**]: Design Tools and Techniques—*Software libraries*

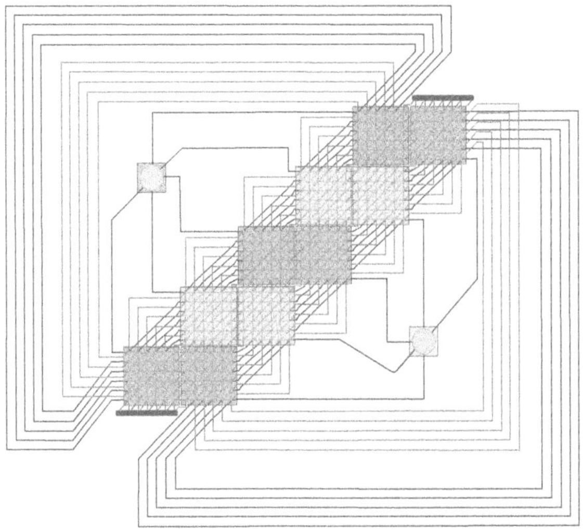

Figure 1: Connectivity of the Icosahedral grid. Each circular point in the figure represents a piece of data; the two large circles in the top-left and bottom-right corners represent data nodes for the north and south poles. Each of the blue rectangular regions represents a collection of data that is stored in an array. We illustrate six by six nodes in each non-polar array but in practice these arrays contain several thousands of nodes. The lines between nodes show connectivity. The lines going into and out of the red bars are connected.

Keywords

Programming models; Domain-specific languages; Compilers; High-performance computing; Parallel programming; Earth simulation; Atmospheric science

1. INTRODUCTION

Applications that simulate the Earth's atmosphere, land, and oceans are used to study problems in Geophysics, Climatology, Oceanography, and related fields. These simulation applications often require large amounts of computing and programmer resources. One of the main hurdles programmers face when developing Earth simulations is implementing globe discretization details in an efficient manner. The need for efficiency leads to a distributed memory parallel implementation and semi-regular grids, which are a patchwork quilt of regular arrays that connect in irregular ways. This causes the parallelization and grid connectivity details to

```
x2(:,:,:) = zero

! Iterate through subgrids, local blocks of data,
! vertical, and horizontal nodes.
DO g=1,10
 DO blk=lclBlk(g),lclBlk(g+1)
  DO j = 2,jm-1
   DO i = 2,im-1
     x2(blk,i,j) = area_inv(blk,i,j) * &
       ((x1(blk,i+1,j  )-x1(blk,i,j)) *
         weight(1,blk,i,j) + &
        (x1(blk,i+1,j+1)-x1(blk,i,j)) *
         weight(2,blk,i,j) + &
          ...
   END DO
  END DO
 END DO

 ! UPDATE NORTH POLE
 i = 2; j = jm; blk=1
 x2(blk,i,j) = area_inv(blk,i,j) *
               pweight(blk,i,j) * ...

 ! UPDATE SOUTH POLE
 i = im; j = 2
 x2(blk,i,j) = area_inv(blk,i,j) *
               pweight(blk,i,j) * ...
END DO
```

Figure 2: Fortran source code for stencil in SWM proxy application (extracted from GCRM).

```
real function x2(x1, i, j)
  ! ** Input parameters and local variables: **
  real, intent(inout) :: array(:, :)
  integer, intent(in) :: i, j

  x2 = &
    area_inv(i,j) * &
    ((x1(i+1,j  )-x1(i,j)) * weight(1,i,j) + &
     (x1(i+1,j+1)-x1(i,j)) * weight(2,i,j) + &
      ...
end function
```

Figure 3: Fortran source code for a simple stencil. The function x2 calculates the stencil for position (i,j) reading values from x1.

permeate application code. This paper introduces abstractions that enable an orthogonal specification of the stencil algorithm, the grid connectivity, and the grid decomposition for parallelization.

Figure 1 illustrates the semi-regular connectivity pattern of the icosahedral grid [17, 31], which is used in the Global Cloud Resolution Model (GCRM) [5]. As can be seen in the figure, the grid consist of twelve subgrids. Ten of these subgrids store data for pairs of triangular faces of an icosahedron and two of these subgrids store data for the north and south poles of the Earth.

Once the Earth is discretized and stored, applications iteratively perform operations on the discretized data to simulate some physical change over time. These operations typically take the form of a stencil computation. Stencil computations iterate over every point in a grid updating each value using values from neighboring nodes.

Figure 2 shows an example stencil from the Shallow Water Model (SWM) proxy application for GCRM. The code is executed in each process of an SPMD MPI program, where each process is responsible for computing over a subset of the blocks within the ten main subgrids.

Each block includes an extra layer (or halo) of array elements in all directions so that the stencil computation in the for loop can be the same at every location on the inside of the array except for the possible north and south pole nodes, which have their own specialized code.

As detailed on the icosahedral grid webpage [4], the software architects of GCRM have taken great care to map large chunks of the icosahedral grid to regular arrays and to keep the amount of special code needed for the stencil computations to a minimum. To handle nodes in the mesh that have five neighbors instead of the typical six, nodes with five neighbors have one of their neighboring halo values filled with a zero. In this manner the same six neighbor stencil can be used throughout the whole subdomain. The north and south pole singularities are mapped into the halo of one subdomain each and their five neighbors are placed so that they do not interfere with the rest of the subdomain. However, the north and south pole still require extra code as can be seen in Figure 2.

Even though the specialized code for the poles reflects a lack of separation of concerns between stencil code and the irregular grid connectivity, we do not show any communication code in Figure 2; this is because GCRM cleanly separates communication from stencil code. Nevertheless, the communication code that is in GCRM is highly tangled with information about the grid connectivity. This tangling of concerns leads to two main issues. (1) Whenever switching an application from one grid to another for scientific modeling reasons, most of the code in the application must be rewritten. The Parallel Ocean Program (POP) [19] provides an example of this. Between versions 1.4.3 and 2.0 the application was significantly rewritten to change from the dipole grid to the tripole grid. (2) The communication code, which is a significant portion of the full application, is currently written by hand for the specific grid and parallel distribution. In the 14,813 line SWM proxy application for GCRM, initializing and conducting communication involves 1,891 lines of code. In CGPOP [30], a 3,214 line miniapp of POP, initializing and conducting communication involves about 1,147 out of 3,214 lines of code. Our lines-of-code values were measured using the SLOCCount tool [2].

Ideally, programmers should be able to specify grid connectivity, stencil code, and parallel distribution orthogonally without having to write any specialized communication code. Figure 3 shows an idealized version of the stencil in the GCRM. Several libraries abstract parallelization details from programmers to enable easier implementation of certain types of code. Stencil libraries and generators such as Patus [11], Mint [32], and Physis [25], can be used to specify a stencil and its parallelization details orthogonally. Mesh based solver libraries such as Liszt [13], also allow for an orthogonalization of algorithm and grid. However, existing programming language work has not focused on the semi-regular grids seen in applications like GCRM or the Parallel Ocean Program. Additionally, some of these approaches would require rewriting full simulation applications in different languages, which is problematic.

To address these issues we introduce a set of abstractions for the orthogonal specification of semi-regular grid connectivity, stencil computations, and grid distribution for parallelism. With these abstractions we are able to maintain a clean separation of grid topology from stencil algorithm and parallel distribution and use a generic communication algo-

Construct a subgrid of size n by m:

```
subgrid_new(n,m)
```

Construct a border map between rectangular region (x1_t, y1_t, x2_t, y2_t) in the halo of subgrid sg_t (target) to rectangular region (x1_s, y1_s, x2_s, y2_s) in the halo of subgrid sg_s (source):

```
bmap_new(x1_t, y1_t, x2_t, y2_t, sg_t,
         x1_s, y2_s, x2_s, y2_s, sg_s)
```

Construct a new grid:

```
grid_new()
```

Add subgrid sg to the a grid g:

```
grid_addSubgrid(g, sg)
```

Add border map b to grid g:

```
grid_addBMap(g, b)
```

Figure 4: Interface for specifying semi-regular grid connectivity in GridLib library

rithm that will work for any semi-regular grid. We implement these abstractions in a Fortran library called GridLib.

A library based approach has the advantage that it can be integrated into existing Fortran programs and work with existing Fortran debugging and development tools. A disadvantage of a library based approach is that it introduces overhead. To alleviate this potential disadvantage we create a source-to-source translation tool called GridWeaver. GridWeaver inlines library calls and user-defined stencil class, removing overhead, and lets us produce code that performs competitively against hand-written code. We evaluate our tool by comparing performance against a benchmark stencil based on the Parallel Ocean Program.

We introduce our semi-regular grid abstractions in Section 2. In Section 3 we formalize these abstractions and describe how they are implemented; we also present an algorithm that calculates what communication must occur for a semi-regular grid. In Section 4 we discuss the need for a translation tool in order to maintain performance. We discuss related work in section 6 and conclude in Section 7.

2. SEMI-REGULAR GRID ABSTRACTIONS

In this section we describe abstractions that can be used to specify and operate on semi-regular grids. We also describe how to use these abstractions via functions calls to our GridLib Fortran library.

To perform a parallel stencil computation in GridLib we require users to specify three things: (1) grid connectivity, (2) grid decomposition, and (3) the stencil algorithm. The following subsections describe the relevant abstractions and library functions for each of these three requirements.

2.1 Specifying Connectivity

There are three main types of abstractions we use to specify connectivity of semi-regular grids: subgrids, border mappings, and grid objects. Subgrids represent a two-dimensional index space where a grid exhibits regular connectivity, border mappings represent connectivity between subgrids, and grids aggregate the subgrids and border mappings together to form a single object.

In Figure 4 we present the interface for defining connectivity in GridLib. Although GridLib is a Fortran 90 library we use an object-oriented approach in its design. The functions `subgrid_new`, `bmap_new`, and `grid_new` construct new subgrid, border-mapping, and grid objects respectively.

When constructing a new subgrid the user specifies the width and height of the subgrid. It is not necessary that all subgrids in a grid have the same width and height. For example, the connectivity of the Icosahedral grid depicted in Figure 1 consists of ten N by M subgrids representing the sides of an icosahedron and two one by one subgrids that represent the north and south poles.

Our current interface only supports subgrids that are two-dimensional, although our approach could be generalized to handle greater dimensionality. It should be noted that this limitation does not prevent stencils from operating on higher dimensional data: for example, an array of values, rather than a scalar, could be associated at each point of the grid. This limitation does prevent a grid from having differing connectivity along the higher dimensions or being decomposed along these dimensions; however, for the CGPOP and SWM applications two-dimensional subgrids are sufficient. In other Earth science applications there might be a column of data associated with each cell or node in the two-dimensional subgrid, but the connectivity between subgrids is still two dimensional in nature

In GridLib, subgrids are connected to one another via border mappings. Border mappings are based on the idea of specifying a layer of nodes, called a halo, that surrounds a subgrid and then indicating connectivity by specifying a target and source rectangular region. The target region lies in the halo of a given subgrid, the source region lies along the border of another (or potentially the same) subgrid. The mapping specifies that the region occupied by the target should be filled with values from the source region. For example, in Figure 5a the border mapping `bmap_new(3,1, 3,4, sg1, 1,1, 1,4, sg2)` indicates that the target rectangle in the halo of the left hand subgrid should be filled with the rectangle from the border of the right hand subgrid. With border mappings we are able to model the complex connectivity patterns seen along array borders in semiregular grids (see Figures 5b and 5c for more examples).

Typically the halo stores copies of data from neighboring subgrids. Once a halo's nodes are populated (copied) a stencil computation may be performed on a given subgrid without requiring access to any values outside the subgrid. In practice, subgrids are further divided into blocks that contain their own halos so that a finer granularity of parallelism can be achieved; however, for specification purposes the user only need think about a halo of nodes existing around the subgrid. In this paper and in our current implementation of GridLib we limit halos to be of single element depth. An implication of this is that stencil operations that work on the grid are required to be compact (only accessing nearest neighbor values). Future work will focus on relaxing this assumption.

Figure 5 illustrates different patterns of mapping that occur in Earth grids In this figure we also illustrate how each pattern is specified with border mappings and provide code that uses the interface in Figure 4 to specify the mapping. One thing to note is that the rectangular regions specified by the mappings have an orientation. In Figure 5 this orientation is illustrated using small triangles in one of the four

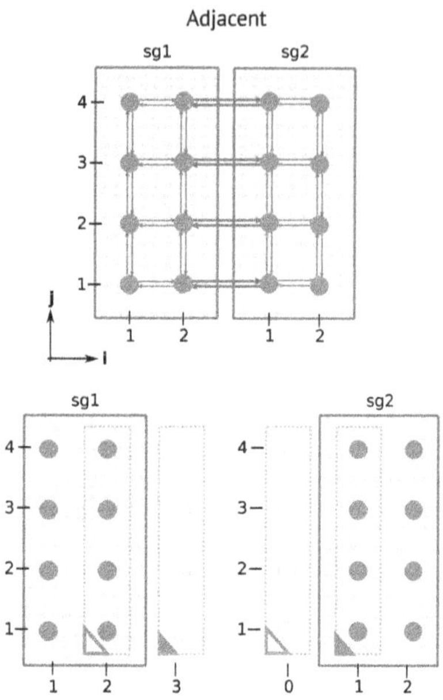


```
type(Grid) :: g
type(SubGrid) :: sg1, sg2
type(BMap) :: bm1, bm2

g = grid_new()
sg1 = subgrid_new(2, 4)
sg2 = subgrid_new(2, 4)

bm1 = bmap_new(3,1, 3,4, sg1,
               1,1, 1,4, sg2)
bm2 = bmap_new(0,1, 0,4, sg2,
               2,1, 2,4, sg1)

grid_addSubgrid(g, sg1)
grid_addSubgrid(g, sg2)
grid_addBMap(g, bm1)
grid_addBMap(g, bm2)
```

(A)

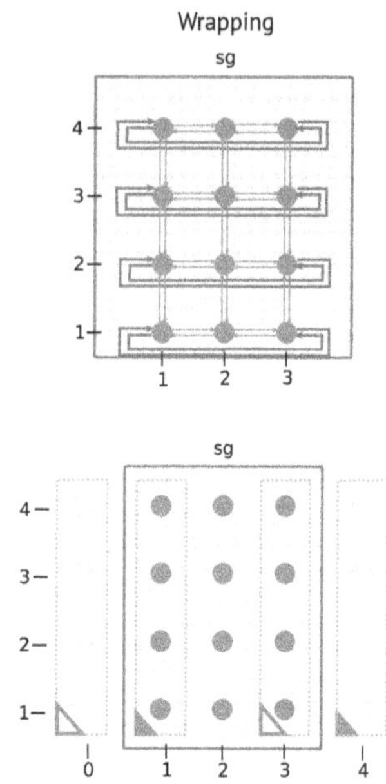


```
type(Grid) :: g
type(SubGrid) :: sg
type(BMap) :: bm1, bm2

g = grid_new()
sg = subgrid_new(3, 4)

bm1 = bmap_new(4,1, 4,3, sg,
               1,1, 1,4, sg)
bm2 = bmap_new(0,1, 0,4, sg,
               3,1, 3,4, sg)

grid_addSubgrid(g, sg)
grid_addBMap(g, bm1)
grid_addBMap(g, bm2)
```

(B)

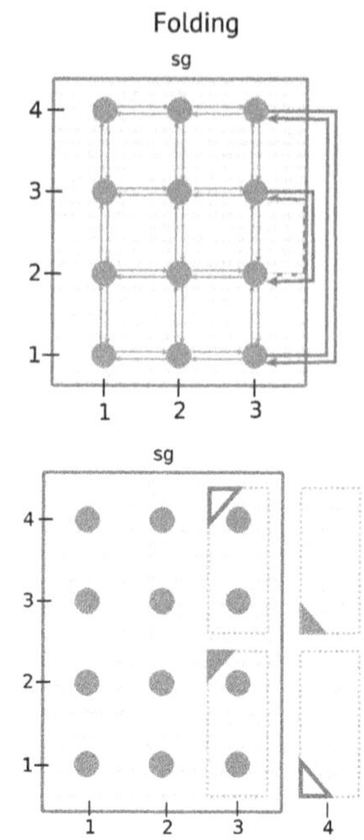


```
type(Grid) :: g
type(SubGrid) :: sg
type(BMap) :: bm1, bm2

g = grid_new()
sg = subgrid_new(3, 4)

bm1 = bmap_new(4,3, 4,4, sg,
               3,2, 3,1, sg)
bm2 = bmap_new(4,1, 4,2, sg,
               3,4, 3,3, sg)

grid_addSubgrid(g, sg)
grid_addBMap(g, bm1)
grid_addBMap(g, bm2)
```

(C)

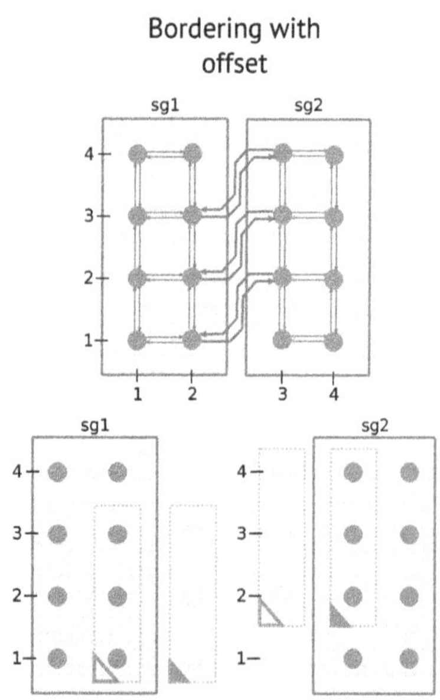


```
type(Grid) :: g
type(SubGrid) :: sg1, sg2
type(BMap) :: bm1, bm2

g = grid_new()
sg1 = subgrid_new(2, 4)
sg2 = subgrid_new(2, 4)

bm1 = bmap_new(3,1, 3,3, sg1,
               1,2, 1,3, sg2)
bm2 = bmap_new(0,2, 0,4, sg2,
               2,1, 2,3, sg2)

grid_addSubgrid(g, sg1)
grid_addSubgrid(g, sg2)
grid_addBMap(g, bm1)
grid_addBMap(g, bm2)
```

(D)

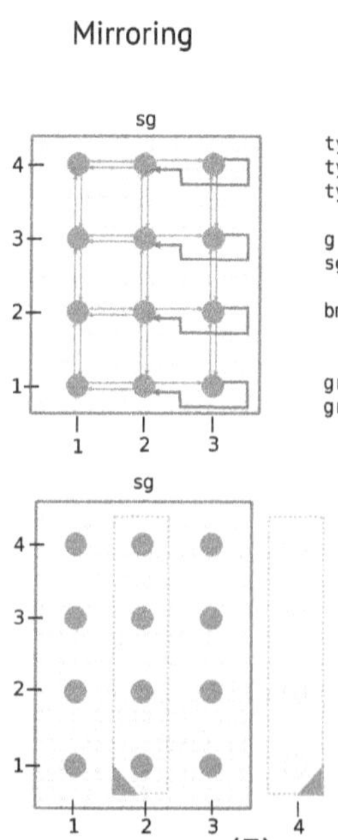


```
type(Grid) :: g
type(SubGrid) :: sg
type(BMap) :: bm

g = grid_new()
sg = subgrid_new(3, 4)

bm1 = bmap_new(4,1, 4,4, sg,
               2,1, 2,4, sg)

grid_addSubgrid(g, sg)
grid_addBMap(g, bm)
```

(E)

Figure 5: Examples of border connectivity patterns. In each subfigure we include an illustration of the connectivity pattern between nodes in the subgrid. Below each connectivity pattern illustration we show how the connectivity is represented using border mappings (the dashed rectangles). Below (in a,b, and c) or next (in d and e) to that we show code using the GridLib interface from Figure 4 that specifies the connectivity.

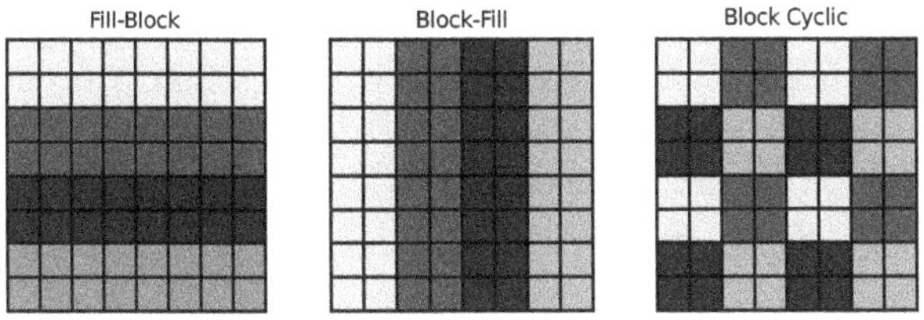

Figure 6: GridLib includes functions for decomposing an array into blocks in the typical block and cyclic combinations. Each color in this figure represents a different process.

corners of each source and target rectangle. The first coordinate of the specified target region corresponds to the first coordinate of the specified source region. Using the notation of the parameters passed to the `bmap_new` function in Figure 4, target point (`x1_t`, `y1_t`) corresponds to source point (`x1_s`, `y1_s`), target point (`x1_t`, `y1_t`) corresponds to source point (`x1_s`, `y1_s`), and `x1_s`, `y1_s`, `x1_t`, `y1_t` are not necessarily greater than `x2_s`, `y2_s`, `x2_t`, `y2_t` respectively.

The connectivity illustrated in a, b, c, and d in Figure 5 are seen in actual grids. The adjacency pattern in Figure 5a is seen in the cubed-sphere [28] and icosahedral grids [17, 31]. The wrapping pattern in 5b appears in toroidal and dipole grids [29]. The folding pattern in 5c appears in the tripole grid and the offset pattern seen in 5d appears in the icosahedral grid [26]. We include the mirroring pattern in 5e since it is seen in array-based languages such as ZPL [10].

2.2 Specifying Decomposition

Once a grid's connectivity is specified it is possible to assign values to each of its nodes. If a stencil computation is to run in serial then an array can be allocated for each subgrid and there is no need for further decomposition. On the other hand, if the stencil is to run in parallel then the grid must be decomposed into chunks that are distributed to each processing elements. In a shared memory environment this ownership identifies what nodes a processor is responsible for updating when conducting the stencil; in a distributed memory environment this ownership identifies both what nodes a processor is responsible for updating as well as what nodes that processor is responsible for storing.

A naive decomposition would be to assign ownership of one entire subgrid to each processing element. This decomposition does not scale since large machines contain several thousands more processing elements than there are subgrids; the most complex grid we have studied, the Icosahedral grid, consists of only twelve subgrids.

To address this concern GridLib provides several functions for decomposing a grid into blocks. Each of these functions will decompose the subgrids into equally sized blocks and assign ownership according to some pattern. In Figure 6 we illustrate three different decomposition patterns; these patterns are based on the array decomposition features of High Performance Fortran [23]. Users may also manually assign or modify the decomposition.

In line 45 of Figure 7 we use the `new_block_fill` function to specify a block-fill decomposition with blocks of size 64 by 64 on the tripole grid. In lines 9 through 28 we use the grid connectivity functions described in Section 2.1 to define the connectivity of the tripole grid.

```
1 module Stencils; contains
2     real function fivePtAvgStencil(A, i, j)
3         fivePtAvgStencil = 0.2 * &
4             (A(i, j) + A(i-1, j) + &
5             (i+1, j) + A(i, j-1) + A(i, j+1))
6     end function
7 end module
8 program StencilOnTripole
9     type(SubGrid) :: sg
10    type(BMap) :: w2e, e2w, fold1, fold2
11    type(Grid) :: g
12    type(Decomposition) :: dcmp
13    type(Data) :: data_in, data_out
14    integer :: N, M
15
16    ! Create subgrid
17    N = 2048; M = 2048
18    call subgrid_new(sg, N, M)
19
20    ! Create mappings for tripole connectivity
21    call bmap_new(w2e,    0, 1,    0, M,  sg,
22                        N+1, 1,  N+1, M,  sg);
23    call bmap_new(e2w, N+1, 1,  N+1, M,  sg,
24                          1, 1,    1, M,  sg);
25    call bmap_new(fold1, 1, M+1,   N/2,M+1, sg
26                          N, M,    N/2+1,M,   sg)
27    call bmap_new(fold2, N/2+1, M+1,  N, M+1, sg,
28                            N/2, M,    1, M,   sg)
29
30    ! Create a tripole grid
31    call grid_new(g)
32    call grid_addSubgrid(sg)
33    call grid_addBMaps(w2e, e2w, fold1, fold2);
34
35    ! Specify a decomposition and input data
36    dcmp = decomposition_new_block_fill(g, 64, 64)
37    data_in = data_new_from_file("input.dat", dcmp)
38    data_out = data_new(dcmp)
39
40    ! Perform stencil operation
41    data_out =
42        data_apply(data_in, fivePtAvgStencil)
43 end program StencilOnTripole
```

Figure 7: GridLib code for stencil on tripole grid. The `decomposition_new_block_fill` function applies a block-fill decomposition (illustrated in Figure 6) to grid g where each block is 64 by 64 nodes. The call to `data_new_from_file` reads in a data object from `"input.dat"` and stores the data using the previously defined decomposition. The `data_apply` function performs the stencil operation specified in the fivePtAvgStencil function using `data_in` for input values and `data_out` for output values.

2.3 Specifying Algorithm

Once decomposition is specified values may be assigned to grid node and stencil operations can be used to update these values. Figure 7 shows a complete example program that uses GridLib to perform a stencil operation on the tripole grid [26]. From a GridLib user's perspective there are two things that must be specified in order to perform a stencil operation: (1) instantiating data objects and (2) applying a stencil function.

Data objects map values to grid nodes. GridLib includes functions for reading and writing data objects to and from files. The functions that construct data objects are passed a decomposition object that specifies how to distribute the data. The `data_apply` function applies a stencil operation to every point in a data object. This function is passed (1) a data object that is referenced when grabbing values for a stencil operation and (2) a reference to a function that performs the stencil operation for a given point. We apply this function in lines 41 through 42 in Figure 7.

The function that performs the stencil operation is specified by the user. This stencil function is passed the coordinates of a given point `(i, j)` and a function `A` that is used to retrieve the values of nodes neighboring `(i, j)`. Despite the fact that we implement A as a function we encourage users to think of it as though it what an array. In this fashion the stencil code appears similar to what would be in the loop body of a serial stencil implementation on a purely regular grid. Note the similarity in the simplicity of the specification of the **`fivePtAvgStencil`** function and the code in Figure 3.

3. IMPLEMENTING ABSTRACTIONS

In the previous section we introduced abstractions for specifying the connectivity of semi-regular grids. These abstractions, which we have implemented in the GridLib library, enable a separate specification of grid topology from stencil code. In this section we describe issues that emerge when implementing these abstractions. Specifically we look at: (1) how to handle stencil nodes that have less than the typical number of neighbors, and (2) how to automate communication.

3.1 Handling Non-Standard Stencil Nodes

Due to the fact that subgrids represent regular portions of a grid, all elements in a subgrid that are not along one of its four borders will have the same connectivity pattern. Nodes along a border have at most the same number of neighbors. For example, the poles seen in Figure 1 have five neighbors while most other nodes in the grid have six.

When a stencil computation attempts to access a nonexistent neighbor GridLib will return a value of zero. The user is responsible for writing the stencil computation so that it computes the correct value given this behavior. Since most stencils are written as linear combinations where the value of each neighboring node is multiplied by some coefficient the product for a non-existent neighbor will also be zero. We have found this behavior correctly implements the stencils in GCRM and CGPOP across all nodes. To ensure this behavior, prior to conducting communication, we initialize all values in a halo to be zero.

3.2 Communication Planning for Halos

We have found one of the most complicated portions of implementing semi-regular grid computations to be handling communication. Communication code is typically long and specialized for the grid used: in SWM (a 14,813 line proxy application of GCRM) communication takes 1,891 lines of code; in CGPOP [30] (a 3,214 line miniapp of POP) communication takes 1,147 lines of code.

Communication in these applications and in GridLib is cleanly separated by making use of halo regions around blocks of data. However, in SWM and CGPOP this code is written to be specific to the grid used. In GridLib we have implemented a generic communication algorithm that will populate block halos for any semi-regular grid. Once the halo is populated a stencil computation may update the values within a block without conducting any additional communication.

In this section we introduce an algorithm, used by GridLib, that will properly populate halo values for a semi-regular grid. To do this we begin by formalizing the semi-regular grid abstractions introduced in Section 2. The way GridLib stores and constrains its abstractions is based on these formalisms. We write the communication algorithm (shown in Algorithm 1) in terms of these formalisms.

3.2.1 Formalisms for semi-regular grid abstractions

We define a subgrid σ as an index space

$$\sigma = \{s, \langle i,j\rangle \mid s,i,j \in \mathbb{Z} \wedge 1 \le i \le N \wedge 1 \le j \le M\}, \quad (1)$$

where N and M are bounds on the index space, and s is an integer used to uniquely identify the subgrid. Thus all nodes in the same σ have the same value for s.

All subgrids have an associated halo and border-point index space. The halo of a subgrid σ of size N by M with identifier s is $h(\sigma)$ where

$$\begin{aligned} h(\sigma) = \{s, \langle i,j\rangle \mid\ & s,i,j \in \mathbb{Z} \wedge \\ & 0 \le i \le N+1 \wedge \\ & 0 \le j \le M+1\} - \sigma \end{aligned} \quad (2)$$

Border mappings are used to determine how nodes in a subgrid σ_1's halo $h(\sigma_1)$ map to nodes that lie within subgrid σ_2. Note that border mappings can apply to the same subgrid (that is σ_1 may equal σ_2). A border mapping β (equation 7) is defined in terms of two rectangular regions ρ_{tgt} and ρ_{src} (equations 5 and 6) that respectively lie in $h(\sigma_1)$ and σ_2 (equations 3 and 4) where

$$(s_1, p_i, p_j), (s_1, q_i, q_j) \in h(\sigma_1) \quad (3)$$

$$(s_2, v_i, v_j), (s_2, w_i, w_j) \in \sigma_2 \quad (4)$$

$$\rho_{\text{tgt}} = (s_1,\ p_i, p_j,\ q_i, q_j) \quad (5)$$

$$\rho_{\text{src}} = (s_2,\ v_i, v_j,\ w_i, w_j) \quad (6)$$

$$\beta = (\rho_{\text{tgt}}, \rho_{\text{src}})\,. \quad (7)$$

It is also necessary that ρ_{tgt} and ρ_{src} to have the same size.

When mapping nodes to ρ_{tgt} from ρ_{tgt} we may need to deal with regions that are oriented differently. To translate a point from one orientation to another we multiply it by an orientation matrix. The orientation function o returns the matrix for a given rectangle. We define o as

$$o(\rho) = \begin{cases} \begin{pmatrix} 1 & 0 \\ 0 & 1 \end{pmatrix} & \text{if } q_i \ge p_i \wedge q_j \ge p_j \\ \begin{pmatrix} -1 & 0 \\ 0 & 1 \end{pmatrix} & \text{if } q_i \le p_i \wedge q_j \ge p_j \\ \begin{pmatrix} -1 & 0 \\ 0 & -1 \end{pmatrix} & \text{if } q_i \le p_i \wedge q_j \le p_j \\ \begin{pmatrix} 1 & 0 \\ 0 & -1 \end{pmatrix} & \text{if } q_i \ge p_i \wedge q_j \le p_j \end{cases} \quad (8)$$

For a given border mapping β there is a border mapping function $m : \beta \times \mathbb{Z}^3 \to \mathbb{Z}^3$ where

$$m(\beta, s_1, \langle i,j\rangle) = (s_2, \langle i', j'\rangle) \quad (9)$$

such that

$$\begin{pmatrix} i' \\ j' \end{pmatrix} = \begin{pmatrix} v_i \\ v_j \end{pmatrix} + o(\rho_h)o(\rho_b)\left(\begin{pmatrix} i \\ j \end{pmatrix} - \begin{pmatrix} p_i \\ p_j \end{pmatrix}\right). \quad (10)$$

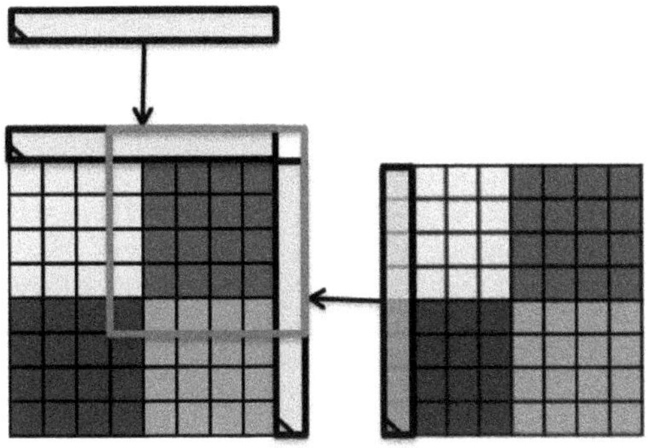

Figure 8: Halo of a block in a sub-grid. When populating the red block's halo some values come from neighboring blocks in the same sub-grid, other come from outside the subgrid.

This mapping function takes a point in a halo $(s_1, \langle i, j \rangle)$ and determines the location $(s_2, \langle i', j' \rangle)$ of the value that should be copied into the halo point.

We define a grid as a tuple $\gamma = (S, B)$ where S is a set of subgrids and B is a set of border mappings. All subgrids $\sigma \in S$ have a unique id s. A grid defines a global index space g such that

$$g(\gamma) = \bigcup_{\sigma \in S} \sigma. \tag{11}$$

The abstraction we use for assigning grid nodes to processes is the decomposition. Our decomposition abstraction consists of a set of blocks. We define a block θ as a tuple:

$$\theta = (b, p, s, \langle u_i, u_j \rangle, \langle v_i, v_j \rangle), \tag{12}$$

where $\langle u_i, u_j \rangle$ to $\langle v_i, v_j \rangle$ is a rectangular region in subgrid s. All blocks are given a unique identifier b and are assigned to a process p.

We define B to be a set of blocks. To simplify later abstractions and their implementations we constrain all blocks to be the same size and require that the union of blocks in B span the space $g(\gamma)$ of some grid γ.

Now that we have defined formalisms for grid connectivity and data decomposition we can describe the formalisms used to perform a stencil operation.

For a given grid γ we may define one or more data objects δ over that grid. Each point in the grid's index space $x \in g(\gamma)$ has an assigned value $\delta(x)$. The function δ has the signature

$$\delta(x) : \mathbb{Z}^3 \rightarrow \mathbb{R}. \tag{13}$$

To store data we use a three dimensional array where two of the dimensions correspond to values in the two-dimensional block and the third dimension corresponds to a block's local ID.

3.2.2 *Algorithm and formalisms for communication*

Around each of the stored blocks we include a single-node depth halo. The halo stores a copy of data from surrounding blocks. Once the halo is populated stencil operations can be applied independently to all nodes in each block. The GridLib library is currently limited to computations that have a single layer of halo depth. Due to the complex connectivity patterns that exist between grids handling larger

Input: A Grid G and distribution D
Output: A communication plan for each (MPI) rank r
$\pi(r) = (\mu_r(r), \mu_s(r))$.

let μ_r(r) be receiving messages for rank r
let μ_s(r) be sending messages for rank s
let B be the set of border mappings

! Determine the communication that occurs to populate
! each block's halo.
foreach *block* b_{tgt} *in the grid* **do**
  s = the subgrid b resides in
  r_r = the rank that owns block b_{tgt}
  b_{i1} = global i coordinate of block b_{tgt}
  b_{j1} = global j coordinate of block b_{tgt}
  b_{i2} = global i extent of block b_{tgt}
  b_{j2} = global j extent of block b_{tgt}

  ! Construct a region that includes all internal and
  ! halo nodes for block b_{tgt}
  $\rho_{\text{blkHalo}} = (s, \langle b_{i1} - 1, b_{j1} - 1 \rangle, \langle b_{i2} + 1, b_{j2} + 1 \rangle)$

  ! Determine the blocks that b_{tgt} *communicates with*
  O = set of blocks overlapping with ρ_{blkHalo}

  ! For each of the neighboring blocks create a message
  ! for the region in $\rho_{blkHalo}$ *that it overlaps with.*
  foreach $b_{src} \in O$ **do**
    r_{tgt} = rank that owns block b_{tgt}
    r_{src} = rank that owns block b_{src}
    ρ_{blk} = region spanned by block b_{src}
    ρ_o = region of ρ_{blkHalo} intersecting with ρ_{blk}

    if ρ_o *is contained in* s **then**
      ! Create a message within the subgrid
      $\mu_r(r_r) = \mu_r(r_r) \cup (b_{\text{tgt}},\ \text{tr}(\rho_o, b_{\text{tgt}}),\ r_{\text{src}})$
      $\mu_s(r_s) = \mu_s(r_s) \cup (b_{\text{src}},\ \text{tr}(\rho_o, b_{\text{src}}),\ r_{\text{tgt}})$
    else
      ! Create a message for each portion of
      ! ρ_o *that is in a border mapping*
      foreach $\beta \in B$ **do**
        if ρ_o *intersects with* β **then**
          ρ_m = intersection of β and ρ_o
          $\mu_r(r_r) = \mu_r(r_r) \cup$
            $(b_{\text{tgt}},\ \text{tr}(\text{rm}(\rho_m, \beta), b_{\text{tgt}}),\ r_s)$
          $\mu_s(r_s) = \mu_s(r_s) \cup$
            $(b_{\text{src}},\ \text{tr}(\text{rm}(\rho_m, \beta), b_{\text{src}}),\ r_r)$
        end
      end
    end
  end
end

Algorithm 1: Algorithm to generate a communication plan. The function $\text{tr}(\rho, b)$ returns a region that translates the global indices used in ρ into the local indices used in block b. The function $\text{rm}(\rho, \beta)$ returns a region where each of the four coordinates of ρ are passed through the border mapping function m.

halo depths is a more difficult and the algorithms presented in this paper do not easily scale to multi-depth halos. In Figure 8 we illustrate the halo region for a single block in a subgrid. Notice that some of the values needed to populate the halo come from blocks within the same subgrid and other values come from values on a different subgrid.

Prior to conducting communication we initialize values in the halo to zero. In this manner if an (n+1)-point stencil operation is applied to a point with less than n neighbors it will return zeroes for the missing neighbors. We have found this behavior correctly implements the stencils in GCRM and CGPOP across all nodes.

To populate the halo we conduct communication GridLib uses an abstraction internal to itself called a communication plan. This object is used to guide a message passing communication between processes. In this communication plan we identify each process with a rank r.

Each rank has a communication plan π, which is a tuple

$$\pi_r = (\mu_r, \mu_s), \tag{14}$$

where μ_r is the set of messages to receive and μ_s is the set of messages to send. A message μ is a tuple

$$\mu = (b, r, \rho), \tag{15}$$

where r is a rank that the message is received from if $\mu \in M_s$ or sent to if $\mu \in M_r$, b is the block to place data into if $\mu \in M_s$ or send data from if $\mu \in M_s$, and ρ is a rectangular region in block b. In Algorithm 1 we present a method for generating a communication plan object.

In our GridLib implementation we then populate a halo by simply posting MPI receive calls for each message in $\mu_r(r)$ on a given rank r, and post MPI sending calls for each message in $\mu_s(r)$ and copying the values read in from the received calls into the specified region of the specified block's halo. We perform this update halo operation each time a stencil is performed.

The algorithm will iterate through each block in the grid, calculate what region of a subgrid its halo covers, then determine what neighboring blocks overlap with this halo. If any portion of the block's halo extends beyond the boundary of a subgrid it will iterate through border mappings to determine if any of them intersect with the halo. After determining what blocks are neighboring a given block we construct messages in $\mu_r(r)$ and $\mu_s(r)$ to copy the neighboring data into the halo.

4. GRIDWEAVER TRANSLATION TOOL

We have developed a library called GridLib, which implements the abstractions introduced in this paper. The GridLib library enables a separate specification of semi-regular grids topology details from stencil algorithms. This specification enables users to specify a parallel stencil computation without requiring the user to write any parallel code.

A disadvantage of a library based approach is that libraries necessarily introduce overhead. In GridLib this overhead is introduced due to the fact that whenever a stencil computation is performed the user-defined function that encapsulates the stencil operation will be called for every point in the grid. Furthermore, within this function another function will be called whenever accessing the point's value or the value of any of its neighbors.

For example, the function `fivePtAvgStencil` will be called once for every point in the grid, and, although it syntactically appears like an array, the symbol `A` is actually function that returns the value associated with some grid point from data-structures internal to GridLib.

To address this overhead we have developed a code generation tool called GridWeaver that preprocesses programs written with GridLib andn inlines GridLib calls. To parse and translate Fortran programs we use the Rose source-to-source translation framework [27]. The name GridWeaver comes from both the notion of tying several subgrids together to form a single grid and the idea of weaving the GridLib library code into a user's program. An analogy can be drawn between this weaving process and the weaving of advice to joinpoints done by Aspect Oriented Programming [22] compilers.

More specifically, GridWeaver replaces calls to `data_apply` with a loop nest that will iterate over all locally owned nodes and will embed the contents of the stencil function within this loop nest. Gridweaver then replaces calls to the function `A` with code that directly accesses data from the array GridLib uses internally to store grid data. The inlining optimization is not performed automatically by Fortran compilers due to the fact that the stencil operation is specified outside of GridLib by its user but is invoked internally.

5. EVALUATION RESULTS

In Figure 9 we show a performance comparison of GridLib and GridWeaver against a stencil computation extracted from CGPOP. The extracted stencil is representative of CGPOP. In experiments run on a 2.8 GHZ Intel Core2 Machine CGPOP's kernel ran at performance of 2.35 GFLOP/s while the extracted stencil performed at 2.41 GFLOP/s. We performed this stencil for 100 iterations on a 3600 by 3600 dipole-grid with a row-blocked distribution.

We performed our scalability experiments on two machines at Colorado State University: Bacon, a 16 core, 2.13 GHz, Intel XeonE7 machine with 128 GB of memory; and the ISTeC Cray HPC system, a Cray XT6m with 1248 cores across 52 compute-node, and 1.6 TB of memory. There are 24 cores per node on the ISTeC Cray. This evaluation demonstrates that (1) GridLib introduces library overhead that reduces performance, particularly when run on small number of cores, and (2) GridWeaver is able to produce code that performs similarly to hand-written code. The GridWeaver tool is able to produce the efficient code by inlining the GridLib library calls as described in Section 4.

6. RELATED WORK

Several tools have been developed to aid with implementing stencil computations on structured or unstructured grids. These tools differ in terms of what types of grids they operate on, how grids and stencils are specified, and what platform and languages they target. For example, the framework from Kamil et al. [21], Mint [32], Patus [12], Physis [25], and Pochoir [24] work on regular grids, while Liszt [14], MPAS [3], and OP2 [15] work on irregular grids. Some grids, such as the torus, are mostly regular but include simple wrap-around (periodic) boundaries. Many allow periodic boundaries [11, 32, 25] but are unable to handle the other types of boundaries illustrated in Figure 5. Parallel array languages such as ZPL [10] also have the ability to express periodic boundaries.

The Chombo toolkit has the ability to work with grids that are composed of multiple subgrids. In Chombo a por-

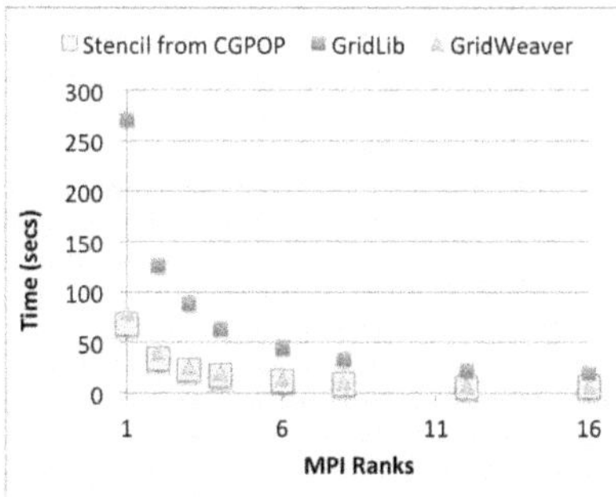

(a) Performance on multicore

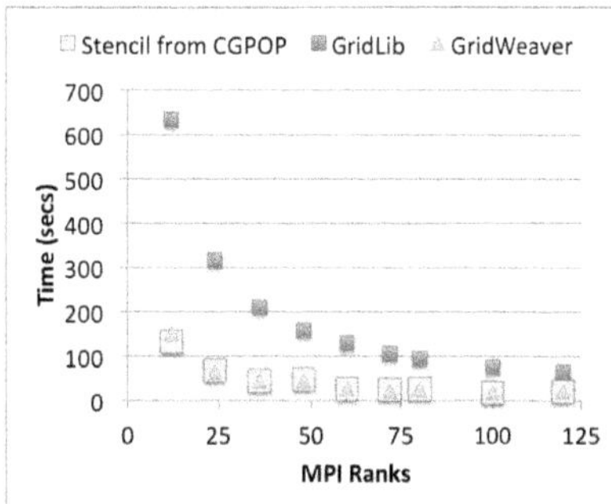

(b) Performance on cluster

Figure 9: Performance comparison of GridLib and GridWeaver against the stencil extracted from CGPOP

tion of a regular grid may be adaptively refined to form an embedded, finer grained, subgrid. In such a case the coarser, enclosing, grid will copy data from the neighbor points in the finer, enclosed, grid; an averaging operator is used to translate between the finer and coarser data [6]. Chombo also the ability to allocate subgrids next one another through its Mapped Multiblock Grids abstraction. In this abstraction a series of grids in a two-dimensional domain is mapped to a three-dimensional range. Chombo will automatically determine how to interpolate and communicate values between subgrids that are adjacent in the three-dimensional range [1]. GridLib uses a different approach by having the user specify connectivity between subgrids directly

The Overture system also has the ability to work on grids that are composed of several subgrids. In Overture [7] users specify a geometry; Overture then discretizes that geometry with overlapping regular grids. As part of the discretization process connections between grids are determined and communication plans between grids are developed. It is unclear how one might adapt established semi-regular grids such as the icosahedral grid, cubed sphere, and tripole would be specified within the Overture framework. overture, More generally, to address software engineering concerns seen in Earth Science computations, researchers have developed component based software frameworks such as Cactus [16] and the Earth System Modeling Framework
(ESMF) [18]. These packages address the issues raised when composing different components of an Earth simulation application to one another (for example: how to compose a given sea model with an atmosphere model), and how to convert data from one gridded model to another (the regridding problem). However, these frameworks do not introduce to address the data-layout problem seen for a grid within a given component, which we address with this work.

The concept of using an abstraction to specify an array's decomposition is not unique to the GridLib and GridWeaver tools. The high-performance Fortran language [23] allows users to specify regular, block, cyclic, and block-cyclic distributions along each of an arrays dimensions. HPCS languages such as Chapel [8, 9] includes a first class distribution object that enable a separate specification of an array from its decomposition.

Other work has used the term semi-regular grid to refer to a regular grid that is then refined in places using a triangular mesh [33].

The GridWeaver code generator replaces calls to `data_apply` with a loop nest that iterates over grid nodes then embeds the body of the stencil function within the loop nest. Embedding the stencil function is similar to how iterators are inlined in Chapel and other languages [20].

7. CONCLUSIONS

In this paper we introduce abstractions for representing semi-regular grids. Semi-regular grids are used in Earth simulation programs and can be stored using one or more arrays. If these arrays are expanded to include a halo region then stencil computations can be applied without requiring any communication code within the stencil. We present a communication creation algorithm that determines how to populate the halos when the grid and the block distribution for the grid have been specified with orthogonal abstractions Communication plans are metadata used to direct send and receive calls. Using these abstractions and this communication plan generation algorithm GridLib enables users to specify grid connectivity separately from algorithm and alleviates the need to write communication code.

GridLib is a Fortran library. A Fortran library based approach is convenient in that it does not require users to rewrite their code if it is already in Fortran and in the fact that it will operate with existing Fortran debugging tools. A disadvantage of a library based approach is overhead introduced by the library. To alleviate the overhead we introduce a tool called GridWeaver that replaces the library calls with more efficient code. Existing libraries and tools for stencils have not focused on the class of semi-regular grids.

Current limitations of our approach include that it assumes that grid connectivity only differs along two dimensions and that halo size is one. Even with these limitations all of the stencils in CGPOP are expressible and all of the stencils except for one in SWM are expressible The abstractions could be relaxed to remove the first assumption without too much difficulty; however, we believe relaxing the second assumption will require more work due the fact that outgoing edges of subgrids often change directions. We intend our future work to focus on generalizing our abstractions to enable larger halos.

Acknowledgements

We would like to especially thank John Dennis and Ross Heikes for their help with the CGPOP and SWM proxy applications. The authors gratefully acknowledge the use of the ISTeC Cray at Colorado State University. This project is supported by a Department of Energy Early Career Grant DE-SC0003956.

8. REFERENCES

[1] Chombo: Mapped multiblock grids. https://commons.lbl.gov/display/chombo/Mapped+Multiblock+Grids.

[2] Sloccount tool website. http://www.dwheeler.com/sloccount/.

[3] MPAS: Model for prediction across scales. http://mpas.sourceforge.net/, December 2011.

[4] Spherical geodesic grids: A new approach to modeling the climate. http://kiwi.atmos.colostate.edu/BUGS/geodesic/, July 2012.

[5] Website: Design and testing of a global cloud resolving model. http://kiwi.atmos.colostate.edu/gcrm/, July 2012.

[6] M. Barad, P. Colella, D. T. Graves, T. J. Ligocki, D. Modiano, P. O. Schwartz, and B. V. S. and. EBChombo software package for cartesian grid, embedded boundary applications. Technical report, Lawrence Berkeley National Laboratory, February 2000.

[7] D. Brown, W. Henshaw, and D. Quinlan. Overture: An object-oriented framework for solving partial differential equations. In Y. Ishikawa, R. Oldehoeft, J. Reynders, and M. Tholburn, editors, *Scientific Computing in Object-Oriented Parallel Environments*, volume 1343 of *Lecture Notes in Computer Science*, pages 177–184. Springer Berlin Heidelberg, 1997.

[8] B. Chamberlain, D. Callahan, and H. Zima. Parallel programmability and the chapel language. *Int. J. High Perform. Comput. Appl.*, 21(3):291–312, Aug. 2007.

[9] B. L. Chamberlain, S. J. Deitz, D. Iten, and S.-E. Choi. User-defined distributions and layouts in chapel: philosophy and framework. In *Proceedings of the 2nd USENIX conference on Hot topics in parallelism*, HotPar'10, pages 12–12, Berkeley, CA, USA, 2010. USENIX Association.

[10] B. L. Chamberlain, S. eun Choi, S. J. Deitz, and L. Snyder. The high-level parallel language zpl improves productivity and performance. In *In Proceedings of the IEEE International Workshop on Productivity and Performance in High-End Computing*, 2004.

[11] M. Christen, O. Schenk, and H. Burkhart. Automatic code generation and tuning for stencil kernels on modern shared memory architectures. *Computer Science - Research and Development*, 26(3-4):205–210, Apr. 2011.

[12] M. Christen, O. Schenk, and H. Burkhart. Automatic code generation and tuning for stencil kernels on modern shared memory architectures. *Comput. Sci.*, 26:205–210, June 2011.

[13] Z. DeVito, N. Joubert, F. Palacios, S. Oakley, M. Medina, M. Barrientos, E. Elsen, F. Ham, A. Aiken, K. Duraisamy, E. Darve, J. Alonso, and P. Hanrahan. Liszt: a domain specific language for building portable mesh-based PDE solvers. In *Proceedings of 2011 International Conference for High Performance Computing, Networking, Storage and Analysis*, SC '11, pages 9:1—-9:12, New York, NY, USA, 2011. ACM.

[14] Z. DeVito, N. Joubert, F. Palacios, S. Oakley, M. Medina, M. Barrientos, E. Elsen, F. Ham, A. Aiken, K. Duraisamy, E. Darve, J. Alonso, and P. Hanrahan. Liszt: a domain specific language for building portable mesh-based pde solvers. In *Proceedings of 2011 International Conference for High Performance Computing, Networking, Storage and Analysis*, SC '11, pages 9:1–9:12, New York, NY, USA, 2011. ACM.

[15] M. B. Giles, G. R. Mudalige, Z. Sharif, G. Markall, and P. H. J. Kelly. Performance Analysis and Optimization of the OP2 Framework on Many-Core Architectures. *The Computer Journal*, 55(2):168–180, July 2011.

[16] T. Goodale, G. Allen, J. Lanfermann, Gerd Masso, T. Radke, E. Seidel, and J. Shalf. The Cactus Framework and Toolkit: Design and Applications. In *Proceedings of the 5th international conference on High performance computing for computational science*, pages 197—-227, 2003.

[17] R. Heikes and D. A. Randall. Numerical Integration of the Shallow-Water Equations on a Twisted Icosahedral Grid. Part II. A Detailed Description of the Grid and an Analysis of Numerical Accuracy. *Monthly Weather Review*, 123(6):1881–1887, 1995.

[18] C. Hill, C. DeLuca, M. Suarez, and A. Da Silva. The architecture of the earth system modeling framework. *Computing in Science & Engineering*, 6(1):18–28, Jan. 2004.

[19] P. Jones. Parallel Ocean Program (POP) user guide. Technical Report LACC 99-18, Los Alamos National Laboratory, March 2003.

[20] M. Joyner, B. L. Chamberlain, and S. J. Deitz. Iterators in chapel. In *Eleventh International Workshop on High-Level Parallel Programming Models and Supportive Environments (HIPS 2006)*, 2006.

[21] S. Kamil, C. Chan, S. Williams, L. Oliker, J. Shalf, M. Howison, and E. W. Bethel. A generalized framework for auto-tuning stencil computations. In *In Proceedings of the Cray User Group Conference*, 2009.

[22] G. Kiczales, J. Lamping, A. Mendhekar, C. Maeda, C. Lopes, J. marc Loingtier, and J. Irwin. Aspect-oriented programming. In *ECOOP*. SpringerVerlag, 1997.

[23] C. Koelbel, D. B. Loveman, R. S. Schreiber, L. S. J. Guy, and M. E. Zosel. *The High Performance Fortran Handbook.* MIT Press, September 1996.

[24] C.-k. Luk, B. C. Kuszmaul, and C. E. Leiserson. The Pochoir Stencil Compiler. *Artificial Intelligence*, 36:117–128, 2011.

[25] N. Maruyama, T. Nomura, K. Sato, and S. Matsuoka. Physis: an implicitly parallel programming model for stencil computations on large-scale gpu-accelerated supercomputers. In *Proceedings of 2011 International Conference for High Performance Computing, Networking, Storage and Analysis*, SC '11, pages 11:1–11:12, New York, NY, USA, 2011. ACM.

[26] R. J. Murray. Explicit Generation of Orthogonal Grids for Ocean Models. *Journal of Computational Physics*, 126(2):251–273, 1996.

[27] D. Quinlan. Rose: Compiler support for object-oriented frameworks. In *Proceedings of Conference on Parallel Compilers (CPC2000), Aussois, France*, volume 10 of *Parallel Processing Letters*. Springer Verlag, 2000.

[28] R. Sadourny. Conservative Finite-Difference Approximations of the Primitive Equations on Quasi-Uniform Spherical Grids. *Monthly Weather Review*, 100(2):136–144, Feb. 1972.

[29] R. D. Smith and S. Kortas. Curvilinear coordinates for global ocean models. Technical report, Los Alamos National Laboratory, LA-UR-95-1146, 1995.

[30] A. Stone, J. Dennis, and M. M. Strout. The cgpop miniapp, version 1.0. Technical Report Technical Report CS-11-103, Colorado State University, July 1 2011.

[31] H. Tomita, M. Tsugawa, M. Satoh, and K. Goto. Shallow Water Model on a Modified Icosahedral Geodesic Grid by Using Spring Dynamics. *Journal of Computational Physics*, 174(2):579–613, 2001.

[32] D. Unat, X. Cai, and S. B. Baden. Mint. In *Proceedings of the international conference on Supercomputing - ICS '11*, page 214, New York, New York, USA, 2011. ACM Press.

[33] Z. J. Wood, P. Schröder, D. Breen, and M. Desbrun. Semi-regular mesh extraction from volumes. In *Proceedings of the conference on Visualization '00*, VIS '00, pages 275–282, Los Alamitos, CA, USA, 2000. IEEE Computer Society Press.

A Stencil Compiler for Short-Vector SIMD Architectures

Tom Henretty
The Ohio State University
henretty@cse.ohio-state.edu

Richard Veras
Carnegie Mellon University
rveras@cmu.edu

Franz Franchetti
Carnegie Mellon University
franzf@ece.cmu.edu

Louis-Noël Pouchet
Univ. California, Los Angeles
pouchet@cs.ucla.edu

J. Ramanujam
Louisiana State University
jxr@ece.lsu.edu

P. Sadayappan
The Ohio State University
saday@cse.ohio-state.edu

ABSTRACT

Stencil computations are an integral component of applications in a number of scientific computing domains. Short-vector SIMD instruction sets are ubiquitous on modern processors and can be used to significantly increase the performance of stencil computations. Traditional approaches to optimizing stencils on these platforms have focused on either short-vector SIMD or data locality optimizations. In this paper, we propose a domain-specific language and compiler for stencil computations that allows specification of stencils in a concise manner and automates both locality and short-vector SIMD optimizations, along with effective utilization of multi-core parallelism. Loop transformations to enhance data locality and enable load-balanced parallelism are combined with a data layout transformation to effectively increase the performance of stencil computations. Performance increases are demonstrated for a number of stencils on several modern SIMD architectures.

Categories and Subject Descriptors

D.1.3 [**Programming Techniques**]: Concurrent Programming—*Parallel Programming*; D.3.4 [**Programming Languages**]: Processors—*Code Generation, Compilers*

Keywords

DSL, Multicore, SIMD, Split Tiling, Stencils

1. INTRODUCTION

There is increasing interest in developing domain-specific frameworks for high-performance scientific computing due to the diversity of current/emerging parallel architectures. In addition to the benefit of a DSL (Domain Specific Language) on user productivity, a significant advantage is that semantic properties derived from the high-level abstractions can be utilized to develop powerful specialized compiler transformations that can be tailored to the characteristics of different architectural platforms. Using the Stencil Domain Specific Language (SDSL) [11], this paper describes a set of compiler transformations that are needed to generate efficient code for multicore processors with short-vector SIMD ISAs such as SSE, AVX, VSX, LRBNi etc.

Stencil computations involve arithmetic operations on physically contiguous data elements, e.g., c0*(A[i-1]+A[i]+A[i+1]). Since vector operations with ISAs like SSE require the loading of physically contiguous data elements from memory into vector registers and the execution of identical and independent operations on the components of vector registers, stencil computations pose challenges to efficient implementation on these architectures, requiring the use of redundant and unaligned loads of data elements from memory into different slots in different vector registers. We [12] had previously addressed this issue through a *dimension-lifting-transpose (DLT)* data layout transformation. However, only sequential execution was addressed. Further, the approach was only evaluated on data sets that fit in L1 cache. Tiling over spatial and the time dimensions is essential in conjunction with DLT for high performance on large data sets. However, as elaborated in detail in the next section, standard time-tiling of stencil codes via skewing introduces inter-tile dependences that are incompatible with the form of vector parallelism used by the DLT transformation. In this paper, we develop an integrated approach to perform tiling in conjunction with DLT transformation to generate efficient parallel code for stencil computations over large data sets on shared memory multiprocessors. We compare performance with code generated by the Pochoir stencil compiler [18] and Pluto [2, 4] for several benchmarks on multiple target multicore processors, demonstrating strong performance benefits for 1D and 2D stencils. The paper makes the following contributions:

- It presents a stencil DSL compiler that integrates data layout transformation for short-vector SIMD ISAs with load-balanced tiled parallel execution for multi-statement stencils.
- It demonstrates significant performance improvement on several multi-core platforms for a number of benchmarks, over Intel's ICC compiler and state-of-the-art research compilers like Pochoir and Pluto.

The paper is organized as follows. In Sec. 2 we use an illustrative example to explain the main problem to be addressed in integrating DLT with tiling. Sec. 3.1 describes the stencil DSL and Sec. 3.4 provides a high-level overview of the compiler algorithms developed. Sections 4 and 5 provide details of the compiler algorithms. Experimental results are presented in Sec. 6 and related work is covered in Sec. 7.

2. PROBLEM DESCRIPTION

In this section we first provide some background on the DLT data layout transformation of Henretty et al. [12] that was developed to overcome the fundamental data access inefficiency on current

ICS'13, June 10–14, 2013, Eugene, Oregon, USA.

short-vector SIMD architectures with stencil computations. We then describe why standard time-tiling is infeasible in conjunction with the DLT transformation and a different form of tiling – split-tiling – can be used effectively in conjunction with DLT.

2.1 Overview of DLT Transformation

Fig. 1 illustrates the DLT transformation for a one-dimensional vector of 24 elements for an ISA with a vector length of 4. Whereas B[0:3] form an aligned vector before transformation, after the DLT transformation, B[0], B[6], B[12], and B[18] form the first four elements Bdlt[0:3] in the transformed layout. The next four contiguous elements Bdlt[4:7] in the transformed layout correspond to B[1], B[7], B[13], and B[19], etc. Thus the sum of aligned vectors, Bdlt[0:3]+Bdlt[4:7]+Bdlt[8:11], computes $< B[0]+B[1]+B[2], B[6]+B[7]+B[8], B[12]+B[13]+B[14], B[18]+B[19]+B[20] >$. Thus the fundamental problem with vectorized addition of contiguously located elements in memory is overcome in the transformed layout where operands that need to be combined are located in the same slot of different vectors rather than in different slots of the same vector.

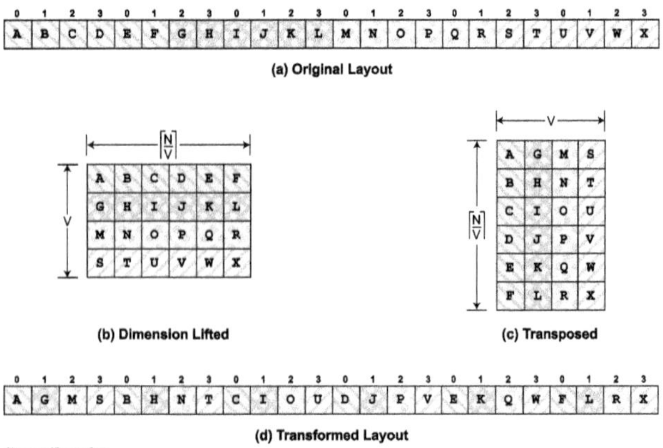

Stencil code:

```
for (i = 1; i < 24; ++i)
  A[i] = B[i-1]+B[i]+B[i+1];
```

Figure 1: Data layout transformation for SIMD vector length of 4

2.2 Standard Tiling and DLT Transformation

We next use a Jacobi 1D stencil example to explain the problem with the use of standard time-tiling in conjunction with DLT layout transformation. Although the input to our stencil compiler uses a special DSL language (described in Sec. 3.1), we use standard loop notation in C to motivate the problem since this lower-level view makes it easier to discuss issues pertaining to loop fusion and time-tiling when compiling general multi-statement stencils for high performance – something that to the best of our knowledge is not addressed by other stencil compilers such as PATUS [5] and Pochoir [18].

Fig. 2(a) shows code for a 1D Jacobi 3-point stencil with a sequence of two spatial loops within an outer time loop, where S1 performs the stencil computation over the spatial domain and S2 copies the output array into the input array for use in the next time step. In order to enhance data locality, time-tiling may be employed, but will first require some transformations in order to create atomic tiles that compute forward for several time steps over a subset of the spatial domain that is small enough to fit within cache. Fig. 2(b) shows a fused form that creates a unified 2D iteration

```
for (t=0; t<T; t++) {
  for (i=1; i<N-1; i++) {
    B[i] = 0.33*(A[i-1] + A[i] + A[i+1]); // S1
  for (i=1; i<N-1; i++)
    A[i] = B[i]; // S2
}
```

(a) Unfused

```
for (t=0; t<T; t++) {
  B[1]=0.33*(A[0]+A[1]+A[2]);
  for (i=2; i<N-1; i++) {
    B[i] = 0.33*(A[i-1] + A[i] + A[i+1]);
    A[i-1] = B[i-1];
  }
  A[N-1] = B[N-1];
}
```

(b) Fused

Figure 2: Jacobi 1D stencil

space with a statement body including both S1 and S2 (along with peeling of an iteration at the boundaries of the *i* loop).

Further skewing of this unified iteration space will be required to create valid "rectangular" tiles, which can equivalently be viewed as parallelogram-shaped tiles in an unskewed iteration space, as shown in Fig. 3(a). Because of the shape of valid tiles (they cannot be rectangular in an unskewed iteration space due to forward and backward dependences along the spatial dimension), there are inter-tile dependences between adjacent tiles along both the time and spatial dimensions. This inter-tile dependence along the spatial dimension makes it infeasible to use DLT because DLT causes spatially separated data elements (for example, B[0], B[6], B[12], B[18] in Fig. (1)) to be gathered together in a single vector and therefore must be operated upon concurrently. The circled value in each tile of Fig. 3(a) represents the logical time at which the tile can be executed, such that all tiles it depends on have been previously computed.

Fig. 3(b) shows a different form of tiling – split-tiles. Here, upright and inverted tiles alternate and the inter-tile dependences are only from an upright tile to its two neighboring inverted tiles. As a result, concurrent execution of all upright tiles over a given time range is feasible, followed by concurrent execution of the inverted tiles over the same time range. Again, the circled values within the tiles indicate the sequence of execution of the tiles, where tiles with the same sequence number can be executed concurrently. With such a tiling strategy, it is now feasible to use DLT, as long as all data elements grouped into each vector are all within upright tiles or all within inverted tiles. Further, unlike execution required with standard tiling, the schedule for parallel tile execution with split-tiles is fully load balanced and does not have a sequential start and gradual build up of inter-tile parallelism as required for wavefront-parallel standard tiling.

In the next section, we provide a description of the stencil DSL and a high-level overview of the compiler algorithm for code generation.

3. OVERVIEW OF APPROACH

Before delving into the details of the algorithms, in this section we first describe the stencil DSL we translate. Next, we provide overviews of two methods used to tile SDSL codes, nested and hybrid split-tiling. Finally, a high-level overview of the approach to

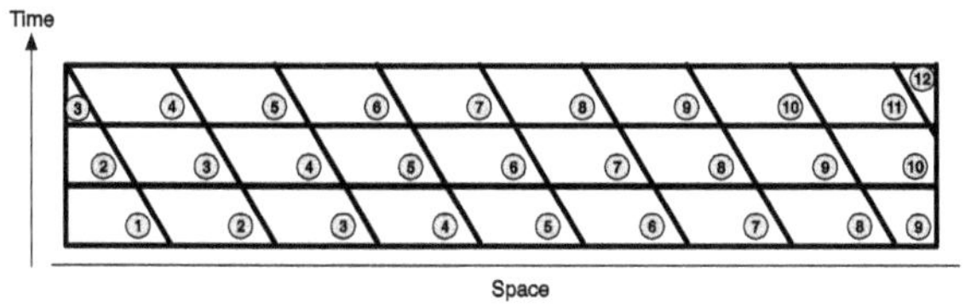

(a) Standard Tiling

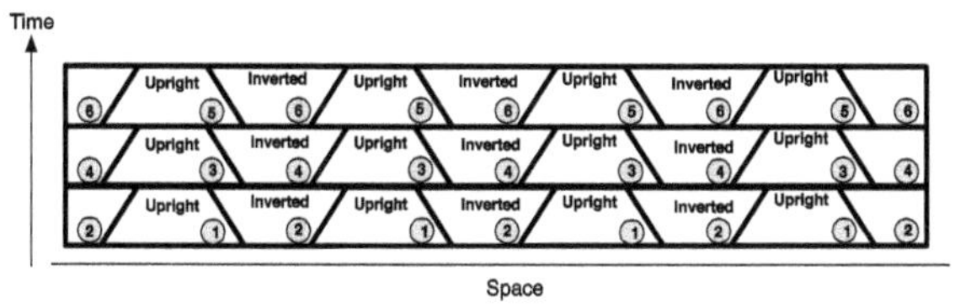

(b) Split-Tiling

Figure 3: Tiled iteration space for 1D space, 1D time

transform an input SDSL program into an semantically equivalent split-tiled DLT program is provided.

3.1 SDSL – Stencil Domain Specific Language

A stencil computation can be summarized as one or more functions being identically applied to points on a regular grid, where the values of some groups of neighboring elements are used for each function, and this process is repeated multiple times. The Stencil Domain Specific Language (SDSL) enables the concise description of stencil computations and is briefly described in the following sections.

3.1.1 *Program Description*

The computation shown in Fig. 4 is a standard Jacobi 2D computation, which averages the value of the 5 neighboring points (up, down, left, right, and center) to compute the new value of the center point.

```
grid g[dim1][dim0];
double griddata a on g at 0,1;

iterate 100 {
  stencil five_pt {
    [1:dim1-2][1:dim0-2] : [1]a[0][0] =
                     0.2*([0]a[-1][0]+
           [0]a[0][-1]+[0]a[ 0][0]+[0]a[0][1]+
                          [0]a[ 1][0]);
  }
}
```

Figure 4: A simple Jacobi 2D example in SDSL

Structural Mesh (`grid`). The first line of Fig. 4 defines `g`, the grid where stencil computations may be defined. It is an n-dimensional Cartesian coordinate space (a subset of $\mathbb{Z}^2$ here), and the computations operate on a subset of this grid. We note that grid size can be a parameter, that is a program constant whose value is not known at compile-time.

Data Elements (`griddata`). The second line of Fig. 4 defines `a`, a double precision data field with the same structure as grid `g`. This field holds data values used in stencil functions, and multiple fields may be defined over a grid. The grid `g` is used to define the size of `a` and sets limits on field indices. The `at` clause specifies that there should be two copies of the field, one associated with the current outermost loop iteration and another at the next outermost loop iteration.

Computation (`iterate` *and* `stencil`). The last eight lines of Fig. 4 define a stencil computation. Three key concepts are defined: (1) outer loop trip count, (2) subgrid(s) over which to apply a stencil function and (3) stencil function(s).

The outer loop trip count is defined in the `iterate` construct, and is 100 in the example. The stencil construct is given a unique identifier, `five_pt`, and contains the definition of a subgrid over which to apply the stencil function definition that follows. In the example the subdomain `[1:dim1-2][1:dim0-2]` defines a subset of the grid `g` that contains all elements except a single cell border on all four sides.

A stencil function is defined after the subdomain definition. This function averages the current point and four of its neighbors in `a` at the current timestep and places the resluts in `a` at the next timestep. References to `griddata` consist of the offset from the current iteration in brackets, followed by the the name of the referenced field, followed by offsets from the current point in each spatial dimension in brackets.

3.1.2 *General Form of an SDSL Program*

In general, an SDSL program contains one `grid`, one or more `griddata`, one `iterate`, and one or more `stencil` definitions, where each `stencil` may define one or more subdomains and the stencil functions that operate upon them.

The abstract form of an SDSL program is represented in Fig. 5. The program is constrained to be a collection of M K-dimensional grid data and N stencils, with each stencil applying some stencil function f on one or more grid data. Each stencil function is executed on a rectangular subdomain $Z \subset \mathbb{Z}^K | 0 \leq lb_Z^k, ub_Z^k < dim_k \forall k \in \{1..K\}$. While an SDSL program may have multiple subdomains and stencil functions defined inside one `stencil`, the abstract version in Fig. 5 is semantically equivalent.

```
grid g[dimK]...[dim1];

griddata g1,g2...,gM on g;

iterate T {
  stencil s1 {
    [lb_s1_K:ub_s1_K]...[lb_s1_1:ub_s1_1] : f1(...);
  }
  stencil s2 {
    [lb_s2_K:ub_s2_K]...[lb_s2_1:ub_s2_1] : f2(...);
  }
  ...
  stencil sN {
    [lb_sN_K:ub_sN_K]...[lb_sN_1:ub_sN_1] : fN(...);
  }
}
```

Figure 5: General form of an SDSL program

SDSL programs are parallelized and optimized for data locality using nested and hybrid split-tiling, described in the next two sections.

3.2 Nested Split-Tiling

In nested split-tiling, a d-dimensional loop spatial loop nest is recursively split-tiled along each dimension. The outermost spatial loop at level d is split-tiled, producing a loop over upright tiles and a loop over inverted tiles. Inside each of these loops, loop level

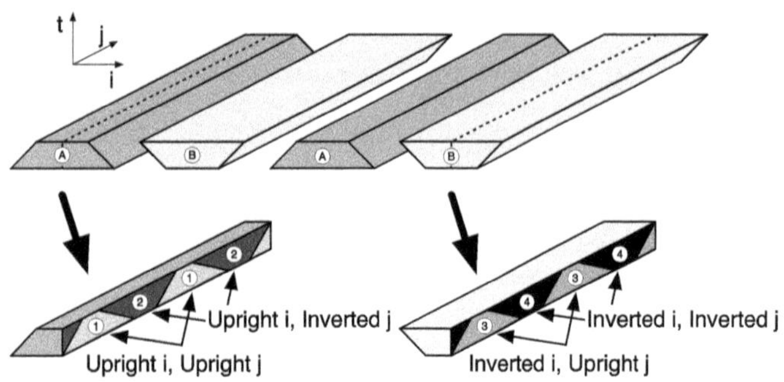


```
for tt
  parfor ii // (A) Upright i
    parfor jj // (1) Upright j
      for t { for i { for j {}}};
    barrier();
    parfor jj // (2) Inverted j
      for t { for i { for j {}}};
    barrier();
  parfor ii // (B) Upright j
    parfor jj // (3) Upright j
      for t { for i { for j {}}};
    barrier();
    parfor jj // (4) Inverted j
      for t { for i { for j {}}};
    barrier();
```

(a) 2D nested split-tiling

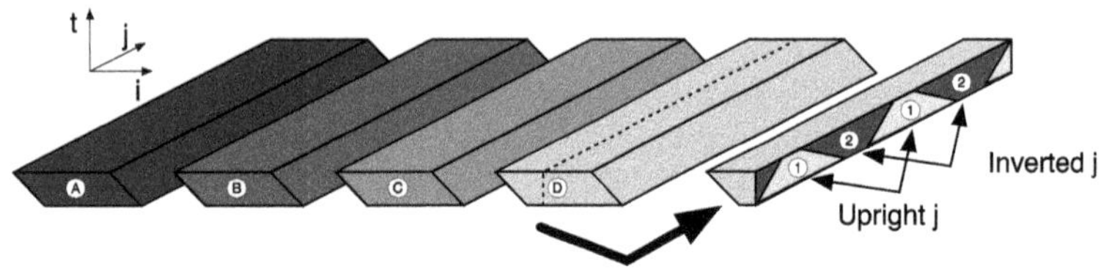


```
for tt
  for ii // (A) (B) (C) (D) Traditional i
    parfor jj // (1) Upright j
      for t { for i { for j {}}};
    barrier();
    parfor jj // (2) Inverted j
      for t { for i { for j {}}};
    barrier();
```

(b) 2D hybrid split-tiling

Figure 6: 2D nested and hybrid split-tiling.

$d-1$ is split-tiled, giving four tile loop nests. Split-tiling is performed recursively in each new loop nest until the base loop level 1 is reached and there are 2^d total loop nests corresponding to all possible combinations of upright and inverted tiles on each dimension. Nested split-tiling of a 2D code is illustrated in Fig. 6(a).

Fig. 6(a) depicts, on the left, a series of upright ('A') and inverted ('B') tiles in the i dimension. All upright 'A' tiles may be executed concurrently, followed by all inverted 'B' tiles. Below these tiles are representative cross-sections of an upright and inverted tile showing the nested split-tiles in the j dimension. These tiles are labeled such that all tiles with the same number, ('1', '2', '3', or '4') may be executed concurrently, and tiles with a lower number must be executed before tiles with a higher number.

The pseudocode in Fig. 6(a) shows the loop nests responsible for producing the diagram. Nested inside the sequential tt loop are two parallel ii loops corresponding to the 'A' and 'B' tiles shown in the diagram. Nested inside the 'A' loop are parallel jj upright ('1') and inverted ('2') tile loops corresponding to the tiles shown in the left cross-section, Similarly, the 'B' loop contains nested parallel '3' and '4' loops corresponding to the right cross-section. A barrier follows each jj tile loop to enforce tile execution order and ensure that no dependences are violated.

Nested split-tiling enables parallelization of all spatial loop nests in a stencil, however (1) it imposes a lower bound on the size of upright tiles for a given time tile size, or equivalently, (2) it imposes an upper bound on the time tile size given an upright tile's size.

In nested split-tiling, upright tiles must be sized such that they retain their characteristic trapezoidal shape, as in Fig. 3(b). If the base of the upright tile is not large enough for a given time tile size, the sloping lines will eventually form a tip. At this point tile execution cannot extend any further in time.

Given an upright tile with a base size of T_U^d, maximum absolute value of slopes in d s_{max}^d, maximum offset of all statements o_{max}^d, and time tile size T_T the following constraint can be stated:
$T_U^d \geq 2 * T_T * s_{max}^d + 2 * o_{max}^d$

For higher dimensional problems, the lower bound on upright tile size causes tiles to overflow cache for even small time tile sizes. Consider a 3-dimensional stencil with, for all dimensions, maximum slope $s_{max}^d = 2$, maximum offset $o_{max}^d = 0$, and $T_T = 8$. This requires $T_U^d \geq 32$. For an upright tile in all dimensions, including the innermost vector dimension, this is at least 32K vector elements, enough to overflow L1 and L2 cache on most modern architectures.

3.3 Hybrid Split-Tiling

We overcome the tile size constraints of nested split-tiling with a hybrid of standard tiling on the outermost space loops and split-tiling on the inner loops. Hybrid split-tiling for a 2D stencil is illustrated in Fig. 6(b). The pseudocode contains a single ii loop nested in the tt loop which corresponds to the four traditional i dimension tiles 'A', 'B', 'C', and 'D' shown in the diagram. These tiles must be executed in sequence from 'A'–'D'. Nested inside the ii loop is the split-tiled jj loop which has the same upright / inverted tile structure as the split-tiled inner loops described in the previous section.

Standard tiling does not impose any constraint on tile sizes along spatial dimensions as a function of the time tile size. Thus, standard tiles may be compacted to a much smaller size to compensate for the larger tile sizes required by split-tiled dimensions. This allows for a substantially reduced multidimensional tile footprint. In the example at the end of Sec. 3.2, we may reduce the tile size of the outermost dimension to 2, thereby reducing the the tile size to 2K elements. Since inner loops are split-tiled, we retain adequate parallelism.

3.4 Overview of the Optimization Algorithm

In order to perform combined data layout transformations for SIMD vectorization with parallel tiling for data locality, we use a multi-stage process to integrate dimension-lift-and-transpose (DLT) with multi-level split-tiling. The overall transformation flow is summarized in Fig. 7.

```
Input
  P: input SDSL program
  dsplit: number of dimensions to split-tile
Output
  O: optimized C program

  O ← performDLT(P)
  (α⃗,β⃗,o⃗_L,u⃗) ← backslice(P)
  O ← performSplitTiling(O, α⃗, β⃗, o⃗_L, u⃗, dsplit)
  O ← finalizeTiling(O, α⃗, β⃗, o⃗_L, u⃗, dsplit)
  return O
```

Figure 7: Overview algorithm

Function `performDLT` applies DLT on all inner-most vectorizable loops, following the method presented in Henretty et al. [12]. We remark that programs that can be modeled in SDSL all have vectorizable inner-loops, so that DLT can be applied for all stencil functions. Details of this function are provided later in Sec. 5. Function `backslice` performs backslicing analysis to compute the exact shape of the split-tiles (that is, computing for each stencil function the offsets and slopes of a split-tile, to be translated on the entire spatial domain). This is detailed in Section 4. Function `performSplitTiling` uses the split-tile shape information computed to generate split-tile code for the *d* split inner spatial dimensions. This is detailed in Section 5. Finally, function `finalizeTiling`completes code generation, by applying standard tiling on the remaining dimensions, if any. The integration as well as the complete algorithm is discussed in Section 5.

4. BACKSLICING ANALYSIS

Split-tiling requires the computation of sets of iteration space points that can be executed atomically – that is a valid tiling – while preserving parallelism between tiles of the same category (i.e., upright tiles have to be parallel with each other). In order to compute the *shape* of the split-tile that satisfies those properties, we first highlight the main ideas using a Jacobi 1D stencil, before describing the general algorithm for higher dimensional stencils with an arbitrary number of stencil functions.

4.1 Split-Tiling Jacobi 1D

We illustrate the main ideas behind split-tiling using a Jacobi 1D example. Fig. 8 shows the corresponding input SDSL program.

```
grid g[1000];
double griddata a on g at 0,1;

iterate 100 {
  stencil f1 {
    [1:998] : [1]a[0] =
          0.33*([0]a[-1]+[0]a[0]+[0]a[1]);
  }
}
```

Figure 8: A simple Jacobi 1D example in SDSL

In the SDSL intermediate representation, an explicit copy of the field `a1` into the field `a0` is added after each time iteration, leading to a program equivalent to the C code shown in Fig. 9.

Statement `f1` performs the actual stencil computation, producing the `a1` field, statement `f2` copies the `a1` field to the `a0` field. This sequence is repeated 100 times.

```
for (t = 0; t < 100; t++) {
  for (i = 1; i <= 998; i++) {
    f1: a1[i] = 0.33*(a0[i-1] + a0[i] + a0[i+1]);
  }
  for (i = 0; i <= 999; i++) {
    f2: a0[i] = a1[i];
  }
}
```

Figure 9: Jacobi 1D example with explicit copy

4.1.1 *Examining an Upright Tile*

Let us consider the top segment of an upright tile for `f2`, over a span $[P,Q]$, that corresponds to the iterations of `f2` performed at time T. In order to correctly compute those iterations, we need the values $[P-1,Q+1]$ of `a1` that were computed by executing `f1` on the segment $[P-1,Q+1]$ time T, which in turn depends on the values of `a0` over $[P-2,Q+2]$ copied by `f1` at time $T-1$. Based on data dependences between the statements `f1` and `f2`, we can compute precisely which iterations must have been computed at previous time steps for each of the statements in order to compute the segment $[P,Q]$ of `f2` at time step T. This is illustrated in Fig. 10.

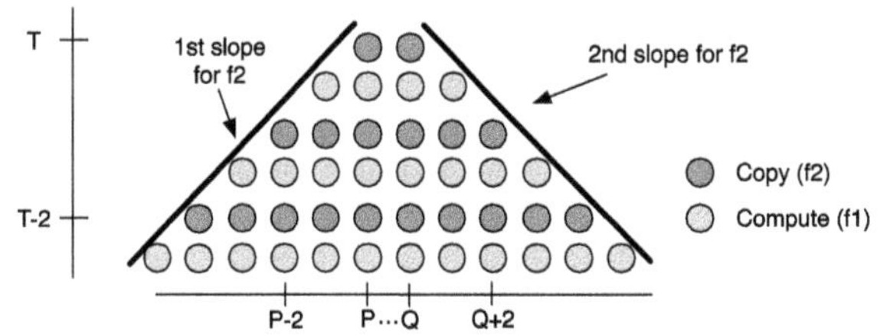

Figure 10: Upright split-tile for Jacobi 1D

Fig. 10 shows the set of preceding iterations, for both `f1` and `f2`, that must be computed in order to obtain the segment $[P,Q]$ at time T. We show here a time tile size of 3, that is, we build a split-tile that computes over three time steps.

The dependences are analyzed from the SDSL representation. Due to the restriction on stencil shapes to be constant integer offsets (e.g., -1, 2, etc.), the dependences are simple integer relations between time and the access functions. In the next sections we show how data dependences are used to construct a *dependence summary graph* and formulate validity constraints on the split-tiles for the slopes and statement offsets.

4.1.2 *Building the Dependence Summary Graph*

We begin by creating the dependence summary graph (DSG), a multigraph with vertices for each stencil function and edges that summarize flow and anti dependence information between stencil functions. In general, a vector of 2*d+1 components is used to model data dependence in an imperfectly nested loop with maximum loop depth d, with d components representing the distances along the loops, and the other d+1 components being used to mark the relative textual ordering within a loop level. However, the structure of an SDSL program always has the form of an outer time loop surrounding a sequence of perfectly nested loops. For generation of valid split-tiled code, the exact textual position of a sequence of statements is not significant, but only whether a dependence is from a textually preceding or succeeding statement within the time loop. Further, when several dependences exist between a pair of statements due to multiple array read references it is only necessary to identify the maximal spatial extent of dependences along the different directions at each time step. Therefore, instead of using the standard general representation of dependence vectors, we separate out the distance vector component along the time (outermost) dimension and the components along the spatial dimensions.

For the Jacobi 1D example, we have the following dependences:

$$\mathcal{D}_{\text{f1}\rightarrow\text{f2}} = \begin{cases} \text{flow: f1}(t,i) & \rightarrow & \text{f2}(t,i) \\ \text{anti: f1}(t,i) & \rightarrow & \text{f2}(t,i-1) \\ \text{anti: f1}(t,i) & \rightarrow & \text{f2}(t,i) \\ \text{anti: f1}(t,i) & \rightarrow & \text{f2}(t,i+1) \end{cases}$$

$$\mathcal{D}_{\text{f2}\rightarrow\text{f1}} = \begin{cases} \text{flow: f2}(t,i) & \rightarrow & \text{f1}(t+1,i-1) \\ \text{flow: f2}(t,i) & \rightarrow & \text{f1}(t+1,i) \\ \text{flow: f2}(t,i) & \rightarrow & \text{f1}(t+1,i+1) \\ \text{anti: f2}(t,i) & \rightarrow & \text{f1}(t+1,i) \end{cases}$$

The spatial components of the dependence vectors between dependent statements are computed by subtracting the target iteration from the source iteration, yielding the following vectors:

$$d_{\text{f1}\rightarrow\text{f2}} = \begin{cases} \delta_T = 0, \delta_i = <0> \\ \delta_T = 0, \delta_i = <-1> \\ \delta_T = 0, \delta_i = <0> \\ \delta_T = 0, \delta_i = <1> \end{cases} \qquad d_{\text{f2}\rightarrow\text{f1}} = \begin{cases} \delta_T = 1, \delta_i = <-1> \\ \delta_T = 1, \delta_i = <0> \\ \delta_T = 1, \delta_i = <1> \\ \delta_T = 1, \delta_i = <0> \end{cases}$$

The spatial components of the distance vectors are then coalesced into a tuple for each dependence such that the coalesced tuple $C^{fs\rightarrow ft} = <\delta_L, \delta_U>$ where δ_L is the maximum spatial distance and δ_U is the minimum spatial distance between two dependent statements fs and ft. For the Jacobi 1D example the tuples for each dependence are identical, $C^{\text{f1}\rightarrow\text{f2}} = C^{\text{f2}\rightarrow\text{f1}} = <1,-1>$. These tuples are used to label edges in the DSG, along with a separate label for the time distance δ_T. Assembling the coalesced tuples, time distances, dependences, and statements leads to the DSG shown in Fig. 11 for the Jacobi 1D example.

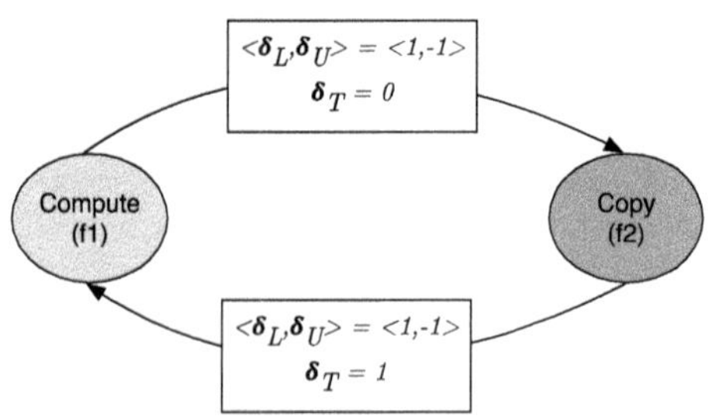

Figure 11: Dependence Summary Graph (DSG) for Jacobi 1D

This DSG is subsequently used in Sec. 4.1.3 to build validity constraints for split-tiles and in Sec. 4.1.4 to compute slopes and statement offsets.

4.1.3 Building Validity Constraints

We seek to constrain the legal values of tile slope and statement offsets by assembling a system of linear inequalities based upon the DSG and the loop bounds of the split-tiled code we will generate. Pseudocode for the loop nests of Jacobi 1D upright tile is shown in Fig. 12. Informally, the validity constraints state that, for any pair of dependent statements, given a region over which the target

```
for (tt = ...)
  for (ii = ...)
    for (t = 0; t < T_T; t++)
      for (i = ii + o_L^f1 + α*t; i ≤ ii + T_U + o_U^f1 + β*t; i++)
        f1: a1[i] = 0.33*(a0[i-1] + a0[i] + a0[i+1]);
      end for
      for (i = ii + o_L^f2 + α*t; i ≤ ii + T_U + o_U^f2 + β*t; i++)
        f2: a0[i] = a1[i];
      end for
    end for
  end for
end for
```

Figure 12: Loop nests for Jacobi 1D upright tile. Time tile size is T_T; upright space tile size is T_U. Offsets from lower bound are o_L^{f1} and o_L^{f2}; offsets from upper bound are o_U^{f1} and o_U^{f2}. Slope of lower bound is α; slope of upper bound is β.

statement is executed, the source statement will be executed over a region that is, *at minimum*, large enough to satisfy the dependence.

From the DSG, we note that to compute statement `f2` over some range $[A,B]$ at timestep T we require that statement `f1` be executed over the range $[A-1, B-(-1)]$ at timestep T. Similarly, to compute statement `f1` over some range $[C,D]$ at timestep T we require that statement `f1` be executed over the range $[C-1, D-(-1)]$ at timestep $T-1$.

Combining the dependence information from the DSG with the loop bounds of Fig. 12 gives us validity constraints on values the loop bounds may take, and results in the following system of inequalities for lower bounds:

$$\begin{aligned} ii + o_L^{\text{f1}} + \alpha * t &\leq ii + o_L^{\text{f2}} + \alpha * t - 1 \\ ii + o_L^{\text{f2}} + \alpha * (t-1) &\leq ii + o_L^{\text{f1}} + \alpha * t - 1 \end{aligned}$$

The following system constrains the upper bounds:

$$\begin{aligned} ii + T_U + o_U^{\text{f1}} + \beta * t &\geq ii + T_U + o_U^{\text{f2}} + \beta * t + 1 \\ ii + T_U + o_U^{\text{f2}} + \beta * (t-1) &\geq ii + T_U + o_U^{\text{f1}} + \beta * t + 1 \end{aligned}$$

Simplifying and rearranging these systems of inequalities yields the following system of difference constraints for lower bounds:

$$\begin{aligned} o_L^{\text{f1}} - o_L^{\text{f2}} &\leq -1 \\ o_L^{\text{f2}} - o_L^{\text{f1}} &\leq \alpha - 1; \end{aligned}$$

the corresponding constraints for upper bounds are shown below:

$$\begin{aligned} o_U^{\text{f2}} - o_U^{\text{f1}} &\leq -1 \\ o_U^{\text{f1}} - o_U^{\text{f2}} &\leq -\beta - 1. \end{aligned}$$

These systems are used in Sec. 4.1.4 to compute valid offsets for all statements.

4.1.4 Computing Slopes and Offsets

To determine legal values for slopes α and β we compute, respectively, maximum and minimum cycle ratios [1,7] on the DSG. A cycle ratio $\rho_L(C)$ on the DSG is computed by finding a cycle C, summing δ_L values over the cycle, and dividing by the sum of δ_T values. A cycle ratio $\rho_U(C)$ is calculated in a similar fashion with δ_U values. We set $\alpha = max(\rho_L(C))$ and $\beta = min(\rho_U(C))$ for all cycles C in the DSG.

We examine the only cycle in our example DSG, C_0, between `f1` and `f2`. The DSG tells us that computing `f1` on some interval $[A,B]$ at time T allows us to compute `f2` on the interval $[A + \delta_L^{f1\rightarrow f2}, B + \delta_U^{f1\rightarrow f2}]$ at time $T + \delta_T^{f1\rightarrow f2}$ without violating any dependences. Continuing along the cycle, computing `f2` on the interval $[A+\delta_L^{f1\to f2}, B+\delta_U^{f1\to f2}]$ at time $T+\delta_T^{f1\to f2}$ allows us to compute `f1` on the interval $[A+\delta_L^{f1\to f2}+\delta_L^{f2\to f1}, B+\delta_U^{f1\to f2}+\delta_U^{f2\to f1}]$ at time $T+\delta_T^{f1\to f2}+\delta_T^{f2\to f1}$.

Substituting in known values for the various δ variables shows us that computing `f1` over the interval $[A,B]$ at time T allows us to compute `f1` over the interval $[A+2, B-2]$ at time $T+1$. Thus, we see a slope of 2 on the lower bound and a slope of -2 on the upper bound.

Equivalently, summing δ_L values and dividing by the sum of δ_T values gives us $\rho_L(C_0)=2$; a similar calculation gives us $\rho_U(C_0)=-2$. Since there is only one cycle in the DSG, these values are $max(\rho_L(C))$ and $\min(\rho_U(C))$, and we set $\alpha = max(\rho_L(C)) = 2$ and $\beta = \min(\rho_U(C)) = -2$.

These values for α and β are substituted into the systems of difference constraints, and a solution to each of these systems is obtained using the Bellman-Ford algorithm [1, 6]. For the Jacobi 1D example we obtain $o_L^{f1} = -1$, $o_U^{f1} = 1$, and $o_L^{f2} = o_U^{f2} = 0$.

4.2 General Method

Our general algorithm closely follows the principles we have explained for Jacobi 1D. Since stencils may be multidimensional slopes and offsets are separately computed for each dimension. Further, different stencil functions may apply to different subdomains, which may be disjoint, overlapping, or identical. Because of this we conservatively assume all stencil functions are executed at all points in the problem domain when calculating dependences. This is an over-approximation of data dependences and has no impact on the final correctness of the generated code.

We present in Fig. 13 a general algorithm for computing slopes and offsets for a given input program. This algorithm produces lower/upper slope vectors with one slope per dimension, and lower/upper offset vectors with one offset per stencil statement.

```
Input
  P: input SDSL program
Output
  (α⃗, β⃗, o⃗_L, o⃗_U): Vectors of slopes alpha, beta.
                   Vectors of lower and upper offsets in each
                   spatial dimension for each stencil statement

  D ← calculateDependences(P)
  s ← calculateDependenceDistances(D)
  DSG ← buildDSG(s,P)
  foreach dimension d of P do
     α_d ← computeMaxCycleRatio(DSG,d)
     β_d ← computeMinCycleRatio(DSG,d)
     α⃗[d] ← α_d
     β⃗[d] ← β_d
     (v⃗_L,v⃗_U) ← buildValidityConstraints(DSG,α_d,β_d)
     o⃗_L[d] ← solveForOffsets(v⃗_L)
     o⃗_U[d] ← solveForOffsets(v⃗_U)
  end do
  return (α⃗, β⃗, o⃗_L, o⃗_U)
```

Figure 13: Algorithm `backslice`

The algorithm in Fig. 13 takes an arbitrary SDSL program as input. Dependence analysis is performed on this program to determine all flow and anti dependences, and dependence distance vectors are calculated. The dependence distance vectors are used to build the DSG, where each vertex is an SDSL statement and each edge is labeled with a time distance. Edges are also labeled with coalesced distances, computed for each spatial dimension as in Sec. 4.1.2 and placed in vectors $(\vec{\delta_L}, \vec{\delta_U})$.

After the DSG is built, slopes and offsets are computed along each dimension d. For each dimension of the DSG we compute α and β using maximum and minimum cycle ratios. The α_d and β_d values are then added to $\vec{\alpha}$ and $\vec{\beta}$ as the slopes for d. Once the slopes have been computed for a dimension, validity constraints are constructed as shown in Sec. 4.1.3. Once the slopes and validity constraints are known for a given dimension, `solveForOffsets()` rearranges the validity constraints into a system of differences and solves for offset values using the Bellman-Ford algorithm. Offsets for each statement in the current dimension are appended to the offset vectors. This process is repeated until slopes and offsets have been computed for all dimensions.

4.3 Proof of Correctness

Upright Tiles: The validity constraints guarantee that no dependences in an upright tile will be violated. In this section we prove that lower bound slopes calculated with the maximum cycle ratio always lead to a system of constraints that has a solution; the proof for the upper bound and minimum cycle ratio is identical.

A system of difference constraints not solvable by the Bellman-Ford algorithm would contain a negative weight cycle. We show that this is not possible.

We begin by constructing a graph isomorphic to the DSG where each vertex is a statement and each directed edge is labeled with its corresponding validity constraint for the lower bound v_L^e on some dimension d.

All validity constraints take one of the following forms:

$$o^s \le o^t - \delta_e \quad \Rightarrow \quad o^s - o^t \le -\delta_e \tag{1}$$

$$o^s \le o^t - \delta_e + \alpha \quad \Rightarrow \quad o^s - o^t \le -\delta_e + \alpha \tag{2}$$

In (1) the dependence associated with the constraint has source and target statements at the same timestep; in (2) the statements are 1 timestep apart. The unknown source statement offset is o^s, the unknown target statement offset is o^t, the dependence distance/edge weight is δ_e, and α is the unknown slope.

We next show that any cycle of length k on this graph restricts the possible values of α to be of the following form:

$$\alpha \ge \frac{1}{t}\sum_{i=1}^{k} \delta_i. \tag{3}$$

Note that the maximum cycle ratio simply maximizes α subject to the constraint in (3). In (3), δ_i is the weight of an edge in the cycle and t is the number of edges where source and target are separated by 1 timestep. Every vertex n in the cycle is entered through an edge f and exited through an edge g. On edge e, vertex n is the target of the dependence; on edge g, vertex n is the source of the dependence. Summing validity constraints $v_L^f + v_L^g$ eliminates the offset o^n. The accumulated sum $\sum_{i=1}^{k} v_L^i$ eliminates all offsets and leaves $0 \ge \sum_{i=1}^{k} \delta_i - t * \alpha$, which is equivalent to (3).

We now show that a negative weight cycle in the graph used by the Bellman-Ford algorithm to solve the system of difference constraints requires a value of α that violates (3).

All constraints in the system of differences we are solving take one of two forms, Equation 1 or Equation 2. The graph used in Bellman-Ford, after removing the start vertex and zero-weight edges emanating from it, is isomorphic to the DSG and the validity constraint graph described above. Each vertex is a statement offset, and each edge is weighted by the difference between the source and the target offset. The weight of any length k cycle is shown in (4).

$$\sum_{i=1}^{k} -\delta_i + t * \alpha \tag{4}$$

Assume there is a negative weight cycle of length k. This requires (5) to be true:

$$\sum_{i=1}^{k} -\delta_i + t * \alpha < 0 \quad (5)$$

Rearranging (5), we have α constrained by (6):

$$\alpha < \frac{1}{t} \sum_{i=1}^{k} \delta_i \quad (6)$$

The same cycle, on the validity graph, shows that α is constrained by (3). This is a contradiction as we know α was constructed by maximized subject to (3) thus our assumption of a negative weight cycle in the graph used to compute offsets was wrong and the system of differences constraints used to solve for offsets will always have a solution.

Inverted Tiles: The loop bounds for each statement in an inverted tile are set to fully span the gap between adjacent upright tiles (or a domain boundary). The proof of satisfaction of all dependences during execution of an inverted tile is a direct consequence of this "completeness" property of the span of spatial loops of an inverted tile. Consider all instances at time t, of an arbitrary statement S_q in an inverted tile. Any dependence on instances of any statement S_p mean that S_p textually precedes S_q, or that the dependence is from instances of S_q at some earlier time step. There are three possibilities for any such statement instance from which there exists a dependence: i) it belongs in some upright tile, ii) it belongs in the same inverted tile, iii) it belongs in some other inverted tile. If we have case (i), the dependence is satisfied since all upright tiles are executed before any inverted tiles. If we have case (ii), again the dependence is satisfied since statements are executed in textual order within the inverted tile for a time step, and in increasing time order across time steps. Finally, case (iii) is impossible since other inverted tiles are separated from the current inverted tile by at least one upright tile, whose slopes are guaranteed to prevent any dependence edge crossing their boundaries.

Multiple Spatial Dimensions: In the proof of correctness, so far we have focused on the case of a single spatial dimension. For multi-dimensional stencils, as explained in Sec. 3, tiles may have different characteristics along the different spatial dimensions. For example, with two spatial dimensions and nested split tiling, there are four possibilities: Upright-Upright, Upright-Inverted, Inverted-Upright, Inverted-Inverted. With hybrid split tiling, one or more spatial dimensions may be tiled using standard parallel tiles (using the slope β computed for the right boundary in that dimension by the back-slicing analysis). The proof of validity of execution in the multi-dimensional case is a consequence of the fact that the loop bounds along each spatial dimension are independent of iterators of other spatial dimensions. Consider, for example, a stencil with three spatial dimensions i, j, and k, where standard tiling is used along k, and split tiling along i, and j. Let a particular tile be upright along i, and inverted along j. At some time step t, the set of all instances of a statement S_q will necessarily correspond to a cross product of ranges along the three spatial extents: [kl:ku,jl:ju,il:iu]. The instances of any statement S_p that S_q depends upon, can be expressed as $[kl+\delta_L^k : ku+\delta_U^k, jl+\delta_L^j : ju+\delta_U^j, il+\delta_L^i : iu+\delta_U^i]$. We can prove that all such dependences are satisfied by proving that the extents along each dimension are satisfied. For upright or inverted tiles along any dimension, we have proved that the required extents will be covered by the generated slopes/offsets. For a standard tiled dimension too, the dependences will be satisfied: on the lower side, the instances will either lie in the same tile or in an earlier numbered tile that would have been executed before this tile; on the upper side, the instance will necessarily lie within the same tile because the slope and offset from the back-slicing computation is used.

5. CODE GENERATION

Before detailing the code generation algorithm, the structure of generated code is shown in Figure 14. The example shows code for a single-statement 1D stencil. Upright and inverted inter-tile loops can be found, respectively, at lines 11 and 26. Note that the upright tile loop covers an extent from the lowest bound of any stencil function to the highest bound of any stencil function, and the inverted tile tile loop extends beyond this on both sides. This is needed to ensure that boundary cells are computed as upright tiles slope away from them. It is enabled by the `max()` and `min()` expressions that prevent intra-tile loop bounds from taking values outside of the original loop's domain (lines 17 and 32). Constraints on tile size values such as `UPR_TILE_SIZE` and `INV_TILE_SIZE` are imposed as needed to ensure correctness of generated code; this is explained below.

```
1  // Time tile loop
2  for (tt = 0; tt < T; tt += TT_SIZE) {
3    // Upright tile loop
4    // F1 is a stencil function, lb_F1 (ub_F1) is the lower (upper) bound of
5    // the grid coordinate where F1 is applied
6    upr_lb = lb_F1; // for multiple stencil functions F1, F2, ..., it is
7                    // actually  min(lb_F1,lb_F2,...)
8    upr_ub = ub_F1; // Similarly max(lb_F1, lb_F2...)
9    // UPR_TILE_SIZE (INV_TILE_SIZE) is the size of the upright (inverted)
10   // tile base
11   for (ii = upr_lb; ii < upr_ub; ii += UPR_TILE_SIZE + INV_TILE_SIZE) {
12     // Time loop
13     for (t = tt; t < min(tt+TT_SIZE,T); t++) {
14       tile_lb_F1 = ii + offset_F1_lb + upr_alpha*(t-tt);
15       tile_ub_F1 = ii + UPR_TILE_SIZE +
16       offset_F1_ub + upr_beta*(t-tt) - 1;
17       for (i = max(tile_lb_F1, lb_F1); i <= min(tile_ub_F1, ub_F1); i++) {
18           // 1D stencil function code.
19       }
20     }
21   }
22   // Inverted tile loop
23   inv_lb = upr_lb - INV_TILE_SIZE;
24   inv_ub = ub_F1 + INV_TILE_SIZE; // for multiple stencil functions
25                                   // F1, F2, ... it is max(ub_F1,ub_F2,...)
26   for (ii = inv_lb; jj <  inv_ub; ii += UPR_TILE_SIZE + INV_TILE_SIZE) {
27     // Time loop
28     for (t = tt; t < min(tt+TT_SIZE,T); t++) {
29       tile_lb_F1 = ii + inv_offset_F1_lb + inv_alpha*(t-tt);
30       tile_ub_F1 = ii + INV_TILE_SIZE +
31       inv_offset_F1_ub + inv_beta*(t-tt) - 1;
32       for (i = max(tile_lb_F1, lb_F1); i <= min(tile_ub_F1, ub_F1); i++) {
33          // 1D stencil function code
34       }
35     }
36   }
37 }
```

Figure 14: Illustration of structure of generated code for 1D case

Algorithm 15 is the overall algorithm to perform DLT and split-tiling on a program that can be expressed in SDSL. It is a more detailed version of the overview algorithm shown earlier.

Functions `GetXXX` retrieve properties of the SDSL program required for code generation (e.g., name of arrays, number of dimensions, etc.). Functions `GenCopyXXXLoop` copies the data from the original layout to the DLT layout. Function `vectorize` generates a sequence of vector intrinsics call (SSE or AVX in our experiments) to compute the same arithmetic operation as the corresponding statement in the stencil function, using SIMD vectors. Function `ChangeBoundsToDLT` adapts/creates the loop structure scanning the dimension-lifted data arrays. Functions `GenMaskedXXX` use SIMD masked write operations to cope with vectors in the generated code where one of the vector slot (necessarily the first or last slot only) contains ghost data. The reader may refer to [12] for

```
Input
    P: Stencil program
    L_vec: Integer length of a vector (in elements)
Output
    P_sdlt: C code for Split-tiled, DLT version of the input
        SDSL program

  P_sdlt ← Copy(P)
  // Convert arrays to DLT.
  A ← GetArrays(P_sdlt)
  l_time ← GetTimeLoop(P_sdlt)
  foreach array a in A do
    dims ← GetDimensions(a, P_sdlt)
    l_copyin ← GenCopyInLoop(a, dims, L_vec)
    l_copyout ← GenCopyOutLoop(a, dims, L_vec)
    l_time.Prepend(l_copyin)
    l_time.Append(l_copyout)
  end do
  // Vectorize statements.
  S ← GetStatements(P_sdlt)
  foreach statement s in S do
    s_vec ← Vectorize(s, L_vec)
    l_enc ← GetEnclosingLoop(s_vec, P_sdlt)
    ChangeBoundsToDLT(l_enc)
    s_vec^start ← GenMaskedWriteStartStmt(s_vec, L_vec)
    l_start ← GenMaskedStartLoop(s_vec^start, l_enc)
    l_enc.Prepend(l_start)
    s_vec^end ← GenMaskedWriteEndStmt(s_vec, L_vec)
    l_end ← GenMaskedEndLoop(s_vec^end, l_enc)
    l_enc.Append(l_end)
  end do
  // Backslice original code.
  (x⃗) ← computeOffsetSlopes(P)
  AddBacksliceResults(P_sdlt, x⃗)
  // Create nested split-tile loops
  l_tt ← CreateTimeTileLoop()
  d ← GetSpaceDimensionCount(P_sdlt)
  GenNestedSplitTileLoops(l_tt, d)
  GenTileBodies(l_tt, P_sdlt, d)
  ReplaceTimeLoop(l_tt, P_sdlt)
```

Figure 15: Algorithm `LayoutTransformAndSplitTile`

more details. Functions `GenNestedSplitTileLoops` and `GenTileBodies` are described below.

Algorithm 16 provides detail for the code generation of split-tiled code, in the context of a program on which DLT has been performed first. We remark that in order for the code generation of the `masked writes` required by DLT to be correct, we impose a constraint relating the size of the innermost dimension to the tile sizes:

$$|d_{innermost}| \mod (upr\_tile\_size + inv\_tile\_size) = 0$$

Adding this constraint greatly simplifies the code generation, avoiding the need to handle complex corner cases at the tile boundaries. This limitation is not a problem in practice, since padding can be used to comply with this constraint.

Function `GenInvertedFullBndryTileCondition` generates a conditional to determine whether to execute a full inverted tile or an boundary inverted tile that includes two loop nests for the start and end boundaries of DLT codes. Function `AdjustTimeAndSpaceLoopBounds` alters the loop boundaries of the loops copied from the original code to tile loop boundaries using the results of backslicing. Function `TrimMaskedWriteLoops` removes the masked write loops at the start and end of the inverted boundary tile loops, leaving the masked writes between them.

We conclude by presenting the algorithm for generating split-tiled loop nests shown in Algorithm 17. Hybrid split-tiling code generation requires minimal changes to Algorithms 16 and 17. Algorithm 17 requires a conditional to check if it is generating code for the outermost loop. If so, a standard tile loop is generated instead of a split-tiled loop. Algorithm 16 requires a change to the `AdjustTimeAndSpaceLoopBounds()` procedure to correctly traverse the standard tile dimension.

```
Input
    l: A time tile loop with empty nested split-tile loops inside
    P_sdlt: Stencil program with DLT performed and backslicing
        results inserted
    d: Integer representing current loop depth (1 innermost)
Output
    l: with split-tile loop bodies generated
  if d == 1 then
    l_orig ← GetOriginalLoopBody(P_sdlt)
    //Generate upright tile body
    l_upr ← GetUprightTileLoop(l)
    CopyTimeAndSpaceLoops(P_sdlt, l_upr, 1)
    RemoveMaskedWriteLoops(l_upr)
    AdjustTimeAndSpaceLoopBounds(l_upr, P_sdlt)

    l_inv ← GetInvertedTileLoop(l)
    (l_inv^full, l_inv^bndry) ← l.GenInvertedFullBndryTileCondition()
    //Generate inverted full tile body
    CopyTimeAndSpaceLoops(P_sdlt, l_inv^full, 1)
    RemoveMaskedWriteLoops(l_inv^full)
    AdjustTimeAndSpaceLoopBounds(l_inv^full, P_sdlt)

    //Generate inverted boundary tile body
    CopyTimeAndSpaceLoops(P_sdlt, l_inv^bndry, 2)
    AdjustTimeAndSpaceLoopBounds(l_inv^bndry, P_sdlt)
    TrimMaskedWriteLoops(l_inv^bndry)
  else
    l_upr ← GetUprightTileLoop(l)
    GenTileBodies(l_upr, P_sdlt, d − 1)
    l_inv ← GetInvertedTileLoop(l)
    GenTileBodies(l_inv, P_sdlt, d − 1)
  end if
```

Figure 16: Algorithm `GenTileBodies`

```
Input
    l: Loop to add nested upright and inverted tile loops to
    d: Integer representing current loop depth (1 innermost)
Output
    l: with nested upright and inverted tile loops added

  if d == 1 then
    l_upr ← l.AddUprightTileLoop()
    l_inv ← l.AddInvertedTileLoop()
  else
    l_upr ← l.AddUprightTileLoop()
    GenNestedSplitTileLoops(l_upr, d − 1)
    l_inv ← l.AddInvertedTileLoop()
    GenNestedSplitTileLoops(l_inv, d − 1)
  end if
```

Figure 17: Algorithm `GenNestedSplitTileLoops`

6. EXPERIMENTAL EVALUATION

The effectiveness of the both nested split-tiling and hybrid split-tiling applied in conjunction with the dimension-lifting transformation was experimentally evaluated on several hardware platforms using a variety of stencil kernels. We compare performance to the diamond-tiling system used by Pluto [2], the cache-oblivious tiling system used by Pochoir [18], and the Intel C Compiler v13.0.

6.1 Experimental Setup

Hardware: Experiments were performed on three hardware platforms with DVFS features disabled on all of them. *AMD Phenom II X6 1100T* (K10 micro-architecture) is a 6-core x86-64 chip, clocked at 3.3GHz; single-precision peak performance of 26.4 GFlop/s/-core (158.4 GFlop/s aggregate); double-precision peak performance of 13.2 GFlop/s/core (79.2 GFlop/s aggregate). *Intel Core i7-920* (Nehalem micro-architecture) is a quad-core x86-64 chip running at 2.66 GHz; single-precision peak performance of 21.28 GFlop/s/-core (85.12 GFlop/s aggregate); double-precision peak performance of 10.64 GFlop/s/core (42.56 GFlop/s aggregate). *Intel Core i7-2600K* (Sandy Bridge micro-architecture) is a quad-core core x86-64 chip running at 3.4 GHz; single-precision peak performance of 54.4 GFlop/s/core (217.6 GFlop/s aggregate); double-precision peak performance of 27.2 GFlop/s/core (108.8 GFlop/s aggregate).

Programs were compiled using the Intel C Compiler v13.0 with the '`-O3 -ipo -xHost`' optimization flags was used for split-tiled, Pluto, and Pochoir codes on all machines. Auto-parallelization and auto-vectorization was enabled for ICC results with the '`-parallel -O3 -ipo -xHost`' optimization flags and appropriate vectorization pragmas.

Benchmarks: The following stencil codes were used (with the names used to refer to them in parentheses): Jacobi 1D (jac-1d-3), Jacobi 2D (jac-2d-5), Jacobi 3D (jac-3d-7); Laplacian, Gradient and Poisson 2D; FDTD 2D [16]; Heat 1D/2D/3D distributed with Pochoir [18].

All array dimensions were set to be significantly larger than last level cache on all micro-architectures. For all stencils, the footprint of each array was set to 244.14MB for single precision and 488.28MB for double precision; this was achieved using 1D arrays with $64 * 10^7$ scalar elements, 2D arrays with 8000^2 elements, and 3D arrays with 400^3 elements. The number of time steps was set to 100 for all benchmarks.

Tile sizes were autotuned for Pluto with diamond tiling, as well as for our split-tiling work. The autotuning was done over a sampling of the set of tile size combinations that respect the various constraints (i.e., multiple of vector length) of each framework. Autotuning runs were performed for a maximum of 4 hours per SIMD unit / benchmark combination (how to speed up tile size autotuning, for instance using acceleration/search heuristics is beyond the scope of this paper, we simply tested all tile sizes in our subset). For split-tiled codes all threads (one thread per core) were assigned to the outermost parallel loop using OpenMP parallel for pragmas.

6.2 Experimental Results

Absolute performance for single and double precision experiments across all platforms and codes are given in Figures 18–20.

In all cases Pochoir, nested split-tiled, and hybrid split-tiled codes are significantly faster than sequential C code auto-parallelized and vectorized by Intel's ICC compiler. Not all benchmarks could be optimized by Pochoir, which can only generate optimized tiled parallel code for single statement stencil codes. Multi-statement, multi-loop stencil codes like FDTD, with three inter-related stencils updating Ex[t] using Ex[t-1] and Hz[t-1], Ey[t] using Ey[t-1] and Hz[t-1], and Hz[t] using Hz[t-1], Ex[t], and Ey[t]), cannot be expressed in Pochoir.

1D Benchmarks: Having only one split-tiled dimension allowed tiles to fit in cache and provided ample parallelism. High performance was expected of these codes and was observed. Nested split-tiling + DLT outperformed ICC, Pochoir, and Pluto on both 1D benchmarks across all platforms. Improvement over Pochoir ranged from a low of 1.27× for double precision Jacobi-1D on Nehalem to a high of 2.2× for single precision Heat-1D on Sandy Bridge. Hybrid split-tiling does not apply to 1D benchmarks as the inner loop is split-tiled for both fine grain vector parallelism and coarse grain thread-level parallelism.

2D Benchmarks: Across all 2D benchmarks hybrid split-tiling outperformed ICC, Pochoir, Pluto, and nested split-tiling on both quad core Intel platforms. For the hexacore AMD, performance

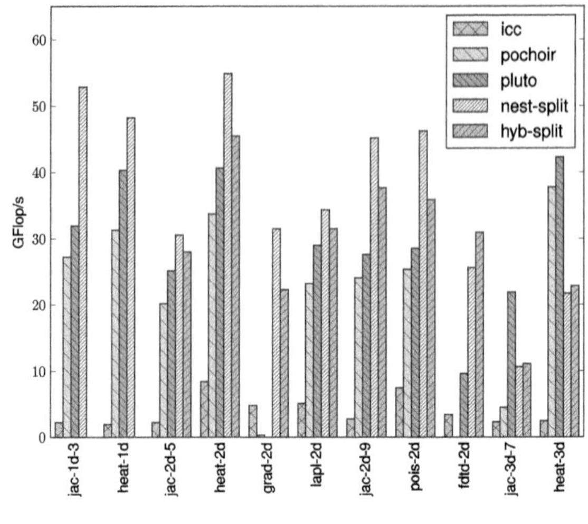

(a) Single-precision

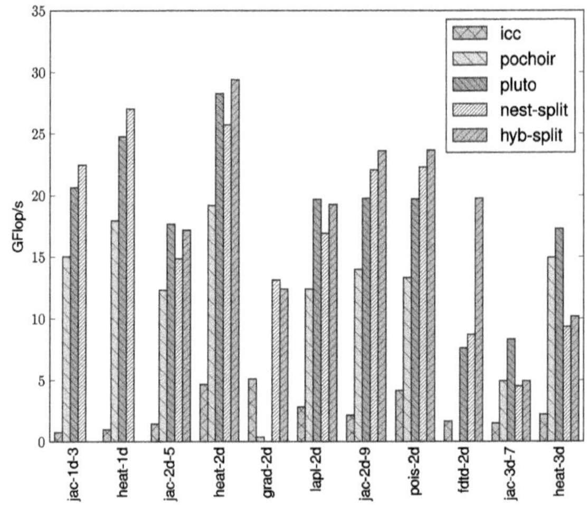

(b) Double-precision

Figure 18: AMD Phenom II X6 SSE2 Performance

of hybrid split-tiling + DLT fell behind both nested split-tiling and Pluto on several benchmarks, both single and double precision.

This performance anomaly is due to load balancing issues. DLT effectively turned the dimension of the arrays involved from 8000 × 8000 float/double scalars to 8000 × 2000 float vectors and 8000 × 4000 double vectors. With hybrid split-tiling, tiles from the smaller dimension (subject to the constraints described in Sec. 3.2) had to be distributed across threads. Smaller tiles with better load balancing characteristics limited reuse, while larger tiles with significant reuse were not plentiful enough to adequately distribute load across cores.

Nested split-tiling exhibited better load balancing because only tiles along the larger dimension were distributed across cores. The outer dimension was large enough to allow both large tiles for significant reuse and a large quantity of tiles for load balancing. Hybrid split-tiling on quad core Intel platforms did not have any load balancing issues because the smallest dimension was divisible by 4, allowing for the same number of tiles to be distributed across all cores.

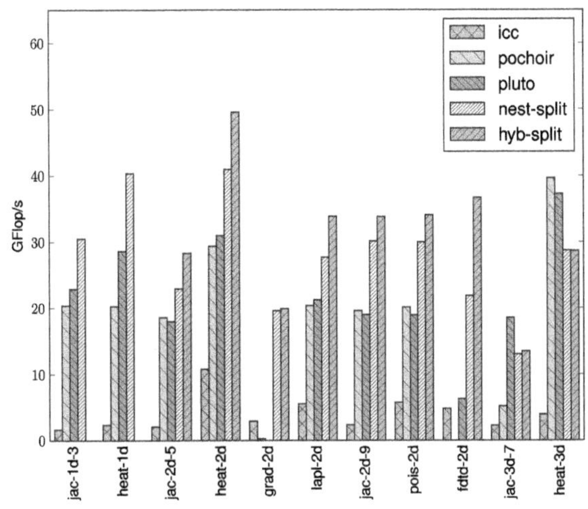

(a) Single-precision

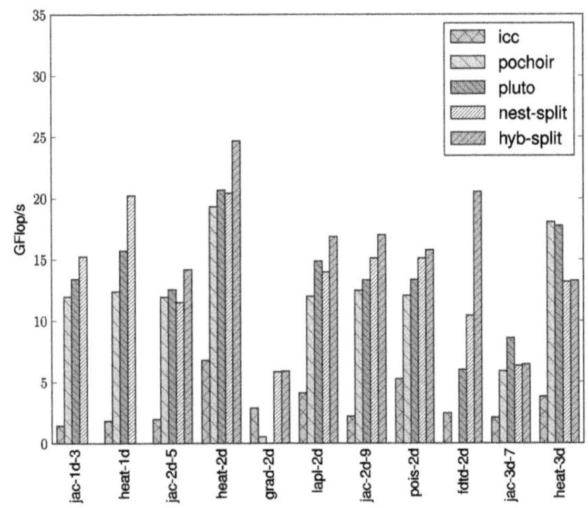

(b) Double-precision

Figure 19: Intel Core i7-920 SSE4 Performance

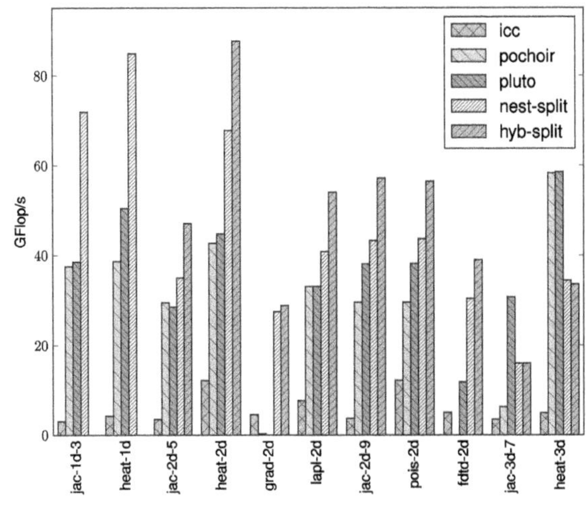

(a) Single-precision

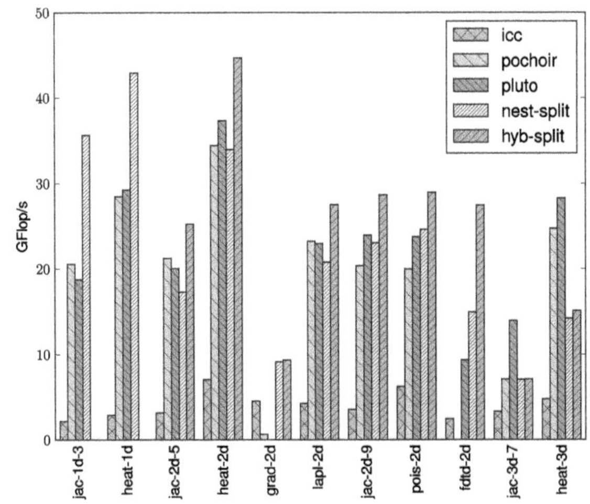

(b) Double-precision

Figure 20: Intel Core i7-2600K AVX Performance

3D Benchmarks: Both hybrid and nested split-tiling fell behind Pochoir and Pluto on both 3D benchmarks across all platforms. While hybrid split-tiling was able to significantly reduce the pressure on the memory system for 2D benchmarks, its benefit was not seen when adding a third dimension. In 3D, both inner dimensions are split-tiled, thus spatial tile sizes in both inner dimensions must increase when time tile size is increased.

For both the Heat-3D and Jacobi-3D benchmarks, an increase of one in the time tile size leads to an upright tile size increase of four in each dimension. Tile sizes grow fast enough that by the time significant gains can be achieved from data reuse, the code is bound by memory latency and bandwidth consumption from spatial tiles that have grown significantly larger than L1 cache.

The diamond tiles used by Pluto overcome this limitation by halving the amount of data required for a given time tile size. For a time tile size of 16 and slopes of 2 on either side, an upright tile used in nested and hybrid split-tiling must be at least 64 elements at its base. A diamond tile with a time tile size of 16 begins at a point, expands to 32 elements at its widest and narrows to a point again. Pluto is able to reuse data significantly more than both Pochoir and nested and hybrid split-tiling.

Further exacerbating the problem is the fact that DLT causes tile sizes in the innermost dimension to be multiplied by vector size. Coupled with the constraints on tile size described in Sec. 3.2 this leads to split-tiling + DLT tile sizes (in KB) that are much larger than similar tile sizes (size of each dimension). In Heat-3D both Pluto and Pochoir are able to achieve high performance across all platforms. It is likely that the smaller tile sizes (in KB) enable Pochoir to achieve very high performance on this code.

7. RELATED WORK

A number of recent efforts have targeted the optimization of stencil computations for multicore CPUs and GPUs [2, 5, 8–10, 13, 15, 17–19]. Strzodka et al. [17] used time skewing and cache-size oblivious parallelograms to improve the memory system pressure and parallelism in stencils on CPUs. Micikevicius et al. [15] hand-tuned a 3-D finite difference computation stencil and achieved an order of magnitude performance increase over existing CPU implementations on GT200-based Tesla GPUs. Datta et al. [8] developed an optimization and auto-tuning framework for stencil computations, targeting multi-core systems, NVidia GPUs, and Cell SPUs.

Tiling is a critical transformation for optimizing stencil computations since they typically perform repeated sweeps over large multi-dimensional arrays that are much too large to fit within cache. In order to benefit from both intra-step reuse as well as data reuse across several successive sweeps over the domains, so called "time tiling" is essential. The standard approach to time-tiling of stencil computations requires skewing of the iteration space and introduces inter-tile dependences along the spatial dimensions and thereby restricts parallelism to wavefront parallelism in the tile space. Alternate approaches to tiling using overlapped tiles [13], split-tiles [9] or "diamond" tiles [2, 14] enable a greater degree of inter-tile parallelism. In this paper we have developed compiler algorithms for enabling split-tiling in conjunction with a dimension-lifted-transpose data layout transformation. Grosser et al. [9] utilize a variant of split-tiling for GPGPU with substantially different tile shaping, analysis, and code generation techniques than this work.

Among the numerous research efforts to optimize stencil computations, a few of them have developed a specialized DSL compiler for stencils. PATUS [5] is a stencil compiler developed by Christen et al. that uses both a stencil description and a machine mapping description to generate efficient CPU and GPU code for stencil programs. A stencil-DSL compiler for GPUs that uses overlapped tiling for parallel execution was recently reported [13].

Tang et al. [18] have developed and publicly released the Pochoir stencil compiler that uses a DSL embedded in C++ to produce high-performance code for stencil computations using cache-oblivious parallelograms for parallel execution on shared-memory systems. In this paper, we compare performance on several multi-core systems of the code generated using DLT and split-tiling with the code generated by Pochoir, showing that we achieve comparable or better performance. But unlike the DSL compiler we have described in this paper, neither PATUS nor Pochoir can generate optimized time-tiled code for multi-statement stencil computations such as the FDTD (Finite Difference Time Domain) stencil.

The use of Chapel for the description of dense and sparse stencils was investigated by Barrett et al. [3]. The Chapel work enables automated distributed memory parallelization of stencils but does not address time-tiling or vectorization. Very recent work by Bandishti et al. [2] enhanced the Pluto compiler to incorporate a strategy for "diamond" tiling, that is particularly effective in parallelizing stencil computations. However, our approach to combining data layout transformation in conjunction with split-tiling provides significant performance advantages over Pluto for a range of stencil benchmarks, as seen from our experimental results.

8. CONCLUSIONS

In this paper, we have described compiler algorithms for a a stencil DSL incorporating two key transformations – dimension-lifted-transpose data layout transformation to optimize vector loads / stores, and split-tiling for enhanced inter-tile concurrency. Experimental results on a number of stencil benchmarks on multiple target multicore platforms demonstrate significant performance improvements achievable over state-of-the-art production compilers such as Intel's ICC, but also significant improvements over Pochoir and recent work on diamond tiling in Pluto. Our compiler has greater scope of applicability than Pochoir, effectively optimizing arbitrary multi-statement stencils.

Acknowledgments. This work was supported in part by the U.S. National Science Foundation through awards 0926687 and 0926688, by the Center for Domain-Specific Computing (CDSC) funded by NSF "Expeditions in Computing" award 0926127, and the Department of Energy through award DE-SC0005033.

9. REFERENCES

[1] R. K. Ahuja, T. L. Magnanti, and J. B. Orlin. *Network Flows: Theory, Algorithms, and Applications*. Prentice-Hall, 1993.

[2] V. Bandishti, I. Pananilath, , and U. Bondhugula. Tiling stencil computations to maximize parallelism. In *SC*, 2012.

[3] R. F. Barrett, P. C. Roth, and S. W. Poole. Finite difference stencils implemented using chapel. ORNL TM-2007/122, 2007.

[4] U. Bondhugula, A. Hartono, J. Ramanujam, and P. Sadayappan. A practical automatic polyhedral program optimization system. In *PLDI*, 2008.

[5] M. Christen, O. Schenk, and H. Burkhart. PATUS: A code generation and autotuning framework for parallel iterative stencil computations on modern microarchitectures. In *IPDPS*, 2011.

[6] T. H. Cormen, C. E. Leiserson, R. L. Rivest, and C. Stein. *Introduction to Algorithms*. 2001.

[7] G. B. Dantzig, W. Blattner, and M. Rao. Finding a cycle in a graph with minimum cost to time ratio with application to a ship routing problem. 1966.

[8] K. Datta, M. Murphy, V. Volkov, S. Williams, J. Carter, L. Oliker, D. Patterson, J. Shalf, and K. Yelick. Stencil computation optimization and auto-tuning on state-of-the-art multicore architectures. In *SC*, 2008.

[9] T. Grosser, A. Cohen, P. H. Kelly, J. Ramanujam, P. Sadayappan, and S. Verdoolaege. Split tiling for GPUs: automatic parallelization using trapezoidal tiles. In *Proc. GPGPU-6*, 2013.

[10] D. Han, S. Xu, L. Chen, and L. Huang. PADS: A pattern-driven stencil compiler-based tool for reuse of optimizations on GPGPUs. In *ICPADS*, 2011.

[11] T. Henretty, J. Holewinski, N. Sedaghati, L.-N. Pouchet, A. Rountev, and P. Sadayappan. Stencil Domain Specific Language (SDSL) User Guide 0.2.1 draft. OSU TR OSU-CISRC-4/13-TR09, 2013.

[12] T. Henretty, K. Stock, L.-N. Pouchet, F. Franchetti, J. Ramanujam, and P. Sadayappan. Data layout transformation for stencil computations on short-vector SIMD architectures. In *CC*, 2011.

[13] J. Holewinski, L.-N. Pouchet, and P. Sadayappan. High-performance code generation for stencil computations on GPU architectures. In *ICS*, 2012.

[14] S. Krishnamoorthy, M. Baskaran, U. Bondhugula, J. Ramanujam, A. Rountev, and P. Sadayappan. Effective automatic parallelization of stencil computations. In *PLDI*, 2007.

[15] P. Micikevicius. 3d Finite difference computation on GPUs using CUDA. In *GPGPU-2*, 2009.

[16] D. Orozco and G. R. Gao. Mapping the FDTD Application to Many-Core Chip Architectures. In *ICPP*, 2009.

[17] R. Strzodka, M. Shaheen, D. Pajak, and H.-P. Seidel. Cache oblivious parallelograms in iterative stencil computations. In *ICS*, 2010.

[18] Y. Tang, R. A. Chowdhury, B. C. Kuszmaul, C.-K. Luk, and C. E. Leiserson. The Pochoir stencil compiler. In *SPAA*, 2011.

[19] J. Treibig, G. Wellein, and G. Hager. Efficient multicore-aware parallelization strategies for iterative stencil computations. *ArXiv e-prints*, 2010.

Exploiting Domain Knowledge to Optimize Parallel Computational Mechanics Codes

Chenyang Liu[1], M. Hasan Jamal[1], Milind Kulkarni[1], Arun Prakash[2] and Vijay Pai[1]
[1]School of Electrical and Computer Engineering
[2]School of Civil Engineering
Purdue University
West Lafayette, IN, USA
{liu441, jamal0, milind, aprakas, vpai}@purdue.edu

ABSTRACT

An important emerging problem domain in computational science and engineering is the development of *multi-scale computational methods* for complex problems in mechanics that span multiple spatial and temporal scales. An attractive approach to solving these problems is *recursive decomposition*: the problem is broken up into a tree of loosely coupled sub-problems which can be solved independently and then coupled back together to obtain the desired solution. However, a particular problem can be solved in myriad ways by coupling the sub-problems together in different tree orders. As we argue in this paper, the space of possible orders is vast, the performance gap between an arbitrary order and the best order is potentially quite large, and the likelihood that a domain scientist can find the best order to solve a problem on a particular machine is vanishingly small.

In this paper, we present a system that uses domain-specific knowledge captured in computational libraries to optimize code written in a conventional language (C). The system generates efficient coupling orders to solve computational mechanics problems using recursive decomposition. Our system adopts the inspector-executor paradigm [9], where the problem is inspected and a novel heuristic finds an effective implementation based on domain properties evaluated by a cost model. The derived implementation is then executed by a parallel run-time system (Cilk) which achieves optimal parallel performance. We demonstrate that our cost model is highly correlated with actual application runtime, that our proposed technique outperforms non-decomposed and non-multiscale methods. The code generated by the heuristic also outperforms alternate scheduling strategies, as well as over 99% of randomly-generated recursive decompositions sampled from the space of possible solutions.

Categories and Subject Descriptors

D.3.4 [**Processors**]: Compilers, Optimization; G.1.8 [**Partial Differential Equations**]: Finite element methods

ICS'13, June 10–14, 2013, Eugene, Oregon, USA.

General Terms

Algorithms; Performance

Keywords

Domain-specific Optimization; Multi-scale Method; Recursive Decomposition

1 Introduction

Multi-scale methods for computational mechanics have been an area of significant research interest in recent years [11, 12, 18]. These methods allow mechanical systems, both static and dynamic, to be simulated with vastly differing spatial and temporal scales in different parts of the domain. This allows areas of interest to be investigated at fine granularity but at high computational cost, while other portions of the problem can be approximated with a much coarser-grain simulation. Multi-scale methods thus hold the promise of simulating complex systems at the necessary level of resolution without incurring the cost of such fine-grained simulation throughout the problem domain. The multi-scale strategy is thus even more targetted towards achieving computational efficiency than well-studied strategies such as adaptive mesh refinement (AMR) that only adopt multiple spatial scales.

An attractive approach to multi-scale simulation that has been investigated in recent work is *recursive domain-decomposition* [3, 5, 13, 16, 20, 26]. A large problem is broken up into a set of loosely-coupled subdomains; these subdomains can be solved independently, except for points on potential shared *interfaces* that connect them. These shared interfaces require that the solutions of each individual subdomain be coupled to ensure that their solutions at the interface are consistent. As long as the interfaces are small relative to the subdomain sizes, it is computationally advantageous to decompose a large system versus solving the system as a single entity. For the particular case of recursive bisection adopted in this study, coupling is a pair-wise operation, and as subdomains are coupled, a solution is obtained for the combined, larger domain. Hence, by hierarchically coupling the subdomains, the solution for the overall system can be obtained. We describe this coupling order using a *coupling tree*. Figure 1 shows a sample decomposition, where the problem domain is decomposed into six subdomains that are solved independently and coupled together according to the coupling tree depicted in the figure.

A critical point about this hierarchical approach to solving multi-scale problems is that the *structure* and *topology*

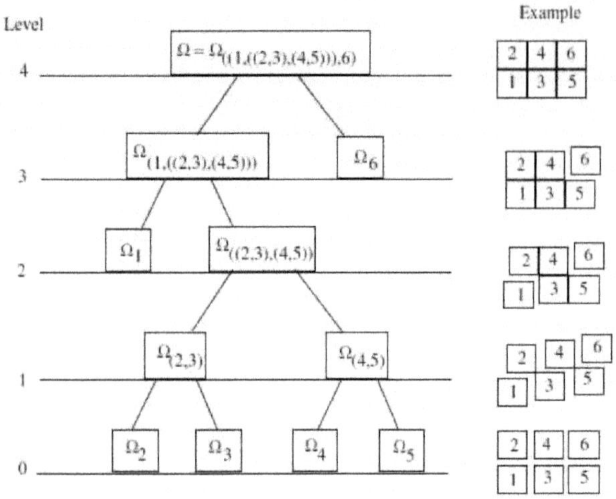

Figure 1: A Decomposed Problem Domain and Corresponding Recursive Coupling Order

of the coupling tree has a significant effect on the performance of the algorithm. Because the coupling operation is both commutative and associative, a vast number of unique coupling trees are possible (945 for a problem with just 6 subdomains), making it highly unlikely for all but the simplest problems that a domain scientist will adopt an effective coupling order. Furthermore, because the various relevant parameters associated with computational costs are problem-dependent, finding the optimal coupling tree becomes even more difficult, as no single approach for finding an optimal tree coupling order may work for all different problems.

To tackle this problem, we have developed a run-time optimization system based on the inspector-executor approach. We first inspect the original program to infer the high level computational structure of the problem. We then use semantic properties of the coupling operation, as well as a domain-specific cost model to obtain cost values that reflect the coupling of multi-scale subdomains. Next, we generate an optimal coupling order based on those cost values. Finally, the optimized schedule is run using the Cilk framework to exploit available parallelism. We find that our approach yields sequential and parallel performance that is significantly better than other available techniques.

Finally, we discuss how our overall approach to optimizing domain applications might be generalized, both in terms of other computational algorithms that can benefit from our system in particular, and more broadly how similar semantics-exploiting approaches might be applicable in other domains.

2 Background

In this section we provide a general description of the physical problems encountered in mechanics that we will be solving using parallel recursive domain decomposition. The dynamical behavior of almost all mechanical systems is generally governed by laws of physics expressed as partial differential equations (PDEs) of continuum mechanics. These PDEs are most commonly solved by expressing them in integral forms and using numerical methods, such as finite elements, finite volumes, finite differences etc. to evaluate these integrals. For instance, the PDE:

$$-\rho\ddot{\boldsymbol{u}} + \mathrm{div}\boldsymbol{\sigma} + \boldsymbol{b} = \boldsymbol{0} \qquad \forall \boldsymbol{x} \in \Omega \tag{1}$$

describes the displacement $\boldsymbol{u}$ and stresses $\boldsymbol{\sigma}$ at *all* points $\boldsymbol{x}$ in a body Ω, being acted upon by forces $\boldsymbol{b}$. The density is denoted by ρ and a superimposed dot ($\dot{}$) represents a derivative with respect to time ($\frac{d}{dt}$). The "div" operator represents vector divergence, or the sum of partial derivatives in each spatial dimension ($\mathrm{div}\boldsymbol{\sigma} = \frac{\partial \sigma}{\partial x} + \frac{\partial \sigma}{\partial y} + \frac{\partial \sigma}{\partial z}$) . Note that Equation (1) is simply an expression of Newton's 2nd law for every point $\boldsymbol{x}$ in Ω. Upon writing this time-dependent PDE in integral form and numerically *discretizing*, one obtains a *system* of ordinary differential equations (ODEs):

$$\boldsymbol{M}\,\ddot{\boldsymbol{u}}(t) + \boldsymbol{D}\,\dot{\boldsymbol{u}}(t) + \boldsymbol{K}\,\boldsymbol{u}(t) = \boldsymbol{p}(t) \tag{2}$$

where $\boldsymbol{M}$, $\boldsymbol{D}$ and $\boldsymbol{K}$ represent the mass, damping and stiffness matrices respectively, associated with the discretization, $\boldsymbol{p}(t)$ is a vector of time-dependent forces acting on the body, and $\boldsymbol{u}(t)$ is the vector of displacements that needs to be solved for. Most commonly, these ODEs are solved by finite-difference schemes by approximating the time derivatives using difference formulas. This allows one to solve for the state $\boldsymbol{u}_{n+1} \approx \boldsymbol{u}(t_{n+1})$ of the system at some time t_{n+1} from a known state $\boldsymbol{u}_n \approx \boldsymbol{u}(t_n)$ by advancing through a small time-step Δt where $t_{n+1} = t_n + \Delta t$.

$$\mathbb{M}\,\mathbb{U}_{n+1} = \mathbb{P}_{n+1} - \mathbb{N}\,\mathbb{U}_n \tag{3}$$

This process can be repeated successively to advance the solution in a *time-stepping* manner [19]. However, depending on the problem, the size of the this system of equations can be very large making its solution as a single complete system very computationally intensive. One way to avoid solving this system as a whole is by using domain decomposition. This approach divides the problem into smaller sub-domains, solves them independently (possibly in parallel), and couples them back by enforcing continuity constraints on the interfaces between the sub-domains.

2.1 Solving a Recursively Decomposed Domain

In this section we illustrate a non-iterative hierarchical implementation of the *recursive* domain decomposition method. Given a finite element mesh partitioned into S subdomains, a hierarchy of subdomains can be built by combining two subdomains at a time until the original undecomposed mesh is recreated. Such a hierarchy can be effectively represented by the *tree* structure as shown in Figure 1. The *leaf* nodes in the *tree* represent the subdomains that are not further subdivided. The original undecomposed structure Ω is called the *root* node. In general, for any node $\Omega_{(A,B)}$ in the tree, the problem is substituted with two coupled sub-problems for Ω_A and Ω_B replacing Equation (3) with:

$$\left[\begin{array}{cc|c} \mathbb{M}^A & & \mathbb{C}^A \\ & \mathbb{M}^B & \mathbb{C}^B \\ \hline \mathbb{B}^A & \mathbb{B}^B & \mathbf{0} \end{array}\right] \left[\begin{array}{c} \mathbb{U}^A_{n+1} \\ \mathbb{U}^B_{n+1} \\ \hline \mathbf{\Lambda}^{(A,B)}_{n+1} \end{array}\right] = \left[\begin{array}{c} \mathbb{P}^A_{n+1} - \mathbb{N}^A\mathbb{U}^A_n \\ \mathbb{P}^B_{n+1} - \mathbb{N}^B\mathbb{U}^B_n \\ \hline \mathbf{0} \end{array}\right] \tag{4}$$

Note that the matrices $\mathbb{C}_A, \mathbb{B}_A$ and $\mathbb{C}_B, \mathbb{B}_B$ represent connectivity matrices associated with the subdomains Ω_A and Ω_B respectively for the interface $\Gamma^{(A,B)}$ between them exclusively. The matrix system (4) can be solved in a decomposed

manner (instead of as solving it as a whole), using the following sequence of operations at each time step:
(i) Solve the smaller *uncoupled* problems

$$\mathbb{M}^s \, \mathbb{V}^s_{n+1} = \mathbb{P}^s_{n+1} - \mathbb{N}^s \mathbb{U}^s_n \quad (5)$$

for both subdomains $s = \{A, B\}$.
(ii) Solve for the *interface* Lagrange multipliers $\boldsymbol{\Lambda}^{(A,B)}_{n+1}$:

$$\boldsymbol{H}^{(A,B)} \, \boldsymbol{\Lambda}^{(A,B)}_{n+1} = \boldsymbol{f}^{(A,B)}_{n+1} \quad (6)$$

where the matrix $\boldsymbol{H}^{(A,B)}$, that represents the interface operator required to enforce continuity of the solutions $\mathbb{U}^A_{n+1}$ and $\mathbb{U}^B_{n+1}$ across the interface $\Gamma^{(A,B)}$, is computed only once as discussed in the remark below. The vector $\boldsymbol{f}^{(A,B)}_{n+1}$ is obtained from the uncoupled solution in step (i) above as $\boldsymbol{f}^{(A,B)}_{n+1} = \mathbb{C}^A \mathbb{V}^A_{n+1} + \mathbb{C}^B \mathbb{V}^B_{n+1}$.
(iii) *Update* the individual subdomain solutions:

$$\mathbb{U}^s_{n+1} = \mathbb{V}^s_{n+1} - \mathbb{Y}^s \boldsymbol{\Lambda}^{(A,B)}_{n+1} \quad (7)$$

again for both subdomains $s = \{A, B\}$, and where the matrices $\mathbb{Y}^s$ are also precomputed once as discussed in the remark below.
Remark: The $\mathbb{Y}^s$ matrices are precomputed once for both subdomains as:

$$\mathbb{M}^s \, \mathbb{Y}^s = \mathbb{C}^s \quad (8)$$

and do not change during the rest of the computation (for linear problems), so they are saved and used for every time-step. The interface operator $\boldsymbol{H}^{(A,B)}$ is then simply obtained by matrix multiplication:

$$\boldsymbol{H}^{(A,B)} = \mathbb{B}^A \, \mathbb{Y}^A + \mathbb{B}^B \, \mathbb{Y}^B \quad (9)$$

and it also does not change for the duration of the computation.

A representative pseudocode for solving a general node $\Omega_{(A,B)}$ in the tree is given by the *recursive* subroutine TreeSolve presented in Figure 2(a), where the inputs are $\Omega_{(A,B)}$ (the node to be solved), $\mathbb{P}^{(A,B)}$ (applied external forces to the mechanical system) and $\mathbb{U}^{(A,B)}_n$ (the current state of the subdomain at time-step t_n), and the output is $\mathbb{U}^{(A,B)}_{n+1}$ (the desired state of the subdomain at the next time-step t_{n+1}). Note that each call to TreeSolve requires computation involving the $\mathbb{Y}$ matrices, which are computed with the recursive BuildY subroutine presented in Figure 2(b). This function uses the various degrees of freedom (dof) on the interface $\Gamma^{(A,B)}$ to calculate the $\mathbb{Y}$ matrices. Input to the subroutine is a tree node $\Omega_{(A,B)}$ and the outputs are the $\mathbb{Y}$ matrices for coupling its two daughter nodes Ω_A and Ω_B.

The coupling tree is solved with a single call to the recursive function: TreeSolve(Ω, $\mathbb{P}$, $\mathbb{U}_n$, $\mathbb{U}_{n+1}$) for a given load $\mathbb{P}$ and initial conditions $\mathbb{U}_n$. Leaf nodes are solved for their responses to external forces using a conventional time integration scheme using the Newmark method [19] and these responses are later coupled in the hierarchy to obtain the full system solution. As for the coupling operations, they only require one multiplication on a smaller (interface-sized) matrix $\boldsymbol{H}^{(A,B)}$ and vector $\boldsymbol{\Lambda}^{(A,B)}_{n+1}$. The subroutine BuildY makes calls to TreeSolve which requires the $\mathbb{Y}$ matrices to have already been computed apriori. With our ordering of the recursive calls in the subroutines, we ensure that all $\mathbb{Y}$ matrices below the particular coupling node have already been computed before we attempt to couple its children.

```
TreeSolve(Ω_(A,B), P^(A,B), U_n^(A,B), U_{n+1}^(A,B))
    If Ω_(A,B) is a Leaf Node then
        Solve Ω_(A,B)
    Else
        Call TreeSolve(Ω_A, P^A, U_n^A, V_{n+1}^A)
        Call TreeSolve(Ω_B, P^B, U_n^B, V_{n+1}^B)
        Compute Λ_{n+1}^(A,B) from H^(A,B) Λ_{n+1}^(A,B) = f^(A,B)
        Update U_{n+1}^A = V_{n+1}^A − Y_A^(A,B) Λ_{n+1}^(A,B)
        Update U_{n+1}^B = V_{n+1}^B − Y_B^(A,B) Λ_{n+1}^(A,B)
    End if
END TreeSolve
```

(a) Subroutine to solve a general node $\Omega_{(A,B)}$ in the tree.

```
BuildY(Ω_(A,B), Y_A^(A,B), Y_B^(A,B))
    Do for K = A, B
        If Ω_K is NOT a Leaf Node :
            Call BuildY(Ω_K, Y^K_LeftChild(K), Y^K_RightChild(K))
        Do for each dof J in Γ_b^(A,B)
            If K = A : P^K = +1 load on dof J in Ω_K
            If K = B : P^K = −1 load on dof J in Ω_K
            Call TreeSolve(Ω_K, P^K, 0, column J of Y_K^(A,B))
        End do
    End Do
END BuildY
```

(b) Subroutine to build the $\mathbb{Y}$ matrices for a general node.

Figure 2: Subroutines for Recursive Solution Procedure

The final algorithm for solving a linear dynamics problem can be summarized in the following steps:

1. Construct the hierarchy of subdomains and build their interface matrices.
2. Form the individual subdomain system matrices.
3. Call BuildY(Ω, $\mathbb{Y}_{left}$, $\mathbb{Y}_{right}$).
4. Form and factorize $\boldsymbol{H}$ matrices for all coupling levels.
5. Compute initial acceleration on the global mesh.
6. Loop over number of time steps FOR n = 1:N
    - Call TreeSolve(Ω, $\mathbb{P}$, $\mathbb{U}_n$, $\mathbb{U}_{n+1}$).

It is important to note here that the initial acceleration calculations and BuildY routines are required to be performed only once at the beginning of the computation. Especially in the case of the BuildY routine, these *initialization* functions are quite costly in terms of computational cost compared to the final TreeSolve routine. However, long term simulation of physical models may require running thousands or millions of timesteps, which amortizes all other costs aside from TreeSolve. Later, when discussing performance of our TreeSolve algorithms, we omit the time taken by other routines.

2.2 Multiple Time Scales

In section 2.1 we discussed a method that utilizes the same time-step for discretizing all the different subdomains in a tree. However, this approach is most beneficial when different subdomains are solved at different timescales. The inclusion of multiple timescales allows for a more fine-grained simulation of specific subdomains within the global problem which contain physically interesting features. The use of different timescales for different subdomains necessitates some key modifications to the TreeSolve algorithm. The main difference is that subdomains with smaller timescales are solved multiple times in a single TreeSolve to advance by a large timestep. We will briefly discuss how two subdomains with different timestep granularities are coupled together. Finer details of the multi-time-scale method can be obtained from the references [22–24].

We describe the method to couple two subdomains, subdomain A at timestep ΔT and subdomain B at timestep Δt where $\Delta T = m\Delta t$, m being an integer timestep ratio. This method can be extended for more layers of coupling of subdomains at different timestep ratios. Using the Newmark method, we wish to advance both subdomains A and B from time t_0 to $t_0 + \Delta T$, shown in Figure 3. However, subdomain A will only require advancing by one large timestep ΔT, whereas subdomain B needs to advance m times by the small timestep Δt. In the context of our TreeSolve algorithm, this means that subdomain B will perform the leaf solve m times while subdomain A performs it a single time. We handle the different timestep ratios by keeping track of the largest ΔT at each coupling node, and calling TreeSolve m times depending on the timestep ratio between its left and right subtrees.

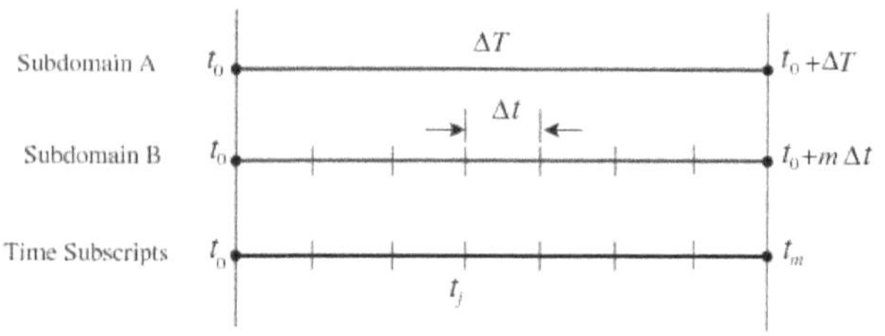

Figure 3: Representation of Time Steps for two Subdomain Case

The multi-time scale coupling requires one other modification in the algorithm which we call *load transfers*. These load transfers are required when there is a common interface between subdomains with different timesteps. Because coupling only occurs at the larger timesteps, linear interpolation is used to approximate the interface reactions at the smaller timesteps. When advancing at a smaller Δt timestep, these load transfers are introduced to preserve equilibrium with the subdomain at the larger time step ΔT. The following equation defines these load transfers $\boldsymbol{S}_j$:

$$\boldsymbol{S}_j = \left(1 - \frac{j}{m}\right)\boldsymbol{\Lambda}_0 \qquad \forall j \in [1, 2, \cdots, m] \tag{10}$$

where m is the time step ratio ($\Delta T/\Delta t$) for the coupling, j is the intermediate timestep of subdomain B, and $\boldsymbol{\Lambda}_0$ is the value of $\boldsymbol{\Lambda}^{(A,B)}$ obtained from the coupling operation in Equation (6) for the previous timestep. Since the $\boldsymbol{\Lambda}$ vector is computed in our initial acceleration calculation at time zero and at each coupling operation, we are guaranteed $\boldsymbol{S}_j$ will be available at every timestep for every subdomain solve, to allow simultaneous solution of different subdomains in parallel.

The final solution algorithm is presented in Figure 4, where subtrees are solved multiple times depending on their timestep ratio at an interior node, and load transfers are saved at each

```
RecursiveSolve(Node)
  If Leaf(Node)
    LeafSolve(Node) [with load transfers]
  Else
    For(Timestep ratio on Left)
      RecursiveSolve(Left)
    For(Timestep ratio on Right)
      RecursiveSolve(Right)
    Couple(Left, Right)
    Save Load Transfer Matrix Λ
  End If
```

Figure 4: Pseudocode for Multi-Timestep TreeSolve

subdomain and handled correctly at every leaf solve. Due to the additional complexity of handling multiple timescales, additional constraints are placed to make our solver feasible. In our problems, we ensure that timestep values are all a fixed ratio of a base timestep value. We also constrain our tree so that child nodes are always at a lower or equivalent time step of its parent node. Finally, in order to correctly handle load transfers required by the multi-timescale method, we require that all subdomains at each timescale be coupled as separately, and each tree then coupled together with the tree of the next smallest timescale, and so forth in the final coupling tree. Although, this restricts the space of trees in the solution space, the entire space still grows exponentially with the number of subdomains.

3 Semantics of Coupling Trees

In this section we describe the properties of our coupling trees, which lays the foundation for creating valid tree orderings. Our inspector phase takes these contraints to find a suitable objective function which is optimized to find the best coupling order. We show that the number of distinct valid trees is exponentially large and that it is not an easy task to find an optimal ordering. To obtain a good solution, we introduce a cost model which correlates with the computational time taken to complete the TreeSolve routine, which becomes the target of our optimization.

The important properties of a coupling operation are that they are both associative and commutative. Coupling two subdomains A and B is identical regardless of order, and coupling (A B) with C is no different than coupling A with (B C). Thus, given a particular coupling tree, we can create a new, equivalent tree by re-associating the coupling operations. This is equivalent to performing tree-rotations on any pair of coupling operations, as shown in Figure 5(a) or by performing commutative swaps of the tree, as shown in Figure 5(b).

By performing a series of these commutative and associative manipulations, we see that *any* binary tree with a particular set of leaf nodes represents a valid coupling order for a given problem. However, trees with only their left and right children swapped will have the same behavior in terms of coupling, and will hence have the same performance. The question we ask is "How many possible distinct trees $\mathcal{T}(s)$ are there for a given number of subdomains s?" It can be shown that the number of possible trees for s subdomains, $\mathcal{T}(s)$, is given by:

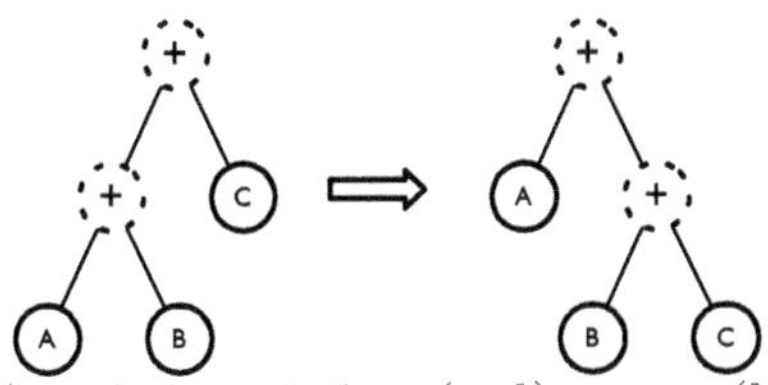

(a) Associative rotation: $(a \cdot b) \cdot c \equiv a \cdot (b \cdot c)$

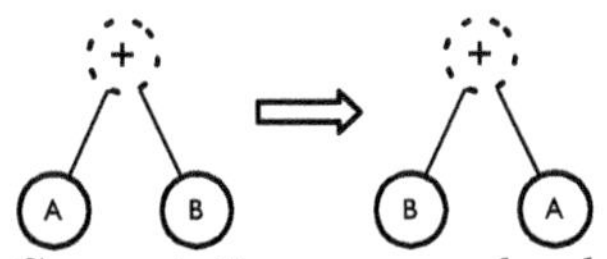

(b) Commutative swap: $a \cdot b \equiv b \cdot a$

Figure 5: Possible Optimizing Operations on Trees

$$\mathcal{T}(s) = \frac{(2s-2)!}{2^{s-1}(s-1)!}$$

Intuitively, this is related to the Catalan numbers, which represent (among other things) the total possible configurations for a binary tree. For a tree with s leaves, we start with the $s-1^{th}$ Catalan number, $\frac{(2s-2)!}{s!(s-1)!}$. This must then be multiplied by $s!$ to account for all possible commutative reorderings, and then divided by $2^{(s-1)}$ to disregard left-right reflections that have no impact on performance. This quantity grows very quickly: $\mathcal{T}(8) = 135{,}135$, and for any reasonable number of subdomains (even small problems may have 32 subdomains), the space of possible trees is too large to exhaustively search for an optimal solution. In the multi-time-scale case, the constraint that trees of different timescales must be coupled at a single point somewhat reduces the possible number of orderings, as not all trees adhere to the coupling constraints. Nevertheless, the above expression reflects the number of orderings present in each of the subtrees.

Given the large number of trees, how might we select the correct tree for a given problem? In this paper, we adopt an approach that is based on the inspector-executor model for program optimization. In this approach, an inspector evaluates the given tree coupling order by a user, and uses heuristics to find an optimal tree coupling order that minimizes computational cost, thus reducing execution time and gaining performance. In order to set a performance-based objective, we modeled the computational cost after the sequence of computations being carried out by the algorithm.

4 Cost Model & Heuristics

To automatically find optimal coupling schedules for our decomposed problems, we adopt a model to quantify the cost of any particular coupling configuration. Using this model, we develop an optimization scheme that selects from the configuration space of all coupling schedules one that produces a low cost. This section discusses the cost model and the optimization system we developed based on these models.

4.1 Cost Model

A cost model was developed to accurately reflect the execution time of the TreeSolve code prior to solving the coupling tree. This is done by inspecting the coupling tree and modeling its costs based on the properties of the input, namely the interface and subdomain sizes. Once the tree structure

Cost per leaf	Cost per interior node	
n_i^3	$\sum_{i \in C} n_i^2 m_{i:v}$	Update of Y
	$\sum_{i \in C} n_i m_{i:v}^2$	Calculating H
	m_v^3	Calculating λ
	$\sum_{i \in C} n_i m_{i:v}$	Updating X
	$\sum_{v' \in C} \sum_{i \in v'} n_i m_{i:v'} m_{i:v}$	Solving F
	$\sum_{v' \in C} m_{v'}^2 m_v$	Calculating Λ
	$\sum_{v' \in C} \sum_{i \in v'} n_i m_{i:v'} m_{i:v}$	Updating Y

Table 1: Cost Model Contributions from Coupling Tree

is determined, we then measure the matrix sizes for all operations to estimate the time it will take to run during actual execution. There are several different cost components that contribute to the TreeSolve cost. Most of them are matrix-matrix or matrix-vector multiplications as well as a few matrix-matrix and matrix-vector solves. We characterize their costs based on the sizes of the matrices and the amount of work necessary to compute their solutions. The following variable definitions are used to come up with the costs:

1. $\boldsymbol{n_i}$: number of equations in subdomain $\boldsymbol{S}_i$
2. $\boldsymbol{m_v}$: number of equations in the coupling interface for interior node v
3. $\boldsymbol{m_{i:v}}$: number of equations in interface of v that are associated with subdomain $\boldsymbol{S}_i$
4. $\boldsymbol{C}$: Descendant leaf nodes of an interior node
5. $\boldsymbol{v}, \boldsymbol{v}'$: interior nodes

For a given tree (or subtree), the total cost of that tree comes from the leaf nodes in that (sub)tree, which represent the decomposed subdomains, and the interior nodes of the (sub)tree, which represent the coupling cost of the tree. The values of these costs are given in Table 1.

The different matrices $\boldsymbol{Y}, \boldsymbol{H}, \boldsymbol{\lambda}, \boldsymbol{X}, \boldsymbol{F}$ and $\boldsymbol{\Lambda}$ (some temporary) are used in the final TreeSolve and BuildY subroutines. Details of the equations and computations for these matrices can be found in the reference [22]. We note one important fact: each interior node's cost is determined by the number of leaf nodes under that interior node, and hence interior nodes higher in the tree (*i.e.*, coupling operations higher in the tree) have higher costs than those lower in the tree.

With this cost model, our inspector can access cost values of different trees without having to solve them. In our results, we show that the cost values correlate well with actual runtimes, enabling us to use heuristics based on the models to create effective coupling trees.

Figure 6 shows CDF of tree cost for 1000 randomly generated trees, for a given computational mechanics problem decomposed into 8 subdomains. It is observed that by picking only 1000 randomly coupled trees out of the whole tree space (< 1% of the space), the costs vary substantially, and between two coupling configurations, the costs can differ by an order of magnitude. Our work presents a way to find a configuration that obtains a near-optimal runtime among the space of coupling trees.

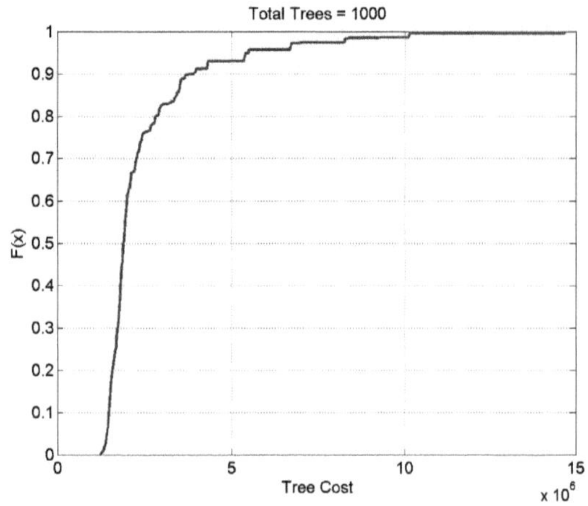

Figure 6: CDF of 1000 Random Trees based on tree costs

4.2 Tree Building Heuristics

With a large space of existing possible trees for a given problem, the probability of a domain scientist choosing a low cost tree is small. A domain scientist with limited computing knowledge might couple subdomains based simply on the partition ordering of the subdomains (*i.e.*, the order in which partitioners such as METIS [14] produce mesh partitions). We call this the Default approach, and it represents the baseline coupling order for a problem. As described above, our system adopts the inspector-executor paradigm that analyzes the input of a given hierarchical multi-scale computational mechanics problem and automatically determines effective coupling orders based on our cost model before solving the coupling tree.

Given that the cost model developed in the previous section computes costs on a per-subtree basis, an intuitive approach would be to develop a greedy algorithm that builds the coupling tree from the bottom up. Recall that when two subdomains are coupled after being solved for a time step, their coupled solution is similar to first joining together the equations and then solving the larger, merged subdomain. As a result, a greedy approach might proceed by coupling together subdomains based on some heuristic such as coupling subdomains with the largest shared interface, and then treating the coupled subtree as a new, larger subdomain and repeating the process. At each step, the cost model can be used to evaluate the coupling heuristic for the current set of subdomains to be coupled.

We experimented with several greedy heuristics; however, there is a fundamental drawback with this greedy approach. Although it optimizes the cost for each instance of coupling, it ignores the future cost of coupling subtrees necessary to solve the decomposed system, causing poor performance. Recall that coupling operations higher in the tree inherently cost more than coupling operations lower in the tree. Hence, bottom-up algorithms, which cannot even predict what the costs higher in the tree will be until the lower levels have been assembled, are not appropriate.

Instead, we adopt a *top down* approach, focusing on minimizing the coupling costs at higher levels of the tree. Beyond this, we would also like to maintain the balance of the tree, with both left and right subtrees for any node having roughly equal solution times; this will improve the potential parallelism of the resulting tree.

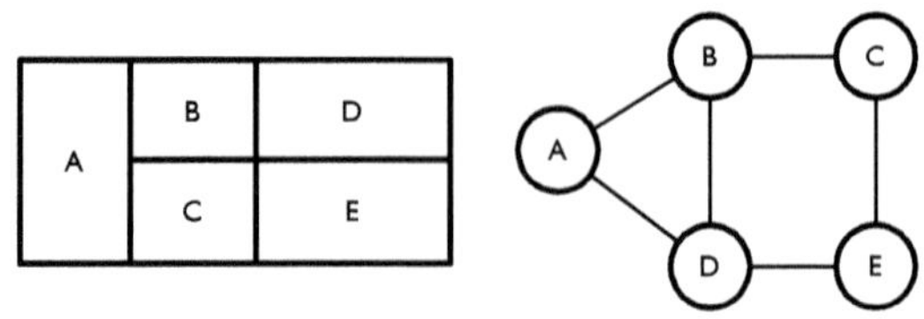

Figure 7: Graph Representing a 5 Subdomain System

To implement our top-down approach, the inspector phase analyzes the input problem and views the partitioned mesh as an undirected graph, as shown in Figure 7. In the graph, each node represents a subdomain, and edges represent shared interfaces between them. In other words, the graph represents the topology of the subdomains. One approach to building a tree top-down given this abstraction is to simply perform a series of graph bisections. The graph is divided into two partitions, with nodes from each partition representing the subdomains that will be in the left and right subtrees of the root. This process can be repeated recursively to construct the entire subtree. In the multi-time-scale case, we produce multiple graphs, one for each timestep in the problem (as subdomains at each time step must be coupled together before moving on to larger time steps).

Note that even performing this top-down bisection relies on domain knowledge: because this tree-building approach can produce arbitrary results, it is only legal *because we know the domain semantics allow for any coupling order.* Nevertheless, despite leveraging domain semantics to build the tree, this approach does not consider that leaf solve and coupling costs are based on properties of the operations such as the number of equations and interface sizes. This bisection technique is what an application programmer might think as optimal for decomposing meshes in a top-down fashion. However, this method (labeled cost-agnostic in our experiments) does not take into account *domain specific cost information.*

One of the key contributions of this work, labeled our domain-specific heuristic, is a scheduling procedure that not only integrates domain-specific semantic information, but also domain-specific cost information. We use domain knowledge obtained from our cost model and apply the coupling and subdomain costs to the edge and node weights in our graph prior to partitioning. In particular, a node's weight is calculated based on the leaf-node cost model, and is the cube of the number of equations in the subdomain. Precise edge weights are harder to determine, as they rely on the overall structure of the subtree rooted at a coupling node. However, the primary cost of a coupling operation is proportional to the size of the interface between the domains being coupled. Hence, edge weights are set to the interface size of the two subdomains connected by that edge.

We then use METIS to perform repeated bisections of this graph, as in the cost-agnostic approach. There are two key differences, however. METIS attempts to create balanced partitions while minimizing the weight of cut edges. The cost of a coupling operation is proportional to the interface size between the two domains being coupled. When the graph is bisected, the two sets of nodes representing the two domains that will be coupled, and the interface between those domains is exactly captured by the edges that are cut. Hence, because edge weights are determined by interface size, by minimizing the weight of cut edges, METIS naturally produces low-cost coupling operations. Second, the dominant cost in the TreeSolve algorithm is the cost of solving leaf nodes for a tree. Because these costs are exactly captured by the weights on nodes, by attempting to balance the two partitions of a graph, METIS naturally produces balanced trees. Hence, by incorporating knowledge of our domain-specific cost models into the top-down tree-building framework, we can produce low-cost, well-balanced trees. This tree building strategy focuses on minimizing total work, but still performs well for both parallel and serial execution. Intuitively, the domain-specific heuristic produces well balanced trees. Provided with sufficient parallelism, minimizing the total work also reduces the total parallel runtime, resulting in optimal parallel performance as well.

After producing a coupling tree, the inspector transforms this tree into an execution schedule, which is passed on to the executor phase for execution. Our approach provides two executors: a sequential executor and a parallel executor. Both executors use platform-optimized BLAS [6] and LAPACK [2] routines to efficiently compute the matrix solutions for a system using the hierarchical method. For our parallel implementation, we use Cilk [7] to obtain optimal parallel performance. Section 5 describes the parallel execution strategy.

5 Parallelization

This section describes the details of the TreeSolve parallel executor. We briefly discuss the semantics of Cilk and its role in our parallel execution scheme. We then provide details on how TreeSolve is parallelized, highlighting specific issues that arise when running in parallel and how we overcome them.

Cilk is an algorithmic multithreaded language used to optimize parallel programs. We chose to use Cilk because it is a minimally intrusive parallelization tool which can deal with irregular codes without introducing large synchronization overheads. The parallel TreeSolve calls the Cilk multithreaded runtime system using fork-join parallelization at each tree node. This allows each subtree path to run concurrently, while Cilk's work-stealing mechanism effectively handles any load balance issues that arises due to complexities of the the recursive algorithm and multiple timescales.

Running the TreeSolve along with Cilk requires adding some minimally intrusive code to our existing algorithm. Two Cilk constructs, spawn and sync, are used to direct the parallel execution. The following pseudocode shows the modified TreeSolve algorithm using Cilk.

Figure 8 captures the overall structure required by Cilk to run the TreeSolve algorithm in parallel. Running the Cilk version of TreeSolve will spawn new threads to concurrently execute the left and right paths at each interior node of the tree. Threads eventually reach a leaf node, where it then runs the routine for a subdomain solve to advance a timescale. Once threads finish from both the left and right paths, they arrive at the sync point, where the atomic coupling operation updates the subdomains from the left and right subtrees. Additional bookkeeping is required to correctly couple subdomains of different timescales. Static timescale values are stored at each node in our tree structure to validate coupling of subtrees. Since subtrees are decoupled from other subtrees from other paths, we can execute them in parallel; however, each path may be executed different number of times depending on their assigned timescales.

```
Cilk TreeSolve(Node)
    If Leaf(Node)
        LeafSolve(Node) [with load transfers]
    Else
        Spawn TreeSolve(Left)
        Spawn TreeSolve(Right)
        Sync
        Couple(Left, Right)
        Save Load Transfer Matrix Λ
    End If
```

Figure 8: TreeSolve Algorithm using Cilk

5.1 Difficulties

Optimal parallelization of TreeSolve is not an easy task. Due to the recursive nature of the TreeSolve and multiple timescales, algorithms using a typical fork-join model performs poorly due to load imbalance. Previous versions of TreeSolve which used these methods saw unpredictable parallel performance. Depending on the input and its coupling order, parallel execution was extremely inefficient, sometimes taking an additional order of magnitude for extreme cases. We also implemented a dynamic parallel algorithm which did not use a fork-join model. This dynamic execution scheme maintained a task queue composed of coupling and subdomain operations, and executed them as it became available, then enqueuing new tasks once dependencies were satisfied. This scheme resolved issues caused by load imbalance, but required locks to synchronize at every coupling operation of execution. Our Cilk implementation is very similar to that approach; however, Cilk uses synchronization methods which incur a lower overhead than traditional locks, while using a work-stealing method to remedy load imbalance. For most inputs, Cilk is able to outperform other parallel implementations of the TreeSolve algorithm.

6 Evaluation

In this section, we validate our cost model against actual runtime performance and evaluate the performance of the cost-agnostic and domain-specific heuristics running both sequential and parallel TreeSolve algorithms. We focus on the results of three physical systems, represented as finite element meshes of hexahedral elements, as testing systems: 1) a 128 subdomain cube mesh with 15625 elements 2) a 128 subdomain rocket mesh with 3632 elements and 3) a 128 subdomain stargrain mesh with 37152 elements. Each mesh is partitioned by METIS to give an optimal partitioning. These systems are simulated using the multi-scale solver running on an AMD Opteron 6176 SE system configured with four 12-core processors (a total of 48 cores) running at 2.3 GHz. Each input contains two timescales, with an eighth of the subdomains assigned to run at a smaller timestep and the rest of the system at a larger timestep. The timestep ratio is 10 for the cube and stargrain input, while it is 100 for the rocket input. The timestep values are arbitrarily chosen; however, for the rocket input, the smaller timesteps are assigned to the subdomains of interest, containing cracked regions of the physical system. Figure 9 shows the three meshes after partitioning, as seen from the various colors.

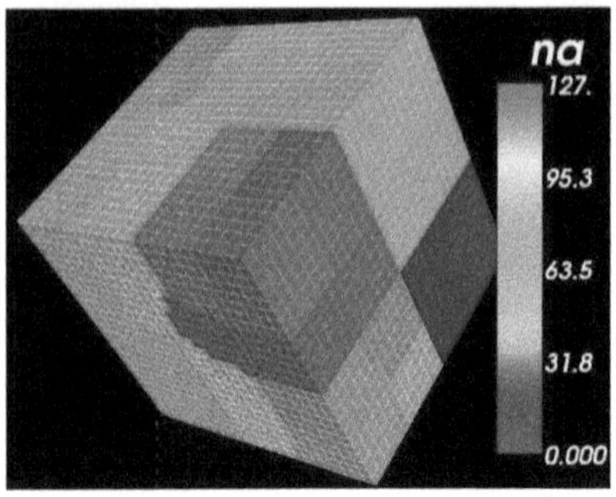

(a) Example of a Partitioned Cube Mesh

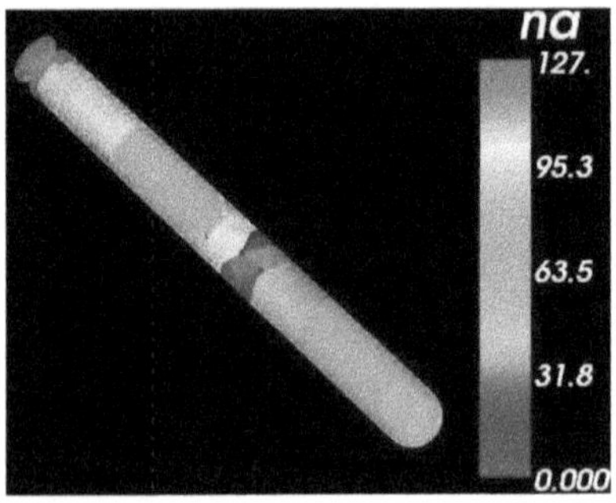

(b) Example of a Partitioned Rocket Mesh

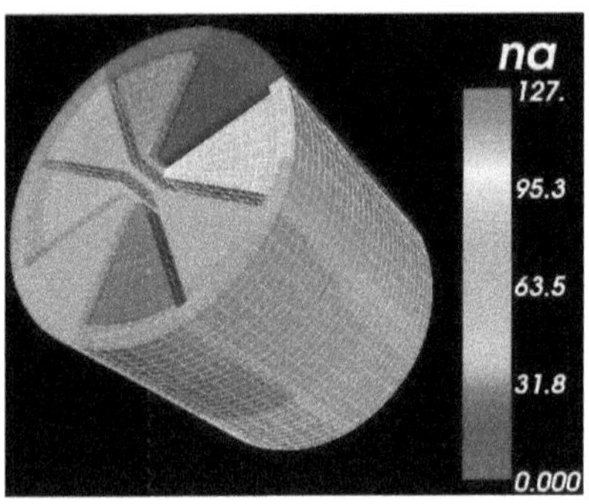

(c) Example of a Partitioned Stargrain Mesh

Figure 9: Visualization of Finite Element Mesh Models

6.1 Cost model validation

To validate our cost model, a set of 500 randomly generated coupling trees was used to represent a sample of the entire space of coupling trees. These trees are created by starting with all subdomains in separate subtrees and randomly selecting two subtrees to be coupled together until the full tree is obtained. Note that this random coupling means that occasionally two subdomains that do not share an interface will be coupled. This schedule is mathematically and semantically correct: the final solution will be computed correctly. Nevertheless, such coupling orders are nonsensical from a performance perspective, as there is no benefit in reduced work to be gained from coupling subdomains that are not adjoining.

The rocket input shown in Figure 9(b), partitioned into a 32 subdomain mesh (as a sample input), was used to explore the space of trees. Figure 10 illustrates the correlation of our cost model with the actual runtimes for solving the 32 subdomain mesh on single and multiple threads. For various number of cores, actual runtimes are plotted against the projected cost of the corresponding trees. The results show that the correlation between the projected cost and expected runtime has an average correlation coefficient of 0.77–0.85 for single and multiple threads. We estimate the parallel costs using the same sequential model. We justify that the parallel runtime correlates with total work during parallel execution. Although we see that correlation does decrease for higher number of threads, our cost model does strongly reflect the execution time of the TreeSolve code. For the remaining test inputs, the cost model shows similar results with high correlation.

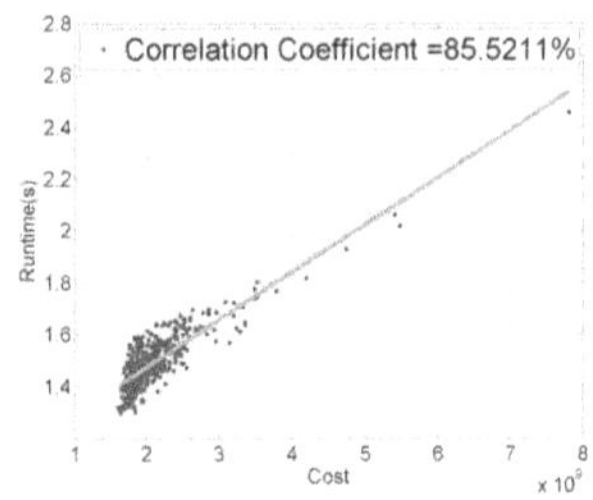

(a) 1 Core

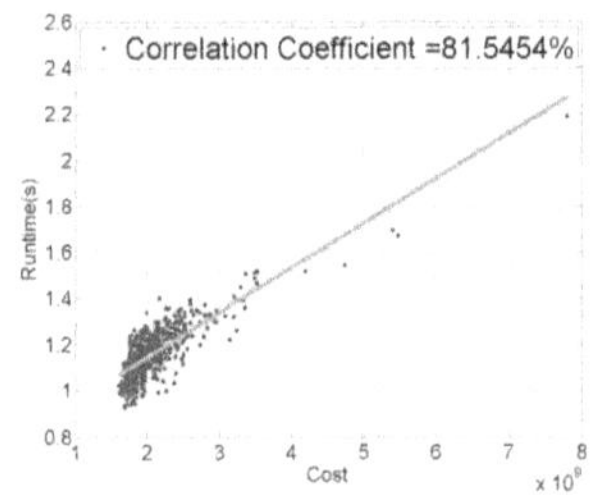

(b) 2 Cores

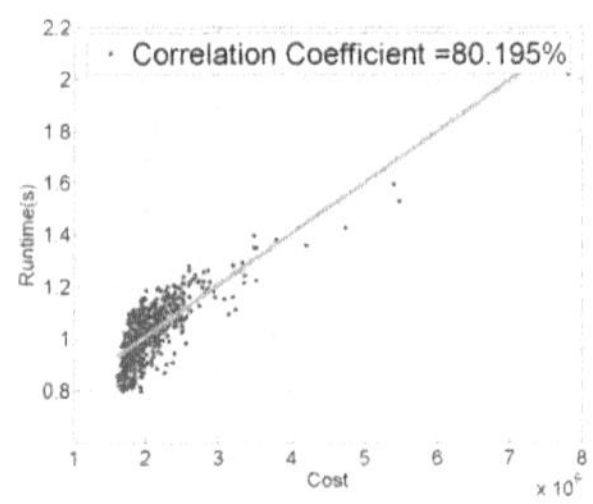

(c) 4 Cores.

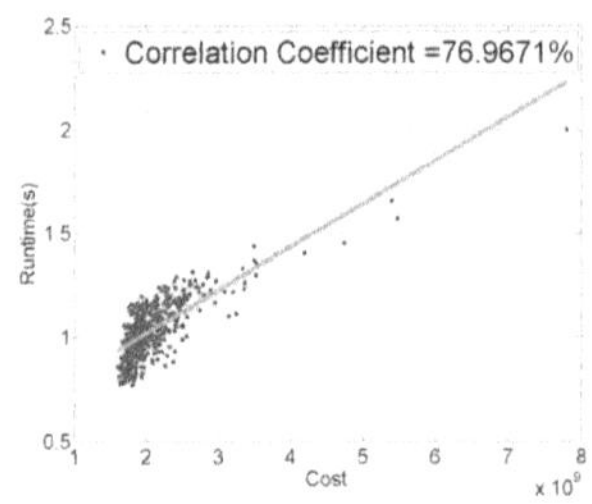

(d) 8 Cores.

Figure 10: Rocket: Cost vs Runtime Correlation of 500 Random Trees

6.2 Performance comparisons

We next compare the execution times for running our heuristics on our three testing inputs. Given each partitioned mesh, our heuristics generate new coupling orders to solve each problem, subject to multiple timescales. In addition to our domain-specific heuristic DS, we evaluate the cost-agnostic tree CA and the Default DT, which is based on the initial METIS numbering. As described in Section 4.2, DT serves as a baseline; the initial coupling schedule produced after METIS is used to partition the initial mesh into subdomains. This coupling schedule also serves as the input to our inspector-executor system. CA uses a top-down approach to produce a new tree, but does not incorporate the domain-specific cost models, while our DS heuristic refines the top-down approach by incorporating knowledge of leaf solve and coupling costs. For each input, we evaluate all three schedules.

Figure 11 shows a CDF of the runtimes for running the 32 subdomain rocket input for various numbers of threads. We compare the execution times of DS, CA, and DT, along with the 500 randomly generated trees for single and multiple threads. Here we observe that DS outperforms all the trees that we tested and we achieved a significant speedup

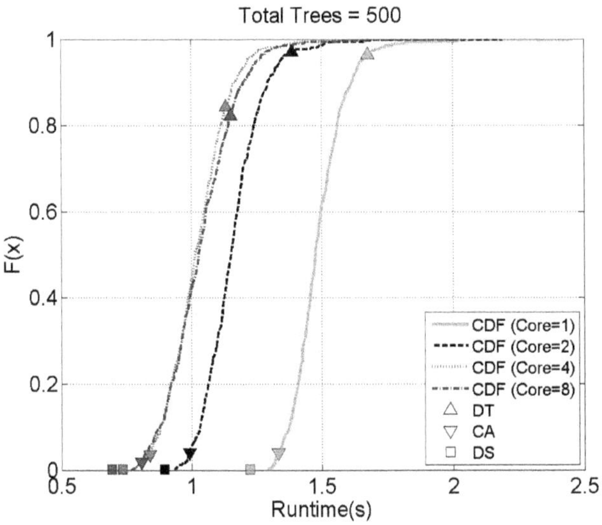

Figure 11: Rocket: CDF of Runtimes for 500 Random Trees with Heuristics

over randomly selected trees in the configuration space. In other words, despite the vast configuration space, by incorporating domain-specific semantic and cost knowledge, we are able to infer a very effective coupling order. We also note that the other evaluated schedules, DT and CA perform worse than our domain-specific schedule. We see that the default schedule is quite slow, while CA yields better results. Nevertheless, our DS approach outperforms the CA schedule by 7 to 20%.

6.3 Parallel performance

Figure 12 compares the execution times for each heuristic across different number of threads for the cube, rocket and stargrain input meshes. We note that in all cases, the DS approach delivers noticeably better performance than the CA and DT. While the specific amount of improvement when using our DS heuristic is problem-dependent, we see that incorporating domain knowledge provides a consistent edge across multiple inputs. Table 2 shows the speedup of CA and DS over the baseline, DT, for each of the inputs at both one and eight threads. Not only does the DS schedule perform the best in single-threaded execution, the advantage increases at higher thread counts; DS provides better scalability.

	No. Thread = 1		No. Thread = 8	
	CA	DS	CA	DS
Cube	0.94	1.33	1.04	1.52
Rocket	1.35	1.47	1.65	1.95
Stargrain	1.26	1.52	1.93	2.62

Table 2: Speedups of CA and DS schedules over baseline DT

For all of the schedules, performance scales up to 4 threads and speedup is obtained when increasing the number of threads. For 8 threads and beyond, the results do not scale well. Using the Cilk profiling tool, we found that for each input, past 4 cores, the runtime of critical path equals the runtime of the solver. This indicates that the parallelism saturates at 8 threads and not much more parallelism can be exploited. Increasing communication costs and parallel overhead plays a role here. This lack of scalability is understandable because the structure of the input is inher-

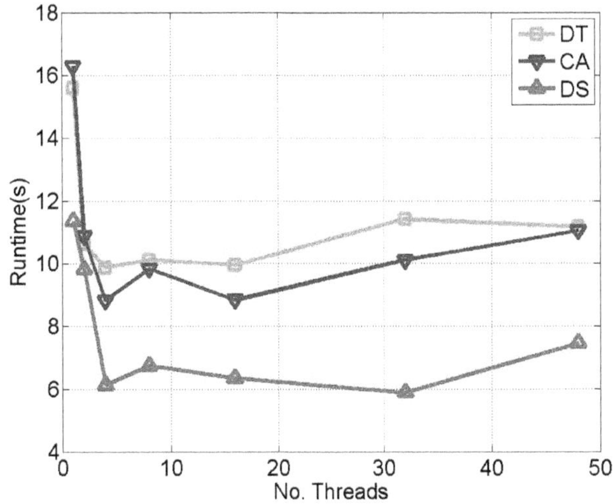

(a) 128 Subdomain Cube Mesh

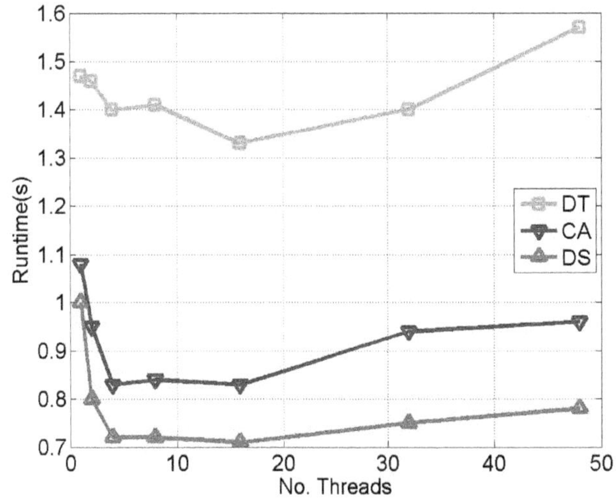

(b) 128 Subdomain Rocket Mesh

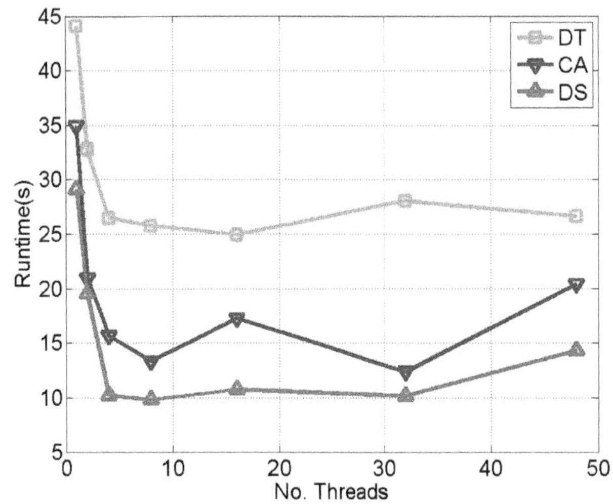

(c) 128 Subdomain Stargrain Mesh

Figure 12: Execution times across different number of threads

ently imbalanced. Figure 13 shows a tree generated using top-down heuristic using sample 32 subdomain rocket input. We see that the left side of the tree has 4 subdomains and the right side has 28 subdomains. This imbalance is due to the fact that a small number of subdomains are at a lower time scale, which requires fine grain calculations as compared to other parts of the mesh and, due to limitations of the coupling algorithm must be solved separately from the rest of the mesh. In other words, there is a certain amount of inevitable, application-specific load imbalance, especially when there are only a few subdomains run at small time scales. Additionally, the tree-based nature of the algorithm and the fact that coupling occurs atomically limit available parallelism.

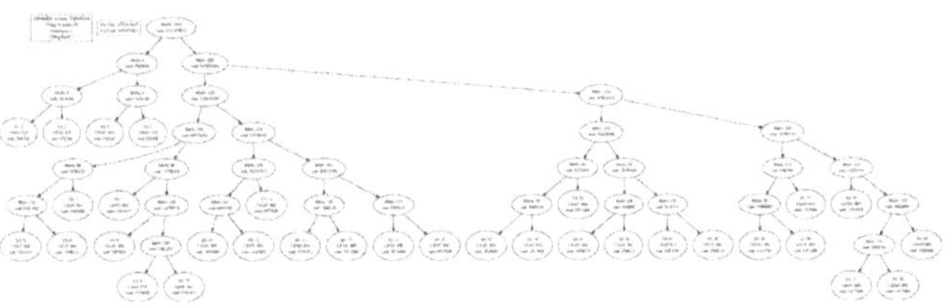

Figure 13: A typical form of a tree generated from input meshes

Available parallelism and scalability across heuristics

A natural question, given the inherent lack of scalability, is whether our scheduling heuristics negatively impact the available parallelism of the program. To investigate this question, we used Cilk to profile the total work, critical path length (span), and amount of parallelism (work/span) afforded by each schedule across all of the inputs. Table 3 summarizes these results.

There are two key take-aways from these results. First, as expected, the DS scheduling heuristic, which incorporates domain-specific semantic and cost information, yields the best single-threaded performance (work), often by a significant margin. This is consistent with the raw performance numbers shown above. Second, despite the heuristics focusing on work minimization, with parallelism only of secondary importance, parallelism is not adversely affected. In fact, on two of the three inputs, DS provides better parallelism than the other two schedules, and on the third input, DS exhibits the same amount of parallelism as CA. The advantage of DS in available parallelism is reflected in the scalability results of Table 2, where DS scales better in practice than the alternative schedules.

Input	Schedule	Work (sec)	Critical Path (sec)	Parallelism
Cube	DT	16.54	10.65	1.55
	CA	17.60	10.02	1.76
	DS	11.94	5.98	2.00
Rocket	DT	2.18	1.55	1.41
	CA	1.93	1.29	1.50
	DS	1.27	0.67	1.90
Stargrain	DT	44.09	23.77	1.85
	CA	34.91	11.12	3.14
	DS	29.12	9.23	3.15

Table 3: Inherent parallelism in coupling schedules

6.4 Inspector phase overhead

The inspector phase, which consists of analyzing the mesh topology and creating the coupling tree, takes approximately as much time as reading the input file. However, long term simulation of physical models may require running thousands or millions of timesteps, which amortizes all other costs aside from the TreeSolve iterations, which is what we measured. Depending on the problem, the time taken by the inspector phase is 0.1% to 1% that of the total executor phase time and less than the time it takes to run TreeSolve for one timestep.

7 Related Work

Domain-specific languages There have been many projects that have leveraged semantic properties of domains to perform domain-specific optimizations on applications that could not be performed by traditional compilers. In the Spiral project, digital signal processing applications are written in a domain-specific language, SPL, and then manipulated using algebraic transformations before optimized code is generated [29]. In the Tensor Contraction Engine, a domain-specific language is used to specify computational chemistry problems as a series of operations on tensors [4]. Because these operations possess simple semantic properties such as commutativity and associativity, the number of possible tensor contraction "schedules" is vast; at compile time, a search procedure identifies the minimal-cost implementation of the given problem and passes that implementation to code-generation routines that perform further optimizations. Other projects have exploited semantic properties in numerically intensive codes written in Matlab—Falcon [25], MaJIC [1, 17] and Telescoping Languages [8, 15]. The key unifying factor in all of these approaches is that they operate at compile-time. In contrast, our optimization approach operates at run-time, as the structure of the problem is not known until the input is seen. Section 8 discusses additional key differences between our approach and prior work, and explores the ramifications of these differences.

Inspector-executor approaches The inspector-executor approach has been used to perform parallelization and optimization in numerous situations where the computational structure of a program is not known until run time. It is often used for parallelization, where the dependence structure of an application is inspected, and a parallelization schedule is determined [21]. In other settings, the dependence structure of a sparse-matrix application can be unfolded to drive *runtime reordering transformations* that aim to improve locality [10, 27]. To our knowledge, most inspector-executor approaches focus on identifying dependences so that an existing computational schedule can be restructured to improve performance. Nevertheless, the underlying algorithm (*i.e.*, the operations performed and the dependence structure) remains the same. In contrast, we use inspection to unfold the computational structure and then *transform* the computation, producing a new computation with an entirely new data flow and dependence structure. Note that because our transformations change the dependence structure, they *necessarily* must exploit semantic properties of the operations (since they violate existing dependences).

8 Lessons Learned

While the study presented in this paper is specific to one method for solving computational mechanics problems, we note that this same general approach applies to a large number of recursive-decomposition-based computational science problems, which arise in domains ranging from computational mechanics to fluid dynamics to peridynamics. Hence, we expect that our inspector-executor system can readily be applied to these other problems.

Moreover, we feel that the approach we took to transforming the problem leads to general lessons that can be applied more broadly. In most instances of domain-specific transformation systems (*e.g.*, [1, 4, 8, 15, 17, 25, 29]), the initial program is written in a domain-specific, high-level language where the semantics needed to drive the optimizations are explicit in the language. In contrast, in our work the computational solver is written in a traditional language (C). The routines that unfold the computational structure are associated with the library interface, and hence can work with any *implementation* of that interface, as well as any application that uses the library.

At a high level, one can view the traditional approach of performing domain-specific optimizations as *optimize-lower*. That is, write an application in a domain-specific language, *optimize* the application using the semantic properties exposed by the DSL then *lower* the program into the target low-level language where other domain-agnostic optimizations can be performed. In contrast, in this work we *started* with an application written in a low-level language. Routines associated with the domain library were used to *lift* the program into a high-level representation that was then transformed and subsequently lowered back into calls to the low-level library routines. Hence, our approach is more aptly termed *lift-optimize-lower*. The primary advantage to a lift-optimize-lower approach is that the source program need not be written in a domain-specific language, but instead can be written using domain libraries familiar to domain scientists.

Another interesting point about our approach is that the transformation routines are completely general. The transformations performed on the computation tree merely take advantage of commutativity and associativity. While these properties are related to the semantics of the domain, the transformations themselves are by no means domain-specific. In fact, the very simplicity of these properties makes them much more broadly applicable. Indeed, the same properties are exploited in systems like the tensor contraction engine (TCE) [4].

This commonality presents an attractive possibility. Consider developing a *high level* intermediate representation, which could represent programs as a composition of abstract operations with domain-agnostic properties such as commutativity and associativity. A program can be lifted into this high level representation, with its domain-specific operations mapped to the appropriate abstract operations (*e.g.*, in our domain, the Couple operation would be mapped to an associative and commutative abstract operation). At this point, a generic transformation engine can act on the high level representation, and the transformed program can be lowered back to the original representation. Even though the transformations are generic, they can be driven by domain-specific cost models as in our application study, effectively performing domain-specific optimizations while remaining domain agnostic. This is similar in spirit to the approach of Willcock *et al.* [28], where compiler transformations that deal with basic types are extended to work on more complex types, allowing for the same transformation pattern to be used in multiple domains; the key difference is that in our scenario, transformations are driven by domain-specific cost models, rather than syntax.

Essentially, rather than performing domain-specific transformations, with new systems being built for each new domain, the kernel of the proposed optimization framework would be completely domain-independent, instantiated only with cost models for operations and routines to translate back and forth from the intermediate representation. Such an approach would lead to a clean separation of concerns, as domain scientists need only consider the high level properties of the operations in their domains, while systems writers can focus on efficient transformations and effective search heuristics. Our case study of a computational mechanics solver is an important proof-of-concept of this approach, as the transformations and search heuristics are oblivious to the details of the domain, relying only on the domain-specific cost model to drive the search. Future work will be to map other domains (such as tensor contraction, fluid dynamics, etc.) to the same run-time transformation framework.

9 Conclusions

This paper presents an effective algorithm for optimizing computational mechanics codes based on recursive domain decomposition for static and dynamic systems. Solving a decomposed problem is represented as solving a binary tree, and the structure of the tree dictates the performance of the solver. We show that the number of possible tree coupling orders is exponentially large for systems even with a moderate number of subdomains. Among the various trees, many do not perform well, and it is not obvious which trees have good performance.

We demonstrate for real problems that our heuristic can generate near optimal coupling trees and execute them efficiently. We show that the inspector's heuristics for building coupling trees consistently produce trees that rank in the 99th percentile of possible trees for problems. Finally, we show that the executor is able to deliver scalable performance on multiple cores as long as there is parallelism to be exploited, providing solutions in less time than randomly selected coupling trees. It automatically provides optimized, parallel implementations of multi-scale computational mechanics problems, allowing domain scientists to take advantage of novel computational techniques without devoting substantial time to the tedious process of optimizing a parallel implementation on a problem-by-problem basis.

Acknowledgments

We would like to thank the anonymous reviewers for their feedback and suggestions. This research is supported by the Department of Energy under contract DE-FC02-12ER26104. M. Hasan Jamal is supported by a Fullbright Fellowship.

References

[1] G. Almási and D. Padua. MaJIC: Compiling MATLAB for speed and responsiveness. In *Proceedings of the ACM SIGPLAN 2002 Conference on Programming Language Design and Implementation*, PLDI '02, pages 294–303, 2002.

[2] E. Anderson, Z. Bai, C. Bischof, J. Demmel, J. Dongarra, J. D. Croz, A. Greenbaum, S. Hammarling, A. McKenney, S. Ostrouchov, and D. Sorensen. *LAPACK's user's guide.* SIAM, 1992.

[3] P. Arbenz, U. L. Hetmaniuk, R. B. Lehoucq, and R. S. Tuminaro. A comparison of eigensolvers for large-scale 3d modal analysis using amg-preconditioned iterative methods. *International Journal for Numerical Methods in Engineering*, 64:204–236, 2005.

[4] G. Baumgartner, D. E. Bernholdt, D. Cociorva, R. Harrison, S. Hirata, C.-C. Lam, M. Nooijen, R. Pitzer, J. Ramanujam, and P. Sadayappan. A high-level approach to synthesis of high-performance codes for quantum chemistry. In *Proceedings of the 2002 ACM/IEEE conference on Supercomputing*, Supercomputing '02, pages 1–10, 2002.

[5] J. K. Bennighof and R. B. Lehoucq. An automated multilevel substructuring method for eigenspace computation in linear elastodynamics. *SIAM Journal on Scientific Computing*, 25:2084–2106, 2004.

[6] S. Blackford, J. Demmel, J. Dongarra, I. Duff, S. Hammarling, G. Henry, M. Heroux, L. Kaufman, A. Lumsdaine, A. Petitet, R. Pozo, K. Remington, and C. Whaley. An updated set of Basic Linear Algebra Subprograms (BLAS). *ACM Transactions on Mathematical Software*, 28(2):135–151, June 2002.

[7] R. D. Blumofe, C. F. Joerg, B. C. Kuszmaul, C. E. Leiserson, K. H. Randall, and Y. Zhou. Cilk: An efficient multithreaded runtime system. In *Proceedings of the 5th ACM SIGPLAN Symposium on Principles and Practice of Parallel Programming*, PPOPP '95, pages 207–216, 1995.

[8] A. Chauhan and K. Kennedy. Optimizing strategies for telescoping languages: Procedure strength reduction and procedure vectorization, year = 2001. In *ICS '01: Proceedings of the 15th International Conference on Supercomputing*, pages 92–101.

[9] R. Das, M. Uysal, J. Saltz, and Y.-S. Hwang. Communication optimizations for irregular scientific computations on distributed memory architectures. *Journal of Parallel and Distributed Computing*, 22:462–479, 1993.

[10] C. Ding and K. Kennedy. Improving cache performance in dynamic applications through data and computation reorganization at runtime. In *Proceedings of the ACM SIGPLAN 1999 Conference on Programming Language Design and Implementation*, PLDI '99, pages 229–241, 1999.

[11] J. Fish. Bridging the scales in nano engineering and science. *Journal of Nanoparticle Research*, 8(5):577–594, 2006.

[12] V. Gravemeier, S. Lenz, and W. A. Wall. Towards a taxonomy for multiscale methods in computational mechanics: Building blocks of existing methods. *Computational Mechanics*, 41(2):279–291, 2008.

[13] W. Hackbush. On the computation of approximate eigenvalues and eigenfunctions of elliptic operators by means of a multigrid method. *SIAM Journal on Numerical Analysis*, 16:201–215, 1979.

[14] G. Karypis and V. Kumar. Metis - unstructured graph partitioning and sparse matrix ordering system, version 2.0. Technical report, Department of Computer Science, University of Minnesota, 1995.

[15] K. Kennedy, B. Broom, K. Cooper, J. Dongarra, R. Fowler, D. Gannon, L. Johnsson, J. Mellor-Crummey, and L. Torczon. Telescoping languages: A strategy for automatic generation of scientific problem-solving systems from annotated libraries. *Journal of Parallel and Distributed Computing*, 61(12):1803–1826, 2001.

[16] Z. Li, Y. Saad, and M. Sosonkina. pARMS: a parallel version of the algebraic recursive multilevel solver. *Numerical Linear Algebra with Applications*, 10:485–509, 2003.

[17] V. Menon and K. Pingali. A case for source-level transformations in MATLAB. In *Proceedings of the 2nd conference on Domain-Specific Languages*, DSL '99, pages 53–65, 1999.

[18] J. Michopoulos, C. Farhat, and J. Fish. Modeling and simulation of multiphysics systems. *Journal of Computing and Information Science in Engineering*, 5:198, 2005.

[19] N. M. Newmark. A method of computation for structural dynamics. *Journal of Engineering Mechanics, ASCE*, 85:67–94, 1959.

[20] C. Papalukopoulos and S. Natsiavas. Dynamics of large scale mechanical models using multilevel substructuring. *Journal of Computational and Nonlinear Dynamics, ASME*, 2:40–51, 2007. Transactions of the ASME.

[21] R. Ponnusamy, J. Saltz, and A. Choudhary. Runtime compilation techniques for data partitioning and communication schedule reuse. In *Supercomputing '93: Proceedings of the 1993 ACM/IEEE Conference on Supercomputing*, 1993.

[22] A. Prakash. *Multi-time-step domain decomposition and coupling methods for non-linear structural dynamics.* PhD thesis, University of Illinois at Urbana-Champaign, 2007.

[23] A. Prakash and K. D. Hjelmstad. A FETI based multi-time-step coupling method for Newmark schemes in structural dynamics. *International Journal for Numerical Methods in Engineering*, 61:2183–2204, 2004.

[24] A. Prakash and K. D. Hjelmstad. A multi-time-step coupling method for Newmark schemes in structural dynamics. In *proceedings of McMat2005: Joint ASME/ASCE/SES Conference on Mechanics and Materials*, June 2005.

[25] L. D. Rose and D. Padua. A MATLAB to Fortran 90 Translator and its Effectiveness. In *International Conference on Supercomputing*, pages 309–316, 1996.

[26] Y. Saad and J. Zhang. BILUTM: A domain-based multilevel block ILUT preconditioner for general sparse matrices. *SIAM Journal on Matrix Analysis and Applications*, 21:279–299, 1999.

[27] M. M. Strout, L. Carter, and J. Ferrante. Rescheduling for locality in sparse matrix computations. In *Proceedings of the International Conference on Computational Sciences-Part I*, ICCS '01, pages 137–148, 2001.

[28] J. J. Willcock, A. Lumsdaine, and D. J. Quinlan. Reusable, generic program analyses and transformations. In *Proceedings of the 8th International Conference on Generative Programming and Component Engineering*, GPCE '09, pages 5–14, 2009.

[29] J. Xiong, J. Johnson, R. W. Johnson, and D. Padua. SPL: A language and compiler for DSP algorithms. In *Proceedings of the Programming Languages Design and Implementation (PLDI)*, pages 298–308, 2001.

TEAPOT: A Toolset for Evaluating Performance, Power and Image Quality on Mobile Graphics Systems

Jose-Maria Arnau
Computer Architecture Department
Universitat Politecnica de Catalunya
jarnau@ac.upc.edu

Joan-Manuel Parcerisa
Computer Architecture Department
Universitat Politecnica de Catalunya
jmanel@ac.upc.edu

Polychronis Xekalakis
Intel Labs
Intel Corporation
polychronis.xekalakis@intel.com

ABSTRACT

In this paper we present TEAPOT, a full system GPU simulator, whose goal is to allow the evaluation of the GPUs that reside in mobile phones and tablets. To this extent, it has a cycle accurate GPU model for evaluating performance, power models for the GPU, the memory subsystem and for OLED screens, and image quality metrics. Unlike prior GPU simulators, TEAPOT supports the OpenGL ES 1.1/2.0 API, so that it can simulate all commercial graphical applications available for Android systems.

To illustrate potential uses of this simulating infrastructure, we perform two case studies. We first turn our attention to evaluating the impact of the OS when simulating graphical applications. We show that the overall GPU power/performance is greatly affected by common OS tasks, such as image composition, and argue that application level simulation is not sufficient to understand the overall GPU behavior. We then utilize the capabilities of TEAPOT to perform studies that trade image quality for energy. We demonstrate that by allowing for small distortions in the overall image quality, a significant amount of energy can be saved.

Categories and Subject Descriptors

C.1.4 [**Parallel Architectures**]: Mobile Processors; C.4 [**Performance of Systems**]: Modeling techniques

Keywords

Mobile GPU; low-power graphics; simulation infrastructure

1. INTRODUCTION

Mobile devices such as smartphones and tablets have been widely adopted in recent years, emerging as one of the most rapidly spread technology [14]. At the same time, mobile user interfaces have evolved from simple text-based displays to a point where interactive high definition 3D graphics is becoming the standard [11]. Mobile software excels in providing very rich user interfaces powered by graphics hardware, including a plethora of 2D/3D games, applications for maps or web browsing, and even hardware acceleration of the desktop [21]. Not surprisingly, previous studies have identified the GPU and the screen as the main battery consumers on a smartphone for many use cases [1, 3]. As the demand for more visually compelling graphics on mobile devices continues to grow, understanding the performance and power aspects of the graphics subsystem grows in importance.

Prior work on GPU simulation tools [2, 4, 10, 13] is mainly focused on accurately modelling desktop-like GPUs. Unfortunately, these simulators are not tailored towards the mobile segment. In fact, to the best of our knowledge, none of them have support for the OpenGL ES API [29], which means that they cannot run smartphone applications. Furthermore, most of them do not provide a power model. This is an important impediment, as all of the mobile segment devices are battery operated and thus power consumption is key design aspect. Moreover, none of the existing simulators provide energy estimations for the OLED screens. This is an important aspect of graphics simulation as the screen is one of the main battery consumers and its energy depends on the output generated by the GPU [5].

Full system GPU simulation is another important benefit provided by our simulator, that is not available in any existing GPU simulation infrastructure. This means that frequent GPU-related tasks such as image composition [21], or rendering of background applications (e.g., advertisements), are usually not taken into consideration. As we will show in a later section, this accounts for non-negligible discrepancies in the simulated use of the GPU. More specifically, we show that the OS GPU usage is non-negligible, representing up to 52% of GPU time and up to 48% of GPU energy for a set of commercial Android games.

In this paper we present TEAPOT, a toolset for evaluating the performance, energy and image quality of a mobile graphics subsystem. TEAPOT provides full-system simulation of Android applications. It includes a cycle-accurate GPU simulator, a power model for mobile GPUs, based on McPAT [8], and a power model for OLED screens [5]. Furthermore, it is able to provide image quality assessment using the models presented in [17].

In terms of the GPU microarchitecture, TEAPOT models both Tile-Based Deferred Rendering (TBDR) [35] and Immediate-Mode Rendering (IMR) [10]. While IMR is more

ICS'13, June 10–14, 2013, Eugene, Oregon, USA.

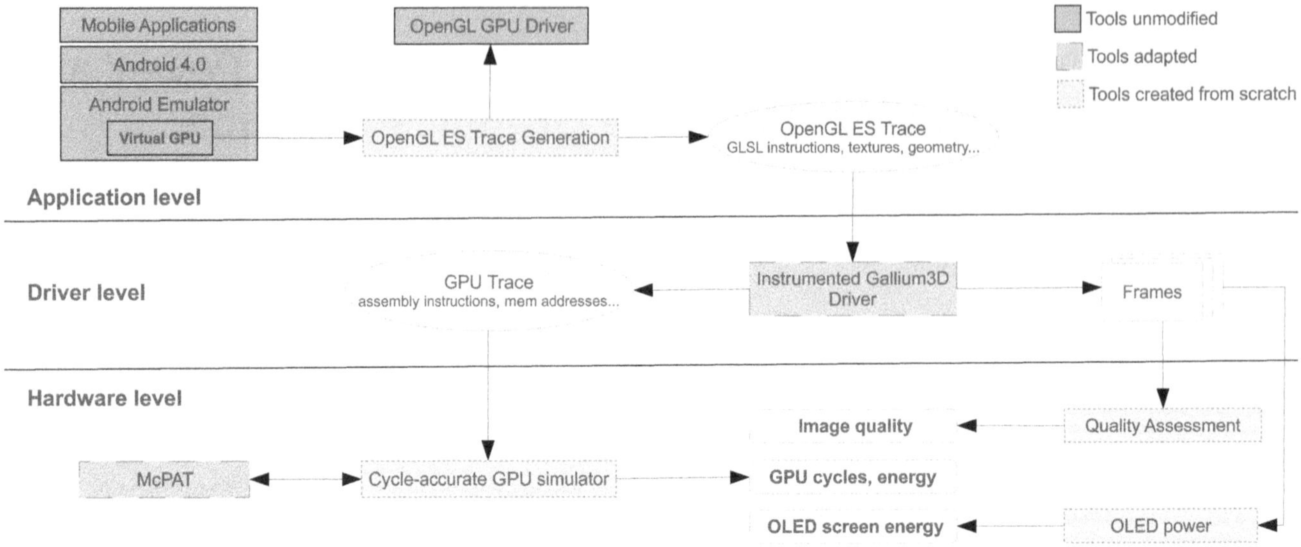

Figure 1: Mobile GPU simulation infrastructure.

popular for desktop GPUs, for GPUs targeting energy efficiency TBDR seems to be the design of choice (ARM Mali [24] and PowerVR [33] are TBDR). Prior work only focused on the IMR approach, which as it will be shown in Section 2.3.1 is significantly different from TBDR both in terms of performance and power.

This paper focuses on GPU simulation tools. Its main contributions are the following:

- We describe TEAPOT, a new toolset for analyzing mobile graphics systems in 4 dimensions: GPU execution time, GPU energy, OLED screen energy and image quality.
- We show how TEAPOT can be employed to evaluate energy saving techniques that trade quality for energy. Our results demonstrate that up to 90% of GPU energy can be saved by reducing screen resolution, losing less than 13% image quality for a set of commercial Android games.
- We argue that full-system GPU simulation is crucial to achieve accurate results, since common OS tasks such as image composition consume 26% of GPU time and 24% of GPU energy on average for a set of Android games.

The remainder of this paper is organized as follows: The next section describes TEAPOT. In Section 3 we present our evaluation methodology. In Section 4 we illustrate the benefits of using full-system GPU simulation, analyzing the OS GPU usage. In Section 5 we evaluate different energy saving techniques that trade quality for energy. Section 6 contains a discussion of related work on GPU simulation tools. Finally, in Section 7 we provide some conclusions.

2. SIMULATION INFRASTRUCTURE

TEAPOT is a set of tools that can be used for evaluating mobile graphics systems. Figure 1 illustrates the overall infrastructure. TEAPOT leverages existing tools (e.g, McPAT or Gallium3D) that have been coupled with our GPU models and adapted for the low-power segment. The goal of TEAPOT is to drive the evaluation of new energy saving techniques for low power graphics.

TEAPOT is able to run and profile unmodified commercial Android applications. We have modified the Gallium3D driver in order to profile OpenGL ES commands and collect a complete GPU instruction and memory trace. This trace is then fed to our cycle-accurate GPU simulator with which we estimate the power and performance for the given application.

As mentioned earlier, TEAPOT also includes a power model for OLED screens. This is crucial for mobile devices as the energy consumed by the screen is a significant part of the overall energy, while it also depends on the images rendered by the GPU. Therefore, the tasks performed by the GPU driver and the GPU can significantly affect the energy consumed by the OLED screen. Thus, when analyzing an energy saving technique for mobile GPUs we must ensure that possible energy savings in the GPU are not compensated by an increment in screen energy and vice versa.

TEAPOT provides several image quality metrics, based on per-pixel errors or based on the human visual perception system. These metrics are useful when evaluating aggressive energy saving techniques that trade image quality for energy. Significant energy savings can be achieved by allowing small distortions on the output images, as shown in Section 5, and the visual quality metrics are necessary for evaluating the magnitude of the distortion. The next sections illustrate the workflow of the simulation infrastructure and provide more insights into the components of TEAPOT.

2.1 Application Level

TEAPOT uses the Android Emulator available in the last version of the Android SDK [18] for running mobile applications on a desktop computer. The Android Emulator is based on QEMU [34] and supports GPU virtualization [37]. Hardware acceleration is thus available for the guest Operating System running inside the emulator, Android in that case. When enabling GPU virtualization, the OpenGL ES

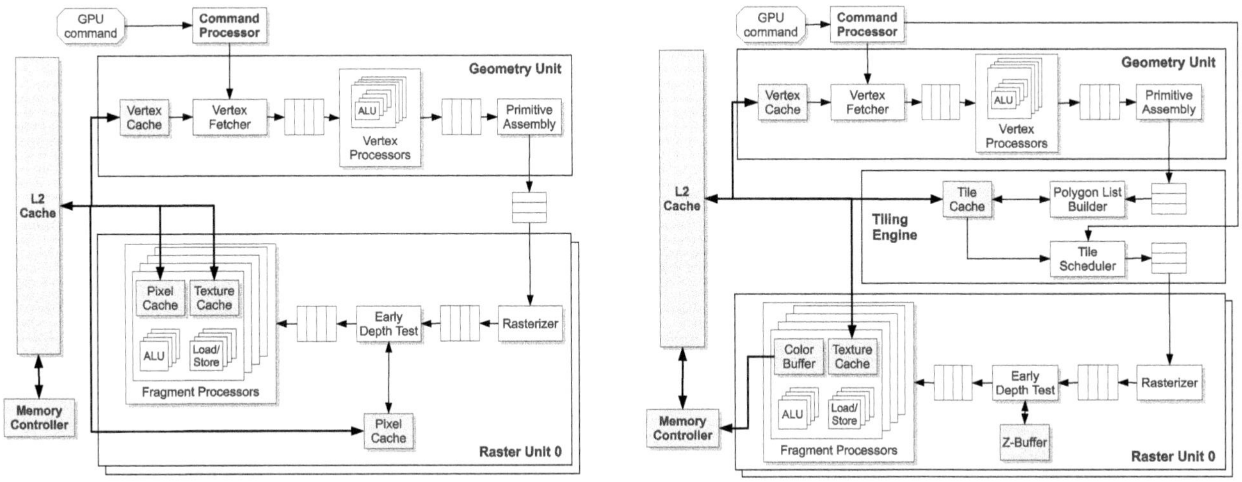

(a) Immediate Mode Renderer. (b) Tile-Based Deferred Renderer.

Figure 2: Mobile GPU architectures implemented in the simulator. Tile-Based Deferred Renderers are also referred in the literature as sort-middle architectures [9], whereas Immediate Mode Renderers are also named sort-last fragment [6].

commands issued by the applications are redirected to the GPU driver of the desktop machine. Since OpenGL ES is hardware accelerated, state-of-the-art 3D games run at high frame rates on the emulator. This also simplifies the GPU profiling since the OpenGL ES commands are not processed inside the emulator but they are redirected to the desktop GPU driver and, hence, they are completely visible to the host system.

The *OpenGL ES trace generator* component captures the OpenGL ES command stream generated by the Android applications. It saves the GPU commands in a trace file, and redirects them to the appropriate GPU driver. It consists on a library interposed between the Android Emulator and the desktop GPU driver that contains replacements for all the functions in the OpenGL ES API, so when a graphical application calls some OpenGL ES function, the one in the trace generator is selected instead of the one in the GPU driver. Hence the *OpenGL ES trace generator* is completely transparent for the emulator and it just causes a small frame rate decrease due to the time necessary for logging and redirecting the GPU commands.

The OpenGL ES trace file contains the GLSL vertex and fragment shaders [30], i. e. the code executed by the GPU, and all the data employed for rendering including textures, geometry and state information. Therefore, it contains all the necessary data for reproducing the OpenGL ES command stream. Furthermore, the thread identifier is stored in the trace together with each OpenGL ES command, so the cycle-accurate simulator can report per-thread statistics. Note that the *OpenGL ES trace generator* captures commands not from just one application but from all the applications concurrently using the GPU, including the Android OS, so TEAPOT provides full-system GPU simulation.

2.2 Driver Level

The Gallium3D [22] driver provides GPU functional emulation in TEAPOT. Gallium3D is an infrastructure for developing GPU drivers. It includes several front-ends for different graphics APIs, including OpenGL ES, and multiple back-ends for distinct GPU architectures. A modified version of Gallium3D is employed for executing the commands stored in the OpenGL ES trace file. A software-based backend is selected for rendering since it can be easily instrumented in order to get a complete GPU instruction and memory trace.

Gallium3D translates the high level GLSL shaders into an intermediate assembly code, TGSI [36]. The software backend of Gallium3D consists of an emulator for this TGSI assembly language. By instrumenting the TGSI emulator all the instructions executed by the GPU and all the memory addresses referenced are collected and stored in a GPU trace file. Note that a software renderer is different from real hardware, so special care is taken in order to trace just the addresses that would be issued in a real GPU. On the other hand, off-screen rendering is employed so the frames are written into an image file instead of being displayed on the screen.

2.3 Hardware Level

A cycle-accurate GPU simulator is employed for estimating the GPU execution time taking as input the instruction and memory traces generated by Gallium3D. GPU energy estimations are also provided by using a modified version of McPAT. The output frames generated by Gallium3D are then used for computing the energy consumed by the OLED screen. Finally, the image quality assessment module estimates the visual quality of the output images.

2.3.1 Cycle-Accurate GPU Simulator

Our GPU simulator is able to model low-power GPUs based on conventional Immediate Mode Rendering (IMR), such as the GeForce inside the NVIDIA Tegra 2 SoC [19], and Tile-Based Deferred Rendering (TBDR), such as the ARM Mali [24]. Figure 2a illustrates the IMR model modeled in TEAPOT. First, the *Command Processor* receives a command from the CPU and it sets the appropriate control signals so the input triangle stream is processed through the pipeline. Next, the *Geometry Unit* converts the input world-space triangles into a set of transformed 2D screen-space triangles. Finally, the *Raster Unit* computes the color

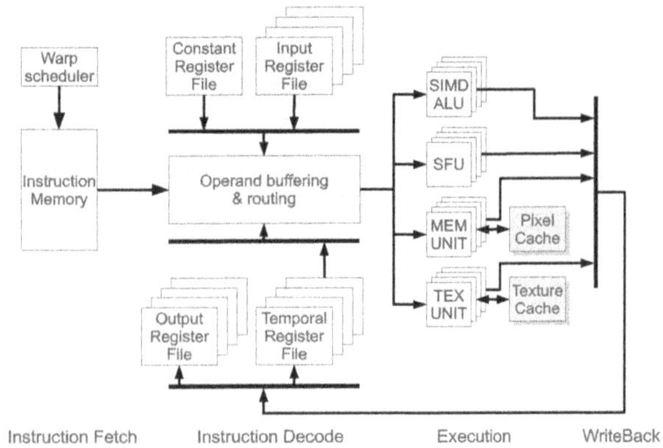

Figure 3: Fragment processor architecture. Vertex processors are similar but they do not include Pixel/Texture Caches and MEM/TEX units.

of the pixels overlapped by the triangles. This architecture is called "Immediate Mode" because once a triangle has been transformed it is immediately sent down the graphics pipeline for further pixel processing. The main problem of this architecture is *overdraw*: the colors of some pixels are written multiple times into memory because of pixels from younger triangles replacing pixels from previously processed triangles.

In TBDR, shown in Figure 2b, the screen is divided into tiles, where a tile is a rectangular block of pixels. Transformed triangles are not immediately sent to the *Raster Unit*. Instead, the *Tiling Engine* stores the triangles in memory and sorts them into tiles, so that for each tile that a triangle overlaps a pointer to that triangle is stored. Once all the geometry for the frame have been fetched, transformed and sorted, the rendering starts. Just one tile is processed at a time in each *Raster Unit*, so all the pixels for the tile can be stored in local on-chip memory and they are transferred just once to the off-chip color buffer in system memory when the tile is ready, avoiding the *overdraw*. However, transformed triangles have to be stored in memory and fetched back for rendering, so there is a trade-off between memory traffic for geometry and memory traffic for pixels. TBDR is becoming increasingly popular in the mobile GPU segment as shown in Table 1.

Regarding the memory hierarchy, the mobile GPU employs several first level caches for storing vertices, pixels or textures. These caches are connected through a bus to a second level shared cache. In TBDR, local on-chip memories are employed for storing all the pixels for a tile. This information is not cached in the L2 but it is directly transferred to main memory.

Figure 3 shows the architecture for the programmable units of the GPU pipeline, the vertex and fragment processors. It consists of a fairly simple 4-stage in-order pipeline. A form of SMT is employed to hide the memory latency by interleaving the execution of several warps. A warp is a group of threads executed in lockstep mode, that is the same instruction is executed by all the threads but each thread operates on a different fragment/vertex. The *Warp Scheduler* determines from which warp to fetch an instruction by using a Round Robin policy. Next, the source operands are fetched from the register file. Each thread has available a set of input registers, for storing input parameters such as screen coordinates or texture coordinates, a set of temporal registers, for intermediate computations, and a set of output registers for storing the result of the fragment program. Furthermore, a set of constant registers is shared by all the threads, these registers contain global state information such as the number of lights enabled. Four types of functional units are included in each Fragment Processor: the SIMD ALU, the Special Functions Unit (reciprocal, square root), the Memory Unit and the Texture Unit (computes the color of a texture at a given coordinates). The warps that are stalled waiting for a long latency operation are marked as blocked and are not selected for execution by the *Warp Scheduler*. In the last pipeline stage the result of the instruction is written in the temporal or in the output register file. No forwarding mechanism is present. However, consecutive instructions usually belong to different warps since Round Robin is employed.

Table 1: Unlike in the desktop segment, TBDR has a remarkable presence in the mobile GPU market.

Manufacturer	**Chipset**	**GPU Architecture**
NVIDIA	Tegra	Immediate-Mode [19]
ARM	MALI	Tile-Based [24]
Imagination	PowerVR	Tile-Based [33]
Qualcomm	Adreno	Hybrid [31]

Vertex Processors are similar to Fragment Processors, but they do not have to handle memory or texture instructions so they do not include Memory units, Textures Units or Pixel/Texture caches. We assume a non-unified architecture as opposite to a unified architecture where all the processors can handle both vertices and fragments. Usually, unified architectures offer better workload balance, whereas non-unified architectures can exploit the difference between vertex and fragment processing to build more specialized and optimized processors. For instance, the results obtained by using McPAT indicate that a Vertex Processor has just 64% of the area of a Fragment Processor. TEAPOT reports statistics per-frame and per-thread. Since GPU commands are tagged with the thread identifier, TEAPOT is able to assign fractions of GPU execution time and energy to each application.

2.3.2 Power Model

A modified version of McPAT [8] is used for estimating GPU energy consumption. During start-up, the GPU simulator calls to McPAT passing all the microarchitectural parameters, such as the number of processors or the cache sizes, so it can build the internal chip representation. McPAT estimates the dynamic energy required to access each one of the hardware structures and the leakage power. During simulation, the cycle-accurate GPU simulator collects statistics for each unit and, at the end of every frame, it submits all the activity factors to McPAT. The dynamic energy is computed by accounting for events in the GPU simulator and then multiplying these events by a given energy cost estimated by McPAT. The static energy is obtained by multiplying the total GPU leakage by the execution time. McPAT has been slightly modified so it can better model a low-power GPU. For instance, McPAT allows just for one private data cache for each core, whereas the Fragment Processors contain two data caches (Pixel and Texture caches).

Table 2: Android games employed for the experiments.

Game	Description
angrybirds	2D puzzle game
badpiggies	2D puzzle game
captainamerica	3D beat'em up game
chaos	3D helicopter simulator
crazysnowboard	3D snowboarding simulator
hotpursuit	3D racing game
ibowl	3D bowling game
sleepyjack	3D action game
templerun	3D arcade game

Table 3: General purpose mobile applications.

Application	Description
anatomy	Interactive 3D human anatomy model
citysurf	3D GIS/Mapping System
desktop	Android desktop with 3D widgets
droidiris	Image browser
facebook	Android facebook client
globaltime	3D world clock
k9mail	E-mail client

Furthermore, data caches are considered to be read/write, whereas Texture caches are read-only so they do not need some hardware structures such as the write-back buffer. Finally, we have extended McPAT in order to model Texture sampling units. The texture sampler is implemented by using a combination of Load units, for fetching the texels (texture pixels) from memory, and FP units, for applying the texture filtering.

On the other hand, TEAPOT employs the power model presented by Dong et. al [5] for estimating the energy consumed by the OLED screen. OLED-based displays consume significantly different energy when displaying different colors due to their emissive nature. This characteristic creates a dependence between the GPU and the screen, since the energy consumed by the display depends on the images generated by the graphics hardware. The OLED power model provides three functions f(R), f(G) and f(B) that map pixel intensity into energy consumption for the red, green and blue components of a pixel based on [5].

2.3.3 Image Quality Assessment

Generating high quality images comes at the cost of significant energy consumption which sometimes is not desirable in the mobile segment, specially for low-battery conditions. Significant energy savings can be achieved by allowing small distortions on image quality, as shown in Section 5. When trading quality for energy we need some way of evaluating the magnitude of the visual quality decrease. To this extent, TEAPOT provides several metrics for automatic image quality assessment. Image quality is evaluated by comparison with a reference image, usually as a result of a high quality rendering. The error is then estimated by comparing the high quality image with the distorted image. Two types of metrics are typically employed for image quality assessment, ones based on per-pixel errors and the other based on the human visual perception system.

Regarding the metrics based on per-pixel errors, TEAPOT implements the MSE (Mean Squared Error) [25] and the PSNR (Peak Signal-to-Noise Ratio) [32].

TEAPOT also includes the MSSIM (Mean Structural SIMilarity Index) presented in [17], a metric based on the human visual perception system. This metric is more desirable since the images generated by the GPU are interpreted by users. Hence, an error in a pixel is a problem just if it can be perceived by the human visual system, i. e. if it causes a degradation of structural information, since the human visual perception system is highly adapted for extracting structural information from a scene. An MSSIM value of 100% means perfect image fidelity, whereas a value of, for example, 90% indicates 10% of perceivable differences between the reference image and the distorted image. The original MSSIM metric only works on gray-scale images, but it can be adapted for RGB format [12].

Table 4: GPU parameters employed for the experiments. We model mobile GPUs based on Immediate Mode Rendering and Tile-Based Deferred Rendering.

Parameter	Value
Architecture	IMR, TBDR
Frequency	600 Mhz
Num. of Vertex Procs.	4
Num. of Frag. Procs.	4
Num. of threads per Proc.	16 (4 warps, 4 threads/warp)
Tile Cache	32 KB, 4-way, 64 bytes/line
L2 Cache	128 KB, 8-way, 64 bytes/line
Pixel/Texture Caches	8 KB, 2-way, 64 bytes/line
Vertex Cache	16 KB, 2-way, 64 bytes/line
Main memory	1 GB, 100 cycles latency, 64 bytes/line
Tile Size	16 x 16 pixels

3. EVALUATION METHODOLOGY

In order to illustrate how TEAPOT can be employed for analyzing mobile graphics systems we have generated traces for several Android applications. We have first focused on games since they represent an important segment of the market and games are applications that typically stress the GPU significantly. Table 2 shows all the games we have selected. We have tried to provide a good representation of commercial smartphone games, covering both simple 2D games and more complex 3D games. We have also included a set of general purpose applications shown in Table 3. Again, we have covered a wide range of commonly used applications for smartphones, including maps, a mail client, an image browser or the Android desktop. Although general purpose applications do not tend to be so GPU intensive as games, they also rely on hardware accelerated graphics for displaying very rich user interfaces. Table 4 shows the GPU configuration employed for the experiments. We have set up the timing simulator to model an Immediate-Mode Renderer similar to that of the NVIDIA Tegra 2 chipset [19] (shown in Figure 2a), and a Tile-Based Renderer similar to the ARM Mali GPU [24] (shown in Figure 2b).

3.1 Performance characterization

We have conducted several experiments to measure the overhead introduced by our instrumentation in the Android

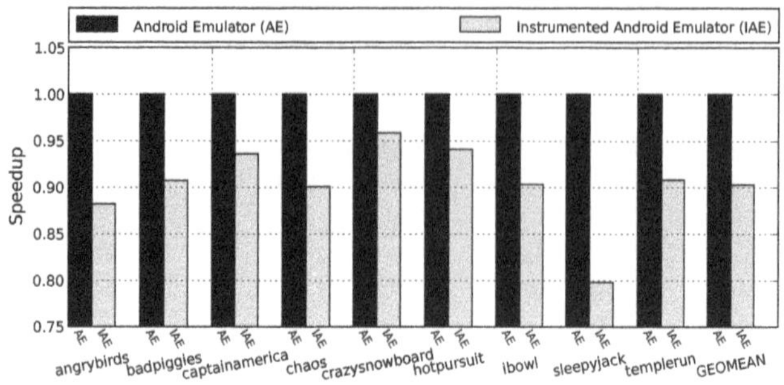

Figure 4: Overhead introduced in the Android Emulator. The *OpenGL ES Trace Generator* of TEAPOT produces a slowdown of 10% on average for our set of commercial Android games. Hence, the frame rate is not drastically reduced and games are still playable when generating traces.

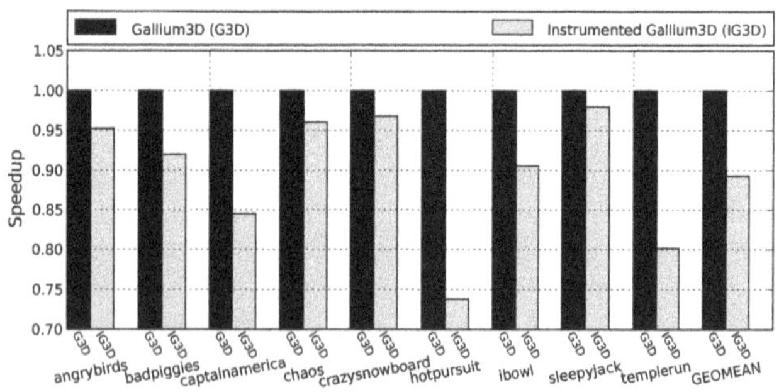

Figure 5: Overhead introduced in the Gallium3D *softpipe* driver. The instrumentation of the software renderer causes a slowdown of 11% on average in our set of commercial Android games.

Emulator and Gallium3D. Furthermore, we have analyzed the slowdown caused by the GPU functional and timing simulators included in TEAPOT, compared to the performance offered by a mobile GPU.

Figure 4 shows the performance slowdown produced by the *OpenGL ES Trace Generator* of TEAPOT. The numbers were collected on an Intel i5-3210M 2.5 GHz, with 4 GB of main memory and an Intel HD Graphics 4000 GPU. The generation of the OpenGL ES trace produces a slowdown between 4% (*crazysnowboard*) and 20% (*sleepyjack*), with an average overhead of just 10% for our set of commercial Android games. Hence, the games are still playable in the Android Emulator despite all the OpenGL ES commands are saved in a trace file.

Figure 5 shows the overhead introduced by the instrumentation of the Gallium3D software renderer. Frames are rendered at WVGA resolution (800x480). The generation of the GPU instruction and memory traces causes a slowdown between 2% (*sleepyjack*) and 26% (*hotpursuit*), with an average overhead of 11% for our set of Android games.

Finally, Figure 6 shows the performance of the GPU functional simulator, the Gallium3D *softpipe* driver, and the performance of the timing simulator compared with a real GPU. We assume a frame rate of 40 FPS for the comparison, which is common on current mobile GPUs. The simulations were executed on a cluster where each node features an Intel Xeon E5-2630L CPU and 64 GB of RAM. The software renderer,

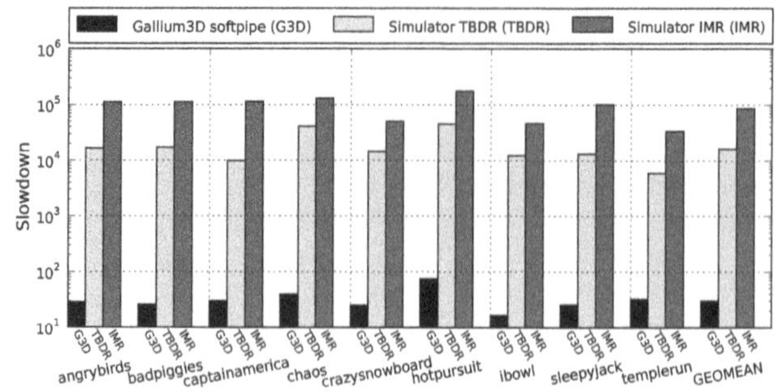

Figure 6: Slowdown of the functional simulator, Gallium3D, and the timing simulators for IMR and TBDR. We assume a frame rate of 40 FPS for the real GPU hardware.

Gallium3D, is an order of magnitude slower than real hardware. On the other hand, the GPU timing simulator causes an overhead between four and five orders of magnitude with respect to a real mobile GPU, for both architectures IMR and TBDR. These slowdowns are common for cycle-accurate microarchitectural simulations.

4. ANDROID GPU USAGE

Image composition is the process of merging the output surfaces from multiple sources together into a single surface, where a surface is a memory area to hold an image. In a multi-tasking mobile device many of the activities taking place simultaneously generate images for display on the screen. One of the components of Android, the *SurfaceFlinger*, takes care of merging all the application surfaces into a final image that is sent to the display. Composition is a compute intensive task that involves complex operations such as scaling, rotation, handling transparencies or color space conversions [20]. The *SurfaceFlinger* utilizes OpenGL ES to boost this process via hardware accelerated graphics. Using the GPU for image composition significantly improves the performance of the *SurfaceFlinger*, making it possible to display complex user interfaces at high frame rates in a smartphone. However, it can potentially reduce the performance of the graphical applications since the same GPU is employed for both rendering and composition.

Figure 7 shows the overhead of hardware accelerated image composition for several Android games. The graph depicts the percentage of GPU time and energy devoted to rendering the game and the image composition. *SurfaceFlinger* represents up to 41% of the total GPU execution time, with an average of 26% for a GPU based on IMR. Regarding the energy, *SurfaceFlinger* accounts for a non-negligible 24% of the GPU energy on average. For a GPU based on TBDR, the image composition represents 27% of the GPU execution time and 25% of the GPU energy on average.

Image composition is even more important for general purpose applications. As shown in Figure 8, it consumes 56% of the GPU time and 55% of its energy on average for IMR. These applications are not displayed in full screen, hence widgets from multiple applications are visible in the screen, increasing the number of surfaces that have to be merged during composition. For TBDR, 52% of GPU time and 51% of GPU energy are spent on average for image composition.

The Android GPU usage is non-negligible at all, representing an important percentage of GPU time and energy.

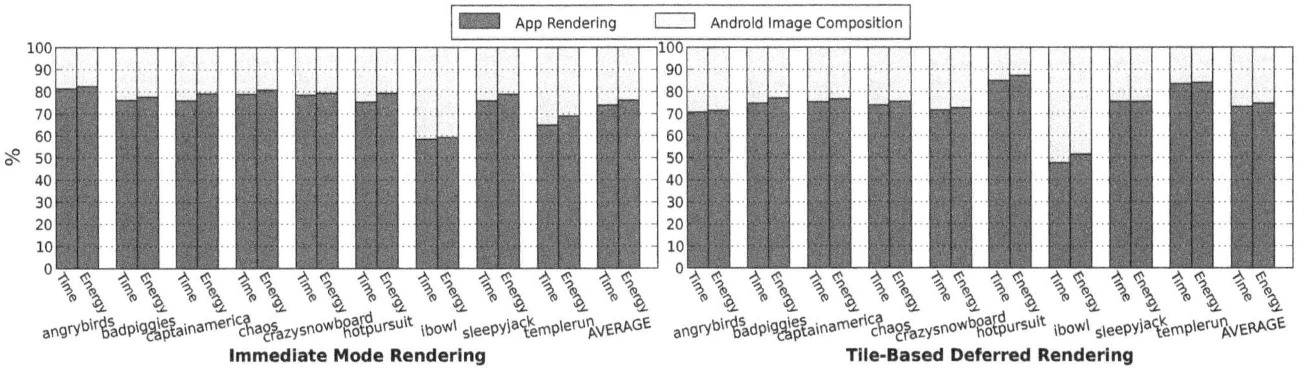

Figure 7: Percentage of GPU time and GPU energy (static and dynamic energy) for rendering and image composition, for several Android games.

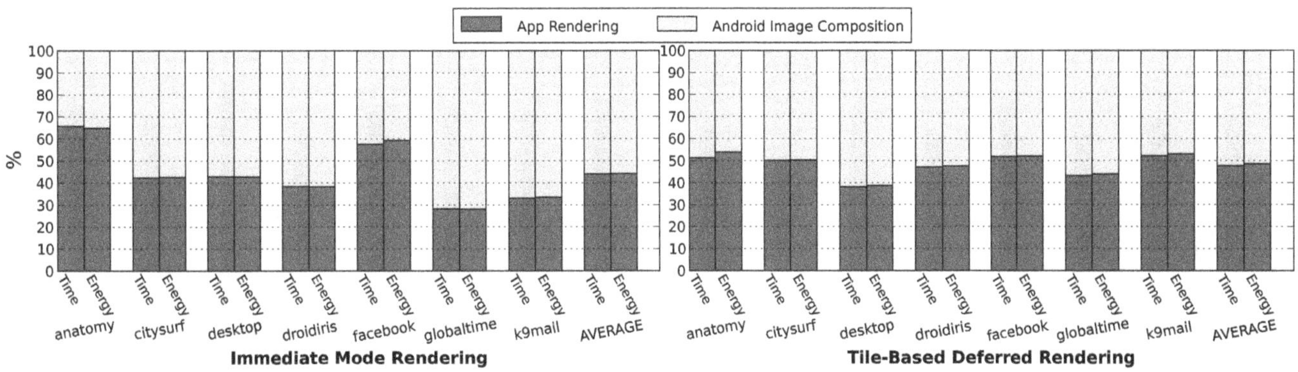

Figure 8: Percentage of GPU time and GPU energy (static and dynamic energy) for rendering and image composition, for several Android general purpose applications.

Therefore, full-system GPU simulation is a hard requirement for achieving accurate results when evaluating a mobile GPU. Profiling just one target application provides fairly incomplete information, since multiple applications utilize the GPU concurrently and image composition makes intensive use of graphics hardware. Note that composition is still necessary even if there is just one graphical application running in full screen [21]. The GPU usage of each application can be evaluated in TEAPOT, since it captures all the OpenGL ES calls in an Android system and reports per-thread statistics.

5. TRADING QUALITY FOR ENERGY

Current trends for mobile devices indicate a sustained increase of image quality and resolution. Image quality strongly depends on the amount of graphics processing, so it comes at the expense of higher energy consumption. Actually, the graphics subsystem consumes an important fraction of total energy on such devices [1, 3]. On the other hand, energy is a main constraint for battery-powered devices like smartphones. Hence, both image quality and operating time per battery charge are important design features, but these are unfortunately conflicting goals. Whether one or the other should prevail may depend on circumstances and even on personal preferences. For instance, when our device has recently been charged, we likely want it to operate at its best video quality. However, when battery is close to be exhausted, we may prefer to keep the phone alive and preserve most of its functionality (e.g. to avoid losing important phone calls), at least until we can plug it to recharge. In that case, we may likely be happy to sacrifice some video quality for energy. There is a large body of research on techniques for reducing GPU energy consumption, such as texture compression [15], prefetching [16], access/execute decoupling [1], etc.

As a way to illustrate the utility of TEAPOT, we have conducted a case study to evaluate the energy saving usefulness of trading image quality for energy. One simple way of trading video quality for energy is by reducing screen resolution. We have performed a series of experiments measuring both the energy consumed by the GPU (static and dynamic energy) and the quality of the produced images at different screen resolutions. TEAPOT calculates several well established image quality metrics (MSSIM [17], PSNR [32], and MSEv[25]). These metrics assess the quality of an image by computing its similarity to a given reference image. For the following experiments, the reference image frames are generated at HD resolution (1280x720), as illustrated in Figure 13, and the images under test are produced at WVGA (800x480), VGA (640x480), HVGA (420x380) and QVGA (320x240) resolutions.

Figure 9 shows the normalized GPU energy, including both static and dynamic energy, spent when running several games at these four different image resolutions. We found 55%, 64%, 81% and 90% average energy savings respectively, for a GPU based on IMR, and 54%, 63%, 78% and 88% average energy savings for Tile-Based Deferred Render-

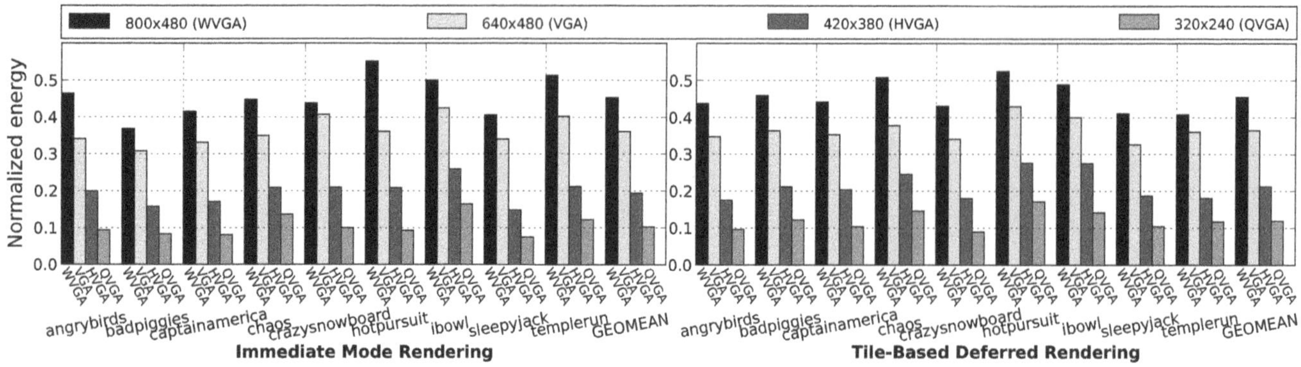

Figure 9: Normalized GPU energy (static and dynamic), in relation to the energy consumed when using HD resolution, for several Android games. The graph includes results for IMR (left) and TBDR (right).

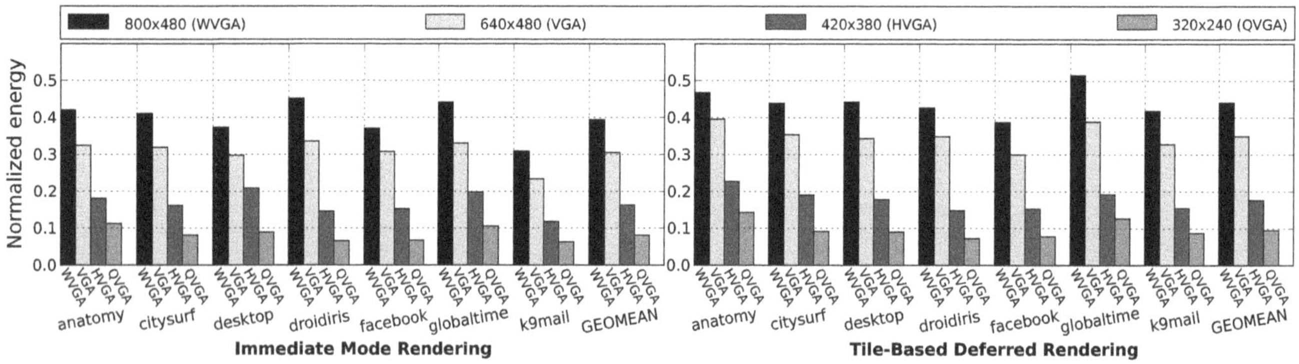

Figure 10: Normalized GPU energy (static and dynamic), in relation to the energy consumed when using HD resolution, for several general purpose applications. The graph includes the numbers for IMR (left) and TBDR (right).

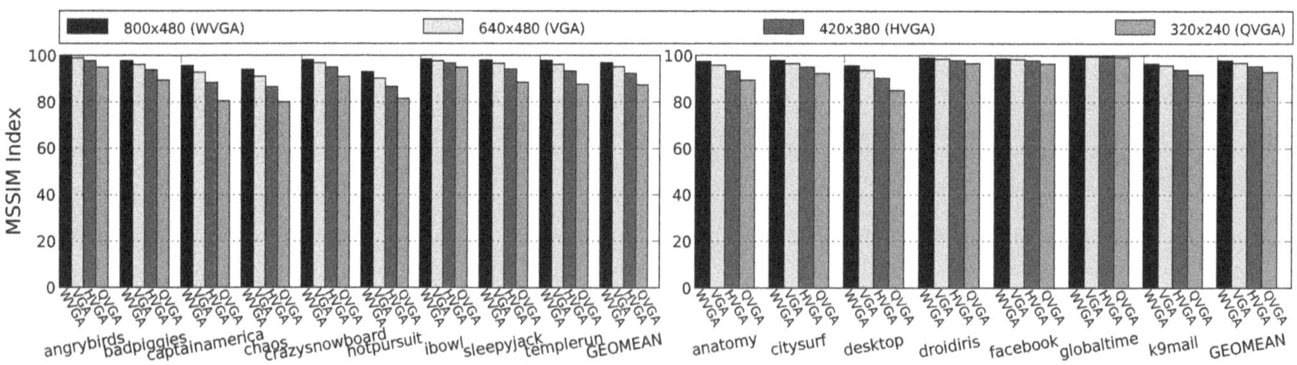

Figure 11: Image quality, compared with HD resolution, for several Android games (left) and general purpose applications (right). The MSSIM index [17] is employed as the metric for automatic image quality assessment.

ing. Figure 10 shows similar energy results for the general purpose applications, we found 60%, 70%, 83% and 92% average energy savings respectively for IMR, and 56%, 65%, 82% and 90% average energy savings for TBDR.

Figure 11 shows the corresponding image qualities, evaluated by using the MSSIM index. We found 3%, 5%, 7% and 13% of average quality loss for the Android games, respectively. The worst case image quality losses are around 20%, and they are observed by *captainamerica*, *chaos* and *hotpursuit* at QVGA resolution. However, the general purpose applications are less sensitive to the screen resolution than games. We observed just 2%, 3%, 5% and 7% of average quality loss, respectively. Games tend to render more complex objects than the general purpose applications so they are more sensitive to screen resolution.

Figure 12 plots average quality versus energy, it includes just the numbers for IMR since very similar results were obtained for TBDR. The graph shows that reducing image quality provides at first a huge energy reduction, but further quality sacrifices tend to produce progressively lower energy savings. The main energy savings are obtained by the first reduction step (from HD to WVGA), which saves 55%

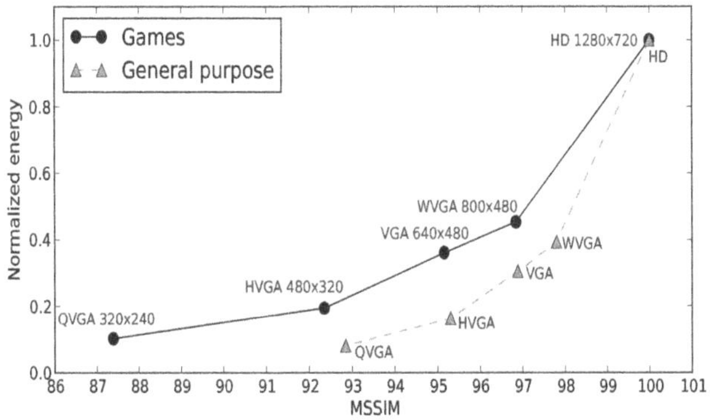

Figure 12: Image quality vs energy for different screen resolutions. The x coordinate for each point is the geometric mean of the MSSIM for all the applications, the y coordinate is the geometric mean of the normalized energy.

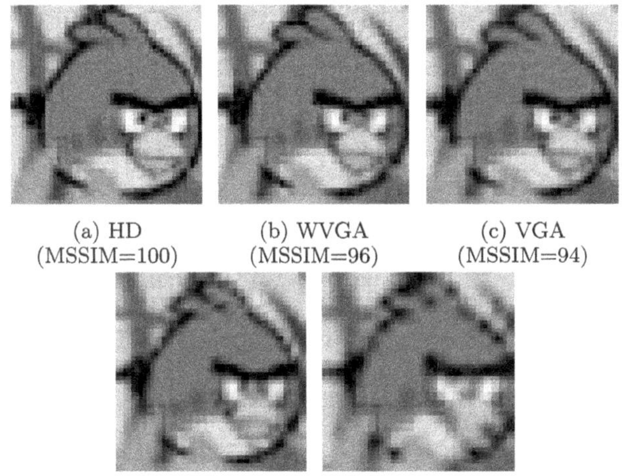

(a) HD (MSSIM=100) (b) WVGA (MSSIM=96) (c) VGA (MSSIM=94)

(d) HVGA (MSSIM=88) (e) QVGA (MSSIM=73)

Figure 13: Image quality is evaluated by comparison with a HD reference image. (a) is a 50x50 pix. sample crop of the HD frame. (b)-(e) show the same frame region at smaller screen resolutions (scaled up to highlight the differences).

the energy by just 3% loss in quality (Android games). In other words, it reduces 18,3% of energy for each 1% in quality, while further successive downgrading steps (to VGA, HVGA and QVGA) provide only additional reductions of 5.4%, 5.9%, and 1.8% of energy for each 1% in quality. Similar results are observed for general purpose applications. Moving from HD to WVGA provides 30% energy savings on average for each 1% in quality, whereas downgrading to VGA, HVGA and QVGA achieves just additional energy reductions of 9.7%, 8.9% and 3.3% for each unit of quality respectively.

Overall, this study shows that the graphics driver could save up to 90% of GPU energy by sacrificing less than 13% of quality for games, and up to 92% of GPU energy by losing less than 7% image quality for general purpose applications. Of course, this ability could be controlled by software so that it is activated only under predefined circumstances (e.g. battery level), or enabled by the user on demand.

6. RELATED WORK

The development of tools for evaluating the GPU has attracted the attention of the architectural community the last few years. Recent simulators, such as GPGPUSim [2] or Barra [4], model General Purpose GPU (GPGPU) architectures. These tools support CUDA [27] or OpenCL [28], but they do not support graphics APIs such as OpenGL. GPGPUSim includes a power model, GPUWattch [23], which is also based on McPAT as in TEAPOT. Both power models are similar, but GPUWattch focuses on GPGPU specific features whereas TEAPOT models more specialized graphics hardware. For instance, GPGPUSim models FP units that can be combined to execute 1 double-precision (DP) or 2 single-precision (SP) operations, but TEAPOT relies on SP units since DP is common in scientific workloads but not in games. On the contrary, TEAPOT models specialized Texture Sampling units since texture fetching instructions are frequent in graphical workloads.

ATTILA [10] provides an OpenGL framework for collecting traces of desktop games and a cycle-accurate GPU simulator. A Direct3D [26] driver is also included in the last versions. Although ATTILA provides full support for desktop games, it cannot run applications for smartphones. Furthermore, its GPU simulator models a desktop-like immediate-mode renderer, whereas TBDR [35] is very popular in the low-power segment. Finally, ATTILA does not include a power model. Qsilver [13] can also collect and simulate traces from desktop OpenGL games, and it includes a power model. GRAAL [7] also provides OpenGL support and a power model for GPUs. Furthermore, it models a low-power GPU based on TBDR. However, OpenGL ES support is not available in any of these simulators so they cannot run mobile applications for smartphones and tablets. Unlike the aforementioned tools, TEAPOT additionally provides image quality metrics for automatic image quality assessment and includes a power model for OLED screens, since it has been designed for analyzing graphical workloads in the low-power segment. In addition, TEAPOT supports full-system GPU simulation, being able to profile multiple applications accessing the GPU concurrently.

7. CONCLUSIONS

This paper presents TEAPOT, a toolset for evaluating mobile graphics systems. Unlike previous GPU simulators, TEAPOT is tailored towards the low-power segment. It provides full-system cycle-accurate GPU simulation for mobile workloads and a power model for both the GPU and the OLED screen. Moreover, it employs image quality metrics, allowing for image quality assessment. We have conducted two case studies in order to demonstrate some of the potential uses of TEAPOT. First, we have analyzed the importance of full-system GPU simulation, showing that the OS GPU usage is non-negligible. Our results demonstrate that Android image composition takes 26% of GPU time and 24% of GPU energy on average for a set of commercial games. We then turned our focus into analyzing techniques that trade quality for energy. We showed that significant amounts of energy can be saved by allowing for small distortions in image quality. Our results indicate that by reducing the quality of the graphics by 13%, energy savings of 90% are attainable.

8. ACKNOWLEDGMENTS

This work has been supported by the Generalitat de Catalunya under grant 2009SGR-1250, the Spanish Ministry of Economy and Competitiveness under grant TIN 2010-18368, and Intel Corporation. Jose-Maria Arnau is supported by an FI-Research grant.

9. REFERENCES

[1] J.-M. Arnau, J.-M. Parcerisa, and P. Xekalakis. Boosting Mobile GPU Performance with a Decoupled Access/Execute Fragment Processor. In *Proc. of ISCA*, pages 84–93, 2012.

[2] A. Bakhoda, G. Yuan, W. Fung, H. Wong, and T. Aamodt. Analyzing CUDA Workloads Using a Detailed GPU Simulator. In *Proc. of ISPASS*, pages 163–174, 2009.

[3] A. Carroll and G. Heiser. An Analysis of Power Consumption in a Smartphone. In *Proc. of USENIX*, pages 21–21, 2010.

[4] S. Collange, M. Daumas, D. Defour, and D. Parello. Barra: A Parallel Functional Simulator for GPGPU. In *Proc. of MASCOTS*, pages 351–360, 2010.

[5] M. Dong, Y.-S. K. Choi, and L. Zhong. Power Modeling of Graphical User Interfaces on OLED Displays. In *Proc. of DAC*, pages 652–657, 2009.

[6] M. W. Eldridge. *Designing Graphics Architectures Around Scalability and Communication*. PhD thesis, 2001.

[7] B. Juurlink, I. Antochi, D. Crisu, S. Cotofana, and S. Vassiliadis. GRAAL: A Framework for Low-Power 3D Graphics Accelerators. *IEEE Computer Graphics and Applications*, 28(4):63–73, 2008.

[8] S. Li, J. H. Ahn, R. D. Strong, J. B. Brockman, D. M. Tullsen, and N. P. Jouppi. McPAT: An Integrated Power, Area, and Timing Modeling Framework for Multicore and Manycore Architectures. In *Proc. of MICRO*, pages 469–480, 2009.

[9] S. Molnar, M. Cox, D. Ellsworth, and H. Fuchs. A Sorting Classification of Parallel Rendering. *IEEE Comput. Graph. Appl.*, 14(4):23–32, July 1994.

[10] V. Moya, C. Gonzalez, J. Roca, A. Fernandez, and R. Espasa. ATTILA: A Cycle-level Execution-Driven Simulator for Modern GPU Architectures. In *Proc. of ISPASS*, pages 231–241, 2006.

[11] K. Pulli, T. Aarnio, K. Roimela, and J. Vaarala. Designing Graphics Programming Interfaces for Mobile Devices. *IEEE Comput. Graph. Appl.*, 25(6):66–75, Nov. 2005.

[12] J. Rasmusson, J. Hasselgren, and T. Akenine-Möller. Exact and Error-Bounded Approximate Color Buffer Compression and Decompression. In *Proc. of EUROGRAPHICS Conf. on Graphics Hardware*, pages 41–48, 2007.

[13] J. W. Sheaffer, D. Luebke, and K. Skadron. A Flexible Simulation Framework for Graphics Architectures. In *Proc. of the EUROGRAPHICS Conf. on Graphics Hardware*, pages 85–94, 2004.

[14] A. Shye, B. Scholbrock, and G. Memik. Into the Wild: Studying Real User Activity Patterns to Guide Power Optimizations for Mobile Architectures. In *Proc. of MICRO*, pages 168–178, 2009.

[15] J. Ström and T. Akenine-Möller. iPACKMAN: High-Quality, Low-Complexity Texture Compression for Mobile Phones. In *Proc. of the EUROGRAPHICS Conf. on Graphics Hardware*, pages 63–70, 2005.

[16] J. Tang, S. Liu, Z. Gu, C. Liu, and J.-L. Gaudiot. Prefetching in Embedded Mobile Systems Can Be Energy-Efficient. *IEEE Comput. Archit. Lett.*, 10(1):8–11, Jan. 2011.

[17] Z. Wang, A. Bovik, H. Sheikh, and E. Simoncelli. Image Quality Assessment: from Error Visibility to Structural Similarity. *IEEE Transactions on Image Processing*, 13(4):600–612, 2004.

[18] Android SDK. `http://developer.android.com/sdk/index.html`.

[19] Bringing High-End Graphics to Handheld Devices. `http://www.nvidia.com/content/PDF/tegra_white_papers/Bringing_High-End_Graphics_to_Handheld_Devices.pdf`.

[20] Color Space Conversions. `http://www.poynton.com/PDFs/coloureq.pdf`.

[21] Composition with Snapdragon. `https://developer.qualcomm.com/sites/default/files/composition-with-snapdragon.pdf`.

[22] Gallium3D. `http://en.wikipedia.org/wiki/Gallium3D/`.

[23] GPUWattch. `http://www.gpgpu-sim.org/gpuwattch/`.

[24] Mali-400 MP: A Scalable GPU for Mobile Devices. `http://www.highperformancegraphics.org/previous/www_2010/media/Hot3D/HPG2010_Hot3D_ARM.pdf`.

[25] Mean Squared Error. `http://en.wikipedia.org/wiki/Mean_squared_error`.

[26] Microsoft Direct3D. `http://en.wikipedia.org/wiki/Microsoft_Direct3D`.

[27] NVIDIA CUDA Programming Guide. `http://docs.nvidia.com/cuda/cuda-c-programming-guide/`.

[28] OpenCL. `http://www.khronos.org/opencl/`.

[29] OpenGL ES. `http://www.khronos.org/opengles/`.

[30] OpenGL Shading Language. `http://en.wikipedia.org/wiki/GLSL`.

[31] Qualcomm Adreno 320. `http://www.anandtech.com/show/6112/qualcomms-quadcore-snapdragon-s4-apq8064adreno-320-performance-preview`.

[32] Peak signal-to-noise ratio. `http://en.wikipedia.org/wiki/Peak_signal-to-noise_ratio`.

[33] PowerVR Technology Overview. `http://www.imgtec.com/factsheets/SDK/PowerVR%20Technology%20Overview.1.0.2e.External.pdf`.

[34] QEMU. `http://wiki.qemu.org/Main_Page`.

[35] Tile-Based Deferred Rendering. `http://en.wikipedia.org/wiki/Tiled_rendering`.

[36] Tungsten Graphics Shader Infrastructure. `http://people.freedesktop.org/~csimpson/gallium-docs/tgsi.html`.

[37] Using hardware acceleration in the Android Emulator. `http://developer.android.com/tools/devices/emulator.html#acceleration`.

Scaling Data Race Detection for Partitioned Global Address Space Programs

Chang-Seo Park, Koushik Sen
EECS Department
University of California, Berkeley
{parkcs,ksen}@cs.berkeley.edu

Costin Iancu
Computational Research Division
Lawrence Berkeley National Laboratory
cciancu@lbl.gov

ABSTRACT

Contemporary and future programming languages for HPC promote hybrid parallelism and shared memory abstractions using a global address space. In this programming style, data races occur easily and are notoriously hard to find. Existing state-of-the-art data race detectors exhibit $10\times - 100\times$ *performance degradation and do not handle hybrid parallelism. In this paper we present the first complete implementation of data race detection at scale for UPC programs. Our implementation tracks local and global memory references in the program and it uses two techniques to reduce the overhead: 1) hierarchical function and instruction level sampling; and 2) exploiting the runtime persistence of aliasing and locality specific to Partitioned Global Address Space applications. The results indicate that both techniques are required in practice: well optimized instruction sampling introduces overheads as high as 6500% (65× slowdown), while each technique in separation is able to reduce it only to 1000% (10× slowdown). When applying the optimizations in conjunction our tool finds all previously known data races in our benchmark programs with at most 50% overhead when running on 2048 cores. Furthermore, while previous results illustrate the benefits of function level sampling, our experiences show that this technique does not work for scientific programs: instruction sampling or a hybrid approach is required.*

Categories and Subject Descriptors

D.2.5 [**Software**]: Software Engineering—*Testing and Debugging*

Keywords

Data Race, Tracing, Sampling, Instrumentation Overhead

1. INTRODUCTION

Attaining good performance and efficacy on contemporary and future large scale High Performance Computing systems requires using hybrid programming models: OpenMP+MPI, UPC+MPI, Intel TBB + MPI or OpenMP+UPC. With multiple levels, *intra-node* parallelism is usually exploited using shared memory programming models, while *inter-node* parallelism is exploited using message passing or shared memory abstractions.

Bugs due to non-deterministic execution and conflicting memory accesses are fairly common and notoriously hard to detect in a parallelism rich environment. Previous work demonstrates the ability of dynamic program analyses to find concurrency bugs (data race [33], atomicity violations [22], deadlock [7]) in shared memory programs. Dynamic program analyses have been also used to find *heisenbugs* in distributed memory programs: DAMPI [39] for MPI wildcard receives and UPC-Thrille [29] for data races in Unified Parallel C [10].

Data race detectors for shared memory programming [31, 33] trace individual memory references (load/store instructions) and reason about program semantics using a centralized analysis. The implementations are optimized to reduce the instrumentation overhead and reportedly slow down the execution by less than 10× at small concurrency. Bug finding for distributed memory programming models is made scalable by using a distributed analysis, but the current approaches illustrated by DAMPI and UPC-Thrille [29, 39] track only calls into communication libraries. Tools that can handle hybrid programming have not been demonstrated yet. Furthermore, while acceptable when testing programs on workstations, the current overhead of dynamic program analyses is hard to stomach at the contemporary HPC concurrencies of tens of thousands of cores. Large scale analyses face the additional challenge to provide the lowest achievable overhead while still providing good coverage.

In this paper we present the first complete dynamic analysis for distributed memory programs able to track both memory references and communication calls. Our main design goal is attaining very low overhead at scale. We extend the UPC-Thrille data race detection tool with tracking of individual memory references and validate it using implementations of the NAS Parallel Benchmarks [6], as well as other fine-grained dynamic programming and tree search applications. UPC-Thrille, detailed in Section 2, implements a dynamic program analysis where the program is executed with additional instrumentation and data about memory accesses, communication and synchronization operations is gathered and analyzed.

Performance degradation caused by instrumentation is a well recognized challenge for dynamic program analyses. The most widely used technique to reduce overhead is sampling [3, 4, 23, 17, 39, 29] of the program execution. Tools for shared memory use instruction level sampling while the distributed

ICS'13, June 10–14, 2013, Eugene, Oregon, USA.

memory tools [39, 29] implement its equivalent by sampling the communication operations. For shared memory, Marino et al [23] recently introduced LiteRace which coarsens the granularity of the sampling at function boundaries. LiteRace showed better scalability and coverage than instruction level sampling when applied on several Microsoft programs, as well as Apache and Firefox.

We have experimented with both instruction level sampling and function level sampling. Contrary to LiteRace, the results presented in Section 3 indicate that instruction level sampling performs better than function level sampling for scientific programs. Instruction level sampling adds runtime overhead as high as 65× while many runs using function level sampling did not terminate, even when instrumenting only the first execution of a function.

The scalability and efficacy of our tool is determined solely by the instrumentation overhead. We have performed experiments to determine a "default" sampling frequency that provides both coverage and low performance degradation. Our results indicate that manipulating the sampling frequency is not enough to attain acceptable slowdown on the workload under consideration.

We propose a combination of techniques to minimize the tool overhead. In Section 4.1 we describe how to use program semantic information such as aliasing to prune the number of events traced. In Section 4.2 we propose a hierarchical sampling approach where the instrumentation granularity is dynamically controlled both at the function level and at the instruction level. Applying each technique in isolation is able to reduce the maximum tool overhead from 65× with instruction sampling to roughly 10×. When combining aliasing based pruning with hierarchical sampling, we were able to reduce the maximum overhead from 10× (i.e. 1000%) to only 50% while finding the same races using 2048 cores. We believe that our findings are widely applicable to any tool for data race detection in Partitioned Global Address Space languages: Chapel, Titanium, Co-Array Fortran. This paper makes the following contributions:

- We develop the first complete dynamic analysis for distributed memory programs which is able to track both memory references and communication calls with significantly low overhead.
- We show that state-of-the-art sampling techniques for data race detection do not scale for scientific programs.
- We propose a hierarchical sampling technique which is able to reduce instrumentation overhead from 65× to 10×.
- We propose a novel aliasing based pruning heuristics, which when combined with hierarchical sampling, further reduces overhead from 10× to 0.5× .

2. UNIFIED PARALLEL C

UPC is a parallel extension of the ISO C programming language for high performance computing. UPC uses the Single-Program-Multiple-Data (SPMD) programming model and provides a Partitioned Global Address Space: each task has access to a private address space and to a global shared address space. The language extends the C type system with the qualifier of `pointer-to-shared` to denote accesses to the global address space. `Pointers-to-shared` can be casted to proper C pointers, but not vice-versa. This is widely used in practice for performance reasons and for calling into native libraries such as Intel MKL. In addition, the language provides synchronization primitives (`lock, barrier`), bulk memory transfers (`memput, memget`), as well as a memory consistency [41, 21] model.

Together with Chapel, X10, Co-Array Fortran and Titanium, UPC belongs to the family of Partitioned Global Address Space languages. These PGAS languages distinguish between local and global references and provide support for logical data layouts, such as block-cyclic array distribution. As a result, they implement complicated memory management and a reference to a global object is orders of magnitude slower [18] than a load/store instruction due to complex addressing rules.

2.1 Finding Data Races with UPC-Thrille

A *data race* occurs in parallel programs when two threads access the same memory location with no ordering constraints between them, and at least one of the accesses is a write [1, 27].

In our previous work, we developed a data race detector for UPC called UPC-Thrille. UPC-Thrille was able to find only data races between accesses performed using variables with the `pointer-to-shared` data type (e.g. `shared int *`) and communication calls (e.g. `memget`). It instruments communication calls and implements an active testing [19] methodology which works in two phases:

- A predictive analysis phase which uses a distributed lock-set-based algorithm [33, 29] to identify data races. The data races reported by the predictive analysis could be real or infeasible. The results reported show that UPC-Thrille is able to predict potential data races with good scalability and overhead lower than 15%.
- A confirmation phase, where the program is re-executed under a controlled schedule that attempts to make the potential races manifest, i.e. create a state by manipulating the schedule where two threads are about to access the same memory location and at least one of the accesses is a write. Races that are not reproduced are unlikely to be false positives.

Well optimized UPC programs usually cast `pointers-to-shared` (e.g. `shared int *`) to C proper pointers (e.g. `int*`) and the released UPC-Thrille cannot detect data races introduced by memory aliases. Furthermore, the presence on non-blocking communication operations [8] introduces another class of data races. As non-blocking communication is a "background" asynchronous activity that can be overlapped with computation, memory accesses within a task can race with the communication operations initiated by the same task. A complete data race detection solution needs to track all the memory references, including those using C pointers, as well as communication calls. Therefore, our released UPC-Thrille was prone to false-negatives, i.e. it could miss to report real data races during an execution.

In the rest of this paper we discuss the implementation and optimizations required for the complete UPC-Thrille data race detector. The tool is publicly available under a BSD license.

3. THE OVERHEAD OF DATA RACE DETECTION

Instrumentation overhead is recognized as a problem that dynamic race detectors have to address. Commercial tools for C programs such as the Intel Thread Checker or the Sun Thread Analyzer, usually instrument all load/store instructions at the expense of 600× execution slowdown [36] on scientific OpenMP programs with small memory footprints. Average overheads on other scientific programs for the Intel Thread Checker have been reported [32] around 200× and as high as 485×.

Sampling techniques have been introduced by Arnold and Ryder [3] and later adopted in other bug finding tools [4, 23] for parallel programs. The efficacy of these techniques is determined by the granularity of the instrumented code region and the sampling strategy. Tools [4] for finding bugs in programs running on managed runtimes (e.g. Java) tend to use instruction level sampling; the additional instrumentation overhead is not perceived as unacceptable since the runtime already manages object metadata and access. These systems usually observe up to $3X\times$ slowdowns for non-scientific applications and data is not available for HPC applications. Distributed memory tools such as DAMPI [39] sample only communication calls.

Recently, Marino et al [23] proposed a technique to coarsen the sampling control from instruction level to function level. They use a compiler to generate instrumented and un-instrumented versions of functions and select the appropriate copy at runtime. The instrumented version of a function monitors every memory reference during its execution. Their LiteRace tool introduces up to 3× overhead while providing good coverage on non-scientific programs; it has not been evaluated on scientific programs. In the rest of this paper we refer to this technique as function sampling. One reason that function sampling outperforms instruction sampling is that it amortizes better the cost of tracking memory references: function sampling executes one branch/decision per application level function call while instruction sampling executes one branch/decision per instruction traced.

Several sampling strategies have been proposed and evaluated for non-scientific programs. Random sampling has been shown to provide poor coverage. SWAT [17] detects memory leaks and uses an approach where the execution of code segments is sampled at a rate inversely proportional to their execution frequency. LiteRace uses a bursty sampler, where the execution of a function is sampled initially at a 100% rate and the sample rate is progressively reduced until it reaches a lower bound. Both approaches try to give priority to regions of code rarely executed and give priority to the first execution of any code region.

The implementation of UPC-Thrille described in [29] instruments `memget/memput` communication operations with a bursty sampling similar to LiteRace.

In order to provide a complete data race detection solution we have modified UPC-Thrille and the Berkeley UPC compiler to track all memory references, including all references through C proper pointers. We provide a well optimized implementation of instruction sampling that makes extensive use of C macro-definitions to eliminate function call overheads for the instrumentation code. Every memory reference is examined using a bursty sampling strategy. We have also implemented function sampling with the same bursty strategy.

For any sampled memory reference, the implementation has to check whether the address resides within a thread's private address space or within the global address space. This requires integration with the UPC runtime memory management module and it is an expensive operation, common to PGAS languages. References to the private address space are ignored as they cannot race. Global references are inserted into the UPC-Thrille internal data structures and further checked against other references.

We distinguish three types of overhead: 1) *instrumentation overhead* is introduced by the checks to prune the non-interesting data accesses; 2) *computation overhead* is introduced by the operations on internal data structures to manage the interesting accesses; and 3) *communication overhead* introduced by the exchange of conflicting accesses between tasks. Thus, private references contribute only to instrumentation overhead while global references also contribute to the computation and communication overhead.

3.1 Benchmarks

We evaluate UPC benchmarks using fine-grained and bulk communication. Table 1 presents statistics about the benchmark characteristics. For implementations using bulk communication primitives we use the NAS Parallel Benchmarks (NPB) [25, 26, 6], releases 2.4 and 3.3. We have performed experiments with the problem classes A, B and C and D; overall, the memory footprint of the workload varies from tens of MBs to tens of GBs. Asanović et al [5] examined six different promising domains for commercial parallel applications and report that a surprisingly large fraction of them use methods encountered in the scientific domain. In particular, all methods used in the NAS benchmarks (multigrid, sparse-matrix operations, sorting, Fast Fourier Transformation, dense linear algebra) appear in at least one commercial domain. Thus, beside their HPC relevance, these benchmarks are of interest to other communities.

The fine-grained benchmarks reflect the type of communication/synchronization that is present in larger applications during data structure initializations, dynamic load balancing, or remote event signaling. The *guppie* benchmark performs random read/modify/write accesses to a large distributed array, a common operation in parallel hash table construction, graph algorithms and data mining. The amount of work is static and evenly distributed among tasks at execution time. The *psearch* benchmark performs parallel unbalanced tree search [28]. The benchmark is designed to be evaluation tool for dynamic load balancing strategies.

The selected programs provide a good sample of different programming and software engineering styles, dynamic application behavior and scalability characteristics. The NAS benchmarks contain many function calls and have a structure common to any large application. The fine-grained benchmarks contain few or no user defined function calls, a structure common to many scientific libraries and their unit testing. In the NAS benchmarks, the ratio of local memory accesses to communication calls performed at runtime is large ($O(10^5)$ or above) , while in the fine grained benchmarks they are roughly equal. The NAS benchmarks implement iterative methods, while the code in the fine-grained benchmarks represents a "direct" solve executed only once.

Due to the randomness of the access pattern and the fre-

				Overhead				
Bench	LoC	Runtime(s)	#Races	NL	HA.5	IA	FA0	I
guppie	271	19.070	2(2) + 0(0)	54.9%	54.2%	53.7%	DNF	74.9%
psearch	803	0.697	3(1) + 2(2)	2.48%	10.8%	666%	8.01%	6490%
BT 3.3	9698	189.48	7(0) + 3(1)	0.574%	1.16%	77.6%	DNF	-
CG 2.4	1654	39.573	0(0) + 1(1)	1.09%	27.6%	57.6%	DNF	2579%
EP 2.4	678	54.453	0(0) + 0(0)	-0.618%	0.805%	2.09%	4.74%	111%
FT 2.4	2289	62.663	2(2) + 0(0)	0.601%	30.1%	121%	DNF	2744%
IS 2.4	1426	5.130	0(0) + 0(0)	0.376%	119%	159%	DNF	1201%
LU 3.3	6348	155.997	0(0) + 44(2)	-0.425%	-	75.7%	DNF	-
MG 2.4	2229	18.687	2(2) + 4(0)	0.336%	176%	632%	DNF	2020%
SP 3.3	5740	247.937	10(0) + 3(1)	0.160%	0.861%	29.1%	DNF	-

Table 1: *Statistics for the NAS Parallel Benchmarks class C, guppie and psearch running on 16 cores. We report the races found as A(B) + C(D), where A represents the number of races detected by the original UPC-Thrille tool with B of them confirmed, and C represents the additional number of races detected with our extensions with D of them confirmed through phase II. Some execution overheads are omitted (-), due to configuration errors.*

quency of execution, these benchmarks require the tool to provide good program coverage. NAS FT exhibits a race between the initialization code and the subsequent computation: initialization is executed only once. *guppie* performs random updates to a global table and it exhibits two races: read-write and write-write. *psearch* implements a work stealing strategy that exhibits random data races.

3.2 Comparison of Function and Instruction Sampling

The experimental results are obtained on a Cray XE6 system composed of nodes containing two twelve-core AMD MagnyCours 2.1 GHz processors. The system has two nodes attached to a Gemini network interface card, forming an overall 3-D torus network with 6,384 nodes. The network is providing a bandwidth of 9.375 GBytes/sec per direction in 10 directions. The maximum injection bandwidth per node is 20GB/s. Our implementation extends UPC-Thrille as contained in the Berkeley UPC release 2.14.2.

Table 2 describes the experiment labeling scheme and summary of results is shown in Table 1. Instruction sampling is denoted by **I** and we use the setting of 0.9 instruction back-off factor as our baseline, as indicated in [29]. Function sampling is denoted by **F**. For a given setting of the sampling frequency for **I**, we are interested in determining a sampling frequency for **F** that provides similar coverage.

We will use the behavior of the CG benchmark to illustrate the differences between the different configurations. These CG trends are representative for the whole suite of benchmarks we examined. Figure 1 presents the tool performance when applied to CG classes A and D running on 16 and 2048 cores respectively. The benchmark implements an iterative method and Class A solves a problem with a small memory footprint (MBs) in few iterations, while class D solves a large (GBs) problem. For reference, the original UPC-Thrille tool adds 8% runtime overhead when instrumenting only communication calls (labeled as **NL** in the graphs for No-Local). Our implementation finds one new race in the implementation of this benchmark when compared to the original UPC-Thrille.

Instruction level sampling **I** of all memory references adds a 3600% overhead to the CG class A benchmark execution. Function level sampling **F.5** introduces a 2900% overhead, lower than the 3600% overhead of **I**. For problem larger than class A, function level sampling exhibits very large overheads or the execution does not finish (DNF): some runs exhaust the available memory while some were manually terminated after observing 1000× slowdown.

A comparison of the overhead breakdown for **F** and **I** illustrates the fundamental differences between the two methods. **I** introduces almost all overhead (3600%) in instrumentation, with less than 3% for computation and communication overhead combined, while **F.5** adds only 112% instrumentation overhead. This large difference validates the common intuition that function level sampling amortizes better the cost of deciding what references to track. On the other hand, **F.5** exhibits a large 2800% computation overhead to record and reason about the memory references that are actually tracked. The computation overhead for **I** is very small at less than 2%. This behavior is explained by the temporal distribution of tracked memory accesses during the program execution. UPC-Thrille uses a combination of lock-set based and happens-before analysis that requires tracking all memory references between two `barrier` statements. Function level sampling exhibits a clustered behavior, where many memory references are tracked for a short period of time. Instruction sampling spreads the tracking of memory references more evenly over the program execution. Thus, the behavior of function sampling is determined by the scalability of the tool internal data structures, while the behavior of instruction sampling is determined the speed of "classifying" a memory access.

3.3 Instrumentation and Computation Overheads

Previous work on data race detection focuses on word-level memory accesses and require only keeping track of conflicting addresses. These tools usually use hash table data structures internally. For scientific programs with bulk communication operations (PGAS or MPI), data races on full memory ranges can occur during execution. UPC-Thrille uses an efficient Interval Skiplist [16] data structure to represent memory ranges that demonstrated good performance when sampling only communication operations.

As the performance of function sampling is clearly hampered by the internal data structure overhead, we evaluate the scalability using micro-benchmarks for the insertion and search operations. The time complexity of these algorithms is dependent on the number of elements in the data structure and the distribution of the intervals. We evaluate performance across a range of list sizes and interval distributions: sequential, reverse sequential, strided and uniform random.

Format	S[A][F]
Sampling	H: hierarchical, I: instruction-level, F: function-level NL: no instrumentation on local accesses
Alias	Indicates the use of the persistence alias heuristic
Factor	Back-off factor for sampling at function level
Example	HA.5: Hierarchical sampling with alias heuristic and back-off factor of 0.5

Table 2: *Key for the experiment naming scheme.*

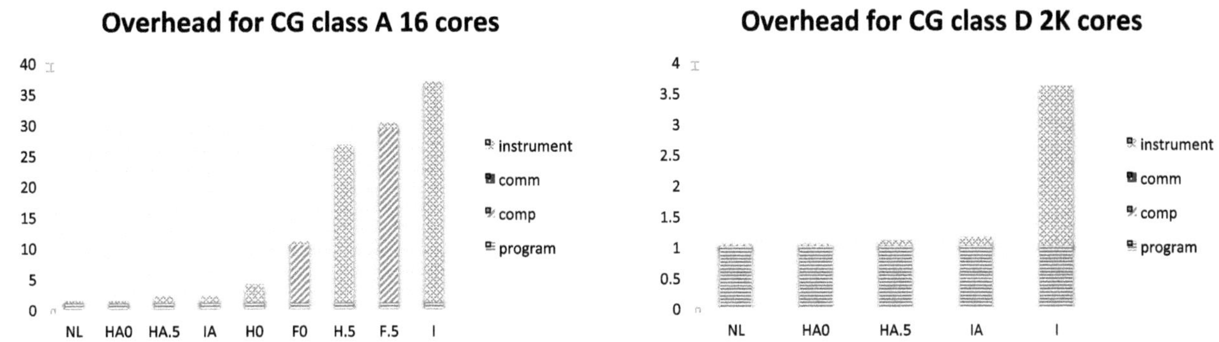

Figure 1: *Breakdown of data race detection overhead for the CG class A benchmark running on 16 cores and class D running on 2048 cores. The* **F** *and* **FA** *configurations did not finish for the class D experiment. At the mid-point* **HA.5** *the probability of sampling a function invocation decays from 1 to 0, by 0.5 each time a function invocation is instrumented.*

Sequential streams are often encountered in code that performs data structure initialization, and are present in all of our benchmarks. They are also the holy-grail of cache optimizations. Strided accesses occur in the Fast Fourier Transform code NAS FT, while random accesses of the form `a[b[i]]` appear in sparse methods of NAS CG and sorting in NAS IS, as well as *guppie*. For a real-world perspective, we also measure the average number of memory intervals that are recorded in our benchmarks.

Figures 2 and 3 present the measured performance on one core of the Cray XE6 system. For a uniform random distribution of 20,000 ranges, the average insert time is 12 μs and the average search time is 1.3 μs. For a more regular distribution of ranges such as a sequential one (e.g. [0, 10), [10, 20), [20, 30), ...), the insertion and search times were higher at 114 μs and 2.4 μs, respectively. This is a weakness of the Interval Skiplist which relies on randomness of data for balancing link levels. In practice, the effect can be easily offset by adding some irregularity, such as the implementation inserting random benign addresses with low frequency. In the application benchmark, the memory access stream does have irregularity, and as illustrated by the results for MG inserts are on average 45 μs and searches 0.54 μs.

When using instruction sampling for the application benchmarks, the Interval Skip-lists never grew too large. They remained at under 1000 unique ranges, thus the insert and search times of the Interval Skiplist do not contribute largely to the overhead. On the other hand, when using function sampling the data structures grew above 10^6 entries, at which point we stopped the execution due to the very large overheads already accumulated.

Instruction sampling pays a higher cost for classifying a memory reference but it naturally throttles the number of references recorded at any time. Function sampling performs a fast classification while having to record a large number of references. Reference classification has a constant overhead independent of the number of references already recorded, while recording overhead scales with the number of references. This difference explains why function sampling scales worse than instruction sampling for scientific programs. For reference, when running on the Cray XE6, the average instrumentation overhead per reference is 1ns, the average memory classification is 45ns, the average computation overhead per reference is 500ns while the average communication overhead per reference is 60μs.

3.4 Sampling for Scientific Applications

Our results indicate that for the workload considered function sampling is not a feasible strategy. Function sampling is indeed faster than instruction sampling for problems using small datasets, such as class A of the NAS Parallel Benchmarks. When increasing the data set size to B, C and D, function sampling in any flavor does not terminate, while the highest slowdown introduced by instruction sampling is 65×. From all benchmarks considered, the only exception happens for *psearch* and EP where **F** is roughly twice as fast than **I**. *psearch* is a tree search benchmark which performs a constant and small amount of work per function, independent of the problem size: this is a common characteristic to many commercial applications. EP is an "Embarrassingly Parallel" benchmark with no global memory accesses.

Our results contradict the intuition that function sampling scales better than instruction sampling. The performance reversal is caused by having only coarse grained control over instrumentation: as loops within scientific applications execute billions of references, function sampling tracks billions of references. In the PGAS case, this is compounded by the fact that classifying the locality of a reference is expensive.

As we have evaluated codes widely used in the scientific domain using small and large datasets running at small and large concurrency, we believe that our finding is widely applicable. In contrast, previous shared memory data race

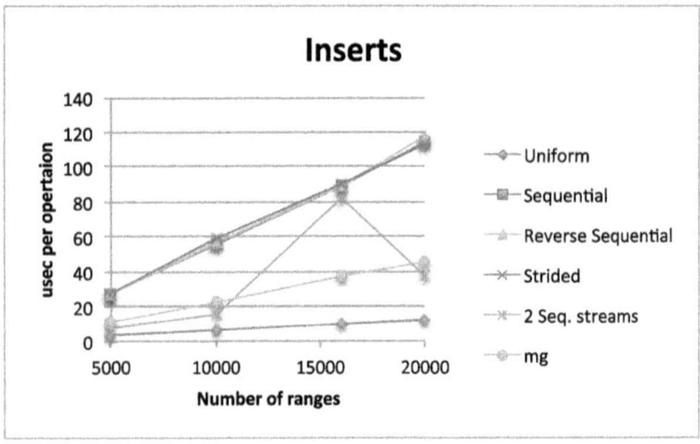

Figure 2: *Average time for the insert operation in Interval Skiplist.*

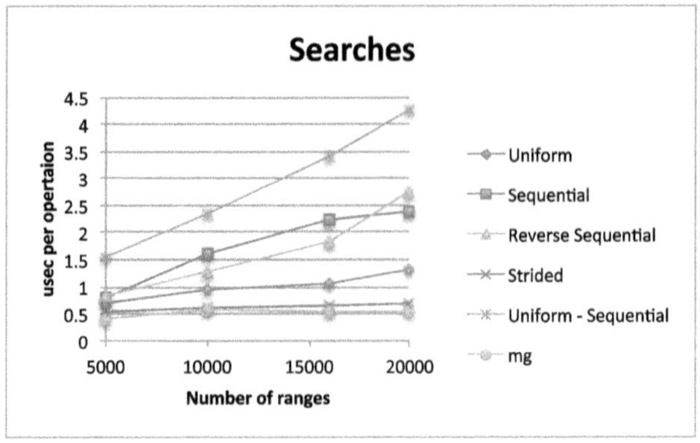

Figure 3: *Average time for the search operation in Interval Skiplist.*

detectors [33, 23, 31, 14] have been scaled at most up to 16 cores and on applications using small data sets. LiteRace is validated on a four core system, while the tool presented by Raman et al [31] has been scaled up to 16 cores.

4. TECHNIQUES TO REDUCE OVERHEAD

As the slowdown of data race detection is caused by instrumentation, additional techniques are required when low overhead is mandatory. This can be achieved by: 1) reducing the number of events traced with better filtering techniques; and 2) better control over the instrumentation granularity.

The most obvious approach is lowering the sampling frequency. We have performed a search over this space, detailed results omitted for brevity. Our results indicate that acceptable behavior at scale cannot be attained solely by tuning the sampling frequency and additional optimizations to reduce the number of references tracked are required for scientific applications. We propose two such techniques that improve scalability without sacrificing analysis precision.

The first optimization filters events by exploiting program semantic information such as aliasing. We improve the analysis performance by exploiting the insight that *aliases are persistent* in PGAS programs: once one is created it will point in the same region (private or global) for a long period of time. Using this we can eliminate the overhead introduced by looking up the physical memory layout inside the language runtime.

The second optimization reduces overhead by providing more control over the instrumentation granularity. We use a hierarchical sampling approach that combines function and instruction sampling to amortize the instrumentation cost while retaining fine grained control over the number of events sampled.

4.1 Exploiting the Persistence of Locality

PGAS languages, such as UPC, Titanium, CAF, Chapel and X10, provide the abstraction of a shared memory address space. Data residing in this space is accessible through references to variables that have a particular type, e.g. "`pointer-to-shared`" type in UPC or "global" in Titanium[1].

The memory management inside any PGAS language runtime is complex due to the need to provide globally addressable memory and to support data layouts, e.g. block cyclic layouts. Thus, references to global object and pointer arithmetic operations translate into runtime operations orders of magnitude [18] more expensive than operations on local references, through a C pointer in the UPC case. Application developers aggressively cast global references to local for performance reasons, including the need to call external libraries such as Intel MKL.

For every local memory reference, the data race detection code needs to perform the inverse up-cast operation and check whether the address is globally visible. This operation is also orders of magnitude more expensive than a regular memory load/store.

For portability reasons, we implement a runtime approach that does not require compiler support. We limit the number of runtime up-casts using the intuition that aliases/locality are persistent. Once initialized, a local reference will access only the private space or only the global space during the program execution. This assumption allows the analysis to dynamically determine the "locality" of any reference only once and cache the result for the rest of the execution. In our implementation, we add a shadow variable to cache the locality of every memory reference expression.

The persistence of locality assumption is valid in all of our test programs and it does not decrease the precision of the analysis. Eight of the ten benchmarks (except EP and guppie) have C pointers aliased to the global heap and the tool finds the same races found by an analysis that "checks" every local memory reference. These races are shown in Table 1 in the column '#Races as "+ C (D)" .

When the underlying assumption is not valid during the execution, the heuristic as implemented may lead to false negatives (miss real data races). However, as casts of global references are complicated and are implemented as runtime "calls", the technique can be trivially generalized for programs with a more dynamic behavior. Any runtime casting call can be extended to invalidate the cached locality information. For casting of proper C pointers, the compiler can easily generate the invalidation calls at the operation site. The performance of this extension is determined by the ratio of casts to memory references performed by the program at runtime. The additional overhead for realistic programs is likely to be negligible in practice

4.2 Hierarchical Sampling

For every memory reference there are two sources of runtime overhead. Instrumentation overhead is introduced to decide whether the reference should be recorded and compu-

[1]Actually, in Titanium any reference is global by default and the language provides local qualifiers.

tation overhead is introduced when recording the reference in the tool internal data structures. By reducing the instruction sampling rate one can clearly reduce overhead, but at the expense of program coverage. To provide both low overhead and good coverage we propose a hierarchical sampling approach which combines the fine grained control of instruction sampling with the overhead amortization provided by function sampling. By using a good hierarchical sampling strategy, we can reduce the instrumentation overhead while retaining the ability to sample from a diverse context with less redundancy. Using the concept of code regions, we formally define instrumentation and hierarchical sampling.

DEFINITION 1 (CODE REGIONS). *We inductively define code regions. By definition, the smallest unit of a code region is a memory reference (read or write). A code region is a reference or a sequence of one or more code regions. The entire program is the largest code region. Each code region R has a label, denoted as #R.*

Functions, loop bodies, basic blocks etc. are examples of code regions. We assume structured code, i.e. that all code regions are properly nested.

DEFINITION 2 (REGION STACK). *During program execution, a region stack RS is maintained. Similar to a call stack, when a region is entered, the label of the region #R is pushed to RS. When exiting a region, the last label is popped from the stack. At the beginning of a program execution, RS is initially empty.*

DEFINITION 3 (INSTRUMENTATION). *Instrumentation is a transformation of a code region* $R \rightarrow R^{inst}$.
If R is a memory reference (base case)

$$R^{inst} = \begin{array}{l} \textbf{if } \textit{check-reference}(\#R :: RS) \textbf{ then} \\ \quad | \ \textit{log}(\#R) \\ R \end{array}$$

Else, if R is a sequence of regions $[R_1, R_2, \ldots, R_n]$,

$$R^{inst} = \begin{array}{l} \textbf{if } \textit{check-region}(\#R :: RS) \textbf{ then} \\ \quad RS = \#R :: RS; \\ \quad [R_1^{inst}, R_2^{inst}, \ldots, R_n^{inst}]; \\ \quad RS = tail(RS) \\ \textbf{else} \\ \quad | \ [R_1, R_2, \ldots, R_n] \end{array}$$

By specializing the *check-reference* and *check-region* and choosing the region granularity, we can implement multiple sampling algorithms. For example, instruction sampling with an exponential back-off (strategy **I** in the experiments presented in Section 3.2), is implemented as the following functions. The map $p : label \rightarrow \mathbb{R}$ contains the (dynamic) sampling probabilities of regions.

$\forall \#R \in Statements.\ p(\#R) = 1.0$

```
check-reference(#R :: RS) =
if rand() < p(#R) then
  | p(#R) *= BACKOFF_FACTOR;
  | return true
else
  | return false
```

check-region(x) = true

Function sampling as introduced by the LiteRace [23] implementation is defined as follows. The region is a whole function and the *sample-strategy* function depends on the strategy of sampling, such as a fixed probability, random or an adaptive strategy.

check-reference(x) = true

check-region#R :: RS) = sample-strategy(#R)

Intuitively, the *check-reference* function decides what events should be logged at runtime, while the *check-region* function provides control over the granularity of these decisions. We propose a hierarchical sampling strategy that combines instruction sampling with function sampling. The combination of hierarchical sampling with the aliasing runtime heuristic is referred to as **HA** and described as:
$\forall \#R \in Statements \cup Functions.\ p(\#R) = 1.0$

```
check-reference(#R :: RS) =
if p > 0 ∧ rand() < p(#R) then
  | if is-local-access(R) then
  |   | // locality persistence heuristic
  |   | p(#R) = 0;
  |   | return false;
  | else
  |   | p(#R) *= STMT_BACKOFF_FACTOR;
  |   | return true;
else
  | return false
```

```
check-region(#R :: RS) =
if p > 0 ∧ rand() < p(#R) then
  | p(#R) *= FUNC_BACKOFF_FACTOR;
  | return true
else
  | return false
```

This implementation uses exponential back-off at both individual reference and function granularity.

4.3 Scalable Data Race Detection

In the following, the letter **A** in the configuration name denotes composing the aliasing heuristic to that particular sampling method. We denote the configuration using hierarchical instruction sampling by **H**, where we control instrumentation at the function and the instruction level. Instructions are sampled with the baseline 0.9 value for **I**, while the numbers in the title denote the function back-off factor. Thus, **H1** is identical to **I** (always samples functions), while with **H0** we sample only the first invocation of any function. At the mid-point **H.5** the probability of sampling a function invocation decays from 1 by 0.5 each time the function is sampled; for long running programs the sampling probability converges to 0. Selected results are presented in Table 1 and Figures 1 and 4.

Composing the aliasing optimization with any of the tool instrumentation methods greatly improves performance. As illustrated in Figure 1, the overhead of instruction sampling is reduced from 3600% to 105% with **IA** for CG class A. Similar trends are observable when scaling the problem and running class D on 2048 cores. For this particular configuration, the **FA** method does not terminate due to out of memory errors or excessive slowdown. **I** exhibits a 259% overhead, while **IA** exhibits less than 15% slowdown.

Composing aliasing with function and instruction sampling does not change the overall trends. For problems using small datasets, such as class A of the NAS Parallel Benchmarks, **F** or **FA** is faster than **I** or **IA**, respectively. When increasing the data set size to B, C and D, **FA** still does not terminate. Overall, the maximum **IA** slowdown is 10×.

Hierarchical sampling **H** performs better than both instruction and function sampling. For CG, **H.5** exhibits a 2550% slowdown, significantly better than both **F** and **I**. Overall, with hierarchical sampling we still observe slowdowns as high as 20×, which is still unacceptable when running at scale. With the hierarchical sampling approach, the instrumentation overhead contributes the most to the program slowdown.

Composing the aliasing heuristic with the hierarchical sampling strategy provides best performance. For CG, the overhead of hierarchical sampling is reduced from 2550% with **H.5** to 99% with **HA.5** and from 294% with **H0** to 17% with **HA0**. In the case of the NAS Parallel Benchmarks class C on 16 cores, the weighted average overhead for all the benchmarks with **HA.5** was 11.9%.

Figure 4 shows the performance when running strong scaling experiments for the classes C and D of the NAS Parallel Benchmarks. For all experiments, the lowest overhead is introduced by the **HA** configuration and we are able to find all the races with less than 50% runtime overhead when running up to 2048 cores.

Overall, instrumentation overhead contributes the most to the slowdown caused by data race detection. The computation overhead in the scalable versions of **IA** and **HA** is small. At large scale the communication overhead is also small due to the techniques presented in [29].

5. BUGS FOUND

The column labeled '#Races' in Table 1 shows the data races found by our tool. The data is presented as A(B) + C(D), where A(B) denotes races found by the original UPC-Thrille and C(D) the *additional* C races found in phase I and reproduced (D) in phase II by this new implementation. All the additional races are uncovered due to the ability to track global to local memory aliases.

We detect a previously unknown race in NAS CG where memory is initialized using "local" pointers and distributed without synchronization to other tasks using global pointers. The races reproduced in *psearch*, BT, SP and LU are benign and are intended by the programmer. In *psearch* they occur on a counter used for work-stealing, while the races confirmed in BT, SP and LU occur when executing custom synchronization code:

`signal (v = 1);` || `wait ( while( v == 0););`.

The races reported as potential but not reproduced in BT, SP and LU occur between memory accesses separated by the custom synchronization code. Note that reporting infeasible data races in the presence of custom synchronization code is a common limitation of data race detection tools. Our 2nd phase tries to remove this limitation—it never confirms the feasibility of these data races. This is a possible indication that these data races are false positives.

6. DISCUSSION

We believe that our techniques and findings are widely applicable to other languages or programming models. The alias heuristic is applicable to any PGAS language since they provide a global address space and performance and software engineering concerns require programmers to aggressively identify references that are local to a given "task". Hierarchical sampling is a generic technique orthogonal to the language, programming model employed in the application, or the data race detection algorithm. It is clearly required for SPMD parallelism (UPC, CAF, MPI) or OpenMP parallel loops, where work per function scales with the problem size. When using structured parallelism as present in Habanero-C or OpenMP tasking, some applications may perform a constant amount of work per function and the overall behavior approximates commercial applications or that of our *psearch* benchmark. In this case, hierarchical sampling performs at least as well as function sampling. The benefits of hierarchical sampling are also orthogonal to the choice of data race detection algorithm: lock-set-based or happens-before.

In PGAS languages, global addresses have associated object metadata and casting and address arithmetic operations require calls into the language runtime. Thus, a runtime only implementation of the aliasing heuristic works well. Static analysis may be able to complement or supplant our runtime analysis approach. Besides the obvious engineering challenges to implement alias and escape analysis in a multi-language, multi-programming model environment, there is a practical expectation on performance improvements. The implementation of our alias heuristic adds one extra branch instruction per memory reference. Static analysis will eliminate some of these branches. Qualitatively, this is similar to the effects of function sampling when compared to instruction sampling. In our experiments, function sampling outperformed instruction sampling by at most 3×.

As our hierarchical approach considers only two granularities at function and instruction level, an interesting question is whether further refinement improves performance. One obvious solution is to consider loop nests as the unit of instrumentation. Our tool did not finish when instrumenting only the first execution of any function, which indicates that any strategy that instruments whole loops is likely to exhibit high overhead. Thus, a strategy that peels off few instrumented loop iterations is required to limit slowdown. In our opinion, any such strategy is likely to produce equivalent behavior to the hierarchical sampling we implemented.

Performance can be further improved by reducing computation overhead with data structures with better scalability characteristics than Interval Skiplist. The results provide little incentive as for our workload instrumentation overhead directly determines slowdown.

For our future work we plan to extend the data race detection implementation to provide maximum coverage on a time budget: our goal is to find the maximum number of data races with no more than a guaranteed application slowdown. Our preliminary experiences indicate that we are likely to be able to guarantee no more than 2× slowdown. Toward controlling time, the scalability analysis of the internal data structures has already yielded valuable insights which allows us to derive space/state bounds. Toward improving coverage, we plan to use the concept of region stacks introduced in the formalism presented in Section 4.2. We plan to experiment with several other strategies besides exponential back-off at reference and function level: i) proportional sampling per unique region stack; ii) k-region context sampling (similar to k-CFA [34] and k-object-sensitive [24] analyses; and iii) proportional sampling at functions and exponential back-off at statements.

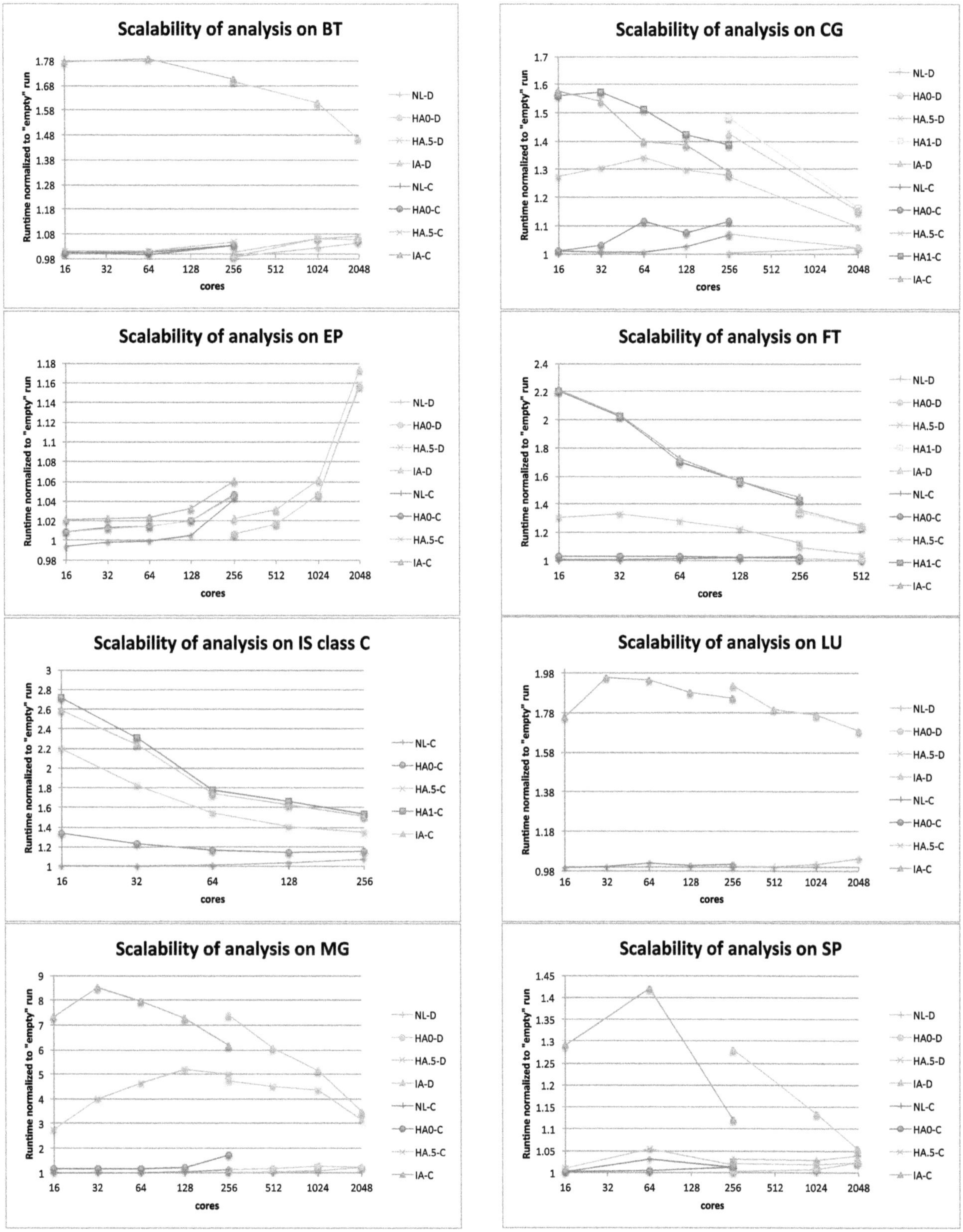

Figure 4: *Scalability of the different sampling methods when running the tool on the NAS Parallel Benchmarks, classes C and D. The overhead of instruction sampling* **I** *is very high compared to the others and it has been omitted for presentation purposes.*

7. OTHER RELATED WORK

Data race detection tools can be broadly classified as using static or dynamic techniques. Static techniques [30, 9] are scalable and complete, i.e. find all the races in the program. On the other hand, they report a very large number of false positives which need to be filtered by users and can handle only limited types of synchronization primitives such as locks or barriers.

Dynamic techniques for finding concurrency bugs can be classified into two classes: predictive techniques and precise techniques Predictive dynamic techniques [33, 11] could predict concurrency bugs that did not happen in a concurrent execution; however, such techniques still report false warnings. UPC-Thrille implements a predictive dynamic technique, followed by automatic filtering of false positives. Precise dynamic techniques, such as happens-before race detection [2, 12, 14] and atomicity monitoring [22, 15], are capable of detecting concurrency bugs that actually happen in an execution. Therefore, these techniques are precise, but they cannot give good coverage as predictive dynamic techniques.

Dynamic techniques have to address the challenge of high runtime overhead. Sampling approaches to reduce instrumentation overhead have been discussed throughout this paper. Techniques to reduce the computation overhead have been explored as well. Choi et al [11] discuss static analysis techniques to reduce the overhead of data race detection for Java programs. As alias and pointer analysis for C based programs is notoriously conservative, these techniques need to be supplemented by the runtime techniques presented in Section 4.1. Recently, Raman et al [31] describe a scalable implementation for data race detection in Habanero Java programs implemented using fine-grained structured parallelism. Their benchmarks are equivalent to our fine-grained benchmarks, while our NAS benchmarks use coarse grained interactions. They report analysis overheads as high as 10× and provide valuable data about the scalability of other state of the art race detectors for multi-threaded programs: Eraser [33] and FastTrack [14]. They report slowdowns as high as 100× for the latter.

So far there have been a lot of research effort to verify and test concurrent and parallel programs written in Java and C/pthreads for non-HPC platforms; the literature listed above supports this fact. There have also been efforts to test and verify HPC programs, mostly focused on C/MPI programs. ISP [37] is a push-button dynamic verifier capable of detecting deadlocks, resource leaks, and assertion violations in C/MPI programs. DAMPI [39, 40] overcomes ISP's scalability limitations and scales to thousands of MPI processes. Like ISP, DAMPI only tests for MPI Send/Recv interleavings, but runs in a distributed way. In contrast to our work, DAMPI instruments and reasons only about the ordering of Send/Recv operations with respect to the MPI ranks, and not about the memory accessed by these operations. Both ISP and DAMPI assume that program input is fixed. TASS [35] removes this limitation by using symbolic execution to reason about all possible inputs to a MPI program, but it is work only at inception. MPI messages can be intercepted and analyzed for bugs and anomalies. Intel MessageChecker [13] does a post-mortem analysis after collecting message traces, while MARMOT [20] and Umpire [38] check at runtime.

8. CONCLUSION

To our knowledge, we discuss the first implementation of a data race detector for distributed memory programs that tracks both memory references and communication operations. The main design goal of our implementation is to provide low overhead with good program coverage when running at scale.

Dynamic program analysis tools face the challenge of instrumentation overhead and sampling techniques have been shown to be effective in reducing program slowdown. The state-of-the-art technique to reduce overhead is considered to be function sampling. We use a workload containing UPC programs and experiment with function and instruction level sampling. Our results indicate that function level sampling is not feasible for scientific programs: increasing the input set increases the amount of work per function invocation in these applications and the analysis does not terminate. Instruction sampling works better for scientific programs and our implementation finds races with up to 65× slowdown.

In order to obtain acceptable program slowdown we experiment with tuning the sampling frequency. For the workload considered, the performance degradation for settings required to find all the "known" bugs is still high.

We propose two techniques to improve the scalability of data race detection: 1) hierarchical function and instruction level sampling; and 2) exploiting the runtime persistence of aliasing and locality in UPC applications. The results indicate that both techniques are required in practice: any stand-alone technique is able to reduce overhead only to 1000% (10× slowdown). When applying the optimizations in conjunction our tool finds races with at most 50% overhead when running on 2048 cores of a CrayXE6 system.

Acknowledgements

Support for this work was provided through the X-Stack program funded by U.S. Department of Energy, Office of Science, Advanced Scientific Computing Research under collaborative agreement number DE-SC0008699 and through a gift from Oracle. Additional support to LBNL was provided by the U.S. Department of Defense. This research also supported in part by Microsoft (Award #024263) and Intel (Award #024894) funding and by matching funding by U.C. Discovery (Award #DIG07-10227).

9. REFERENCES

[1] S. Adve and K. Gharachorloo. Shared Memory Consistency Models: A Tutorial. *IEEE computing*, December 1996.

[2] S. V. Adve, M. D. Hill, B. P. Miller, and R. H. B. Netzer. Detecting Data Races on Weak Memory Systems. In *18th International Symposium on Computer architecture (ISCA)*, pages 234–243. ACM, 1991.

[3] M. Arnold and B. G. Ryder. A Framework for Reducing the Cost of Instrumented Code. In *Proceedings of the ACM SIGPLAN 2001 conference on Programming language design and implementation*, PLDI '01, 2001.

[4] M. Arnold, M. T. Vechev, and E. Yahav. QVM: An Efficient Runtime for Detecting Defects in Deployed Systems. *ACM Trans. Softw. Eng. Methodol.*, 21(1), 2011.

[5] K. Asanovic, R. Bodik, B. C. Catanzaro, J. J. Gebis, P. Husbands, K. Keutzer, D. A. Patterson, W. L. Plishker, J. Shalf, S. W. Williams, and K. A. Yelick.

The Landscape of Parallel Computing Research: A View from Berkeley. Technical Report UCB/EECS-2006-183, EECS Department, University of California, Berkeley, Dec 2006.

[6] D. Bailey, T. Harris, W. Saphir, R. Van Der Wijngaart, A. Woo, and M. Yarrow. The NAS Parallel Benchmarks 2.0. *Technical Report NAS-95-010, NASA Ames Research Center*, 1995.

[7] S. Bensalem and K. Havelund. Dynamic Deadlock Analysis of Multi-threaded Programs. In *Haifa Verification Conference*, pages 208–223, 2005.

[8] D. Bonachea. Proposal for Extending the UPC Memory Copy Library Functions and Supporting Extensions to GASNet. Technical Report LBNL-56495, Lawrence Berkeley National Lab, 2004.

[9] S. Burckhardt, R. Alur, and M. M. K. Martin. CheckFence: Checking Consistency of Concurrent Data Types on Relaxed Memory Models. In *Programming Language Design and Implementation (PLDI)*, pages 12–21, 2007.

[10] W. W. Carlson, J. M. Draper, D. E. Culler, K. Yelick, and K. W. E. Brooks. Introduction to UPC and Language Specification, 1999.

[11] J.-D. Choi, K. Lee, A. Loginov, R. O'Callahan, V. Sarkar, and M. Sridharan. Efficient and precise datarace detection for multithreaded object-oriented programs. In *Programming language design and implementation (PLDI)*, pages 258–269, New York, NY, USA, 2002. ACM.

[12] J.-D. Choi, B. P. Miller, and R. H. B. Netzer. Techniques for Debugging Parallel Programs With Flowback Analysis. *ACM Trans. Program. Lang. Syst.*, 13(4):491–530, 1991.

[13] J. DeSouza, B. Kuhn, B. R. de Supinski, V. Samofalov, S. Zheltov, and S. Bratanov. Automated, scalable debugging of MPI programs with Intel Message Checker. In *Software engineering for high performance computing system applications*, SE-HPCS '05, pages 78–82, 2005.

[14] C. Flanagan and S. N. Freund. FastTrack: efficient and precise dynamic race detection. In *Programming language design and implementation (PLDI)*, 2009.

[15] C. Flanagan, S. N. Freund, and J. Yi. Velodrome: a sound and complete dynamic atomicity checker for multithreaded programs. In *Programming language design and implementation (PLDI)*, pages 293–303. ACM, 2008.

[16] E. N. Hanson and T. Johnson. The interval skip list: A data structure for finding all intervals that overlap a point. In *Workshop on Algorithms and Data Structures*, pages 153–164. Springer, 1992.

[17] M. Hauswirth and T. M. Chilimbi. Low-overhead memory leak detection using adaptive statistical profiling. In *Proceedings of the 11th international conference on Architectural support for programming languages and operating systems*, ASPLOS-XI, 2004.

[18] P. Husbands, C. Iancu, and K. Yelick. A performance analysis of the berkeley upc compiler. In *Proceedings of the 17th annual international conference on Supercomputing*, ICS '03, 2003.

[19] P. Joshi, M. Naik, C.-S. Park, and K. Sen. An extensible active testing framework for concurrent programs. In *Computer Aided Verification (CAV)*, Lecture Notes in Computer Science. Springer, 2009.

[20] B. Krammer, M. Müller, and M. Resch. Runtime checking of MPI applications with MARMOT. In *Mini-Symposium Tools Support for Parallel Programming, ParCo 2005, Malaga, Spain.*

[21] W. Kuchera and C. Wallace. The UPC memory model: Problems and prospects. In *the 18th International Parallel and Distributed Processing Symposium (IPDPS)*, April 2004.

[22] S. Lu, J. Tucek, F. Qin, and Y. Zhou. AVIO: detecting atomicity violations via access interleaving invariants. *SIGARCH Comput. Archit. News*, 34(5):37–48, 2006.

[23] D. Marino, M. Musuvathi, and S. Narayanasamy. LiteRace: Effective Sampling for Lightweight Data-Race Detection. In *PLDI*, 2009.

[24] A. Milanova. Parameterized object sensitivity for points-to analysis for java. *ACM Trans. Softw. Eng. Methodol*, 14:2005, 2005.

[25] The NAS Parallel Benchmarks. Available at http://www.nas.nasa.gov/Software/NPB.

[26] The UPC NAS Parallel Benchmarks. Available at http://upc.gwu.edu/download.html.

[27] R. H. B. Netzer and B. P. Miller. What are race conditions? some issues and formalizations. *LOPLAS*, 1992.

[28] S. Olivier and J. Prins. Scalable dynamic load balancing using UPC. In *International Conference on Parallel Processing (ICPP)*, 2008.

[29] C.-S. Park, K. Sen, P. Hargrove, and C. Iancu. Efficient Data Race Detection for Distributed Memory Parallel Programs. In *Proceedings of the Supercomputing Conference (SC11)*, 2011.

[30] S. Qadeer and D. Wu. KISS: keep it simple and sequential. In *Programming language design and implementation (PLDI)*, pages 14–24. ACM, 2004.

[31] R. Raman, J. Zhao, V. Sarkar, M. Vechev, and E. Yahav. Scalable and Precise Dynamic Datarace Detection for Structured Parallelism. In *Proceedings of the 33rd ACM SIGPLAN conference on Programming Language Design and Implementation (PLDI)*, 2012.

[32] P. Sack, B. E. Bliss, Z. Ma, P. Petersen, and J. Torrellas. Accurate and efficient filtering for the intel thread checker race detector. In *Proceedings of the 1st workshop on Architectural and system support for improving software dependability*, ASID '06, 2006.

[33] S. Savage, M. Burrows, G. Nelson, P. Sobalvarro, and T. Anderson. Eraser: a dynamic data race detector for multithreaded programs. *ACM Trans. Comput. Syst.*, 15(4):391–411, 1997.

[34] O. Shivers. *Control-Flow Analysis of Higher-Order Languages*. PhD thesis, 1991.

[35] S. F. Siegel and T. K. Zirkel. Automatic formal verification of MPI-based parallel programs. In *Principles and practice of parallel programming*, PPoPP '11, 2011.

[36] C. Terboven. Comparing intel thread checker and sun thread analyzer. In *PARCO'07*, pages 669–676, 2007.

[37] S. S. Vakkalanka, S. Sharma, G. Gopalakrishnan, and R. M. Kirby. ISP: a tool for model checking MPI programs. In *Principles and practice of parallel programming*, PPoPP '08, 2008.

[38] J. S. Vetter and B. R. de Supinski. Dynamic software testing of MPI applications with Umpire. In *Supercomputing*, SC '00, Washington, DC, USA, 2000. IEEE Computer Society.

[39] A. Vo, S. Aananthakrishnan, G. Gopalakrishnan, B. R. d. Supinski, M. Schulz, and G. Bronevetsky. A Scalable and Distributed Dynamic Formal Verifier for MPI Programs. In *Supercomputing (SC10)*, 2010.

[40] A. Vo, G. Gopalakrishnan, R. M. Kirby, B. R. de Supinski, M. Schulz, and G. Bronevetsky. Large scale verification of mpi programs using lamport clocks with lazy update. In *Proceedings of the 2011 International Conference on Parallel Architectures and Compilation Techniques*, PACT '11, pages 330–339, Washington, DC, USA, 2011. IEEE Computer Society.

[41] K. Yelick, D. Bonachea, and C. Wallace. A Proposal for a UPC Memory Consistency Model. Technical Report LBNL-54983, Lawrence Berkeley National Laboratory, May 2004.

Elastic and Scalable Tracing and Accurate Replay of Non-Deterministic Events *

Xing Wu, Frank Mueller
North Carolina State University
mueller@cs.ncsu.edu

ABSTRACT

SCALATRACE represents the state-of-the-art of parallel application tracing for high performance computing (HPC). This paper presents SCALATRACE II, a next generation tracer that delivers even higher trace compression capability, even when events are not always regular. In this work, we contribute a spectrum of novel compression and replay techniques that are fundamentally different from our past approaches. SCALATRACE II features a redesigned low-level encoding scheme of trace data such that data elements are *elastic* and self-explanatory. With this new encoding scheme, trace compression is enhanced by introducing innovative intra-node and inter-node trace compression algorithms that guarantee high compression rates in a loop structure agnostic fashion. In practice, the improved compression scheme is particularly efficient for scientific codes that demonstrate inconsistent behavior across time steps and nodes. A novel approach is further contributed to probabilistically replay sequences of non-deterministic events. To assess the compression efficacy of SCALATRACE II, we conduct experiments not only with computational kernels but also a real-world application, the Parallel Ocean Program (POP). Compared to the first generation SCALATRACE, we observe key improvements on trace compression for benchmarks with inconsistent time step behavior and diverging task level behavior while retaining timing accuracy even under probabilistic replay.

Categories and Subject Descriptors

C.4 [**Performance of Systems**]: Measurement techniques

Keywords

SCALATRACE, Trace Compression, Performance

1. INTRODUCTION

The compute power of supercomputers has been doubling each year in the past two decades. The era of exascale computing is projected to arrive in the near future. With such large systems, recording the program behavior of parallel applications for post-mortem performance analysis is becoming increasingly difficult. On the one hand, analyzing complicated scientific applications requires complete and accurate performance data. On the other hand, the large number of processors/cores and the increasing gap between computational power and I/O performance pose great challenges in terms of efficiency and scalability of performance analysis tools. Consequently, traditional analysis tools either collect lossless traces by sacrificing scalability [23] or report only aggregated statistical information that might be insufficient for in-depth performance analysis and debugging [32]. To address this discrepancy, we designed SCALATRACE, a scalable parallel communication and I/O tracing library that features on-the-fly trace compression [26, 29]. For single program, multiple data (SPMD) parallel applications, SCALATRACE is able to collect lossless traces that are much more space-efficient than the past approaches.

SCALATRACE is one tool that represents the state-of-the-art of parallel application tracing for high performance computing (HPC), specifically for communication events. In this paper, we present SCALATRACE II, the next generation SCALATRACE that features a fundamental redesign in every aspect. SCALATRACE II is designed to address the shortcomings of previous work. It targets inefficiencies in the compression of communication traces for applications with inconsistent program behavior across time steps and diverging parallel control flow. For example, coupled large-scale scientific codes such as the Community Earth System Model (CESM) [5] exhibit multiple program, multiple data (MPMD) behavior. They perform multi-physics simulation with different modules using diverse inputs, executing a multitude of algorithms, and running on different sets of processors. To generate scalable traces for these applications, methodologies that better exploit trace similarities across time steps and MPI tasks are in demand.

With SCALATRACE II, we contribute a spectrum of novel compression and replay techniques that are fundamentally different from our past approaches. In SCALATRACE II, MPI parameters and loop information are stored as elastic data element representations, a redesigned low-level encoding scheme that is automatically evolving and self-explanatory. By annotating loop information with participant information, we designed a loop agnostic inter-node compression scheme that ensures perfect event matching for applications with task-specific communication patterns. We also redesigned the task-level loop compression to perform approximate loop iteration matching, which is particularly effective for applications with inconsistent behavior across time steps.

SCALATRACE II inherits the lossy philosophy proposed in our previous work [37]. In essence, SCALATRACE II can be configured to compress MPI parameters to the utmost using probabilistic methods while still preserving most of the advantages of the lossless approach. We further developed SCALAREPLAY II, a brand-new probabilistic replay engine that is compatible with the loop agnostic trace format. With SCALAREPLAY II, we improved the coordinated random value selection of the trace replay algorithm. Optimizations such as multi-context traversal are also designed to boost the robustness, accuracy, and scalability of the replay engine.

We evaluated SCALATRACE II with regard to two aspects: (1) effectiveness of trace compression and (2) correctness and timing accuracy of the probabilistic replay. We conducted experiments with a subset of the NAS Parallel Benchmark suite, the Sweep3D neutron-transport kernel, and the Parallel Ocean Program (POP). Experimental results demonstrate that SCALATRACE II achieves

*This work was supported in part by NSF grants CCF-1217748, CNS-0958311, and HECURA-0937908.

ICS'13, June 10–14, 2013, Eugene, Oregon, USA.

key improvements on trace compression for benchmarks exhibiting task-specific communication patterns, inconsistent loop behavior, and/or diverging parallel control flow. Results on probabilistic replay show that SCALAREPLAY II is able to accurately re-produce the execution times of the original applications. Across all the test cases, the mean absolute percentage error of the replay times is only 5.7%. Given such accuracy, we conclude that the lossy compression scheme, powerful in reducing trace sizes, is equally applicable to scenarios where timing accuracy is required.

This work makes the following contributions:

- We propose SCALATRACE II, a fundamental redesign of SCALATRACE that features a spectrum of novel compression techniques to improve trace compression for applications with inconsistent loop-level and task-level behavior.
- We designed SCALAREPLAY II, a probabilistic replay engine compatible with SCALATRACE II that significantly improves robustness, accuracy, and scalability.
- By comparing the compression ratio of two generations of SCALATRACE with computational kernels and real-world applications, we investigate the causes of compression inefficiency and demonstrate potential solutions to obtain better compression.

2. PREVIOUS WORK

This section summarizes our previous work on the last generation SCALATRACE and provides the background for the improvements and redesigns discussed in Section 3.

2.1 Intra-node and Inter-node Compression

SCALATRACE is a communication tracing framework for parallel applications using the Message Passing Interface (MPI), the *de facto* standard for scientific computing. It utilizes the MPI profiling layer (PMPI) to intercept MPI calls. It collects lossless, order-preserving, and space-efficient communication traces by exploiting the program structure and performing a two-stage trace compression, i.e., intra-node and inter-node compression.

SCALATRACE utilizes Extended Regular Section Descriptors (RSDs) to capture loop structures of one or multiple communication events. Power-RSDs (PRSDs) are utilized to recursively specify RSDs in nested loops. To perform intra-node loop compression, SCALATRACE constantly searches for repeating event sequences ending with the current tail event. In order for two event sequences to be considered matching, SCALATRACE requires not only equal lengths but also identical call stack signatures, loop structures, and equivalent MPI parameter values for events at corresponding positions in the two sequences. When a new loop iteration (a repeating sequence of events) is identified, SCALATRACE eagerly compresses it with the previous iteration by inserting a new outer loop or increasing the trip count of an existing RSD/PRSD by one. As such, SCALATRACE is able to generate scalable traces with respect to the number of time steps if loop trip counts are consistent.

At program completion, SCALATRACE performs an inter-node compression along a radix tree rooted in rank 0. During this reduction, internal nodes combine their traces with other task-level traces received from child nodes. To perform compression, two task-level event sequences are compared at the granularity of a loop structure, i.e., matching standalone events and whole loops are merged. Subsequently, diverging subsequences bounded by matching preceding and succeeding events are concatenated. For applications with regular SPMD behavior, SCALATRACE generates near constant sized traces irrespective of the number of nodes of a parallel job.

2.2 The Ranklist Representation

Inter-node compression identifies events that are executed by multiple MPI tasks. To perform the compression for one such event, SCALATRACE attaches a *ranklist,* i.e., a list of the ranks of the participating MPI tasks, to the event. Ranklists are constructed in a recursive manner. Using the EBNF meta-syntax, a ranklist is represented as

$$< dimension\ start\ iters\ stride\ \{iters\ stride\} >,$$

where *dimension* is the dimension of the group, *start* is the rank of the starting node, and the $< iters\ stride >$ pair is the iteration and stride of each dimension. With the ranklist representation, SCALATRACE is able to capture the spatial characteristics of a set of nodes and to describe it succinctly.

2.3 Histogram-based Compression

SCALATRACE preserves the timing information of an execution by recording the delta times, i.e., relative times between successive communication and computational stages. In the case where a single communication/computational stage in the source code generates multiple delta times due to loop and/or parallel execution, these delta times are merged using histograms during loop compression and/or cross-node reduction. The histogram-based compression is a lossy approach that captures the distribution of a set of values instead of memorizing the exact values. While the histogram approach is particularly effective for scalable compression of performance data in the form of numerical values, it is also applicable to MPI parameters, such as DEST and SOURCE, to more closely capture the communication pattern.

3. TRACE COMPRESSION AND REPLAY

3.1 Elastic Data Element Representation

SCALATRACE II features a complete redesign of SCALATRACE, ranging from the very low-level data structures to the core trace compression algorithms. In this section, we introduce the novel elastic data element representation.

A SCALATRACE trace file is a human-readable text file. A data element in the trace file is an integer that represents the value of either an MPI event parameter, such as the destination of a send, or a program control flow parameter, such as the trip count of a loop. From our experience with the previous version of SCALATRACE, we learned that even though a data element is apparently simple as an integer, it may become complicated when the trace is compressed to a high degree. For example, assume a scalar integer value d represents the destination of an MPI_Send operation. When the same MPI_Send is called twice with destinations d_1 and d_2 in consecutive loop iterations, the two events will be compressed due to SCALATRACE's loop compression mechanism (see Section 3.2). Thus, the scalar value d evolves into a vector (d_1, d_2). When the same loop has multiple iterations, the destination vector may grow in a non-scalable fashion. Hence, a vector compression mechanism is activated. Finally, the inter-node compression further imposes another level of complexity on the data element representation. In a nutshell, a compressed data element ought to contain not only the parameter value, but also loop details and participant information.

In SCALATRACE II, we introduce the elastic data element representation and apply this representation to all the data elements in the trace. The elastic data element representation is a list of $< value\ vector, ranklist >$ pairs, where a *value vector* is simply a C++ vector of primitive integer values. On initialization, there is only one such pair in the list consisting of a value vector of a single parameter value and a ranklist of a single participant. During loop compression, new values are appended to the value vector in the order that they are generated so that the replay engine or other trace analyzers can traverse the values in the correct order. During inter-node reduction, we merge the ranklists when the value vectors fully match, otherwise a new < *value vector, ranklist* > pair is added to the list. As such, the data element is fully self-explanatory; no additional information is required to resolve a data element for a particular rank and loop iteration.

To keep the size of the value vector scalable, we constantly perform a loop compression against the entries in the vector. Whenever possible, a vector of $m \cdot n$ elements is represented as a vector of m elements and n iterations. Note that the choice of the vector compression algorithm is not set in stone. For example, run-length encoding might be more efficient for loop parameters when an MPI event is specific only to certain loop iterations (see Section 3.2.1). Since the vector compression mechanism is encapsulated in the elastic data element representation, it is possible to intelligently choose the best compression strategies and convert to the most space-efficient format when necessary.

As the fundamental data structure of SCALATRACE II, it is vital to guarantee its scalability even under extreme circumstances. We realized that there always exist cases where even a sophisticated algorithm fails to compress the value vectors. We therefore further enhanced the elastic data element representation to exploit probability-based compression using histograms (see Section 2.3) for selected parameter types, such as SOURCE, DEST, and COUNT of point-to-point communication routines. Nonetheless, utilizing such lossy compression techniques poses challenges for the trace replay. We have updated our past probabilistic trace replay technique to address these challenges. The new approach is discussed in detail in Section 3.5.

3.2 Compressing Partially Matching Loops

SCALATRACE utilizes the MPI profiling layer (PMPI) to intercept MPI calls during application execution. It performs loop detection and compression by searching for consecutive repeating patterns in the MPI event sequence. In contrast to the instruction-level binary instrumentation, which is able to pinpoint the entry and exit points of loop structures, the SCALATRACE approach relies heavily on recognizing repeating patterns. With SCALATRACE II, we redesigned the task-level loop compression algorithm from the ground up to support the compression of loops with iteration-specific behavior.

3.2.1 Handling Iteration-specific Behavior

Production-grade scientific applications such as the Parallel Ocean Program (POP) demonstrate inconsistent behavior across time steps. POP performs a set of computations and communications of an inner loop in multiple iterations in each time step. Due to inconsistent data-dependent convergence in the computation, the trip counts of the inner loop vary across different time steps. In addition, branches inside loop structures also lead to loop iterations with different event counts and unmatching event sequences. This behavior can also be observed in many Adaptive Mesh Refinement (AMR) applications in which the input set is dynamically rebalanced on a periodic basis. Due to the iteration-specific behavior, SCALATRACE's task-level loop compression fails to compress loop iterations because the loop detection algorithm requires identical event sequences for loop iterations with matching inner loop structures.

In SCALATRACE II, we overcome the shortcoming by loosening the iteration matching criteria. In order for two consecutive sequences of events $E1,...,Ea$ and $Eb,...,En$ to be considered a match, SCALATRACE II only requires their beginning and ending events to match, i.e., $E1 == Eb$ and $Ea == En$. Under such criteria, once two matching loop iterations are identified, SCALATRACE II's aggressive longest common subsequence (LCS) based loop compression algorithm will merge the rest of the events, irrespective of the loop lengths or the inner loop structures. As an example, if a certain node executes the following code,

```
for(int i=0; i<2; i++){
    MPI_Barrier(); // E1
    if(i == 0)
        MPI_Isend(); // E2
    if(i == 1)
        MPI_Irecv(); // E3
    MPI_Barrier(); // E4
}
```

Figure 1: Loop with Iteration-specific Behavior

the trace after loop compression will be

$$E1_{(4,2)}\ E2\ E3\ E4,$$

where the subscript of $E1$ indicates that $E1$ is the beginning event of a loop structure of with 4 members events and 2 iterations. In general, we use the following mnemonic to describe the loop stack associated with a loop head event E:

$E_{(m_1,i_1)(m_2,i_2)...(m_n,i_n)}$: *E is the head event of a series of n-nested loops, where the outermost loop has a loop length (member event count) of* m_1 *and an iteration count of* i_1*, the second outermost loop has a loop length of* m_2 *and an iteration count of* i_2*, and so on.*

A unique challenge of forcibly merging partially matching loop iterations is to preserve the information of in which iteration a certain event was actually called. As in the example above, a mechanism is needed to tell that $E2$ was only called in the first iteration whereas $E3$ was only called in the second iteration. To address this problem, we represent the loop information as elastic data elements. Recall that the value vector grows as more values are appended to the vector due to loop compression. For example, assuming event E is the head event of loop L, $E_{(a_1\ a_2, b_1\ b_2)}$ indicates that when the first time loop L is executed, it has a_1 member events and b_1 iterations, whereas for the second time, it has a_2 member events and b_2 iterations. (This is possible when loop L is executed during two different iterations of its parent loop). We hence treat every event as a loop of length 1 and iteration 1. During loop compression, we merge events according to the results of the longest common subsequence analysis and manipulate the loop information according to the following rules:

1. An event $E_{(1,0)}$ is called a *dummy event* because the loop information indicates that it is executed zero times.
2. For event $E_{(a_1\ a_2...,b_1\ b_2...)(c_1\ c_2...,d_1\ d_2...)...}$, adding an outer loop $E_{(a_1\ a_2...,1\ 1...)(a_1\ a_2...,b_1\ b_2...)(c_1\ c_2...,d_1\ d_2...)...}$ does not change the loop structure in terms of the iteration times and event order w.r.t. execution in nested loops. The added outer loop is thus called a *pseudo-loop* with just one iteration.
3. If event $E1_{(a_1\ a_2...,b_1\ b_2...)(c_1\ c_2...,d_1\ d_2...)...}$ in iteration $I1$ matches with $E2_{(i_1\ i_2...,j_1\ j_2...)(k_1\ k_2...,l_1\ l_2...)...}$ in iteration $I2$, merge $E1$ and $E2$ by merging the loop information at corresponding levels. Merging the value vectors is accomplished by appending the value vector of $I2$ to that of $I1$. If the loop stack depth d_1 at $E1$ does not match the depth d_2 at $E2$, e.g., $d_1 > d_2$, align the loop stacks by adding pseudo-loops to the top of the loop stack at $E2$ as placeholders to avoid mismatches between the extra outer loops at $E1$ and $E2$ during traversal.
4. If event E is in iteration $I1$ but not in iteration $I2$, create a dummy event E' of E and insert it into $I2$ immediately before the matching event M of $I1$ and $I2$ returned by the longest common subsequence analysis. The loop stack of E' is created according to that of E by adding pseudo-loops. The vector values at each nest level of E' are generated by referring to M for the number of times it would be encountered if it were in $I2$. As such, E' acts as a placeholder to avoid mistakenly calling E when executing $I2$. After

the insertion of all the iteration-specific events, merge iterations $I1$ and $I2$ according to the third rule.

5. When merging iteration $I2$ into iteration $I1$, if the outermost loop of the head event E of $I1$ is not a loop of the entire event sequence of $I1$, a new outer loop is identified and a new loop descriptor $(n,2)$ is added to the top of the loop stack of E, where n equals to number of events in both $I1$ and $I2$.

In essence, the rules above ensure that the iteration-specific events will only be executed in the correct iterations. The introduction of pseudo-loops as placeholders guarantees that 1) iteration-specific events are evaluated but not executed in loop iterations they do not belong to, and, therefore, 2) meaningful loop information is evaluated and fetched in the correct loop iteration. Nevertheless, the core of the loop compression algorithm is still the longest common subsequence analysis performed against the two sequences of MPI events. The matching event pairs returned by the LCS analysis are the basis for loop information adjustment. Therefore, the complexity of this algorithm is $O(m \cdot n)$, where m and n are the numbers of events in the two event sequences, respectively.

By applying the aforementioned loop compression guidelines, SCALATRACE II is able to compress loops with iteration-specific behavior. For example, the MPI code shown in Figure 1 is eventually compressed as follows:

$$E1_{(4,2)}\, E2_{(1,1\ 0)}\, E3_{(1,0\ 1)}\, E4$$

3.2.2 Handling Trailing Iterations

The NAS Parallel Benchmarks (NPB) BT code exemplifies a pattern of an MPI event sequence that a multitude of stencil codes share at the end of a time step. Each MPI task communicates with its neighbors with a series of send, receive, and wait operations in a loop, as illustrated in the simplified example of Figure 2.

```
/* m time steps */
for(int i=0; i<m; i++){
    ... // MPI events
    for(int j=0; j<n; j++){
        MPI_Isend();
        MPI_Irecv();
        MPI_Waitall();
    }
}
```

Figure 2: Loop with Trailing Iterations

The original SCALATRACE compresses the outer loop only if n, the trip count of the inner loop, is a constant. In contrast, SCALATRACE II's more aggressive loop compression discussed in Section 3.2.1 can always compress the outer loop even if n is not a constant, e.g., $n = f(i)$. However, since SCALATRACE II eagerly compresses detected loops, the second iteration of the outer loop will be compressed immediately when the first iteration of the inner loop terminates. As a result, the remaining $n-1$ iterations of the inner loop cause the *trailing iterations* problem.

To address the trailing iterations problem, we redesigned the entire loop detection and compression algorithm to perform a delayed merge, as shown by Algorithm 1. Essentially, Algorithm 1 does not eagerly merge a newly identified loop iteration. It rather marks it as a *pending iteration* so that a potential trailing iteration can be merged with the pending iteration later without having to perform any decompression. Specifically, after an event E is appended to the trace, DETECTLOOP() is called to find the *target_head*, *merge_tail*, and *merge_head* for two matching loop iterations ending with *target_tail* $== E$. Assuming a loop structure is found, the sequence *merge_head*, ..., *merge_tail* can be 1) the ending subsequence of a pending iteration detected previously, 2) a pending iteration whose match has already been found, or 3) a sequence independent of any prior loop structures. In the first case, the sequence *target_head*, ..., *target_tail* is identified as a trailing iteration. An event sequence can simultaneously be the trailing iteration of multiple pending iterations in a nested manner, i.e., line 16 - 21 of Algorithm 1 updates all the pending iterations by appending the trailing iteration to each of them. In the second case, where the sequence *merge_head*, ..., *merge_tail* is itself a pending iteration, the sequence *target_head*, ..., *target_tail* is then identified as the next iteration of the pending iteration. Since it is now safe to conclude that there will be no more trailing events for the pending iteration *merge_head*, ..., *merge_tail*, Algorithm 1 performs a delayed iteration merge by calling MERGEPENDINGITERATION() (line 22 - 24). Finally, the newly detected iteration *target_head*, ..., *target_tail* is always marked as a pending iteration in either case. The function MERGEPENDINGITERATION() merges the iteration between the events *pending_head* and *pending_tail* with the iteration between the memorized events *head* and *tail*. Before calling LCSLOOPCOMPRESSION() which implements the algorithm introduced in Section 3.2.1, MERGEPENDINGITERATION() first compresses pending iterations of all nested inner loops (line 32 - 51) by recursively calling itself. Finally, when MPI_Finalize is called, all loops either have zero or one pending iteration. To eventually merge them, the function FINALIZEPENDINGITERATIONS() is called, which treats the entire trace as an iteration and recursively merges inner loops by calling MERGEPENDINGITERATION().

3.3 Approximate Stack Signature Matching

SCALATRACE preserves a call stack signature by logging the call sites of the calling stack for each event. Using these stack signatures, SCALATRACE is able to distinguish MPI calls of the same type by their locations in the program. The stack signature therefore serves as the only basis for comparison of events, which then makes loop detection possible. Nonetheless, strictly enforced stack signature comparison may not always benefit trace compression. For example, POP wraps MPI_Bcast of different data types with different functions, which are then invoked in 36 different files at approximately 400 different locations. Experimental results show that due to such usage, the size of the trace of the initialization stage — a stage that is usually less important for performance analysis — accounts for 26% of the size of the final trace. More commonly, a number of scientific applications, including POP and the NPB BT and SP codes, are coded according to the data decomposition, their communication topology, or their simulation stages, with the MPI events hidden deep in the call stack, as shown in Figure 3. As a result, these applications also create trace events with various stack signatures even though they are functionally symmetric. In both cases, there exists the need to trade the call stack information for better compression.

```
simulate(){          solve_x(){          solve_y(){
  while(i<s){          // compute            // compute
    solve_x();         MPI_Isend();          MPI_Isend();
    solve_y();         MPI_Irecv();          MPI_Irecv();
    i++;               MPI_Wait();           MPI_Wait();
  }                    MPI_Wait();           MPI_Wait();
}                    }                     }
```

Figure 3: The Simplified NPB BT Code

In SCALATRACE II, we loosened the stack signature comparison criteria to tolerate a pre-defined number of different frames. When comparing two stack signatures, we start from the first call site (the *main* function) and compare the call sites in corresponding frames one by one. The comparison returns *true* only if the number of different frames is less than the user-defined threshold. As an ongoing improvement, we also allow users to specify a range of instruction addresses, so that the call sites within it will always be

Algorithm 1 Loop Compression with Delayed Merge

Precondition: T: the trace after a new event was appended as the new tail

```
function DetectLoop(T)
    target_tail ← T.tail
    merge_tail ← T.FindMatch(target_tail)
    target_head ← merge_tail.next
    while true do
        merge_head ← T.FindMatch(TARGET_HEAD)
        if merge_head.isPendingMember == true then        ▷ potential trailing iteration, more checks
            pending_tail ← FindPendingTail(merge_head)
            if pending_tail == merge_tail then    ▷ trailing iteration of a pending iteration must follow the pending iteration immediately
                break
            end if
        else                                   ▷ not a trailing iteration, no more check
            break
        end if
    end while

    if target_head...target_tail is a trailing iteration then
        PIs ← FindPendingsForTrailing(target_head, target_tail)
        for pendingIteration ← PIs.first, PIs.last do
            pendingIteration.AddTrailing(target_head, target_tail)
        end for
    end if

    if merge_head...merge_tail is a pending iteration then        ▷ perform the delayed merge: merge a pending iteration only when the next iteration (namely, target_head...target_tail) is found
        MergePendingIteration(merge_head, merge_tail)
    end if

    for event ← target_head, target_tail do
        event.isPendingMember ← true
    end for
end function

function MergePendingIteration(pending_head, pending_tail)
    head ← FindKnownMergeHead(pending_head)
    tail ← FindKnownMergeTail(pending_tail)

    for event ← head, tail do
        if event.IsKnownMergeHead() == true then
            h ← FindPendingHead(event)
            t ← FindPendingTail(event)
            new_tail ← MergePendingIteration(h, t)
            if tail == t then
                tail ← new_tail
            end if
        end if
    end for

    for event ← pending_head, pending_tail do
        if event.IsKnownMergeHead() == true then
            h ← FindPendingHead(event)
            t ← FindPendingTail(event)
            new_tail ← MergePendingIteration(h, t)
            if pending_tail == t then
                pending_tail ← new_tail
            end if
        end if
    end for

    LCSLoopCompression(head, tail, pending_head, pending_tail)
    DeleteEvents(pending_head, pending_tail)
    return tail
end function

function FinalizePendingIterations(T)
    ...
end function
```

considered a match. During loop compression, we compare event $E1$ in iteration $I1$ with event $E2$ in iteration $I2$ in term of both event type and stack signature. If their signatures differ less than the predefined limit, we replace $E2$'s signature with that of $E1$ and update all the signature-annotated statistics of $E2$'s succeeding events accordingly. With such user-configurable stack signature imprecision, ScalaTrace II is able to better exploit the potential of trace compression than the original ScalaTrace for applications like POP or BT, as illustrated in Figure 3. The user-defined limit serves as a tuning parameter to trade off compression against accuracy.

3.4 Loop Agnostic Inter-node Compression

ScalaTrace performs inter-node trace compression to exploit the single-program multiple-data (SPMD) paradigm of scientific applications. However, the compression capability of the original ScalaTrace is limited by the fact that loop structures must be treated as an indivisible unit. For example, the code in Figure 4 cannot be compressed across nodes because the *for* loops on different nodes have mismatching trip counts and event sequences. The strong dependence on the perfect matching of loop structures is partially alleviated by the recursive loop matching algorithm proposed in our previous work [37], but it still cannot handle the case where loop trip counts do not match.

```
Rank 0:                      Rank 1:
for(i=0;i<5;i++){            for(i=0;i<6;i++){
    MPI_Isend(1);                MPI_Isend(0);
    MPI_Irecv(1);                MPI_Irecv(0);
}                                MPI_Waitall(2);
MPI_Isend(1);                }
MPI_Irecv(1);
MPI_Waitall(12);
```

Figure 4: Code Needs Loop Agnostic Inter-node Compression

The restrictions on loop structures for inter-node compression are eliminated in ScalaTrace II due to the introduction of the elastic data element representation. Close examination shows that the crux of the compression problem stated above is the coupling of the loop information and the event participants information. Specifically, the loop structure is formed during task-level loop compression and only applies to the same task. Given two loop head events from different MPI tasks, they cannot be merged if the loop structures diverge, because there is no mechanism to recover the task-specific loop information once it is compressed. By representing the loop information as elastic data elements, a separate ranklist is attached for each loop data element (including trip count and loop length). When merging two loop head events, we simply merge the loop structures at each corresponding loop level by following the general rules of compression of the elastic data element representation. Namely, if the loop structures match, they are compressed by merging their ranklists. If the loop structures at a certain loop level do not match, they are merged by adding another $< value\ vector, ranklist >$ pair to distinguish their task-specific loop information.

By decoupling loop information from event participant information, ScalaTrace II is able to perform loop structure agnostic inter-node compression. During inter-node compression, the longest common subsequence is determined by evaluating only the stack signatures of the events originating from different MPI tasks, and the events are then merged accordingly. For example, the events of the code shown in Figure 4 will be merged into the trace shown in Figure 5, where the number in brackets shows the ranklist of the loop information prior to merging, and the MPI parameters are ignored.

Rank	Event
0 1	$MPI\_Isend()_{(2,5)[0](3,6)[1]}$
0 1	$MPI\_Irecv()$
0	$MPI\_Isend()$
0	$MPI\_Irecv()$
0 1	$MPI\_Waitall()$

Figure 5: Final Trace of the Code in Figure 4

Lastly, since the new inter-node compression algorithm is loop agnostic, it does not have to perform LCS analysis recursively for each level of nested loops. Hence, assuming m and n are the lengths of two task-level traces, the complexity of the inter-node compression algorithm is $O(m \cdot n)$.

3.5 Replaying Non-deterministic Traces

For scalability reasons, SCALATRACE II's elastic data element representation may internally transform from a lossless $<$ *value vector, ranklist* $>$ pair representation to a lossy histogram representation for pre-configured parameters including SOURCE, DEST, and COUNT. As was discussed in our prior work, representing non-performance data, such as DEST, as histograms still preserves meaningful information regarding the communication topology [37]. However, it poses a great challenge to the re-creation of the program behavior from the probabilistic trace because critical communication parameters are not accurate anymore.

SCALAREPLAY II is the new replay engine designed to cope with probabilistic traces. In contrast to the previous version of SCALAREPLAY, we redesigned the trace traversal algorithm to support SCALATRACE II's loop agnostic traces. We have also made key improvements in SCALAREPLAY II to boost the robustness and replay accuracy. SCALAREPLAY II utilizes a coordinated random value selection approach described in our previous work. In essence, during replay, nodes parse send events but skip receive events in the trace. At send events, senders select receivers from the DEST histograms by referring to random numbers. In order to generate matching receives for the send operations, each node parses the traces of other nodes to locate send operations addressed to itself. This is made possible by the fact that senders and their potential receivers agree on the random number used for value selection (by generating an identically seeded sequence of random numbers). In this way, the overhead of exchanging control messages via back-channel communication is avoided.

Improvements for SCALAREPLAY II center around a novel trace traversal strategy. In the past approach, each node used a single pointer to traverse a global trace; whenever there is a loop structure, the node traverses it as a participant. However, this is impossible with SCALATRACE II's new trace format because loop structures interleave in the final trace, as shown in Figure 5. In addition, traversing with a single pointer also causes timing accuracy problems. With the previous approach, a node parsed every event in the order it was seen during the traversal. However, due to a stack signature mismatch, events that happened simultaneously may be recorded far apart in the trace, as shown in Figure 6. With the single pointer approach, task 0 will not issue MPI_Irecv(1) until it reads event 4 after having performed some computation for 10 seconds at event 2. As a result, task 1 will be blocked on the blocking send (event 4) for 10 seconds and the total runtime of the program approaches 20 seconds, i.e., almost twice as much as it ought to be.

```
if(rank==0){
      MPI_Irecv(1);
      compute(10s);
      MPI_Wait();
}else if(rank==1){
      MPI_Send(0);
      compute(10s);
}
```

ID	Rank	Event
1	0	*MPI_Irecv*(1)
2	0	*compute*(10*s*)
3	0	*MPI_Wait*()
4	1	*MPI_Send*(0)
5	1	*compute*(10*s*)

Figure 6: Trace Needs Multiple Context Pointers for Replay

To address these issues, SCALAREPLAY II utilizes multiple traversal context pointers during replay. Intuitively, a trace reflects the result of a parallel execution, where the parallel processes progress concurrently through potentially distinct control flows with occasional synchronizations. The replay engine mimics this process by replaying with one primary traversal pointer while keeping track of the other nodes' parallel executions with multiple additional traversal context pointers. In SCALAREPLAY II, a traversal context is a lightweight data structure that keeps track of the progress of the traversal on behalf of a certain MPI task. It consists of an event pointer, a loop information manager, a random number manager, and a timer. The event pointer always points to the next event to be replayed/evaluated. It supports operations such as *hasNext*() and *next*(). The loop information manager keeps track of the traversal by memorizing the current loop stack as well as iteration counts at each loop level. The random number manager guarantees that contexts of the same rank on different nodes always agree on the same series of random numbers. Lastly, the timer is used to calculate the aggregated execution time at a certain event according to the recorded times of events traversed so far.

During replay, each node progresses according to its primary context, i.e., the context with the rank of a node. It issues all the events other than receives, and sleeps for all recorded computational phases within its context as a normal replay. To post matching receives for potential senders, each node also traverses the trace of the other nodes by maintaining secondary traversal contexts for them. When traversing secondary contexts, all non-send events and computations are ignored so that the current node can quickly identify send operations addressed to itself. However, the current node does not post a receive immediately when a send is identified. Instead, it postpones the receive to approximately the time that a corresponding send operation is issued on the sender side, which can be estimated by referring to the timer of the sender's secondary context. By posting receives in this way, SCALAREPLAY II manages to clear the system receiving buffer in a timely manner and thus improves replay time accuracy.

To further improve the performance and scalability of SCALAREPLAY II, additional optimizations are implemented. In practice, most parallel applications are designed such that each node only has a limited number of point-to-point communication destinations (otherwise, collectives are used). We therefore have introduced a negotiation stage before the replay in which each node calculates a destination set of a configurable size and informs selected receivers so that each node only has to maintain a limited number of traversal contexts during replay. In addition, we also improved the performance of the replay engine by overlapping context management with simulated compute times that the primary context has to perform anyhow. With these optimizations, the replay engine manages to scale to a large number of nodes.

4. EVALUATION

We evaluated SCALATRACE II with regard to two aspects: (1) its effectiveness of trace compression, as well as the advantages of different compression optimizations, and (2) correctness and timing accuracy of probabilistic replay. For experiment (1), we used a subset of the NAS Parallel Benchmark suite (version 3.3 for MPI) [2], including BT, CG, LU, MG, and SP, the Sweep3D neutron-transport kernel [33], and the Parallel Ocean Program [28]. We chose these benchmarks because they exercise both collectives and point-to-point communications in multiple time steps. Besides, some of these benchmarks either do not have consistent loop behavior or do not show strict SPMD regularity. Consequently, these benchmarks poses great challenges to the existing trace compression libraries, including the last generation SCALATRACE. In these experiments, we configured SCALATRACE II to use different compression algorithms and we study the impact of each option. In experiment (2), we assessed SCALATRACE II's and SCALAREPLAY II's capabilities of preserving and re-producing computational performance with respect to wall clock execution times. Particularly, we conducted all replay experiments with probabilistic traces, which is significantly more challenging than replaying with lossless traces. The second experiment used the same benchmarks as in experiment (1).

All experiments were conducted on ARC, a 1,728 core cluster with 108 compute nodes, 32 GB memory per node, and Infiniband QDR interconnect. Due to limited access to the system, our experiments run on a subset of nodes sufficient to reflect trends of trace size growth with respect to increasing execution scale.

4.1 Trace File Size

The first experiment evaluates SCALATRACE II's compression effectiveness with the NPB BT, CG, LU, MG, SP codes, Sweep3D, and POP. We chose these benchmarks because they are stencil codes exhibiting multi-dimensional communication topologies and complicated loop structures. Among these benchmarks, MG, SP, and POP demonstrate inconstant message sizes and irregular SPMD behavior, and are hence particularly challenging for lossless and structure-preserving trace compression. In these experiments, we compared SCALATRACE II with our past approach. In order to demonstrate the effect of different configurations, we itemize the optimizations (as explained below) and collected traces by applying the options in an incremental manner:

• *ScalaTrace II*: features only the loop agnostic inter-node compression enabled by the elastic data element representation;

• *LCS Loop Compression*: additionally performs the longest common subsequence based loop compression;

• *Approximate Signature Matching*: adds a finer-grained optimization that matches and merges events when stack signatures differ by no more than a pre-defined threshold;

• *Parameter Histogram*: adds lossy compression that converts overlong value vectors into histograms.

According to the improvements achieved with SCALATRACE II, benchmarks are divided into three categories and results are depicted in Figure 7.

The first category consists of BT and CG. These benchmarks either demonstrate perfectly matching loop iterations or regular SPMD behavior that leads to structurally identical task-level traces. Hence, our past approach is able to capture the loop structures and has little difficulty merging time step loops across tasks. Consequently, SCALATRACE II only shows limited reduction in trace size for BT and CG when configured to be fully lossless. Nevertheless, there is still room for improvement when fuzziness is allowed. For example, by applying the approximate stack signature matching, SCALATRACE II manages to deliver another 22% trace size reduction for BT on average. More importantly, when parameter histograms are enabled for elastic data elements, we eventually obtained constant sized traces for BT and CG — a critical improvement that makes a key difference at large scale.

LU and Sweep3D constitute the second category for which SCALATRACE II improves trace compression by forcibly merging task-level traces in a loop agnostic way. Both LU and Sweep3D are stencil codes with a 2D task layout. Depending on the location in the 2D communication topology, a node may have a different number of neighbors, and thus follow a communication pattern that is unique to one of the nine communication groups (4 corners, 4 boundaries, and interior nodes). Because the past approach matches the loop structures as an entirety during inter-node reduction, it fails to exploit the similarities in time step loops across communication groups. SCALATRACE II takes advantages of these similarities. Consequently, by applying loop agnostic inter-node compression alone, SCALATRACE II manages to reduce trace sizes by 28% and 41% for Sweep3D and LU, respectively. By enabling

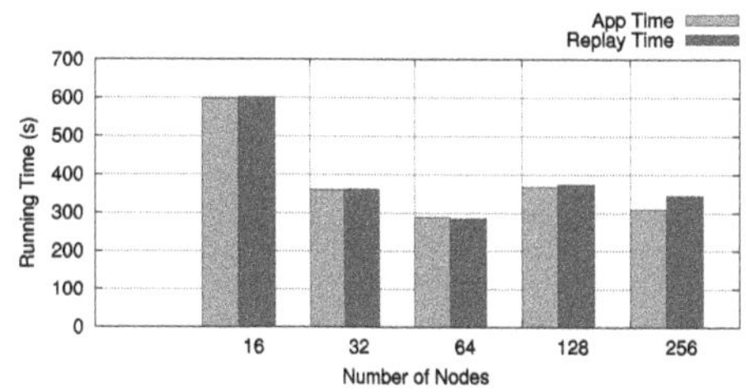

Figure 9: Probabilistic Replay Time Accuracy of POP

extra optimizations, SCALATRACE II eventually generates traces that are 43% and 65% smaller for LU and Sweep3D, respectively.

The most compelling improvement, however, is observed for the NPB MG and SP codes, and the Parallel Ocean Program. Among these benchmarks, SP sends messages with fluctuating sizes in loops. This prevents loop compression of the last generation SCALATRACE but can be handled with SCALATRACE II where all parameters are represented as elastic data elements. MG is the most challenging test case of the NAS Parallel Benchmark suite. It features a complicated communication pattern consisting of a primary 7-point 3D torus and a secondary nested 3D torus among nodes at particular positions in the topological space. Due to the interleaving of these two patterns, MG demonstrates both iteration-specific behavior and task-specific behavior, and thus poses great challenges for both intra-node and inter-node compression. By utilizing approximate loop iteration matching and loop agnostic inter-node compression, SCALATRACE II produces lossless traces that are orders of magnitude smaller for MG and SP, as depicted in Figure 7(f) and 7(g) on a logarithmic y axis. To further compress the varying message sizes for SP, we enabled lossy tracing with parameter histograms and thus obtained near constant sized traces that are collectively only 0.5% of the trace size of the past approach.

POP performs ocean simulations for multiple time steps. It features both inconsistent loop behavior across time steps and diverging task-level behavior that hinders inter-node compression. In previous work, we applied probabilistic compression techniques at the MPI parameter level and managed to greatly reduce POP's trace size [37]. With SCALATRACE II, we improve our previous work by more systematically exploiting structural properties of the trace. As shown in Figure 7(h), by utilizing loop agnostic inter-node compression, we reduced the trace size by a maximum of two orders of magnitude. This is almost as much of an improvement as we obtained with the previous lossy approach, yet we still maintain lossless traces. Furthermore, after additional optimizations are enabled, we eventually obtained near constant sized traces that are 48 to 351 times smaller. Besides, we also conducted experiments to assess the time step scalability, namely how efficient SCALATRACE II's longest common subsequence based loop compression can detect and compress time step loops. For this experiment, we keep the execution scale at 64 MPI tasks and increase the number of time steps. Experimental results in Figure 7(i) show that, by utilizing the LCS based approximate loop matching, SCALATRACE II is able to produce a constant sized trace. In contrast, the traditional approach is sensitive to iteration-specific events and thus is not time step scalable for POP. From these experimental results, we conclude that even with parameter-level probabilistic compression techniques, it is still possible to analyze structural properties in the trace systematically and perform compression in a top-down manner.

4.2 Probabilistic Replay Time Accuracy

The second set of experiments assesses SCALATRACE II's and SCALAREPLAY II's capabilities of preserving and re-producing computational times. We focus on 1) checking if SCALAREPLAY II is able to correctly coordinate the random value selection across nodes to replay probabilistic traces without deadlock, and 2) de-

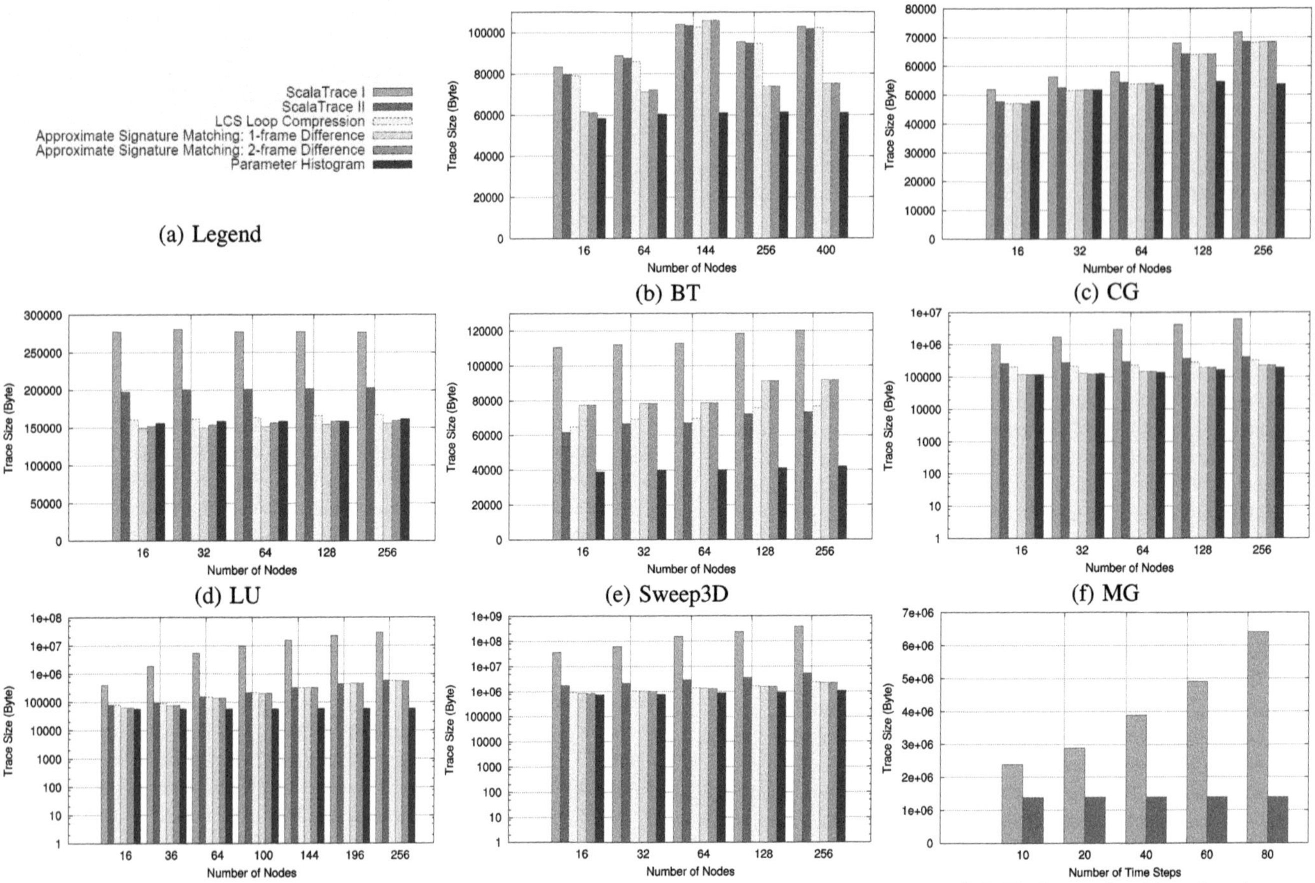

(a) Legend (b) BT (c) CG (d) LU (e) Sweep3D (f) MG (g) SP (h) POP (Increasing Node Counts) (i) POP (Increasing Time Steps)

Figure 7: Trace File Sizes [Bytes] for Varying Number of Nodes of NPB BT, CG, LU, MG, SP, Sweep3D, and POP

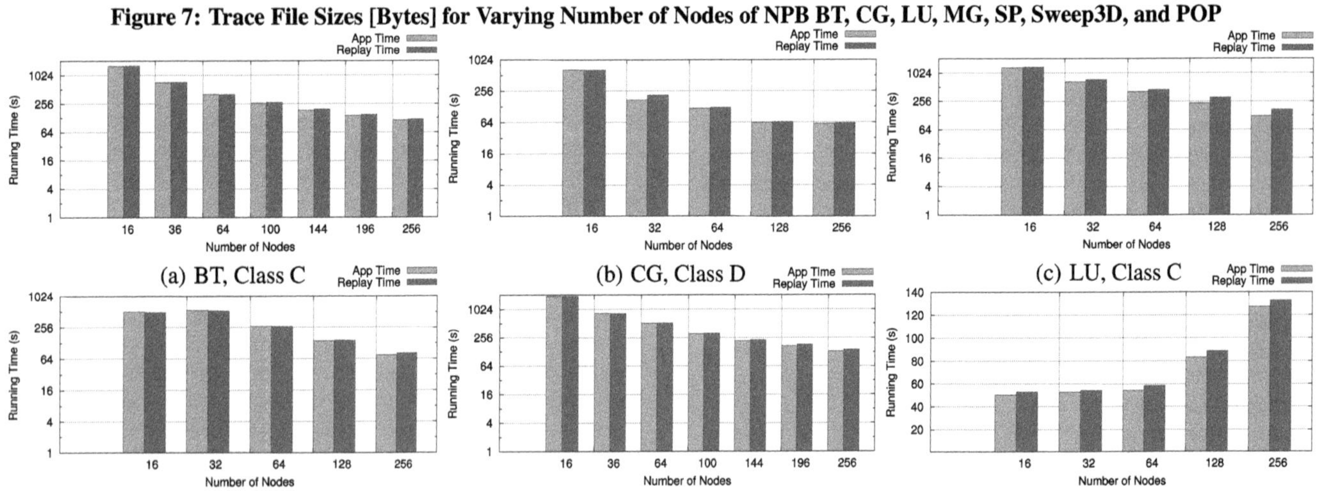

(a) BT, Class C (b) CG, Class D (c) LU, Class C (d) MG, Class D (e) SP, Class C (f) Sweep3D

Figure 8: Accuracy of Probabilistic Replay Time [Sec] for Varying # Nodes of BT,CG,LU,MG,SP,Sweep3D (see below for POP)

termining how accurate probabilistic replay can re-produce execution times of an original application. We conducted these experiments with the same set of benchmarks used for the first experiment. Among these benchmarks, the NAS Parallel Benchmarks and POP are strong-scaling codes while Sweep3D is a weak-scaling code. Problem sizes were chosen for strong-scaling benchmarks to ensure that a reasonable amount of computation exists across all tested scales. To provide input for the replay engine, we configured SCALATRACE II to collect probabilistic traces where critical MPI parameters (e.g., SOURCE, DEST, COUNT) are represented as histograms. Particularly, we set the histogram-triggering threshold to 1 to forcibly convert all elastic data elements into histograms irrespective of how concise lossless value vectors actually are.

Figures 8,9 compare the probabilistic replay times with the execution times of the original applications. First, being able to obtain these results allows us to validate that the coordinated random value selection of the replay algorithm is deadlock free for the evaluated benchmarks. Besides, the experimental results also show that SCALAREPLAY II can accurately re-produce the computational performance of the original applications. Quantitatively, the mean absolute percentage error of the replay times (i.e., $100\% \times |(T_{\text{replay}} - T_{\text{app}})/T_{\text{app}}|$) across all test cases in Figures 8,9 is only 5.7%. Such high replay timing accuracy indicates that 1) the execution times are accurately preserved within lossy traces and 2) the probabilistic replay approach is able to re-produce the runtimes of the original applications without introducing unmanageable control overhead. Overall, given the accurately preserved and re-produced performance characteristics, we conclude that the histogram-based lossy compression, which has been shown to produce powerful reductions in the trace size, is equally viable in scenarios where timing accuracy is required.

5. RELATED WORK

Our work is closely related to prior research in the area of parallel application tracing and profiling [23, 27, 13, 31]. Traditional tracing tools such as Vampir [23], Extrae [8], and Paraver/Dimemas [27] collect plain application traces that are not scalable due to the sheer size of the performance data gathered. The Open Trace Format (OTF) aims at scalable tracing [17]. But OTF utilizes regular zlib compression, and tools based on it generally lack structure-aware compression. Hence, these tools cannot fully exploit structural similarities, nor are they suitable for trace-based scalability analysis and code generation [35, 36, 34].

SEQUITUR exploits hierarchical structures in sequences of discrete symbols for compression [24, 25]. It constructs a context-free grammar for a given sequence by representing repeating diagrams as non-terminals. Because SEQUITUR excels in both data compression and structural inference, it is employed by an array of algorithms and tools as the compression infrastructure for a variety of purposes. For example, Marathe et al. utilize SEQUITUR to compress data access instructions in their memory tracing work [22]. Larus proposes whole program paths (WPP) to capture a program's dynamic control flow, where an enhanced SEQUITUR algorithm is designed to compress acyclic path traces [19]. Krishnamoorthy et al. present a trace compression algorithm that is largely based on SEQUITUR [18]. To fully exploit the pattern detection capability of SEQUITUR, this work performs trace compression at argument level instead of event level. While this optimization is effective in improving the compression, it also makes the final trace unreadable and not structure-preserving. In general, if the program structure is not preserved at the event level, most post-processing or trace-based performance analysis becomes difficult or even infeasible because decompressing and effectively rendering the trace may require large amounts of memory and computing power that are not available on commodity desktops or laptops.

Recent advances in online trace compression utilize domain-specific techniques to achieve trace size reduction. SCALATRACE performs task-level loop compression and cross-node trace compression in a memory-efficient manner [26]. It generates near constant sized or orders of magnitude smaller traces for SPMD codes. Xu et al. construct coordinated performance skeletons from traces to estimate application execution time in new hardware environments [38, 39]. They adapt a pattern analysis algorithm from bioinformatics to perform loop analysis. Nonetheless, due to the lack of on-the-fly loop compression, this tool is subject to limitations on time step scalability. Knupfer et al. utilize Complete Call Graph (CCG) to hierarchically store an application trace according to the call stack [16]. By comparing and merging similar subgraphs, the trace is compressed in a bottom-up fashion. In contrast to our work, CCGs cannot handle inconsistent program behavior that leads to mismatching low-level sub-structures in CCGs.

Besides lossless or near lossless tracing techniques, our work is also related to the work that provides lightweight application profiling functionalities. For example, mpiP collects aggregated statistical information about MPI functions and computation times [32]. Gprof measures the durations and frequencies of procedures using a hybrid approach of instrumentation and sampling [14]. HPC-Toolkit collects call path profiles [9, 1]. To further reduce the overhead involved in profiling, Gamblin et al. utilize statistical sampling and parallel clustering techniques to reduce the number of parallel processes from which performance data is collected, and thus improve the scalability of parallel profiling tools [12, 11, 10]. In contrast to the lossless tracing approach, tools like mpiP generally report simple and high-level information that is only suitable for a superficial understanding of performance problems. For in-depth performance debugging or complicated analysis, application tracing is still necessary. As an instrumentation framework for both communication event tracing and performance data collection, SCALATRACE II can employ the statistical methods proposed in prior research to improve its numerical performance data collection and compression. This is subject to future work.

A unique approach for quick acquisition of communication traces involves program slicing. Program slicing is a source code analysis technique that effectively reduces a program to a subset of the statements (a program slice) that is relevant to a target statement or variable. As an example, Zhai et al. proposed the FACT approach [42]. This approach constructs a program slice for MPI calls and strips out the computation. With the communication-only program slice, it then becomes feasible to obtain the communication trace readily without executing the computational part. While it is possible to combine program slicing with existing communication trace compression techniques, an inherent shortcoming of slicing is that it neither captures execution times, nor can it handle data-dependent control flows. Consequently, this technique is only applicable in limited scenarios.

In addition to techniques on communication tracing and profiling, our work is also relevant to prior research on parallel replay. For example, Rolt^{MP} proposes a Lamport timestamp-based approach for deterministic replay of programs with non-deterministic receives [30]. MPIWIZ is a deterministic replay method that can only replay a subset of the tasks of an MPI application [40]. PHANTOM employs deterministic replay and cross-node performance clustering techniques to predict the performance of parallel applications on future systems [41].

In a broader sense, prior research on memory tracing and memory trace-based performance analysis supplements this work. As the next generation of SCALATRACE, SCALATRACE II continues to utilize Regular Section Descriptors (RSDs) and Power-RSDs (PRSDs) to describe nested loop structures in a trace. RSDs were originally proposed to track inter-procedural side effects on common substructures of arrays to promote compiler-aided parallelization [15]. Marathe et al. adapted the RSD representation and proposed PRSDs for memory trace compression [21, 20]. Budanur et al. further designed Extended-PRSDs to perform multi-level scalable parallel memory tracing in SCALAMEMTRACE [3]. SIGMA employs online trace compression to collect lossless memory traces for simulation and performance tuning [6]. Elnozahy et al. utilize loop detection and reduction for address trace compression [7]. VPC3 employs value predictors to compress events comprising program counter values and extended data fields [4].

6. CONCLUSION

Application tracing is one of the most important and useful vehicles for performance analysis and debugging of parallel applications. Yet, designing scalable and efficient parallel tracing tools for exascale systems and grand-challenge HPC applications remains an open problem. In this work, we contribute SCALATRACE II, a fundamental redesign of SCALATRACE that features a spectrum of innovative lossless compression techniques aiming at scalable trace compression of large-scale scientific codes with irregular SPMD behavior or even MPMD characteristics. We designed an elastic data element representation to address compression inefficiencies of previous work. Enabled by the new encoding scheme, novel algorithms are devised to perform approximate loop matching and loop agnostic cross-node trace compression. We also incorporated parameter histogram-based lossy compression capabilities into SCALATRACE II and adapted the replay subsystem to enable more accurate probabilistic trace replays. We evaluated SCALATRACE II with the NAS Parallel Benchmarks, Sweep3D, and a real-world application, the Parallel Ocean Program. Experimental results demonstrate that the redesigned trace compression algorithms are particularly effective for applications with inconsistent behavior across time steps and MPI tasks. In comparison to prior research, we deem SCALATRACE II a solid improvement towards exascale performance analysis.

7. REFERENCES

[1] L. Adhianto, S. Banerjee, M. Fagan, M. Krentel, G. Marin, J. Mellor-Crummey, and N. R. Tallent. Hpctoolkit: tools for performance analysis of optimized parallel programs http://hpctoolkit.org. *Concurr. Comput. : Pract. Exper.*, 22(6):685–701, Apr. 2010.

[2] D. H. Bailey, E. Barszcz, J. T. Barton, D. S. Browning, R. L. Carter, D. Dagum, R. A. Fatoohi, P. O. Frederickson, T. A. Lasinski, R. S. Schreiber, H. D. Simon, V. Venkatakrishnan, and S. K. Weeratunga. The NAS Parallel Benchmarks. *The International Journal of Supercomputer Applications*, 5(3):63–73, Fall 1991.

[3] S. Budanur, F. Mueller, and T. Gamblin. Memory trace compression and replay for SPMD systems using Extended PRSDs. *SIGMETRICS Perform. Eval. Rev.*, 38(4):30–36, Mar. 2011.

[4] M. Burtscher. Vpc3: A fast and effective trace-compression algorithm. In *SIGMETRICS Conference on Measurement and Modeling of Computer Systems*, pages 167–176, N.Y., June 2004.

[5] Community earth system model. http://www.cesm.ucar.edu/index.html.

[6] L. DeRose, K. Ekanadham, J. K. Hollingsworth, and S. Sbaraglia. SIGMA: A simulator infrastructure to guide memory analysis. In *Supercomputing*, Nov. 2002.

[7] E. N. Elnozahy. Address trace compression through loop detection and reduction. In *SIGMETRICS Conference on Measurement and Modeling of Computer Systems*, pages 214–215, 1999.

[8] Extrae. http://www.bsc.es/computer-sciences/extrae.

[9] N. Froyd, J. Mellor-Crummey, and R. Fowler. Low-overhead call path profiling of unmodified, optimized code. In *Proceedings of the 19th annual international conference on Supercomputing*, pages 81–90, 2005.

[10] T. Gamblin, B. R. de Supinski, M. Schulz, R. Fowler, and D. A. Reed. Scalable load-balance measurement for spmd codes. In *Supercomputing*, pages 1–12, 2008.

[11] T. Gamblin, B. R. de Supinski, M. Schulz, R. Fowler, and D. A. Reed. Clustering performance data efficiently at massive scales. In *Int'l Conf. on Supercomputing*, pages 243–252, 2010.

[12] T. Gamblin, R. J. Fowler, and D. A. Reed. Scalable methods for monitoring and detecting behavioral equivalence classes in scientific codes. In *IPDPS*, pages 1–12, 2008.

[13] M. Geimer, F. Wolf, B. J. N. Wylie, E. Abraham, D. Becker, and B. Mohr. The scalasca performance toolset architecture. In *International Workshop on Scalable Tools for High-End Computing*, June 2008.

[14] S. L. Graham, P. B. Kessler, and M. K. McKusick. gprof: A call graph execution profiler. In *Symposium on Compiler Construction*, pages 276–283, June 1982.

[15] P. Havlak and K. Kennedy. An implementation of interprocedural bounded regular section analysis. *IEEE Transactions on Parallel and Distributed Systems*, 2(3):350–360, July 1991.

[16] A. Knupfer. Construction and compression of complete call graphs for post-mortem program trace analysis. In *International Conference on Parallel Processing*, pages 165–172, 2005.

[17] A. Knüpfer, R. Brendel, H. Brunst, H. Mix, and W. E. Nagel. Introducing the Open Trace Format (OTF). In *Int'l Conf. on Computational Science*, pages 526–533, May 2006.

[18] S. Krishnamoorthy and K. Agarwal. Scalable communication trace compression. In *Conference on Cluster, Cloud and Grid Computing*, pages 408–417, 2010.

[19] J. R. Larus. Whole program paths. *SIGPLAN Not.*, 34(5):259–269, May 1999.

[20] J. Marathe, F. Mueller, and B. R. de Supinski. A hybrid hardware/software approach to efficiently determine cache coherence bottlenecks. In *Int'l Conf. on Supercomputing*, pages 21–30, June 2005.

[21] J. Marathe, F. Mueller, T. Mohan, B. R. de Supinski, S. A. McKee, and A. Yoo. METRIC: Tracking down inefficiencies in the memory hierarchy via binary rewriting. In *International Symposium on Code Generation and Optimization*, pages 289–300, Mar. 2003.

[22] J. Marathe, F. Mueller, T. Mohan, S. A. McKee, B. R. de Supinski, and A. Yoo. Metric: Memory tracing via dynamic binary rewriting to identify cache inefficiencies. *ACM Transactions on Programming Languages and Systems*, 29(2):1–36, Apr. 2007.

[23] W. E. Nagel, A. Arnold, M. Weber, H. C. Hoppe, and K. Solchenbach. VAMPIR: Visualization and analysis of MPI resources. *Supercomputer*, 12(1):69–80, 1996.

[24] C. G. Nevill-Manning and I. H. Witten. Compression and explanation using hierarchical grammars. *The Computer Journal*, 40(2/3), 1997.

[25] C. G. Nevill-Manning and I. H. Witten. Linear-time, incremental hierarchy inference for compression. In *Proceedings of the Conference on Data Compression*, DCC '97, pages 3–, Washington, DC, USA, 1997. IEEE Computer Society.

[26] M. Noeth, F. Mueller, M. Schulz, and B. R. de Supinski. Scalatrace: Scalable compression and replay of communication traces in high performance computing. *Journal of Parallel Distributed Computing*, 69(8):969–710, Aug. 2009.

[27] V. Pillet, V. Pillet, J. Labarta, T. Cortes, and S. Girona. PARAVER: A tool to visualize and analyze parallel code. In *Proceedings of the 18th Technical Meeting of WoTUG-18: Transputer and Occam Developments*, pages 17–31, 1995.

[28] The parallel ocean program (POP), 1996. http://climate.lanl.gov/Models/POP/.

[29] P. Ratn, F. Mueller, B. R. de Supinski, and M. Schulz. Preserving time in large-scale communication traces. In *Int'l Conf. on Supercomputing*, pages 46–55, June 2008.

[30] M. Ronsse and D. Kranzlmueller. Roltmp-replay of lamport timestamps for message passing systems. *Euromicro Conference on Parallel, Distributed, and Network-Based Processing*, page 0087, 1998.

[31] S. S. Shende and A. D. Malony. The tau parallel performance system. *Int. J. High Perform. Comput. Appl.*, 20(2):287–311, May 2006.

[32] J. Vetter and M. McCracken. Statistical scalability analysis of communication operations in distributed applications. In *ACM SIGPLAN Symposium on Principles and Practice of Parallel Programming*, 2001.

[33] H. Wasserman, A. Hoisie, and O. Lubeck. Performance and scalability analysis of teraflop-scale parallel architectures using multidimensional wavefront applications. *The International Journal of High Performance Computing Applications*, 14:330–346, 2000.

[34] X. Wu, V. Deshpande, and F. Mueller. ScalaBenchGen: Auto-generation of communication benchmarks traces. In *International Parallel and Distributed Processing Symposium*, pages 1250–1260, 2012.

[35] X. Wu and F. Mueller. ScalaExtrap: Trace-based communication extrapolation for spmd programs. In *ACM SIGPLAN Symposium on Principles and Practice of Parallel Programming*, pages 113–122, Feb. 2011.

[36] X. Wu, F. Mueller, and S. Pakin. Automatic generation of executable communication specifications from parallel applications. In *Int'l Conf. on Supercomputing*, pages 12–21, 2011.

[37] X. Wu, K. Vijayakumar, F. Mueller, X. Ma, and P. C. Roth. Probabilistic communication and i/o tracing with deterministic replay at scale. In *International Conference on Parallel Processing*, pages 196–205, 2011.

[38] Q. Xu, R. Prithivathi, J. Subhlok, and R. Zheng. Logicalization of MPI communication traces. Technical Report UH-CS-08-07, Dept. of Computer Science, University of Houston, 2008.

[39] Q. Xu and J. Subhlok. Construction and evaluation of coordinated performance skeletons. In *International Conference on High Performance Computing*, pages 73–86, 2008.

[40] R. Xue, X. Liu, M. Wu, Z. Guo, W. Chen, W. Zheng, Z. Zhang, and G. Voelker. Mpiwiz: subgroup reproducible replay of mpi applications. In *ACM SIGPLAN Symposium on Principles and Practice of Parallel Programming*, pages 251–260, 2009.

[41] J. Zhai, W. Chen, and W. Zheng. Phantom: predicting performance of parallel applications on large-scale parallel machines using a single node. In *ACM SIGPLAN Symposium on Principles and Practice of Parallel Programming*, pages 305–314, 2010.

[42] J. Zhai, T. Sheng, J. He, W. Chen, and W. Zheng. FACT: Fast communication trace collection for parallel applications through program slicing. In *Proceedings of SC'09*, pages 1–12, 2009.

A New Approach for Performance Analysis of OpenMP Programs

Xu Liu
Rice University
Dept. of Computer Science
MS 132
P.O. Box 1892, Houston, TX
77251-1892
xl10@rice.edu

John Mellor-Crummey
Rice University
Dept. of Computer Science
MS 132
P.O. Box 1892, Houston, TX
77251-1892
johnmc@rice.edu

Michael Fagan
Rice University
Dept. of Computer Science
MS 132
P.O. Box 1892, Houston, TX
77251-1892
mfagan@rice.edu

ABSTRACT

The number of hardware threads is growing with each new generation of multicore chips; thus, one must effectively use threads to fully exploit emerging processors. OpenMP is a popular directive-based programming model that helps programmers exploit thread-level parallelism. In this paper, we describe the design and implementation of a novel performance tool for OpenMP. Our tool distinguishes itself from existing OpenMP performance tools in two principal ways. First, we develop a measurement methodology that attributes blame for work and inefficiency back to program contexts. We show how to integrate prior work on measurement methodologies that employ directed and undirected blame shifting and extend the approach to support dynamic thread-level parallelism in both time-shared and dedicated environments. Second, we develop a novel deferred context resolution method that supports online attribution of performance metrics to full calling contexts within an OpenMP program execution. This approach enables us to collect compact call path profiles for OpenMP program executions without the need for traces. Support for our approach is an integral part of an emerging standard performance tool application programming interface for OpenMP. We demonstrate the effectiveness of our approach by applying our tool to analyze four well-known application benchmarks that cover the spectrum of OpenMP features. In case studies with these benchmarks, insights from our tool helped us significantly improve the performance of these codes.

Categories and Subject Descriptors

C.4 [**Performance of systems**]: Measurement techniques, Performance attributes; D.2.8 [**Metrics**]: Performance measures.

Keywords

OpenMP, performance measurement, performance analysis, software tools.

ICS'13, June 10–14, 2013, Eugene, Oregon, USA.

1. INTRODUCTION

Developing multithreaded programs for shared memory systems can be tedious, especially if one directly uses a primitive threading library. To simplify development of multithreaded programs, the high performance computing community has developed the OpenMP Application Program Interface (OpenMP API) [15]. The compiler directives, library routines, and environment variables collectively known as the OpenMP API define a portable model for shared-memory parallel programming. OpenMP is the preferred model for adding threading to MPI applications for recent supercomputers based on highly-threaded processors.

Given the importance of OpenMP, it is necessary to develop effective tools that pinpoint and quantify causes of performance losses in OpenMP applications. To address that goal, our research aims to develop effective performance analysis strategies and techniques for OpenMP, prototype these strategies and techniques in a tool to evaluate their utility, and ensure that these strategies and techniques are embodied in a general OpenMP performance tools API that is suitable for inclusion in the OpenMP standard. This paper describes the results of our research.

There are several challenges for building effective performance tools for OpenMP. First, a tool must have low runtime overhead. Otherwise, any measurements it records will be suspect. Second, one must attribute performance measurements back to the program. In previous work [1], we have shown that attributing performance metrics to full calling contexts in parallel programs is essential to understand context-dependent performance bottlenecks, such as synchronization delays. Third, in parallel programs, identifying *symptoms* of performance losses is easy; gaining insight into their *causes* requires a more sophisticated approach.

To address these challenges, we developed a novel framework for measurement and analysis of OpenMP programs. Our approach supports *all* OpenMP features including nested parallel regions, work-sharing constructs, synchronization constructs, and OpenMP tasks. We have developed two novel methods to measure and analyze the performance of OpenMP programsm. First, we developed a measurement methodology that attributes blame for work and inefficiency back to program contexts. We show how to adapt prior work on measurement methodologies (blame shifting, see section 2) to OpenMP programs. We extended these methods to support dynamic thread-level parallelism in both time-shared and dedicated environments. Furthermore, we describe a more space-efficient mechanism for handling locks. Second, we developed a novel deferred context resolution method that supports on-the-fly attribution of performance metrics to full calling contexts within an OpenMP program execution. This approach enables us to collect compact call path profiles for OpenMP program executions *without* the need for traces.

We demonstrate the utility of our tool in case studies of four well-known application benchmarks using a version of the GNU OpenMP (GOMP) implementation, augmented with lightweight instrumentation and an API to support our measurement approach. Using insights provided by our tool, we were able to significantly improve the performance of these codes.

The next section of the paper surveys major OpenMP profiling tools and distinguishes their various approaches from our approach. Section 3 describes how we attribute blame for performance losses in OpenMP programs. Section 3 also explains our online deferred context resolution method for attributing performance metrics to full calling contexts in OpenMP programs. Section 4 discusses implementation issues for our tool. Section 5 demonstrates the effectiveness of our solution by studying four OpenMP benchmarks and identifying nontrivial improvement opportunities. Section 6 summarizes our conclusions and describes our ongoing work.

2. RELATED WORK

Tools for profiling and tracing OpenMP programs use either instrumentation or sampling as their principal measurement approach.

Tools such as TAU [18], ompP [7] and Scalasca [24] use the OPARI [14] source-to-source instrumentation tool to insert monitoring code around OpenMP constructs and the POMP [14] monitoring API to support measurement. POMP was proposed as a potential standard tool API for OpenMP; however, it was not embraced by the standards committee. Concerns about POMP include its reliance on instrumentation, the complexity of the API, and its runtime overhead. IBM provides a nearly complete implementation of the POMP API as part of their High Performance Computing Toolkit (HPCT) [3] and uses binary rewriting to add POMP calls to application executables. Due to concerns about overhead, IBM does not support the POMP API in optimized versions of their OpenMP runtime.

In contrast, tools such as Intel Vtune Amplifier XE 2013 [9], PGI's Group PGPROF [22], and OpenSpeedShop [17] use sampling to monitor OpenMP programs with low measurement overhead. While Cray's CrayPat [4] principally uses sampling, it relies on Cray and PGI compilers to add tracepoints to record entry/exit of parallel regions and worksharing constructs. However, none of these tools pinpoint code regions that cause idleness or lock waiting in an OpenMP program. With the exception of PGPROF, which relies on special characteristics of PGI's OpenMP runtime, these tools cannot attribute performance information to user-level calling contexts and instead present an implementation-level view that separates a main thread from OpenMP worker threads.

The tool most similar to ours is Oracle Solaris Studio (OSS) [16]. OSS is a full-featured, sampling-based performance tool that supports analysis of OpenMP programs built using Oracle's OpenMP compiler and runtime [23]. A key component of Oracle's OpenMP runtime is an API that provides information to support sampling-based performance tools [10]. Using the API requires no compiler support. Oracle's API confers two important advantages to OSS. First, it enables OSS to collect intricate performance metrics like overhead, idleness and work. Second, it enables OSS to attribute these metrics to full user-level calling contexts. A drawback of OSS, however, is that to collect profiles, OSS must record sample *traces* and then resolve full calling contexts from these traces during post-mortem analysis. Such traces quickly grow large as a program executes. A significant difference between OSS and our work is the approach for measurement and attribution of waiting and idleness. OSS attributes idle or spinning threads to contexts in which waiting occurs rather than trying to relate the idleness back to its causes. For example, OSS does not blame sequential regions for thread idleness. Consequently, it does not highlight sequential regions as opportunities for improving program performance.

To address the generic problem of attributing performance losses to their causes, Tallent and Mellor-Crummey [19] proposed a method for performance analysis now known as *blame shifting*. Their approach is based on the insight that an idle thread is a symptom of a performance problem rather than the cause. They describe a strategy for sampling-based performance analysis of Cilk programs executed by a work stealing runtime. Rather than a thread attributing samples to itself when it is idle, it announces its idleness to working threads using two shared variables. These two variables count the number of idle and working threads separately. At any asynchronous sample event, a working thread reads both variables and computes its share of the blame, which is proportional to the number of idle threads divided by the number of working threads, for not keeping idle threads busy. We refer to this strategy as *undirected* blame shifting as a thread has no knowledge of what other thread or threads will share the blame for its idleness.

Later, Tallent at el. [21] proposed a different blame shifting technique for lock spin waiting. In the extended technique, A thread waiting for a lock shifts blame for its waiting to the lock holder. We refer to this strategy as *directed* blame shifting, since an idle thread arranges to transfer blame to a specific thread. When OpenMP programs execute, various circumstances require either a directed or undirected blame shifting strategy to attribute idleness or lock waiting to its underlying causes.

In this paper, we integrate and extend both directed and undirected blame shifting to handle the full range of OpenMP programs. We elaborate our approach in the next section.

3. APPROACH

Providing insight into the performance of OpenMP programs requires careful design and implementation of mechanisms for measuring and attributing execution costs. To achieve low overhead, we use a measurement approach principally based on asynchronous sampling. The efficacy of sampling-based profiling for analyzing program performance is well known, e.g., [20]. A sampling-based performance tool can collect a flat profile that identifies source lines and routines where an OpenMP program spends its time without any special support from an OpenMP runtime system. Such an approach can identify *symptoms* of inefficiencies, such as spin waiting at barriers or for locks. However, providing insight into *causes* of inefficiencies in OpenMP programs requires designing tool measurement capabilities for this purpose and assistance from OpenMP runtime systems. We designed and prototyped lightweight instrumentation for OpenMP runtime systems that enables our tool to attribute idleness to causes. To make our approach attractive as a potential standard OpenMP tools API, important goals of our work were to minimize the runtime overhead of our instrumentation and developer effort needed to add it to any OpenMP runtime.

The following two sections elaborate our approach. Section 3.1 discusses how to attribute performance metrics to their causes for OpenMP programs. Section 3.2 describes how to attribute metrics to full calling contexts on the fly for OpenMP programs.

3.1 Attributing idleness and lock waiting

Our tool measures and attributes an OpenMP thread's execution time into four categories:

- *Idleness*: The time a thread is either spin waiting or sleep waiting at a barrier for work. For example, OpenMP threads waiting at a barrier inside or outside a parallel region are idle. If a thread is not idle, the thread is busy.
- *Work*: The time a busy thread spends executing application code, including both serial and parallel regions.
- *Overhead*: The time a busy thread spends executing code in the OpenMP runtime system.
- *Lock waiting*: The time a thread spends spin waiting for locks.

These four metrics reflect different aspects of an OpenMP program execution. Depending on which metrics are prominent, different tuning strategies apply. If idleness dominates work attributed to a code region, that code region is insufficiently parallelized. If lock waiting associated with a code region is high, that code is associated with significant lock contention and the use of mutual exclusion in that code region needs review. If overhead for a code region is high but idleness is low, increasing the granularity of parallelism may reduce the overhead. If overhead is low and idleness is high, then decreasing the granularity of parallelism may reduce the idleness. Finally, if the overhead and idleness for a region are both high, then changing the granularity of parallelism will not help performance and the parallelization of the code region merits review.

To collect these four metrics, we modified a version of the GNU OpenMP runtime to explicitly maintain a state variable for each thread. When a thread takes a sample, it can query the runtime to determine which metric should be adjusted. It is worth of noting that the sum of these four metrics represents the aggregate execution time across all threads.

Finally, we use different techniques to attribute these metrics to their causes. Since work and overhead belong to the threads performing them, we attribute both metrics to a thread receiving a sample. For idleness, we apply an *undirected blaming* technique to attribute it to busy threads, highlighting the fact that threads suffering from excessive work are the causes of idleness. For lock waiting, we apply a *directed blaming* technique to attribute it to lock holders to identify problematic locks.

Section 3.1.1 and 3.1.2 discuss the challenge and our solution for the undirected and directed blaming technique in OpenMP programs respectively. Section 3.1.3 describes how we integrate undirected and directed blaming to attribute idleness and lock waiting in OpenMP programs.

3.1.1 Undirected blaming for idleness

As discussed in Section 2, previous work by Tallent and Mellor-Crummey [19] considers how to blame idleness among threads in a static thread pool. Their approach is insufficient for OpenMP, because OpenMP allows the number of worker threads to change dynamically during execution. In contrast, our undirected blaming technique supports attribution of idleness for OpenMP programs in the presence of dynamic thread-level parallelism in both time-shared and dedicated environments. Equation 1 shows how we compute idleness for a program context in the presence of dynamic parallelism.

$$\begin{aligned} I_c &= \sum_{k=1}^{s_c} I_{c,k} = \sum_{k=1}^{s_c} p\frac{i_{c,k}}{b_{c,k}} = p\sum_{k=1}^{s_c}(\frac{i_{c,k}+b_{c,k}}{b_{c,k}} - 1) \\ &= p\sum_{k=1}^{s_c}(\frac{t_{c,k}}{b_{c,k}} - 1) \qquad (1) \end{aligned}$$

I_c is the total idleness attributed to a specific context c in the program over time. I_c is measured in processor cycles or microseconds and represents the aggregate idleness across all threads while one or more threads executed code in context c. $I_{c,k}$ is the idleness attributed to context c for the kth sample. p is the sampling period, which is constant during program execution. s_c is the total number of samples taken in the context c. $i_{c,k}$ is the number of idle threads in the system when sample k occurs in context c. $b_{c,k}$ is the number of busy threads in the system when sample k occurs in context c. Like Tallent and Mellor-Crummey [19], we apportion the blame for instantaneous idleness in the system among the busy threads at the time. $t_{c,k}$, shown as the sum of $i_{c,k}$ and $b_{c,k}$, is the total number of threads considered by our undirected blaming technique in the context c when sample k is taken. Equation 1 shows how we transform our idleness method to compute total idleness for a context by replacing the need for $i_{c,k}$, a measure of instantaneous idleness, with $t_{c,k}$, a measure of instantaneous thread-level parallelism. After the transformation, there is no need for our tool to maintain a shared variable reflecting the number of idle threads in the system.

Note, however, that choosing an appropriate value for $t_{c,k}$ depends on the environment. To see why, consider the appropriate action concerning sequential code occurring *before* the first OpenMP parallel region. In a time-shared environment, an OpenMP program should *not* be charged for idleness outside a parallel region. In contrast, in a dedicated environment, this sequential code *should* be charged for the idleness of allocated cores even if threads have not yet been allocated to run on them. In the text that follows, we will elaborate the details of how our tool automatically chooses the appropriate value of $t_{c,k}$, depending on the environment.

For a time-shared environment, we should compute the idleness incurred by OpenMP threads required by each code region. If a code region in an OpenMP program does not use all hardware threads, these threads are available to other co-running programs and the OpenMP program should not be charged for unused threads. Thus, a sequential code region of an OpenMP program is not charged for idleness because it requires only one thread and keeps it busy. To handle this case, in a time-shared environment, we let $t_{c,k}$ to be the number of threads in use when sample k is received in context c. In this case, $t_{c,k}$ is a variable of c and k. Fortunately, OpenMP provides an API to query the number of threads in use at any time. Thus, we can compute $I_{c,k}$ eagerly at each sample k and accumulate it to I_c.

For a dedicated environment, we propose two ways to choose $t_{c,k}$ values to compute two different idleness metrics to reflect inefficiency with respect to different viewpoints. To compute *core idleness*, we set $t_{c,k}$ to be the total number of cores[1] in a dedicated system. This setting blames working threads in an OpenMP program if a core in the system is unused. For this case, the value of $t_{c,k}$ is constant during execution and can be read from system configuration information. Alternatively, to compute *thread idleness*, we want $t_{c,k}$ to be the maximum number of threads ever in use during a program's execution. This idleness metric is useful when assessing the scalability of an OpenMP program on different numbers of threads. In this case, the maximum number of threads used by a program will be unknown until the program terminates because an OpenMP program can dynamically adjust its thread count using an API. To handle this case, we add two callbacks to the OpenMP runtime system so our tool is notified when a thread is created or destroyed. In these callbacks, our tool maintains an instantaneous global thread count using atomic increment/decrement. During execution, our tool records the maximum instantaneous thread count observed. When computing *thread idleness*, $t_{c,k}$ represents the maximum instantaneous thread count during execution. Since our tool won't know its value until the end of an execution, we separately accumulate two terms in Equation 1, $p \sum_k \frac{1}{b_{c,k}}$ and $-ps_c$, for each context. At the end of an execution, we compute *both* core and thread idleness metrics for each context c according to Equation 1 by simply multiplying $\sum_k \frac{1}{b_{c,k}}$ through by the appropriate value of $t_{c,k}$, which is constant for all k samples in both cases, and adding it to the second term, which is proportional to the number of samples in c. Both of the aforementioned methods attribute idleness to sequential code regions in OpenMP programs, but relative to different baselines. In our case studies, we use the thread idleness metric to identify performance bottlenecks for benchmarks running in a dedicated environment.

3.1.2 Directed blaming for lock waiting

Tallent at el. [21] developed a version of directed blaming for pthread programs, described in Section 2. Their method, which uses function wrapping to override pthread locking primitives, is not applicable to OpenMP runtime systems for three reasons. First, OpenMP runtimes have several different mutual exclusion implementations: locks, critical, ordered, and atomic sections. There is no defined interface that a tool can wrap. Second, efficiently wrapping a locking primitive requires intimate knowledge about the representation it uses. However, OpenMP runtime vendors are unwilling to commit to a fixed lock representation—they want the freedom to use whatever representation they deem best for a particular architecture because the choice of lock representation may affect a program's speed and scalability. Third, the approach in [21] associates extra state with each live lock to store blame information. Here, we describe a new approach for directed blaming for OpenMP programs that efficiently supports directed blaming for all mutual exclusion constructs in an OpenMP runtime system. Furthermore, it requires only modest additional space for managing blame; namely, proportional to the maximum number of concurrently contended locks rather than the maximum number of live locks.

Our directed blaming technique works in three parts: lock acquisition, asynchronous samples, and lock release. To minimize the overhead of lock acquisition, we do not require that any code be added to the critical path of an uncontended lock acquisition in an OpenMP runtime. Only if a lock acquisition fails and a thread is forced to wait does our tool record the lock we are trying to acquire in a thread-local variable. In this case, recording the lock will have little or no effect on execution time since this operation is done only when a thread begins to wait.

When a thread receives an asynchronous sample, our performance tool's signal handler queries the thread state maintained in the OpenMP runtime. Besides returning the thread state, if the thread is currently in the *lockwait* state, the state query API we defined for the OpenMP runtime will also return the address of the lock that the thread is awaiting. If the thread is in the *lockwait* state, the signal handler uses the lock address as the key for a hash table. Our tool uses a hash table of fixed, modest size, e.g. 1024 entries, to maintain a map of blame that must be charged to the thread holding any particular lock.[2] The hash table is initialized when our tool is first attached to the program. When the signal handler tries to accumulate blame for a lock in the hash table, it allocates an entry for the lock in the table on demand if one doesn't already exist. Hash table entries are tagged with the lock address. If two held locks hash to the same entry, blame for one will be discarded. When monitoring is enabled and a lock release callback is registered with the OpenMP runtime, then every lock release will invoke the callback with the lock address as an argument. At this point, we look up the lock in the hash table, accept any blame that has accumulated in the table for the lock, and reset the table entry's state to free so that it is available to be reallocated on demand. If the blame accumulated in the table is greater than 0, then our tool unwinds the call stack and attributes the accumulated blame for lock waiting to the calling context of the lock release.

When designing the protocol for concurrently maintaining the hash table to accumulate blame, we considered two types of implementations: a heavyweight algorithm that carefully handles any data race that might arise when two locks hash to the same table entry, and a lighter weight implementation that doesn't use atomic operations to manage data races. The heavyweight approach uses atomic operations and has higher runtime overhead. The lighter weight method might cause a lock to receive additional blame or some blame to be lost. The odds of this happening in practice are extremely

[1]Alternatively, one could do this for SMT hardware thread contexts.

[2]The idea of only maintaining blame for *actively contended* locks in a hash table is due to Alexandre Eichenberger (IBM T.J. Watson Research Center).

small. As a result, we opted for the lighter weight protocol. It works exceptionally well in practice because (a) the number of locks actively contended at the same time is much smaller than the size of hash table so collisions are rare, and (b) only locks with very large sample counts charged to them are worthy of attention by an analyst. While data races can change sample counts slightly, infrequent errors of this sort are extremely unlikely to change an analyst's assessment as to whether a particular lock is a problem or not.

3.1.3 *Integrating directed and undirected blaming*

When an OpenMP program has threads in both idle and lockwait states at the same time, it suffers performance losses from both thread idleness and lock contention. To handle this case properly, directed and undirected blaming techniques need to coordinate. The *lockwait* metric needs no special care because we can always blame it directly to the context of lock holders. However, the attribution of *idleness* in such circumstances deserves careful attention.

Consider an OpenMP program execution at a point in time when there are n_i threads idle, n_w threads working, and n_l thread waiting for locks. There are three reasonable ways to consider attributing blame for *idleness* among these threads. First, we consider using undirected blaming to only charge idleness of the n_i idle threads to the n_w working threads. Any working thread that receives an asynchronous sample in this execution state charges itself for $\frac{n_i}{n_w}$ units of idleness. This blaming scheme highlights code regions being executed by working threads as contributing to the idleness of other threads, but it ignores threads holding locks as deserving extra attention. The second method uses undirected blaming to charge an equal fraction of idleness to each thread that is working or waiting for a lock. This method attributes $\frac{n_i}{n_w+n_l}$ idleness to the context that receives an asynchronous sample in a working or waiting thread. This scheme charges idleness not only to the context of each working thread that receives an asynchronous sample, but also to the context of any thread waiting for a lock. The rationale of this scheme is that an idle thread is waiting for all working and waiting threads. Note, however, that each thread waiting for a lock is waiting for a lock holder. Our third method uses undirected blaming technique to charge idleness to threads both in working and lock waiting state, and then uses directed blaming to charge idleness inherited by a thread waiting for a lock to its lock holder. For example, if all n_l waiting threads are spinning at the same lock, this method attributes $\frac{n_i}{n_w+n_l}$ idleness to each context that receives an asynchronous sample in a working thread, $\frac{n_i n_l}{n_w+n_l}$ idleness to the lock release, and no idleness to the context in each waiting thread. We choose the third of these methods because it transfers any blame for idleness received while waiting for a lock directly to the lock holder.

3.2 Deferred context resolution

Attributing metrics to full calling context is essential for understanding the performance of parallel programs and the underlying causes of inefficiencies. Consequently, interpreting the runtime stack for both master and worker threads in an OpenMP program is paramount. Most OpenMP runtimes manage master and worker threads separately. In fact, too our knowledge, only PGI's OpenMP runtime uses a cactus stack to readily provide both master and worker threads with a unified call stack view.

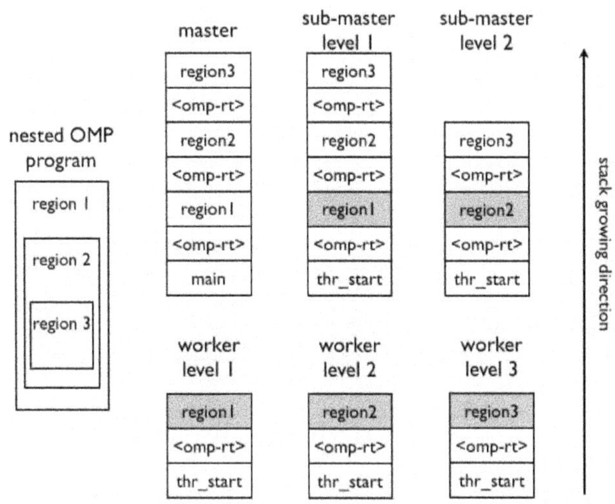

Figure 1: The call stack for master, sub-master and worker threads in an OpenMP program with three levels of nested parallelism. As shown, stacks grow from bottom to top. The calling contexts for the parallel regions shown in grey are scattered across two or more threads.

To illustrate the problem tools face interpreting call stacks of OpenMP threads, consider Figure 1, which shows the call stacks of several threads in the presence of nested parallelism. When a worker thread in an outer parallel region encounters nested parallelism, it becomes a master thread for the inner region. Threads other than the master thread lack full calling context for computations they perform. Assembling the complete user-level calling context for work in a parallel region requires information about the calling context for the region itself, as well as that of any enclosing regions. Thus, to assemble the full calling context for region 3 being executed by the level 3 worker, the level 3 worker requires the location in region 3 from its own stack, the context in which region 3 was invoked by the level 2 sub-master thread, the context in which region 2 was invoked by the level 1 sub-master thread, and finally the context in which region 1 was invoked by the master thread.

A straightforward way to support assembly of distributed context information involves the following steps when encountering a parallel region:

1. Create a unique ID for the parallel region instance.
2. If the master thread encounters a parallel region, unwind its call stack to capture the region's creation context and store the resulting context in a region table where it can be looked up by region ID.
3. If a sub-master thread or a worker encounters a new parallel region, unwind its call stack to the parallel region at the base of its stack, look up the calling context for that parallel region in the region table, assemble the full calling context of the new region instance, and register it in the region table.

When a thread receives an asynchronous sample as the program runs, the thread merely needs to unwind its own call stack, determine the parallel region at the base of its stack, look up the prefix of its calling context in the region table, and assemble the final result. To support this approach, the OpenMP runtime system needs to supply a callback at the entry of each parallel region instance and an API that the tool can use to query a parallel region instance ID.

Capturing the context using the outlined approach, however, is more expensive than it needs to be. The overhead of this approach can be reduced in some cases. If a parallel region is small and worker threads in the region run quickly enough so that no asynchronous samples are taken while they are executing work in the region, then there is no need to recover the full calling context for the region. To avoid the cost of context capture when no worker thread has been sampled in the region, Itzkowitz [10] proposed a *deferred* context resolution technique that is used in Oracle Solaris Studio [16].

Rather than capturing the calling context context for a new a parallel region instance as it is entered, Oracle Solaris Studio defers capturing context until the end of the region instance. They maintain a global map that indicates whether a thread received an asynchronous sample within a parallel region instance. If not, then one can skip capturing the region's context. While the deferred context resolution can dramatically reduce measurement overhead for small, but frequently called parallel regions, it introduces a new problem: a thread can no longer immediately assemble the full context for its work when it receives an asynchronous sample. The context for any enclosing parallel regions will only become available *after* the regions exit. In Oracle Solaris Studio, Itzkowitz et al. cope with this by recording available partial context information for each sample in a trace. Then, in a post mortem phase, full context is reconstructed using context for enclosing parallel regions that later becomes available. Supporting deferred context resolution places an additional constraint on an OpenMP runtime system—a callback from region *exit* is required.

To avoid the need for large traces and post-mortem context assembly when using deferred context resolution, we devised an approach for *online* deferred context resolution. Whenever the master thread receives an asynchronous sample, it unwinds its call stack and enters its call path into the reference calling context tree (CCT). Whenever an OpenMP worker thread receives an asynchronous sample, the thread queries its parallel region ID. Its full calling context won't be known at this point because the context of the enclosing parallel region won't be known until after the region exits. Let us denote the call stack suffix the worker thread recovers at this point as s. Since the calling context for the enclosing parallel region is not yet known, s will have a placeholder at its base associated with its enclosing parallel region instance ID r_1. The thread next records s in a thread-private CCT rooted at r_1. This CCT is stored in a *thread CCT map* indexed by r_1. When the thread receives a subsequent sample, it again unwinds its call stack. If it is still in in the parallel region instance with ID r_1, it adds its new call stack suffix to its calling context tree rooted at r_1 in the *thread CCT map*.

When a master or sub master exits a parallel region r, it checks the *region instance sample map* to see if a sample was processed by any worker or sub-master thread in that parallel region instance. If so, the thread unwinds its call stack to acquire the calling context s_2 of the parallel region instance. s_2 is entered in the *resolved region map* indexed by the parallel region ID r.

When a worker or sub-master thread receives an asynchronous sample, if it finds itself in a parallel region different than the one for the previous sample, it inspects the *thread CCT map* to see if any context information for its CCTs is available from the *resolved region map*. If so, it prepends context information from the *resolved region map* to its relevant CCTs. Any CCT whose context is now fully resolved is taken out of the *thread CCT map* and placed into the reference CCT. When a thread exits or a process terminates, all remaining deferred contexts are resolved and any remaining information in the *thread CCT map* is folded into the reference CCT.

We compare our online method for deferred context resolution with the offline method used by Oracle Solaris Studio using the LULESH application benchmark, which is one of our case studies described in Section 5.2. For a 48-thread execution of LULESH using the same program input and sampling rate, Oracle Solaris Studio records a 170MB performance data file to perform deferred context resolution postmortem. Using our online deferred context resolution strategy, our tool records a compact profile for each thread, 8MB total—a reduction in data volume of more than 20x.

Like Oracle Solaris Studio, our prototype tool distinguishes OpenMP runtime frames on the call stack from others by simply identifying that they belong to the shared library for the OpenMP runtime. For the OpenMP standard, a solution suitable for statically-linked programs is needed as well. We are part of the OpenMP standards committee working group designing a new tools API that provides the necessary support. The new API has the OpenMP runtime record stack addresses for procedure frames that enter and exit the OpenMP runtime. When one uses call stack unwinding, this interface will enable one to identify sequences of procedure frames on the stack that belong to the OpenMP runtime rather than user code, even for statically linked programs. We are in the process of evaluating this design to provide feedback to the OpenMP tools API subcommittee.

A note about context resolution for OpenMP tasks.

OpenMP 3.0 tasks [2] support work stealing execution. With respect to context resolution, this introduces an additional consideration. Since task creation may be separated from task execution, tasks have an additional component to their context—the *creation* context.

To record the creation context of a task, we add an 8-byte field in the OpenMP task data structure maintained by the runtime system. Once a non-immediate-run task is created, a callback function is invoked to pass the 8-byte field to the performance tool. The performance tool unwinds the call stack to collect the task creation context in the callback function invoked at each task creation point. It then updates the 8-byte field in the task structure with the task creation context. When a task is executed, the performance tool uses two query APIs to get the task creation context and the root frame of the executing task. We combine the two to get the full context of the task. One complicated but practical case is that one task can be nested in another task. We can concatenate the outer task creation context with the inner task creation context to resolve the full context of the inner task. However, if the program recursively creates nested tasks, the call site of inner-most tasks may be deep in the call stack. Long recursive call paths aren't typically of much interest to a performance analyst. For that reason, we collapse the call stack for recursive tasks. If the root frame of one task is the same as that of its parent, we fold the performance data of the task into its parent and skip its frames on the call stack.

Incorporating the creation context into the complete context for every OpenMP task is expensive. The overhead of eagerly gathering this information cannot be tied to the sampling rate, and therefore it is uncontrolled. Consequently, we do not employ *creation-extended* task context construction by default. Rather than providing a full creation context for a task by default, we simply associate the task with its enclosing parallel region. If a performance analyst needs the full creation context for tasks, our tool will collect it upon request, though this extra information increases monitoring overhead. Our case studies in Section 5 did not require full creation contexts for tasks to provide performance insights.

4. TOOL IMPLEMENTATION

To evaluate our ideas, we implemented them in the HPCToolkit [1] performance tools. HPCToolkit is an open-source, multi-platform, sampling-based performance tool for measurement and analysis of application performance on parallel systems. We extended HPCToolkit's existing call path profiler to support the techniques described in the previous section. Using these techniques, our extended HPCToolkit is able to analyze the performance of OpenMP and OpenMP+MPI programs by both collecting measures of work, idleness, overhead, and lock waiting; and then attributing these measures to full calling contexts in a unified user-level view. To analyze performance data, we use HPCToolkit's `hpcviewer` graphical user interface. `hpcviewer` associates both measured and derived metrics to full calling contexts, thereby representing a unified view reconstructed using our online deferred context resolution strategy.

The implementation of our techniques, however, requires support from the OpenMP runtime system. Consequently, we took special care to minimize the required support. Our initial prototype was based on an open-source OpenMP implementation — GNU OpenMP (GOMP) [6]. To support both our blaming strategies and online deferred context resolution, we modified GOMP source code to insert necessary callbacks, query functions, and data structures associated with parallel regions and tasks. Our modification encompassed 5 files and less than 50 lines of code. The software development cost to add the necessary OpenMP runtime support for our methods is quite low. Also, as we show in Section 5, the runtime impact of our proposed support is similarly low.

To quantify the improvement one can obtain after optimization, we compute two derived metrics from each raw metric we defined in Section 3.1. For example, we derive *absolute idleness* and *relative idleness* metrics from the raw *idleness* metric. Absolute idleness quantifies the idleness in a given context relative to the entire effort of the program. It shows the maximum possible (percentage) improvement if the idleness is eliminated for that context. Relative idleness reflects the parallel efficiency for the context. A high relative idleness value means the context is making poor use of parallel resources. A good rule of thumb is to focus optimization efforts on contexts with both high absolute idleness and high relative idleness.

Note that both derived metrics are computed after the raw data has been collected. The defining equations are shown in equation 2. The notation key in equation 2 is as follows: $I_{c,abs}$ is the absolute idleness computed for context c; $I_{c,rel}$ is the relative idleness computed for context c; I_c, W_c, O_c, and L_c are idleness, work, overhead, and lock waiting respectively attributed to the context c; I_r, W_r, O_r, and L_r are idleness, work, overhead, and lock waiting respectively aggregated for the whole program.

$$\begin{aligned} I_{c,abs} &= \frac{I_c}{I_r + W_r + O_r + L_r} \times 100\% \\ I_{c,rel} &= \frac{I_c}{I_c + W_c + O_c + L_c} \times 100\% \end{aligned} \quad (2)$$

It is worth noting that analogous derived metrics exist for *work*, *overhead* and *lock waiting* as well.

5. CASE STUDIES

In this section, we evaluate the utility and overhead of our measurement approach using a set of application benchmarks that employ OpenMP parallel loops with and without nested parallel regions, OpenMP tasking, and OpenMP in conjunction with MPI. Below, we briefly describe the benchmarks that we studied.

- AMG2006 [13], one of the Sequoia benchmarks developed by Lawrence Livermore National Laboratory, is a parallel algebraic multigrid solver for linear systems arising from problems on unstructured grids. The driver for this benchmark builds linear systems for various 3D problems. It consists of sequential and parallel regions that both affect its performance. AMG2006 is a MPI-OpenMP hybrid benchmark written in C.
- LULESH [12] is an C++ application benchmark developed by Lawrence Livermore National Laboratory, solving the Sedov blast wave problem for one 3D material. LULESH is implemented using a variety of parallel programming models; here, we study the performance of its OpenMP version. The OpenMP implementation of LULESH contains parallel regions inside deep loop nests so the number of parallel region instances in an execution is more than 20K.
- NAS BT-MZ [11] is a multi-zone parallel benchmark written in Fortran that employs two levels of nested OpenMP parallelism. It divides the data into several zones which are computed in the first level parallel regions. In each zone, computation is also parallelized in second level parallel regions. This benchmark manages load balance in the outer-level parallel regions.
- HEALTH [5] is a benchmark that is part of the Barcelona OpenMP Tasks Suite. With the medium input, it creates more than 17 million untied tasks during execution. The benchmark is used to evaluate task creation and scheduling policies inside an OpenMP runtime system.

We compiled each of these benchmarks using the GNU 4.6.2 compiler with `-O3` optimization and linked with our modified version of GOMP library from GCC 4.6.2. We measured the performance of these codes on a system with four 12-core AMD Magny-Cours processors and 128 GB

Benchmark	native GOMP	modified GOMP	profiling
AMG2006	54.02s	54.10s	56.76s
LULESH	402.34s	402.56s	416.78s
NAS BT-MZ	32.10s	32.15s	34.23s
HEALTH	71.74s	72.20s	74.27s

Table 1: Running times for our case study applications with (a) the unmodified GOMP runtime library (no sampling), (b) the modified GOMP library with lightweight instrumentation to support blame shifting (no sampling), and (c) the modified GOMP library while profiling at 200 samples per second per thread. Execution times represent the average over three executions.

memory. For AMG2006, we studied executions consisting of 4 MPI processes and 8 OpenMP threads per process. For LULESH, we studied executions with 48 OpenMP threads. For NAS BT-MZ, we studied executions that used 4 threads for outer parallel region and 8 threads for inner parallel regions. For HEALTH, we studied runs on 8 OpenMP threads. We measured the performance of these codes using asynchronous sampling at a rate of 200 samples/s per thread.

We first evaluate the measurement overhead associated with our modified GOMP library and profiler. Table 1 compares the execution time of each benchmark code using the native GOMP library, our modified GOMP library with performance measurement hooks, and the modified GOMP library with our profiler attached. The capabilities employed by our profiler include using undirected, directed as well as integrated blaming for *idleness*, *work*, *overhead* and *lock waiting*, and using online deferred context resolution for parallel regions, resolving task contexts to their enclosing parallel region. By comparing the times in the first and second columns of the table, we see that our GOMP modifications to support performance tools add almost no overhead. Comparing the first and third columns shows that the measurement overhead using our profiler is less than 5% for each of these codes.

Note that if we resolve the *full* creation context for tasks to their creation contexts in HEALTH, the run time of a profiled execution jumps from 74.27s to 431.48s. This is more than a 6x slowdown compared to its unmonitored execution. Resolving the full creation context for tasks in HEALTH is so expensive because HEALTH creates 17 million tiny tasks as it executes, with each task requiring a call stack unwind to recover its full creation context. To keep measurement overhead low, our profiler's default measurement approach is to only resolve task contexts to their enclosing parallel region.

In the following four sections, we illustrate the effectiveness of our profiling approach by describing insights it delivered for each of our benchmark applications and how they helped us identify optimizations that yielded non-trivial improvements to these codes.

5.1 AMG2006

Figure 2 shows a time-centric view of traces of AMG2006 executing on 8 MPI ranks with 8 OpenMP threads per rank. Trace lines for each of the MPI processes and OpenMP threads are stacked along the Y axis and time flows left to right. The color at each point in a thread's time line represents the procedure executing at that time. An execution of AMG2006 consists of three phases: MPI initialization, problem setup, and solve.

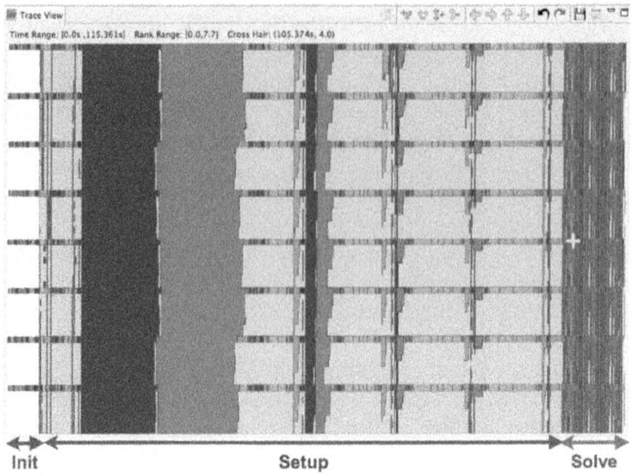

Figure 2: HPCToolkit's time-centric view rendering of a complete execution of AMG2006 on 64 cores – 8 MPI ranks with 8 OpenMP threads/rank.

During initialization, only the master thread in each MPI rank is active. The initial white space in the traces of OpenMP worker threads shows that they are idle before they are created. During the setup phase shown in Figure 2, the light gray color for OpenMP worker threads represents worker threads blocked in `pthread_cond_wait`. This view illustrates that OpenMP threads are idle most of the time; the largest component of that idleness occurs while the master thread in each MPI rank executes serial code for `hypre_BoomerAMGCoarsen`. Our code-centric view for the full execution (not shown) reports that 34.9% of the total effort in the execution corresponds to idleness while `hypre_BoomerAMGCoarsen` executes; the relative idleness our tool attributes to this routine is 87.5%—exactly what we would expect with one of 8 cores working within an MPI rank. Our tool's quantitative measure for idleness attributed to this serial code is a result of our blame shifting approach. Neither VTune nor Oracle Solaris Studio directly associates idleness with serial code. During the setup phase, short bursts of activity by OpenMP worker threads separate long gray intervals of idleness. However, the intervals of activity by the worker threads are of unequal lengths, which indicates that even when threads are working, their work is imbalanced. While the setup phase in this benchmark execution accounts for a large fraction of the total time, the solve phase dominates in production computations. For that reason, we focus the rest of our analysis on the performance of the solve phase. Figure 3 shows an expanded view of one iteration of the solve phase. The imbalanced intervals of gray indicate idleness caused by a severe load imbalance in OpenMP loops employed by `hyper_BoomerAMGRelax`.

To analyze the solver phase in more detail, we use HPCToolkit's code-centric *hpcviewer* to analyze measurement data collected for just the solve phase of the benchmark in an execution by 4 MPI ranks with 8 OpenMP threads per rank. Figure 4 attributes *idleness*, *work* and *overhead* to the com-

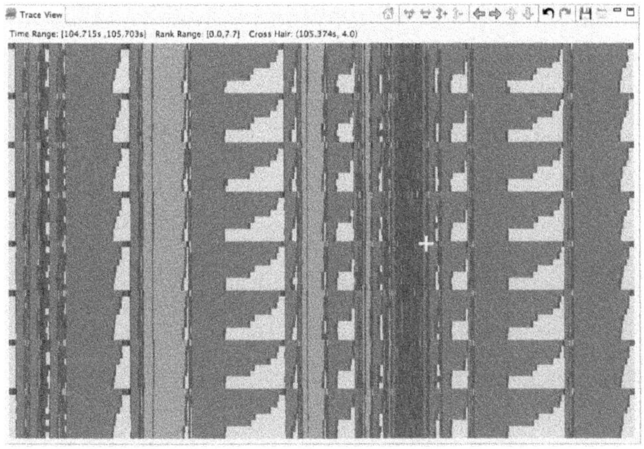

Figure 3: HPCToolkit's time-centric view rendering of a single iteration of AMG2006's solver on 64 cores – 8 MPI ranks with 8 OpenMP threads/rank.

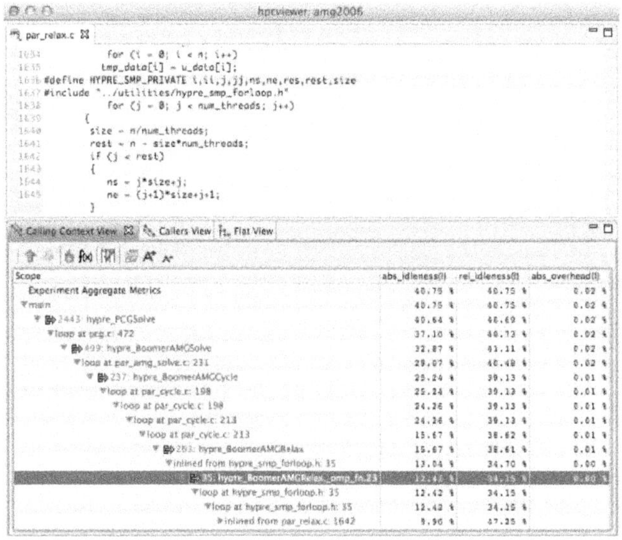

Figure 4: A calling context view of AMG2006's solver phase. More than 12% of the execution time of all threads is spent idling in the highlighted parallel region.

plete calling context of parallel regions. *hpcviewer* consists of three panes. The top one is the source code pane; the bottom left one shows program contexts such as routines, loops and statements; the bottom right one shows the metrics associated with each program context. Both inclusive and exclusive values are computed for all metrics. Figure 4 shows only inclusive metric values. The 40.75% aggregate absolute idleness metric for the solve phase means that threads are working only about 60% of the time. The OpenMP runtime overhead for the solve phase is negligible—only 0.02%. Drilling down the call path from `main`, we find that a large part of the idleness in the solve phase is attributed to a parallel region—`hyper_BoomerAMGRelax._omp_fn.23`, which is highlighted in Figure 4. Work by that routine (and routines it calls) accounts for 12.42% of the idleness in the solve phase. The relative idleness measure of 34.15% for this program context indicates that this parallel region is active, roughly one third of the threads are idle. The discussion in Section 3.1 indicates that if overhead is low and idleness is high, one should reduce the granularity of parallel work to increase parallelism and improve load balance.

To apply this optimization, we examined the source code corresponding to `hyper_BoomerAMGRelax._omp_fn.23` in the source pane of Figure 4. We found that this parallel region decomposes the computation into one piece of work for each thread and each thread is statically assigned a piece of work. Since each piece of work computes an equal number of iterations in the parallel loop, it would appear that each thread has equal amount of work. However, the execution time of iterations differs significantly due to characteristics of the input dataset, resulting in load imbalance. To reduce the load imbalance that causes the high *idleness* in this parallel region, we decomposed the work into a number of smaller pieces and used dynamic scheduling to balance the work among threads. Decomposing the work into five chunks per thread provided enough flexibility for dynamic scheduling to reduce load imbalance without adding too much overhead for the scheduling itself. The optimization reduced the *idleness* of `hyper_BoomerAMGRelax._omp_fn.23` from 3.05e+11 to 4.53e+09 CPU cycles, reducing the running time of the solve phase by 11%.

5.2 LULESH

In Figure 5, we analyze measurements from a 48-thread execution of LULESH using a bottom-up view which attributes metric consumption to routines and their calling contexts. We sorted the results to identify routines with the highest exclusive absolute idleness. The top routine is the `madvise` system call, which is called by `free` from both the application and the OpenMP runtime. The idleness associated with `free` amounts to 4.6% of the total thread execution time. The percentage of relative idleness indicates that only the master thread calls `free` and the other 47 threads are idle. It is worth noting that the performance tool reports that `free` accounts for only 0.1% of total execution time. Without idleness blame shifting, it would not appear that memory management is a potential performance problem. To see if we could improve performance by using a better memory allocator, we used Google's TCMalloc [8] (a high-performance threaded allocator) instead of `glibc`'s implementations of `malloc` and `free`. Surprisingly, the execution time drops from 402s to 102s—a 75% improvement!

To understand the improvement, which was well beyond our expectations, we compared profiles of the original and optimized versions of LULESH. As we expected, the absolute idleness associated with `free` drops from 4.6% to less than 0.1%. However, we also found that the work associated with some parallel regions shrank by a factor of 20. Further examination showed that data is allocated immediately before entering these regions on each iteration of an enclosing loop. Pseudo code in Figure 6 shows the structure of these problematic parallel regions. Because `glibc`'s `free` releases memory pages to the operating system, a subsequent `malloc` causes pages to be added back to the application's address space. As threads attempt to write these newly-allocated pages in the parallel region, they fault and stall as the operating system lazily zero-fills the pages. Repeatedly freeing, reallocating, and zero-filling pages is surprisingly costly. Un-

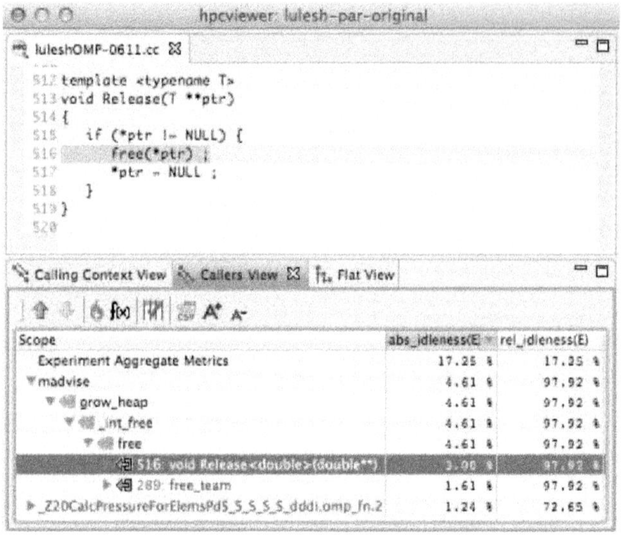

Figure 5: A bottom-up view of call path profiles for LULESH. madvise, which is called while freeing memory, is identified as the routine with the most idleness.

```
for( ... ) {
    malloc a[n], b[n], c[n];
    #pragma parallel for
    for(i=0; i<n; i++)  {
        a[i] = ...;
        b[i] = ...;
        c[i] = ...;
    }
    free a, b, c;
}
```

Figure 6: Pseudo code showing how memory is allocated, initialized, and freed in LULESH.

like glibc, TCMalloc does not return deallocated pages to the operating system so it avoids the cost of repeated zero-filling, leading to a 75% speedup.

While our idleness measure didn't help us predict the full benefit of changing the memory allocator, it did uncover the "tip of the iceberg," which helped us improve the performance of LULESH. The high overhead of zero-filling pages that we missed with our measurements was masquerading as work since it was incurred in parallel regions. An analysis based on sampling measurements of real time and graduated instructions might have provided some additional insight into operating system overhead that was unobserved.

5.3 NAS BT-MZ

To evaluate HPCToolkit's support for measurement and analysis of OpenMP programs with nested parallel regions, we used it to study the performance of the NAS BT-MZ benchmark. Figure 7 shows the unified calling contexts that HPCToolkit recovers for nested parallel regions in BT-MZ. In the figure, the parallel region `MAIN__._omp_fn.3` is nested inside `MAIN__._omp_fn.0`, showing that our method properly reconstructs calling contexts for nested parallel regions. The aggregate *absolute idleness* is larger than *absolute work*, which means that threads are idle more than half of the time during execution. Examination of the inclusive idleness measurements for the calling context of the nested parallel regions shows that most of the idleness comes from the innermost region. To optimize BT-MZ, we refactored the `exch_qbc` routine highlighted in Figure 7 because it has 1.55% *absolute work* but 11.1% *absolute idleness*. The *relative idleness* for this routine is more than 87%. Looking deeper along the call path inside the innermost parallel region, we see that `pthread_create` is responsible for idleness that amounts to roughly 3% of the overall execution cost. This cost is incurred because GOMP does not use a persistent thread pool for threads in nested parallel regions. Threads used in nested parallel regions are created at region entry and destroyed at region exit. For a nested parallel region in a loop, frequent thread creation and destruction can degrade performance.

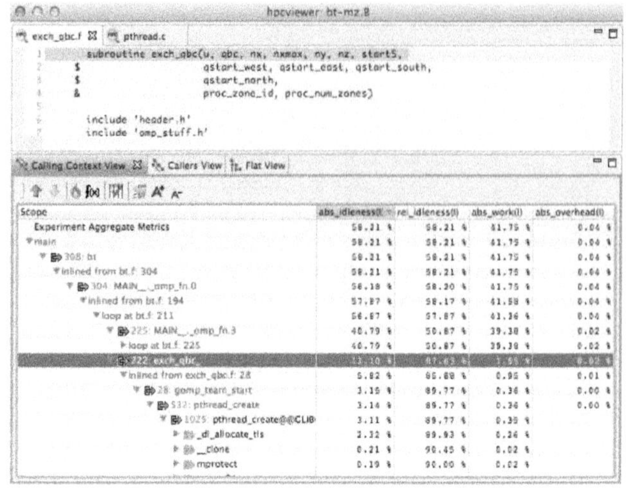

Figure 7: A calling context view of call path profiles for BT-MZ shows that the amount of idleness reported for exch_qbc is over seven times larger than the work it performs.

Changing the inner parallel region inside `exch_qbc` to a sequential region eliminated the *idleness* caused by thread creation and destruction, improving performance by 8%.

5.4 HEALTH

To evaluate HPCToolkit's support for measurement and analysis of programs based on OpenMP tasking, we studied the HEALTH benchmark. In this execution, we used HPCToolkit's (low-overhead) default context resolution for tasks, which attributes tasks back only to their enclosing parallel region rather than their full creation context. In experiments with HEALTH on eight threads, we found that its absolute idleness was much less than 1%, indicating that each thread was working on a parallel task most of the time. However, severe lock contention in the benchmark caused threads to spend much of their time spin waiting. Figure 8 shows a bottom-up view of the lock waiting metrics for an execution of HEALTH. The absolute lock wait metric shows threads in HEALTH spent roughly 75% of their total execution time waiting for locks. As described in Section 3.1.2,

Figure 8: Bottom up view of HEALTH benchmark showing lock contention in the GOMP library.

blame for lock waiting gets attributed to the context where the lock holder releases the lock. Figure 8 shows blame being attributed up call paths from lock release to contexts where the lock was released.

The highly contended locks are released on line 201 of `GOMP_task` and line 348 of `GOMP_taskwait`. Locks released at these points account for significant waiting—roughly 41% and 33% of the thread execution time respectively. The OpenMP task `sim_village_par._omp_fn_2` is the common caller of `GOMP_task` and `GOMP_taskwait`, where lock contention leads to significant waiting. The lock release highlighted in the source code pane shows the problematic lock—`task_lock`. Note that `task_lock` is used in the GOMP library, not the user's code. `task_lock` is the lock used to manipulate the task queue created in a parallel region. It causes excessive contention in `sim_village_par._omp_fn_2`, as this routine recursively spawns 17 million tiny tasks and all threads contend for the lock to access the task queue. The `task_lock` used by `sim_village_main_par._omp_fn.1` causes little contention, so there is no need to optimize this parallel region. The best way to reduce contention for the task queue inside `sim_village_par._omp_fn_2` is to reduce the number of tasks by increasing task granularity. Another version of the program achieves this objective by using a cutoff to stop spawning tasks once granularity falls below a threshold. This improvement reduced program execution time by 82%, which is consistent with what our lock waiting measurements predicted.

6. CONCLUSIONS & ONGOING WORK

This paper proposes mechanisms to support low-overhead, sampling-based performance analysis of OpenMP programs. We demonstrate that an implementation of these techniques in HPCToolkit provides deep insight into the performance of threaded program executions by measuring and attributing informative metrics including idleness, work, overhead, and lock waiting. Our OpenMP profiler employs online deferred context resolution to efficiently and accurately attribute these metrics to full calling contexts in compact profiles, avoiding the space overhead of traces required by prior tools. Reducing the space overhead is an important aspect of our strategy that will enable it to scale to large parallel systems. The case studies reported in this paper validate the effectiveness and low overhead of our approach. Table 2 indicates the problems we identified using our tool in each of the application benchmarks, summarizes the optimizations we applied to improve each program, and shows the percent improvement that we achieved.

app	problem	optimization	improvement
AMG2006	high idleness in parallel regions	use dynamic scheduling to eliminate load imbalance	11%
LULESH	high idleness caused by a sequential routine `free`	use Google's tcmalloc threaded allocator	75%
BT-MZ	high idleness caused by frequent thread creation and exit in nested parallel regions	eliminate unnecessary inner parallel regions	8%
HEALTH	high lock contention for the task queue in OpenMP runtime	coarsen the task granularity	82%

Table 2: Summary of performance bottlenecks identified using our tool and our code optimizations in response.

We are presently working with the OpenMP standards committee to define a standard tools API for OpenMP. The emerging interface developed with the committee provides full support for our blame shifting approach. This includes interfaces that enable us to attribute performance metrics to full calling contexts as well as to pinpoint and quantify root causes of thread idleness and lock waiting. The new tools API provides support sufficient for analysis of both statically and dynamically linked applications. IBM has added support for a draft of this interface to a new lightweight OpenMP runtime system for their XL compilers for Blue Gene/Q. An implementation of HPCToolkit employs this draft interface to measure OpenMP programs executed by this runtime.

In the future, we plan to generalize our approach for deferred context resolution to support assembly of global view call path profiles on a heterogeneous system that offloads computation from a host node populated with conventional multicore chips to attached manycore accelerators, such as Intel MIC chips.

Acknowledgments

We thank Laksono Adhianto and Mark Krentel for their contributions to HPCToolkit. Without their efforts, this work would not have been possible. We thank Alexandre Eichenberger for his enthusiastic collaboration on the emerging OMPT OpenMP tools API. This research was supported in part by the DOE Office of Science under cooperative agreement number DE-FC02-07ER25800, by Sandia National Laboratories under purchase order 1293383, and Lawrence Livermore National Laboratory under subcontract B602160.

7. REFERENCES

[1] L. Adhianto, S. Banerjee, M. Fagan, M. Krentel, G. Marin, J. Mellor-Crummey, and N. R. Tallent. HPCToolkit: Tools for performance analysis of optimized parallel programs. *Concurrency and Computation: Practice and Experience*, 22:685–701, 2010.

[2] E. Ayguadé et al. The design of OpenMP tasks. *IEEE Trans. Parallel Distrib. Syst.*, 20(3):404–418, Mar. 2009.

[3] I.-H. Chung. IBM high performance toolkit, 2008. `https://computing.llnl.gov/tutorials/IBM.HPC.Toolkit.Chung.pdf`.

[4] Cray Inc. Using Cray performance analysis tools, April 2011. Document S-2376-52, `http://docs.cray.com/books/S-2376-52/S-2376-52.pdf`.

[5] S. R. Das and R. M. Fujimoto. A performance study of the cancelback protocol for time warp. *SIGSIM Simul. Dig.*, 23(1):135–142, July 1993.

[6] Free Software Foundation. GOMP—an OpenMP implementation for GCC. `http://gcc.gnu.org/projects/gomp`, 2012.

[7] K. Fürlinger and M. Gerndt. ompP: A profiling tool for OpenMP. In *Proc. of the First and Second International Workshops on OpenMP*, pages 15–23, Eugene, Oregon, USA, May 2005. LNCS 4315.

[8] Google Inc. TCMalloc: Thread-Caching Malloc. `http://goog-perftools.sourceforge.net/doc/tcmalloc.html`. Last accessed April 3, 2013.

[9] Intel. Intel VTune Amplifier XE . `http://software.intel.com/en-us/articles/intel-vtune-amplifier-xe`, July, 2012.

[10] M. Itzkowitz, O. Mazurov, N. Copty, and Y. Lin. An OpenMP runtime API for profiling. `http://www.compunity.org/futures/omp-api.html`.

[11] H. Jin and R. F. V. der Wijngaart. Performance characteristics of the multi-zone NAS parallel benchmarks. *J. Parallel Distrib. Comput.*, 66(5):674–685, May 2006.

[12] Lawrence Livermore National Laboratory. Livermore Unstructured Lagrangian Explicit Shock Hydrodynamics (LULESH). `https://computation.llnl.gov/casc/ShockHydro`. Last accessed April 3, 2013.

[13] Lawrence Livermore National Laboratory. ASC Sequoia Benchmark Codes. `https://asc.llnl.gov/sequoia/benchmarks`, 2012.

[14] B. Mohr, A. D. Malony, S. Shende, and F. Wolf. Design and prototype of a performance tool interface for OpenMP. *The Journal of Supercomputing*, 23:105–128, 2002.

[15] OpenMP Architecture Review Board. OpenMP application program interface, version 3.0. `http://www.openmp.org/mp-documents/spec30.pdf`, May 2008.

[16] Oracle. Oracle Solaris Studio. `http://www.oracle.com/technetwork/server-storage/solarisstudio/overview/index.html`.

[17] M. Schulz et al. OpenSpeedShop: An open source infrastructure for parallel performance analysis. *Scientific Programming*, 16(2-3):105–121, Apr. 2008.

[18] S. Shende and A. D. Malony. The TAU parallel performance system. *International Journal of High Performance Computing Applications, ACTS Collection Special Issue*, 2005.

[19] N. R. Tallent and J. Mellor-Crummey. Effective performance measurement and analysis of multithreaded applications. In *Proc. of the 14th ACM SIGPLAN Symposium on Principles and Practice of Parallel Programming*, pages 229–240, New York, NY, USA, 2009. ACM.

[20] N. R. Tallent, J. Mellor-Crummey, and M. W. Fagan. Binary analysis for measurement and attribution of program performance. In *Proc. of the 2009 ACM SIGPLAN Conf on Programming Language Design and Implementation*, pages 441–452, New York, NY, USA, 2009. ACM.

[21] N. R. Tallent, J. Mellor-Crummey, and A. Porterfield. Analyzing lock contention in multithreaded applications. In *Proc. of the 15th ACM SIGPLAN Symposium on Principles and Practice of Parallel Programming*, 2010.

[22] The Portland Group. PGPROF Profiler Guide Parallel Profiling for Scientists and Engineers. `http://www.pgroup.com/doc/pgprofug.pdf`, 2011.

[23] R. van der Pas. OpenMP Support in Sun Studio. `https://iwomp.zih.tu-dresden.de/downloads/3.OpenMP_Sun_Studio.pdf`, 2009.

[24] F. Wolf et al. Usage of the SCALASCA toolset for scalable performance analysis of large-scale parallel applications. In *Tools for High Performance Computing*, pages 157–167. Springer Berlin Heidelberg, 2008.

Conservative Row Activation to Improve Memory Power Efficiency

Kun Fang
Dept. of ECE
University of Illinois at Chicago
Chicago, USA
kfang2@uic.edu

Zhichun Zhu
Dept. of ECE
University of Illinois at Chicago
Chicago, USA
zzhu@uic.edu

ABSTRACT

With the fast improvement on memory bandwidth and capacity, the memory power consumption has become a major contributor to the overall system power profile. Due to the increasing importance of memory-level parallelism at the multi-core era, most memory scheduling schemes eagerly exploit such parallelism to optimize performance. A common policy used by memory controllers today is, whenever possible, always trying to open memory banks for pending requests to maximize bank-level parallelism and throughput. However, we find that this is neither power optimal nor necessary for maintaining performance because usually many banks are open while waiting for the data bus ownership.

To address this issue, we propose a "Conservative Row Activation" scheme that delays the row activation operation of a request to an idle rank until its corresponding column access will not be blocked by the busy data bus. This can reduce the memory power with negligible performance impact by allowing a rank to stay at the low-power mode longer. To minimize performance impact, our scheme monitors the data bus transactions and reserves bus slots for column commands at the earliest possible time. The detailed simulation results indicate that our scheme can reduce the memory power consumption of a group of quad-core multiprogramming memory-intensive workloads with SPEC2006 applications by 5.6% on average. It may even improve the performance slightly (by 0.3% on average), because the data bus utilization can be improved by giving column accesses higher priority than other commands.

Categories and Subject Descriptors

B.3.1 [**Hardware**]: MEMORY STRUCTURES—*DRAM*; C.1 [**Computer Systems Organization**]: Multiple Data Stream Architectures (Multiprocessors)

Keywords

Multi-core processor; Memory access scheduling; Power optimization

1. INTRODUCTION

In recent years, the memory bandwidth and capacity has been improved steadily to meet the user demands on higher bandwidth and larger capacity. A negative side-effect is the continuous increase on memory power consumption, which has become a first-order design consideration for memory systems. In this study, we propose a new scheme to reduce memory power consumption with negligible performance impact.

As we enter the era of multi-core systems, memory-level parallelism has become a very important performance factor. This is because multiple concurrently running processes generate multiple memory access streams and they tend to destroy locality appeared at the memory side. To support multiple concurrent requests, a typical memory system has multiple ranks and banks, which can serve requests in parallel. The memory controller will schedule device and bus transactions for those concurrent requests to meet timing constraints and avoid resource contentions. A common strategy used by today's controllers is, whenever possible, always trying to open a memory bank for a pending request to maximize bank-level parallelism and thus throughput. However, we find that this is neither power optimal nor necessary for maintaining good performance. Since memory requests tend to cluster together, it is common that several banks are open but most of them are just stay idle, waiting for the data bus to become free. That wastes unnecessary power and contributes little to extra performance.

Figure 1 shows an example of two concurrent read requests going to two banks in different ranks. Each request has an activation command followed by a column access command. Once an activation command is sent out, after a delay of tRCD, the corresponding rank enters the active state, the bank is open, and the row containing the required data is fetched to the row buffer. The first request (mapped to Rank0 in the example) can immediately issue its column access command once its bank is open because the data bus is free at that time. However, the second request (mapped to Rank1 in the example) has to wait three more bus cycles for the data bus becoming free after its bank is open and ready to serve column accesses. This is because the data bus is shared among all the ranks connected to a channel and can only serve one data transfer at a time. The extra three cycles of Rank1 in the high-power, active state is not necessary for delivering the maximal performance. If the activation of Rank1 is delayed by three cycles as shown in Figure 2, the second request can issue its column access command right after a delay of tRCD once its activation command is issued,

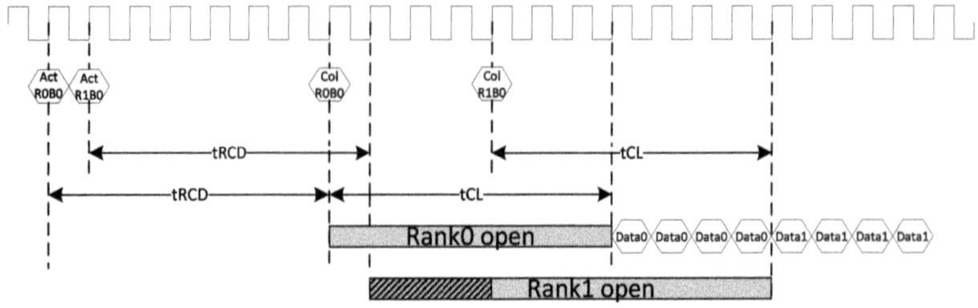

Figure 1: Conventional timing diagram of two concurrent requests going to different ranks. (The shaded bar represents the wasted cycles due to data bus contention.)

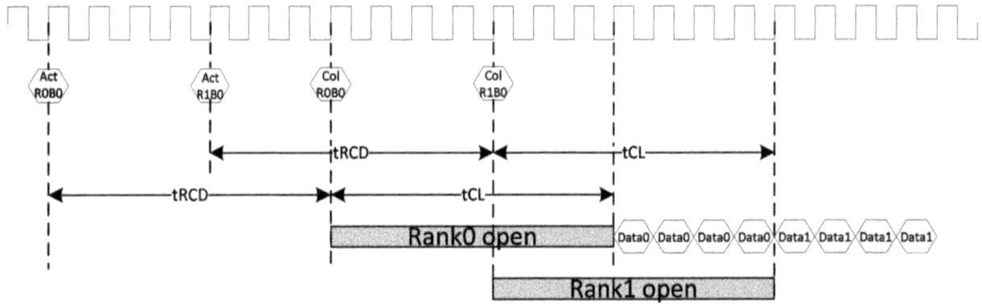

Figure 2: Timing diagram of Conservative Row Activation for two concurrent requests going to different ranks.

and there are no cycles for Rank1 to be wasted in the high-power, active state. This example shows delaying bank/row activation until its corresponding column access not being blocked by the busy data bus can reduce the time that a rank stays at the high-power, active state to save memory power without compromising performance.

There are two questions to be answered before the idea of delaying row activation can be applied in real systems to improve memory power efficiency. The first one is whether the optimal delay time of a row activation can be determined efficiently. The answer to this question is yes. Because the memory controller knows the status and timing of each bank and each pending request, and it also knows when the command and data buses become free. Thus, for a given request, the controller knows the earliest time that the column access command can be sent out. It can use that information to calculate backward the latest time when the row activation command should be sent out, since the row activation and column access commands must be separated by at least a time of tRCD.

The second question is whether it happens frequently in real systems that several banks are open but idle waiting for data bus becoming free. We further verify with experiments that such situation does happen frequently in real systems. We collect the statistics of the number of cycles that a bank is in active state but cannot issue its column command because the data bus is not free. Then we calculate the metric of "possibility that a bank open but waiting for free data bus". The metric can give us an idea of how often that a bank stays at the unnecessary open state wasting energy. For instance, we find out that for a memory-intensive workload consisting of SPEC2006 applications *lbm*, *gemsFDTD*, *leslie3d* and *libquantum*, the experimental result on a dual-channel configuration with two DIMMs per channel and two ranks per DIMM shows that on average a bank wastes 11.5% of time in active state but waiting for a free data bus to issue column commands. Note that a rank usually contains four or eight banks. So a rank will be more likely to stay at the active state but the data bus is used by other ranks.

Based on those analysis and observations, we propose a "Conservative Row Activation" memory access scheduling scheme to improve memory system power efficiency with minimal performance impact. Instead of activating a bank at the earliest possible time, it activates a bank only when the follow-up column access will not wait for the data bus ownership. The scheme monitors the data bus transactions and reserves bus slots for each pending column command at the earliest possible time. Then the optimal time to issue the corresponding row activation is calculated as tRCD cycles before the column command. In this way, more banks can stay in idle state longer and ranks will get a better chance to stay in the low-power, precharge state to save power. In addition, because the column commands can still be issued almost at the same time as before, the performance impact would be minimal.

We build a detailed memory model and integrate it to the MARSS [24] simulator. Running the quad-core workloads with SPEC2006 [27] benchmark, the experiment indicates that our proposed scheme can effectively improve memory system power efficiency with little performance impact. The memory power is saved by 5.6%, 3.3% and 5.8% on average for MEM, ILP and MIX workloads, respectively (up to 7.0%). The performance is even slightly improved for MEM workloads because our scheme can slightly improve the bus utilization by giving column access commands higher priority than others. The weighted speedup for MEM workloads is improved by 0.3% on average (up to 1.0%). For ILP and MIX workloads, the performance loss is less than 1.0%.

2. BACKGROUND

2.1 DDR SDRAM Memory System

A conventional memory system may consist of a few memory channels. Each channel can operate independently and connect with one to four DIMMs. Each DIMM consists of several DRAM devices that are organized as ranks to serve requests. In desktop and server environment, the data bus in a channel is usually 64-bit wide and is shared by all devices connected to the channel. Using the most widely used x8 devices as an example, eight devices will form a rank to match the bus width and serve memory requests together. For a typical memory system with a last-level cache block size of 64 bytes, the 64-byte data of each cache line filling request will be spread onto eight devices, with each holding 64-bit data.

There are usually four or eight banks in a DRAM device and each has a row buffer. When a row activation command and corresponding row address are received, the row decoder translates the row address and selects a row from the corresponding DRAM bank. Then the contents of the selected row are fetched to the row buffer. When there are valid data in the row buffer, the bank is open to accept subsequent column access requests. A column access command can be issued to an open bank to transfer data to or from the column selected by the column decoder. If data in any row other than the one currently in the row buffer need to be accessed, a precharge command will be issued to the bank, which stores the data in row buffer back to DRAM core. After that, a new set of row activation and column access can be performed. All the read and write operations on DRAM devices are accomplished by scheduling these basic commands.

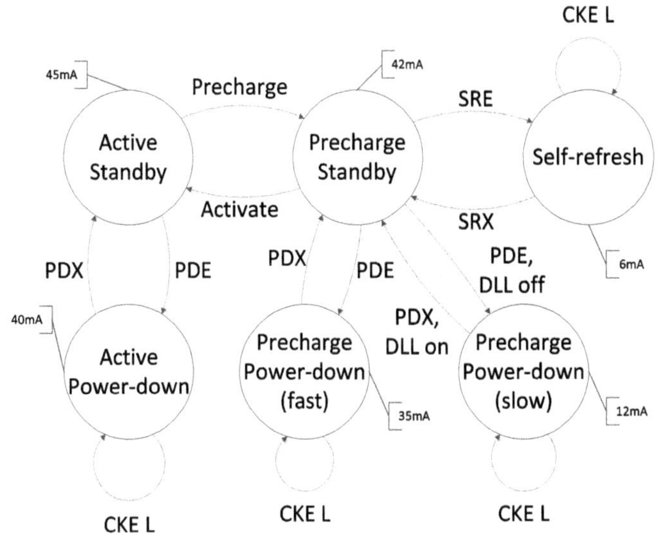

Figure 3: Low power modes for DDR3-1600 memory device and the current under each mode. PDE: Power-Down Enter; PDX: Power-Down eXit; SRE: Self-Refresh Enter; SRX: Self-Refresh eXit.

2.2 DDR SDRAM Power Modes

The DRAM device can enter into several different power modes to reduce its power consumption if there is no access to the device. Figure 3 shows different power modes of a typical DDR SDRAM device and the transition between each mode. When there is one or more banks open in a rank, the rank is in the Active Standby mode. The rank can enter the Active Power-down mode by putting the CKE (clock enable) signal to low. If there is no bank open in a rank, the rank is in the Precharge Standby mode (fast or slow). When only the CKE is put to low, the rank can be put into the Precharge Power-down (fast) mode. If the DLL (delay-locked loop) is also disabled, it will be put into the Precharge Power-down (slow) mode, which consumes less power than the fast mode but requires longer time to return to the standby mode and then serve incoming requests. The rank can also be put into the Self-refresh mode that just performs the periodic refresh operation to maintain the data and consumes the least power. The current value of each mode is also shown in the figure. The data is based on the Micron 2GB DDR3-1600 x8 device [19]. We can see that at the Active/Precharge Standby mode, the current (determine power consumption) is higher than that at the Precharge Power-down fast/slow modes (45/42 mA vs. 35/12 mA). The power mode determines the background power. When the rank is performing an activation or a precharge operation, the operation power is consumed. When the rank is bursting data in/out, the I/O and termination power is consumed. Background power, operation power and I/O and termination power are three sources of power consumed by a rank during normal operations.

3. CONSERVATIVE ROW ACTIVATION

As described in Section 1, conventional memory schedulers usually open a row at the earliest possible time to maximize memory-level parallelism and to minimize memory access latency. However, we find that although such scheduling policy is simple and performance-optimal, it wastes unnecessary energy. For today's memory systems, it is common that several requests are served by the memory system at the same time since multiple threads/applications are running concurrently on the multi-core processors. We find that when there exist multiple concurrent memory requests, some of the row activation operations can be delayed to save memory power without performance penalty.

In a typical desktop/server system with DDRx memory system, the memory bus is eight-byte wide and the block size of the last level cache is 64 bytes. Each cache miss request from the last level cache will fetch 64-byte data in a burst, whose length is eight. Thus, each burst occupy the DDRx data bus for four bus cycles to transfer its data. Because each memory bus/channel can only transfer one burst at a time, all data transfers must be serialized by the bus. In general, the data bus is the performance bottleneck instead of the command/address bus. A typical memory request occupies the data bus for four cycles (with additional cycles for read/write turn-around), while its row activation and column access commands each occupies the command bus for one cycle. Thus, when the row activation commands of two concurrent requests to different banks are sent out back to back, the bank to serve the second request will sit in the open state waiting for the data bus becoming free to perform its column access. Such waiting in the high-power open state is unnecessary. It consumes extra power but contributes little to performance.

To address this issue, we propose a memory scheduling scheme called "**Conservative Row Activation**". It delays the row activation of a pending request until its subsequent column access does not need to wait for the data bus becoming free. This allows memory ranks to stay in the low-power idle state longer to save memory power. At the same time, our scheme tries to avoid delaying column accesses to minimize the performance impact.

3.1 Basic Scheme

Memory system performance should always be considered at the highest priority because it directly affects the overall system performance. Bear this in mind, we propose the "Conservative Row Activation" memory scheduling scheme to save memory power with minimal performance impact. To maximize the rank idle time for memory power saving, our scheme delays the row activation command as late as possible. However, a row has to be opened for column access to get the data transferred. Moreover, a column cannot be immediately read from or written to after the row activation command, a delay of tRCD (row access to column access delay) must be expired between the row activation and its column access. Thus, to minimize the performance impact, our scheme should avoid delaying the column access when the row access is delayed. In order to achieve the goal, our scheme would carefully calculate and then schedule the row command so that a bank will be opened at the latest time without delaying the column command.

for *Every memory cycle at best available bank* **do**
    if *This cycle is reserved* **then**
        Issue the column command;
    else
        if *Bank Idle* **then**
            Check timing for activation and column access at tRCD memory cycles later;
            if Success then: Reserve cmd bus for column access at tRCD memory cycles later AND Issue activation for this bank;
        else
            Check timing for column access at tRCD memory cycles later for row hits;
            And reserve bus slots if available;
end

Algorithm 1: Conservative Row Activation algorithm.

Algorithm 1 describes the scheduling of row activation and column access demands by our proposed scheme. The basic idea is to look ahead for data bus availability and reserve the time slot on the bus for a pending column access. Once the time slot of the column access is determined, the timing of its associated row activation can be calculated using the value of tRCD, and the activation command can be scheduled accordingly. When a pending request goes to a bank, whether an activation can be issued must satisfy the following constraint: *Its column command can be issued immediately after the bank enters the open state.*

To ensure this, the scheduler looks ahead for tRCD memory cycles and tries to reserve command bus slots for the column command first. If there is no timing conflicts, the memory controller will mark the command bus for this request's column access at tRCD cycles in the future and issue the row activation at this cycle. Otherwise, the row activation will not be issued now, and such procedure will repeat the next cycle. In this way, most of the banks can be put at idle state and let the rank enter precharge standby low-power mode to save memory power. For row-buffer hits, the memory controller will also look ahead for tRCD memory cycles and reserve the slot for its column access. This is because the looking ahead and reserving scheme implicitly prioritizes reserved column accesses. The row-buffer hits

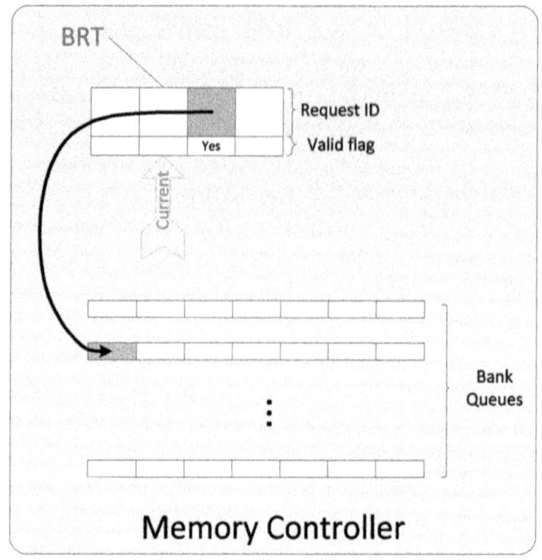

Figure 4: BRT and bank queues in memory controller. The reserved BRT entry will point to the request in bank queue.

should be given the same privilege to acquire the data bus as the row-buffer misses; otherwise, they will be starved.

To avoid modification on the memory device and DDR command and also ensure the correctness of memory access scheduling, a reserved column access must be issued at its designated cycle and cannot be issued on any other time. Thus, at each memory cycle, the memory controller will first check if the current cycle is reserved for any column access. If so, the reserved column command is issued. Otherwise, this cycle can be used to test a new activation and make reservation for its column command.

3.2 Implementation

The hardware implementation of our scheme in the memory controller is simple. An array called "Bus Reservation Table" (BRT) is added for each memory channel to record the reserved command bus slots for pending column accesses. The data bus reservation does not need to be recorded because the timing of a data bus transfer is determined once its corresponding column access command is issued. For DDRx memory devices, once a column access command is issued, depending on whether the request is a read or a write, after a delay of tRL (column command to read data delay) or tWL (column command to write data delay) cycles, the data bus will be occupied for four memory cycles by the request.

Each entry of the BRT (Bus Reservation Table) will record a request ID for whom the time slot has been reserved. It also contains a valid bit to tell the memory controller if the entry is a valid reserve or the entry should be ignored. The BRT is referenced as a circular queue and a pointer is used to indicate which entry of BRT stands for the current cycle. The pointer will increase by one every memory cycle, and it will be wrapped around and pointing to the BRT head when reaching the tail of BRT.

Figure 4 shows the structure of the BRT and the bank queues in the memory controller. The bank queues are structures in the memory controller that buffer and schedule requests for each bank. As the simple example shown in the figure, a BRT slot is reserved for a column access (its associated activation has already been served). The *current* pointer points to one slot ahead of the reserved slot, which

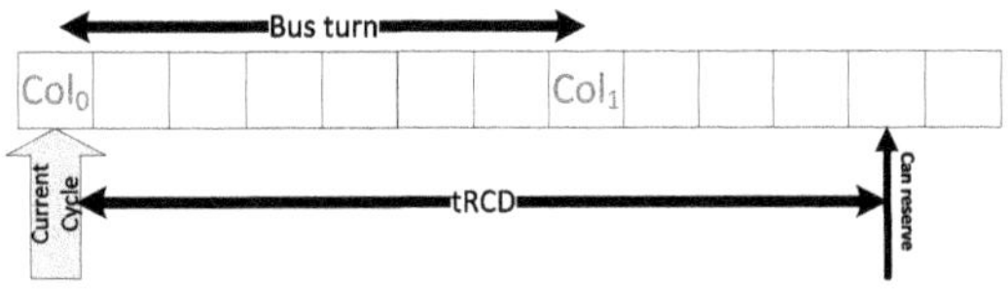

Figure 5: An example of row and column command conflicts at the same cycle.

means a column access is reserved for the next memory cycle. Then at the next memory cycle, the *current* pointer will point to the reserved entry. The valid flag is set for the entry. Thus, the entry is valid and the Request ID field will tell the memory controller to find the corresponding request in the memory bank queues and issue corresponding command for it.

3.3 Hardware Overhead

As discussed in Section 3.2, the additional hardware to support the Conservative Row Activation scheme is BRT. Every time when a reservation is made, the memory controller will look ahead for tRCD cycles and try to reserve a command bus slot there. So the minimum number of entries for BRT is tRCD + 1 (11 + 1 for DDR3-1600 memory device). The maximum number of entries should depend on how many slots that it would like to reserve in the future. Because the memory controller can update the BRT on every memory cycle, there is no need to reserve more than two requests. Given that each request is separated by four or five cycles if they satisfy the requirement stated in Section 3.1, the maximum number of BRT entries is 32. The valid flag will need one bit. The Request ID can either be the request number if the memory controller has a central facility to keep tracking every pending memory requests or the rank and bank index of each request otherwise. Considering a typical memory system today, the estimated size of one BRT entry is no more than six bits. So the total size of BRT per channel would be 192 bits.

The memory controller should remember the reserved requests so that it will not reschedule a reserved request. A rescheduling may change the bank state and waste the reserved time slot. Thus, we propose to add a one-bit "reserved" flag for each entry of the bank queues. The additional storage overhead will be within several hundred bits depending on the size of the bank queues for a memory controller implementation. In summary, the hardware cost to implement our scheduling algorithm is trivial.

3.4 Improvements from Basic Scheme

The basic Conservative Row Activation scheme is simple but strictly requires a column access be immediately scheduled after its bank is open, which sometimes introduces conflicts on command bus and thus decreases the command bus utilization and performance. Figure 5 shows a simple example of conflicts on the command bus.

As shown in the figure, Col_0 and Col_1 are previously reserved command bus slots for column accesses to Bank 0 and Bank 1, respectively. Col_0 and Col_1 are at the turning point from a read burst to a write burst. Due to bus turnaround delay, they are apart by seven memory cycles. The closest next available time slot for a new column access is at Cycle 11. However, the cycle cannot be reserved for a new column access because that would require an activation to be issued at the current cycle to open the row. However, the current cycle has already been reserved for the column access to Bank 0. As a result, the memory controller will choose to issue the column command for Bank 0 and delay the activation for the new request to the next cycle, and reserve Cycle 12 for its column access. There will be a bubble on the data bus, which reduces the data bus utilization. The schedule of DRAM commands is very dynamic and complex. There will be many cases that commands may conflict with each other and cause bubbles on the data bus. This will reduce memory system performance.

To resolve the problem, we modify the original scheme and relax a little bit on the constraint stated in Section 3.1 to: *The column command can be issued immediately or one memory cycle after the bank enters the open state.*

The relaxed rule allows a bank to stay in the open state for one more memory cycle. The modification gives the activation command a two-memory-cycle window to minimize the performance loss. Choosing a window wider than two memory cycles may further reduce command bus conflicts. However, that will reduce memory power saving and complicate the scheduling algorithm. From experiments, we find that the two-cycle window is a good design choice.

Another optimization is done to further reduce memory power. The scheme saves memory power mainly by reducing the time that each rank stays at the active state. If requests are spread across several ranks, it is better to schedule requests in the same rank together and then go to the next rank instead of jumping across ranks frequently. Thus, our revised scheme will give higher priority to requests going to the current rank than those to different ranks.

```
for Every memory cycle at best available bank in the
same rank; Then different rank do
    if This cycle is reserved then
        Issue the column command;
    else
        if Bank Idle then
            Check timing for activation and column
            access at tRCD memory cycles later;
            (Relax 1 memory cycle if fails);
            if Success then: Reserve cmd bus and data
            bus for column access at tRCD memory
            cycles later AND Issue activation for this
            bank;
        else
            Check timing for column access at tRCD
            memory cycles later for row hits;
            And reserve bus slots if available;
end
```

Algorithm 2: Modified Conservative Row Activation algorithm that allows a two-cycle window for activation command to avoid timing conflict.

Algorithm 2 shows the improved Conservative Row Activation scheme. Compared with the basic scheme, the revised one can improve the data bus utilization and thus memory performance. The side effect is that a rank may stay in the high-power open state slightly longer.

We also want to point out that our scheme works on a page policy that auto-precharge a row if there is no pending request on it. It is also the most widely used page policies in today's computer systems. With multi-core processors, the locality among memory access streams is much lower than

Table 1: Major simulation parameters.

Parameter	Value
Processor	4core, 3.2GHz, 4-issue per core, 14-stage pipeline
Functional units	2 IntALU, 4 LSU, 2 FPALU,
IQ, ROB and LSQ size	IQ 32, ROB 128, LQ 48, SQ 44
Physical register num	128 Int, 128 FP, 128 BR, 128 ST
Branch prediction	Combined, 6k bimodal + 6k two level, 1K RAS, 4k-entry and 4-way BTB
L1 caches (per core)	64KB Inst/64KB Data, 2-way, 16B line, hit latency: 3-cycle Inst/3-cycle Data
L2 cache (shared)	4MB, 8-way, 64B line, 13-cycle hit latency
Memory	2 channels, 2 DIMMs/channel, 2 ranks/DIMM, 8 banks/rank
Memory controller	64-entry buffer, 15ns overhead
DDR3 DRAM latency	DDR3-1600:11-11-11: precharge/ row access/ column access: 13.75ns

that with a single memory access stream. The page policy we use tends to perform better than open page policy.

For the open page policy, it lets the bank stay in active state until it must be precharged to serve a conflict memory request, our scheme would have smaller impact on memory power and performance because memory ranks will have little chance to be at precharge low-power state.

4. EXPERIMENTAL METHODOLOGIES

We have built a detailed DDR3 DRAM memory model and integrated it into MARSSx86 [24] simulator. The simulator is capable of keeping track of each request and the state of every memory channel, rank and bank. The simulated memory controller will issue commands according to the current memory status and pending requests. The memory transactions are pipelined whenever possible. Also the XOR-based mapping [30] is used. Table 1 shows the major simulation parameters.

4.1 Memory Power Calculation and Performance Metrics

We follow the Micron power calculation methodology [19] to estimate the power consumption of DDR3 DRAM devices. At the end of every memory cycle, the energy consumption of the current cycle is calculated based on the state of each device, and the result is recorded and accumulated. The parameters used for calculating the DRAM power are listed in Table 2. For cases that the electrical current values presented in data-sheet are from the maximum device voltage, they are de-rated by the normal voltage[19].

The performance is characterized using weighted speedup [26] $\sum_{i=1}^{n}(IPC_{multi}[i]/IPC_{single}[i])$, where n is the total number of applications running, $IPC_{multi}[i]$ is the IPC value of the application running with other instances and $IPC_{single}[i]$ is the IPC value of the same application running alone.

4.2 Workloads

Our experiments simulate a quad-core x86-64 system with Linux 2.6.31.4 (64-bit) running on it. We use applications from SPEC2006 [27] benchmarks to form quad-core multi-programming workloads for evaluation and pin each application in a workload to a processor core. We use the same method described in a previous work [13] to group SPEC benchmarks into two categories: MEM (memory-intensive) and ILP (compute-intensive) based on their L2 cache misses per 1000 instructions (L2 MPKI). The MEM applications are those with larger than ten L2 MPKI and the ILP applications are those with smaller than ten L2 MPKI. Table 3 shows fourteen quad-core multi-programming workloads randomly formed based on their categories. The MEM-x workloads contain applications from the MEM group and the ILP-x workloads are from the ILP group. We then pickup two applications from each group to form the MIX-x workloads to simulate workloads with different memory behavior running in the same system.

Table 2: Parameters used for calculating DRAM Power (2GB, x8, DDR3-1600, 11-11-11).

Parameters	Values
Normal voltage	1.5V
Active precharge current	95mA
Precharge power-down standby current (fast)	35mA
Precharge power-down standby current (slow)	12mA
Precharge standby current	42mA
Active power-down standby current	40mA
Active standby current	45mA
Read burst current	180mA
Write burst current	185mA
Burst refresh current	215mA

Table 3: Experimenting Workloads.

Workloads	Applications
MEM-1	lbm,gemsFDTD,leslie3d,libquantum
MEM-2	bwaves,soplex,sphinx3,cactusADM
MEM-3	mcf,perlbench,zeusmp,milc
MEM-4	libquantum,soplex,lbm,milc
ILP-1	gamess,namd,povray,calculix
ILP-2	tonto,gromacs,astar,omnetpp
ILP-3	sjeng,hmmer,gobmk,xalancbmk
ILP-4	gcc,bzip2,namd,gamess
MIX-1	lbm,libquantum,povray,calculix
MIX-2	leslie3d,gemsFDTD,gamess,namd
MIX-3	bwaves,soplex,tonto,astar
MIX-4	sphinx3,cactusADM,gromacs,omnetpp
MIX-5	mcf,perlbench,sjeng,hmmer
MIX-6	zeusmp,milc,gcc,gobmk

We insert a signal at the starting point of every application's main execution phase and let the application run in the fast forwarding mode until the signal is reached and then let the application sleep. When all the applications in a workload reach their signals, all the applications will be waken up and the detailed simulation and statistic collecting will launch for the following 400 million instructions.

5. EXPERIMENTAL RESULTS

We compare our proposed Conservative Row Activation scheduling scheme with a baseline, a modified version of FR-FCFS [25] (First Read, First Come First Serve) scheduler that groups bank hits together and prioritizes reads over writes, to evaluate the performance and power consumption. Our scheme focuses on the bank activation policy and can be applied with other schedulers targeting fairness or QoS. If not specified, all the results are based on the memory configuration of two Channels, two DIMMs per Channel

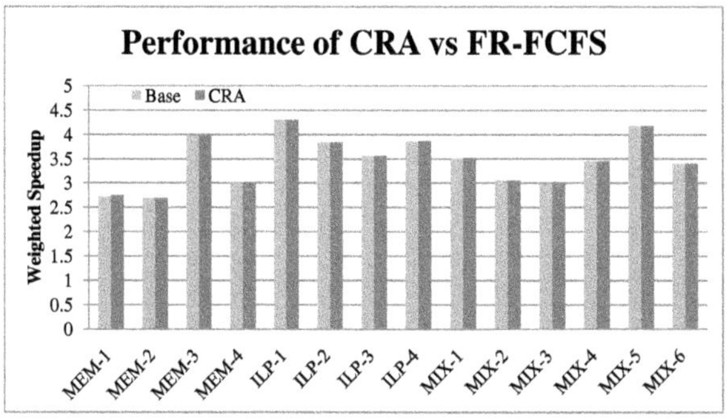

(a) Weighted speedup of Conservative Row Activation compared to baseline.

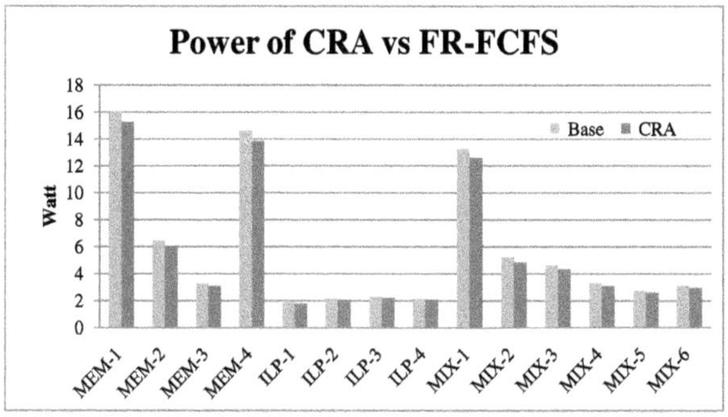

(b) Power consumption of Conservative Row Activation compared to baseline.

Figure 6: Overview of power saving and performance impact of Conservative Row Activation.

and two Ranks per DIMM. We use CRA to stand for our Conservative Row Activation scheme in the figures to reduce title space.

5.1 Overview of Performance and Power Consumption

The proposed scheme can reduce memory power by allowing a rank to stay longer in the precharged state and gives the rank more chances to be put into the low-power mode. Figure 6 compares the performance and memory power consumption of our Conservative Row Activation scheme and the baseline FR-FCFS scheme. From Figure 6a, we can see that in general, the proposed scheme achieves the same performance as the baseline. For MEM workloads, the scheme improves performance by 0.3% on average. Especially for MEM-1, which is the most memory-intensive workload, our scheme outperforms the baseline by 1.0%. For CPU-intensive workloads, our scheme and the baseline almost performs the same. The performance difference is less than 0.09% (our scheme is slightly better). For MIX workloads, we find that for three of them (MIX-2, MIX-4 and MIX-5), our scheme performs worse than baseline. But the difference is negligible (less than 0.02%). This result shows that our scheduling scheme can retain the performance effectively. This is because although the activation is delayed, the scheme looked into the future to place column commands wisely and the latency of a request is determined by when its column access is performed not when its row activation is performed. This mechanism does not change the baseline scheduling sequence of data transfer hence the performance is kept the same.

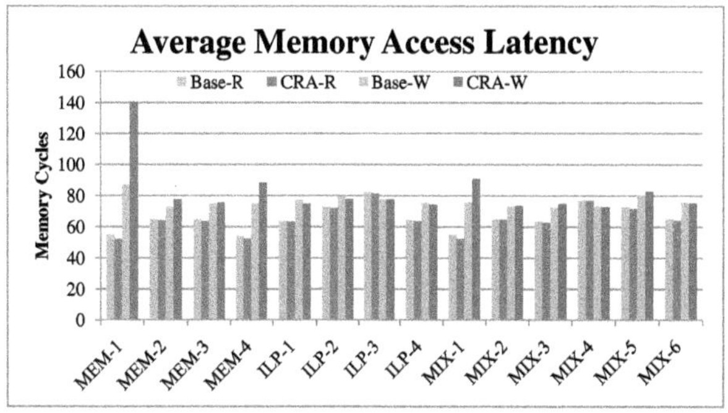

Figure 8: Memory read and write latency for Conservative Row Activation compared to baseline.

Figure 6b shows the memory power consumption of our scheme and the baseline. The average power reduction of using our scheme is 5.6%, 3.3% and 5.8% for MEM, ILP and MIX workloads, respectively. For ILP workloads, the power saving is from 2.1% to 4.1%. This is because for CPU-intensive workloads, the memory traffic is low. The ranks are in the low-power mode for most of the time. Their power consumption ranges from 1.8W to 2.3W, which is far less than that of memory-intensive workloads (16.1W for MEM-1). When ILP workloads are running, concurrent memory requests are few, and thus the chance of banks open but data bus is not available to transfer data is low. Thus, our scheme only has small impact on ILP workloads. For memory-intensive workloads, the power reductions are from 5.1% to 6.4%. Memory-intensive workloads tend to have more concurrent memory requests. Because conventional memory schedulers tries to open as many banks as possible, the possibility of several banks open but data bus being occupied is much higher. Our scheme can prevent banks open unnecessarily early and avoid consuming unnecessary extra power. MIX workloads have medium memory bandwidth requirement. The memory-intensive applications in them generate request concurrency that tends to open many banks at the same time, while the computation-intensive applications put less stress on the memory system. Our scheme can help saving memory power for the concurrent requests, while the total memory power consumption is less than the pure memory-intensive workloads. As a result, their power saving ratio is slightly higher than MEM workloads (from 4.7% to 7.0%).

5.2 Performance Analysis

To further analyze the performance impact of our scheme, we collect the memory system statistics to get an insight of why our scheme can slightly improve performance. Figure 7 shows the utilization rate of read and write requests on the data bus. As shown in the figure, the scheme can slightly improve the data bus utilization. The biggest improvements are on workloads MEM-1, MEM-4, MIX-1 and MIX-3. The data bus utilization of read and write combined are improved by 0.8%, 0.4%, 0.6% and 0.4%, respectively. The reason behind is that our scheme reserves command and data bus slots in advance, which gives higher priority to column accesses, and the memory scheduler can make a better decision on scheduling bus transactions. In this way,

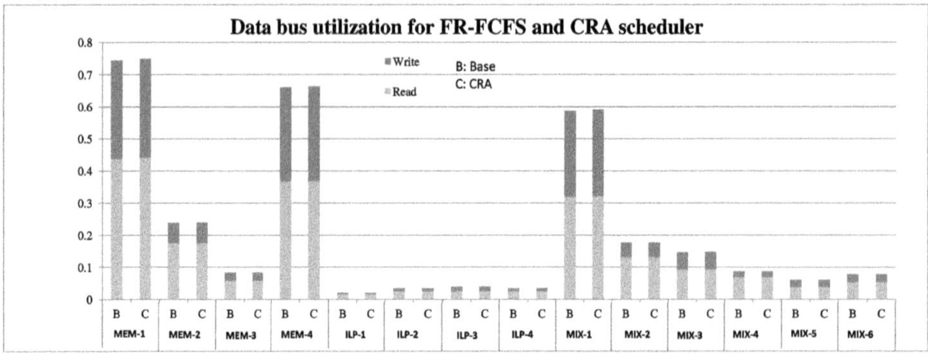

Figure 7: Data bus utilization of Conservative Row Activation compared to baseline.

our scheme can put the data transfers closer to each other and reduce the bubbles on the data bus. For the other workloads, the data bus utilization of our scheme and the baseline is almost the same (the difference is less than 0.1%). The result partly explains why using our scheme performs better than the baseline. Giving higher priority to column accesses can increase the data bus utilization and hence the memory throughput is improved. For memory-intensive workloads, the data bus is the bottleneck. The better the data bus is utilized, the less the CPU will be blocked by outstanding load instructions.

Figure 8 shows the average read and write latency of each workload. We can see that the average read latency is reduced for all of the workloads. For MEM workloads, the read latency is reduced by 2.9% on average. Especially for MEM-1, the most memory-intensive workload, the read latency is reduced by 5.6%. The read requests are on the critical path and directly affect the system performance. The 5.6% of latency reduction leads to the 1.0% of overall performance improvement for this workload. The write latency of some workloads is increased because our proposed algorithm gives column access higher priority than other DRAM commands and it tries to issue all the outstanding reads before writes to minimize bus turn-arounds, which delays writes more. However, since the overall performance only directly depends on read latency, a longer write latency in exchange for a shorter read latency is good for performance. For the other workloads, the change of read and write latency is less obvious. The read latency is reduced by 1.1% and 1.7% for ILP and MIX workloads on average, respectively. For average write latency, the MIX workloads get a 4.1% increase on average, and the ILP workloads have a 1.8% decrease on average. Unlike MEM workloads, ILP workloads have lower memory bandwidth. Our scheme can place the transactions on data bus more compactly and thus both the read and write latency can be reduced for those workloads.

5.3 Power Analysis

We will study the source of power saving of our Conservative Row Activation scheme in this section. Figure 9 breaks down the power consumption of our experiments into three parts as in Micron DDR3 power calculator [19] and as discussed in Section 2:

1. Background power.
2. Operation power.
3. I/O and termination power.

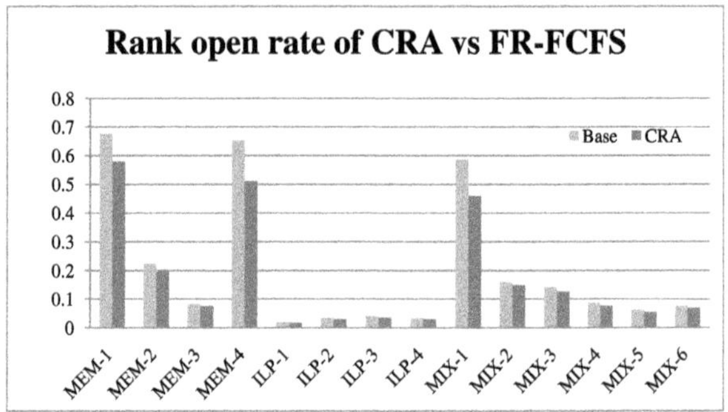

Figure 10: Percentage of average rank active time of Conservative Row Activation compared to baseline.

The figure shows that the major power saving comes from reduction on background power. When using our scheme, the background power dropped by 12.0%, 4.1% and 10.8% on average for MEM, ILP and MIX workloads, respectively. Figure 10 shows the percentage of time that any bank is open in a rank (rank active). If a bank is open, it may transfer data, wait for data bus ownership if another bank is transferring data or wait for DRAM timing constraints (tCL, tRTP, tWR etc) to expire to perform device operation. Our scheme targets the portion of a bank waiting for data bus and tries to minimize it. The result shows that the scheme can reduce the bank open rate by 13.7%, 9.9% and 12.2% on average for MEM, ILP and MIX workloads, respectively. For MEM workloads that have the most memory-intensive applications, the reduction on bank open rate ranges from 8.6% to 21.5%. Thus, the observation of reduction on background power is due to memory ranks staying longer at the precharge low-power state rather than at the active power state. For MEM workloads, the background power can be saved by 9.1% to 13.8%. For ILP workloads, the reduction on bank open rate is small (from 7.9% to 10.9%). This is because for CPU-intensive workloads, the parallel accesses to different memory banks are small. So the reduction on background power is also small (from 2.3% to 5.3%). The power consumption of MIX workloads is between that of the MEM and ILP workloads. The improvement of background power ranges from 6.5% to 14.0% because of the drop of bank open rate ranging from 6.1% to 21.6%.

For operation power, I/O power and termination power, because our scheme does not change the underlying sched-

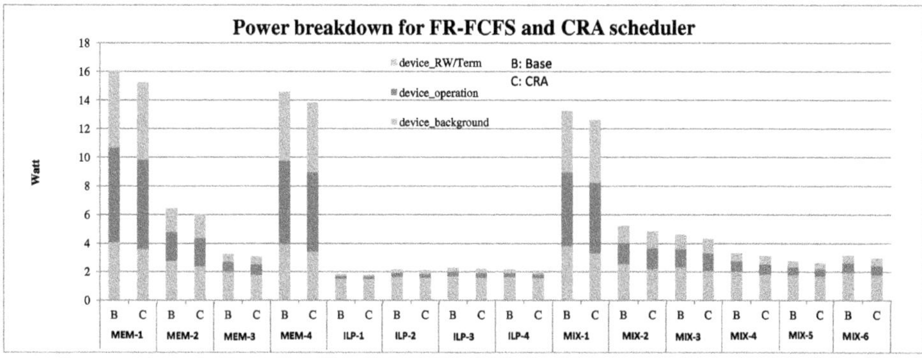

Figure 9: Power breakdown of Conservative Row Activation compared to baseline.

uler, their changes are small. The average difference on I/O and termination power for MEM, ILP and MIX workloads is less than 0.5%. Compared to the baseline, our scheme reduces the operation power by 3.3%, 1.7% and 1.7% for MEM, ILP and MIX workloads on average, respectively. This is due to the slight difference of power consumed by activating the first idle bank and the rest of the idle banks. Our scheme allows more banks to stay at the idle state and will increase the chance of activating a first idle bank in a rank.

6. RELATED WORK

Many studies have been focused on how to utilize low power modes of DRAM. Lebeck et al. proposed power-aware page allocation policy to increase the chance of DRAM chips to be put in low-power modes [15]. Delaluz et al. proposed software and hardware approaches and OS scheduling methods to reduce memory power [3]. Fan et al. studied control policies for memory power [6, 7]. Huang et al. proposed a virtual memory scheme to manage memory power [9] and maximized the chip low-power time by dealing with memory traffic [10]. Li et al. proposed performance guaranteed low-power management schemes [16]. Pandey et al. extended the memory power management aspect by considering DMA access behaviors [23]. Hur and Lin studied power saving potential of memory scheduling and memory power control schemes via throttling [11]. Diniz et al. proposed algorithms to reduce Rambus DRAM power by dynamically adjusting chip power states [4].

There are also studies proposed to modify memory system architecture or management policies to reduce memory power. For instance, Zheng et al. proposed a mini-rank architecture that reduces memory operation power and background power by activating fewer devices for each memory request [31]. Ahn et al. proposed Multi-core DIMM used the rank subset concept with split data bus to reduce the memory power [1]. Udipi et al. proposed to split the DRAM row buffer to reduce memory power consumption via less operation power [28], which will require significant change of commercial device. Mrinmoy et al. studied refreshment algorithms to reduce memory refresh power [8]. Kaseridis et al. proposed DRAM page policy that sets the target of page hit number and schedules memory requests accordingly [12] to optimize page open time and reduce activation power. Several other studies focusing on using low-power DRAM to build low-power memory systems [29, 17]. Our work differs from the above studies by focusing on the scheduling of row and column accesses to reduce the DRAM background power while not hurting the performance.

There have also been many other studies on memory scheduling algorithms. Mckee et al. proposed to reorder memory requests [18] to reduce memory read latency. Rixner et al. proposed the FR-FCFS scheduler [25] to improve memory throughput. Nesbit et al. used fair queueing to schedule memory requests for fairness and QoS [22]. STFM [20] estimated the slowdown of each thread and prioritizes the thread that had been slowed down the most. PAR-BS [21] formed a batch of requests for threads and prioritized the one with fewest requests for performance purpose. The ATLAS scheduler [13] aimed to maximize system throughput by prioritizing threads that have attained the least service. TCM [14] partitioned threads in two groups via memory intensiveness and scheduled them to get the optimal fairness and throughput. The Prefetch-Aware memory scheduler [5] identified the prefetch streams and scheduled non-prefetch and accurate prefetches ahead to improve performance. Ausavarungnirun et al. proposed a staged memory scheduler [2] to co-schedule CPU and GPU accesses.

Our scheduling scheme is not for performance, throughput or fairness and can be combined with the above scheduling policies to further optimize power efficiency.

7. CONCLUSION

In this study, we propose a new memory scheduling scheme called "Conservative Row Activation" that delays the row activation of a request for power optimization by allowing a bank to stay at the low-power mode until further delaying the activation would harm performance. It minimizes the performance impact by looking ahead when the bus becoming free and reserving slots on command/data buses for future column commands. Our simulation results indicate that the memory efficiency can be improved with negligible performance impact. This scheme can be implemented on top of many existing memory schedulers with little hardware overhead.

8. ACKNOWLEDGMENTS

We appreciate the anonymous reviewers for helpful comments on this work. The work is supported in part by the US National Science Foundation (NSF) under grant CCF-0954111.

9. REFERENCES

[1] J. H. Ahn, N. P. Jouppi, C. Kozyrakis, J. Leverich, and R. S. Schreiber. Future scaling of processor-memory interfaces. In *Proceedings of the Conference on High Performance Computing Networking, Storage and Analysis*, pages 1–12, New York, NY, USA, 2009.

[2] R. Ausavarungnirun, K. K.-W. Chang, L. Subramanian, G. H. Loh, and O. Mutlu. Staged memory scheduling: achieving high performance and scalability in heterogeneous systems. In *Proceedings of the 39th Annual International Symposium on Computer Architecture*, pages 416–427, 2012.

[3] V. Delaluz, M. Kandemir, N. Vijaykrishnan, A. Sivasubramaniam, and M. J. Irwin. DRAM energy management using software and hardware directed power mode control. In *Proceedings of the 7th International Symposium on High-Performance Computer Architecture*, pages 159–169, 2001.

[4] B. Diniz, D. Guedes, J. Wagner Meira, and R. Bianchini. Limiting the power consumption of main memory. In *Proceedings of the 34th International Symposium on Computer Architecture*, pages 290–301, 2007.

[5] E. Ebrahimi, C. J. Lee, O. Mutlu, and Y. N. Patt. Prefetch-aware shared resource management for multi-core systems. In *Proceedings of the 38th Annual International Symposium on Computer Architecture*, pages 141–152, June 2011.

[6] X. Fan, C. Ellis, and A. Lebeck. Memory controller policies for DRAM power management. In *Proceedings of the 2001 International Symposium on Low Power Electronics and Design*, pages 129–134, 2001.

[7] X. Fan, C. Ellis, and A. Lebeck. Modeling of DRAM power control policies using deterministic and stochastic Petri nets. In *Proceedings of the 2nd international conference on Power-aware computer systems*, pages 130–140, February 2002.

[8] M. Ghosh and H.-H. S. Lee. Smart Refresh: An enhanced memory controller design for reducing energy in conventional and 3D Die-Stacked DRAMs. In *Proceedings of the 40th International Symposium on Microarchitecture*, pages 134–145, Dec. 2007.

[9] H. Huang, P. Pillai, and K. G. Shin. Design and implementation of power-aware virtual memory. In *Proceedings of the USENIX Annual Technical Conference 2003 on USENIX Annual Technical Conference*, pages 57–70, 2003.

[10] H. Huang, K. G. Shin, C. Lefurgy, and T. Keller. Improving energy efficiency by making DRAM less randomly accessed. In *Proceedings of the 2005 International Symposium on Low Power Electronics and Design*, pages 393–398, 2005.

[11] I. Hur and C. Lin. A comprehensive approach to DRAM power management. In *Proceedings of the 13th International Symposium on High-Performance Computer Architecure*, pages 305–316, 2008.

[12] D. Kaseridis, J. Stuecheli, and L. K. John. Minimalist open-page: a DRAM page-mode scheduling policy for the many-core era. In *Proceedings of the 44th Annual IEEE/ACM International Symposium on Microarchitecture*, pages 24–35, 2011.

[13] Y. Kim, D. Han, O. Mutlu, and M. Harchol-balter. ATLAS: A scalable and high-performance scheduling algorithm for multiple memory controllers. In *Proceedings of the 16th International Symposium on High Performance Computer Architecture*, pages 1–12, 2010.

[14] Y. Kim, M. Papamichael, O. Mutlu, and M. Harchol-Balter. Thread cluster memory scheduling: Exploiting differences in memory access behavior. In *Proceedings of the 2010 43rd Annual IEEE/ACM International Symposium on Microarchitecture*, pages 65–76, 2010.

[15] A. R. Lebeck, X. Fan, H. Zeng, and C. Ellis. Power aware page allocation. In *Proceedings of the Ninth International Conference on Architectural Support for Programming Languages and Operating Systems*, pages 105–116, 2000.

[16] X. Li, Z. Li, F. David, P. Zhou, Y. Zhou, S. Adve, and S. Kumar. Performance directed energy management for main memory and disks. In *Proceedings of the 11th International Conference on Architectural Support for Programming Languages and Operating Systems*, pages 271–283, 2004.

[17] K. T. Malladi, F. A. Nothaft, K. Periyathambi, B. C. Lee, C. Kozyrakis, and M. Horowitz. Towards energy-proportional datacenter memory with mobile DRAM. In *Proceedings of the 39th Annual International Symposium on Computer Architecture*, pages 37–48, 2012.

[18] S. A. McKee, W. A. Wulf, J. H. Aylor, M. H. Salinas, R. H. Klenke, S. I. Hong, and D. A. B. Weikle. Dynamic access ordering for streamed computations. *IEEE Trans. Comput.*, 49(11):1255–1271, Nov. 2000.

[19] Micron Technology, Inc. DDR3 SDRAM System-Power Calculator. `http://download.micron.com/downloads/misc/ddr3_power_calc.xls`.

[20] O. Mutlu and T. Moscibroda. Stall-time fair memory access scheduling for chip multiprocessors. In *Proceedings of the 40th International Symposium on Microarchitecture*, pages 146–160, December 2007.

[21] O. Mutlu and T. Moscibroda. Parallelism-aware batch scheduling: Enhancing both performance and fairness of shared DRAM systems. In *Proceedings of the 35th Annual International Symposium on Computer Architecture*, pages 63–74, 2008.

[22] K. J. Nesbit, N. Aggarwal, J. Laudon, and J. E. Smith. Fair queuing CMP memory systems. In *Proceedings of the 39th International Symposium on Microarchitecture*, pages 208–222, Dec. 2006.

[23] V. Pandey, W. Jiang, Y. Zhou, and R. Bianchini. DMA-aware memory energy management. In *Proceedings of the 12th International Symposium on High-Performance Computer Architecture*, pages 133–144, Feb. 2006.

[24] A. Patel, F. Afram, H. Zeng, and K. Ghose. MARSSx86 - micro-architectural and system simulator for x86-based systems. `http://www.marss86.org/index.php/Home`.

[25] S. Rixner, W. J. Dally, U. J. Kapasi, P. Mattson, and J. D. Owens. Memory access scheduling. In *Proceedings of the 27th International Symposium on Computer Architecture*, pages 128–138, June 2000.

[26] A. Snavely, D. M. Tullsen, and G. Voelker. Symbiotic jobscheduling with priorities for a simultaneous multithreading processor. In *Proceedings of the 2002 ACM International Conference on Measurement and Modeling of Computer Systems*, pages 66–76, 2002.

[27] Standard Performance Evaluation Corporation. *SPEC CPU2006*. http://www.spec.org.

[28] A. Udipi, N. Muralimanohar, N. Chatterjee, R. Balasubramonian, A. Davis, and N. Jouppi. Rethinking DRAM design and organization for energy-constrained multi-cores. In *Proceedings of the 37th Annual International Symposium on Computer Architecture*, pages 175–186, 2010.

[29] D. H. Yoon, J. Chang, N. Muralimanohar, and P. Ranganathan. Boom: Enabling mobile memory based low-power server DIMMs. In *Proceedings of the 39th Annual International Symposium on Computer Architecture*, pages 25–36, 2012.

[30] Z. Zhang, Z. Zhu, and X. Zhang. A permutation-based page interleaving scheme to reduce row-buffer conflicts and exploit data locality. In *Proceedings of the 33rd International Symposium on Microarchitecture*, pages 32–41, 2000.

[31] H. Zheng, J. Lin, Z. Zhang, E. Gorbatov, H. David, and Z. Zhu. Mini-rank: Adaptive DRAM architecture for improving memory power efficiency. In *Proceedings of the 41st International Symposium on Microarchitecture*, pages 210–221, November 2008.

Active Disk Meets Flash: A Case for Intelligent SSDs

Sangyeun Cho[1,2] Chanik Park[3] Hyunok Oh[4]
Sungchan Kim[5] Youngmin Yi[6] Gregory R. Ganger[7]

[1]Memory Solutions Lab., Memory Division, Samsung Electronics Co., Korea
[2]Computer Science Department, University of Pittsburgh, USA
[3]Memory Division, Samsung Electronics Co., Korea
[4]Department of Information Systems, Hanyang University, Korea
[5]Division of Computer Science and Engineering, Chonbuk Nat'l University, Korea
[6]School of Electrical and Computer Engineering, University of Seoul, Korea
[7]Department of Electrical and Computer Engineering, Carnegie Mellon University, USA

ABSTRACT

Intelligent solid-state drives (iSSDs) allow execution of limited application functions (e.g., data filtering or aggregation) on their internal hardware resources, exploiting SSD characteristics and trends to provide large and growing performance and energy efficiency benefits. Most notably, internal flash media bandwidth can be significantly (2–4× or more) higher than the external bandwidth with which the SSD is connected to a host system, and the higher internal bandwidth can be exploited within an iSSD. Also, SSD bandwidth is projected to increase rapidly over time, creating a substantial energy cost for streaming of data to an external CPU for processing, which can be avoided via iSSD processing.

This paper makes a case for iSSDs by detailing these trends, quantifying the potential benefits across a range of application activities, describing how SSD architectures could be extended cost-effectively, and demonstrating the concept with measurements of a prototype iSSD running simple data scan functions. Our analyses indicate that, with less than a 2% increase in hardware cost over a traditional SSD, an iSSD can provide 2–4× performance increases and 5–27× energy efficiency gains for a range of data-intensive computations.

Categories and Subject Descriptors

B.4.2 [**Input/Output and Data Communications**]: Input/output devices; C.4 [**Performance of Systems**]: Design studies; C.5.0 [**Computer System Implementation**]: General

General Terms

Design, Experimentation, Performance

Keywords

Data-intensive computing, energy-efficient computing, storage systems

1. INTRODUCTION

A large and growing class of applications process large quantities of data to extract items of interest, identify trends, and produce models of and insights about the data's sources [1,2]. Increasingly, such applications filter large quantities (e.g., TBs) of semi-structured data and then analyze the remainder in more detail. One popular programming model is Google's MapReduce [3] (as embodied in the open source Hadoop system [4]), in which a data-parallel map function is generally used to filter data in a grep-like fashion. Another builds on more traditional database systems and makes extensive use of select and project functions in filtering structured records. A common characteristic is streaming through data, discarding or summarizing most of it after a small amount of processing.

Over a decade ago, research efforts proposed and explored embedding of data-processing functionality within storage or memory components as a way of improving performance for such applications. For example, there were several proposals for so-called "active disks" [5–9], in which limited application functions could be executed on a disk drive's embedded CPU to increase parallelism and reduce reliance on host bandwidth at marginal cost. Also, there were proposals for executing functions on processing elements coupled with memory banks ("active RAM") [10, 11], with similar goals. In developing these ideas, researchers developed prototypes, programming models, and example application demonstrations. Although interesting, few real systems adopted these proposals, for various technical reasons including manufacturing complexity (especially for active RAM proposals) and independent advances that marginalized the benefits (e.g., distributed storage over commodity multi-function servers [12–14], which end up having conceptual similarities to the active disk concept).

The active disk concepts are poised for a comeback, in the context of flash-based SSDs, which are emerging as a viable technology for large-scale use in systems supporting data-intensive computing. Modern and projected future SSDs have characteristics that make them compelling points for embedded data processing that filters/aggregates. In particular, their internal bandwidths often exceed their external bandwidths by factors of 2–4×, and the bandwidth growth over time is expected to be rapid due to increased internal parallelism. Even without the internal-to-external bandwidth multiplier, the rates themselves are sufficiently high that delivering them all the way to a main CPU requires

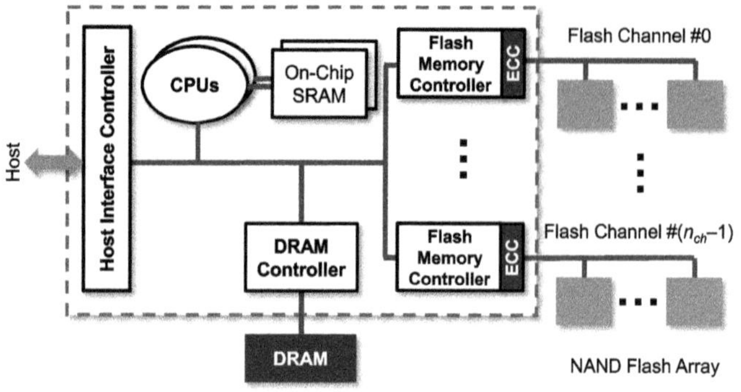

Time frame	Characteristics
2007–2008	4-way, 4 channels, 30–80 MB/s R/W performance; mostly SLC flash based;
2008–2009	8–10 channels, 150–200+ MB/s performance (SATA, consumer); 16+ channels, 600+ MB/s performance (PCI-e, enterprise); use of MLC flash in consumer products;
2009–2010	16+ channels, 200–300+ MB/s performance (SATA 6 Gbps); 20+ channels, 1+ GB/s performance (PCI-e); adoption of MLC in enterprise products;
2010–	16+ channels; wider acceptance of PCI-e;

Figure 1: General architecture of an SSD (left): The dashed box is the boundary of the controller chip. SSD evolution with new host interface standards (right).

substantial energy; filtering most of it near the flash channels would avoid that energy usage.

This paper develops the case for and an architecture for the result, which we refer to as "intelligent SSDs" (iSSDs). We detail the relevant SSD technology characteristics and trends that create the opportunity and discuss their architectural consequences. Combined with analyses of ten data-intensive application kernels, the internal parallelism (via multiple flash memory channels) and bandwidths of modern and future SSDs push for optimized compute elements associated with each flash memory channel. We focus on use of low-power reconfigurable stream processors for this role.

The performance and energy efficiency benefits of iSSDs are substantial. We quantify these benefits and explore the design space via analytical performance and energy models, as well as some demonstration experiments with a prototype iSSD. Compared to the traditional approach of executing the entire application on a primary server CPU, the iSSD approach offers 2–4× higher throughput and 5–27× more energy efficiency. We show that the iSSD approach provides much of this benefit even when compared to alternate approaches to improving efficiency of data-intensive computing, including heterogeneous elements in the server CPU [15] (e.g., GPUs or the same reconfigurable stream processors we envision for iSSDs), reliance on so-called "wimpy" nodes [16], or embedding the processing in the RAM subsystem as in proposals discussed above. All of the bandwidth benefits and half of the energy efficiency can only be achieved by exploiting the SSD-internal bandwidth and avoiding the need to move the data to other components.

2. BACKGROUND AND RELATED WORK

2.1 Active devices for data-intensive computing

The concept of "active devices", in which limited application functionality is executed inside a memory or storage component, has been well-developed over the years. Active disk designs, especially, were motivated and studied extensively. The early proposals laid out the case for exploiting the excess computing cycles of the hard disk drive (HDD) controller's embedded processor for useful data processing, especially filter and aggregation functions. For example, Riedel et al. [9] showed that, by aggregating the bandwidth and computing capabilities of ten (emulated) HDDs, measured performance improves more than 2.2×, 2.2× and 2.8× for workloads like nearest-neighbor search, frequent set mining and image registration, respectively. Substantial benefits have also been demonstrated for a range of other data-intensive workloads, including database scan, select, and aggregation operations, satellite data processing, image processing, and search of complex non-indexed data [5,6,8,17]. Active memory system designs (sometimes called "intelligent RAM") have also been proposed and studied [10,11], allowing simple functions to transform and filter ranges of memory within the memory system without having to move it to the main CPU.

Programming models for active disks were developed and shown to fit such data-parallel processing tasks, addressing both the data delivery and software safety issues; these same models should be suitable for iSSDs. As a representative example, Acharya et al. [5] proposed a stream-based programming framework and the notion of sandboxed "disklets" (disk-resident codes) for processing data ranges as they are made available by the underlying device firmware.

Active devices have not become the norm, for various reasons. In the case of active memories, complex manufacturing issues and memory technology changes arose. In the case of active disks, the demonstrated benefits were primarily from parallelized data-local execution; for many data-intensive computing activities, those benefits have instead been realized by spreading stored data across collections of commodity servers (each with a few disks) and partitioning data processing across those same servers [12–14]. The same approach has been more efficiently implemented with so-called wimpy nodes and low-power CPUs [16], as well. But, we believe that flash-based SSDs have characteristics (e.g., parallel channels and very high internal bandwidths) that make "active-ness" compelling, where it wasn't for these other devices.

There is recent research work studying the impact of adding active-ness to SSDs. Kim et al. [18] accelerate database scan using simple hardware logic within an SSD. Boboila et al. [19] and Tiwari et al. [20] perform data analytics within SSDs in the context of HPC simulation-data analytics pipelines. Like our work, these studies reveal the performance and energy benefits of data processing within SSDs. Our work is unique because we characterize and study general data-intensive kernels, offer a detailed performance and energy modeling framework, give prototyping results using a commercial device, and evaluate architectural trade-offs.

2.2 Architecture and evolution of SSDs

Figure 1 illustrates the general architecture of an SSD and how SSDs have evolved with the introduction of new higher bandwidth host interfaces [21]. Key hardware components in an SSD are the host interface controller, embedded CPU(s),

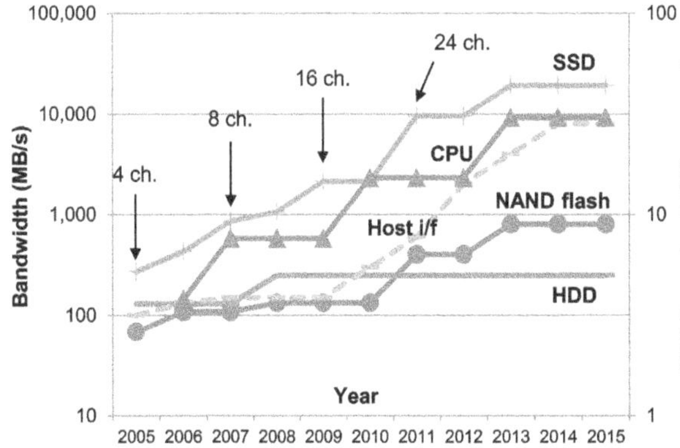

Figure 2: Bandwidth trends of key hardware components.

on-chip SRAM, DRAM and flash memory controllers connected to the flash chips. On top of the hardware substrate runs the SSD firmware commonly referred to as *flash translation layer* (or FTL).

The host interface controller supports a specific bus interface protocol such as SATA, SAS and PCI Express (PCI-e). The host interface bandwidth has steadily increased, from PATA (1.5 Gbps max) to SATA (3 to 6 Gbps) in desktop systems and from SCSI (maxed out at about 5 Gbps) to SAS (about 6 Gbps as of this writing) in enterprise applications. PCI-e has a high bandwidth of 2 to 8 Gbps per lane and shorter latency than other interfaces.

The CPU(s) and SRAM provide the processing engine for running FTL. SRAM stores time-critical data and codes. Typically, the CPU is a 32-bit RISC processor clocked at 200 to 400 MHz. Depending on the application requirements, multiple CPUs are provided to handle host requests and flash management tasks concurrently. DRAM stores user data and FTL metadata, and is operated at 667 MHz or higher.

Flash memory controllers (FMCs) are responsible for data transfer between flash memory and DRAM (or host interface). They also guarantee data integrity based on an error correction code (ECC). As NAND flash memory is continuously scaled down and adopt two-bits- or three-bits-per-cell schemes, the ECC logic has become a dominant part of an SSD controller chip [22]. For high performance, FMCs utilize multi-way interleaving over multiple flash chips on a shared I/O channel as well as multi-channel interleaving.

The NAND flash memory interface has evolved from 40 Mbps single data rate to 400 Mbps double data rate; as higher performance is desired, the bandwidth will be raised even further [21]. Figure 2 plots the bandwidth trends of the HDD, flash memory, SSD, host interface and CPU. The bandwidth improvement in flash, especially resulting from increased use of multiple memory channels (with 8–16 being common today) for parallel data retrieval, results in much higher raw internal and external bandwidth than HDDs.

SSD bandwidth characteristics are what lead us to explore the iSSD concept. The very high bandwidths mean that substantial bandwidth capability and energy is required to deliver all data to an external processing unit, both of which could be reduced by filtering and/or aggregating within the SSD. Indeed, modern external SSD bandwidths lag raw internal bandwidths significantly—differences of 2–4× are common. So, an iSSD could process data 2–4× faster just by being able to exploit the internal data rate. Moreover, the natural parallelism inherent in SSD's use of multiple channels couples well with parallelized data stream processing.

2.3 iSSD-relevant workload characteristics

iSSDs would be expected to provide benefits for data-intensive applications that explore, query, analyze, visualize, and, in general, process very large data sets [1, 2, 25]. In addition to simple data filtering and aggregation, some emerging data mining applications are characterized by substantial computation. This subsection examines a number of common data-intensive application kernels to gain insight into their relevant characteristics.

Table 1 lists the kernels.[1] We show three metrics in the table to characterize and highlight the data processing complexity and the architectural efficiency. Among the three metrics, IPB captures the data processing complexity of a kernel. If IPB is high (e.g., k-means), implying that much work is needed to process a given input data, the workload is compute-intensive. In another example, grep and scan execute well less than ten instructions on average to process a byte. IPB is determined primarily by the specific data processing algorithm, the expressiveness of the instruction set, and the compiler's ability to produce efficient codes.

By comparison, CPI reveals, and is determined by, the hardware architecture efficiency. On the testbed we used, the ideal CPI is 0.20 to 0.25 because the processor is capable of issuing four to five instructions per cycle. The measured CPI values range from 0.60 (ScalParC and Naïve Bayesian) to 1.7 (histogram). Compared with the ideal CPI, the values represent at least 2× and up to 8.5× efficiency degradation. There are three main reasons for the inefficiency: high clock frequency (i.e., relatively long memory latency), poor cache performance, and frequent branch mispredictions. According to Ozisikyilmaz et al. [26] the L2 cache miss rates of the classification kernels in Table 1 are as high as 10% to 68%. Moreover, HOP has a branch misprediction rate of 10%, considerably higher than other workloads in the same benchmark suite.

Another interesting observation is that kernels with a low IPB tend to have a high CPI. Kernels with an IPB smaller than 50 have the average CPI of 1.14 while the the average CPI of kernels with an IPB above 50 is only 0.82. We reason that high-IPB kernels are compute-intensive and utilize the available functional units and reuse the data in the cache memory relatively well. On the other hand, low-IPB kernels spend few instructions per unit data and the utilization of the hardware resources may slide (e.g., cache performs poorly on streams).

Lastly, CPB combines IPB and CPI (CPB = IPB × CPI), and is the data processing rate of a platform. Hence, it is our goal to minimize CPB with the proposed iSSD. For the kernels we examined, CPB ranges from less than ten (scan and grep) to over a hundred (k-means).

3. INTELLIGENT SSDS

iSSDs offer the earliest opportunity to process data after they are retrieved from the physical storage medium. This section describes the iSSD—its hardware architecture and software architecture. Feasible data processing strategies as well as challenges to exploit iSSDs are also discussed.

3.1 Hardware architecture

The main difference in hardware between a regular SSD and

[1]A few kernels were adapted to run on both an x86 and an ARM-based simulator platform described in Section 4.3.

NAME [SOURCE]	DESCRIPTION	INPUT SIZE	CPB*	IPB†	CPI‡
word_count [23]	Counts the number of unique word occurrences	105MB	90.0	87.1	1.0
linear_regression [23]	Applies linear regression best-fit over data points	542MB	31.5	40.2	0.8
histogram [23]	Computes the RGB histogram of an image	1,406MB	62.4	37.4	1.7
string_match [23]	Pattern matches strings against data streams	542MB	46.4	54.0	0.9
ScalParC [24]	Decision tree classification	1,161MB	83.1	133.7	0.6
k-means [24]	Mean-based data partitioning method	240MB	117.0	117.1	1.0
HOP [24]	Density-based grouping method	60MB	48.6	41.2	1.2
Naïve Bayesian [24]	Statistical classifier based on class conditional independence	126MB	49.3	83.6	0.6
grep (v2.6.3)	Searches for a pattern in a file	1,500MB	5.7	4.6	1.2
scan (PostgreSQL)	Database scan	1,280MB	3.1	3.9	0.8

Table 1: Example data-intensive kernels. Measurements were made on a Linux box with a Nehalem-class processor using Intel's VTune. Programs were compiled using `icc` (Intel's C/C++ compiler) at `-O3`. Results do not include the time to handle file I/O. *Cycles Per Byte. †Instructions Per Byte. ‡Cycles Per Instruction.

an iSSD is their compute capabilities; iSSDs must provide substantially higher yet efficient compute power to translate the raw flash memory bandwidth into high data processing rates. In conventional HDDs and SSDs, in-storage compute power is provisioned to meet the firmware performance requirements (e.g., host command processing, block mapping, error handling). The active disk work [5,6,8] optimistically predicted that future storage controller chips (in HDDs) will have increasingly more excess compute capabilities. However, that didn't happen because there is no immediate merit for a storage vendor to add higher horsepower to a device than needed at cost. We argue that the iSSD internal architecture must be designed specially and offer both high raw performance and flexible programmability.

There are at least two ways to add compute resources in the SSD datapath: by integrating more (powerful) embedded CPUs and by augmenting each FMC with a processing element. While we consider both in this work, we note that SSD designers have kept adding more flash memory channels to continue the SSD bandwidth growth. Hence, it is necessary to scale the amount of compute power in the iSSD according to the number of flash memory channels, motivating and justifying the second approach. This approach has an added benefit of not increasing the bandwidth requirements on the shared DRAM. This work proposes to employ a *customized ASIP* and a *reconfigurable stream processor* as the FMC processing element, as shown in Figure 3.

The diagram in the red box shows the components inside an FMC—flash interface, scratchpad SRAM, DMA, embedded processor, reconfigurable stream processor and bus bridge. Raw data from the flash memory are first stored in the scratchpad SRAM before data processing begins. Data are then processed by the per-FMC embedded processor (and the stream processor). The embedded processor has a custom instruction set for efficient data processing and small area cost. However, as Table 1 suggests, certain algorithms may still require many cycles for each input byte and may render the FMC stage a serious bottleneck. For example, word count has an IPB of 87. If the flash memory transfers data at 400 MB/s and the embedded processor is clocked at 400 MHz, the actual achievable data processing rate would be slowed down by the factor of 87, compared to the full raw data bandwidth (assuming a CPI of 1)!

In order to effectively increase the FMC's data processing rate, this work explores incorporating a reconfigurable stream processor, highlighted in the bottom diagram. Once configured, the stream processor performs like dedicated hardware, achieving very high data processing rates and low power [27].

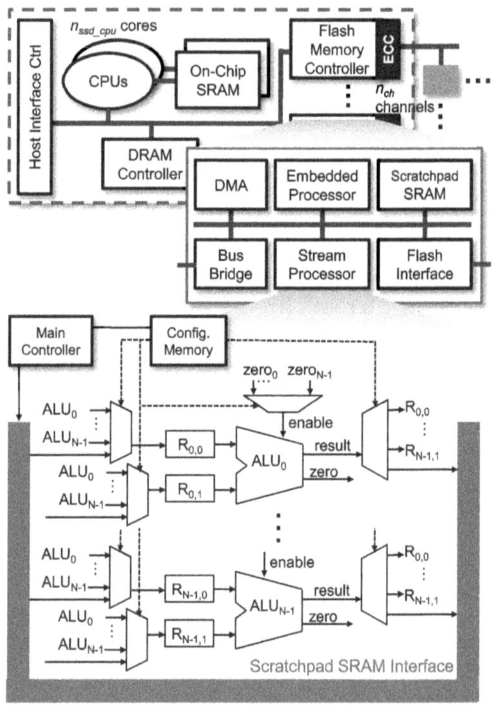

Figure 3: The organization of an iSSD's FMC (in red box) and the reconfigurable stream processor (bottom).

At the heart of the stream processor are an array of ALUs, configurable connections and the main controller. An ALU's output is either stored to the SRAM or forwarded to another ALU. How processed data flow within the processor is configurable (by programming the "configuration memory"). The main controller is responsible for the configuration and sequencing of operations. Figure 4 presents three example instances of the stream processor. For these examples, the CPB improvement rate is 3.4× (linear_regression), 4.9× (k-means) and 1.4× (string_match).

Data processing with the proposed FMC is expected to be efficient. First, the stream processor exploits high fine-grained parallelism with multiple ALUs. Second, the embedded processor and the stream processor feed their data from a scratchpad memory, not cache (i.e., no cache misses). Third, the embedded processor has a shallow pipeline and does not suffer from a high branch misprediction penalty like the host CPU. Hence, the effective average CPB achieved with the FMCs is expected to be very competitive. This observation is revisited in Section 4.

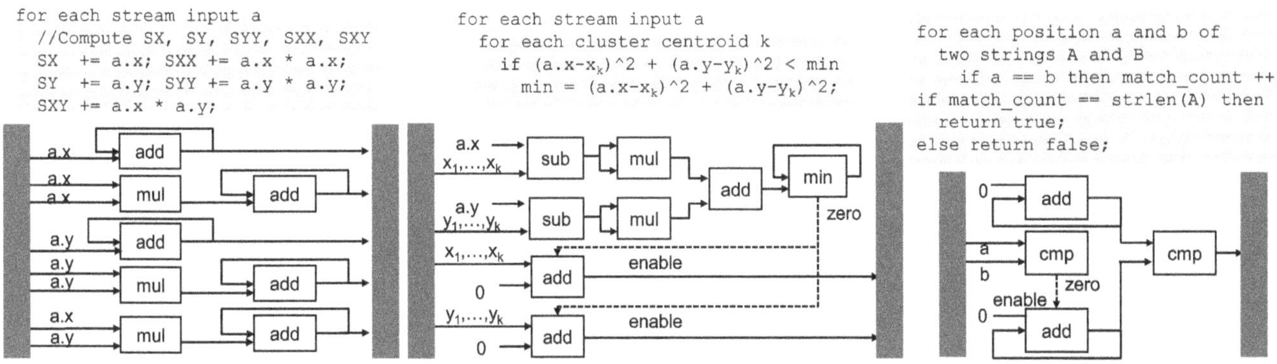

Figure 4: Reconfigurable stream processor instances for linear_regression, k-means and string_match from left.

Beyond FMCs, further data processing can be done by the SSD's main embedded CPUs. The performance of the CPUs can be scaled with the core type (e.g., ARM7 vs. Cortex-A8), core count, and clock frequency. Because the CPUs see data from all flash memory channels, they can perform "wide-scope" tasks like the Reduce stage of a MapReduce job. The performance of the embedded CPUs is limited by the shared DRAM bandwidth, however.

3.2 Software architecture

Since an iSSD platform includes multiple heterogeneous processor cores, its programming framework should be able to express parallelism for heterogeneous processors. Among many frameworks, for example, OpenCL [28] meets the requirements. It not only supports data parallel executions on each parallel device but also provides a unified programming framework to coordinate heterogeneous devices and host CPUs to collaborate. Another framework that is particularly interesting to us and that we delve further into, is MapReduce [3]. It was developed primarily for distributed systems and assumes individual processing units (computers) read data from a storage device.

The MapReduce framework provides two basic primitives: *Map* and *Reduce*. They are user specified and easy to parallelize and distribute on the computing elements (FMC processors and embedded CPUs in the context of the iSSD) with the assistance of the run-time system. In addition, the MapReduce model matches well with the hardware organization of the iSSD as shown in Figure 5(a). Input data are saved in flash memory prior to being transferred to FMCs. They execute the Map phase and the intermediate results are stored in DRAM or flash memory temporarily. The output data are produced and transferred to the host system or flash memory after the Reduce phase is run on the iSSD's CPUs.

The Map and Reduce functions are assigned to the iSSD or the host system depending on the cost and benefit projection. The job partitioning and resource assignment are managed by the MapReduce run-time system that is split to run on the host system and the iSSD. We call the run-time system "Initiator" (on the host) and "Agent" (on the iSSD), as shown in Figure 5(b). Initiator is essentially a run-time library and provides programmers with a programming interface to iSSDs. It hides some iSSD details such as the number of embedded CPUs and FMCs, the capability of stream processors, and flash memory parameters. Agent is responsible for allocating and scheduling Map and Reduce tasks inside the iSSD. It communicates with Initiator through a tunneling mechanism available in storage protocols like SATA, SAS and PCI-e or via an object storage interface [29].[2] An iSSD based job execution scenario using the suggested framework is illustrated in Figure 5(b).

iSSDs face an issue that was thoroughly explored in previous active disk work [5, 6, 8]: enabling applications to target data even though legacy file systems are not aware of underlying active-ness and underlying devices are not aware of file system organization details. One approach is to use a separate partition and direct I/O for the data, which worked for modified databases and work for our MapReduce framework. In our iSSD prototype on a real SSD (Section 4.3), this approach is taken. Another is to modify legacy file systems to allow applications (e.g., Initiator) to obtain block lists associated with files, and request that they do not change for a period of time, which can then be provided to the iSSD.

An issue for iSSDs that was not present for active disks relates to how data is partitioned across the flash memory channels. Striping across channels is used to provide high streaming bandwidth, which could create difficulties for processing of data on individual per-channel processing elements; with striped data, no single processing element would have it all. Fortunately, the stripe unit size is fairly large (e.g., 8KB or 16KB) and consistent with common file system block sizes and database page sizes [5, 6, 8]. For applications that can process individual blocks/pages, one by one, channel striping should present no issue for our proposed iSSD architecture. Fortunately, almost all active disk work found this to hold for applications of interest, which was important because of files being partitioned into independently allocated blocks. Many more recent data mining activities can also be arranged to fit this requirement, given exposure of the internal block (stripe unit) size. When it is not possible, the embedded CPUs can still process data (more slowly), as it sees the unstriped data.

3.3 Data processing strategies with iSSDs

Allocation of Map and Reduce functions to different processing elements affects the system performance significantly. Therefore, one must carefully map tasks onto heterogeneous hardware resources in an iSSD platform. This work explores two data processing strategies: *pipelining* and *partitioning*.

Pipelining. The pipelining strategy assigns tasks to a set of computing resources in a hierarchical manner. For instance, Map functions could be mapped onto processors inside FMCs and Reduce functions onto the iSSD's embedded CPUs. As

[2]There are interesting trade-offs between using a commodity legacy interface like SATA (large installed base) and the object storage interface (rich information within storage). Exploring their trade-offs is not the focus of this paper.

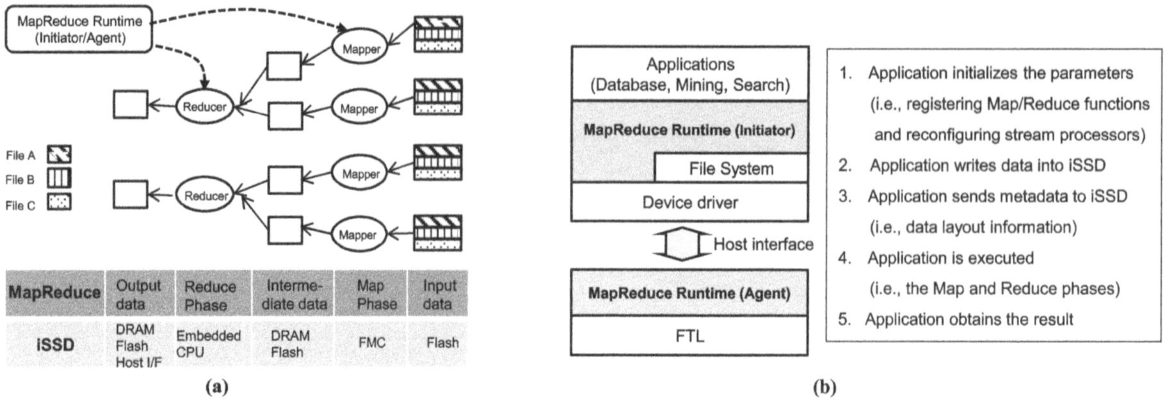

Figure 5: Mapping the MapReduce framework to iSSD. (a) Associating MapReduce phases to iSSD hardware organization. (b) Software structure and execution flow of iSSD.

such, a set of homogeneous processors execute their mapped tasks in parallel and send the computed results to the next layer of processors in a pipeline fashion. For example, FMCs can perform pattern search in parallel. They can then pass the matched values to the shared DRAM buffer. Next, the iSSD's embedded CPUs can accomplish complex operations that require global information, such as Reduce tasks, join in database, and sort over filtered data sets (preprocessed by FMCs). Intermediate data are stored in temporary memory (SRAM, DRAM or, even flash memory) and computation results are passed to the higher level computing stages.

Because the available physical processing resources are organized in a hierarchical manner in an iSSD platform—from FMCs to embedded CPUs (inside the iSSD) to host CPUs—, this data processing strategy fits nicely with the available hardware infrastructure. However, certain applications may not naturally and efficiently exploit this strategy (e.g., lack of low-level parallelism needed to utilize FMCs).

Partitioning. In general, host CPUs are higher performance than any single computing resource in the iSSD. If we map a given data-intensive computing job entirely to an iSSD we may end up under-utilizing the host CPUs. To fully utilize the computing resources in both the host platform and the iSSD, we could assign Map functions to both entities by "partitioning" the job into properly sized sub-jobs. For example, if the input data set is composed of 1,000 files, 400 files could be delegated to the iSSD and the remaining 600 files could be processed by the host CPUs.

For best results, we need to balance the amount of data (computation) the host CPUs and the iSSD take based on their performance. This decision can be made at run time ("dynamic load-balancing") or before the job is launched ("static load-balancing"). For stream oriented applications, the simple, static load-balancing would work well; this is because the execution time of each function varies little in stream applications.

Finally, the pipelining and the partitioning strategies can be used in combination. In fact, combining both strategies will likely lead to better system performance with higher overall resource utilization. Section 5.2 discusses this point.

4. MODELING ISSD BENEFITS

This section develops models to evaluate the benefits of the proposed iSSD approach. We take a data-centric perspective and express performance and energy as a function of *input data size*. In essence, the overall performance (or inversely, total time) and energy are determined by the average time and energy to process a single input byte. We will separately discuss models for pipelining and partitioning.

4.1 Models for pipelining

Performance. A data-intensive workload may involve multiple execution phases. For example, a typical MapReduce workload would go through three phases, namely, *map*, *sort* and *reduce*. Hence, once we compute the times of individual phases, we can combine them to obtain the overall execution time.[3] The execution time of a given phase is, simply put, D/B, where D is the input data size and B the overall processing bandwidth for the phase. Our performance modeling effort accordingly focuses on computing B.

We assume that D is sufficiently large for each phase. Moreover, B is determined primarily by the underlying hardware architecture and the workload characteristics. Then, each phase's execution time is determined by D and the steady data processing bandwidth ($=B$) of the system during the phase. Riedel [8] makes the same assumptions.

With the pipelining workload mapping strategy, data being processed go through multiple steps in a pipelined manner. Each step can be thought of as a pipeline stage and the step that takes the longest amount of time determines the overall data processing bandwidth at the system level. The steps are: (a) Data transfer from NAND flash chips to an FMC on each channel; (b) Data processing at the FMC; (c) Data transfer from the FMC to the DRAM; (d) Data processing with the SSD embedded CPU(s) on the data stored in the DRAM; (e) Data transfer from the SSD (DRAM) to the host via the host interface; and (f) Data processing with the host CPU(s). If the time needed for each of the above steps is $t_{nand2fmc}$, t_{fmc}, $t_{fmc2dram}$, t_{ssd_cpu}, $t_{ssd2host}$ and t_{host_cpu}, respectively, the bandwidth is the inverse of the total time (T_{total}). Hence, we have:

$$T_{total} = (1-p)\cdot t_{conv} + \max(t_*), \quad B = \frac{D}{T_{total}} \qquad (1)$$

where t_* is the list of the time components defined above (for steps (a)–(f)) and $(1-p)$ is the portion of the execution that is not pipelinable [8] using the iSSD scheme, and t_{conv} is the time that would be consumed with the conventional scheme. Let us now tackle each term in t_*.

[3]Tasks of different phases may overlap in time depending on how the "master" coordinates task allocations [3].

(a) Data transfer from NAND flash chips to an FMC on each channel. Given n_{ch} flash channels and the per-channel effective data rate of r_{nand}, $t_{nand2fmc} = D/n_{ch} \cdot r_{nand}$. We assume that data have been split onto the NAND flash chips evenly and all data channels are utilized equally.

(b) Data processing at the FMC. Once data are retrieved from NAND flash chips, they are processed in parallel using n_{ch} FMCs. Each processor at an FMC is assumed to run at the frequency of f_{fmc}. Furthermore, to process a single byte, the processor would require CPB_{fmc} cycles on average. Hence,

$$t_{fmc} = \frac{D \cdot CPB_{fmc}}{n_{ch} \cdot f_{fmc}} = \frac{D \cdot IPB_{fmc} \cdot CPI_{fmc}}{n_{ch} \cdot f_{fmc}}. \quad (2)$$

In the above formulation, IPB_{fmc} exposes the efficiency of the instruction set chosen (and the compiler), CPI_{fmc} the microarchitecture, and f_{fmc} the microarchitecture and the circuit-level processor implementation.

(c) Data transfer from the FMC to the DRAM. We introduce a key parameter α to express the amount of residual data for further processing after FMCs finish processing a batch of data. α can be referred to as *reduction factor* or *selectivity* depending on the workload semantics, and has a value between 0 and 1. The time needed to push the residual data from the FMCs to the DRAM is, then: $t_{fmc2dram} = \alpha \cdot D/r_{dram}$. We assumed that the aggregate data rate of the n_{ch} NAND flash channels is at least r_{dram}, the DRAM bandwidth.

(d) Data processing with the embedded CPU(s). Our formulation here is similar to Equation (2).

$$\begin{aligned} t_{ssd\_cpu} &= \frac{\alpha \cdot D \cdot CPB_{ssd\_cpu}}{n_{ssd\_cpu} \cdot f_{ssd\_cpu}} \\ &= \frac{\alpha \cdot D \cdot IPB_{ssd\_cpu} \cdot CPI_{ssd\_cpu}}{n_{ssd\_cpu} \cdot f_{ssd\_cpu}}. \end{aligned}$$

CPB_{ssd_cpu}, f_{ssd_cpu}, IPB_{ssd_cpu} and CPI_{ssd_cpu} are defined similarly. n_{ssd_cpu} is the number of embedded CPUs.

(e) Data transfer from the SSD to the host. If there remains further processing after step (d), data transfer occurs from the iSSD to the host. With a data reduction factor β, the time to transfer data is expressed as: $t_{ssd2host} = \alpha \cdot \beta \cdot D/r_{host}$, where r_{host} is the host interface data transfer rate.

(f) Data processing with the host CPU(s). In the last step, data processing with the host CPU takes:

$$\begin{aligned} t_{host\_cpu} &= \frac{\alpha \cdot \beta \cdot D \cdot CPB_{host\_cpu}}{n_{host\_cpu} \cdot f_{host\_cpu}} \\ &= \frac{\alpha \cdot \beta \cdot D \cdot IPB_{host\_cpu} \cdot CPI_{host\_cpu}}{n_{host\_cpu} \cdot f_{host\_cpu}}, \end{aligned}$$

where n_{host_cpu} is the number of host CPUs. CPB_{host_cpu}, f_{host_cpu}, IPB_{host_cpu} and CPI_{host_cpu} are CPB, clock frequency, IPB and CPI for the host CPUs.

The above time components ((a) through (f)) are plugged into Equation (1) to obtain the data processing bandwidth of a particular phase in a workload. Note that the effect of parallel processing with multiple computing resources (n_{ch}, n_{ssd_cpu} and n_{host_cpu}) is exposed.

Finally, let us derive the bandwidth of the conventional data processing scheme by adapting the above formulation. Because there is no data processing within the SSD, $\alpha = \beta = 1$ (all data will be transferred to the host). Furthermore, step (b) and (d) are skipped, i.e., $t_{fmc} = t_{ssd\_cpu} = 0$. With these changes, Equation (1) applies to predicting the performance of the conventional data processing scheme.

Energy. The main idea of our energy models is: The overall energy is a function of input data size and energy to process a single byte. Energy consumption of a system is the sum of two components, dynamic energy and static energy ($E_{total} = E_{dyn} + E_{static}$). We assume that E_{static} is simply $P_{static} \cdot T_{total}$ where P_{static} is a constant (static power); accordingly, we focus in this section on deriving E_{dyn}.

Dynamic energy consumption is split into energy due to computation and energy for data transfer. That is, $E_{dyn} = E_{comp}+E_{xfer} = D \cdot (EPB_{comp}+EPB_{xfer})$, where EPB_{comp} is the average energy spent on processing a single byte of input and EPB_{xfer} is the average energy spent on data transfer per single byte. EPB_{comp} can be further decomposed into terms that represent the contributions of different hardware components: $EPB_{comp} = EPB_{fmc} + \alpha \cdot EPB_{ssd\_cpu} + \alpha \cdot \beta \cdot EPB_{host\_cpu}$. Similarly, $EPB_{xfer} = EPB_{nand2fmc} + \alpha \cdot EPB_{fmc2dram} + \alpha \cdot \beta \cdot EPB_{ssd2host}$, where EPB_{A2B} is the energy needed to move a byte from A to B.

To expose the processor design choices and their impact, we can further decompose the terms of EPB_{comp}: $EPB_{fmc} = EPI_{fmc} \cdot IPB_{fmc}$, $EPB_{ssd\_cpu} = EPI_{ssd\_cpu} \cdot IPB_{ssd\_cpu}$, and $EPB_{host\_cpu} = EPI_{host\_cpu} \cdot IPB_{host\_cpu}$, where EPI_* is the average energy per instruction, an architectural and circuit design parameter.

4.2 Models for partitioning

Performance. With the partitioning strategy, data are split between the iSSD and the host for processing. Hence, $D = D_{issd} + D_{host}$. Then, based on the partition, the execution time $T_{total} = \max(D_{issd}/B_{issd}, D_{host}/B_{host})$, where B_{issd} and B_{host} stand for the data processing bandwidth of the iSSD and the host. Clearly, the above formulation captures the importance of "good" partitioning, because T_{total} is minimized when the execution times of the iSSD and the host are equal. B_{issd} and B_{host} can be easily obtained with our formulation of Section 4.1. For example, B_{host} can be expressed as $n_{host\_cpu} \cdot f_{host\_cpu}/CPB_{host\_cpu}$.

Energy. Like before, we assume that E_{static} is $P_{static} \cdot T_{total}$ and focus on deriving the dynamic energy, $E_{dyn} = E_{comp} + E_{xfer} = D_{issd} \cdot EPB_{issd\_comp} + D_{host} \cdot EPB_{host\_cpu} + D_{host} \cdot EPB_{ssd2host}$. EPB_{issd_comp} is the average energy spent on processing a single byte of input within the iSSD and can be computed using our formulation for pipelining with $\beta = 0$. EPB_{host_cpu} and $EPB_{ssd2host}$ were previously defined.

4.3 Validation

The basic performance modeling framework of this work was previously validated by Riedel [8]. They compare the performance of a single server with fast, directly attached SCSI disks against the same machine with network-attached (emulated) active disks. Because the iSSD architecture stresses high data access parallelism inside a single device, the emulation approach is too limiting in our case. Instead, we develop and use two iSSD prototypes to validate our models and evaluate the iSSD approach. Our first prototype is a detailed execution-driven iSSD simulator that runs on SoC Designer [30]. Our second prototype is built on a real SSD product platform provided by Samsung [31]. Let us discuss each in the following.

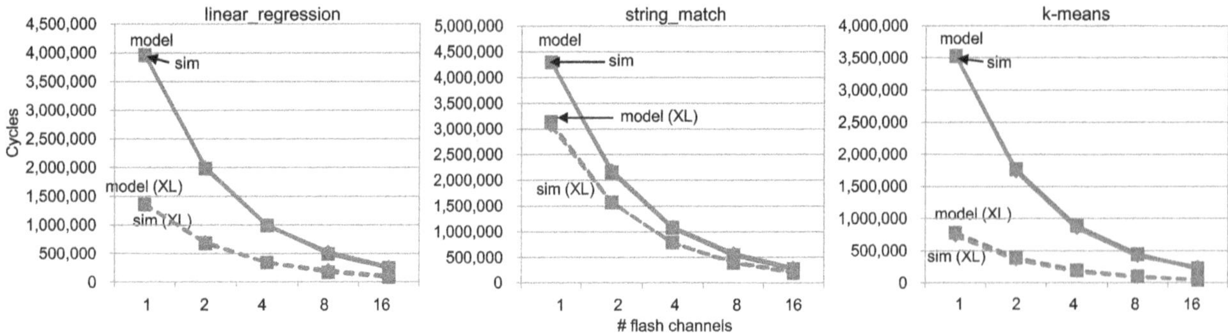

Figure 6: Comparison of cycle counts of three benchmarks obtained with our models and SoC Designer simulation. Dotted lines and solid lines are for iSSD processing with and without stream processor acceleration (XL), respectively.

Model validation through simulation of iSSD hardware. Our simulation is both functional and timing. We describe the hardware components in Figure 3 using SystemC and realistic timings. We use an existing cycle-accurate ARM9 model to simulate embedded CPUs and FMC processors. Additionally, we build a timing-only wrapper simulation component for reconfigurable stream processors to avoid designing a full-fledged stream processor at the RTL level. This component reads program execution traces and generates necessary events (e.g., bus transactions) at specified times.

We have ported a MapReduce framework similar to Stanford Phoenix [23] to natively run on our simulator. An embedded CPU in the iSSD becomes a "master" and triggers FMCs to execute Map tasks (more experimental settings in Section 5.1). It also manages buffers in DRAM to collect intermediate data. If the output buffer in DRAM gets full, the embedded CPU flushes the data and triggers the FMCs for further data processing.

Figure 6 plots how well the results obtained from our analytical model and the simulator agree. Overall, the model is shown to predict the performance trends very well as we change the number of flash memory channels; performance trends are accurately predicted at every flash memory channel count in all examined workloads. The maximum absolute error between the two results was 17.9% and the average error was 5.1%.

Scan experiments with prototype iSSD. We also separately studied how database scan is accelerated and system-level energy consumption is saved with the iSSD approach by porting PostgreSQL's scan algorithm to the Samsung SSD platform, having sixteen 40 MB/s FMCs (i.e., internal bandwidth is 640 MB/s) and a SATA 3 Gbps interface (~250 MB/s on the quad-core system used). The SSD has two ARM processors and 256 MB DRAM. As for software implementation, simple Initiator and Agent were implemented in the host system and the SSD. They communicate with each other through a system call, `ioctl()` with the `ATA_PASS_THROUGH` parameter. A SATA reserved command was used for parameter and metadata passing. The scan algorithm is implemented into a Map function and loaded into the code memory of the SSD.

For input data, a 1 GB TPC-H Lineitem table [32] was written into flash memory with striping. Selectivity was 1% and projectivity was 4 bytes (out of 150 bytes). After input data was stored, the data layout information such as table schema and projected column was delivered to the SSD. As soon as the host system invoked the scan function through Initiator, the input data were read into the internal DRAM and compared with the key value for scan operation.

iSSD parameters	
r_{nand}	400 MB/s
r_{dram}	3.2GB/s (@800 MHz, 32b bus)
n_{ch}	8–64 with the step of 8
f_{fmc}	400 MHz, 800 MHz
n_{ssd_cpu}, f_{ssd_cpu}	4, 400 MHz
System parameters	
r_{host}	600 MB/s (SATA), 4 or 8 GB/s
n_{host_cpu}	4, 8, 16
f_{host_cpu}	3.2 GHz
Workload parameters—linear_regression, string_match, k-means, scan	
p	1
α	0.05 for scan; <0.05 for others;
CPB_{fmc}	33.6, 38.8, 157.6, 4.0
CPB_{fmc} (w/ accel.)	10.1, 28.3, 32.4, 1.0
CPB_{host_cpu}	31.5, 46.4, 117.0, 3.1

Table 2: Parameter values used during evaluation.

Matched data items are transferred to the host periodically by Initiator until there is no more data to be scanned.

The measured performance improvement with the iSSD over the host system was 2.3×. Because database scan is not compute-intensive, this performance improvement came closely by the ratio between the SSD-internal NAND flash bandwidth and the host interface bandwidth (640 MB/250 MB=2.56). Through careful mapping of the scan algorithm, we were able to achieve a near-maximum performance gain with only a single embedded CPU. In particular, scan operation and FTL execution time (tens of microseconds) are effectively hidden by data transfer time between flash memory and the internal DRAM. Our analytical models can capture this effect, and the performance predictions in Figure 7 agree with our measurement result. We also measured dynamic energy improvement (difference of current flowing from the wall outlet to the system) of 5.2× using a multimeter.

5. QUANTITATIVE EVALUATION

To complement the prototype measurements in the previous section, this section uses the analytical models to study the performance and energy benefits of the iSSD approach across a broader range of configurations. Our main focus is to prove the concept of the iSSD and identify conditions when the iSSD obtains the most and least benefit.

5.1 Evaluation setup

Table 2 lists the values of the parameters to plug into our models. Hardware parameters (for the iSSD and the host platform) are based on the technology trends summarized in Section 2.2. For intuitive discussions, we focus on four selected

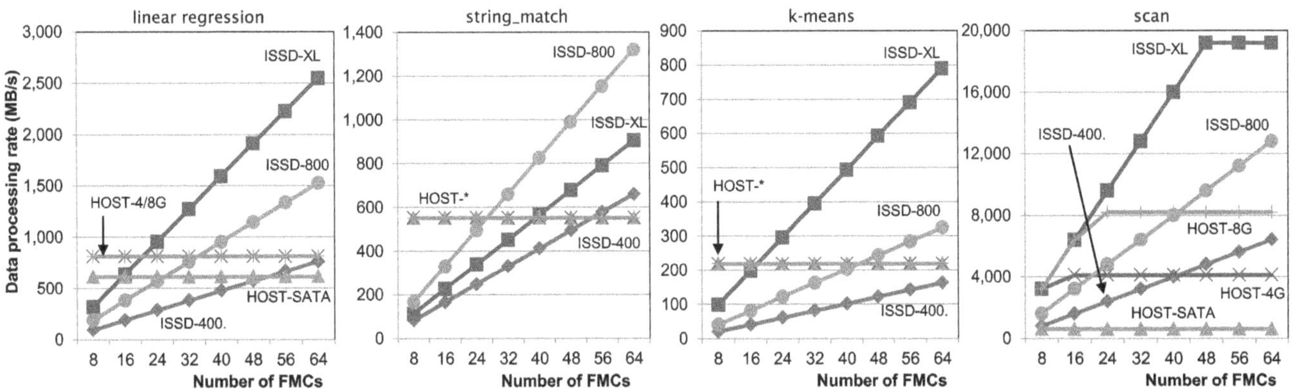

Figure 7: Performance of selected kernels on five system configurations: HOST-SATA, HOST-4G, HOST-8G, iSSD-400, iSSD-800, and iSSD-XL. HOST-"*speed*" represents a conventional, host CPU based processing scheme with the storage interface speed of "*speed*" ("SATA"=600 MB/s, "4G"=4 GB/s, "8G"=8 GB/s). iSSD-400 and iSSD-800 employ FMCs running at 400 MHz and 800 MHz for data processing. iSSD-XL uses reconfigurable stream processors for processing. iSSD-400 uses the SATA interface, iSSD-800 the PCI-e 4 GB/s interface, and iSSD-XL the PCI-e 8 GB/s interface.

kernels that have different characteristics: linear_regression, string_match, k-means, and scan. In terms of computation complexity (expressed in IPB), scan is the simplest and k-means is the most complex. Except scan, which we implement its kernel to directly run on FMCs, we ported the Map stage of the remaining kernels to FMCs. We focus on the Map stage of the kernels only because there are many options for running the Reduce stage (e.g., in iSSD or host? Overlapped or not?) and the Map stage is often the time-dominant phase (76–99% in our examples). We use hardware acceleration to speed up the kernels using the stream processor instances in Figure 4. For scan, we estimate CPBs for iSSD to be 4 and 1 (with hardware support for fast matching) based on our experiments on a real SSD platform (Section 4.3).

Throughout this section, we fix r_{nand} to 400 MB/s to keep the design space to explore reasonably bounded. This way, we focus on n_{ch}, the only parameter to control the internal raw data bandwidth of the storage. In the case of iSSD, n_{ch} also determines the raw data processing throughput. Lastly, we set $p = 1$ [8].

5.2 Results

Performance improvement potential. Figure 7 compares the data processing rate of different iSSD and conventional machine configurations, as we change the number of FMCs. We assume that the host machine has eight CPUs. iSSD configurations are shown to effectively increase the data processing bandwidth as we add more FMCs while conventional machine configurations (having equally fast SSDs) gain little.

Interestingly, the performance of the conventional configurations were compute-bound except for scan. For example, with k-means and string_match (our "compute-intensive" kernels), the host interface speed mattered little. With linear_regression, the 4 GB/s and 8 GB/s host interface speeds made no difference. iSSD configurations show scalable performance in the whole FMC count range, except with scan. In this case, the performance of iSSD-XL was saturated due to the internal DRAM bandwidth wall (not the host interface bandwidth) when the number of FMCs exceeded 48. By comparison, all conventional machine configurations suffered the host interface bandwidth limitation, making scan the only truly storage bandwidth bound workload among the kernels examined. Still, iSSD configurations scale the scan throughput for the most part because the iSSD does not transfer filtered data to the host, reducing the required data traffic substantially. Our results clearly highlight the importance of efficient data handling with optimized hardware, parallel data processing and data filtering.

Among the examined kernels, string_match and k-means have an IPB larger than 50 and are compute-intensive (see Table 1). In both cases, the data processing rate on the host CPUs is not bounded by the host interface bandwidth at all. Interestingly, their performance behavior on the iSSD is quite different. k-means was successfully accelerated and performs substantially better on the iSSD than host CPUs with 24 or more FMCs. In contrast, string_match required as many as 40 FMCs to outperform host CPUs. The main reason is that the stream processor is not as effective for this kernel as other kernels and produced a small gain of only 37% compared with the 400 MHz FMC processor (also indirectly evidenced by the large improvement with the 800 MHz FMCs). If the iSSD has insufficient resources, one would execute workloads like string_match on host CPUs [8]. Still, the particular example of string_match motivates us to investigate (in the future) a broader array of workload acceleration opportunities, especially to handle unstructured data streams efficiently.

In a conventional system, parallelism is exploited by involving more CPUs in computation. To gain further insight about the effectiveness of parallel processing inside the iSSD (with FMCs) as opposed to on the host platform (with multiple CPUs), Figure 8 identifies *iso-performance* configurations of the iSSD and conventional systems in two plots, each assuming a different host interface speed (600 MB/s vs. 8 GB/s).

Both plots show that hardware acceleration makes iSSD data processing much more efficient by increasing the effective per-channel throughput. Consider linear_regression for example: When r_{host} is 600 MB/s, the iSSD obtains the performance of the 16-CPU host configuration with 52 FMCs (without acceleration) and 15 FMCs (with acceleration). Note that there is a large difference between the maximum raw instruction throughput between the iSSD and the host configurations; the 4-CPU host configuration (4×3.2 GHz×4 instructions/cycle) corresponds to twice the computing capacity of the 64-FMC iSSD configuration (64×400 MHz×1 instruction/cycle). The fact that we find iso-performance points in each column reveals the strength of the iSSD ap-

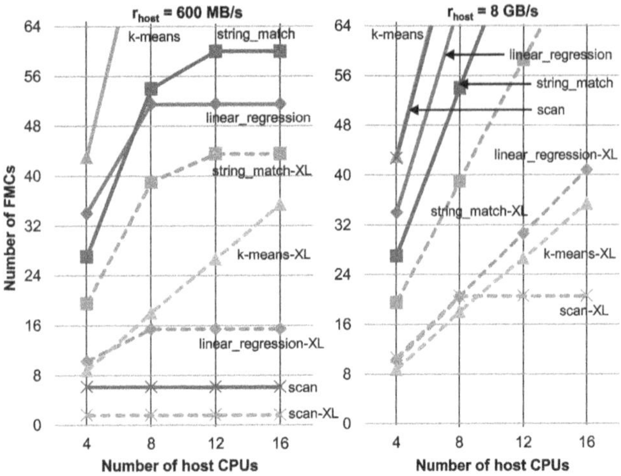

Figure 8: Iso-performance iSSD (Y axis) and host (X) configurations.

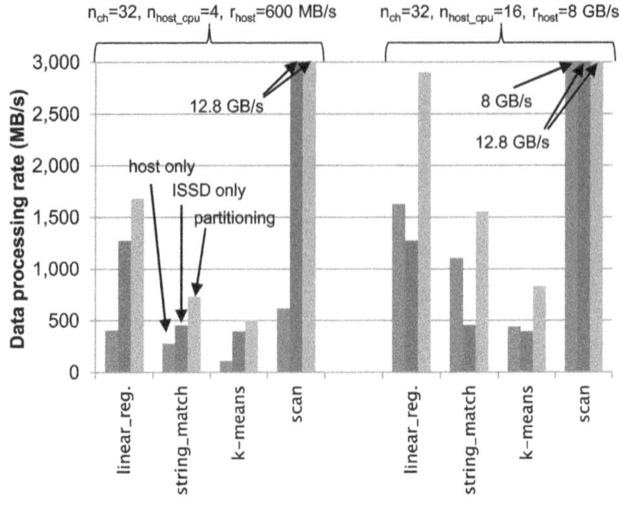

Figure 9: Performance of host only, iSSD only, and partitioning based combined configuration.

proach. Simple kernels like scan and linear_regression perform much more efficiently on the iSSD. Moreover, relatively complex kernels like k-means will also be quite suitable for running on the iSSD, given adequate hardware acceleration support.

With a high-bandwidth host interface, the host CPU configurations gain on performance, and hence, the curves are pushed toward the upper-left corner. Still, the iSSD provides robust performance with acceleration for scan, k-means and linear_regression. With fewer than 41 FMCs, the iSSD performed as well as 16 CPUs for these kernels.

We also gain from above results an insight that having more powerful embedded CPUs in an iSSD (e.g., Cortex-A8s at 1.2 GHz) will not produce equivalent cost-effective performance benefits because they are subject to the same architecture inefficiency issues that plague host CPUs. Moreover, with significantly more compute power in the embedded CPUs, the shared DRAM bandwidth will become a new bottleneck. Attacking data at FMCs—the front line of computing resources—appears essential for scalable data processing in iSSDs.

Lastly, we explore the potential of applying both partitioning and pipelining strategies in the iSSD architecture. We employ all computing resources, including FMCs and host CPUs, to maximize data processing throughput. Figure 9 presents the result, assuming optimal work partitioning between the iSSD and host CPUs (i.e., the host CPUs and the iSSD finish execution simultaneously). It is shown that higher data processing throughput is achievable with partitioning, compared with either the host only or the iSSD only configuration. Except for scan, the maximum achievable throughput is the sum of the throughputs of the host CPUs and the iSSD. This is because the ample internal flash memory bandwidth ($n_{ch} = 32$) can feed the host CPUs and the FMCs simultaneously. This is why data processing throughput of nearly 1,700 MB/s is achieved with linear_regression when the host interface bandwidth is merely 600 MB/s. In case of scan, pipelining with the iSSD already achieves the highest possible data throughput (12.8 GB/s) that matches the raw flash memory bandwidth and partitioning brings no additional benefit. In this case, the host CPUs may perform other useful computation or enter into a low power mode.

The partitioning strategy brings practical benefits because partitioning is relatively straightforward when the input data is large and the partitioning overhead becomes relatively small. We are encouraged by our result, and specific research issues of static and dynamic partitioning (and load balancing) are left for future work.

Energy reduction potential. To investigate potential energy savings of the iSSD approach, we compute EPB for three configurations: conventional host processing, iSSD without acceleration, and iSSD with acceleration. The examined configurations follow the setup of Section 5.1 and $n_{ch} = 8$. We break down energy into key system components. In case of host processing, they are: CPUs, main memory, chipset, I/O bus and SSD. For iSSD, we consider: FMC processor, stream processor, DRAM, NAND flash and I/O.

We use the widely practiced event-based energy estimation method (e.g., [33, 34]). We determine our energy parameters based on publicly available information. For example, energy of the host CPU and the in-iSSD processors are derived from [27, 35, 36]. SRAM scratchpad memory and DRAM energy are estimated using [37] and [38]. Flash memory energy is obtained from data books and in-house measurement. For fair comparison, we assume that the host CPU is built with a 22-nm technology while the SSD/iSSD controllers are built with a 45-nm technology (i.e., two technology generations apart). Figure 10 is the result and the parameters used.

It is shown that overall, the iSSD configurations see large energy reduction in all examined kernels by at least 5× (k-means) and the average reduction was over 9×. Furthermore, energy is significantly smaller when the stream processor was used—the maximum reduction was over 27× for linear_regression (9× without the stream processor). The stream processor was very energy-efficient, consuming only 0.123 nJ/byte in the worst case (string_match), compared with 63.0 nJ/byte of the host CPU for the same kernel. Clearly, hardware acceleration proves to be effective for both performance improvement and energy saving in iSSDs.

In host processing, typically more than half of all energy is consumed for data transfer (I/O, chipset and main memory). iSSD addresses this inefficiency by migrating computation and eliminating unnecessary data transfer. In this sense, the iSSD approach is in stark contrast with other approaches toward efficient data processing, such as intelligent mem-

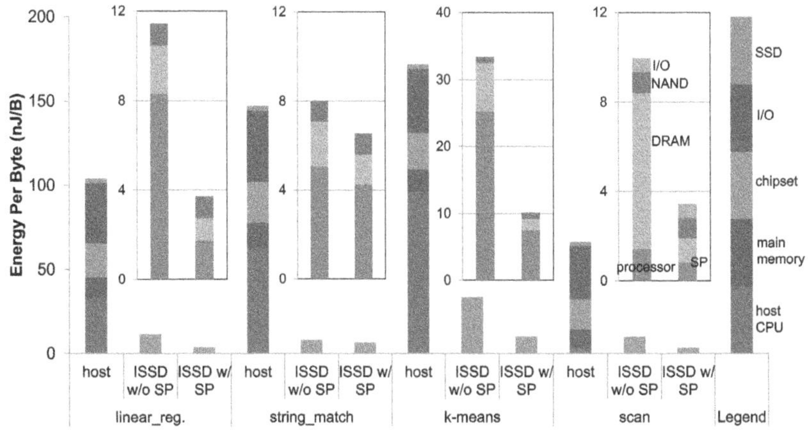

Category	Energy Parameters
Host system	$E_{CPU} = 0.82$ nJ/inst. [35] $P_{DRAM} = 420$ mW [38] $P_{chipset} = 5.49$ W [34] $P_{I/O} = 9.61$ W [34]
SSD & ISSD	$E_{NAND,8kB\ read} = 3.31\ \mu J$ $E_{NAND,8kB\ write} = 64.94\ \mu J$ $P_{DRAM} = 154$ mW [38] $E_{host\ i/f} = 1.05$ nJ/B [40] $E_{proc.} = 192$ pJ/inst. [36] $E_{stream\ ALU} = 2.11$ pJ/op. [27] $E_{stream\ MUL} = 67.6$ pJ/op [27] $E_{stream\ Reg.} = 4.23$ pJ/access [27] $E_{proc.\ SRAM} = 89.3$ pJ/read [37] $E_{stream\ SRAM} = 21.1$ pJ/read [37]

Figure 10: Breakdown of energy into key system components (left) and input parameters to the energy model (right).

ory [10], on-CPU specialization [15], GPGPUs [39] and low-power CPUs [16]; they offer more efficient computing than powerful CPUs but do not (fully) eliminate the overheads of data transfer. For example, even if these approaches employ the same energy-efficient reconfigurable stream processors, their energy improvement would be limited to 1.04× to 1.60× (when iSSD achieves 17× to 27× with acceleration).

Cost analysis. Finally, we estimate and compare the hardware cost of an SSD and an iSSD. Standard components like flash and DRAM chips are identical in both designs. With that the main cost difference comes from the controller chip. We break down the chip cost in gate count (details not shown) and estimate the die cost difference to be 25%.[4]

The SSD bill of material (BOM) is dominated by the NAND flash chips. 5or example, commodity 512 GB SSDs are priced at as low as $399 in on-line stores as of June 2012, whereas 64 Gbit MLC NAND flash chips are sold at $4.36 (obtained at `www.dramexchange.com` on June 10, 2012).[5] According to this price, the cost for the flash memory chips is $279, accounting for 70% of the SSD end user's price. Assuming a small end margin and logistics cost of 15% and manufacturing costs of $5, the total BOM is $334.

After deducting other miscellaneous costs like DRAM ($4), mechanical/electro-mechanical parts ($20) and box accessary ($5), we estimate the controller chip cost to be $26. Hence, even if the new iSSD-capable controller chip costs 25% more than a conventional controller chip, the additional cost of an iSSD *will not exceed 2% of a similarly configured SSD.* We believe that this cost is substantially smaller than upgrading the host system (e.g., CPUs with more cores) to get the same performance improvement the iSSD can bring and is well exceeded by the expected energy savings over the system lifetime.

6. CONCLUSIONS

Intelligent solid-state drives (iSSDs) offer compelling performance and energy efficiency benefits, arising from modern and projected SSD characteristics. Based on analytic models and limited experimentation with a prototype iSSD, we show that iSSDs could provide 2–4× higher data scanning throughput and 5–27× better energy efficiency relative to today's use of commodity servers. Based on analysis of ten data-intensive application kernels, we describe an architecture based on reconfigurable stream processors (one per internal flash memory channel) that could provide these benefits at marginal hardware cost increases (<2%) to traditional SSDs. Most of these benefits would also be realized over non-iSSD approaches based on efficient processing outside of SSDs, because they do not exploit SSD-internal bandwidth or avoid costly high-bandwidth transfers of all processed data.

[4]The main contributors to the iSSD chip cost increase include: embedded CPU cores (more capabilities and more cores), more scratchpad RAM (from more cores) and more complex FMCs.

[5]Contract prices could be higher or lower than the spot price shown here, depending on seasonal and macro price trends.

Acknowledgment

We thank the reviewers for their constructive comments, which helped improve the quality of this paper. Hyunjin Lee (now with Intel Labs) and Juyoung Jung at the University of Pittsburgh assisted with early data collection. Sang Kyoo Jeong of Memory Division, Samsung Electronics Co. proofread and offered detailed comments on a draft of this paper. We appreciate the help of these individuals.

This work was supported in part by the US National Science Foundation (CCF-1064976 and CNS-1012070), the Semiconductor Industry Collaborative Project between Hanyang University and Samsung Electronics Co., the Basic Science Research Program of the National Research Foundation of Korea (NRF) funded by the Ministry of Education, Science and Technology (2010-0005982, 2011-0013479), IT R&D program MKE/KEIT (10041608), the Seoul Creative Human Development Program (HM120006), and the companies of the PDL Consortium.

7. REFERENCES

[1] R. E. Bryant, "Data-intensive supercomputing: The case for disc," Tech. Rep. CMU-CS-07-128, School of Computer Science, Carnegie Mellon University, Pittsburgh, PA, May 2007.

[2] A. Halevy, P. Norvig, and F. Pereira, "The unreasonable effectiveness of data," *IEEE Intelligent Systems*, vol. 24, pp. 8–12, March 2009.

[3] J. Dean and S. Ghemawat, "Mapreduce: Simplified data processing on large clusters," in *OSDI*, pp. 137–150, 2004.

[4] T. White, *Hadoop: The Definitive Guide (Chapter 6: How MapReduce Works)*. O'Reilly, 2009.

[5] A. Acharya, M. Uysal, and J. Saltz, "Active disks: programming model, algorithms and evaluation," ASPLOS-VIII, pp. 81–91, 1998.

[6] K. Keeton, D. A. Patterson, and J. M. Hellerstein, "A case for intelligent disks (idisks)," *SIGMOD Record*, vol. 27, no. 3, pp. 42–52, 1998.

[7] E. Riedel, G. A. Gibson, and C. Faloutsos, "Active storage for large-scale data mining and multimedia," VLDB '98, pp. 62–73, 1998.

[8] E. Riedel, *Active Disks–Remote Execution for Network-Attached Storage*. PhD thesis, Carnegie Mellon University, Pittsburgh, PA, 1999.

[9] E. Riedel, C. Faloutsos, G. Gibson, and D. Nagle, "Active disks for large-scale data processing," *Computer*, vol. 34, pp. 68–74, June 2001.

[10] D. Patterson, T. Anderson, N. Cardwell, R. Fromm, K. Keeton, C. Kozyrakis, R. Thomas, and K. Yelick, "A case for intelligent ram," *Micro, IEEE*, vol. 17, pp. 34–44, March/April 1997.

[11] M. Oskin, F. Chong, and T. Sherwood, "Active pages: a computation model for intelligent memory," in *Computer Architecture, 1998. Proceedings. The 25th Annual International Symposium on*, pp. 192–203, June 1998.

[12] L. Barroso, J. Dean, and U. Holzle, "Web search for a planet: The google cluster architecture," *IEEE Micro*, vol. 23, pp. 22–28, March-April 2003.

[13] Open Compute Project. `http://opencompute.org`.

[14] B. F. Cooper, E. Baldeschwieler, R. Fonseca, J. J. Kistler, P. P. S. Narayan, C. Neerdaels, T. Negrin, R. Ramakrishnan, A. Silberstein, U. Srivastava, and R. Stata, "Building a cloud for yahoo!," *IEEE Data Eng. Bull.*, vol. 32, no. 1, pp. 36–43, 2009.

[15] G. Venkatesh, J. Sampson, N. Goulding, S. Garcia, V. Bryksin, J. Lugo-Martinez, S. Swanson, and M. B. Taylor, "Conservation cores: reducing the energy of mature computations," in *Proceedings of the fifteenth edition of ASPLOS on Architectural support for programming languages and operating systems*, ASPLOS '10, pp. 205–218, ACM, 2010.

[16] D. G. Andersen, J. Franklin, M. Kaminsky, A. Phanishayee, L. Tan, and V. Vasudevan, "Fawn: a fast array of wimpy nodes," in *Proceedings of the ACM SIGOPS 22nd symposium on Operating systems principles*, SOSP '09, pp. 1–14, ACM, 2009.

[17] L. Huston, R. Sukthankar, R. Wickremesinghe, M. Satyanarayanan, G. R. Ganger, E. Riedel, and A. Ailamaki, "Diamond: A storage architecture for early discard in interactive search," FAST, pp. 73–86, 2004.

[18] S. Kim, H. Oh, C. Park, S. Cho, and S.-W. Lee, "Fast, energy efficient scan inside flash memory solid-state drives," ADMS, September 2011.

[19] S. Boboila, Y. Kim, S. Vazhkudai, P. Desnoyers, and G. Shipman, "Active flash: Performance-energy tradeoffs for out-of-core processing on non-volatile memory devices," MSST, April 2012.

[20] D. Tiwari, S. Boboila, Y. Kim, X. Ma, P. Desnoyers, and Y. Solihin, "Active flash: Towards energy-efficient, in-situ data analytics on extreme-scale machines," FAST, pp. 119–132, February 2013.

[21] R. Schuetz and S. Jeong, "Looking ahead to higher performance ssds with hlnand," in *Flash Memory Summit*, 2010.

[22] W. Wong, "A chat about micron's clearnand technology," *electronic design*, December 2010.

[23] R. M. Yoo, A. Romano, and C. Kozyrakis, "Phoenix rebirth: Scalable mapreduce on a large-scale shared-memory system," IISWC, pp. 198–207, 2009.

[24] R. Narayanan, B. Ozisikyilmaz, J. Zambreno, G. Memik, and A. Choudhary, "Minebench: A benchmark suite for data mining workloads," IISWC, pp. 182–188, 2006.

[25] M. Cannataro, D. Talia, and P. K. Srimani, "Parallel data intensive computing in scientific and commercial applications," *Parallel Comput.*, vol. 28, pp. 673–704, May 2002.

[26] B. Ozisikyilmaz, R. Narayanan, J. Zambreno, G. Memik, and A. Choudhary, "An architectural characterization study of data mining and bioinformatics workloads," IISWC, pp. 61–70, 2006.

[27] W. J. Dally, U. J. Kapasi, B. Khailany, J. H. Ahn, and A. Das, "Stream processors: Progammability and efficiency," *Queue*, vol. 2, pp. 52–62, March 2004.

[28] Khronos Group, "Opencl." `http://www.khronos.org/opencl/`.

[29] M. Mesnier, G. R. Ganger, and E. Riedel, "Object-based storage," *IEEE Communication Magazine*, vol. 41, pp. 84–90, August 2003.

[30] Carbon SoC Designer Plus. `http://carbondesignsystems.com/SocDesignerPlus.aspx`.

[31] Samsung Electronics Co. `http://www.samsung.com/global/business/semiconductor/Greenmemory/Products/SSD/SSD_Lineup.html`.

[32] TPC, "Tpc-h." `http://www.tpc.org/tpch/default.asp`.

[33] D. Brooks, V. Tiwari, and M. Martonosi, "Wattch: a framework for architectural-level power analysis and optimizations," ISCA '00, pp. 83–94, 2000.

[34] W. Bircher and L. John, "Complete system power estimation: A trickle-down approach based on performance events," ISPASS, pp. 158–168, 2007.

[35] E. Grochowski and M. Annavaram, "Energy per instruction trends in intel microprocessors." Tech.@Intel Magazine, March 2006.

[36] ARM Ltd., "Cortex a9 processor." `http://www.arm.com/products/processors/cortex-a/cortex-a9.php`.

[37] HP Labs., "Cacti 5.3." `http://quid.hpl.hp.com:9081/cacti/`.

[38] Micron Technology, Inc., "Sdram power calculator." `http://download.micron.com/downloads/misc/SDRAM_Power_Calc_10.xls`.

[39] B. He, W. Fang, Q. Luo, N. K. Govindaraju, and T. Wang, "Mars: a mapreduce framework on graphics processors," PACT '08, pp. 260–269, 2008.

[40] NXP, "Nxp x1 phy single-lane transceiver px1011." `http://ics.nxp.com/products/pcie/phys/`.

Design of a Large-Scale Storage-Class RRAM System

Myoungsoo Jung[1,2], John Shalf[2,3] and Mahmut Kandemir[1]
[1] Department of Computer Science and Engineering, The Pennsylvania State University
[2] Computational Research Division, Lawrence Berkeley National Laboratory
[3] National Energy Research Scientific Computing Center, Lawrence Berkeley National Laboratory
mj@cse.psu.edu, jshalf@lbl.gov, kandemir@cse.psu.edu

ABSTRACT

Resistive Random Access Memory (RRAM) is a promising next generation non-volatile memory (NVM) technology, thanks to its performance potential, endurance and ease-of-integration with standard silicon CMOS processes. While prior work has evaluated RRAM as a replacement for DRAM or even cache memory, to our knowledge there is no prior study that has investigated whether RRAM could be a viable NAND flash replacement in building large-scale storage-class memory systems. Motivated by this observation, our paper first discusses and quantifies the main problems associated with RRAM that prevent it from replacing NAND flash. The main solution we propose, "slab-based memory access with local/global bitlines," enables dense RRAM islands but can also cause performance related problems. To compensate for the latter, we also propose exploiting internal resource parallelism in RRAM and employing optimized data movement interfaces. Our extensive experimental evaluation using a cycle-level NVM simulator and real workloads under diverse computing domains indicate that the proposed architecture can provide 2.95 $\sim$ 8.28 times better bandwidth and 66 % $\sim$ 88 % shorter latency as compared to the conventional NAND flash, and improve the system-level performance of our workloads by 5x, with a storage capacity similar to that of the state-of-the-art NAND flash.

Categories and Subject Descriptors

B.3.1 [**Hardware**]: Memory Structures—*Semiconductor Memories*; C.0 [**Computer System Organization**]: General—*Modeling of computer architecture*

General Terms

Design, Measurement, Performance.

Keywords

Non-Volatile Memory, Resistive Random Access Memory, Crossbar Array, Macro-architecture, Micro-architecture.

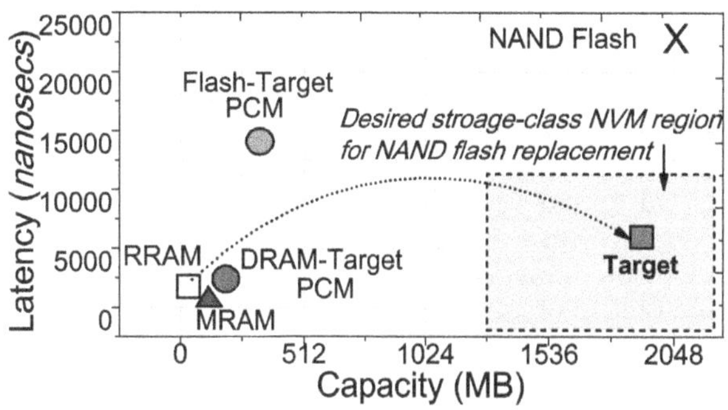

Figure 1: Design and optimization goal of a large-scale storage-class RRAM based system. Our design goal is to provide a similar storage capacity, but much better performance compared to state-of-the-art NAND flash.

1. INTRODUCTION

NAND flash is becoming a very popular storage-class memory and one of the conventional data storage mediums, thanks to its small form factor, low power consumption and performance superiority over spinning disks. However, it is quickly approaching its physical limits; as NAND flash scales down in feature size, it is becoming either too slow or too unreliable [8, 13]. Furthermore, NAND flash has been considered to be the main performance bottleneck in many handheld devices [14] and read-intensive scientific applications [12] since its performance is worse than network speed and exhibits significant variations. Even though different non-volatile memory (NVM) technologies are proposed to substitute NAND flash, currently, there exists *no* NVM that can directly replace NAND flash, as shown in Figure 1. Magnetic RAM (MRAM) and Spin-Transfer Torque RAM (STT-RAM) provide fast latency for switching their magnetic tunneling junction with the small size of storage capacity, which make them more suitable for SRAM or DRAM replacement, not NAND flash. Industry predicts that Phase-Change RAM (PCRAM), another attractive NVM technology, cannot directly replace NAND flash or DRAM [17] either, due to switching power related issues, which lead to slower latency than DRAM and lower storage capacity than NAND flash. In contrast to the complicated I/O process of conventional NVM technologies (e.g., PCRAM needs to heat up a storage material and NAND/NOR flash injects electrons into their floating gates), resistive RAM (RRAM) can store bits by simply changing resistance with voltage [22, 19, 15]. This memristor characteristic enables RRAM cells

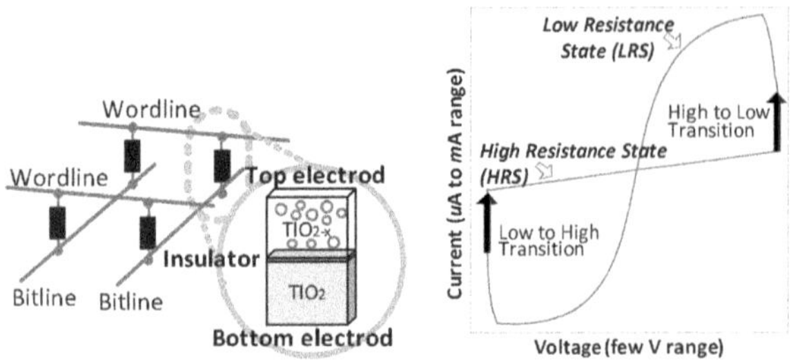

(a) Crosspoint array structure (b) I-V characteristic

Figure 2: Resistive switch I-V characteristic and a conceptual view of the RRAM cell on a crosspoint. RRAM can simply change resistance state with voltage, which is more reliable and faster than other NVM options.

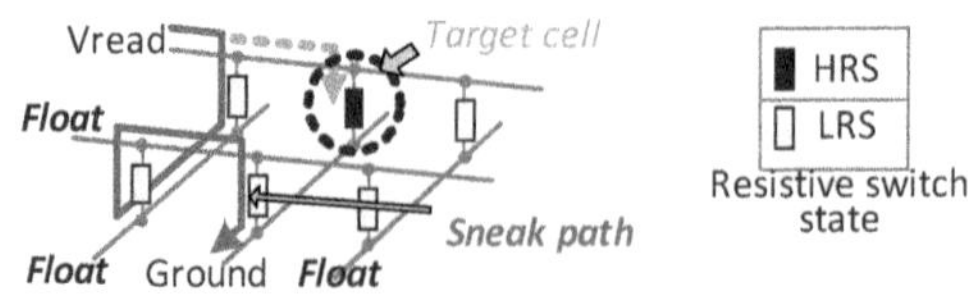

Figure 3: The sneak path problem associated with the crossbar architecture. The sneak path is an essential problem with the crossbar, which can lead to read and write failures.

switch among different resistance values within very short times like 7∼100 *ns* and be more reliable [2, 17] than other NVM technologies. In addition, RRAM can be constructed as a crossbar array which in turn makes it extremely dense, a promising alternative to replace NAND flash [16, 10]. Recently, various studies targeting RRAMs have been carried out, but they mainly target replacing caches [18, 6] or conventional main memory [23, 21] by capitalizing on different RRAM characteristics.

However, we *found that RRAM will have difficulty in directly replacing NAND flash memory because of its array level architectural limitations.* Specifically, our experimental data shows that, with RRAM, the maximum memory island size that could be accommodated is 64 ∼ 256 times smaller than the current NAND flash blocks. The main reason behind this limit is the "read sensing margin problem", which causes read failures on large-scale RRAM arrays.

In this paper, we present and evaluate the design of a large-scale storage-class RRAM system that can replace NAND flash memory by providing comparable storage capacity, but with much better performance. To alleviate the read sensing margin problem, we propose a *slab-based memory access scheme*, which divides a page-based I/O request into multiple memory accesses phases at the array level. This scheme sacrifices some memory-level performance, but achieves higher storage capacity and better reliability. To compensate the performance loss caused by the slab-based memory access, we also propose to exploit the internal parallelism at a macro-architecture level. Our experimental results using a cycle-level NVM simulator indicate that the storage-class RRAM can successfully take NVM medium off the critical path in Android-based handheld devices and High Performance Computing (HPC) I/O server nodes in National Energy Research Scientific Computing Center (NERSC) Clusters at Lawrence Berkeley National Laboratory (LBNL), and it is able to directly replace NAND flash. The **main contributions** of this paper can be summarized as follows:

• *Enabling storage-class RRAM.* We observed that, when using RRAM, the number of bits which can be placed into a single wordline is four times smaller than what a prior study [23, 21] claims, due to the read sensing margin problem. This small size of the crossbar structure makes it difficult for RRAM to replace the current NAND flash technology. With our proposed slab-based memory access scheme however, RRAM can be eight times denser compared to an unoptimized crossbar array architecture, which in turn leads to a storage capacity similar to NAND flash, even under smaller memory island areas.

• *Designing RRAM macro-architecture.* In addition to exploring a slab-based memory access scheme, we introduce the "local bitline" and "global bitline" concepts that help us form very large memory islands when using our slab-based memory access scheme. We also incorporate memory islands into multiple planes and dies, thereby taking advantage of the macro-level parallelism. Lastly, we analyze the main bottlenecks in our proposed architecture, and optimize them by introducing high-frequency data movement interfaces.

• *A system-level RRAM performance evaluation.* We perform a simulation based evaluation of our design targeting both a handheld device and a high performance I/O server node [20]. In this early evaluation, we show how RRAM can help us remove the performance bottlenecks caused by the NAND flash medium in diverse computing domains. Specifically, our results indicate that the proposed storage-class RRAM system can improve, on an average, the handheld system bandwidth and shorten I/O latency by 2.95 times and 66%, respectively.

2. BACKGROUND

2.1 Resistive Switching Effect

A resistive switch in RRAM consists primarily of *two metal electrodes*, which are separated by a functional isolator, as shown in Figure 2a. This metal-insulator-metal (MIM) structure can possess two different ohmic resistance states, referred to as *high resistance state* (HRS) and *low resistance state* (LRS). As shown in Figure 2b, HRS and LRS can be toggled by exceeding threshold voltages (e.g., V_{set} to switch to HRS, V_{reset} to switch to LRS), which is known as the *memory write* process. Since '1' and '0' can be represented by HRS and LRS, respectively, the data can be distinguished by measuring the electronic current when a small read voltage (V_{read}) is applied. This process is referred to as the *memory read*.

Unlike three-terminal devices such as DRAM, this two-terminal characteristic of the resistive switch enables RRAM to be incorporated into nano-crossbar arrays atop of the traditional CMOS components. Further, while the three-terminal devices always require an access transistor, the resistive switch can be implemented as a *zero-transistor one-register (0T1R)* cell on the crossbar. Consequently, an RRAM cell at each crosspoint can have the smallest feature size, $4F^2$ [23, 21, 6], which makes it possible to build a large-scale storage system.

Device Characteristic	Value
Interconnect Resistance	0.65 Ohm
RESET Voltage (V_{reset})	2.0 V
SET Voltage (V_{set})	-2.0 V
Read Voltage (V_{read})	0.5 V
Non-linearity	20 (Kr)
Low Resistance State	10 KOhm
High Resistance State	500 KOhm
Read Sense Resistance	100 Ohm

Table 1: RRAM and crossbar structure parameters and their default values [21] in our HSPICE simulation.

2.2 Crossbar Array Architecture

The crossbar structure perpendicularly overlays two nanowire electrode arrays to each other so that the resistive switch is formed at each crosspoint [16, 10], as shown in Figure 2a. In this crossbar architecture, the row-direction and column-direction nanowires are referred to as *wordline* and *bitline*, respectively. A set of multiple resistive switches, connected to a single wordline, is referred to as a *page*.

Sneak Path. Even though the no-transistor characteristic (0T1R) of the crossbar enables RRAM to form large-scale memory islands with much smaller area than the three-thermal devices, it also introduces the "sneak path" problem. *The sneak path is an unexpected path in the crossbar structure, which can lead to write and read failures.* Considering Figure 3 as an example, when the target cell is HRS (black), a high current might be measured because of the current flowing through the unselected LRS cells (white). Note that this unwanted activity can occur during both reads and writes if the access transistors are not integrated into all resistive switches of the crossbar. Unfortunately, the 0T1R crossbar structure is a necessary feature to have if we are to form a large-scale storage-class memory system using RRAM [4, 5]. In an attempt to address this sneak path problem, there exist two "circuit-level" solutions that do not need extra transistor integration, as explained below.

Page Write. For writing data into a specific page, two different voltages, V_{set} and V_{reset}, can be applied to the target wordline in tandem [3, 23, 21], and 0V needs to be applied to the selected bitlines of the page. To avoid writes to unintended RRAM cells, the half of V_{set} and V_{reset} should be applied to the unselected bitlines as well as wordlines, as depicted in Figure 4a. This *half-selection scheme* enables all cells connected to the target wordline to toggle their resistance states in parallel, which is known as a *page write*. However, V_{set} and V_{reset} cannot be applied simultaneously in the crossbar structure [23]; in reality, write operations are divided into two different steps – writing the cells for indicating '0' with V_{reset} is called a *reset* operation and writing '1' with V_{set} is referred to as a *set* operation.

Page Read. V_{read} is applied to the selected (target) wordline, and all other wordlines are grounded (0V), as shown in Figure 4b. This *biased wordline selection* scheme has been proposed in an attempt to reduce the conventional crossbar read failures, caused by the sneak path [19, 15]. To identify LRS or HRS ('0' or '1'), a *sensing logic*, connected to each bitline, compares the current coming from the memory island with the current from an external reference cell. Because of this parallel access, the state of the page in the target wordline can be captured simultaneously. However,

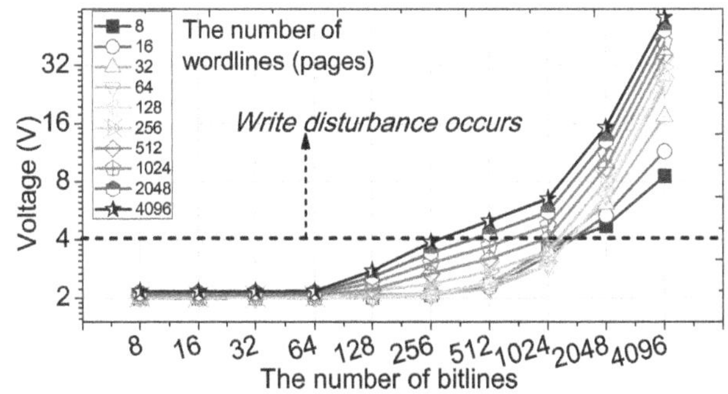

Figure 5: Voltage requirement and write disturbance analysis with varying crossbar configurations. Based on our HSPICE simulation, 1024x512 or 512x512 is the theoretical maximum crossbar size that can avoid unintentional writes. Each curve corresponds to a different number of wordlines in the crossbar.

during the read process, if the sensing margin, defined by the current difference between the target cells and reference cell, is too small, the data read cannot be identified by the sensing logic [5, 6].

3. CROSSBAR ARRAY AND RRAM LIMITATION STUDY

Thanks to the half-selection and biased wordline selection schemes, the crossbar-based RRAM can alleviate the sneak path problem. However, as one increases the number of bitlines and wordlines, these two schemes introduce different challenges for both reads and writes, which make it again difficult for RRAM to replace NAND flash. In this section, we explain the main challenges caused by state-of-the-art selection schemes and discuss their limitation using HSPICE simulation – the characteristics of the RRAM and crossbar structure we tested are given in Table 1.

Write Disturbance. As the page size increases, the half-selection scheme introduces a *write disturbance* problem, which changes the states of the unselected cells in addition to the target cells. The main reason behind these unreliable writes is that the writes with large-sized pages require a higher voltage due to the voltage drop imposed by longer wordlines. As a result, the half of the voltage exceeds the write threshold values (V_{set} or V_{reset}), thereby toggling the resistive switch states of the unselected wordlines. Figure 5 illustrates the voltage requirement that we evaluated using HSPICE when varying the number of wordlines and bitlines (from 8 to 4096). As we increase the number of bitlines, significant voltage drops take place for all the crossbar configurations tested. Even though the point where we reach the write disturbance (in our test, this point is 4V) would be different based on the number of wordlines employed, we noted that the maximum bitlines allowing reliable writes is 1024 with 64 wordlines or 512 with 512 wordlines. It should also be noted that, as shown by our experiments, a larger page size in the crossbar structure can be accommodated by reducing the number of wordlines.

Read Sensing Margin. The biased-selection scheme can avoid the sneak path problem by inducting the sneak current to the zero-biased wordlines, as shown in Figure 4b. Ironically, this current induction also reduces the current flowing

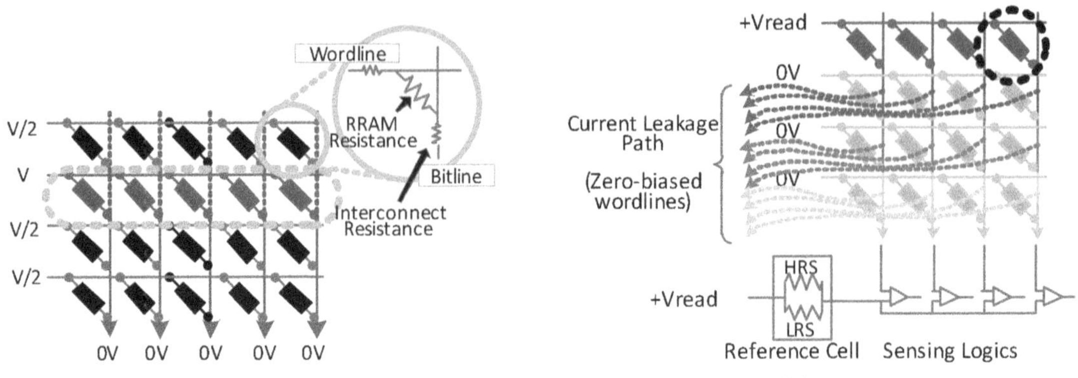

(a) Write (b) Read

Figure 4: Writes and reads on the crossbar structure. The half-selection scheme (a) and biased wordline selection (b) minimize the sneak path at the circuit level, but limit the size of the RRAM crossbar.

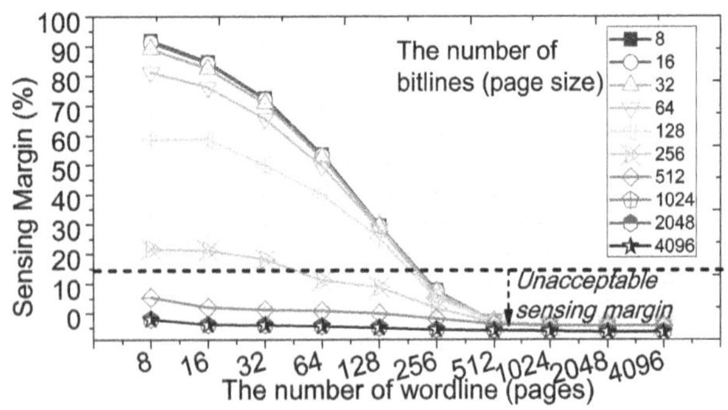

Figure 6: Read sensing margin analysis when varying the number of bitlines and wordlines. Unacceptable sensing margin is a more serious challenge than writes (128x128 is the maximum crossbar size).

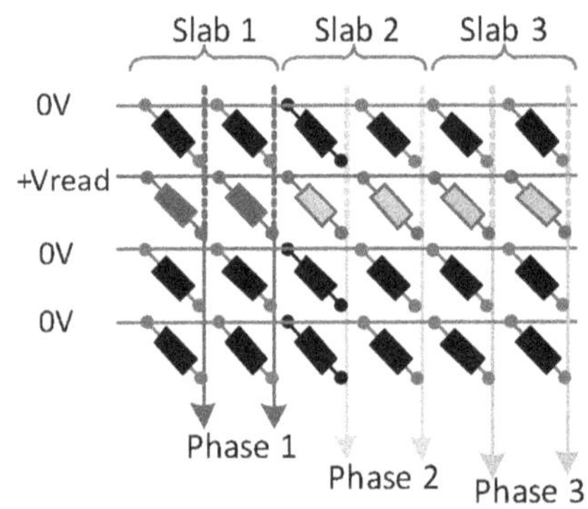

Figure 7: The concept of slab-based memory access in RRAM.

through the target page and introduces poor sensing margin if the size of the crossbar increases. This *leakage current* problem leads to read failures, and gets worse and worse as we increase the page size, as it makes the current significantly shrink by adding more bitlines. Figure 6 plots our HSPICE simulation results that give read sensing margins with the biased selection scheme when varying the number of wordlines and bitlines. Unlike what prior study reported [23, 21], *reads constitute a more problematic challenge than writes and are the dominant factor in deciding the memory array size.* Due to the sensing margin problem, the maximum page size that allows reliable reads is 128 with 128 wordlines per memory island, which is *eight times* smaller than that of writes. Considering the size of the current NAND flash blocks (256KB ~ 2MB), this memory island (2KB) is *too small* to build a large-scale storage-class NVM using RRAM.

4. DESIGNING STORAGE-CLASS RRAM

We first redesign the array-level sensing logic so that the length of wordline for reads can be longer, similar to that of writes. This redesigning is motivated by two critical observations: 1) activating a small number of bitlines for reading page data out can increase the read sensing margin, and 2) a large page size can be achieved by employing a small number of wordlines. We then introduce multiple memory islands and address the peripheral overhead problem through sharing so that RRAM can form a large-scale storage-class memory. Finally, we analyze the main performance bottlenecks in this architecture and optimize them by adopting enhanced interfaces and crossbar configurations.

4.1 Improving Sensing Margin

To overcome the limitations of the biased selection scheme, we propose a *slab-based memory access strategy*, which divides a page-based I/O request into multiple memory access phases at the array-level, as illustrated in Figure 7. A *slab* is a *set of bitlines*, which can be simultaneously activated to access the resistive switches in the target page. This slab-based memory access can minimize the leakage current problem by reducing the amount of current heading towards the biased wordlines for each memory access phase, as shown in Figure 8. In addition, to address the current shrinkage problem, we introduce *multiple reference cells* at the end of each and every wordline, as motivated by [6]. While the baseline sensing scheme uses the current coming from the external reference cell, this sensing logic with the internal reference cells can be aware of the resistance values, which vary based on what data have been stored by leveraging the

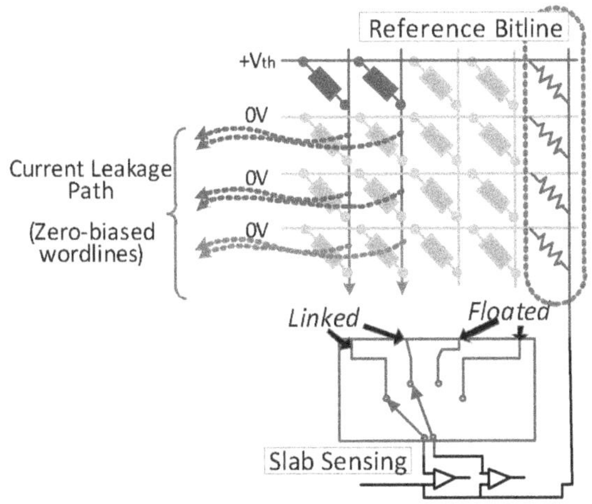

Figure 8: Slab-based memory access schematic.

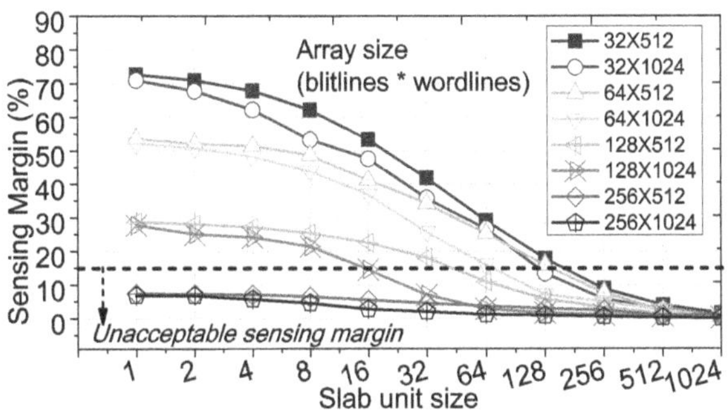

Figure 9: Sending margin with the slab-based memory access. Our proposed slab-based memory access alleviates the sensing margin problem and increases the page size by eight times.

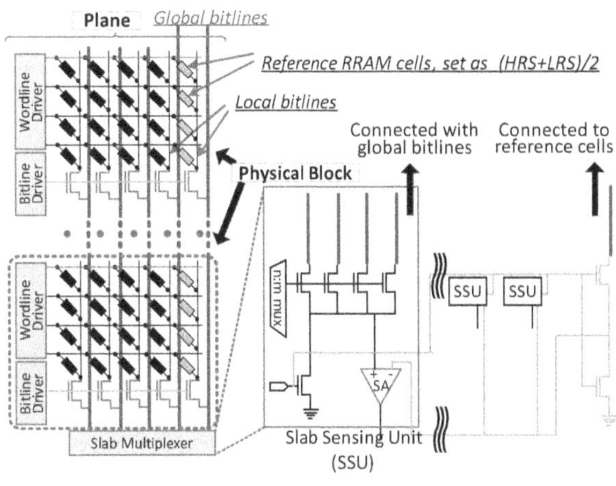

Figure 10: Multi-crossbar schematic. Multi-crossbar enables us place many memory islands into an RRAM plane and reduces the peripheral overheads by introducing global and local bitlines in the plane.

voltage passing through all the cells that are connected to the target wordline.

Figure 9 plots the sensing margin improvement results with our slab-based memory access scheme. We observe that our slab-based memory access scheme increases the sensing margin by five times on average, compared to the baseline sensing scheme, and enables a page size of 1024, which is equal to that of writes, with 64 wordlines. The main downside of our slab-based memory access scheme is its potential *long latency*, caused primarily by the multi-phase data sensing. To compensate this performance penalty, we take advantage of the macro-architecture parallelism. In addition, since the number of wordlines is smaller than that of writes, we determine the size of a memory island based on the limits imposed by *reads* rather than writes.

4.2 Macro-architecture Design

To build an RRAM plane, the RRAM crossbar architecture has two design optimization issues to be addressed in terms of *space utilization*. First, even though one can achieve a large page size with the proposed slab-based memory access, our memory islands are composed of fewer worldlines, compared to DRAM- or cache-target RRAM islands that have been proposed by [23, 21, 4, 5]. Consequently, to achieve high storage capacity, we also introduce multiple crossbar memory islands into a plane and consider each corresponding crossbar as a physical block. This *multi-crossbar* approach enables us achieve a thousand times larger storage capacity than a single crossbar structure could provide by interconnecting multiple physical blocks in the plane.

4.2.1 Relaxing Peripheral Overheads

One main concern regarding our multi-crossbar might be the peripheral and wiring overheads. The main reason why NAND flash can provide ten times higher storage capacity than NOR flash (even though underlying NVM cell technologies are not different) is that many flash cells are connected in series, referred to as NAND string, which allows a denser layout. Even though the 0T1R cell of RRAM is close to that of NAND flash, each physical block in the multi-crossbar requires their own sensing logic and bitlines, which does not blend well with large-scale NVM.

To address this issue, we first reduce the number of bitlines required to connect physical blocks by introducing the *global bitline* and *local bitline* concepts, and allowing the sensing logic in a plane to be shared by multiple physical blocks (see Figure 10). The slab sensing unit is connected only to the global bitlines in the plane, and these global bitlines are shared by the multiple physical blocks. The global bitlines and local bitlines are connected through the bitline-select transistors. Based on the incoming memory request, the target page in a block is activated by the transistor, which is controlled by the bitline drivers. Despite this overhead of additional transistors per physical block, the reduction in bitlines and sensing units allows a dense physical layout. In addition, the slab-based memory access scheme requires a sense amplifier per slab sensing unit, not per bitline, which can in turn help us achieve a large RRAM plane.

4.2.2 Improving Multi-Crossbar Density

Lastly, we further optimize the memory density of the RRAM plane by adopting a *layered-bipolar array* structure [16, 5], which stacks multiple metal layers and sandwiches the resistive switches between them without any extra isolation layer. The main design concept behind the layered-bipolar array structure is to employ complementary material stack structures composed of the regular memory stack and the one with a reversed deposition order [16]. In fact, this layered array has successfully been implemented on a complete CMOS wafer and stacked four crossbar with five metal layers [7]. In this work, we integrate the layered array into our multi-crossbar as shown on the right portion of Figure 11. In the integrated layered multi-crossbar structure, the wordlines and local bitlines are connected to the top and bottom electrodes of two different vertical bipolar switches. Therefore, a page can be n times larger in size, where n is the number of the layers employed; however, because of the vertically-connected shared resource, only half of a target page can be activated simultaneously [5].

4.2.3 *Introducing Macro Level Parallelism*

To compensate for the performance penalty of the proposed slab-based memory access and layered array, we also employ multiple planes in a die, and package multiple dies in a single chip, as shown in Figure 11. In this macro-architecture, multiple memory requests can be interleaved across multiple dies and served by multiple planes in parallel. Since the switching-speed across the resistance states of RRAM is much faster than the speed of the NAND flash write operation and the macro-architecture of RRAM has more internal resources than other NVMs, memory transactions should be efficiently handled to achieve high levels of internal parallelism. Therefore, data movement is managed by the internal I/O logic, and the address and control commands are handled by the command interface and control logic employing a macro-level command queue. All bus activities related these commands and data movements are brought into the internal logic through a single multiplexed I/O interface in tandem to provide chip interconnection compatibility with conventional NVMs. It should be pointed out that, in cases where the memory operation is very fast, this serialized data movement might be on the critical path in terms of performance.

5. PERFORMANCE STUDY AND OPTIMIZATION

Setup and Latency Modeling. To measure the base-line performance, we simulated a layered multi-crossbar RRAM by modifying a hardware-validated cycle-level NVM simulation model [11]. This simulation framework models the timing and delay of peripherals, page buffer, interface and data bus handling in detail. The read latency for an RRAM operation can be expressed as follows:

$$t_{latency} = \frac{(\delta t_v + t_{sense}) * n_{wl}}{n_{slab} * 0.5 \cdot n_{layer}}, \quad (1)$$

where t_{sense} is the time for sensing, and n_{wl}, n_{slab}, and n_{layer} indicate the number of wordlines, bitlines in a slab, and layers, respectively. Let C_l, R_l, and R_r denote the total line capacitance, resistance and pull-down resistance of the resistive switch, respectively. We then have δt_v, the RC delay time, as follows:

$$\delta t_v = R_l * 0.5 \cdot C_l * (1 + \frac{R_r + R_l/3}{R_r + R_l}). \quad (2)$$

The capacitance (C_l) and resistance (R_l) can simply be obtained as $C_l = 2 \cdot \varepsilon_0 \cdot \varepsilon_r \cdot w_l / h$ and $R_l = \rho \cdot l / A$. The parameter values used in this expression like relative static permittivity (ε_r) can vary significantly based on which nanowire and technology are employed (we use 22nm standard nanowire technology [9]). Also, the write latency can similarly be expressed as $t_{write} = 2 * t_{switch} \cdot n_{slab} \cdot n_{layer}/2$, where t_{switch} is the time for switching resistance. In this paper, we use $t_{switch} = 100$ $n$sec, extracted from [23]. In addition to the main device characteristics (Table 1), the remaining macro-level configuration, simulation parameters and area comparison analysis are given in Table 2.

	RRAM	MLC	SLC
Pages	128	128	64
Page size	4096 (4 layers)	32768	16384
Blocks	4096	8196	4096
Plane	8	2	2
Die	4	2	2
Capacity	8192MB	8192MB	2048MB
Area(F^2)	2.75E+11	2.80E+11	1.07E+09

Table 2: Storage-class RRAM and NAND flash configurations evaluated in our experiments.

5.1 Baseline RRAM vs NAND Flash

We compare two different types of NAND flash with our storage-class RRAM system when varying the number of bitlines in a slab from 1 to 128. In this comparison, I/O request sizes tested vary from 1KB to 4MB for both reads and writes. In our notation, "X" in "RRAM-X" indicates the number of bitlines in a slab (e.g., RRAM-64 means a slab contains 64 bitlines). In addition to understanding the basic performance behavior of our storage-class RRAM, one of the goals behind this study is to find an "ideal" slab-based memory access scheme, which provides better performance (in terms of latency and bandwidth) than NAND flash as well as high read and write reliability.

Write Latency. We observe that the average latencies of all slab-based memory access schemes outperform an MLC NAND flash, as shown in Figure 12a. Specifically, RRAM-128 reduces the average latency of an MLC NAND flash by 96%. The average latency of even RRAM-1 is about 53% of MLC NAND flash.Comparing against SLC NAND flash, we see that the average latency of RRAM exceeds it in cases where the number of bitlines in a slab is more than two. RRAM-128 still reduces write latency of SLC NAND flash by 78%.

Read Latency. The read latency behavior of our slab-based memory access scheme is quite different than its write behavior. As shown in Figure 12b, the performance of RRAM-1 ~ RRAM-8 is worse than both the SLC and MLC NAND flash, and only RRAM-16 ~ RRAM-128 perform better than NAND flash. One of the reasons for this is the relatively faster read performance of NAND flash. More specifically, the memory array structure in NAND flash is well optimized to serve large size of I/Os in parallel. It should also be noted that, unlike writes, the read latency benefits of RRAM under large slab sizes are not as significant.

Bandwidth Analysis. Figure 12c illustrates the bandwidth for all the configurations tested in this work. To make a better comparison, the bandwidth values of NAND flash are shown on the right side of the graph. While the read

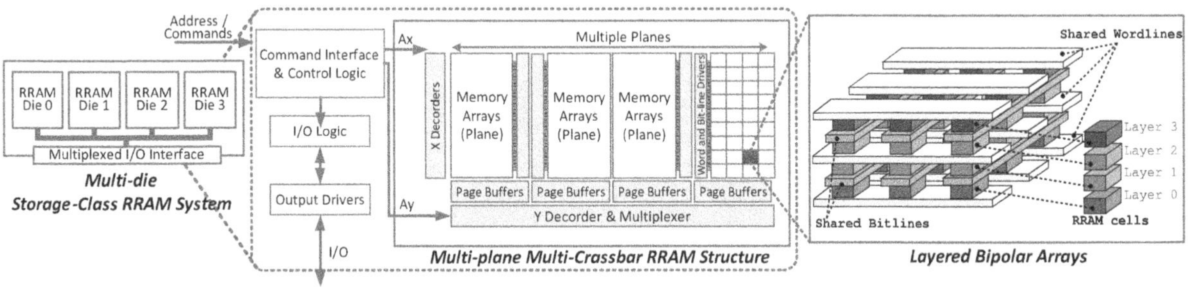

Figure 11: System-level macro-architecture schematic.

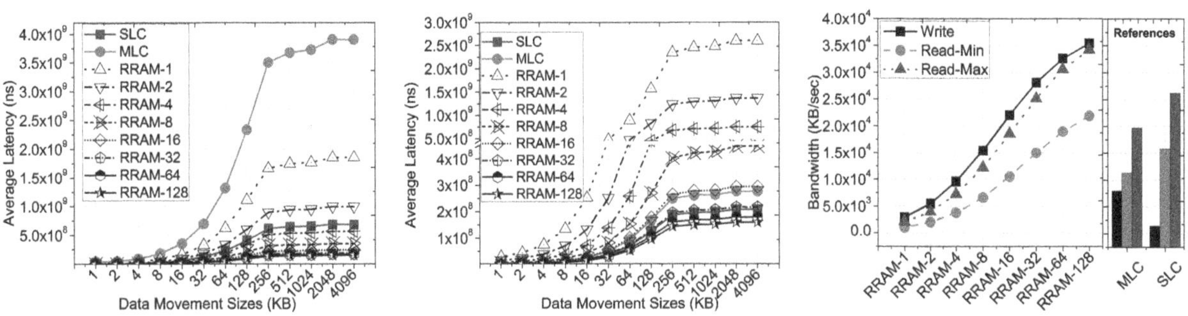

(a) Write Latency (b) Read Latency (c) Bandwidth

Figure 12: Latency and bandwidth comparison.

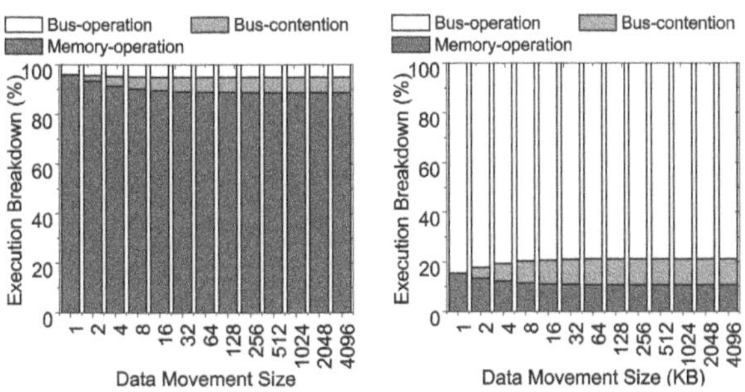

(a) RRAM-1 (b) RRAM-128

Figure 13: Execution time breakdown. Note that unlike RRAM-1, RRAM-128 spends most of its time in taking the data out from the page buffer.

performance of NAND flash is hundred times better than write performance, all our RRAM configurations show better throughput on writes than reads. Specifically, writes are 56.9 % faster than reads, on average, due to the multiplexed I/O interface, which causes slow data movement of the read operations. One can conclude from our analysis that RRAM-32 outperforms the MLC-NAND flash, and, beyond RRAM-64, the performance of the slab-based RRAM configurations exceeds the performance of all NAND flash configurations tested.

Performance Bottleneck Analysis. To better understand the reason behind this performance disparity between reads and writes, we breakdown the total execution time into tree different I/O activities: memory operation, bus operation and bus contention, as shown in Figure 19. The memory operation component captures the time it takes for the data coming from the target memory island to arrive at the page buffer, and the bus operation component represents the time taken in command and date movement handing through the multiplexed interface. A bus contention occurs when I/O requests in the macro-level queue are executed in an out-of-order fashion. One can see from our results that, while RRAM-1 fully utilizes the execution time for handing memory operations, RRAM-128 spends most of its time in taking the data out from the page buffer (20% of the total execution) via the multiplexed interface. We believe that this is the main reason why the latency benefits of RRAM-32 $\sim$ RRAM-128 are not good, compared to NAND flash, and their read throughput is lower than their write throughput. This performance bottlenecks can be mitigated by adopting an enhanced interface, which would make storage-class RRAMs (RRAM-32 $\sim$ RRAM-128) more attractive. The next section describes such an interface.

5.2 Optimizing Data Movement Interface

In this section, we optimize the multiplexed interface using various clock frequencies ranging from 40 MHz (a common interface bus clock for the current NVM technology) to 1333MHz (a popular bus clock for the main memory), and study how different frequency interfaces impact read performance.

Performance Analysis. Figure 14b plots the change in the read latency with varying frequency. For better comparison, the latencies of SLC NAND flash and MLC NAND flash with different frequency interfaces are added to the right side of the figure, as a reference. One can see from this figure that, the latency improvement brought by a higher frequency interface is higher than the case where we employ a larger slab size with a slow interface. For example, RRAM-64 with 1333MHz interface provides 3.56 times shorter latency than

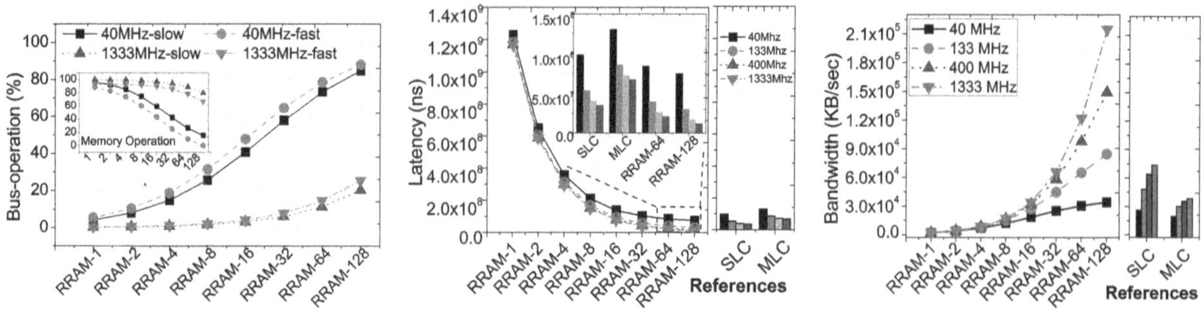

(a) Bus-operation activity change (b) Latency change (c) Bandwidth change

Figure 14: Latency and bandwidth comparison between RRAM and NAND flash with enhanced interface and bus frequency.

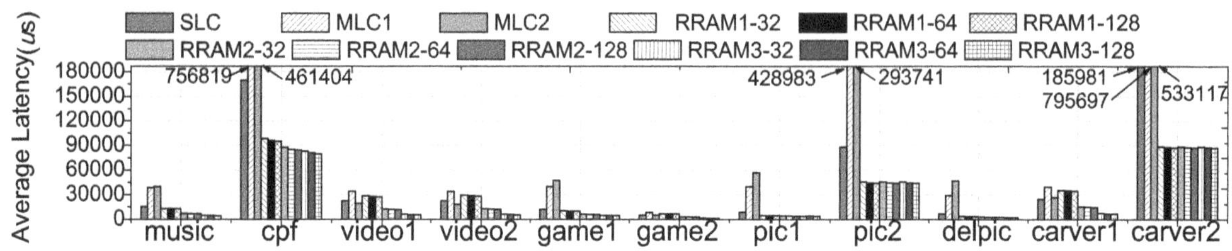

Figure 15: Average latency per I/O request (system-level).

RRAM-128 employing a 40 MHz interface. Figure 14c shows bandwidth improvement as one increases the clock frequency of the interface. While RRAM-128 employing 133MHz interface improves bandwidth by only about 2x, it improves the bandwidth by 8x under a 1333 MHz interface.

Based on these results, we conclude that the conventional storage-class interface should be removed from RRAM, and a high frequency clock, which is typically used for main memories, needs to be adopted. We see that, by employing a high frequency interface, RRAM-128, on average, exhibits shorter latency by 66% and 2.95 times better bandwidth than NAND flash.

Utilization Analysis. The main reason why an RRAM configuration with high frequency interface exhibits much better bandwidth and latency can be explained by studying resource utilization. Figure 14a depicts the time taken by data movement and memory operations as a fraction of the total I/O time when varying the slab size and clock frequency. While the contribution of data movement with the 40 MHz interface keeps growing as the slab size increases, with a 1333MHz bus clock, data movement for all RRAM systems accounts for a small fraction of the total execution (under 20%). In contrast, while an RRAM with 40MHz devotes only 20% of the total I/O time to handling memory operations, an RRAM employing 1333 MHz spends most of its time in handling the memory operations, irrespective of the slab size employed, which in turn allows the RRAM to exhibit true resistive switch performance.

6. SYSTEM-LEVEL PERFORMANCE EVALUATION

To evaluate our storage-class RRAM, we first explain our mobile system setup, workload characteristics and storage configurations regarding three different NAND flash types and our storage-class RRAMs. We then compare the performance behaviors of the NAND flash and the RRAMs under the different workloads. The performance metrics that we used for the comparison are as follows: bandwidth, IOPS – IO operation per second, and average latency. In addition, we provide time series and resource utilization comparisons between NAND flash and storage-class RRAMs. Lastly, we quantify macro-level parallelism that SLC flash and RRAM-128 exhibit in order to demonstrate how the proposed macro-architecture of the large-scale storage-class RRAM compensates for the potential performance loss, caused by the slab-based memory access scheme.

	Total Size (KB)	Avg Size (KB)	Read Fraction (%)	Write Rand. (%)	Read Rand. (%)
music	12072	131	94.6	84.4	94.1
cpf	492704	420	44.9	79.2	79.5
video1	1201613	115	99.8	93.7	88.6
video2	10750486	115	99.9	93.8	92.3
game1	81696	87	88.2	86.6	85.1
game2	952804	27	99.7	98.9	92.2
pic1	1799	26	38.2	96.8	86.9
pic2	134168	56	0.1	91.9	86.6
delpic	5973	25	74.7	95.8	92.9
carver1	153884297	127	99.9	45.8	80.6
carver2	512000	128	0.1	16.4	–

Table 3: Main characteristics of our Android and HPC (Carver) cluster I/O node workloads.

6.1 Evaluation Setup

We use the cycle-level NVM simulation model described in Section 5. To simulate storage medium and measure the system-level performance accurately, we collected diverse

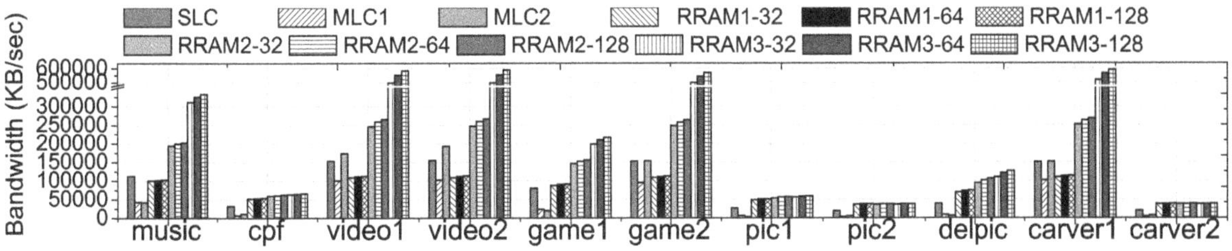

Figure 16: Bandwidth.

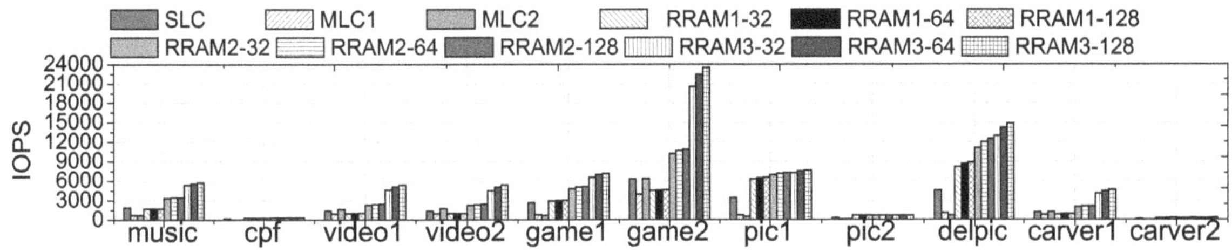

Figure 17: IOPS (I/O Operations Per Second).

workloads from a real mobile machine and HPC I/O node, as explained below.

Mobile Device Setup. To collect traces, we chose Samsung Galaxy S2 (SHW-M250S) employing Android Gingerbread 2.3.3 as its operating system; we believe that similar results could also be achieved under other mobile devices such as Google Nexus One and LG G2X. In order to collect block-level storage access information, we used *blktrace* [1], which is a widely-used Linux I/O tracing tool.

HPC I/O Node Configuration. We collected workloads from an out-of-core eigensolver code [24, 25] running under Global Parallel File System (GPFS), which is installed in Carver cluster [20] in NERSC at LBNL. The testbed is composed of 50 nodes: 40 computational nodes and 10 I/O nodes. Each node is equipped with two Intel Xeon X5550 processors clocked at 2.67 GHz (4 cores each, hyper-threading is disabled) and 24GB of DDR3 memory. Each node runs on Red Hat 5.5 with Linux kernel 2.6.18-238.12.1.el5.

System-Level Workloads. We now describe the important characteristics of the block-level workloads used in this study. We originally collected 24 different handheld workloads by executing the most frequently-used mobile applications to serve as benchmarks and 10 HPC I/O nodes by running the out-of-core Eigensolver code, but then omitted some results that indicate similar behavior to those shown here to save space.The *music* workload is collected by periodically playing a MP3 file (3.04 MB); the *cpf* workload includes a 45MB file copy process on the Linux EXT4 file system; *video1* and *video2* are workloads obtained by playing a 45MB video file for 1 and 10 minutes, respectively; *game1* and *game2* are collected by executing two popular mobile game applications, AngryBird and Asphalt 6 HD, for about 10 minute, respectively; and, finally, *pic1*, *pic2* and *delpic* are collected by performing a series of image file processes, taking 80MB size images and deleting them from the default Gallery. The *carver1* and *carver2* are collected by executing our out-of-core eigensolver code (writing sparse matrix-vector data structures once as the initial phase (carver2) and repeatedly reading the vector for a nuclear computation (carver1)). The important characteristics of our workloads are given in Table 3.

NVM Storage Configuration. We prepared three different types of NAND flash and storage-class RRAMs, as shown in Table 4. The SLC NAND flash device provides faster read latency than MLC1 and MLC2 (by 2x and 8x, respectively). The main difference between the MLC1 and MLC2 configurations is the page size they employ. Even though the page-based read latency of MLC2 is much longer than that of MLC1, MLC2 generally exhibits better system-level performance under our workloads, mainly due to the larger page size it employs.

Even though all these NAND flash devices typically employ 40 MHz $\sim$ 55 MHz interfaces, for better comparison against our RRAM, we introduced 400 MHz interface to them – we observed that there is no additional performance gain when we employ a 1333 MHz interface in NAND flash, irrespective of the underlying NAND flash type. For the storage-class RRAM simulation, we leveraged the same resistive switch characteristics used in Section 5 (Table 1). It should be noted that all the NVM technologies we tested are applied as a package device. Even though the performance of package device is much poorer than that of a form of solid state disk, it allows us to fairly compare each NVM system with our storage-class RRAM systems.

6.2 I/O Performance

Throughput. We observed that our storage-class RRAMs significantly improve system throughput (in terms of both bandwidth and IOPS) for all the workloads tested, as indicated by Figure 16. Specifically, they improve bandwidth by 8.28 times and IOPS by 8.57 times, on average, for both write-intensive and mixed workloads (e.g., cpf, pic1, pic2, delpic), as compared to MLC1. Further, compared even against the SLC NAND flash, our RRAMs provide by 2.95 times better bandwidth and 2.84 times better IOPS.

In read-intensive workloads (e.g., music, video1, video2, game2), performance improvement brought by our RRAMs is more significant, except for RRAM1; RRAM3 gives about 500 $\sim$ 600 MB/sec while SLC NAND flash (with the 400MHz

Device Type	Feature	Value
Single Level Cell (SLC)	Page Size(Bytes)	2048
	Write Latency(us)	250
	Read Latency(us)	25
	Erase Latency(us)	1500
	Memory Area(F^2)	1.07E+09
Multi-Level Cell 1 (MLC1)	Page Size(Bytes)	2048
	Write Latency(us)	250∼2200
	Read Latency(us)	50
	Erase Latency(us)	2500
	Memory Area(F^2)	2.80E+11
Multi-Level Cell 2 (MLC2)	Page Size(Bytes)	8192
	Write Latency(us)	440∼5000
	Read Latency(us)	200
	Erase Latency(us)	2500
	Memory Area(F^2)	1.07E+09
Storage-Class RRAM	Nanowire	22 nm [9]
	Die & Plane	4 & 8
	Memory Area(F^2)	2.75E+11
	slab size	32 ∼ 128
RRAM1	Interface clock	133MHz
RRAM2		400MHz
RRAM3		1333MHz

Table 4: NAND flash device and storage-class RRAM characterization. Note that all of the NAND flash configurations tested employ a fast toggle interface (400MHz) and dual die and dual plane architecture.

interface) provides about 130 MB/sec, and MLC1 and MLC2 result in 62 MB/sec and 99 MB/sec, respectively. The reason why the performance of RRAM1 is worse than SLC or even MLC2 NAND flash is its slow interface (133MHz) and smaller page unit size, as already explained in Section 5.2.

Latency. Figure 15 plots system-level average latency, measured by the time taken by the storage system to return the requested data per I/O request (not per page-based memory request). As shown in the figure, the storage-class RRAMs reduce the average latency by 66% compared to the SLC NAND flash, and provide 88% and 75% shorter average latency, respectively, than MLC1 and MLC2 NAND flash. Similar to the case with throughput, RRAM1 exhibits worse behavior than SLC NAND flash under the read-intensive workloads. One interesting performance behavior on this average latency study is the performance of MLC2 NAND flash. Even though MLC2 provides about 4x worse latency than MLC1 NAND flash at a device-level, the average latency experienced with MLC1 is better than that of MLC2 in the following workloads: cpf, video1, video2, and pic2. This performance behavior can be explained with the help of two observations: 1) the average request sizes of such workloads are larger than other workloads (56KB ∼ 420KB), and 2) MLC2 NAND flash can serve them with 4x larger page-sized I/O operations. It should be noted that, even though the page size of the storage-class RRAMs is 8x smaller than MLC1, the average latency of RRAM2 and RRAM3 is better than all NAND flash configurations tested. The main reason for this is that our RRAM can take advantage of the macro-level parallelism in serving large size I/O requests.

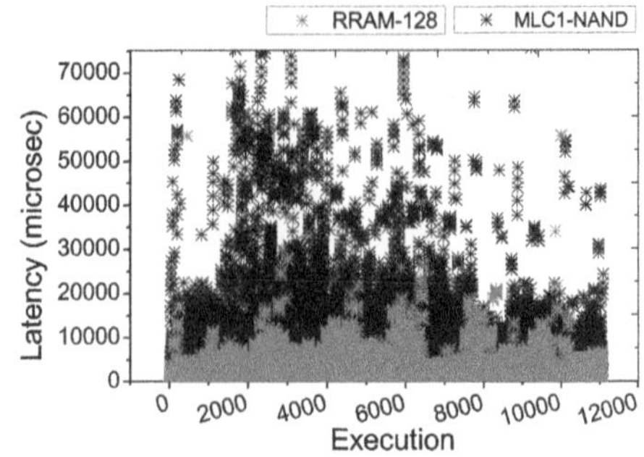

(a) RRAM-128 vs. MLC1

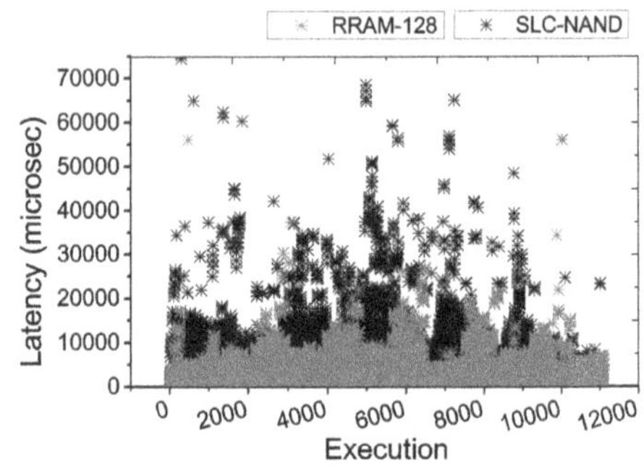

(b) RRAM-128 vs. SLC

Figure 18: Latency time series comparison (video1).

6.3 Time Series

Figure 18 shows the time series of two different types of NAND flashes (MLC1 and SLC) and RRAM-128 under a read-intensive workload (video1). In this figure, we only show the latencies under 70 ms for the sake of brevity. As illustrated in Figure 18a, RRAM-128 reduces the system latency by 84% compared to the MLC1 NAND flash, and outperforms it when executing all incoming I/O requests. Similarly, as compared to the SLC NAND flash (Figure 18b), RRAM-128 provides, on average, 76 % shorter system latency, and guarantees faster response time in all twelve thousand I/O requests. We believe that these results form a clear evidence that the storage-class RRAMs can (with proper optimizations) replace the current NAND flash technology with better performance, and take the storage medium bottleneck off the critical path in mobile device applications.

6.4 Resource Utilization

In this section, we compare the resource utilization characteristics of SLC and RRAM-128 by employing the same frequency in interface. Figures 19a and 19b decompose the total I/O execution times of the SLC NAND flash and RRAM-128 into bus-operation, bus-contention and memory-operation activities, described in Section 5.2. These two figures explain the memory-level performance difference between NAND flash and storage-class RRAM. While the memory operation activities of the SLC NAND flash are already well balanced with data movement (bus-operation) activities under by the 400 MHz interface, RRAM-128 fully devotes its time to handling memory operations, and still requires a faster interface to bring its data out. This observation means that our storage-class RRAM is fundamentally capable of providing shorter latency and better throughput than NAND flash,

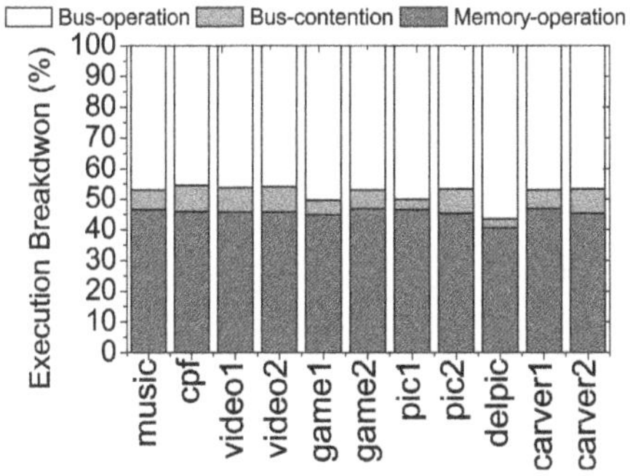

(a) SLC NAND

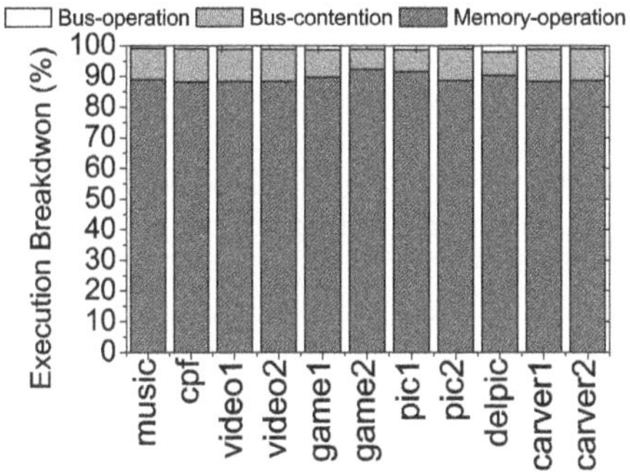

(b) RRAM-128

Figure 19: Execution time breakdown with a 400MHz interface (page-based I/O access).

even though its slab-based memory access strategy sacrifices some performance in order to guarantee circuit-level I/O reliability.

6.5 Quantifying Parallelism

Figure 20 illustrates the different degrees of macro-level parallelism in SLC NAND flash and RRAM-128. In this figure, *PAL0* indicates the I/O requests served by the memory system without any parallelism; *PAL1* means all planes associated to the same page offset are activated to serve an I/O request; and *PAL2* means that the incoming I/O requests are interleaved across multiple dies. Lastly, *PAL3* means that I/O requests are scattered among all internal resources (dies, plane, and layered crossbar), and simultaneously served by them. Note that the high levels of parallelism (PAL3 and PAL2) improve system bandwidth and shorten system latency as well.

As shown in Figures 20a and 20b, the SLC NAND flash serves I/O requests through PAL1 and PAL2 by about 90% of time. In contrast, RRAM-128 serves reads and writes through PAL3 by 43.2% (see Figure 20c) and 28.1% (see Figure 20d), on average, respectively. Further, RRAM-128 enjoys about 15.7% more PAL2 compared to the SLC NAND flash. The main reason behind this high degree of parallelism is that, in RRAM, 4x many planes and 2x many dies compose a single page (as compared to conventional NAND flash), and the size of incoming I/O requests for most workloads tested are large enough to span all macro-level resources. Consequently, RRAM-128 successfully compensates for the potential performance loss caused by the slab-based memory access strategy.

7. RELATED WORK

We found very few published papers on system-level RRAM, and most prior studies focus on resistive cell technology or circuit-level optimizations. [19, 15] proposed a device structure for RRAM, which can overcome the sneak path problem by employing an additional select transistor or diode. [3, 23, 21] proposed circuit-level solutions to avoid the sneak path problem by applying half of voltage or zero-biased voltages on unselected worldlines, and studied the memory array limitations by mainly focusing on addressing the write disturbance problem. [4, 5] suggested a 3D-stacked RRAM memory array that can exploit the characteristics of a bipolar resistive switch to mitigate the sneak path problem.

Even though these studies gave us great insights to build a large-scale storage class RRAM, they primarily aimed to replace the main memory or even cache memory with *a small size of memory island.* Further, none of these prior studies proposed a macro-architecture to build large-scale RRAM or evaluated *system-level performance* of RRAMs.

To the best of our knowledge, this paper is the first one that proposes a storage-class RRAM architecture that can replace NAND flash, and presents a detailed system-level performance evaluation by comparing diverse NAND flash technologies and storage-class RRAMs using various real application workloads. In contrast to previous RRAM-based studies, our investigation reveals the crossbar structure limitations to address both the read and write reliability problems using HSPICE simulation, and mitigates them by employing both system-level and circuit-level solutions. We also studied various high frequency interfaces to extract maximum RRAM performance from memory islands.

8. ACKNOWLEDGEMENTS

We would like to express thanks to Sanghyun Lee (Corelinks), Kuk-Hwan Kim (University of Michigan), Yi-Chung Chen (University of Pittsburgh), Cy Chan (LBNL), and Naveen Muralimanohar (HP Labs), Con Xu (PennState), for technical discussion on RRAM technologies. We also would like to express thanks Erik Saule (Ohio State University), H. Metin Aktulga (LBNL), Shane Canon (LBNL) and Chao Yang (LBNL) for collecting HPC workloads in the out-of-core eigensolver application for nuclear computation. We are grateful to many anonymous reviewers for their detailed comments which have greatly improved the quality of our paper. This research is supported in part by NSF grants 1017882, 0937949, and 0833126 and DOE grant DE-SC0002156 as well as used resources of the National Energy Research Scientific Computing Center, which is supported by the Office of Science of the U.S. Department of Energy under Contract No. DE-AC02-05CH11231.

9. CONCLUDING REMARKS

The three main contributions of this paper can be summarized as follows. First, we propose a novel memory access strategy that works well with dense RRAM islands, making them competitive with NAND flash capacities. Second, we incorporate memory islands into multiple planes and dies, thereby taking advantage of macro-level parallelism in RRAMs. Third, we analyze the main bottlenecks in this architecture, and optimize them by introducing high-frequency data movement interfaces. To quantify the effectiveness of our proposed system and optimizations, we evaluate them

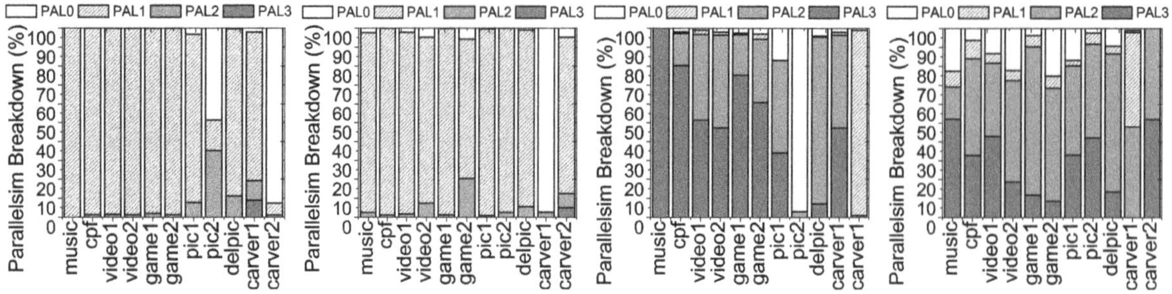

(a) SLC read (b) SLC write (c) RRAM-128 read (d) RRAM-128 write

Figure 20: Parallelism breakdown.

under various real Android workloads and high performance computing workloads with different values of major system parameters. The results from this experimental analysis indicate that the proposed architecture can provide 2.95 $\sim$ 8.28 times better bandwidth and 66 % $\sim$ 88 % shorter latency as compared to the conventional NAND flash, and improve the system-level performance of our workloads by 5x, with a storage capacity similar to that of the state-of-the-art NAND flash.

10. REFERENCES

[1] Brunelle, A. *Block I/O Layer Tracing.* 2006.

[2] Chang, M.-F., et al. A 4MB embedded slc resistive-ram macro with 7.2ns read-write random-access time and 160ns MLC-access capability. In *ISSCC* (2011).

[3] Chen, Y.-C., et al. An access-transistor-free (0t/1r) non-volatile resistance random access memory (rram) using a novel threshold switching, self-rectifying chalcogenide device. In *IEDM* (2003).

[4] Chen, Y.-C., et al. 3D-him: A 3D high-density interleaved memory for bipolar rram design. In *NANOARCH* (2011).

[5] Chen, Y.-C., et al. 3D-ICML: A 3D bipolar reram design with interleaved complementary memory layers. In *DATE* (2011).

[6] Chen, Y.-C., et al. A look up table design with 3D bipolar RRAMs. In *ASP-DAC* (2012).

[7] Chevallier, C., et al. A 0.13 um 64Mb multi-layered conductive metal-oxide memory. In *ISSCC* (2010).

[8] Grupp, L. M., et al. The bleak future of nand flash memory. In *FAST* (2012).

[9] ITRS. International technology roadmap for semiconductors 2009 edition. In *http://www.itrs.net/Links/2009ITRS/Home2009.htm.*

[10] Jo, S. H., et al. High-density crossbar arrays based on a si memristive system. In *Nano Letter* (2009).

[11] Jung, M., et al. NANDFlashSim: Intrinsic latency variation aware NAND flash memory system modeling and simulation at microarchitecture level. In *MSST* (2012).

[12] Jung, M., et al. Physically addressed queueing (PAQ): Improving parallelism in solid state disks. In *ISCA* (2012).

[13] Jung, M., and Kandemir, M. Revisiting widely held ssd expectations and rethinking system-level implications. In *Proc. of SIGMETRICS* (2013).

[14] Kim, H., et al. Revisiting storage for smartphones. In *FAST* (2012).

[15] Kim, K.-H., et al. A functional hybrid memristor crossbar-array/cmos system for data storage and neuromorphic applications. In *Nano Letters* (2011).

[16] Kugeler, C., et al. High density 3D memory architecture based on the resistive switching effect. *Solid-State Electronics* (2009).

[17] Lammers, D. Resistive ram gains ground. In *IEEE Spectrum* (2010).

[18] Lewis, D., et al. Architectural evaluation of 3D stacked RRAM caches. In *3DIC* (2009).

[19] Linn, E., et al. Complementary resistive switches for passive nanocrossbar memories. In *Nature Materials* (2010).

[20] NERSC. In *http://www.nersc.gov/users/computational-systems/carver/.*

[21] Niu, D., et al. Design trade-offs for low-power, high density cross-point resistive memory. In *ISLPED* (2012).

[22] Strukov, D. B., et al. The missing memristor found. *Nature* (2009).

[23] Xu, C., et al. Design implications of memristor-based rram cross-point structrues. In *DATE* (2011).

[24] Zhou, Z., et al. An out-of-core dataflow middleware to reduce the cost of large scale iterative solvers. In *P2S2* (2012).

[25] Zhou, Z., et al. An out-of-core eigensolver on ssd-equipped clusters. In *Proceedings of the 2012 IEEE International Conference on Cluster Computing* (2012), CLUSTER '12.

Memorage: Emerging Persistent RAM based Malleable Main Memory and Storage Architecture

Ju-Young Jung
Computer Science Department
University of Pittsburgh
Pittsburgh, PA, USA
juyoung@cs.pitt.edu

Sangyeun Cho
Memory Solutions Lab., Memory Division,
Samsung Electronics Co., Korea
Computer Science Department,
University of Pittsburgh
Pittsburgh, PA, USA
cho@cs.pitt.edu

ABSTRACT

This paper addresses new system design issues that will occur when a large quantity of emerging persistent RAM (PRAM) is put on the main memory bus of a platform. First, we anticipate that continued technology advances will enable us to integrate (portions of) the system storage within the PRAM modules on a system board. This change calls for comprehensive re-examination of the system design concepts that assume slow disk and the block I/O concept. Next, we propose *Memorage*, a system architecture that virtually manages all available physical resources for memory and storage in an integrated manner. Memorage leverages the existing OS virtual memory (VM) manager to improve the performance of memory-intensive workloads and achieve longer lifetime of the main memory.

We design and implement a prototype system in the Linux OS to study the effectiveness of Memorage. Obtained results are promising; Memorage is shown to offer additional physical memory capacity to demanding workloads much more efficiently than a conventional VM manager. Under memory pressure, the performance of studied memory-intensive multiprogramming workloads was improved by up to 40.5% with an average of 16.7%. Moreover, Memorage is shown to extend the lifetime of the PRAM main memory by 3.9 or 6.9 times on a system with 8 GB PRAM main memory and a 240 GB or 480 GB PRAM storage.

Categories and Subject Descriptors

C.0 [**Computer Systems Organization**]: General—*System architectures*; D.4.2 [**Operating Systems**]: Storage Management—*Main memory, Secondary storage*

Keywords

Emerging persistent RAM; Memory hierarchy; Management; Performance; Write endurance

ICS'13, June 10–14, 2013, Eugene, Oregon, USA.

1. INTRODUCTION

DRAM has been exclusively used as a platform's main memory for decades, thanks to its high performance and low cost per bit. However, DRAM main memory already accounts for 20% to 40% of the system power consumption and its portion is growing [4]. Furthermore, according to the ITRS 2011 report [23], there is no known path for the DRAM technology to scale below 20nm. Eventually, DRAM may no longer be the best technology for main memory, with new memory technologies emerging to take over its role.

Indeed, researchers have recently started exploring the use of emerging persistent RAM (PRAM) as a DRAM replacement [28, 33, 43]. They focus on overcoming the relatively low performance and write endurance of phase change memory (PCM), a type of PRAM, with clever architectural techniques. Due to its non-volatility, PRAM is also expected to provide an adequate medium for high performance storage systems. Condit et al. [16] describe a file system that takes advantage of byte-addressable PCM and Dong et al. [17] address the design issues of a PCM-based storage device. However, most prior work, including the above, emphasizes only one aspect of PRAM: random accessibility (main memory) or persistence (storage and file system). These proposals maintain the traditional main memory and storage dichotomy in resource management.

We argue in this paper that *future PRAM based systems will have to manage the PRAM main memory resource and the PRAM storage resource in an integrated manner to make the best performance and cost trade-offs.* In a realization of the idea, the physical memory resource manager will need to book-keep the status of the storage resources as well as the memory resources. The integration of resource management will allow the system to flexibly provision the available resources across the memory and storage boundary for better performance and reliability. The following technology trends support this argument:

• **There will be little characteristic distinctions between main memory resources and storage resources.** Note that there are independent research and development efforts on scalable PRAM main memory and fast "PRAM storage devices" (or "PSDs") using high-density PRAM chips. If scaling predictions of ITRS [23] are realized (from 22nm flash half pitch in 2011 to 8nm in 2024) and given that the PCM cell density is comparable to that of NAND flash (see Table 1), a single PCM die can pack 256 Gbits by year 2024. This chip capacity, estimated conservatively, enables build-

	Latency			Program energy	Allowable access unit	Retention on power-off	Write endurance	Cell density*
	read	write	erase					
PCM	20ns	100ns	N/A	100 pJ	byte	Yes	$10^8 \sim 10^9$	$5F^2$
STT-MRAM	10ns	10ns	N/A	0.02 pJ	byte	Yes	10^{15}	$4F^2$
ReRAM	10ns	20ns	N/A	2 pJ	byte	Yes	10^6	$6F^2$
DRAM	10ns	10ns	N/A	2 pJ	byte	No	10^{16}	$(2/3)F^2$
NAND flash	25μs	200μs	1.5ms	10 nJ	page/block	Yes	$10^4 \sim 10^6$	$4 \sim 5F^2$
HDD	8.5ms	9.5ms	N/A	N/A	sector	Yes	N/A	$2 \sim 3F^2$

Table 1: Comparison of emerging PRAM and existing memory/storage technologies [27]. ***F* is the minimum feature size of a given process technology.**

ing a small form-factor memory module carrying hundreds of gigabytes. Stacked multi-chip packaging techniques have matured and packages containing 8 to 16 chips are already commercially feasible [35].

In addition, fully exploiting the high bandwidth of the PRAM modules in a platform requires that all the capacity be interfaced via the main memory bus. Researchers have already explored the benefit of placing flash memory on the main memory bus [25]. Suppose that both main memory and system storage are comprised of PRAM and are on the same memory bus; then the main memory and storage resources are no more heterogeneous than DRAM and hard disk drive (HDD) in today's systems, but are quite homogeneous. This offers an unprecedented, practical opportunity for the system to manage the resources in an integrated manner.

• **Reducing I/O software overhead becomes even more important than in the past.** Many software artifacts have been incorporated in a conventional OS to deal with the slow, block-oriented HDDs. For example, complex I/O scheduling algorithms have been implemented in the block I/O layer of the Linux OS [10]. If the current software stack is unchanged, however, the major difference in data access latency between PRAM main memory and a PSD will be dominated by the overhead of the software stack that handles I/O requests. For example, a 4-KB data transfer between a PSD and main memory can be done in hardware in a microsecond, whereas the software overhead of an I/O operation—from a user I/O request to the OS file system to the block I/O layer to the device driver and vice versa—amounts to tens of microseconds [11, 15, 27, 28]! This software overhead has been acceptable because the same data transfer operation with a HDD typically takes milliseconds and the software overhead is only a fraction of the latency.

• **Storage density grows exponentially and a typical user underutilizes the available storage capacity.** HDD and NAND flash density improvement rates have outpaced Moore's Law [22, 26]. While there are different storage usage scenarios such as PC, embedded and server environments, the entire capacity of a given storage device is rarely filled up, leaving some space unused during its lifetime. Agrawal et al. [5] measured the file system fullness and quantified the annual file system size growth rate to be only 14% on average. Moreover, the storage administrator usually performs careful storage capacity provisioning to ensure there is room for the stored data set to grow. Provisioned but unused storage capacity is, in a sense, a lost resource.

In this paper, based on the above observations, we make a case for *Memorage*, a system architecture that utilizes the system's PRAM resources in an integrated manner. With its capability to address all PRAM resources in the system, Memorage can improve the main memory performance by granting more directly accessible physical PRAM capacity of the PSD to the main memory. Moreover, it increases the lifetime of the PRAM resource by spreading writes to all PRAM capacity without being limited by the main memory-storage wall. Effectively, Memorage achieves higher system performance, higher PRAM resource utilization, and longer lifetime through *virtual over-provisioning*. Our experiments based on a prototype system find that Memorage's performance improvement potential is large; the performance of individual programs in a memory-intensive multiprogrammed workload was improved by up to 40.5%, under a high memory pressure. Our analytical analysis finds that the lifetime improvement potential is also high. For example, we obtain 3.9× or 6.9× lifetime increase when a system has 8 GB main memory and a 240 GB or 480 GB PSD.

In what follows, Section 2 will first discuss emerging PRAM technologies and anticipated architectural changes from both hardware and software perspectives. Section 3 then introduces Memorage and discusses how it can be incorporated in the Linux kernel. Proposed Memorage concepts are studied experimentally and analytically in Section 4. Lastly, related work and conclusions are summarized in Section 5 and 6.

2. BACKGROUND

2.1 Emerging Persistent RAM Technologies

There are a handful of PRAM (also called storage class memory or SCM [18]) technologies being actively developed by industry. Table 1 lists and compares three promising PRAM technologies with DRAM, NAND flash and HDD technologies: PCM, STT-MRAM (spin-transfer-torque magnetoresistive RAM) and ReRAM (Resistive RAM) [34, 38, 39, 41]. Basically, PRAMs' operations are based on sensing the resistance of a cell material rather than electrical charge. PCM is considered to be the closest (among all PRAM technologies) to mass production, with commercial and sample chips available at high densities (1 to 8 Gbits) [3, 14, 18, 34].

PRAMs have several desirable properties in common. Unlike DRAM, they are non-volatile. Compared with NAND flash, they are byte-addressable and have faster speeds. On the other hand, PRAMs have known shortcomings; PRAMs like PCM and ReRAM have limited write cycles, requiring aggressive wear-leveling in write-intensive applications. Moreover, their access latencies are longer than DRAM, and in certain cases, write latency is much longer than read latency. Likewise, write energy can be disproportionately large. Therefore, system designers must pay extra caution to hiding and reducing writes [13].

Meanwhile, ITRS [23] is anticipating multi-level cell (MLC) solutions of PRAMs. The MLC designs effectively reduce the cost per bit by packing more bits per memory cell. While

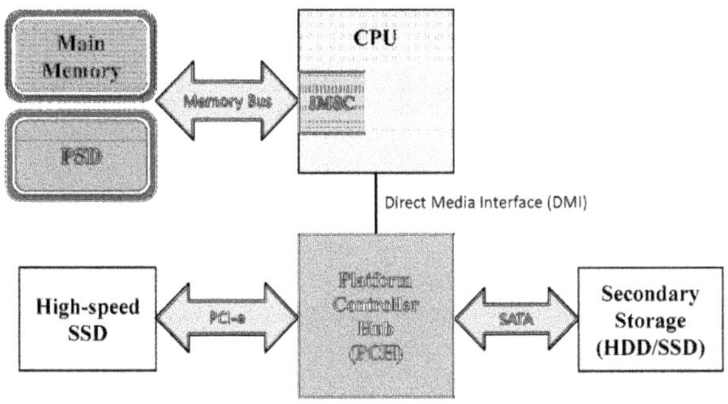

Figure 1: PRAM main memory and a PSD share the memory bus. IMSC represents Integrated Memory and Storage Controller. Note that not all storage devices in this figure have to be present simultaneously.

a single-level cell (SLC) can represent two logic values, '0' and '1' (with two resistance levels), an MLC cell stores more than two logical symbols. Future high-density MLC PRAMs may store more than two bits per cell [15, 23, 31].

Introducing MLC PRAM to a platform has several implications. First, MLC PRAM will be slower than SLC PRAM. Reportedly, MLC PCM read and write are 2 to 4 times slower [17, 32]. This is mainly due to more sensing levels for read and an iterative programming process for write [8]. The second implication is the lower write endurance of MLC PRAM because: (1) the iterative write process accelerates cell wearing; and (2) reduced resistance margins between different symbols make it harder to precisely control programming, especially when the cell is partially worn out.

Because of its higher density and lower performance, MLC PRAM is more suitable for use in a PSD than in main memory. If a PSD employs MLC PRAM and main memory uses SLC PRAM, there is a latency gap between the two resources. Still, this gap ($<10\times$) is not as significant as the gap between DRAM and HDD ($10^5\times$). There are also techniques to opportunistically enhance the speed of MLC PRAM, e.g., by treating an MLC PCM device like an SLC device when the system's capacity demand is low [8, 17, 20, 32].

2.2 Storage Attachable Hardware Interfaces

In today's commodity platforms, HDDs are the slowest hardware component connected through a relatively slow serial ATA (SATA) interface. With SATA, a disk access request must pass through multiple chips and buses (front-side bus to North Bridge to South Bridge to SATA) before it reaches the storage medium, incurring long latency. Early NAND flash SSD offerings provide a direct migration path from HDDs based on the legacy interface like SATA. However, both enterprise and consumer SSDs have quickly saturated the SATA bandwidth. Recent high-speed SSDs are attached via the higher-bandwidth PCI Express (PCI-e) interface [19].

Likewise, it is reasonable to predict that PSDs will interface with faster buses than PCI-e because PRAMs have superior performance to flash memory. To accommodate fast PSDs, a new higher-performance I/O standard may be created. However, in this case, or with legacy interfaces, the byte-addressability of a PSD could be lost. In addition, the memory bus is the highest-bandwidth bus of a platform. Hence, a PSD will be most likely and best co-located with PRAM main memory modules on a platform's memory bus.

We expect that future platforms will continue supporting legacy PCI-e and SATA interfaces. It is quite conceivable that multiple heterogeneous storage devices may co-exist. For instance, the HDD could provide ample capacity to store large file data while the PSD provides fast I/O for hot data. A particular storage configuration will be chosen based on the cost, performance and capacity trade-offs made by the user. Figure 1 illustrates a possible future computing platform with a PSD on the memory bus.

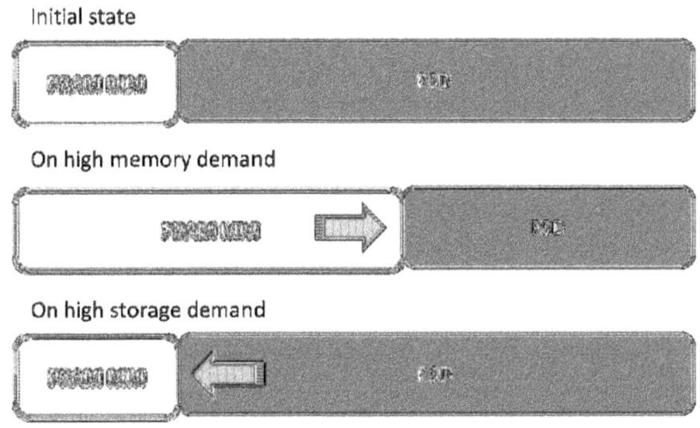

Figure 2: Illustration of the Memorage concept. The Memorage dynamically expands or shrinks the capacity of main memory (denoted "MM") and PSD on demand.

2.3 OS I/O Software Stack

Traditional OS I/O software stack and file systems have been designed for rotating HDDs. Hence, storage optimizations are mainly devoted to reducing disk seek time through efficient I/O scheduling. However, SSDs benefit little from such HDD-centric optimizations. Accordingly, as an outgrowth, system designers customize the OS I/O software stack with SSDs in mind [11, 36] and design new file system [24].

In a conventional OS I/O stack, a read or write request must first go to the block I/O layer that is responsible for I/O scheduling. The request then waits (in anticipation) for other requests that can be merged together to reduce accesses to the slow HDD. The Linux's default "completely fair queuing" (CFQ) scheduler [10] is an example of doing this. By comparison, with a fast SSD, it is not always beneficial to merge requests. Depending on the target configuration, it makes sense to bypass the block I/O scheduler and the block device driver (e.g., SCSI subsystem) all together.

Since PSDs are byte-addressable and even faster than SSDs, we expect further changes to occur. Especially, trade-offs between different access granularities (block vs. byte) must be examined closely as many small updates will not require forming and handling blocks. Ultimately, adopting the PSD architecture warrants designing a new file system to fully exploit the fine access granularity as opposed to conventional block-based file systems. File caching policies also need close re-examination. While it is not our goal to study all possible changes, we believe our work presents an interesting first step in this direction.

3. MEMORAGE

3.1 Memorage Philosophy

Memorage tackles the inefficiency of PRAM resource utilization by collapsing the traditional static boundary between main memory and storage resources (see Figure 2). The Memorage approach is motivated by the fact that fast PRAM storage resources will likely remain underutilized if a system is designed based on the traditional dichotomy of memory and storage. It also enables us to mitigate the problem of PRAM's limited endurance with a global wear-leveling strategy that involves all available PRAM resources.

Storage capacity in a drive has increased with the improvement in storage density. Studies like Meyer et al. [30] and Agrawal et al. [5] show however that storage utilization has not been growing with the increasing storage capacity. Meyer et al. analyzed vast file system content data collected for over four weeks in 2009 in a large corporation. Agrawal et al. collected their data from 2000 to 2004 in the same company. According to their results, storage capacity has increased by almost two orders of magnitude, but the mean utilization of the capacity has actually decreased by 10% from 53% to 43%. Furthermore, 50% of the users had drives less than 40% full while 70% of the users had their drives no more than 60% full. These studies clearly suggest that a storage device in a system is likely to have *substantial unused space* during its lifetime.

Memorage aims to effectively address the above wastefulness by suggesting the following two principles:

1. Don't swap, give more memory. Under high memory pressure, a conventional OS virtual memory (VM) manager swaps out previously allocated pages into the storage to respond to memory requests. Significant performance penalty is incurred when frequent swap in and swap out operations occur. In Memorage, main memory borrows directly accessible memory resources from the PSD to cope with memory shortages. Offering more memory capacity effectively eliminates the need for costly swap operations.

2. Don't pay for physical over-provisioning. To guarantee reasonable lifetime, reliability and performance of the PRAM main memory, robust wear-leveling and garbage collection with over-provisioned capacity is required. Flash SSDs commonly resort to over-provisioning of as much as 20% of the (advertised) capacity. Over-provisioned capacity is typically hidden from the user, and may remain inefficiently utilized. In Memorage, as long as capacity planning of the PSD allows, the PSD can donate its free capacity to the main memory to relax the limited write endurance problem and facilitate wear-leveling. Effectively, Memorage offers "logical" or "virtual" over-provisioning without hiding any capacity from the user or incurring additional cost for physical over-provisioning.

To summarize, we expect two important benefits from the Memorage principles. First, by granting more directly accessible memory capacity to the physical memory pool (principle 1), the system can decrease the frequency of page faults. Because PRAM is orders of magnitude faster than traditional HDDs, avoiding the software overheads of page faults can lead to significant performance improvement. Second, by dynamically trading resources between the main memory and the storage (principle 2), lifetime becomes more manageable because the write traffic to the main memory and the storage can be re-distributed with software control.

3.2 Key Design Goals

In this subsection, we discuss three goals that have guided the design and implementation of Memorage.

- **Transparency to existing applications.** It is impractical to require re-compiling all existing applications for a new system feature to be enabled. To ensure its seamless adoption, we encapsulate Memorage inside the OS kernel and do not modify application-level interfaces. While not required, the user may configure Memorage parameters to tune resource management policies according to particular system-level objectives. Our goal is to have a Memorage system autonomously and intelligently manage the underlying PRAM resources, considering user preferences.
- **Small development efforts.** Meeting the transparency goal may impose additional complexities on system software design, especially the memory and storage subsystem of an OS. The complexities hinder the fast adoption of Memorage architecture. Thus, we aim at avoiding long development time by reusing the existing system software infrastructure whenever possible. This paper describes our prototype design in detail so that other researchers and developers can easily implement Memorage in their systems.
- **Low system overheads.** An implementation of Memorage may incur performance and memory overheads because it adds a new layer of resource control. The performance overheads are incurred when PRAM resources are transferred from the storage side to the main memory side, and vice versa. The space overheads come from book-keeping and sharing resource usages across the two sides. In this work, we design a prototype Memorage system by reusing kernel-level functions and data structures to achieve this goal. We note that the performance overheads are paid fairly infrequently, only when PRAM resources are exchanged under memory pressure situations.

3.3 Memorage Design and Implementation

We now discuss our Memorage prototype, integrated in a recent Linux kernel. The prototype Memorage system runs on a non-uniform memory architecture (NUMA) platform with a large system memory that emulates a PSD, as will be explain in Section 4.1. The general strategies used in our implementation will also apply to other OSes.

We focus on how the first principle—*Don't swap, give more memory*—is incorporated in our implementation because the current Linux kernel has no provisions for memory wear-leveling. However, we will separately study via analytical modeling how Memorage helps improve the efficiency of wear-leveling in Section 4.4. That said, incorporating the first Memorage principle requires two major changes in an OS: (1) managing the status of PRAM resources in both memory and storage together; and (2) developing a strategy to dynamically expand and shrink the main memory capacity. We subsequently expatiate our design approaches to accommodate the two changes.

3.3.1 Managing Resource Information

As we discussed in the previous section, the Memorage prototype extensively reuses the existing memory management infrastructure of Linux. For example, key data structures to keep track of the state of a node (representing per-CPU memory resources), a zone (expressing a memory region in a node) or a page remain unchanged. The existing node descriptor, *struct pglist_data*, still contains the information of a node that includes the Memorage zone, while the zone descriptor, *struct zone*, keeps holding the information of the list of active and inactive pages in the Memorage zone. Besides, the status of a page is recognized by the page descriptor, *struct page* as usual (see [10] for more details).

To acquire the status information of resources in the Memorage zone, VM manager works closely with the PSD device driver and the file system. The PSD device driver builds on a

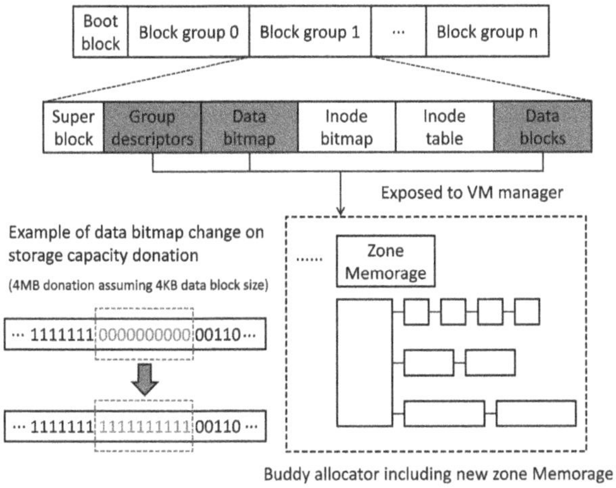

Figure 3: Memorage exposes free data blocks from a (mounted) file system to VM manager as a new zone. Buddy allocator treats the new Memorage zone the same way as other zones.

ramdisk driver to emulate the PSD with the system DRAM and can perform both block I/O operation and page-level allocation from the designated node resources. It takes as input the size of the Memorage zone, the resource amount to lend/reclaim at a time, and the memory node ID to contain the Memorage zone. The PSD device driver utilizes the Linux memory hotplug facility [1], which significantly simplifies the task of updating the OS-level information of available memory resources as they are traded between the main memory and the PSD.

PSD resource detection. An important design question that arose is: *When should the Memorage zone be prepared?* Linux for the x86 architecture obtains the memory resource information from the BIOS during the boot process and sets the memory related system-wide parameters like maximum number of page frames accordingly. To keep a system's resource discovery process consistent, our prototype system assumes that PSD resources are similarly detected at boot time and the OS book-keeps the PSD's physical resource information in addition to system memory resources. However, resource information relevant to PSD is marked to be unavailable (or offlined) on loading the PSD device driver that is also performed as a part of the boot process. As a result, OS's VM manager has the full information of PSD resources but cannot allocate a page from it until Memorage explicitly pumps in the predefined amount of PRAM resources from the PSD under memory pressure. Our prototype PSD device driver carries this out by hot-removing the PSD region (which is a memory node) during its initialization. However, the offlined PSD region is logically removed from VM manager rather than physically.

File system metadata exposure. When Memorage donates some capacity to main memory by transferring its resource to VM manager, the file system must catch and log such resource allocation events so that it does not allocate donated resources for new file data. For further illustration, Figure 3 depicts the basic on-disk layout of a file system (e.g., ext3) as well as its interaction with the buddy allocator system. The file system partitions the storage space into block groups, and each block group is comprised of *superblock, group descriptors, data block bitmap, inode bitmap, inode table* and *data blocks*. From each block group information, the following field information should be passed to the buddy memory allocator:

1. *Group descriptors* that specify the status of individual block groups such as the number of free blocks;
2. *Data block bitmap* that identifies which blocks within a block group are free blocks; and
3. *Data blocks* that stores file data in the file system.

The inode-related information does not have to be changed because blocks or pages in the PSD are free blocks with no file data on them. Given this information from the file system, the buddy allocator manages the Memorage zone just as other zones during memory allocation and deallocation. In our prototype, the Memorage zone is conceptually a node in the NUMA model that most modern OSes support. Thus, the memory allocator can utilize the fact that cost of accessing main memory nodes may be different according to the geometric distance from the requesting core.

Clean up on system reboot. In response to normal system shutdown request, Memorage mandates the file system to nullify the bitmap information previously marked for PSD donations because we assume data lifetime is over along with system reboot. By doing so, a file system consistency checker (e.g., *fsck*) can avoid reporting unwanted check result in a subsequent boot process. However, to address unexpected power failure, our prototype further needs to modify current *fsck* implementation to invalidate the inconsistent bitmap rather than fixing it up.

3.3.2 Memory Expansion and Shrinkage

When a system has little free memory pages, Memorage's VM manager dynamically expands the effective memory capacity by allocating pages from the PSD and marking the data block bitmap accordingly. Then, the file system treats the pages as if they hold file data and keeps them from being allocated. Likewise, when the file system notices a storage capacity shortage, Memorage's VM manager deallocates pages in the Memorage zone and returns them to the storage resource pool. Once the file system secures a safe number of pages, it resumes allocating them to file data. Note that Memorage's VM manager may not release the PSD pages immediately after they enter into either the inactive list or free list. This design choice helps Memorage's VM manager avoid frequent file system metadata manipulation.

The net effect of Memorage's flexible capacity sharing can be explained clearly by examining how a VM manager handles high memory pressure situations. Commodity Linux has three *watermarks* (i.e., *pages_high*, *pages_low*, and *pages_min*) used to control the invocation and sleeping of *kswapd*, the kernel swap daemon [10]. When the number of available physical page frames falls below *pages_low*, *kswapd* is invoked to swap out virtual pages and reclaim their page frames. When sufficient page frames have been reclaimed (above *pages_high*), *kswapd* is put into sleep. Essentially, *Memorage lowers the watermarks* by pumping in physical page frames borrowed from the storage capacity. As a result, *kswapd* will run less frequently with the same series of memory allocation requests. The difference between two points (1 and 2) in the figure captures the "expanded" margin to tolerate memory shortage with Memorage.

Allocator modifications for resource sharing. To realize the capacity sharing, our implementation modifies the buddy memory allocator in two ways. First, it adds a new watermark (WMARK_MEMORAGE) between *page_high* and

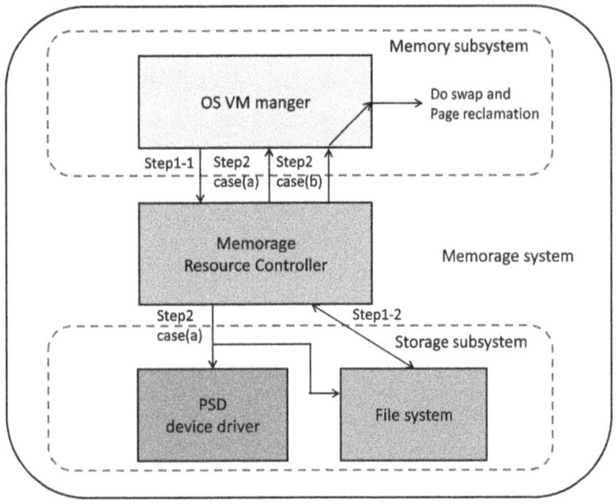

Figure 4: Cooperation between OS VM manager and storage subsystem to implement Memorage's flexible capacity sharing.

page_low. In particular, the watermark is set to one page lower than the value of *page_high* to minimize the chance of page swap and reclamation. Second, it endows the allocator with the ability to inquire about Memorage zone's resource availability when the number of allocatable pages reaches the new watermark. Figure 4 further illustrates the interaction between the memory allocator and the storage system under Memorage. Different from the conventional memory allocator, which starts page swap and reclamation under memory pressure, Memorage checks the possibility of borrowing resources from PSD before it allows the OS VM manager to swap the extant pages (Step 1-1 and 1-2). In response to this inquiry, Memorage either grants the memory allocator to allocate PSD resources (Step 2 case (a)) or suggests the allocator to follow the normal swap and reclamation process due to the unavailability of PSD resources (Step 2 case (b)).

Resource transfer size. What amount of resources the PSD provides to main memory at one time is an important knob to control Memorage's overhead associated with updating file system metadata and kernel data structures. To mitigate the overhead, Memorage allocates PSD pages in large chunks (but not all excess pages) at a time. Whereas the transfer size is a tuning parameter dependent on the system platform, our prototype system uses 2 GB granularity based on measurement results (see Figure 6). If a system later undergoes more severe memory demands that cannot be met with the current Memorage zone, then Memorage "dynamically" appends another chunk of PSD pages to the zone. By doing so, Memorage manipulates file system metadata as well as memory pool-related data structures less frequently, and sidesteps the potentially large resource exchange overhead. This mechanism is similar to a mixture of the pre-allocation feature in xfs or ext4 file system and the thin-provisioning scheme for dynamic storage growth [21].

Memorage zone shrinkage. An aggressive reclamation strategy returns the donated storage resources to storage resource pool immediately after the memory resource deficit has been resolved. Even if this choice can make a right resource provisioning, it may increase resource transfer overhead in a situation of bursty memory pressure which needs previously reclaimed storage resources again. On the other hand, a lazy reclamation strategy requests Memorage to reclaim the donated storage resources only when a storage notifies its resource shortage. Although this strategy can help Memorage avoid frequent resource transfer, it may leave the memory system in an undesirable over-provisioned state. Therefore, we leverage a balanced approach which is neither aggressive nor lazy. It shrinks Memorage zone with the help of a kernel thread which reclaims the donated PSD pages when a system is not under memory pressure. Also, it considers reclaiming frequently referenced pages first because keeping those pages on the donated slower (MLC) PSD resources will degrade system performance.

3.4 Comparison with Possible Alternatives

Memorage provides a future PRAM system with a seamless evolving path to overcome the inefficient resource utilization of the traditional "static" memory management strategy. There are other possible alternative strategies to utilize the PRAM resources.

First, a platform may feature only fast SLC PRAMs on the main memory bus and the system partitions the memory space into main memory and storage capacity. This way, the system may grow and shrink each space dynamically to respond to system demands. In a sense, this approach throws away the traditional notions of main memory and storage dichotomy completely. Unfortunately, this strategy may not result in the most cost-effective platform construction because it does not exploit the cost benefits of MLC PRAMs. Moreover, deciding when to control the growth of a particular space, especially the storage, is not straightforward. By comparison, Memorage honors the traditional notion of main memory and storage capacity (that a user perceives) but manages the underlying PRAM resources such that overheads for swapping and main memory lifetime issues are effectively addressed.

Second, in lieu of dynamically reacting to memory pressure, a system may statically "give" PSD resources that correspond to the traditional swap space to main memory. In essence, the main memory capacity is increased by the swap space. When the system's memory usage does not exceed the total main memory capacity, this static approach may result in better performance than Memorage. However, since it sets apart the fixed amount of PRAM resources for main memory, it does not adapt to dynamic changes of working set sizes like Memorage does; it brings about the over- and under-provisioned memory resource problem again.

Yet another approach may create a file and delegate the file system to handle memory shortage situations with the capacity occupied by the file. This approach is analogous to giving a swap file that dynamically adjusts its size. However, since this approach must always involve the file system layer to get additional pages on memory deficit, it cannot achieve raw PRAM performance of the PSD due to unnecessary file operations unrelated to page resource allocation.

3.5 Further Discussions

Caveat for reclaiming the donated PSD pages. All pages are not reclaimable immediately on request. If the donated pages have a page reference count greater than zero when storage shortage is reported, they cannot be reclaimed shortly. Instead, those pages can be reclaimed only after their contents first migrate onto other pages. To make matters worse, not all pages can be migrated. For example, direct mapped kernel pages are not. Therefore, it is im-

System Component	Specification
Platform	HP Proliant SL160g6 Server
CPU	Two 2.4 GHz Intel Xeon E5620 processors (4 cores/processor)
Hyper-threading	8 hardware threads/processor
Last-Level Cache (L3)	12MB
Main Memory	192 GB DDR3-1066 SDRAM
Operating System	Linux kernel 3.2.8
File System	Ext3

Table 2: Experimental platform.

portant to take into account the fact that reclamation of donated pages may not be instant (reporting an error such as -EBUSY) and PSD pages should not be used for non-migratable kernel pages.

Handling a race condition between VM manager and file system. Since VM manager can manipulate the metadata of file system, designers must carefully handle potential race conditions that may be caused by accessing shared information such as block bitmap simultaneously. One possible way to address the problem is to use a conventional locking scheme that mandates serializing accesses to the shared information. Alternatively, one can design a new file system dedicated for PRAM, e.g., Wu et al. [42] delegates storage resource management to VM manager entirely. However, this requires compromising the compatibility with existing file systems. For this reason, we prefer the locking strategy to avoid modifications to file systems.

Determining lifetime ratio of main memory to PSD. How global wear-leveling is done in Memorage determines the relative lifetime of PRAM main memory and the PSD. For example, if we treat all the PRAM resources indifferently, we could make both main memory and PSD have an equal lifetime. Others may want the PSD to live longer than main memory and limit the amount of PSD capacity used in Memorage's over-provisioning. Such decisions rely on the preference of a user as well as the system upgrade period; it is hard to say simply which strategy is better. Section 4.4 examines the effect of lifetime ratio of main memory to PSD.

4. EXPERIMENTAL RESULTS

This section evaluates Memorage's benefits. After describing methodology, we will discuss separately (1) software latency of a page fault (Section 4.2); (2) application performance improvement (Section 4.3); and (3) main memory lifetime improvement (Section 4.4).

4.1 Evaluation Methodology

We employ a number of methods for evaluation. To obtain the software latency of a page fault, we measure the actual latency using fine-grained instrumentation of the Linux kernel. For application-level performance measurements, we use the Memorage prototype described in Section 3.3. Lastly, to evaluate the lifetime improvement with Memorage, we develop intuitive analytical models.

We employ two different platforms for experiments. Our latency measurement is performed on a desktop platform. The platform runs Linux kernel 2.6.35.2 with the ext3 file system and features an Intel Core i7 quad processor, 8 MB L3 Cache, and 9 GB DDR3-1066 DRAM. Our Memorage prototype runs on a dual-socket Intel Xeon-based platform

Configuration	Description
Baseline	4.4 GB effective memory available. This size causes significant memory shortage.
Memorage	In addition to 4.4 GB (Baseline), Memorage provide an additional 2 GB capacity on low memory. Thus, the workload sees 6.4 GB total, and this capacity is larger than the aggregate memory footprint of the workload.

Table 3: Evaluated memory configurations. Each configuration has a distinct effective memory capacity.

and a newer kernel. This platform has a large memory capacity organized in NUMA and eases emulating the PSD capacity. We perform application performance evaluation on this platform. Table 2 summarizes the platform's specification.

To form our workload, we select eight benchmarks from the SPEC CPU2006 suite because they are memory-bound applications [32]. The applications and their memory footprint (dynamic resident set size or RSS) are *bwaves* (873 MB), *mcf* (1,600 MB), *milc* (679 MB), *zeusmp* (501 MB), *cactusADM* (623 MB), *leslie3d* (123 MB), *lbm* (409 MB), and *GemsFDTD* (828 MB). Thus, the aggregate RSS of our multiprogrammed workload is 5.6 GB. Since our experimental platform has eight hardware threads, all applications in our workload can run simultaneously.

The first set of experiments focus on measuring the software latency of page fault handling and use *mcf*, whose RSS is 1.6 GB and is the largest of all applications. To ensure we observe many page faults (opportunities for measurements), we run *mcf* after seizing all physical memory capacity but only 1.3 GB. Measurement was done with the Linux kernel function tracer *Ftrace* [9], which instruments the entry and exit points of target functions with a small overhead.

For application performance studies, we assume that main memory is built with SLC PRAM whereas the PSD uses MLC PRAM. This assumption implies that the target system is built cost-effectively—fast, small capacity main memory and large capacity, yet slightly slow storage. As discussed in Section 2.1, this construction does not necessarily imply much longer access latency to the PSD-provided memory capacity because MLC PRAM can be read and programmed like SLC PRAM. We assume that the PRAM capacity donated to the main memory realm (Memorage) and the PSD capacity reserved for swap space (conventional system) are operating in the fast SLC mode. Given the assumptions, we emulate both the PRAM main memory and the PRAM PSD with the host machine's DRAM. In particular, all applications are pinned to run on the first NUMA node only. The PSD capacity is offered by the second NUMA node. The swap partition is implemented using a ramdisk.

As the primary metric for performance comparison, we use the program execution time to complete each of eight applications in our workload, started at once. Given the multi-core CPU with eight hardware contexts, this simple metric is intuitive and relevant. Co-scheduling of applications also ensures that platform resources are not underutilized. To reduce the effect of measurement noises, we repeat experiments three times and average the results. We also reboot the system after each experiment to keep the system state fresh and ensure that our workload runs under as much identical system conditions as possible.

We consider two target machine configurations shown in Table 3: Baseline and Memorage. The Baseline configura-

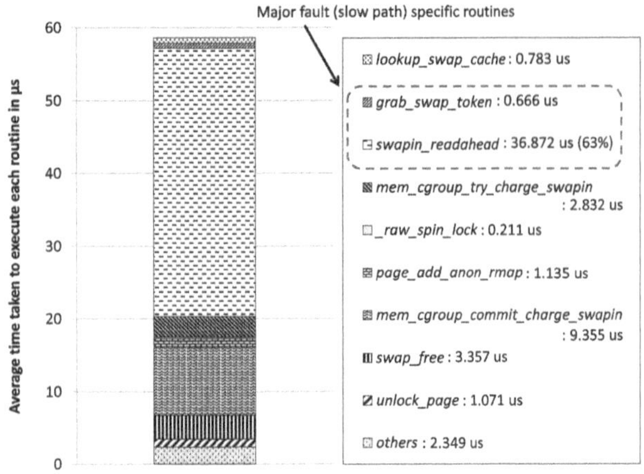

Figure 5: Breakdown of software latency of the Linux page fault handler. Routines in the legend are invoked in order.

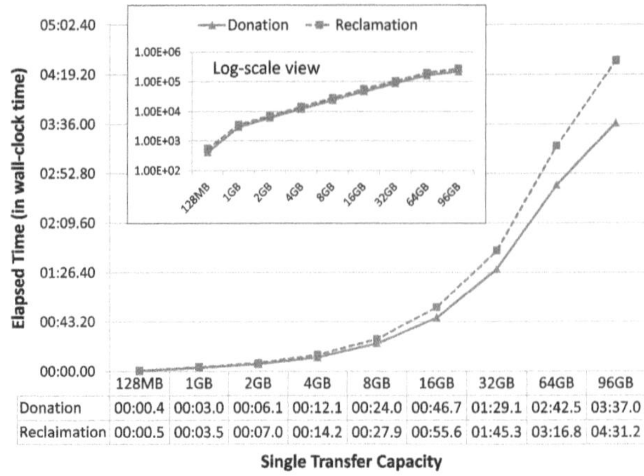

Figure 6: The latencies (in min:sec.ms) needed for Memorage to offer and retrieve PSD resources as the transfer size changes.

tion offers the total physical memory capacity of 4.4 GB. Note that this capacity is smaller by about 20% than the studied workload's aggregate footprint (5.6 GB). Accordingly, this configuration exposes the impact of frequent swap operations in a conventional system under memory pressure. The Memorage configuration offers 2 GB of additional memory capacity from the PSD.

4.2 Software Latency of a Page Fault

In this section, we obtain and report two latencies, one for "fast path" (taken for a minor fault) and another for "slow path" (major fault). A minor fault happens when the swap-in operation finds the missing page in the in-memory cache. On the other hand, a major fault requires fetching the missing page from the swap space on the storage device (PSD). On our platform, the fast path latency was measured to be 21.6 μs and the slow path latency was 58.6 μs. We find that even the fast path places nontrivial software latency on the critical path. Considering the capabilities of the underlying hardware, 21.6 μs is not a small number at all. For instance, the latency to read a 4 KB page can be as small as 0.47 μs with the 8.5 GB/sec DDR3-1066 DRAM in our platform.

Figure 5 breaks down the page fault handling latency according to the routines involved. Most routines are executed on both the fast path and the slow path. Two routines are executed only on the slow path, `grab_swap_token()` and `swapin_readahead()`, and they account for a dominant portion in the entire latency of the slow path—37.5 μs of 58.6 μs. The `swapin_readahead()` turns out to be the most time-consuming; it reads the missing page from the swap area and performs DRAM copying. This routine's latency grows with the number of pages that should be brought in, because the page reclaiming routine must first make enough room for the pages under high memory pressure. Another major contributor, responsible for 12.18 μs, is a family of "memory control group" routines (prefixed with `mem_cgroup`). Their main goal is to reduce the chances of swap thrashing.

After all, given the long latency required on each page fault, a memory-bound application's performance will suffer if its memory requirements are not fully satisfied due to memory shortage. The situation can be considerably relieved with Memorage because it grants more physical memory capacity to the system and satisfies memory demands from applications directly without involving time-consuming page fault handling.

4.3 Application Performance

The result of the previous section suggests that even if we provide a very fast swap space with a PSD, the page fault overhead will remain high because of the long software latency. Let us now turn our attention to evaluating the benefit of Memorage by comparing the application-level performance measured under different memory configurations.

Before we evaluate the application performance, we first examined the achievable memory bandwidth of our experimental platform by running STREAM benchmark [29]. This allows us to quantify the performance difference between main memory (on the local node) and the emulated PSD (on the remote node). Our result shows that main memory achieves higher bandwidth than the PSD by about 15% on average. We consider this difference to be a reasonable artifact of our experimental environment, as reading from and writing to MLC PRAMs (even if they are operating in the SLC mode) could take slightly longer than SLC PRAMs.

Next, we measure the time needed for our Memorage implementation to offer physical resources from the PSD to main memory or vice versa. This latency represents an artifact of Memorage that applications would not experience if sufficient memory were given to them initially, and is paid only when the physical resources are transferred between main memory and the PSD, not on each (minor) page fault. Figure 6 presents our result, as a function of the amount of memory capacity to donate or reclaim at one time. The plot clearly shows that the measured latency increases linearly, proportional to the transferred data size. Based on the result, we determined that a 2 GB transfer size is a reasonable choice during our application-level performance study.

Figure 7 presents the performance of Memorage normalized to that of Baseline. We show results for individual benchmark applications in the workload. Performance improvement rate varies among the applications. Six out of eight applications gained significant performance improvement. Memorage improves the total execution time by 16.5% on average and by up to 40.5% in mcf, compared to Baseline. mcf is the most memory demanding application in the workload and it benefited the most. On the other hand, leslie3d saw little performance improvement.

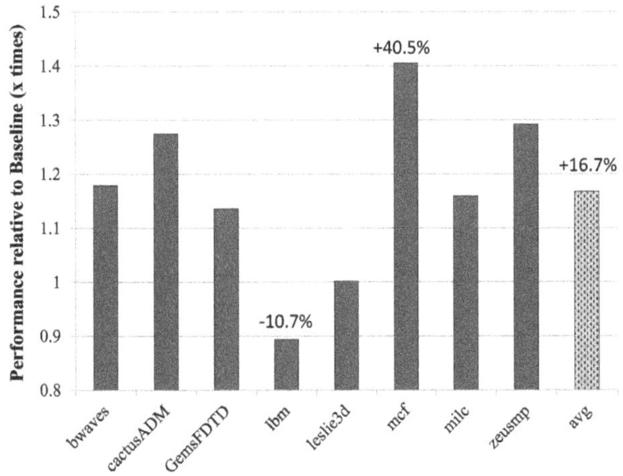

Figure 7: Relative performance of benchmarks with Memorage (based on wall clock time measurement). Performance improvement can be identified with a value greater than 1.

The plot also shows that all applications achieved performance improvement with the additional memory capacity offered by Memorage, except one application; lbm actually loses performance with more memory. This seemingly counter-intuitive result is caused by the uncontrolled resource contention in the processor core (hyper-threading) and the shared cache. lbm has a relatively small memory footprint that can easily be cached. Hence, when other more memory-demanding applications are blocked waiting for memory allocation (in Baseline), it actually gets more CPU cycles. As a result, lbm grabs shared cache capacity it needs and executes faster. We also find that slight memory shortage (e.g., several dozens of MBs) is successfully handled by *kswapd*, whereas the large gap between the total required memory size and the currently available memory size (20% in our experiment) is hard to overcome with the Linux page reclamation capability, resulting in crawling software latencies very often.

Figure 8 shows that Memorage dramatically reduces the portion of system time in the total execution time of the studied benchmarks. The programs spend a large portion of their execution time in system execution under heavy memory pressure because they have to block (in the sleep state) and yield the CPU to other processes until the faulting page becomes available through page fault handling. Because this handling is slow, the faulting process may be blocked for a long time. The increase of user time with Memorage implies that CPU cycles are spent on useful work of the user application. More user time results in fast program execution time and gives the system more chances to serve other user applications, improving the overall system throughput.

Finally, Figure 9 depicts the average number of dynamic memory instructions executed between two successive major or minor page faults. In Memorage—having generous memory capacity—the system rarely experiences a major fault. Baseline suffers a sizable number of major faults, as many as three to six orders of magnitude more major faults than Memorage. It also shows that minor page faults occur more frequently than major faults. They occur even when there is enough memory capacity to elude memory pressure because modern OSes implement many in-memory cache structures and resource management schemes. For example, the widely used copy-on-write mechanism may cause a minor page fault

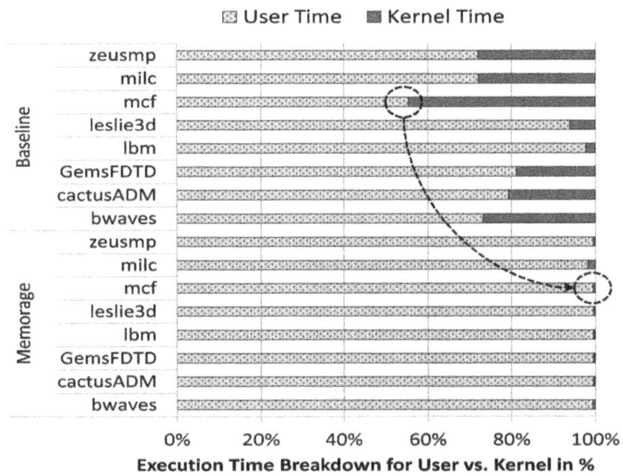

Figure 8: Total execution time is normalized to highlight the relative time spent in user applications and system routines.

due to a write on a shared page. Therefore, it is not surprising that Memorage is relatively insensitive to the number of minor faults, which have smaller impact on system performance compared to major faults. Nonetheless, Memorage decreases the number of minor faults as well because page faults often incur additional minor faults (e.g., swap cache hit) during fault handling but Memorage avoids them.

4.4 Main Memory Lifetime

Main memory lifetime improvement when system lifetime is maximized. In a typical platform use scenario where main memory update rate is substantially higher than storage update rate, the system lifetime would be determined by the main memory lifetime. In this section, we analytically obtain the lifespan improvement of PRAM main memory with Memorage's virtual over-provisioning. Let us first focus on the case when the system lifetime is maximized (i.e., main memory lifetime equals storage lifetime).

Let L_m and L_s be the lifespan of PRAM main memory and PSD in the conventional system, respectively. They represent the time taken until all PRAM cells are worn out through memory and storage writes. Also, let C_m and C_s be the main memory capacity and the PSD capacity and let E_m and E_s be the specified write endurance of PRAM resources for main memory and PSD. Then, in the conventional system, the total data volume, D_m and D_s, writable to the main memory or the PSD before their write endurance limit is reached, are: $D_m = E_m \cdot C_m$ and $D_s = E_s \cdot C_s$.

Now, let B_m and B_s denote the average data update rate or write data bandwidth, for the main memory and the PSD, respectively. Then the lifetime of the two entities are calculated by: $L_m = D_m/B_m$ and $L_s = D_s/B_s$. At this point, we assume that perfect wear-leveling is in place for both the main memory and the PSD.

In order to relate the resources initially dedicated to main memory and PSD, we introduce α and β. Then, $C_s = \alpha \cdot C_m$ and $B_m = \beta \cdot B_s$. Because storage capacity is in general larger than that of main memory ($C_s > C_m$) and the data update rate of main memory is higher than that of storage ($B_m > B_s$), $\alpha > 1$ and $\beta > 1$ would normally hold. Similarly, we introduce γ to relate the endurance limit of the main memory and the PSD. That is, $E_m = \gamma \cdot E_s$. We normally expect γ to be greater than 1.

On a system with Memorage, let L_{new} be the lifespan

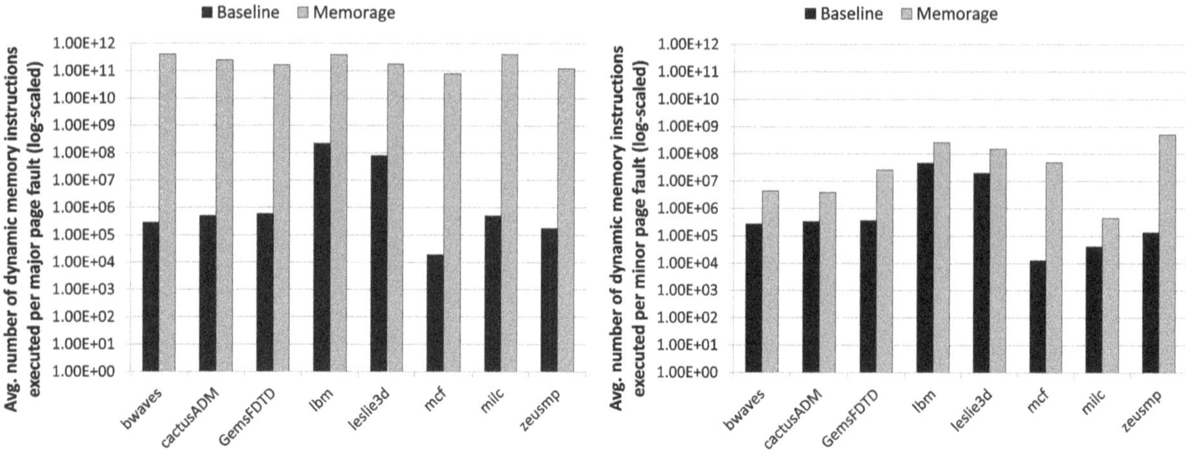

(a) Avg. number of memory instructions per major fault (b) Avg. number of memory instructions per minor fault

Figure 9: Memorage reduces the impact of major and minor page faults by increasing the average number of memory instructions between two faults. A larger value means that more memory references are made without a page fault.

of the main memory. Ideally, Memorage could expose the whole PRAM resource capacity to global wear-leveling because it manages all PRAM resources. If we define D_{new} and B_{new} to be the total writable data volume and the data update rate for the total, Memorage-managed PRAM capacity, we have $L_{new} = D_{new}/B_{new}$, where $D_{new} = E_m{\cdot}C_m{+}E_s{\cdot}C_s$ and $B_{new} = B_m + B_s$. Finally, by rewriting L_{new} we obtain:

$$L_{new} = \frac{E_m \cdot C_m + E_s \cdot C_s}{B_m + B_s} = \frac{E_m \cdot (C_m + \frac{\alpha}{\gamma} \cdot C_m)}{B_m + \frac{1}{\beta} \cdot B_m} = \frac{E_m \cdot C_m \cdot (1 + \frac{\alpha}{\gamma}) \cdot \beta}{B_m \cdot (1+\beta)} = L_m \cdot \frac{(1+\frac{\alpha}{\gamma}) \cdot \beta}{(1+\beta)} \quad (1)$$

Equation (1) captures the key trade-offs that determine the new lifetime. For example, with a higher α (i.e., storage is larger than memory), the main memory lifetime increases. If γ is larger, implying that the write endurance of the main memory is better than the write endurance of the PSD, the relative benefit of global wear-leveling of PRAM resource decreases. Finally, given that α/γ is reasonably greater than 0 (e.g., PSD capacity is large enough and/or the write endurance of the PSD is close to that of the main memory), β determines the overall lifetime gain. With a larger β, the lifetime improvement increases.

Suppose for example a platform that has 8 GB main memory and a 240 GB or 480 GB PSD (α is 30 or 60, common in high-end notebooks). Figure 10 illustrates how the lifetime improvement of PRAM main memory changes as we vary the relative data write bandwidth to main memory and PSD (β). We assumed γ is 10. The lifetime improvement is shown to rapidly reach a maximum value, even when β is small—write bandwidth difference is small (e.g., see the points near $\beta = 10$). Even in an unrealistic worst-case scenario of $\beta = 1$, Memorage achieves 2× and 3.5× longer lifetime than the conventional system. Realistically, write bandwidth seen by the main memory tends to be much larger (β is large) [2,33], and hence, we expect that the large main memory lifetime improvement of Memorage will be effectively achieved.

Understanding trade-offs in global wear-leveling. Our formulation so far assumed that $L_m = L_s = L_{new}$ and a perfect, global wear-leveling method with zero overhead. To gain insights about realistic wear-leveling, we consider a hypothetical wear-leveling method where the main memory borrows an extra capacity of η from the PSD constantly. This borrowed capacity resides within the main memory realm for time τ and is then returned back. The PSD immediately lends a fresh capacity of η to replace the returned capacity. To improve lifetime, the main memory "rests" its own capacity of η, covered by the borrowed capacity.

The hypothetical wear-leveling method follows the spirit of Memorage in two ways. First, it involves the available physical resources in the main memory and the PSD only, without assuming any over-provisioned physical resources. Second, it uses borrowed capacity from the PSD to improve the main memory lifetime, across the traditional memory and storage boundary. Furthermore, the method exposes two important trade-offs (η and τ) a realistic wear-leveling scheme may also have. η captures the amount of provisioned capacity and determines the degree of lifetime improvement. On the other hand, τ dictates the frequency of resource exchange, and hence, reveals the overhead of resource management and the potential wear amplification.

Let us assume that $\eta < C_m < C_s$ (i.e., the borrowed capacity is relatively small, compared with C_m and C_s) and let L'_m and L'_s denote the new lifetime of the main memory and the PSD under the hypothetical wear-leveling scheme. Deriving the new lifetimes is fairly straightforward.

$$L'_m = (D_m{\cdot}C_m)/(B_m{\cdot}(C_m - \eta)),\; L'_s = D_s/(B_s + \frac{\eta}{C_m}{\cdot}B_m + \frac{2\eta}{\tau})$$

The effect of exchanging resource is manifested by the transfer of bandwidth from the main memory to the PSD ($\eta \cdot B_m/C_m$). The overhead of resource trading is revealed by the added bandwidth ($2\eta/\tau$) to the PSD side.
Introducing a new variable $h = \eta/C_m$, main memory lifetime improvement and PSD lifetime degradation are:

$$L'_m/L_m = \frac{1}{(1-h)}, \quad L_s/L'_s = 1 + \beta \cdot h + \frac{2h \cdot C_m}{\tau \cdot B_s} \quad (2)$$

As expected, the memory side lifetime improvement is a function of h (h is the relative size of η to C_m). It is also shown that h and β (B_m/B_s) plays a role in the PSD lifetime. Intuitively, the PSD's lifetime degrades faster if: (1) the main memory bandwidth is relatively large and (2) larger capacity is delegated from the PSD to the main memory. Lastly, the wear-leveling overhead becomes larger with the

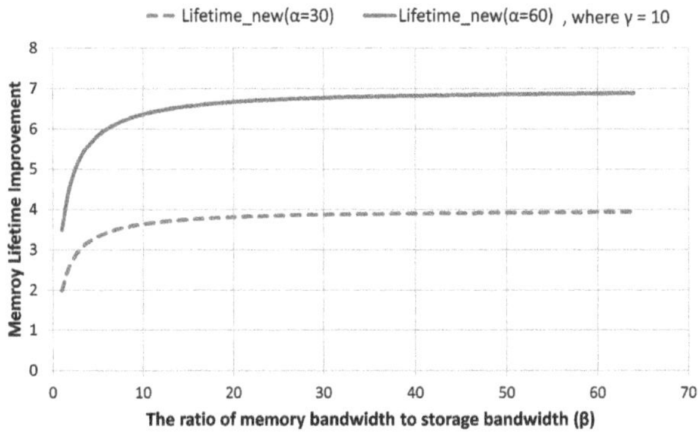

Figure 10: Main memory lifetime improvement.

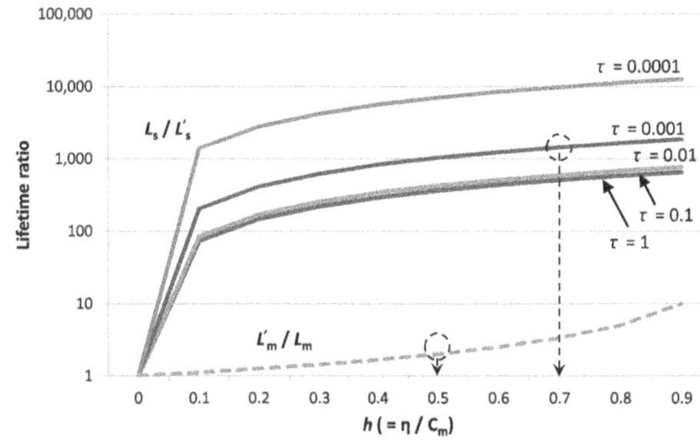

Figure 11: Main memory lifetime improvement and PSD lifetime degradation as a function of h and τ.

traded capacity size and decreases with a longer capacity trading period and higher storage side bandwidth.

To express the above as a function of h and τ only, let us fix other variables. Like before, imagine a platform with 8 GB main memory and a 480 GB PSD. Also, assume $B_s =$ 12 GB/day [2] and $\beta = 720$ (large bandwidth difference between main memory and PSD).

Figure 11 plots Equation (2). It is shown that the main memory lifetime increases with h while the lifetime of PSD decreases. Furthermore, the degradation of PSD lifetime is affected substantially by the choice of τ (expressed in "days"). For example, the degradation ratio difference between $\tau = 1$ (resource exchange occurs once a day) and $\tau = 0.01$ (hundred times a day) was more than an order of magnitude. Given the trend, how would the user choose h and τ? A feasible strategy would consider the lifetime improvement or degradation ratio target. For example, if the user desires at least 2× main memory lifetime improvement, h need to be 0.5 or larger (shown in the lower circle on the plot). If the same user would like the maximum PSD lifetime degradation of 1,500, he/she could choose $\tau = 0.0001$ and ensure $h = 0.7$ or less (upper circle). The user could use any value between 0.5 and 0.7 for h. This concrete example demonstrates that the developed model is powerful and can guide wear-leveling management policies.

The improvement of main memory lifetime comes at a high cost of degrading the PSD lifetime. In the previous example, obtaining 2× improvement in the main memory lifetime corresponds to 1,000× PSD lifetime degradation. This cost may appear excessive. However, in fact, the cost is justified when the system lifetime is limited by the main memory lifetime. For example, if $E_s = 10^5$, the expected lifetime of the 480 GB PSD is over 10,000 years when $B_s = 12$ GB/day. When $E_m = 10^6$, the lifetime of the 8 GB PRAM main memory, even with perfect wear-leveling, is only 2.5 years at $B_m = 100$ MB/s. In this case, reducing the PSD lifetime from 10,000 years to 10 years (1,000× degradation) to increase the main memory lifetime to 5 years makes perfect sense. Our analysis demonstrates that Memorage's ability to trade resources between PSD and main memory is extremely valuable toward improving not only the performance but also the lifetime of a platform.

5. RELATED WORK

The work by Freitas et al. [18] gives an excellent overview of the PRAM technologies. They suggest that a PRAM is a "universal memory," providing capacity to both main memory and storage of a platform. They also suggest that the PCM technology is closest to mass production. However, they do not discuss in detail the notion of system-wide, dynamic co-management of memory and storage resources in an integrated framework and how the notion can be realized.

Recently the computer architecture community paid due attention to building PCM main memory [28, 33, 43]. Because PCM has lower performance and smaller write endurance than DRAM, the focus was on developing techniques to hide the long PCM access latency, reduce write operations, and distribute wearing among PCM cells. These studies looked only at the main memory architecture.

On the other hand, Caulfield et al. [11, 12] and Akel et al. [6] evaluated the potential of PRAM as a storage medium. They studied the performance of a block storage device that employs PRAM and is connected to the host system through the high bandwidth PCI-e interface. Furthermore, like our work, Caulfield motivated the need to revamp the key OS components like the block I/O layer; however, they assume a conventional DRAM main memory and stick to the traditional main memory and storage dichotomy. Accordingly, their work focused only on streamlining the storage access path in the OS and the storage hardware built with PRAM.

Work done by other researchers also reveals that the maximum SSD performance is not realized without streamlining the traditional I/O software layers. Accordingly, they propose specific techniques to optimize the OS I/O stack and file system [24, 36, 37]. However, their concerns so far are for NAND flash SSDs on a legacy interface rather than byte-addressable PSDs. Even if these changes are applicable to the PSD, the techniques are strictly for the storage side of the PRAM technology.

Badam et al. [7] proposed to use SSD as main memory extension rather than storage by providing users with new set of APIs to explicitly allocate pages from SSD. While the method improves the performance of large memory footprint applications, it requires applications using the APIs to be recompiled. Also, they treat SSD just as memory resources without considering the role as file storage. In our proposal, PSD is not only used as memory extension without modifications to an application, but also keeps performing its innate duty to store files.

Qureshi et al. [32] and Dong et al. [17] proposed to improve the access latency of MLC PCM by adaptively changing the operating mode from slow MLC to fast SLC mode. While the former focused only on main memory, the latter dealt only with storage. By comparison, Memorage makes use of both main memory and storage resources together to obtain the best system performance. Memorage is a flexible architecture in that it neither binds itself to the PCM technology, nor does it require the use of fast page mode in MLC.

Finally, there are two inspiring studies that address the inefficient resource utilization in main memory and the storage system. Waldspurger [40] shows that memory usages are uneven among co-scheduled virtual machines and proposes "ballooning" to flexibly re-allocate excess memory resources from a virtual machine to another. This technique helps manage the limited main memory resources more efficiently. Similarly, Hough et al. [21] present "thin provisioning" to enhance the storage resource utilization by allocating storage capacity on demand. While both proposals tackle an important problem, their focus is limited to a single resource—main memory or storage (but not both).

Compared to the above prior work, we address the system-level performance and resource utilization issue of a future platform whose main memory and storage capacity collocated at the memory bus are both PRAM. A Memorage system collapses the traditional main memory and the storage resource management and efficiently utilizes the available PRAM resources of the entire system to realize higher performance and longer lifetime of the PRAM resources.

6. CONCLUSIONS

Emerging persistent RAM (PRAM) technologies have the potential to find their place in a computer system and replace DRAM and (a portion of) traditional rotating storage medium. This paper discussed potential architectural and system changes when that happens. Furthermore, we proposed Memorage, a novel system architecture that synergistically co-manages the main memory and the storage resources comprised of PRAM. Our experimental results using a prototype system show that Memorage has the potential to significantly improve the performance of memory-intensive applications (by up to 40.5%) with no additional memory capacity provisions. Furthermore, carefully coordinated PRAM resource exchange between main memory and PRAM storage is shown to improve the lifetime of the PRAM main memory (by up to 6.9×) while keeping PSD lifetime long enough for the studied system configurations. Memorage presents a practical, plausible evolution path from the long-standing memory-storage dichotomy to integration and co-management of memory and storage resources.

Acknowledgements

This work was supported in part by the US NSF grants: CCF-1064976 and CNS-1012070.

7. REFERENCES

[1] Memory hotplug. http://www.kernel.org/doc/Documentation/memory-hotplug.txt, 2007.

[2] Nand evolution and its effects on solid state drive (ssd) usable life. http://www.wdc.com, 2009.

[3] Micron announces availability of phase change memory for mobile devices. http://investors.micron.com/releasedetail.cfm?ReleaseID=692563, 2012.

[4] N. Aggarwal et al. Power-efficient DRAM speculation. *HPCA*, pages 317–328, 2008.

[5] N. Agrawal et al. A five-year study of file-system metadata. *TOS*, 3(3):1553–3077, Oct. 2007.

[6] A. Akel et al. Onyx: A protoype phase-change memory storage array. *HotStorage*, pages 2–2, 2011.

[7] A. Badam and V. Pai. Ssdalloc: hybrid ssd/ram memory management made easy. *NSDI*, pages 16–16, 2011.

[8] F. Bedeschi et al. A bipolar-selected phase change memory featuring multi-level cell storage. *JSSC*, 44:217–227, 2009.

[9] T. Bird. Measuring function duration with Ftrace. *Japan Linux Symposium*, 2009.

[10] D. Bovet and M. Cesati. *Understanding the Linux Kernel*. O'Reilly, 2005.

[11] A. Caulfield et al. Moneta: A high-performance storage array architecture for next-generation, non-volatile memories. *MICRO*, pages 385–395, 2010.

[12] A. Caulfield et al. Providing safe, user space access to fast, solid state disks. *ASPLOS*, pages 387–400, 2012.

[13] S. Cho and H. Lee. Flip-N-write: a simple deterministic technique to improve PRAM write performance, energy and endurance. *MICRO*, pages 347–357, 2009.

[14] Y. Choi et al. A 20nm 1.8V 8gb PRAM with 40MB/s program bandwidth. *ISSCC*, pages 46–48, 2012.

[15] G. F. Close et al. A 512mb phase-change memory (pcm) in 90nm cmos achieving 2b/cell. *VLSIC*, pages 202–203, 2011.

[16] J. Condit et al. Better I/O through byte-addressable, persistent memory. *SOSP*, pages 133–146, Oct. 2009.

[17] X. Dong and Y. Xie. AdaMS: Adaptive MLC/SLC phase-change memory design for file storage. *ASP-DAC*, pages 31–36, 2011.

[18] R. Freitas and W. Wilcke. Storage-class memory: The next storage system technology. *IBM J. of R & D*, 52(4-5):439–448, 2008.

[19] FusionIO. ioDrive2 datasheet. http://www.fusionio.com/platforms/iodrive2, 2012.

[20] L. Grupp et al. Characterizing flash memory: anomalies, observations, and applications. *MICRO*, pages 24–33, 2009.

[21] G. Hough. 3par thin provisioning: Eliminating allocated-but-unused storage and accelerating roi. Technical report, 3PAR Coporation, 2003.

[22] C. Hwang. Nanotechnology enables a new memory growth model. *the IEEE*, 91(11):1765 – 1771, 2003.

[23] ITRS. 2011 edition. http://public.itrs.net, 2011.

[24] W. Josephson et al. Dfs: A file system for virtualized flash storage. *TOS*, 6(3):14:1–14:25, Sept. 2010.

[25] D. Kim et al. Architecture exploration of high-performance PCs with a solid-state disk. *Trans. Computers*, 59(7):878–890, 2010.

[26] D. Klein. The future of memory and storage: Closing the gaps. Microsoft WinHEC, 2007.

[27] M. Kryder and C. Kim. After hard drives–what comes next? *Trans. Magnetics*, 45:3406 – 3413, 2009.

[28] B. Lee et al. Architecting phase change memory as a scalable DRAM alternative. *ISCA*, June 2009.

[29] J. McCalpin. Stream: Sustainable memory bandwidth in high performance computers. http://www.cs.virginia.edu/stream/, 1995.

[30] D. Meyer and W. Bolosky. A study of practical deduplication. *TOS*, 7(4):14, 2012.

[31] H. Pozidis et al. Enabling technologies for multi-level phase change memory. *E\PCOS*, 2011.

[32] M. Qureshi et al. Morphable memory system: A robust architecture for exploiting multi-level phase change memories. *ISCA*, pages 153–162, June 2010.

[33] M. Qureshi et al. Scalable high performance main memory system using phase-change memory technology. *ISCA*, June 2009. IBM T.J. Watson RC.

[34] S. Raoux et al. Phase-change random access memory: A scalable technology. *IBM J. of R & D*, 52(4-5):465–480, 2008.

[35] Samsung. Fusion Memory. http://www.samsung.com, 2010.

[36] M. Saxena and M. Swift. Flashvm: virtual memory management on flash. *USENIXATC*, pages 14–14, 2010.

[37] E. Seppanen et al. High performance solid state storage under linux. *MSST*, pages 1–12, 2010.

[38] A. Smith and Y. Huai. STT-RAM - a new spin on universal memory. *Future Fab International*, 23:28–32, 2007.

[39] D. Strukov et al. The missing memristor found. *Nature*, 453(7191):80–83, 2008.

[40] C. Waldspurger. Memory resource management in vmware esx server. *SIGOPS OSR*, 36(SI):181–194, Dec. 2002.

[41] Z. Wei et al. Highly reliable taox reram and direct evidence of redox reaction mechanism. *IEDM*, pages 1–4, 2008.

[42] X. Wu and N. Reddy. SCMFS: a file system for storage class memory. *SC*, pages 39:1–39:11, 2011.

[43] P. Zhou et al. A durable and energy efficient main memory using phase change memory technology. *ISCA*, 2009.

Function, Latency, Bandwidth, Power: Towards A Better Computer

Keynote Talk

Steve Teig
Tabula, Inc.
Santa Clara, California
steve@tabula.com

ABSTRACT

Computation in practice consists of executing functions, usually with the intention of achieving all three of correctness, high throughput, and low latency. Unfortunately, the most popular ways to specify functions - e.g., C++, Java, etc. - have not advanced significantly in 20 years. Mainstream software is hard to reason about and lacks any means of even expressing throughput or latency requirements, much less satisfying them. On the hardware front, the throughput of uniprocessors has barely increased in 10 years, yet developing efficient algorithms for multi-core processors remains ad hoc and frequently fails. Latency is no longer improving either – because multiple cores now compete for limited, off-chip memory bandwidth, and each core needs access to lots of off-chip memory. Finally, the ever-increasing need for communications throughput for datacenters, the Internet, and mobile devices is at odds with the importance of decreasing power consumption. What is a supercomputing community to do? (Hint: I believe that it is neither multi-core microprocessors nor GPUs.)

Categories and Subject Descriptors

I.0 [**Computing Methodologies**]: General

Keywords

latency, throughput

ICS'13, June 10–14, 2013, Eugene, Oregon, USA.
ACM 978-1-4503-2130-3/13/06.

Short Biography

Steve Teig is the President and Chief Technology Officer of Tabula and the inventor of Tabula's Spacetime 3-Dimensional Programmable Logic Architecture. In 2012, Tabula has been recognized with an Edison Award, an American Business Gold Award, inclusion in MIT's "TR50" list of the 50 most innovative companies worldwide, and as #3 in the Wall Street Journal's "Next Big Thing" list of the most promising venture-backed startup companies. Prior to founding Tabula, Steve was CTO of Cadence Design Systems, having joined Cadence through its acquisition of Simplex Solutions, where he was also CTO. Prior to Simplex, he was CTO of two successful biotechnology companies: CombiChem and BioCAD. Earlier in his career, he developed foundational logic simulation and place-and-route technologies that continue to have far-reaching influence. Steve received a B.S.E. degree in Electrical Engineering and Computer Science from Princeton University and holds over 250 patents. In 2011, he was awarded the World Technology Award for IT hardware innovation.

Improving Communication in PGAS Environments: Static and Dynamic Coalescing in UPC

Michail Alvanos[∓†]
Programming Models
Barcelona Supercomputing Center
malvanos@bsc.es

Montse Farreras[‡]
Dep. of Computer Architecture
Universitat Politècnica de Catalunya
mfarrera@ac.upc.edu

Ettore Tiotto
Static Compilation Technology
IBM Toronto Laboratory
etiotto@ca.ibm.com

José Nelson Amaral
Dep. of Computing Science
University of Alberta
jamaral@ualberta.ca

Xavier Martorell[‡]
Dep. of Computer Architecture
Universitat Politècnica de Catalunya
xavim@ac.upc.edu

Abstract

The goal of Partitioned Global Address Space (PGAS) languages is to improve programmer productivity in large scale parallel machines. However, PGAS programs may have many fine-grained shared accesses that lead to performance degradation. Manual code transformations or compiler optimizations are required to improve the performance of programs with fine-grained accesses. The downside of manual code transformations is the increased program complexity that hinders programmer productivity. On the other hand, most compiler optimizations of fine-grain accesses require knowledge of physical data mapping and the use of parallel loop constructs.

This paper presents an optimization for the Unified Parallel C language that combines compile time (static) and runtime (dynamic) coalescing of shared data, without the knowledge of physical data mapping. Larger messages increase the network efficiency and static coalescing decreases the overhead of library calls. The performance evaluation uses two microbenchmarks and three benchmarks to obtain scaling and absolute performance numbers on up to 32768 cores of a Power 775 machine. Our results show that the compiler transformation results in speedups from 1.15X up to 21X compared with the baseline versions and that they achieve up to 63% the performance of the MPI versions.

[†]Also, with the Department of Computer Architecture, Universitat Politècnica de Catalunya, Cr. Jordi Girona 1-3, 08034 Barcelona, Spain

[‡]Also, with the Barcelona Supercomputing Center, Cr. Jordi Girona 29, 08034 Barcelona, Spain

[∓]Also, with IBM Canada CAS Research, Markham, Ontario, Canada

ICS'13, June 10–14, 2013, Eugene, Oregon, USA.

Categories and Subject Descriptors

C.4 [**Performance of Systems**]; D.3.4 [**Compilers**]; D.1.3 [**Parallel programming**]; D.3.2 [**Concurrent, distributed, and parallel languages**]

Keywords

Unified Parallel C, Partitioned Global Address Space, One-Sided Communication, Performance Evaluation

1. INTRODUCTION

With the advent of multi-core processors, next-generation architectures and large scale parallel machines are not only increasing in size but also in complexity. In such a scenario, productivity is becoming crucial for software developers. Parallel languages and programming models need to provide simple means for developing applications that can run on parallel systems without sacrificing performance. To improve programmer productivity in distributed memory architectures, Partitioned Global Address Space (PGAS) languages appeared. PGAS languages, such as Unified Parallel C [12], Co-Array Fortran [21], Chapel [13], X10 [8], and Titanium [27], extend existing languages with constructs to express parallelism and data distribution. These languages provide a shared-memory-like programming model, where the address space is partitioned and the programmer has control over the data layout.

Regardless of all research community efforts, the de facto programming model for distributed memory architectures is still the Message Passing Interface (MPI) [20]. One reason is that PGAS programs deliver scalable performance only when they are carefully tuned. This limitation contradicts the philosophy of PGAS languages: ease of programming and productivity. In PGAS languages, the programmer accesses the data using individual reads and writes to the shared space. However, in a distributed environment this coding style translates into fine-grained communication, which has poor efficiency and hinders performance of PGAS applications. Due to the poor performance of fine-grained accesses, PGAS programmers optimize their applications by using large data transfers, whenever possible.

To cope with the fine-grained messages, the research community proposed the coalescing of shared accesses to improve performance. However, the existing solutions [9, 11, 5] have two important limitations: (i) They require the knowledge of physical data mapping at compile time. The programmer must specify the number of threads, the number of processing nodes, and the data distribution at compile time. (ii) The compiler can optimize shared accesses when occurring inside work-sharing constructs: *upc_forall* in UPC. However, passing the number of processing nodes as a compiler flag is not usually a practical solution, because it requires different binaries for different number of processors. Moreover, a number of available UPC benchmarks do not use the *upc_forall* loop structure. Thus, the automatic static coalescing is not possible in many realistic scenarios.

The IBM Power 775 supercomputer [22] (PERCS: Productive, Easy-to-use, Reliable Computing System) is a distributed-memory machine that features as many as 16384 32-Core compute nodes. Designed for 0.948 Teraflop/s peak performance per node, the machine is the IBM's answer for the DARPA's High Productivity Computing Systems (HPCS) initiative. The strength of the machine is its network architecture: a two-level direct-connect interconnect topology that fully connects every element in each of the two level through the Hub chip [3]. This topology improves the bisection bandwidth over other topologies and eliminates the need for external switches. New [12, 8] and traditional [20] programming models exploit the characteristics of the architecture for fast and reliable performance.

This paper presents a compiler optimization with the proper runtime support to tolerate the latency of fine-grained accesses, through a combination of runtime (dynamic) and compile time (static) coalescing techniques. The inspector-executor technique [7, 19, 23, 25] is used to discover the affinity between accesses and data allocation in the absence of explicit compile time affinity information, and thus to enable the runtime to coalesce fine-grained accessed. Regarding the novelty of our work, to the best of our knowledge, we are the first to apply the inspector-executor technique to the UPC language and redesign it to make it scalable to large core counts. Furthermore, there is no previous work that combines the compile time and runtime data coalescing techniques. Our contributions are:

- We present a combination of dynamic and static coalescing techniques [5, 9] to increase the communication efficiency, tolerate the network latencies, and decrease the runtime overhead. We demonstrate that the runtime and static coalescing can improve the performance of fine-grained accesses inside loops.
- We present a thorough, quantitative performance analysis of the benchmarks. We compare our optimization with the manual optimized version of the benchmarks, achieving from 15% up to 63% the performance of the hand tunned versions. The experimental results indicate that the lack of collective communications and the overhead of the inspector loops have tremendous impact on the performance.
- We evaluate the scalability of UPC language using benchmarks that contain fine-grained communication on the PERCS architecture. We point out that the interconnection network burdens the performance with certain data-access patterns.

The rest of this paper is organized as follows. Section 2 provides an overview of the Unified Parallel C language, and introduces the fine-grained accesses problem. Section 3 presents the implementation details of the optimization. Section 4 presents the methodology used. Section 5 presents the evaluation and section 6 presents the related work. Section 7 presents the conclusions.

2. BACKGROUND

PGAS programming languages use the same programming model for local, shared and distributed memory hardware. The programmer sees a single coherent shared address space, where shared variables may be directly read and written by any thread, but each variable is physically associated with a single thread.

2.1 Unified Parallel C

The Unified Parallel C (UPC) language follows the PGAS programming model. It is an extension of the C programming language designed for high performance computing on large-scale parallel machines. UPC uses a Single Program Multiple Data (SPMD) model of computation in which the amount of parallelism is fixed at program startup time.

```
 1  typedef struct { uint8_t r[IMGSZ];} RowOfBytes;
 2  shared [*] RowOfBytes orig[IMGSZ], edge[IMGSZ];
 3  void Sobel_upc(void){
 4   int i,j,d1,d2; double magn;
 5   upc_forall(i=1; i<IMGSZ-1; i++; &edge[i]){
 6    for (j=1; j<IMGSZ-1; j++){
 7     d1 = (int) orig[i-1].r[j+1] - orig[i-1].r[j-1];
 8     d1+=((int) orig[ i ].r[j+1] - orig[i].r[j-1])<<1;
 9     d1+= (int) orig[i+1].r[j+1] - orig[i+1].r[j-1];
10     d2 = (int) orig[i-1].r[j-1] - orig[i+1].r[j-1];
11     d2+=((int) orig[i-1].r[ j ] - orig[i+1].r[j])<<1;
12     d2+= (int) orig[i-1].r[j+1] - orig[i+1].r[j+1];
13     magn=sqrt((double)(d1*d1+d2*d2));
14     edge[i].r[j]=(magn>255) ? 255:(uint8_t)magn;
15    }
16   }
17  }
```

Listing 1: UPC version of Sobel kernel.

Listing 1, presents the computation kernel of the Sobel edge detection benchmark. Arrays `orig` and `edge` are declared as shared (line 2). Data are stored into single dimensional arrays of rows In this parallel version of the kernel, each thread is responsible for the computation of n consecutive picture rows. Where $n = IMGSZ/THREADS$ as specified by the `[*]` blocking factor. The construct `upc_forall` distributes loop iterations among the UPC threads. The `&edge[i]` expression in the `upc_forall` construct is the affinity expression. The affinity expression specifies that the owner thread of the specified element `&edge[i]` will execute the ith loop iteration.

The UPC compiler translates the shared accesses to runtime calls to fetch and store data. Runtime calls are responsible for fetching, or modifying the requested data. Each runtime call may imply communication of one element of the array, leading to fine-grained communication which leads to poor performance. When the physical data mapping is unknown at compiler time, the compiler does not apply the shared data coalescing or privatization optimizations.

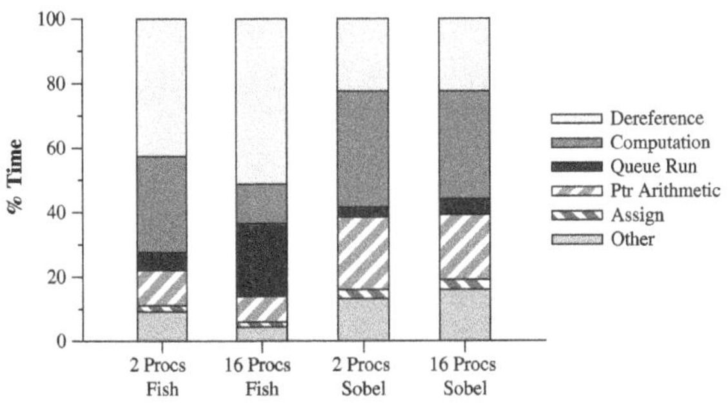

Figure 1: Normalized execution time breakdown of gravitational *fish* and *sobel* benchmarks using 2 and 16 UPC threads.

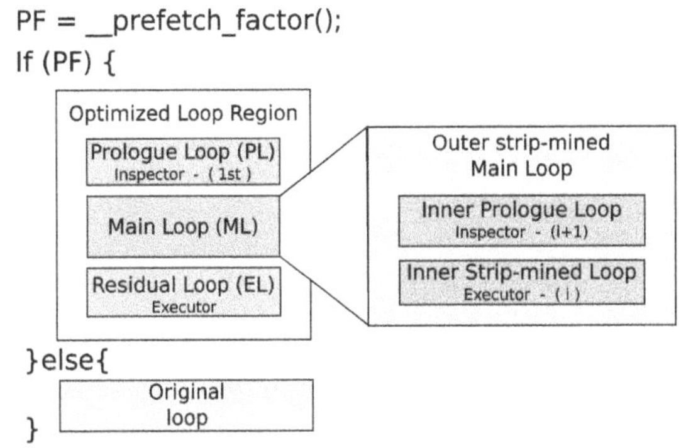

Figure 2: The final form of transformed loop using the inspector-executor transformation.

2.2 Motivating Examples

This section presents the execution time breakdowns for two different benchmarks: *Sobel* [17] and *fish* [1]. The profiles in figure 1 show that little time is spent on the actual computation (30% in *fish* and 35% in *Sobel* with two UPC threads). Several sources of overhead are identified: (i) time spent in accessing shared data (*dereference* phase) shows the impact of the communication latency for fine-grained accesses where communication is necessary for each dereference call; (ii) Shared pointer arithmetic (*Ptr Arithmetic*) has an impact because shared pointers contain more information than plain pointers and operating with them is expensive. This impact is greater in Sobel (20%) because it contains more shared accesses (nine) per loop iteration. Overall, two problems arise from these codes with fine-grained accesses to shared data: (i) the low communication efficiency because of the use of small messages, and (ii) the high overhead due to the large number of runtime calls created.

2.3 UPC Framework

The experimental prototype for the code transformations described in this paper is built on top of the XLUPC compiler framework [26]. The XLUPC compiler has three main components: (i) the `Front End (FE)` transforms the UPC source code to an intermediate representation (W-Code); (ii) the `Toronto Portable Optimizer (TPO)` high-level optimizer performs machine independent optimizations; (iii) a low-level optimizer performs machine-dependent optimizations. TPO contains optimizations for UPC and other languages including C and C++. The XLUPC runtime supports shared-memory multiprocessors using the Pthreads library and the Parallel Active Messaging Interface (PAMI).

3. DESIGN & IMPLEMENTATION

This section presents an improved version of the inspector-executor optimization and its combination with the static coalescing. The compiler applies the loop transformations and inserts the calls between different parts of the loop structure. The runtime is responsible for profitability analysis, keeping the list of shared accesses, message aggregation, and retrieving the data from local buffers.

3.1 Inspector-executor optimization

Previous research has focused on optimizing fine-grained accesses using static coalescing optimizations [5, 11, 9]. The biggest disadvantage of that approach is that the compiler must know the physical data mapping to be able to coalesce accesses or privatize the shared pointers. This requirement implies that the programmer must specify the number of threads at compile time.

Other researchers proposed the use of inspector-executor technique [23, 19] to allow the coalescing of shared accesses when the physical data mapping is unknown. The core idea is to collect the shared addresses that are accessed in a loop, analyze, coalesce, and fetch them ahead of time, before the data is required. The compiler creates a prologue (inspector) loop before the actual (executor) loop. The inspector loop collects the addresses for later analysis. After the inspector loop, the runtime analyzes the collected addresses and aggregates the messages. The executor loop reads the data from local buffers and performs the actual computation. However, the generic inspector-executor approach has two problems that we address in our work: (i) the *pause issue*: the execution of the actual program is paused to analyze shared accesses and to fetch corresponding data; (ii) the *resource issue*: the number of iterations of the loop may be so high that the memory requirements are increased to unacceptable levels.

To cope with these problems, the compiler strip-mines the main loop breaking the loop's iteration space into smaller chunks of size PF. The inspector loop analyzes PF iterations at a time. PF is the `prefetch factor`, it is chosen by the runtime to maximize benefit without exhausting the resources, solving the *resource issue*. To address the *pause issue*, the compiler shifts the inspector loops by one block, creating a pipelining effect. The inspector loop collects the elements for the $(i+1)$th block of iterations while the executor loop reads the coalesced data from a local buffer of the ith block of iterations. Next, the compiler applies loop versioning and creates two loops variants: the transformed and the native. Figure 2 presents the transformed loop structure.

In the final step of the transformation the compiler inserts the necessary runtime calls: (i) *__add_access* to collect shared accesses in the inspector loop; (ii) *__schedule* to analyze, coalesce the accesses, and issue network communication, before the main loop; (iii) *__dereference* to translate the shared pointer to the pointer to local data in the main loop. Alvanos *et al.* describe an earlier prototype and a preliminary evaluation of the use of the inspector-executor approach [2].

3.2 Static coalescing

The inspector-executor optimization increases the network efficiency over the unoptimized version of the benchmark. On the other hand, this approach increases the overhead due to additional runtime calls. To overcome the aforementioned overhead, we extend the inspector-executor approach by applying the static coalescing optimization in the inspector and the executor loops. The algorithm coalesces shared accesses when the compiler can prove that the remote data belong to the same thread. When the number of threads is dynamic, this is only possible when accessing members of shared structures that belong to the same thread. Therefore, the compiler applies the optimization when the program uses shared arrays with data structures.

```
AnalyseSharedRefs(Procedure p)

 1: RefList ← collectSharedReferences();
 2: BucketRefList ← ∅;
 3: for each shared mem ref R_s in RefList do
 4:    isInserted ← FALSE;
 5:    for each shared Bucket bck_s in BucketRefList do
 6:       if R_s is compatible with Bck_s then
 7:          Bck_s.Add(R_s);
 8:          isInserted ← TRUE;
 9:          break;
10:       end if
11:    end for
12:    if isInserted = FALSE then
13:       Bck_s ← newShrReferenceBucket();
14:       Bck_s.Add(R_s);
15:       BucketRefList.Add(Bck_s)
16:    end if
17: end for
```

Algorithm 1: Analysis of shared references.

The static coalescing requires additional compiler analysis and runtime modifications. Algorithm 1 presents the analysis algorithm. First, the compiler analyzes the shared accesses that are fields of shared structures. The compiler classifies the shared addresses in buckets containing compatible shared addresses (line 6). A shared reference is compatible with one bucket when the containing shared references use the same base symbol (array), the same array index, same element access size, but different offset inside the structure. If the compiler is not able to find any compatible bucket, then it creates a new bucket and adds the shared reference (line 14). Finally, the compiler sorts the shared references during the addition to the bucket, based on the local offset.

For each bucket the compiler inserts the dereference call on the first occurrence of a shared reference of the bucket and replaces each shared reference with the local buffer, by increasing the index of the local buffer based on the order of shared references.

Figure 3 exemplifies the static coalescing optimization. The example program on the Figure 3(a) shows a simple reduction of the `a` and `c` struct fields, from a shared array of structures written in UPC. Figure 3(b) presents the physical mapping of the shared array running with two UPC threads. The array is distributed cyclically among the UPC threads. Figure 3(c) presents the final code transformation. The transformation places the accesses on the `a` and `c` struct fields in the same bucket. Thus, it generates the appropriate runtime call (*__add_access_strided*) in the inspector loop to pass along the information about the stride between these access and the number of elements in the bucket. At runtime, the coalescing optimization fetches the `a` and `c` fields and places them in consecutive memory locations in the local buffer.

3.3 Runtime support

The runtime provides functionality for the inspector-executor optimization. The runtime: (a) decides if the optimization is profitable, (b) stores information for the shared references, (c) coalesces shared references, and finally (d) retrieves the data from the local buffers.

The runtime analyzes the profitability based on an heuristic that takes into account the number of iterations, the number of shared elements the loop accesses, and the number of processes. First, the runtime checks if the number of processes is more than one. Next, the runtime calculates the actual number of iterations for the inspector loops, using the following equation: $PF = MIN(\frac{MAX\_FETCH}{loop\_nelems}, upper\_bound)$;

The second task of the runtime is to collect and store the information about shared accesses in the inspector loops. For each shared access the runtime stores information about the shared variable, the offset, and the remote thread. For each pair of variable and UPC thread the runtime inserts an entry on a hash table. Each entry of this hash table contains an array of the offsets. The runtime does not issue any communication during the collection phase. The coalescing algorithm requires an additional library call for the inspector loops to support the collection of the shared references. The new library call has two additional arguments: the stride and the number of elements.

The third task is to analyze, coalesce and prefetch shared accesses. The runtime first sorts the collected offsets using the quicksort algorithm, removes duplicates, and prepares the vector of offsets to fetch. There are two reasons for sorting and removing duplicates from the offset list. First, the sorting makes the translation from shared index to local index for the buffer in the executor loops faster. Second, removing duplicates decreases the transfer size in applications that have duplicates, such as stencil computation. Finally, the runtime prepares a vector of offsets for fetching data. The transport library uses one-sided communication to achieve high throughput with low overhead.

The final task is the data retrieval from the local buffers. The runtime returns a pointer to the local buffer and sets the index value. Internally the runtime first tries to calculate the index value directly by using an auxiliary table. If the index value is not found, the runtime searches for the index value in the offset table using a binary search algorithm.

3.4 Local data optimization

One of the key runtime optimizations is the efficient access management of shared data that belong to the same UPC thread. The runtime identifies and ignores the local shared accesses, avoiding the overhead of unnecessary analysis. The runtime returns a pointer to the local data in the dereference calls to avoid memory copies. However, the presented static coalescing optimization requires symmetrical physical data mapping between the buffers. Thus, the constraint of the optimization is violated because local shared data have different memory mapping, in contrast with the prefetched buffers that contain only the prefetched elements.

The data locality is known at runtime. Therefore, we address this challenge by modifying the *__dereference* run-

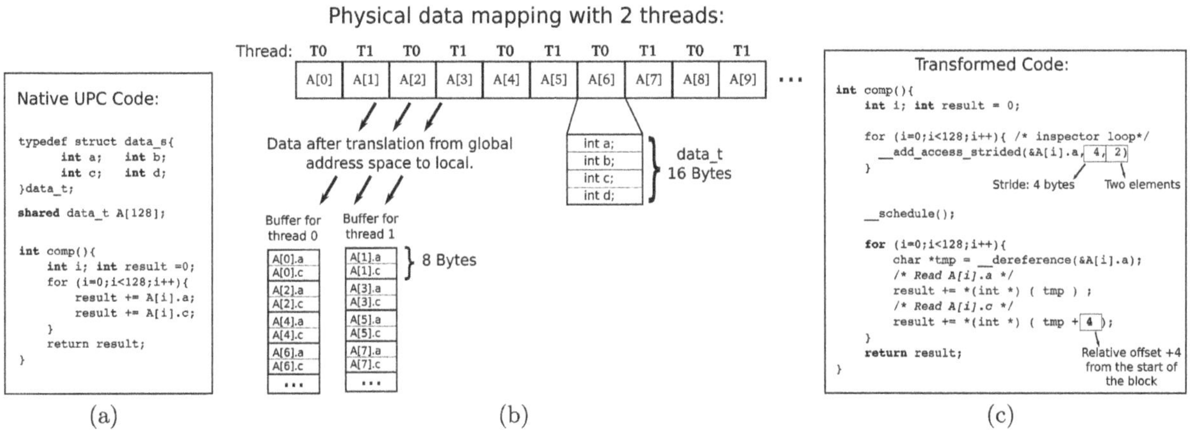

Figure 3: Example of Static data coalescing: native UPC source code (left), physical data mapping (middle), and transformed code (right). Transformed code is simplified for illustrative purposes.

Final Transformed Code:

```
int comp(){
    int i; int result =0 ; size_t stride;
    for (i=0;i<128;i++){
        stride = 4;    /* Compiler sets default stride */
        char *tmp = __dereference(&stride, &A[i].a);

        result += *(int *) ( tmp ) ;  /* Read A[i].a */
        /* Read A[i].c  */
        result += *(int *) ( tmp + 1*stride );
    }                                          Relative offset
    return result;                           from the start of
}                                                   the block
```

Runtime Dereference Call

```
void *__dereference(struct fat_ptr *ptr, int *stride){

    if ( ptr->node == CURRENT_NODE){
       /* No need to change the stride */
       return __get_local_data(ptr);
    }

    /* Change the distance of elements */
    *stride = ptr->elem_size;
    return __get_prefetched_data(ptr);
}
```

Figure 4: Final code modification and a high level implementation of the runtime.

time call to return the stride between the accesses. Figure 4 presents the generated code and a part of the dereference call in the runtime. In this example the distance between the fields is four bytes. The runtime sets the stride when the data are prefetched and stored in local buffer. On the other hand, the runtime returns a pointer to local data and does not change the default stride between elements (eight in the example), when the shared data are local. The compiler generates code for accessing different fields of the structure by multiplying the relative offset according to the order of shared references.

3.5 Resolving Data Dependencies

In a parallel loop with references and assignments the compiler may not be able to statically determine the data dependencies and must assume alias dependencies between the shared pointers. To guarantee memory consistency, the compiler creates the shared write calls with an additional argument that notifies the runtime to make additional checks for outstanding transfers. The compiler will set this flag to true if there is an overlapping between shared addresses or if the compiler fails to resolve the alias dependencies. The runtime handles the stores to shared data in one of three different ways:

- Compiler signals that there is no overlapping with other shared objects that application modifies. In this case, the runtime does not execute any additional code.
- Program writes on shared data and there is a copy of the shared data on a local buffer. Runtime issues the remote store and updates the local buffer to maintain the consistency.
- There is overlapping between the shared stores and the transferred data from a remote node. In this case the runtime waits for the transfer to complete and overwrites the prefetched data.

4. METHODOLOGY

This evaluation uses an IBM Power 775 supercomputer [22] with 1024 nodes with 32 Power7 cores on each node, running at 3.856 GHz, totaling 32768 cores. The size of available main memory is 128 GBytes. The machines are grouped in drawers consisted of eight nodes. Four drawers are connected to create a SuperNode (SN). The nodes are equipped with the Power7 Hub chip interconnect [3] for communication. The SuperNodes use eight links to communicate together. The Hub chip is connected with the four Power7 chips using four links, of 24GB/s each. The Hub chip contains seven links for intra-drawer communication, 24 links for intra-SuperNode communication, and 16 links for inter-SuperNode communication. The full system consists of 56 SuperNodes (SNs), totaling 1742 nodes.

All runs use one process per UPC thread and schedule one UPC thread per Power7 core. At most 4096 iterations are prefetched (*MAX_FETCH*). Each UPC thread communicates with other UPC threads through the network interface or interprocess communication. The UPC threads are grouped in blocks of 32 per node and each UPC thread is bound to its own core. The results presented in this evaluation are the average of the execution time for the five runs. In all experiments the execution time variation is less than 5%. One iteration of the optimized loop is always run before the actual measurement to warm-up the internal structures of the runtime. All benchmarks are compiled using the '-qarch=pwr7 -qtune=pwr7 -O3 -qprefetch' compiler flags.

4.1 Benchmarks and Datasets

The optimizations described in this paper aim at benchmarks that contain fine-grained accesses of field members on shared structures. Table 1 presents the list of the benchmarks and the communication pattern.

Microbenchmark: The microbenchmark is a loop that accesses a shared array of structures. There are two variations of this microbenchmark. In both versions an access to an element of the array accesses all four elements of the data structure. In the **stream-like** microbenchmark the loop accesses consecutive array elements (Listing 2). In the **random** microbenchmark the loop accesses randomly selected array elements.

```
typedef struct d{double var0; double var1;
                   double var2; double var3; } data_t;

#define SIZE (1<<31)
shared data_t Table[SIZE];

double bench_stream_4_fields(){
  uint64_t i;
  double result0 = 0.0, result1 = 0.0;

  for (i=MYTHREAD; i<SIZE-1; i+=THREADS){
   result0 = Table[i+1].var0 + Table[i+1].var1;
   result1 = Table[i+1].var2 + Table[i+1].var3;
  }
  return result0 + result1;
}
```

Listing 2: Microbenchmark kernel that reads four structure fields from a shared array sequentially.

Sobel: The Sobel benchmark computes an approximation of the gradient of the image intensity function, performing a nine-point stencil operation. In the UPC version [17], shown in listing 1, the image is represented as a one-dimensional shared array of rows and the outer loop is a parallel *upc_forall* loop. The evaluation uses different data set size per number of UPC threads (weak scaling), starting from 32768×32768 as input image size in 32 UPC threads, up to 1048576×1048576 using 32768 UPC threads.

Gravitational fish: The gravitational UPC fish benchmark emulates fish movements based on the gravity. The benchmark is N-Body gravity simulation, using parallel ordinary differential equations [1]. A different data set size is used for different number of UPC threads, starting from 16K objects for 32 threads until to 512K for 32768 UPC threads.

WaTor: The benchmark simulates the evolution over time of predators and preys in an ocean [14]. The ocean is represented by a two-dimensional matrix where each cell can either be empty or contain an individual: a predator or prey. In each time step predators and preys move, replicate or die following certain rules. This implementation assigns four lines of the ocean per UPC thread.

Benchmark	Communication Type
Microbenchmark_i	Stream-like from neighbour thread
Microbenchmark_ii	Random access
Sobel	Nine-point Stencil
Fish Grav	All-to-all/Reduction
WaTor	Rand. updates/reduction/25-point stencil

Table 1: Benchmarks and Communication type.

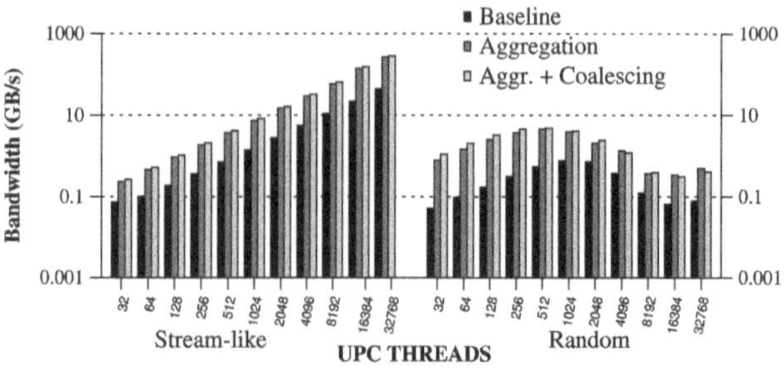

Figure 5: Performance in GB/s for the microbenchmark reading four fields from the same data structure in streaming fashion (left), and random reads using four fields (right).

A number of other benchmarks, such as Mcop (chain multiplication problem) and K-Means, also benefit from the coalescing optimization because they contain fine-grain accesses that can be coalesced at runtime. These benchmarks achieve a speedup from 4X up to 15X using our optimization. They were excluded from the evaluation because the purpose of this paper is to show the benefits of combining dynamic and static coalescing techniques.

4.2 Benchmark versions

The evaluation uses five different benchmark versions:

- The *Baseline* version, compiled with dynamic number of threads and disabled the inspector-executor optimization.
- The *Aggregation* version, where the compiler applies the inspector-executor optimization that prefetches and coalesces shared references at runtime.
- The *Aggregation + Coalescing* combines the inspector-executor and the static coalescing optimization.
- The *hand-optimized* shows the performance of the benchmarks using coarse-grained communication and manual pointer privatization.
- The *MPI* version contains coarse-grained communication. It uses collective communication when possible and does not use the non-blocking mechanisms.

5. EXPERIMENTAL RESULTS

This experimental evaluation assesses the effectiveness of the inspector-executor and static coalescing optimizations by presenting the following: (1) the performance on microbenchmarks to help understand the maximum speedup that can be achieved and the potential performance bottlenecks; (2) the performance of real applications; (3) bottlenecks and limitations of the inspector-executor approach;

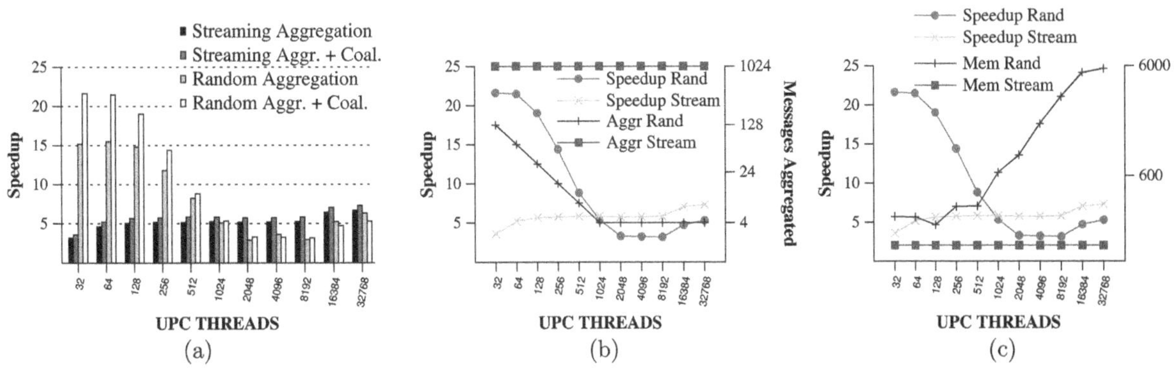

Figure 6: Achieved speedup for the two microbenchmark variations reading four fields (left), speedup compared with the number of messages aggregated (middle), and speedup compared with the memory consumption of the runtime (right).

(4) a comparison of the inspector-executor optimization with the manually optimized and the MPI versions of the benchmarks; (5) measurements of the optimization cost in terms of code increase, compilation time, and execution time.

5.1 Microbenchmark Performance

In the stream-like microbenchmark the bandwidth increases linearly with the number of UPC threads — notice the log-log scale in Figure 5. The stream-like microbenchmark reads data from the neighbouring UPC threads. The runtime creates one entry in a hash table resulting in very low memory overhead. On average, 4096 elements were coalesced into a single message. The speedup for this stream-like benchmark is between 3.1x and 6.7x as shown in the dark bars of Figure 6(a). The slight increase in the achieved speedup for more than 16384 UPC threads is most likely due to higher latency and network contention.

On the other hand, when reading elements in random order, the speedup varies from 3.2x up to 21.6x. The combination of the inspector-executor and the static coalescing optimizations give a speedup of 10% over the simple inspector-executor approach in stream-like workloads and around from 10% up to 25% for the random one.

The random-access benchmark achieves better bandwidth (4.5 GB/s) than the stream-like variation (2.1 GB/s) when the prefetching is enabled and the benchmarks runs with 256 or less UPC threads. The Hub Chip architecture explains this result. The Hub Chip has 7 different links for connecting nodes on the same drawer. These links have unidirectional bandwidth of 3 GB/s point-to-point between cores with a maximum of 24 GB/s aggregated unidirectional bandwidth [4]. In the streaming benchmark only one of the threads in the node communicates with a neighbouring node and therefore only one of the Hub links is used, decreasing the maximum bandwidth that is available. In contrast, in the random case, all nodes may communicate, with the communication potentially going through the 7 available links.

The performance gain (speedup) of the random access decreases while it remains constant in the stream-like benchmark. There are two reasons for this behaviour: (i) The number of coalesced messages, and (ii) the memory consumption of the runtime. The right-side vertical axis of Figure 6(b) is the number of coalesced messages. As expected, there is a correlation between the speedup and the aggregation of the messages. In the stream-like benchmark all shared accesses come from the neighbour thread, therefore the number of coalesced messages remains constant, being only limited by the number of iterations we inspect, the prefetch factor (which is $\frac{MAX\_FETCH}{loop\_num\_elems} = \frac{4096}{4} = 1024$). In the random-access benchmark, if we assume a uniform distribution, the number of random accesses that hit the same thread is decreasing with the number of threads to the minimum of one array entry that contains 4 shared accesses for each element of the structure. Figure 6(c) presents the correlation between memory consumption and the speedup. In the stream-like benchmark memory consumption is kept constant because all accesses come from the same thread and only one entry of the hash table is required while a random distribution leads to a more populated hash table and therefore memory consumption increases with the number of threads.

Finally, there is a performance decrease in the random reads for more than 1024 UPC threads, with or without prefetch. The reason for this performance decrease is the interconnect between SuperNodes. The network architecture has a two-level direct-connect interconnect topology that fully connects every element in each of the two levels. With only two levels in the topology, the longest direct route can have at most three hops consisted from no more than two L hops and at most one D hop [22]. The total amount of traffic that uses the inter-SuperNode links is: $\frac{\#THREADS - \#SN * \#INTER - \#INTRA}{\#THREADS} = \frac{16384 - 16*8 - 1024}{16384} = 92.96\%$ of the traffic. The remaining traffic uses local links for the communication. Overall, the interconnection of the SuperNodes limits the performance in random access patterns due to saturation of the remote links for more than 1024 UPC threads.

5.2 Applications Performance

Figure 7(a) presents the performance numbers for the **Sobel benchmark** in mega-pixel per second. The inspector-executor (*aggregation*) optimization achieves a performance gain between +10% and +90%. The relatively low performance gain compared with the microbenchmark and the gravitational fish benchmark, is due to good shared data locality. For example only the 1.6% of shared accesses are remote, running with 2048 UPC threads. The Sobel benchmark communicates with the neighbouring UPC threads

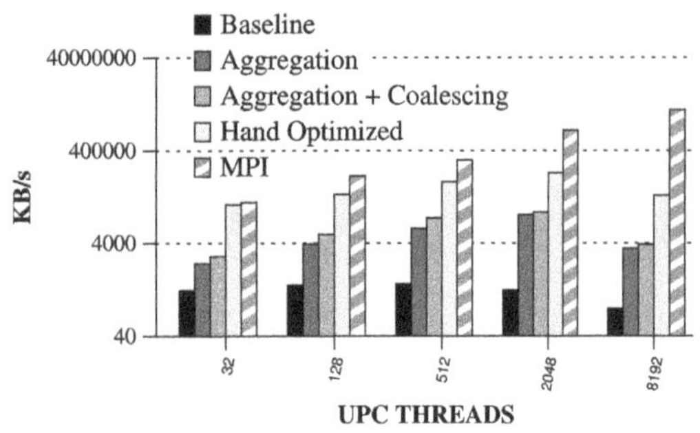

Figure 8: Performance of the WaTor benchmark.

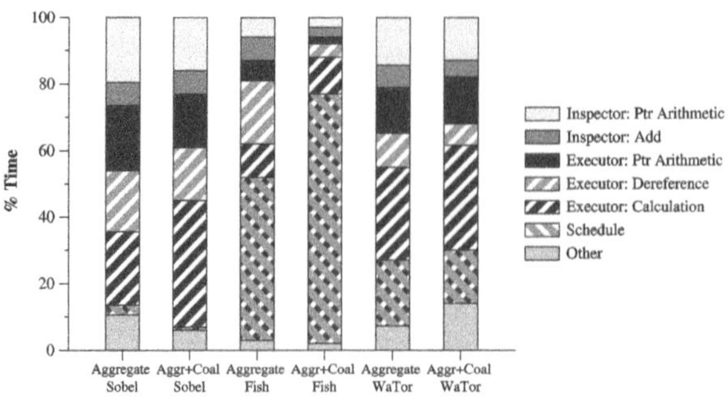

Figure 9: Normalized execution time breakdown of the benchmarks using 128 UPC threads.

only in the start and in the end of the computation. The *Aggregation + Coalescing* technique achieves from 2.4x up to 3.3x speedup over the *baseline* because the static coalescing is decreases the number of library calls. Furthermore, one interesting characteristic of the Sobel benchmark is that the runtime coalesces 258 packets into one remote message, independent the number of the UPC threads.

Figure 7(b) reports the number of objects computed per second in the **fish benchmark**. The static coalescing gives and additional speedup between 9x up to 26x compared with the baseline version. Furthermore, the performance drops significantly for more than 2048 UPC threads. The evaluation is limited to 8192 UPC threads, because runs with 16K or more threads are not practical. There are two issues that limit the performance of the application: (i) the architecture limitations of the interconnect network and (ii) the way the data are stored and accessed. First, for the same reasons that *random access microbenchmark* has bad performance for more than 1024 UPC threads, the fish benchmark saturates the inter-SuperNode links. Secondly, all UPC threads access data in streaming fashion starting from the first UPC thread. Thus, for the first iterations of the loop, all the UPC threads try to access at the same time the data on the first UPC thread.

Figure 8 presents the performance numbers for the **WaTor benchmark** in KB/s. The aggregation and the static coalescing gives a speedup from 3.8x up to 15.6x compared with the baseline version. Furthermore, the combination of aggregation and static coalescing is from 5.3x up to 25.1x faster than the baseline. The performance decreases for more than 1024 UPC threads because of the communication pattern. The benchmark reads 25 points of the neighbouring cells of the grid, in order to calculate the forces. Thus, 30% of the shared accesses are remote in this part of the benchmark. The large number of remote shared references saturates the remote links for more than 2048 UPC threads. The compiler optimizes most of the accesses in the remaining part using the remote update optimization [6].

5.3 Where does the time go?

The most important drawback from the inspector-executor optimization is the overhead added by the inspector loops and the analysis of accesses at runtime. Figure 9 presents a breakdown of the normalized execution time. The shared pointer arithmetic (*Ptr Arithmetic*) translates the offset to the relative offset inside the thread.

The inspector loops take 31% and 18% of the execution time in the Sobel and gravitational fish benchmarks, respectively. The static coalescing optimization decreases the overhead from the inspector and the executor loops from 20% up to 30%. The trend is similar for the gravitational fish benchmark. The proposed optimization decreases the overhead created from the inspector and the executor loops. One the other hand, the WaTor benchmark behaves almost identically with a small decrease on the overhead of the inspector and executor loops. The compiler optimizes only the force calculation part in the WaTor benchmark. Thus, the relative contribution of the other parts of the benchmark to the execution time increases. One interesting characteristic of the fish benchmark is the poor performance of the scheduling algorithm (*Schedule*) which is due to the all-to-all communication pattern. Thus, a better scheduling algorithm that exploits collective communication is necessary to achieve good performance in the fish benchmark (Figure 7(b)).

5.4 Comparing against hand-optimized & MPI

One of the goals for this optimization is to provide comparable performance to the hand-optimized version. The Sobel benchmark achieves (*Aggregation + Coalescing*) from 27% up to 63% of the performance of the MPI version. Figure 9 shows the source of performance difference: the overhead from the inspector and executor loops. One interesting observation is that the UPC hand-optimized version is from 1.05x up to 1.45x faster than MPI version, because of the better overlap of one-sided communication. In contrast with UPC language, the MPI requires the synchronization of the two processes to transfer the data.

Regarding the fish benchmark, the compiler-optimized version (*Aggregation + Coalescing*) achieves from 8% up to 32% of the speed of the UPC hand-optimized version. The advantage of the UPC-optimized and MPI versions is the use of collective communication.

Concerning the WaTor benchmark, the MPI version is faster but requires additional code before and after the force calculation and objects movement. The compiler does not create additional calls for accessing the data in contrast with the UPC versions. Overall, one weakness of this implementation is that it is missing the identification and exploitation of collective communication patterns.

5.5 Cost of the optimization

The inspector-executor and static coalescing come at a cost: (a) compile time increase, (b) code increase, and (c) runtime memory consumption.

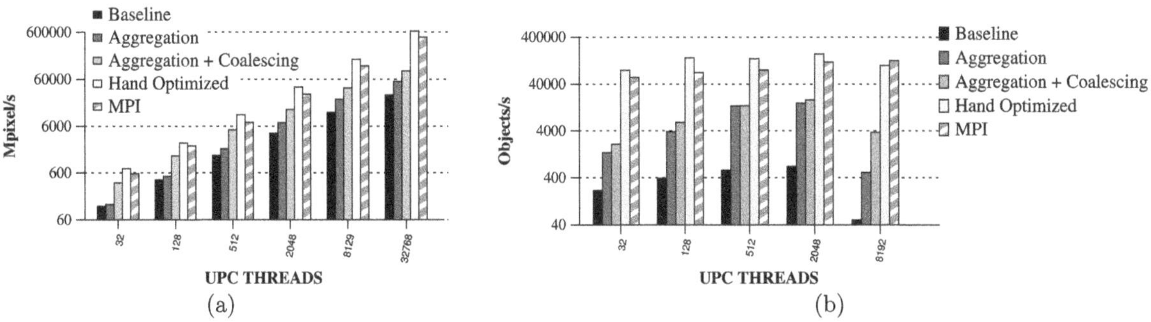

Figure 7: Performance numbers for the Sobel benchmark (a), and fish benchmark (b) for different versions.

Benchmark	Base	Aggr.	Aggr. & Coal.	Cost/access
Sobel	13702	17966	16270	+856
Fish Grav	15619	19755	19179	+890
WaTor	34872	37432	36792	+960

Table 2: Object file increase increase in bytes. We consider only the transformed file.

The increase in compilation time varies from 15% to 30%. The main reason for such a large increase is the data and control flow rebuild of the transformed loops.

The second drawback of the inspector-executor transformation is the code increase. The transformation requires the creation of three additional loops and the strip mining of the main loop. Moreover, it inserts some runtime calls for inspecting and managing the shared accesses. Table 2 presents the code increase for the three benchmarks. The Sobel benchmark with the inspector-executor optimization (*Aggregation*) approach has the biggest code increase, due to its large number of shared accesses. On average each prefetched shared access adds 900 bytes of additional code.

Finally, the inspector-executor transformation increases the memory requirements. The runtime must keep information about the shared accesses and about the use of local buffers for fetching the data. To address this challenge, we limit the value of the prefetch factor to avoid the allocation of large amounts of memory. Limiting the additional allocated memory to less than six MBytes, because ensures that the local buffers and the meta-data fit in the cache hierarchy.

5.6 Summary

The evaluation indicates that the combination of inspector-executor and static coalescing optimizations is an effective technique for decreasing the overhead of fine-grained accesses. The static coalescing optimization has a performance gain from 5% up to 210% compared to the simple inspector-executor loop optimization. The impact is more pronounced in random accesses benchmarks rather than stream-like, due to higher latency. The inability to discover collective access patterns limits the performance in some benchmarks, such as the fish gravitational, to from 4% up to 13% the speed of the MPI version. There are three factors that limit the performance. First, there is the overhead of the inspector loop and the analysis. Second, the absence of collective communication limits the performance in certain data-access patterns.

6. RELATED WORK

Optimizations for data coalescing using static analysis exist in Unified Parallel C [11, 5] and High Performance Fortran [9, 18]. A compiler uses data and control flow analysis to identify shared accesses to specific threads and creates one runtime call for accessing the data from the same thread. However, the existing locality analysis algorithms either only apply to *upc_forall* loops, or they require information for the physical data placement at compile time.

Another approach for minimizing the communication latency in the PGAS programming model is to split request and completion of shared accesses. The technique is called either "split-phase communication" [10] or "scheduling" [15, 18]. However, these approaches have limited opportunities with a loop structure, because of the data flow complexity.

The inspector-executor strategy is a well-know optimization technique in PGAS languages. There are approaches [19] for compiler support using a global name space programming model, or language-targeted optimizations such as: High Performance Fortran [7], Titanium language [25], X10 [16], and Chapel [24]. In contrast, our approach applies the strip-mining transformation on the original loop to achieve overlapping of communication with computation.

7. CONCLUSIONS AND FUTURE WORK

This paper presents an optimization to reduce the latency of fine-grained shared accesses and to increase the overall performance of programs written under the UPC language. The optimization combines the static coalescing optimization and the inspector-executor approach, with proper runtime support. The evaluation indicates that the combination of these two optimizations is an effective technique to decrease the impact of fine-grained accesses and to increase the network efficiency. Even though the communication efficiency increased, there is still room for further optimizations. For instance the overhead of the inspector loops may decrease by describing the index expression and the index ranges to the runtime using a runtime call. Nevertheless, this paper makes a significant contribution to improve the performance of programs written in PGAS languages, while keeping the promise of higher programmer's productivity.

Acknowledgments

Authors would like to thank George Almási and Ilie Gabriel Tanase for their support during the runtime development. The authors would like to thank Ioannis Manousakis, Ivan Tanasic, and Bo Wu for their valuable comments.

The researchers at Universitat Politècnica de Catalunya and Barcelona Supercomputing Center are supported by the IBM Centers for Advanced Studies Fellowship (CAS2012-069), the Spanish Ministry of Science and Innovation (TIN2007-60625, TIN2012-34557, and CSD2007-00050), the European Commission in the context of the HiPEAC3 Network of Excellence (FP7/ICT 287759), and the Generalitat de Catalunya (2009-SGR-980). IBM researchers are supported by the Defense Advanced Research Projects Agency under its Agreement No. HR0011-07-9-0002. The researchers at University of Alberta are supported by the NSERC Collaborative Research and Development (CRD) program of Canada.

8. REFERENCES

[1] S. Aarseth. *Gravitational N-Body Simulations: Tools and Algorithms*. Cambridge Monographs on Mathematical Physics. Cambridge University Press.

[2] M. Alvanos, M. Farreras, E. Tiotto, and X. Martorell. Automatic Communication Coalescing for Irregular Computations in UPC Language. In *Conference of the Center for Advanced Studies*, CASCON '12.

[3] B. Arimilli, R. Arimilli, V. Chung, S. Clark, W. Denzel, B. Drerup, T. Hoefler, J. Joyner, J. Lewis, J. Li, N. Ni, and R. Rajamony. The PERCS High-Performance Interconnect. *High-Performance Interconnects*, 0:75–82, 2010.

[4] K. J. Barker, A. Hoisie, and D. J. Kerbyson. An early performance analysis of POWER7-IH HPC systems. In *Proceedings of 2011 International Conference for High Performance Computing, Networking, Storage and Analysis*, SC '11, pages 42:1–42:11.

[5] C. Barton, G. Almasi, M. Farreras, and J. N. Amaral. A Unified Parallel C compiler that implements automatic communication coalescing. In *14th Workshop on Compilers for Parallel Computing*, 2009.

[6] C. Barton, C. Cascaval, G. Almasi, Y. Zheng, M. Farreras, S. Chatterje, and J. N. Amaral. Shared memory programming for large scale machines. *Programming Language Design and Implementation (PLDI)*, pages 108–117, June 2006.

[7] P. Brezany, M. Gerndt, and V. Sipkova. SVM Support in the Vienna Fortran Compilation System. Technical report, KFA Juelich, KFA-ZAM-IB-9401, 1994.

[8] P. Charles, C. Grothoff, V. Saraswat, C. Donawa, A. Kielstra, K. Ebcioglu, C. von Praun, and V. Sarkar. X10: an object-oriented approach to non-uniform cluster computing. 40(10):519–538, 2005.

[9] D. Chavarria-Miranda and J. Mellor-Crummey. Effective Communication Coalescing for Data-Parallel Applications. In *In Proceedings of the 10th ACM SIGPLAN Symposium on Principles and Practice of Parallel Programming (PPoPP)*, pages 14–25, 2005.

[10] W.-Y. Chen, D. Bonachea, C. Iancu, and K. Yelick. Automatic nonblocking communication for partitioned global address space programs. In *Proceedings of the 21st annual international conference on Supercomputing (ICS '07)*, pages 158–167.

[11] W.-Y. Chen, C. Iancu, and K. Yelick. Communication Optimizations for Fine-Grained UPC Applications. In *Proceedings of the 14th International Conference on Parallel Architectures and Compilation Techniques*, PACT '05, pages 267–278, 2005.

[12] U. Consortium. UPC Specifications, v1.2. Technical report, Lawrence Berkeley National Lab LBNL-59208.

[13] Cray Inc. Chapel Language Specification Version 0.8. `http://chapel.cray.com/spec/spec-0.8.pdf`.

[14] A. K. Dewdney. Computer recreations sharks and fish wage an ecological war on the toroidal planet Wa-Tor. *Scientific American*, pages 14–22, 1984.

[15] Y. Dotsenko, C. Coarfa, and J. Mellor-Crummey. A Multi-Platform Co-Array Fortran Compiler. In *Proceedings of the 13th International Conference on Parallel Architectures and Compilation Techniques*, PACT '04, pages 29–40.

[16] K. Ebcioglu, V. Saraswat, and V. Sarkar. X10: Programming for hierarchical parallelism and non-uniform data access. In *Proceedings of the International Workshop on Language Runtimes, OOPSLA*, 2004.

[17] T. El-Ghazawi and F. Cantonnet. UPC performance and potential: a NPB experimental study. In *Proceedings of the 2002 ACM/IEEE conference on Supercomputing*, Supercomputing '02, pages 1–26.

[18] M. Gupta, E. Schonberg, and H. Srinivasan. A Unified Framework for Optimizing Communication in Data-Parallel Programs. *IEEE Transactions on Parallel and Distributed Systems*, 7:689–704, 1996.

[19] C. Koelbel and P. Mehrotra. Compiling Global Name-Space Parallel Loops for Distributed Execution. *IEEE Trans. Parallel Distrib. Syst.*, 2, 1991.

[20] MPI Forum. MPI: A Message-Passing Interface Standard. `http://www.mpi-forum.org`.

[21] R. Numwich and J. Reid. Co-array fortran for parallel programming. Technical report, 1998.

[22] R. Rajamony, L. Arimilli, and K. Gildea. PERCS: The IBM POWER7-IH high-performance computing system. *IBM Journal of Research and Development*, 55(3):3–1, 2011.

[23] J. H. Saltz, R. Mirchandaney, and K. Crowley. Run-time parallelization and scheduling of loops. *IEEE Transactions on Computers*, 40(5):603–612, 1991.

[24] A. Sanz, R. Asenjo, J. Lopez, R. Larrosa, A. Navarro, V. Litvinov, S.-E. Choi, and B. L. Chamberlain. Global data re-allocation via communication aggregation in Chapel. In *SBAC-PAD*. IEEE Computer Society, 2012.

[25] J. Su and K. Yelick. Automatic Support for Irregular Computations in a High-Level Language. In *Proceedings of the 19th IEEE International Parallel and Distributed Processing Symposium (IPDPS)*, 2005.

[26] G. Tanase, G. Almási, E. Tiotto, M. Alvanos, A. Ly, and B. Daltonn. Performance Analysis of the IBM XL UPC on the PERCS Architecture. Technical report, 2013. RC25360.

[27] K. A. Yelick, L. Semenzato, G. Pike, C. Miyamoto, B. Liblit, A. Krishnamurthy, P. N. Hilfinger, S. L. Graham, D. Gay, P. Colella, and A. Aiken. Titanium: A High-performance Java Dialect. *Concurrency - Practice and Experience*, 10(11-13):825–836, 1998.

Bandwidth-optimal All-to-all Exchanges in Fat Tree Networks

Bogdan Prisacari
IBM Research
bpr@zurich.ibm.com

German Rodriguez
IBM Research
rod@zurich.ibm.com

Cyriel Minkenberg
IBM Research
sil@zurich.ibm.com

Torsten Hoefler
ETH Zurich
htor@inf.ethz.ch

ABSTRACT

The personalized all-to-all collective exchange is one of the most challenging communication patterns in HPC applications in terms of performance and scalability. In the context of the fat tree family of interconnection networks, widely used in current HPC systems and datacenters, we show that there is potential for optimizing this traffic pattern by deriving a tight theoretical lower bound for the bandwidth needed in the network to support such communication in a non-contending way. Current state of the art methods require up to twice as much bisection bandwidth as this theoretical minimum. We propose a set of optimized exchanges that use exactly the minimum amount of resources and exhibit close to ideal performance. This enables cost-effective networks, i.e., with as little as half the bisection bandwidth required by current state of the art methods, to exhibit quasi optimal performance under all-to-all traffic. In addition to supporting our claims by mathematical proofs, we include simulation results that confirm their correctness in practical system configurations.

Categories and Subject Descriptors

C.2.1 [**Computer-Communication Networks**]: Network Architecture and Design—*Network communications*

Keywords

all-to-all; fat tree networks; bandwidth optimality

1. INTRODUCTION AND MOTIVATION

Today's parallel computations are often arranged in a bulk synchronous programming (BSP) model [36] in which communication and computation steps alternate. For example, in the Message Passing Model as implemented by MPI [25], one can realize communication steps by sending messages between processes. Several common communication patterns, such as broadcast, are available as collective communications in MPI. This high-level specification enables a clean separation of concerns between the algorithm, that requires certain semantics, and the network architecture, that implements communication. This enables performance-portability of programs to a wide variety of different architectures and systems. Indeed, a collective programming model has enormous benefits for programmability as well as performance [9] and is thus also adopted by many other parallel programming environments [2, 21].

Of those collective communications, all-to-all is certainly the most demanding operation for the network because it needs to move $\Omega(p)$ data between p processes; it is thus also often considered the least scalable of MPI's collective operations [3]. Yet, there are many applications that require this communication pattern: Spectral codes, such as Direct Numerical Simulation [23] perform a 3D Fast Fourier Transform, utilizing large all-to-all communications for transposing the y direction over the network together with shared-memory on-node transforms of the x direction [6]. Even at the other end of the spectrum of scientific applications, data-driven parallel graph computations, such as betweenness centrality, essentially perform full all-to-all exchanges over the network [37].

All-to-all has thus been the subject of multiple research efforts optimizing it for different theoretical network models, such as LogP [29] or Postal [4], or technologies, such as InfiniBand [19] or Myrinet [39]. Our approach, however, is mostly oblivious to the network technology and current theoretical network models because we optimize for a certain network *topology*.

One important topology today is the family of fat trees [17], which form the base of several Petascale computer architectures (e.g., [38]). Fat trees con be configured in terms of bandwidth, rack layout, and cost. At the heart of the cost/performance trade-off, and thus a critical decision in supercomputer design, is the number of resources towards the root, which determines the *bisection bandwidth*. As computations requiring all-to-all exchanges are important, and as it is commonly believed that all-to-all bandwidth is bounded by the bisection bandwidth (cf. [16]), most fat tree networks are designed with full bisection bandwidth.

In this paper, we show that all-to-all only requires half bisection bandwidth due to its inherent locality. We then demonstrate how to design slimmed fat trees that have optimal cost while still providing full all-to-all bandwidth and

ICS'13, June 10–14, 2013, Eugene, Oregon, USA.
Copyright 2013 ACM 978-1-4503-2130-3/13/06 ...$15.00.

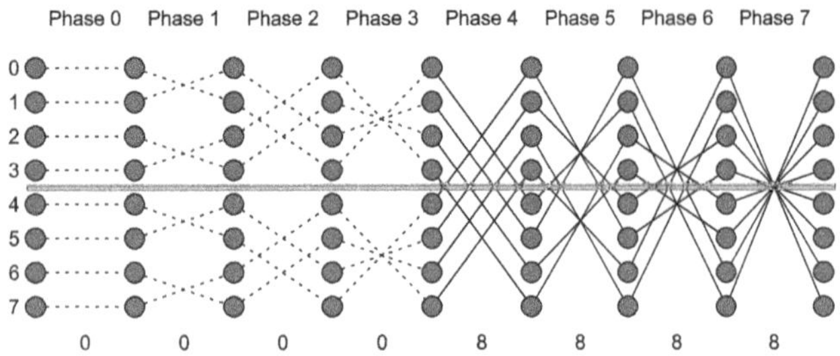

Figure 1: XOR exchange pattern between 8 communicating tasks. The first half of the phases are local and no traffic crosses the network bisection (horizontal line), whereas during the last half of the phases, all the messages cross the bisection (continuous lines). This requires a bisection bandwidth equal to the aggregate injection bandwidth.

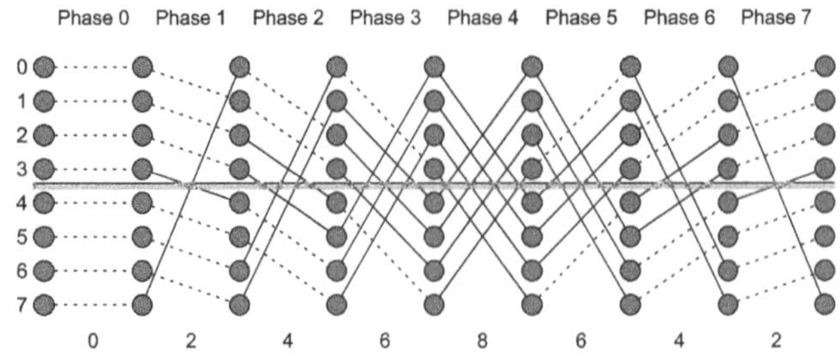

Figure 2: Linear exchange pattern between 8 communicating tasks for shift = 0. The uneven distribution of the number of messages (continuous lines) crossing the network bisection requires a bisection bandwidth equal to the aggregate injection bandwidth to enable contention-free traffic in all phases.

how to schedule all-to-all communications on general trees optimally. The main contributions of our work are:

- A general discussion of locality in the all-to-all problem.
- A construction of cost-optimal fat trees delivering full all-to-all bandwidth.
- An algorithm to compute optimal exchange patterns for a given fat tree.

We start with a description of the locality within all-to-all and intuitive examples for mappings to fat trees. We then present generic lower bounds for all-to-all communications on fat trees followed by a construction of optimal all-to-all schedules. We conclude our study with a set of simulated real-world examples.

2. THE ALL-TO-ALL PROBLEM

In this section we will discuss the intuition behind the bounds for all-to-all. The full proof and the algorithm to compute the send permutations for a given fat tree will be presented in Sections 3.1 and 3.4.

All-to-all is often referred to as "bisection-bound" (cf.[16]). While this is true asymptotically, i.e., a full-bandwidth all-to-all requires a $\Omega(p)$ bisection bandwidth on p processes, we will show that it only requires half of the actual bisection bandwidth *if one can take advantage of the inherent locality of the all-to-all problem.*

Consider an all-to-all schedule where each process $p \in P$ exchanges a single message with each other process. Let P_1 and P_2 form an arbitrary bisection of the process set P, such that $b = |P_1| = |P_2| = \frac{|P|}{2}$. In an all-to-all, each process in the set P_1 has b peers in P_1 and b peers in P_2, such that only $b = \frac{|P|}{2}$ exchanges leave each set. If P_1 and P_2 were arbitrary bisections of processes mapped to endpoints in an arbitrary topology, then only half of the messages cross any bisection of this topology. Thus, intuitively, all-to-all exchanges require only half bisection bandwidth for arbitrary topologies.

The argument can be applied recursively, i.e., partitioning P_1 into P_{11} and P_{12} etc., yielding a bandwidth-minimal construction. We now demonstrate that current all-to-all algorithms do not take advantage of this observation and thus require full bisection bandwidth for a full-bandwidth all-to-all. We then show how to utilize our observation by optimally scheduling all-to-all communications such that they require only half bisection bandwidth and cause less congestion than today's algorithms.

A typical [40] way of performing an all-to-all exchange between N processes or tasks, especially when there is no possibility of message aggregation (such as is the case for large messages), is to schedule the exchange as a set of N phases. Every process sends a single message and receives a single message in each phase (we consider that a process sends a message to itself as well). In this case, the exchange pattern can be entirely defined by a function that maps a given phase p and source task s to a unique destination task d (all three numbered from 0 to $N-1$), meaning that during phase p, the message sent by task s is destined to task d. The two widely used exchange patterns are the binary XOR exchange and the linear shift exchange [40].

In the case of XOR (Figure 1), the function is $d_{\text{XOR}} = s \,\text{XOR}\, p$, where the exclusive or operation is performed bit by bit on the binary representations of s and p.

In the case of the linear shift exchange [30] (Figure 2), the function is $d_{\text{LIN}} = (s+p+\text{shift}) \bmod N$, where N is the total number of communicating tasks and shift is a parameter that takes a constant integer value between 0 and $N-1$.

If we partition the 8 nodes in the example all-to-all in the two equal halves separated by the horizontal median line it is obvious that both exchanges exhibit an uneven distribution of the amount of traffic traversing this bisection of the network across the different phases, with a peak required bisection bandwidth, in both cases, equal to the aggregate injection bandwidth.

Looking at the two examples, it is equally obvious that the average number of messages crossing the bisection as we have defined it in every phase is only half the total number of communicating tasks. Furthermore, there is a way to ensure that in every phase no more than this average number of messages crosses the bisection (Figure 3). This makes it possible to have uncontended per phase traffic with only half the full bisection bandwidth.

We will show in the following sections that the observations for this small example hold in general. We will prove tight lower bounds on the bandwidth required for uncontended all-to-all traffic. Furthermore, for fat tree networks in particular we will introduce a bandwidth-optimized exchange pattern that satisfies these bounds.

3. ALL-TO-ALL OPTIMIZATION

First, we define the model of the interconnection network we are considering, the *fat tree* network. Fat trees are one of the most popular indirect network topologies used in current supercomputers.

The term fat tree has been used to refer to a broad class of different interconnection layouts. All fat trees can be described as a multi-stage tree-like topology where the width (bandwidth) of the connections increases towards the root of the tree.

An *ideal fat tree* would be a single binary tree interconnection network where the bandwidth of each link towards the root can always accommodate the aggregate capacity of the sub-tree connected to that link. These *ideal fat tree* networks are not realizable for large clusters, as the bandwidth needs to double at each level towards the root, which would require switches with either exponentially increasing number of ports or exponentially increasing bandwidth per link. The CM-5 [17] was the first machine to implement a variant of the ideal fat tree network.

However, it is possible to construct a tree-like network with an equivalent link bandwidth property by using fixed-radix switches, i.e., without increasing the number of connections per switch or their bandwidth [28, 27]. It is furthermore possible to construct networks [26] where the bandwidth towards the root can be tuned to almost arbitrary values, from the full-bisection bandwidth characteristic of ideal fat-trees to reduced bandwidth realizations that have a correspondingly reduced cost. We will discuss these and other practical implications of our method in Section 4.

For the time being, we will assume the following fat-tree model. We consider a layered single rooted tree structure that is homogeneous in that every node on a given layer has the same number of descendants. Using a notation similar to [26], we denote by $FT(L; M_1, M_2, ..., M_L)$ a tree of $L+1$ consecutively numbered layers, with 0 being the layer of the leaves and L that of the single root. Given a layer l, M_l then denotes the number of descendants that every node on layer l has. The tasks that send and receive messages are located at the leaf nodes, whereas the nodes on the other levels serve as message routers. We will assume a single task per node (The case where several tasks are present on the same node is equivalent to extending the fat tree with an additional leaf level, where every leaf corresponds to a task). Furthermore, we will assume that every upward link starting on a node on a given layer has a fixed bandwidth dependent only on the layer index. In the context of this abstract model of the network, we will now prove that the requirement of uncontended all-to-all traffic induces a tight lower bound on the bandwidth of every fat tree link.

3.1 Bandwidth-optimal link occupation in all-to-all communication over a fat tree

Given a fat tree $FT(L; M_1, ..., M_L)$ defined as above, we will show in this section that uncontended all-to-all traffic requires that every upward link originating on a layer l node as well as every downward link ending on a layer l node needs to be able to accommodate at least $B_{\min}(l)$ messages, with:

$$B_{\min}(l) = M_1 \cdot M_2 \cdot ... \cdot M_l - \left\lfloor \frac{M_1 \cdot M_2 \cdot ... \cdot M_l}{M_{l+1} \cdot M_{l+2} \cdot ... \cdot M_L} \right\rfloor . \quad (1)$$

To this end, we denote by Π_l the product $M_1 \cdot M_2 \cdot ... \cdot M_l$. Given that every leaf node corresponds to a single task, the total number of tasks is $N = \Pi_L$. Let us consider one of the nodes on level l, denoted by μ. The total number of messages originating from layer 0 descendants of this node

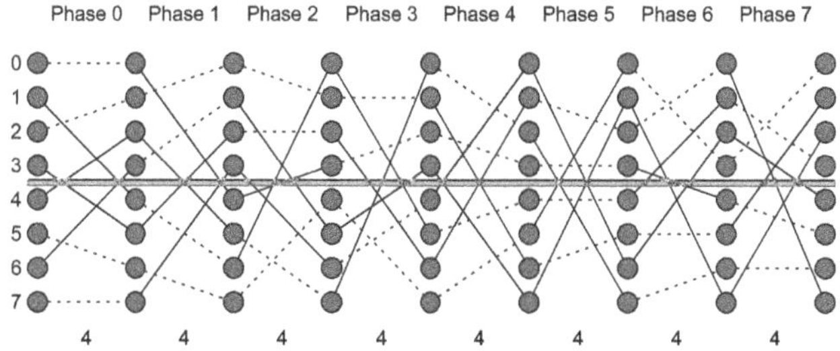

Figure 3: Optimized exchange pattern obtained for a fat tree with 2 levels and with $M_2 = 2$ and $M_1 = 4$. The link occupation optimization ensures that in every phase exactly half of the messages (continuous lines) cross the network bisection, thus making contention free traffic possible with only half the full bisection bandwidth.

during the all-to-all exchange is equal to the number of such descendants (which equals Π_l) multiplied by the total number of destinations (which equals Π_L). Out of these Π_L destinations, Π_l are located in the subtree rooted in μ and thus messages destined to these "local" tasks need *not* be routed on the link going upward from μ. All messages destined to the other tasks, located outside the subtree rooted in μ, *must* be routed on μ's upward link. Consequently, during the complete all-to-all exchange, the number of messages passing through the upward link originating on any node on level l equals $U(l) = \Pi_l \cdot (\Pi_L - \Pi_l)$.

As the exchange comprises Π_L phases, the average per-phase number of messages passing through the upward link originating on a given node on level l therefore equals $\overline{U}(l) = \Pi_l \cdot \left(1 - \frac{\Pi_l}{\Pi_L}\right)$

Given an arbitrary exchange pattern and an arbitrary phase of that exchange, the maximum number of messages passing through an upward link at level l is equal to or greater than $\overline{U}(l)$. This is equivalent to saying that at least one link will have $\overline{U}(l)$ or more messages passing through it in that phase. Thus, a prerequisite for uncontended single-phase traffic is to provide every upward link with sufficient bandwidth to transfer at least this number of messages. As such, contention-free traffic imposes a lower bound of $\lceil \overline{U}(l) \rceil$ on the number of messages that every upward link starting on a layer l node must be able to accommodate, bound that is equal to $B_{\min}(l)$ as defined in Equation (1).

Through a similar analysis, we can compute the minimum bandwidth necessary on downward links. Considering again one arbitrary node μ on level l, the total number of messages destined to level 0 descendants of this node during the entire exchange is equal to $\Pi_l \cdot \Pi_L$. Out of the Π_L sources of these messages, Π_l are located in the subtree rooted in μ and thus none of the messages originating from them traverse the downward link ending in μ. Consequently, during the complete exchange, the number of messages passing through the downward link ending on any node on level l equals $D(l) = \Pi_l \cdot (\Pi_L - \Pi_l)$, which leads to an average per-phase number of downward messages equal to $\overline{D}(l) = \Pi_l \cdot \left(1 - \frac{\Pi_l}{\Pi_L}\right)$.

Applying the same argument as before, we conclude that every downward link ending on a layer l node must be able to accommodate at least $\lceil \overline{D}(l) \rceil$ messages, which is again exactly equal to $B_{\min}(l)$ defined in Equation (1).

Next, we will introduce an exchange pattern that requires

no more than this minimum capacity, thus effectively proving that the bounds are tight. We will start by intuitively explaining the construction of the new pattern, then proceed to rigorously define it and prove its optimality.

3.2 Intuitive bandwidth-optimal exchange

Let us consider the example all-to-all exchange among 8 tasks presented in Section 2on a $FT(2;4,2)$ topology. For simplicity, let's start by optimizing the load induced by all tasks, on the two upward links ending in the root node.

As shown in Section 3.1, the key to optimizing bandwidth utilization is to balance the load on each link across all phases. Obtaining a bandwidth utilization of $B_{\min}$ across all phases is only possible if every phase exhibits this utilization. In our specific example, we are interested in $B_{\min}(1) = M_1 - \lfloor M_1/M_2 \rfloor = 2$. Thus, we must find a way to ensure that an arbitrary upward link ending on the root is used by exactly two messages in each phase. One way to achieve this is for every source task s to choose in any two consecutive phases a destination that is in the same layer 1 subtree as itself and a destination that is in the other layer 1 subtree. However, this is not enough, as all 4 tasks in a subtree could all choose to send messages outside of the subtree in the same phases. Therefore it is also necessary that the source tasks belonging to the same subtree are desynchronized among themselves in their choice of the destination subtree. A simple subtree selection function that achieves this is $((s \bmod 2)+(p \bmod 2)) \bmod 2$. Once we have selected the subtree, we also need to ensure that the actual destination within that subtree is unique over the set of sources. This can be achieved by selecting among the 4 choices in a specific subtree via the formula $((s/2) + (p/2)) \bmod 4$, where / yields the quotient of integer division. The complete destination selection function can then be defined as: $d = (((s \bmod 2)+(p \bmod 2)) \bmod 2)*4+((s/2)+(p/2)) \bmod 4$. This exchange is illustrated in Figure 3 and it is bandwidth optimal as exactly 4 messages cross the bisection in each phase.

We extend this to the general case of a $FT(L; M_1, ..., M_L)$ topology using the same principles. To balance load on the highest layer links, every source will send in M_L consecutive phases to M_L different subtrees. This approach is reused recursively from top to bottom.

The formalization and rigorous generalization of the approach follows in the next subsections. We first define a generic family of exchanges based on a *variable base representation* of numbers, then proceed to select among this set an exchange that we will prove to be bandwidth-optimal.

3.3 Permuted variable base exchanges

Given an ordered set of strictly positive integer numbers $(\Theta_1, \Theta_2, ..., \Theta_K)$ and given a number x with $0 \le x < \Pi_{k=1}^{K}\Theta_k$, we define the following notation:

$$x = \Sigma_{k=1}^{K}\left(\theta_k^x \cdot \Pi_{k'=1}^{k-1}\Theta_{k'}\right), \quad 0 \le \theta_k^x < \Theta_k, \quad 1 \le k \le K. \quad (2)$$

Basically, this equation defines a way of representing positive integers in "variable base". Unlike a normal base-n representation where each digit can take any value between 0 and $n-1$, in this case each digit may have a different range. The θ_k digits define a representation in base $(\Theta_1, \Theta_2, ..., \Theta_K)$, where the least significant digit's base is Θ_1. This representation, which applies solely to non-negative integers strictly smaller than $\Pi_{k=1}^{K}\Theta_k$, can be easily proven to be unique and uniquely identifying a certain value. That is to say:

$$\begin{aligned} &\forall x, y \text{ s.t. } 0 \le x, y < \Pi_{k=1}^{K}\Theta_k, \\ &x = y \Leftrightarrow (\theta_k^x = \theta_k^y, \quad 1 \le k \le K). \end{aligned} \quad (3)$$

In the context of fat trees, we will assign a variable base representation to every leaf node, and consequently, to every task. For this, we will assign tasks with indices ranging from 0 to $\Pi_L - 1$ and choose appropriate variable bases to represent those indices in.

Given a fat tree $FT(L; M_1, ..., M_L)$, let $K = L$ and let $(\Theta_1, \Theta_2, ..., \Theta_L) = (M_{\sigma(1)}, M_{\sigma(2)}, ..., M_{\sigma(L)})$, where σ is an arbitrary permutation of $(1, 2, ..., L)$. Additionally, we denote by α_k^x the digits of an arbitrary number x in the variable base $(M_1, M_2, ..., M_L)$. With these notations, we propose the following exchange pattern, which we will refer to as a *permuted-variable-base* exchange pattern. Let d be the destination of the message generated by source s in phase p. All three values s, d and p are numbers between 0 and $\Pi_{k=1}^{K}M_k - 1$. Then the function defining the pattern is:

$$\alpha_{\sigma(k)}^d = (\theta_k^s + \theta_k^p) \bmod \Theta_k, \quad 1 \le k \le K. \quad (4)$$

We will now show that this exchange model satisfies the two key properties of a valid all-to-all exchange pattern composed of phases: a source never sends to the same destination twice and no two sources send to the same destination in the same phase.

For the first property, let p_1 and p_2 be two distinct phases and let s be a certain source. We seek to prove that in this case, d_1 and d_2 obtained with Equation (4) are distinct.

Because p_1 and p_2 are positive and strictly smaller than $\Pi_{k=1}^{K}M_k$, they have a θ-representation. Furthermore, since they are distinct, according to Equation (3) there exists at least one $\tilde{k}$ with $1 \le \tilde{k} \le K$ such that $\theta_{\tilde{k}}^{p_1} \ne \theta_{\tilde{k}}^{p_2}$. According to Equation (4):

$$\theta_{\tilde{k}}^s + \theta_{\tilde{k}}^{p_1} = q_1 \cdot \Theta_{\tilde{k}} + \alpha_{\sigma(\tilde{k})}^{d_1}$$

where q_1 is an integer. Given that

$$0 \le \theta_{\tilde{k}}^s + \theta_{\tilde{k}}^{p_1} < 2 \cdot \Theta_{\tilde{k}}$$

and

$$0 \le \alpha_{\sigma(\tilde{k})}^{d_1} < \Theta_{\tilde{k}}$$

it follows that

$$-\Theta_{\tilde{k}} < q_1 \cdot \Theta_{\tilde{k}} < 2 \cdot \Theta_{\tilde{k}}.$$

As q_1 is an integer, it can only be 0 or 1. Similarly, q_2 has the same property. In the case where both are 0 or both are 1 ($q_1 = q_2 = q$), it immediately follows that $\alpha_{\sigma(\tilde{k})}^{d_1} \ne \alpha_{\sigma(\tilde{k})}^{d_2}$ from:

$$\theta_{\tilde{k}}^s + \theta_{\tilde{k}}^{p_1} - q \cdot \Theta_{\tilde{k}} = \alpha_{\sigma(\tilde{k})}^{d_1}$$

$$\theta_{\tilde{k}}^s + \theta_{\tilde{k}}^{p_2} - q \cdot \Theta_{\tilde{k}} = \alpha_{\sigma(\tilde{k})}^{d_2}$$

$$\theta_{\tilde{k}}^{p_1} \neq \theta_{\tilde{k}}^{p_2}$$

In the case where q_1 is 1 and q_2 is 0, we obtain

$$\theta_{\tilde{k}}^{p_1} - \theta_{\tilde{k}}^{p_2} = \alpha_{\sigma(\tilde{k})}^{d_1} - \alpha_{\sigma(\tilde{k})}^{d_2} + \Theta_{\tilde{k}}.$$

If $\alpha_{\sigma(\tilde{k})}^{d_1}$ were equal to $\alpha_{\sigma(\tilde{k})}^{d_2}$, then $\theta_{\tilde{k}}^{p_1} - \theta_{\tilde{k}}^{p_2} = \Theta_{\tilde{k}}$, which would lead to $\theta_{\tilde{k}}^{p_1} \geq \Theta_{\tilde{k}}$, which would constitute a contradiction. Therefore, in this case as well, $\alpha_{\sigma(\tilde{k})}^{d_1}$ must be different from $\alpha_{\sigma(\tilde{k})}^{d_2}$. The symmetric case ($q_1$ is 0 and q_2 is 1) is similar. As we proved that there exists a $\tilde{k}$ for which $\alpha_{\sigma(\tilde{k})}^{d_1} \neq \alpha_{\sigma(\tilde{k})}^{d_2}$, we proved that $d_1 \neq d_2$.

The proof of the second property is similar as the computation of the destination task as given by Equation (4) is symmetric with respect to the phase number p and the source number s.

This shows that every permutation σ of $(1, 2, ..., L)$ induces a valid exchange pattern. However, not all of these patterns optimize the maximum traffic traversing the upward links in the fat tree. In the following subsection, we will prove that the specific exchange pattern corresponding to $\overline{\sigma} = (L, L-1, ..., 2, 1)$ is bandwidth-optimal.

3.4 Bandwidth-optimal exchange pattern

As explained above, let $(\Theta_1, \Theta_2, ..., \Theta_L) = (M_{\overline{\sigma}(1)}, M_{\overline{\sigma}(2)}, ..., M_{\overline{\sigma}(L)}) = (M_L, M_{L-1}, ..., M_1)$.

We will prove that the bandwidth requirements induced at layer l by the variable-base-exchange corresponding to this particular base is equal to $B_{\min}(l)$.

We will start with the per phase bandwidth requirement per upward link. First note that all the descendants of a given node on level $\tilde{k}$ share the same α_k values for all k such that $\tilde{k} < k \leq L$.

Let p be a given phase of the all-to-all exchange. Let μ be an arbitrary node at level $\tilde{k}$. The total number of messages originating in level 0 descendants of this node during phase p is $\Pi_{\tilde{k}}$. Among these messages, some will be destined to nodes that are descendants of μ and some to nodes that are not. For a message to be destined to a descendant of μ, as noted above, its destination d must have certain fixed values for some of its α coefficients, values that depend exclusively on the position of μ. Specifically:

$$\alpha_k^d = \alpha_k(\mu), \quad \tilde{k} < k \leq L.$$

As d is obtained via Equation (4) this leads to:

$$(\theta_{L+1-k}^s + \theta_{L+1-k}^p) \bmod M_k = \alpha_k(\mu), \quad \tilde{k} < k \leq L.$$

As for a given p, the θ representation of p is fixed, and θ_{L+1-k}^s, θ_{L+1-k}^p and $\alpha_k(\mu)$ are all strictly smaller than M_k, this means that the θ representation of s needs to satisfy:

$$\theta_{L+1-k}^s = t_k(\mu, p), \quad \tilde{k} < k \leq L$$

where $t_k(\mu, p)$ is a set of factors independent of s. So for a descendant s of μ to send a packet to another descendant of μ in phase p of the exchange, the θ coefficients of s from rank 1 to rank $L - \tilde{k}$ must all have values that depend exclusively on μ and p, but not on s. According to the θ representation definition in Equation (2), this is equivalent to:

$$s = r(\mu, p) + q(s, \mu, p) \cdot \Pi_{k=1}^{L-\tilde{k}} \Theta_k$$

where $0 \leq r(\mu) < \Pi_{k=1}^{L-\tilde{k}} \Theta_k$. Thus, the only sources s that send messages to other descendants of μ are those whose index yields a fixed remainder (dependent of μ and p) when divided by $\Pi_{k=1}^{L-\tilde{k}} \Theta_k$. Because the s values are consecutive among the descendants of μ and because in total there are $\Pi_{\tilde{k}}$ such descendants, the minimum number of sources that send to a destination that is also a descendant of μ is:

$$N_{min}(\tilde{k}) = \left\lfloor \frac{\Pi_{\tilde{k}}}{\Pi_{k=1}^{L-\tilde{k}} \Theta_k} \right\rfloor$$

which according to the definition of the base is equal to:

$$N_{min}(\tilde{k}) = \left\lfloor \frac{\Pi_{\tilde{k}}}{\Pi_{k=\tilde{k}+1}^{L} M_k} \right\rfloor. \quad (5)$$

The rest of the messages could potentially go outside of the subtree rooted in μ. Therefore, the maximum bandwidth (in terms of number of messages) necessary on the upward link starting on any node on level $\tilde{k}$ is:

$$B_{max}(\tilde{k}) = \Pi_{\tilde{k}} - \left\lfloor \frac{M_1 \cdot M_2 \cdot ... \cdot M_{\tilde{k}}}{M_{\tilde{k}+1} \cdot M_{\tilde{k}+2} \cdot ... \cdot M_L} \right\rfloor \quad (6)$$

which exactly equals the value we previously found for the minimum bandwidth theoretically necessary in a fat tree for contention-free all-to-all messaging.

The per-phase bandwidth requirement per downward link can be computed analogously. During a given phase, at most $\Pi_{\tilde{k}}$ messages in total are sent to the $\Pi_{\tilde{k}}$ level 0 descendants of a node μ of the fat tree on level $\tilde{k}$. It can be shown with an argument analogous to the one above that among these messages, a minimum number must originate from these same descendants, and that that minimum number is equal to $N_{min}(\tilde{k})$ in Equation (5). As such, by the same argument as before, we obtain the same upper bound as that given by Equation (6) for the bandwidth required on the downward links.

3.5 Discussion

In this section, we have derived tight lower bounds on the bandwidth requirement of the all-to-all exchange in fat tree networks. We have also introduced an optimal exchange pattern that uses no more than the minimal bandwidth.

This new exchange pattern allows for a better use of network resources, freeing bandwidth for other traffic if the tree was designed with bandwidth in excess of the minimal bound, or, alternatively, allowing for reduced-cost fat trees that perform optimally under the all-to-all.

Compared to a standard fat tree that offers full bisection bandwidth at every level, the amount of bandwidth that is left unused, or, alternatively can be removed altogether from the tree is given, for a layer l link, by $\Pi_l - B_{\min}(l)$. This bandwidth surplus is largest at the top of the tree and decreases rapidly with the layer index. Nonetheless, at the highest level we can leave unused as much as $\frac{1}{M_L}$ of the full bisection bandwidth. Given certain conditions (specifically $M_L = 2$), this means we can achieve optimal all-to-all traffic with only half the full bisection bandwidth.

Because the amount of redundant bandwidth at lower layers of the tree decreases exponentially, in practice only a few top levels will allow significant reduction of bandwidth usage while some lower levels will allow no reduction at all. This, coupled with the fact that the fully optimized pattern as described above is highly intricate, leads to an interest in performing the optimization only at the levels where reduction occurs. We have developed methods similar to the one presented above to tune the complexity of the pattern while maintaining optimality but these will be discussed in a subsequent work.

4. PRACTICAL CONSIDERATIONS

In this section we will address some issues that arise from the fact that, in practice, fat tree networks are not implemented by means of ideal fat trees. This is because in practice the exponential increase in link bandwidth that is typical of multi-layered fat trees can only be achieved by means of having an exponentially increasing number of links between a single pair of nodes. This in turn leads to a necessity of switches with a very large port count, which are not feasible.

Therefore, in practice, fat tree topologies are approximated by means of k-ary n-trees [28, 27] or more generally by means of Extended Generalized Fat Trees (XGFTs) [26]. These network designs offer an alternative that only needs fixed small-radix switches and still provides many of the properties of ideal fat trees. However, the advantages come at the expense of reduced flexibility in bandwidth configuration and, more importantly, at the expense of needing more complicated routing algorithms.

The following two subsections briefly outline how the routing needs to be adapted to take full advantage of the optimal exchange pattern and provide an estimate of the cost saving that can be achieved by reducing the bandwidth to the theoretical lower bound for optimal all-to-all exchanges.

4.1 Routing in XGFTs

In practical fat tree realizations, optimizing the exchange pattern is not sufficient to benefit from contention-free traffic. The optimal exchange pattern introduced in Section 3.4 only ensures that, in each phase, the *aggregate* bandwidth at each fat-tree-equivalent-node of the network matches the aggregate number of messages traversing that node.

This is a necessary but not a sufficient condition for contention-free message routing. In addition, the routing strategy must ensure that the messages indeed use the available bandwidth evenly, i.e., it must assign conflict-free paths for all messages in each phase.

In XGFT networks, the typical way to establish minimal deadlock-free paths is simple up*/down* routing [33]. Given a (source, destination) pair, paths are constructed by routing upwards to any of the Nearest Common Ancestor (NCA) nodes and then downwards to the destination. Once a specific NCA is chosen, the routing choices from source to NCA and from NCA to destination are uniquely determined. The specificity of a certain routing strategy then lies in the approach used to select a specific NCA for every (source, destination) pair.

Several traffic-pattern-oblivious approaches exist, from random [10, 7] or adaptive [8, 20] route selection to deterministic (e.g., modulo based) approaches such as *S*ource-*mod-k* [26, 17, 14] or *D*estination-*mod-k* [18, 31, 41].

For complex patterns such as ours however, oblivious routing can prove insufficient. A pattern-aware routing approach takes advantage of information about the communicating pairs in a network and information about the network itself and uses it to find an optimized set of routes that will minimize contention for the set of (source, destination) pairs. Pattern-aware schemes solve in some way or another a *max-flow* network problem. A variety of approaches to achieve this are presented by Kinsy et. al [15]. Among these approaches, we were able to derive optimal conflict-free routes for the bandwidth-optimal exchange that we are proposing by means of Mixed Integer-Linear Programming.

4.2 Cost effective fat tree networks

Since the optimized exchange exhibits contention free all-to-all phases in reduced bandwidth topologies, we consider the network cost savings that this exchange allows.

Given an XGFT$(h : m_1, m_2, ..., m_h : w_1, w_2, ..., w_h)$ [26], the number of switches necessary to build the layer l of the topology is $S(l) = w_1 \cdot ... \cdot w_l \cdot m_{l+1} \cdot ... \cdot m_h$. The number of bidirectional links that connect layer l to layer $l-1$ is $E(l) = S(l) \cdot m_l$.

To simplify the analysis, consider a simple cost reduction scenario. Let's start with a full bisection bandwidth XGFT (i.e., where $w_{l+1} = m_l, 1 \leq l < h$ and $w_1 = 1$) that additionally has $m_h = 2$. This is the case we have shown to have the highest potential for bandwidth reduction. The reduced tree, XGFT$'(h : m_1, m_2, ..., m_h : w_1, w_2, ..., w'_h)$, has exactly the same parameters as the full bisection bandwidth tree, with the exception of w'_h which equals $w_h/2$.

Given the properties shown above, we can see that, for $1 \leq l < h$, $E(l) = E'(l) = E = w_1 \cdot m_1 \cdot ... \cdot m_h$ and $S(l) = S'(l) = E/m_l$. For $l = h$ we have $E(h) = E$, $E'(h) = w_1 \cdot m_1 \cdot ... \cdot m_h/2 = E/2$, $S(h) = E/m_h$ and $S'(h) = E/(2m_h)$.

The saving potential in the number of switches equals

$$1 - \frac{\sum_{l=1}^{h} S'(l)}{\sum_{l=1}^{h} S(l)} = 1 - \frac{1/(2m_h) + \sum_{l=1}^{h-1} 1/m_l}{1/m_h + \sum_{l=1}^{h-1} 1/m_l}$$

and in the number of links equals

$$1 - \frac{\sum_{l=1}^{h} E'(l)}{\sum_{l=1}^{h} E(l)} = 1 - \frac{(h - 1/2) \cdot E}{h \cdot E} = \frac{1}{2h}.$$

For typical XGFTs interconnecting 16 to 1024 leaf nodes, we can thus *achieve a reduction in the number of switches of* 25% − 30% *and a reduction in the number of necessary links of* 12% − 16%.

5. EXPERIMENTS

The following results were obtained by means of a simulation framework that is able to accurately model custom networks (including XGFTs) at a flit level [22]. The simulator provides a high level of customization and modularity, allowing the configuration of the desired model in detail. Several tests have been performed on XGFTs of 16, 32, 64, 128, 256, 512 and 1024 leaf nodes and up to 4 non-leaf levels. All these fat tree topologies had the M parameter of the topmost level equal to two ($M_L = 2$) and half bisection bandwidth. Table 1 shows the exact configurations used.

The simulations were performed using output-buffered switches with 4 kbytes of buffer space per port. The links had a bandwidth of 10 Gbit/s while their latency was either

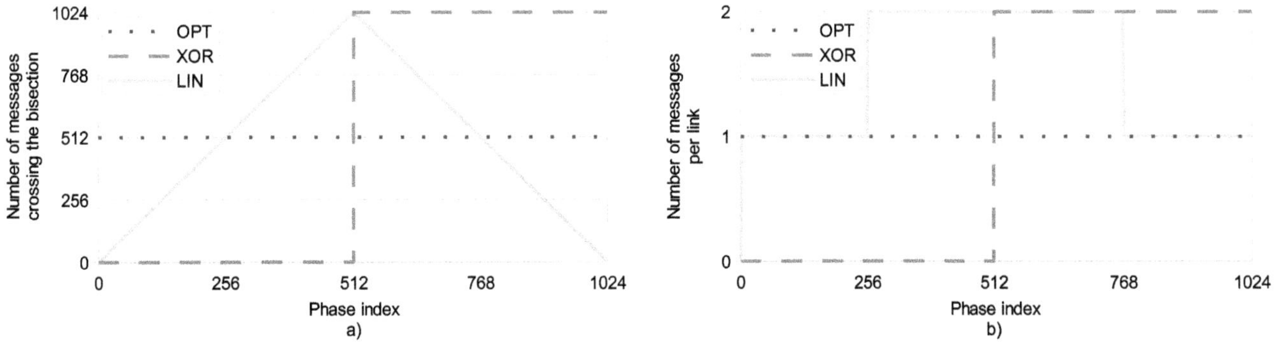

Figure 4: Bisection (top level) occupation induced by XOR, LIN and OPT exchange patterns. The topology is an XGFT with $M_L = 2$ with half bisection bandwidth and total number of leaf nodes equal to 1024. Figure a) shows the total number of messages crossing the bisection in each phase, while Figure b) shows the best value for maximum link contention (in number of messages), or best contention level, that can be obtained in each phase.

N	Network topology
16	$XGFT[3:4,2,2:1,4,1]$
32	$XGFT[3:4,4,2:1,4,2]$
64	$XGFT[3:8,4,2:1,8,2]$
128	$XGFT[3:8,8,2:1,8,4]$
256	$XGFT[4:8,4,4,2:1,8,4,2]$
512	$XGFT[4:8,8,4,2:1,8,8,2]$
1024	$XGFT[4:8,8,8,2:1,8,8,4]$

Table 1: Benchmarked topological configurations, using the notation from [26].

set to an ideal value of zero (to validate theoretical estimations) or to a realistic value of 100 ns (to estimate performance on real-life systems). In this same realistic latency scenario, switch traversal was considered to have a latency of 50 ns while adapter latency (the time between a message is issued in the MPI library and the time its first bit leaves the adapter) was set to 500 ns. Credit based flow control was used as well as wormhole switch traversal.

The messages have a constant size which, depending on the scenario, took values between 64 bytes (a single flit) and 32 kbytes, while the flit size was fixed to 64 bytes. Each acknowledgement consisted of a single flit.

The traffic pattern is that of a single all-to-all collective exchange performed by one task on each of the leaf nodes of the XGFT. The exchange is split into consecutive phases in each of which every node sends a single message and receives a single message and acknowledges it. No explicit synchronization or separation of the phases is enforced. The exact structure of each phase (the set of (source, destination) pairs) is defined according to one of three exchange models, all defined in Sections 2 and 3.4:

- XOR: the binary XOR model,
- LIN: the linear shift model with a shift value of 0,
- OPT: the optimized exchange given by Equation (4).

The metric we used is that of the time necessary for the traffic pattern to complete. However, these completion times can amount to very different values when looking at different sized networks and even at the same network with messages of different size. We are not interested in how these parameters influence the completion time, but rather in the influence of the exchange pattern within each given (network size, message size) configuration. As such, all results show the relative completion time compared to an ideal completion time that we will define in the following.

5.1 Ideal all-to-all performance

We use the following model to compute a best-case expectation for the completion time of the all-to-all exchange. Ideally, the messages travel through the network with no contention and simply incur the cumulative latency of the links, switches and adapters that they traverse. During the exchange, a given source sends $M_1 \cdot M_2 \cdot \ldots \cdot M_{l-1} \cdot (M_l - 1)$ messages to sources in its layer l subtree but not in its layer $l-1$ subtree, for every l. These messages need to first arrive at the root of the subtree, passing through 1 adapter, l links and $l-1$ switches, then cross the root, then travel again through 1 adapter, l links and $l-1$ switches to get to their destination. The cumulative latency for the entire path is thus $t_{\text{path}}(l) = 2 \cdot t_{\text{adapter}} + (2 \cdot l - 1) \cdot t_{\text{switch}} + 2 \cdot l \cdot t_{\text{link}}$.

Given a message that is made up of F flits, each of size S, and a link bandwidth of B, uncontended wormhole switch traversal ensures that the time it takes end-to-end, from message generation to message delivery, equals $t_{\text{path}}(l) + F \cdot S/B$.

The message needs to be acknowledged, which is equivalent to an extra one-flit message being sent along the reverse path. This leads to the total message time being: $T(l) = 2 \cdot t_{\text{path}}(l) + (F+1) \cdot S/B$.

Given the message distribution we described above, the ideal exchange time is given by

$$T = \sum_{l=1}^{L} M_1 \cdot M_2 \cdot \ldots \cdot M_{l-1} \cdot (M_l - 1) \cdot T(l)$$

5.2 Ideal latency analysis and measurements

To validate our simulation framework, we analyze the network contention induced by the three approaches when other performance limiting factors such as latency and latency-induced phase overlapping are factored out.

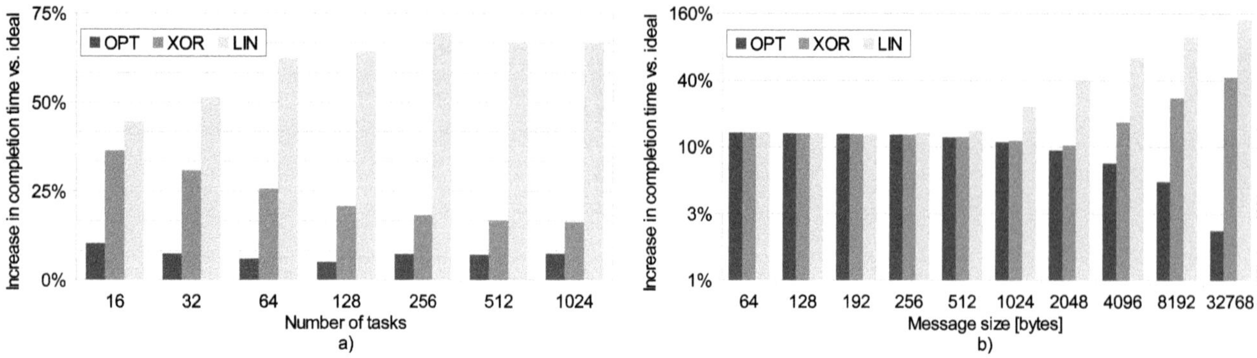

Figure 5: Completion time comparison between the three exchange patterns for varying networks sizes under fixed 4 KB message size (Fig. a) and for varying message size under fixed 512 leaf nodes network size (Fig. b). Please note the linear scale for the y axis in a) and the logarithmic scale for the y axis in b).

The XOR exchange exhibits no contention in half of its phases, namely in the phases where messages do not reach the top level of the fat tree. In the other half, N messages cross the top level, but have only half bisection bandwidth available, leading to a contention level of exactly two conflicts in every one of these $N/2$ phases. We defined the contention level as being the maximum number of messages that need to use a common link.

In the case of the LIN exchange, exactly $N - |2p - N|$ messages cross the top level of the tree in phase p, leading to a contention level of 2 yet again in exactly $N/2$ phases (the phases where $N - |2p - N| > N/2$).

In the case of the OPT exchange, exactly $N/2$ messages cross the top level of the tree in every phase, leading to uncontended traffic in every phase (Figure 4).

This implies that, in absence of latency and latency-induced phase overlapping, we can estimate theoretically that OPT will have a completion time close to the optimum, while LIN and XOR will incur a doubling of the completion time of half the phases, leading to at least a 50% increase in all-to-all completion time. This is confirmed accurately by our simulator, which yields completion times for OPT within 1% of the ideal time and completion times for XOR 50% – 55% longer than ideal, both irrespective of the message size. LIN performs even worse, with completion times between 70% and 140% larger than ideal (the performance loss increases with both the network and the message size). This is due to additional phase overlapping induced by intra-phase differences in message delivery time caused by different flows exhibiting different levels of contention (which is not the case for OPT and XOR).

5.3 Realistic latency results

We performed two sets of benchmarks to predict OPT performance on real systems. The first one is aimed at studying the influence of the network size on the performance gain induced by the optimized exchange pattern. The second on the other hand studies the influence of the size of the exchanged messages on the same performance gain.

Figure 5 a) illustrates the relative completion time of the three exchange patterns for a fixed message size of 4 kbytes and for different network sizes. We observed that in the realistic latencies configuration OPT managed to achieve completion times less than 10% higher than ideal, surpassing XOR (which is between 15% and 35% worse than ideal) and LIN (which is between 50% and 70% worse than ideal). The advantage of the optimized exchange versus XOR was especially strong for smaller topologies.

Figure 5 b) illustrates the relative completion time of the three exchange patterns for a fixed number of 512 communicating tasks (and a fixed network size) and for different sizes of the exchanged messages. We observed that for messages smaller than approximately 512 bytes, where the completion time is latency dominated, the optimization of the exchange doesn't help too much, because the impact of contention was small. For messages larger than this threshold, where the completion time was congestion dominated, OPT achieved an increasingly closer to ideal level of performance (reaching only a 2% – 5% difference for very large messages), while the non-optimized exchanges became progressively worse as the message size increased, reaching as much as a 40% performance decrease for XOR and as much as 140% for LIN, for very large messages. This confirms that our approach is asymptotically bandwidth optimal.

6. RELATED WORK

Collective optimizations are increasingly important in large-scale high-performance computing. Thus, numerous research works deal with the optimization of collective operations in general and all-to-all in particular. Most traditional approaches assume theoretical network models, such as the Postal model or the LogP model. Well-tuned algorithms exist for both models [4, 1]. However, all theoretical models (with the notable exception of LoGPC [24], which has not been used to model all-to-all algorithms due to its complexity), do not consider the network topology and thus only optimize endpoint congestion. Our work, however, uses a simple topology-specific model for optimizing all-to-all communications. Our model can be combined with existing network models to model endpoint congestion more accurately and can also be used as a blue-print for optimizing other collectives on fat trees. However, our contribution lies in the scheduling algorithm rather than the model.

Topology becomes more important with growing system size and several researchers acknowledge the fact that algorithms purely based on the mentioned theoretical models do not perform well on real systems. For example, Chan et al. [5] provide a general abstract framework for topology-aware collective communication. However, the abstract nature of this framework makes it hardly applicable to the recursive structure of fat trees. Zahavi et al. [42, 40] show that a particular routing function (a variant of up*/down*) guarantees under certain placement conditions full-bandwidth all-to-all exchanges implemented using typical collective permutation sequences on full bisection bandwidth fat trees. We improve upon this result by a factor of two, in that our methods applied to networks with half the full bisection bandwidth exhibit no or negligible decrease in performance by comparison. Sack and Gropp present a small set of topology-aware collectives for fat tree and torus networks in [32], however, in this latest work, they do not consider all-to-all and their approach of adding communication does not lead to improvements for all-to-all. In previous work [35], targeted at the implementation of optimized collectives in MPICH, the authors proposed the selection among a pool of implementations of different collective algorithms depending on message size and number of communicating processes, but not on any specific topology.

Other approaches for optimizing collectives, for example, improving the lower-level send/receive primitives [19], non-blocking collectives [12, 11], or hierarchical exchanges [13, 34] are completely orthogonal to the scheduling of messages. Those techniques can use our message-scheduling algorithm for improving the bandwidth of all-to-all.

7. CONCLUSIONS

The goal of this paper was to show that the current state of the art exchange patterns for the personalized all-to-all collective message exchange can be optimized in fat tree topologies to the point of using half of the bisection bandwidth required by previous proposals. To this end, we have derived a theoretical bound on the network link occupation that is intrinsically necessary and sufficient for any all-to-all exchange and we have shown that current approaches require as much as twice that proven optimally minimum. Furthermore, we introduced a message exchange pattern that we demonstrated to be bandwidth-optimal and that thus uses exactly the minimum required amount of network resources. Finally, by conducting network simulations benchmarking the proposed method against established approaches, we confirmed that in practical scenarios the optimizations we proposed achieve important reductions in network utilization, or alternatively network complexity and cost (by reducing the top level of the network such that only half the bisection bandwidth remains available), with little impact on performance. Furthermore, we demonstrated that in the half-bisection network scenario, where a cost-effective network with only the minimum amount of necessary resources was used, current methods incurred significant performance penalties, (in the 12% to 40% range for XOR and in the 12% to 140% range for LIN) whereas our method only diverged by at most 12% from optimal performance.

In conclusion, our method enables new design options for fat tree networks and offers a viable way of maintaining close to ideal application performance levels with important reductions in cost.

8. REFERENCES

[1] A. Alexandrov, M. F. Ionescu, K. E. Schauser, and C. Scheiman. LogGP: incorporating long messages into the LogP model - one step closer towards a realistic model for parallel computation. In *Proceedings of the 7th annual ACM symposium on Parallel algorithms and architectures (SPAA)*, pages 95–105, NY, USA, 1995. ACM.

[2] G. Almasi, P. Hargrove, I. Gabriel, and T. Y. Zheng. UPC collectives library 2.0. In 5th *Conference on Partitioned Global Address Space Programming Models*, 2011.

[3] P. Balaji, D. Buntinas, D. Goodell, W. Gropp, T. Hoefler, S. Kumar, E. Lusk, R. Thakur, and J. L. Traeff. MPI on Millions of Cores. *Parallel Processing Letters (PPL)*, 21(1):45–60, Mar. 2011.

[4] J. Bruck, C.-T. Ho, E. Upfal, S. Kipnis, and D. Weathersby. Efficient algorithms for all-to-all communications in multiport message-passing systems. *IEEE Trans. Parallel Distrib. Syst.*, 8(11):1143–1156, Nov. 1997.

[5] E. Chan, M. Heimlich, A. Purkayastha, and R. van de Geijn. On optimizing collective communication. In *Cluster Computing, 2004 IEEE International Conference on*, pages 145 – 155, sept. 2004.

[6] R. Fiedler. Preparing Applications for Sustained Petascale Performance, 2011.

[7] J. Flich, M. P. Malumbres, P. López, and J. Duato. Improving routing performance in Myrinet networks. In *Proc. of the 14th International Parallel and Distributed Processing Symposium*, pages 27–32, Los Alamitos, CA, USA, 2000. IEEE Computer Society.

[8] P. Geoffray and T. Hoefler. Adaptive routing strategies for modern high performance networks. In *High Performance Interconnects, 2008. HOTI '08. 16th IEEE Symposium on*, pages 165–172, Aug. 2008.

[9] S. Gorlatch. Send-receive considered harmful: Myths and realities of message passing. *ACM Trans. Program. Lang. Syst.*, 26(1):47–56, Jan. 2004.

[10] R. I. Greenberg and C. E. Leiserson. Randomized routing on fat-trees. In *Proc. of the 26th Annual Symposium on the Foundations of Computer Science*, pages 241–249, 1985.

[11] T. Hoefler and A. Lumsdaine. Optimizing non-blocking collective operations for InfiniBand. In *IEEE International Symposium on Parallel and Distributed Processing, IPDPS 2008*, pages 1 –8, 2008.

[12] T. Hoefler, A. Lumsdaine, and W. Rehm. Implementation and performance analysis of non-blocking collective operations for MPI. In *Proceedings of the 2007 ACM/IEEE Conference on Supercomputing, SC '07*, pages 1 –10, nov. 2007.

[13] P. Husbands and J. C. Hoe. MPI-StarT: delivering network performance to numerical applications. In *Proceedings of the 1998 ACM/IEEE conference on Supercomputing (CDROM)*, Supercomputing '98, pages 1–15, Washington, DC, USA, 1998.

[14] H. Kariniemi. *On-Line Reconfigurable Extended Generalized Fat Tree Network-on-Chip for Multiprocessor System-on-Chip Circuits.* PhD thesis, Tampere University of Technology, 2006.

[15] M. A. Kinsy, M. H. Cho, T. Wen, E. Suh, M. van Dijk, and S. Devadas. Application-aware deadlock-free oblivious routing. In *Proceedings of the 36th annual international symposium on Computer architecture*, ISCA '09, pages 208–219, New York, NY, USA, 2009. ACM.

[16] C. Kurmann, F. Rauch, and T. M. Stricker. Cost/performance tradeoffs in network interconnects for clusters of commodity PCs. In *Proceedings of the*

17th International Symposium on Parallel and Distributed Processing, IPDPS '03, pages 196.2–, Washington, DC, USA, 2003. IEEE Computer Society.

[17] C. Leiserson et al. The network architecture of the Connection Machine CM-5. In *Proc. of the Fourth Annual ACM Symposium on Parallel Algorithms and Architectures*, pages 272–285, San Diego, CA, USA, June 1992.

[18] X.-Y. Lin, Y.-C. Chung, and T.-Y. Huang. A multiple LID routing scheme for fat-tree-based InfiniBand networks. *Proc. of the 18th International Parallel and Distributed Processing Symposium*, pages 11–, 2004.

[19] A. Mamidala, R. Kumar, D. De, and D. Panda. MPI collectives on modern multicore clusters: Performance optimizations and communication characteristics. In *Cluster Computing and the Grid, 2008. CCGRID '08. 8th IEEE International Symposium on*, pages 130 –137, may 2008.

[20] J. C. Martínez, J. Flich, A. Robles, P. López, and J. Duato. Supporting fully adaptive routing in InfiniBand networks. In *Proceedings of the 17th International Symposium on Parallel and Distributed Processing*, IPDPS '03, pages 44.1–, Washington, DC, USA, 2003. IEEE Computer Society.

[21] J. Mellor-Crummey, L. Adhianto, W. N. Scherer, III, and G. Jin. A new vision for coarray fortran. In *Proceedings of the 3th Conference on Partitioned Global Address Space Programing Models*, PGAS '09, pages 5:1–5:9, New York, NY, USA, 2009. ACM.

[22] C. Minkenberg, W. Denzel, G. Rodriguez, and R. Birke. End-to-end modeling and simulation of high-performance computing systems. *Springer Proceedings in Physics: Use Cases of Discrete Event Simulation: Appliance and Research*, page 201, 2012.

[23] P. Moin and K. Mahesh. Direct numerical simulation: a tool in turbulence research. *Annual Review of Fluid Mechanics*, 30(1):539–578, 1998.

[24] C. A. Moritz and M. I. Frank. LoGPC: modeling network contention in message-passing programs. *SIGMETRICS Perform. Eval. Rev.*, 26(1):254–263, June 1998.

[25] MPI Forum. MPI: A Message-Passing Interface Standard. Version 3.0, September 2012.

[26] S. R. Öhring, M. Ibel, S. K. Das, and M. J. Kumar. On generalized fat trees. In *Proceedings of the 9th International Parallel Processing Symposium*, page 37, Washington, DC, USA, 1995. IEEE Computer Society.

[27] F. Petrini and M. Vanneschi. A comparison of wormhole-routed interconnection networks. In *Proc. 3th International Conference on Computer Science and Informatics*, NC, USA, Mar. 1997.

[28] F. Petrini and M. Vanneschi. k -ary n -trees: High performance networks for massively parallel architectures. *IPPS*, 00:87, 1997.

[29] J. Pješivac-Grbović, T. Angskun, G. Bosilca, G. Fagg, E. Gabriel, and J. Dongarra. Performance analysis of mpi collective operations. *Cluster Computing*, 10(2):127–143, 2007.

[30] S. Ranka, J.-C. Wang, and G. C. Fox. Static and run-time algorithms for all-to-many personalized communication on permutation networks. *IEEE Trans. Parallel Distrib. Syst.*, 5(12):1266–1274, Dec. 1994.

[31] C. G. Requena, F. G. Villamón, M. E. Gómez, P. López, and J. Duato. Deterministic versus adaptive routing in fat-trees. *Proc. of the 21st Parallel and Distributed Processing Symposium, 2007*, pages 1–8, Mar. 2007.

[32] P. Sack and W. Gropp. Faster topology-aware collective algorithms through non-minimal communication. In *Proceedings of the 17th ACM SIGPLAN symposium on Principles and Practice of Parallel Programming*, PPoPP '12, pages 45–54, New York, NY, USA, 2012. ACM.

[33] M. Schroeder, A. Birrell, M. Burrows, H. Murray, R. Needham, T. Rodeheffer, E. Satterthwaite, and C. Thacker. Autonet: a high-speed, self-configuring local area network using point-to-point links. *Selected Areas in Communications, IEEE Journal on*, 9(8):1318 –1335, oct 1991.

[34] S. Sistare, R. vandeVaart, and E. Loh. Optimization of MPI collectives on clusters of large-scale SMP's. In *Proceedings of the 1999 ACM/IEEE conference on Supercomputing (CDROM)*, Supercomputing '99, New York, NY, USA, 1999. ACM.

[35] R. Thakur, R. Rabenseifner, and W. Gropp. Optimization of collective communication operations in MPICH. *IJHPCA*, 19(1):49–66, 2005.

[36] L. G. Valiant. A bridging model for parallel computation. *Commun. ACM*, 33(8):103–111, Aug. 1990.

[37] J. J. Willcock, T. Hoefler, N. G. Edmonds, and A. Lumsdaine. Active pebbles: parallel programming for data-driven applications. In *Proceedings of the international conference on Supercomputing*, ICS '11, pages 235–244, New York, NY, USA, 2011. ACM.

[38] M. Xie, Y. Lu, L. Liu, H. Cao, and X. Yang. Implementation and evaluation of network interface and message passing services for TianHe-1A supercomputer. In *Proceedings of the 2011 IEEE 19th Annual Symposium on High Performance Interconnects*, HOTI '11, pages 78–86, Washington, DC, USA, 2011. IEEE Computer Society.

[39] W. Yu, D. K. Panda, and D. Buntinas. Scalable, high-performance nic-based all-to-all broadcast over Myrinet/GM. In *Proceedings of the 2004 IEEE International Conference on Cluster Computing*, CLUSTER '04, pages 125–134, Washington, DC, USA, 2004. IEEE Computer Society.

[40] E. Zahavi. Fat-trees routing and node ordering providing contention free traffic for MPI global collectives. In *IPDPS Workshops*, pages 761–770. IEEE, 2011.

[41] E. Zahavi, G. Johnson, D. J. Kerbyson, and M. Lang. Optimized InfiniBand fat-tree routing for shift all-to-all communication pattern. In *International Supercomputing Conference (ISC07)*, Dresden, Germany, June 2007.

[42] E. Zahavi, G. Johnson, D. J. Kerbyson, and M. Lang. Optimized InfiniBand(TM) fat-tree routing for shift all-to-all communication patterns. *Concurr. Comput. : Pract. Exper.*, 22(2):217–231, Feb. 2010.

An Automatic Input-Sensitive Approach for Heterogeneous Task Partitioning

Klaus Kofler, Ivan Grasso, Biagio Cosenza and Thomas Fahringer
Institute of Computer Science
University of Innsbruck, Austria
{klaus,grasso,cosenza,tf}@dps.uibk.ac.at

ABSTRACT

Unleashing the full potential of heterogeneous systems, consisting of multi-core CPUs and GPUs, is a challenging task due to the difference in processing capabilities, memory availability, and communication latencies of different computational resources.

In this paper we propose a novel approach that automatically optimizes task partitioning for different (input) problem sizes and different heterogeneous multi-core architectures. We use the Insieme source-to-source compiler to translate a single-device OpenCL program into a multi-device OpenCL program. The Insieme Runtime System then performs dynamic task partitioning based on an offline-generated prediction model. In order to derive the prediction model, we use a machine learning approach based on Artificial Neural Networks (ANN) that incorporates static program features as well as dynamic, input sensitive features. Principal component analysis have been used to further improve the task partitioning. Our approach has been evaluated over a suite of 23 programs and respectively achieves a performance improvement of 22% and 25% compared to an execution of the benchmarks on a single CPU and a single GPU which is equal to 87.5% of the optimal performance.

Categories and Subject Descriptors

D.3.2 [**Language Classifications**]: Concurrent, distributed, and parallel languages; D.3.4 [**Processors**]: Code generation/Compilers; C.1.3 [**Other Architecture Styles**]: Heterogeneous (hybrid) systems

General Terms

Languages, Algorithms, Performance

Keywords

heterogeneous computing, compilers, GPU, task partitioning, code analysis, machine learning, runtime system

1. INTRODUCTION

In the past few years, heterogeneous computing systems have emerged as mainstream and cost-effective means for scaling. Compared to traditional homogeneous systems, they offer high peak performance and energy efficiency. Not surprisingly, three of the ten fastest supercomputers in the world are heterogeneous systems [5], consisting of nodes with multi-core CPUs and GPUs. The transition from homogeneous to heterogeneous architectures is challenging with respect to the efficient utilization of the hardware resources and the reuse of the software stack. This problem has drawn great interest from researchers and industry, leading to the proposal of several programming models including HMPP [2], OpenACC [3], CUDA [27] and OpenCL [22]. OpenCL (Open Computing Language) is the first open standard for cross-platform parallel computing, supported by many hardware vendors such as AMD, ARM, IBM, Intel, and NVIDIA. OpenCL supports a wide range of hardware through a low-level high performance abstraction layer, supporting the development of programs without knowledge of the underlying architecture. Nevertheless, writing programs for heterogeneous systems remains a challenging task due to the difference in processing capabilities, memory availability, and communication latencies of different computational resources (called *devices* in OpenCL).

1.1 Motivation

As heterogeneous computing opens many new opportunities for developing parallel algorithms, our work is motivated by the additional challenges and complexity that it also introduces. One of the challenges is the distribution of tasks (i.e. task partitioning) among the available OpenCL devices in order to maximize the system performance. Task partitioning defines how the total workload (all threads of a program) is distributed among several computational resources.

It is important to understand that the best performing task partitioning is likely to change with different applications, different (input) problem sizes, and different hardware configurations. We justify our statement presenting a case study with two programs which are part of our test cases: *linear regression* and *reduction*. The programs have been executed with different problem sizes and varying task paritionings. We measured the execution times on two heterogeneous target architectures, consisting of one CPU and two GPUs (the target architecture configurations are detailed in Table 3). The results of these experiments are shown in Figure 1.

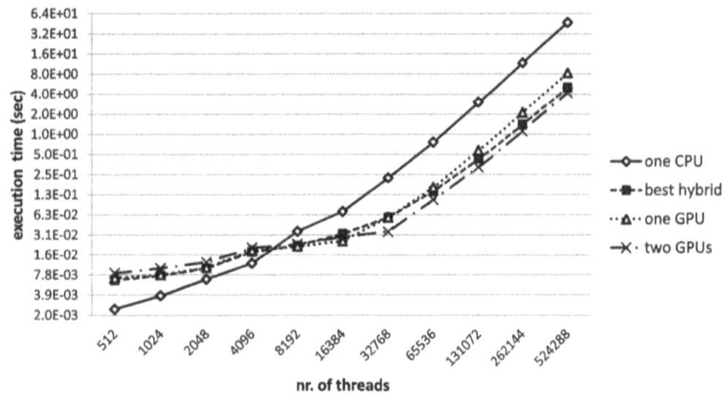

(a) Linear regression on *mc1*

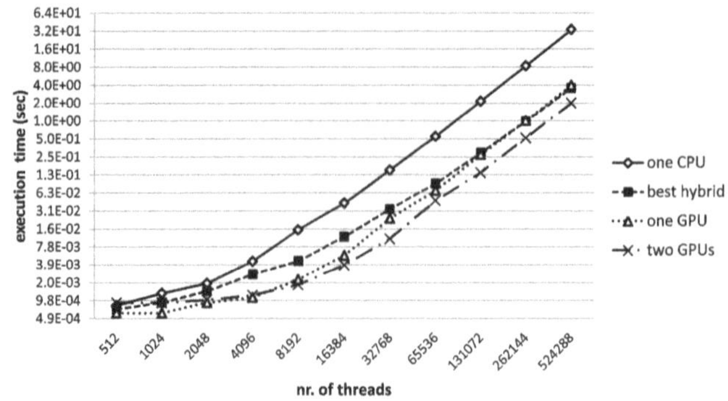

(b) Linear regression on *mc2*

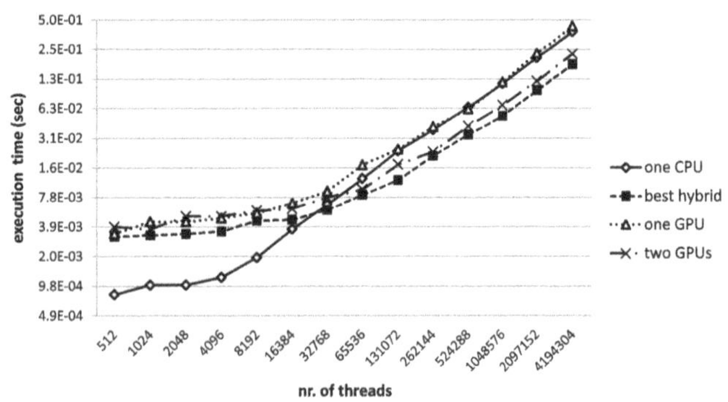

(c) Reduction on *mc1*

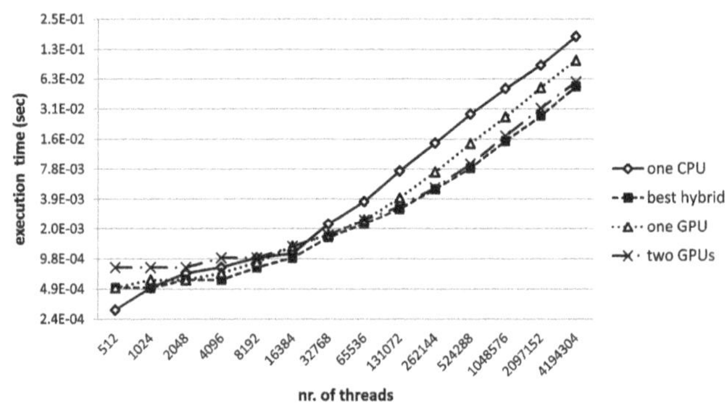

(d) Reduction on *mc2*

Figure 1: Performance behavior of two programs on different target architectures with varying problem size (i.e. the number of threads). Each chart shows execution times (in seconds) in logarithmic scale (y-axis) with different number of threads (*work items* in OpenCL) (x-axis). Detailed hardware descriptions of the target architectures *mc1* and *mc2* are shown in Table 3.

On the first target architecture (*mc1*, see Table 3) for small problem sizes, the GPU is less effective and the *one CPU* task partitioning delivers the best performance for both applications. However, for specific problem sizes, a *hybrid* task partitioning (using the CPU as well as one or two GPUs) or a *GPU only* task partitioning is preferable. On the second target architecture (*mc2*, see Table 3), *linear regression* performs best on one GPU for smaller problem sizes while *reduction* reaches the best performance with one CPU. For increasing problem sizes the GPUs become more effective and *linear regression* should be distributed over two GPUs for both *mc1* and *mc2*. The *reduction* program exhibits a different behavior for larger problem sizes, favoring hybrid solutions which outperform any homogeneous configuration by up to 44% and 19% on *mc1* and *mc2*, respectively.

These experiments demonstrate that even for a single application, the optimal partitioning considerably depends on the problem size and the capabilities of the hardware.

Another important aspect of heterogeneous computing is the difficulty of writing *multi-device* programs (i.e. a single program which can be executed on multiple devices concurrently). Since current state-of-the-art compilers are not capable of automatizing this complex task, new tools are needed in order to facilitate the conversion of existing programs to heterogeneous systems.

In this paper we present an automatic, problem size sensitive compiler-runtime method for task partitioning of OpenCL programs on heterogeneous systems. Our work is based on machine learning which effectively combines compile time analysis with runtime feature evaluation to predict the optimal task partitioning for every combination of program, problem size and hardware configuration.

The contributions of this paper are as follows:

- We propose and implement a novel compiler-runtime framework for auto-generation of multi-device OpenCL code and optimized task partitioning on heterogeneous systems. Our framework is portable to any OpenCL environment with an arbitrary number of devices. Our task partitioning approach is based on an offline generated problem size sensitive model, which is capable of outperforming the CPU/GPU only strategy by 22% and 25%, respectively. Our experimental results demonstrate the capabilities of our approach using 23 different applications on two different heterogeneous multi-device systems.
- We show that Principal Component Analysis (PCA) does improve the performance of dynamic task partitioning system by 2% to 7%, depending on the used machine learning technique and target architecture.

(a) Training phase

(b) Deployment phase

Figure 2: Framework Overview

- We present an analysis of different machine learning techniques suitable to solve the automatic task partitioning problem and show that Artificial Neural Networks (ANN) outperform Support Vector Machines (SVM) for the presented use case.
- We empirically demonstrate the benefits of our machine learning based approaches compared to traditional static task partitioning techniques.

The remainder of this paper is organized as follows. The next section gives an architectural overview of the Insieme Compiler and Runtime framework. Section 3 describes the partitioning problem and the generation of the machine learning models. Section 4 presents the experimental methodology. Section 5 discusses the experimental results. Section 6 presents related works and Section 7 concludes the paper.

2. FRAMEWORK OVERVIEW

Heterogeneous systems are difficult to program, and moreover the performance capability of individual devices can vary significantly across different applications and problem sizes which often makes static, problem size insensitive distribution techniques unsuitable. The Insieme Compiler and Runtime framework [1] relieves the developer from this difficult task. It consists of a source-to-source compiler and a runtime system. The Insieme Compiler translates single-device OpenCL programs (i.e. OpenCL programs which use only one computational resource) into multi-device OpenCL programs. The Insieme Runtime System distributes the computation among the available devices to effectively exploit the performance capabilities of a heterogeneous system.

2.1 Architecture

Figure 2 illustrates the architecture of the proposed framework, highlighting two main phases: *training* and *deployment*. The labels (1-7) in Figure 2(a) and Figure 2(b) explain the processing of a program within the Insieme framework.

The goal of the training phase is to build a task partitioning prediction model. Any previously unseen target architecture can be supported by generating a new model for it. Since the model generation is done automatically, our approach can be ported to any heterogeneous system without user intervention. To build a model, a set of OpenCL programs are provided to the system and translated into the Insieme parallel intermediate representation (INSPIRE, see Section 2.2) by the code analyzer (1). From this representation, the features of the program (*static program features*) are extracted and stored in a database (2). The intermediate representation of the program is then passed to the backend which generates multi-device OpenCL code (3). Once generated, the new program will be executed with various problem sizes and the available task partitionings. The obtained performance measurements (4), together with the problem size dependent features of the program (i.e. *runtime features*), are collected and added to the database (5). After these steps have been accomplished for all programs, the trainer uses the features and the performance measurements stored in the database (6) to generate a task partitioning prediction model (7).

In the deployment phase a new OpenCL program is provided to the analyzer (1) for optimizations, the static features are extracted (2) and the intermediate representation is passed to the backend (3) which generates a multi-device OpenCL program (4). When the program is executed, the runtime features are provided to the previously trained model (5), which combines them with the static program features to predict the best task partitioning for the current program with the selected problem size (6). Finally, the runtime system executes the program on the given hardware using the predicted task partitioning (7).

2.2 Implementation

We have implemented a powerful framework for code transformations and program analysis for heterogeneous parallel systems as part of Insieme [1]. It consists primarily of two components: a source-to-source compiler and a runtime system. The compiler translates OpenCL input code to an Intermediate Representation (IR) and back to OpenCL. This IR offers a formal and compact representation of programs that facilitates code analysis and transformation. The Insieme Runtime System is responsible for the execution and scheduling of the generated programs. It is capable of partitioning and distributing tasks over heterogeneous computing devices using interchangeable scheduling policies.

The Insieme Compiler's input is a single-device OpenCL program. An OpenCL program consists of a host and a device part. The host part runs on the CPU and is responsible for setting up the OpenCL devices (e.g. a GPU or the CPU itself). The device part (called *kernel*) is a data-parallel task and describes the computations performed by a single thread (called *work item* in OpenCL). During the program execution, a certain number of work items is generated and executed in parallel. The number of work items generated increases with the input problem size. The exchange of data between the host and the compute devices is implemented through *memory buffers*, that are passed as separate arguments to the kernel.

The translation of the OpenCL input code into IR code occurs in two distinct steps. In the first step, the Insieme Compiler uses the open source Clang C frontend [7] to generate an Abstract Syntax Tree (AST) from the input code. In a second step, the AST is transformed to the Insieme parallel intermediate representation (INSPIRE [1]) on which analyses and transformations are performed.

In order to distribute a task, the Insieme Compiler analyzes the generated IR of the input program. It collects the subscripts of all buffer accesses in order to derive the buffer's access pattern. This analysis identifies whether a buffer should be replicated or distributed evenly among several devices. After collecting all the access patterns, the analysis checks if the access expression is (a) a constant, (b) the result of a convex function depending on the thread id, or (c) something else. If only accesses of type (b) occur, the buffer is split among all devices (i.e. buffer is splittable). If accesses of type (a) or (c) happen, part of it (a) or the entire buffer (c) has to be copied to every device (i.e. the buffer is non-splittable). In case of (a) and (c), the amount of data to be transferred increases linearly with the number of devices used. Obviously, copying the same data to each device is only feasible if there are only read accesses to these buffers. When write accesses of type (a) or (c) occur, our framework is not capable of distributing the kernel. A kernel can be distributed over several devices if and only if all its buffers with write accesses are splittable. However, due to the limited synchronization capabilities of OpenCL, in most kernels use access pattern (b) for their write accesses, which means they are splittable.

The access pattern analysis is based entirely on the device code. However, also the host code has to be adapted according to the results of the access pattern analysis in order to guarantee the correct distribution of data. For this reason, the Insieme Compiler connects host and device code during the translation of the Clang AST into IR, enabling the analysis of the entire program.

After the analysis, the IR is translated by the backend to a multi-device OpenCL program. The generated code is semantically equivalent to the input code, but its kernels can be distributed among a generic number of devices by the Insieme Runtime System. This implies that some buffers are replicated while others are distributed over the selected devices, depending on their access pattern inside the kernel. To select the task partitioning *a priori*, the runtime system employs a model generated by machine learning. This model is based on static program features extracted at compile time and problem size sensitive features collected at runtime. A detailed description of how we extract features and build this model can be found in Section 3.

2.3 Limitations

While the Insieme framework can be used to optimize the performance of many programs on heterogeneous systems, it also has limitations that leave room for future improvement. At the current stage, the buffer analysis and task partitioning are executed individually on each kernel. In programs with multiple kernels, this can cause unnecessary data transfers since the output of each of them must be copied back to the host in order to be redistributed with a new task partitioning.

Device-specific optimizations are not in the scope of this publication, although our machine learning guided task partitioning could potentially support it. We are aware of the opportunities that this approach can offer and we will investigate it in future work.

Other restrictions are related to scattered data accesses and atomic operations, both performed on buffers in global memory. For scattered accesses on buffers, the analysis distinguishes two cases: read-only and read-write buffers. In the first case, the entire buffer will be copied to each device including data that is not needed. In the second case the kernel will be not distributed, since the gathering and merging of writes from different devices is not yet supported. Regarding the use of atomic operations on buffers, OpenCL does not provide any means to implement such operations over multiple devices, therefore Insieme currently does not support kernels with atomic operations.

Our approach cannot deal with irregular workloads due to the difficulty to statically predict an optimized task partitioning for such cases.

3. PARTITIONING PARALLEL TASKS

Data-parallel tasks can often be split into smaller subtasks and distributed across multiple devices. However, finding an efficient partitioning is not trivial. As will be explained in Section 5 and also pointed out by other studies [18], a dynamic scheduling approach may not lead to an optimal solution, mostly due to the large difference in performance and transfer bandwidth of the individual devices. Therefore our approach, based on analysis of the program structure and input data, tries to predict the optimal partitioning for an OpenCL program *a priori*. This section describes the extraction of features and the construction of the machine learning model, used to predict a partitioning.

3.1 Predicting the Optimal Partitioning

Our overall approach requires to build a model using machine learning in order to predict a task partitioning p from a vector of features that describes the essential characteristics of a program as well as the current problem size. Each task partitioning is characterized by a tuple of n integer values for a target architecture with n devices. Each value represents the percentage of work that is executed on a particular device. The set P contains all possible partitionings over the available devices with a granularity of 10% and the predicted task partitioning p should be as near as possible to the best task partitioning in terms of performance. As done in [18] we choose a granularity of 10% since this is a good compromise between granularity and number of task partitionings.

3.2 Extracting Features

The feature extraction consists of two phases. In the first phase, all the features that can be statically inferred from the intermediate representation are extracted. This is done during the source-to-source compilation step of the Insieme Compiler. In the second phase, the Insieme Runtime System determines the values of all problem size dependent runtime features. This phase takes place when a program is executed, since the problem size is unknown at compile time.

(a) Features selected by Greedy Feature Selection for *mc1*

Rk.	static program features	MSE
2	OpenCL built-in functions	76.3
3	Number of branches / number of statements	64.4
4	Scalar float operations /number of statements	61.1
Rk.	**Runtime features**	**MSE**
1	Data transfer size for *splittable buffer* (device to host)	99.7
5	Number of global work items	60.0
6	Data transfer size for *splittable buffer* (host to device)	47.6
7	Runtime feature Nr. 3 / total number of arith. operations	47.5

(b) Features selected for *mc2*

Rk.	static program features	MSE
1	Number of branches / number of statements	91.6
2	Scalar float operations / number of statements	75.8
4	OpenCL built-in functions / number of statements	66.9
6	Scalar int operations / number of statements	56.5
7	Vector float operations / number of statements	52.2
8	Number of loops / number of statements	48.6
9	Scalar int operations	47.5
10	Vector float operations	46.9
Rk.	**Runtime features**	**MSE**
3	Data transfer size for *splittable buffer* (host to device)	69.6
5	Data transfer size for *splittable buffer* (device to host)	64.0

Table 1: Static program and runtime features used by our approach determined using the Greedy Feature Selection [30] ranked with their selection order along with the mean squared error (MSE) on the training dataset using an SVM.

The feature extractor needs to know the execution count of each feature relevant statement. If it is not possible to derive the execution count at compile time (for instance, if loop bounds depend on input data), the feature extractor assumes a loop iteration count of 100. This means that every static feature that appears in a loop is multiplied by 100. If loops are nested, this rule is applied recursively. The resulting value may not be realistic in many cases. However, our goal is not to estimate the absolute execution times but instead compare relative execution times for different devices. Therefore, it is sufficient to consider whether feature relevant statements occur outside, inside or within nested loops. The compiler is also responsible for the generation of one univariant linear polynomial for each runtime feature, which takes the problem size as input. The generated polynoms are evaluated during the second phase of the feature extraction to calculate the actual values of the runtime features.

The features we used to train our framework are subdivided in static program features (extracted from the intermediate representation during the source-to-source translation process) and runtime features (calculated by the runtime system when the program is executed). Most static program features count the occurrence of certain activities, like arithmetic operations, memory accesses, or OpenCL built-in functions (e.g. *log* or *cos*). Others describe the ratio between two characteristics (e.g. the ratio between computation and memory accesses or the ratio between number of branches and all instructions).

All runtime features depend on the problem size. Apart from the problem size itself, they describe how much data has to be transferred between the host and the devices. We differ between device-to-host and host-to-device transfers and between the size of splittable and non splittable buffers. Since splittable buffers are distributed over all devices, the amount of data to be copied is independent from the number of devices used. In contrast, the transfer size of non splittable buffers scales with the number of devices, since each device must hold a copy of the entire buffer in its memory.

We used the Greedy Feature Selection described in [30] and illustrated by Algorithm 1 to select the most important features out of a set of 24 static code features and 9 dynamic runtime features. To select the most important features, a separate model is trained for each single feature $s \in S$. The one of the model which yields the lowest error mse is added to the set of selected features F. In the next step, a separate model for each remaining feature s and the already selected

Algorithm 1 Greedy Feature Selection. The features to be used are collected in the set F.

$S \leftarrow$ non empty set of all features
$F \leftarrow \emptyset$; $mse \leftarrow \infty$; $improved \leftarrow true$
while $improved$ **do**
    $improved \leftarrow false$
    for all $s \in S$ **do**
        $model \leftarrow trainModel(\{s\} \cup F)$
        $mse_{tmp} \leftarrow evaluate(model)$
        if $mse_{tmp} < mse$ **then**
            $mse \leftarrow mse_{tmp}$
            $f \leftarrow s$ ▷ feature selected to be used
            $improved \leftarrow true$
        end if
    end for
    if $improved$ **then**
        $S \leftarrow S \setminus \{f\}$
        $F \leftarrow F \cup \{f\}$
    end if
end while

ones in set F is trained. Again, the feature which gives the lowest error is added to the set of selected features F. We repeat this step until adding another feature will not further improve the error.

We performed this greedy algorithm on both target architectures using an SVM. For the feature selection, static code features and dynamic runtime features were treated equally. Table 1 lists the features that we used to train models for our two target architectures. The column Rk. indicates the order in which the features where added. The column MSE shows the means squared error of the model using the current feature and the ones with a lower Rk. The selected features clearly show that on *mc1* the dynamic runtime features have a bigger influence on the result, while on *mc2* the static features are more important. This underlines the necessity to select the features individually for different target architectures. As shown in Section 5, the combination of the selected static program features and runtime features apparently carry enough information to characterize the behavior of our tested programs.

3.3 Generating Training Data

To train and validate our model we use the set of codes listed in Table 2. As shown in Figure 2(a), all training codes

Training codes description	Performance[1] on *mc1*				Performance[1] on *mc2*			
Application	CPU	GPU	SVM	ANN	CPU	GPU	SVM	ANN
Data Transfer to/from Device	90	37	92	**98**	84	72	88	**94**
Vector Addition	77	40	93	**94**	71	69	**87**	85
Matrix Multiplication	64	49	78	**87**	45	79	**98**	90
Black-Scholes Option Pricing	82	41	91	**93**	65	76	93	**95**
Vertex positions in Sine Wave Pattern	15	**70**	34	47	7	70	83	**95**
2D 3x3 Convolution	70	50	94	**98**	38	82	95	**96**
Molecular Dynamics Simulation	81	57	94	**99**	68	87	83	**94**
Sparse Matrix Vector Multiplication	96	59	97	**100**	82	93	**98**	96
Linear Regression	51	59	51	**60**	22	74	70	**83**
K-Means clustering	86	48	97	**98**	76	80	85	**88**
K-Nearest-Neighbor Classification	22	**68**	45	48	5	68	69	**87**
Symmetric Rank-2k Operations	**95**	24	87	78	**94**	49	51	54
Sobel Filter	75	58	91	**97**	51	**90**	85	85
Median Filter	82	54	96	**98**	56	93	90	**96**
Ray-triangle Intersection	90	62	94	**97**	74	**98**	89	94
Finite-time Lyapunow Exponent Field Calculation	77	56	**95**	94	59	82	**85**	84
Flow Map Calculation	91	35	60	**92**	75	81	81	**88**
Chunked Reduction	72	41	84	**89**	61	73	**88**	87
Perlin Noise Generator	**94**	17	81	73	83	49	84	**85**
Chunked Calculation of the Geometric Mean	68	45	81	**92**	54	81	**94**	93
Mersenne Twister Random Number Generator	79	41	**91**	89	67	72	90	**91**
Bytewise Integer Compression	77	39	90	**94**	70	69	89	**95**
Simulation of a Swinging Pendulum	20	**75**	20	20	19	70	58	**76**

[1] Achieved performance compared to the maximum performance as percentage values as described in Section 5.

Table 2: Description of test cases used for model training and performance of various task partitioning strategies.

are compiled with the Insieme source-to-source compiler and their static program features are collected in a database. After the compilation, the programs are executed with various problem sizes (9 to 18 problem sizes, depending on the program) and task partitionings, adding to the database information about runtime features and execution times. The set of explored task partitionings depends, as described in Section 3.1, on the number of available devices in the system.

In order to generate the training patterns needed for the model generation, we perform an exhaustive search on that set, finding the task partitioning with the best execution time. The size of the search space is defined by the number of experiments multiplied with the number of possible task partitionings.

For the number of training codes and the target architectures considered in our study, the search space consists of $355 \times 21 = 7455$ elements, where 355 corresponds to all problem size/program combinations and 21 is the number of task partitionings.

For each combination of test case and problem size we generate one training pattern that combines static and dynamic program features with the best performing task partitioning. Such task partitioning will then be used as target value during the training of our model.

3.4 Building the Model

Based on the training patterns we build a model with one input for each feature (listed in Table 1) and one output, which represents the task partitioning predicted by the model. In our framework the user can choose between Support Vector Machines [12] and Artificial Neural Networks [12] (ANN). As shown in Table 4, SVMs have a much lower training time, while ANNs introduce a lower overhead during the deployment phase and show a higher performance.

During the construction of the model we also evaluate the effect of Principal Component Analysis [12] (PCA) on the result. PCA can be described as the linear projection that minimizes the average projection cost, defined as the mean squared distance between the data points and their projections [29]. In our case this means that a certain number of features is reduced to a smaller number of new features in a lossy way, conserving as much of the original features' variance as possible. PCA can help to increase the estimation accuracy of models. However, calculating the PCA, which includes the calculation of the features' eigenvalues and eigenvectors, introduces a notable overhead. This means that applying PCA to all our features, which include some values only available at runtime, would substantially increase the execution time. In order to eliminate this additional overhead, we apply PCA only to the static program features, leaving the runtime features unchanged. In this way we move the overhead of calculating the principal components from runtime to the source-to-source compilation phase. The effect of PCA on our models' performance is described in Section 5.2.

4. EXPERIMENTAL METHODOLOGY

This section describes the test cases and the target architectures used in our experiments as well as the evaluation methodology.

4.1 Test Cases

To evaluate the performance of our approach we used a selection of 23 programs (see Table 2). These programs have been drawn from OpenCL vendors example codes, applications from our department and VRC at the Universität Stuttgart [28], and benchmark suites [13, 16, 10]. After translating the OpenCL input program with the Insieme Compiler, the Gnu Gcc Compiler version 4.6.3 was used to convert the resulting code to binary.

In order to examine the impact of problem sizes on task partitioning we executed each benchmark with varying prob-

	Machine	
Name	*mc1*	*mc2*
CPU manufacturer	AMD	Intel
CPUs	2x Opteron 6168	2x Xeon X5650
#CPU cores (HT)	24	12 (24)
CPU frequency	1.9 GHz	2.67 GHz
#Parallel Ops (SP)	96	48
Peak Performance	364 GFLOPS	256 GFLOPS
Memory	32 GB	24 GB
Memory Bandwidth	83 GB/s	62 GB/s
Compiler	GCC 4.6.3 w/ "-O3"	
Operating System	CentOs 5.8	
OpenCL version	AMD APP SDK 2.7	
GPU manufacturer	Ati	NVIDIA
GPUs	Radeon HD5870	GeForce GTX480
#GPU cores	20	15
Core frequency	850 MHz	1401 MHz
#Parallel Ops (SP)	1600	480
Peak Performance	2.7 TFLOPS	1.3 TFLOPS
Memory	2 GB	1.5 GB
Memory Bandwidth	153 GB/s	177 GB/s
Connection	PCIe 2.0 x16	PCIe 2.0 x16
OpenCL version	AMD APP SDK 2.7	CUDA 4.1.1

Table 3: Experimental target architectures.

lem sizes on two target architectures. For each test case we examined 9 to 18 different problem sizes (depending on the amount of memory needed by the program), resulting in 355 training patterns. Each training pattern consists of the static features of a program, its runtime features for a certain problem size as well as the best task partitioning for the given program with the current problem size. To ensure a fair comparison between different task partitionings, we measured the execution time of the kernels including the memory transfer overhead [17]. For each task partitioning, we executed a series of five experiments, recording the average execution time. The result has been validated with the *Student's t test* [4], ensuring reliable results with a confidence level of 95%.

4.2 Experimental Setup

The experiments were performed on two different heterogeneous target architectures composed of three OpenCL devices: two GPUs and two multi-core CPUs in a dual-socket infrastructure. While both GPUs represent a separate device, the two CPUs are reported as a single OpenCL device. The first platform, *mc1*, consists of two AMD Opteron CPUs and two Ati Radeon GPUs, while the second, *mc2*, holds two Intel Xeon CPUs and two NVIDIA GeForce GPUs. Table 3 gives a more detailed listing of the two systems' characteristics.

As already mentioned in Section 3.1 we use a set of task partitionings. For the target architectures used in this study, consisting of one CPU device and two GPU devices, we characterize each task partitioning with a tuple of three numbers representing the percentage of the workload executed on a specific device. The first number represents the portion to be executed on the CPU while the second and third number represent the percentage for the first and second GPU, respectively. Task partitioning $(100, 0, 0)$, for example, means that the entire workload is assigned to the CPU, while $(0, 50, 50)$ means that the work is distributed evenly among the two GPUs while nothing is assigned to the CPU. The entire set of task partitionings P is constructed as follows:

$$X = \{0, 10, 20, ..., 100\}$$
$$P = \bigcup_{x \in X} \{(x, 100 - x, 0), (x, \tfrac{100-x}{2}, \tfrac{100-x}{2})\}$$

Where X is the set of different percentage values of the workload considered to be executed by the CPU. The remaining workload is then executed by the first GPU or it is distributed evenly among the two GPUs. The resulting set P consists of 21 different task partitionings.

From this set P our runtime system tries to select the optimal task partitioning using the prediction model as described in Section 3. To evaluate the performance of our approach we compare the execution times of a program with two different task partitionings. The first task partitioning is proposed by the Insieme Runtime System and the second one is found by an exhaustive search over all task partitionings over the set P.

In order to evaluate the quality of our models we do a leave-one-out cross validation [14] on all our training programs of the set C listed in Table 2. To evaluate the model's performance for a particular program $c \in C$, we train the model with all programs except c. Obviously, this means not leaving out only one training pattern, but all training patterns related to program c (all different problem sizes).

5. EXPERIMENTAL RESULT

In this Section we report the performance result of our approach. As performance metric we use the achieved percentage of the maximum performance, which can be reached by applying the best task partitioning. We calculate it as follows

$$s = t_{best}/t_{actual} * 100$$

where s is the achieved performance in percentage, t_{best} is the execution time of the best task partitioning (identified with an exhaustive search over all task partitionings used) and t_{actual} is the actual execution time of the selected task partitioning. To combine the performance for several experiments in one value (e.g. the performance for a specific test case using different problem sizes), we simply calculate the average of the performance across these experiments.

5.1 Performance Results

Depending on the target architecture, the problem size and the program, it can be important to select a certain task partitioning, whereas in other cases, several different task partitionings may deliver similar good performance. For instance, as can be seen in Figures 3(a) and 3(b), when executing *matrix multiplication* with large problem sizes it is very important to distribute the workload over both GPUs. Furthermore, for hybrid solutions it is not important if one or two GPUs are used, since the CPU is always the limiting factor. For smaller problem sizes, in particular for *mc2*, several task partitionings yield good performance. In contrast to that, on *mc1* small matrices should be multiplied on the CPU alone. The penalty for selecting a non-optimal task partitioning for intermediate problem sizes on *mc1* is less severe than on *mc2*.

The situation is different when running our *integer compression* implementation. Figure 3(c) shows that on *mc1*

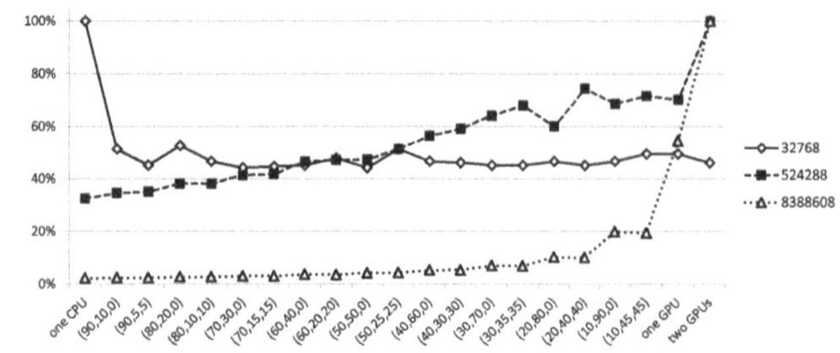

(a) Matrix Multiplication on *mc1*

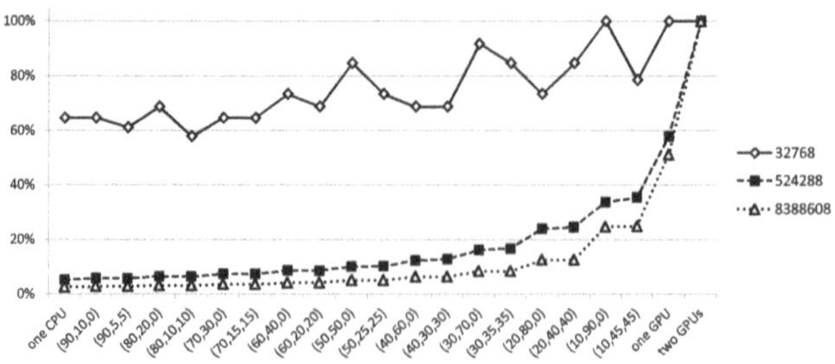

(b) Matrix Multiplication on *mc2*

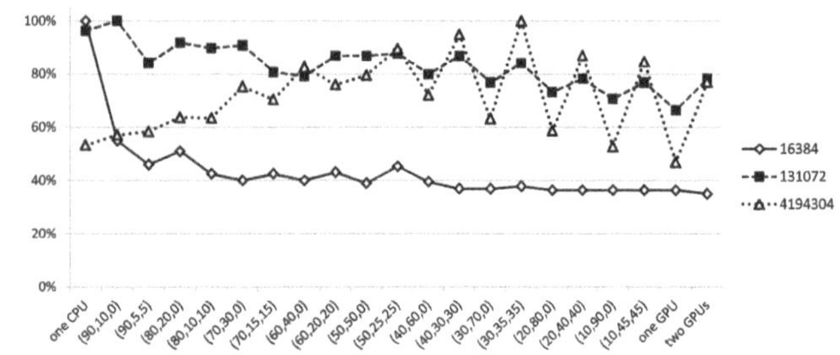

(c) Bytewise Integer Compression on *mc1*

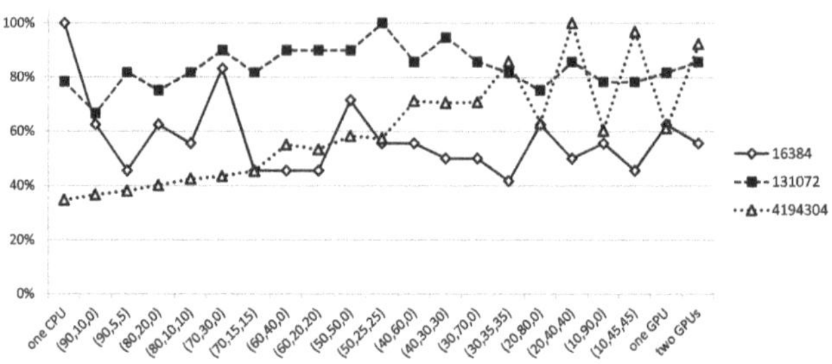

(d) Bytewise Integer Compression on *mc2*

Figure 3: Performance behavior of different programs on two target architectures with different problem sizes (e.g. 32768 work items). On the x-axis the various task partitionings are listed while the y-axis shows the achieved performance in %, relative to the best task partitioning (see Section 5).

with a problem size of 16384 work items, the CPU substantially outperforms all other task partitionings, while on *mc2* the difference is much smaller and all task partitionings deliver 40% or more of the maximum performance, as revealed in Figure 3(d). For the larger problem sizes, on both target architectures a hybrid task partitioning delivers the best performance. However, the best performing task partitioning is different for each problem size and target architecture. In this test case, using a heterogeneous distribution can reduce the execution time by up to 23% over any homogeneous task partitioning (including the dual GPU task partitioning).

As shown in Figure 1, there are cases in which a single GPU performs better than two GPUs. This behavior can be observed for some data transfer dominated scenarios and is mainly related to the shared connection of the GPUs to the CPU's main memory.

From the 355 training patterns considered for this study, more than 25% deliver best performance when using a hybrid task partitioning.

5.2 Comparison of Different Techniques

For the Insieme Runtime System we tested a variety of models, generated either with a Support Vector Machine [12] (SVM) or an Artificial Neural Network [12] (ANN). For both techniques we used the implementation provided by the Shark library [20]. In this section, we compare the performance of our model-guided runtime system with the performance of the two default strategies which use either one CPU or one GPU. These are the only available options when using the unchanged input programs, without the generation of multi-device code by the Insieme Compiler.

Furthermore, without using the Insieme framework, the challenging task of choosing the most appropriate device is left to the user.

Task Partitioning Approach	Execution Time				Performance[1]		
	Training (sec)		Deployment (ms)				
	mc1	*mc2*	*mc1*	*mc2*	*mc1*	*mc2*	**Avg.**
CPU only	-	-	-	-	73	58	**65.5**
GPU only	-	-	-	-	48	77	**62.5**
Random	-	-	0.12	0.09	44	55	**59.5**
SVM[2]	8	8	0.31	0.23	80	78	**79.0**
ANN[2]	248	421	0.07	0.07	84	84	**84.0**
SVM[3]	22	19	0.28	0.18	82	85	**83.5**
ANN[3]	317	201	0.07	0.06	86	89	**87.5**

[1] Percentage of maximum performance as described in Section 5.
[2] Using all static features listed in Table 1
[3] Using static features generated form the static features listed in Table 1 with PCA

Table 4: Properties and performance of different machine learning algorithms.

We also show the advantage of our approach over the expected performance of a random scheduler, calculated by taking the average execution time over all task partitionings in our set P (described in Section 4.2).

Table 4 shows the average performance for a cross validation over all test cases in Table 2 using different scheduling approaches. On *mc1* the CPU-only strategy outperforms the GPU-only strategy while on *mc2* we observe the opposite behavior. This underlines the complexity of choosing the most appropriate device in a heterogeneous environment. On average, over the two target architectures, both default strategies fail to reach 70% of the maximum performance. In most cases there are only few well performing task partitionings while the others show rather poor performance. Therefore, the random scheduler is not a good solution and even lags behind the two default strategies.

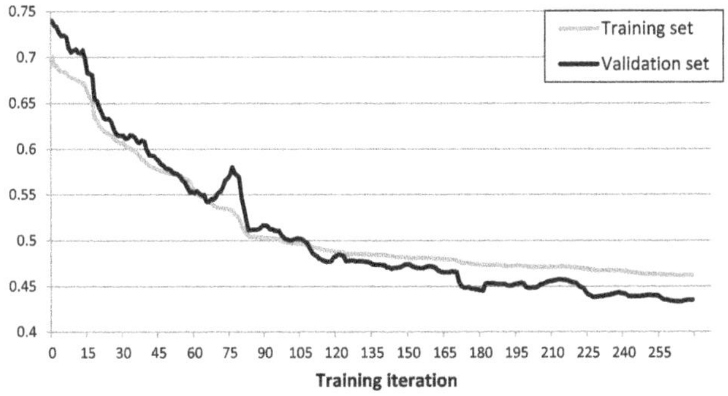

(a) *mc1*

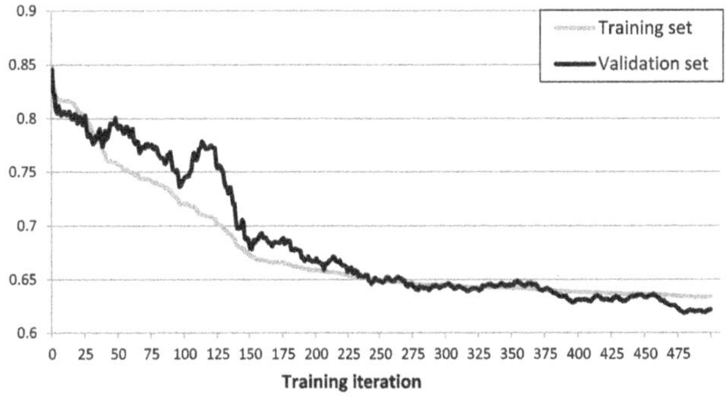

(b) *mc2*

Figure 4: Error curves showing the means squared error after each training iteration of our best performing ANNs on our two experimental target architectures.

Our SVM approach uses the MulticlassSVM implementation of [20]. As kernel function we used Radial Basis Function [12] (RBF). This kernel function is the most widely used for classification with SVMs. The parameter γ of the RBF was set to 2.5, the regularization parameter c was set to 15 for both positive and negative examples. We observed, that the performance does not vary more than 4 - 5% when changing these values, which demonstrates the robustness of SVMs with regard to these parameters.

The ANNs used for our study are three-layer feed-forward perceptron networks with a sigmoid activation function and fife neurons in the hidden layer [12]. All three layers are fully connected with their neighboring layers. For our ANN we use the FFNet implementation of [20]. All weights inside an ANN are initialized randomly within the same range, equal to $+/-0.125$.

As training algorithm we used the conjugate gradient method provided by Shark, which automatically adapts the training rate. To determine the number of training iterations for the neural network, we use the *early stopping* method which terminates the training automatically after a certain level of convergence is reached. The training data is split into a training set, used to train the model, and a validation set which is not used for training. The level of convergence is measured by observing how the error on the validation set evolves over consecutive training iterations [12]. Depending on what test case is removed from the training set to perform the cross validation, the training is stopped after 36 to 749 iterations. The training times shown in Table 4 refer to the training for all test cases without cross validation. Figure 4 shows how the mean squared error evolves on the training set and the validation set during the training (without cross validation) on both of our target architectures using our best performing ANN. In both cases the error curves on the training set are very smooth and converge to a minimum. As usual, the error curves on the validation set are more uneven, but they also converge during the training. Surprisingly, in both cases the mean squared error on the validation set was lower than the one on the training set when the training was stopped.

As explained in Section 3.4, we apply PCA to our static program features. On both target architectures we use the first n principal components of the static code features listed in Table 1 in order cover 100% of the static program features' total variance (calculated in single precision floating point). For the static features used on *mc1*, this resulted in using only the first principal component. For the ones used on *mc2*, two principal components were needed to cover all their variance. Our results in Table 4 clearly show that PCA improves the accuracy of our models and shortens the deployment times. PCA is only applied to static code features, so it is not part of the execution time of the programs. It is noticeable that the models used on *mc2* benefit more from the PCA than the models used on *mc1*. This is most likely related to the higher number of static code features used on *mc2*, which can be reduced to one quarter of the original number using PCA without loosing any information.

Our task partitioning approach which assigns one portion of the task to each device, has some significant advantages over a dynamic scheduler. A dynamic scheduler has to split a task into a large amount of small chunks. At the beginning of the execution, each device receives one chunk. When a device has finished its assigned work, it will receive another chunk until the entire task has been processed. The chunk size is a very important factor for such an approach. Smaller chunks are better for load balancing, but they reduce the parallelism inside one chunk and suffer from higher data transfer and kernel invocation overhead. Larger chunks reduce the load balancing, but also the number of kernel invocations and data transfers, resulting in a lower overall overhead. On the one hand, a scheduler for OpenCL task partitioning should use large chunks, because the kernel invocation and data transfer overhead are relatively high, compared to the execution time. For example, executing two *vector addition* chunks with a size of 65536 on a GPU in *mc1* takes 71% longer than running one chunk of twice the size. On the other hand, a scheduler for OpenCL task partitioning requires small chunks, due to the high differences in performance of the heterogeneous devices. As it can be seen in Figure 3(a), with a problem size of 838868 running only 10% of the task on the CPU reduces the performance to 20% of the performance that can be reached by distributing the task evenly over both GPUs. Based on this observation, we believe that dynamic schedulers cannot efficiently solve the task partitioning problem as described in this paper.

5.3 Analysis of the Results

In Table 2 we compare the performance of the task partitionings predicted by the Insieme Runtime System based on an SVM and ANN using PCA (listed in Table 4), with the performance delivered by the CPU/GPU only strategy for each code and each target architecture individually. For almost all test cases, the CPU-only strategy delivers a higher performance on *mc1* than on *mc2*, while the GPU-only strategy usually performs better on *mc2*. This is related to the weaker performance of the GPU (Ati Radeon HD5870) in *mc1*. Its VLIW architecture with very wide instruction width and high branch miss penalty would require specific fine-tuning of each code to perform well [33]. However, none of our test cases was tuned for a specific device.

On average considering both target architectures, our machine learning guided approaches deliver a significant better performance than the two default strategies for most test cases. Our models are capable of representing the target architecture's characteristics in order to find performance efficient task partitionings. Our approaches also determine which device is to be favored for every specific target architecture. This is underlined by the fact that our machine learning guided approaches show their worst performance for atypical test cases, i.e. test cases which perform better on the GPU than on the CPU on *mc1* (e.g. Simulation of a Swinging Pendulum) or vice versa on *mc2* (e.g. Symmetric Rank-2k Operations on *mc2*).

In most cases the ANN achieves better performance than the SVM. The ANN is also faster to predict the task partitioning of a program, as shown in Table 4. For both of our approaches the time to predict the task partitioning is negligible (in the range of 0.06 to 0.31 ms). The downside of ANN is the corresponding relatively long training time as well as the associated sensitivity regarding the tuning parameters like network structure or weight initialization range. SVMs do not have this many tuning parameters and the quality of the result does not depend that much on the parameters' value.

6. RELATED WORK

In recent years, heterogeneous systems have received great attention from the research community. Several projects [32, 6, 9, 31, 24, 23] mainly focused on OpenMP, CUDA, and OpenCL extensions, investigated how to facilitate the programming of clusters with heterogeneous nodes. Our work, while following the same idea, targets an automatic management of multiple devices in a single node. A similar study was done by Chen et al. [11]. The authors introduce an automatic parallelization process to use multiple GPUs. This work targets mainly the analysis of access patterns for data decomposition, showing that many applications can be parallelized automatically. Our approach, based on a similar analysis, not only derives the data partition schemes, but also provides a solution for optimal task partitioning on heterogeneous devices.

Extensive work has been done to address mapping or scheduling of tasks to heterogeneous systems. Several frameworks [32, 8, 25] have been created to support the developer in the use of all available computing resources of a heterogeneous system. Although these studies propose several possible solutions to the problem, they are mostly based on performance estimations provided by the user. On the contrary, our approach is automatic and does not require any additional user-supplied information. Furthermore, these approaches focus on optimizing the scheduling of multiple tasks, assuming that several parallel tasks are available. Our system is designed to optimize the execution of a single task and can therefore optimize also programs with a single task.

Other works have investigated the problem of automatic task partitioning. Luk et al. [26] introduced an adaptive mapping approach based on a regression model. Their system considers every first run of a program as a training run that can be then used to determine the computation-to-processor mapping for the same program with a new input problem. This approach expects that a program is trained once and then used many times afterward. In contrast to our work, they only show results of one target architecture equipped with only one CPU and one GPU.

A similar approach was adopted by Kai et al. [21]. They proposed a holistic energy management framework for heterogeneous architectures which dynamically splits and distributes the workload over GPU and CPU based on the observed performance. Their algorithm dynamically adjusts the task partitioning based on the runtime difference between devices. Our approach, on the other hand does not require any profiling or training runs of the program to optimize it. We can derive an optimized task partitioning during the first run of a new program by using a previously, offline trained model.

Hong et al. [19] proposed MapCG, a framework that supports source code level portability between CPU and GPU. By incorporating a MapReduce programming model, a program can be compiled and executed on either CPUs or GPUs without modification. However, they observed that CPU/GPU combinations did not yield significant performance improvement for the 8 test cases they examined. In contrast to this work, as already described in Section 5.1, on our target architectures, we observed the important role of the hybrid task partitioning to achieve the best performance for our test cases.

Grewe et al. [18] developed a purely static task partitioning approach based on predictive modeling and program features. Starting from a multi-device OpenCL code, the authors predict the partitioning of a task with a machine learning model based on static features analysis for fixed problem sizes. Our work uses a similar machine learning approach, but combines static program features detected at compile time with dynamic features collected at runtime that allow the adaptation of the task partitioning to different problem sizes. We test our approach for different target architectures emphasizing the importance of the problem size and the hardware configuration for the tuning of the task partitioning. Furthermore, our system is not limited to a CPU-GPU configuration but can handle an arbitrary number of heterogeneous devices in a single node.

7. CONCLUSION

In this paper we proposed a novel approach for the automatic distribution of OpenCL programs on heterogeneous systems. It consists of a source-to-source compiler, which translates a single-device OpenCL program into a multi-device OpenCL program and a runtime system which distributes the workload over all heterogeneous resources using a machine learning based, offline generated prediction model.

Our measurements demonstrate that the optimal task partitioning depends on the program, the target architecture, and the problem size. To accommodate this observation, we use two classes of features: static program features, whose values can be extracted from the source code at compile time, and problem size dependent runtime features, whose values are collected during program execution.

We compared different machine learning techniques, showing that ANNs can reach a higher overall performance, while SVMs can be trained much faster and are less sensitive with respect to their intrinsic parameters. We observed, that the importance of features varies between different platforms. We also demonstrated that PCA applied to the static program features increases the models' accuracy while reducing its runtime overhead.

To demonstrate the portability of our system, all tests were performed on two different target architectures. On average, over those target architectures, the Insieme framework achieves up to 87.5% of the optimal performance across 23 programs. Our approach outperforms the default strategies of using only the CPU or only the GPU, which achieve 65.5% and 62.5% of the optimal performance, respectively. In addition, we outperform a random heterogeneous scheduler which yields to only 49.5% of the optimal performance.

Future work will extend our approach with the capabilities to accurately analyze and efficiently distribute device-optimized multi-kernel OpenCL programs on heterogeneous systems. Furthermore our findings can be extended beyond the single computing node by taking advantage of the libWater distributed runtime system [15] which allows OpenCL programs to transparently address devices within a distributed cluster system like if they were local.

8. ACKNOWLEDGMENT

This project was funded by the FWF Austrian Science Fund as part of the FWF Doctoral School CIM Computational Interdisciplinary Modelling under contract W01227 and by the Austrian Research Promotion Agency under contract nr. 834307 (AutoCore).

9. REFERENCES

[1] Insieme Compiler Runtime Framework. `http://insieme-compiler.org/`.

[2] HMPP, Hybrid Multicore Parallel Programming. `http://www.openhmpp.org`, 2012.

[3] OpenACC Application Program Interface. `http://openacc.org/`, 2012.

[4] R-manual:Student's t-Test. `http://stat.ethz.ch/R-manual/R-patched/library/stats/html/t.test.html`, 2012.

[5] Top 500 Supercomputer site. `http://www.top500.org/`, 2012.

[6] R. Aoki, S. Oikawa, T. Nakamura, and S. Miki. Hybrid opencl: Enhancing opencl for distributed processing. In *ISPA*, pages 149–154, 2011.

[7] Apple Inc. Clang/LLVM. `http://clang.llvm.org/`, 2012.

[8] C. Augonnet, S. Thibault, R. Namyst, and P.-A. Wacrenier. Starpu: A unified platform for task scheduling on heterogeneous multicore architectures. In *Euro-Par*, pages 863–874, 2009.

[9] A. Barak and A. Shilo. The Virtual OpenCL (VCL) Cluster Platform. In *Proc. Intel European Research & Innovation Conference*, page 196, 2011.

[10] S. Che, M. Boyer, J. Meng, D. Tarjan, J. W. Sheaffer, S.-H. Lee, and K. Skadron. Rodinia: A benchmark suite for heterogeneous computing. In *IISWC*, pages 44–54, 2009.

[11] D. Chen, W. Chen, and W. Zheng. Cuda-zero: a framework for porting shared memory gpu applications to multi-gpus. *SCIENCE CHINA Information Sciences*, 55(3):663–676, 2012.

[12] Christopher M. Bishop. *Pattern Recognition and Machine Learning*. Springer-Verlag New York, Inc., Secaucus, NJ, USA, 2006.

[13] A. Danalis, G. Marin, C. McCurdy, J. S. Meredith, P. C. Roth, K. Spafford, V. Tipparaju, and J. S. Vetter. The scalable heterogeneous computing (shoc) benchmark suite. In *GPGPU*, pages 63–74, 2010.

[14] Ethem, Alpaydin. *Introduction to Machine Learning*. The MIT Press, Cambridge, MA, USA, 2004.

[15] I. Grasso, S. Pellegrini, B. Cosenza, and T. Fahringer. libwater: Heterogeneous distributed computing made easy. In *ICS*, 2013.

[16] S. Grauer-Gray, L. Xu, R. Searles, S. Ayalasomayajula, , and J. Cavazos. Auto-tuning a high-level language targeted to gpu codes. In *InPar*, 2012.

[17] C. Gregg and K. M. Hazelwood. Where is the data? why you cannot debate cpu vs. gpu performance without the answer. In *ISPASS*, pages 134–144, 2011.

[18] D. Grewe and M. F. O'Boyle. A static task partitioning approach for heterogeneous systems using opencl. In *CC*, 2011.

[19] C. Hong, D. Chen, W. Chen, W. Zheng, and H. Lin. Mapcg: writing parallel program portable between cpu and gpu. In *PACT*, pages 217–226, 2010.

[20] Institut für Neuroinformatik, Ruhr-University Bochum. Shark Machine Learning Library. `http://shark-project.sourceforge.net/`, 2012.

[21] M. Kai, L. Xue, C. Wei, Z. Chi, and W. Xiaorui. Greengpu: A holistic approach to energy efficiency in gpu-cpu heterogeneous architectures. In *ICPP*, 2012.

[22] Khronos OpenCL Working Group. The OpenCL 1.2 specification. `http://www.khronos.org/opencl`, 2012.

[23] J. Kim, S. Seo, J. Lee, J. Nah, G. Jo, and J. Lee. Opencl as a unified programming model for heterogeneous cpu/gpu clusters. In *PPoPP*, pages 299–300, 2012.

[24] J. Kim, S. Seo, J. Lee, J. Nah, G. Jo, and J. Lee. Snucl: an opencl framework for heterogeneous cpu/gpu clusters. In *ICS*, pages 341–352, 2012.

[25] M. D. Linderman, J. D. Collins, H. Wang, and T. H. Y. Meng. Merge: a programming model for heterogeneous multi-core systems. In *ASPLOS*, pages 287–296, 2008.

[26] C.-K. Luk, S. Hong, and H. Kim. Qilin: exploiting parallelism on heterogeneous multiprocessors with adaptive mapping. In *MICRO*, pages 45–55, 2009.

[27] NVIDIA Corporation. CUDA Programming Model. `https://developer.nvidia.com/cuda-toolkit`, 2012.

[28] A. Panagiotidis, D. Kauker, F. Sadlo, and T. Ertl. Distributed computation and large-scale visualization in heterogeneous compute environments. In *Proceedings of the 11th International Symposium on Parallel and Distributed Computing*, 2012.

[29] K. Pearson. On lines and planes of closest fit to a system of points in space. In *Philosophical Magazine, Series 6, vol. 2, no. 11*, pages 557–572, 1901.

[30] M. Stephenson and S. Amarasinghe. Predicting unroll factors using supervised classification. In *Proceedings of the international symposium on Code generation and optimization*, CGO '05, pages 123–134, Washington, DC, USA, 2005. IEEE Computer Society.

[31] M. Strengert, C. Muller, C. Dachsbacher, and T. Ertl. Cudasa: Compute unified device and systems architecture. In *EGPGV*, pages 49–56, 2008.

[32] E. Sun, D. Schaa, R. Bagley, N. Rubin, and D. Kaeli. Enabling task-level scheduling on heterogeneous platforms. In *Proceedings of the 5th Annual Workshop on General Purpose Processing with Graphics Processing Units*, pages 84–93, 2012.

[33] P. Thoman, K. Kofler, H. Studt, J. Thomson, and T. Fahringer. Automatic opencl device characterization: guiding optimized kernel design. In *Euro-Par*, pages 438–452, 2011.

libWater: Heterogeneous Distributed Computing Made Easy

Ivan Grasso, Simone Pellegrini, Biagio Cosenza, and Thomas Fahringer
Institute of Computer Science, University of Innsbruck, Austria
{grasso, spellegrini, cosenza, tf}@dps.uibk.ac.at

ABSTRACT

Clusters of heterogeneous nodes composed of multi-core CPUs and GPUs are increasingly being used for High Performance Computing (HPC) due to the benefits in peak performance and energy efficiency. In order to fully harvest the computational capabilities of such architectures, application developers often employ a combination of different parallel programming paradigms (e.g. OpenCL, CUDA, MPI and OpenMP), also known in literature as hybrid programming, which makes application development very challenging. Furthermore, these languages offer limited support to orchestrate data and computations for heterogeneous systems.

In this paper, we present libWater, a uniform approach for programming distributed heterogeneous computing systems. It consists of a simple interface, compliant with the OpenCL programming model, and a runtime system which extends the capabilities of OpenCL beyond single platforms and single compute nodes. libWater enhances the OpenCL event system by enabling inter-context and inter-node device synchronization. Furthermore, libWater's runtime system uses dependency information enforced by event synchronization to dynamically build a DAG of enqueued commands which enables a class of advanced runtime optimizations. The detection and optimization of collective communication patterns is an example which, as shown by experimental results, improves the efficiency of the libWater runtime system for several application codes.

Categories and Subject Descriptors

C.1.3 [**Other Architecture Styles**]: Heterogeneous (hybrid) systems; D.3.2 [**Language Classifications**]: Concurrent, distributed, and parallel languages; D.3.4 [**Processors**]: Runtime Environments

Keywords

OpenCL, MPI, distributed computing, heterogeneous computing, programming model, runtime system

ICS'13, June 10–14, 2013, Eugene, Oregon, USA.

1. INTRODUCTION

Recently, the major chip manufacturers have faced the problem of three walls [7]: the power wall, the instruction level parallelism wall, and the memory wall. This turned the development of hardware design towards multi- and many-core CPUs, next to special purpose hardware and accelerators such as GPUs. As a result, engineers and academics are pervasively embracing the use of heterogeneous architectures to attain the highest performance possible from a single compute node.

However, heterogeneous computing also poses the new challenge of how to handle the diversity of execution environments and programming models. The Open Computing Language [19] introduces an open standard for general-purpose parallel programming of heterogeneous systems. An OpenCL program may target any OpenCL-compliant device and today many vendors such as Adapteva, Altera, AMD, IBM, Intel and NVidia provide an implementation of the OpenCL standard. An OpenCL program comprises a *host* program and a set of *kernels* intended to run on a compute device. It also includes a language for kernel programming, and an API for transferring data between host and device memory and for executing kernels.

Single node hardware design is shifting to a heterogeneous nature. At the same time many of today's largest HPC systems are clusters that combine heterogeneous compute device architectures [4]. Although OpenCL has been designed to work with multiple devices, it only considers local devices available on a single machine. However, the host-device semantics can be potentially applied to remote, distributed devices accessible on different compute nodes.

Porting single-node multi-device applications to clusters that combine heterogeneous compute device architectures is not straightforward and, in addition, it requires the use of a communication layer for the data exchange between nodes (e.g. MPI [25]). Writing programs for such platforms is error prone and tedious. Therefore new abstractions, programming models and tools are required to deal with this problem.

This paper introduces *libWater*, a library-based extension of the OpenCL programming paradigm that simplifies the development of applications for distributed heterogeneous architectures. *libWater* aims to improve both productivity and implementation efficiency when parallelizing an application targeting a heterogeneous platform by achieving two design goals: (*i*) transparent abstraction of the underlying distributed architecture, such that devices belonging to a remote node are accessible like a local device; (*ii*) access to performance-related details since it supports the OpenCL kernel logic.

The main contributions of this paper are:

- The presentation of the *libWater* programming model, which extends the OpenCL standard by replacing the host code with a simplified interface. The definition of a novel device query language (DQL) for OpenCL device management and discovery.

- A lightweight distributed runtime environment which dispatches the work between remote devices, based on asynchronous execution of both communications and OpenCL commands. *libWater* runtime also collects and arranges dependencies between commands in the form of a powerful representation called *command DAG*.

- A demonstration of how the *command DAG* can be effectively exploited to improve the scalability. For this purpose we introduce a collective communication pattern recognition analysis and optimization that matches multiple single point-to-point data transfers and dynamically replaces them with a more efficient collective operation (e.g. *scatter*, *gather* and *broadcast*) supported by MPI.

- A study of the scalability of *libWater* on a real production cluster using up to 64 homogeneous compute nodes. Results show that an efficiency of around 64% is achieved, on average, for 6 application codes. Finally we demonstrate the suitability of *libWater* for a heterogeneous GPU cluster for two codes.

The rest of the paper is organized as follows. Section 2 and 3 provide an introduction to OpenCL and libWater programming model. Section 4 describes the distributed runtime system and the underlying command DAG representation. The runtime optimizations are treated in Section 5 and the experimental evaluation is presented in Section 6. Section 7 and 8 discuss related work and conclusions.

2. THE OPENCL PROGRAMMING MODEL

OpenCL is an open industry standard for programming heterogeneous systems. The language is designed to support devices with different capabilities such as CPUs, GPUs and accelerators. The platform model comprises a *host* connected to one or more *compute devices*. Each device logically consists of one or more compute units (CUs) which are further divided into processing elements (PEs). Within a program, the computation is expressed through the use of special functions called *kernels* that are, for portability reason, compiled at runtime by an OpenCL driver. Interaction with the devices is possible by means of *command-queues* which are defined within a particular OpenCL *context*. Once enqueued, commands – such as the execution of a kernel or the movement of data between host and device memory – are managed by the OpenCL driver which schedules them on the actual physical device.

Commands can be enqueued in a blocking or non-blocking way. A non-blocking call places a command on a command-queue and returns immediately to the host, while a blocking-mode call does not return to the host until the command has been executed on the device. For synchronization purpose, within a context, *event* objects are generated when kernel and memory commands are submitted to a queue. These objects are used to coordinate execution between commands and enable decoupling between host and devices control flows.

Despite being a well designed language that allows the access to the compute power of heterogeneous devices from a single, multi-platform source code base, OpenCL has some drawbacks and limitations. One of the major drawbacks is that, because being created as a low-level API, a significant amount of boilerplate code is required even for the execution of simple programs. Developers have to be familiar with numerous concepts (i.e. *platform*, *device*, *context*, *queue*, *buffer* and *kernel*) which make the language less attractive to novice programmers. Another important limitation is that, although it was designed to address heterogeneous systems, in case of devices from different vendors, objects belonging to the context of one vendor are not valid for other vendors. This limitation clearly becomes a problem when synchronization of command queues across different contexts is needed.

3. THE LIBWATER PROGRAMMING INTERFACE

libWater is a C/C++ library-based extension of the OpenCL programming paradigm that simplifies the development of distributed heterogeneous applications. It inherits the main principles from the OpenCL programming model trying to overcome its limitations. While maintaining the notion of host and device code, *libWater* exposes a very simple programming interface based on four key concepts: *device*, *buffer*, *kernel* and *event*. A *device* represents a compute device, but differently from the original paradigm this single object is an abstraction of the OpenCL platform, device, queue and context concepts. Such simplification reduces the number of source code lines necessary for the initialization of the devices, and thus avoids the boilerplate configuration code that is usually present in every OpenCL program. Furthermore, the library is not restricted to a single node but, taking internally advantage of the message passing model, it provides access to devices on remote nodes as if they were locally available.

Since *libWater* can grant access to a large number of distinct devices, the selection of a particular one can be cumbersome. In order to simplify this important aspect, *libWater* introduces a novel domain specific language for querying devices. A *device query language* (DQL) query statement follows an SQL-like structure, that is composed of 4 basic clauses with the following syntax:

```
SELECT          [ALL | TOP k | POS i]
    FROM NODE   [n [, ...]]
    WHERE       [restrictions attribute values]
    ORDER BY    [attribute [, ...]]
```

The `SELECT` clause (the only one which is mandatory) respectively allows the selection of all the devices, the first top *k*, or a particular device from the device list generated under the restrictions on the following clauses. With `FROM NODE` a single node or a list of nodes can be specified narrowing the range of selectable devices to those particular nodes. The clauses `WHERE` and `ORDER BY` allow the control of the device restrictions on attribute values and the order in which the devices will be returned. The possible attribute values are currently those exposed by the OpenCL `clGetDeviceInfo` function. A DQL use case is shown and discussed in Section 4.2. DQL

Device Management (wtr_)	
void **init_devices**('DQL', ...)	device **get_device**('DQL', ...)
int **get_num_devices**()	void **release_devices**()
void **print_device_infos**(device)	
Buffer Management (wtr_)	
buffer **create_buffer**(device, mem_flag, size, evt)	
void **write_buffer**(buffer, size, source_ptr, wait_evt, evt)	
void **read_buffer**(buffer, size, dest_ptr, wait_evt, evt)	
void **release_buffer**(buffer, wait_evt, evt)	
Kernel Management (wtr_)	
kernel **create_kernel**(device, name, kernel_name, build_options, flag, evt)	
void **run_kernel**(kernel, work_dim, global_work_size, local_work_size, wait_evt, evt, num_args, ...)	
void **release_kernel**(kernel, wait_evt, evt)	
Event Management (wtr_)	
event **create_event**()	void **release_event**(evt)
event **merge_events**(num, ...)	void **wait_for_events**(num, ...)
void **init_event_array**(num, evt)	
void **release_event_array**(num, evt)	

Table 1: The complete *libWater* API.

queries can be used for both device initialization and device selection. The latter must be a subset of the former and since *libWater*'s device concept represents a single device only, the function `wtr_get_device` only accepts queries that make use of the `POS` clause.

Table 1 presents the *complete* API of the *libWater* library. The prefix `wtr_` and the C language pointer syntax has been removed from the table for readability reasons. Initialization and selection of devices is done, respectively, by using the `wtr_init_devices` and the `wtr_get_device` routines. Once a *device* is created, it is possible to allocate data and execute computation on it. In *libWater*, this is done through the use of the *buffer* and the *kernel* concepts. These two objects are similar to their respective OpenCL versions, with the main difference that, during their creation, they are bound to a specific device. For this reason no device must be specified for buffer and kernel related functions. The principal kernel functions are `wtr_create_kernel` and `wtr_run_kernel`. The former receives as parameter a `flag` that specifies whether the `name` input argument contains the kernel code or it is the name of a file containing the OpenCL kernel. The latter is used for executing a kernel in the previously bound device. The parameters `work_dim`, `global_work_size` and `local_work_size` are the same specified in the OpenCL `clEnqueueNDRangeKernel`. The `num_args` parameter states the number of input arguments accepted by the kernel. This parameter is followed by a list of a variable number of pairs. Each pair consists of a size (in bytes) and a pointer to the corresponding kernel argument. The first value of the pair distinguishes between buffers – when is equal to 0 – or a valid address in the host memory. The fourth concept in *libWater* is the *event* object. Most of *kernel* and *buffer* functions have one or two parameters called `wait_evt` and `evt`. The latter is an output argument which is used by the invoked command to generate an event object. If not specified, *libWater* assumes blocking semantics for the routine. The former specifies the event object on which the execution of the command depends. If not present, the command has no dependencies and thus it can be immediately executed. Since there can be a dependency between several commands, the `wtr_merge_events` function can be used to merge multiple event objects into one.

The last major difference between *libWater* and the OpenCL model is the fact that initialization and release of buffers and kernels can be invoked using a non-blocking semantics. The main reason for this is to increase the amount of operations that the runtime system can overlap. In the next section we explain how dependency information enforced by events are then exploited by *libWater*'s runtime system.

4. THE LIBWATER DISTRIBUTED RUNTIME SYSTEM

While the main focus of the programming interface of *libWater* is on simplicity and productivity, the underlying runtime system aims at low resource utilization and high scalability. Calls to *libWater* routines are forwarded to a distributed runtime system which is responsible for dispatching the OpenCL commands to the addressed devices and for transparently and efficiently moving data across the cluster nodes. The *libWater* distributed runtime is written in C++ and internally uses several paradigms, such as pthreads, OpenMP and MPI for parallelization.

4.1 Runtime System Architecture

Figure 1 shows the organization of the *libWater* distributed runtime system. The *host code*, which directly interacts with *libWater*'s routines, runs on the so called *root node*, which by default is the cluster node with rank 0. This thread will be referred to as the *host thread.* In the background, a second thread, i.e. the *scheduler thread*, is allocated to execute an instance of the `WTRScheduler`. On the remaining cluster nodes, a single *scheduler thread* is spawned independently of the number of available devices (only one MPI process is allocated per node). This thread executes an instance of the `WTRScheduler` which represents the backbone of *libWater*'s distributed runtime system.

Each `WTRScheduler` continuously dequeues `wtr_commands` from the local command queue. `wtr_commands` in the system are generated in two ways, either by (*i*) *libWater*'s routines (step 1), or (*ii*) by delegation from the root scheduler (step 3). Calls to the *libWater*'s interface are converted into command descriptors (i.e. command design pattern) and immediately enqueued into the root node local command queue (step 1) of Figure 1. Since all `wtr_commands` are generated by the root node itself, we refer to its queue as the runtime *global* command queue.

`wtr_commands` are either wrappers for OpenCL commands or data transfer jobs (i.e. `send_job` or `recv_job`) which are generated by the library routines whenever the device addressed by a read or write buffer operation is located in a remote (i.e. *rank* $\neq$ 0) compute node. The descriptor of a `wtr_command` is *self-contained* since it carries all the information necessary for its execution . To be portable across cluster nodes, OpenCL objects such as kernels, buffers and events are identified, within the `wtr_command` object, by a unique ID. The root scheduler continuously fetches the `wtr_commands` from the global command queue, decodes its content and – depending on the targeted device – dispatches the command to the correct node. When the `wtr_command` addresses

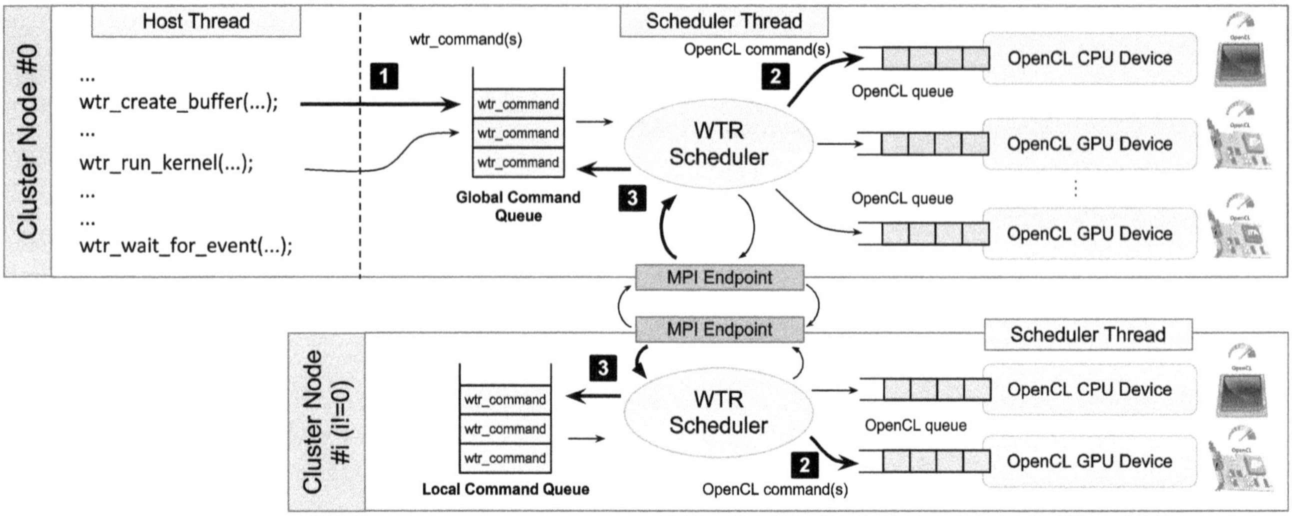

Figure 1: *libWater*'s distributed runtime system architecture.

one of the local OpenCL devices, the corresponding OpenCL command is created and enqueued into the device command queue (step 2). When a remote OpenCL device is addressed, an MPI message is generated – serializing the content of the `wtr_command` descriptor – and dispatched to the cluster node hosting the requested device. The `WTRScheduler` of the target node then de-serializes the `wtr_command` and, instead of immediately executing it, enqueues the `wtr_command` instance into the local command queue (step 3). The same `WTRScheduler` is then responsible to dispatch the corresponding OpenCL command into one of its local device queues (step 2).

The heartbeat of the `WTRScheduler` is an advanced event system which allows the management of an entire compute node – hosting multiple OpenCL devices – using only a single application thread. Indeed, because one instance of the `WTRScheduler` runs on every cluster node, trying to keep the resource usage as low as possible is of paramount importance in order to avoid wasting CPU cycles which can be used to run an OpenCL kernel. Different from related work, e.g. the SnuCL runtime system [20], which exclusively reserves an entire cluster node and a physical CPU core in each compute node only for scheduling purposes, our system does not exclusively reserve any user resources for scheduling. Furthermore, using a single thread, for both executing local `wtr_commands` and for performing scheduling decisions, reduces the amount of synchronization since accesses to event and the command queues do not need to be synchronized.

Relying on a single thread can however easily become a performance bottleneck. An interesting example is the interaction with MPI routines. By default many MPI implementations implement blocking behaviour with a *spin-lock* mechanism in order to minimize latency. This means for example that a blocking receive, waiting for a message from the communication channel, continuously checks for incoming data usually saturating the cycles of a CPU core. In an environment like ours, where CPU cores may be used to run OpenCL kernels, this behaviour must be avoided. Our solution is to avoid in every event handler routine any call to blocking MPI or OpenCL routines and always use the non-blocking semantics. The main idea is the creation of periodic events, handled by the event system using a priority queue based on timestamps, to check for the completion of pending operations. For OpenCL routines, we exploit the OpenCL event system and the associated callback mechanism. In this way, the `WTRScheduler` is able to dispatch several commands on the OpenCL devices, or MPI data transfers, which although being issued sequentially (by the single flow of the execution) are concurrently executed by the available resources (i.e. OpenCL devices and the network controller). The same event-based technique utilized to manage multiple OpenCL devices in a single node is also exploited on the large scale across cluster nodes.

4.2 Event-based Command Scheduling

As already explained in the previous section, *libWater* puts a strong emphasis on events. Following the semantics of OpenCL, dependency information enforced by programmers are used to select `wtr_commands`, which can be safely enqueued into one of the cluster nodes. *libWater* provides an event object, i.e. `wtr_event`. Internally, `wtr_events` are mapped either to an OpenCL `cl_event` object, or to a `wtr_command` identifier which is automatically generated for each `wtr_command` enqueued into the system. These dependencies allow the runtime system to organize enqueued `wtr_commands` into a DAG.

A complete multi-device *libWater*-based host program is shown in Listing 1. This code initializes all the available NVidia GPU devices. It then selects two devices belonging respectively to node rank 0 and 1, with a global memory larger than 1024MB. For each device the code in Listing 1 does the following: create a kernel (i.e. `kern`, in line 10) and a read/write buffer (i.e. `buff`, line 11). Then the contents from the host memory is written into the device buffer by the `wtr_write_buffer` command (line 12) and the `wtr_run_kernel` command is issued providing `buff` as an input argument (lines 14-16). The computed result is then retrieved by the `wtr_read_buffer` command (line 17) which moves data from the device memory back to the host memory. From the runtime system point of view, the execution of the previous code generates a set of dependent commands structured as the DAG depicted in Figure 2. The DAG $G(V, E)$ is composed of vertices, i.e. `wtr_commands` $\in V$, interconnected

```
wtr_init_devices(
  "SELECT ALL WHERE (type = gpu AND vendor = nvidia)");
wtr_event* evts[2];
for (int i=0; i<2; ++i) {
  size_t offset=size/2*i;
  wtr_device* dev = wtr_get_device("SELECT POS 1 FROM
       NODE %d WHERE global_memory > 1024MB",i);
  assert(dev != NULL && "Device does not exist!");
  wtr_event* e[8];
  wtr_init_event_array(7,e);
  wtr_kernel* kern = wtr_create_kernel(dev,"kernel.cl","fun"
       , "", WTR_SOURCE, e+0);
  wtr_buffer* buff = wtr_create_buffer(dev,
       WTR_MEM_READ_WRITE, size/2, e+1);
  wtr_write_buffer(buff, size/2, ptr+offset, e+1, e+2);
  e[7] = wtr_merge_events(2, e+0, e+2);
  wtr_run_kernel(kern,1,(size_t[1]){size/2},NULL,e+7,e+3,2,
                 0, buff,
                 sizeof(size_t), &offset);
  wtr_read_buffer(buff, size/2, ptr+offset, e+3, e+4);
  wtr_release_buffer(buff, e+4, e+5);
  wtr_release_kernel(kern, e+3, e+6);
  evts[i] = wtr_merge_events(2, e+5, e+6);
  wtr_release_event_array(8, e);
}
/* Blocks until buffers and kernels are released */
wtr_wait_for_events(2, evts+0, evts+1);
wtr_release_event_array(2, evts);
```

Listing 1: A complete multi-device program example using *libWater*'s routines

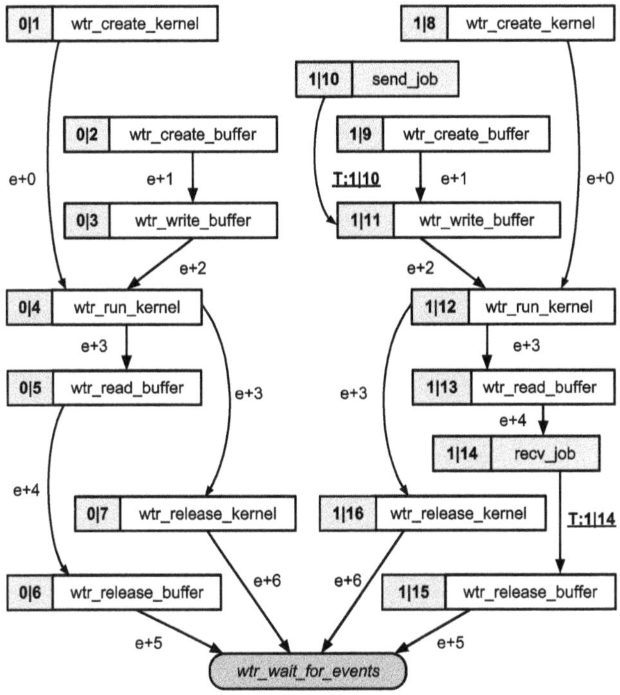

Figure 2: DAG of `wtr_commands` generated during the execution of the code snippet in Listing 1.

through directed edges $(a,b) \in E \,|\, a,b \in V$, or *events*, which guarantee that the correct order of execution, and therefore the semantics of the input program, is maintained. The *set* of dependencies associated with a command $c \in V$ is defined as $c.deps = \{v \in V \,|\, (v,c) \in E\}$. It is worth mentioning that not all *libWater* library routines generate a corresponding `wtr_command`. For example, creation, merging and release of events are only meaningful in the root node, therefore there is no need for serializing them. In Figure 2, each `wtr_command` carries a descriptor in the form $x|y$ where x represents the node rank, *c.node_id*, on which the targeted device, *c.dev_id*, is hosted and y is the unique command identifier assigned by the runtime system. As already mentioned, for buffer operations on remote devices (i.e. device on node 1) explicit data transfers are automatically inserted by the *libWater* library (e.g. `wtr_commands` 10 and 14).

Events determine when a `wtr_command` can be scheduled for execution. The scheduler uses a *just-in-time* strategy to select the next `wtr_command` from the local command queue. The logic works as follows: enqueued `wtr_commands` are analyzed in a FIFO fashion and, for each ready command, the scheduler checks whether dependencies – explicitly specified by event objects – are satisfied. If a command has no dependencies, it can be executed. Since the host program generates all the commands solely on the root node, scheduling is done at this node. However, a centralized scheduler on a single node is not an effective strategy since it limits command throughput and thus the overall scalability of the system.

In order to solve this problem, we rely on the fact that the OpenCL runtime system already has the capability of scheduling commands and handling dependencies by using events. It is worth noting that in OpenCL this mechanism is limited since events cannot be used to perform command synchronization across different contexts. *libWater* unifies event handling through `WTRScheduler` instances which manage inter-context synchronization and offload intra-context synchronization to the OpenCL driver.

We implemented a *three-level hierarchal scheduling* approach as described in Algorithm 1. At the top level, the root node of the *libWater* runtime system *pro-actively* schedules `wtr_commands` from the global queue to the targeted cluster nodes. *cmd*, fetched from the command queue, is sent to the target node (i.e. *cmd.node_id*) only if each of its dependent commands (i.e. the set *cmd.deps*) are to be executed on the same remote node (lines 6–9). The second level scheduling is local to each node (lines 11–14). The scheduler checks whether *cmd* only depends on `wtr_commands` addressing the same OpenCL device. In such case, the command is enqueued into the corresponding device queue (i.e. *dev.dev_id*) and dependencies are mapped to local OpenCL events. Alternatively, if a `wtr_command` C_1 depends on a second `wtr_command` C_2, scheduled in another context (of the same node), the local `WTRScheduler` ensures that C_1 is not enqueued into the OpenCL device queue before C_2 is completed. The third-level scheduling is implemented by the OpenCL runtime system itself which is responsible of managing single device queues. If *cmd* cannot be scheduled, due to unsatisfied dependencies, then it is pushed back in the command queue.

Command dependencies are automatically updated when a `wtr_command` c completes. Locally, a *command completion event* is generated. The associated *callback* function is depicted in Algorithm 2. The function removes, for every command in the local queue, any dependence on c. Additionally, nodes notify the root scheduler with a message (lines 5–7) triggering

Algorithm 1 The WTR_Scheduler's algorithm

```
cmd_queue                                  ▷ Local FIFO wtr_command queue
my_rank                                    ▷ MPI process rank
while true do
  cmd ← cmd_queue.pop();
  if cmd.node_id ≠ my_rank then
    if ∀ d ∈ cmd.deps | d.node_id = cmd.node_id then
      send(cmd, cmd.node_id, SCHED)        ▷ Delegates cmd to node
      continue
    end if
  else
    if ∀ d ∈ cmd.deps | d.dev_id = cmd.dev_id then
      issue(cmd.cl_cmd, cmd.deps)          ▷ Delegates to corresp. dev.
      continue
    end if
  end if
  cmd_queue.push(cmd)                      ▷ Failed to schedule event due to deps.
end while
```

Algorithm 2 Update wtr_command dependencies

```
function CALLBACK_CMD_COMPLETION(c)
  for cmd in cmd_queue do
    cmd.deps.remove(c)                     ▷ Removes c from the dependencies
  end for
  if my_rank ≠ 0 then
    send(c, 0, DONE)                       ▷ Notifies the root node of c completion
  end if
end function
```

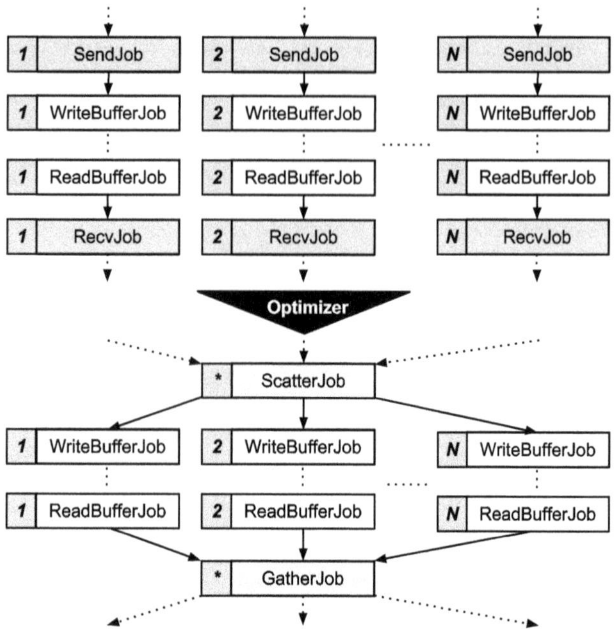

Figure 3: Dynamic collective communication pattern replacement (DCR) optimization.

a similar completion event internally at node 0. In such a way, commands in the global queue waiting for the completion of c can be scheduled – depending on the targeted device – either to a local device or to a remote node.

This multi-level scheduling allows the runtime system to hide the costs of the scheduling, as well as data transfers, with the actual work being done by the devices in the background. The main idea is to use non-blocking semantics when OpenCL commands are scheduled in the corresponding devices. In this way, the WTRScheduler can continuously dispatch commands to other devices or move data from and to the root node. In the example in Figure 2, commands 0|1 and 0|2 can be executed in parallel. Events at addresses $e + 0$ and $e + 1$ are handled by the root WTRScheduler since the OpenCL standard does not allow non-blocking semantics for these operations. The remaining commands (i.e. 0|3, 0|4 and 0|5) are inserted asynchronously into the OpenCL device queue of node 0, upon completion of commands 0|1 and 0|2. Events e+2 and e+3 are therefore handled directly by the OpenCL runtime system. Following the same logic, wtr_commands addressing the second OpenCL device (i.e. 1|*) are sent to the node with rank 1. The blocking function wtr_wait_for_events stops the execution of the host until the release operations on both nodes have completed.

5. THE DYNAMIC COLLECTIVE REPLACEMENT (DCR) OPTIMIZATION

The underlying architecture of the *libWater* runtime system and the emphasis on events, promoted by its interface, enables several runtime optimizations which are transparent to the user. This capability is a direct consequence of adhering to the OpenCL queuing semantics. Indeed, while commands are being enqueued into the system, a command DAG (as shown in Figure 2) is internally created. Since OpenCL issues commands to the appropriate device only when an explicit flush is invoked by the programmer, the runtime system can analyze large portions of the application DAG and optimize it for improving scalability.

An optimization which has been implemented in the *libWater* runtime system is the dynamic detection and replacement of collective communication patterns (DCR). Whenever the addressed device is not hosted in the root node, a call to wtr_write_buffer and wtr_read_buffer respectively generates an MPI send and receive operation. When an OpenCL application is distributed among all available devices, input buffers are usually either split or replicated between compute nodes. This parallelization strategy is common and it results in a DAG containing several send/receive transfer operations for every device of the cluster. An example is depicted in Figure 3 which represents a realistic DAG resulting from the splitting of an input and output buffer among a set of N OpenCL devices.

Point-to-point data transfers performed by the *libWater* runtime system imply an increased latency when compared with the native MPI send or receive routines. The reason for that is the polling mechanism implemented by the *libWater* runtime system – mainly employed to save node resources – which replaces the spin-lock mechanism commonly used by MPI libraries. Additionally, the number of required data transfers is directly proportional to the cluster nodes (and thus devices). This results in a large number of commands being dispatched by the runtime system and consecutively negatively impacts the overall scalability. MPI offers a large set of communication patterns called *collective operations* [25]. These routines are highly efficient since nearly all modern supercomputers and high-performance networks provide specialized hardware support for collective operations [23]. Additionally, the implementation of such collective operations employs dynamic runtime tuning techniques which choose, among a set of semantically equivalent algorithms, which best fit the underlying network topology and architecture [9, 27, 28].

Algorithm 3 DCR pattern recognition

```
1: function REPLACE_COLLECTIVE_PATTERNS(G(V, E), root)
2:   for t in BFS(G(V, E), root) do
3:     if t.type ∈ {SendJob, RecvJob} then
4:       jobs[t.node_id].append(t)                    ▷ Orders transfer jobs
5:     end if
6:   end for
7:   for i ← 0 to min({jobs[k].length : ∀ k | 0 ≤ k < N}) do
8:     pattern ← 0
9:     for j ← 1 to N do
10:      if jobs[j][i].type ≠ jobs[j − 1][i].type then break
11:      if jobs[j][i].buf = jobs[j − 1][i].buf ∧
12:        jobs[j][i].size = jobs[j − 1][i].size then
13:        if pattern = 2 then break
14:        pattern ← 1              ▷ Sequence recognized as a broadcast
15:      end if
16:      if jobs[j][i].buf = jobs[j − 1][i].buf + jobs[j − 1][i].size then
17:        if pattern = 1 then break
18:        pattern ← 2      ▷ Sequence can be either scatter or gather
19:      end if
20:    end for
21:    if j ≠ N ∨ pattern = 0 then continue
22:    if pattern = 1 ∧ jobs[0][i].type = SendJob then
23:      replace_with_broadcast(jobs, i)
24:    else
25:      if jobs[0][i].type = SendJob then replace_with_scatter(jobs, i)
26:      else replace_with_gather(jobs, i)
27:    end if
28:  end for
29: end function
```

Related work analyzed the problem of automatic detection of collective patterns from a set of point-to-point communications. This technique is common in MPI performance tools which are capable of detecting such patterns via post-mortem analysis of program traces [21]. The general problem of collective communication pattern detection is NP-hard, however, under particular restrictions the problem can be solved in polynomial time. A more recent work [15] proposed a fast solution, with a complexity of $O(n \log n)$, which makes the approach more suitable for runtime systems.

The goal of our `DCR` optimization algorithm is to analyze the command DAG isolating point-to-point data transfers and detect whether a subset of those resembles one of the collective patterns supported by MPI. This is possible since – if the application is carefully written using events for command synchronization – the command DAG will be available to the runtime system scheduler before the first blocking command is invoked (e.g. `wtr_wait_for_event(s)`). Since data transfers in our environment have all the same root (the node 0), the analysis for patterns is simplified. The pattern recognition is presented in Algorithm 3. The command DAG is traversed once in breadth-first order (lines 1–6), transfer commands are collected into N separate lists (i.e. variable *jobs*), one per device. On the extracted N lists, pattern analysis is performed (lines 7–28). The check is done by considering elements having the same position within the transfer job lists. Furthermore, the check is simplified by the fact that every send and receive `wtr_command` carries information of the buffer location (*buf*) and the amount of bytes being transfered (*size*). The pattern analysis starts by taking the first transfer `wtr_command` from the N lists and by checking against a supported pattern, i.e. *broadcast*, *scatter* or *gather*. For instance, in a broadcast N send operations are expected where $\forall\, i \mid 0 \leq i < N-1,\ buf_i = buf_{i+1} \vee size_i = size_{i+1}$. If the check fails, the transfer jobs are tested against a scatter or gather pattern $\forall\, i \mid 0 \leq i < N-1,\ buf_i + size_i = buf_{i+1}$.

Once a pattern is recognized, single point-to-point transfers are removed from the command DAG and replaced by the corresponding collective communication operation (lines 23, 25 and 26). A visual example of this optimization is depicted in Figure 3, where multiple send operations are collapsed into a single scatter operation and correspondingly, receives are rewritten as a gather operation. By doing so, dependencies between successive commands are updated in order to keep the semantics of the input program unchanged.

Since collective operations must involve all the processes in a communicator, the current implementation of the `DCR` optimization works when all the initialized devices participate in the computation. Therefore, the analysis is limited to regular applications which *must* involve all OpenCL devices in data transfers. This is important to keep the pattern recognition algorithm simple and fast, since this optimization is applied during runtime. In the future, we plan to improve this mechanism by extending the pattern recognition also to sub-groups of devices.

Vienna Supercomputing Cluster 2 (VSC2)

Max # of nodes	1.314
Processors	2 x AMD Opteron 6132 HE
Cores per node	2 x 8
Clock Frequency	2.2 GHz
Memory per Node	32 GB DDR3
Interconnection	Infiniband 4x QDR
Open MPI version	1.6.1
OpenCL version	AMD APP 2.6

Table 2: The VSC2 experimental target architecture.

6. EXPERIMENTAL EVALUATION

We used *libWater* to encode 6 computational kernels, some of them taken from various OpenCL benchmarking suites (i.e. AMD and IBM), and studied their scalability. In four of them, the kernels were optimized for local memory, i.e. `PerlinNoise` (from IBM), `NBody` (from AMD), `Floyd` and `kNN` manually written by us. For the remaining two codes, `MatrixMul` and `LinReg` we used a naive implementation unoptimized for what concern local memory. The table shows, for each kernel, the number of input and output buffers used by the kernel. We define a buffer as *splittable* when its content can be distributed among the devices. The nature of a buffer is strictly related to the algorithm being implemented within the OpenCL kernel, and thus the application. Non splittable buffers are always replicated on every device.

For the strong scalability analysis we used a real production cluster, the Vienna Supercomputing Cluster 2 (VSC2) [3], ranked 162th in the Top500 list [4], whose details are summarized in Table 2. A second study was conducted to test the suitability of *libWater* to exploit the computational capabilities of a heterogeneous cluster configuration. For this purpose we used a cluster, composed of 3 compute nodes (i.e. `mc1`, `mc2` and `mc3`), custom made with *off-the-shelf* GPU accelerators. The hardware details are depicted in Table 3.

The six applications utilized for our study are listed in Table 4. We started from a pure OpenCL implementation and

	mc1	mc2	mc3
CPUs	2 x AMD Opteron(tm) 6168 @1.9GHz	2 x AMD Opteron(tm) 6168 @1.9GHz	2 x Intel(R) Xeon(R) X5650 @2.67GHz
GPUs	2 x ATI Radeon HD 5870	1 x NVIDIA GTX 480	1 x NVIDIA GTX 460
RAM	24 GB DDR3		
Interconn.	Infiniband QDR		
Open MPI	1.6.1		
OpenCL	AMD APP 2.6	CUDA 5.0	CUDA 5.0

Table 3: The architecture of mc1, mc2 and mc3 heterogeneous compute nodes.

rewrote them using *libWater*. In Table 4, we show the reduction, in terms of lines of code, achieved when the application is written using our library. It is worth mentioning that while the original OpenCL applications were single device codes, the *libWater* based implementation is instead multi-device code. On average, we were able to reduce the lines of the host code by approximately a factor of 2 due to the higher level abstractions provided by *libWater*.

6.1 Homogeneous CPU cluster

The applications shown in Table 4 were executed on the VSC2 homogeneous CPU cluster. We were able to access up to 64 nodes with a total of 1024 CPU cores. Since the 2 AMD CPUs which are hosted per node are considered by the OpenCL driver as a single device, the speedup was computed based on the number of compute nodes (and thus OpenCL devices) instead of single CPU cores. The workload partitioning is implemented, for each test case, by assigning to each OpenCL device an equal amount of work.

The scalability tests were performed in the following way: the original OpenCL version of the applications were executed in a single node and their execution times used as a reference measurement. *libWater* was then used for node numbers ranging from 2 to 64. The main differences between the original version of the application codes and the one written using *libWater* are mainly in the host code. The kernel code was slightly modified only to forward the *offset* value used by the workload partitioning (as shown in Listing 1). We computed the ideal scaling for each application using the reference execution time and dividing it by the number of nodes. We conducted experiments with *libWater* by using two different settings: the first, named *baseline*, uses the runtime system without dynamic optimizations enabled; the second, DCR, uses the collective pattern replacement mechanism as described in Section 5. The results of our experiments are depicted in Figure 4.

For each of the six applications, we show the execution time (in seconds) for up to 64 devices and the corresponding speedup with respect to a single node. Overall, we observe that our approach scales almost linearly, especially for those codes using few input/output buffers. PerlinNoise, Figure 4(a), is an example of those, since it has no dependencies on input buffers and the data produced by the kernel is distributed between the devices. For such code, the baseline configuration of our runtime system achieves a speedup of 53 for 64 nodes, and thus an efficiency of 83%. When the number and size of the input/output buffers increases, the efficiency of our system decreases. The worst case is represented by the LinReg application, Figure 4(f), which stops scaling after 32 nodes. This kernel has 4 input buffers, 2 of them are not splittable (because of dependencies within the kernel code) and therefore must be replicated on every node. The remaining 2 input and output buffers are instead splittable. For such code we have an immediate decrease (75% on two nodes) of the efficiency. This is because the kernel execution is delayed due to the fact that several wtr_commands are executed (and transfered to the target nodes) to create and initialize the input/output buffers. However this delay is a constant and system efficiency remains almost unvaried up to 16 nodes. On 32 and 64 nodes the efficiency of the baseline runtime system starts decreasing significantly.

This problem is largely addressed by the dynamic collective pattern replacement, i.e. DCR, optimization which was introduced in Section 5. This optimization reduces the load on the scheduler since it replaces several single transfer jobs with one collective operation. In LinReg this optimization improves the scalability of the system by a factor of 2 achieving an efficiency of 55%. A small effect of this optimization can be observed for smaller node configurations because collective operations are optimized for a large number of nodes. An interesting result is the effect of the DCR optimization on the PerlinNoise test case. In such a case, the DCR optimization fails to improve performance over the baseline. The reason is that collective operations are blocking while point-to-point communications in the runtime system are non-blocking thereby allowing overlapping of multiple transfers. The synchronization costs introduced by the gather operation is therefore not properly compensated by the amount of exchanged data. We believe that this problem can be eliminated by using *non-blocking collective* routines which have been introduced in the latest MPI standard [25] and will soon be available in mainstream MPI libraries. Additionally, since this optimization is done dynamically, and therefore the amount of data being transfered is known by the scheduler, heuristics can be integrated to decide when such optimization should be applied.

On average, *libWater* achieves an efficiency of 80% on 32 nodes and 64% when 64 nodes are used. Without the DCR optimization the system has an efficiency of 47% on 64 nodes. This means that the DCR optimization improves the system efficiency by 17% on 64 nodes and we expect this value to increase proportionally with the number of nodes.

6.2 Heterogeneous GPU cluster

Since OpenCL allows access to heterogeneous devices we conducted a second experiment which demonstrates *libWater* on a heterogeneous GPU cluster as described in Table 3. In order to run applications on such environment, the input code was rewritten so that the workload distribution was controllable via command line arguments. It is worth mentioning that workload partitioning for heterogeneous architectures is an active research problem [13, 22, 17, 14]. However, this aspect is completely orthogonal to our library and for the sake of this experiment, we derive workload partitionings in an empirical way.

We ran the MatrixMul and the Floyd test cases using different combinations of devices. For each device configuration, several different workload splittings were tested and the fastest one was chosen. The partitionings and their corresponding execution times, are shown in Table 5. For exam-

Application	OpenCL LOC	*libWater* LOC	Input size	Input/Output buffers (*splittable*)	Short Description
`PerlinNoise`	412	**301**	20K x 20K	0(0) / 1(1)	Gradient noise generator
`Nbody`	450	**324**	600K bodies	2(0) / 2(2)	N-body simulation
`kNN`	234	**101**	*ref*: 8M, *query*: 80K	2(1) / 2(1)	k-nearest neighbor
`Floyd`	222	**113**	Vertices 8K, Adjacency matrix 64K	1(0) /1(0)	Floyd-Warshall
`MatrixMul`	219	**104**	7K x 7K ($A = B = C$)	2(1) / 1(1)	Matrix Multiplication
`LinReg`	298	**149**	1000K	4(2) / 1(1)	Linear regression

Table 4: Application codes used for *libWater* evaluation.

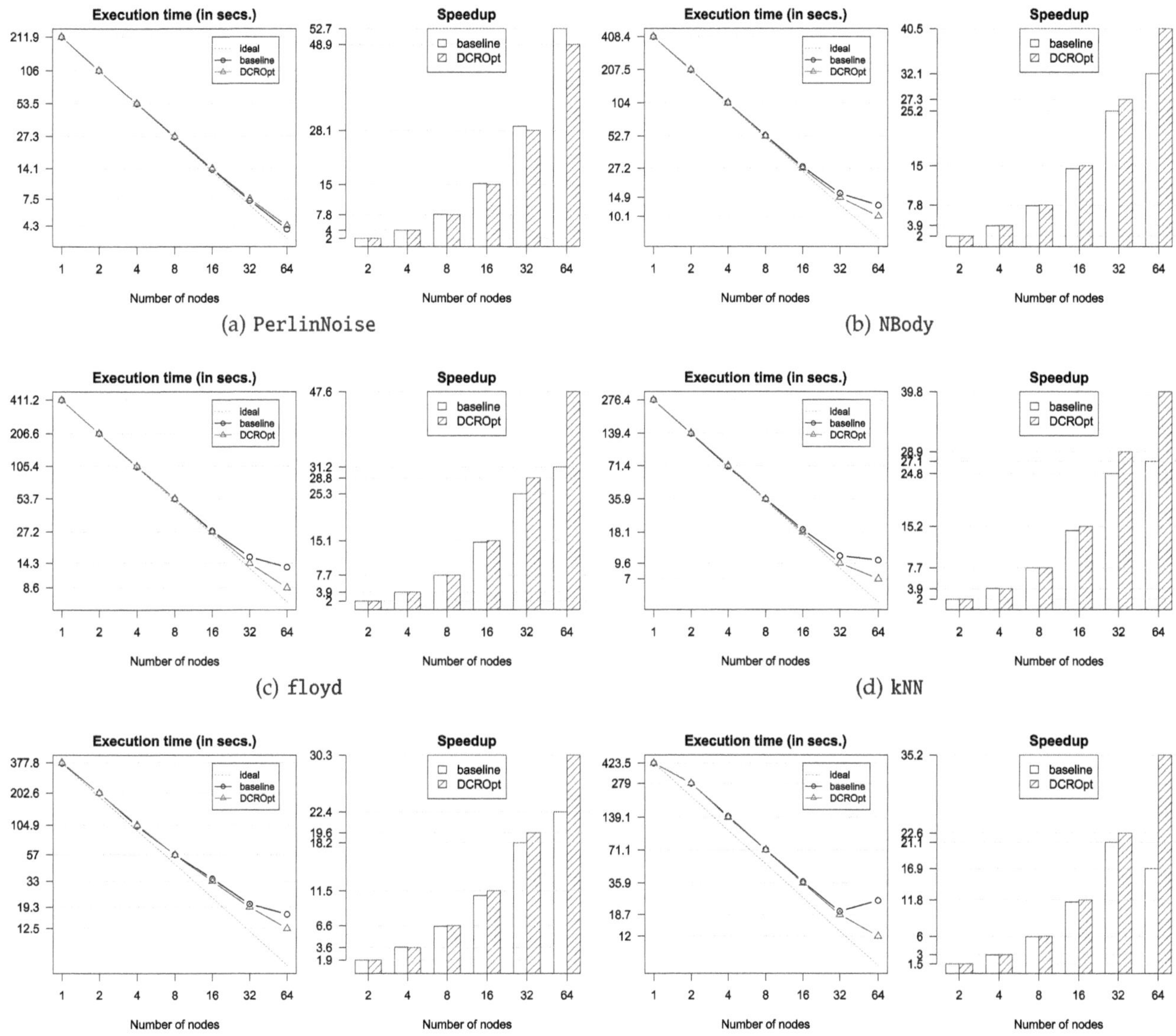

(a) `PerlinNoise` (b) `NBody` (c) `floyd` (d) `kNN` (e) `MatrixMul` (f) `LinReg`

Figure 4: Strong scaling of *libWater* on the VSC2

ple, in `MatrixMul`, configuration `C1` assigns all the workload to the first GPU of node `mc1`. The execution time for this configuration is 63.3 seconds. By equally splitting the workload between the two accelerators on the same node, i.e. `C2`, we double the performance. Between the GPUs, the NVidia GTX 480 is the fastest device requiring only 29.4 seconds to complete the work. However *libWater* can be used to improve the execution time even further. The overall execution time can be reduced by 50% by using the workload partition as described by configuration `C8` which assigns 22% to each GPU in `mc1`, 44% to the NVidia GTX 480 and the remaining 12% to the NVidia GTX 460 accelerator. For `Floyd` results are different. Its execution on the GTX 480 is 8 times faster than the AMD GPU and 4 times better than the GTX 460. However, performance can still be improved by splitting the workload between the two NVidia accelerators by assigning

	Device	Workload Partition Configurations							
		C1	C2	C3	C4	C5	C6	C7	C8
MatrixMul	mc1-GPU1	100%	50%	-	-	35%	25%	-	22%
	mc1-GPU2	-	50%	-	-	-	25%	-	22%
	mc2-GPU3	-	-	100%	-	65%	50%	75%	44%
	mc3-GPU4	-	-	-	100%	-	-	25%	12%
	Exec. time (in secs.)	63.3	32.5	29.4	68.4	23.7	19.0	26.6	**17.3**
Floyd	mc1-GPU1	100%	50%	-	-	2%	1%		0.5%
	mc1-GPU2	-	50%	-	-	-	1%	-	0.5%
	mc2-GPU3	-	-	100%	-	98%	98%	99%	98%
	mc3-GPU4	-	-	-	100%	-	-	1%	1%
	Exec. time (in secs.)	101.6	51.3	14.9	58.3	17.3	16.0	**13.1**	16.3

Table 5: Performance of `MatrixMul` and `Floyd` on the heterogeneous cluster for different combination of GPUs.

99% of the work to the faster GTX 480 and 1% to the GTX 460. This experiment demonstrates, despite higher latencies caused by additional data transfers between host and device memory, non-blocking communication yields good scalability behaviour even for heterogeneous architectures. However, scalability on such environments depends on several factors and we plan to investigate this issues in future work.

7. RELATED WORK

In recent years, heterogeneous systems have received a great amount of attention from the research community. Although several projects have been recently proposed to facilitate the programming of clusters with heterogeneous nodes [20, 8, 6, 5, 18, 12, 26, 31], none of them combines support for high performance inter-node data transfer, support for a wide number of different devices and a simplified programming model. Our work takes into account all this aspects through the development of the *libWater* library.

Kim et al. [20] proposed the *SnuCL* framework that extends the original OpenCL semantics to heterogeneous cluster environments. Their work is closely related to ours. SnuCL relies on the OpenCL language with few extensions to directly support collective patterns of MPI. Indeed, in SnuCL is the programmer responsibility to take care of the efficient data transfers between nodes. In that sense, end users of the SnuCL platform need to have an understanding of MPI collective calls semantics in order to be able to write scalable programs. This deeply differs from our system where such optimizations are transparently applied by the *libWater* runtime system. Furthermore, SnuCL poses a limit to the number of devices which can be addressed by their runtime system, i.e. NVidia accelerators and CPUs. Differently, *libWater* can interface with every OpenCL driver making the list of supported platforms virtually unlimited.

Also other works have investigated the problem of extending the OpenCL semantics to access a cluster of nodes. The Many GPUs Package (*MGP*) [8] is a library and runtime system that using the MOSIX VCL layer enables unmodified OpenCL applications to be executed on clusters. *Hybrid OpenCL* [6] is based on the FOXC OpenCL runtime and extends it with a network layer that allows the access to devices in a distributed system. The *clOpenCL* [5] platform comprises a wrapper library and a set of user-level daemons. Every call to an OpenCL primitive is intercepted by the wrapper which redirects its execution to a specific daemon at a cluster node or to the local runtime. *dOpenCL* [18] extends the OpenCL standard, such that arbitrary compute devices installed on any node of a distributed system can be used together within a single application. *Distributed OpenCL* [12] is a framework that allows the distribution of computing processes to many resources connected via network using JSON RPC as communication layer. *OpenCL Remote* [26] is a framework which extends both OpenCL's platform model and memory model with a network client-server paradigm. *Virtual OpenCL* [31], based on the OpenCL programming model, exposes physical GPUs as decoupled virtual resources that can be transparently managed independent of the application execution.

While the objectives of these approaches are similar to ours, none of them provides an abstraction layer to reduce the complexity associated with the OpenCL development and, furthermore, they show a very limited scalability in clusters of 4 to 8 compute nodes. In particular, none of them employs dynamic communication optimizations as we do.

Besides OpenCL-based approaches, also CUDA solutions have been proposed to simplify distributed systems programming. *CUDASA* [29] is an extension of the CUDA programming language which extends parallelism to multi-GPU systems and GPU-cluster environments. *rCUDA* [11] is a distributed implementation of the CUDA API that enables shared remote GPGPU in HPC clusters. *cudaMPI* [24] is a message passing library for distributed-memory GPU clusters that extends the MPI interface to work with data stored on the GPU using the CUDA programming interface. All of these approaches are limited to devices that support CUDA, i.e. NVidia GPU accelerators, and therefore they cannot be used to address heterogeneous systems which combines CPUs and accelerators from different vendors.

Other projects have investigated how to simplify the OpenCL programming interface. Sun et. al [30], proposed a task queueing extension for OpenCL that provides a high-level API based on the concepts of work pools and work units. *Intel CLU* [16], *OCL-MLA* [1] and *SimpleOpencl* [2] are lightweight API designed to help programmers to rapidly prototype heterogeneous programs. Beside the simplified interface, *libWater* provides fine-grained control over device selection (i.e. DQL) and an improved device synchronization based on events.

A more sophisticated approach was proposed in [10]. OmpSs relies on compiler technologies to generate host and kernel code from a sequential program annotated with pragmas. The runtime of OmpSs internally uses a DAG similar to ours with the scope of scheduling. However, to our knowledge, the DAG is not dynamically optimized like in our approach. Additionally, by relying on the user for kernel code, *libWater* allows for fine-grained performance tuning.

8. CONCLUSIONS

In this paper, we introduced *libWater*, a library for simplifying the programming of heterogeneous distributed systems.

The proposed interface demonstrates that raising the abstraction level of the OpenCL programming model is possible without losing control over performance. We showed, with an example, how a multi-device distributed host program can be written using approximately 25 lines of code. By defining a simple, but powerful, device query language (DQL), *libWater* simplifies the management and discovery of a large number of OpenCL devices. The simple API makes the library a perfect target for automatic code generation tools, thus it can be easily integrated in compilers.

libWater's interface is tightly bound to a lightweight distributed runtime system which is designed from scratch for high scalability and low resource usage. Because of the non-blocking semantics promoted by the library interface, commands can be organized by the runtime system into a DAG to be used for dynamic analysis and optimizations.

We studied the strong scalability on a homogeneous production cluster using up to 64 nodes, for which our system achieves an efficiency of 64%. We also demonstrated the effectiveness of how *libWater* addresses highly heterogeneous configurations by running two test cases on a cluster system composed by 4 different GPU accelerators.

libWater will be released as an open-source project with the goal of becoming a research platform to investigate performance aspects of heterogeneous and distributed HPC architectures.

Acknowledgments

This project was funded by the FWF Austrian Science Fund as part of project TRP 220-N23 "Automatic Portable Performance for Heterogeneous Multi-cores" and by the FWF Doctoral School CIM Computational Interdisciplinary Modelling under contract W01227. The computational results presented have been achieved in part using the Vienna Scientific Cluster 2 (VSC2).

9. REFERENCES

[1] OCL-MLA. http://tuxfan.github.com/ocl-mla/.

[2] Simple-opencl. http://code.google.com/p/simple-opencl/.

[3] The Vienna Scientific Cluster 2. http://www.vsc.ac.at/, 2012.

[4] Top 500 Supercomputer sites. http://www.top500.org/, 2012.

[5] A. Albano, R. Jose, P. Antonio, and S. L. Paulo. clOpenCL - Supporting Distributed Heterogeneous Computing in HPC Clusters. In *10th International Workshop HeteroPar*, 2012.

[6] R. Aoki, S. Oikawa, T. Nakamura, and S. Miki. Hybrid OpenCL: Enhancing OpenCL for Distributed Processing. In *ISPA*, pages 149–154, 2011.

[7] K. Asanovic, R. Bodik, B. C. Catanzaro, J. J. Gebis, P. Husbands, K. Keutzer, D. A. Patterson, W. L. Plishker, J. Shalf, S. W. Williams, and K. A. Yelick. The Landscape of Parallel Computing Research: A View from Berkeley. Technical report, EECS Department, University of California, Berkeley, 2006.

[8] A. Barak, T. Ben-Nun, E. Levy, and A. Shiloh. A Package for OpenCL Based Heterogeneous Computing on Clusters with Many GPU Devices. In *Workshop PPAC*, pages 224–231, 2010.

[9] J. Bruck, C.-T. Ho, S. Kipnis, and D. Weathersby. Efficient Algorithms for All-to-All Communications in Multi-Port Message-Passing Systems. In *SPAA*, pages 298–309, 1994.

[10] J. Bueno, J. Planas, A. Duran, R. M. Badia, X. Martorell, E. Ayguade, and J. Labarta. Productive Programming of GPU Clusters with OmpSs. In *IPDPS*, pages 557–568, 2012.

[11] J. Duato, A. J. Peña, F. Silla, R. Mayo, and E. S. Quintana-Ortí. rCUDA: Reducing the number of GPU-based accelerators in high performance clusters. In *HPCS*, pages 224–231, 2010.

[12] B. Eskikaya and D. T. Altilar. Distributed OpenCL Distributing OpenCL Platform on Network Scale. In *IJCA*, volume ACCTHPCA 2, pages 26–30, 2012.

[13] I. Grasso, K. Kofler, B. Cosenza, and T. Fahringer. Automatic problem size sensitive task partitioning on heterogeneous parallel systems. In *PPoPP*, 2013.

[14] D. Grewe and M. F. O'Boyle. A static task partitioning approach for heterogeneous systems using opencl. In *CC*, 2011.

[15] T. Hoefler and T. Schneider. Runtime Detection and Optimization of Collective Communication Patterns. In *PACT*, pages 263–272, 2012.

[16] Intel Corporation. Computing Language Utility. http://software.intel.com/.

[17] M. Kai, L. Xue, C. Wei, Z. Chi, and W. Xiaorui. Greengpu: A holistic approach to energy efficiency in gpu-cpu heterogeneous architectures. In *ICPP*, 2012.

[18] P. Kegel, M. Steuwer, and S. Gorlatch. dOpenCL: Towards a Uniform Programming Approach for Distributed Heterogeneous Multi-/Many-Core Systems. In *IPDPS Workshops*, pages 174–186, 2012.

[19] Khronos OpenCL Working Group. The OpenCL 1.2 specification. http://www.khronos.org/opencl, 2012.

[20] J. Kim, S. Seo, J. Lee, J. Nah, G. Jo, and J. Lee. SnuCL: an OpenCL framework for heterogeneous CPU/GPU clusters. In *ICS*, pages 341–352, 2012.

[21] A. Knüpfer, D. Kranzlmüller, and W. E. Nagel. Detection of Collective MPI Operation Patterns. In *PVM/MPI*, pages 259–267, 2004.

[22] K. Kofler, I. Grasso, B. Cosenza, and T. Fahringer. An automatic input-sensitive approach for heterogeneous task partitioning. In *ICS*, 2013.

[23] S. Kumar, G. Dozsa, G. Almasi, P. Heidelberger, D. Chen, M. E. Giampapa, M. Blocksome, A. Faraj, J. Parker, J. Ratterman, B. Smith, and C. J. Archer. The deep computing messaging framework: generalized scalable message passing on the blue gene/p supercomputer. In *ICS*, pages 94–103, 2008.

[24] O. S. Lawlor. Message passing for GPGPU clusters: CudaMPI. In *CLUSTER*, pages 1–8, 2009.

[25] MPI Forum. MPI: A Message-Passing Interface Standard. Version 3. http://www.mpi-forum.org, 2012.

[26] R. Özaydin and D. T. Altilar. OpenCL Remote: Extending OpenCL Platform Model to Network Scale. In *HPCC-ICESS*, pages 830–835, 2012.

[27] J. Pjesivac-Grbovic, T. Angskun, G. Bosilca, G. E. Fagg, E. Gabriel, and J. Dongarra. Performance analysis of MPI collective operations. *Cluster Computing*, 10(2):127–143, 2007.

[28] P. Sanders, J. Speck, and J. L. Träff. Two-tree algorithms for full bandwidth broadcast, reduction and scan. *Parallel Computing*, 35(12):581–594, 2009.

[29] M. Strengert, C. Müller, C. Dachsbacher, and T. Ertl. CUDASA: Compute Unified Device and Systems Architecture. In *EGPGV*, pages 49–56, 2008.

[30] E. Sun, D. Schaa, R. Bagley, N. Rubin, and D. Kaeli. Enabling task-level scheduling on heterogeneous platforms. In *Workshop GPGPU*, pages 84–93, 2012.

[31] S. Xiao and W. chun Feng. Generalizing the Utility of GPUs in Large-Scale Heterogeneous Computing Systems. In *IPDPS Workshops*, pages 2554–2557, 2012.

Exploring Hardware Overprovisioning in Power-Constrained, High Performance Computing

Tapasya Patki
Dept. of Computer Science
The University of Arizona
tpatki@cs.arizona.edu

David K. Lowenthal
Dept. of Computer Science
The University of Arizona
dkl@cs.arizona.edu

Barry Rountree
Lawrence Livermore
National Laboratory
rountree@llnl.gov

Martin Schulz
Lawrence Livermore
National Laboratory
schulzm@llnl.gov

Bronis de Supinski
Lawrence Livermore
National Laboratory
bronis@llnl.gov

ABSTRACT

Most recent research in power-aware supercomputing has focused on making individual nodes more efficient and measuring the results in terms of flops per watt. While this work is vital in order to reach exascale computing at 20 megawatts, there has been a dearth of work that explores efficiency at the whole system level. Traditional approaches in supercomputer design use *worst-case* power provisioning: the total power allocated to the system is determined by the maximum power draw possible per node. In a world where power is plentiful and nodes are scarce, this solution is optimal. However, as power becomes the limiting factor in supercomputer design, worst-case provisioning becomes a drag on performance.

In this paper we demonstrate how a policy of *overprovisioning* hardware with respect to power combined with intelligent, hardware-enforced power bounds consistently leads to greater performance across a range of standard benchmarks. In particular, leveraging overprovisioning requires that applications use effective *configurations*; the best configuration depends on application scalability and memory contention. We show that using overprovisioning leads to an average speedup of more than 50% over worst-case provisioning.

Categories and Subject Descriptors

C.4 [**Computer Systems Organization**]: Performance of Systems

General Terms

Measurement, Performance

Keywords

Power; High-Performance Computing; Overprovisioned; RAPL

1. INTRODUCTION

The reality of power-limited supercomputing has begun to transform the community's understanding of performance. The still highly influential standard has been flops measured on the Linpack benchmark [4]. *Flops per watt*, epitomized by the Green 500 [11] list of supercomputers, is a new metric that may soon carry more importance. However, flops-per-watt varies widely across applications, and designing a system that optimizes it for any single benchmark leads to inefficient and suboptimal performance for other benchmarks.

The architecture community has addressed a similar design problem on single nodes (and embedded systems) by a process of *overprovisioning* hardware [19]. For example, in recent chip designs (e.g., Nehalem), more cores exist on the processor than can simultaneously run at the highest CPU clock frequency (due to power constraints). The user (or system, or hardware) has a choice among several different combinations of clock frequency and active core counts, with smaller core counts allowing higher frequencies.

The U.S. Department of Energy's goal of exascale computing with 20 megawatts or less means that the power that can physically be brought to the machine room will constrain future systems. Further, typical estimates are that each MW-year costs $1M so supercomputing centers can only afford a limited amount of power. Thus, we should also consider overprovisioning for high-performance computing (HPC).

With such constraints, we can guarantee full power to a restricted number of nodes (*worst case provisioning*) or we must limit the power to more nodes (*overprovisioning*). While an overprovisioned supercomputer cannot execute each node at full power, it could achieve better overall performance in terms of application execution time than a system with fewer fully-powered nodes. However, to achieve better performance on overprovisioned systems, we require new strategies to manage applications such that the best overall performance is achieved—while not exceeding the system-wide power bound. In particular, we must understand how different applications behave under enforced power limitations and how application configurations influence the utilization of the available power. For instance, under a power bound, an application's scalability characteristics determine whether we want to use fewer nodes at higher power per node or more nodes at lower power per node. Future systems are even likely to go a step further and allow power to be directed to individual components; e.g., if the code is CPU-bound, then cores can be run faster while reducing power to memory and other node componenents.

In this paper we provide, as far as we know, the first extensive study on real hardware that explores how HPC applications behave under a power bound and how application configurations influence the performance in overprovisioned systems. We analyze strongly-scaled HPC benchmarks on the *rzmerl* cluster at LLNL, which has 162 Intel Sandy Bridge nodes. We use Intel's RAPL interface to enable and to enforce power limits and to study their effects on performance using several benchmarks.

This paper makes the following contributions:

- We study the effect of a power bound on a set of high performance computing applications;
- We show that the optimal configuration for a given application depends on its parallel efficiency and memory intensity as well as the particular power bound;
- We show that using overprovisioning leads to an average speedup of more than 50% over worst-case provisioning on four applications (BT-MZ, LU-MZ, SP-MZ, and SPhot).

The rest of this paper is organized as follows. Section 2 provides the overall approach for our study. Section 3 introduces Intel's RAPL interface for power clamping, Sections 4, 5, and 6 describe our experimental details, baseline power results, and multiple-node results, respectively. Next, Section 7 describes related work, Section 8 discusses future opportunities in overprovisioned supercomputing, and Section 9 provides concluding remarks.

2. OVERPROVISIONING

As mentioned above, an overprovisioned system is one in which we cannot simultaneously power all components at peak power. Overprovisioned systems will become more common as we hit what Venkatesh et al. term the *utilization wall* [35]. We expect that as transistor switching speeds increase, we will not be able to dissipate the heat at the same rate. Thus, the fraction of the chip that can be executed at full speed is monotonically decreasing; the part of the chip that must remain unused is referred to as *dark silicon* [2]. This fact has given rise to dynamic overclocking features in modern processor architectures, such as Intel's Turbo Boost [15] and AMD's Turbo CORE [5]. Processors are now designed to be *overprovisioned* with respect to power— the CPU frequency at which a core executes depends on the number of active cores, and not all cores can simultaneously run at the highest frequency.

The same idea should be applied to supercomputing. Exascale systems will have a power budget; the current bound set by DoE is 20 MW. Overprovisioning in the supercomputing context means that not all nodes in the facility can execute at peak power simultaneously. As opposed to worst-case provisioning, overprovisioning is advantageous because it can allow, for example, both highly scalable and less scalable jobs to perform well. In particular, an application's scalability determines whether we should use fewer nodes at higher power per node or more nodes at lower power per node. Also, when only a few nodes in the application are on the critical path, running all nodes at peak power might be wasteful. In addition, depending on an application's CPU and memory usage, we can choose to use fewer cores per node or to allocate component power within a node (that is, power to the packages and the memory subsystem) based on utilization. While overprovisioning means that the supercomputing center buys more compute capacity can be used, it allows the user to customize the system to an application and thereby to achieve better performance.

As overprovisioning becomes more common, the HPC community will need to address the performance challenges that arise. Power must be scheduled more carefully among the hardware resources in an HPC cluster. These resources include the racks in the machine room, the nodes within the racks, the components within a node and the interconnect; and, a fixed system-level power-constraint on the cluster will hierarchically translate to a node-level power-constraint, possibly in a non-uniform manner.

In order to explore overprovisioning and its effect on application performance, we address the following question in this paper: given a machine with n nodes and c cores per node, a cluster-level power bound P on the machine, and a strongly-scaled HPC application, how important is choosing the optimal *configuration*? We define a configuration as: (1) a value for n, (2) a value for c, (3) an amount of power p to be allocated to each node. The constraint is that the total power consumed must be no more than the bound P, and the goal is to minimize application runtime.

We explore this issue through a series of experiments on a 162 node Intel Sandy Bridge cluster at LLNL and use Intel's RAPL interface to enforce various power bounds on a wide range of HPC applications and benchmarks. Thus, the cluster is effectively an overprovisioned system.

3. INTEL'S RAPL INTERFACE: RUNNING AVERAGE POWER LIMIT

The Intel Sandy Bridge processor family supports onboard power measurement and power clamping at a fine granularity through a novel interface named Running Average Power Limit (RAPL) [16]. The architecture has four power *domains—Package* (PKG), *Power Plane 0* (PP0), *Power Plane 1* (PP1) and *DRAM*. The PKG domain represents the processor die, and the DRAM domain includes directly attached memory. PP0 covers mostly the cores, while PP1 covers uncore devices (like the off-chip last-level cache or the Intel QuickPath Interconnect). The Sandy Bridge architecture has two processor *models*, the *client* (family=0x06, model=0x2A) and the *server* (family=0x06, model=0x2D). The client model supports the PKG, PP0 and the PP1 domains, and the server model supports the PKG, PP0 and DRAM domains.

A series of Machine Specific Registers (MSRs) implement RAPL. To access these MSRs, developers can use the *msr* kernel module. This module exports a file interface that can be used to read from or write to the MSRs given appropriate permissions using the `readmsr` and `writemsr` instructions. The RAPL interface includes the `MSR_RAPL_POWER_UNIT` read-only register that exposes the units for power, energy and time in Watts, Joules and Seconds respectively, at architecture-specific precision. We use server model Sandy Bridge nodes with units of 0.125W, 0.0000152J and 0.000977 seconds.

Power Measurement.

Each domain has a 32-bit, read-only `ENERGY_STATUS` MSR, which is updated approximately every millisecond. Because the unit of joules is small, this is expected to roll over within hours. Average power can be calculated using this MSR and the elapsed time.

Power Clamping.

Each domain has a `POWER_LIMIT` MSR that can specify a time window and a maximum average-power value. The hardware ensures that the average power over the specified time window does not exceed the power value by adjusting the processor P- and T- states and using other undocumented techniques.

The `POWER_INFO` set of registers provide information on the *thermal specification power*, the lowest power bound and the largest time window supported. For our system, for the PKG domain, the lowest power bound is 51W, the thermal specification is 115W, the largest possible time window is 0.0459 seconds, and the maximum power rating is 180W.

The `librapl` library.

To analyze HPC applications under a power bound, we developed the *librapl* library to facilitate safe user-space access of Intel's RAPL MSRs. This library uses the MPI profiling layer to intercept `MPI_Init()` and `MPI_Finalize()` calls to set up the necessary MSRs. Thus, we do not modify application source code. The library can also sample MPI programs at a desired time interval and intercept every MPI call in the application to gather timing and energy/power information. It further infers the operating frequency for each core using the `APERF` and `MPERF` MSRs [16]. Our library can be downloaded from `https://github.com/tpatki/librapl` and is currently in use at Purdue University, the University of Illinois at Urbana-Champaign, LLNL, and the University of Arizona.

4. EXPERIMENTAL AND APPLICATION DETAILS

In all results in this paper, we report power values in Watts and timing information in seconds. We conduct our experiments on the *rzmerl* cluster at LLNL, which is a 162-node Sandy Bridge cluster. Each node is a 062D server model with two PKG domains, and 8 cores per package. The memory per node is 32GB. The clock speed is 2.6 GHz, and the maximum turbo frequency is 3.3 GHz. The cluster has a 32-node per job limit. We use MVAPICH2 version 1.7 and compile all codes with the Intel compiler version 12.1.5. OpenMP threads were scheduled using the scatter policy by setting the `KMP_AFFINITY` environment variable. The scatter policy distributes threads on a node as evenly as possible. This determines the number of threads running on each socket and in turn determines cache performance and node power.

Power clamping for PP0 and DRAM was disabled by default. We run all experiments with power clamping on the PKG domain with a single clamping window and the shortest possible time window (0.000977 seconds). Thus, we avoid any potential power spikes that might result when using larger time windows. We use four PKG power caps: 51 W; 65 W; 80 W; and 95 W. We run each configuration at least three times to eliminate noise. We disable Turbo Boost when power capping. In addition, we assumed that unused nodes in the cluster took zero power.

We also run experiments with turbo enabled without using any RAPL-enforced power bounds. A cap of 115 W in our results represents this *turbo mode*. 115 W corresponds to the thermal limit on the PKG and, when we use turbo mode, this thermal limit becomes our power cap by default.

Our experiments use a hybrid MPI/OpenMP model. Hybrid models have low intra-node communication overhead and are more flexible in terms of configurations that we can test. Also, future architectures are likely to have many integrated cores on a single chip (for instance, Intel's MIC [14]). Because MPI processes have significant memory and communication overhead, the hybrid model is more likely than a flat MPI model.

HPC Applications.

We used four HPC applications: SPhot [1] from the ASC Purple suite [20] and BT-MZ, SP-MZ, and LU-MZ from the NAS suite [3]. SPhot is a 2D photon transport code that uses a Monte Carlo approach to solve the Boltzmann transport equation by mimicking the behavior of photons as they are born in hot matter and move through different materials. SPhot is a CPU-bound, embarrassingly parallel application. For our multiple-node experiments, Nruns was set to 8192. For the single-node experiments, Nruns was set to 1024. The NAS Multi-zone parallel benchmarks (NAS-MZ) are derived from Computational Fluid Dynamics (CFD) applications and are designed to evaluate the hybrid model. We use all three NAS-MZ benchmarks: Block Tri-diagonal solver, or BT-MZ; Scalar Penta-diagonal solver, or SP-MZ; and Lower-Upper Gauss-Seidel solver, or LU-MZ. We use the Class C inputs.

Synthetic Benchmarks.

In order to cover the extreme cases in the application space, we developed four MPI/OpenMP synthetic benchmarks. These tests are (1) CPU-bound and scalable (SC); (2) CPU-bound and not scalable (NSC); (3) Memory-bound and scalable (SM); (4) Memory-bound and not scalable (NSM). The CPU-bound benchmarks run a simple spin loop, and the Memory-bound benchmarks do a vector copy in reverse order. We control scalability by adding communication using `MPI_Alltoall()` (i.e., fewer calls to `MPI_Alltoall()` means better scalability).

5. BASELINE POWER RESULTS

We first present details on the effect of power on our applications to understand the impact of power limitations. We run our benchmarks on one node, varying the core count from 4 to 16, to study application characteristics and their impact on configurations.

Figure 1 shows the average PKG and DRAM power measured across the two sockets of the node for our benchmarks, at 4 and 16 cores and in turbo mode. We observe that some applications are more memory-intensive than others and hence consume more DRAM power. Examples of these are BT-MZ, SP-MZ, LU-MZ, and SM. At 16 cores per node, SP-MZ used 10.3% of its socket power for memory. Similarly, BT-MZ and LU-MZ used about 7-8% of their socket power for memory. SPhot, on the other hand, is relatively CPU intensive. We also observe that moving from 4 to 16

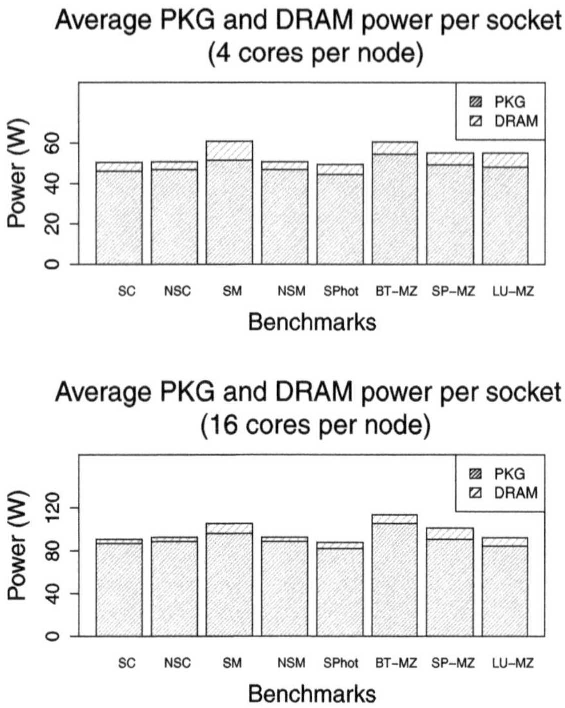

Figure 1: Average PKG and DRAM power consumption per socket

cores affects PKG power more than DRAM power. For instance, SPhot used 44.6 W of PKG power at 4 cores and 82.1 W of PKG power at 16 cores; DRAM power increased from 4.9 W to 5.7 W. Similarly, for BT-MZ, PKG power increased by 93% from 54.5 W to 105.7 W, but DRAM power only increased by 31%.

Figure 1 also shows that applications do not always use their allocated power. While the thermal limit on the PKG in turbo mode is 115 W, none of the applications actually use this much power, even when using all 16 cores. Most applications need between 80 and 90 W, except for BT-MZ, which uses nearly 106 W when running 16 cores. This important observation calls for efficient power allocation.

Figure 2 shows the impact of varying the PKG power bound on the node on application performance at 4 and 16 cores per node for SPhot and SP-MZ. At 4 cores per node, none of the applications use more than 51 W of PKG power. Thus, at all power bounds except 115 W, the highest non-turbo frequency (2.6 GHz) can be chosen. The only way to achieve a higher frequency and improve application performance is to engage Turbo. Despite identical (non-Turbo) frequencies across different power bounds, we observe a slight slowdown in performance of about 1-2% for our applications from 51 W to 100 W with 4 cores per node. As we run each experiment at least three times to eliminate noise, overhead introduced by Intel's RAPL algorithm (which is different at different power bounds) may cause this slowdown. At 16 cores per node, application performance improves with an increase in power, as the impact of DVFS and other undocumented RAPL techniques is seen. Our

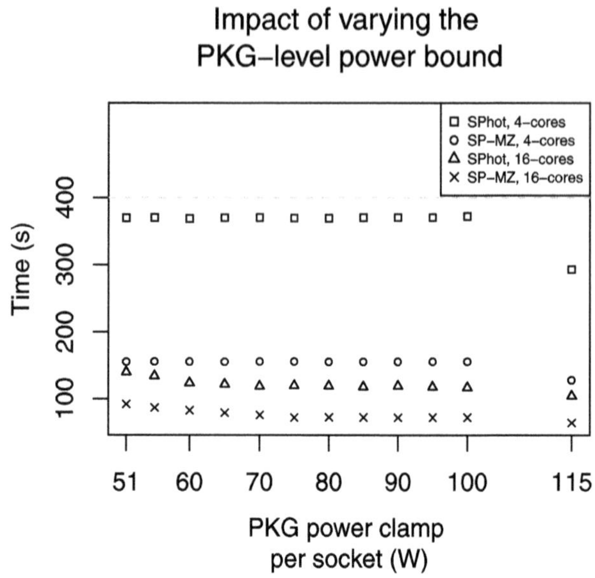

Figure 2: Impact of varying the PKG power clamp on execution time.

applications benefit from higher power up to about 85 W. Performance improved by 21.3% for SP-MZ and by 17.1% for SPhot. In turbo mode (115 W), all applications perform significantly better as they run at a higher CPU frequency. Performance for SPhot improved more than SP-MZ, primarily because SPhot is CPU-bound and less memory intensive.

Next, we run single-node and multiple-node experiments with Turbo Boost to determine its effect on configurations. We collect samples every second with *librapl* and measure the frequency ratio by reading the `APERF` and `MPERF` MSRs [16]. Figure 3 shows our results on a single-node with varying core count on our CPU-bound, scalable synthetic benchmark. We multiply the median frequency ratio value from the samples with the maximum non-turbo frequency (2.6 GHz) to determine the effective turbo frequency. Frequency ratios vary little across our samples. Our results indicate that the effective turbo frequency depends on the number of active cores. Intel documentation [15] confirms this observation and also mentions that the turbo frequency varies with temperature. We run our experiments at LLNL, where the machine room temperature was fairly constant over time and do not encounter any variation in the turbo frequency that could be attributed to temperature.

We also run multiple-node experiments with Turbo Boost enabled and collect frequency samples every second with *librapl*. In these experiments, we use the same number of cores per node. All nodes reach the same turbo frequency, which is stable throughout the application's execution. All nodes engage in turbo mode similarly.

Summary.

Power utilization varies between applications and power affects them differently. Thus, multiple-node overprovisioning could improve performance.

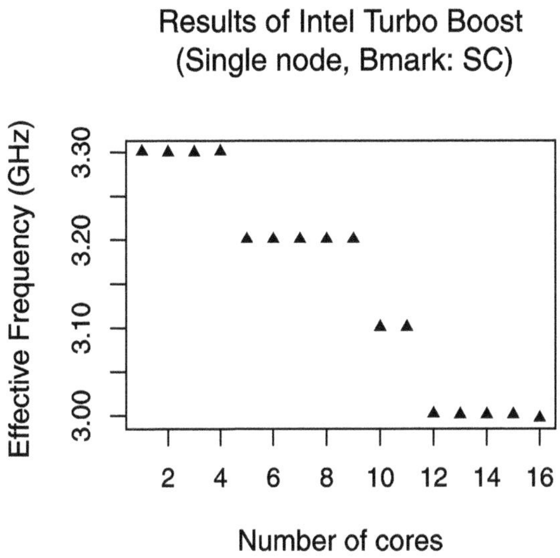

Figure 3: Turbo Boost on a single node with the CPU-bound, scalable benchmark.

6. MULTIPLE NODE OVERPROVISIONING

This section presents and analyzes multiple-node results of the HPC applications and synthetic benchmarks that we listed in Section 4. Because we could not feasibly run every possible configuration and because *rzmerl* has a 32-node limit per job, we run experiments with 8 to 32 nodes and 4 to 16 cores per node, in increments of 2. For the scope of this paper, we assume uniform power allocation per node and that the applications are perfectly load-balanced.

6.1 Configurations

As discussed in Section 2, we define a configuration as: (1) a value for number of nodes, n, (2) a value for number of cores per node, c, and (3) power allocated per node, p, in Watts. We denote a configuration as $(n \times c, p)$. Because power capping is unavailable on DRAM and PP0, we use p to represent the PKG power that is allocated to the node. We measure DRAM power along with PKG power, and our results report their sum on each socket across all nodes when we report total power.

For comparison purposes, we define four special configurations: *packed-max*; *packed-min*; *spread-max*; and *spread-min*. The term *packed* denotes that a configuration uses all cores on one node before using an additional node, while *spread* denotes that processes are spread as evenly as possible across all nodes, with 4 being the fewest cores per node used. When we append *max* is appended, we use the maximum power (i.e., turbo mode) on each node, while *min* means we use the minimum power (i.e., clamp at 51 Watts). In all four special configurations, we continue to add cores and/or nodes until we reach the global power bound (or until we cannot add more nodes).

6.2 Results

We run our benchmarks on multiple nodes under various overprovisioned scenarios. Our cluster of 32 nodes consumed about 6350 W of power when running all cores as fast as possible. We investigate four overprovisioned scenarios; in each we have 32 nodes at our disposal, but power limits of 2500 W, 3000 W, 3500 W, and 4000 W. For comparison purposes, we also look at the case with unlimited power.

Figure 4 displays the potential speedup that overprovisioning can provide. This graph compares the best performance of any configuration that is under the respective power bound, compared to using *packed-max* (which is worst-case provisioning). If no bar exists then *packed-max* is optimal.

The average speedup of BT-MZ, LU-MZ, SP-MZ, and SPhot when using overprovisioning compared to worst-case provisioning is 73.8%, 55.6%, 67.2%, and 50.9% for a 2500 W, 3000 W, 3500 W, and 4000 W bound, respectively. Clearly, overprovisioning can lead to large performance improvements. For four cases, using a configuration other than *packed-max* is best even with unlimited power; this is due to memory contention that degrades performance when using all cores.

Overprovisioning essentially allows applications to utilize the machine as a reconfigurable architecture, which allows for better performance than worst-case provisioning. For example, consider the global power bound of 3500 W. Here, SP-MZ executes 2.49 times faster when using the optimal configuration of $(26 \times 12, 80)$ than the *packed-max* configuration associated with worst-case provisioning, $(20 \times 16, 115)$. With worst-case provisioning, the facility would only have 20 nodes. We study the *potential* speedup that overprovisioning can support. We leave the question of *how* to determine configurations that realize this speedup for future work.

6.2.1 Comparing Different Configurations

Figure 5 (page seven) shows in-depth results for three of our power bounds (2500 W, 3500 W, and unlimited) for all applications. The y-axis represents performance of the four canonical configurations, normalized to the performance of the optimal configuration under the global power bound (higher is better). The x-axis lists our eight benchmarks. Each figure includes a table that provides the actual configurations. The figure also contains the total power consumed (packages and memory power) and the time taken.

First, the figure shows some applications perform best using *packed* configurations compared to the *spread* configurations and that execution time can vary substantially between *packed* and *spread* configurations. This trend can be observed across all the benchmarks as well as power bounds. For example, at a global power bound of 2500 W, the *spread-min* configuration for SPhot runs 64.5% slower than *packed-min*. For SP-MZ at the same power bound, the *spread-max* configuration runs 2.16 times faster than the corresponding *packed-max* configuration. For SC, the *spread-min* runs more than twice as slow when compared to the *packed-min* configuration. In addition, for NSC, *spread-max* runs 2.36 times slower than *packed-max*.

The difference between the *packed-max* and *packed-min* configurations can also be significant. For example, with SPhot the *packed-max* configuration runs 29.8% slower than *packed-min* at 2500 W because the *packed-min* configuration utilizes more nodes and thus more total cores at lower power per node, as can be seen from the corresponding table. For SP-MZ and BT-MZ, the execution time difference between the *spread-max* and *spread-min* configurations is negligible. However, for LU-MZ this difference is 8% under a power

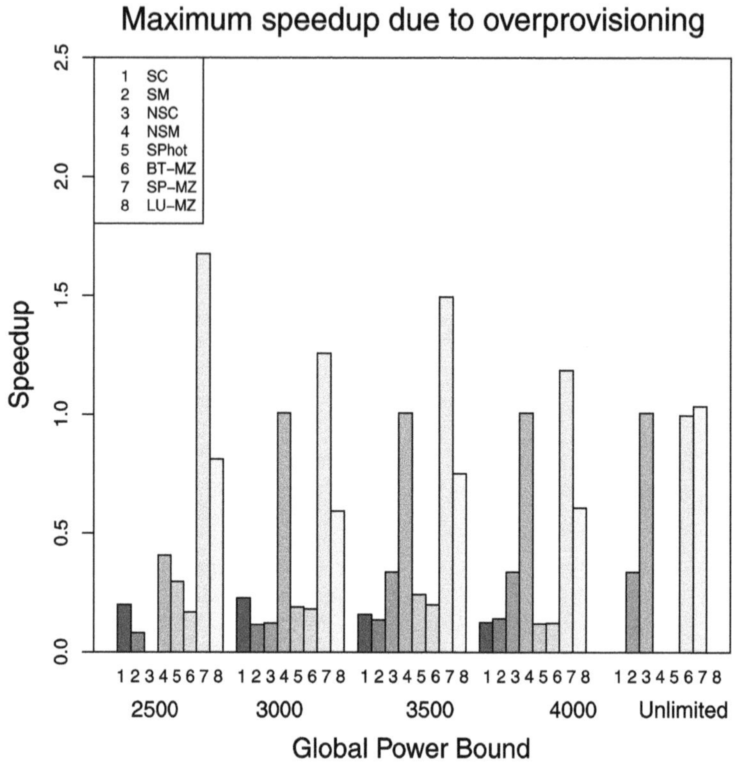

Figure 4: Speedup due to overprovisioning

bound of 2500 W and 16% under a power bound of 3500 W. When we vary the power bound, the execution time difference as well as the trend followed by the canonical and optimal configurations varies. At each global power bound, the configurations associated with the same canonical form can be different with an increase in the nodes and cores. For example, with SP-MZ *packed-max* is $(12 \times 16, 115)$ at 2500 W and $(20 \times 16, 115)$ at 3500 W.

Second, the best configuration is not always one of *packed-max*, *packed-min*, *spread-max*, or *spread-min*. For example, at 2500 W, BT-MZ, SP-MZ, LU-MZ and NSM have an optimal configuration that is different than the four canonical configurations. As the corresponding table shows, the optimal configuration for SP-MZ was $(22\times 8, 80)$, which was 22% faster than the fastest canonical configuration, $(28 \times 4, 51)$. Running fewer nodes at higher power per node performs better than running more nodes at lower power per node in this case, as opposed to SPhot.

Third, the best configuration for an application depends on the particular global power bound. For instance, at a power bound of 2500 W, the best configuration for SP-MZ is $(22 \times 8, 80)$. On the other hand, when the power bound is 3500 W, it is $(26 \times 12, 80)$—one expects more nodes with a higher power bound, but the number of cores per node is different.

Application characteristics determine whether better execution times result from using more nodes, with fewer cores per node and at lower power; or fewer nodes, with more cores per node, and at a higher power. For instance, SPhot and BT-MZ always perform better when running more cores per node, and fewer nodes at higher power (i.e., *packed*), primarily because they are more CPU intensive than SP-MZ and LU-MZ. The *spread* configurations perform better for SP-MZ and LU-MZ because they are more memory intensive, and using more cores per node for such applications causes memory contention. For example, at 2500 W and 3500 W, the *spread* configurations are close to optimal for LU-MZ. Application scalability also plays an important role in determining the right configuration. SP-MZ, LU-MZ, NSC, and NSM have an optimal configuration that is neither *packed* nor *spread*, but somewhere in between because running as few as 4 cores per node and as many nodes as possible under the power bound increases communication.

Importantly, blindly choosing the configuration that takes the maximum amount of power under the enforced global power bound is in some cases a bad decision. For example, the optimal configuration for SPhot at 2500 W is not the one that takes the maximum amount of power under the 2500 W limit. Another example of this is LU-MZ at 6500 W. Even when the configuration with highest power leads to best performance, Figure 5 shows that competing configurations that take slightly less power (less than 0.1% of the power associated with the optimal configuration) are sometimes significantly worse in performance (for example, SP-MZ at 3500 W). A variation in power of 0.1% could result from experimental variance.

6.2.2 Using Fewer Cores

Cases exist in which using *fewer* total cores results in better execution time. This result is not unexpected, since sim-

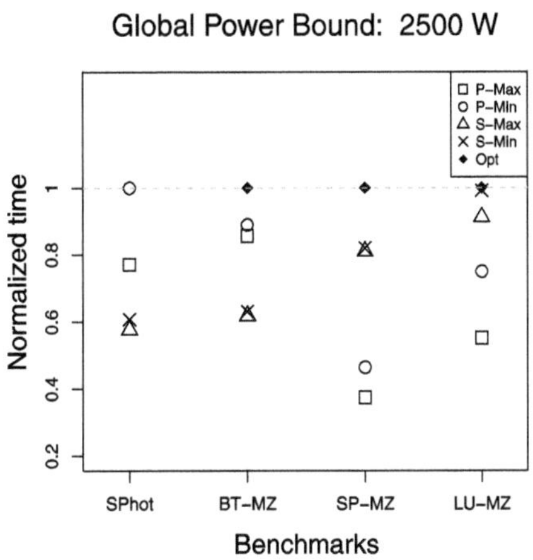

Bmark	Configuration $(n \times c, p)$	Total Power (W)	Time (s)
SPhot	$(12 \times 16, 115)$	2181.29	74.27
	$(22 \times 16, 51)$	2388.51	57.24
	$(24 \times 4, 115)$	2459.74	99.18
	$(32 \times 4, 51)$	2472.33	94.19
	$(22 \times 16, 51)$	2388.51	57.24
SP-MZ	$(12 \times 16, 115)$	1974.66	13.88
	$(20 \times 16, 51)$	2179.92	11.16
	$(22 \times 4, 115)$	2449.71	6.40
	$(28 \times 4, 51)$	2337.83	6.34
	$(22 \times 8, 80)$	2452.81	5.19
LU-MZ	$(12 \times 16, 115)$	2227.95	25.29
	$(20 \times 16, 51)$	2350.36	18.61
	$(22 \times 4, 115)$	2409.92	15.31
	$(28 \times 4, 51)$	2383.34	14.08
	$(22 \times 8, 80)$	2412.42	13.95

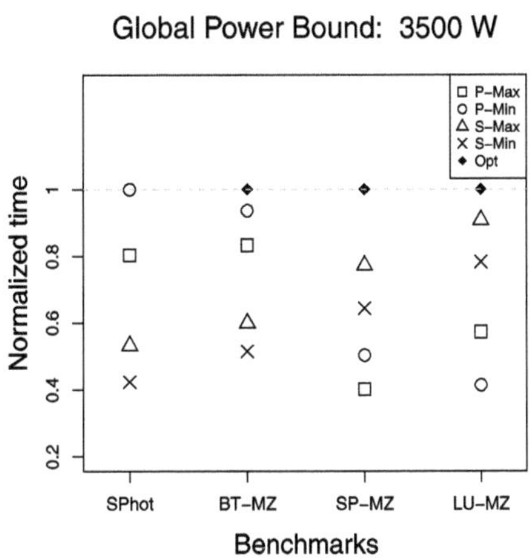

Bmark	Configuration $(n \times c, p)$	Total Power (W)	Time (s)
SPhot	$(18 \times 16, 115)$	3263.74	49.52
	$(32 \times 16, 51)$	3477.62	39.81
	$(32 \times 4, 115)$	3252.82	74.79
	$(32 \times 4, 51)$	2472.33	94.19
	$(32 \times 16, 51)$	3477.62	39.81
SP-MZ	$(20 \times 16, 115)$	3240.22	9.10
	$(32 \times 16, 51)$	3494.16	7.26
	$(32 \times 4, 115)$	3431.63	4.72
	$(32 \times 4, 51)$	2647.40	5.67
	$(26 \times 12, 80)$	3497.16	3.65
LU-MZ	$(18 \times 16, 115)$	3308.11	16.46
	$(30 \times 16, 51)$	3379.74	22.78
	$(32 \times 4, 115)$	3492.11	10.37
	$(32 \times 4, 51)$	2730.48	12.03
	$(32 \times 8, 95)$	3497.34	9.42

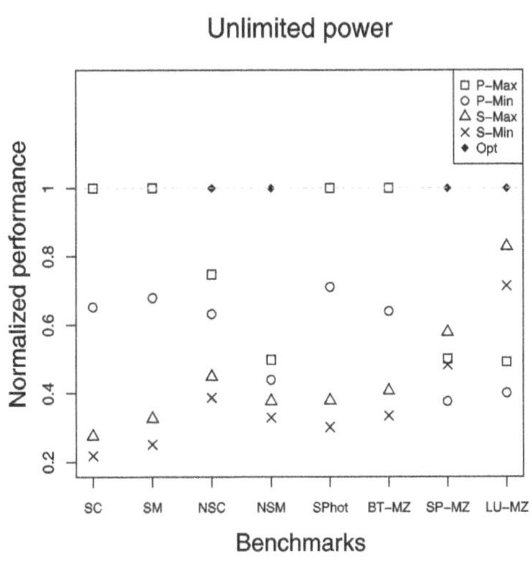

Bmark	Configuration $(n \times c, p)$	Total Power (W)	Time (s)
SPhot	$(32 \times 16, 115)$	5768.41	28.30
	$(32 \times 16, 51)$	3477.62	39.81
	$(32 \times 4, 115)$	3252.82	74.79
	$(32 \times 4, 51)$	2472.33	94.19
	$(32 \times 16, 115)$	5768.41	28.30
SP-MZ	$(32 \times 16, 115)$	4978.38	5.45
	$(32 \times 16, 51)$	3494.16	7.26
	$(32 \times 4, 115)$	3431.63	4.72
	$(32 \times 4, 51)$	2647.40	5.67
	$(32 \times 14, 115)$	5590.13	2.73
LU-MZ	$(32 \times 16, 115)$	5487.03	17.48
	$(32 \times 16, 51)$	3608.65	21.43
	$(32 \times 4, 115)$	3492.11	10.37
	$(32 \times 4, 51)$	2730.48	12.03
	$(32 \times 8, 115)$	4458.88	8.59

Figure 5: Multiple node experiments at a global power bound of 2500 W (top), 3500 W (middle) and unlimited (bottom). The left-hand side shows normalized performance (to the optimal) per benchmark, and the right-hand side shows the configuration and execution time for each point for SPhot, SP-MZ and LU-MZ. The last (shaded) row shows the optimal configuration.

ilar results have been shown for worst-case provisioning [9]. For example, as the table corresponding to unlimited power shows, both SP-MZ and LU-MZ perform better with fewer total cores with the same PKG-level power bound. With SP-MZ, the *spread-max* configuration, $(32 \times 4, 115)$ is about 15% faster than the *packed-max*, $(32 \times 16, 115)$ (which runs four times as many cores). Two reasons lead to this behavior: first, in turbo mode, running fewer cores per node results in a higher effective turbo frequency; and, second, memory contention at 16 cores causes performance degradation. However, the optimal configuration is $(32 \times 14, 115)$, which uses more total cores than the *spread-max* configuration, but fewer cores per node than the *packed-max* configuration. The result is significantly better memory performance. The optimal configuration runs 72% faster than the fastest canonical one, which cannot be attributed to turbo mode because having 14 or 16 active cores per node results in the same effective turbo frequency.

In the case of LU-MZ, though, the effect of turbo mode as well as reduced memory contention can be seen more prominently. The optimal configuration, $(32 \times 8, 115)$ runs more than twice as fast as the *packed-max*, and 17% faster than the fastest canonical configuration, *spread-max*.

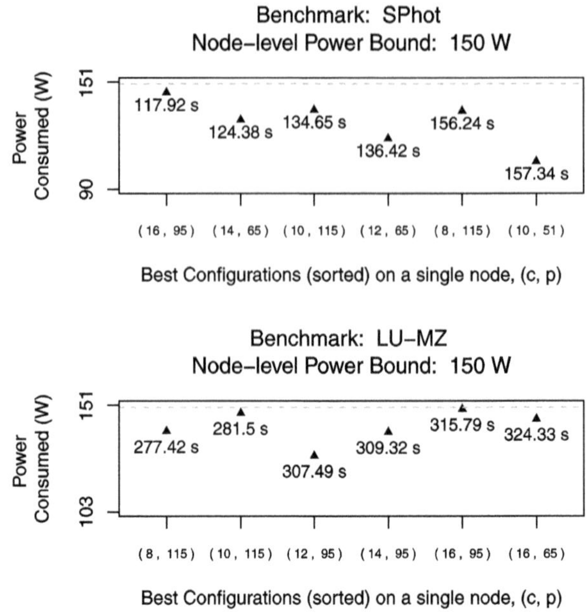

Figure 6: Configurations for SPhot and LU-MZ on a single node.

7. RELATED WORK

To the best of our knowledge, our work is the first study of HPC on power-constrained clusters and the first to explore optimal configurations under power bounds in the context of overprovisioned systems. Little work exists on HPC under a power bound. Rountree et al. [28] were the first to explore the idea using a dynamic, hardware-enforced power-bound in the HPC environment and to propose RAPL as an alternative to DVFS. They also examined power variation across processors and demonstrated that variation in processor power translates to variation in processor performance under a power bound. Springer et al. [32] studied computing under an energy bound for HPC applications, but this older work used DVFS instead of power clamping; they also used only eight single-core nodes and thereby avoided any scaling issues due to limited on-node memory bandwidth. Femal and Freeh [10] developed a technique for safe overprovisioning, but they focused on sets of CGI programs executed by web servers in data centers. In contrast, our work is focused on improving the performance of a single HPC program that has access to the entire cluster.

Curtis-Maury introduced Dynamic Concurrency Throttling, which controls the number of active threads that execute parallel regions to optimize for power and performance dynamically [7–9]. Li et al. [21] further extended this work to hybrid programming models. While these teams looked at configurations for general power minimization, they did not consider and study the impact of hardware-enforced or system-level power bounds on configurations.

Prior work has explored saving power/energy under a time bound in both the HPC and real-time communities. In the HPC arena, work has used linear programming to find near-optimal energy savings with zero time increase [29] as well as a run-time system that implements these ideas [27]. In the real-time community, several have used mixed integer linear programming to solve the DVFS scheduling problem [17,30, 33,34] but are limited to a single processor. Several other real-time approaches save energy [24–26,36,37].

Additionally, there also is work in DVFS to trade execution time for lower power/energy [6,13] as well as several analytic models to predict or to understand energy consumption in the context of scalability [12,22,31]. There are several other DVFS algorithms, including thrifty barriers [23], CPUMiser [12], and Jitter [18].

Overall, while significant work exists on optimizing or minimizing power, our work is the first to study the impact of power bounds, not only within a node, but also at larger-scale installations. Thus, we provide a first peek into the behavior of future generations of supercomputing systems, where such a scenario will be reality.

8. FUTURE WORK

Future work will proceed in multiple directions. One avenue is to investigate nonuniformity in power allocation. In this paper we studied *uniform* overprovisioned supercomputing. That is, while we showed that using more nodes with reduced power often leads to better performance, each node has a uniform configuration. While common for today's HPC applications, future applications are expected to be more heterogeneous.

In particular, assigning nonuniform power per node may improve performance, especially if the application exhibits load imbalance. However, a naive power assignment to each node (e.g., proportional increase in power based on amount of work) may produce poor results. For example, consider results on a single node in Figure 6. For SPhot, using more cores at lower power is profitable. On the other hand, for LU-MZ, running fewer cores at higher power is better.

Clearly, if we allocate power to nodes in a nonuniform manner, we should understand how power bounds impact performance through a node-level power-performance model.

In past work we have used nonuniform DVFS settings to save energy with negligible performance loss [27].

A second avenue will develop models to predict the optimal configuration given a system-level power-constraint and a strongly-scaled application. We envision involve multiple steps, including (1) developing a single-node model to predict the optimal number of cores and power allocation for the components within a node (packages and memory subsystem) and (2) a model to allocate inter-node power based on the critical path of the application and its load imbalance.

A third avenue is to study the impact of using dynamic overclocking techniques such as Turbo Boost. We will experiment with clamping DRAM power and explore how best to utilize clamping in the PKG domain. RAPL is one of the technologies that will eventually enable us to schedule power more intelligently on a power-constrained cluster.

9. CONCLUSION

In this paper we identified an emerging problem in the HPC arena: how to leverage overprovisioning in HPC installations. With power becoming a first order design constraint on our road to exascale, such overprovisioned systems will be commonplace, i.e., we will no longer be able to fully power all nodes all the time. In such a scenario, we need to understand how we can configure our applications to best exploit the overall system while adhering to a global power bound.

Our experiments show that the optimal configuration under a cluster power bound for a strongly-scaled HPC application performs much better than the configuration corresponding to the naive, worst-case provisioned scenario. We also presented some early results on package power clamping and discussed its impact on application performance as well as on configurations. Overall, our experiments show that we can obtain substantial application speedup when carefully exploiting overprovisioned systems—over 50% on average.

10. ACKNOWLEDGEMENTS

We would like to extend our thanks to Livermore Computing and their support staff for providing us with the appropriate permissions required to access the MSRs. This material is based upon work supported by the National Science Foundation under Grant No. 1216829. Part of this work was performed under the auspices of the U.S. Department of Energy by Lawrence Livermore National Laboratory under Contract DE-AC52-07NA27344 (LLNL-CONF-634672).

11. REFERENCES

[1] SPhot- Monte Carlo Transport Code, Lawrence Livermore National Laboratory.

[2] Ucsd center for dark silicon. `http://darksilicon.org/`.

[3] NASA Advanced Supercomputing Division, NAS Parallel Benchmark Suite v3.3, 2006.

[4] Top500 Supercomputer Sites, November 2012.

[5] AMD. AMD Turbo CORE Technology.

[6] K. W. Cameron, X. Feng, and R. Ge. Performance-constrained distributed DVS scheduling for scientific applications on power-aware clusters. In *Supercomputing*, Seattle, Washington, November 2005.

[7] Matthew Curtis-Maury, Filip Blagojevic, Christos D. Antonopoulos, and Dimitrios S. Nikolopoulos. Prediction-based power-performance adaptation of multithreaded scientific codes. *IEEE Trans. Parallel Distrib. Syst.*, 19(10):1396–1410, October 2008.

[8] Matthew Curtis-Maury, James Dzierwa, Christos D. Antonopoulos, and Dimitrios S. Nikolopoulos. Online power-performance adaptation of multithreaded programs using hardware event-based prediction. In *International Conference on Supercomputing*, New York, NY, USA, 2006. ACM.

[9] Matthew Curtis-Maury, Ankur Shah, Filip Blagojevic, Dimitrios S. Nikolopoulos, Bronis R. de Supinski, and Martin Schulz. Prediction models for multi-dimensional power-performance optimization on many cores. In *International Conference on Parallel Architectures and Compilation techniques*, New York, NY, USA, 2008. ACM.

[10] Mark E. Femal and Vincent W. Freeh. Safe overprovisioning: using power limits to increase aggregate throughput. In *International Conference on Power-Aware Computer Systems*, Dec 2005.

[11] Wu-Chun Feng and Kirk W. Cameron. The Green500 list: Encouraging sustainable supercomputing. *IEEE Computer*, 40(12):50–55, 2007.

[12] R. Ge, X. Feng, W. Feng, and K. W. Cameron. CPU Miser: A performance-directed, run-time system for power-aware clusters. In *International Conference on Parallel Processing*, Xi'An, China, 2007.

[13] Chung-Hsing Hsu and Wu-Chun Feng. A power-aware run-time system for high-performance computing. In *Supercomputing*, November 2005.

[14] Intel. Intel Many Integrated Core Architecture.

[15] Intel. Intel Turbo Boost Technology 2.0.

[16] Intel. Intel-64 and IA-32 Architectures Software Developer's Manual, Volumes 3A and 3B: System Programming Guide, 2011.

[17] Tohru Ishihara and Hiroto Yasuura. Voltage scheduling problem for dynamically variable voltage processors. In *International Symposium on Low power Electronics and Design*, pages 197–202, 1998.

[18] Nandani Kappiah, Vincent W. Freeh, and David K. Lowenthal. Just in time dynamic voltage scaling: Exploiting inter-node slack to save energy in MPI programs. In *Supercomputing*, November 2005.

[19] Rakesh Kumar, Dean M. Tullsen, Norman P. Jouppi, and Parthasarathy Ranganathan. Heterogeneous chip multiprocessors. *IEEE Computer*, 38(11):32–38, Nov 2005.

[20] Lawrence Livermore National Laboratory. The ASCI Purple benchmark codes. `http://www.llnl.gov/asci/purple/benchmarks/limited/code_list.html`.

[21] Dong Li, Bronis R. de Supinski, Martin Schulz, Dimitrios S. Nikolopoulos, and Kirk W. Cameron. Strategies for energy efficient resource management of hybrid programming models. *IEEE Transaction on Parallel and Distributed Systems*, 2012.

[22] Jian Li and José F. Martìnez. Dynamic power-performance adaptation of parallel computation on chip multiprocessors. In *12th International Symposium on High-Performance Computer Architecture*, Austin, Texas, February 2006.

[23] Jian Li, José F. Martínez, and Michael C. Huang. The thrifty barrier: Energy-aware synchronization in shared-memory multiprocessors. In *10th International Symposium on High Performance Computer Architecture*, Madrid, Spain, February 2004.

[24] Bren Mochocki, Xiaobo Sharon Hu, and Gang Quan. A realistic variable voltage scheduling model for real-time applications. In *Proceedings of the 2002 IEEE/ACM International Conference on Computer-Aided Design*, 2002.

[25] Bren Mochocki, Xiaobo Sharon Hu, and Gang Quan. Practical on-line DVS scheduling for fixed-priority real-time systems. In *11th IEEE Real Time and Embedded Technology and Applications Symposium*, 2005.

[26] M. Angels Moncusí, Alex Arenas, and Jesus Labarta. Energy aware EDF scheduling in distributed hard real time systems. In *Real-Time Systems Symposium*, December 2003.

[27] B. Rountree, D. Lowenthal, B.R. de Supinski, M. Schulz, V. Freeh, and T. Bletch. Adagio: Making DVS Practical for Complex HPC Applications. In *International Conference on Supercomputing*, June 2009.

[28] Barry Rountree, Dong H. Ahn, Bronis R. de Supinski, David K. Lowenthal, and Martin Schulz. Beyond DVFS: A First Look at Performance under a Hardware-Enforced Power Bound. In *IPDPS Workshops*, pages 947–953. IEEE Computer Society, 2012.

[29] Barry Rountree, David K. Lowenthal, Shelby Funk, Vincent W. Freeh, Bronis de Supinski, and Martin Schulz. Bounding energy consumption in large-scale MPI programs. In *Supercomputing*, November 2007.

[30] H. Saputra, M. Kandemir, N. Vijaykrishnan, M.J. Irwin, J.S. Hu, C.-H. Hsu, and U. Kremer. Energy-conscious compilation based on voltage scaling. In *Joint Conference on Languages, Compilers and Tools for Embedded Systems*, 2002.

[31] Rob Springer, David K. Lowenthal, Barry Rountree, and Vincent W. Freeh. Minimizing execution time in MPI programs on an energy-constrained, power-scalable cluster. In *ACM Symposium on Principles and Practice of Parallel Programming*, March 2006.

[32] Robert C. Springer IV, David K. Lowenthal, Barry Rountree, and Vincent W. Freeh. Minimizing execution time in MPI programs on an energy-constrained, power-scalable cluster. In *ACM Symposium on Principles and Practice of Parallel Programming*, March 2006.

[33] Vishnu Swaminathan and Krishnendu Chakrabarty. Investigating the effect of voltage-switching on low-energy task scheduling in hard real-time systems. In *Asia South Pacific Design Automation Conference*, January 2001.

[34] Vishnu Swaminathan and Krshnendu Chakrabarty. Real-time task scheduling for energy-aware embedded systems. In *IEEE Real-Time Systems Symposium*, November 2000.

[35] Ganesh Venkatesh, Jack Sampson, Nathan Goulding, Saturnino Garcia, Vladyslav Bryksin, Jose Lugo-Martinez, Steven Swanson, and Michael Bedford Taylor. Conservation cores: reducing the energy of mature computations. In *ASPLOS*, 2010.

[36] Yumin Zhang, Xiaobo Sharon Hu, and Danny Z. Chen. Task scheduling voltage selection for energy minimization. In *Proceedings of the 39th annual Design Automation Conference*, 2002.

[37] Dakai Zhu, Rami Melhem, and Bruce R. Childers. Scheduling with dynamic voltage/speed adjustment using slack reclamation in multi-processor real-time systems. *IEEE Transactions on Parallel and Distributed Systems*, 2003.

The Power 775 Architecture at Scale

Ramakrishnan Rajamony, Mark W. Stephenson, Evan Speight
rajamony@us.ibm.com, mstephen@us.ibm.com, speight@us.ibm.com
IBM Research, 11501 Burnet Road, Austin, TX, USA

ABSTRACT

We describe the IBM Power 775, a supercomputing system that was designed to provide high performance at very large scales. The system recently attained world record performance numbers for three important, communication-heavy supercomputing benchmarks: RandomAccess, PTRANS, and Global FFT. At the heart of the Power 775's performance is the "hub module", which is a high-radix router containing forty-seven copper and optical links with a switching capacity of over 1.1 Tbyte/second. This level of bandwidth is unprecedented for typical systems of the scale we discuss in this paper. As a result, we were forced to develop a complete software stack to fully leverage the communication capabilities of the system. In this paper we evaluate the Power 775 server at scales up to 2 Petaflops (63,360 POWER7 cores), discuss hardware and software tradeoffs considered during the design process, and finally present some lessons learned.

Categories and Subject Descriptors: C.4 [Computer Systems Organization]: Performance of Systems

General Terms: Performance, Design, Experimentation

Keywords: Design studies; Performance attributes; Measurement techniques

1. INTRODUCTION

The design of the Power 775 (henceforth referred to as P775) began in 2001 as part of the DARPA PERCS program [22], and centered around the premise that high-performance communication would be the significant challenge for large-scale computing systems.

It is well known that several real-world analytics and supercomputing problems are communications bound. These problems spend more time moving data than they do operating on data. Indeed, we can see this effect today even on relatively small GPU systems with high-bandwidth connections to memory [17]. The problem of operand delivery is only exacerbated as we increase system size.

Consider an operation as conceptually simple as matrix transposition on which many algorithms rely. A parallel implementation of transpose may require a large fraction of the system to communicate, including potentially requiring every process to communicate with every other process. This is clearly a situation that becomes more expensive as the number of processes increases, and the maximum spatial distance between any two processes increases.

Much of the design effort for the P775 focused on the *hub module*, which is the heart of the system's communication fabric. The hub module is a high-radix router that switches data between sixteen 10 Gbyte/s optical links, twenty-four 5 Gbyte/s optical links, and seven 24 Gbyte/s copper links, with each link delivering the stated capacity in each direction. The hub chip switches *raw* data in excess of 1.1 Tbyte/second.

As demonstrated in November 2012, the P775 is over 3× faster than its nearest competitor in parallel matrix transposition, and over 4× faster on RandomAccess, a global memory performance benchmark [3]. On Global FFT, the P775 is only 1.6× worse than the K computer while being 5.5× smaller in peak capacity. These differences are even starker when the comparison is normalized and done on a per unit FLOP basis.

In this paper we describe the design of the P775 and evaluate it on three communication-heavy HPCC benchmarks [3] commonly used to gauge supercomputers. More specifically, we make the following contributions:

- We evaluate the P775 server "at scale" on workloads that traditionally perform poorly. This is the first paper to evaluate the P775 system at large scales.
- We describe how we attained world record performances for the communication heavy HPCC benchmarks: RandomAccess, PTRANS, and Global FFT.
- We learned many lessons through the course of this decade-long project. Of particular importance to this community, we describe system architectural features that we found useful, that we found detrimental, and that we wished we had.

The next section walks the reader through the system level design, starting with the microarchitecture. We also describe the compute node, other building blocks, and culminate with a description of an at-scale P775 server. Section 3 describes the communication-heavy, high-performance-computing workloads we use to analyze the P775, and we perform the analysis in Section 4. Section 5 is a retrospective discussion of lessons learned. We review related work in Section 6, and finally, Section 7 concludes the paper.

ICS'13, June 10–14, 2013, Eugene, Oregon, USA.

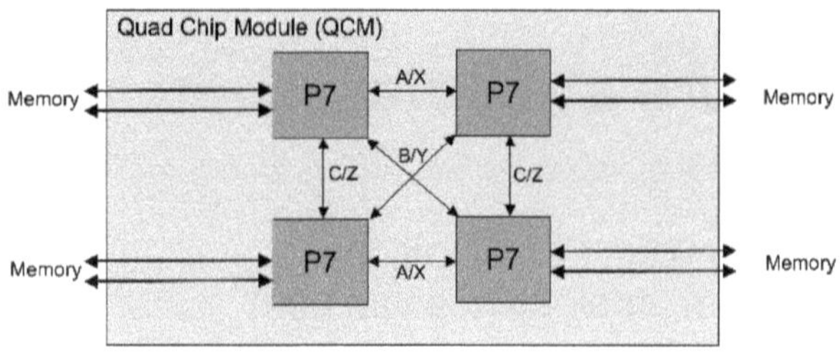

Figure 1: The XYZABC links in a QCM.

2. THE ARCHITECTURE

This section provides a bottom-up view of the system architecture. We start by describing the main compute engine of the P775, the POWER7 chip. Then we introduce the *compute node*, which is a collection of tightly interconnected POWER7s and a *hub chip*. We finally describe the P775's interconnection topology and routing schemes.

The entire system, including the processors, memories, and hub chips, is water cooled. Thermal waste dissipated by purified water circulating over the system components is exchanged with the facility chilled water through a set of four water conditioning units at the bottom of each rack.

2.1 The POWER7

The POWER7 chip is the main compute engine of the P775. The POWER7 processor has been thoroughly described elsewhere [7, 15, 16], so we only discuss some of its most pertinent features here. The POWER7 chip has eight cores and each core has an independent set of inclusive L1, L2, and L3 caches [1]. The cores are superscalar, highly speculative, and support up to 4-way simultaneous multithreading (SMT). The microarchitecture also implements a set of integer and floating point SIMD instructions, referred to as VSX (Vector Scalar eXtension). Using VSX, each core can process up to eight double precision floating point operations per cycle. There are two memory controllers in every POWER7 chip, which connect through eight memory channels to multi-ported DDR3 1333MHz DIMMs. The POWER7 hardware prefetchers maintain enough state to prefetch up to twelve concurrent memory streams.

2.2 The Compute Node

With the computational building block of the P775 in place, we can discuss the *compute node*, which contains a *Quad Chip Module* (QCM) and a *hub chip*. The QCM, shown in Figure 1, contains four tightly connected POWER7 chips providing 32 SMP cores. The tight connection is provided by the XYZABC links. This name makes more sense in the context of Figure 1, where we can see the direct communication channel between all pairs of POWER7 chips in the QCM. The bandwidth of each of these links is 48 Gbyte/s in each direction.

A compute node supports up to 256 Gbytes of memory, and its 32 cores run at 3.84GHz, attaining a peak performance of 0.98 Tflop/s.

From a management perspective, a QCM runs a single Linux or AIX operating system image [22]. Programmers can use posix threads and shared memory to orchestrate communication and computation within this image.

2.2.1 The Hub Chip

The compute node contains a fifth chip, the *hub chip*, that is the heart of the P775 architecture. The hub chip is a high-radix router that enables system sizes up to 16,384 compute nodes. The hub chip uses L_{local}, L_{remote}, and D links to connect to other compute nodes. We discuss these later.

The hub chip performs several important I/O functions and optimizations. It uses a high-performance coherent bus, called the *PowerBus*, to fully participate in coherence operations that take place among the four POWER7 chips. Software can register portions of a process' effective address space with the hub chip's memory management unit. Consistency can then be maintained with the translation look-aside buffers (TLBs) on the QCM's cores. This important feature is the building block for using a global address space across the entire system. Specific packet types exist that can instruct a hub chip to atomically perform certain operations on registered memory without involving the local cores.

The hub chip also has PCI connections (two 16× and a single 8×) that are used to connect to storage adapters. Storage disk enclosures are integrated into the P775 rack. Storage server functions are executed on QCMs set aside for that purpose. A description of the storage performance of the P775 is outside the scope of this paper.

Hub chips are the gateways for global communications. All *collective* operations (*e.g.*, barrier, reduce, broadcast, prefix sums, etc.) necessarily funnel through hub chips. To improve the performance of collective operations, the hub chip contains a *Collective Acceleration Unit* (CAU), which reduces the involvement of the POWER7 cores for many collective operations [25]. In the work we present here, we found the synchronization acceleration provided by the CAU to be especially useful.

Figure 2 (best viewed in color) shows a broader view of the QCM links (QCMs are on the blue planes). The links that connect the hub chip to the POWER7 chips are called W links, and they provide a bandwidth of 24 Gbyte/s in each direction.

The hub chip is 582 mm^2 in size, is implemented using 45 nm Cu SOI lithography, and contains 440 million transistors and 13 levels of metal [10].

2.3 Drawers

Figure 2 shows the P775 architecture at scales larger than a single compute node. A *drawer* is a collection of eight compute nodes (the green boxes in the figure). Physically, a drawer is 3.6" high (2U), 34.4" wide, and 54" deep, and weighs close to 350 lbs. The 256 cores in a drawer attain a peak performance of 7.86 Tflop/s.

Within a drawer, a set of copper $\mathrm{L_{local}}$ links provides direct connectivity between each pair of the eight compute nodes. These links operate at 24 Gbyte/s in each direction.

2.4 Supernodes

In canonical form, four drawers comprise a supernode (the yellow boxes in the figure). A supernode therefore contains 32 nodes for a total of 1024 cores, and a peak performance of 31.4 Tflop/s. A rack can be configured to house two or three supernodes, with fewer supernodes per rack permitting more storage.

Within a supernode, $\mathrm{L_{remote}}$ links connect each pair of

[1]The L3 can also be shared among the cores, as noted in [8].

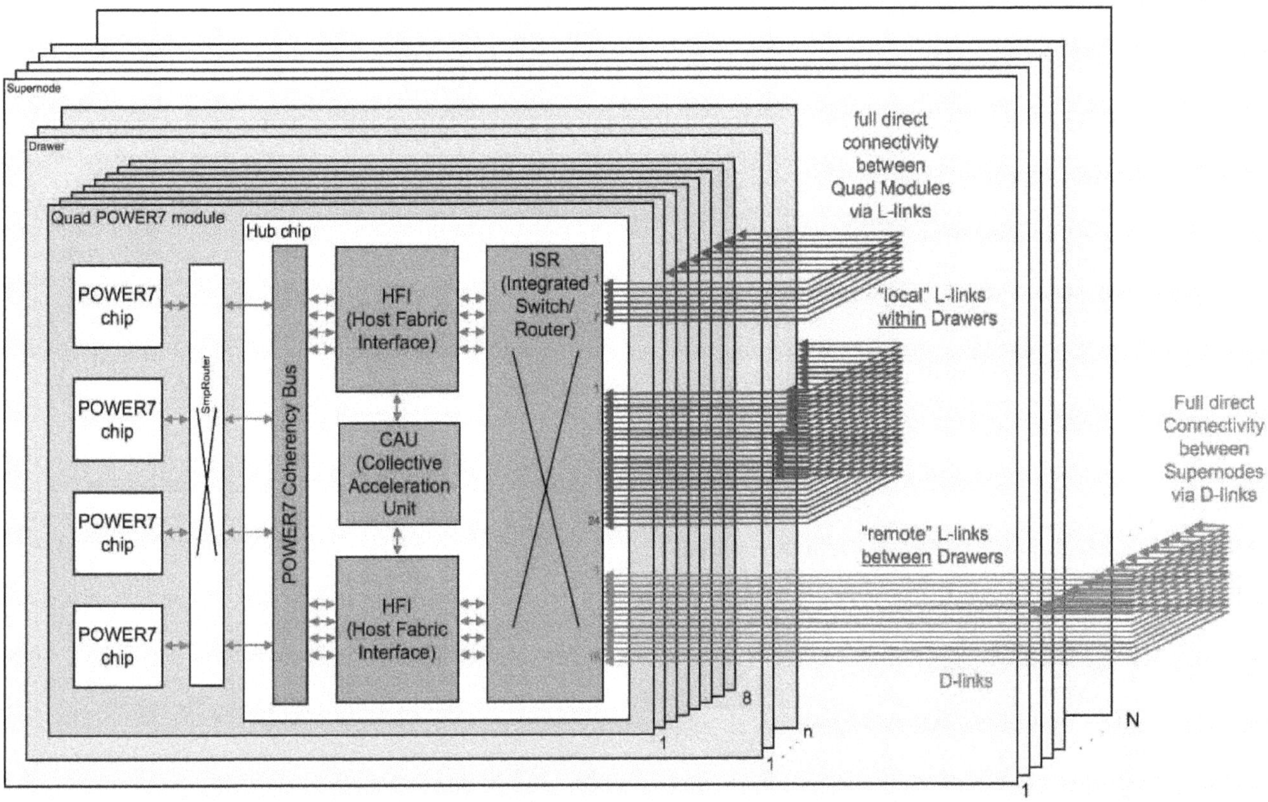

Figure 2: The P775 topology. A *compute node* consists of four POWER7 chips and a hub chip. A *drawer* contains up to eight compute nodes, and a *supernode* contains up to four drawers. There is full, direct connectivity between the compute nodes within a drawer (via local *L*-links), and between drawers (via remote *L*-links). Supernodes also have full, direct connectivity (via optical *D*-links). Best viewed in color.

compute nodes in different drawers with a bandwidth of 5 Gbyte/s in each direction. The combination of L_{local} and L_{remote} links fully connects a compute node within a supernode to every other compute node within that supernode.

2.5 At Scale

The maximal configuration supported by the architecture is 512 supernodes, resulting in 16,384 nodes, 512K cores, and a peak performance of 16 Pflop/s.

Optical *D*-links provide full connectivity between each pair of supernodes. The bandwidth of each link is 10 Gbyte/s in each direction, and they can be combined for increased bandwidth. Because it is not obvious from the figure, we specifically point out that the topology was designed as a two-level interconnect that fully connects any two compute nodes in at most three hops [22].

2.6 Routing

The P775 moves packets using *direct* and *indirect* routes [6]. A direct route employs one of potentially many shortest paths between any two compute nodes in the system. With only two levels in the topology, the longest direct route can have at most three hops.

Indirect routes provide increased point-to-point bandwidth and guard against potential hot spots in the interconnect. An indirect route has an intermediate compute node in the route that resides on a different supernode from that of the source and destination compute nodes. Thus, it is a composition of a shortest path from the source compute node to the chosen intermediate node, and a shortest path from the intermediate node to the destination node.

3. COMMUNICATION-HEAVY HPC WORKLOADS

This section describes three communication-heavy workloads from the HPC Challenge benchmark suite [3, 20]. The motivations for using these in our evaluation are:

- These workloads are communication heavy and memory intensive. It is a common observation in the computer architecture literature that memory and interconnection bandwidths are not scaling nearly as fast as compute capabilities. These workloads nicely highlight the widening capability gap.
- These workloads can be heavily modified to take advantage of special features of the target platform. We were able to leverage the P775's architecture to elegantly tune these applications from the algorithm level down to the assembly level.
- Because these are standardized benchmarks, vendors and researchers can conveniently compare our results to those for other systems.

3.1 RandomAccess (GUPS)

Whereas some benchmarks, such as LINPACK, are primarily designed to measure the compute capabilities of a system, RandomAccess is designed to stress memory and interconnect performance.

Conceptually, a "global address space" is created that is made up of the memories of all the compute elements participating in the execution. Each compute element then launches a series of operations that update the values of locations within this global address space. The locations are chosen at random and could point to a location local or remote to the current compute element. An update consists of performing an "exclusive-or" operation between the existing contents of the memory location and a random value. The contents of the memory location do not have to be retrieved. Performance is measured in terms of Giga Updates Per Second (GUPS).

3.2 PTRANS

PTRANS (parallel matrix transpose) is a conceptually simple benchmark that performs the matrix operation

$$A = A^T + B \quad (1)$$

where A and B are random, double precision n by n matrices (*i.e.*, $A, B \in \mathbb{R}^{nxn}$). The stated purpose of PTRANS is to measure "the total communications capacity of the system interconnect" [20]. The data transfer rate is simply the size (in bytes) of matrix A divided by the time it takes to perform the operation in Equation 1. Note that the many memory operations present in PTRANS (read A, read B, write A) necessitate more work than a cache-contained all-to-all benchmark designed purely to stress the interconnect.

The benchmark imposes strict requirements on the way data is distributed between the system's processes. The rules ensure that communication cannot be circumvented through an artful mapping between processes and compute elements. Figure 3 shows the salient points of the PTRANS data distribution including the notions of P and Q that determine how the data is tiled [9]. For the cases considered in this paper, we chose P and Q to be relatively prime, necessitating that every process communicate data to every other process in the system.

3.3 Global Fast Fourier Transform (FFT)

The Fast Fourier Transform (FFT) is one of the most widely used computations in the world. It is used in a diverse set of fields, for computations as varied as convolution to solving partial differential equations. The FFT computes the Discrete Fourier Transform in time $\Theta(n \log n)$ [11].

In this work we consider the widely used Cooley-Tukey algorithm, which is stated recursively in Matlab in Algorithm 1. Of particular importance for large-scale multiprocessor systems, note that there are three *global* transposes (requiring all-to-all communication), and two *local* compute-intensive phases.

The algorithm treats the 1D input f as a 2D $n1 \times n2$ matrix M, where $n1 \cdot n2 = length(f)$.[2] Thereafter, all of the local computation, including the recursive calls on lines 6 and 11, operates along the rows of the intermediate matrices. The explicit transpositions on lines 4, 8, and 13 optimally localize the data for subsequent computation [12]. With this view in mind, it becomes more evident how to map this algorithm to processes: each process "owns" a contiguous slab of the intermediate matrices so that all computation is process-local.

Algorithm 1 The six-step recursive FFT algorithm.

```
function F = FFT(f)
1   n = length(f)
2   [n1, n2] = factor(n)
3   M = reshape(f, n1, n2)
4   M1 = transpose(M)               % Step 1: global all-to-all
5   for k = 1:n2                    % Step 2: local computation
6       M2(k,:) = FFT(M1(k,:))      % Compute the FFTs along
7   end                                 % the rows of M1
8   M3 = transpose(M2)              % Step 3: global all-to-all
9   M4 = M3 .* V_{n1 x n2}          % Step 4: twiddle factors [11]
10  for k = 1:n1                    % Step 5: local computation
11      M5(k,:) = FFT(M4(k,:))      % Compute the FFTs along
12  end                                 % the rows of M4
13  F = transpose(M5)               % Step 6: global all-to-all
```

Notice that we do not include the bottom-out condition of the recursion. In the multiprocessor setting it is typical to relegate the recursive steps (lines 6 and 11) to a highly-tuned FFT library. Again, this is feasible because the memory required for these steps is local to the process.

4. RESULTS

This section discusses results obtained on a 64-supernode P775 system named Hurcules [3] with a peak performance of 2 Pflop/s. For each of the workloads, we highlight important aspects of the system's design, including software considerations, that were necessary for attaining high performance. Performance data on additional workloads is available on the HPC Challenge website [3, 2].

We obtained a first set of results at the full Hurcules size involving 1,980 compute nodes running Linux.[4] In addition, we measured the scalability of RandomAccess and PTRANS on up to 1,472 compute nodes, equating to 48 supernodes. We then infer the scalability of Global FFT using the measured PTRANS scalability and the performance of serial FFT on a single compute node.

4.1 RandomAccess

RandomAccess rules forbid sorting that transforms the random updates into regular (non-random) operations. Furthermore, no more than 1,024 updates can be buffered at a compute element at any given time. On large systems, the buffered updates are almost all bound for distinct destinations. The traditional high-performance solution to RandomAccess introduces software-based dimension-ordered routing that aggregates individual updates into larger packets bound to the same region of the larger system [14]. Such a scheme uses more interconnect bandwidth than truly required and suffers from the software overheads of breaking up and reassembling packets at intermediate destinations.

On the P775, we implement RandomAccess as a multithreaded program running concurrently on all compute nodes.

[2] Without loss of generality, we assume row-major order. We also assume *length*(f) is not prime.

[3] The machine name is indeed (mis)spelled Hurcules [*sic*].

[4] Even though a 64-supernode system contains $64 \times 32 = 2,048$ compute nodes, a small number of these are set aside for storage, login, and fail-in-place.

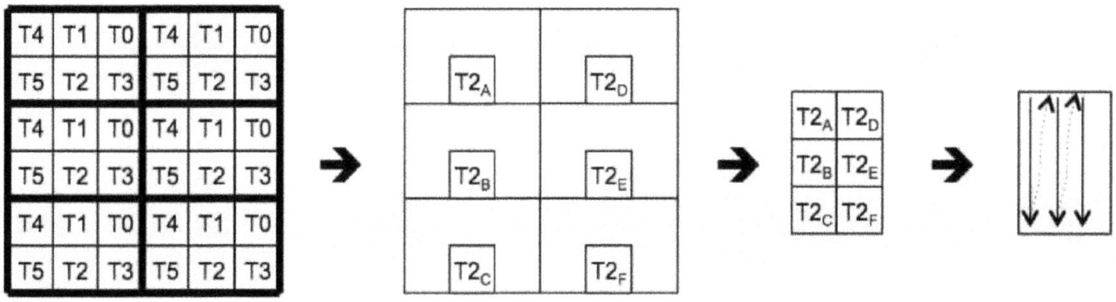

Figure 3: The A and B matrices are block-cyclic distributed with a randomized assignment of matrix chunks to processes. The processes are arranged as a $P \times Q$ grid (2×3 here). The three sub-figures on the right-hand side show the data "owned" by process T2 and how it is stored in column major order within its address space.

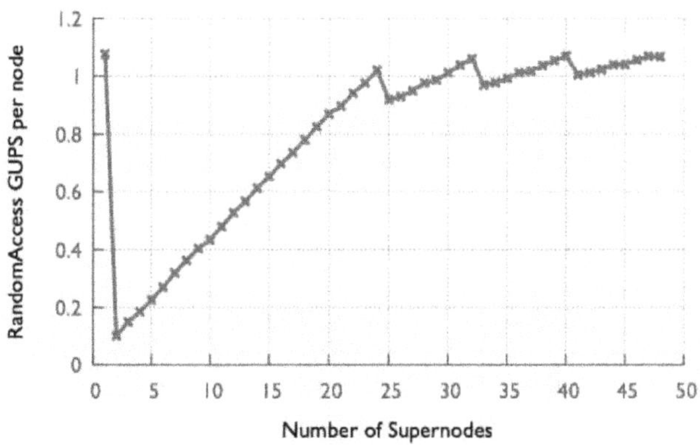

Figure 4: RandomAccess scaling on Hurcules. The Y-axis is in terms of GUPS per compute node (System GUPS performance *divided* by the number of nodes used) The 1.08 GUPS/node asymptote indicates linear performance scaling.

At startup, the software "registers" the local portion of the RandomAccess table with the local hub chip. The threads craft packets (each specifying a distinct update operation) placing them in send FIFOs, which are data structures from where the hub chip picks up packets. Each packet is 32-bytes in size and specifies the effective address of the remote location, the compute node housing the location, and the operand to be used in the update. The local hub chip sends the packets to the remote compute node's hub chip, where the update is performed. The hub chip hardware is optimized to move 32-byte atomic read-modify-write packets that are aggregated (dis-aggregated) into (from) 128-byte network *flits* at intermediate hub chips.

Figure 4 shows the performance of RandomAccess as the number of supernodes is varied. The Y-axis shows the system performance in Giga Updates Per Second (GUPS) divided by the number of compute nodes. A flat line on this graph indicates that an incremental increase of compute power yields a linear increase in performance. Indeed, the graph asymptotes to a performance of 1.08 GUPS per compute node. No known previous system has exhibited this level of performance.

The P775 has an abundance of interconnect links and interconnect bandwidth. Every pair of supernodes on Hurcules is connected by eight D optics links, providing a bandwidth of 80 Gbyte/s per supernode pair in each direction. However, the achievable bisection bandwidth of a two-supernode subset of Hurcules is far higher, since indirectly routed traffic can bounce off any of the remaining 62 intermediate supernodes in the system (see Section 2.6). An express goal of our scaling studies was to determine where the interconnect stops becoming a bottleneck. We achieve this by deliberately considering only direct routing.

Thus, a dramatic performance drop can be seen when going from one supernode (where the performance is 1.08 GUPS per compute node) to two supernodes (where the performance is 0.1 GUPS per compute node). RandomAccess performance steadily increases *linearly* as more supernodes are added to the system, continuing until the interconnect is no longer the bottleneck at 24 supernodes.

Beyond 24 supernodes, the performance starts oscillating in a "sawtooth" pattern that gradually trends upwards. The reason for the drop in GUPS per compute node from 24 to 25 supernodes, from 32 to 33 supernodes, and from 40 to 41 supernodes as well as the rising trend of the overall GUPS per compute node has to do with how non-local RandomAccess traffic is routed.

The first hop taken by a non-local RandomAccess flit (i.e., a RandomAccess flit that is destined for a different supernode) is always a L_{local} hop. This link also has a limit on how much traffic it can carry. When switching from 24 to 25 supernodes, there is one L_{local} link that has to carry twice the traffic as the other links within that drawer. As the number of supernodes increases, the excess traffic to be carried by the one L_{local} link as compared to the other links in the drawer decreases. In other words, the imbalance in L_{local} link traffic reduces as the number of supernodes increases. We expect the asymptote to eventually become the 1.08 GUPS obtained on a single supernode.

4.2 PTRANS

The P775 has a very high raw interconnect bandwidth. The main challenge with obtaining high-performance on parallel matrix transpose is in delivering that bandwidth through the communications stack to the workload. We achieved this by implementing an elegant solution for dealing with the boundary condition of packet losses.

In the absence of fully reliable hardware packet transport, protocol stacks typically make a local copy of all transmitted data, and use a timer-driven, acknowledgment-based mechanism to perform re-transmissions and garbage collect copies of the sent data. On the P775, there are two reasons why a data packet sent to/from the hub chip FIFOs [6] can be lost. First, the hardware optical laser transceiver can itself fail. This is rare event (with a predicted MTTF of around a week) for which an out-of-band checkpoint-restart technique is apt. The more prevalent reason for packet losses is due to the receive FIFO into which the hub chip deposits packets [6] becoming full. This happens when the receiving software is not emptying a receive FIFO as fast as the hub chip is filling it. Packets are dropped in this situation to prevent traffic from backing up and unfairly causing other parts of the system (perhaps executing other workloads) to get congested.

Rather than add a re-transmission protocol to handle such dropped packets, we devise a solution to eliminate the possibility of the receive FIFO ever getting full. We break up the data transfer into "rounds" that only transfer as much data as can fit into pre-allocated receive FIFO buffers. We set aside 4 Gbytes of buffer space on every compute node, equal to slightly over 3% of the node's physical memory. Because the size of the data being transferred is known a priori, each process is able to precompute the exact receive FIFO at the destination for each packet it will send. The receivers can also calculate exactly how much data will arrive on each FIFO.

After all data is sent for a round and after it has all been received, each process enters a global barrier that precludes buffer overruns. Upon exit from the barrier, all processes begin the procedure again until all rounds are completed. This algorithm makes use of the fact that on the P775, the time to carry out a round (i.e., pump out 4 Gbytes) far exceeds the time to perform a global barrier using the CAU.

To eliminate hot spotting in the interconnect, we would like to randomize the destinations to which packets are sent. Interestingly, the data distribution adopted by PTRANS already randomizes the mapping of data blocks to tasks; although this was adopted to discourage solutions that reduce data transfer through clever mappings of tasks to physical system nodes. Traversing the A matrix in order is therefore sufficient to ensure that the packets being sent are bound for different destinations. We revisit this aspect when discussing the transpose phase of the Global FFT.

We further simplify our implementation by eliminating the need to maintain state beyond that which can be encapsulated in a single packet. The largest packet that can be sent on the P775 interconnect is 2048 bytes (of course, software can always compose longer messages using multiple packets). We limit ourselves to sending no more that 2048 bytes of data and metadata, which a receiver uses to deposit received data into the correct places within its address space. More specifically, we use a PTRANS block size of 15×15 to ensure that each such block can be both transported within an indivisible P775 packet and dealt with independently by the receiver. Each block and its associated metadata fits within a single 1920-byte packet.

Figure 5 shows the scalability of PTRANS between one and forty-eight supernodes. As in the case of RandomAccess, the Y-axis on the graph shows the system performance divided by the number of compute nodes. A flat line on this graph indicates that an incremental increase of compute power yields a linear increase in performance. The graph asymptotes to a performance of over 30 Gbyte/s per compute node. This level of performance is far superior to

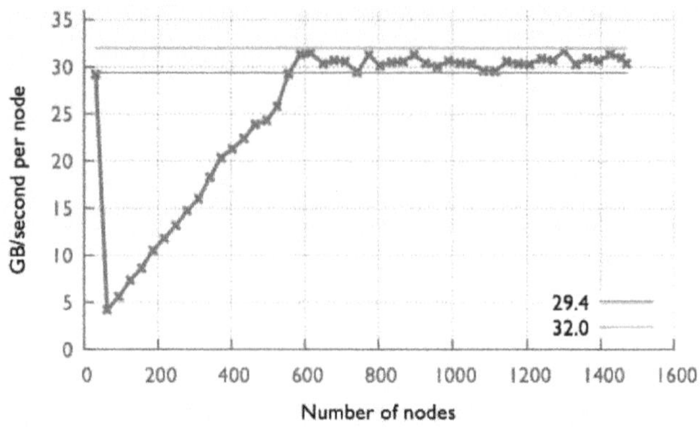

Figure 5: PTRANS scaling on Hurcules. The Y-axis is in terms of PTRANS per compute node (system PTRANS performance *divided* by the number of compute nodes used). Linear scaling is clearly evident from the performance asymptote.

that exhibited by other high performance computing systems [3, 2].

As with RandomAccess, performance falls dramatically when going from one to two supernodes *simply because in Hurcules, directly routed traffic can only use the eight physical wires connecting the two supernodes.*

At one supernode, the system performs at 919 Gbyte/s corresponding to 29.7 Gbyte/s/node. At two supernodes, the performance falls to 260 Gbyte/s, which corresponds to 4.2 Gbyte/s/node. As the number of supernodes increases beyond two, PTRANS performance steadily increases on a *per-supernode basis.* This happens until we reach 19 supernodes at which point the system has sufficient bisection bandwidth such that the D-link capacity is no longer a bottleneck.

Beyond 19 supernodes, there is performance variation at different supernode levels, but the per-node PTRANS performance stabilizes to be ≈ 30 Gbyte/s/node. The sawtooth shaped performance behavior is not seen in G-PTRANS because the local L-links offer the full link capacity for carrying data, as opposed to being gated by the packet recombination rate for 32-byte RandomAccess packets.

4.3 Global FFT

The Global FFT in HPC Challenge requires a single-dimensional double-precision complex–to–complex FFT to be performed by all compute elements. The input vector is distributed over all nodes and the result vector is required to be deposited back in–place. As mentioned in Section 3.3, we treat the large single-dimensional input vector as a two-dimensional matrix, and we follow Algorithm 1. We choose HPC Challenge parameters such that the matrix is approximately square.

We use FFTW 3.2 [13] to compute the row FFTs (lines 6 and 11 in the algorithm), which we modified to support POWER7's VSX SIMD instruction set [7]. Load balancing while computing the row FFTs is achieved by having the cores compete for work.

The three global transpositions (lines 4, 8, and 13 in the algorithm) are similar to that used in PTRANS. We use an internal block size of 8×8 (16 byte) double-precision complex numbers during the transpose operation. Note that $8 \times 8 \times 16 = 1024$, which is again smaller than the 2048-byte packet limit even after accounting for necessary software headers. Interestingly, the P775 interconnect performs as well for packets of this size compared to larger 2 Kbyte packets.

During the transpose phase of the Global FFT, each process must communicate with every other process in the system. To avoid interconnect hot spots, we use a software architected pseudo-randomized routing scheme. Each process randomly traverses the set of all processes with which it must communicate— care being taken to ensure that every node uses a different pseudo-random traversal through the node set. Our implementation is particularly simple. Let N be the total number of tasks with which a given task must communicate. We provide each task with a number P (taken from a large statically constructed list of prime numbers) that is both relatively prime to N as well as different from the value of P used on any other task. The task set is ordered exactly the same way on each node, but in iteration i each node picks task $P \cdot i \bmod N$ in the ordered set with which to communicate. Of course, many other randomization schemes are possible. We also experimented with a regular routing scheme where every node traverses the task set starting with the node to its "right". Such a scheme is oft-advocated but performed 12% worse than our randomized scheme on the single supernode upon which we were able to test.

Table 1: Measured Global FFT performance on Hurcules

System size (compute nodes)	Raw performance (Gflop/s)	Percentage of peak
8	512.1	6.52%
1,458	94855.8	6.63%
1,944	132658.1	6.95%

Table 1 shows the measured performance of Global FFT at different system sizes of Hurcules (HPCC constrains node counts to be expressible as $2^i \cdot 3^j \cdot 5^k$ for integer i, j, k.). Unlike RandomAccess and PTRANS, we were unable to obtain a full scaling curve due to the prohibitive time it would have taken to plan the FFTW component at each of the different data set sizes.

The asymptotic Global FFT performance on large P775 systems can be calculated as a composition of the performance for each stage of Algorithm 1. The performance for the two compute phases (lines 5–7 and 10–12) depends on how long FFTW takes to compute the associated "slabs" of rows on the POWER7 compute node. The performance for the three transpose phases is determined by the asymptotic PTRANS performance of 30 Gbyte/s/compute node. Note that the extra floating point operations in line 9 for performing the so-called "twiddle" multiplications get transparently folded in to the transpose operation before data blocks are written out. These operations can be trivially overlapped with the memory loads that bring data into the caches.

Let n be the size of the Global FFT being solved. FFT efficiency calculations assume that the FFT itself requires $5 \cdot n \cdot \lg n$ floating point operations. Let P be the number of nodes, F be the floating point execution rate (flops/s) per node when executing the serial compute phases, η_s be the efficiency when computing the serial portion of the FFT, and B represent the bandwidth that each node can sustain during the transpose phase (we know from figure 5 that B asymptotes to 30 Gbyte/s). Note that each FFT data point is double-precision complex and 16 bytes in size. Then:

$$
\begin{aligned}
\text{Time for each compute phase} &= 5 \cdot n \cdot \lg n/(F \cdot P) \\
\text{Time taken by each transpose} &= 16 \cdot n/(B \cdot P) \\
\text{Total time} &= 3 \times \text{TransposeTime} + 2 \times \text{ComputeTime} \\
&= 48 \cdot n/(B \cdot P) + 10 \cdot n \cdot \lg n/(F \cdot P) \\
\text{FLOP rate} &= \text{Floating point operations /Time taken} \\
&= 5 \cdot \lg n \cdot B \cdot F \cdot P/(48 \cdot F + 10 \cdot B \cdot \lg n) \\
\text{Efficiency} &= 5 \cdot \lg n \cdot B \cdot \eta_s/(48 \cdot F + 10 \cdot B \cdot \lg n)
\end{aligned}
$$

For the weakly scaled case, the size of the FFT is proportional to the number of nodes used in the computation. Then, $\lg n = k + \lg P$, where k is some constant. Assume that each node can contribute 2^{30} data points, corresponding to 16 Gbytes of data. We can later observe that our results are not sensitive to this assumption. Each node or compute node can also compute at a peak rate of 982 Gflop/s. We can then compute the efficiency for the global FFT:

$$
\begin{aligned}
\eta_g &= (5 \cdot 30 \cdot (30 + \lg P \cdot \eta_s)/(48 \cdot 982 \cdot \eta_s + 300 \cdot (30 + \lg P)) \\
&\approx 6.8\% \text{ when } P = 1000
\end{aligned}
$$

A few interesting observations can be made from the above equation. First, since we compute the serial FFT on only either the row or the column, and since the 1D vector is structured as a roughly square matrix, an increase in the 1D vector length by a factor of f only increases the size of the serial FFT by $\sqrt{f}$. On the POWER7, η_s is around 30% for n corresponding to what will fit in the memory of up to a few thousand nodes. Solving the above equation, we see that the efficiency of the global FFT changes very slowly as the number of nodes is changed; the insensitivity to the constant k can also be immediately grasped. This rationalizes the slightly superlinear performance of a weakly scaled Global FFT on the P775.

4.4 Analysis

Hurcules, the largest P775 system we were able to access, was made up of 64 supernodes with a peak performance of 2 Pflop/s. At this scale, the RandomAccess, PTRANS, and Global FFT performances were 2,021 GUPS, 60.5 Tbyte/s, and 132.7 Tflop/s respectively. By itself, the raw performance on RandomAccess and PTRANS places the P775 at the number one spot in the world. However, comparing the 2 Pflop/s Hurcules system we experimented upon against larger production systems such as the K computer[5] or the Cray XT5 system at ORNL[6] is inherently unfair.

A better technical comparison would be to normalize the performance on these workloads against peak system performance, especially since we have empirically shown linear performance scaling on these three workloads. Figure 6 does exactly that for systems over 150 TFLOPS peak. The dramatically improved efficiency of the P775 is very clear

[5]http://www.aics.riken.jp/en/
[6]http://www.olcf.ornl.gov/

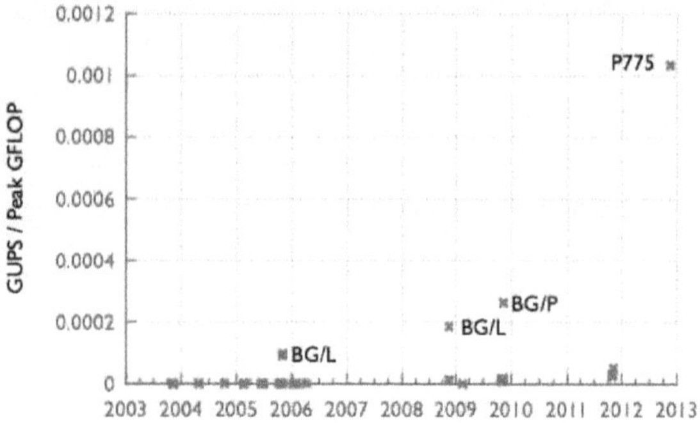

(a) Normalized performance for RandomAccess.

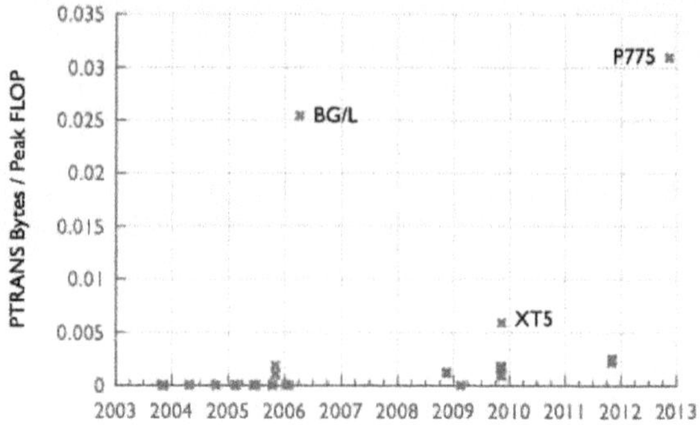

(b) Normalized performance for PTRANS.

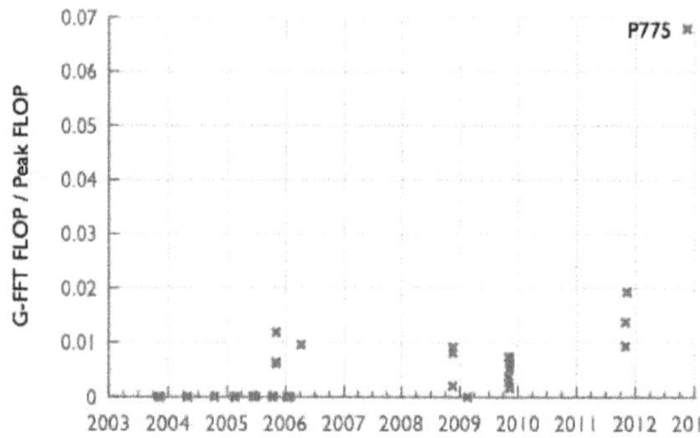

(c) Normalized performance for G-FFT.

Figure 6: Historical normalized performance per peak flop for a variety of different systems.

in this figure, which shows normalized performance against peak flops that various systems have been able to achieve over time, on the HPC Challenge benchmarks.[7]

The results in Figure 6(b) contain a notable outlier for PTRANS. The relatively high 0.025 bytes/peak FLOP score measured on an IBM BG/L system was attained before version 1.2.0 of the HPC Challenge benchmark was released. As such, this outcome was obtained on a benchmark version that does not mandate the randomization necessary to ensure global communication.

The P775 system was designed from the outset to yield fixed increments of communication performance for incremental additions of hardware, with linear weak scaling becoming a consequence of this design criteria. A considerable amount of hardware simulations were used to mitigate performance losses that might arise due to implementation bugs. Up to its maximal size of 512 supernodes, we expect the P775 to perform linearly on communication intensive workloads such as those discussed in this paper.

5. HEROIC PROGRAMMER'S RETROSPECTIVE

This section describes some interesting observations and lessons learned while designing, developing, and evaluating the system. We mention up front that our goal was to tease as much performance out of the system as possible. From a software point of view, this involved continuous tweaking, and redesign. A common theme among the lessons we learned is that architectural and software features designed to aid programmer productivity can severely inhibit performance for heroic programmers. In a few cases we decided to bypass architectural features that are in place to relax the burden on software. Likewise, we also avoided some programmer productivity libraries such as MPI and PAMI. Given the context of this paper, this should not be viewed as a condemnation of these features. Rather, we hope this discussion leads to a more automatic middle ground that strikes a better balance between programmer productivity and optimal performance.

5.1 Core Architecture Observations

Somewhat surprisingly, simultaneous multi-threading was not useful for any of the workloads we ran, and in many cases hurt performance. Traditionally, SMT helps performance by permitting the core to overlap instruction execution with high latency instructions. We designed our codes with appropriate software–inserted prefetches to make demand load latencies to generally not be a performance bottleneck. Consequently, the resource division that occurs with simultaneous multithreading [24, Page 1:3 "POWER7 Core"] far outweighed any latency hiding advantages. For less carefully designed code, SMT is likely to be beneficial.

Reinforcing much related work (*e.g.*, [21]), we found the VSX SIMD extensions to be useful for the FFT (as well as for HPL and DGEMM, which we have not addressed in this paper). For the sizes of FFTs we consider in this paper,

[7] BG/Q's recently published results of 858 GUPS on a 3.36 Pflop/s system still place it at only 0.00026 GUPS/Peak GFLOP.

our VSX-enabled FFTW-3.2 library is ~18% faster than its scalar counterpart on POWER7.

For the benchmarks on which we have evaluated the P775, hardware prefetching was not strictly required and was often a hindrance. Specifically, for the benchmarks surveyed in this paper, RandomAccess is random by design, and therefore hardware prefetchers hurt performance by squandering memory bandwidth on data that will never be referenced. PTRANS and FFT do have predictable strides for which it seems reasonable to presume that hardware prefetching will prove useful. In fact, the POWER7 architecture somewhat impressively maintains enough hardware state for prefetching up to 12 different streams.

However, we discovered that in the case of PTRANS, array sub-tiles larger than 12 $\times$ 12 were necessary in order to obtain sufficient communications performance; such sub-tiles rendered the 12–stream hardware prefetcher useless as each new stream (started above the maximum number of twelve) kicked out an active prefetch stream from the prefetch engine. An execution of PTRANS on a 1.7 Pflop/s subset of Hurcules with hardware prefetching enabled *realized a 15% performance loss*, showing how system–level issues can outweigh micro-level design decisions. A more beneficial approach was to explicitly prefetch required data through hand-inserted software prefetch instructions. The interaction of software and system-level issues is often very complicated, making a compelling argument that hardware focus more on providing strong support for explicit software prefetching.

On the positive side, the POWER7 architecture provides a mechanism to change the mode of the core hardware prefetcher on-the-fly. We used this feature to great effect in the case of Global FFT, where we turned on full hardware prefetching during the sequential compute phases and then turned it off during the transpose phases. We found the combination of the hardware prefetcher control and Linux kernel support that achieved this to be particularly elegant and eminently useful.

5.2 Large-scale Observations

While communications libraries such as MPI simplify programming, using them incurs a significant amount of overhead. In particular, the copy and garbage collection overheads involved in the use of such stacks (see Sections 4.2 and 4.3) eats away precious memory bandwidth that is no longer available to the application. We used a custom designed software stack that more tightly integrates communication with the application logic; such stacks need to be further explored.[8]

When evaluating all-to-all communications, we noticed that naively communicating between all pairs of processes creates hotspots. Others have argued for support for randomized routing in hardware for reducing hotspots [18]. We instead advocate moving the complexity to software. Our all-to-all communications randomize the $\langle source, dest \rangle$ pairs involved in communication at the algorithm level to avoid network contention. The approach performs well and is quite practical, as it still relies on deterministic routing (see Sections 4.2 and 4.3). To the best of our knowledge, this approach to alleviating hotspots is novel.

[8]We have also used such an integrated stack in the design of our Graph500 implementation [1], a non-trivial workload.

6. RELATED WORK

Various aspects of the P775 system have previously been discussed. The POWER7 chip has been described in [15, 16]; the network characteristics of the system are discussed in [6, 25]. Finally, the performance of an early, drawer-level version of the P775 has been previously evaluated [8, 22]. At 64 supernodes and 2 Pflop/s, this system is significantly larger than those in earlier studies [8, 22]. Furthermore, the benchmarks we consider in this paper significantly stress the interconnect.

The P775 hub chips are high-radix routers: Even for the largest supported configurations, the shortest path between any two nodes is at most three hops. Other notable implementations of high-radix routers include Cray's BlackWidow system [4, 23], and the Cray Dragonfly network [5, 18]. As Kim et. al note in [18] where they introduce the Dragonfly topology, high-radix routers simultaneously reduce the diameter and the latency of interconnection networks.

To further improve the interconnect performance, the P775 hub chip has hardware support for collective communication operations, and supports several high-performance computing protocols [6, 25]. The Blue Gene/Q interconnect also has hardware acceleration for collective operations [19].

Unlike the Dragonfly topology, the P775 does not employ dynamic routing. Instead, the hub chip implements deterministic and hardware-directed randomized indirect routing [6]. We use deterministic routing for the experiments presented in this paper; however, we developed a randomized algorithm for the all-to-alls in PTRANS and FFT that substantially reduces network congestion.

7. CONCLUSION

We rigorously evaluated and analyzed large-scale configurations of the IBM P775 on three HPC Challenge benchmarks. The benchmarks particularly stress a system's interconnect, and require optimization from the algorithm level down. Several interesting features of the P775 allowed us to extract a high level of performance resulting in linear performance with weak scaling. In fact, the P775 currently holds the top spot for PTRANS and RandomAccess. As we have seen for these applications, the P775 especially shines when we consider system efficiency.

Enabling peak performance of these benchmarks on the P775 taught us much about the system. We opted to write our own application-specific communication layers to avoid the overhead of libraries such as MPI. Though the effort involved was non-trivial, the protocols we devised were highly effective; further improvements were gained by crafting randomized versions of our protocols. In a couple of cases we were surprised to discover that for our carefully written code, ordinarily beneficial hardware features consistently hindered performance. Though we couch our lessons learned in the context of heroic programmers, they are hopefully of interest to the broader architecture community.

8. ACKNOWLEDGEMENTS

The PERCS project has been supported by the U. S. Defense Advanced Research Projects Agency (DARPA) under its Agreement No. HR0011-07-9-0002. Any opinions, findings and conclusions or recommendations expressed in this material are those of the authors and do not necessarily reflect the views of DARPA.

The P775 system exists because of the efforts of a large number of IBM staff, including architects, designers, implementors, verification engineers, software developers, project managers, and system administrators. None of the work described in this paper would have been possible without the dedicated hard work of this team.

9. REFERENCES

[1] Graph500 Results. *https://ibm.biz/BdxpWQ.*

[2] HPC Challenge 2012 Awards. *https://ibm.biz/Bdxgfa.*

[3] HPC Challenge Results. *https://ibm.biz/BdxpWC.*

[4] D. Abts, A. Bataineh, S. Scott, G. Faanes, J. Schwarzmeier, E. Lundberg, T. Johnson, M. Bye, and G. Schwoerer. The Cray BlackWidow: a highly scalable vector multiprocessor. In *Proceedings of ACM/IEEE Supercomputing (SC)*, 2007.

[5] B. Alverson, T. Johnson, J. Kopnick, M. Higgins, and J. Reinhard. Cray Cascade: a Scalable HPC System based on a Dragonfly Network. In *Proceedings of ACM/IEEE Supercomputing (SC)*, 2012.

[6] B. Arimilli, R. Arimilli, V. Chung, S. Clark, W. Denzel, B. Drerup, T. Hoefler, J. Joyner, J. Lewis, Jian Li, Nan Ni, and R. Rajamony. The PERCS High-Performance Interconnect. In *2010 IEEE 18th Annual Symposium on High Performance Interconnects (HOTI)*, pages 75 –82, Aug 2010.

[7] R. X. Arroyo, R. J. Harrington, S. P. Hartman, and T. Nguyen. IBM POWER7 systems. *IBM Journal of Research and Development*, 55(3):2:1 –2:13, May-June 2011.

[8] Kevin J. Barker, Adolfy Hoisie, and Darren J. Kerbyson. An early performance analysis of POWER7-IH HPC systems. In *Proceedings of ACM/IEEE Supercomputing (SC)*, 2011.

[9] Jaeyoung Choi, Jack Dongarra, and David Walker. Parallel matrix transpose algorithms on distributed memory concurrent computers. *ORNL Tech Report ORNL/TM-12309*, October 1993.

[10] Scott Clark et al. The IBM Hub Module in 45nm CMOS SOI: A Terabyte Interconnect Switch for High-Performance Computer Systems. *Hot Chips 22*, August 2010.

[11] Thomas H. Cormen, Charles E. Leiserson, Ronald L. Rivest, and Clifford Stein. *Introduction to Algorithms.* MIT Press, 2nd edition, 2001.

[12] M. Frigo, C.E. Leiserson, H. Prokop, and S. Ramachandran. Cache-oblivious algorithms. In *Proceedings of the 40th Annual FOCS Symposium* . IEEE, 1999.

[13] Matteo Frigo and Steven G. Johnson. The Design and Implementation of FFTW3. In *Proceedings of the IEEE*, pages 216–231, 2005.

[14] Rahul Garg and Yogish Sabharwal. Optimizing the HPCC randomaccess benchmark on blue Gene/L Supercomputer. In *Proceedings of SIGMETRICS/Performance*, 2006.

[15] R. Kalla and B. Sinharoy. POWER7: IBM's Next Generation Server Processor. *Hot Chips 21*, August 2009.

[16] R. Kalla, B. Sinharoy, W.J. Starke, and M. Floyd. POWER7: IBM's next-generation server processor. *IEEE Micro*, 30(2):7–15, 2010.

[17] S.W. Keckler, W.J. Dally, B. Khailany, M. Garland, and D. Glasco. GPUs and the Future of Parallel Computing. *IEEE Micro*, 31(5):7 –17, Sep-Oct 2011.

[18] John Kim, Wiliam J. Dally, Steve Scott, and Dennis Abts. Technology-Driven, Highly-Scalable Dragonfly Topology. In *Proceedings of the 35th Annual International Symposium on Computer Architecture (ISCA)*, 2008.

[19] S. Kumar, A.R. Mamidala, D.A. Faraj, B. Smith, M. Blocksome, B. Cernohous, D. Miller, J. Parker, J. Ratterman, P. Heidelberger, Dong Chen, and B. Steinmacher-Burrow. PAMI: A Parallel Active Message Interface for the Blue Gene/Q Supercomputer. In *26th International Parallel and Distributed Processing Symposium (IPDPS),*, May 2012.

[20] Piotr R Luszczek, David H Bailey, Jack J Dongarra, Jeremy Kepner, Robert F Lucas, Rolf Rabenseifner, and Daisuke Takahashi. The HPC Challenge (HPCC) benchmark suite. In *Proceedings of ACM/IEEE Supercomputing (SC)*, 2006.

[21] Huy Nguyen and Lizy Kurian John. Exploiting SIMD parallelism in DSP and multimedia algorithms using the AltiVec technology. In *Proceedings of the 13th International Conference on Supercomputing (ICS)*, pages 11–20. ACM, 1999.

[22] R. Rajamony, L. B. Arimilli, and K. Gildea. PERCS: The IBM POWER7-IH High-Performance Computing System. *IBM Journal of Research and Development*, 55(3):233–244, May 2011.

[23] Steve Scott, Dennis Abts, John Kim, and William J. Dally. The BlackWidow High-Radix Clos Network. In *Proceedings of the 33rd International Symposium on Computer Architecture (ISCA)*, 2006.

[24] Balaram Sinharoy and et. al. IBM POWER7 multicore server processor. *IBM Journal of Research and Development*, 55(3):1:1 –1:29, May-June 2011.

[25] Gabriel Ilie Tanase, Gheorghe Almási, Hanhong Xue, and Charles Archer. Composable, non-blocking collective operations on POWER7 IH. In *Proceedings of the 26th ACM International Conference on Supercomputing (ICS)*, ICS '12, pages 215–224. ACM, 2012.

Bubble Coloring: Avoiding Routing- and Protocol-induced Deadlocks With Minimal Virtual Channel Requirement

Ruisheng Wang Lizhong Chen Timothy Mark Pinkston
Ming Hsieh Department of Electrical Engineering
University of Southern California
Los Angeles, California, USA
{ruishenw, lizhongc, tpink}@usc.edu

ABSTRACT

Handling routing- and protocol-induced deadlocks is a critical issue in designing a reliable communication system. Generally, to avoid these two types of deadlocks without losing routing freedom requires a large amount of virtual channels (VCs), which imposes significant negative effects on router power, energy and frequency. In this paper, we propose a virtual cut-through switched Bubble Coloring (BC) scheme, which can avoid both routing- and protocol-induced deadlocks and allow fully adaptive routing on any topology without the need for multiple virtual channels. Results from both synthetic and full-system simulation show that, compared to a conventional deadlock-free scheme with 4VCs (i.e., XY_adaptive_4VC), our BC scheme with the minimal 1VC (i.e., BC_1VC) can reduce router energy and area by up to 51.2% and 58.3%, respectively, and has comparable performance at the same time. As the proposed BC scheme does not require multiple virtual channels, it also reduces the complexity of router arbitration logic, which brings the opportunity to increase router frequency and further improve system performance.

Categories and Subject Descriptors

C.1.2 [**Computer Systems Organization**]: Multiprocessors—*Interconnection architectures*

General Terms

Design, Experimentation, Performance

Keywords

Bubble flow control; Routing-induced deadlock; Protocol-induced deadlock; Minimal virtual channel requirement

1. INTRODUCTION

As the number of processors integrated in a system continues to grow, networks on-chip (NoCs) and interconnection networks more generally have become essential components of modern chip multiprocessors (CMPs) and parallel processing systems. In order to provide efficient and reliable communication through the networks, routing- and protocol-induced deadlocks, which are catastrophic to the communication system, should be efficiently handled.

Routing-induced deadlocks occur when there is a cyclic dependency between resources created by the packets transported through various paths in the network. To break such cyclic dependence, the turn model and its extensions [15, 7, 13] have been proposed, which reduce the degree of routing freedom by disallowing certain paths between source and destination nodes. In order to maintain full routing freedom (i.e., to support fully adaptive routing), Duato's Protocol [11] is proposed to avoid routing-induced deadlock by using an additional virtual channel.

Deadlock freedom provided by the schemes mentioned above is based on the consumption assumption [17] where the end node will consume all packets from the network once the destination is reached. However, when interactions and dependencies are created between packets of different message classes at network endpoints, that assumption may not be valid and protocol-induced deadlocks (also known as message-dependent deadlocks) may occur [17]. The conventional solution for protocol-induced deadlocks is to have separate virtual networks for each message class [18]. As the number of message classes increases, the virtual channel (VC) requirement rises proportionally. Thus, current approaches for designing routing- and protocol-induced deadlock-free schemes with complete routing freedom require a large number of VCs. However, implementing such a large number of VCs in routers has considerable negative impacts on router area, power and frequency. Hence, it is important to provide a scheme to avoid routing- and protocol-induced deadlocks with minimal requirement on the number of virtual channels.

In this paper, we propose a virtual cut-through (VCT) switched Bubble Coloring scheme that enables fully adaptive routing on any topology without the need for multiple virtual channels while still avoiding both routing- and protocol-induced deadlocks.

Our contributions are summarized as follows:

1. A topology-agnostic fully adaptive Bubble Ring (BR) scheme is proposed to avoid routing-induced deadlocks without the need for multiple virtual channels.

2. A Bubble Coloring (BC) scheme, an extension of the Bubble Ring scheme, is proposed to avoid protocol-induced deadlocks without the need for multiple virtual channels.

3. The results from both synthetic and full system simulation show that, compared to a conventional deadlock-

ICS'13, June 10–14, 2013, Eugene, Oregon, USA.

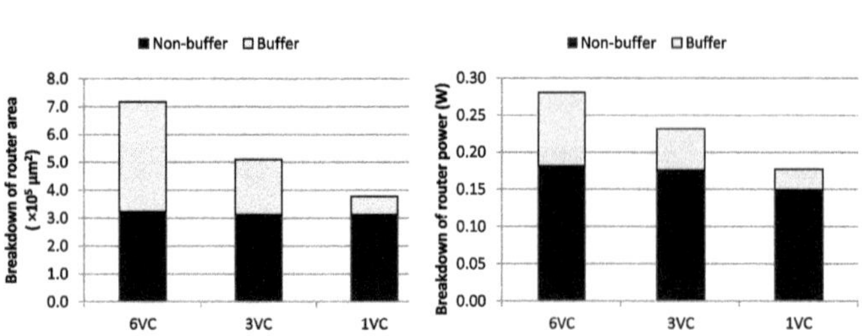

(a) Router area (b) Router power

Figure 1: Breakdown of router area and power

free scheme with 4VCs (i.e, XY_adaptive_4VC), our BC scheme with the minimal 1VC (i.e., BC_1VC) can reduce router energy and area up to 51.2% and 58.3%, respectively, and has comparable performance at the same time. As the proposed BC scheme does not require multiple virtual channels, it also reduces the complexity of router arbitration logic which brings the opportunity to increase router frequency and further improve system performance.

The rest of the paper is organized as follows. Section 2 provides motivation for reducing VC cost and background for bubble flow control. Section 3 proposes our Bubble Ring and Bubble Coloring schemes to avoid routing- and protocol-induced deadlocks, providing a proof sketch for deadlock freedom. Section 5 describes our evaluation methodology, and Section 6 presents simulation results. Related work is discussed in Section 7. We conclude the paper and discuss some future work in Section 8.

2. BACKGROUND AND MOTIVATION

2.1 Need for Reducing Virtual Channel Cost

Deadlocks in interconnection networks include routing-induced deadlocks that are caused by cyclic dependence in routing functions and protocol-induced deadlocks that are caused by dependencies among different types of messages (e.g., a reply message depends on a request message). To avoid these network abnormalities, virtual channels (VCs) [9, 10] have been used extensively in many deadlock-avoidance schemes. For example, messages in the MOESI directory cache protocol [14] can be classified into three dependent classes. Within each message class, two VCs can be used to implement deadlock-free adaptive routing in a 2-D mesh, for instance, by applying Duato's Protocol [11] – one VC employs deterministic routing (e.g., XY-routing) to provide escape paths while the other VC acts as an adaptive resource to enable fully adaptive routing. Then, to avoid protocol-induced deadlocks, at least three independent virtual networks (VNs) are needed to separate different dependent message classes.

The above typical way of avoiding deadlocks, however, is achieved at a large overhead of high VC count manifested in router area, power and frequency. To illustrate the overhead, Figure 1 plots the breakdown of router area and power for different number of VCs at 45nm with 3GHz frequency and 1.1V operating voltage (more details of the simulation infrastructure are described in Section 5). The first bars in Figure 1 (a) and (b) correspond to the above example using 6 VCs to avoid routing- and protocol-induced deadlocks. As can be seen, over 54% of the router's area and 35% of the

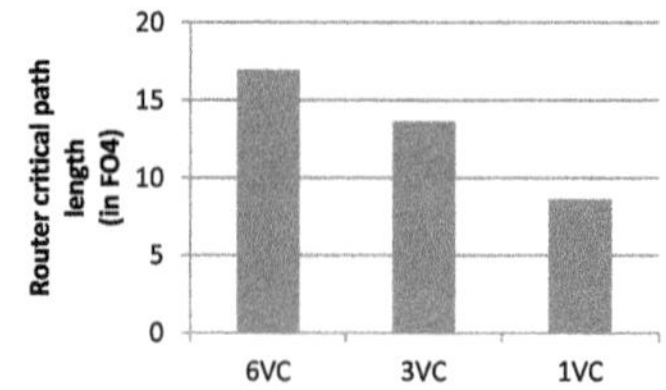

Figure 2: Router critical path length

router power are consumed by the virtual channel buffers, demonstrating a great need to minimize VC requirements.

The overhead of VCs can be reduced in both routing- and protocol-induced deadlock avoidance schemes. Consider first the impacts of reducing VC requirement in avoiding routing-induced deadlocks. The second bars (i.e., the 3VC bar) in Figure 1 (a) and (b) show that, if a deadlock-free scheme only needs one VC per VN to avoid deadlocks in the routing algorithm, the overall buffer area and power can be reduced by 50% and 43%, respectively (which corresponds to a savings of 29% and 18% of total router area and power, respectively). However, to compensate for the performance degradation with fewer VCs, the design of such deadlock-free schemes becomes very challenging in order to provide a higher degree of routing freedom, in particular, to support fully adaptive routing with only 1 VC per VN. In Section 3.1, the Bubble Ring scheme is proposed to achieve the potential benefits of reducing VCs while being able to preserve full adaptivity in routing algorithms.

Another effective but more challenging way to reduce VC requirement is to devise schemes to handle protocol-induced deadlocks more efficiently. In the ideal form, such schemes should avoid all possible deadlocks with minimally 1 VC in total, regardless of the number of dependent message classes. The rightmost bars in Figure 1 (a) and (b) highlight the advantages. Compared to the scheme with 6VCs, the buffer area and power is reduced by 83% and 74%, respectively (which corresponds to a savings of 47% and 37% of the router area and power, respectively). However, to realize those schemes, significant modifications are needed from previous approaches. Section 3.2 proposes a new innovative scheme (i.e., Bubble Coloring) which can avoid protocol-induced deadlocks without requiring multiple virtual channels.

In addition to saving resources, the number of VCs also has a considerable impact on the complexity of router control logic, particularly the VC allocator (VA) and switch allocator (SA). The SA is affected as the input-arbitration step in SA is to select one VC from multiple VCs within the same physical channel to participate in the output-arbitration step in SA. The VA and SA stages typically lie on the critical path of the router pipeline and determine the router frequency [24]. Figure 2 compares the length of the router critical path, calculated from the delay model proposed by Peh and Dally [19]. As shown in the figure, the router critical path can be shortened by 19% and 48% in schemes with 3VCs and 1VC, respectively, indicating a considerable reduction in router latency and increase in throughput when configured at maximum achievable frequency.

In summary, considering the direct impacts of reducing the number of VCs on router area, power and frequency, as well as the indirect impact on network and overall system performance, it is imperative to devise efficient deadlock-free schemes that minimize the VC requirement in avoiding routing- and protocol-induced deadlocks.

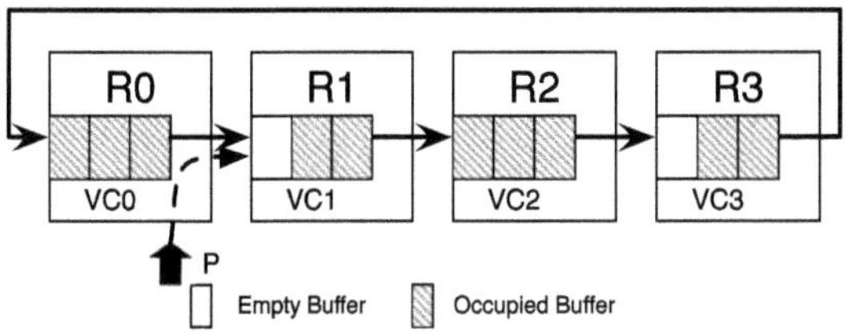

Figure 3: Bubble flow control

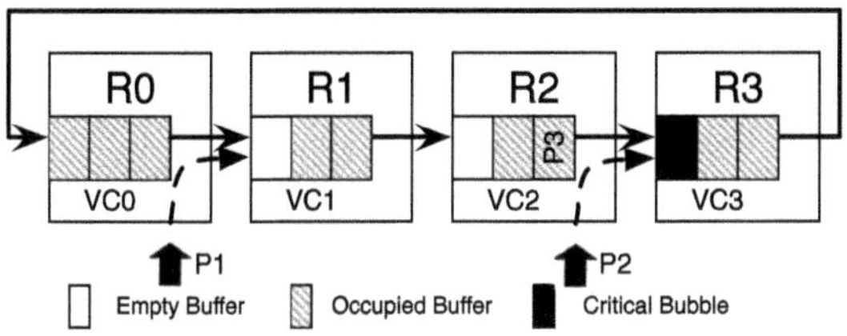

Figure 4: Critical bubble scheme

2.2 Bubble Flow Control and Critical Bubble Scheme

Deadlocks can be handled by the routing algorithm and/or the flow control mechanism. Prior work [21, 6, 5] has been proposed to use flow control instead of routing restrictions on additional virtual channels as a means of avoiding deadlocks to reduce VC cost. But these works have some limiting constraints.

Bubble Flow Control (BFC) [21] has been proposed to avoid routing-induced deadlocks in any embedded ring in tori. A bubble in BFC is an empty packet-sized buffer. According to the theorem of BFC, for any unidirectional ring in a given dimension of a torus network, the ring is deadlock-free if there is at least one bubble located anywhere in the ring after packet injection. Figure 3 depicts an example for a unidirectional ring of an arbitrary dimension in a torus. Each small rectangle represents a packet-sized buffer. Packet P is allowed to inject into VC1, as after the injection there is still a bubble in VC3 which ensures deadlock freedom within the ring. Along with Dimension-Order Routing (DOR) that avoids deadlocks across dimensions by restricting the routes provided to packets, BFC is free from routing-induced deadlock in tori.

To implement the theorem of BFC, global information needs to be communicated at each local node. Otherwise, as in the above example, packet P at R0 has only the information of VC1 (which is stored in the upstream router R0) but is not aware of the buffer utilization of any other node. As a result, P does not have sufficient information to make an optimal decision. The Critical Bubble Scheme (CBS) proposed in [6] solves this difficulty by using the notion of a *critical bubble* to convey the global information locally. As shown in Figure 4, an empty packet-sized buffer in any router along the directional ring is marked as the critical bubble for the entire ring (e.g., the black rectangle in VC3). This critical bubble can only be used by packets that are already in the ring, but cannot be used by injecting packets. For instance, P1 is allowed to inject as there is at least one non-critical bubble in VC1, whereas P2 is not allowed to inject as the only bubble in VC3 is the critical bubble. Essentially, the absence of the critical bubble at VC1 indicates the existence of a bubble (i.e., the critical bubble) elsewhere in the ring, thus providing implicit global information.

The CBS only needs each buffer to be at least one packet-size, and if more than one packet is injecting simultaneously (e.g., P1 and P2 are injecting in the same cycle), it is clear which one should be injected and which one should not, based only on local information. In addition, the critical bubble can be displaced backward in the ring either proactively (e.g., if VC2 is empty and P2 is waiting for injection), or by the incoming packet (e.g., P3 occupying the critical bubble will mark the newly freed buffer in VC2 as the critical bubble so that logically the critical bubble is simply transferred backwards rather than consumed). In both cases, the existence of the critical bubble in the ring is always maintained, ensuring that not all buffers are fully occupied. However, like BFC, CBS is applicable only to torus-like topologies. Moreover, two VCs per VN are needed to implement adaptive routing and separate VNs are required to avoid protocol-induced deadlocks, making both CBS and BFC susceptible to high VC count.

In this paper, we extend the basic notion of bubble flow control and critical bubbles as the basis for our proposed approach to provide an efficient deadlock-free scheme on any topologies but without the need for multiple VCs.

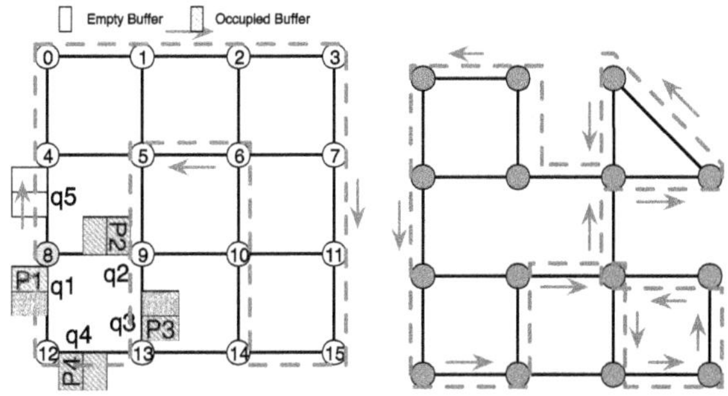

(a) A 4 × 4 mesh (b) An irregular network

Figure 5: Topologies with virtual rings

3. PROPOSED SCHEME

3.1 Avoiding Routing-induced Deadlocks

The Bubble Ring (BR) scheme is comprised of a bubble flow control mechanism and a routing algorithm.

The basic idea of Bubble Ring flow control is first to construct a unidirectional virtual ring that connects all the nodes in the network. Figure 5 shows two examples of virtual rings (represented by dash lines) for a 4×4 mesh and an irregular topology[1]. The ring is "virtual" because there is no additional links or queues for implementing the ring. Only nominal control logic is needed for the routers to associate the input ports and output ports that are in this virtual ring. Note that this ring is not necessarily a Hamiltonian cycle since a node can be visited more than once as is shown in Figure 5 (b). For performance reasons, the virtual ring should be as short as possible. Intuitively, such a virtual ring can always be constructed if the topology is strongly connected. With that, the critical bubble scheme [6] can be applied in such a way to make sure there is always at least one free buffer in the virtual ring. In this way, packets in the ring can always be able to move along the ring to reach any destination.

[1]This is one of many possible topologies which could be formed by construction or due to faults occurring in a base network such as a 2D mesh with express links.

The routing algorithm can use the virtual ring as an escape path. The packet will first try to use its preferred output port based on a specified adaptive routing subfunction which provides a subset of the total routing options supplied by the routing algorithm. If there is no preferred output port available, the packet can be forwarded to the escape outport (i.e., the outport in the virtual ring) provided by the escape routing subfunction also defined by the routing algorithm. For example, in Figure 5 (a), packets P1, P2, P3 and P4 are at the head of queue q1, q2, q3 and q4, respectively. Each queue is in the associated router R8, R9, R12 and R13. Assume that all these four queues are full. With the specified adaptive routing subfunction, a cyclic dependency on these queues may occur. For example, the adaptive routing subfunction may supply only q2, q3, q4 and q1 to packet P1, P2, P3 and P4, respectively. In this situation, our Bubble Ring routing subfunction can avoid deadlocks by providing a way of escape from such knotted cyclic dependency. In this example, since P1 cannot choose its preferred output port supplied by the adaptive routing subfunction (i.e., q2), it can be forwarded to the output port in the virtual ring, i.e., q5. Note that because BR flow control guarantees that there is always at least one free buffer in the virtual ring, P1 can move to q5 eventually even if q5 is temporally full. After P1 moves to q5, packets P2, P3 and P4 can continue to move to their preferred output ports so that this deadlock is avoided. Note that in order to allow packets from any direction to move into the virtual ring, we assume that packets can make U turns. Different from Duato's Protocol [11] where the escape path consists of the resources from an additional set of virtual channels, the escape path in our BR scheme is comprised of the same set of resources used for the adaptive paths. For example, q3, q4 and q1 are the queues for both the escape path and the preferred adaptive output queues for P2, P3 and P4.

The formal description is as follows. To facilitate the discussion throughout the paper, we first introduce some basic definitions derived from [11, 12, 21].

Definition 1. An *interconnection network*, I, is a strongly connected directed graph $I = G(N, Q)$. The vertices of the graph, N, represent the set of processing nodes. The arcs of the graph, Q, represent the set of queues associated to the communication links interconnecting the nodes. Each queue $q_i \in Q$ has capacity of $cap(q_i)$ measured in the number of packets, and the number of packets currently stored in the queue is denoted as $size(q_i)$.

The set of queues Q is divided into three subsets: injection queues Q_I, delivery queues Q_D, and network queues Q_N. Each node uses a queue from Q_I to send packets that travel through the network employing queues from Q_N, and when they reach their destination they enter a queue from Q_D. Therefore, packets are routed from a queue in the set $Q_{IN} = Q_N \cup Q_I$ to a queue in the set $Q_{ND} = Q_N \cup Q_D$. Let Q_{VR} be a subset of Q_N consisting of all the network queues along some minimal virtual ring that spans all nodes of I.

Definition 2. A routing function, $R : Q_{IN} \times N \rightarrow \wp\{Q_{ND}\}$, provides a set of alternative queues to route a packet p located at the head of any queue $q_i \in Q_{IN}$ to its destination node $n_d \in N$. $\wp\{Q_{ND}\}$ denotes the power set of Q_{ND}. A deterministic routing function provides only one alternative queue, $R(q_i, n_d) = q_j$, $q_j \in Q_{ND}$. A routing subfunction, R_s, for a given routing function R is a routing function defined in the same domain as R but its range (i.e., set of alternative next queues) is restricted to a subset $Q_{NDs} \subseteq Q_{ND}$. Let R_{VR} be the routing subfunction that provides a next-hop queue in the virtual ring, i.e., $R_{VR}(q_i, n_d) = q_j$, $q_j \in Q_{VR}$.

Definition 3. A flow control function, $F : Q_{IN} \times Q_{ND} \rightarrow \{true, false\}$, determines the access permission for a packet p located at the head of queue q_i to enter queue $q_j \in R(q_i, n_d)$. Thus, the packet p is allowed to advance from q_i to q_j if $F(q_i, q_j) = true$.

Let $cb(q_j)$ be the number of critical bubbles at q_j. In this paper, we assume there is only one critical bubble in the virtual ring, so $\sum_{q_i \in Q_{VR}} cb(q_i) = 1$.

To keep one free packet-sized buffer in the virtual ring at all times, our flow control on the bubble ring, F_{BR}, is based on critical bubble flow control:

$$F_{BR}(q_i, q_j) = true$$
$$if \begin{cases} size(q_j) \le cap(q_j) - 1 & \text{when } q_i \in Q_{VR} \text{ or } q_j \notin Q_{VR} \\ size(q_j) \le cap(q_j) - cb(q_j) - 1 & \text{when } q_i \notin Q_{VR} \text{ and } q_j \in Q_{VR} \end{cases} \quad (1)$$

When a packet outside the virtual ring wants to move into the ring (i.e., $q_i \notin Q_{VR}$ and $q_j \in Q_{VR}$), it cannot occupy the critical bubble. In other words, if the critical bubble is present at q_j (i.e., $cb(q_j) = 1$), the packet needs at least two free buffers to move into q_j (i.e., $size(q_j) \le cap(q_j) - 2$). Otherwise, it just needs at least one free buffer.

For the rest of the conditions, if the packet wants to (1) travel outside the ring (i.e., $q_i \notin Q_{VR}$ and $q_j \notin Q_{VR}$), or (2) go out of the ring (i.e., $q_i \in Q_{VR}$ and $q_j \notin Q_{VR}$), or (3) stay in the ring (i.e., $q_i \in Q_{VR}$ and $q_j \in Q_{VR}$), it only needs at least one free buffer at q_j. Note that based on the Critical Bubble Scheme [6], if a packet in the ring occupies the critical bubble, the newly freed buffer in the upstream router will be marked as the the new critical bubble, which guarantees that there is still at least one free buffer marked as a critical bubble in the ring.

This flow control mechanism will guarantee that there is always a free bubble inside the virtual ring. Due to this free buffer, the packets in the ring cannot be blocked so that the routing algorithm can use this ring as its escape path to avoid routing-induced deadlocks. The formal description of a routing function based on our BR scheme is the following:

$$R(q_i, n_d) = R_{adaptive}(q_i, n_d) \cup R_{VR}(q_i, n_d) \quad (2)$$

The packet will try to choose its preferred queues based on a given adaptive routing subfunction $R_{adaptive}(q_i, n_d)$ (e.g., Region Congestion Aware routing [16]) first, and use the queue in the virtual ring (i.e., $q_j \in Q_{VR}$) supplied by the escape routing subfunction (i.e., R_{VR}) as its alternative escape path.

LEMMA 1. *Packets in virtual ring queues provided by the routing subfunction R_{VR} can always make forward progress under F_{BR} flow control.*

PROOF SKETCH. This can be proved by contradiction. Assume a deadlock occurs, such that no packet in the virtual ring can move to the next queue. F_{BR} flow control keeps the critical bubble inside the ring. Without losing generality, assume the critical bubble is at router i (i.e., R_i). If there is a packet in the upstream router (i.e., R_{i-1}) along the virtual ring, the routing function supplies a path for the packet to move to router R_i when there is no other preferred output ports for this packet available. Due to the presence of the critical bubble (i.e., one free bubble) at router i, bubble ring flow control will guarantee the packet can move to router R_i. This contradicts with the deadlock assumption. If there is no packet in the upstream router R_{i-1}, we can continue

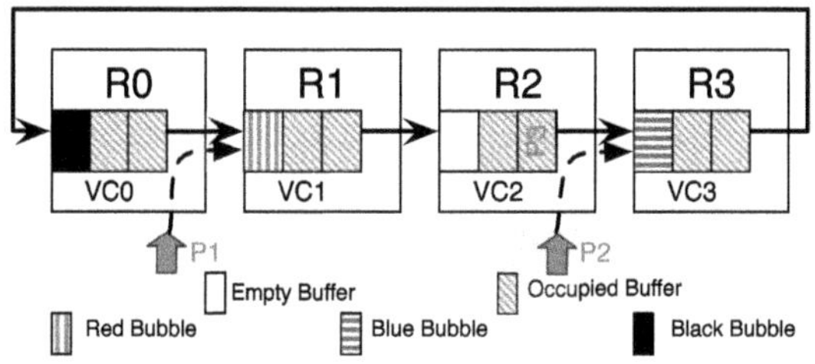

Figure 6: Bubble Coloring flow control

to search backward along the ring until we find a packet at router R_{i-j}. Due to the free buffer available at that downstream router, this packet can move. □

THEOREM 1. *An interconnection network I with a routing function R and flow control F_{BR} is free from routing-induced deadlocks if there exists a virtual ring queue supplied by R_{VR} and controlled by F_{BR} such that, for each cycle, at least one packet occupying the head of a queue can be allocated to the virtual ring queue.*

PROOF SKETCH. If there are packets in the virtual ring, based on Lemma 1, we can always find a packet able to move along the ring. If the ring is empty, the packets outside the ring can make progress by injecting into the queues in the virtual ring as provided by the routing algorithm. □

3.2 Avoiding Protocol-induced Deadlocks

Although our proposed BR scheme is able to avoid routing-induced deadlocks, it is still susceptible to protocol-induced deadlocks. For example, assume there are two message classes A and B, where class A depends on class B (e.g., request-reply classes). Also assume that all the queues in the network are full except for one critical bubble in the ring and that all the packets in the virtual ring are from message class A. In this situation, packets from class A cannot be consumed because they are waiting for the completion of packets from class B. Packets from class B cannot move forward either, because the virtual ring is fully occupied by packets from class A, and there is no room for them to inject. Hence, it is possible for protocol-induced deadlocks to occur under the BR scheme.

To avoid protocol-induced deadlocks, we propose Bubble Coloring which is a novel extension of our Bubble Ring scheme. The Bubble Coloring (BC) scheme guarantees that packets in one message class can always reach their destinations even though packets of other message classes are blocked from being consumed at end nodes. The basic idea is to reserve one additional bubble (i.e., one free packet sized buffer) in the virtual ring for each message class besides the original critical bubble used for avoiding routing-induced deadlocks. These bubbles are represented by different colors corresponding to distinct message classes. The colored bubble for a given message class serves as a normal free buffer for the packets from its own message class (i.e., it can be used for injection), but it serves as a critical bubble for all other message classes (i.e., it cannot be used for injection).

Figure 6 provides an example of the BC scheme. As is shown, VC0, VC1, VC2 and VC3 form the virtual ring. The red packet, $P1$, which is out of the ring can move into the ring (i.e., into VC1) because it can occupy the bubble having the same color (i.e., red). However, Packet $P2$ with red color cannot move into the ring (i.e., into VC3) because it cannot occupy a bubble with a different color (i.e., blue). Packet P3 already inside the virtual ring can move to VC3 and pull the blue bubble to VC2 at the same time even it has a different color from the bubble. This is because it is already in the virtual ring as opposed to trying to inject into the ring. By reserving such a colored bubble in the virtual ring for every message class, packets from the same message class can always have a chance to move into the ring, i.e., not be blocked by packets from the other message classes. Since the packets in the ring cannot be blocked due to the existence of the original critical bubble, no protocol-induced deadlocks can happen.

To make sure colored bubbles will always stay in the virtual ring, the BC scheme has two additional rules beyond the BR scheme: (1) Once a colored bubble is occupied by a packet with the same color at injection into the virtual ring, the packet will be marked as having consumed the colored bubble and carry forward the color mark for that message class as it travels along the ring. (2) When the packet marked as having consumed a colored bubble moves out of the ring, it will leave the color mark to the newly freed buffer so that the colored bubble will reappear in the ring. These two rules will continue a colored bubble in the virtual ring for reuse by other packets having the same color at the injection into the ring.

We assign a distinct color to the original critical bubble, i.e., black, such that there is no black message class. Therefore, no packet can use the black bubble for injection. In this sense, our Bubble Ring scheme can be considered as a special case of our Bubble Coloring scheme.

The formal description of the proposed BC scheme is as follows:

Let $cb_k(q_j)$ be the number of bubbles with color k at queue j and $color(q_i)$ be the color of the packet at the head of q_i. Assume there are $M+1$ colors for M different message classes, where one color (i.e., black) is designated as the original critical bubble. In this paper, we assume there is only one bubble for each color, so for each message class k, $k = 1, 2, ..., M+1$, $\sum_{q_j \in Q_{VR}} cb_k(q_j) = 1$. With this, BC flow control is given by the following:

$$F_{BC}(q_i, q_j) = true$$
$$if \begin{cases} size(q_j) \leq cap(q_j) - 1, \text{ when } q_i \in Q_{VR} \text{ or } q_j \notin Q_{VR} \\ size(q_j) \leq cap(q_j) - \sum_{k=1, k \neq color(q_i)}^{M+1} cb_k(q_j) - 1, \\ \quad \text{when } q_i \notin Q_{VR} \text{ and } q_j \in Q_{VR} \end{cases} \tag{3}$$

If a packet at the head of queue q_i with $color(q_i)$ wants to move into the virtual ring (i.e., $q_i \notin Q_{VR}$ and $q_j \in Q_{VR}$), it needs one additional free buffer besides all the bubbles at q_j it cannot occupy (i.e., all the bubbles with a different color, $\sum_{k=1, k \neq color(q_i)}^{M+1} cb_k(q_j)$).

If a packet occupies a colored bubble, it will take the color mark of this bubble with it when it travels inside the ring and leave the color mark to the newly freed buffer when it moves out of the ring. In this way, all the colored bubbles will be kept in the ring.

A routing function based on our proposed bubble coloring scheme is the same as that based on our BR scheme in Eq. (2). That is, packets will be supplied with queues in the virtual ring if their preferred output ports are not available.

THEOREM 2. *An interconnection network I with a routing function R and flow control F_{BC} is free from protocol-induced deadlocks if there exists a virtual ring queue supplied by R_{VR} and controlled by F_{BC} such that, packets from any message class cannot persistently be blocked by packets from other message classes.*

PROOF SKETCH. The BC scheme reserves one bubble (i.e., free buffer) in the ring for each message class so that packets from different message classes have a chance to move into the ring at sometime. According to Lemma 1, due to the existence of the original critical bubble (i.e., black bubble), packets in the ring can make forward movement eventually, which means packets from any message class can never be blocked by packets from other message classes, thus no protocol-induced deadlocks can form. □

3.3 Discussion

3.3.1 Misroutes

Our adaptive routing algorithm may cause misroutes when packets need to move to the escape output ports that do not lie on the minimal path to break the knotted cyclic dependencies. To reduce the chance of misroutes, we set a waiting time threshold T_w. With this, a packet will not move to its escape port unless it cannot be allocated any of the queues in its preferred output ports in the successive T_w cycles. The longer T_w is, the less chance the packet will be misrouted. However, increasing T_w will also increase the blocking time of the packets when cyclic dependencies occur. Empirically, we set the T_w to be 5 cycles .

Note that the escape outports may be on the minimal path for a packet which avoids misroutes. Also, packets that are deflected to the virtual ring and misrouted can return to their minimal paths (i.e., they do not need to stay in the ring) once there are resources available. It is also possible to minimize the misroutes with more advanced virtual ring structures for some particular topology. For example, for a mesh with bidirectional links, two virtual rings with opposite directions can be constructed to provide more escape output ports, so that packets will have higher chance to choose the escape output ports that are on the minimal paths. Different types of virtual rings (e.g., hierarchical rings) at the different virtual networks can also be constructed to further improve the performance. These are topology-specific optimizations which can be explored for the specific network structures.

3.3.2 Livelock

A pathological problem that could arise with misrouting is livelock. When a packet continues to be misrouted, it may not be able to move closer to its destination. To solve this livelock problem, we set a threshold for the maximum number of allowed misroutes (T_m). If a packet has been misrouted for more than T_m times, the packet will be forced to stay in the virtual ring until it reaches its destination.

3.3.3 Starvation

Similar to original bubble flow control [21], our scheme is also susceptible to the starvation problem. Some routers may continually inject packets into the virtual ring, which cause other routers to lose the ability to inject their own packets into the ring. We apply the same starvation prevention design as the original bubble follow control mechanism [21]. If a router detects starvation, it will send a '*starve*' signal to its upstream router along the ring. If a router receives a '*starve*' signal, it will stop injecting packets into the ring and propagate this '*starve*' signal to the next upstream router. Once the packet in this router gets served, the '*starve*' signal will be de-asserted and propagated to the rest of the routers, so that other routers can resume to inject packets into the ring.

4. IMPLEMENTATION

The block diagram in Figure 7 shows the micro-architecture of a typical four-stage virtual cut-through router. Arriving

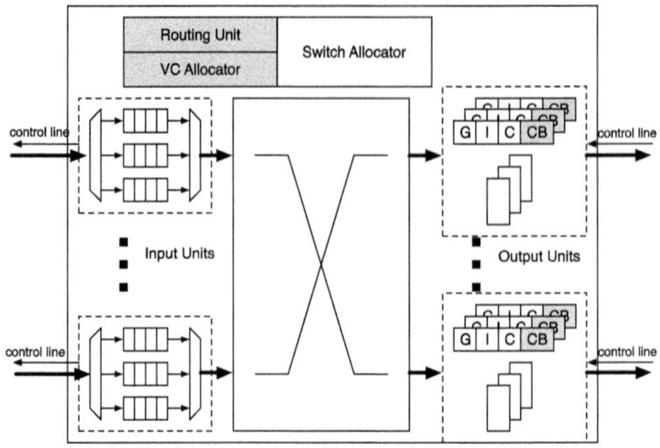

Figure 7: Router micro-architecture

packets will first be written into the input buffer, and then travel through the stages of Virtual channel Allocation (VA), Switch Allocation (SA), Switch Traversal (ST), and finally move out to the next router through Link Traversal (LT) stage. Note that the VA stage is not required unless additional VCs are used for mitigating head-of-line (HOL) blocking. That is, multiple VCs are not required by our proposed schemes to avoid deadlocks but can be used to reduce congestion. Look-ahead routing is adopted to reduce the zero-load latency.

The modifications needed to implement BC scheme is indicated as the shaded areas in Figure 7. The Routing Unit is modified to support BC routing algorithm (i.e., Eq. (2)). To support the rules of BR/BC flow control, Virtual channel Allocation (VA) logic is slightly modified based on Eq. (1) or Eq. (3.2). Some control logic is also added to associate the input and output ports in the virtual ring.

At the output units, the fields of the output virtual channel state are extended. Besides the conventional fields, such as global state (G), input VC (I) and credit count (C) [8], a new field for counting number of bubbles in each color (CB) is added.

To exchange the information about colored bubbles between routers, one control signal for each color is added. To prevent starvation, one '*starve*' signal is also included. Note that these extra control signals are only needed for the input and output ports along the virtual ring.

5. METHODOLOGY

The proposed scheme is evaluated experimentally under a full-system simulation using GEM5 [4], with Garnet [2] for detailed timing of the interconnection network. DSENT [22] configured with a model of an industrial standard 45nm CMOS process is used for router power and area estimation. All the additional hardware described in Section 4 is modeled in the simulator and accounted for in the evaluation. A canonical four-stage Virtual Cut-Through (VCT) switched router with credit-based flow control is assumed. We use a routing algorithm conforming to Eq. (2) where the adaptive routing subfunction provides output ports along all minimal paths to the destination of the packet. Output ports with more credits are prioritized over those with lower credits. Table 1 lists the key parameters of the simulation configuration. We compare all the schemes with mesh networks, on which various deadlock-free schemes have been studied extensively in prior works [11, 10].

Table 1: Full system simulation configuration

Network topology	4x4 or 8x8 Mesh
Router	4-stage VCT, 2GHz
Input buffer	10 flits per VC
Link bandwidth	128 flit/cycle
Cores	Alpha EV5 Core, 2GHz
L1 cache (I & D)	Private, 2-way, 32kB, 2 cycle
L2 cache	Private, 8-way, 512kB each, 6 cycle
Coherence protocol	directory MOESI with 3 message classes
Memory controller	4, located one at each corner
Memory latency	128 cycles

With a typical 128-bit link width, short packets of 16-bits only contain a single flit while long packets carrying 64 byte data plus addition control information have 5 flits. The depth of the buffer for each virtual channel is 10 flits which can hold at most two long packets. A directory MOESI coherence protocol with three message classes [14] are used in the simulation.

We compare the following different deadlock-free schemes with varying number of VCs in our experiments:

1. XY_3VC: XY routing is used to avoid routing-induced deadlocks and 1 VC for each message class is assigned to avoid protocol-induced deadlocks. This scheme requires three VCs in total.

2. XY_adaptive_4VC: Compared to XY_3VC, this scheme adds one additional adaptive virtual channel shared by all message classes and uses XY_3VC as its escape path. It requires four VCs in total.

3. BR_3VC: The Bubble Ring scheme is used to allow fully adaptive routing with routing-induced deadlock-freedom, but it requires one VC for each message class to avoid protocol-induced deadlocks. This scheme requires three VCs in total.

4. BR_adaptive_4VC: Compared to BR_3VC, this scheme adds one additional adaptive virtual channel shared by all message classes and uses BR_3VC as its escape path. It requires four VCs in total.

5. BC_xVC: This group of schemes applies the Bubble Coloring (BC) scheme to avoid both routing- and protocol-induced deadlocks. The number of virtual channels is x (x = 1, 2, 3 or 4).

Both synthetic traffic and multi-threaded applications are used as workloads. For synthetic traffic, the simulator is warmed up for 10,000 cycles and the statistics are collected over another 100,000 cycles. Four traffic patterns are simulated: uniform random (UR), transpose (TP), bit complement (BC) and Hotspot [8]. For Hotspot traffic, the four nodes at the corner of the mesh network have four times higher probability to be chosen as destinations than all other nodes. We assume there are three message classes. The first two message classes send short 1-flit packets, and the third one sends long 5-flit packets. The third message class has twice the injection rate as the first two (i.e., measured in packets/node/cycle).

For real applications, we use the multi-threaded PARSEC benchmark suite [3]. Each core is warmed up for sufficiently long time (with a minimum of 10 million cycles) and then run until the end of the parallel region. All PARSEC benchmarks use the simsmall input set.

6. EVALUATION

6.1 Synthetic Workload

Figure 8 shows the performance comparison of different deadlock avoidance schemes with varying number of VCs on a 4×4 mesh. As can be seen, XY_3VC scheme has the worst performance under adversarial traffic, i.e., TP, among all the schemes. Under TP traffic, XY routing is not able to balance the traffic between the X dimension and the Y dimension, which leads to the situation where network queues in the X dimension are saturated, while ones in the Y dimension are only lightly loaded. However, by adding one additional adaptive channel over XY_3VC, XY_adaptive_4VC can largely avoid such unbalanced saturation and improve the saturation throughput significantly (over 109%)[2]. This additional virtual channel also helps XY_adaptive_4VC to achieve higher throughput under UR (29.4%), BC (9.1%) and Hotspot (16.7%) due to less head-of-line (HOL) blocking.

Compared to XY_3VC, the proposed BR scheme (BR_3VC) has worse performance under UR and BC traffic patterns. The performance degradation results from the misrouting penalty. When the injection rate increases, packets are more likely to go along the unidirectional virtual ring instead of using preferred outports. When the network is saturated, the throughput of BR_3VC is almost equivalent to the throughput of a unidirectional ring since the majority of packets need to travel along the ring to reach their destinations. However, for TP traffic, the full routing adaptivity that the BR scheme provides enables higher throughput than XY_3VC (145%). The throughput is better than XY_adaptive_4VC (17%) because it allows more VCs to be used adaptively. By adding one adaptive VC on BR_3VC, BR_4VC has its throughput improved even more (83.3%, 18% and 66.7% under UR, Hotspot and BC respectively). This is because that the fourth adaptive channel can be used to relieve the misrouting that would otherwise occur in the first three adaptive channels.

The proposed BC schemes have overall better throughput than XY_3VC and BR_3VC even with only one virtual channel under most of the traffic patterns. With the same number of VCs, BC_3VC outperforms both XY_3VC and BR_3VC under all the traffic patterns. Compared to BR_3VC, the existence of multiple bubbles in the virtual ring can accelerate packet flow in the ring, which increases its throughput. BC_3VC provides 83%, 3.8%, 18.1% and 66.7% throughput improvement over BR_3VC under traffic patterns of UR, TP, Hotpot and BC, respectively. Compared to XY_3VC, BC_3VC has better routing adaptivity, which yields higher throughput (i.e., 29%, 118%, 18% and 10% under UR, TP, Hotspot and BC, respectively). By employing more VCs to reduce HOL blocking, BC schemes can gain higher throughput. Different from XY_3VC and BR_3VC where packets from different message classes can only occupy the assigned virtual channel, the BC scheme allows packets from different message classes to share any virtual channel freely, which allows the traffic to be balanced efficiently among all the virtual channels for the situations where different message classes have different injection rates. This is another source of throughput improvement. From the figure, we can see that no significant throughput improvement can be gained, when the number of VCs in the

[2]Saturation throughput corresponds to the load rate at which the average latency is three times that of the zero-load latency.

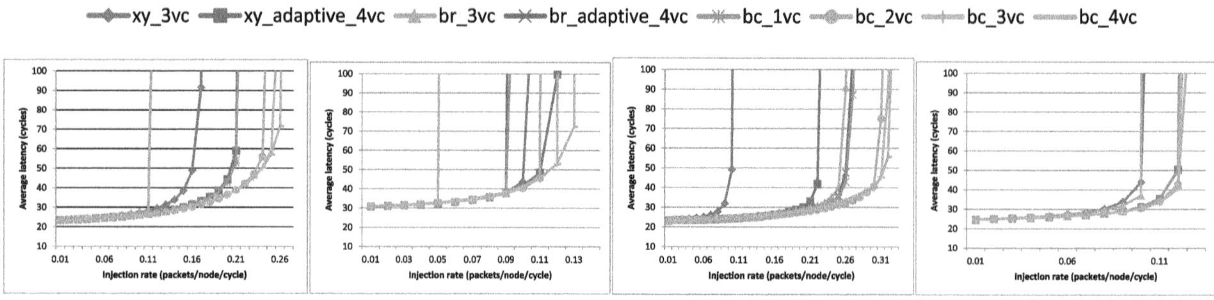

(a) uniform random (b) bit complement (c) transpose (d) hotspot

Figure 8: Performance comparison for 4x4 mesh

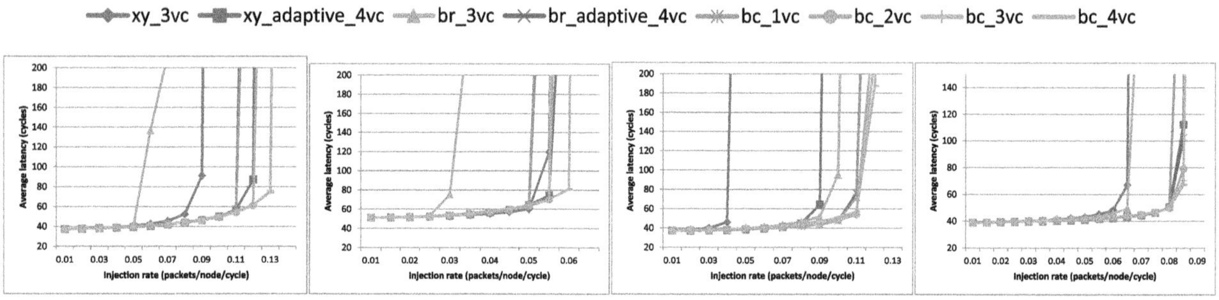

(a) uniform random (b) bit complement (c) transpose (d) hotspot

Figure 9: Performance comparison for 8x8 mesh

BC schemes increases from 2 to 4, which indicates that the most cost-effective design is the BC scheme with 2 VCs.

In evaluating scalability of the proposed schemes, Figure 9 compares the performances of the same set of schemes mentioned above on an 8x8 mesh. A similar trend of the BC schemes performing better than XY and the BR schemes can be observed for all traffic patterns. Compared to the XY and BR schemes with the same number of VCs, BC_3VC achieves higher throughput over XY_3VC by 40%, 140%, 28% and 9% and over BR_3VC by 133%, 9%, 28.5% and 71.4% under UR, TP, Hotspot and BC, respectively. Thus, as the network scales, the proposed BC scheme continues to outperform other schemes significantly which implies it has good scalability.

In summary, better routing adaptivity provided by the BR and BC schemes enables them to have significant performance improvement under adversarial traffic like TP. The BC scheme is able to use virtual channels more efficiently by freely balancing traffic of different message classes among all VCs. Our BC scheme can outperform other schemes with the same number of VCs and can provide comparable performance even with minimally only one VC.

6.2 PARSEC Benchmark Workloads

6.2.1 Execution time

Figure 10 shows the normalized execution time for six PARSEC workloads. The results are normalized to the execution time of the workloads using the XY_3VC scheme. For real workloads such as PARSEC benchmarks, their load rates are relative low, i.e., no more than 0.1 packet per node per cycle on average, which makes little performance differences between various schemes with the same router frequency since all the schemes have the same zero-load latency. The biggest difference in execution time among all the schemes for a single benchmark (i.e., ferret) is within 5%. On average, even the best scheme (i.e., BC_4VC) has

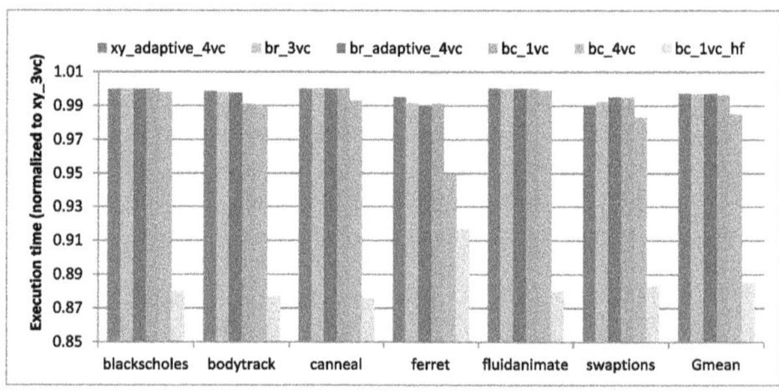

Figure 10: Execution time for PARSEC

only less than 2% execution time reduction over the worst scheme (i.e., XY_3VC). However, as we discussed in Section 2.1, reducing the number of VCs can reduce the length of the router critical path, which gives the opportunity to increase the router frequency. The BC_1VC_HF scheme, which has the same core frequency (2GHz) as the rest of schemes but increases router frequency slightly from 2Ghz to 2.3Ghz (i.e., 15%), can achieve significant performance improvement, i.e., 12% execution time reduction on average. These results show the ability of our BC scheme with minimal number of VCs to provide an increased opportunity of improving overall system performance.

6.2.2 Energy

Figure 11 shows the normalized router energy consumption for six PARSEC benchmarks with different deadlock-free schemes. The results are normalized to XY_3VC. From the figure, we can see that the total router energy is largely affected by the number of virtual channels. The more virtual channels are needed, the more buffers that will be used, which causes more static power consumption. Compared to the schemes with 4VCs (e.g., XY_adaptive_4VC), BC_1VC

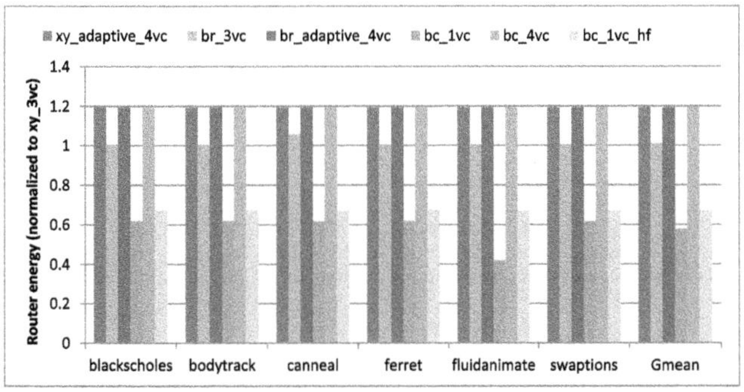

Figure 11: Router energy consumption

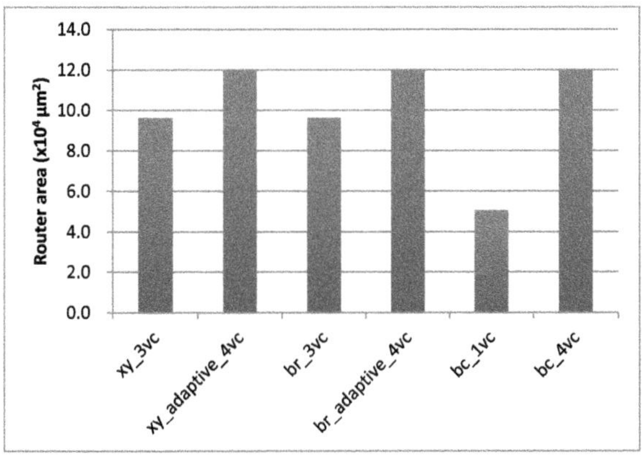

Figure 12: Comparison of per router area

can reduce router energy by up to 51.2%. Under the relatively low traffic load rate, all the schemes will have similar total hop counts since packets in all schemes will likely travel the minimal paths. Therefore, dynamic router energy among different schemes with the same router frequency has no significant differences since the total amount of router activities (e.g., buffer writes, VA/SA arbitrations) is largely dependent on the average packet hop count (i.e., number of packets being forwarded through a router on average). BC_1VC_HF has a higher router energy consumption than BC_1V since the dynamic power has been increased when router frequency becomes higher. In sum, on the one hand, our BC scheme can save a large amount of router energy (shown in Figure 11) without significantly degrading the system performance (shown in Figure 10). On the other hand, our BC scheme provides the opportunity to gain significant performance improvement by increasing router frequency with comparable energy consumption.

6.2.3 Area

Figure 12 shows the comparison of per router area for different schemes. The router area consumption can be divided into buffer or non-buffer (e.g., control logic). Although different schemes have relatively the same non-buffer area, the different number of VCs among different schemes largely affects router buffer area. As expected, the BC scheme with the minimal one virtual channel (i.e., BC_1VC) consumes the least router area. Compared to schemes with 4VCs (e.g., XY_adaptive_4VC), BC_1VC can save router area by up to 58.3%. Considering the fact that there is little performance degradation with reduced number of VCs (shown in Figure 10), it is clear that BC_1VC is most area-efficient among all the schemes.

In summary, by comparing performance, router energy and router area consumption, the simulation results for real multithreaded applications show that the proposed Bubble Coloring scheme with minimal VC requirement can achieve significant improvements in terms of router energy/area efficiency. Compared to conventional XY routing schemes, BC schemes can achieve comparable performance with significant router energy/area savings. The BC scheme also provides the opportunities to significantly improve the system performance by increasing router frequency with no more energy consumption than other schemes.

7. RELATED WORK

Several foundational theories have been established in [11, 12], on which many deadlock-free routing algorithms are based. To improve the effectiveness of routing, previous research has also investigated various selection metrics that utilize local and/or regional information [16]. However, as all these routing algorithms are based on Duato's Protocol [11], at least two virtual channels are needed to implement fully adaptive routing.

The turn model and its extensions [7, 13, 15] avoid routing-induced deadlocks using minimally one VC by disallowing certain paths between the source and destination. Therefore, these schemes can only provide partially adaptive routing as opposed to the fully adaptive routing supported in our proposed approach that can better balance traffic load and reduce contention latency.

While the schemes above can avoid routing-induced deadlocks, they all rely on separate virtual networks to avoid protocol-induced deadlocks, which have considerable negative impacts on area, power and frequency as described in Section 2.1. A formal model of protocol-induced deadlocks is derived in [23], and a recovery-based approach is proposed in [17] to achieve deadlock-freedom; whereas our approach is avoidance-based. Detailed comparison and discussion between the two types of approaches are provided in [20].

Another way of avoiding routing-induced deadlocks is to use bubble flow control mechanisms. Bubble flow control (BFC) was proposed in [21] and adopted in the IBM Blue Gene/L [1]. Recently, more efficient implementations of BFC have been proposed to increase buffer resource utilization [6, 5]. As briefly mentioned before, these works are different from our scheme in two distinct ways. First, these works are applicable only to torus-like topologies whereas our scheme can be applied to a general set of topologies including both regular networks, such as meshes, and irregular networks. Second, existing BFC and its implementations still require separate VNs to avoid protocol-induced deadlocks while our scheme reduces the number of virtual networks to the theoretical minimal value of one.

8. CONCLUSION AND FUTURE WORK

The common way to avoid routing- and protocol-induced deadlocks without losing routing freedom is to use additional virtual channels. However, implementing a large number of VCs in routers has considerable negative impacts on router area, power and frequency. The contribution of this paper is to enable fully adaptive routing on any topology with minimally one virtual channel while still avoiding both routing- and protocol-induced deadlocks. The proposed Bubble Ring flow control mechanism is applied to avoid routing-induced deadlocks through a virtual ring that spans all nodes in the network by maintaining a free packet-sized buffer inside the ring. Routing algorithms, with full routing adaptivity can leverage this deadlock-free virtual ring as its escape path to avoid routing-induced deadlocks. Based on the BR scheme, the Bubble Coloring scheme is proposed to further avoid protocol-induced deadlocks by maintaining one additional free buffer (i.e., colored bubble) in the virtual ring for each message class so that packets from each message class can always reach their destinations through the virtual ring no matter whether other message classes blocked or not. Simulation results for both synthetic traffic and real multi-threaded applications show that, compared to a conventional deadlock-free scheme with 4VCs (i.e, XY_adaptive_4VC), our BC scheme with the minimal 1VC (BC_1VC) can reduce router energy and area by up to 51.2% and 58.3%, respectively, and have comparable performance at the same time. As the proposed BC scheme does not require multiple virtual channels, it also reduces the complexity of the router arbitration logic which brings the opportunity to increase router frequency and further improve system performance.

In the future, the proposed BC scheme can be further extended in promising directions. If a particular topology is given, more virtual rings can be constructed. For example, for meshes with bidirectional links, two unidirectional rings with opposite directions can be constructed, which will reduce the chances of misroutes. The number of misroutes could be further reduced by constructing more advanced rings (e.g., hierarchical rings) on separate virtual channels so that more escape ports along the minimal paths can be found. Our BC scheme can also be used to control network congestion status by adjusting the number of colored bubbles in the virtual rings. The increasing number of bubbles reserved in the virtual ring can accelerate the packet flow along the ring and relieve the congestion status. Considering that the ring is "virtual" and can be easily reconfigured, a class of intelligent congestion control mechanisms with the adaptivity of both virtual ring structures and the number of bubbles in the rings can be derived from our BC scheme in future research.

9. ACKNOWLEDGMENTS

We sincerely thank José Duato for his helpful comments and suggestions. This research was supported, in part, by the National Science Foundation (NSF), grant CCF-0946388.

10. REFERENCES

[1] N. Adiga, G. Almasi, G. Almasi, Y. Aridor, R. Barik, et al. An overview of the bluegene/l supercomputer. In *Proceedings of the 2002 ACM/IEEE conference on Supercomputing*, pages 1–22. IEEE Computer Society Press, 2002.

[2] N. Agarwal, T. Krishna, L.-S. Peh, and N. Jha. Garnet: A detailed on-chip network model inside a full-system simulator. In *Proceedings of the 2009 IEEE International Symposium on Performance Analysis of Systems and Software*, ISPASS '09, pages 33–42, 2009.

[3] C. Bienia and K. Li. Parsec 2.0: A new benchmark suite for chip-multiprocessors. In *Proceedings of the 5th Annual Workshop on Modeling, Benchmarking and Simulation*, June 2009.

[4] N. Binkert, B. Beckmann, G. Black, S. K. Reinhardt, A. Saidi, et al. The gem5 simulator. *ACM SIGARCH Computer Architecture News*, 39(2):1–7, Aug. 2011.

[5] L. Chen and T. M. Pinkston. Worm-bubble flow control. In *Proceedings of the 19th International Symposium on High Performance Computer Architecture*, HPCA '13, pages 366–377, 2013.

[6] L. Chen, R. Wang, and T. M. Pinkston. Critical bubble scheme: An efficient implementation of globally aware network flow control. In *Proceedings of the 25th IEEE International Parallel Distributed Processing Symposium*, IPDPS '11, pages 592–603, 2011.

[7] G.-M. Chiu. The odd-even turn model for adaptive routing. *IEEE Transactions on Parallel and Distributed Systems*, 11(7):729–738, 2000.

[8] W. Dally and B. Towles. *Principles and Practices of Interconnection Networks.* Morgan Kaufmann Publishers Inc., San Francisco, CA, USA, 2003.

[9] W. J. Dally. Virtual-channel flow control. *IEEE Transactions on Parallel and Distributed Systems*, 3(2):194–205, 1992.

[10] W. J. Dally and H. Aoki. Deadlock-free adaptive routing in multicomputer networks using virtual channels. *IEEE Transactions on Parallel and Distributed Systems*, 4(4):466–475, 1993.

[11] J. Duato. A necessary and sufficient condition for deadlock-free routing in cut-through and store-and-forward networks. *IEEE Transactions on Parallel and Distributed Systems*, 7(8):841–854, 1996.

[12] J. Duato and T. Pinkston. A general theory for deadlock-free adaptive routing using a mixed set of resources. *IEEE Transactions on Parallel and Distributed Systems*, 12(12):1219–1235, 2001.

[13] B. Fu, Y. Han, J. Ma, H. Li, and X. Li. An abacus turn model for time/space-efficient reconfigurable routing. In *Proceedings of the 38th International Symposium on Computer architecture*, ISCA '11, pages 259–270, New York, NY, USA, 2011. ACM.

[14] GEM5. Cache coherence protocols, http://gem5.org/cache_coherence_protocols#moesi_cmp_directory.

[15] C. J. Glass and L. M. Ni. The turn model for adaptive routing. In *Proceedings of the 19th International Symposium on Computer Architecture*, pages 278–287, 1992.

[16] P. Gratz, B. Grot, and S. Keckler. Regional congestion awareness for load balance in networks-on-chip. In *Proceedings of the 14th International Symposium on High Performance Computer Architecture*, pages 203–214, 2008.

[17] Y. Ho Song and T. M. Pinkston. A progressive approach to handling message-dependent deadlock in parallel computer systems. *IEEE Transactions on Parallel and Distributed Systems*, 14(3):259–275, Mar. 2003.

[18] S. S. Mukherjee, P. Bannon, S. Lang, A. Spink, and D. Webb. The alpha 21364 network architecture. In *Proceedings of the Ninth Symposium on High Performance Interconnects*, HOTI '01, pages 113–117, Washington, DC, USA, 2001. IEEE Computer Society.

[19] L.-S. Peh and W. J. Dally. A delay model and speculative architecture for pipelined routers. In *Proceedings of the 7th International Symposium on High-Performance Computer Architecture*, HPCA '01, pages 255–266, Washington, DC, USA, 2001. IEEE Computer Society.

[20] T. M. Pinkston and S. Warnakulasuriya. On deadlocks in interconnection networks. In *Proceedings of the 24th International Symposium on Computer Architecture*, ISCA '97, pages 38–49, New York, NY, USA, 1997. ACM.

[21] V. Puente, C. Izu, R. Beivide, J. Gregorio, F. Vallejo, and J. Prellezo. The adaptive bubble router. *Journal of Parallel and Distributed Computing*, 61(9):1180–1208, 2001.

[22] C. Sun, C.-H. O. Chen, G. Kurian, L. Wei, J. Miller, et al. Dsent - a tool connecting emerging photonics with electronics for opto-electronic networks-on-chip modeling. In *Proceedings of the 2012 IEEE/ACM Sixth International Symposium on Networks-on-Chip*, NOCS '12, pages 201–210, Washington, DC, USA, 2012. IEEE Computer Society.

[23] S. Wamakulasuriya and T. Pinkston. A formal model of message blocking and deadlock resolution in interconnection networks. *IEEE Transactions on Parallel and Distributed Systems*, 11(3):212–229, 2000.

[24] Y. Xu, B. Zhao, Y. Zhang, and J. Yang. Simple virtual channel allocation for high throughput and high frequency on-chip routers. In *Proceedings of the 16th International Symposium on High Performance Computer Architecture*, HPCA '10, pages 1–11, 2010.

Evaluating On-Die Interconnects for a 4 TB/s Router

Keith D. Underwood
Intel Federal
keith.d.underwood@intel.com

Eric Borch
Intel Federal
eric.borch@intel.com

John Sizer
Open-Silicon, Inc
johnsizer61@gmail.com

Timothy Stremcha
Open-Silicon, Inc
stremcha@superiontech.com

Michael Strom
Open-Silicon, Inc
mstrom2@gmail.com

ABSTRACT

Future high performance computing networks will exploit routers with both high port counts and high port bandwidth. Scalable on-die interconnects will be needed to insure that the router can sustain its full bandwidth for a variety of traffic patterns. Otherwise, blocking behavior *within a router* can be encountered by a variety of challenging HPC traffic patterns. We examine the router on-die interconnect problem in the context of a hypothetical 4 TB/s router, including throughput on various traffic patterns and die area considerations. The results indicate that the on-die topologies that have been used in the past require either too much area, or achieve too little performance. We present three topologies (two adaptations of existing topologies, and one new topology) that can deliver area-efficient sustained performance.

Categories and Subject Descriptors

C.2.1 [**Computer Systems Organization**]: Computer Communications Networks—*Network Architecture and Design*

Keywords

HPC router, on-die interconnect

1. INTRODUCTION

In high performance computing, the performance of the network is critically important. It is the mechanism by which applications access remote memory through message passing or partitioned global address space (PGAS) models, and the mechanism by which tasks synchronize. At the core of network performance is a key component: the router. Within each router, there is an on-die interconnect (ODI) that attempts to mimic a crossbar as closely as possible[11]. Improvements in both electrical[9] and optical[6, 5] signaling technology are driving up the total bandwidth into a router and, consequently, the total port count. As router port counts increase, it becomes impossible to build a true crossbar due to both the wiring and arbitration challenges[11]. Thus, new on-die interconnect topologies are needed to enable the next generation of routers.

ICS'13, June 10–14, 2013, Eugene, Oregon, USA.

In the field of on-die interconnects (ODI), most of the research is focused on the ODI problem for multi-core processors. In many ways, the ODI for a processor and a router have fundamentally different requirements. A single core in a chip multi-processor (CMP) typically consumes a fraction of the bandwidth that can be delivered by a port on the ODI; thus, hierarchical or concentrated topologies are commonly sufficient[7, 4]. In contrast, the goal of a router is to support every port at full bandwidth. Whereas cores tend to make accesses on a cache line granularity to numerous peers, routers must support both small packets and much larger packets with much longer flows. Perhaps most importantly, the ODI for a CMP must be optimized for area. HPC routers, on the other hand, are frequently I/O limited and the interior of the design only needs to be balanced between buffering and the ODI. Despite their dissimilarities, routers may be able to leverage concepts from CMP ODI research. Both have high port counts, and high total on-die bandwidth. And, both tend to want to achieve high all-to-all on-die bandwidth in some usage models.

In this paper, we investigate options for the on-die interconnect of a future generation of HPC routers. We have chosen a hypothetical router technology point to examine in depth — a 4 TeraByte per second (TB/s) router that provides 64 ports of 32 GB/s per direction. This is similar to the bandwidth that an InfiniBand HDR switch might provide with nearly double the ports of today's FDR products. Since even a summary analysis of many CMP ODI proposals indicates they have insufficient bisection bandwidth for an HPC router, we evaluate promising topologies and topologies from router microarchitecture research as well as a new topology proposal that is designed to be layout friendly.

Each topology is evaluated on several metrics. Performance on various classic HPC router traffic patterns is compared, as well as the performance of a variety of permutation traffic patterns. On-die interconnects for the router are also evaluated on the basis of their tolerance for a fraction of the ports becoming congested and sinking traffic at a drastically slower rate. Finally, die area is compared — not as a first order metric, but as a practical constraint. The results show that a direct extrapolation of prior work in router on-die interconnects[12] would not be practical from an area perspective, but that several of the adaptations of existing topologies that we propose would be feasible and achieve high performance as would a more layout friendly symmetric topology.

2. RELATED WORK

Numerous efforts have evaluated topologies for on-die interconnects for processors. Even designs with moderate core counts still use ring variants[3], but meshes and concentrated meshes are now popular options as a baseline in many works[4, 14, 10]. Indeed, many full chip designs have used a variant of a mesh[13, 15] or a concentrated mesh[8]. Similarly, the flattened butterfly topology has been evaluated in numerous efforts[10, 7, 4], with concentrated versions of the topology typically being considered. One of the few published examples of a product router architecture — the YARC design[12] — leveraged a topology very similar to a flattened butterfly, but did not use concentration so that the router on-die interconnect could sustain nonblocking behavior. Finally, general express cubes have been considered as an option[7] for processor on-die interconnects and have some promising features. The best case of each of these topology concepts was evaluated and extended to be suitable for a router microarchitecture.

The most similar previous work is [1]. While the goals and technology motivators for our work are the same, our approach is quite different. We focused on area estimates based on extrapolations from actual physical design experiments in 45 nm technology to improve the quality of the estimates. In addition, we assumed a 1 GHz clock instead of the 5 GHz clock in [1]. This yields wider datapaths and increases the importance of wiring area in the analysis. We also focused on the ability of the switch to handle arbitrary traffic patterns and do not attempt to exploit the communication characteristics of the higher level topology. We do this because commercial switches are often deployed in multiple topologies (e.g. current InfiniBand hardware exists in fat tree, hypercube, and bristled torus configurations among others). On this metric, the topologies we present appear to behave favorably relative to topologies explored in [1].

3. ADAPTATIONS OF EXISTING TOPOLOGIES

Existing on-die interconnects for CMPs and router designs can broadly be grouped in three categories. CMPs have been produced with ring[3] and 2D mesh topologies[13, 8, 15] and represent a broad category of meshes and torii (and their concentrated variants). A recent router design[12] leveraged a flattened butterfly variant, which represents another class of topologies that have been studied. A similar work in CMPs used multidrop express channels[7], which forms the basis for a third category of on-die interconnects.

In each of the design points discussed below, the router has 64 ports with each port consisting of an input port and output port. Each input port directs flits to some number of sub-switches, which are the functional block for moving data through the on-die interconnect. After passing through one or more sub-switches, the flit arrives at an output port to leave the router.

3.1 Meshes and Torii

A 2D mesh or torus is the most obvious topology after moving away from a crossbar. Its layout matches the approximate 2D structure of a chip while being simple to implement. However, the lack of bisection bandwidth would be a severe limitation to support a higher port count router, which needs full bisection bandwidth. A basic 3D mesh (without concentration) is nominally a full bisection topology at 64 nodes, while a 3D torus adds symmetry and dramatically reduces the average hop count. At 64 nodes, a 3D torus is far superior to typical ODI evaluations in terms of total bandwidth, bisection bandwidth, link utilization symmetry, and blocking behavior. We chose to evaluate a 3D torus due to the bandwidth potential, minimal wiring area, and simplicity.

3.2 Flattened Butterfly Based Topologies

The previously published YARC router design[12] utilizes a topology that is similar to an 8x8 flattened butterfly without concentration. However, when only one input port is connected to each on-die sub-switch, the wiring in the X dimension of a flattened butterfly is heavily overprovisioned. First, wires bring the data in from the input port to a specific sub-switch, and then that sub-switch would send out 7× as many wires to have point to point connections with a sub-switch in each column. Therefore, as with YARC, we first modified the flattened butterfly to have a multi-drop bus in the first dimension (the X dimension) in which the inputs multi-drop into the sub-switch in the correct colum, as shown in Figure 1. This delivers the data to the correct column on the first hop. The multi-drop bus allows every input port to receive one flit per cycle from the link and deliver one flit per cycle into any sub-switch in the first stage (a given row).

We then examined various concentration levels (numbers of output ports per sub-switch) for the flattened butterfly. A concentration of four led to extensive blocking (and poor performance) in numerous traffic patterns; thus, only a concentration of two was evaluated. Given a concentration of 2, we were forced to choose a layout of 32 sub-switches to reach 64 ports. We found that an 8x4 arrangement with a multi-drop bus in X (fan-out in X) meant that a quite tractable amount of routing was required in the Y dimension (4 x (4-1) buses instead of the 8 x (8-1) buses for a concentration of one).

Although 2× concentration improves the wiring requirements by over 4× while maintaining the nominal bisection bandwidth, blocking behavior is still possible. Two packets could attempt to use the same Y link in the same cycle. We also evaluate doubling the number of Y links to achieve nonblocking behavior. To illustrate all of these aspects, we show a 4×4 flattened butterfly in Figure 1. This smaller version makes it easier to see the multi-drop bus in the X dimension and the doubled links in the Y dimension. For simplicity, we are not showing the output ports (in any of our topology figures), so the 2× concentration is not explicitly shown. However, note that a 4×4 array has 32 output ports (2 output ports per tile) and 32 input ports (four rows of 8 multi-drop inputs in the X dimension).

3.3 Multidrop Express Channels Based Topologies

The Multidrop Express Channels (MECS)[7] topology was designed as a scalable on-die interconnect (ODI) for chip multi-processors (CMP) that maintains the hop count of a flattened butterfly while reducing the overall channel count. To evaluate MECS, we started by assuming one of the 64 router ports was connected where a processor was in MECS. The initial MECS design used a concentration of four (four cores per sub-switch). Careful analysis of the baseline MECS

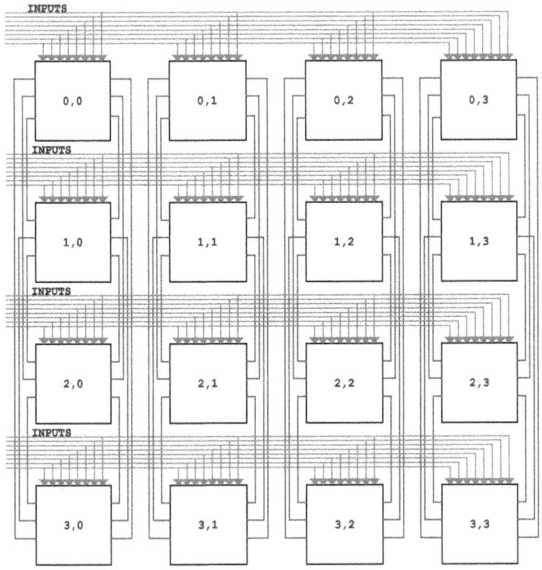

Figure 1: Flattened Butterfly Variant

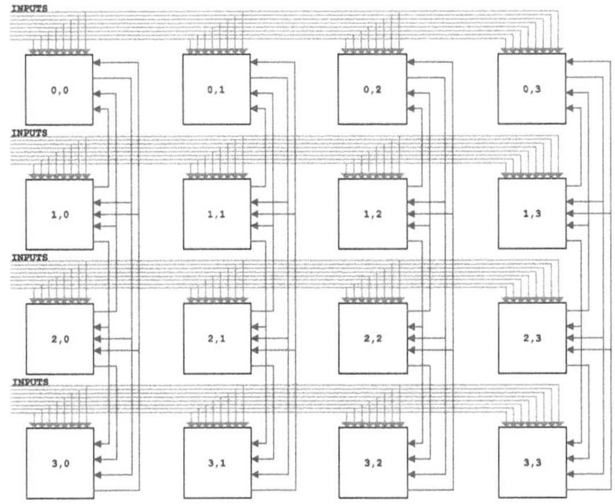

Figure 2: Initial Multidrop Express Channels

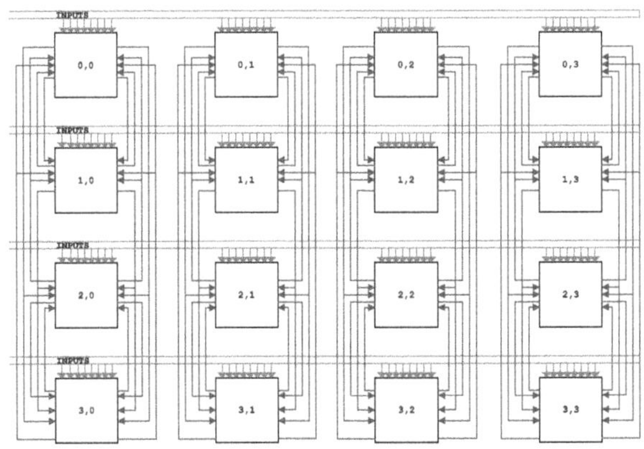

Figure 3: MECS Symmetric w/doubled Y paths

topology indicates two things. First, there is a significant bottleneck due to the concentration. To deal with this, we increased the routing resources and decreased the concentration considered (we considered 8x4 with 2× concentration and 8x8 with no concentration). Second, given those changes, there was relatively little difference between the X dimension routing required for MECS and the X dimension routing required for a flattened butterfly; thus, MECS was extended to use a multi-drop bus from the input ports in the X dimension. Figure 2 shows a small version (32 port, 4×4 with 2× concentration) of our initial MECS topology.

A second modification to the baseline MECS is also evaluated. There is a clear asymmetry to the MECS topology (see Figure 2). The sub-switches in the interior of a column have outbound ports in two directions in the Y dimension. This splits the outbound traffic onto two total multi-drop buses. Outer nodes at the top and bottom, however, have all peers in one direction and thus, only a single outbound port in that dimension. This makes for asymmetric channel loading and non-homogeneous sub-switch design. The modification to MECS (labeled MECS-Symmetric) uses two ports in the Y dimension for all of the sub-switches. Sub-switches at the top and bottom of a column split their connections into the "near half" and the "far half" of sub-switches in that dimension (see Figure 3). This only adds one additional path to each routing track. As with the flattened butterfly topology, we also evaluated doubling the links in the Y dimension to increase throughput. The MECS-Symmetric topology is illustrated in Figure 3 for a 4×4 array of sub-switches (as in 2) with a concentration of 2 (2 output ports attached to each sub-switch, which are not shown).

4. NEW TOPOLOGIES CONSIDERED

When considering the baseline version of the options, the multi-drop bus architectures leveraged in both YARC and the MECS architectures were quite attractive; however, the flattened butterfly portion of YARC required enormous on-die routing resources at extremely high bandwidth, and the MECS architecture has an unfortunate asymmetry at the edges of the topology. Thus, in addition to considering more direct variations on the flattened butterfly and MECS concepts, we considered 2 new topologies.

4.1 Multi-drop Bypass Array (MBA)

The Multi-drop Bypass Array (MBA) topology was proposed as an alternative to MECS. It leverages a multi-drop bus in both the X and Y dimensions of a 2D array of sub-switches. For clarity, a 16 port, 4x4 array is shown in Figure 4. Like our variations on the flattened butterfly and MECS topologies, it uses a multi-drop bus in the X dimension from the input ports on the router into the sub-switches within a row. Each sub-switch then drives a single multi-drop bus to the entire column of sub-switches. Each sub-switch has one output port associated with it. As illustrated in Figure 4, MBA is quite symmetric. It also has X and Y dimension routing requirements that scale linearly with the number of ports on the router. While MBA has abundant X dimension routing, corner-turn traffic patterns can become a bottleneck on the Y dimension routing resources. To alleviate this, variants of MBA were considered that double the Y routing channels, as shown in Figure 4.

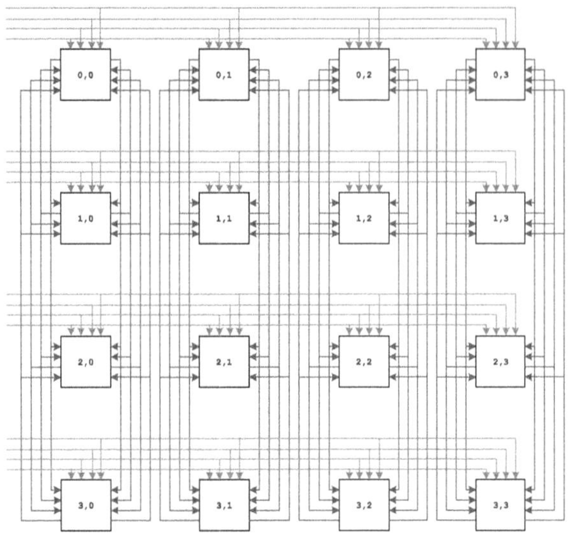

Figure 4: Multidrop Bypass Array w/doubled Y paths

4.2 FanFair

Many of the other topology choices suffer from three problems that can make the physical layout challenging:

- They are asymmetric. They have significantly more routing tracks consumed in either the X or Y dimension.
- They involve large crossbars in the sub-switch.
- The paths from the input ports on the top and bottom of the die have to route down/up to reach a horizontal multi-drop bus that spans the router core.

The FanFair array was created to address these issues. FanFair is a 4x4 array of tiles with 4 output ports at each tile, as shown by the short, unconnected lines. The arrangement enables the use of smaller crossbars than the other topologies by using a hierarchical arrangement of sub-switches, as seen in Figure 5. Each sub-switch receives data from 8 vertical multi-drop buses and 8 horizontal multi-drop buses coming from the input ports. The figure shows these 16 inputs to the sub-switch as 4 groups of 4, each coming into a separate 4x4 cross-bar within the sub-switch. Each sub-switch then drives 6 horizontal point-to-point links and 6 vertical point-to-point links (both are connected in a flattened butterfly style with doubled connectivity). These are shown as 4 groups of 3 outputs of each 4:4 crossbar. Thus, each sub-switch receives 12 point-to-point links from other sub-switches as well (6 each in X and Y, shown as 4 groups of 3 inputs to the 16:4 crossbar). Traffic is segregated into groups such that a group of 4 input ports share 3 point-to-point links in the orthogonal direction from which they arrived. The only large crossbar is the 16:4 crossbar that combines inputs from four smaller 4:4 local crossbars and the 12 point-to-point links received. The full 4x4 FanFair array is shown in Figure 6. While it seems complex, it is highly symmetric and actually composed of smaller crossbars than the other topologies. FanFair has a maximum of a 16:4 crossbar instead of a 16:8 in a flattened butterfly or 16:6 in a MECS topology. FanFair also uses four 4:4 crossbars, which are comparable to the 8:2 crossbars that are also used withing both the flattened butterfly and MECS configurations.

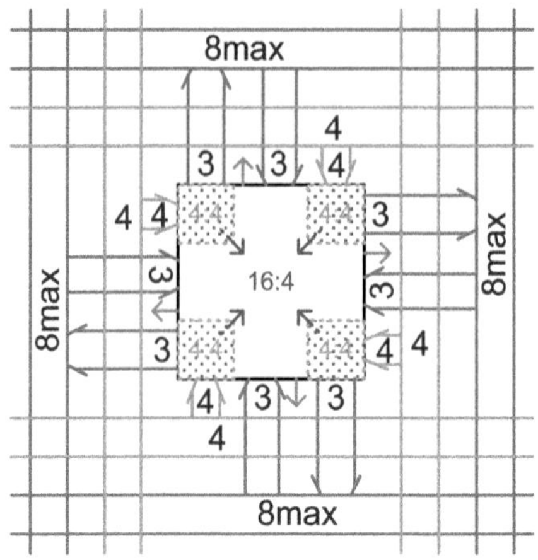

Figure 5: Single FanFair sub-switch

5. METHODOLOGY

Parameterizable simulation models were created for the torus, flattened butterfly, MECS, MBA, and FanFair topologies. The parameters allow the models to be configured for the size and shape of the network, the concentration at each router in the network, and, in many cases, the bandwidth in the X and Y dimensions.

To leverage more realistic buffering and arbitration, multi-drop bus models were developed. These models accurately reflect the connectivity and buffering patterns associated with the target topologies. The YARC design is modeled as an 8x8 flattened butterfly with multi-drop inputs. It supports a concentration of 1 using input and output queuing in the sub-switches and an output speedup of 8. This was only practical in the YARC design because each of the 64 ports in YARC are over ten times less bandwidth than the per-port targets for this router.

The simulation models leverage a relatively simple arbitration scheme (output first) in which the "target" of packets selected a winner from among the requesters for that port. Many of the performance details that are most heavily impacted by the subtleties of more advanced arbitration algorithms would only be seen when the router microarchitecture is integrated into a full network topology simulation.

Two types of workloads have been used for evaluating the on-die topology. First, the standard suite of traffic patterns (bit complement, bit reverse, random, shuffle, and transpose) from prior research is applied to each of the topologies. These patterns apply well-known stress tests to the topology. Second, we ran 10,000 random point-to-point traffic permutations and created a histogram of the aggregate router throughput. In each permutation, every source sends a steady stream of traffic to a single unique, random target. This gives us a sampling of contention between independent paths through the router. In practice, the bit complement, bit reverse, shuffle, and transpose traffic patterns are well

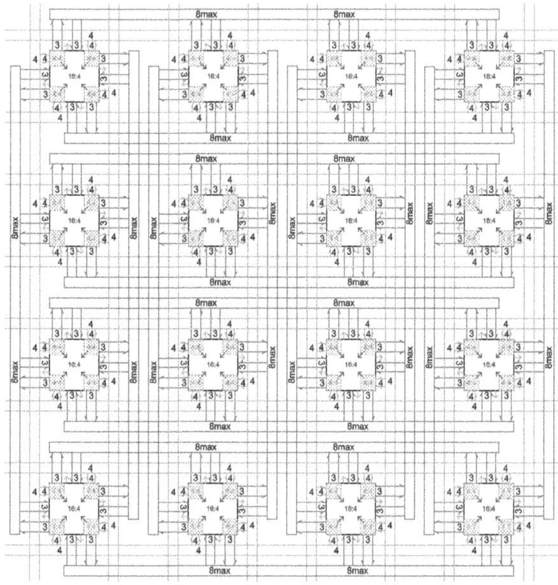

Figure 6: FanFair topology

known points in the random permutation space. Unless otherwise noted, all data shown use single flit packets.

5.1 Traffic variations and contention modeling

Modeling appropriate traffic for a router microarchitecture is quite different from modeling a system-level traffic pattern. The goal is to determine how the worst-case router will perform under the loads that will be provided by the application. Ultimately, this tends not to look like a workload model simply applied to a small topology. Instead, it experiences different mixes of traffic and, most importantly, blocking behavior from downstream contention (e.g. two packets downstream attempting to use the same output port).

The first variable we explored in the workload model is the size of the packets moving through the router. As packet sizes increase, additional contention (blocking behavior) is often encountered in topologies. For the random traffic pattern, we varied the size of the packets used to see the impact on the on-die throughput. Note that varying the packet size on the fixed traffic patterns would have no impact, since flows through the router are managed on a flit level. The blocking behavior occurs when two flows contend for one path on a dynamic basis, and the path is reserved for the life of a packet (i.e., a form of head-of-line blocking). In fixed traffic patterns, the contention is static and appears the same in a long-term average for any reasonable packet size.

Another parameter that was evaluated is the number of virtual channels (VC) that are used. Increasing the number of virtual channels can reduce the head-of-line blocking effects within the router; thus, we modeled traffic being distributed on 1 VC, 2 VCs, and 8 VCs. The 1 VC case is a worst-case behavior, while the 2 VC case is the worst likely scenario in a typical requests/response network. Uniform distribution of traffic across all 8 VCs is a best-case scenario, since perfect VC balance within the network is extremely difficult to achieve.

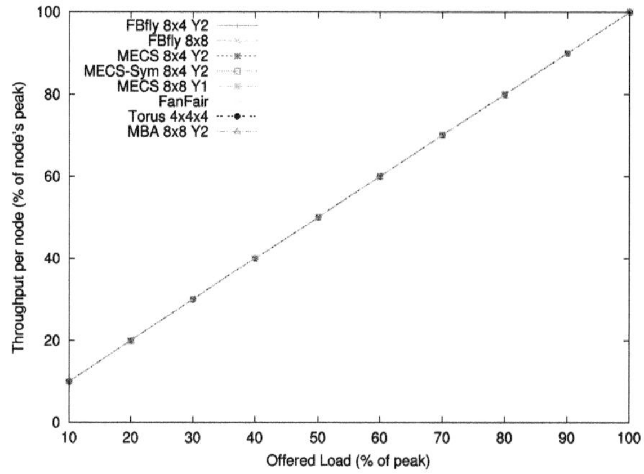

Figure 7: Bit Complement Traffic

The final key parameter we evaluated is the output port throughput. Real networks sometimes have contended paths, which appear to the router as a link with reduced throughput. One key behavior of the router is how it reacts to an output port with reduced throughput and whether that creates congestion that propagates through the ODI and impacts unrelated flows. For this scenario, our focus is on the behavior of the router on-die interconnect; thus, we have not modeled the impacts of adaptive routing. Instead, we have modeled the interference effects that occur in the router in the absence of an effective adaptive routing scheme. We used the random permutation traffic patterns for this evaluation.

6. RESULTS

Results are first presented for several classic patterns to see how the on-die interconnect responds to these patterns. These specific patterns highlight some performance challenges for some of the topologies; hence, the permutation traffic patterns are shown to illustrate what fraction of static permutations are likely to see these performance impacts. In each case, average throughput across all ports is shown. Finally, the congestion response of each on-die topology option is presented for various contention scenarios.

6.1 Classic Traffic Patterns

Five standard traffic patterns that are commonly used for network evaluations were applied to the various topologies. These included bit complement, bit reverse, random, shuffle, and transpose. Each traffic pattern consists of a source injecting a stream of single flit messages in a distribution determined by the traffic pattern. In each graph, the X-axis is the offered load while the Y-axis is the sustained throughput. Ideal throughput is represented by a diagonal line with a pitch of one.

As seen in Figure 7 and Figure 8, all of the topologies sustain approximately full throughput on bit complement and random traffic. In both the flattened butterfly and MECS 8x8 configurations with a concentration at the sub-switch of one, it is not necessary to double the Y links for these traffic patterns.

In contrast, the bit reverse traffic pattern (Figure 9) and transpose pattern (Figure 10) highlight the differences between the topologies. The 8x4 flattened butterfly with doubled Y paths demonstrates its nonblocking nature, while the

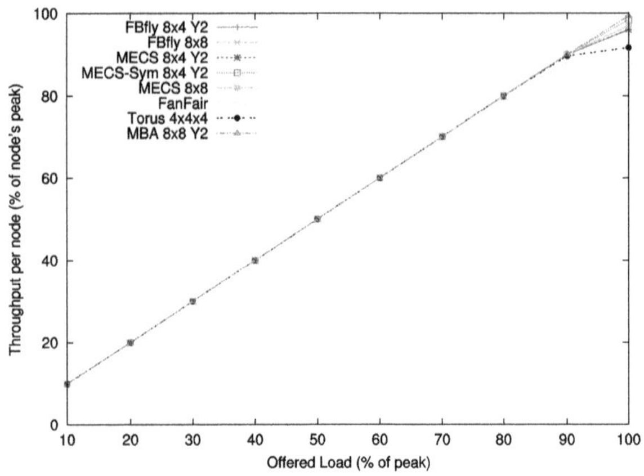

Figure 8: Random Traffic

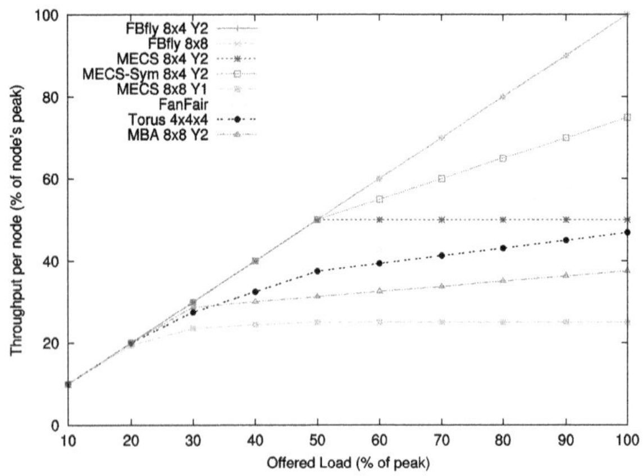

Figure 9: Bit Reverse Traffic

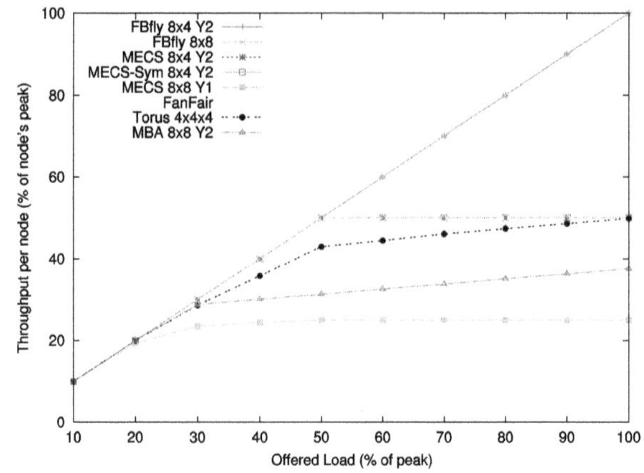

Figure 10: Transpose Traffic

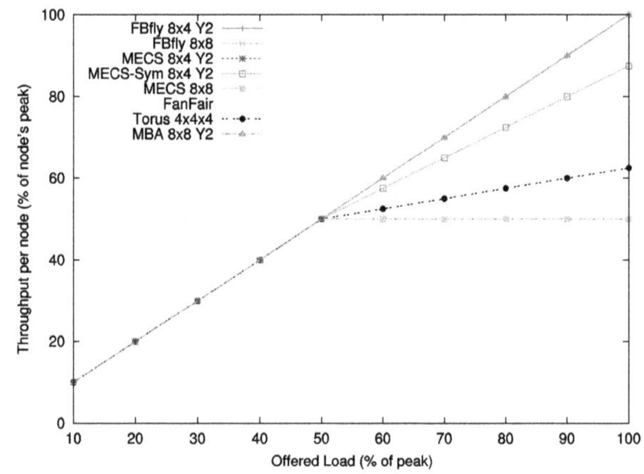

Figure 11: Shuffle Traffic

variants of the 8x4 MECS stand out as the second best. Bit reverse and transpose do highlight that some traffic patterns will be bottlenecked on topologies other than the flattened butterfly. The fraction of traffic patterns that are impacted will be a key determining factor in what is acceptable.

The MECS-Symmetric topology clearly distinguishes itself above the standard 8x4 MECS with doubled Y channels. The transpose-like patterns place particular stress on the relatively limited Y channel resources in topologies that do not double the Y paths.

One of the surprises in these evaluations was the poor performance of the torus topology. The 4x4x4 Torus nominally has sufficient bisection bandwidth for all nodes in any one half of the topology to send all of their traffic to nodes in the other half of the topology. However, the torus is one of the worst performing topologies for 3 out of these 5 traffic patterns. This occurs because the routing algorithm (dimension ordered routing) overload certain links in the torus, which it may be possible to address using adaptive routing across the ODI. Unfortunately, adaptive routing over the ODI would require at least two additional virtual channels inside the torus for every network level virtual channel, which is untenable.

6.2 Traffic Permutations

The traffic patterns shown above are known to stress networks; however, a key question for router microarchitectures is: what fraction of traffic patterns place the microarchitecture under a stress that leads to a reduction in sustained throughput? To begin answering this question, we ran 10,000 traffic permutations through each router on-die interconnect topology. In each pattern, each input port sent a steady stream of traffic to a single output port, and all of the destinations were unique. The results of this experiment are the histograms of average throughput plotted in Figure 12. The X-axis has the traffic band (average sustained throughput) in 5% increments starting at 50%, while the Y-axis shows the percentage of traffic that fell into each band.

As with the previous traffic patterns, the 4x4x4 Torus performs poorly, and in fact is by far the worst performer. It has a distribution that peaks around the 65-70% throughput band. At the other end of the spectrum, the results for the 8x8 flattened butterfly and 8x4 flattened butterfly with doubled Y paths clearly indicate the behavior of nonblocking topologies. The 8x8 MECS topology with a single Y channel is centered on the 80-85% throughput band, while an 8x4 MECS with a concentration of 2 and doubled Y paths yields a permutation histogram that is encouraging — especially when the asymmetry for the edge nodes is removed by moving to the MECS-Symmetric variant. Finally, FanFair performs comparably to the 8x4 MECS.

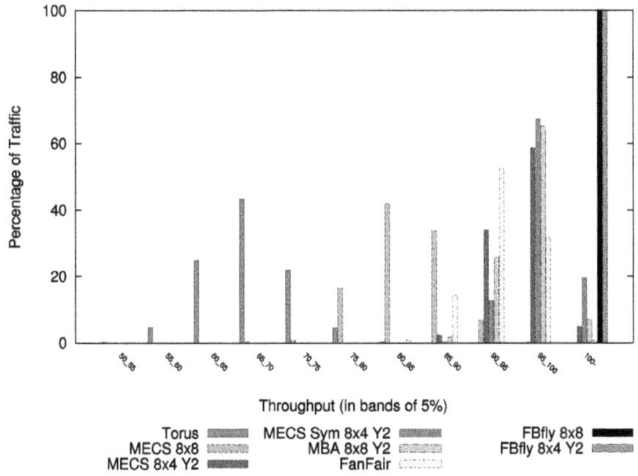

Figure 12: Topology Histograms

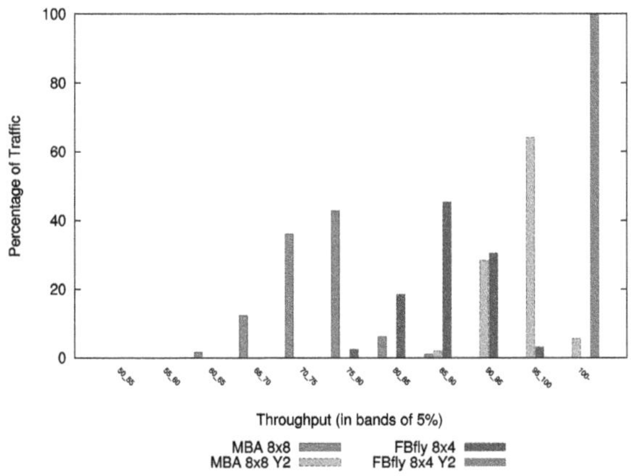

Figure 13: Varying the number of Y Paths

6.3 Doubling the Y path

Several of the topologies shown (8x4 flattened butterfly, 8x4 MECS, 8x8 MBA) have doubled the Y paths to increase throughput, and in the case of an 8x4 flattened butterfly, creates a nonblocking network. This is a significant increase in wiring in the Y dimension, one that necessitates an examination of the benefits of the additional wiring. Figure 13 is a histogram of random permutation runs that shows the affect of doubling the Y paths on 2 of the topologies, an 8x4 flattened butterfly and an 8x8 MBA. Each topology is shown with a single Y path, and a doubled Y path. The center of the distributions is shifted up by 3 bins (15%) for both topologies with the second Y path. It is clear from the figure that the additional Y path is a worthwhile enhancement for both topologies.

The results to this point clearly indicate that many of the topologies do not perform well enough to continue pursuing (Torus, MECS 8x8, MECS 8x4, and MBA). As such, we concentrate our evaulations on the more promising topologies (YARC-like baseline, FanFair, Flattened Butterfly 8x4 with a concentration of 2 and doubled Y, MECS-Symmetric 8x4 with a concentration of 2 and doubled Y).

6.4 Impact of increasing packet size

Figure 8 highlighted the behavior of the various topologies under random traffic using single flit packets. The random permutation patterns showed the fraction of static, non-blocking traffic patterns that sustain high performance on the given topologies. However, in many cases, traffic is neither single flit nor static (where packet size does not matter). Figure 14a shows the performance of the various topologies as the packet size is increased (shown along the X axis) when using uniform random traffic. In this case, traffic is evenly spread across two VCs. In all of the cases, however, contention arises as the buffering is not deep enough to capture the full packet when two inputs collide on a single resource. In this example, the 8x8 flattened butterfly with a concentration of 1 (YARC-like) and the 8x4 flattened butterfly with a concentration of 2 and doubled Y resources show comparable performance and consistently exceed the performance of the other topologies.

Figure 14b replicates the experiment of Figure 14a, but increases the number of virtual channels over which traffic is spread to 8. In this case, the increased use of virtual channels mitigates the head-of-line blocking scenarios and provides additional buffers to absorb traffic in cases of transient conflicts. All the topologies do well, but the flattened butterfly topologies continue to meet or exceed the performance of other topologies.

6.5 Propagation of Network Congestion

One of the challenges in network performance at the system level is congested links. Inevitably, some link in the network (or some collection of links) will become oversubscribed due to imbalances in the traffic pattern. When this happens, it is important to understand the impact on the router design.

One way that an on-die interconnect can demonstrate pathological behavior when a slow output port is encountered is if that slow output port creates congestion that propagates to input ports that never target that output port. To investigate the behavior of the on-die topologies under these scenarios, we again ran random permutation traffic and varied the number of slow output ports and how slow those output ports were.

When running the slow output port cases for random permutation, we varied the number of slow ports (1 or 16), the size of a packet (1 or 16 flits), and the VC usage (1 or 8 VCs used). We ran 1,000 permutations of the cross product of these options with each input port set to inject at 100% throughput and each slow output port set to drain at 10% throughput. What we found was that for the leading candidates, the size of the packet and the number of VCs used had no meaningful impact on the response of the ODI to slow output ports. Thus, we only present the histograms of throughputs for 1 and 16 slow ports with a packet size of 1 flit and using 1 VC.

The 8x8 flattened butterfly (YARC-like), 8x4 flattened butterfly, and FanFair topologies all showed the same behavior under this test (Figures 16 and 15): the histogram for the average throughputs was shifted down by approximately 1.5% for a single slow port and approximately 22% for the case where there are 16 slow ports. Given that each slow port is slowing traffic down to 10% of the peak rate, these are the results one would expect if the slow output port only slows down its corresponding input port (that is, the input port that sends its traffic to that output port). This is the desired behavior for a router.

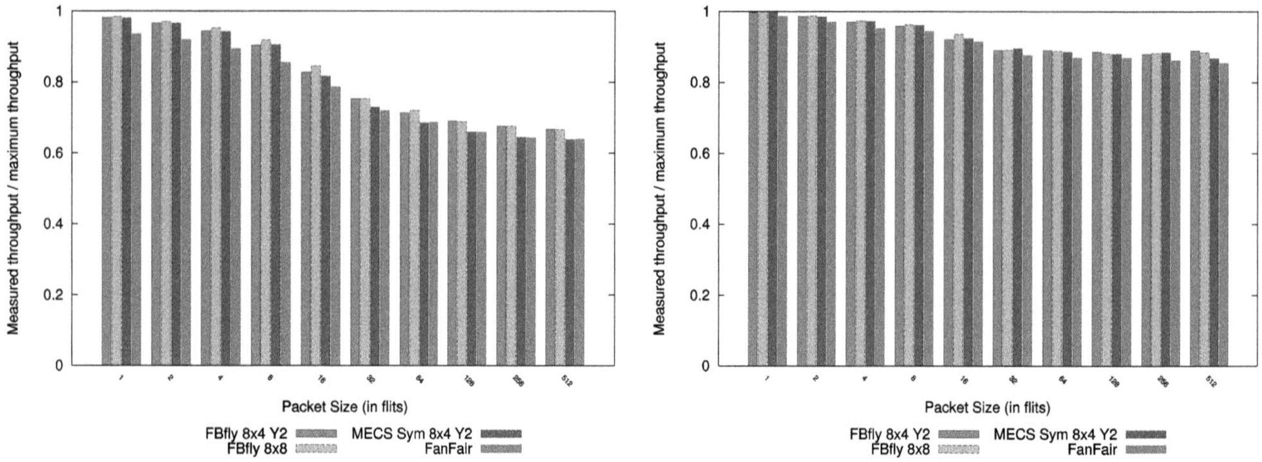

(a) Two VCs (b) Eight VCs

Figure 14: Impact of varying packet size

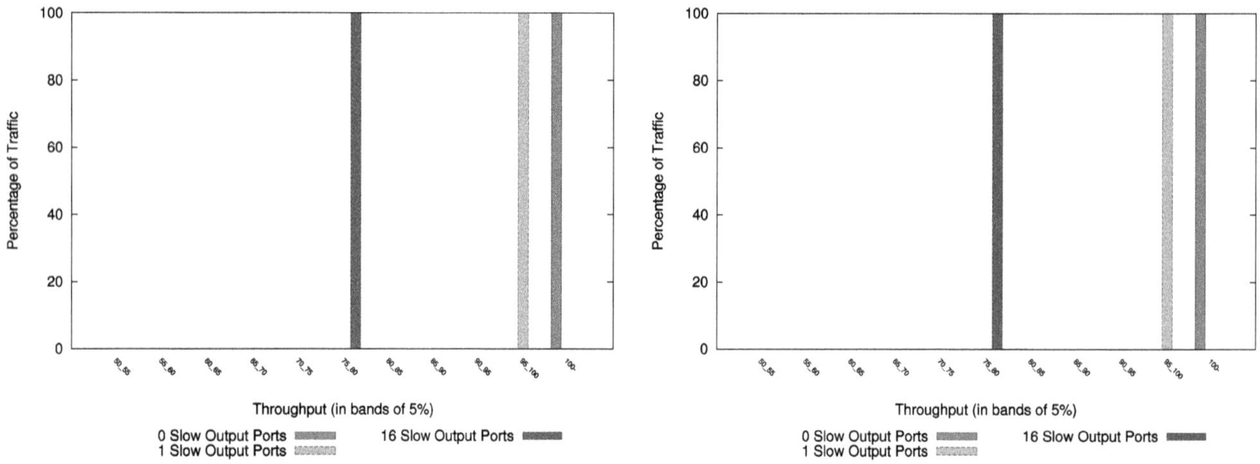

(a) 8x4 Y2 Flattened Butterfly (b) 8x8 Flattened Butterfly

Figure 15: Slow Output Ports for Flattened Butterfly

In contrast, for the MECS Symmetric 8x4 topology (Figure 17) the center of the distribution is shifted down by 3 bins (15%) when one output port is slow. This indicates that a slow output port can negatively impact other input ports that use the same vertical paths. In the case of 16 slow output ports, the drop is greater than the 4-5 bins that would be expected for 25% of the output ports running at 10% of the target rate; however, the drop from 1 slow output port to 16 slow output ports is less than the 4 bins that might be expected. This is because the probability increases dramatically that the other port that a slow output port interferes with is also already slow.

7. DIE AREA ANALYSIS

A commercially available 45 nm process technology was scaled forward to the 22 nm generation assuming 0.7× per generation wire pitch scaling and 0.6× per generation RAM cell scaling. Four metal layers were assumed to be available for on-die interconnect routing, and the four layers were assumed to have a uniform minimum pitch. All routing area results were based on double-spaced routes, which was a conservative approach to minimize cross talk, account for unknown characteristics of future geometries, and accommodate overhead for things like power grid vias. Horizontal channels used two layers (e.g. 4 and 6) and vertical channels used two layers (e.g. 3 and 5), and the area beneath the channels was only used for buffering and registering the datapath. Layout trials were done in a 45 nm process for a horizontal channel and then the area was extrapolated to the vertical channels and to the 22 nm process using the assumptions above. A memory compiler was used to generate memory area estimates for buffers in each sub-switch. Using these assumptions, an area estimate for each on-die topology was constructed.

We evaluated the area for the best performing five topologies. The area targets for the on-die interconnect were set to $75mm^2$, which is consistent with prior commercial prod-

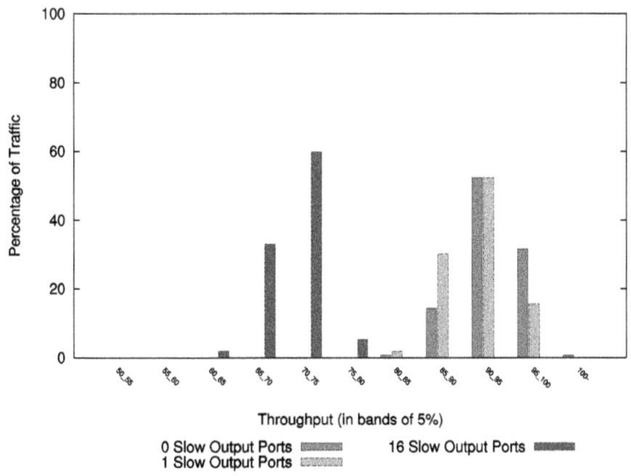

Figure 16: Slow Output Ports on FanFair

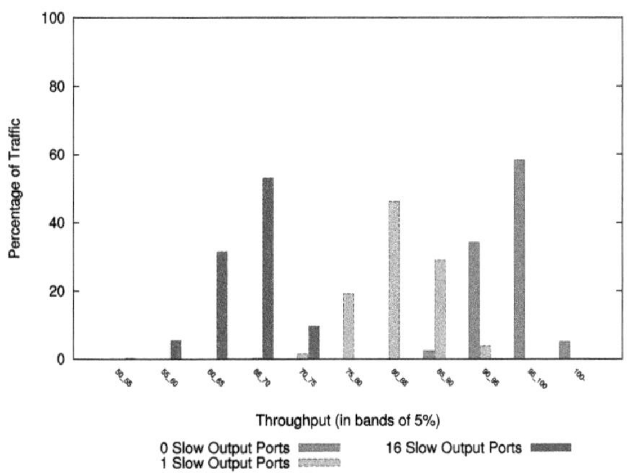

Figure 17: Slow Output Ports on MECS Symmetric

Topology	Routing Column	Routing Row
FBfly 8x8	256	96
MBA 8x8 Y2	128	82
FBfly 8x4 Y2	96	76
MECS-Sym. 8x4 Y2	64	76
FanFair	80	80

Table 1: Routing channels

ucts[12]. In that design point, a $289mm^2$ router was built with approximately 1/3 ($91.32mm^2$) of the area used for SERDES. Our target was to use approximately 25% for the on-die interconnect with the remaining area going to large memory structures, such as input buffers and routing tables.

Area models assumed each datapath was 32 bytes wide plus ECC and control and ran at 1 GHz. Buffers and registers were spaced to meet this timing. Since the I/O arrives at the edge of the router die, it needed to be routed in to the multidrop bus used to reach each of the router sub-switches. Table 7 shows the number of routing channels in both the column and the row.

Clearly, the total number of column channels for the 8x8 flattened butterfly (similar to YARC) is unrealistic given the datapath width, and this shows up in the total routing

Topology	RAM Area(mm^2)	Routing Area(mm^2)
FBfly 8x8	14	75
MBA 8x8 Y2	20	46.5
FBfly 8x4 Y2	10.5	39
MECS-Sym. 8x4 Y2	10.5	32
FanFair	7	36

Table 2: Required Area

area in Table 7. In this case, each column (8 of them) has 56 point to point datapaths connecting the rows (8 rows, which each have paths to each of the 7 other rows). In addition, some vertical channels are needed to bring data in from the top and bottom of the die. Some of the datapaths only span part of the chip and can share vertical channels, which is why it *only* requires 256 vertical channels. Surprisingly, the 8x8 MBA configuration with doubled Y channels has the worst routing performance to routing area of the remaining configurations (average throughput over routing area). This is because all of the vertical datapaths are multidrop buses that span the entire height of the die. Because the 8x4 flattened butterfly only has half as many rows, it had over 4× fewer routing columns; however, this number grew when the vertical channels had to be doubled. FanFair was designed to balance the routing requirements between horizontal and vertical tracks and it excelled in this domain, though it gave it only a modest advantage over the 8x4 flattened butterfly configuration in total die area devoted to routing.

Each sub-switch in the router was assumed to have RAM for 8 virtual channels. Each virtual channel buffer was 8 elements deep to cover the credit loop to the output port that was assumed to be outside the ODI. RAM to buffer vertical channels were also assumed to include 8 elements for each of 8 VCs. While some RAMs could have been shallower, the design symmetry is more important than the micro-optimization. Each element was 32 bytes wide (plus ECC) to capture the datapath. Different ODI topologies yielded different total buffer numbers, since each channel had to be buffered when it entered the sub-switch. FanFair has the minimum buffer area, at $7mm^2$ as extrapolated to 22 nm technology, which gives it an equivalent total area to the symmetric MECS configuration. The 8x4 MECS and flattened butterfly configurations have identical total buffering requirements, but the 8x8 MBA configuration with doubled Y channels requires dramatically more. This is because each MBA sub-switch is receiving from 14 incoming datapaths in the vertical direction and 8 in the horizontal direction for 64 sub-switches. In comparison, both MECS and flattened butterfly receive from 16 in the horizontal direction and 8 in the vertical direction.

8. CONCLUSIONS

The derivative of the 8x8 flattened butterfly that was used for the YARC router clearly offers stellar nonblocking behavior; however, it is impractical to continue to implement that topology as bandwidths increase. Although the narrow channels of YARC allowed it to implement a full 8x8 flattened butterfly without concentration, a similar arrangement with wider channels is not feasible due to the wiring complexity. Furthermore, maintaining the narrow channel width of YARC would have driven the topology out to a much larger port count, which would have again faced the issue of the quadratic growth in the width of the Y channels.

Switching to a concentrated flattened butterfly topology and doubling the vertical (Y) channels can decrease the required die area for the on-die interconnect by over 40% while maintaining equivalent nonblocking behavior. Every comparison of throughput shows that this configuration matches the performance of the YARC configuration. Two other topologies showed good performance while having somewhat better area characteristics. When the MECS topology is configured with 2× concentration, double the vertical channels, and edge channels to improve the symmetry, it has relatively little blocking in most static patterns. It also achieves comparable throughput on uniform random traffic with larger packets. Because it requires fewer routing channels, it saves an additional 15% in ODI area. In addition, the FanFair topology has equivalent total area to the symmetric MECS topology, with only slightly more blocking behavior than the best MECS configuration for static permutation traffic, and, it matches MECS throughput for uniform random traffic as the packet size increases. In addition, the FanFair topology is substantially more layout friendly than either the MECS or concentrated flattened butterfly topology in terms of routing symmetry.

This creates three feasible on-die interconnect topologies for a 4 TB/s router in 22 nm technology, with each offering somewhat different trade-offs. This is almost 4 times the published bandwidth of the IBM PERCS router[2] and would match the required bandwidth for a 64 port InfiniBand HDR router. This should provide the required router scalability for several years.

9. REFERENCES

[1] J.-H. Ahn, S. Choo, and J. Kim. Network within a network approach to create a scalable high-radix router microarchitecture. In *High Performance Computer Architecture (HPCA), 2012 IEEE 18th International Symposium on*, pages 1–12, 2012.

[2] B. Arimilli, R. Arimilli, V. Chung, S. Clark, W. Denzel, B. Drerup, T. Hoefler, J. Joyner, J. Lewis, J. Li, N. Ni, and R. Rajamony. The percs high-performance interconnect. In *Proceedings of the 2010 18th IEEE Symposium on High Performance Interconnects*, HOTI '10, pages 75–82, Washington, DC, USA, 2010. IEEE Computer Society.

[3] G. Chrysos. Knights Corner, Intels first Many Integrate Core (MIC) Architecture Product. In *Hot Chips 24*, August 2012.

[4] R. Das, S. Eachempati, A. Mishra, V. Narayanan, and C. Das. Design and evaluation of a hierarchical on-chip interconnect for next-generation cmps. In *High Performance Computer Architecture, 2009. HPCA 2009. IEEE 15th International Symposium on*, pages 175 –186, feb. 2009.

[5] P. Dong, S. Liao, D. Feng, H. Liang, D. Zheng, R. Shafiiha, X. Zheng, G. Li, K. Raj, A. Krishnamoorthy, and M. Asghari. High speed silicon microring modulator based on carrier depletion. In *Optical Fiber Communication (OFC), collocated National Fiber Optic Engineers Conference, 2010 Conference on (OFC/NFOEC)*, pages 1 –3, march 2010.

[6] W. M. Green, M. J. Rooks, L. Sekaric, and Y. A. Vlasov. Ultra-compact, low RF power, 10 Gb/s silicon Mach-Zehnder modulator. *Optical Express*, 15:17106–17113, 2007.

[7] B. Grot, J. Hestness, S. Keckler, and O. Mutlu. Express cube topologies for on-chip interconnects. In *High Performance Computer Architecture, 2009. HPCA 2009. IEEE 15th International Symposium on*, pages 163 –174, feb. 2009.

[8] J. Howard, S. Dighe, Y. Hoskote, S. Vangal, D. Finan, G. Ruhl, D. Jenkins, H. Wilson, N. Borkar, G. Schrom, F. Pailet, S. Jain, T. Jacob, S. Yada, S. Marella, P. Salihundam, V. Erraguntla, M. Konow, M. Riepen, G. Droege, J. Lindemann, M. Gries, T. Apel, K. Henriss, T. Lund-Larsen, S. Steibl, S. Borkar, V. De, R. Van Der Wijngaart, and T. Mattson. A 48-core ia-32 message-passing processor with dvfs in 45nm cmos. In *Solid-State Circuits Conference Digest of Technical Papers (ISSCC), 2010 IEEE International*, pages 108 –109, feb. 2010.

[9] J. Jaussi, M. Leddige, B. Horine, F. O'Mahony, and B. Casper. Multi-gbit i/o and interconnect co-design for power efficient links. In *Electrical Performance of Electronic Packaging and Systems (EPEPS), 2010 IEEE 19th Conference on*, pages 1 –4, oct. 2010.

[10] J. Kim, J. Balfour, and W. Dally. Flattened butterfly topology for on-chip networks. In *Proceedings of the 40th Annual IEEE/ACM International Symposium on Microarchitecture*, MICRO 40, pages 172–182, Washington, DC, USA, 2007. IEEE Computer Society.

[11] J. Kim, W. J. Dally, B. Towles, and A. K. Gupta. Microarchitecture of a high-radix router. In *Proceedings of the 32nd annual international symposium on Computer Architecture*, ISCA '05, pages 420–431, Washington, DC, USA, 2005. IEEE Computer Society.

[12] S. Scott, D. Abts, J. Kim, and W. J. Dally. The BlackWidow high-radix Clos network. In *Proceedings of the 33rd Annual International Symposium on Computer Architecture*, ISCA '06, pages 16–28, Washington, DC, USA, 2006. IEEE Computer Society.

[13] S. Vangal, J. Howard, G. Ruhl, S. Dighe, H. Wilson, J. Tschanz, D. Finan, P. Iyer, A. Singh, T. Jacob, S. Jain, S. Venkataraman, Y. Hoskote, and N. Borkar. An 80-tile 1.28tflops network-on-chip in 65nm cmos. In *Solid-State Circuits Conference, 2007. ISSCC 2007. Digest of Technical Papers. IEEE International*, pages 98 –589, feb. 2007.

[14] H. Wang, L.-S. Peh, and S. Malik. A technology-aware and energy-oriented topology exploration for on-chip networks. In *Proceedings of the conference on Design, Automation and Test in Europe - Volume 2*, DATE '05, pages 1238–1243, Washington, DC, USA, 2005. IEEE Computer Society.

[15] D. Wentzlaff, P. Griffin, H. Hoffmann, L. Bao, B. Edwards, C. Ramey, M. Mattina, C.-C. Miao, J. Brown, and A. Agarwal. On-chip interconnection architecture of the tile processor. *Micro, IEEE*, 27(5):15 –31, sept.-oct. 2007.

Improving Numerical Accuracy for Non-Negative Matrix Multiplication on GPUs using Recursive Algorithms

Matthew Badin
University of California Irvine
Irvine, CA 92697
mbadin@uci.edu

Paolo D'Alberto
FastMMW
paolo@FastMMW.com

Lubomir Bic
University of California Irvine
Irvine, CA 92697
bic@ics.uci.edu

Michael Dillencourt
University of California Irvine
Irvine, CA 92697
dillenco@ics.uci.edu

Alexandru Nicolau
University of California Irvine
Irvine, CA 92697
nicolau@ics.uci.edu

ABSTRACT

Scientific computing is only bound by the limits of Moore's Law and the scalability of high performance mathematical library implementations. Most mathematical libraries however tend to focus only on general inputs, limiting their potential performance and scalability by not tailoring their implementation to specific inputs, such as non-negative inputs. By removing this limitation it is possible to improve the performance and accuracy of a range of problems. In this paper we explore the limitations of hardware to improve accuracy of non-negative matrix multiply by specifically comparing implementations on the GPU and CPU and propose algorithmic solutions to improve accuracy. Next, we demonstrate a matrix multiply implementation that takes advantage of asymptotically fast matrix multiply algorithms, which have been shown to scale better than $O(N^3)$ matrix multiply implementations, and improve accuracy by up to a whole digit while increasing performance by up to 27% for matrices where the input is positive. Finally, we propose to extend the BLAS level 3 specification to non-negative matrices to allow easy integration of our solution and allow other library authors to implement their own solutions as part of an existing standard.

Categories and Subject Descriptors

G.4 [**Mathematical Software**]: Algorithm Design and Analysis

General Terms

Algorithms, Performance

Keywords

GPGPU, Hybrid Matrix Multiply, BLAS, Accuracy

1. INTRODUCTION

The adoption of parallel processors, and in particular graphics cards (GPUs), are becoming increasingly popular in scientific computing because of their low price and high performance [17]. This has lead researchers to offer high performance matrix multiply implementations for the GPU [22] along with BLAS 3 (Basic Linear Algebra Subroutines) for use in general scientific computing [1]. GPUs and GPU like devices though, with idiosyncratic architecture and a flat memory hierarchy, will yield drastically different matrix multiply implementations [22] than their CPU counterparts [23]. Architectural limitations such as the size or even availability of a cache not only change how matrix multiply is implemented [12, 1], but also affects the overall accuracy of the computation as it dictates how the computation is decomposed [5, 13], resulting in poorer accuracy on the GPU. This deviation in accuracy due to algorithmic differences is true even though the GPU uses an FMA (Fused-Multiply-Add) [20] which produces fewer rounding errors than the CPU implementation [13, 12]. This is analyzed and discussed in Section 3 and demonstrated empirically in Section 5. To solve this accuracy problem, we approach solutions by breaking apart the problem into two subclasses, matrices with positive inputs and those with both positive and negative inputs. Specifically, we will use uniform random between $[0, 1]$ for the input matrices. We place no restriction on the result matrix. This is natural as uniform random matrices with inputs between $[0, 1]$ and $[-1, 1]$ are considered representative of real world inputs and are widely used [11, 13, 3]. In particular, problems that are represented by the $[0, 1]$ range include Markov chains [9], computational biology [2] and pattern recognition [8]. Knowing this and knowing the input allows us to specifically tailor algorithmic solutions, combined with our understanding in how subtle differences in the computation can be broken up to transcend the architectural limitations of the GPU, we are able to not only improve performance by up to 27%, we can also improve accuracy when the matrix input is positive. In addition, because of the quantity of problems represented by the $[0, 1]$ input range and the ability and availability of algorithmic solutions that cater to problems of this type, we propose to extend the BLAS 3 specification to allow other library authors to likewise provide solutions for these types of problems instead of always implementing solutions that cater to the worst case, general inputs. We go into detail about the

BLAS 3 extension proposal in Section 6. This will all be presented through the lens of a new scalable GEMM implementation for the GPU. The rest of the paper is organized as follows: We will start by briefly covering previous work in the area of high performance matrix multiply and BLAS 3 implementations along with hybrid matrix multiply implementations. We will then discuss how the decomposition of the problem affects the overall numerical accuracy of the result, demonstrating this difference empirically by comparing different matrix multiply implementations on different architectures, namely the CPU and the GPU. Next we will demonstrate how this information can be used to build a hybrid matrix multiply implementation that improves performance on the GPU by up to 27% over the native implementation and also improves accuracy by exploiting asymptotically fast matrix multiply algorithms, such as Winograd's variant of Strassen's algorithm [24], that behaves like the canonical $O(N^3)$ matrix multiply algorithm in terms of accuracy when the input is non-negative. Finally, capitalizing on this insight, we propose an extension to the BLAS 3 specification to allow other library authors to take advantage of other asymptotically fast matrix multiply algorithms with similar properties.

2. PREVIOUS WORK

Matrix multiply is ubiquitous in scientific computing. Consequently, considerable effort has been spent on improving its performance. One of the first BLAS 3 implementations to be widely available was ATLAS [23]. ATLAS was unique in that instead of writing architectural specific implementations it would attempt to automatically find the best implementation for a given architecture through an exhaustive search of standard optimization techniques such as blocking and loop unrolling. Various combinations of these techniques would be compiled and tested on a given architecture, the fastest implementation being saved and then used as the basis for all other BLAS 3 functions. Further performance could be found though by ignoring the L1 cache and instead targeting the L2 cache. This insight became the basis of Goto's BLAS implementation [12]. Goto's implementation is widely considered the most efficient on x86 based machines and is even used in official vendor provided libraries such as Intel's Math Kernel Library [16]. With Goto's BLAS implementation, high performance implementations on x86 based machines reached their limit in terms of efficient use of the processor. In order to further increase performance hybrid matrix multiply implementations had to be considered. Hybrid matrix multiply implementations work by first decomposing a problem using matrix multiply algorithms that are asymptotically faster than the canonical $O(N^3)$ algorithm (An example of the canonical matrix multiply algorithm can be found in Section 3.4 Figure 4). The hybrid matrix multiply algorithm then solves the decomposed parts using a high performance implementation like the previously mentioned ATLAS [23] or Goto BLAS [12]. The current state of the art for hybrid matrix multiply algorithms on x86 based machines is the implementation by D'Alberto and Nicolau [10].

Unlike x86 based machines, GPU implementations vary widely due to constantly changing architecture. Within the Nvidia family of GPUs, the best currently available implementation for the Tesla chipset is that offered by Volkov and Demmel [22]. The Fermi chipset, a more modern chipset offered by Nvidia, the best implementation is that offered through MAGMA BLAS [1]. Both implementations though, like all high performance matrix multiply implementations, are limited in terms of their efficient use of the architecture. The only hybrid implementation on the GPU is that by Li, Ranka and Sahni [18]. This implementation demonstrated the performance hybrid matrix multiply algorithms on the GPU. The accuracy analysis of their hybrid matrix multiply algorithm however was fundamentally limited by hardware implementation choices made by Nvidia for that chipset. On the Tesla chipset, the FMADD (floating point multiply and add) did not conform to the IEEE 754 standard, the intermediate result was truncated instead of rounded [20]. The effect of which was exhaustively measured in our previous work [4]. High performance CPU implementations were also not compared, which are well known to be more accurate than the canonical $O(N^3)$ matrix multiply implementation [5]. Additionally, with the Fermi chipset Nvidia replaced the FMADD operation with FMA (fused-multiply-and-add) which halves the number of rounding errors committed [13]. In the next section we will explore the consequences of FMADD versus FMA in terms of theoretical bounds. We will then show empirically how algorithmic decisions play a larger overall role in the accuracy of high performance matrix multiply implementations than whether an FMA or an FMADD is used to compute individual partial products. We will then show in Section 4 how high performance matrix multiply implementations on the GPU can be improved using asymptotically fast implementations, both in terms of performance and accuracy.

3. NUMERICAL ACCURACY

As discussed in Section 2, there are a number of high performance matrix multiply implementations that exist for both the CPU and the GPU. In order to compare the different matrix multiply implementations in terms of numerical stability it becomes useful to have a way of modeling individual rounding errors created by individual operations. The operations of primary concern are those associated with the innermost dot product of each matrix multiply implementation, namely multiplication and addition. Though the model also captures subtraction and division. This model is discussed in Section 3.1.

Empirical results are also useful as they help to not only validate a model and bring to light hidden constants in any error analysis but they can also sometimes illustrate just how pessimistic a model can be. This is the case when comparing asymptotically fast matrix multiply implementations as their accuracy in terms of their error analysis is usually much worse than they are in practice [5, 11]. The empirical results are measured in terms of relative error and absolute error. Relative error is useful as it attempts to capture the error independently of the magnitude of the input, thus allowing for direct comparison of different implementations and architectures. Absolute error is useful if the input matrices are between $[0, 1]$ and $[-1, 1]$ as one can simply scale this difference relative to the magnitude of the input matrices they commonly use. Though other metrics for measuring error exist [25, 21], they do not appear to be commonly used.

For the rest of the paper we also define blocking to mean breaking apart the computation on a single dimension. For instance, by using the canonical three nested loop version of matrix multiply from Section 3.4 Figure 4 as an example, there are three different loops, or rather, dimensions that can be blocked on. Blocking puting a certain number of elements of a gi together instead of computing all elements av dimension. For example, given three matrice with dimensions $M \times K$, $K \times N$ and $M \times N$, re: a matrix product $A \times B = C$. If we were to wr blocking on M and N, we would be blocking matrix C. This means that all of K would for a given block of M and N. Blocking on dimensions, also known as blocking on the re is a common strategy for parallelization as ea can be computed independently. For instance size was $M/2$ by $N/2$, four independent sub could be computed in parallel. It is importar blocking on the K dimension is the only dime affect accuracy. A more detailed blocking e) found in Section 3.4 as well as an analysis of on K affects accuracy in Section 3.3.

3.1 Measuring Rounding Error

Before discussing the standard model, some notation must first be introduced, namely t "unit roundoff". Unit roundoff, also known a *silon*, is defined as β^{1-p} where β is the base, in we are dealing with binary arithmetic and p i being used. This means that unit roundoff wil precision used in the computation. For the re: we will represent unit roundoff with the lett assume round to nearest in all our analysis ar is the IEEE default rounding mode. In the n we will cover the notation we will be using various matrix multiply implementations.

3.2 Notation

In this paper we will use identical notation as that used in "Accuracy and Stability of Numerical Algorithms" by Higham [13]. To briefly cover the important ideas from the book that are relevant to this paper: If x and y are values, and their product is expressed as xy, then $fl(xy)$ would be the product rounded to the precision of the machine. Likewise, if we assign $z = xy$ then we can represent the machine computed result using $\widehat{z}$ so that $\widehat{z} = fl(xy)$. The difference between the compute result and the actual result can then be expressed simply as $|z - \widehat{z}|$. To quantify exactly how much that difference is, we turn to the standard model as presented in Higham's book [13] as the model is widely used and holds for IEEE standard arithmetic. In this model, the result of an individual floating point operations is:

$$fl(x \; op \; y) = (x \; op \; y)(1 + \delta) \qquad (3.1)$$

Here δ represents the relative error of an individual operation and is assumed to be $|\delta| \leq u$. This means that equation 3.1 says that the real answer, rounded to machine precision, is equal to the real answer plus some small relative error, less than or equal to machine epsilon.

3.3 Analysis

Using the standard model represented by equation 3.1, the following forward error bound for the inner product of

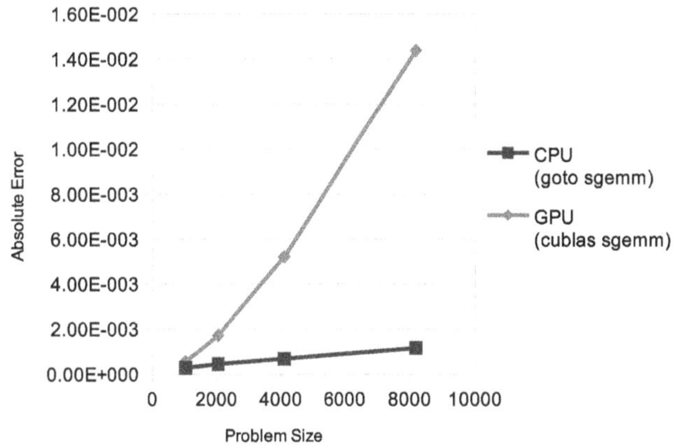

Figure 1: Single - Uni Random [0,1] - Absolute Error

matrix multiply is derived in [13]:

$$|x^T y - fl(x^T y)| \leq \gamma_K \sum_{i=1}^{K} |x_i y_i| = \gamma_K |x|^T |y|, \qquad (3.2)$$

where $\gamma_K = Ku/(1 - Ku)$. Simplified, this becomes:

$$|s_K - \widehat{s_K}| \leq \gamma_K |x|^T |y|, \qquad (3.3)$$

where s_K is the correct result and $\widehat{s_K}$ is the computed result. This model holds for the canonical $O(N^3)$ matrix multiply (or specifically $O(MNK)$), however it no longer holds when the computation is broken up, the normal result of implementing a blocking strategy. If the inner product is broken up into K/b strips, where K is the problem size and each strip contains b summands, the forward error bound becomes:

$$|s_K - \widehat{s_K}| \leq \gamma_{\frac{K}{b}+b-1} |x|^T |y| \qquad (3.4)$$

The benefit of blocking on K is empirically demonstrated in Figures 1 and 2 by comparing SGEMM (single precision general matrix multiply) implementations from Nvidia's CUBLAS on a Nvidia Tesla C2070 as compared to GotoBLAS on a Q9450 Penryn Intel Quad Core processor. For both Figures 1 and 2 the input is uniform random between $[0, 1]$, the result is computed using single precision (SGEMM) and the standard the result is compared against is computed using double precision on the CPU. There are no restrictions on the result. Individual points on the graph are the max of the max for 10 runs for each problem size. Figure 1 is the absolute error and Figure 2 is the relative error. The relative error for GotoBLAS in Figure 2 appears to improve because the tile size chosen by GotoBLAS is targeting a larger problem size, effecting the way the computation is broken up. One interesting side effect of (3.4) is when $b = \sqrt{K}$, which is being illustrated in Figure 2 as the problem size approaches b^2. These results are particularly striking since the CPU implementation is using a floaing-point-multiply-and-add (FMADD) [12, 14, 15] whereas the GPU implementation is using a fused-multiply-and-add (FMA) [20]. How peculiar this result at first appears becomes more apparent when directly comparing the two operations using the standard model. In the standard model, an FMA is modeled as [13]:

$$fl(x + y \times z) = (x + y \times z)(1 + \delta), \qquad (3.5)$$

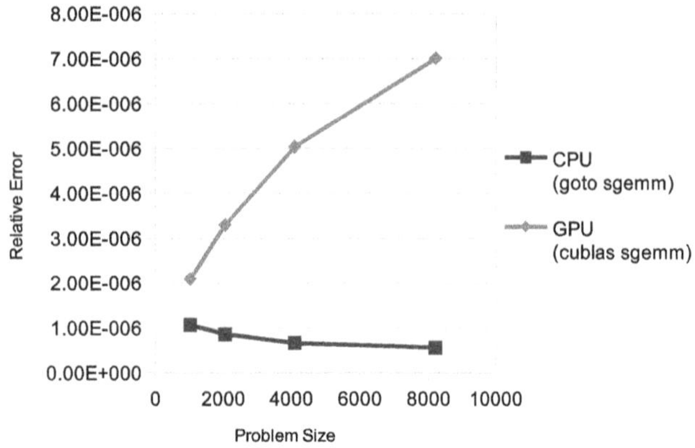

Figure 2: Single - Uni Random [0,1] - Relative Error

where $|\delta| \leq u$. What this means is that an FMA effectively commits roughly half as many rounding errors as the FMADD since the result is only rounded once, after the addition, instead of twice as is the case with the FMADD (once after the multiplication, once after the addition). However, the worst case forward error for a dot product computed using an FMA is still the same as 3.3. A simple analysis is as follows:

Let us assume we have two vectors, y and z, both of length n and a scalar variable x. Using the standard model, an FMA can be expressed with equation 3.5. Applying this model to the first two products we have as follows:

$$\widehat{s_K} = (x + y_1 \times z_1)(1+\delta)$$

$$\widehat{s_K} = [(x + y_1 \times z_1)(1+\delta) + (y_2 \times z_2)](1+\delta)$$

$$\widehat{s_K} = (x + y_1 \times z_1)(1+\delta)^2 + (y_2 \times z_2)(1+\delta)$$

It is easy to see that if this pattern was carried out to n elements, the result would be:

$$\widehat{s_K} = (x + y_1 \times z_1)(1+\delta)^K + (y_2 \times z_2)(1+\delta)^{K-1} ... + (y_K \times z_K)(1+\delta)$$

Using the same analysis that was used to derive the inner product forward error bound for the canonical matrix multiply algorithm [13], we end up with the same forward error bound as represented by equation 3.3. What this means is that the inner product computed using an FMADD and the inner product computed using an FMA have the same worst case forward error bound. More importantly, both are clearly worse than the forward error bound represented by equation 3.4, which is empirically demonstrated in Figures 1 and 2 by comparing the CUBLAS SGEMM implementation against the SGEMM implementation in GotoBLAS [12]. This is because the SGEMM implementation in GotoBLAS is broken up along the K dimension of the matrix product whereas the computation is not broken up along the K dimension in the CUBLAS implementation. This is because the GotoBLAS implementation is blocked on all three dimensions of the matrix product whereas the GPU implementation is only blocked on the result matrix, dimensions M and N. (For reference, GotoBLAS[1], the Tesla chipset implementation by Volkov and Demmel[2] as well as the MagmaBLAS implementation[3] for the Fermi chipset are publicly available.) This means the accuracy difference between the two SGEMM implementations is almost entirely algorithmic and not architectural. In the next subsection we offer a simple example to help illustrate this analysis.

[1] http://www.tacc.utexas.edu/tacc-projects/gotoblas2

```
ALGORITHM: Blocked Matrix Multiply
procedure blockedMultiply(A, B, C, M, K, N, bSize)
for (i = 0, i < M, i = i + bSize)
  for (j = 0, j < N, j = j + bSize)
    for (k = 0, k < K, k = k + bSize)
      AOffset = i * K + k
      BOffset = k * N + j
      COffset = i * N + j
      leafMultiply(A+AOffset, K, B+BOffset, N,
                   C+COffset, N, bSize, bSize, bSize)
```

Figure 3: Blocked Matrix Multiply

```
ALGORITHM: Direct Matrix Multiply (Preload)
procedure leafMultiply(A, ldA, B, ldB, C, ldC, M, K, N)
begin
for (i = 0, i < M, i + +)
  for (j = 0, < N, j + +)
    for (k = 0, k < K, k + +)
      C[i * ldC + j] += A[i * ldA + k] * B[k * ldB + j]
```

Figure 4: Preload Matrix Multiply

3.4 Matrix Multiply Blocking Example

Blocking is a common strategy within high performance matrix multiply kernels. The primary goal of blocking is to maximize reuse of the data in the cache and hence improve performance. Subtleties in how the individual blocks are added to the whole greatly impact the forward error bound on the inner product [13]. This difference is sometimes referred to as *preload* versus *postload* [7]. We adopt this terminology in this paper.

Preload and postload are best discussed in the context of a specific blocking strategy. Consider the code shown in Figure 3, which multiplies the $M \times K$ matrix A by the $K \times N$ matrix B to produce the $M \times N$ matrix C. The matrices are stored in row-major order. The blocks are square, of size $bSize \times bSize$. For simplicity, we assume that the matrix dimensions are all even multiples of the block size. The strategy in Figure 3 is to compute C one column of blocks at a time, always keeping in memory a $bSize \times k$ strip of A along with the block of C currently being computed. The code repeatedly multiplies a block of A by a block of B and adds the result to a block of C. Each partial block computation is performed by calling the procedure

`leafMultiply(A,ldA,B,ldB,C,ldC,M,K,N)`

where A,B, and C are the addresses of the start of the blocks; the blocks are of sizes $M \times K$, $K \times N$, and $M \times N$ respectively; and ldA, ldB, and ldC are the *strides* (i.e., the row lengths) of the three matrices.

The error of the algorithm shown in Figure 3 depends on

[2] http://www.cs.berkeley.edu/~volkov/

[3] http://icl.cs.utk.edu/magma/software/index.html

```
ALGORITHM: Direct Matrix Multiply (Postload)
procedure leafMultiply(A, ldA, B, ldB, C, ldC, M, K, N)
begin
for (i = 0, i < M, i++)
   for (j = 0, < N, j++)
      sum = 0
      for (k = 0, k < K, k++)
         sum += A[i * ldA + k] * B[k * ldB + j]
      end for
      C[i * ldC + j] += sum
   end for
end for
```

Figure 5: Postload Matrix Multiply

how the inner kernel (i.e., the `leafMultiply()` procedure) is implemented. If the implementation is the preload code shown in Figure 4, the summation of the inner product is the standard summation of K terms, for which the forward error bound is modeled by equation 3.3. In contrast, the postload code shown in Figure 5 computes the contribution of the block to the inner product in a temporary variable and adds this sum to the inner product. When the code of Figures 3 and 5 is combined, the net effect is to compute the dot product as the sum of $K/bSize$ partial sums, each of which is the sum of $bSize$ terms. As discussed in the previous subsection, breaking apart the summation affects the accuracy. By applying equation 3.4, the forward error bound for the postload implementation becomes:

$$|s_K - \widehat{s_K}| \le \gamma_{\frac{K}{bSize}+bSize-1}|x|^T|y| \qquad (3.6)$$

Which obviously produces a smaller forward error than the preload implementation for values of $bSize$ that are not equal to 1 or K.

Current GPU implementations on both the Tesla chipset and the Fermi chipset effectively use a preload implementation [1, 22], as illustrated in Figure 4. The forward error bound for the preload implementation is exactly the same as a standard summation, represented by equation 3.3 in Section 3.3. Notice that there is no difference in error between blocking on k and using a preload implementation versus using a postload implementation and changing the update rule in the inner most loop of Figure 3 from "$k = k + bSize$" to "$k = k + 1$". This is what GPU implementations do[2,3]. This implementation detail is in contrast to CPU implementations that effectively use a postload implementation [12, 23], as illustrated in Figure 5. The forward error bound for the postload implementation is represented by equation 3.4 in Section 3.3. This difference has a significant effect on the forward error bound, as was analyzed in Section 3.3 and demonstrated empirically in Figures 1 and 2. In the next section we will discuss algorithmic solutions to improve accuracy on the GPU.

4. ALGORITHMIC SOLUTIONS

As we discussed in Section 3, in order to improve the accuracy of a dot product the computation must be broken up. The most obvious way to break up the inner product is by blocking on k [7]. This is the preferred method for processors with deep memory hierarchies like the CPU as it maximizes cache hits which maximizes reuse of the data, thus avoiding costly trips to main memory [12, 23]. As we demonstrated in our previous work on the CPU, a similar effect can be achieved by breaking up the computation by using the outer product [5]. In general though, and in particular for flat memory hierarchy machines such as that provided by the GPU, blocking on k general leads to poorer performance since any resources allocated for blocking along k could be used to further improve performance as blocking on k has to be simulated with additional registers. Likewise, if the high performance matrix multiply implementation on the GPU is anywhere near 100% utilization of the GPU, you must steal resources from the implementation, reducing performance to increase accuracy. Applying the outer product recursively though requires no additional resources nor does it apply additional operations. The overhead of recursion is entirely limited to how the GPU driver handles multiple kernel launches, namely, if it inserts barriers between kernel launches that access disparate pieces of data. We discuss outer product recursion in detail in the following subsection.

4.1 Outer Product - Recursion

An alternative approach to breaking up the computation is by recursively breaking apart the matrix and computing the outer product. This can be accomplished as follows, given the following matrices:

$$A = \begin{bmatrix} A11 & A12 \\ A21 & A22 \end{bmatrix}, \quad B = \begin{bmatrix} B11 & B12 \\ B21 & B22 \end{bmatrix}, \text{ and}$$

$$C = \begin{bmatrix} C11 & C12 \\ C21 & C22 \end{bmatrix}$$

the entries of C are given by

$$\begin{aligned} C11 &= A11 \times B11 + A12 \times B21, \\ C12 &= A11 \times B12 + A12 \times B22, \\ C21 &= A21 \times B11 + A22 \times B21, \text{ and} \\ C22 &= A21 \times B12 + A22 \times B22. \end{aligned}$$

Each submatrix of A, B and C can likewise be broken up, yielding:

$$A11 = \left[\begin{array}{cc|cc} A11_{11} & A11_{12} & A11_{13} & A11_{14} \\ A11_{21} & A11_{22} & A11_{23} & A11_{24} \\ \hline A11_{31} & A11_{32} & A11_{33} & A11_{34} \\ A11_{41} & A11_{42} & A11_{43} & A11_{44} \end{array}\right],$$

where the first half of $C11_{11}$ is now computed by

$$C11_{11} = (A11_{11} \times B11_{11}) + (A11_{12} \times B11_{21}) + (A11_{13} \times B11_{31}) + (A11_{14} \times B11_{41})$$

In this way, you are effectively halving the error with each additional level of recursion, a special case of this being pairwise summation [13, 5]. What is important here to realize is that this recursive decomposition need not be done with simply the canonical $O(N^3)$ matrix multiply algorithm, this can be done with any asymptotically fast matrix multiply algorithm that can be expressive recursively. Normally this is not pursued because as seen in Figures 1 and 2 Goto's implementation of SGEMM is very accurate and simply reducing the leaf size to even $\frac{K}{8}$, the result of applying a recursive matrix multiply implementation to a depth of three, is not

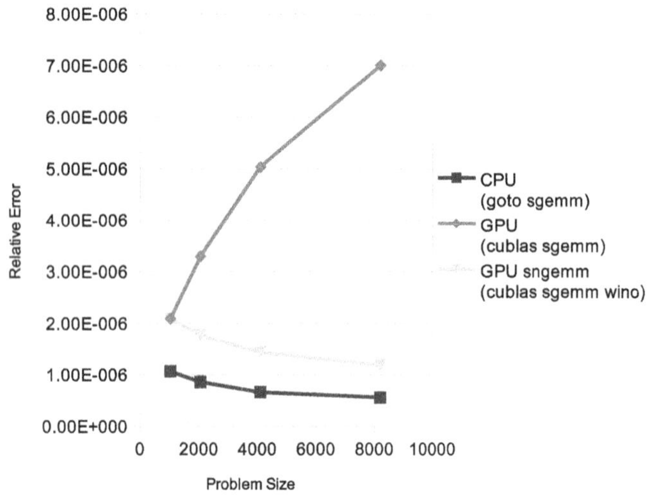

Figure 7: Single - Uni Random [0,1] - Relative Error

enough to out run the constant error that an asymptotically fast matrix multiply algorithm multiplies for each level of recursion. However, this is not the case for preload implementations like those found on GPUs, as we will discuss in the next subsection.

4.2 Winograd

Winograd's variant of Strassen's algorithm, which will be referred to as Winograd's algorithm, is an asymptotically fast matrix multiply algorithm that changes the schedule of operations in Strassen's algorithm, thereby reducing the number of additions in Strassen's algorithm [24]. Additionally, both algorithms only require 7 matrix multiply operations whereas the canonical $O(N^3)$ algorithm requires 8, making them asymptotically faster than the canonical matrix multiply algorithm. Given the same matrices as in Subsection 4.1, the specific schedule we use for Winograd's algorithm (as there are many different schedules and each one has different effects on accuracy) is described in Table 1. The important thing to notice is that for each multiplication in Winograd's algorithm, when the final value is written to matrix C it is done so with either an assignment or through addition, never subtraction. This includes the temporary value U. What this means is that if Winograd's algorithm is applied to input matrices that are all of the same sign, or in this case, every element in both matrix A and B is non-negative, then there is only cancellation if the sub-product is negative. This is commonly referred to as lacking "true" subtraction, as subtraction only occurs if the submatrix being added contains elements of a different sign than the matrix it is being added to. This means that though the overall worst case accuracy bound of Winograd's algorithm has not changed (as the bound makes no assumption on the input), in practice, the error is contained within the least significant bits as catastrophic cancellation through subtraction (actually using the subtraction operator when applying the partial sum to the result matrix C) is generally avoided. This allows Winograd's algorithm, in practice, to behave more like the canonical matrix multiply algorithm when the input is uniform (in this case, uniformly random in $[0, 1]$). Winograd's algorithm has been demonstrated to be, in practice, more accurate than Strassen's algorithm in previous work [5, 11] when the input is uniform random in $[0, 1]$. The key difference here is that since the underlying high performance implementation on the GPU is a preload implementation, the recursive decomposition of Winograd's algorithm breaks up the chains of additions. This effect is not as pronounced when the high performance implementation blocks on K, as most CPU implementations do [12, 23]. The reason for this is there is only really one source of rounding errors but two ways it can be exposed. The first way is if there is some small error in the least significant digits that is suddenly exposed by subtraction, that the least significant digits become the most significant digits (this is commonly referred to as catastrophic cancellation). The second way, and only true source of rounding errors, is the slow accumulation of rounding errors from each individual operation. The pace of this march can be slowed though by breaking up the chains of operations, as we explained in Subsection 4.1.

The implication of this insight can be clearly seen in Figures 6 and 7, (performance for which is provided in Figure 8), where Winograd's variant of Strassen's algorithm (labeled as 'GPU sngemm' and 'GPU dngemm', respectively) is applied to a leaf size of 1024 and the input is between $[0, 1]$. Additional levels of Winograd's algorithm actually improve the accuracy as compared to the implementation offered by Nvidia's CUBLAS. This improvement gives back a digit of accuracy over using Nvidia's CUBLAS, as seen in Figure 6. Though the accuracy of working on the GPU is still worse than that of the CPU, it is much improved over all other implementations offered on the GPU. It is also important to note that blocked postload CPU implementations like Goto's are amongst the most accurate high performance implementations [5]. In order to improve accuracy beyond that provided by blocked postload high performance implementations, such as that provided by GotoBLAS [12], requires a three level hybrid to maintain performance [5] or can be done using pairwise summation at the cost of performance [13, 5].

The benefit of choosing to use Winograd's algorithm over the canonical $O(N^3)$ algorithm is also obvious as seen by the performance gained in Figure 8. The GPU in the general case is faster than the CPU for matrix multiply [1] and we further extend this lead. In the next section we will

Winograd's Algorithm	
Multiplication #	Operations
1	$S = A21 + A22, T = B$ $U = S \times T,$ $C12 = U, C22 = U$
2	$U = A11 \times B11$ $C11 = U$
3	$C11+ = A1 \times B21$
4	$S = S - A11, T = B2$ $U+ = S \times T$ $C12+ = U$
5	$S = A12 - S$ $C12+ = S \times B22$
6	$T = B21 - T$ $C21 = A22 \times T$
7	$S = A11 - A21, T = I$ $U+ = S \times T$ $C22+ = U, C21+ = U$

Table 1: Winograd's Variant of Strassen

demonstrate and discuss the benefits to botl and accuracy to using Winograd's algorithm

5. EMPIRICAL RESULTS

In this section we will demonstrate empiri possible to get both performance and accu ing hybrid matrix multiply algorithms, we de on the GPU. The results were computed on I with CUDA version 4.1 using a Nvidia Tesl CPU is a Q9450 Penryn Intel Quad Core p GotoBLAS2 version 1.13. The performance by comparing the various implementations to plementation, assuming $2 \times N^3$ operations. Ti by using CUDA Events. The matrices compu for convenience. Accuracy was measured usi ror and absolute error [13], which is discusse Section 3.1. Winograd's variant of Strassen's a beled as 'GPU sngemm' for single precision m and 'GPU dngemm' for double precision m An explanation of this naming scheme is pr tion 6. For our implementation we wrote c kernels for assignment, addition and subtra gorithm is implemented recursively using tl Table 1, calling the CUBLAS GEMM impl the leaves for the multiplications. In the ne tions we will provide and discuss additional pe accuracy data, including for problems comp precision.

5.1 Performance

As seen in Figures 8 and 9, the Winograd va algorithm clearly scales better than the canoni tation offered by Nvidia, offering up to 26% better performance in single precision and up to 27% better performance in double precision. The key difference though between the single and double precision implementation is that of the crossover point. As seen in Figure 8, the break even point is a leaf of 1k whereas the break even point for double precision is 2k, as seen in Figure 9. This makes perfect sense given the size difference between single and double precision,

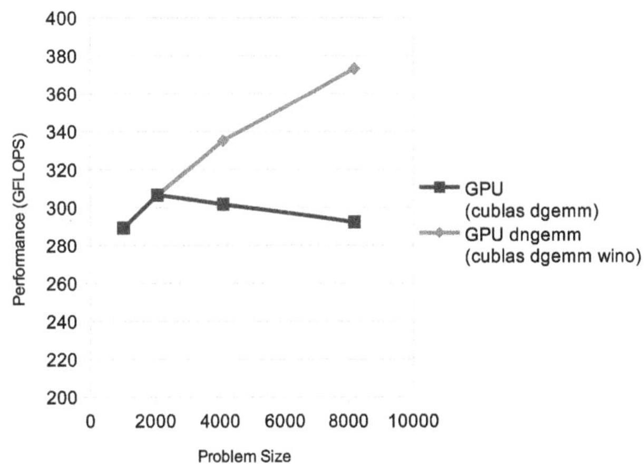

Figure 9: Double - Performance (GFLOPS)

namely, the cost associated with trading multiplications for additions and the additional overhead in bandwidth associated with the additions. To be explicit, it costs more to add matrices in double precision than it does if they are stored in single precision, so the time saved on the multiplication needs to be greater to offset the time lost doing the additions. Thus the crossover point for double precision is a leaf size of 2k whereas the crossover point for single precision is 1k. In either case though, the performance benefit of applying Winograd's variant of Strassen's algorithm is obvious.

5.2 Accuracy

As seen in Figures 10 and 11, double precision behaves identically in terms of absolute and relative error to that of single precision, as introduced in Subsection 4.2 and seen in Figures 6 and 7. Though the overall accuracy of this solution is not better than that of the CPU, if one is choosing to use the GPU for performance reasons, the solution provided in this paper is much more accurate than simply using the standard matrix multiply implementation provided. This difference can be quite large, as seen in Figure 10, for a problem size of 8k, a whole digit of accuracy is returned. In

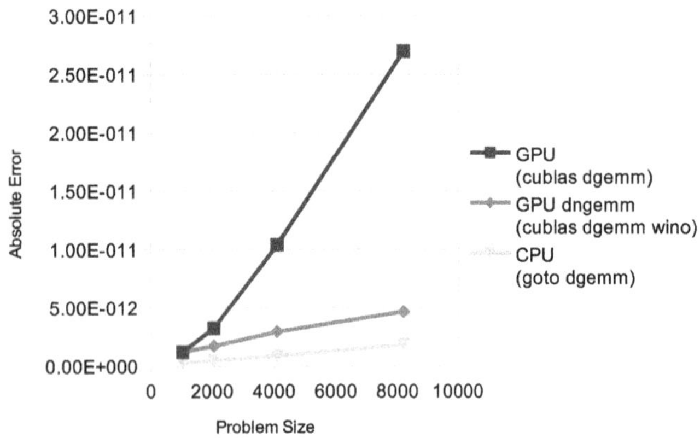

Figure 11: Double - Random [0,1] - Absolute Error

the next section we will discuss expanding the Basic Linear Algebra Subroutines level 3 (BLAS 3) specification in order to offer a standardized method for library authors to implement, as opposed to forcing the general scientific community to reimplement various solutions, or worse, to constantly reorganizing the structure of their programs as new algorithms are implemented using different, incompatible standards.

6. BLAS EXTENSION

It should be clear by now that there are many problems that have non-negative matrix inputs and would benefit from solutions like those offered in this paper. The problem however is the lack of a standard makes adoption unlikely as new implementations will offer new function definitions, forcing the general scientific community to constantly update their program to match the new implementation. In addition, simply replacing an existing BLAS (Basic Linear Algebra Subroutines) level 3 function introduces confusion and creates a conflict with the existing function and limits the new implementation to programs that do not require both the new and original functionality of the method being replaced. The current BLAS level 3 specification is organized as follows:

In the existing BLAS level 3 specification, the functions are named according to the following scheme: One letter for type, followed by two letters specifying something special about the input, for instance, if the input is symmetric, followed by two letters specifying the operation performed. The types supported are 'S' for single precision, 'D' for double precision, 'C' for single complex and 'Z' for double complex. The options that specify something about the input are:

GE General Matrix

HE Hermitian Matrix

SY Symmetric Matrix

TR Triangular Matrix

To give an example, this means a function called DGEMM would translate into a function that performs an operation on Double precision, on a GEneral matrix input, and the operation performed is Matrix Multiply. What we wish to do is provide a narrow extension to the input specification. Over the years, several broader extensions to BLAS have been proposed and implemented [19, 6]. What we aim to do is simply avoid confusion with the existing methods already provided. Keeping with the existing nomenclature, we propose the addition of 'N' to specify non-negative inputs. This 'N' would be inserted between the type of input and the two letter option that further specifies something about the input. In this way, we can allow for both non-negative and symmetric inputs, for instance. Using the DGEMM example from before, this means a new function would be available called DNGEMM, translating into a function that performs on an input that is Double precision, Non-Negative and performs GEneral Matrix Multiply. The benefit of adapting this existing standard as opposed to proposing an entirely new standard is that current scientific programs need only change the name of the function being called in order to gain the benefit of implementations like those provided in this paper as the rest of the function prototype is identical.

7. CONCLUSION

In this paper we have explained and demonstrated empirically that the simple addition of an FMA (Fused-Multiply-Add) will not necessarily result in better accuracy, specifically with regards to matrix multiply. We demonstrated this by comparing high performance implementations on two different architectures, a GPU that provided an FMA, and a CPU that did not. In Subsection 3.3 we showed that surprisingly, the architecture that lacked an FMA, the CPU, actually had better accuracy with regards to matrix multiply than that of the architecture that did have an FMA, the GPU. Next, we analyzed why using the standard model in Section 3, and explored algorithmic solutions to improve the accuracy of matrix multiply on the GPU in Section 4, proposing Winograd's variant of Strassen's algorithm in Subsection 4.2 for improving the accuracy of non-negative matrices. Next, in Section 5, we empirically verified our solution, demonstrating that not only can our solution improve accuracy over the standard high performance implementation provided by Nvidia, it can also improve performance by up to 26% in single precision and 27% in double precision. Finally, in Section 6, we proposed to extend the BLAS (Basic Linear Algebra Subroutines) level 3 specification to include non-negative matrix inputs, 'N', thus allowing library authors to offer their own solutions under an already accepted standard, thereby enabling the general scientific community to easily transition existing programs to using this new solution.

8. ACKNOWLEDGMENTS

We wish to thank the reviewers for their thorough and thoughtful comments and suggestions. In particular, reviewer 1 for the extremely helpful and insightful comments which greatly improved the quality of the paper. We would also like to thank the National Science Foundation for partial support of this research, NSF Grant # 1249449.

9. REFERENCES

[1] E. Agullo, J. Demmel, J. Dongarra, B. Hadri, J. Kurzak, J. Langou, H. Ltaief, P. Luszczek, and S. Tomov. Numerical linear algebra on emerging architectures: The plasma and magma projects. In *Journal of Physics: Conference Series*, volume 180, 2009.

[2] T. Akutsu, S. Miyano, and S. Kuhara. Algorithms for identifying boolean networks and related biological networks based on matrix multiplication and fingerprint function. *Journal of Computational Biology*, 7(3-4):331–343, 2000.

[3] I. J. Anderson. A distillation algorithm for floating-point summation. *SIAM J. Sci. Comput.*, 20(5):1797–1806, 1999.

[4] M. Badin, L. Bic, M. B. Dillencourt, and A. Nicolau. Pretty good accuracy in matrix multiplication with gpus. In *ISPDC*, pages 49–55. IEEE Computer Society, 2010.

[5] M. Badin, P. D'Alberto, L. Bic, M. Dillencourt, and A. Nicolau. Improving the accuracy of high performance BLAS implementations using adaptive blocked algorithms. In *Proceedings of 23rd International Symposium on Computer Architecture and High Performance Computing (SBAC-PAD)*, pages 120–127, 2011.

[6] L. Blackford, J. Demmel, J. Dongarra, I. Duff, S. Hammarling, G. Henry, M. Heroux, L. Kaufman, A. Lumsdaine, A. Petitet, R. Pozo, K. Remington, and R. C. Whaley. An updated set of basic linear algebra subprograms (blas). *ACM Trans. Math. Softw.*, 28(2):135–151, June 2002.

[7] A. M. Castaldo, R. C. Whaley, and A. T. Chronopoulos. Reducing floating point error in dot product using the superblock family of algorithms. *SIAM J. Sci. Comput.*, 31(2):1156–1174, 2008.

[8] E. Cohen and D. D. Lewis. Approximating matrix multiplication for pattern recognition tasks. In M. E. Saks, editor, *SODA*, pages 682–691. ACM/SIAM, 1997.

[9] B. A. Craig and P. P. Sendi. Estimation of the transition matrix of a discrete-time markov chain. *Health Economics*, 11(1):33–42, 2002.

[10] P. D'alberto, M. Bodrato, and A. Nicolau. Exploiting parallelism in matrix-computation kernels for symmetric multiprocessor systems: Matrix-multiplication and matrix-addition algorithm optimizations by software pipelining and threads allocation. *ACM Trans. Math. Softw.*, 38(1):2:1–2:30, Dec. 2011.

[11] P. D'Alberto and A. Nicolau. Adaptive Winograd's matrix multiplications. *ACM Trans. Math. Softw.*, 36:3:1–3:23, March 2009.

[12] K. Goto and R. van de Geijn. On reducing TLB misses in matrix multiplication. Working Note 9, The University of Texas at Austin, November 2002.

[13] N. J. Higham. *Accuracy and Stability of Numerical Algorithms*. SIAM, 2nd edition, 2002.

[14] Intel. *Intel 64 and IA-32 Architectures Software Developer's Manual - Volume 2A: Instruction Set Reference A-M*. Intel Corporation, June 2010.

[15] Intel. *Intel 64 and IA-32 Architectures Software Developer's Manual - Volume 2B: Instruction Set Reference N-Z*. Intel Corporation, June 2010.

[16] Intel. Intel math kernel library (intel mkl) 10.2, 2010.

[17] V. V. Kindratenko, J. Enos, G. Shi, M. T. Showerman, G. W. Arnold, J. E. Stone, J. C. Phillips, and W. mei W. Hwu. Gpu clusters for high-performance computing. In *CLUSTER*, pages 1–8. IEEE, 2009.

[18] J. Li, S. Ranka, and S. Sahni. Strassen's matrix multiplication on gpus. In *Proceedings of 17th International Conference on Parallel and Distributed Systems (ICPADS)*, pages 157–164. IEEE, December 2011.

[19] X. S. Li, J. Demmel, D. H. Bailey, G. Henry, Y. Hida, J. Iskandar, W. Kahan, S. Y. Kang, A. Kapur, M. C. Martin, B. Thompson, T. Tung, and D. J. Yoo. Design, implementation and testing of extended and mixed precision blas. *ACM Trans. Math. Softw.*, 28(2):152–205, 2002.

[20] Nvidia. *NVIDIA CUDA C Programming Guide*. NVIDIA, 4.1 edition, November 2011.

[21] F. W. J. Olver. A new approach to error arithmetic. *SIAM Journal on Numerical Analysis*, 15(2):368–393, April 1978.

[22] V. Volkov and J. Demmel. Benchmarking gpus to tune dense linear algebra. In *Proceedings of the ACM/IEEE Conference on High Performance Computing*, page 31. IEEE/ACM, November 2008.

[23] R. C. Whaley and J. Dongarra. Automatically tuned linear algebra software. In *PPSC*, 1999.

[24] S. Winograd. On the multiplication of 2 x 2 matrices. *Linear Algebra and its Applications*, 4(4):381 – 388, October 1971.

[25] A. Ziv. Relative distance - an error measure in round-off error analysis. *Mathematics of Computation*, (160):563–569, October 1982.

Toward a Scalable Multi-GPU Eigensolver via Compute-Intensive Kernels and Efficient Communication

Azzam Haidar
Electrical Engineering and Computer Science
University of Tennessee
Knoxville, Tennessee, USA
haidar@eecs.utk.edu

Mark Gates
Electrical Engineering and Computer Science
University of Tennessee
Knoxville, Tennessee, USA
mgates3@eecs.utk.edu

Stanimire Tomov
Electrical Engineering and Computer Science
University of Tennessee
Knoxville, Tennessee, USA
tomov@eecs.utk.edu

Jack Dongarra[*] [†]
Computer Science and Mathematics Division
Oak Ridge National Laboratory
dongarra@eecs.utk.edu

ABSTRACT

The enormous gap between the high-performance capabilities of GPUs and the slow interconnect between them has made the development of numerical software that is scalable across multiple GPUs extremely challenging. We describe a successful methodology on how to address the challenges—starting from our algorithm design, kernel optimization and tuning, to our programming model—in the development of a scalable high-performance tridiagonal reduction algorithm for the symmetric eigenvalue problem. This is a fundamental linear algebra problem with many engineering and physics applications. We use a combination of a task-based approach to parallelism and a new algorithmic design to achieve high performance. The goal of the new design is to increase the computational intensity of the major compute kernels and to reduce synchronization and data transfers between GPUs. This may increase the number of flops, but the increase is offset by the more efficient execution and reduced data transfers. Our performance results are the best available, providing an enormous performance boost compared to current state-of-the-art solutions. In particular, our software scales up to 1070 Gflop/s using 16 Intel E5-2670 cores and eight M2090 GPUs, compared to 45 Gflop/s achieved by the optimized Intel Math Kernel Library (MKL) using only the 16 CPU cores.

[*]University of Tennessee, USA

[†]School of Mathematics & School of Computer Science, University of Manchester, United Kingdom

ICS'13, June 10–14, 2013, Eugene, Oregon, USA.

Categories and Subject Descriptors

G.1.3 [**Numerical Analysis**]: Numerical Linear Algebra—*Singular value decomposition, Eigenvalues and eigenvectors*

Keywords

Eigenvalue, GPU Communication, GPU Computation, Performance, Reduction to tridiagonal, Singular Value Decomposition, heterogeneous programming model, task parallelism

1. INTRODUCTION

An exponentially increasing gap over the years of processor speed vs. memory and interconnect speeds has established the notion that "flops are free" compared to the cost of fetching data. Indeed, if we consider the speed of current GPUs vs. bandwidth of CPU-to-GPU communications, the cost of sending one double-precision floating-point (DP) number through PCIe 3.0, disregarding latency, can be the same as 1,000 DP flops on the latest NVIDIA Kepler K20 GPU. In other words, a computation in this setting is bound by the CPU-to-GPU bandwidth, unless data reuse exceeds 1,000. To address this issue, algorithms must be redesigned in order to increase the computational intensity of their major compute kernels, and to reduce synchronization and data transfers between processors. We describe how to achieve this in the development of a scalable high-performance multi-GPU tridiagonal reduction for the symmetric eigenvalue problem.

Eigenvalue problems are fundamental for many engineering and physics applications. For example, image processing, compression, facial recognition, vibrational analysis of mechanical structures, and computing energy levels of electrons in nanostructure materials can all be expressed as eigenvalue problems. There are many ways to formulate mathematically and solve these problems numerically [11], but in all cases, designing an efficient computation is challenging because of the nature of the algorithms. In particular, the basic transformations (orthogonal similarity transformations) applied to the matrix are two-sided, i.e., transformations are applied on both the left and right side of the matrix. This creates data dependencies that prevent the use of standard techniques to increase the computational intensity of the computation [26], such as blocking and look-ahead, which are used extensively in the one-sided LU, QR, and Cholesky factorizations [27]. New algorithms are needed in order to overcome the bottlenecks associated with the standard techniques, as described in Section 4.

Besides the algorithmic design, the development of high-performance scalable software is linked to the programming model and languages used in the implementation. Our development is done in C/C++ and, when available, we rely on existing routines in numerical libraries like CUBLAS and MAGMA BLAS (for GPUs), MKL, ACML, and PLASMA (for multicore CPUs), or MAGMA (for hybrid CPU-GPU systems) to provide the basic building blocks for our algorithms. Our programming model is based on task parallelism where the computation is split into tasks and data dependencies among the tasks, and the execution is scheduled over all available heterogeneous hardware components without violating the dependencies. This model has been successfully used in the development of dense linear algebra libraries [3], and is self-evident in the presentation.

2. RELATED WORK

LAPACK [4] and ScaLAPACK [10] are the standard linear algebra libraries for dense and banded matrices that include eigensolver routines. LAPACK is for shared-memory systems, while ScaLAPACK is its extension to distributed-memory systems. Neither of them supports GPUs. Hardware vendors in general provide well tuned LAPACK and ScaLAPACK versions based on optimized BLAS — the building block for these libraries.

Recent work specifically on eigenvalue problems has concentrated on accelerating separate components of the solvers, and in particular, the reduction to condensed form, which is the most time consuming phase. This includes reductions to Hessenberg, tridiagonal, and bidiagonal forms, each of which is the result of a similarity transformation for general eigenvalues, symmetric eigenvalues, or the singular value decomposition, respectively. The standard one-stage reduction algorithms have been challenged by the method of splitting the reduction phase into multiple stages.

One of the first uses of a two-stage reduction occurred in the context of out-of-core solvers for generalized symmetric eigenvalue problems [16]. Then, a multi-stage method was used to reduce a matrix to tridiagonal, bidiagonal and Hessenberg forms [22]. With this approach, it was possible to recast the expensive memory-bound operations that occur during the panel factorization into a compute-bound procedure. Consequently, a framework called Successive Band Reduction (SBR) was designed [8], that integrated some of the multi-stage work. The SBR toolbox applies two-sided orthogonal transformations based on Householder reflectors and successively reduces the matrix bandwidth size until a suitable bandwidth is reached. The off-diagonal elements are then annihilated, which produces fill-in blocks or bulges that need to be chased down toward the bottom right corner of the matrix, hence this stage is termed "bulge chasing." If eigenvectors are required in addition to the eigenvalues, the bulge chasing transformations can be efficiently accumulated through Level 3 BLAS operations and used to generate the eigenvectors. Communication bounds for such two-sided reductions have been established under the Communication Avoiding framework [6]. A multi-stage approach has also been applied to the Hessenberg reduction [21] as well as the QZ algorithm [20] for the generalized non-symmetric eigenvalue problem.

Tile algorithms have recently seen a rekindled interest when applied to the two-stage tridiagonal [17, 24] and bidiagonal reductions [23]. The first stage is implemented using high performance kernels combined with a data translation layer to execute on top of the tile data layout format. The second stage is implemented based on cache-aware kernels and a task coalescing technique [17]. The performance achieved is far greater than other available implementations. These approaches, in contrast to our own, are not for hybrid GPU-CPU systems.

With the emergence of high-bandwidth, high-performance GPUs, memory-bound and compute-bound operations can be accelerated by an order of magnitude or more. Tomov et al. [26] presented novel hybrid reduction algorithms for the two-sided factorizations, which take advantage of the high bandwidth of the GPU by offloading the expensive Level 2 BLAS operations of the panel factorization to the GPU. Bientinesi et al. [7] instead accelerated the two-stage approach of the SBR toolbox by offloading the compute-bound kernels of the first stage to the GPU. The computation of the second stage (reduction from band to tridiagonal) still remains on the host though. Vomel et al. [28] extended the tridiagonalization approach in [26] to the symmetric standard eigenvalue problem, and Dong et al. [12] to multi-GPUs.

ELPA [5], a recent distributed-memory eigensolver library, was developed for electronic structure codes. ELPA is based on ScaLAPACK and does not support GPUs. It includes one-stage and two-stage tridiagonalizations, the corresponding eigenvector transformation, and a modified divide and conquer routine that can compute the entire eigenspace or a part of it. Haidar et al. [18] developed a two-stage approach for multicore and single GPU. The main thrust of the work presented here is the extension of this two-stage approach to multi-GPUs.

3. MAIN CONTRIBUTIONS

We developed the following new algorithms, software, and techniques for heterogeneous multi-GPU computing:

- **Efficient and scalable multi-GPU BLAS**, including the HER2K and HEMM Level 3 BLAS kernels;
- **Multi-GPU two-stage tridiagonalization**, utilizing techniques to map computational tasks to the strengths of heterogeneous hardware components, and to overlap computation on GPUs with computation on CPUs;
- **Hierarchical multi-GPU communication model** to optimize communication for multi-GPUs, which can be applied in general, beyond the scope of the algorithms developed;
- **Examining trade-offs between communication and extra computation** to reduce overall execution time, which we believe will become increasingly important for current and up-coming hardware.

Further, the algorithms presented are included in MAGMA [1], an open source library of next generation LAPACK-compliant linear algebra routines for hybrid GPU-CPU architectures.

4. BACKGROUND

To solve a Hermitian (symmetric) eigenproblem of the form $Ax = \lambda x$, finding its eigenvalues Λ and eigenvectors Z such that $A = Z\Lambda Z^*$, where * denotes conjugate-transpose, the standard algorithm follows three steps [2, 15, 25]. First, reduce the matrix to tridiagonal form using an orthogonal transformation Q such that $A = QTQ^*$, where T is a tridiagonal matrix (called the "reduction phase"). Note that when a two-sided orthogonal transformation is applied to generate T, the eigenvalues of the tridiagonal matrix are the same as those of the original matrix. Second, compute eigenpairs (Λ, E) of the tridiagonal matrix (called the "solution phase"). Third, back transform eigenvectors of the tridiagonal matrix to eigenvectors of the original matrix, $Z = QE$ (called the "back transformation phase"). Due to the computational complexity and data access patterns, it is well known that the reduction phase is considerably more time consuming than the other two phases combined. Thus, in this paper, we will focus on improving the reduction to tridiagonal step, and present a multi-GPU implementation of it.

4.1 Tridiagonal reduction

Several approaches exist to compute the tridiagonalization of a dense matrix.

4.1.1 Standard approach

Standard software for reducing a symmetric dense matrix to tridiagonal form is available in LAPACK [4] and in MAGMA [1] through the ZHETRD (DSYTRD) routine. This approach suffers from a lack of efficiency, and so it is important to first identify the bottlenecks of this standard one-stage approach. It is characterized by iterating two computational phases: the panel factorization and the update of the trailing submatrix. The panel factorization computes the transformations (reflectors) to introduce zeros below the subdiagonal within a block column using memory-bound Level 2 BLAS operations. The trailing submatrix update applies the accumulated block reflector using compute-bound Level 3 BLAS operations. The parallelism in this approach resides primarily within the trailing submatrix update phase. Synchronization points are required between each panel factorization and trailing submatrix update, preventing overlap of the computational phases and memory transfers between the CPU and GPU. The panel factorization step is actually the critical phase because computing each reflector column of the panel requires a substantial symmetric matrix-vector product involving the trailing submatrix. Although this approach scales on multi-GPUs, the performance is memory-bound [12].

4.1.2 Two-stage approach

Because of the expense of the reduction step, renewed research has focused on improving this step, resulting in a novel technique based on a two-stage reduction [17]. We developed a two-stage algorithm for one GPU [18] which achieved good performance compared to the standard approach [12, 26, 28], motivating us to focus in this paper on developing and optimizing a multi-GPU two-stage approach.

The two-stage reduction is designed to increase the utilization of compute-intensive operations. Many algorithms have been investigated using this two-stage approach [8, 9]. The idea is to split the original one-stage approach into a compute-intensive phase (first stage) and a memory-bound phase (second or "bulge chasing" stage). The first stage reduces the original symmetric dense matrix to a symmetric band form, while the second stage reduces from band to tridiagonal form.

First stage.

The first stage applies a sequence of block Householder transformations to reduce a symmetric dense matrix to a symmetric band matrix. This stage uses compute-intensive matrix-multiply kernels, eliminating the memory-bound matrix-vector product in the one-stage panel factorization, and has been shown to have a good data access pattern and large portion of Level 3 BLAS operations [8, 13, 14, 18]. It also enables the efficient use of GPUs by minimizing communication and allowing overlap of computation and communication. Given a dense $n \times n$ symmetric matrix A, the matrix is divided into $nt = n/b$ block-columns of size b. The algorithm proceeds panel by panel, performing a QR decomposition for each panel to generate the Householder reflectors V (i.e., the orthogonal transformations) required to zero out elements below the bandwidth b. Then the generated block Householder reflectors are applied from the left and the right to the trailing symmetric matrix, according to

$$A = A - WV^* - VW^*, \quad (1)$$

where V and T define the block of Householder reflectors and W is computed as

$$\begin{aligned} W &= X - \tfrac{1}{2}VT^*V^*X, \text{ where} \quad (2)\\ X &= AVT. \end{aligned}$$

Second stage.

The second stage involves memory-bound operations and requires the band matrix to be accessed from multiple disjoint locations. In other words, there is an accumulation of substantial latency overhead each time different portions of the matrix are loaded into cache memory, which is not compensated for by the low execution rate of the actual computations (the so-called surface-to-volume effect). To overcome these critical limitations, we use the novel bulge chasing algorithm (reduction from band to tridiagonal) developed in [17]. This algorithm is designed to extensively use cache friendly kernels combined with fine grained, memory aware tasks in an out-of-order scheduling technique which considerably enhances data locality. This reduction has been designed for multicore architectures, and results have shown its efficiency. This step has been well optimized such that it takes between 5% to 10% of the global time of the reduction from dense to tridiagonal. We refer the reader to [17, 18] for a detailed description of the bulge chasing algorithm.

We decide to develop a hybrid CPU-GPU implementation of only the first stage of this algorithm, and leave the second stage executed entirely on the CPU. The main motivation is that the first stage is the most expensive computational phase of the reduction. Results show that 90% of the time is spent in the first stage reduction. Another motivation for this direction is that accelerators perform poorly when dealing with memory-bound fine-grained computational tasks (such as bulge chasing), limiting the potential benefit of a GPU implementation of the second stage.

5. MULTI-GPU ALGORITHM

Our hybrid CPU-GPU algorithm is similar to the two-stage tridiagonal reduction developed for multicore CPUs [17]. However, a hybrid CPU-GPU implementation needs to take advantage of the GPUs by offloading expensive operations to the GPUs, while overlapping the CPU and the GPU computation and minimizing communication. In other words, our goal is to keep the GPUs busy, making the CPUs wait for the GPUs, and not the reverse. The relatively slow CPU computation and the communications with the GPUs are hidden by overlapping them with the GPU computation. To characterize our work, we start by describing the single GPU implementation of the reduction to banded form.

5.1 Hybrid CPU–single GPU band reduction

The hybrid CPU-GPU algorithm is illustrated in Figure 1. We first run the QR decomposition (GEQRT kernel) of a panel on the CPUs. Once the panel factorization of step i is finished, then we compute W on the GPU, as defined by equation (2). This kernel is called xPNCXW. Its computation involves a matrix-matrix multiplication (GEMM) to compute VT, then a Hermitian matrix-matrix multiplication to compute $X = AVT$ (HEMM), which is the dominant cost of computing W, consisting of 95% of the time spent in computing W, and finally another inexpensive GEMM. Once W is computed, the trailing matrix update (applying transformations on the left and right) defined by equation (1) can be performed using a rank-$2k$ update (HER2K). Note that for real symmetric matrices, the operations corresponding to HEMM and HER2K are SYMM and SYR2K.

However, to allow overlap of CPU and GPU computation, the trailing submatrix update is split into two pieces. First, the next panel for step $i + 1$ (green panel of Figure 1) is updated using two GEMMs on the GPU. The corresponding kernel is called xPNRFB. Next, the remainder of the trailing submatrix (orange triangle of Figure 1) is updated using a HER2K. While the HER2K is executing, the CPUs receive the panel for step $i+1$, perform the next panel factorization (GEQRT), and send the resulting V_{i+1} back to the GPU. In this way, the factorization of panels $i = 2, \ldots, nt$ and the associated communication are hidden by overlapping with GPU computation, as demonstrated in Figure 2.

This is similar to the look-ahead technique typically used in the one-sided dense matrix factorizations. Figure 2 shows a snapshot of the execution trace of the reduction to band form, where we can easily identify the overlap between CPU and GPU computation. Note that the high-performance GPU is continuously busy, either computing W or updating the trailing matrix, while the lower performance CPUs wait for the GPU as necessary. We compare hybrid GPU-CPU implementations of the one-stage and two-stage algorithms in Figure 3, where the two-stage algorithm is about six times faster than the standard one-stage approach. Also, both hybrid implementations are significantly faster than the CPU-only implementation available in the Intel MKL.

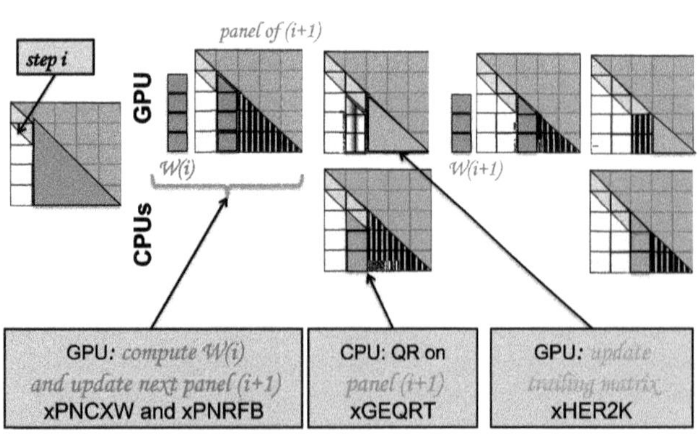

Figure 1: Description of the reduction to banded form, stage 1.

5.2 Hybrid multi CPU-GPU band reduction

In this section, we describe the development of our multi-GPU algorithm, including the constraints to consider, how to deal with communication, and how to achieve good scalability over both CPUs and GPUs. Our target algorithm, the first stage reduction to band form, involves two main multi-GPU kernels: the computation of W and the trailing submatrix update.

Recall that the computation of W involves two small GEMMs (5% of the time to compute W), and one expensive HEMM (95% of the time). Rather than computing the two small GEMMs on one GPU and broadcasting the results to the other GPUs, it is faster to duplicate these two small computations on all the GPUs. A scalable implementation of the multi-GPU HEMM, in which a data distribution is chosen in order to minimize communications, is described below.

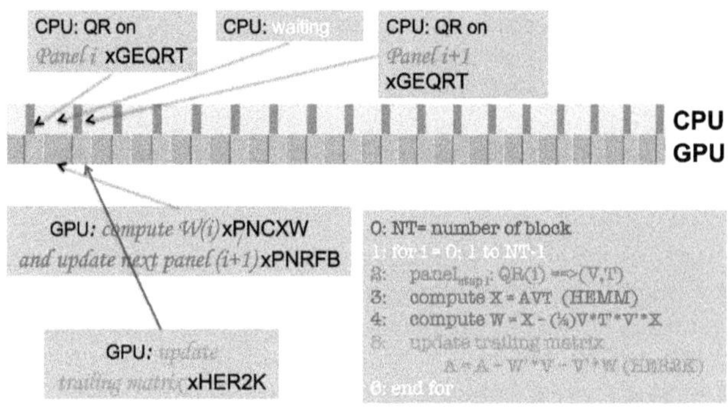

Figure 2: Execution trace of reduction to banded form.

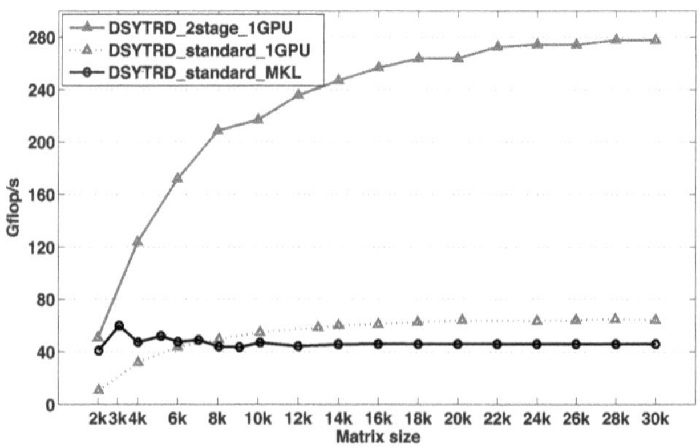

Figure 3: Comparison between the standard and the two-stage approaches for the reduction to tridiagonal. The reference Gflops formula is $4n^3/3$ for all.

As previously described for the single GPU implementation, the trailing submatrix update is split into two parts. First we update the next panel, which is a block column belonging to a single GPU, so it can be updated with two GEMMs on a single GPU. Then a multi-GPU HER2K updates the rest of the trailing matrix, which is distributed across multiple GPUs.

5.2.1 Data distribution

In the LAPACK storage for Hermitian and symmetric matrices, only one of the lower or upper triangles of A has valid entries; the other triangle is not referenced. We shall assume that the lower triangle of A is referenced. Due to the low communication bandwidth between GPUs relative to their high floating point performance, a 1-D block-column cyclic distribution of the matrix was chosen, as shown in Figure 4. However, the block size for distribution does not need to be the same as the bandwidth. It may be more efficient to have a larger block size for distribution than the bandwidth. This only slightly complicates the code, as the first and last block can be partial blocks.

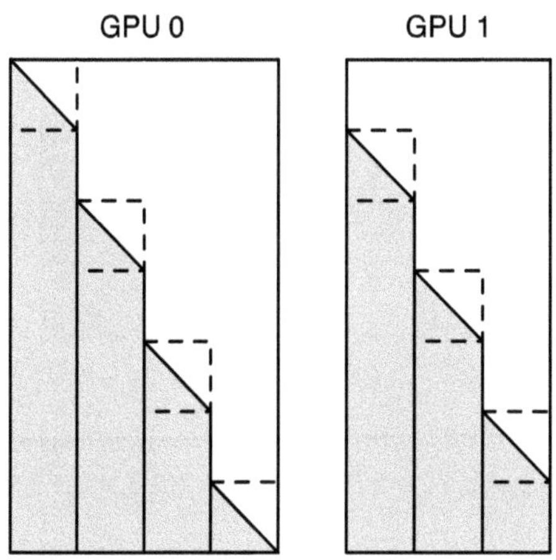

Figure 4: Block-cyclic data distribution. Shaded areas contain valid data. Dashed lines indicate diagonal blocks.

5.2.2 Multi-GPU HER2K (SYR2K)

The Hermitian rank-$2k$ update implements the operation $A = A - VW^* - WV^*$, where A is an $n \times n$ Hermitian matrix, and V and W are $n \times k$ matrices. After distribution, the portion of A on each GPU no longer appears as a symmetric matrix, but instead has a stepped appearance, as in Figure 4. Because of this stepped storage, the multi-GPU HER2K cannot be assembled purely from regular HER2K calls on each GPU. Instead, each block column must be processed individually. The diagonal blocks require special attention. In the BLAS standard, elements above the diagonal are not accessed; the user is free to store unrelated data there and the BLAS library will not touch it. To achieve this, one can use a HER2K to update each diagonal block, and a GEMM to update the remainder of each block column below the diagonal block. However, these small HER2K operations have little parallelism and so are inefficient on a GPU. This can be improved to some degree by using multiple streams to execute several HER2K updates simultaneously. However, because we have copied the data to the GPU, we can consider the space above the diagonal to be a scratch workspace. Thus, we update the entire block column, including the diagonal block, writing extra data into the upper triangle of the diagonal block, which is subsequently ignored. We do extra computation for the diagonal block, but gain efficiency overall by launching fewer BLAS kernels on the GPU and using the more efficient GEMM kernels, instead of small HER2K kernels.

for $i = 1$ to nt **do**
    if this GPU owns block-column i **then**
        $A_{i:nt,i} \mathrel{-}= V_{i:nt} W_i^*$
    end if
end for
for $i = 1$ to nt **do**
    if this GPU owns block-column i **then**
        $A_{i:nt,i} \mathrel{-}= W_{i:nt} V_i^*$
    end if
end for

Algorithm 1: Multi-GPU Hermitian rank-$2k$ update.

We replicate the V and W matrices on all the GPUs. Each block column of A, denoted $A_{i:nt,i}$, is updated with two GEMMs, as shown in Algorithm 1. These can be done in multiple streams, to allow multiple simultaneous GEMMs when a single GEMM does not fill up the GPU. The code loops over all block columns and executes the required GEMMs on the GPU that owns each block column. Other than broadcasting V and W to all GPUs, there is no additional communication required during the HER2K operation, so it scales well to multiple GPUs, as demonstrated in Figure 5.

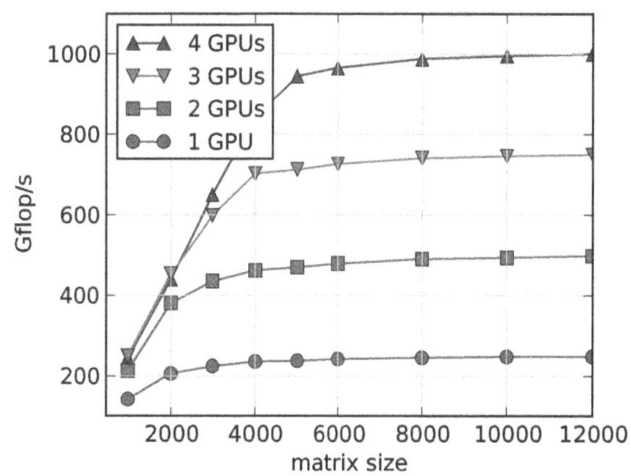

Figure 5: Multi-GPU DSYR2K scales perfectly with number of GPUs.

5.2.3 Multi-GPU HEMM (SYMM)

In this section, we will discuss the different implementations for the HEMM kernel, which is one of the two primary kernels of the reduction to band algorithm. We recall that the role of HEMM is to compute $X = AVT$, where A is an $n \times n$ Hermitian matrix and $B = VT$ is a block-column matrix of size $n \times nb$. We mention that only the lower or the upper triangle of the matrix A is referenced, the opposite

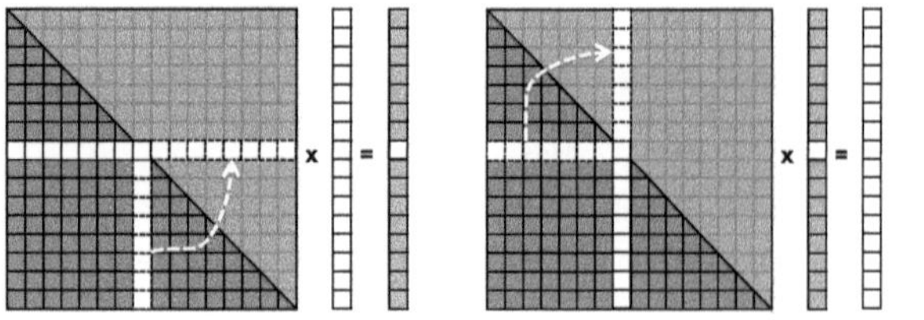

(a) Row-oriented schema (b) Column-oriented schema

Figure 6: Representation of a one GPU HEMM for both Row or Column oriented schema.

triangle being obtained by symmetry. Two loop orderings can be considered when implementing this kernel.

Row-oriented.

A row-oriented HEMM multiplies block-row $A_{i,:}$ by B to compute each block X_i, for $i = 1$ to nt, as illustrated in Figure 6a. Elements of A right of the diagonal are obtained by transposing block-column i below the diagonal (assuming lower-triangular storage). The multi-GPU implementation of this design is given in Algorithm 2 and diagrammed in Figure 7. This implementation suffers from a lack of parallelism due to the small size of its output (small square $nb \times nb$ block) which is known as an *inner product* GEMM and cannot perform efficiently on GPUs (compared to *outer product* GEMM). Because the data is distributed over the GPUs, each GPU computes a partial $X^{(g)}$. A sum-allreduce across the GPUs is then required to accumulate $X = \sum_{g=1}^{\text{ngpu}} X^{(g)}$ and distribute the final result back to all the GPUs.

$X = 0$
for $i = 1$ to nt **do**
  X_i += $A_{i,\text{myblk}} B_{\text{myblk}}$,
  if this GPU owns block-column j **then**
    X_i += $A^*_{i:nt,i} B_{i:nt}$,
  end if
end for
sum–allreduce X

Algorithm 2: Row-oriented multi-GPU HEMM. myblk denotes blocks owned by current GPU.

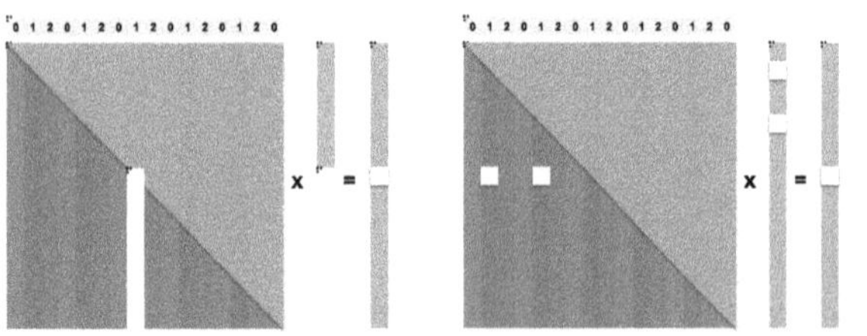

(a) X_i += $A^*_{i:nt,i} B_{i:nt}$ (b) X_i += $A_{i,\text{myblk}} B_{\text{myblk}}$

Figure 7: Block-row i of row-oriented multi-GPU HEMM writes small result with little parallelism. Each color represents different GPU.

Column-oriented.

A column-oriented HEMM multiplies block-column $A_{:,j}$ by block B_j to compute a partial sum $X^{(j)}$, for $j = 1$ to nt, as illustrated in Figure 6b. Elements of A above the diagonal are obtained by transposing block-row j left of the diagonal. The multi-GPU implementation of this design is given in Algorithm 3 and diagrammed in Figure 8. It has a large amount of parallelism because each block-column GEMM results in a large $(n - j * nb) \times nb$ block. Again, each GPU computes a partial $X^{(g)}$, which requires a sum-allreduce across the GPUs to accumulate X and distribute the final result back to all the GPUs. This HEMM algorithm is used in our multi-GPU implementation (version 1 and 2), as detailed in Section 5.2.4.

$X = 0$
for $j = 1$ to nt **do**
  X_{myblk} += $A^*_{j,\text{myblk}} B_j$,
  if this GPU owns block-column j **then**
    $X_{j:nt}$ += $A_{j:nt,j} B_j$
  end if
end for
sum–allreduce X

Algorithm 3: Column-oriented multi-GPU HEMM.

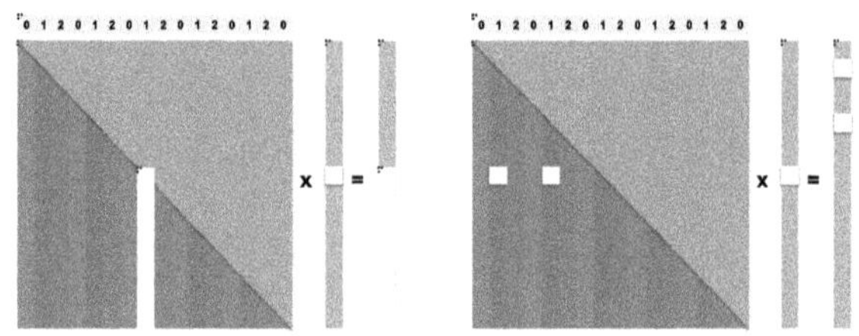

(a) $X_{j:nt}$ += $A_{j:nt,j} B_j$ (b) X_{myblk} += $A^*_{j,\text{myblk}} B_j$

Figure 8: Block-column j of column-oriented multi-GPU HEMM writes large result with significant parallelism.

5.2.4 Communication schema

Reducing communication or overlapping communication with computation is critical in order to maximize the time GPUs spend in compute-intensive kernels, especially for multi-GPU implementations. In the context of our algorithm, the assembly of $X^{(g)}$ of the HEMM described above becomes a synchronization point because the HER2K depends on the result of the HEMM, preventing overlap of communication and computation. Our goal is therefore to minimize the communication time. We investigate various implementations of the communication model that could be used for the sum-allreduce and discuss the trade-offs in each.

Model 1.

In our first implementation, all the GPUs send their $X^{(g)}$ to the CPU, which does the sum-allreduce and then broadcasts the final result X back to all the GPUs. Figure 9 shows an execution trace of the HEMM and its communication with this approach on three GPUs.

To understand the communication behavior requires understanding the underlying hardware topology. Systems with multiple GPUs often use PCIe switches or I/O hubs, with several GPUs connected to each switch. This is the case, for instance, with an NVIDIA S2070, which has four GPUs connected, in pairs, to two PCIe switches. GPUs connected to a PCIe switch share bandwidth to the host CPU. As a result, sending data from multiple GPUs requires the same total time, whether sent in parallel or sequentially.

In the context of our HEMM, we choose to send the data sequentially, so that once the CPU receives data from the first two GPUs, it can start performing the sum-allreduce while receiving the next data. However, the communication time increases linearly with the number of GPUs, creating a severe bottleneck that limits the scalability of this approach. While adding GPUs decreases the HEMM compute time, this is not sufficient to offset the increased communication time. This serialization of communication is easily observed in Figure 9, and from this understanding of the communication behavior, we expect poor performance as the number of GPUs increases. We refer to our implementation of the column-oriented HEMM using this communication model as version 1.

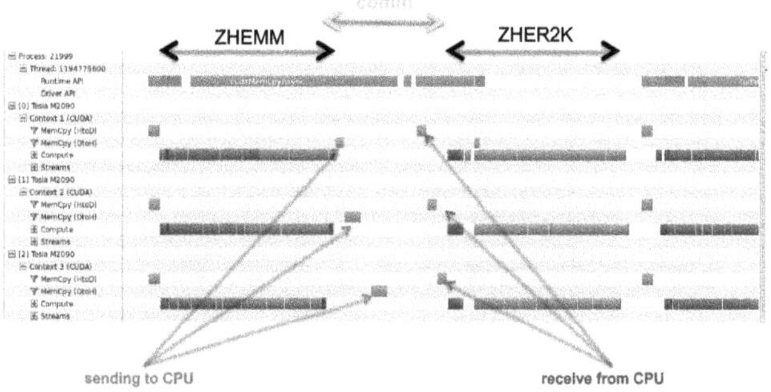

Figure 9: Trace of the execution of ZHEMM using communication model 1 when the CPU is responsible for the communication.

Model 2: **Hierarchical Communication Model.**

To address this increase in communication time, we developed a second, hierarchical, communication schema. Each PCIe switch is viewed as a node in a distributed system, with one GPU in each node assigned to be the master. Within each node, GPUs communicate locally in a "free GPU-GPU mode" with each other or with the master; between two nodes, the master GPUs communicate directly together. This hierarchical communication model is easily adaptable to a distributed environment where the communication between masters of different nodes should be done via the CPU using MPI. This communication model is depicted in Figure 10. Thus, in the context of our HEMM, the sum-allreduce is first done independently by the master GPU within each node, where all the GPUs send their $X^{(g)}$ to the master GPU, which does the addition. After receiving contributions from GPUs within each node, the master GPUs exchange data and each, redundantly, makes the final addition. Then, each master independently broadcasts the final result X to all GPUs within its node.

We refer to our implementation of the column-oriented HEMM using this communication model as version 2. Similarly to version 1, we depict in Figure 11 the execution trace of the HEMM with this communication schema. Here, GPU 0 belongs to node 0, while GPU 1 and GPU 2 belong to node 1. Hence, within each node the communication is

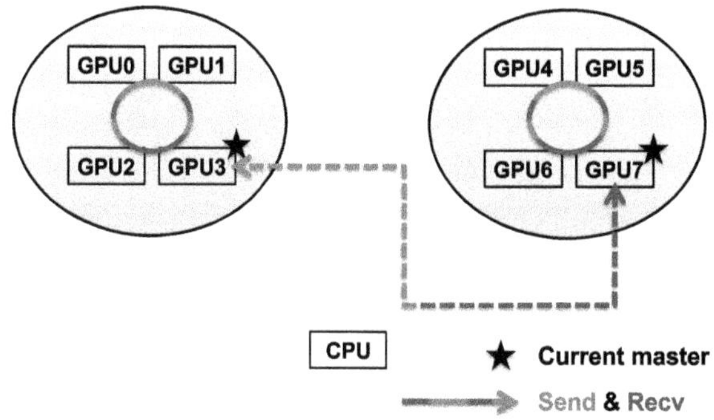

Figure 10: Mapping communication to hardware.

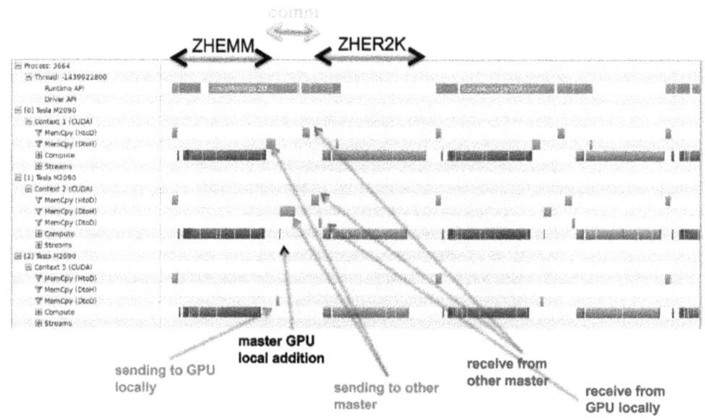

Figure 11: Trace of the execution of ZHEMM using the Hierarchical Communication Model.

done independently and the exchange of data between nodes is reduced to master communication, significantly reducing the communication time.

In Table 1, we report the time in seconds needed by the reduction from dense to band form using these two communication models when varying the number of GPUs. As expected, the second model of communication has good performance and good scalability compared to the first one. We note here that the size of the matrix is too small to achieve linear scaling up to five GPUs.

	1 GPU	2 GPUs	3 GPUs	4 GPUs	5 GPUs
version 1	60.1	43.2	36.7	34.0	33.2
version 2	60.0	29.1	21.8	21.2	20.4
version 3	67.3	30.2	21.7	19.4	16.3

Table 1: Comparison of three versions of reduction to band algorithm, showing time in seconds while varying number of GPUs for matrix of size $n = 15000$ in double complex precision.

5.2.5 Alternative implementation

An alternative third implementation that minimizes the communication can be of interest. Assume that the Hermitian matrix is available in both its lower and upper part. Thus a row-oriented large HEMM can be applied as a single GEMM operation on each GPU. Because the matrix is assumed to be full, then the result of this HEMM is large, of size $n \times n/ngpu$, and thus the resulting parallelism is enough to get good performance. The resulting X_{myblk} is the final result of X for the blocks belonging to each GPU, and thus there is no need for a sum-allreduce. Each GPU needs to broadcast only its computed blocks of X to the other GPUs. The amount of communication is divided by the number of GPUs, resulting in significantly less communication than the two approaches described above. Each GPU must broadcast $n/(nb \times \text{ngpu})$ blocks instead of n/nb blocks. We use the same hierarchical communication model described above in Figure 10 to organize this communications in an optimized fashion. The assembly inside each node is done by local GPU-GPU communication independently from other nodes, while assembly between nodes is done via the master GPU of each node. In Figure 12, we depict a representation of this implementation of HEMM. Note that the number of operations remains the same; the only requirement is that the symmetric part of the matrix needs to be available.

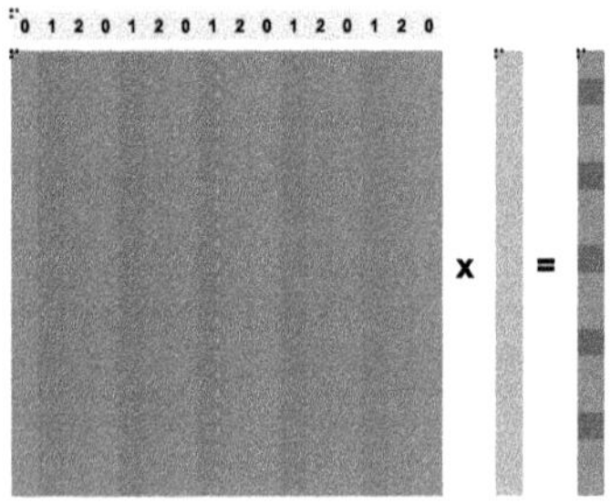

$$X_{\text{myblk}} = A^*_{:,\text{myblk}} B$$

Figure 12: A fast multi-GPU implementation of an HEMM minimizing communication and increasing parallelism.

The main difficulty here is to have the symmetric part of the matrix. To do this we have two choices. First is to symmetrize the matrix just before starting the HEMM kernel. However, this requires significant communication and we would lose any gains we achieved, so we disregard this choice. Second is to symmetrize the matrix *once*, and modify the HER2K so that it maintains the symmetry by updating both the lower and upper parts of the matrix. This incurs no extra communication but does twice the number of operations. We trade off extra computation in the HER2K for a large reduction in communication cost in the HEMM, particularly for a large number of GPUs. This is further justified because the HER2K is overlapped with the panel factorization on the CPUs; with enough GPUs, the HER2K becomes faster than the panel, so the GPUs must wait for the panel instead of the HER2K. Thus, adding extra work to the HER2K will not impact the overall execution time so long as it is faster than the panel.

In Figure 13, we depict the execution trace of this approach, showing that the communication time becomes marginal. We also report in Table 1 the time in seconds for the reduction to band form, and compare it to the previous two versions defined above. We see that for more than three GPUs, the extra work needed by this approach is hidden, and it is able to reach better performance than the two previous versions. For one GPU, it is normal that version 3 is slower, as no communication is needed while the HER2K has twice as many operations, but it is a good example to show

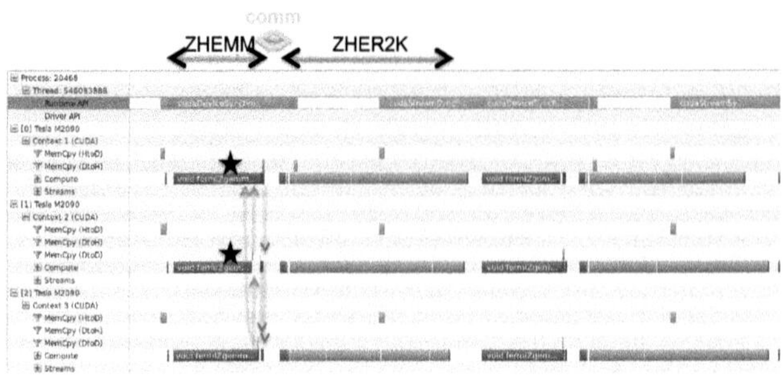

Figure 13: Trace of the execution of ZHEMM using the Hierarchical Communication Model.

that the extra cost is not prohibitive. It is 12% of the time on one GPU, and so becomes less than 6% on two GPUs and so on. Thus we consider version 3 also as interesting as version 2.

6. EXPERIMENTAL RESULTS

This section presents the performance comparisons of our hybrid multi CPU-GPU two-stage TRD against the multi-GPU standard TRD approach, and against the state-of-the-art multicore numerical linear algebra libraries.

6.1 Experimental Environment

Our experiments were performed on the largest shared-memory system we could access at the time of writing this paper. It is representative of a vast class of servers and workstations commonly used for computationally intensive workloads. We benchmark all implementations on an Intel multicore system with dual-socket, 8 core Intel Xeon E5-2670 (Sandy Bridge) processors, each running at 2.6 GHz. Each socket has a 24 MB shared L3 cache, and each core has a private 256 KB L2 and 64 KB L1. The system is equipped with 52 Gbytes of memory. The theoretical peak for this architecture in double precision is 20.8 Gflop/s per core. The system is also equipped with eight NVIDIA M2090 cards with 6 Gbytes per card running at 1.3 GHz, connected to the host via PCIe I/O hubs at 8 Gbytes/s bandwidth.

There are a number of software packages that implement the tridiagonal reduction. For comparison, we used the MKL (Math Kernel Library) [19] which is a commercial software from Intel that is a highly optimized programming library. It includes a comprehensive set of mathematical routines implemented to run well on multicore processors. In particular, MKL includes the LAPACK-equivalent routine performing the tridiagonal reduction DSYTRD. The MAGMA [1] library is used for the multi-GPU standard approach. We recall that the algorithmic complexity of the standard full tridiagonal reduction is $\frac{4}{3}N^3$ and this is used as a reference to draw the performance of all the graphs we show.

6.2 Effect of block size or bandwidth

Both stages in the two-stage reduction to tridiagonal form algorithm depend strongly on the bandwidth size. The reduction to band form can be achieved with efficient Level 3 BLAS operations for large bandwidth size, e.g., $kb > 40$, while the bulge chasing is a memory-bound algorithm, meaning that it performs better for small kb rather than for large kb. The bulge chasing stage has been implemented [17] with cache-friendly kernels and smart scheduling to allow good performance for large $kb > 40$, but it is recommended to keep kb as small as possible. Thus, the choice of bandwidth is a compromise between these two competing factors. Overall, a bandwidth of 64 was found to be a good compromise.

6.3 Performance results

We compare the performance of our hybrid multi-GPU two-stage TRD algorithm against the one-stage approach from optimized state-of-the-art numerical linear algebra libraries. In particular, Figure 14 shows the comparison with (1) the DSYTRD routine from the Intel MKL, and (2) the hybrid multi-GPU DSYTRD from MAGMA. Our implementation asymptotically achieves more than a 7× speedup on one GPU and more than a 20× speed up on six GPUs against MKL. It also achieved a significant performance compared to its multi-GPU counterpart using the standard one-stage approach. It is around 4 times faster than the multi-GPU standard approach. The fact that the first stage is a compute intensive stage, and the fact that the implementation design maps both the algorithm and the communication to the hardware, allows this algorithm to achieve good scalability. We believe that this attractive behavior makes our algorithm a good candidate for the next generation of distributed multi-GPU machines.

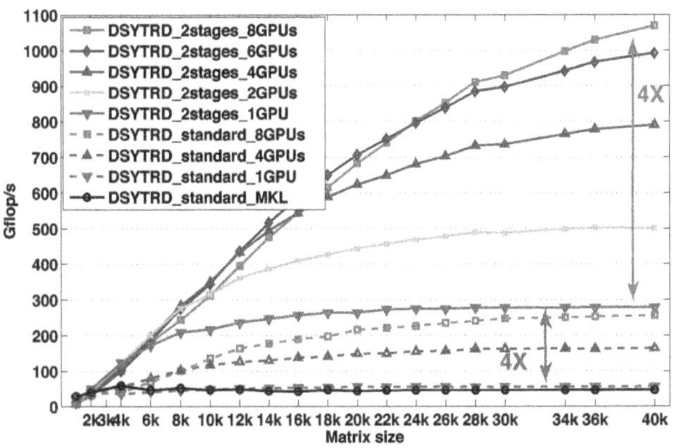

Figure 14: Performance comparison of our two-stage multi-GPU implementation to standard one-stage MKL and MAGMA implementations, in double precision.

6.4 Scalability

Figure 15 shows the performance scalability of the reduction from dense to band. The curves show performance in terms of Gflop/s. We note that this also reflects the elapsed time, e.g., a performance that is two times higher, corresponds to an elapsed time that is two times less. The multi-GPU implementation shows very good scalability. We mention here that Figure 15 shows the performance for only the reduction to band form. We show this graph here only to highlight the scalability of the multi-GPU implementation of the reduction to band. The performance shown in Figure 14 (the full reduction to tridiagonal form) drops slightly compared to Figure 15, because it consists of the time to reduce the matrix to band added to the time to reduce the band to tridiagonal, which, as pointed out earlier, is a multicore only implementation, and so, although it is an efficient CPU code, its elapsed time does not change when the number of GPUs increases. However, the overall performance of our implementation scales very well. We also mention that when integrated into the full eigensystem solver, the second stage will be less than 5% of the time, and so its effect on performance will further decrease.

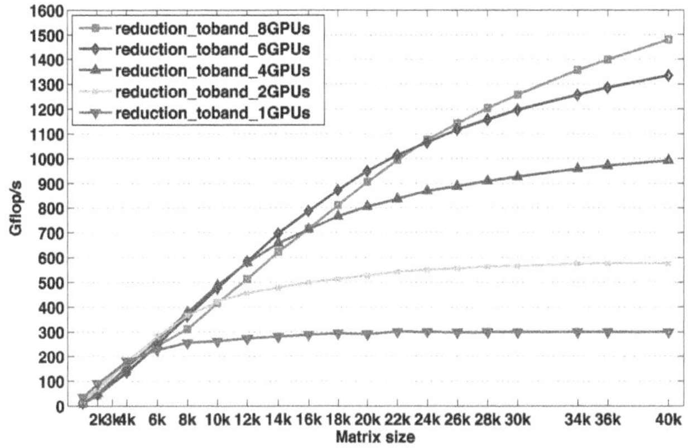

Figure 15: Scalability of our multi-GPU implementation of the reduction to band (first stage) when the number of GPUs increases from one to eight, in double precision.

7. CONCLUSIONS

We demonstrated that it is possible to transform a classical, memory-bound algorithm into a compute-bound algorithm, even on systems with an enormous gap between their computing power and interconnection bandwidth. Moreover, we developed and presented the techniques that make this possible for a highly demanded algorithm that naturally features communication and complex data dependencies. A key technique is to map the algorithm to best take advantage of heterogeneous hardware. In the context of the tridiagonal reduction, we chose a two-stage algorithm due to its richness in compute-intensive kernels, which are scheduled on the GPU, while the memory-bound bulge-chasing stage is scheduled on the CPU using cache-friendly kernels. We also developed a hierarchical communication model for multi-GPUs, based on the underlying communication topology of the host PCIe system.

We believe that these techniques will increase in relevance for upcoming architectures. Indeed, our experience over the last few years, and the results here, show that although GPUs were used to accelerate some standard memory-bound algorithms more than 10×, the improvements stagnated from one generation of GPUs to the next, following the marginal improvements in GPU bandwidth. Thus techniques such as trading-off between communication and extra computation will increase in relevance as computation continues to become exponentially cheaper than communication.

We plan to further study the implementation of multi-GPU algorithms in a distributed computing environment. We believe that the techniques presented will become more popular and will be integrated into dynamic runtime system technologies. The ultimate goal is that this integration will help to tremendously decrease development time while retaining high-performance.

Acknowledgments

The authors would like to thank the National Science Foundation, the Department of Energy, NVIDIA, and MathWorks for supporting this research effort.

8. REFERENCES

[1] MAGMA 1.3. `http://icl.cs.utk.edu/magma/`, 2012.

[2] J. O. Aasen. On the reduction of a symmetric matrix to tridiagonal form. *BIT*, 11:233–242, 1971.

[3] E. Agullo, J. Demmel, J. Dongarra, B. Hadri, J. Kurzak, J. Langou, H. Ltaief, P. Luszczek, and S. Tomov. Numerical linear algebra on emerging architectures: The PLASMA and MAGMA projects. *J. Phys.: Conf. Ser.*, 180(1), 2009.

[4] E. Anderson, Z. Bai, C. Bischof, S. Blackford, J. Demmel, J. Dongarra, J. D. Croz, A. Greenbaum, S. Hammarling, A. McKenney, and D. Sorensen. *LAPACK Users' Guide*. Society for Industrial and Applied Mathematics, Philadelphia, PA, 1999.

[5] T. Auckenthaler, V. Blum, H. J. Bungartz, T. Huckle, R. Johanni, L. Krämer, B. Lang, H. Lederer, and P. R. Willems. Parallel solution of partial symmetric eigenvalue problems from electronic structure calculations. *Parallel Comput.*, 37(12):783–794, 2011.

[6] G. Ballard, J. Demmel, and I. Dumitriu. Communication-optimal parallel and sequential eigenvalue and singular value algorithms. Technical Report EECS-2011-14, EECS University of California, Berkeley, CA, USA, February 2011. LAPACK Working Note 237.

[7] P. Bientinesi, F. D. Igual, D. Kressner, and E. S. Quintana-Ortí. Reduction to condensed forms for symmetric eigenvalue problems on multi-core architectures. PPAM'09, pages 387–395, Berlin, Heidelberg, 2010. Springer-Verlag.

[8] C. H. Bischof, B. Lang, and X. Sun. Algorithm 807: The SBR Toolbox—software for successive band reduction. *ACM Transactions on Mathematical Software*, 26(4):602–616, 2000.

[9] C. H. Bischof and C. V. Loan. The WY representation for products of Householder matrices. *SIAM J. Sci. Statist. Comput.*, 8:s2–s13, 1987.

[10] L. S. Blackford, J. Choi, A. Cleary, E. D'Azevedo, J. Demmel, I. Dhillon, J. Dongarra, S. Hammarling, G. Henry, A. Petitet, K. Stanley, D. Walker, and R. C. Whaley. *ScaLAPACK Users' Guide*. Society for Industrial and Applied Mathematics, PA, 1997.

[11] J. Demmel, J. Dongarra, A. Ruhe, and H. van der Vorst. *Templates for the solution of algebraic eigenvalue problems: a practical guide*. Society for Industrial and Applied Mathematics, PA, 2000.

[12] T. Dong, J. Dongarra, T. Schulthess, R. Solca, S. Tomov, and I. Yamazaki. Matrix-vector multiplication and tridiagonalization of a dense symmetric matrix on multiple GPUs and its application to symmetric eigenvalue problems. *Parallel Comput.*, July 2012. (submitted).

[13] J. J. Dongarra, D. C. Sorensen, and S. J. Hammarling. Block reduction of matrices to condensed forms for eigenvalue computations. *Journal of Computational and Applied Mathematics*, 27(1-2):215 – 227, 1989.

[14] W. Gansterer, D. Kvasnicka, and C. Ueberhuber. Multi-sweep algorithms for the symmetric eigenproblem. In *Vector and Parallel Processing - VECPAR'98*, volume 1573 of *Lecture Notes in Computer Science*, pages 20–28. Springer, 1999.

[15] G. H. Golub and C. F. V. Loan. *Matrix Computations*. The Johns Hopkins University Press, Baltimore, MD, USA, second edition, 1989.

[16] R. G. Grimes and H. D. Simon. Solution of large, dense symmetric generalized eigenvalue problems using secondary storage. *ACM Transactions on Mathematical Software*, 14:241–256, September 1988.

[17] A. Haidar, H. Ltaief, and J. Dongarra. Parallel reduction to condensed forms for symmetric eigenvalue problems using aggregated fine-grained and memory-aware kernels. In *Proceedings of SC '11*, pages 8:1–8:11, New York, NY, USA, 2011. ACM.

[18] A. Haidar, S. Tomov, J. Dongarra, R. Solca, and T. Schulthess. A novel hybrid CPU-GPU generalized eigensolver for electronic structure calculations based on fine grained memory aware tasks. *International Journal of High Performance Computing Applications*, September 2012. (accepted).

[19] Intel. Math Kernel Library. Available at `http://software.intel.com/en-us/articles/intel-mkl/`.

[20] B. Kågström, D. Kressner, E. Quintana-Orti, and G. Quintana-Orti. Blocked Algorithms for the Reduction to Hessenberg-Triangular Form Revisited. *BIT Numerical Mathematics*, 48:563–584, 2008.

[21] L. Karlsson and B. Kågström. Parallel two-stage reduction to Hessenberg form using dynamic scheduling on shared-memory architectures. *Parallel Computing*, 2011. DOI:10.1016/j.parco.2011.05.001.

[22] B. Lang. Efficient eigenvalue and singular value computations on shared memory machines. *Parallel Computing*, 25(7):845–860, 1999.

[23] H. Ltaief, P. Luszczek, and J. Dongarra. High Performance Bidiagonal Reduction using Tile Algorithms on Homogeneous Multicore Architectures. *ACM TOMS*, 2011. Accepted.

[24] P. Luszczek, H. Ltaief, and J. Dongarra. Two-stage tridiagonal reduction for dense symmetric matrices using tile algorithms on multicore architectures. In *IPDPS 2011: IEEE International Parallel and Distributed Processing Symposium*, Anchorage, Alaska, USA, May 16-20 2011.

[25] B. N. Parlett. *The Symmetric Eigenvalue Problem*. Prentice-Hall, Englewood Cliffs, NJ, USA, 1980.

[26] S. Tomov, R. Nath, and J. Dongarra. Accelerating the reduction to upper Hessenberg, tridiagonal, and bidiagonal forms through hybrid GPU-based computing. *Parallel Comput.*, 36(12):645–654, 2010.

[27] S. Tomov, R. Nath, H. Ltaief, and J. Dongarra. Dense linear algebra solvers for multicore with GPU accelerators. In *Proc. of the IEEE IPDPS'10*, pages 1–8, Atlanta, GA, April 19-23 2010. IEEE Computer Society. DOI: 10.1109/IPDPSW.2010.5470941.

[28] C. Vomel, S. Tomov, and J. Dongarra. Divide and conquer on hybrid GPU-accelerated multicore systems. *SIAM Journal on Scientific Computing*, 34(2):C70–C82, 2012.

High Quality Real-Time Image-to-Mesh Conversion for Finite Element Simulations

Panagiotis Foteinos
Department of Computer Science
College of William and Mary
Old Dominion University
pfot@cs.wm.edu

Nikos Chrisochoides
Department of Computer Science
Old Dominion University
nikos@cs.odu.edu

ABSTRACT

In this paper, we present a parallel Image-to-Mesh Conversion (I2M) algorithm with quality and fidelity guarantees achieved by dynamic point insertions and removals. Starting directly from an image, it is able to recover the isosurface and mesh the volume with tetrahedra of good shape. Our tightly-coupled shared-memory parallel speculative execution paradigm employs carefully designed contention managers, load balancing, synchronization and optimizations schemes which boost the parallel efficiency with little overhead: our single-threaded performance is faster than CGAL, the state of the art sequential mesh generation software we are aware of. The effectiveness of our method is shown on Blacklight, the Pittsburgh Supercomputing Center's cache-coherent NUMA machine, via a series of case studies justifying our choices. We observe a more than 82% strong scaling efficiency for up to 64 cores, and a more than 95% weak scaling efficiency for up to 144 cores, reaching a rate of 14.7 Million Elements per second. To the best of our knowledge, this is the fastest and most scalable 3D Delaunay refinement algorithm.

Categories and Subject Descriptors J.6 [Computer Applications]: Computer-Aided Engineering

Keywords Delaunay refinement; parallel; Image to-Mesh Conversion; quality; fidelity

1 Introduction

Image-to-mesh (I2M) conversion enables patient-specific Finite Element modeling in image guided diagnosis and therapy. The ability to tessellate a medical image of multiple tissues into tetrahedra enables Finite Element (FE) Analysis on patient-specific models [6, 38]. This has significant implications in many areas, such as imaged-guided therapy, development of advanced patient-specific blood flow mathematical models for the prevention and treatment of stroke, patient-specific interactive surgery simulation for training young clinicians, and study of bio-mechanical properties of collagen nano-straws of patients with chest wall deformities, to name just a few.

The sequential volume mesh generation methods can be divided into two categories: *PLC-based* and *Isosurface-based*. The PLC-based methods assume that the *surface* $\partial\mathcal{O}$ of the volume $\mathcal{O}$ (about to be meshed) is given as a *Piecewise Linear Complex* (PLC) which contains linear segments and polygonal facets embedded in 3 dimensions [19, 21, 41, 51]. The limitation of this method is that the success of meshing depends on the quality of the given PLC: if the PLC forms very small angles, then termination might be compromised [51, 53].

The Isosurface-based methods assume that $\mathcal{O}$ is known through a function $f : \mathbb{R}^3 \to \mathbb{R}$, such that points in different regions of interest evaluate f differently. This assumption covers a wide range of inputs used in modeling and simulation, such as parametric surfaces/volumes [45], level-sets and segmented multi-labeled images [15, 36, 46]. Function f can also represent PLCs [36] (albeit without topological guarantees), a fact that makes the Isosurface-based method a general approach. Isosurface-based methods ought to recover and mesh both the *isosurface* $\partial\mathcal{O}$ and the volume. Also, since the isosurface is not already meshed into a PLC but it is recovered and meshed during refinement, this method does not suffer from any angle constraints.

In this paper, we present a parallel high quality Delaunay Image-to-Mesh Conversion (PI2M) Isosurface-based algorithm which, starting from a multi-labeled segmented image, recovers the isosurface(s) $\partial\mathcal{O}$ of the object(s) $\mathcal{O}$ and meshes the volume concurrently. Our method is able to produce millions of high-quality elements within seconds respecting at the same time the exterior and interior boundaries of tissues. As far as we know, PI2M is the first parallel Isosurface-based method.

In the parallel mesh generation literature, only PLC-based methods have been considered. That is, either $\mathcal{O}$ is given as an initial mesh [17, 23, 32, 56] or $\partial\mathcal{O}$ is already represented as a polyhedral domain [29, 33, 37, 42]. We, on the contrary, mesh both the volume and the isosurface directly from an image and not from a polyhedral domain. This flexibility offers great control over the trade-off between quality and fidelity: parts of the isosurface of high curvature can be meshed with more elements of better quality. Moreover, our technique avoids the undesired "stair-case" effect [15, 46] that occurs to algorithms that treat the surface voxels as the PLC of the domain [19] (since those input planar facets meet always at 0 or 90 degrees) or to algorithms that heuristically recover the isosurface [40] without topological guarantees.

PI2M recovers the tissues' boundaries and generates quality meshes through a sequence of dynamic insertion and deletion of points which is computed on the fly and in parallel during the course of refinement. Note that none of the parallel Delaunay refinement algorithms we know of support point removals. Point removal, however, offers new and rich

ICS'13, June 10–14, 2013, Eugene, Oregon, USA.

refinement schemes which are shown in the sequential meshing literature [26, 34] to be very effective in practice.

In our previous work [27], we implemented a parallel *Triangulator* able to support fully dynamic insertions and removals. Our parallel Triangulator, however, has one major limitation: as is the case with all Triangulators [8, 11, 12, 27], it tessellates only the convex hull of a set of points, and it is not concerned with any quality or fidelity constraints imposed by the input geometry and the user. Also, in parallel triangulation literature [8, 11, 12], the pointset (whose convex hull is to be constructed) is static and given before the algorithm starts. In this paper, we extend our previous work [27], such that the "discovery" of the (dynamically changing) set of points to be inserted or removed (that will eventually force the final mesh to satisfy the quality and fidelity constraints) is performed in parallel as well: a very dynamic process that increases parallel complexity even more. This is neither incremental nor a trivial extension.

In this paper, we design and implement PI2M, a parallel Isosurface-based Delaunay mesh refinement scheme based on our earlier sequential prototype [26, 28]. Our implementation employs low level locking mechanisms, carefully designed contention managers, and well-suited load balancing schemes that not only boost the parallel performance, but they exhibit very little overhead: our single threaded performance is more than 10 times faster than our previous sequential code and it is consistently 35% faster than CGAL [2], the state of the art Isosurface-based meshing tool.

Parallel Delaunay refinement is a highly irregular and data-intensive application and as such, it is very dynamic in terms of resource management. Implementing an efficient parallel Delaunay refinement would help the community gain insight into a whole family of problems characterized by unpredictable communication patterns [7]. We test and show the effectiveness of PI2M on the challenging cc-NUMA architecture; specifically, we used the Pittsburgh Supercomputing Center's Blacklight, employing BoostC++ threads. We observe a more than 82% strong scaling efficiency for up to 64 cores, and also a more than 95% weak scaling efficiency for up to 144 cores, reaching a rate of 14.7 Million Elements per second. We are not aware of any 3D parallel Delaunay refinement method achieving such a performance, on either distributed or shared-memory architectures. For a higher core count, however, our method exhibits considerable performance degradation. We show that this deterioration is not because of load imbalance or high thread contention, but because of the intensive and hop-wise slower communication traffic involved in increased problem sizes. This problem could be potentially be alleviated by using hybrid approaches to explore network hierarchies [22]. However, this is outside the scope of the paper. Our goal is to develop the most efficient and scalable method on a moderate number of cores. Our long term goal is to increase scalability by exploiting concurrency at different levels [22].

In summary, the method we present (PI2M): **(1)** exhibits the best single-threaded performance, to the best of our knowledge, **(2)** supports parallel Delaunay insertions and removals; past methods including ours dealt only with point insertions, a much easier task, **(3)** conforms to user-specified quality, and most importantly, to the newly added fidelity constraints, **(4)** recovers and meshes the isosurface with topological and geometric guarantees from the beginning of mesh refinement, and thus exploits parallelism earlier (see Figure 4), and **(5)** fills the volume of the domain $\mathcal{O}$ with millions of high-quality tetrahedra within seconds.

Section 2 presents the related work. Section 3 briefly describes the Sequential Delaunay Refinement for Smooth Surfaces and Section 4 outlines the basic building blocks of our parallel implementation. Section 5 presents the Contention Managers. Section 6 presents the strong and weak scaling results together with load balancing improvements. Section 7 is dedicated to single-threaded evaluation. Section 8 summarizes our findings and concludes the paper.

2 Related Work

There is extensive previous work on parallel mesh generation, including various techniques, such as: Delaunay, Octree, or Advancing Front meshing. Note that parallel Delaunay mesh generation/refinement should not be confused with parallel Delaunay triangulation [8, 11, 12, 27]. Delaunay triangulation tessellates the convex hull of a given, static set of points. Mesh generation focuses on element quality and the conformity to the tissues' boundary, which necessitates the parallel insertion or removal of points which are gradually and concurrently discovered through refinement.

One of the main differences between our method and the other parallel mesh generation algorithms in the literature is that they either have the surface of the domain given as a polyhedron, or the extraction of the polyhedron is done sequentially, or they start by an initial background octree. As explained in Section 1, our method constructs the polyhedral representation of the object's surface in parallel, together with the volume meshing, thus taking advantage of another degree of parallelism.

Given an initial mesh, de Cougny and Shephard [23] dynamically repartition the domain such that every processor has equal work. They also describe "vertex snapping", a method that can be used for the representation of curved boundaries, but they give no guarantees about the achieved fidelity (both geometrically and topologically). In [42], the authors implement a tightly-coupled method like ours. We, however, take extra care to greatly reduce the number of rollbacks (see Section 5), and thus achieve excellent speedups for a higher core count. In [18] and [37], a partially-coupled and a decoupled method for distributed systems is developed based on medial axis decomposition. Medial axis decomposition in 3D inputs, however, is a very challenging and still unsolved task. In contrast, our method does not rely on any domain decomposition, and as such, it is flexible enough to be extended to arbitrary dimensions. Kadow [33] starts from a polygonal surface (PSLG) and offers tightly coupled refinement schemes in 2D, respectively. In our case, the polyhedral representation of the object's surface is done in parallel, which adds extra functionality. In [20], the authors present a method which allows the safe insertion of points independently without synchronization. The extension, however, of their method for point removal support is not straightforward. Galtier and George [29] compute a smooth separator and distribute the subdomains to distinct processors. However, the separators they create might not be Delaunay-admissible and thus they need to restart the process from the beginning. Weatherill *et al.* [49] subdivide the domain into decoupled blocks. Each block then is meshed with considerably less communication and synchronization. Tu *et al.* [56] describe a parallel octree method that interacts with the solver in parallel and efficiently. The work of Zhou *et*

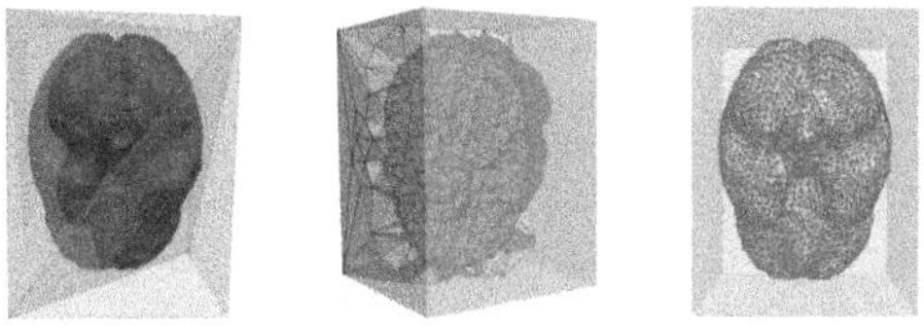

Figure 1: (a) The virual box is meshed into 6 tetrahedra. It encloses the volumetric object. (b) During refinement, the final mesh is gradually being carved according to the Rules. (c) At the end, the set of the tetrahedra whose circumcenter lies inside $\mathcal{O}$ is the geometrically and topologically correct mesh $\mathcal{M}$.

al. [58], and the *Forest-of-octrees* method of Burstedde *et al.* [17] offer techniques for fair and efficient data migration and partitioning in parallel. Load balancing and data migration is also used by Okusanya and Peraire [43] to distribute bad elements across processors. Ito *et al.* [32] start from an initial mesh and Löhner [39] from a PLC for subsequent parallel mesh generation in advancing front fashion. Oliker and Biswas [44] employ three different architectures to test the applicability of 2D adaptive mesh refinement. They conclude that unstructured mesh refinement is not suitable for cc-NUMA architectures: irregular communication patterns and lack of data locality deteriorate performance sometimes even on just 4 cores. In this paper, we show that this becomes a problem in a much higher core count; i.e., with this work, we push the envelop even further. Clearly, this approach has its own limitations, but a highly scalable and efficient NUMA implementation combined with the decoupled and partially coupled approaches we developed in the past can allow us to explore concurrency levels in the order of at least 10^8 to 10^{10} [22].

3 Delaunay Refinement for Smooth Surfaces

Sequential Delaunay Refinement for smooth surfaces is presented in detail in the literature [45, 46] and in our previous work [26, 28]. In this Section, we briefly outline the main concepts.

As is usually the case in the literature [3, 36, 46], we assume that the surface of the object $\partial\mathcal{O}$ to be meshed is a closed smooth 2-manifold. To prove that the boundary $\partial\mathcal{M}$ of the final mesh $\mathcal{M}$ is geometrically and topologically equivalent with $\partial\mathcal{O}$, we make use of the *sample theory* [3]. Omitting the details, it can be proved [3, 4] that the Delaunay triangulation of a dense pointset lying precisely on the isosurface $\partial\mathcal{O}$ contains (as a subset) the correct mesh $\mathcal{M}$. That mesh consists of the tetrahedra t whose circumcenter $c(t)$ lies inside $\mathcal{O}$. Formally, the sample theorem could be stated as follows [4, 14, 25]:

THEOREM 1. *Let V be samples of $\partial\mathcal{O}$. If for any point $p \in \partial\mathcal{O}$, there is a sample $v \in V$ such that $|v - p| \leq \delta$, then the boundary triangles of $\mathcal{D}_{|\mathcal{O}}(V)$ is a provably good topological approximation of $\partial\mathcal{O}$. Also, the 2-sided Hausdorff distance between the mesh and $\partial\mathcal{O}$ is $O(\delta^2)$.*

Typical values for δ are usually fractions of the *local feature size* of $\partial\mathcal{O}$. See [4, 14, 25, 45] for well defined δ parameters. In our application, δ values equal to multiples of the voxel size is sufficient.

Therefore, one of the goals of the refinement is to sample the isosurface densely enough. To achieve that, our algorithm first constructs a *virtual box* which encloses $\mathcal{O}$. The box is then triangulated into 6 tetrahedra, as shown in Figure 1. This is the only sequential part of our method. Next, it dynamically computes new points to be inserted into or removed from the mesh maintaining the Delaunay property. This process continues, until certain fidelity and quality criteria are met. Specifically, the vertices removed or inserted are divided into 3 groups: *isosurface* vertices, circumcenters, and *surface-centers*.

The isosurface vertices will eventually form the sampling of the surface so that Theorem 1 holds together with its theoretical guarantees about the fidelity of the mesh boundary. Let $c(t)$ be the circumcenter of a tetrahedron t. In order to guarantee termination, our algorithm inserts the isosurface vertex which is the closest to $c(t)$. In the sequel, we shall refer to the *Closest IsoSurface* vertex of a point p as $\mathrm{cis}(p) \in \partial\mathcal{O}$. The isosurface vertices (like the circumcenters) are computed during the refinement dynamically with the help of a parallel Euclidean Distance Transformation (EDT) presented and implemented in [54]. Specifically, the EDT returns the *surface voxel* p which is closest to p. A surface-voxel is a voxel that lies inside the foreground and has at least one neighbor of different label. Then, we traverse the ray $\overrightarrow{pp'}$ on small intervals and we compute $\mathrm{cis}(p) \in \partial\mathcal{O}$ by interpolating the positions of different labels [40]. The density of the inserted isosurface vertices is defined by the user by a parameter $\delta > 0$. A low value for δ implies a denser sampling of the surface, and therefore, according to Theorem 1, a better approximation of $\partial\mathcal{O}$.

The circumcenter $c(t)$ of a tetrahedron t is inserted when t has low quality (in terms of its radius-edge ratio [51]) or because its circumradius $r(t)$ is larger than a user-defined size function $\mathrm{sf}(\cdot)$. Circumcenters might also be chosen to be removed, when they lie close to an isosurface vertex, because in this case termination is compromised.

Consider a facet f of a tetrahedron. The *Voronoi* edge $V(f)$ of f is the segment connecting the circumcenters of the two tetrahedra that contain f. The intersection $V(f) \cap \partial\mathcal{O}$ is called a *surface-center* and is denoted by $c_{\mathrm{surf}}(f)$. During refinement, surface-centers are computed similarly to the isosurfaces (i.e., by traversing $V(f)$ on small intervals and interpolating positions of different labels) and inserted into the mesh to improve the planar angles of the boundary mesh triangles [52] and to ensure that the vertices of the boundary mesh triangles lie precisely on the isosurface [45].

In summary, tetrahedra and faces are refined according to the following *Refinement Rules*: **(R1)** Let t be an intersecting tetrahedron. Compute the closest isosurface point $z = \mathrm{cis}(c(t))$. If z is at a distance not closer than δ to any other isosurface vertex, then z is inserted. **(R2)** Let t be an intersecting tetrahedron. Compute the closest isosurface point $z = \mathrm{cis}(c(t))$. If its radius $r(t)$ is larger than $2 \cdot \delta$, then $c(t)$ is inserted. **(R3)** Let f be a facet whose Voronoi edge $V(f)$ intersects $\partial\mathcal{O}$ at $c_{\mathrm{surf}}(f)$. If either its smallest planar angle is less than 30° or a vertex of f is not an isosurface vertex, then $c_{\mathrm{surf}}(f)$ is inserted. **(R4)** If t is an interior tetrahedron whose radius-edge ratio is larger than 2, then $c(t)$ is inserted. **(R5)** Let t be an interior tetrahedron. If its radius $r(t)$ is larger than $\mathrm{sf}(c(t))$, then $c(t)$ is inserted. **(R6)** Let t be incident to an isosurface vertex z. All the already inserted circumcenters closer than 2δ to z are deleted.

Rules R1 and R2 are responsible for creating the appropriate dense sample so that the boundary triangles of the resulting mesh satisfies Theorem 1 and thus the fidelity guarantees. R3 and R4 deal with the quality guarantees, while R5 imposes the size constraints of the users. R6 is needed so termination can be guaranteed. See [26,28,45] for more details. When none of the above rules applies, then refinement is complete. In our previous work [26,28], we prove that termination is guaranteed, the radius-edge ratio of ell elements in the mesh is less than 2, and the planar angles of the boundary mesh triangles is less than 30°.

4 Parallel Delaunay Refinement for Smooth Surfaces

In this Section, we outline the main concepts of our parallel implementation. Note that our tightly-coupled parallelization does not alter the fidelity (Theorem 1) and the quality guarantees described in the previous section.

1) Poor Element List (PEL): Each thread T_i maintains its own *Poor Element List (PEL)* PEL_i. PEL_i contains the tetrahedra that violate the Refinement Rules and need to be refined by thread T_i accordingly.

2) Operation: An operation that refines an element can be either an insertion of a point p or the removal of a vertex p. In the case of insertion, the cavity $\mathcal{C}(p)$ needs to be found and re-triangulated according to the well known Bowyer-Watson kernel [16, 57]. Specifically, $\mathcal{C}(p)$ consists of the elements whose circumsphere contains p. These elements are deleted (because they violate the Delaunay property) and p is connected to the vertices of the boundary of $\mathcal{C}(p)$. In the case of a removal, the ball $\mathcal{B}(p)$ needs to be re-triangulated. As explained in [24], this is a more challenging operation than insertion, because the re-triangulation of the ball in degenerate cases is not unique which implies the creation of illegal elements, i.e., elements that cannot be connected with the corresponding elements outside the ball. We overcome this difficulty by computing a *local Delaunay triangulation* $\mathcal{D}_{\mathcal{B}_{(p)}}$ (or $\mathcal{D}_{\mathcal{B}}$ for brevity) of the vertices incident to p, such that the vertices inserted earlier in the shared triangulation are inserted into $\mathcal{D}_{\mathcal{B}}$ first. In order to avoid races associated with writing, reading, and deleting vertices/cells from a PEL or the shared mesh, any vertex touched during the operation of cavity expansion, or ball filling needs to be locked. We utilize GCC's atomic built-in functions for this goal, since they perform faster than the conventional pthread try_locks. Indeed, replacing pthread locks (our first implementation) with GCC's atomic built-ins (current implementation) decreased the execution time by 3.6% on 1 core and by 4.2% on 12 cores.

In the case a vertex is already locked by another thread, then we have a *rollback*: the operation is stopped and the changes are discarded [42]. When a rollback occurs, the thread moves on to the next bad element in its PEL.

3) Update new and deleted cells: After a thread T_i completes an operation, new cells are created and some cells are invalidated. The new cells are those that re-triangulate the cavity (in case of an insertion) or the ball (in case of a removal) of a point p and the invalidated cells are those that used to form the cavity or the ball of p right before the operation. T_i determines whether a newly created element violates a rule. If it does, then T_i pushes it back to PEL_i (or to another thread's PEL, see below) for future refinement. Also, T_i removes the invalidated elements from the PEL they have been residing in so far, which might be the PEL of another thread. To decrease the synchronization involved for the concurrent access to the PELs, if the invalidated cell c resides in another thread T_j's PEL_j, then T_i removes c from PEL_j only if T_j belongs to the same socket with T_i. Otherwise, T_i raises cell c's invalidation flag, so that T_j can remove it when T_j examines c.

4) Load Balancer: Right after the triangulation of the virtual box and the sequential creation of the first 6 tetrahedra, only the main thread might have a non-empty PEL. Clearly, Load Balancing is a fundamental aspect of our implementation. Our base (not optimized) Load Balancer is the classic *Random Work Stealing* (RHW) [13] technique, since it best fits our implementation design. In Section 6.1, we implement an optimized work stealing balancer that takes advantage of the NUMA architecture and achieves an excellent performance.

If the poor element list PEL_i of a thread T_i is empty of elements, T_i "pushes back" its ID to the *Begging List*, a global array that tracks down threads without work. Then, T_i is busy-waiting and can be awaken by a thread T_j right after T_j gives some work to T_i. A running thread T_j, every time it completes an *operation* (i.e., a Delaunay insertion or a Delaunay removal), it gathers the newly created elements and places the ones that are poor to the PEL of the first thread T_i found in the begging list. The classification of whether or not a newly created cell is poor or not is done by T_j. T_j also removes T_i from the Begging List.

To decrease unnecessary communication, a thread is not allowed to give work to threads, if it does not have enough poor elements in its PEL. Hence, each thread T_i maintains a counter that keeps track of all the poor and *valid* cells that reside in PEL_i. T_i is forbidden to give work to a thread, if the counter is less than a threshold. We set that threshold equal to 5, since it yielded the best results. When T_i invalidates an element c or when it makes a poor element c not to be poor anymore, it decreases accordingly the counter of the thread that contains c in its PEL. Similarly, when T_i gives extra poor elements to a thread, T_i increases the counter of the corresponding thread.

5) Contention Manager (CM): In order to eliminate livelocks caused by repeated rollbacks, threads talk to a Contention Manager (CM). Its purpose is to pause on run-time the execution of some threads making sure that at least one will do useful work so that system throughput can never get stuck [50]. See Section 5 for approaches able to greatly reduce the number of rollbacks and yield a considerable speedup, even in the absence of enough parallelism. Contention managers avoid energy waste because of rollbacks and reduce dynamic power consumption, by throttling the number of threads that contend, thereby providing an opportunity for the runtime system to place some cores in deep low power states.

5 Contention Manager

The goal of the Contention Manager (CM) is to reduce the number of rollbacks and guarantee the absence of rollbacks, if possible [31, 50].

We implemented and compared three contention techniques: the *Aggressive Contention Manager* (Aggressive-CM) [50], the *Random Contention Manager* (Random-CM), and the *Global Contention Manager* (Global-CM).

The Aggressive-CM and Random-CM are non-blocking schemes. As is usually the case for non-blocking schemes [5, 31, 35, 42, 50], we do not prove absence of livelocks for these techniques. Nevertheless, they are useful for comparison purposes as Aggressive-CM is the simplest to implement, and Random-CM has already been presented in the mesh generation literature [5, 35, 42].

Note that none of the earlier Transactional Memory techniques [31, 50] and the Random Contention Managers presented in the past [5, 35, 42] solve the livelock problem. In this section, we show that if livelocks are not provably eliminated in our application, then termination is compromised on high core counts.

5.1 Aggressive-CM

The Aggressive-CM is a brute-force technique, since there is no special treatment. Threads greedily attempt to apply the operation, and in case of a rollback, they just discard the changes, and move on to the next poor element to refine (if there is any). The purpose of this technique is to show that reducing the number of rollbacks is not just a matter of performance, but a matter of correctness. Indeed, experimental evaluation (see Section 5.4) shows that Aggressive-CM very often suffers from livelocks.

5.2 Random-CM

Random-CM has already been presented (with minor differences) in the literature [5, 35, 42] and worked fairly well, i.e, no livelocks were observed in practice. This scheme lets "randomness" choose the execution scenario that would eliminate livelocks. We implement this technique as well to show that our application needs considerably more efficient CMs. Indeed, recall that in our case, there is no much parallelism in the beginning of refinement and therefore, there is no much randomness that can be used to break the livelock.

Each thread T_i counts the number of consecutive rollbacks r_i. If r_i exceeds a specified upper value r^+, then T_i sleeps for a random time interval t_i. If the consecutive rollbacks break because an operation was successfully finished then r_i is reset to 0. The time interval t_i is in milliseconds and is a randomly generated number between 1 and r^+. The value of r^+ is set to 5. Other values yielded similar results. Note that lower values for r^+ do not necessarily imply faster executions. A low r^+ decreases the number of rollbacks much more, but increases the number of times that a contented thread goes to sleep (for t_i milliseconds). On the other hand, a high r^+ increases the number of rollbacks, but randomness is given more chance to avoid livelocks; that is, a contented thread has now more chances to find other elements to refine before it goes to sleep (for t_i milliseconds).

Random-CM cannot guarantee the absence of livelocks. As noted in [10], this randomness can rarely lead to livelocks, but it should be rejected as it is not a valid solution. We also experimentally verified that livelocks are not that rare (see Section 5.4).

5.3 Global-CM

Global-CM maintains a global *Contention List* (CL). If a thread T_i encounters a rollback, then it writes its id in CL and it busy waits (i.e., it blocks). Threads waiting in CL are potentially awaken (in FIFO order) by threads that have made a lot of progress, or in other words, by threads that have not recently encountered many rollbacks. Therefore, each thread T_i computes its "progress" by counting how many consecutive successful operations s_i have been performed without an interruption by a rollbacks. If s_i exceeds a upper value s^+, then T_i awakes the first thread in CL, if any. The value for s^+ is set to 10. Experimentally, we found that this value yielded the best results.

Table 1: Comparison among Contention Managers (CM). Global-CM greatly reduced the number of rollbacks and the overhead time.

	128 cores		256 cores
	Random-CM	Global-CM	Global-CM
execution time	64s	23s	22s
rollbacks	25×10^6 (52.9%)	728,087 (3.1%)	883,768 (3.6%)
contention overhead	4,317s	1,049	3,054s
load balance overhead	869s	130s	281s
rollback overhead	595s	3s	3s
total overhead	5,703s	1,183s	3,339s
speedup	16.9	47.0	49.1

Global-CM can never create livelocks, because it is a blocking mechanism as opposed to random-CM which does not block any thread. Nevertheless, the system might end up to a deadlock, because of the interaction with the Load Balancing's Begging List BL (see the Load Balancer in Section 4).

Therefore, at any time, the number of *active threads* needs to be tracked down, that is, the number of threads that do not busy wait in either the CL or the Begging List. A thread is forbidden to enter CL and busy wait, if it sees that there is only one (i.e., itself) active thread; instead, it skips CL and attempts to refine the next element in its Poor Element List. Similarly, a thread about to enter the Begging List (because it has no work to do) checks whether or not it is the only active thread at this moment, in which case, it awakes a thread from the CL, before it starts idling for extra work. In this simple way, the absence of livelocks and deadlocks are guaranteed, since threads always block in case of a rollback and there will always be at least one active thread.

5.4 Comparison

For this case study, we evaluated each CM on the CT abdominal atlas of IRCAD Laparoscopic Center (http://www.ircad.fr/) using 128 and 256 Blacklight cores (see Table 2 for its specification). The final mesh consists of about 150×10^6 tetrahedra. The single-threaded execution time on Blacklight was 1,080 seconds. See Table 1.

There are three direct sources of wasted cycles in our algorithm, and all of them are shown in Table 1. The **contention overhead time** is the total time that threads spent busy-waiting on a Contention List (or busy-waiting for a random number of seconds as is the case of Random-CM) and accessing the Contention List (in case of Global-CM). The **load balance overhead time** is the total time that threads spent busy-waiting on the Begging List waiting for more work to arrive (see Section 4) and accessing the Begging List. Lastly, the **rollback overhead time** is the total time that threads had spent for the partial completion of an operation right before they decided that they had to discard the changes and roll back.

The Aggressive-CM is missing for both core counts, and the Random-CM is missing from the 256-core experiment, because they were stuck in a livelock. Indeed, we experimentally found that they did not make any progress for more than 1 hour, a scenario of livelock.

Observe that Global-CM greatly reduced the number of rollbacks and the associated wasted cycles, as compared to the standard Contention Manager used in the literature. Random-CM encounters a rollback 50% of the total oper-

Table 2: The specifications of the cc-NUMA machines we used.

	Model	cores per socket	sockets per blade	blades	memory per socket	max hops
Blacklight	Intel Xeon X7560	8	2	128	64GB	5
CRTC	Intel Xeon X5690	6	2	1	48GB	0

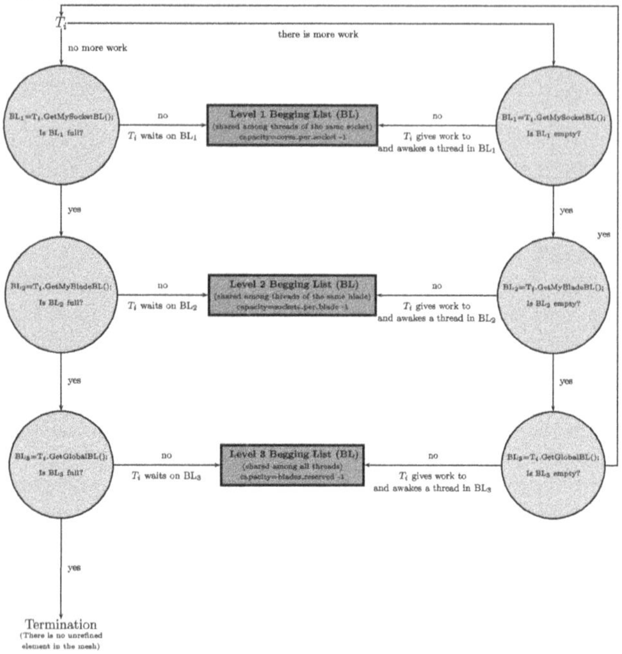

Figure 2: The 3-layer Hierarchical Work Stealing design. Threads ask work from their closest candidates first.

ations attempted, while Global-CM decreased it down to 3% on 128 cores. See the speedup achieved by these two CMS (over the single-thread execution): Global-CM is 2.7 times faster. Even on 256 cores, where both Aggressive-CM and Random-CM failed to terminate, Global-CM achieved a (slight) improvement over its 128-core performance.

Although there are other elaborate and hybrid contention techniques [31, 50], none of them guarantees the absence of livelocks. Therefore, we chose Global-CM because of its simplicity and efficiency.

6 Performance

In this Section, we describe a load balancing optimization and present the strong and weak scaling performance on Blacklight. See Table 2 for its specifications.

6.1 Hierarchical Work Stealing (HWS)

In order to further decrease the communication overhead associated with remote memory accesses, we implemented a *Hierarchical Work Stealing* scheme (HWS) by taking advantage of the cc-NUMA architecture.

We re-organized the Begging List into three levels: BL1, BL2, and BL3. See Figure 2. Threads of a single socket that run out of work place themselves into the first level begging list BL1 which is shared among threads of a single socket. If the thread realizes that all the other socket threads wait on BL1, it skips BL1, and places itself to BL2, which is shared among threads of a single blade. Similarly, if the thread realizes that BL2 already accommodates a thread from the other socket in its blade, it asks work by placing itself into the last level begging list BL3. When a thread completes an operation and is about to send extra work to an idle thread, it gives priority to BL1 threads first, then to BL2, and lastly to BL3 threads. In other words, BL1 is shared among the threads of a single socket and is able to accommodate up to *number_of_threads_per_socket* − 1 idle threads (in Blacklight, that is 7 threads). BL2 is shared among the sockets of a single blade and is able to accommodate up to *number_of_sockets_per_blade* − 1 idle threads (in Blacklight, that is 1 thread). Lastly, BL3 is shared among all the allocated blades and can accommodate at most one thread per blade. In this way, an idle thread T_i tends to take work first from threads inside its socket. If there is none, T_i takes work from a thread of the other socket inside its blade, if any. Finally, if all the other threads inside T_i's blade are idling for extra work, T_i places its id to BL3, asking work from a thread of another blade.

6.2 Strong Scaling Results

Figure 3 shows the strong scaling experiment demonstrating both the Random Work Stealing (RWS) load balance and the Hierarchical Work Stealing (HWS). The input image we used is the CT abdominal atlas obtained by IRCAD Laparoscopic Center (http://www.ircad.fr/). The final mesh generated consists of 147×10^6 elements. On a single Blacklight core, the execution time was 1300 seconds.

Observe that the speed-up of RWS deteriorates by a lot for more than 64 cores (see the green line in Figure 3a). In contrast, HWS manages to achieve a (slight) improvement even on 176 cores. This could be attributed to the fact that the number of inter-blade (i.e., remote) accesses are greatly reduced by HWS (see Figure 3b), since begging threads are more likely to get poor elements created by threads of their own socket and blade first. Clearly, this reduces the communication involved when a thread reads memory residing in a remote memory bank. Indeed, on 176 cores, 98% of all the number of times threads asked for work, they received it from a thread of their own blade, yielding a 42% reduction in inter-blade accesses, as Figure 3b shows.

Figure 3c shows the breakdown of the overhead time per thread for HWS across runs. Note that since this is a strong scaling case study, the ideal behavior is a linear increase of the height of the bars with the respect to the number of threads. Observe, however, that the overhead time per thread is always below the overhead time measured on 16 threads. This means that Global-CM and the Hierarchical Work Stealing method (HLB) are able to serve threads fast and tolerate congestion efficiently on runtime.

6.3 Weak Scaling Results

In this section, we present the weak scaling performance of PI2M on the CT abdominal atlas (http://www.ircad.fr/softwares/3Dircadb/3Dircadb2/3Dircadb2.2.zip). Other inputs (the knee [48] and the brain atlas [55] for example) exhibit similar results on comparable mesh sizes. We do not report them here, because of space limitations.

We measure the number of tetrahedra created per second across the runs. Specifically, let us define with Elements (n) and Time (n), the number of elements created and the time elapsed, when n threads are employed. Then, the speedup is defined as $\frac{\text{Elements}(n) \times \text{Time}(n)}{\text{Time}(n) \times \text{Elements}(1)}$. With n threads, a perfect speedup would be equal to n [30].

We can directly control the size of the problem (i.e., the number of generated tetrahedra) via the parameter δ (see Section 3). This parameter sets an upper limit on the volume of the tetrahedra generated. With a simple volume

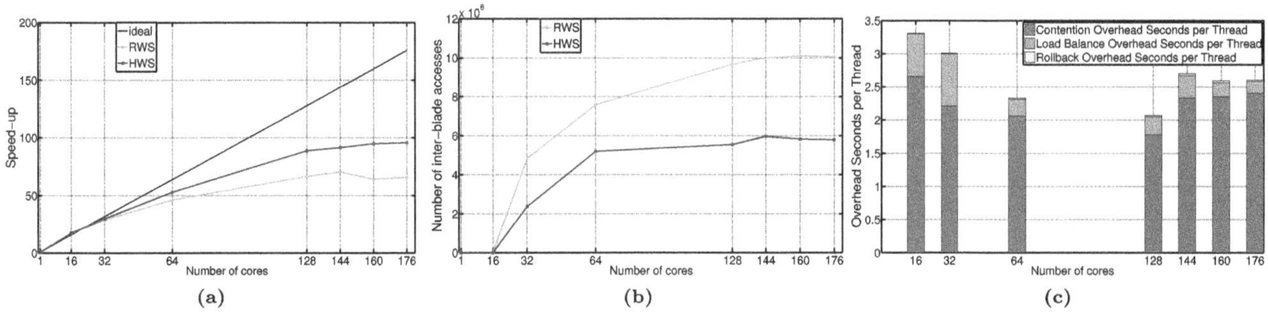

Figure 3: Strong scaling performance achieved by the classic Random Work Stealing (RWS) and Hierarchical Work Stealing (HWS). (a)-(b) Comparison between RWS and HWS on speed-up ($\frac{time_1}{time_{\#Threads}}$) and on the number of inter-blade accesses. (c) Breakdown of the overhead time for HWS.

Table 3: Weak scaling performance. Across runs, the number of elements per thread remains approximately constant.

#Threads	1	32	64	128	144	160	176
#Elements	1.08E+07	3.49E+08	7.44E+08	1.32E+09	1.51E+09	1.67E+09	1.85E+09
Time (secs)	100.80	92.25	102.27	95.91	102.98	135.81	180.96
Elements per second	1.07E+05	3.79E+06	7.28E+06	1.37E+07	**1.47E+07**	1.23E+07	1.02E+07
Speedup	1.00	35.41	68.05	**128.34**	137.24	115.06	95.71
Efficiency	1.000	1.107	1.063	**1.003**	**0.953**	0.719	0.544
Overhead secs per thread	0.00	2.28	3.74	4.62	4.66	6.85	8.54

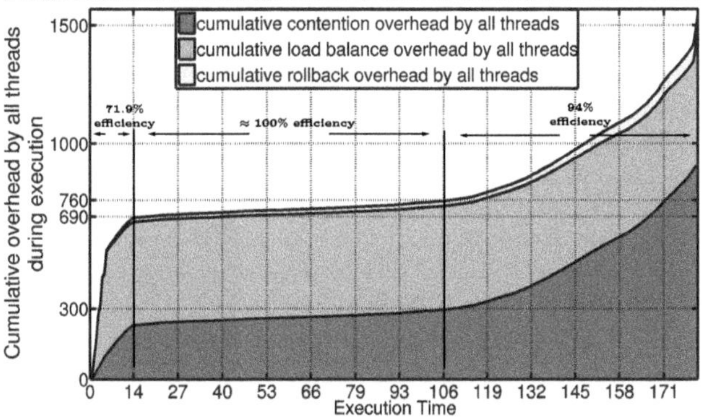

Figure 4: Overhead time breakdown with respect to the wall time for the experiment on 176 cores of Table 3. A pair (x, y) tells us that up to the xth second of execution, threads have not been doing useful work so far for y seconds all together.

argument, we can show that a decrease of δ by a factor of x results in an x^3 times increase of the mesh size, approximately.

See Table 3. The observed speedup is super-linear for up to 128 threads. On 144 cores, we achieve an unprecedented efficiency of 95%, and a rate of 14.7 Million Elements per second. It is worth mentioning that CGAL [2], the fastest sequential publicly available Isosurface-based mesh generation tool, on the same CT abdominal (http://www.ircad.fr/softwares/3Dircadb/3Dircadb2/3Dircadb2.2.zip) image input, is 81% slower than our single-threaded performance. Indeed, CGAL took 548.21 seconds to generate a similarly-sized mesh (1.00×10^7 tetrahedra) with comparable quality and fidelity to ours (see Section 7 for a more thorough comparison case study). Thus, compared to CGAL, the speedup we achieve on 144 cores is 746.39.

Nevertheless, our performance deteriorates beyond this core count. We claim that the main reason of this degradation is not the overhead cycles spent on rollbacks, contention lists, and begging lists (see Section 5.4), but the congested network responsible for the communication. Below, we support our claim.

First of all, notice that the total overhead time per thread increases. Since this is a weak scaling case study, the best that can happen is a constant number overhead seconds per thread. But this is not happening. The reason is that in the beginning of refinement, the mesh is practically empty: only the six tetrahedra needed to fill the virtual box are present (see Figure 1). Therefore, during the early stages of refinement, the problem does not behave as a weak scaling case study, but as a strong scaling one: more threads, but in fact the same size, which renders our application a very challenging problem. See Figure 4 for an illustration of the 176-core experiment of Table 3. X-axis shows the wall-time clock of the execution. The Y-axis shows the total number of seconds that threads have spent on useless computation (i.e., rollback, contention, and load balance overhead, see Section 5.4) so far, cumulatively. The more straight the lines are, the more useful work the threads perform. Rapidly growing lines imply lack of parallelism and intense contention. Observe that in the first 14 seconds of refinement, there is high contention and severe load imbalance. Nevertheless, even in this case, $\frac{176\times14-690}{176\times14} \approx 71.9\%$ of the time, all 176 threads were doing useful work, i.e., the threads were working on their full capacity.

However, this overhead time increase cannot explain the performance deterioration. See for example the numbers on 176 threads. 176 threads run for 180.96s each, and, on the average, they do useless work for 8.54s each. In other words, if there were no rollbacks, no contention list overhead, and no load balancing overhead, the execution time would have to be 180.96s-8.54s =172.42s. 172.42s, however, is far from the ideal 100.8s (that the first column with 1 thread shows) by 172.42s-100.8=71.62s. Therefore, while rollbacks, contention management, and load balancing introduce a merely 8.54s overhead, the real bottleneck is the 71.62s overhead spent on memory (often remote) loads/stores. Nevertheless, we verified that the number of remote accesses, LLC, and TLB misses remain constant per thread across runs, which is the ideal scenario: our Hierarchical Load Balancer (HLB) suppresses successfully excessive remote accesses thus achieving better data locality. Since, however, the problem size increases linearly with respect to the number of threads, either the communication traffic per network switch increases across runs, or it goes through a higher number of hops (each of which adds a 2,000 cycle latency penalty [1]), or both. It seems that after 144 cores, this pressure on the switches slows performance down. A hybrid approach [22] able to scale for larger network hierarchies is left for future work.

Table 4: **The single-threaded performance of our algorithm. It includes the extra overhead introduced by synchronization, contention management, and load balancing to support the (potential) presence of other threads.**

	PI2M	CGAL
#tetrahedra / seconds	51,968	33,462
time	7.1 secs	11.0 secs
#tetrahedra	368,974	368,077
max radius-edge ratio	2	2
smallest boundary planar angle	30°	30°
(min, max) dihedral angles	(4.6°, 170.2°)	(3.5°, 174.7°)
Hausdorff distance	10.7 mm	10.3 mm

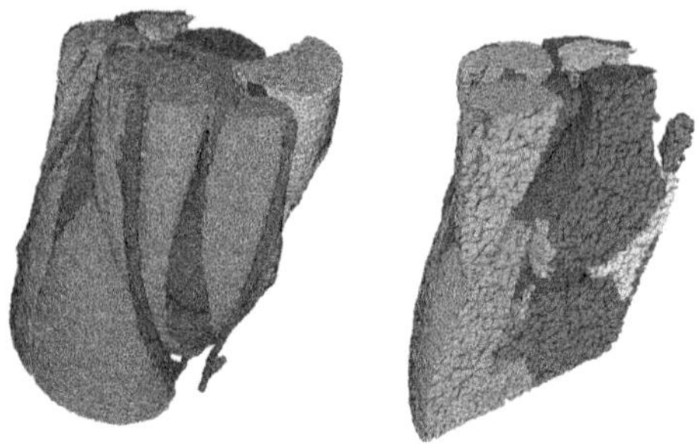

(a) whole mesh (b) cross section

Figure 5: The 368,974 element mesh generated by PI2M with input image the MRI knee atlas [48].

Hyper-threading suffers from the same memory congestion with one exception: the slow-down happens in a lower core count, a fact that needs further investigation. Nevertheless, for low core counts, we obtain a considerable improvement: on 64 cores (128 threads), the execution time is 70.8s, a 30% time decrease compared to the 64 non hyper-threaded core experiment of Table 3.

7 Single-threaded evaluation

In this section, we show that our single-threaded execution time, although it introduces extra overhead due to locking, synchronization, contention management bookkeeping (see Section 5), and hierarchical load balance (see Section 6.1), it is faster than and has similar quality to CGAL, the quickest state-of-the-art Delaunay Isosurface-based mesh generator we are aware of.

See Table 4. For this case study, we set the sizing parameters of CGAL to values that produced meshes of similar size with ours. Observe that the resulting meshes are of similar quality and that the single-threaded PI2M is 35% faster than CGAL. Our timing includes the 1.2 seconds needed for the computation of the Euclidean Distance Transform (see Section 3).

The input image used in this study is the 48-tissue MRI knee atlas freely available at [48]. Other input images yielded the same results: PI2M generates meshes of similar quality to CGAL's and 35% faster. Figure 5 illustrates the mesh generated by PI2M. We used CRTC (see Table 2 for its specifications) for this case study.

8 Discussion, Conclusions, and Future Work

In this paper, we present PI2M: the first parallel Image-to-Mesh (PI2M) Conversion Isosurface-based algorithm and its implementation. Starting directly from a multi-label segmented 3D image, it is able to recover and mesh both the isosurface $\partial\mathcal{O}$ with geometric and topological guarantees (see Theorem 1) and the underlying volume $\mathcal{O}$ with quality elements.

This work is different from parallel Triangulators [8, 11, 12, 27], since parallel mesh generation and refinement focuses on the quality of elements (tetrahedra and facets) and the conformal representation of the tissues' boundaries/isosurfaces by computing on demand the appropriate points for insertion or deletion. Parallel Triangulators tessellate only the convex hull of a set of points.

Our tighly-coupled method greatly reduces the number of rollbacks and scales up to a much higher core count, compared to the tighly-coupled method our group developed in the past [42]. The data decomposition method [20] does not support Delaunay removals, a technique that it is shown to be effective in the sequential mesh generation literature [26, 28]. The extension of partially-coupled [18] and decoupled [37] methods to 3D is a very difficult task, since Delaunay-admissible 3D medial decomposition is an unsolved problem. On the contrary, our method does not rely on any domain decomposition, and could be extended to arbitrary dimensions as well. Indeed, we plan to extend PI2M to 4 dimensions and generate space-time elements (needed for spatio-temporal simulations [9, 47]) in parallel, thus, exploiting parallelism in the fourth dimension.

Our code is highly optimized through carefully designed contention managers, and load balancers which take advantage of NUMA architectures. Our Global Contention Manager (Global-CM) provably eliminates deadlocks and livelocks and, at the same time, reduces the number of rollbacks by a factor of 17 compared to the standard Random technique found in the literature. Global-CM also reduced the number of wasted cycles by a factor of 4.8, improving energy-efficiency by avoiding energy waste because of rollbacks. Our Hierarchical Load Balancer (HLB) sped up the execution by a factor of 1.44 on 176 cores, as a result of a 42% remote accesses reduction.

All in all, PI2M achieves a strong scaling efficiency of more than 82% on 64 cores. It also achieves an excellent weak scaling efficiency of more than 95% on up to 144 cores. Other image inputs yielded very similar results. Because of the limited space, we do not report them here. We are not aware of any 3D parallel Delaunay mesh refinement algorithm achieving such a performance.

It is worth noting that PI2M exhibits excellent single-threaded performance. Despite the extra overhead associated with synchronization, contention management, and load balancing, PI2M generates meshes 35% faster than CGAL and with similar quality.

Recall that in our method, threads spend time idling on the contention and load balancing lists. And this is necessary in our algorithm for correctness and performance efficiency. This fact offers great opportunities to control the power consumption, or alternatively, to maximize the $\frac{\text{Elements}}{\text{second}\times\text{Watt}}$ ratio. Since idling is not the time critical component in our algorithm, the CPU frequency could be decreased during such an idling. Nevertheless, the appropriate frequency drop, the amount of idling, and performance is a trade-off, and its investigation is left as future work.

As already explained, for core counts higher than 144, weak scaling performance deteriorates because communication traffic (per switch) is more intense and passes through a larger number of hops. In the future, we plan to increase scalability by employing a hierarchically layered (distributed and shared memory) implementation design [22] and combine this tightly-coupled method with the decoupled and partially coupled methods we developed in the past, exploring in this way different levels of concurrency.

Acknowledgments

The authors are deeply grateful to PSC's system group for its priceless and prompt support. Special thanks to Dimitris Nikolopoulos, Andrey Chernikov, and Andriy Kot, for their instructive comments and insightful discussions. This work is supported in part by NSF grants: CCF-1139864, CCF-1136538, and CSI-1136536 and by the John Simon Guggenheim Foundation and the Richard T. Cheng Endowment.

9 References

[1] SGI UV 100/1000 system specifications. http://www.sgi.com/products/servers/uv/specs.html, 2012. available online.

[2] CGAL, Computational Geometry Algorithms Library. http://www.cgal.org, v4.0.

[3] N. Amenta and M. Bern. Surface reconstruction by Voronoi filtering. In *SCG '98: Proceedings of the fourteenth annual symposium on Computational geometry*, pages 39–48, New York, NY, USA, 1998. ACM.

[4] N. Amenta, S. Choi, and R. K. Kolluri. The power crust. In *Proceedings of the sixth ACM symposium on Solid modeling and applications*, SMA '01, pages 249–266, New York, NY, USA, 2001. ACM.

[5] C. Antonopoulos, X. Ding, A. Chernikov, F. Blagojevic, D. Nikolopoulos, and N. Chrisochoides. Multigrain parallel delaunay mesh generation: Challenges and opportunities for multithreaded architectures. In *ACM International Conference on Supercomputing*, number 19, pages 367–376, 2005.

[6] N. Archip, O. Clatz, A. Fedorov, A. Kot, S. Whalen, D. Kacher, N. Chrisochoides, F. Jolesz, A. Golby, P. Black, and S. K. Warfield. Non-rigid alignment of preoperative MRI, fMRI, DT-MRI, with intra-operative MRI for enchanced visualization and navigation in image-guided neurosurgery. *Neuroimage*, 35(2):609–624, 2007.

[7] K. Asanovic, R. Bodik, J. Demmel, T. Keaveny, K. Keutzer, J. Kubiatowicz, N. Morgan, D. Patterson, K. Sen, J. Wawrzynek, D. Wessel, and K. Yelick. A view of the parallel computing landscape. *Commun. ACM*, 52:56–67, Oct. 2009.

[8] V. H. Batista, D. L. Millman, S. Pion, and J. Singler. Parallel geometric algorithms for multi-core computers. *Computational Geometry*, 43(8):663–677, 2010.

[9] M. Behr. Simplex space-time meshes in finite element simulations. *International Journal for Numerical Methods in Fluids*, 57:1421–1434, 2008.

[10] M. Ben-Ari. *Principles of concurrent programming, Chapter 3, pages 30-43*. Prentice-Hall, Englewood Cliffs, NJ, 1982.

[11] D. K. Blandford, G. E. Blelloch, and C. Kadow. Engineering a compact parallel delaunay algorithm in 3d. In *Proceedings of the 22nd Symposium on Computational Geometry*, SCG '06, pages 292–300, New York, NY, USA, 2006. ACM.

[12] G. E. Blelloch, G. L. Miller, J. C. Hardwick, and D. Talmor. Design and implementation of a practical parallel delaunay algorithm. *Algorithmica*, 24(3):243–269, 1999.

[13] R. D. Blumofe, C. F. Joerg, B. C. Kuszmaul, C. E. Leiserson, K. H. Randall, and Y. Zhou. Cilk: an efficient multithreaded runtime system. In *Proceedings of the fifth ACM SIGPLAN symposium on Principles and practice of parallel programming*, PPoPP '95, pages 207–216, New York, NY, USA, 1995. ACM.

[14] J.-D. Boissonnat and S. Oudot. Provably good sampling and meshing of surfaces. *Graphical Models*, 67(5):405–451, 2005.

[15] D. Boltcheva, M. Yvinec, and J.-D. Boissonnat. Mesh Generation from 3D Multi-material Images. In *Medical Image Computing and Computer-Assisted Intervention*, pages 283–290. Springer, September 2009.

[16] A. Bowyer. Computing Dirichlet tesselations. *Computer Journal*, 24:162–166, 1981.

[17] C. Burstedde, O. Ghattas, M. Gurnis, T. Isaac, G. Stadler, T. Warburton, and L. Wilcox. Extreme-scale amr. In *Proceedings of the 2010 ACM/IEEE International Conference for High Performance Computing, Networking, Storage and Analysis*, SC '10, pages 1–12, 2010.

[18] A. Chernikov and N. Chrisochoides. Algorithm 872: Parallel 2d constrained delaunay mesh generation. *ACM Transactions on Mathematical Software*, 34:6–25, January 2008.

[19] A. Chernikov and N. Chrisochoides. Multitissue tetrahedral image-to-mesh conversion with guaranteed quality and fidelity. *SIAM Journal on Scientific Computing*, 33:3491–3508, 2011.

[20] A. N. Chernikov and N. P. Chrisochoides. Three-dimensional delaunay refinement for multi-core processors. In *Proceedings of the 22nd annual international Conference on Supercomputing*, ICS '08, pages 214–224, New York, NY, USA, 2008. ACM.

[21] A. N. Chernikov and N. P. Chrisochoides. Generalized insertion region guides for delaunay mesh refinement. *SIAM Journal on Scientific Computing (SISC)*, 2011. under revision.

[22] N. Chrisochoides, A. Chernikov, A. Fedorov, A. Kot, L. Linardakis, and P. Foteinos. Towards exascale parallel delaunay mesh generation. In *International Meshing Roundtable*, number 18, pages 319–336, Salt Lake City, Utah, October 2009.

[23] H. L. D. Cougny and M. S. Shephard. Parallel refinement and coarsening of tetrahedral meshes. *International Journal for Numerical Methods in Engineering*, 46(7):1101–1125, 1999.

[24] O. Devillers and M. Teillaud. Perturbations and vertex removal in a 3d delaunay triangulation. In *Proceedings of the 14th ACM-SIAM Symposium on Discrete algorithms*, SODA '03, pages 313–319, 2003.

[25] T. K. Dey and W. Zhao. Approximate medial axis as a voronoi subcomplex. *Computer-Aided Design*, 36(2):195–202, 2004.

[26] P. Foteinos, A. Chernikov, and N. Chrisochoides. Guaranteed Quality Tetrahedral Delaunay Meshing for Medical Images. In *Proceedings of the 7th International Symposium on Voronoi Diagrams in Science and Engineering*, pages 215–223, June 2010.

[27] P. Foteinos and N. Chrisochoides. Dynamic parallel 3d delaunay triangulation. In *International Meshing Roundtable*, pages 9–26, Paris, France, October 2011.

[28] P. Foteinos and N. Chrisochoides. High-quality multi-tissue mesh generation for finite element analysis. In *MeshMed, Workshop on Mesh Processing in Medical Image Analysis (MICCAI)*, pages 18–28, September 2011.

[29] J. Galtier and P.-L. George. Prepartitioning as a way to mesh subdomains in parallel. In *Special Symposium on Trends in Unstructured Mesh Generation*, pages 107–122. ASME/ASCE/SES, 1997.

[30] J. L. Gustafson. Reevaluating Amdahl's law. *Communications of the ACM*, 31:532–533, 1988.

[31] M. Herlihy, V. Luchangco, and M. Moir. Obstruction-free synchronization: Double-ended queues as an example. In *Proceedings of the 23rd International Conference on Distributed Computing Systems*, ICDCS '03, 2003.

[32] Y. Ito, A. Shih, A. Erukala, B. Soni, A. Chernikov, N. Chrisochoides, and K. Nakahashi. Parallel mesh generation using an advancing front method. *Mathematics and Computers in Simulation*, 75:200–209, September 2007.

[33] C. M. J. Kadow. *Parallel Delaunay Refinement Mesh Generation*. 2004. PhD Thesis, Carnegie Mellon University.

[34] B. M. Klingner and J. R. Shewchuk. Aggressive tetrahedral mesh improvement. In *Proceedings of the International Meshing Roundtable*, pages 3–23. Springer, 2007.

[35] M. Kulkarni, P. Carribault, K. Pingali, G. Ramanarayanan, B. Walter, K. Bala, and L. P. Chew. Scheduling strategies for optimistic parallel execution of irregular programs. In *Proc. Symp. on Parallelism in algorithms and architectures (SPAA)*, pages 217–228, New York, NY, USA, 2008.

[36] F. Labelle and J. R. Shewchuk. Isosurface stuffing: fast tetrahedral meshes with good dihedral angles. *ACM Transactions on Graphics*, 26(3):57, 2007.

[37] L. Linardakis and N. Chrisochoides. Graded delaunay decoupling method for parallel guaranteed quality planar mesh generation. *SIAM Journal on Scientific Computing*, 30(4):1875–1891, March 2008.

[38] Y. Liu, C. Yao, L. Zhou, and N. Chrisochoides. A point based non-rigid registration for tumor resection using imri. In *IEEE International Symposium on Biomedical Imaging: From Nano to Macro*, pages 1217–1220, April 2010.

[39] R. Löhner. A 2nd generation parallel advancing front grid generator. In X. Jiao and J.-C. Weill, editors, *Proceedings of the 21st International Meshing Roundtable*, pages 457–474, 2013.

[40] W. E. Lorensen and H. E. Cline. Marching cubes: A high resolution 3d surface construction algorithm. *SIGGRAPH Computer Graphics*, 21(4):163–169, 1987.

[41] G. L. Miller, D. Talmor, S.-H. Teng, and N. Walkington. A delaunay based numerical method for three dimensions: generation, formulation, and partition. In *Proceedings of the 27th Annu. ACM Sympos. Theory Comput*, pages 683–692. ACM, 1995.

[42] D. Nave, N. Chrisochoides, and P. Chew. Parallel delaunay refinement for restricted polyhedral domains. *Computational Geometry: Theory and Applications*, 28:191–215, 2004.

[43] T. Okusanya and J. Peraire. 3d parallel unstructured mesh generation, 1997. http://citeseerx.ist.psu.edu/viewdoc/summary?doi=10.1.1.48.7898.

[44] L. Oliker and R. Biswas. Parallelization of a dynamic unstructured algorithm using three leading programming paradigms. *IEEE Trans. Parallel Distrib. Syst.*, 11(9):931–940, Sept. 2000.

[45] S. Oudot, L. Rineau, and M. Yvinec. Meshing volumes bounded by smooth surfaces. In *Proceedings of the International Meshing Roundtable*, pages 203–219. Springer-Verlag, September 2005.

[46] J.-P. Pons, F. Ségonne, J.-D. Boissonnat, L. Rineau, M. Yvinec, and R. Keriven. High-Quality Consistent Meshing of Multi-label Datasets. In *Information Processing in Medical Imaging*, pages 198–210, 2007.

[47] T. C. S. Rendall, C. B. Allen, and E. D. C. Power. Conservative unsteady aerodynamic simulation of arbitrary boundary motion using structured and unstructured meshes in time. *International Journal for Numerical Methods in Fluids*, 70(12):1518–1542, 2012.

[48] J. Richolt, M. Jakab, and R. Kikinis. Spl knee atlas. January 2011. Available at: http://www.spl.harvard.edu/publications/item/view/1953.

[49] R. Said, N. Weatherill, K. Morgan, and N. Verhoeven. Distributed parallel delaunay mesh generation. *Computer Methods in Applied Mechanics and Engineering*, 177(1-2):109–125, 1999.

[50] W. N. Scherer, III and M. L. Scott. Advanced contention management for dynamic software transactional memory. In *Proceedings of the 24th annual ACM symposium on Principles of distributed computing*, PODC '05, pages 240–248. ACM, 2005.

[51] J. R. Shewchuk. Tetrahedral mesh generation by delaunay refinement. In *Proceedings of the 14th ACM Symposium on Computational Geometry*, pages 86–95, Minneapolis, MN, 1998.

[52] J. R. Shewchuk. Delaunay refinement algorithms for triangular mesh generation. *Computational Geometry: Theory and Applications*, 22(1-3):21–74, May 2002.

[53] H. Si. Constrained delaunay tetrahedral mesh generation and refinement. *Finite Elements in Analysis and Design*, 46:33–46, 2010.

[54] R. Staubs, A. Fedorov, L. Linardakis, B. Dunton, and N. Chrisochoides. Parallel n-dimensional exact signed euclidean distance transform. September 2006.

[55] I. Talos, M. Jakab, R. Kikinis, and M. Shenton. SPL-PNL Brain Atlas. March 2008.

[56] T. Tu, D. R. O. Hallaron, and O. Ghattas. Scalable parallel octree meshing for terascale applications. In *Proceedings of the 2005 ACM/IEEE conference on Supercomputing*, SC '05, 2005.

[57] D. F. Watson. Computing the n-dimensional Delaunay tesselation with application to Voronoi polytopes. *Computer Journal*, 24:167–172, 1981.

[58] M. Zhou, O. Sahni, T. Xie, M. S. Shephard, and K. E. Jansen. Unstructured mesh partition improvement for implicit finite element at extreme scale. *J. Supercomput.*, 59(3):1218–1228, Mar. 2012.

Tuning the Continual Flow Pipeline Architecture

Komal Jothi and Haitham Akkary
Department of Electrical and Computer Engineering
American University of Beirut
Beirut, Lebanon
+961 1 350 000
{kmj04, ha95}@aub.edu.lb

ABSTRACT

Continual Flow Pipelines (CFP) allows a processor core to process instruction windows of hundreds of instructions without increasing cycle-critical pipeline resources. When a load misses the data cache, CFP checkpoints the processor register state and then moves all miss dependent instructions into a low complexity non-critical waiting buffer to unblock the pipeline. Meanwhile, miss independent instructions execute normally and update the processor state. When the miss data returns, CFP replays the miss dependent instructions from the waiting buffer and then merges the miss dependent and the miss independent execution results.

CFP was initially proposed for cache misses to DRAM. Later work focused on reducing the execution overhead of CFP by avoiding flushing the pipeline before replaying miss dependent instructions, and on allowing these instructions to execute concurrently with miss independent instructions. The goal of these improvements was to gain performance by applying CFP to L1 data cache misses that hit the last level on chip cache. However, many applications or execution phases of applications incur excessive amount of replay and/or rollbacks to the checkpoint. This frequently cancels any benefits from CFP or even causes performance degradation.

In this paper, we improve the CFP architecture by using a novel virtual register renaming substrate, and by tuning the replay policies to mitigate excessive replays and rollbacks to the checkpoint. We describe these new design optimizations and show, using Spec 2006 benchmarks and microarchitecture performance and power models of our design, that our Tuned CFP architecture improves performance and power consumption over previous CFP architectures by ~15% and ~9%, respectively.

Categories and Subject Descriptors

C.1.1 [**Processor Architectures**]: Single Data Stream Architectures – *pipeline processors.*

General Terms

Performance, Design.

Keywords

Superscalar Processors, Instruction Level Parallelism, Continual Flow Pipelines, Latency Tolerant Processors, Virtual Register Renaming.

1. INTRODUCTION

The current era of multi-core processors presents microprocessor architects a difficult design challenge: How to design a processor core that would give good single thread performance on applications with limited thread-level parallelism, yet consume less power, therefore making it possible to integrate more cores on a single die for high throughput performance.

To improve superscalar processor performance on difficult to parallelize applications, architects have been increasing the capacity of reorder buffers, reservation stations (RS), physical register files, and load and store queues [22] with every new out-of-order processor core. For two decades, increasing instruction buffer sizes has provided good performance improvement. However, this approach does not work anymore. First, there is little instruction level parallelism left to justify further increase in instruction buffer size. Second, trying to reduce execution stalls from cache misses with larger conventional cores is impractical. Current buffer sizes are sufficient for code that hits the L1 data cache and way too small for code that misses the last level cache. Load latency to the last level cache on current processors is more than 20 clock cycles, and latency to DRAM, even with on-chip DRAM controller, exceeds hundred cycles. It is not possible to increase the sizes of power hungry and cycle critical buffers, like reorder buffers, reservation stations and physical register files to the capacity necessary to handle long load latencies to the last level cache or DRAM.

A different design strategy is to size the instruction buffers to the minimum capacity necessary to handle the common case of L1 data cache hit and to use new scalable out-of-order execution algorithms to handle code that misses the L1 data cache.

The Continual Flow Pipeline architecture (CFP) [23] was proposed as an energy-efficient large instruction window architecture for reducing the impact of data cache misses on performance, without having to increase instruction buffers and physical register files sizes. CFP breaks away from the conventional reorder buffer mechanisms for managing speculative out-of-order execution. Instead of using a reorder buffer for tracking, buffering and sequentially committing one by one the current set of in-flight instructions, also called the instruction window, CFP uses bulk commit of execution results, and register state checkpoints to recover from branch mispredictions and exceptions [1][14][17].

Instead of residing completely in the hardware instruction buffers, the instruction window becomes virtual and composed physically of a partial, discontiguous subset of the conventional instruction window. As such, instructions that do not encounter cache misses enter the instruction window, execute and commit quickly, freeing all their hardware resources. On the other hand, instructions that depend on cache miss data enter the physical instruction window and wait as long as necessary for their input operands without blocking the execution pipeline.

CFP handles data cache misses as follows. When a load misses the data cache, a poison bit is set in the destination register of the load. Load dependent instructions in the reservation stations (RS) are then woken up, as if the load completed. Poison bits propagate through instruction dependences, and identify all instructions that depend on the load miss and their descendants. The miss load and its dependents, identified by the poison bits in the ROB, pseudo-commit in program order and move from the ROB into a waiting buffer (WB) outside the pipeline. Since dependent instructions do not tie pipeline resources, the core can execute ahead far into the program without stalling due to the cache miss.

When the miss data is fetched, the dependent instructions wake up and replay from the WB into the pipeline to complete their execution. When the WB is emptied and all miss dependent instructions complete, independent and dependent instruction results are merged using a flash copy operation in the retirement register file. Execution then resumes normally.

CFP was originally proposed to tolerate long latencies of L2 cache misses that go to DRAM [23]. In that work, the miss independent and dependent instructions execute at different times, based on the timing of the load miss event and the data arrival event. Switching between the two executions is costly because it involves a pipeline flush, making this proposal unsuitable for L1 misses that hit the on-chip cache. In a more recent work, simultaneous CFP (S-CFP) [15] executes the independent and dependent instructions simultaneously to avoid the costly pipeline flush, thus making S-CFP more suitable for first level data cache misses. However, in S-CFP, many applications or execution phases of applications incur excessive amount of replay and/or rollbacks to checkpoints because of branch mispredictions during CFP execution. The reason is that CFP recovers from replayed mispredicted branches by rolling back execution to checkpoints taken at the load misses. Excessive replay increases the chance of replaying mispredicted branches and consequently rollbacks to the checkpoints. This frequently cancels any desired improvement resulting from S-CFP handling of L1 data cache misses or even causes performance degradation.

1.1 Paper Contribution

In this paper, we focus on the excessive replays and checkpoint rollbacks to improve CFP performance and reduce its power consumption. For this, we use a novel virtual register renaming substrate [21] and fine tune the replay policies to mitigate excessive replays and rollbacks to the checkpoint.

The key contributions of this paper over prior CFP work are:

- On previous CFP architectures, all load miss dependent instructions have to be moved into the waiting buffer and then replayed, once the load miss is moved into the waiting buffer. This is necessary because the miss load releases its renamed destination register when it pseudo-commits and moves to the WB. This breaks the dependence links between the miss load and its dependents, requiring the full dependent thread to be replayed and renamed again to re-establish the dependence relation. In this work, we use virtual register names, which persist for the full life time of the instructions, to specify the dependences between instructions. This allows partial replay of only those dependents moved into the waiting buffer while the miss is outstanding, significantly reducing the number of replayed instructions and the total execution time.
- It introduces an improved CFP policy that keeps miss dependent instructions in the reservation stations as long as they do not block the pipeline. However, when the instruction buffers become full with miss dependent instructions, thus stalling the pipeline, CFP moves the miss dependent instructions into the waiting buffer. Moving instructions into the waiting buffer on resource need basis significantly reduces the amount of replay and costly rollbacks to the checkpoints resulting from branch mispredictions that depend on load misses.
- It introduces a hardware predictor to predict miss dependent branches likely to mispredict. This predictor is used as a branch confidence estimation mechanism to reduce the runahead distance of CFP and the corresponding increase in checkpoint rollback risk. This prediction mechanism improves performance by 5% and reduces by 4 % the power resulting from checkpoint rollbacks due to mispredicted branches that depend on load misses.
- Our optimized CFP architecture removes the reorder buffer from the replay loop, which reduces the replay loop latency of miss dependent instructions evicted into the waiting buffer and thus reduces execution time and dynamic power.

The rest of this paper is organized as follows. Section 2 presents, as background to this work an overview of the simultaneous CFP architecture. Section 3 follows with a description of virtual register renaming and our Tuned CFP architecture and its optimizations. We outline our simulation methodology in Section 4. Section 5 evaluates power and performance of the new CFP design and compares with previous CFP architectures as well as conventional baseline core of equivalent instruction buffers capacity. Section 6 discusses related work and we conclude in Section 7.

2. Continual Flow Pipeline Architecture

This section gives a brief overview of the latest Continual Flow Pipeline architecture called Simultaneous CFP (S-CFP) [15] and illustrates with execution examples, some of its drawbacks. It also explains the new mechanisms we use to tune S-CFP and overcome its drawbacks.

2.1 S-CFP Architecture Overview

The simultaneous continual flow pipeline (S-CFP) core microarchitecture [15] was based on Intel P6 architecture [19].

Figure 1 shows a block diagram of S-CFP microarchitecture [15]. Unlike previous latency tolerant out-of-order architectures, the S-CFP core executes cache miss dependent and independent instructions concurrently using two different hardware thread contexts. The S-CFP hardware is similar to simultaneous multithreading architectures (SMT) [25], except that the two S-CFP simultaneous threads are formed of the miss dependent and miss independent instructions constructed dynamically from the

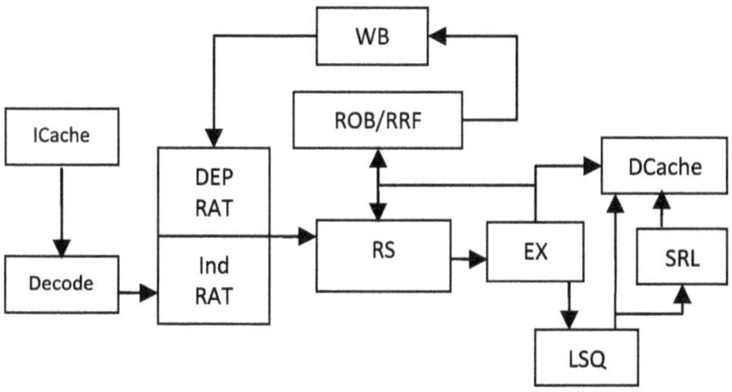

Figure 1. Simultaneous CFP architecture block diagram

same program, instead of being two different programs that run simultaneously on the same core. In order to support two hardware threads, S-CFP has two register alias tables (RAT) for renaming the independent and the dependent thread instructions. S-CFP also has two retirement register file contexts (RRF), one for retiring miss independent instruction results and the other for retiring miss dependent instruction results. The two threads share the reorder buffer, load queue, store queue, reservation stations and data cache read/write ports.

The independent hardware thread is the main execution thread. It is responsible for instruction fetch and decode of all instructions, branch prediction, memory dependence prediction, identifying miss dependent instructions and moving them into the waiting buffer (WB). The dependent thread execution starts when the load miss data is brought into the cache, waking up the load instruction in the WB, and continues until the WB empties. At the end of dependent execution, when all the instructions from the WB have retired (i.e. committed) without any mispredictions or exceptions, the independent and dependent execution results are merged together with a flash copy of the dependent and independent register contexts within the retirement register file. To maintain proper memory ordering of loads and stores from the independent and dependent threads execution, S-CFP uses load and store queues (LSQ), a Store Redo Log (SRL) [10] and a store-set memory dependence predictor [5].

S-CFP renames instructions using the reorder buffer (ROB) [22]. When a load miss reaches the head of the ROB, it is pseudo-retired and moved into the WB immediately. The load miss instruction releases all its pipeline resources including its ROB ID before entering the waiting buffer, breaking its links with its readers that are still in the pipeline. For this reason, the entire dependence chain of the load miss and its dependents needs to renamed and replayed from the WB until all miss dependent instructions complete execution and their results are merged. This can last for a long distance forward in the program, causing excessive replays and rollbacks. We show next in more detail examples that illustrate the drawbacks of S-CFP that are targeted by our optimizations.

2.2 S-CFP Execution Examples

Figures 2(a) and 2(b) show snapshots of the ROB and WB states in S-CFP at different execution times. All shaded instructions correspond to either a load miss or a load miss dependent, both of which are potential candidates to move into the WB. In Figure 2(a), the WB has a load miss *X* at the head waiting for its wakeup.

Instruction *A* misses the first level cache and is marked as a potential candidate to be moved into the WB. When *A* reaches the head of the ROB, there are still free entries available in the ROB. Nevertheless, S-CFP eagerly pseudo-retires and moves *A* into the WB. In order to execute when the miss data is fetched, *A* has to be replayed from the WB back into the pipeline to be renamed again and allocated resources for execution.

Figure 2(b) shows that the load miss hits the L2 data cache and *A* is woken up from the L1 data cache shortly after it enters the WB. However, it is stuck in the WB behind instruction *X* that has missed to DRAM. For a long time afterwards, and until the miss data of load *X* is fetched from DRAM, many of the dependents of *A* will be poisoned and moved into the WB. Therefore, even though *A* has hit the L2 cache, it is replayed with its dependents from the WB as if it has encountered a miss in the L2 data cache and has needed to go all the way to DRAM for the data.

Figures 3(a)-3(c) show an execution sequence to illustrate a situation in S-CFP that leads to a rollback to the checkpoint. Similar to the earlier example, the WB has a load instruction *X* that has missed. Instruction *A* misses the L1 cache. In this example, *F* is a branch that depends on *A*. *A* is moved into the WB from the head of the ROB as shown in Figure 3(a). *F* also follows *A* into the waiting buffer, even though the wakeup for *A* arrives while *F* is still in the ROB/RS, as shown in Figure 3(b). Both *A* and *F* are replayed behind instruction *X* as shown in Figure 3(c). On replay, branch *F* is found to be mispredicted and branch misprediction recovery has to be performed by rolling back execution to the checkpoint, since by then, the sequential state in the register file has been corrupted by the out-of-order pseudo-retirement of instructions during the cache miss processing.

Figures 4(a)-4(d) show another execution sequence to illustrate why S-CFP needs to replay a load and all its dependents once the load enters the WB. In this example, *A* is a load miss and *B* is dependent on *A*. The two instructions are separated by miss independents shown as dotted lines. The figures show only the miss dependents in the pipeline for clarity. The renamed physical source and destination register tags (*src1, src2 -> dest*) are shown alongside the instruction. Also shown below their ROB entries are the ROB IDs or physical destination registers of *A* and *B*. The waiting buffer, initially empty, is also shown in the figures.

In Figure 4(a), *A* reaches the head of the ROB. It pseudo-retires and moves into the WB, releasing all its pipeline resources including its *ROB ID #3*, as shown in Figure 4(b). When *A* wakes up and replays, it is allocated a new entry at the tail of the ROB as shown in Figure 4(c). Notice that *A* gets a new *ROB ID #24* when it is reintroduced into the pipeline. Because of this new ID, even though *B* is still in the RS and the ROB while *A* is being replayed, *A's* data writeback cannot wakeup *B*, because *B* still has the physical register destination *ID #3* as its source operand. *B* reaches the ROB head, pseudo-retires, and moves into the WB. When *B* is replayed and reintroduced into the pipeline, it goes through the rename stage, gets a new *ROB ID #28* and receives the correct physical source register *ID # 24*, re-establishing its link with *A* from the dependent RAT, as shown in Figure 4(d). Notice that an 'x' is shown for the other source IDs to indicate that the IDs of these sources are 'don't care' for illustrating this example.

2.3 Tuned CFP Execution Examples

As illustrated in the above examples, S-CFP results in excessive replays and rollbacks, negatively impacting performance and energy consumption. Our Tuned CFP architecture presented in this paper handles these cases differently as explained below.

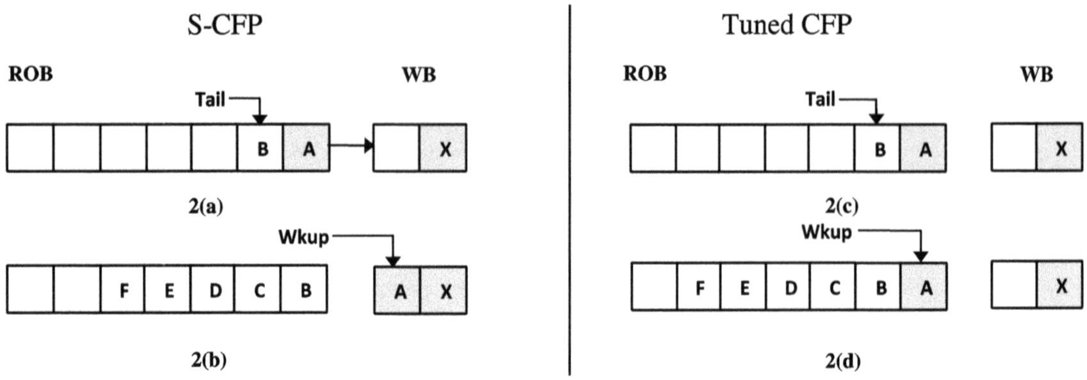

Figure 2. Execution sequence showing S-CFP moving a dependent into WB eagerly

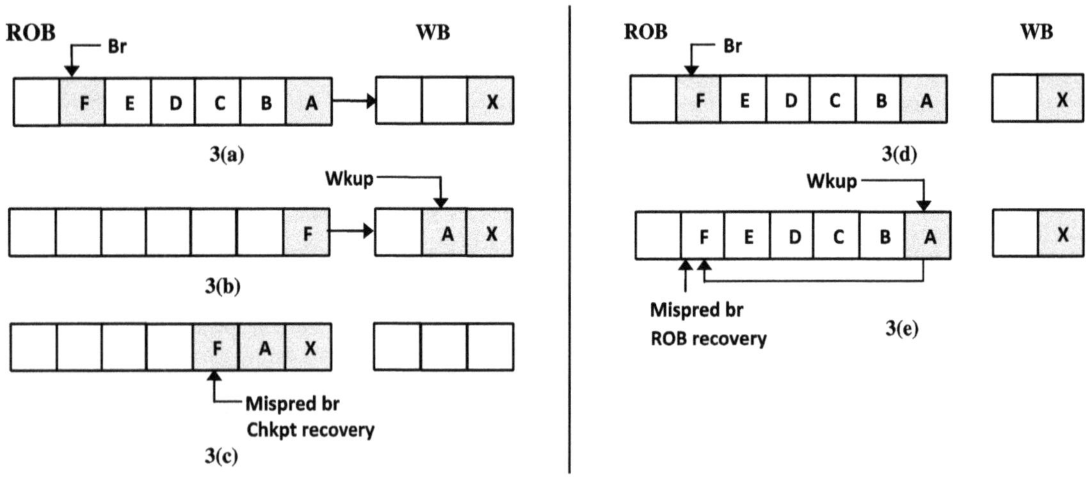

Figure 3. Execution sequence showing a scenario leading to rollback in S-CFP which is avoided in Tuned CFP

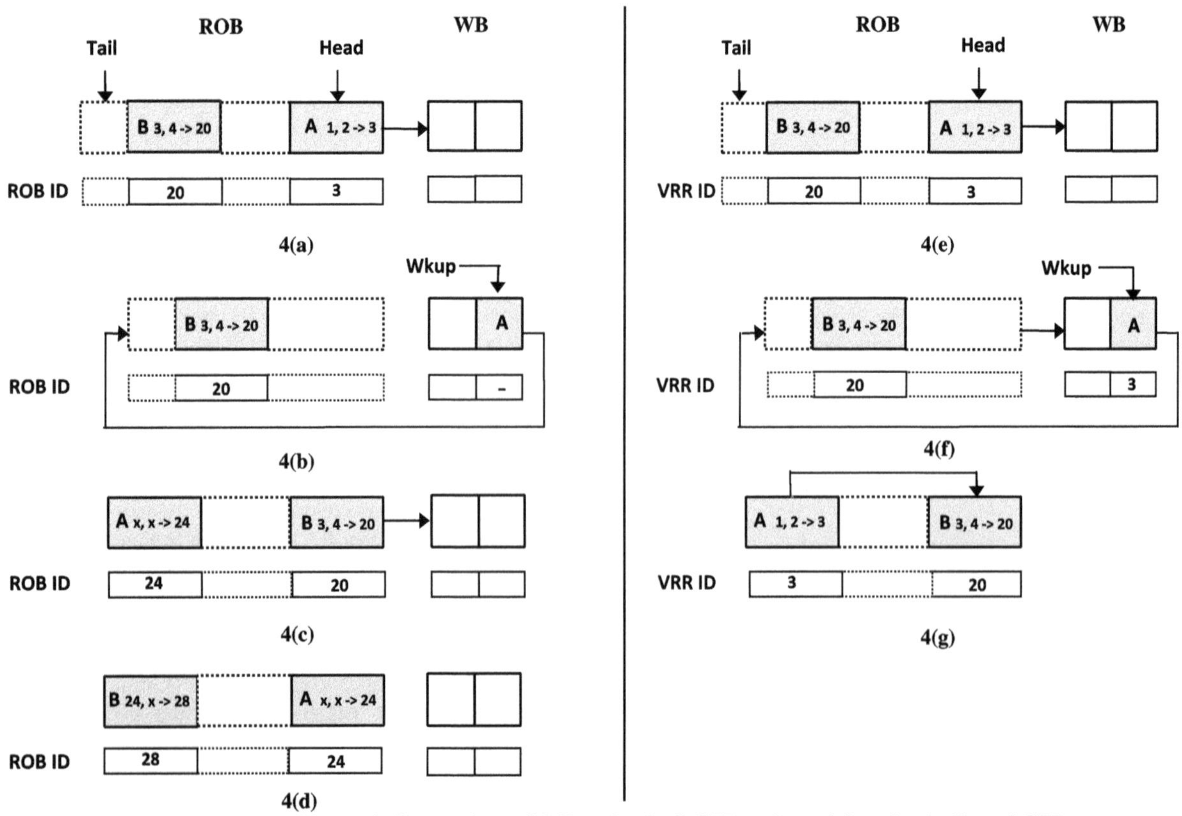

Figure 4. Comparison of full replay in S-CFP and partial replay in Tuned CFP

Figures 2(c) and 2(d) show the ROB and WB states in the Tuned CFP architecture. Instruction *A* misses the first level cache and is marked as poisoned. However, unlike in S-CFP, it does not release its RS entry until it becomes a blocking instruction, just in case the load hits the L2 cache providing the miss data to the CFP core shortly. *A* may reach the head of the ROB before the L2 data cache loads the data, but it will still be kept in the RS and ROB by stalling pseudo-retirement as long as there are free entries in the ROB and other instruction buffers for the pipeline to continue execution of other instructions without blocking. If the miss data arrives before the pipeline blocks, *A* is woken up from the RS and ROB by clearing its poison bits, as shown in Figure 2(d). *A* and its dependents do not require to go through the replay loop at all in this example, saving significant time delay and energy.

Figures 3(d) and 3(e) show how the rollback situation is avoided in the Tuned CFP architecture. Similar to the previous example, instruction *A* stays in the ROB, even if it reaches the head, as long as it is not blocking execution. *A* gets its wakeup before it moves into the WB, as shown in Figure 3(e). Even though *F* is a miss dependent and mispredicted branch, it executes before it pseudo-retires. When it reaches the head of the ROB, the ROB flushes the pipeline to clear all the wrong path instructions that have been fetched after the branch, and signals to the fetch unit to restart fetch and execution from the corrected target. The costly S-CFP branch recovery from the checkpoint has been avoided.

Figures 4(e)-4(g) illustrate a partial replay in the Tuned CFP architecture, representing the same scenario discussed earlier in Figure 4(a). In Tuned CFP, virtual register IDs that are not associated with any physical locations are used for register renaming and in the RS wakeup and scheduling logic. The virtual register IDs of instructions *A* and *B* are shown under their ROB entries in addition to the renamed source and destination virtual register IDs. As before, when *A* reaches the head of the ROB, it pseudo-retires and moves into the WB, as shown in Figure 4(e). However, unlike in S-CFP, *A* only releases its RS but still carries its virtual register *ID #3* along with it into the WB, as shown in Figure 4(f). Later on, when it wakes up and replays, *A* still carries with it its original virtual register *ID #3*, still maintaining its link with its dependent instruction *B* intact, allowing *B* to be woken up and scheduled by the RS without having to replay to be renamed again, as shown in Figure 4(g).

Avoiding excessive replays and rollbacks not only saves significant execution time by miss dependents but also considerable power consumption.

3. CFP WITH VIRTUAL REGISTER RENAMING

In this section, we describe the core architecture of CFP with virtual registers renaming (Tuned CFP), its key mechanisms, and its differences from previous continual flow pipeline architectures.

3.1 Tuned CFP Architecture Overview

Figure 5 shows a block diagram of the Tuned CFP core. Tuned CFP uses Tomasulo's algorithm [24] and reservation stations to perform data-driven, out-of-order execution.

Like all other superscalar architectures, Tuned CFP uses a reorder buffer to commit instructions and update architecture register and memory state in program order. However, Tuned CFP does not use the reorder buffer for register renaming. Instead, it performs register renaming using virtual register IDs generated by a special

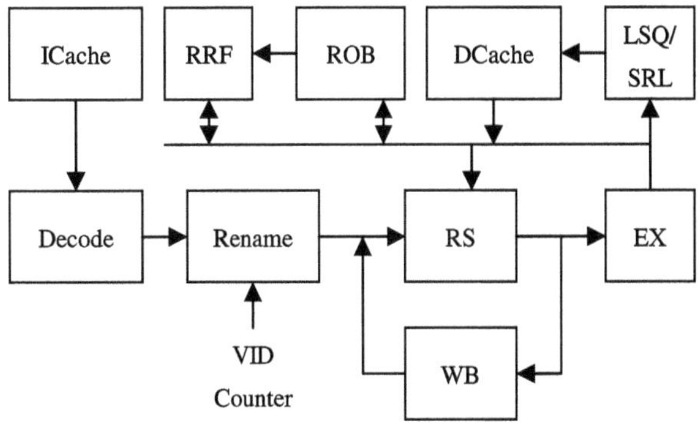

Figure 5. Tuned CFP block diagram

counter. These virtual register IDs are not mapped to any fixed storage locations in the core, and therefore can be large in number and allocated to instructions throughout their life time, including miss dependent instructions evicted to the waiting buffers. Since the virtual register IDs are plentiful and are not associated with actual physical storage, Tuned CFP does not run the risk of execution pipeline buffer-full stalls resulting from miss dependent instructions holding on to their renamed registers for a long time while waiting for the long latency load miss.

The virtual register ID counter is finite in size and cannot be allowed to overflow for correctness reason. Tuned CFP architecture opportunistically resets the virtual register ID counter whenever it can, e.g. when the pipeline is flushed to recover from a mispredicted branch. Otherwise, a pipeline stall and drain is forced to reset the counter when it overflows. With 10-bit virtual ID counter, our simulations show that the impact on performance of forced pipeline stalls to reset the counter is negligible.

Virtual register renaming gives Tuned CFP a significant advantage over previous CFP architectures. Past CFP architectures require all miss dependent instructions to be replayed and renamed again to re-establish dependence links, which is necessary for the reservation stations to re-dispatch the miss dependent instructions in correct data flow order. In contrast, since the virtual register renaming IDs are permanent from the time the miss dependent instructions are renamed until they execute and commit, Tuned CFP can do partial replay of dependent instructions. What this means is that if the load miss data is fetched from memory after the load is moved to the waiting buffer but before its dependents have been moved, Tuned CFP replays only the load. This saves significant execution time that would be spent if all the miss dependent instructions in the reservation stations had to be replayed through the waiting buffer to be renamed again.

3.1.1 Miss Independent Execution

Like previous CFP cores, The Tuned CFP core is capable of executing cache miss dependent and independent instructions concurrently in the pipeline, supported by two retirement register file contexts (RRF), one for retiring miss independent instructions and the other for retiring miss dependent instructions.

In Tuned CFP, execution initially starts using a retirement register file context (RRF) that we call the independent retirement register file. When an L1 data cache load miss occurs, a poison bit is set in the destination reorder buffer entry of the load. Load dependent instructions in the reservation stations (RS) capture the poison bit from the common write back data bus. They are then woken up, as if the load completed, and are scheduled by the reservation stations control logic for pseudo-execution. Pseudo-execution of poisoned instructions does not actually use any execution units. However, pseudo-execution consumes RS dispatch ports and writeback bus cycles to propagate poison bits through instruction dependences and to identify all instructions in the reservation stations that depend on the load miss data. After pseudo-execution, miss dependent instructions stay in their reservation stations until they are waken up for real execution when the load miss data arrives, or until they are moved into the waiting buffer in case their resources are needed to unblock the execution pipeline and execute miss independent instructions.

3.1.2 Replay Loop and Miss Dependent Execution

Figure 5 shows the reduced replay loop in Tuned CFP consisting of two stages: the reservation stations (RS) and the waiting buffer (WB). The waiting buffer basically acts as a second level storage for the reservation stations. With virtual register renaming, entries can be freely evicted from the RS to the WB and then loaded back again to the RS to be scheduled for execution at a later time.

In Tuned CFP, miss dependent instructions are evicted from the reservation stations to the waiting buffer only when their buffer resources are needed to unblock the execution pipeline. Therefore, when a miss is processed and its data fetched to the L1 data cache, the miss dependent instructions may still be in the reservation stations. In this case, when the data is written back, the miss data is captured by all the reservation stations that have instructions that depend on the miss. The captured writeback data sets the source operand "ready" state bits and clears the poison bits of the dependent reservation station entries, making the instructions in these entries ready for scheduling and dispatch to execution.

Evicting miss dependent instructions to the WB on resource need basis significantly reduces the number of replayed instructions, especially in the case of medium latency load misses, which are those that miss the L1 data cache but hit the on-chip L2 cache.

In case of a load miss to DRAM, it is often the case that the long miss latency causes the instruction buffers to fill up and some or all of the in-flight miss dependent instructions to evict to the waiting buffer. When the load miss is serviced, the miss load and its dependents are re-inserted from the waiting buffer back to the reservation stations, from which they are scheduled for execution.

Notice that even though replayed miss dependent instructions do not need to be renamed again, they sometimes, as in Tomasulo's algorithm, need to read source operands that have already been computed and retired from the ROB to the register file (RRF). State bits that track whether the last instructions to write logical registers have been retired are stored in a special storage structure. These state bits are checked during replay to determine if the operands are ready in the RRF, and to read them and move them into the RS with the replayed instructions.

3.1.3 Tuned CFP Reservation Stations

Tuned CFP uses a centralized array of conventional data-capture reservation stations [19]. Each reservation station entry is extended with a poison bit per source operand and L1-DCache-miss bit. The L1-DCache-miss bit is set to 1 if the entry contains a load instruction that has missed the L1 data cache. We say an instruction is poisoned if one of its source poison bits or the L1-DCache-bit is set to 1. A source operand of an instruction is poisoned if and only if it is the destination of another poisoned instruction. In other words, the poison bits propagate the dependences from L1 data cache misses to later instructions in the program to identify instructions that may encounter long data cache miss delays. These instructions are candidates to move to the waiting buffer to avoid pipeline stalls that could occur if any of the reservation stations, reorder buffer load queue or store queue arrays becomes full.

The reservation stations array is augmented with a free list and an order list. Tuned CFP uses the free list to track the occupancy of the reservation stations. The order list tracks the allocation order of the reservation stations, which matches the program order of the instructions, since reservation stations are allocated in the rename pipeline stage. The RS order list could be implemented as part of the reorder buffer by adding the reservation station ID of each instruction to its allocated reorder buffer entry. It also could be implemented as a special array separate from the ROB.

Four conditions are checked to determine if an instruction should be moved to the waiting buffer: 1) the instruction is at the head of the RS order list, 2) the instruction is poisoned, 3) one of the RS, reorder buffer, load queue or store queue arrays is full, and 4) every source operand of the instruction is either poisoned or ready. The last condition ensures that the miss dependent instructions carry their non-poisoned input values with them when they are replayed, since there is no guarantee that these values would not be overwritten in the register file by replay time.

In addition, each reservation station has a state bit that indicates if the instruction in the entry has been replayed once before, i.e. it has been moved earlier in time to the waiting buffer and then back to the RS array. Each reservation station also contains a load miss identifier, in case it has a load instruction that misses the data cache. An implementation could use for this purpose the ID of the L1 data cache fill buffer used to handle the load miss.

3.1.4 Waiting Buffer

The waiting buffer is a wide single ported SRAM array managed as a circular buffer using head and tail pointers. Miss dependent RS entries at the head of the RS array moves to the tail of the waiting buffer when any of the instruction buffers fills up due to data cache misses. When a data cache miss is completed, Tuned CFP replays the miss dependent entries by loading them back from the head of the waiting buffer to the tail of the RS. Ideally, the width of the two buses connecting the RS and the waiting buffer would match the pipeline width. Narrower interconnect can also be used, trading some performance for simpler hardware.

A key to the efficiency of Tuned CFP large window design is the fact that the waiting buffer has no CAM ports, connections to write back buses for capturing data operands or conventional ready/schedule logic. All these functions are handled in the RS array after the data cache miss completes and the miss dependent instructions are replayed. Therefore, the waiting buffer array can be designed using non-tagged SRAM and made significantly larger than the RS array at much lower area and power cost than if the RS array is large enough to hold the full instruction window.

In order to wake up miss dependents from the waiting buffer and replay them, the L1 data cache fill buffer handling a load miss has to receive and save the waiting buffer ID of its load miss. When the miss is completed, Tuned CFP replays the load miss and its dependents in program order, as described earlier, from the head of the waiting buffer back into the RS allocate/write stage of the execution pipeline. These replayed instructions do not need to be renamed again. Their virtual register renames are still valid, thus can be used by the RS to schedule these instructions and to grab their results from the writeback bus into the reservation stations of any dependent instructions, including any instructions that have not been replayed but still waiting in the RS.

3.1.5 Register File and Results Integration

Tuned CFP uses the reorder buffer to recover from miss independent branch mispredictions and to handle exceptions incurred by miss independent instructions. On the other hand, it uses checkpoints to handle branch mispredictions or exceptions encountered by miss dependent instructions.

Like prior CFP proposals [15], Tuned CFP has a specialized register file for checkpointing register state at the load miss, for later use to handle miss dependent branch mispredictions and exceptions. The register file also has special logic for integrating the results of independent and dependent instructions and to restore precise register state after all miss dependent instructions execute.

Figure 6 shows Tuned CFP retirement register file cell with checkpoint flash copy support. Tuned CFP uses a flash copy of the RRF for creating checkpoints. In one cycle every independent RRF state bit (leftmost latch) is shifted into a checkpoint latch within the register cell (center latch). The register file can be restored from the checkpoint in one cycle by asserting RSTR_CLK.

In addition to the checkpoint bit and the independent RRF context bit, Tuned CFP register file cell contains one context bit for the dependent RRF state (rightmost latch). The independent and dependent instruction results integration is a special restore cycle. At the end of dependent execution and when all instructions in the WB have replayed and retired, the RRF has all the live-out registers, some computed by the independent instructions and some computed by the dependent instructions, as determined by the poison bits in the RRF. To integrate these results back into one context, a restore cycle is performed from the dependent context into the independent context. However, not all registers are copied. Figure 6 shows that only poisoned registers are copied by using the poison bits to enable the clock of the copy operation. A 2-to-1 multiplexer in the cell restores either the checkpoint bit or the dependent bit during a RSTR_CLK cycle.

3.1.6 Load and Store Execution in Tuned CFP

To maintain proper memory ordering of loads and stores from the independent and dependent instructions execution, Tuned CFP, like previous CFP proposals, uses load and store queues (LSQ), a Store Redo Log (SRL) [10] and a store-set memory dependence predictor [5]. All stores, dependent and independent, are allocated entries (and IDs) in the SRL in program order at the rename stage of the pipeline. Every load, dependent or independent, carries the SRL ID of the last prior store. The SRL IDs assigned to loads and stores are unique and determine the order of memory instructions.

Tuned CFP performs load-store memory dependence prediction in the front end of the pipeline with a store-set predictor [5] to determine the store on which a load may depend. The predictor uses SRL IDs in the prediction and writes store poison bits in the SRL, thus allowing propagation of poison bits from stores to predicted-dependent loads.

In order to support concurrent, speculative execution of dependent and independent loads and stores, Tuned CFP L1 data

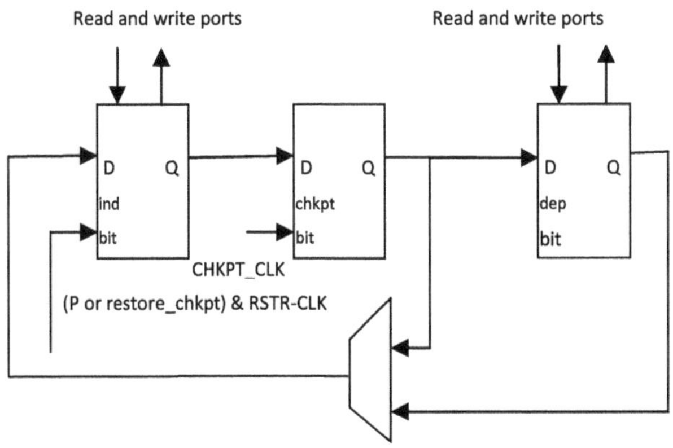

Figure 6. RRF cell with checkpoint and result integration

cache has two new states: Speculative Independent (Spec_Ind) and Speculative Dependent (Spec_Dep). A block that is not in one of these two states is considered to be committed and would be in one of the states defined by the cache coherence protocol, e.g. Shared, Exclusive, or Modified in a MESI coherence protocol.

A detailed description of Tuned CFP Store Redo Log and the speculative L1 data cache is outside the scope of this work but has been described in great detail in previous CFP work [10][15].

4. EVALUATION METHODOLOGY

We built our Tuned CFP architecture model on the Simplescalar ARM ISA simulation infrastructure (www.simplescalar.com) and used all 14 "C" benchmarks from SPEC 2000 and Spec 2006 that we succeeded in compiling using the Simplescalar cross compiler tool. After skipping the initialization code, we simulated 200 million instructions from each benchmark, consisting of four different samples carefully selected from representative execution phases. The selected execution phases display wide variation in the cache miss rate as well as the branch misprediction rate, both of which significantly impact CFP execution behavior. Results in section 5 below show the average performance of these selected samples for each benchmark.

Table 1 shows the simulated machine configurations. We used two-level cache hierarchy of sizes typical of current multicore processors, scaled down proportionally to the number of hardware threads, since we simulate single-thread Tuned CFP core.

Table 1. Simulated machine configurations

Pipeline and buffers	**Baseline core**: 16 stage, 4-wide, 128-entry ROB, 64-entry RS, 64-entry LQ, 48-entry SQ **S-CFP/Tuned CFP core**: 16 stage, 4-wide, 128-entry ROB, 64-entry RS, 64-entry LQ, 48-entry SQ, 256 entry WB, 256 entry SRL
L1 DCache	8KB , 2-way, 3 cycles 64-byte line
L1 ICache	8KB , 2-way, 3 cycles 64-byte line
L2 cache	Unified, 512 KB, 8-way, 16 cycles, 64-byte line
DRAM latency	150 cycles L2 to data return (assuming on-chip Memory Controller)
Branch predictor	Combined bimodal and gshare, 4K Meta, 4K bimodal, 4K gshare, 4K BTB, 16 entry Return Address Stack

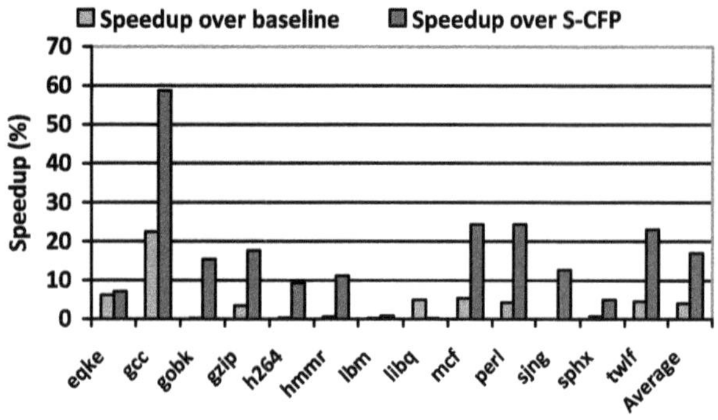

Figure 7. Tuned CFP speedup over baseline and S-CFP

Table 2. Tuned CFP execution statistics

Benchmark	L1 Data cache misses per 1000 instructions	% Speed-up over baseline	% Replayed instructions	Dep. br Mispreds per 1000 instructions
Gcc	31	22.4	3.3	0.38
Sjng	18	~0.0	1.3	0.35
twlf	18	4.5	5.1	0.67
gobk	21	~0.0	2.7	0.28
gzip	13	3.4	1.1	0.46
h264	7	~0.0	0.5	0.1
perl	14	4.2	0.7	0.01
hmmr	6	0.6	0.2	~0.0
eqke	8	6.1	0.6	0.08
sphx	3	0.7	0.1	~0.0
mcf	20	5.3	5.1	0.67
lbm	1	~0.0	~0.0	~0.0
libq	1	5.0	~0.0	~0.0
milc	~0	~0.0	~0.0	~0.0

5. SIMULATION RESULTS

We present in this section two key results. We first compare Tuned CFP instruction/cycle rate (IPC) to S-CFP and the baseline cores. Second, we use a power model of our architecture and evaluate and compare the energy consumption of Tuned CFP to the baseline superscalar core as well as to S-CFP.

5.1 Tuned CFP Performance

In all our simulations, we have used the following branch prediction optimization. In order to limit the risk of a large runahead window of wrong path instructions, it is better to stall the processor when a branch that is likely to mispredict is moved into the waiting buffer. In multiple benchmarks, there is strong correlation between a dependent mispredicted branch and its PC address. A small hardware predictor of 64 entries containing the PC addresses of previous dependent mispredicted branches improves performance by an average of 5% and reduces power by an average of 4%, when used as a branch confidence predictor to stall the pipeline when there is a risk of costly miss dependent branch mispredictions.

Table 2 and Table 3 show various relevant execution statistics of S-CFP and Tuned CFP. Figure 7 shows the speedup of Tuned CFP over S-CFP and over a similar sized conventional superscalar core, when CFP is applied to L1 data cache misses.

First to note, Tuned CFP benefits performance only on benchmarks that frequently miss the cache, as to be expected (see Table 2). Second, Tuned CFP, with the help of significantly reduced replay and rollback (Table 3), outperforms S-CFP by an average of 15%. Tuned CFP, with its latency tolerance to first level cache misses also outperforms the baseline by an average of 4%. Even though the average speedup of all benchmarks over the baseline is modest, Tuned CFP shows considerable performance improvement on benchmarks that frequently miss the data cache, e.g. equake and gcc. Earlier CFP work has similarly shown modest performance improvement on applications like Spec 2006 that do not frequently miss the cache, but significant performance benefit on applications with high cache miss rates, like server and workstations applications [23].

Table 3. S-CFP and Tuned CFP replay, rollback and wrong path statistics

Bench -mark	S-CFP % Replay	Tuned CFP % Replay	S-CFP % Roll back	Tuned CFP % Roll Back	S-CFP % Wrong path insns	Tuned CFP % Wrong path insns
Gcc	30.1	3.3	14.2	1.2	53.8	23.9
Sjng	9.9	1.3	6.7	0.5	64.1	46.7
twlf	15.9	5.1	10.6	4.7	60.4	43.9
gobk	12.9	2.7	12.3	2.3	62.5	43.6
gzip	7.3	1.1	9.4	0.7	52.3	32.4
h264	8.8	0.5	2.0	0.1	19.8	13.2
perl	22.9	0.7	6.6	~0.0	18.0	5.2
hmmr	7.7	0.2	0.1	~0.0	0.8	0.6
eqke	3.8	0.6	1.8	0.7	23.0	20.8
sphx	3.8	0.1	1.5	~0.0	13.4	10.6
mcf	16.1	5.1	11.0	4.7	61.5	44.6
lbm	1.3	~0.0	~0.0	~0.0	0.1	0.1
libq	~0.0	~0.0	~0.0	~0.0	~0.0	~0.0
milc	~0.0	~0.0	~0.0	~0.0	3.8	3.8

Notice that we do not see any performance benefit to S-CFP over a baseline superscalar of equal buffer sizes and caches. This is different from performance gains reported in [15]. Our benchmarks and the samples selected from them are different from those used in [15] and have significantly higher miss dependent mispredicted branches, which exacerbate the excessive rollback drawback of S-CFP, exposing its glass jaw.

Table 3 shows replayed, rollback and wrong path instructions as percentage of total retired instructions for both S-CFP and Tuned

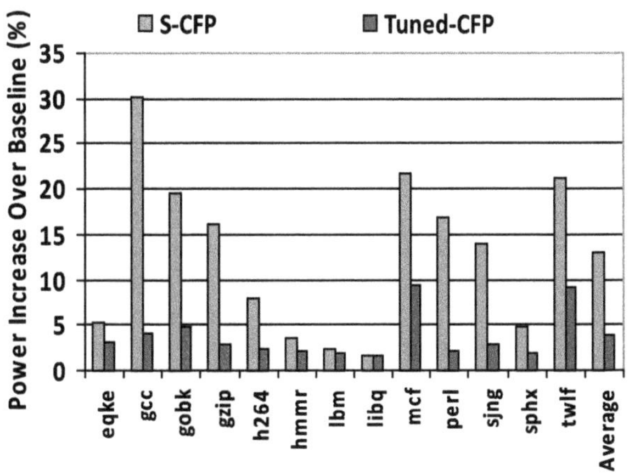

Figure 8. Power increase of S-CFP and Tuned CFP over baseline

CFP. The effectiveness of Tuned CFP optimizations in reducing the excessive replay, rollback and speculative execution is evident and accounts for the significant performance (Figure 7) and power advantage of Tuned CFP over S-CFP. We next quantify Tuned CFP power advantage by presenting results from an architectural level power model of CFP.

5.2. Tuned CFP Power Model and Analysis

We have obtained energy measurements from SPICE circuit simulations, using Cadence tools and 90nm process technology, for all baseline superscalar and CFP core functional blocks. We combined these with logic switching activity measurements from our Simplescalar simulator, creating an Architectural Level Power Simulator (ALPS) [3]. Figure 8 shows the total power consumption increase of S-CFP and Tuned CFP over the baseline for each of our simulated benchmarks. Table 4 shows average power consumption over all our simulated benchmarks of various functional blocks as well as the total baseline, S-CFP and Tuned CFP cores. All the numbers in the table are shown relative to the total power of the baseline core.

The power model accounts for the additional CFP structures, including the SRL, SDB, two thread contexts, checkpoint and result integration support in the RRF. We used 6-transistor SRAM cell design with differential sense amplifiers for the SRL and WB circuits and a single-sided register file cell, augmented with checkpoint and results integration circuit. Accounting for average activity counts and assuming 2GHz clock frequency, the power we measured was 210mW for the SRL, 400mW for the WB, and 1.2W for the CFP RRF.

Tuned CFP shows a reduction of ~9% in power consumption compared to S-CFP due to significant reduction in replay execution, rollback and wrong path instructions. Moreover, Tuned CFP consumes only about 3.9% additional power in return for 4% speedup over the baseline core. This shows that Tuned CFP is a power efficient way to get single thread performance. This and CFP ability to tolerate the increased cache miss rates as more cores are integrated on the same die make our Tuned CFP design a suitable core architecture for future multi-core processors.

Table 4. S-CFP and Tuned CFP power consumption relative to baseline averaged over all benchmarks

Block	Baseline	S-CFP	Tuned CFP
L1 ICache	7.3%	7.6%	7.3%
Decode	15.7%	16.8%	15.9%
RAT	12.8%	13.8%	13.0%
RS	14.3%	16.4%	14.6%
EUs	11.4%	12.2%	11.5%
ROB/RRF	17.0%	20.5%	17.4%
LSQ	14.2%	15.3%	14.5%
L1 DCache	7.3%	7.6%	7.3%
SRL/WB	0%	2.4%	2.4%
Total	100%	112.6%	103.9%

6. RELATED WORK

Proposals for latency tolerant out-of-order cores include the Waiting Instruction Buffer [16], Virtual ROB [8], Cherry [17], Checkpoint Processing and Recovery [1], Continual Flow Pipelines [15][23] and Out of Order Commit Processors [7]. None of these however deal with L1 data cache misses or execute miss dependent and independent instructions simultaneously.

Runahead execution increases memory level parallelism on in-order cores [9] and on out-of-order cores [18] without having to build large reorder buffers. In runahead execution, the processor state is checkpointed at a load miss to DRAM. Execution continues speculatively past the miss for data prefetch benefits. When the miss data returns the execution pipeline is flushed, and execution rolls back to the checkpoint. Except for the prefetch benefit, all work performed during runahead is discarded. SS-CFP executes ahead of L1 data cache misses and does not waste energy by discarding large number of instructions.

Flea-Flicker [2] executes a program on two in-order back-end pipelines coupled by a queue. Flea-flicker executes miss independent instructions in an in-order pipeline, saving all results in a queue. It executes miss dependent instructions in a backup pipeline, merging the results sequentially with the independent results. Flea-flicker and SS-CFP differ in their execution methods, result integration methods and their instruction deferral queues.

The Decoupled Kilo-Instruction Processor [20] executes miss independent instructions on a cache processor and miss dependent instructions on a memory processor. It uses counters in an aging-ROB to identify instructions that depend on a miss. We do not use counting but achieve similar effect to aging by keeping instructions in the RS as long as the pipeline is not blocked.

iCFP [12] tolerates cache misses at all levels in the cache hierarchy, but uses an in-order pipeline, which is less suitable for the performance needs of conventional single-thread applications.

BOLT [13] utilizes additional map tables in Simultaneous Multithreading architecture to re-rename L2 miss dependent slice, combined with a program order slice and a unified physical register file that supports aggressive register reclamation. BOLT reuse of SMT hardware is for improving energy-efficiency, but it does not use virtual register renaming or a streamlined replay loop to improve energy efficiency.

Sun Microsystems Rock is a single die multicore processor for high throughput computing. Rock uses Simultaneous Speculative Threading [4] to defer dependent instructions into a buffer, and executes the deferred instructions from the checkpoint after the miss data returns. The deferred instructions execution uses a simultaneous hardware thread and merges the results into the scout thread future file. Rock uses an in-order pipeline, while Tuned CFP core is out-of-order and thus provides better performance than Rock on single-thread applications.

Gonzalez et al. [11] proposed using virtual registers to shorten the lifetime of physical registers. Kilo instruction processors [6] also used virtual renaming and ephemeral registers to do late allocation of physical registers. In contrast to virtual-physical registers and ephemeral registers, Virtual Register Renaming (VRR) [21] does not require physical registers for any allocation of execution results to physical registers. Our Tuned CFP architecture uses a renaming method similar to VRR.

7. CONCLUSION

This paper presents a Tuned Continual Flow Pipeline architecture that uses virtual register renaming and optimized replay policies to improve performance and reduce replay loop circuit activity and checkpoint rollback execution compared to previous CFP designs. It achieves this by reducing the replay latency associated with the processing of miss dependent instructions after the miss data arrives into the L1 data cache and wakes up the miss load. The architecture achieves this reduction in the miss dependent instructions execution latency by 1) keeping these instructions as long as possible in the reservation stations and moving them to the waiting buffer only when instruction buffer resources are needed and 2) using virtual register renaming which allows partial replay of the miss dependent chain of instructions, requiring only the subset of these instructions that have already moved to the waiting buffer to be replayed. Our Tuned CFP architecture improves performance and power consumption over previous CFP architectures by ~15% and ~9%, respectively.

8. ACKNOWLEDGMENT

This research was supported by a grant from Intel Corporation.

REFERENCES

[1] H. Akkary, R. Rajwar, and S. Srinivasan, "Checkpoint processing and recovery: towards scalable large instruction window processors," in Proc. of MICRO-36, Dec 2003.

[2] R. Barnes, E. Nystrom, J. Sios, S. Patel, N. Navarro, and W. W. Hwu, "Beating in-order stalls with flea flicker two-pass pipelining," in Proc. of MICRO-36, Dec 2003.

[3] D. Brooks, V. Tiwari, and M. Martonosi. "Wattch: a Framework for Architectural-Level Power Analysis and Optimizations," in Proc. of ISCA-27, June 2000.

[4] S. Chaudhry, R. Cypher, M. Ekman, M. Karlsson, A. Landin, S. Yip, H. Zeffer, and M. Tremblay, "Simultaneous speculative threading: a novel pipeline architecture implemented in Sun's Rock processor," in Proceedings of ISCA-36, June 2009.

[5] G. Z. Chrysos and J. Emer, "Memory dependence prediction using store sets," in Proceedings of ISCA-25, June 1998.

[6] A. Cristal, O. Santana, M. Valero and J. Martinez, "Toward kilo-instruction processors," in ACM Transactions on Architecture and Code Optimization, vol. 1, issue 4, pp 389-417, Dec 2004.

[7] A. Cristal, D. Ortega, J. Llosa, and M. Valero, "Out-of-order commit processors," in Proceedings of HPCA-10, Feb 2004.

[8] A. Cristal, M. Valero, J. Llosa, and A. Gonzalez, "Large virtual ROBs by processor checkpointing," Tech. Report, UPC-DAC-2002-39, Department of Computer Science, Barcelona, Spain, July 2002.

[9] J. Dundas and T. Mudge, "Improving data cache performance by pre-executing instructions under a cache miss," in Proc. of the International Conference on Supercomputing, June 1997.

[10] A. Gandhi, H. Akkary, R. Rajwar, S. T. Srinivasan and K. Lai, "Scalable load and store processing in latency tolerant processors," in Proceedings of ISCA-32, June 2005.

[11] A. Gonzalez, M. Valero, J. Gonzalez, and T. Monreal, "Virtual registers," in Proceedings of HPCA-3, Feb 1997.

[12] A. Hilton, S. Nagarakatte, and A. Roth, "Tolerating all-level cache misses in in-order processors," in Proceedings of HPCA-15, Feb 2009.

[13] A. Hilton and A. Roth, "BOLT: energy-efficient out-of-order latency-tolerant execution," in Proc. of HPCA-16, Feb 2010.

[14] W. W. Hwu and Y. N. Patt, "Checkpoint repair for out-of-order execution machines," in Proc. of ISCA-14, June 1987.

[15] K. Jothi, H. Akkary and M. Sharafeddine, "Simultaneous continual flow pipeline architecture," in Proceedings of ICCD-29, Oct 2011.

[16] R. Lebeck, J. Koppanalil, T. Li, J. Patwardhan, and E. Rotenberg, "A large, fast instruction window for tolerating cache misses, "Proceedings of ISCA-29, May 2002.

[17] J. F. Martinez, J. Renau, M. C. Huang, and J. Torrellas, "Cherry: checkpointed early resource recycling in out-of-order microprocessors," in Proc. of MICRO-35, Nov 2002.

[18] O. Mutlu, J. Stark, C. Wilkerson, and Y. N. Patt, "Runahead execution: an alternative to very large instruction windows for out-of-order processors," in Proc. of HPCA-9, Feb. 2003.

[19] D. Papworth, "Tuning the Pentium Pro microarchitecture," in IEEE MICRO, vol. 16, no. 2, April 1996.

[20] M. Pericas, A. Cristal, R. Gonzalez, D. A. Jimenez and M. Valero, "A decoupled kilo-instruction processor," in Proc. of HPCA-12, Feb 2006.

[21] M. Sharafeddine, H. Akkary and D. Carmean, "Virtual register renaming," in Proceedings of the 26th International Conference on Computing Systems, Feb 2013.

[22] J. Smith and G. Sohi, "The microarchitecture of superscalar processors," in Proc. of the IEEE, vol. 83, no. 12, Dec 1995.

[23] S. Srinivasan, R. Rajwar, H. Akkary, A. Gandhi and M. Upton, "Continual flow pipelines," in Proc. of ASPLOS-11, Oct 2004.

[24] R. M. M. Tomasulo, "An efficient algorithm for exploiting multiple arithmetic Units,'' IBM Journal of Research and Development, vol. 11, pp. 25-33, Jan 1967.

[25] D. Tullsen, S. Eggers, and H. M. Levy, "Simultaneous multithreading: maximizing on-chip parallelism," in Proceedings of ISCA-22, June 1995.

Towards More Efficient Execution: A Decoupled Access-Execute Approach

Konstantinos Koukos, David Black-Schaffer, Vasileios Spiliopoulos, Stefanos Kaxiras
Department of Information Technology, Uppsala University
Lägerhyddsvägen 2, 752 37, Uppsala, Sweden
konstantinos.koukos@it.uu.se, david.black-schaffer@it.uu.se,
vasileios.spiliopoulos@it.uu.se, stefanos.kaxiras@it.uu.se

ABSTRACT

The end of Dennard scaling is expected to shrink the range of DVFS in future nodes, limiting the energy savings of this technique. This paper evaluates how much we can increase the effectiveness of DVFS by using a software decoupled *access-execute* approach. *Decoupling* the data *access* from *execution* allows us to apply optimal voltage-frequency selection for each phase and therefore improve energy efficiency over standard *coupled* execution.

The underlying insight of our work is that by decoupling access and execute we can take advantage of the memory-bound nature of the access phase and the compute-bound nature of the execute phase to optimize power efficiency, while maintaining good performance. To demonstrate this we built a task based parallel execution infrastructure consisting of: (1) a runtime system to orchestrate the execution, (2) power models to predict optimal voltage-frequency selection at runtime, (3) a modeling infrastructure based on hardware measurements to simulate zero-latency, per-core DVFS, and (4) a hardware measurement infrastructure to verify our model's accuracy.

Based on real hardware measurements we project that the combination of decoupled access-execute and DVFS has the potential to improve EDP by 25% without hurting performance. On memory-bound applications we significantly improve performance due to increased MLP in the access phase and ILP in the execute phase. Furthermore we demonstrate that our method can achieve high performance both in presence or absence of a hardware prefetcher.

Categories and Subject Descriptors

C.0 [**Computer Systems Organization**]: System architectures

Keywords

Task-Based Execution, Decoupled Execution, Performance, Energy, DVFS

ICS'13, June 10–14, 2013, Eugene, Oregon, USA.

1. INTRODUCTION

Power efficiency has become one of the most important design parameters for hardware, due to limited battery runtime on mobile devices and energy cost on data-center servers and supercomputers. Dennard scaling [2], however, can no longer provide us with constant power density per device, due to the exponential increase of leakage power at lower voltages. As a result, the effective voltage range available for dynamic voltage frequency scaling (DVFS) is expected to shrink in future technology nodes [8]. This undermines DVFS, which has been one of our most powerful techniques to reduce power consumption, due to its quadratic energy savings for at most linear performance degradation. Since the effectiveness of DVFS is threatened by the inability to significantly scale voltage, we must shift our attention to the non-linear relationship between frequency scaling and performance[1] in order to improve DVFS efficiency.

DVFS techniques try to exploit this non-linear relationship in memory-bound programs to reduce power consumption without affecting their performance [10]. This is possible because such programs spend much of their time waiting for memory, and are therefore insensitive to frequency changes. In such cases we can expect an improvement in power-efficiency metrics such as EDP or ED^2P from reducing the frequency. However this is only feasible for programs which are predominantly memory-bound. In most programs, although there are considerable opportunities to scale frequency while waiting for memory, we are unable to benefit from DVFS because memory operations are interspersed with *(or tightly-coupled to)* arithmetic computation, whose performance is tied to frequency.

In such programs, optimal DVFS could be achieved if on a cache miss we could instantly scale down the frequency and instantly scale up after the miss is resolved. Unfortunately, the transition latency for modern CPUs is prohibitive (2000 nsec for the hardware alone), which makes it impossible to apply DVFS at an instruction granularity. The common approach today is to apply a global frequency based on the overall application behavior, which is far from the optimal in many cases. A better approach would be to apply

[1] $Power \propto ACfV^2$ where C is the load capacitance, V is the supply voltage, A is the activity factor and f is the operating frequency. AC is referred as effective capacitance C_{eff}. The relationship between frequency (f) and performance highly depends on the application memory behavior and can range from highly correlated (computation-bound) to uncorrelated (memory-bound). This also creates a non-linear relationship between power consumption and performance.

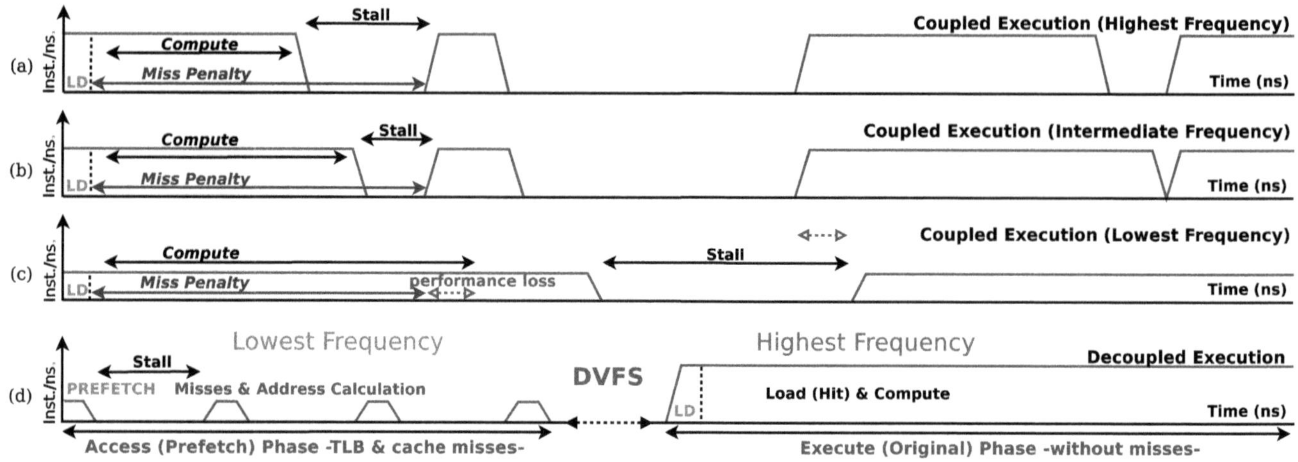

Figure 1: Example of coupled execution under different core frequencies (a,b and c) and decoupled execution (d)

DVFS at a finer granularity than the whole program but coarser than that of a few instructions. If program execution can be divided into distinct phases with homogeneous memory behavior, then the optimal frequency for each phase can be predicted separately [16]. The finer the division, the more effective the DVFS can be (in practice there is a limit due to the DVFS transition latency that adds overhead). Thus in any execution model where memory operations are tightly coupled to arithmetic computations we can only hope to exploit a fraction of the potential DVFS benefit.

To attack this problem, we propose a software *decoupled* access-execute (*DAE*) model [15] in combination with guided DVFS. We execute programs as a series of *tasks*, where each task is split into two fine grain phases: *access* (data prefetching) and *execute* (original computation) where the execute phase is scheduled for immediate execution after the access on the same core. The key idea is that decoupling data access from computation allows us to make different voltage-frequency decisions for each phase (access vs. execute). The access phase prefetches the data, which transforms most cache misses into hits for the execute phase, thereby improving performance of the latter. The access phase spends only a small fraction of its time computing addresses and most of its time waiting for data from memory. As a result it is not affected by core frequency, and we can therefore run it at minimum frequency to save power without hurting performance. In the execute phase most of the cache misses have been eliminated by the prefetching behavior of the access phase. Minimizing stalls on the execute phase makes highest frequency the best fit in terms of EDP.

Figure 1 demonstrates an execution example of coupled (*CAE*) vs decoupled (*DAE*) execution. Diagrams 1a, 1b and 1c show coupled execution under different frequencies, while 1d shows decoupled execution. In any execution model the main source of power inefficiency are the stalls because the processor is spending power waiting for memory. These diagrams show how coupled DVFS methods tries to eliminate stalls and thereby improve power efficiency. Stalls are created when computation cannot hide long miss penalties. Reducing the frequency slows computation down making it overlap more miss penalty and reduce stall length. Figure 1a shows coupled execution at the highest frequency. Although this execution is the fastest available, it is also the least power-efficient due to the energy wasted running the processor at full speed while waiting for DRAM.

DVFS can significantly improve efficiency by scaling down frequency-voltage to save power as shown in Figure 1b. Scaling down frequency will make the execution intervals between stalls longer but because miss penalty overlaps with execution the total execution time remains unaffected until they are fully overlapped. In the case shown in Figure 1c the execution has been unnecessarily slowed down because the execution interval becomes longer than the miss penalty. Additionally, although the stall from the first miss was successfully removed the second miss could not be overlapped by a long computation interval. This demonstrates the inability to choose a global optimal frequency when accesses and execute are interleaved which is common in nearly all applications.

Figure 1d demonstrates decoupled execution to solve this problem. In this case we prefetch data into private caches during the *access* phase and therefore avoid most cache and TLB misses in the *execute* phase due to this prefetching behavior. Decoupling can transform and split an interval of instructions in two phases: one purely memory-bound (access) followed by a purely compute-bound (execute). This allow us to adjust program behavior to DVFS granularity, exploiting more efficiently memory slack by reducing the frequency when waiting for memory and benefit from the future CPU DVFS capabilities.

Obtaining good performance on modern CPUs requires efficiently parallelized, and scalable, code. For this reason our work focuses on parallel workloads. An important question that arises is how to implement a decoupled access-execute model for parallel programs. For this, we turn to task-based programming models, which lead to an elegant solution for implementing DAE. In a task-based programming model, parallelism is expressed through tasks that can be scheduled independently. In our approach a task is defined as a function and because of this, we can easily replicate and transform each task into an access and an execute phase. We do this the simplest way possible: the access phase of a task is the task without any computation or data stores (e.g., just address calculation and loads), while the execute phase is the original unmodified task. Although this leads to redundant execution of all address calculations and memory access instructions, it requires minimal programmer or compiler effort.

The task-based model affords us considerable latitude in exploring decoupled access-execute. By controlling the input data size of the tasks we control the granularity of prefetch and DVFS. Thus, we can amortize the DVFS overhead with how much data we can prefetch into the cache during the access phase. We perform our experiments on state-of-the-art systems using accurate, fine-grain, power measurements taken directly from the processor power rails and project the results as if we had instantaneous per-core DVFS. We are restricted to this approach because state-of-the-art CPUs do not yet feature on chip voltage regulators [11] to enable low-latency, per-core DVFS [12]. Our work shows that decoupling access from execute can improve the effectiveness of DVFS and achieve performance comparable to CAE at max frequency and at the same time maintain optimal EDP.

2. RELATED WORK

The idea of decoupling access from execution was initially proposed by Smith [15] in 1982. In his approach the execution units were unaware of address calculation and were only capable of performing an arithmetic operation on the next available operands. The use of hardware prefetchers in modern architectures to hide memory latencies has a similar effect. Kamruzzaman et. al. [9] presented a technique to parallelize the memory accesses of single-threaded applications, using a decoupled approach with helper threads to speculatively prefetch data. The goal was to reduce execution time compared to the sequential execution with minimal compiler or programmer effort. This approach suffers from reduced efficiency compared to parallel execution because they parallelize only the memory accesses (up to 60% speedup using 4 cores), at the cost of linear power increase when enabling cores (up to 4x power consumption).

Similarly Ibrahim et. al. [6] demonstrate the benefit of a slipstream execution on multiprocessor systems. Keramidas et. al. [10] presented tools and techniques for efficient DVFS on coupled execution while Spiliopoulos et. al. [16] further improve that work and embed it in the Linux kernel, using performance monitoring unit (PMU) based models to detect and scale voltage-frequency on application phases. In our approach, instead of trying to adjust DVFS granularity to program behavior we modify program behavior to DVFS granularity.

3. METHODOLOGY

Our experimental setup consists of (1) the runtime system that handles parallel execution and profiling of workloads using coupled and decoupled execution, (2) applications with manually created access phases, (3) a power model to estimate per task-phase power consumption and simulate low-latency, per-core DVFS, and (4) a hardware infrastructure to verify the accuracy of the model.

As mentioned in Section 1 our method tries to exploit the non-linear relationship between frequency scaling and performance of memory bound applications (or phases). A primary prerequisite of our method is that we can reduce power consumption by reducing the core frequency without compromising the available bandwidth from the main memory (off-core). Thus, we can achieve optimal power savings without any performance degradation in memory-bound phases of the application. Figure 2 shows the aggregate bandwidth delivered from the main memory under different access patterns and CPU frequencies for Intel's state-of-the-art processors with the use of a parallel micro-benchmark we developed. Figure 2a shows that the aggregate bandwidth remains unaffected under different core frequencies, which suggests significant room for EDP improvement for memory bound phases.

The worst performing pattern in Figure 2 is *random*, which uses a random walk with distances mostly larger than a page. In addition to cache misses it also causes TLB misses and irregular accesses to memory pages. This pattern hardly achieves 6 GB/s aggregate bandwidth from all cores which is 85% lower than a *sequential* access pattern that can achieve up to 11 GB/s. The processor though has a peak bandwidth limit of 21 GB/s shared among all 4 cores. This is approached by a linear access micro-benchmark using the *prefetcht0* instruction, which achieves up to 80% of the peak bandwidth. Figure 2b shows the aggregate bandwidth under different number of threads. We observe that bandwidth scales sub-linearly up to 3 threads

3.1 Task parallel runtime system

The runtime system is responsible for the parallel execution, synchronization, scheduling, and load balancing of tasks. For our experiments, the runtime also profiles time and monitors hardware counter events per task using PAPI [13]. In a normal execution the runtime selectively collects statistics using sparse sampling for the IPC and the execution time of each task phase. This information is then used by a power model (discussed in section 3.3) that predicts the optimal execution frequency for each task phase based on previous execution knowledge of the same task. The runtime can then apply the predicted frequency using the *cpufreq utilities* [3] interface. Although the functionality to DVFS each task phase independently is implemented we cannot use it because current processors do not feature per-core DVFS and their DVFS transition latency is too high. We expect that this limitation will be addressed in future processors. Our goal is therefore to predict the benefits of applying DVFS to a decoupled program by using real hardware measurements and model the expected power and performance of per-core, low-latency DVFS.

In our runtime a task is a C/C++ function that can be executed asynchronously by any active core in parallel. Each task can have two phases: execute and (optionally) access, where each one of them is expressed as a different function. The runtime stores the function pointer(s) and the arguments of the function(s) internally and schedules the task for parallel execution. The task is executed as a single unit by the runtime calling the access phase (if available) and immediately after that the execute phase on the same core. The scheduling of the task is a runtime decision that tries to balance load across all cores. We also support manual binding of tasks to cores to enable application defined scheduling policies.

The runtime uses a single (main) thread that issues tasks to multiple queues that other (worker) threads poll. Each active thread has a private and a shared queue to store and schedule task descriptors. Load balancing is enabled by work stealing of tasks through shared queues, while private queues enforce local FIFO execution. The runtime supports two synchronization primitives: *barriers* for global synchro-

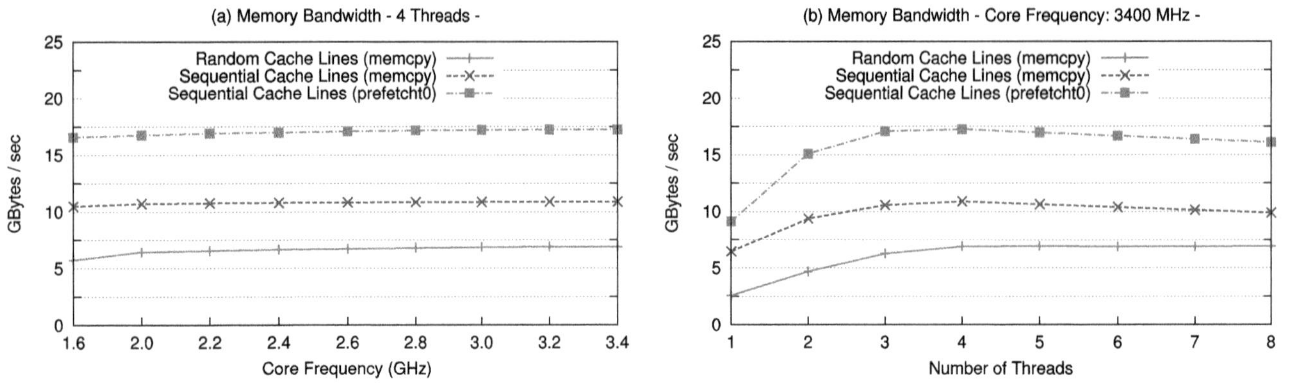

Figure 2: Measured memory bandwidth for Intel Sandybridge using DDR3 at 1333 MHz for: (a) 4 threads at different core frequencies, (b) different number of threads at highest core frequency. We need at least 3 threads to saturate bandwidth.

nization and *point to point* for synchronization across tasks. Synchronization primitives and internal memory allocators use lock free algorithms to reduce overhead. The runtime is designed to have very low execution overheads with total overhead per task of only 400 core cycles on Intel Sandybridge CPU.

3.2 Generating access phase

The access phase serves to prefetch the data for the execute phase into the cache. To create the access phase for a task we remove all stores and arithmetic calculations and keep only the loads and address calculation required for the loads. Eliminating stores guarantees that there will be no side effects from the access phase. To optimize prefetching we replace load instructions with the builtin *prefetcht0* x86 instruction [7] because it does not stall instruction retirement and does not require a destination register. This explains why *prefetcht0* can achieve higher bandwidth over *loads* as shown in Figure 2. The access phase can prefetch both loads and stores into the cache because both are memory accesses. However only loads can stall the pipeline which makes them performance critical. Stores are less likely to create stalls as they are buffered and therefore we don't prefetch them.

In our implementation we have to perform the address calculation once for the access phase and once again for the execute phase. The impact of this is to execute extra instructions compared to the initial coupled execution. In terms of performance, the duplicate address calculation is overlapped with the long latencies of prefetch misses thereby reducing their impact. From an energy perspective increasing the number of instructions executed on the core results in a direct power increase subject to the linear equations shown in Figure 3. In practice the IPC of the access phase is less than 0.5 so it can affect power significantly less than frequency scaling but still remains a source of inefficiency. More sophisticated splitting of tasks to access and execute phases can reduce or even eliminate redundant address calculations and therefore improve our results but it is left for future work.

3.3 Power Model

The fine-granularity of our approach (tasks range from a few microseconds up to a millisecond) and the overlapping of access and execute phases on different cores, prevents

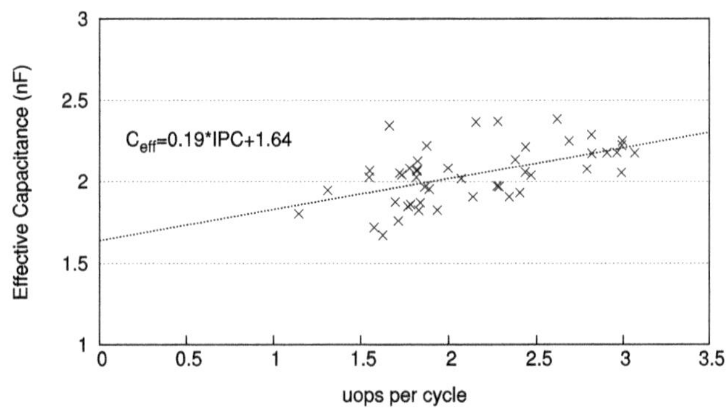

Figure 3: Correlation between effective capacitance and uops executed per cycle for Intel Sandybridge processor. Methodology described in [16]

us from directly measuring per-task power consumption on the hardware. Current power measurement infrastructures (both integrated on-chip power sensors and external measurement hardware) provide sampling periods on the order of milliseconds. Furthermore, current hardware does not provide per-core DVFS, with some machines having all cores under a single clock domain (Intel) and others with multiple clock domains but a single voltage domain (AMD). These hardware restrictions are expected to change with the introduction of on-chip voltage regulators [12] in future generations to support nano-scale DVFS [11].

To overcome these limitations, we employ an IPC-based power model to estimate power consumption. This approach enables us to estimate power consumption of any execution interval, however short in duration. Our model is built by measuring per-core dynamic power, and static power for the whole processor (per-core static plus shared L3 power) using multiple instances of the same workload running independently on different cores. To measure the power consumed by the processor we use the measurement infrastructure described in [17]. We express static power P_{static} as linear function of f, V for each number of active cores. To measure the static power we use a micro-benchmark with an infinite loop and use *nanosleep* system call to run at an IPC close to zero, while this minimum activity prevents the core from entering a deep sleep state.

For the dynamic power (similar to [16]), we assume that effective capacitance C_{eff} correlates linearly with the micro-ops executed per cycle. As shown in Figure 3, we derive a linear approximation to the effective capacitance by measuring the power and IPC across SPEC2006 [4]. Having f, V and C_{eff} (as a function of IPC) we estimate per-core dynamic power using $P_{dynamic} = C_{eff}fV^2$ equation. In a parallel execution the total processor power is the sum of the dynamic per-core power plus the total static power of the processor.

To validate the accuracy of our model we compare the total power estimate against the measured value for each of the SPEC2006 benchmark suit (on all frequencies and number of cores). For the SPEC2006 benchmark suit, the average error is 3.1% while the maximum error is 9.1%[2]. For the applications we use to evaluate DAE, the average and maximum errors for estimating the total energy is 4.5% and 7% respectively. More accurate performance counter-based models, such as those proposed by Spiliopoulos et. al. in [17], could be used to improve accuracy. We have chosen this model as it provides sufficient accuracy and requires just a single performance counter event (for the instructions) which is available in most architectures.

3.4 Putting it all together

The methodology described above for estimating power consumption is necessary for quantifying the energy benefits of our DAE programming model. Using this approach we are able to overcome two key limitations of current hardware, and thereby accurately estimate per task-phase energy. These two limitations are: 1) the inability to measure per task-phase energy consumption due to its fine granularity and the overlapping of different tasks access and execute phases on different cores, and, 2) the inability of current hardware to provide per-core, low-latency DVFS.

State of the art processors feature high overhead for frequency and voltage switching (between 8 and 10 usec[3]), which is prohibitive for applications that require fine-grain tasks. In our workloads the average access-phase duration per task is between 3 and 16 usec as shown in Table 1. Although our runtime is able to DVFS each phase of a decoupled access-execute task as discussed in Section 1, this overhead and the lack for per-core DVFS support prevents us from using this at runtime on current hardware.

To overcome the above restrictions and project our model benefits to future processors we disable per-phase DVFS at runtime and develop a model (Algorithm 1) to simulate zero-overhead, per-core DVFS. For that we execute our workloads both for CAE and DAE at all available frequencies and collect detailed *time* and *IPC* statistics as provided by the runtime. For time statistics we measure T_{access}, $T_{execute}$ per task and the total execution time of the application. For the IPC statistics we measure IPC_{access}, $IPC_{execute}$ respectively. Additionally we measure the number of tasks executed. Providing both *time* and *IPC* to our power model we can estimate per-phase energy for any voltage-frequency combination. Using profiling information for performance and the results of the power model for energy we can accurately estimate the benefit of our technique for future processors with low-latency, per-core DVFS. We also collect coarse grain power measurements and compare the overall power estimate of the model against them to verify its accuracy.

[2]The error shown in Figure 3 refers only to dynamic power. Including static power to estimate total power can improve accuracy since it is deterministic.

Algorithm 1 DAE overall methodology

for all f, V **do**
- Measure average $Time_{access}$ $(AVG(T_A))$
- Measure average $Time_{execute}$ $(AVG(T_X))$
- Measure average IPC_{access} $(AVG(IPC_A))$
- Measure average $IPC_{execute}$ $(AVG(IPC_X))$
- Measure total execution time (T_{total}) and total energy ($E_{measured}$) and verify model accuracy

end for

Naive policy:(Access=f_{min}, Execute=f_{max})

E_A = PowerModel($AVG(IPC_A^{f_{min}})$)*$AVG(T_A^{f_{min}})$

E_X = PowerModel($AVG(IPC_X^{f_{max}})$)*$AVG(T_X^{f_{max}})$

OptEDP policy:

E_A = PowerModel($AVG(IPC_A^{f_{opt}})$)*$AVG(T_A^{f_{opt}})$

E_X = PowerModel($AVG(IPC_X^{f_{opt}})$)*$AVG(T_X^{f_{opt}})$

The goal of the decoupled access-execute model is to provide optimal EDP efficiency through DVFS with minimal performance degradation. For that we implement two DVFS policies: (1) *naive*, where the access phase always runs at the lowest frequency and the execute phase always runs at the highest frequency, and (2) *optEDP* in which the runtime intelligently adjusts the frequency of each phase based on IPC and power model to obtain the best EDP. We expect that the *naive* approach will keep total execution time very close to the execution time of coupled execution at highest frequency because the access phase performance is not affected by DVFS and the execute phase runs at the highest frequency. The EDP improvement for this policy is limited to the energy we can save by running the access phase at lower frequency. In memory-bound applications with irregular memory access patterns, the total execution time can be reduced over coupled execution due to the accuracy of software prefetching and the increased MLP[4] in the access phase, which leads to an additional EDP improvement.

In the *optEDP* policy the runtime tries to intelligently DVFS each phase based on the power model, thus total performance may be reduced because the execute phase is allowed to run slower in order to improve overall EDP. Although in the general case stores can not stall the execution and the address calculation runs on such a low IPC that is not affected by core frequency, there are some rare cases in which the address calculation is very complex and a slightly higher (than the lowest) frequency could improve EDP, or stores have very irregular access pattern followed by TLB misses and therefore a slightly lower (than the highest) frequency could also improve EDP. As a baseline for our experiments we use the original coupled execution at highest frequency.

[3]The DVFS transition latency is 8 usec on AMD (Bulldozer) using *powernow-k8* driver and 10 usec for Intel (Sandybridge and Nehalem) using *acpi-cpufreq* driver

[4]The use of *prefetch{t0-t2}* x86 instructions over normal loads can increase effective bandwidth as explained in section 3.2 and shown in Figure 2

Table 1: Application characteristics and task configuration. $\%T_A$: Average fraction of the application's execution time spent in the access phase and T_A(usec): Average duration of the access phase.

Application	$\% T_A$	T_A(usec)	Task Size(KB)	Access Pattern
Cholesky	5.6	3.09	16 - 48	Tiled
LU	3.3	2.94	16 - 48	Tiled
FFT	10.5	15.89	16 - 128	Butterfly
LBM	51.0	7.94	38	Stream Collide
CG	43.0	3.38	32	Indirection
LibQ	56.9	2.94	8 - 16	Regular
Cigar	66.2	5.88	32	Indirection

4. EVALUATION

4.1 Evaluation framework

For the evaluation framework we ported and optimized using SSE three SPLASH2 [18] kernels: FFT, LU and Cholesky, two SPEC CPU2006 [5] applications: 470.lbm and 462.libquantum, CG from the NAS parallel benchmarks [14] and CIGAR [1]. This set of benchmarks covers a wide range of memory access patterns and behaviors, from compute-bound (LU, Cholesky and FFT) to memory-bound (CIGAR and libquantum). CG and LBM have an intermediate behaviour. Table 1 lists the behavior and configuration used for the evaluation of the applications. Although there is a large variation in the duration of the execute phase across different applications (e.g., 87 usec for Cholesky and 4.5 usec for CG), for the access phase the duration is mostly affected by the data size and only slightly by the access pattern.

4.2 Performance/Energy Evaluation

Increasing parallelism in any class of applications can make the application more memory-bound as it increases the rate of requests to DRAM resulting in longer stalls per request due to memory bandwidth saturation. This limits program scalability. Our technique relieves the execute phase from these stalls by prefetching data in the access phase. Since in the access phase we use *prefetch* vs. *load* instructions, for memory-bound applications we measure an average speedup of 6.9% and 8.4%, for 2 and 4 threads respectively. The improvement in total execution time directly leads to a reduction in EDP. Additionally, decoupled execution gives us the opportunity to lower the core frequency in the access phase in order to further improve power efficiency.

Figure 4 demonstrates the benefit of decoupling using CG as an example. In this figure we show time (left graph) and energy (right graph) as a function of frequency and core count. In each graph we show on the left half coupled access-execute (CAE) at various frequencies (grouped into a cluster) and core counts (3 clusters using 1,2 and 4 cores) and on the right half decoupled access-execute (DAE) in a similar manner. The difference between CAE and DAE is the following: while the whole program in CAE runs at a specific frequency f_k, for DAE this holds only for its execute phase while the access phase runs at a constant minimum frequency f_{min}. This gives rise to the following interesting properties:

Time (figure 4 left): At f_{min}, CAE and DAE exhibit almost same total time. As we scale frequency higher, time in CAE and the execute phase of DAE shrinks. But time in the access phase of DAE remains constant, since the access phase is always executed at f_{min}. Yet, the total time of DAE closely tracks (or even improves on) the total CAE time. This is because memory accesses are *inelastic* to processor frequency scaling regardless of whether they are tightly coupled and embedded within execution or decoupled and separated from it. In other words, waiting for memory in CAE and DAE costs the same and is not affected by scaling the frequency. As a result, scaling frequency in the access phase only marginally affects its time.

Energy (figure 4 right): Energy in CAE is proportional to $T f_k V^2$, for its whole execution, resulting in a steep energy increase when f_k increases. However, a significant part of DAE execution, the access phase, *has a constant energy*, because it runs at constant frequency (f_{min}), costing significantly less than the corresponding CAE part that is interspersed throughout CAE execution. For DAE the total energy is given by $E_A^{f_{min}} + E_X^{f_k}$ and it can be modelled with the methodology described in Algorithm 1. If we were to scale frequency in the DAE access phase in sync with the execute phase we would observe the same steep increase in energy as in the CAE case. It is this difference in the energy increase, and the fact that access phase time is unaffected by frequency, that gives the decoupled-access execute model its advantage.

4.2.1 *Understanding Performance*

The result of DAE is to eliminate cache misses from the execute phase, thereby improving its ILP and allowing it to run with significantly reduced stall time in the pipeline. This makes the highest frequency the more efficient selection in terms of EDP for this phase. On the other hand, the access phase is memory-bound which makes it performance intensive to core DVFS, and therefore the lowest frequency (or one close to that depending on the complexity of address calculations) can be the optimal selection. Ideally the total execution time for the *naive* DAE policy would be very close to the original at max frequency.

Figure 5 verifies this assumption by showing the performance degradation caused by DVFS on a coupled execution and the benefit of decoupling access from execute using both *naive* and *optEDP* policies. Figure 5a shows the results with hardware prefetcher enabled while figure 5b shows the impact of turning off the hardware prefetcher on Intel's Sandybridge processors. Normalization is performed using the execution time of each application at highest frequency with the hardware prefetcher enabled as baseline. In Figure 5a we observe that the *naive* DAE without a hardware prefetcher performs similarly, and in the cases of memory-bound applications significantly better, than a coupled execution at the highest frequency.

The *optEDP* policy chooses the frequency that will achieve the optimal EDP for each phase based on a brute force search. The performance of this policy depends highly on the application. It performs better when there are complex address calculations in the access phase so that the optimal EDP for that phase is achieved at a frequency slightly higher than the minimum frequency. It performs worse than naive when the optimal EDP for the execute phase is at a frequency lower than the maximum. This happens in applications where writes are highly coupled to the execute phase and able to stall the execution.

When disabling the HW prefetcher we observe that coupled execution suffers from significant performance degra-

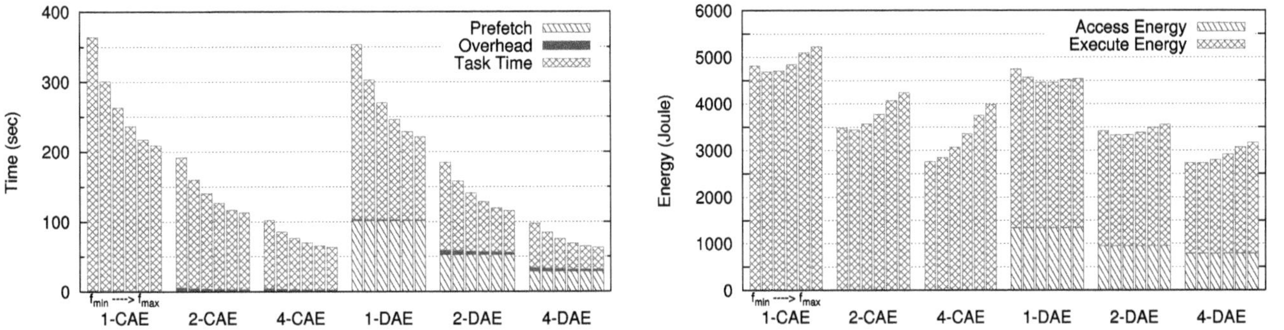

Figure 4: The impact of core frequency on execution time and energy. CG execution using 1,2 and 4 threads. For CAE we use frequencies from f_{min} (1.6 GHz) to f_{max} (3.4 GHz) with a step of 400 MHz while for DAE we use f_{min} for the access phase and f_{min} to f_{max} with a step of 400 MHz for the execute phase.

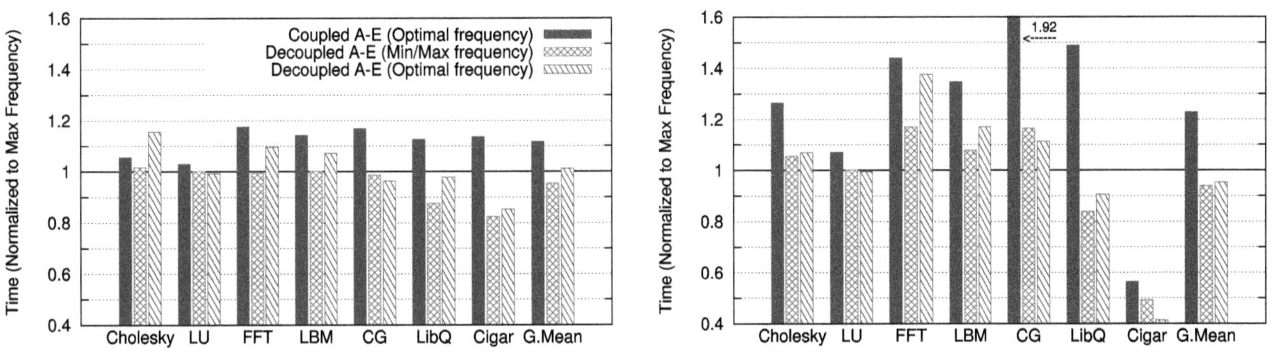

(a) with hardware prefetcher

(b) without hardware prefetcher

Figure 5: Execution runtime of CAE and DAE for Intel Sandybridge using 4 threads. Baseline is coupled execution (CAE) at maximum frequency with the hardware prefetcher enabled.

dation. An exception to this is *cigar* where the hardware prefetcher cannot detect its irregular pattern and therefore consumes bandwidth fetching unnecessary data which reduces performance. DAE performance on the other hand is less susceptible to misbehavior of the hardware prefetcher because the access phase accurately prefetches the data. With the exception of cigar, all other applications perform better when DAE is applied on a machine with hardware prefetcher, mostly because the access phase of DAE can provide hints to the hardware prefetcher and can therefore improve its accuracy.

4.2.2 Understanding Stalls

The key idea of decoupling is to move the memory slack from computation (execute phase) to a separate phase (access) that we can run at lower frequency. Memory slack is defined as the time that execution units are stalled due to off-chip misses. To evaluate how effectively we decouple real applications we need to measure slack in the initial program. For that we need to be able to measure stall cycles in the pipeline due to LLC misses. Unfortunately there is no such hardware counter. Another approach is to use a miss penalty approximation on all cache levels but it is rather inaccurate due to speculative, out-of-order execution. To overcome these limitations we use a combination of available hardware counter events, including stall cycles and hit ratio at each level of the cache.

Figure 6 shows the percentage of stall cycles in the dispatch unit for CAE and the two phases of DAE. These results can (a) characterize how memory-bound each application is and (b) how much of the stall time from coupled execution can be moved to the access phase in decoupled execution. Using Figure 6 we can characterize Cholesky, LU and FFT as compute-bound because they spend most of their execution time in coupled execution keeping the pipeline active while the rest can be characterized as memory-bound. We observe that for the compute-bound applications DAE eliminates only a small amount of the stall existing in the coupled execution. This is because these applications are optimized using SSE which creates pipeline stalls that are not associated with memory accesses.

For memory-bound applications we observe (a) small overall speedup of DAE over CAE and (b) significant amount of stall time moved from CAE to DAE access phase which is the reason for the energy savings achieved. This supports our initial hypothesis that decoupling accesses and scheduling them ahead of the computation can significantly reduce stalls. The percentage of time spent on address calculation (*active(A)*) is relatively larger for memory-bound applications. This can be either because the task duration on these applications is significantly smaller than in compute-bound

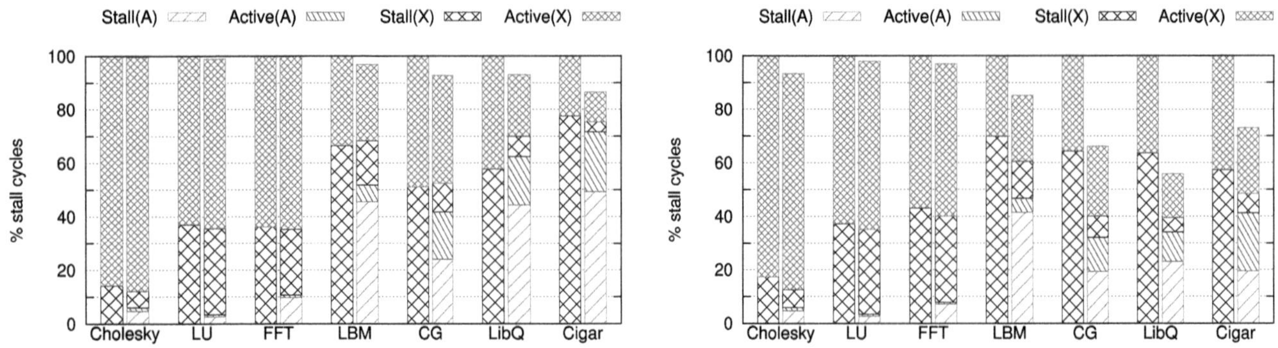

(a) with hardware prefetcher

(b) without hardware prefetcher

Figure 6: Percent pipeline stalls for CAE (left bar) and DAE (right bar) on Intel Sandybridge with 4 threads

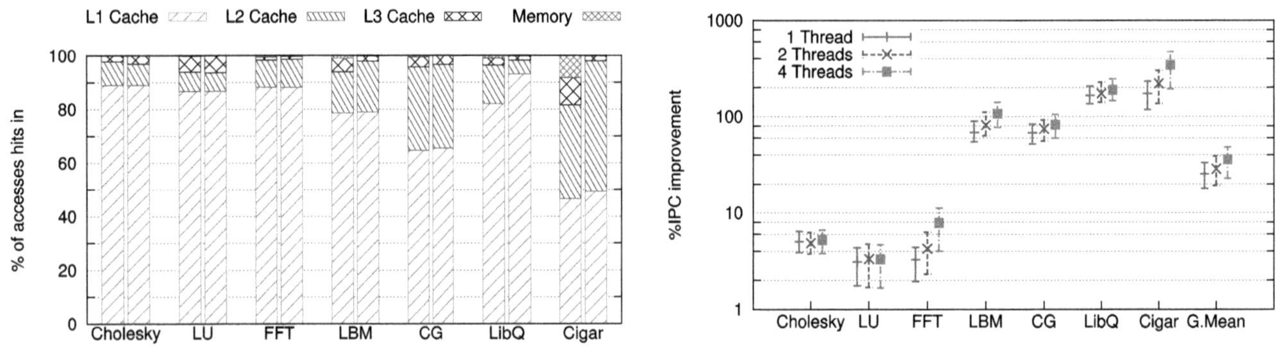

(a) Hit ratio improvement of DAE using 4 threads. Right bar: DAE execute phase. Left bar: coupled execution (CAE).

(b) IPC improvement of DAE execute phase over coupled execution (CAE) for Intel Sandybridge, across all frequencies.

Figure 7: Hit ratio and IPC improvement of decoupled over coupled execution models with hardware prefetcher enabled.

applications (LibQ) or because the access pattern is more irregular (cigar, CG). The key observation for memory-bound applications is that the overall speedup derives from the reduction of the non-stall time of execute phase while the total stall time including address calculation on the access phase in DAE is higher compared to the total stall time in CAE. Figure 6b shows the benefit of DAE without a hardware prefetcher. In this case we observe that the total stall time of DAE vs. CAE is reduced on every application, explaining the performance improvement shown in Figure 5b.

4.2.3 *Understanding cache behavior*

The accurate software prefetching of the access phase improves cache behavior of the execute phase for DAE applications. Figure 7a shows the impact on hit rate from decoupling for each application. Decoupling eliminates off-chip traffic during the execute phase in all applications. In memory-bound applications it also manages to reduce off-core traffic by better utilizing private caches. Therefore for LibQ, LBM, CG and cigar we observe that a significant proportion of L2 misses have been eliminated. Performance improvements come primarily from the reduction of LLC misses because their penalties cannot be hidden by out-of order execution.

4.2.4 *Improving ILP*

In the previous section we have shown that DAE significantly improves the cache hit ratio of memory bound applications and eliminates most of the LLC misses from the execute phase. This reduces stall time and increases the IPC of this phase as shown in Figure 7b. For compute-bound applications such as LU, Cholesky, and FFT, we observe only a slight increase in IPC followed by a small performance improvement. For memory-bound applications, where we eliminate more LLC misses and reduce unnecessary off-chip traffic, we observe an IPC improvement ranging from 100% to 500%. This explains the performance gain of the execute active time, shown in Figure 6.

4.2.5 *Improving MLP*

The two previous sections explain the performance benefit of the execute phase. For the memory bound applications, the prefetch nature of the access phase can also improve memory-level parallelism (MLP). This is because in coupled execution, issuing of loads is limited by the size of the reorder buffer and the number of independent loads present in the reorder buffer. In decoupled execution, it is the prefetching queues (which are significantly larger than the reorder buffer) that limit MLP. Moreover, in DAE execution function units are fully available for performing address calculations, which also contributes to the increase of MLP.

Increased MLP contributes towards the increase of bandwidth utilization (as shown in Figure 9). Figure 2a shows that there is a potential of 30% higher bandwidth by using *prefetch* instructions over *loads*. To measure the bandwidth demands of our workloads we use performance counters and

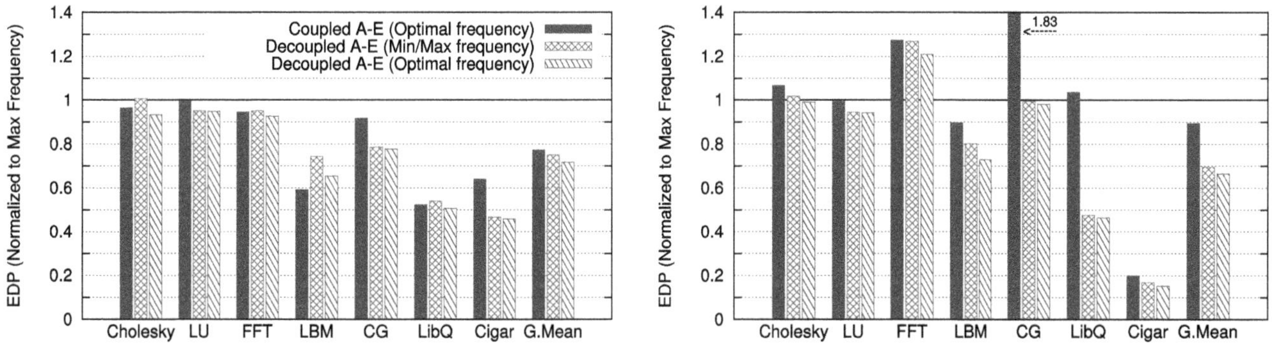

(a) with hardware prefetcher

(b) without hardware prefetcher

Figure 8: EDP of CAE and DAE for Intel Sandybridge using 4 threads, normalized to CAE at maximum frequency

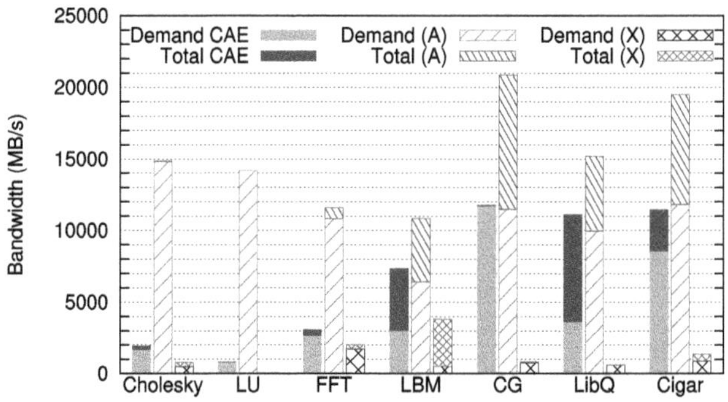

Figure 9: Application bandwidth on CAE and DAE models on Intel Sandybridge. Demand bandwidth does not include bandwidth generated by the hardware prefetcher while total includes it. Left bar shows CAE. Middle and right bars shows access (A) and execute (X) phases of DAE.

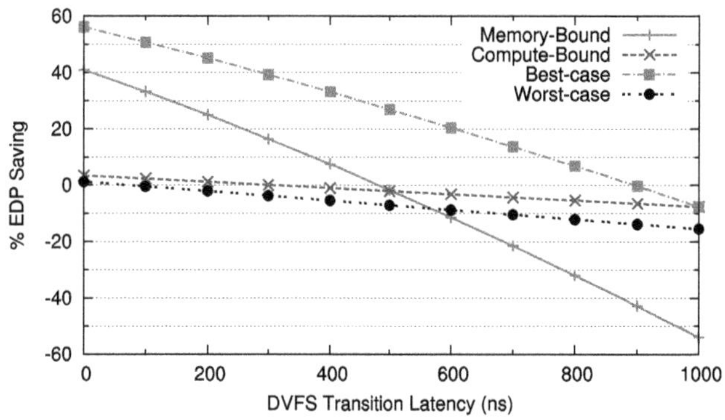

Figure 10: Simulation of future DVFS transition latency using 4 threads for the average of memory bound vs compute bound applications

measure off-chip requests. Figure 9 shows the total traffic generated in each phase of each task on both CAE and DAE executions. "Demand" is the traffic generated by *LLC misses* and *software prefetches* while "total" includes the traffic generated also by the hardware prefetcher. Each triplet of bars corresponds to an application. The leftmost bar refers to coupled execution while the other two refer to access "(A)" and execute "(X)" phases of DAE respectively. The increase in traffic indicates that the access phase of DAE operates at a much higher MLP compared to CAE.

4.2.6 Understanding Power Efficiency

Our method improves EDP by improving both *execution time* (due to ILP improvement in the execute phase and MLP in the access phase) and *power* due to DVFS in the access phase. Figure 8 shows the EDP benefit of decoupled over coupled execution. In compute-bound applications there is limited opportunity for EDP improvement in the range of 10% but both coupled and decoupled executions manage to deliver improvements. The advantage of DAE is that it delivers this EDP benefit without any performance degradation. For the memory-bound applications DAE goes further and improves EDP by more than 50% in some cases. On CG and Cigar there is major advantage of DAE over CAE of 15%, mostly due to the performance gain. On libquantum both CAE and DAE perform similarly while on LBM, CAE delivers better EDP than DAE. The reason is that decoupling helps only with the loads whereas LBM is constrained by stores that are coupled with computation in the execute phase which is amenable to DVFS. Thus, the *optEDP* DAE policy in Figure 8a improves EDP and approaches the optimal CAE. A comparison of Figure 8a with Figure 8b shows a significant contribution of the hardware prefetcher to the EDP improvement of almost 15% in coupled execution. Our method does not rely on the presence of a hardware prefetcher and does not conflict with it, therefore we observe that in both cases we obtain an average EDP improvement of 25%.

5. TOWARDS FUTURE PROCESSORS

As we explained in Ssection 3.4 our runtime is able to DVFS each phase but the benefit is limited, mostly because of the inability of per core DVFS on current processors. To overcome this limitation we modelled zero overhead, per-core DVFS. For that we use detailed time profiling measured by our runtime on all possible core frequencies hardware provides. We measure the number of tasks executed per core and the average duration of each phase (access and execute). Additionally we measure the overhead that the runtime itself creates for scheduling and any possible idle time created by application imbalances.

Having the number of tasks and the duration of each phase allows us to simulate any DVFS transition overhead by simply adding that overhead as shown in Figure 10. For the average of both memory and compute-bound applications we observe that we lose EDP benefit when DVFS transition latency overhead is larger than 500 nsec. Memory-bound applications are more promising for EDP benefit over compute-bound that are also less affected by DVFS transition overhead. The reason is that the execute phase of compute-bound applications is significantly larger than the access phase with the DVFS overhead. Figure 10 also shows the best (cigar) and worst (cholesky) applications behavior. For the best application we observe that we lose the EDP benefit of decoupled DVFS close to 1 usec which is double than the average, while for the worst application we have very limited potential for EDP improvement but also small impact of DVFS transition latency.

6. CONCLUSIONS

In this work we explored the potential of DVFS for decoupled access/execute applications in a task-based parallel environment. For applications with irregular memory accesses decoupling outperforms coupled execution both in terms of performance and power efficiency. For the computation-bound and moderately memory-bound applications, DAE can achieve equal EDP improvements to coupled execution at optimal frequency but without the trade-off of reduced performance. Using models to predict optimal EDP per task phase at runtime we can adjust the application performance and EDP dynamically. We have shown that by decoupling access from execute, a machine with low latency per-core DVFS could achieve on average 25% EDP reduction without sacrificing performance.

7. ACKNOWLEDGEMENTS

This work is supported, in part, by the Swedish Research Council UPMARC Linnaeus Centre and the EU Project: LPGPU FP7-ICT-288653.

References

[1] Cigar - case injected genetic algortihm. http://ecsl.cse.unr.edu/.

[2] R. Dennard, F. Gaensslen, V. Rideout, E. Bassous, and A. LeBlanc. Design of ion-implanted mosfet's with very small physical dimensions. *Solid-State Circuits, IEEE Journal of*, 9(5):256 – 268, oct 1974.

[3] M. Dongili. cpufreq utilities. http://www.kernel.org/pub/linux/utils/kernel/cpufreq/.

[4] J. L. Henning. Spec cpu2006 benchmark descriptions. *SIGARCH Comput. Archit. News*, 34(4):1–17, Sept. 2006.

[5] J. L. Henning. Spec cpu2006 benchmark descriptions. *SIGARCH Comput. Archit. News*, 34(4):1–17, Sept. 2006.

[6] K. Ibrahim, G. Byrd, and E. Rotenberg. Slipstream execution mode for cmp-based multiprocessors. In *High-Performance Computer Architecture, 2003. HPCA-9 2003. Proceedings. The Ninth International Symposium on*, pages 179–190, 2003.

[7] Intel. Intel ® 64 and ia-32 architectures optimization reference manual, pp.366-369, 2012.

[8] ITRS. Design 2011 edition, 2011.

[9] M. Kamruzzaman, S. Swanson, and D. M. Tullsen. Inter-core prefetching for multicore processors using migrating helper threads. In *Proceedings of the sixteenth international conference on Architectural support for programming languages and operating systems*, ASPLOS '11, pages 393–404, New York, NY, USA, 2011. ACM.

[10] G. Keramidas, V. Spiliopoulos, and S. Kaxiras. Interval-based models for run-time dvfs orchestration in superscalar processors. In *Proceedings of the 7th ACM international conference on Computing frontiers*, CF '10, pages 287–296, New York, NY, USA, 2010. ACM.

[11] W. Kim, D. Brooks, and G.-Y. Wei. A fully-integrated 3-level dc-dc converter for nanosecond-scale dvfs. *Solid-State Circuits, IEEE Journal of*, 47(1):206 –219, jan. 2012.

[12] W. Kim, M. Gupta, G.-Y. Wei, and D. Brooks. System level analysis of fast, per-core dvfs using on-chip switching regulators. In *High Performance Computer Architecture, 2008. HPCA 2008. IEEE 14th International Symposium on*, pages 123 –134, feb. 2008.

[13] P. J. Mucci, S. Browne, C. Deane, and G. Ho. Papi: A portable interface to hardware performance counters. In *In Proceedings of the Department of Defense HPCMP Users Group Conference*, pages 7–10, 1999.

[14] NASA. Nas parallel benchmarks, 1999. http://www.nas.nasa.gov/publications/npb.html.

[15] J. E. Smith. Decoupled access/execute computer architectures. *SIGARCH Comput. Archit. News*, 10(3):112–119, Apr. 1982.

[16] V. Spiliopoulos, S. Kaxiras, and G. Keramidas. Green governors: A framework for continuously adaptive dvfs. In *Proceedings of the 2011 International Green Computing Conference and Workshops*, IGCC '11, pages 1–8, Washington, DC, USA, 2011. IEEE Computer Society.

[17] V. Spiliopoulos, A. Sembrant, and S. Kaxiras. Power-sleuth: A tool for investigating your program's power behavior. In *Modeling, Analysis Simulation of Computer and Telecommunication Systems (MASCOTS), 2012 IEEE 20th International Symposium on*, pages 241 –250, aug. 2012.

[18] S. C. Woo, M. Ohara, E. Torrie, J. P. Singh, and A. Gupta. The splash-2 programs: characterization and methodological considerations. In *ISCA '95: Proceedings of the 22nd annual international symposium on Computer architecture*, pages 24–36, New York, NY, USA, 1995. ACM.

Quantifying Performance Bottleneck Cost Through Differential Analysis

Souad Koliaï
Exascale Computing Research
Versailles, France,
souad.koliai@exascale-computing.eu

Zakaria Bendifallah
Exascale Computing Research
Versailles, France,
zakaria.bendifallah@exascale-computing.eu

Mathieu Tribalat
Exascale Computing Research
Versailles, France,
mathieu.tribalat@exascale-computing.eu

Cédric Valensi
Exascale Computing Research
Versailles, France,
cedric.valensi@exascale-computing.eu

Jean-Thomas Acquaviva
Exascale Computing Research
Versailles, France,
jean-thomas.acquaviva@exascale-computing.eu

William Jalby
University of Versailles
Versailles, France,
william.jalby@uvsq.fr

ABSTRACT

Accurate performance analysis is critical for understanding application efficiency and then driving software or hardware optimizations. Although most of static and dynamic performance analysis tools provide useful information, they are not completely satisfactory. Static performance analysis does not provide an accurate view due to the lack of runtime information (eg: cache behavior). On the other hand, profilers, generally mixed with hardware counters, provide a wide range of performance metrics but lack the ability to correlate performance informations with the appropriate code fragment, data structure or instruction. Finally, cycle accurate simulators are too complex and too costly to be used routinely for optimization of real life applications. This paper presents the Differential Analysis method, an approach designed for simple and automatic detection of performance bottlenecks. This approach relies on DECAN, a tool which generates different binary variants obtained by patching individual or groups of instructions. The different variants are then measured and compared, allowing to evaluate the cost of an instruction group and therefore its optimization potential benefit. Differential analysis is illustrated by the use of DECAN on a range of HPC applications to detect performance bottlenecks.

Categories and Subject Descriptors

D.2.8 [**Software Engeneering**]: Metrics—performance measures

Keywords

Bottleneck detection, differential analysis, binary rewriting, performance evaluation

1. INTRODUCTION

A critical problem in High Performance Computing is to bridge the gap between peak and achieved performance. Despite impressive raw performance, the achievable fraction on production computing systems remains a frustration for the application developer. The performance gap has been acknowledged, and numerous tools (cf. Section 5) have been developed to bridge it. In fact, one of the key issues to resolve is not only to find the performance bottlenecks but also to correlate back to the source code, which is the natural place where the application developer has to insert the optimizations. For example, knowing through performance counters that a loop generates a high number of cache misses is not enough. First, the loop may contain ten arrays accessed in different ways and only a few of these accesses are responsible for most of the cache misses. Second, knowing the number of cache misses is not enough, quantifying its impact is also critical. It might happen that most of the cache misses are in fact near hits (apparent latency is less than 10 cycles) while a few of them have a very high latency. Therefore these few cache misses have the largest impact on overall performance. In fact, this last category of misses is the one to be optimized in the first place. This leads to the more general notion of potential performance gain for optimization. Let us assume that routine A consumes 60% of the total execution while routine B consumes 30% and, at the same time, the maximum potential performance gain for A is estimated at 10% (resulting in an overall performance gain of 6%) while performance gain for routine B is estimated at 50% (resulting in an overall performance gain of 15%). In such a case it is clear that more effort should be spent on the optimization of routine B. However, the difficult part is how to evaluate the potential performance gain.

To answer most of the problems listed above, simulation tools might seem the best approach. They are accurate and enable not only bottleneck detection but the correlation of performance issues with the source code as well. They also give a clear quantification of performance impact. Unfortunately, such tools do not take into account all of the system aspects of the target machine such as the memory configuration and the OS. Furthermore they are slow and in general not user friendly for an application developer.

To remedy this situation, we developed the DECAN tool, which relies on differential analysis to identify and quantify performance bottlenecks. The DECAN principle is very similar to standard debugging techniques where programmers remove statements one after another to identify the bug. The basic concept is fairly simple: the original binary is first measured and then several variants, each of them addressing a potential performance bottleneck, are generated and measured. By comparing performance measurements of these variants with the reference timing, we can detect bottlenecks and assert their performance impact. All of the measurements are done on the real target machine, taking into account all of the system aspects and offering decent analysis time when compared with simulation. The DECAN tool performs binary level transformations. It does not consider the arithmetic compliance with the original binary, and it makes sure not to change the control flow. Furthermore, the transformation scope of DECAN is at the instruction level.

1.1 Motivating Example

To illustrate DECAN, let us consider the following piece of code (extracted from a dense Singular Value Decomposition library):

Algorithm 1 Code example

```
real * 8 A(N,16), scal, s(16) {Column oriented storage}
DO i = 1,16 (Parallel loop)
  DO k= 1, N
    A(k,i) = A(k,i)/scal
    s(i) = s(i) + A(k,i) * A(k,i)
  ENDDO
ENDDO
```

We consider different values of N ranging from 200 up to 1000K. The target machine is a 4-core Sandy-Bridge architecture (see section 4.1). The parallelization of the outermost loop is ideal and results in a perfect load balance between the cores. The innermost loop contains a stride 1 access to an array. It results in a very good vectorization. The only two potential issues are: 1) the reduction operation and 2) the division operation which is very costly on Sandy-Bridge architectures. The division operation can not be factored out of the innermost loop because the use of a reciprocal operation followed by a multiply affects numerical properties.

First, DECAN is used to generate two binary variants to detect for which data range the loop is CPU bound or data access bound:

- *LSI_STREAM* is a binary variant in which all of the floating-point (FP) arithmetic operations have been suppressed: only the data access instructions and the address/loop instructions have been kept.
- *FPI_STREAM* is a binary variant in which all of the load / store operations have been suppressed: only the FP instructions and the address/loop instructions have been kept.

Measuring LSI_STREAM (resp. FPI_STREAM) enables the contribution of data access (resp arithmetic) instructions to the overall execution time to be evaluated. Figure 1 shows that for values of N less than 400K the bottleneck is the arithmetic operations while for N values greater than 400K the bottleneck is the data access.

To investigate the performance impact of reduction and division operations, two more variants were generated:

- *ORIG_NODIV* is a binary variant in which only the FP division is suppressed.

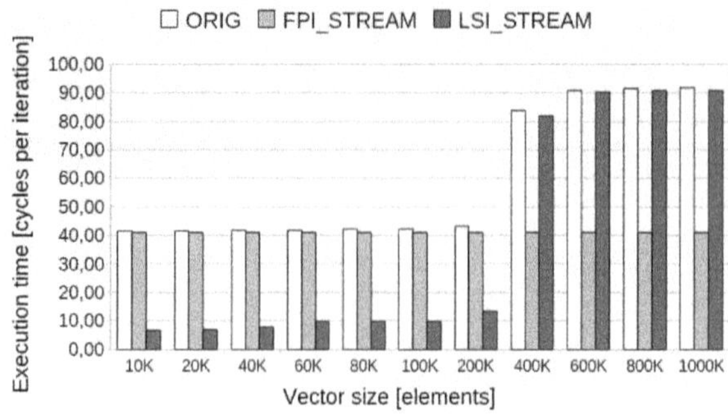

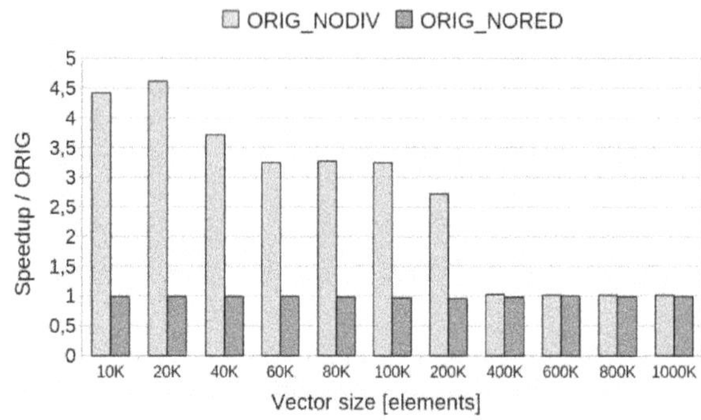

Figure 1: The upper figure shows the streams analysis with the variants FPI and LSI. The lower figure shows the elementary transformations NODIV and NORED. The experiments are performed on 4 cores

- *ORIG_NORED* is a binary variant in which the dependencies between iterations relative to the addition (second statement of the original loop) are suppressed. This is achieved by inserting an XOR (Exclusive OR) instruction which sets to zero the content of the register where the sum is normally accumulated. Inserting such an instruction automatically breaks the dependencies between consecutive executions of the addition instruction.

Figure 1 presents the relative performance gains of these variants with respect to the original. First, it clearly shows that the reduction operation induces no performance penalties across the whole data range (ORIG_NORED performance is identical to the original). Second, the division operation is very costly (i.e. it is the main performance bottleneck) for values of N less than 400K while the division operation cost is hidden by the data access for larger N values. Therefore, the technique of keeping the division operation within the loop to increase numerical accuracy had a performance impact only for smaller N values. A third variant, ORIG_NORED_NODIV, not shown here, was generated to detect potential interaction between the division and the reduction operations. This third variant had exactly the same performance as the ORIG_NODIV variant.

Similar observations for the impact of the division operation could have been achieved at the source code level by suppressing it but the compiler could have then suppressed the original statement from the generated code. Another approach is to replace the division with a multiply operation, yet the compiler may still generate an altered code. Operating with DECAN at the binary level allows "surgical" operations (with minimal intrusion) to be performed, keeping the DECAN variant code very close to the original target code. Now suppressing reductions at the binary level is much more challenging and in most of the cases would result in a code very different from the original one.

1.2 Paper Contributions and Organization

The main contribution of this paper is the DECAN tool which allows at the loop level:

- to quickly and accurately identify key performance limitations
- to quickly assess quantitatively the potential performance gain associated with removing a given performance bottleneck
- to efficiently correlate performance problems with source code.

These three key features allow the efficiency of overall application performance tuning process to be improved considerably.
The paper is organized as follows: Section 2 introduces the general infrastructure of the DECAN tool as well as the techniques used to preserve the original program flow. Section 3 discusses the DECAN framework and describes the instruction transformation process itself; it also deals with DECAN limitations. Section 4 shows the experimental results on different codes. Section 5 briefly reviews other tools used in application performance analysis. Finally the conclusion summarizes and gives an outline of the future works.

2. DECAN INFRASTRUCTURE

First, we describe the global base environment on top of which the tool is built. Then, we discuss the program (and loop) control flow management, which is essential. Indeed, altering the binary has a major impact on the overall program behavior and special care has to be taken so that this remains under control. The section also addresses handling of OpenMP and MPI codes.

2.1 Disassembling and identifying target binary loops

DECAN relies on a software stack composed of two major components:
MADRAS (Multi Architecture Disassembler Rewriter and Assembler) [16], is a tool to disassemble a file in ELF [12] format and to return a sequence of structures containing information about the assembly instructions. MADRAS is also able to patch a file by inserting function calls or assembly instructions, deleting instructions or modifying them by changing their opcode or operands.
MAQAO (Modular Assembly Quality Analyzer and Optimizer) [5] is a framework which performs control and data flow analyses on the list of instructions provided by MADRAS. The resulting high level structure is a control flow graph augmented with an accurately constructed loop hierarchy. Other useful information is provided via dataflow analysis such as the list of registers used and *Use-Def* chains.

The loop hierarchy provided by MAQAO is made available to the user through a loop topology file. Its form is an intermediate representation of the chosen part of the program to study. The representation can be obtained by different kinds of requests. For example, a request could be the loop hierarchy contained between two source lines. The file is updated with the desired transformations and fed into DECAN.

2.2 Control Flow Management

Since DECAN directly modifies loop binaries, the overall program behavior might be affected and the program might even crash. We will distinguish two levels of impact and correspondingly two levels of control flow: outside of the modified loop (*outer control flow*), and within the modified loop (*inner control flow*). In order to keep control of the program behavior, we will use two approaches: first, limit the scope of the loops transformed by DECAN and second, restore correct behavior of the application.

Preserving outer control flow: A more general approach (used in [10]) to tackle this problem is the injection of a recovery loop, right after the loop modified by DECAN, to restore the correct states of registers and memory. Basically, the original loop is not only replaced by the transformed one, but also duplicated; when the DECANNed loop execution completes, the original version is also executed just after it. The following steps summarize the mechanism:

- **Context saving**: All the registers (general purpose, vector, flags and FPU) are saved
- **Monitors activation**: Monitoring activation probes are injected
- **Modified loop execution**: The transformed version of the loop is executed
- **Monitors deactivation**: Monitoring deactivation probes are injected
- **Context restore**: All the registers are restored
- **Original loop execution**: The original version of the loop is executed to recover the correct state of registers and memory

To be entirely correct, this technique also requires that all the stores are deleted in the transformation process because no corrupted data should be written.
In addition to this general mechanism, we also use a more specific technique which is ideal when targeting only one loop at a time. The principle is to insert an exit sequence right after the execution of the modified binary loop to make the program stop without crashing. Exiting right after the execution of the DECAN loop will prevent any propagation of the "incorrect" data generated by the DECANNed loop. This technique is implemented through an instance mode: first a given target binary loop is selected and the program is launched to monitor execution timings of different instances of that target loop. This helps to define an instance number K of interest (usually it corresponds to the largest execution time monitored). DECAN patches the binary to let the program run normally (the original binary code is executed) until the Kth instance of the target loop is detected. This triggers a branch to the timing and execution of the modified binary code of the target loop followed by an early exit.
For most of the performance studies performed so far using DECAN, the two methods have been able to function correctly.

In its current version, DECAN does not modify loops containing subroutine calls: for example, a loop containing an MPI *Send* or *Receive* statement will not be modified. This limitation is essentially motivated by the necessity to narrow the propagation of the "side effects" in the modified binary: a loop modified by DECAN will in general compute incorrect values and therefore parameters passed to the subroutine calls will be incorrect. This "no subroutine" rule will suffer two major exceptions: 1) DECAN will still operate on loops containing calls to intrinsic functions such as exponential. 2) It also handles the calls to the runtime library such as the ones inserted by the compiler for managing the OpenMP parallel constructs. It should be noted that the "no subroutine call" limitation can be easily worked around in most of the practical cases by forcing subroutine inlining.

Preserving inner control flow: First, loops with conditional branches cannot be transformed in a naive manner because the paths' execution ratio and order must be kept unchanged. In order to fulfill this requirement, as a preliminary step (before any transformation is applied) a detailed static analysis is performed to compute *Use-Def* chains involved in the computation of the values governing the conditional branch. The resulting instruction lists are put in a blacklist and skipped during the transformation step. Using such a technique guarantees that the branch behavior will be identical in the original loop and in the DECANNed loop because all of the instructions governing the branch have not been modified.

A more subtle issue can arise with instructions such as divide or square roots. Since "incorrect" numerical values are generated in the DECANNed loop, exceptions (divide by 0, square root of a negative number) can be triggered during the execution of the modified version of the loop. A first partial solution to overcome this difficulty is simply to mask interruptions during DECANNed loop execution but this will not be entirely satisfactory because instruction timing can be affected. To preserve timing properties, we insert load instructions from specific stack locations to provide division/square root operations with operands leading to standard timing. The overall performance impact of these extra load instructions will remain limited, first because across iterations, these extra loads will always access the same stack locations resulting in L1 hits, and second because the cost of these L1 hits is negligible with respect to the cost of a divide or a square root instruction.

2.3 Information Reporting

As DECAN works on small portions of the program it is essential for it to perform an accurate performance monitoring followed by a good source level correlation.

Performance monitoring In order to accurately capture the transformation impact, DECAN places its monitoring probes at the entry and exits of the loop. For that, it creates basic blocks and redirect the control flow coming to and going out of the loop to point to those blocks. Furthermore, several probe types are available:

- Timers by the insertion of RDTSC instructions inside the blocks.
- Iteration counters by the insertion of incrementable global variables with MADRAS.
- Hardware counters by the insertion of functions calls to an API provided by a hardware counter/event monitoring tool. In the case of DECAN we use Likwid [3] whose API functions serve as triggers to start and stop the counters.

As a result the profiling overhead is greatly minimized.

Correlating back to the source code Relating assembly instructions to source code level is straightforward when debug information (DWARF format) is available. Fortunately, INTEL compilers provide such an option without altering the quality, and therefore performance, of the code generated. The option assigns to each instruction its corresponding source line and source file path. In most of the reasonable cases (multidimensional arrays) it is also possible to get information about the array allocation and therefore enable connection between instruction groups and arrays.

2.4 Dealing With Parallel Codes

OpenMP codes: Despite the fact that compilers do not fully follow the code generation structure specified in the OpenMP standard, they remain close enough to it. This enables us to recognize the important OpenMP structures (such as parallel loops) and inject the probes according to their positions. Additionally since the same loop binary can be executed by different threads, the timing probes track down the thread ID and generate a separate report for each of them.

MPI codes: DECAN handles MPI applications in the same manner as it handles sequential ones. The main difference lies in the results reporting mechanism: in the MPI case a report file is generated for each process which runs the loop. As mentioned earlier the "no subroutine call" rule will force DECAN to skip loops containing standard MPI statements such as SEND and RECEIVE.

3. TRANSFORMATION FRAMEWORK

While the previous section dealt with the control flow which might be seen as the skeleton of the program, the current section will walk through the intra-block modifications by addressing the instruction selection and transformation process.

3.1 Overview

The DECAN version presented in this paper targets the x86 instruction set with a focus on SSE/AVX instructions (floating-Point x87 instructions using the stack are not addressed).
DECAN operates on binary loops. It uses a configuration file (called template) to specify how a binary loop is modified. A template consists of two major components:

- *LIST OF INSTRUCTION SUBSETS*: a subset of instructions (extracted from the loop body) on which DECAN will apply the same specific transformation.
- *LIST OF TRANSFORMATIONS*: on a given instruction subset, specific transformations can be applied such as simple deletion, opcode or operand modification and replacement by other instructions or insertion of new instructions.

For the LSI_STREAM template, the subset of instructions to be modified consists of all of the FP SSE/AVX instructions. To this subset, the following transformation process is uniformly applied: FP instructions involving only registers are simply suppressed while FP instructions having one operand coming from memory are replaced by an equivalent LOAD operation using the same operand and the same target register.
A DECAN variant is simply a DECAN template applied to one or several binary loops.
The DECAN operating mode will specify how the DECAN variants are executed (see section 2.3).
Since one of the issues is to deal with binaries, we will first describe how to modify binaries.

3.2 Identifying instruction subsets

For each binary loop, DECAN generates a detailed Data Dependency Graph, as well as the list of addresses and SSE/AVX registers used by the binary.
From that point, DECAN will identify different instruction subsets which are potential candidates for modification (see Table 1).
The *LS SUBSET* aggregates all of the read/write instructions and therefore is not sufficient to distinguish between accesses to different arrays. To achieve that goal, *LS SUBSET* is further subdivided into groups. A group is essentially a set of read/write operations which are addressing close by memory locations. For example, loads to A(I) and A(I+1) are set within the same group. The group generation is detailed in the next subsection.

SUBSET	Definition (instructions listed below are extracted from target loop body)
LS SUBSET	all of the SSE/AVX instructions having one of its operands operating to/from memory (either as destination or source)
L SUBSET	all of the SSE/AVX instructions having one of its source operands coming from memory
S SUBSET	all of the SSE/AVX instructions having as a target operand a memory location
FP SUBSET	all of the SSE/AVX FP arithmetic instructions
DIV SUBSET	all of the SSE/AVX FP divide instructions
RED SUBSET	all of the FP or LOGICAL instructions directly involved in a reduction
LOC SUBSET	all of the instructions involved in the loop branch control operations

Table 1: Instruction subsets

For each group, we also identify the subsets of instructions modifying the address registers (base and index) defining it.

3.3 Grouping

Analyzing performance globally for all memory instructions is too coarse.
The goal is to refine the scope of the analysis to something more meaningful and isolate delinquent instructions. However, discarding a single instruction is misleading in case of *hit under miss*. For instance, if *A[0]* is a miss, then the next access to *A*, *A[1]*, will be a hit. Discarding the access to *A[0]* will simply shift the miss to *A[1]*. To pinpoint the bottleneck accurately, an aggregation scheme to regroup accesses on a cache line basis (*A[0]-A[3]*) has to be designed.
Furthermore, aggregation eases measurement interpretation. Instead of a per cache line analysis, a per data structure analysis is more relevant for an application developer. The ability to discard all the accesses to a given data structure at the same time sorts the different data structures by cost.

	Assembly code	Groups
0	LOOP:	
1	MOVSS (**%RDI, %R8, 4**), %XMM0	1 → G1
2	ADDSS **12(%RDI, %R8, 4)**, %XMM0	2 → G1
3	ADDSS **24(%RDI, %R8, 4)**, %XMM0	3 → G1
4	MOVSS %XMM0, *12(%RDX, %R8, 4)*	4 → G2
5	INC %R8	
6	CMP %R9, %R8	
7	JB LOOP	

Table 2: advanced data-flow analysis tracks the symbolic values of registers. Based on registers value it is then possible to infer which instructions are targeting the same data structure. Such instructions are coalesced within *groups*

Definition: A group is a set of memory accesses to the same data structure. The structure is usually an array, but it can also be a memory area used for spill-fill. Two instructions are considered to belong to the same group if they target an address using the same base and index register values, the only difference being the offset (see Table 2 for an example of groups).

As shown in the example depicted in Table 2 grouping analysis requires a partial knowledge of the execution context, which is evaluated through advanced dataflow analysis. Indeed, for each used register or memory address, an internal representation is used to keep its possible formal values.

3.4 DECAN Transformations

On each instruction subset DECAN can perform different modifications (see Table 3).

Transformation	Operations performed on all of the instructions of the target subset
Transformations applicable to any subset	
DELETION	Delete instruction
N1B	Instructions are replaced by a 1 Byte NOP
NMB	Instructions are replaced by a MultiByte NOP, the size of the NOP in bytes being equal to the size of the instruction replaced
Transformations applicable to L subset or a group	
L_L1_HIT	The memory address of each Load instruction is replaced by a constant address (different for each Load) on the stack. Store instructions are deleted
Transformations applicable to a group	
GROUP_PREFETCH	Before the first instruction of a group a software prefetch instruction is inserted using the base and index registers defining the group
Transformations applicable to S subset	
S2L	This transformation replaces Store opcode by an equivalent Load opcode, the operands being swapped: the source register (resp. memory target address) of the Store becomes the source register (resp. memory source address) for the Load

Table 3: Subset Transformations

The transformations *N1B* and *NMB* are useful because the simple *DELETION* "brutally" modifies the front end pipeline behavior: some instructions being suppressed, the remaining instructions are issued at a higher rate than in the original code. The use of the N1B and NMB transformations helps to keep the issue rate of those instructions close to the issue rate of the original code.
The last three transformations of Table 3 target specific potential performance problems:

- *L_L1_HIT*: The net effect of such a transformation is that across iterations, every load instruction will repeatedly hit the same location: after an initial miss, the subsequent accesses will be L1 hits. By comparing the transformed code timing with the original unchanged code, a quick estimate of performance penalty due to data access can be obtained. Using groups, this performance penalty can be precisely attributed to a given array access.
- *GROUP_PREFETCH*: This transformation assesses the hardware prefetcher efficiency by prefetch distance, thus allowing a precise investigation of memory access behavior.

- *S2L*: This transformation aims to evaluate the cost of false sharing or more generally the cost of coherency operations. Simply suppressing the store will induce a potential reduction of the cache footprint of the code, while replacing the Store by a Load keeps the same cache footprint as the original code.

The transformations listed can have side effects with potentially large impact on performance and this defeats our purpose of tight control of modification impact. For example, deleting a single load instructions can introduce dependencies between two arithmetic instructions which were independent in the original code. To prevent this, specific instructions (zeroing a register) are inserted: the process is exactly similar to the one used for breaking dependencies within reduction constructs.

More complex transformations (not described here for lack of space) are also available: one of particular interest targets the stride associated with a group. In such a case, the stride is replaced by a smaller one to avoid writing out of array bounds. This transformation is particularly useful to assess the cost of strides accesses.

3.5 DECAN limitations

First, DECAN has only been developed and tested on X86 processors. However, most of the techniques can be easily transferred to other ISAs and very likely at a much lower cost because the X86 instruction set is one of the largest and hence one of the most complex.

Second, although DECAN overhead can be precisely controlled, it must be evaluated. When applied to a whole application a single DECAN transformation will at most double the execution time of its target loop due to the replay code inserted after each DECANNed version. If many variants have to be tested, then this factor would be multiplied by their number.

Third, DECAN can be limited by measurement accuracy. Let us consider a loop accessing 50 different arrays, all of them being accessed from the same memory hierarchy level and having similar data access behavior (same stride, same alignment). Using L_L1_HIT on one of the arrays will show at best a 2% variation in execution time, which is within standard measurement margin errors. Therefore, no conclusions can be reached on any individual data array access behavior. Fortunately, most of the loops access less than 20 arrays, making the example mentioned clearly a corner-case.

Fourth, in cases of complex control flows with many branches within the innermost loops, preserving the original flow during execution will limit the number of instructions eligible for modification by DECAN. Therefore, the potential for exploration will be reduced. It should be noted that, in practice, this problem was never encountered for HPC codes. For example, in all of the NAS benchmarks, all of the hot innermost loops have a simple control flow that is easily handled by DECAN.

3.6 DECAN Summary

Table 4 illustrates how DECAN operates on a binary. The leftmost column contains the assembly code of an example loop. Instructions being part of the *LS SUBSET* are in italic and those of the *FP SUBSET* are in bold. The middle and rightmost columns show the loops resulting from the transformation process. Beyond the deleted and replaced instructions we can see the change in the address of the branch instruction in the modified versions which is due to the code being moved by MADRAS.

ORIGINAL CODE	
MOVSD -0x8(%RDX,%R9,8),%XMM0	
INC %R8	
MULSD -0x8(%RCX,%RAX,1),%XMM0	
MOVSD 0(%RDI,%RDX,1),%XMM1	
MOVSD 0x8(%RDI,%RDX,1),%XMM3	
SUBSD %XMM0,%XMM1	
MOVSD %XMM1,0(%RDI,%RDX,1)	
MOVSD -0x8(%RDX,%R9,8),%XMM2	
MULSD -0x10(%RCX,%RAX,1),%XMM2	
ADD $-0x10,%RCX	
SUBSD %XMM2,%XMM3	
MOVSD %XMM3,0x8(%RDI,%RDX,1)	
ADD $0x10,%RDI	
CMP %R10,%R8	
JB 402c40	
LSI_STREAM	**FPI_STREAM**
MOVSD -0x8(%RDX,%R9,8),%XMM0	XORPS %XMM0,%XMM0
INC %R8	INC %R8
MOVSD -0x8(%RCX,%RAX,1),%XMM0	MULSD %XMM0,%XMM0
MOVSD 0(%RDI,%RDX,1),%XMM1	XORPS %XMM1,%XMM1
MOVSD 0x8(%RDI,%RDX,1),%XMM3	XORPS %XMM3,%XMM3
	SUBSD %XMM0,%XMM1
MOVSD %XMM1,0(%RDI,%RDX,1)	XORPS %XMM2,%XMM2
MOVSD -0x8(%RDX,%R9,8),%XMM2	MULSD %XMM2,%XMM2
MOVSD -0x10(%RCX,%RAX,1),%XMM2	
ADD $-0x10,%RCX	ADD $-0x10,%RCX
	SUBSD %XMM2,%XMM3
MOVSD %XMM3,0x8(%RDI,%RDX,1)	
ADD $0x10,%RDI	ADD $0x10,%RDI
CMP %R10,%R8	CMP %R10,%R8
JB 6b897e	JB 6b897e

Table 4: Example of subset transformations. Two variants were generated one for LSI_STREAM and the other for FPI_STREAM. In the leftmost column, instructions in italic correspond to the LS SUBSET and those in bold to the FP SUBSET

4. EXPERIMENTAL RESULTS

4.1 Experimental Setup

All experiments were conducted on a XEON E31240 processor (Sandy-Bridge) with 4 cores running at 3.30GHz. Each core has a private L1(32 KB) and L2 (256 KB) whereas the L3 (8 MB) is shared among all.
All applications were compiled with the Intel Fortran Compiler (ifort 12.1.4) and the -O3 flag and the runs were made under LINUX OS.

4.2 RTM Application: Focusing optimization effort on the right loop

Reverse Time Migration (RTM) [6] is a standard algorithm used for geophysical prospection. The code used in this study is an industrial implementation of the RTM algorithm.

Our RTM code operates on a regular 3D grid. The core of the domain is processed uniformly, but a specific process is applied on the borders of the domain, the skin of the domain, to annihilate potential wave reflections. From a performance perspective, more than 90% of the execution time of the application is spent in two functions, *inner* and *damping*. These two functions are executing similar code on two different parts of the domain, *inner* is devoted to the core of the domain, while *damping* is used on the skin of the domain. Standard domain decomposition techniques are used to spread the workload on multicore target machines. Since the grid is uniform, load balancing is easily achieved by using rectangular sub-domains.

In our study, we focused on the *inner* routine which represents a much larger execution time than *damping*.
In the *inner* function, 3 loops denoted Lapx (resp. Lapy and Lapz) are used to compute the 3 components of the finite difference operator along the 3 axis (X, Y and Z). A fourth loop computes the wave-field. These four loops are themselves surrounded by 2 outermost loops to complete the operator computation over the entire sub-domain. The sub-domain size is too large to fit in the L1 or L2 caches, therefore cache blocking has to be used to optimize cache usage.

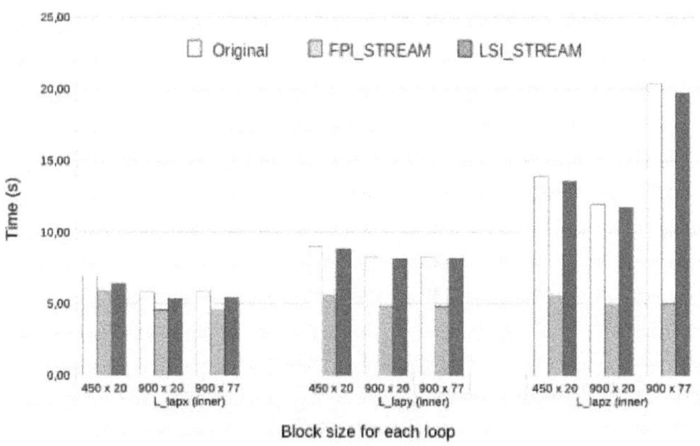

Figure 2: Stream performance comparison for the RTM application. For the three functions *lapx*, *lapy* and *lapz*, histograms represent respectively the speed of arithmetic operations and memory accesses depending on the blocking used for the data.

Figure 2 presents the results obtained by running the original code, the LSI and FPI_STREAM variants. Blocking was performed only along 2 dimensions, X and Y, and 3 different blocking strategies were studied: (Bx = 450, By = 20), (Bx = 900, By = 20), (Bx = 900, By = 77) where Bx (resp. By) denotes block size along the X (resp. Y) axis. The leftmost (resp. center and rightmost) histograms refers to Lapx execution time (resp. Lapy and Lapz). The leftmost and center histograms indicate that FPI_STREAM and LSI_STREAM are very close. This reveals that data access penalty is limited (not worth being optimized) and furthermore not very sensitive to block size. At the opposite, the large gap between FPI_STREAM and LSI_STREAM for Lapz reveals a large data access penalty: therefore the blocking strategy effort should only be focused on Lapz.

4.3 Timing The Access To Individual Memory Structure: EUFLUX application

EUFLUX is a 3D finite element CFD application from Dassault [9], ITRSOL (the iterative solver) represents over 80% of the execution and is the most time consuming routine is EUFLUXm. The EUFLUXm routine implements a sparse matrix-vector product in a quadruply nested loop. Among the four different arrays, three of them, *VECX*(2D), *OMPU*(3D) and *OMPL*(3D), are read-only and the last one *VECY*(2D) is read and written. The code of EUFLUXm is presented in Figure 3.

A quick inspection of the code reveals that most of the array

```
do icb=1,ncbt
  igp   = isg
  isg   = icolb(icb+1)
  igt   = isg - igp
  do ig=1,igt
    e    = ig + igp
    i    = nnbar(e,1)
    j    = nnbar(e,2)
    do k=1,ndof
      do l=1,ndof
        vecy(i,k) = vecy(i,k) + ompu(e,k,l)* vecx(j,l)
        vecy(j,k) = vecy(j,k) + ompl(e,k,l) * vecx(i,l)
      enddo
    enddo
  enddo
enddo
```

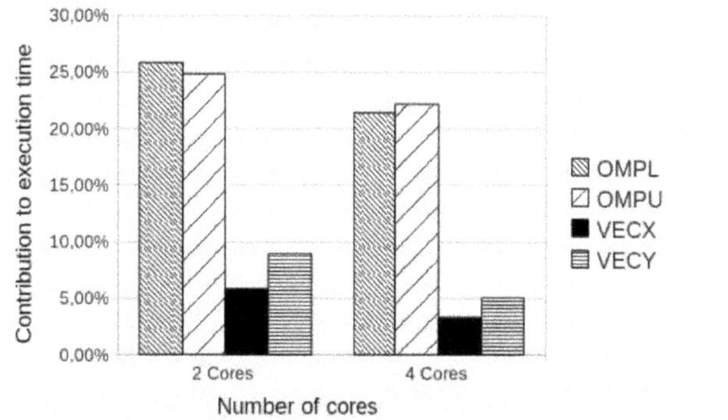

Figure 3: The upper figure presents the source code of the matrix-vector product in EUFLUXm. The lower figure shows the individual contribution in the overall execution time of memory instructions targeting each array of the EUFLUXm routine. Results are presented for 2 and 4 cores.

accesses suffer from bad stride access. The two innermost loops could be interchanged or alternatively arrays could be restructured (transposed). Restructuring an array is a complex and expensive code modification because it has to be propagated throughout the whole application. Therefore the real issue is to determine which arrays should be prioritized for restructuring.

The groups analysis (see Section 3.3) applied on the loop shows that among the 4 arrays, the accesses to *OMPU* and *OMPL* in Figure 3 are the most time consuming. The two arrays represent more than 40% of the total execution time, followed by *VECY* and *VECX* with an individual time share lower than 10%. Any optimization effort has to consider that performance issues in the loop are essentially tied to the *OMPU* and *OMPL* arrays.

4.4 Cache Coherence Protocol Analysis

Cache organization is a critical design decision in multicore processors; we propose to apply differential analysis in order to investigate the cost of cache coherence protocols. This study is conducted on the OpenMP version of the RTM application considered in the first case study. From a coherency perspective RTM is an interesting case: the code consists of iterations over a data parallel loop. Between two consecutive iterations the same array is written then read in the following iteration. First the write operations can generate false sharing: a cache line being simultaneously accessed in write mode by two different cores. Furthermore, the computation on a sub-domain requires access to data from other neighboring sub-domains: typically, all of the data on the border of the sub-domain are first written by a core and then in the next iteration read by a different core. Such writes followed by reads on the same memory location induce coherency traffic.

The methodology of measurements involves a simple transformation (S2L): all the store instructions of one loop are replaced by load instructions without changing either the memory location or the accessed register. Such a transformation will annul all of the coherency actions which would have been normally triggered by the store. Figure 4 denotes the execution time of all the innermost loops executed. The bars corresponding to the S subset with the S2L transformation are all at the same level (one) indicating a zero performance impact. For reference, the variant based on simple store deletion has been run. The results show an almost equivalent performance with the original versions except for two loops which present a non negligible store cost. From these results it can be stated that the cache coherence overhead remains negligible for the RTM application.

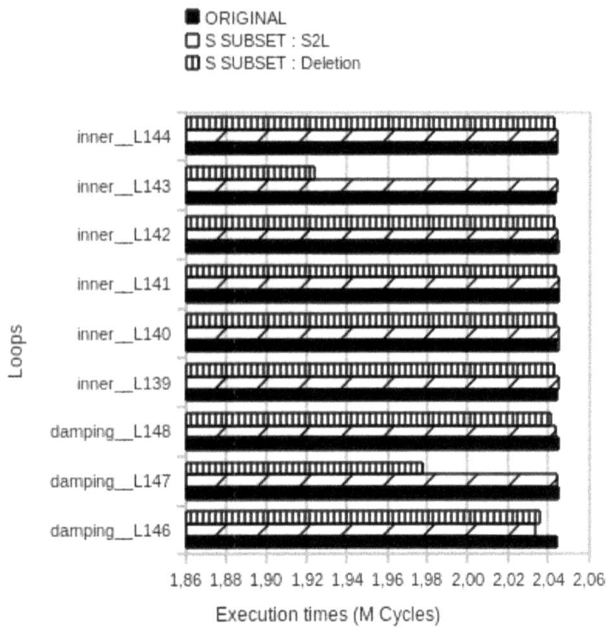

Figure 4: Evaluation of the cost of cache coherence protocol. The S SUBSET with S2L transformation variants show similar performances as their corresponding original versions. The S SUBSET with DELETION transformation variants show similar performances also, except for two loops which present a relatively non negligible store cost.

4.5 NAS Benchmarks Characterization

In order to test the scalability of the DECAN tool regarding complex codes, we chose the NAS Parallel Benchmarks *NPB-OMP3.0* as a test suite and performed a basic characterization of the behavior of its parallel loops. As known, most of the NAS Benchmarks implement iterative algorithms, therefore the alteration of the loops semantic leads to an earlier end of the program. This issue allowed us to use the sampling technique introduced in Section 2.2.
Figure 5 presents the results obtained on five of the benchmarks: *BT*, *CG*, *LU*, *SP* and *EP*. For each of them the hottest functions are selected and only their loops were considered. Two DECAN templates were applied: LSI_STREAM and the FPI_STREAM.

The results provide a clear insight on the trend of each benchmark. In the *BT* benchmark for example, the first two loops are driven by memory operations. As the execution time of the loop decreases we see more balance between the two versions. The loops of *CG* are highly memory bound. The hint for this is given by the big gap between the ratios of the two templates, especially in the upper loops. The only binary loop captured in *EP* performs a series of stores which explains the extremely low ratio for the FPI_STREAM version.

BT			
LOOP	% of Exec time	LSI_ STREAM	FPI_ STREAM
z_solve__L162	**6,87%**	0,96	0,30
y_solve__L155	**5,52%**	0,96	0,45
x_solve__L146	**5,27%**	0,92	0,59
z_solve__L161	**4,20%**	1,00	0,79
y_solve__L154	**4,15%**	1,00	0,79
x_solve__L147	**3,42%**	1,00	0,79
compute_rhs__L134	**0,17%**	0,94	0,87
y_solve__L151	**0,11%**	0,93	0,83
z_solve__L158	**0,10%**	0,94	0,85
x_solve__L143	**0,10%**	0,95	0,90

SP			
LOOP	% of Exec time	LSI_ STREAM	FPI_ STREAM
z_solve_j__L264	**1,92%**	1,00	0,32
z_solve_j__L270	**1,58%**	0,99	0,14
y_solve_k__L243	**1,44%**	1,00	0,77
y_solve_k__L245	**1,34%**	1,00	0,44
x_solve_k__L219	**1,33%**	0,94	0,64
z_solve_j__L266	**1,31%**	0,90	0,79
y_solve_k__L241	**1,27%**	0,92	0,28
x_solve_k__L224	**1,13%**	0,99	0,51
x_solve_k__L222	**1,07%**	0,99	0,76
y_solve_k__L247	**1,04%**	0,92	0,20

EP			
LOOP	% of Exec time	LSI_ STREAM	FPI_ STREAM
MAIN__L6	**100,00%**	1,00	0,01

CG			
LOOP	% of Exec time	LSI_ STREAM	FPI_ STREAM
conj_grad__L25	**26,38%**	1,00	0,02
conj_grad__L13	**24,89%**	1,00	0,10
conj_grad__L3	**24,44%**	1,00	0,05
conj_grad__L16	**12,27%**	0,98	0,09
conj_grad__L9	**7,14%**	1,00	0,13
conj_grad__L23	**2,39%**	0,98	0,50
conj_grad__L19	**0,37%**	0,99	0,30
conj_grad__L6	**0,35%**	1,00	0,39
conj_grad__L12	**0,19%**	0,98	0,78
conj_grad__L14	**0,18%**	0,94	0,85

LU			
LOOP	% of Exec time	LSI_ STREAM	FPI_ STREAM
rhs__L89	**4,33%**	0,98	0,16
rhs__L97	**3,45%**	1,00	0,41
rhs__L107	**3,39%**	0,90	0,39
rhs__L105	**2,94%**	1,00	0,24
rhs__L116	**2,13%**	0,90	0,46
rhs__L106	**1,86%**	0,94	0,89
rhs__L118	**1,39%**	0,94	0,62
rhs__L100	**1,73%**	0,89	0,59
rhs__L96	**1,68%**	0,93	0,83
rhs__L103	**1,36%**	0,95	0,78

Figure 5: Results of the application of the two DECAN templates LSI_STREAM and FPI_STREAM on 5 of the NAS Parallel Benchmarks 3.0. In each table the 10 hottest parallel loops are considered. For the two templates applied on each loop, the ratio of the execution time on the original one is reported.

5. RELATED WORKS

The comparison with previous works needs to be done at two levels: first, the basic mechanisms used for understanding low-level interaction between hardware and software and second how these mechanisms are integrated in a performance evaluation tool.

In terms of basic mechanisms, the closest work to DECAN is the technique proposed by Fursin et al. [10] to determine a lower bound on execution time. In their work, Fursin *et al.* use assembly level instrumentation to determine the lower bound on the execution time. From that bound they derive the potential gain of optimizations. Basically the idea is to transform all memory accesses in order to target a unique memory location. The goal is to lead all memory instructions into triggering cache hits. The timing of such a modified code determines a best case performance where all data accesses are L1 hits. They also introduce the idea of recovery code to overcome the semantic loss. Our DECAN greatly extends this idea by applying instruction suppression/modification to a much larger class of instructions (not only load/store) but also by using much more complex modification schemes (cf. section 3).

Besides modifying the binary as proposed in DECAN, there are two standard approaches for analyzing low-level interactions between hardware and software: 1) hardware performance counters/events and 2) simulation tools.

5.1 Hardware Performance Counters

For two decades hardware counters/events have attracted a large deal of attention [13]. Counters have the ability to monitor various events occurring within the processor at very low overhead without altering the numerical output of the system. Hardware counters are consequently used in a large number of tools; they are now natively supported in the Linux kernel since the version 2.6 through the *perf* subsystem [8].

Hardware events are excellent at capturing how a given piece of hardware is used but very often they fail in evaluating the exact performance impact: for example, hardware events can count cache misses but what matters is not the number of cache misses but the total impact of cache misses on performance i.e. the product of the number of cache misses and the average cost of cache misses. In general, hardware counters fail at evaluating accurately such average costs. In contrast, DECAN can directly provide a detailed estimation on how much a given array access costs.

Another difficulty with hardware counters is the correlation between source code and hardware event counts. Hardware counters can be triggered on and off at the beginning and the end of a loop structure or a function but the results are reported globally for the whole loop/function and not for individual source code statements.

To refine further the link between performance issues and source code, architects have extended the counter monitoring capabilities with Precise Event Based Sampling (PEBS) [11]. PEBS is introduced to link exactly a performance event with the delinquent instructions. First due to the statistical nature of the loop, there must be a sufficient number of samples to get realistic information. In general, this prevents using these mechanisms on too short loops (less than a few ten thousands of cycles). Second, due to the reordering mechanism of most x86 processors, it remains challenging to pinpoint the offending instruction [13].

In contrast to performance counters, DECAN can operate on loops with a very short duration (1000 cycles), the main limitation being the timer accuracy. Furthermore, the transformations are directly performed on a few selected subsets of instructions allowing a direct correlation between performance impact and the binary/source code to be made.

One final difficulty with hardware performance events is their complexity. First, their number is fairly high (in general over a thousand) making them hard to use. Secondly, many of them refer to low-level microarchitectural details which are not publicly available making counter information hard to decipher. For example, knowing that the reservation station is full and generates partial stalls in the front end pipeline does not give a precise clue of what to do to optimize the code. Interestingly enough, when used in conjunction with hardware events, DECAN helps in the identification of the instructions which are causing reservation station overflow.

5.2 Cache Simulators

In order to bridge the gap between the low-level information brought back by hardware counters and the real needs of the optimization, cache simulators are used. The main drawback of these simulators is the large overhead induced by the need to track every memory access. Among the performance analysis tools built on the top of cache simulators two well-known tools are detailed below.

Cachegrind: Cachegrind [4] is the cache profiler included in the Valgrind instrumentation framework. When using Valgrind, the original instructions never run on the host processor. Instead, Valgrind converts instructions on-the-fly to an intermediate representation. Valgrind companion tools can easily and directly manipulate the intermediate representation which is then recompiled for the target architecture. Cachegrind is based on the simulation of configurable L1I, L1D, and L2 caches. It identifies the number of cache misses for each line of the source code, with per-function, per-module and whole-program summaries.

ThreadSpotter: Acumem AG [1] offers the commercial product ThreadSpotter specially targeted at analyzing data access issues. It relies on a statistical analysis of address traces to estimate various potential problems with data access (stride, false sharing).

Both Cachegrind and ThreadSpotter are excellent at capturing general code properties such as temporal and spatial localities. However, since both of them are using very simplified cache models they fail to correctly assess the performance impact of the problems detected. Finally, since they focus only on data access, they are missing all of the potential performance problems relative to the arithmetic units.

5.3 Performance Evaluation Tools

Scalasca: Scalasca mainly focuses on MPI programs and is very efficient for quickly identifying communication problems such as late sender-early receiver. For OpenMP programs, Scalasca can identify load balancing issues in data parallel loops and synchronization issues. Scalsca uses source level instrumentation which is well suited for the communication problems listed above (minimal interference with the compiler). However for more general performance bottlenecks Scalasca does not provide any specific exploration technique besides hardware performance counters which by themselves are not always adequate.

TAU: Tuning and Analysis Utilities (TAU) Performance System [14, 15] is a performance profiling and tracing framework. As

such, it offers much more flexibility in the performance investigation techniques than Scalasca. The TAU framework addresses performance problems on three levels: instrumentation, measurement, and analysis. It provides instrumentation at different levels and performs tracing on parallel programs.
Although TAU offers many possibilities of using (inserting / triggering) various performance counters, it basically inherits all of the key limitations of hardware performance counters and in many cases, it will not be very helpful for performance bottleneck investigation.

PerfExpert [7] goes a step further by trying to analyze performance bottlenecks and provide optimization guidelines. Again, it mostly rely on hardware performance counters to evaluate performance problems and suffers from the same problems as the others. However, the approach of synthesising hardware counter information to derive performance optimization is very powerful.

XE Amplifier: XE Amplifier [2] is an Intel tool for performance analysis. It has different features, including stack sampling, thread analysis and hardware event sampling. Some traditional features, such as identifying the hottest modules and functions in a whole application or tracking call sequences, are also supported. XE Amplifier leverages hardware counters for in-depth analysis of the memory system and architectural tuning and associates performance issues with the source code. If no symbol sources are found in the binary, XE Amplifier navigates through the disassembled code at a basic bloc granularity.

With a reduced set of tests (variants), DECAN can offer the ability to determine the source of issues that are worth investigating (high potential Return On Investment). Complementary analyses such as the ones provided by PerfExpert or XE Amplifier can be used to derive what are the most profitable optimizations.

6. CONCLUSIONS AND FUTURE WORK

This article presents a novel approach based on partitioning the instruction flow according to either the hardware resource accessed or the memory targeted. Generating different variants from the original binary allows the cost of each fraction of the flow to be quantified. We call the general method the "differential" analysis and propose the DECAN tool as an implementation. DECAN by its concept is intrusive and can break the numerical stability of the application; numerical accuracy is not an important matter in terms of performance analysis except in cases where the control flow of the application is altered. However, the tool supports multiple schemes to detect or circumvent control flow hazards introduced by the differential analysis.
Through several case studies, we have demonstrated how DECAN can identify and quantify performance bottlenecks. We have also shown the current main DECAN limitations: sensitivity to timer accuracy, potential difficulties in interpreting the results and finally limitations in dealing with complex code structure.

Future work will first focus on addressing the limitations listed above. Furthermore, we plan to develop a systematic methodology for generating variants and combining the obtained results in a more meaningful manner.

Acknowledgments

This work has been carried out by the Exascale Computing Research laboratory, thanks to the support of CEA, GENCI, Intel, UVSQ, and by the PRiSM laboratory, thanks to the support of the French Ministry for Economy, Industry, and Employment throught the ITEA2 project H4H. Any opinions, findings, and conclusions or recommendations expressed in this material are those of the author(s) and do not necessarily reflect the views of the CEA, GENCI, Intel, or UVSQ.

7. REFERENCES

[1] Acumem. http://www.roguewave.com/.
[2] Amplifier xe. http://software.intel.com/en-us/articles/intel-vtune-amplifier-xe-documentation/.
[3] Likwid: Lightweight performance tools. http://code.google.com/p/likwid/.
[4] Valgrind: instrumentation framework for building dynamic analysis tools. http://www.valgrind.org.
[5] D. Barthou, A. Charif Rubial, W. Jalby, S. Koliai, and C. Valensi. *Performance Tuning of x86 OpenMP Codes with MAQAO*, page 95. 2010.
[6] E. Baysal, D. Kosloff, and J. Sherwood. Rerverse time migration:geophysics, 1983.
[7] M. Burtscher, B.-D. Kim, J. Diamond, J. McCalpin, L. Koesterke, and J. Browne. Perfexpert: An easy-to-use performance diagnosis tool for hpc applications. In *2010 ACM/IEEE*, SC '10, pages 1–11, Washington, DC, USA, 2010. IEEE Computer Society.
[8] A. C. de Melo. Performance counters on linux: the new tools. 2009.
[9] Q. V. Dinh, A. Naim, and G. Petit. rapport final de synthèse sur l'optimisation des logiciels de simulation numérique de l'aéronautique. *Technical report, Dassault Aviation*, pages xii, 51, 53, 54, 70, 71, 83, 2007.
[10] G. Fursin, M. F. P. O'Boyle, O. Temam, and G. Watts. A fast and accurate method for determining a lower bound on execution time: Research articles. *Concurr. Comput. : Pract. Exper.*, 16(2-3):271–292, Jan. 2004.
[11] D. Levinthal. Performance analysis guide for intel® coretm i7 processor and intel® xeontm 5500 processors.
[12] H. Lu. Elf: From the programmer's perspective. *NYNEX Science and Technology Inc*, page 95, 1995.
[13] T. Moseley, N. Vachharajani, and W. Jalby. Hardware performance monitoring for the rest of us: a position and survey. In *Proceedings of the 8th IFIP international conference on Network and parallel computing*, NPC'11, pages 293–312, Berlin, Heidelberg, 2011. Springer-Verlag.
[14] S. Shende, A. Malony, S. Moore, P. Mucci, and J. Dongarra. Integrated tool capabilities for performance instrumentation and measurement. 2007.
[15] S. S. Shende and A. D. Malony. The tau parallel performance system. *The International Journal of High Performance Computing Applications*, 20:287–331, 2006.
[16] C. Valensi and D. Barthou. Madras: Multi-architecture binary rewriting tool. Technical report.

Efficient Sparse Matrix-Vector Multiplication on x86-Based Many-Core Processors

Xing Liu
School of Computational Science and Engineering
Georgia Institute of Technology, Atlanta, Georgia
xing.liu@gatech.edu

Mikhail Smelyanskiy
Parallel Computing Lab, Intel Corporation
Santa Clara, California
mikhail.smelyanskiy@intel.com

Edmond Chow
School of Computational Science and Engineering
Georgia Institute of Technology, Atlanta, Georgia
echow@cc.gatech.edu

Pradeep Dubey
Parallel Computing Lab, Intel Corporation
Santa Clara, California
pradeep.dubey@intel.com

ABSTRACT

Sparse matrix-vector multiplication (SpMV) is an important kernel in many scientific applications and is known to be memory bandwidth limited. On modern processors with wide SIMD and large numbers of cores, we identify and address several bottlenecks which may limit performance even before memory bandwidth: (a) low SIMD efficiency due to sparsity, (b) overhead due to irregular memory accesses, and (c) load-imbalance due to non-uniform matrix structures.

We describe an efficient implementation of SpMV on the Intel® Xeon Phi™ Coprocessor, codenamed Knights Corner (KNC), that addresses the above challenges. Our implementation exploits the salient architectural features of KNC, such as large caches and hardware support for irregular memory accesses. By using a specialized data structure with careful load balancing, we attain performance on average close to 90% of KNC's achievable memory bandwidth on a diverse set of sparse matrices. Furthermore, we demonstrate that our implementation is 3.52x and 1.32x faster, respectively, than the best available implementations on dual Intel® Xeon® Processor E5-2680 and the NVIDIA Tesla K20X architecture.

Categories and Subject Descriptors

D.1.3 [**Programming Techniques**]: Concurrent Programming; C.1.4 [**Processor Architectures**]: Parallel Architectures

Keywords

ESB format, Intel Many Integrated Core Architecture (Intel MIC), Intel Xeon Phi, Knights Corner, SpMV

ICS'13, June 10–14, 2013, Eugene, Oregon, USA.

1. INTRODUCTION

Sparse matrix-vector multiplication (SpMV) is an essential kernel in many scientific and engineering applications. It performs the operation $y \leftarrow y + Ax$, where A is a sparse matrix, and x and y are dense vectors. While SpMV is considered one of the most important computational kernels, it usually performs poorly on modern architectures, achieving less than 10% of the peak performance of microprocessors [7, 26]. Achieving higher performance usually requires carefully choosing the sparse matrix storage format and fully utilizing the underlying system architecture.

Recently, Intel announced the Intel® Xeon Phi™ [1] Coprocessor, codenamed Knights Corner (KNC), which is the first commercial release of the Intel® Many Integrated Core (Intel® MIC) architecture. Unlike previous microprocessors from Intel, KNC works on a PCIe card with GDDR5 memory and offers extremely high memory bandwidth. The first model of KNC has 60 cores, featuring a new 512-bit SIMD instruction set. With a clock speed in excess of 1 GHz, KNC has over 1 Tflops double precision peak performance from a single chip.

In this paper, we consider the design of efficient SpMV kernels on KNC. We first evaluate the new architecture with a simple SpMV kernel using the widely-used Compressed Sparse Row (CSR) format. Our experiments on KNC reveal several performance bottlenecks that diverge from our prior knowledge about SpMV on other architectures. From this experience, we design a novel sparse matrix format, called ELLPACK Sparse Block (ESB), which is tuned for KNC. The new format extends the well-known ELLPACK format with (a) finite-window sorting to improve the SIMD efficiency of the SpMV kernel; (b) a bit array to encode nonzero locations to reduce the bandwidth requirement; and (c) column blocking to improve memory access locality.

With a large number of cores, one critical performance obstacle of SpMV on KNC is load imbalance. To address this problem, we present three load balancers for SpMV on KNC and compare them with other load balancing methods. Using the ESB format and the proposed load balancers, our optimized SpMV implementation achieves close to 90% of the STREAM Triad bandwidth of KNC and is 1.85x faster than the optimized implementation using CSR format. Compared to other architectures, SpMV on KNC is 3.52x faster than on dual-socket Intel® Xeon® Processor E5-2680 and is 1.32x faster than on NVIDIA Tesla K20X.

---

[1] Intel, Xeon, and Intel Xeon Phi are trademarks of Intel Corporation in the U.S. and/or other countries.

2. OVERVIEW OF KNIGHTS CORNER

2.1 Knights Corner Architecture

Knights Corner is a many-core coprocessor based on the Intel® MIC architecture. It consists of x86-based cores, caches, Tag Directories (TD), and GDDR5 Memory Controllers (MC), all connected by a high speed bidirectional ring. An architectural overview of KNC is given in Fig. 1.

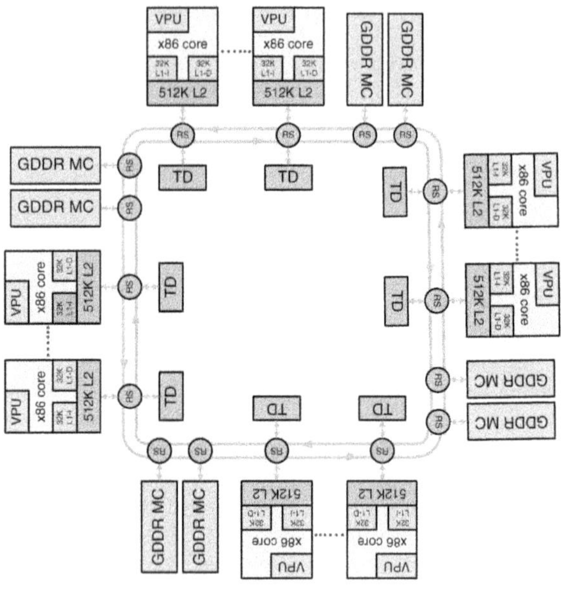

Figure 1: High-level block diagram of KNC.

Each core of KNC is composed of four components: an in-order dual-issue pipeline with 4-way simultaneous multi-threading (SMT), a 512-bit wide SIMD engine called Vector Processing Unit (VPU); 32 KB L1 data and instruction caches; and a 512 KB fully coherent L2 cache. The KNC's L2 caches are fully coherent using a set of tag directories. Each of the tag directories responds to L2 cache misses from a fixed portion of the memory space. As shown in Fig. 1, the memory controllers are symmetrically interleaved with pairs of cores around the ring. The memory addresses are uniformly distributed across the tag directories and memory controllers. This design choice provides a smooth traffic characteristic on the ring and is essential for good bus performance.

Given the large number of cores and coherent caches, L2 cache misses on KNC are expensive compared to those on other x86 processors. On a L2 cache miss, an address request is sent on the ring to the corresponding tag directory. Depending on whether or not the requested address is found in another core's cache, a forwarding request is then sent to that core or memory controllers, and the request data is subsequently forwarded on the ring. The cost of each data transfer on the ring is proportional to the distance between the source and the destination, which is, in the worse case, on the order of hundreds of cycles. Overall, the L2 cache miss latency on KNC can be an order of magnitude larger than that of multi-core CPUs.

2.2 Intel® Initial Many Core Instructions

KNC provides a completely new 512-bit SIMD instruction set called Intel® Initial Many Core Instructions (Intel® IMCI). Compared to prior vector architectures (MMX, SSE, and AVX), Intel® IMCI has larger SIMD width and introduces many new features. One important new feature is *write-mask*, which we use in our SpMV implementations. The write-mask in a SIMD instruction is a mask register coming with the destination vector. After the SIMD instruction is executed, each element in the destination vector is conditionally updated with the results of the instruction, contingent on the corresponding element position bit in the mask register.

The Intel® IMCI also supports irregular memory accesses, which are very useful for SpMV. The *gather* instruction loads sparse locations of memory into a dense vector register, while the *scatter* instruction performs the inverse. In both instructions, the load and store locations of memory are specified by a base address and a vector of signed 32-bit offsets.

2.3 Test Platform

The platform used for experimental tests in this paper is a pre-production part of KNC with codename ES B0, which is installed with Intel® MIC Platform Software Stack (MPSS) Gold 2.1. The pre-production system is equipped with 8 GB GDDR5 memory and includes a 61-core KNC coprocessor running at 1.09 GHz, which is capable of delivering 1.05 Tflops double precision peak performance.[2] In this work, we use 60 cores to test the SpMV implementations, leaving the remaining core to run the operating system and administrative software. The STREAM Triad benchmark on this system achieves a score of 163 GB/s with ECC turned on.

3. UNDERSTANDING THE PERFORMANCE OF SPMV ON KNC

We first implemented a simple SpMV kernel using CSR format on KNC. The CSR format is standard, consisting of three arrays: the nonzero values of the sparse matrix are stored in *val*; the column indices corresponding to each nonzero are stored in *colidx*; and the list of indices giving the beginning of each row are stored in *rowptr*.

3.1 Test Matrices

Table 1 lists sparse matrices used in our performance evaluation. These are all the matrices used in previous papers [26, 21, 9] that are larger than the 30 MB aggregate L2 cache of KNC (using 60 cores). A dense matrix stored in sparse format is also included. These matrices come from a wide variety of applications with different sparsity characteristics. No orderings were applied to these matrices, but our results may be better if we use orderings that promote locality when accessing the vector x.

Table 1: Sparse matrices used in performance evaluation.

Name	Dimensions	nnz	nnz/row
Dense8	8K×8K	64.0M	8000.00
Wind Tunnel	218K×218K	11.6M	53.39
Circuit5M	5.56M×5.56M	59.5M	10.71
Rail4284	4K×1.09M	11.3M	2633.99
Mip1	66K×66K	10.4M	155.77
In-2004	1.38M×1.38M	16.9M	12.23
Si41Ge41H72	186K×186K	15.0M	80.86
Ldoor	952K×952K	46.5M	48.86
Bone010	987K×987K	71.7M	72.63
Rucci1	1.98M×110K	7.8M	3.94
Cage15	5.16M×5.16M	99.2M	19.24
Rajat31	4.69M×4.69M	20.3M	4.33
12month1	12K×873K	22.6M	1814.19
Spal_004	10K×322K	46.1M	4524.96
Crankseg_2	64K×64K	14.1M	221.64
Torso1	116K×116K	8.5M	73.32

[2]Evaluation card only and not necessarily reflective of production card specifications.

3.2 Overview of CSR Kernel

Similar to earlier work on SpMV for multi-core CPUs [26, 7], our CSR kernel is statically load balanced by row decomposition, in which the sparse matrix is partitioned into row blocks with approximately equal numbers of nonzeros. Each thread multiplies one row block with a SIMD kernel. We also applied common optimizations to our CSR kernel, including loop unrolling and software prefetching of nonzero values and column indices.

Algorithm 1: Multiply a row block (from row startrow to endrow) in CSR format (rowptr, colidx, val).

```
1  rowid ← startrow;
2  start ← rowptr [rowid];
3  while rowid < endrow do
4      idx ← start;
5      end ← rowptr [rowid + 1];
6      vec_y ← 0;
       /* compute for a row */
7      while idx < end do
8          rem ← end − idx;
9          writemask ← (rem > 8 ? 0xff : (0xff ≫ (8 − rem)));
10         vec_idx ← load (&colidx [idx],writemask);
11         vec_vals ← load (&val [idx], writemask);
12         vec_x ← gather (vec_idx, &x [0], writemask);
13         vec_y ← fmadd (vec_vals, vec_x, vec_y, writemask);
14         idx ← idx + 8;
15     y [rowid] ← y [rowid] + reduce_add (vec_y);
16     start ← end;
17     rowid ← rowid + 1;
```

Alg. 1 shows the pseudocode of the SIMD kernel, in which the inner loop (lines 7-14) processes a matrix row. In each iteration, at most 8 nonzeros are multiplied as follows. First, the elements from *colidx* and *val* are loaded into vectors (lines 10 and 11). Next, the elements from vector *x* are gathered into *vec_x* (line 12). Finally, *vec_vals* and *vec_x* are multiplied and added to *vec_y* by the fused multiply-add instruction (line 13). When fewer than 8 nonzeros are left in a row, only a portion of the slots in the SIMD instructions will be used. In this case, we only update the corresponding elements in the destination vectors. To achieve this, a write-mask (line 9) is used to mask the results of the SIMD instructions.

3.3 Performance Bounds

We use four performance bounds (measured in flops) to evaluate the performance of our CSR kernel. First, the *memory bandwidth bound performance* is the expected performance when the kernel is bounded by memory bandwidth. It is defined as

$$P_{bw} = \frac{2\,nnz}{M/B}$$

where *nnz* is the number of nonzeros in the matrix, *B* is the STREAM bandwidth of KNC, and *M* is the amount of memory transferred in the SpMV kernel, which is measured by Intel® VTune™.

The *compute bound performance* is measured by running a modified CSR kernel, in which all memory accesses are eliminated. Concretely, the modified kernel only uses the first cache lines of *val* and *colidx*. It also eliminates the memory accesses on vector *x* by setting *colidx* to be {0, 8, 16, 24, 32, 40, 48, 56}.

The *ideal balanced performance* is the achievable performance when SpMV kernels are perfectly balanced, and is computed as

$$P_{balanced} = \frac{2\,nnz}{T_{mean}}$$

where T_{mean} is the average execution time of the threads.

Finally, the *effective bandwidth bound performance* is the best performance one would expect given that (a) the kernel is bandwidth bound; (b) there are no redundant memory accesses to vectors *x* and *y*. It is defined as

$$P_{ebw} = \frac{2\,nnz}{M_{min}/B}$$

where M_{min} is the minimum memory traffic of SpMV assuming perfect reuse of vectors *x* and *y*.

Prior work has shown that SpMV is memory bandwidth bound on modern architectures [7, 26, 6]. Thus, it is expected that for all matrices the compute bound performance is larger than the memory bandwidth bound performance. The ideal balanced performance represents the achievable peak performance of a balanced SpMV kernel. For an efficient SpMV implementation, it should be close to the memory bandwidth bound performance. Additionally, the difference between the ideal balanced performance and the measured performance may quantify the degree of load imbalance.

3.4 Performance Bottlenecks

Fig. 2 shows the performance of our CSR kernel on all test matrices and the corresponding performance bounds. By comparing the measured performance of our CSR kernel to these performance bounds, we discover some unexpected performance issues.

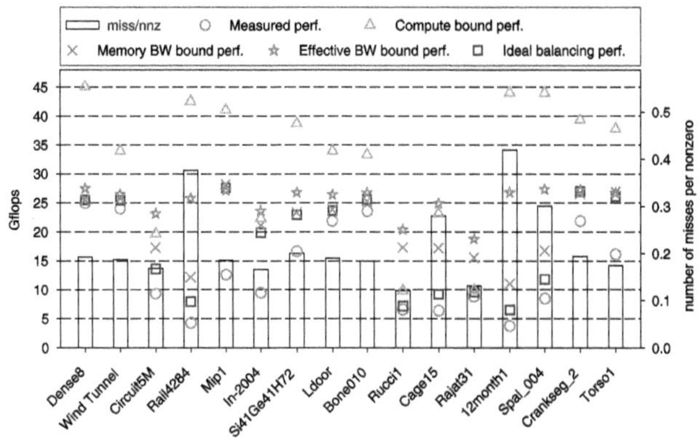

Figure 2: Performance of CSR kernel and performance bounds. The average number of L2 cache misses per nonzero is shown in vertical bar.

3.4.1 Low SIMD Efficiency

As seen in Fig. 2, for some matrices that have very short row lengths, e. g., *Rajat31* and *Rucci1*, the compute bound performance is lower than the bandwidth bound performance, suggesting that their performance is actually bounded by computation. Previous work on SpMV [7, 4] attributes the poor performance of matrices with short rows to loop overheads. For wide SIMD, we argue that this is also because of the *low SIMD efficiency* of the CSR kernel, i. e., low fraction of useful slots used in SIMD instructions.

More precisely, for a matrix with very few nonzeros per row, the CSR kernel cannot fully utilize KNC's 512-bit SIMD instructions. As a result, the CSR kernel on this matrix performs poorly, and if the SIMD efficiency is very low, the compute bound performance of the kernel may be smaller than the memory bandwidth bound performance. For example, the matrix *Rucci1* has on average 3.94 nonzeros per row. Multiplying this matrix using our CSR kernel on KNC can only use half of the SIMD slots. Thus, the SIMD efficiency is only 50%.

Low SIMD efficiency is not a unique problem for CSR. It can be shown that the compute bound performance will be lower than the memory bandwidth bound performance when the SIMD efficiency is lower than some threshold. Given a matrix format, its SpMV implementation on KNC usually includes a basic sequence of SIMD instructions similar to lines 7-14 in Alg. 1, which multiplies at most 8 nonzeros (in double precision). Assuming that the basic SIMD sequence takes C cycles (C accounts for both SIMD instructions and loop overheads) and F is the clock speed (Hz), then the compute time for the SIMD sequence is C/F. The minimum memory transfer time for the SIMD sequence is $(8s \times P \times \eta)/B$, where s is the working set size (in bytes) for one nonzero, where P is the number of cores in use, η is the SIMD efficiency, and B is the STREAM bandwidth. To avoid being bounded by computation, the compute time should be greater than the memory transfer time, thus η needs to satisfy

$$\eta > \eta_{min} = \frac{B}{8s \times P} \times C/F \quad (1)$$

This provides the minimum required SIMD efficiency for the given matrix format. We will revisit this in Section 4.

3.4.2 Cache Miss Latency

Four matrices, *Rail4284*, *Cage15*, *12month1* and *Spal_004*, have ideal balanced performance much lower than both the compute bound performance and the memory bandwidth bound performance. This suggests that, even if the kernel is perfectly balanced, the performance is neither bounded by computation nor bandwidth.

To determine the reason for this, Fig. 2 shows the average number of L2 cache misses (measured by Intel® VTune™) per nonzero for all test matrices. From this figure, we see that those matrices whose ideal balanced performance is lower than the compute and memory bandwidth bound performance have much more L2 cache misses than other matrices (per nonzero). We also notice that their effective bandwidth bound performance is much higher than the memory bandwidth bound performance, which means there are a large number of redundant memory accesses on vector x. This implies that the poor performance of these matrices may be because of excessive cache misses due to accessing vector x. Unlike accesses to matrix values, accesses to x are not contiguous and can be very irregular, and we do not have an effective way to perform prefetching on x to overcome cache miss latency. While KNC has hardware support for prefetching irregular memory accesses, it does have an overhead that often negates its benefits.

Cache miss latency is not a unique problem for KNC. However, it is more expensive on KNC than on other architectures. To better understand the problem, we compare the cache miss latency (memory latency) and memory bandwidth of KNC with those of CPUs and GPUs. Sandy Bridge, an example of recent multi-core CPUs, has an order of magnitude smaller latency and 5x less memory bandwidth than KNC. While the memory latency of Sandy Bridge still affects performance, the SpMV kernels on it tend to be memory bandwidth bound. High-end GPUs have comparable memory bandwidth and latency to KNC. However, memory latency is usually not a problem for GPUs as they have a large number of warps per streaming multiprocessor (vs. 4 threads per core on KNC) so the memory latency can be completely hidden.

3.4.3 Load Imbalance

In the CSR kernel, we statically partition the matrix into blocks with equal numbers of nonzeros. We call this partitioning scheme *static-nnz*. Although *static-nnz* is widely used in previous SpMV implementations on multi-core processors and leads to good performance, it performs poorly on KNC. As shown in Fig. 2, for at least 8 matrices the CSR kernel is highly unbalanced. This results in a significant performance degradation up to 50%.

The poor performance of *static-nnz* in these cases is mainly due to the fact that the sparsity structure of a sparse matrix often varies across different parts of the matrix. In one case, some parts of the matrix may have more rows with shorter row lengths than other parts. The threads assigned to these parts are slower than the other threads because they are burdened by more loop overheads. In another case, some parts of the matrix may have very different memory access patterns on vector x than others. For these parts of the matrix, accessing vector x may cause more cache misses. Considering that KNC has far more cores than any other x86 processor, it is more likely to have some partitions with very different row lengths or memory access patterns from others. As a result, while all partitions in *static-nnz* have the same number of nonzeros, they can have very different performance. This explains why *static-nnz* performs well on previous CPUs but is not effective on KNC.

In summary, the results using our CSR kernel on KNC reveal that, depending on the matrix, one or more of three bottlenecks can impact performance: (a) low SIMD efficiency due to wide SIMD on KNC; (b) high cache miss latency due to the coherent cache system; (c) load imbalance because of the large number of cores. We will first address the low SIMD efficiency and the cache miss latency bottlenecks in the next section by proposing a new matrix format. The subsequent section addresses load imbalance.

4. ELLPACK SPARSE BLOCK FORMAT

4.1 Motivation

From the architectural point of view, KNC bears many similarities with x86-based multi-core CPUs. On the other hand, there are also similarities between KNC and GPUs, for example, both have wide SIMD. Thus, before considering a new matrix format for KNC, it is necessary to first evaluate existing matrix formats and optimization techniques used for CPUs and GPUs.

4.1.1 Register Blocking

Register blocking [8] is one of the most effective optimization techniques for SpMV on CPUs, and is central to many sparse matrix formats [3, 4, 26]. In this section, we explain why this technique is not appropriate for KNC. In register blocking, adjacent nonzeros of the matrix are grouped into small dense blocks to facilitate SIMD, and to reuse portions of the vector x in registers. Given that KNC has wider SIMD and larger register files than previous x86 CPUs, it seems advantageous to use large blocks on KNC. However, sparse matrices in general cannot be reordered to give large dense blocks; zero padding is necessary, resulting in redundant computations with zeros and low SIMD efficiency.

To evaluate the use of register blocking, we measure the *average nonzero density of the blocks* (ratio of the number of nonzeros in a block to the number of nonzeros stored including padding zeros) using various block sizes and compare these with the minimum required SIMD efficiency (η_{min}) in Eq. 1. In general, the SIMD efficiency of SpMV is approximately equal to the average nonzero density. It can be shown that, even when the smallest block sizes for KNC to facilitate SIMD are used, the nonzero densities for many matrices are still smaller than η_{min}. Thus register blocking leads to low SIMD efficiency on KNC. The details are as follows.

First, we calculate η_{min} for register blocking using Eq. 1. In register blocking, all nonzeros within a block share one coordinate index, thus the working set for one nonzero is roughly equal to the number of bytes for storing one double-precision word, i.e.,

8 bytes. To multiply 8 nonzeros using register blocking, an efficient implementation of the basic SIMD sequence requires approximately 6 cycles (1 cycle for loading x, 1 cycle for loading val, 1 cycle for multiplication, and 2-3 cycles for loop overheads and prefetching instructions). Additionally, we use 60 cores at 1.09 GHz, and the STREAM bandwidth on KNC achieves 163 GB/s. Putting these quantities together and using Eq 1, we obtain $\eta_{min} = 23.7\%$. We now measure the nonzero densities for the smallest block sizes that facilitate SIMD on KNC. The results are displayed in Table 2, showing that, for 4×4, 8×2 and 8×8 register blocks, 6, 7 and 8 matrices have nonzero density lower than 23.7%, respectively. We note that this is a crude study because no matrix reordering was used, but the above illustrates the point.

Table 2: Average percent nonzero density of register blocks and ELLPACK slices (slice height 8).

Matrix	Register blocking			SELLPACK
	4×4	8×2	8×4	
Dense8	100.00	100.00	100.00	100.00
Wind Tunnel	69.83	63.47	59.91	98.96
Circuit5M	29.70	21.82	18.39	60.07
Rail4284	20.09	14.00	10.75	38.18
Mip1	82.08	77.52	73.30	90.10
In-2004	37.99	37.59	28.19	66.69
Si41Ge41H72	30.30	25.38	20.45	64.88
Ldoor	59.60	53.64	45.98	89.75
Bone010	58.83	51.71	45.98	94.02
Rucci1	12.26	18.11	9.32	98.55
Cage15	17.25	12.47	9.98	97.16
Rajat31	12.22	10.98	6.67	98.73
12month1	9.82	8.86	5.66	25.39
Spal_004	23.12	14.00	13.66	91.39
Crankseg_2	52.17	48.72	40.33	89.76
Torso1	73.52	69.55	62.85	93.42

4.1.2 ELLPACK and Sliced ELLPACK

The ELLPACK format and its variants are perhaps the most effective formats for GPUs. ELLPACK packs the nonzeros of a sparse matrix towards the left and stores them in a $m \times L$ dense array (the column indices are stored in a companion array) where m is the row dimension of the matrix, and L is the maximum number of nonzeros in any row. When rows have fewer than L nonzeros, they are padded with zeros to fill out the dense array. The dense array is stored in column-major order, and thus operations on columns of the dense array can be vectorized with SIMD operations, making this format very suitable for architectures with wide SIMD.

The efficiency of the ELLPACK format highly depends on the distribution of nonzeros. When the number of nonzeros per row varies considerably, the performance degrades due to the overhead of the padding zeros. To address this problem, Monakov et al. [15] proposed the sliced ELLPACK (SELLPACK) format for GPUs, which partitions the sparse matrix into row slices and packs each slice separately, thus requiring less zero padding than ELLPACK.

Table 2 also shows the average nonzero density of slices in SELLPACK using slice height 8, corresponding to KNC's double precision SIMD width. For matrices with highly variable numbers of nonzeros per row, the SELLPACK format still requires excessive zero padding.

4.2 Proposed Matrix Format

SpMV in the CSR format suffers from low SIMD efficiency, particularly for matrices with short rows. Since SIMD efficiency is expected to be higher in the ELLPACK format, and since the format supports wide SIMD operations, it forms the basis of our proposed matrix format, called *ELLPACK Sparse Block* (ESB). At a high level, ESB effectively partitions the matrix coarsely by rows and columns into large sparse blocks. The row and column partitioning is a type of cache blocking, promoting locality in accessing vector x. The sparse blocks in a block column are appended and stored in a variant of the ELLPACK format.

In practice, matrices generated by an application code may have an ordering that is "local," e. g., rows corresponding to nearby grid points of a mesh are ordered together, which translates to locality when accessing the vector x. Such an ordering may also be imposed by using a bandwidth reducing ordering. The coarse row and column partitionings in ESB are intended to maintain locality, as described below.

4.2.1 SELLPACK Storage with a Bit Array

The original ITPACK-ELLPACK format was designed for classical vector processors which required long vector lengths for efficiency. SIMD processing on GPUs requires vector lengths equal to the number of threads in a thread block, and thus it is natural to store the matrix in slices (i. e., SELLPACK) which requires less zero padding. SIMD processing on CPUs including KNC only requires vector lengths equal to the width of SIMD registers. Again it is natural to store the matrix in slices, and the smaller slice height required on CPUs can make this storage scheme particularly effective at reducing zero padding.

To further reduce the memory bandwidth associated with the padding zeros, we can avoid storing zeros by storing instead the length (number of nonzeros) of each *row*, as done in ELLPACK-R [22] for GPUs. Here, each CUDA thread multiplies elements in a row until the end of the row is reached. For SIMD processing on CPUs, we can store the length of each *column* of the dense ELLPACK arrays, corresponding to the length of the vector operations for processing that column (this assumes that the rows are sorted by length and thus the nonzeros in each column are contiguous).

For KNC, instead of storing column lengths, it is more efficient to store a bit array, with ones indicating nonzero locations in the SELLPACK dense array with slice height 8. (Rows within a slice also do not need to be sorted by length when a bit array is used.) Each 8 bits corresponds to one column of a matrix slice and can be used expediently as a write-mask in KNC's SIMD instructions to dynamically reconstruct the SELLPACK dense array as the SpMV operation is being carried out. Required memory bandwidth is reduced with this bit array technique, but it technically does not increase SIMD efficiency because we still perform arithmetic on padding zeros. We note that earlier work has also used bit arrays for storing the sparsity pattern of blocks of sparse matrices in order to avoid explicitly storing zeros [27, 3].

4.2.2 Finite-Window Sorting

On GPUs, row sorting can be used to increase the nonzero density of slices for SELLPACK [5, 11]. Rows of the sparse matrix are sorted in descending order of number of nonzeros per row. As adjacent rows in the sorted matrix have similar numbers of nonzeros, storing the sorted matrix in SELLPACK format requires less zero padding than without sorting.

The adjacent rows in the sparse matrix in the original ordering often have high temporal locality on accesses to vector x. This is because the matrix either naturally has good locality or has been reordered to reduce the matrix bandwidth. While row sorting increases the nonzero density, it may destroy this locality, which results in extra cache misses. To limit this side effect of row sorting, instead of sorting the entire matrix, we partition the matrix into row blocks with block height w and sort the rows within each block individually. We call this new sorting scheme *Finite-Window Sorting* (FWS). We refer to w as the *window size*. As mentioned, this is a row partitioning that promotes locality when accessing vector x.

To evaluate FWS, we measure the average nonzero density of SELLPACK slices for various window sizes and the corresponding amount of memory transfer due to the accesses on vectors x and y (measured by Intel® VTune™) of the SpMV kernel using SELLPACK format. As an example, the result for *In-2004* is shown in Fig. 3 (results for other matrices are similar). We see that the nonzero density and the amount of memory transfer both increase as the window size increases. However, an important observation is that when the window size is smaller than some value, e. g., 1000 for *In-2004*, the amount of memory transfer appears to grow much more slowly than the nonzero density. This is a positive result since it suggests that we may use FWS to significantly increase the nonzero density while only slightly increasing the amount of memory transfer.

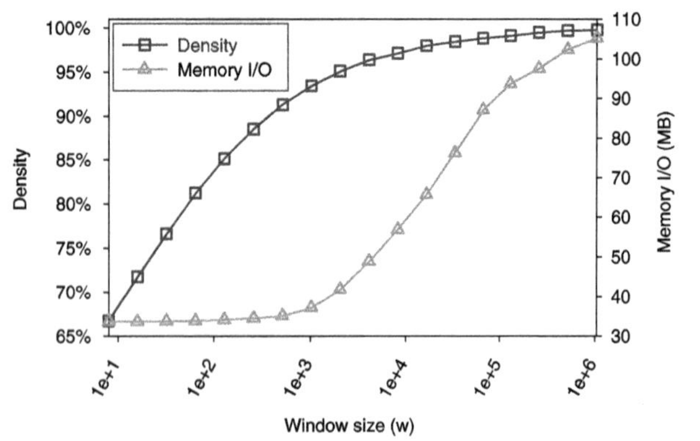

Figure 3: Nonzero density and memory I/O as a function of window size (w) for *In-2004*.

To address the low SIMD efficiency problem of SELLPACK, we use FWS to increase the average nonzero density of slices to be just larger than η_{min}. Since η_{min} is relatively small, a small w is sufficient for most matrices, thus the increase in memory transfer is very slight. We use the same w for the entire matrix.

Fig. 4 illustrates the ESB format for a $m \times n$ matrix. The ESB format consists of six arrays: *val*, the nonzero values of the matrix; *colidx*, the column indices for the nonzeros; *vbit*, an array of bits marking the position of each nonzero in SELLPACK; *yorder*, the row ordering after FWS (c permutation vectors of length m); *sliceptr*, a list of $m/8 \times c$ values indexing where each slice starts in *val*; *vbitptr*, a list of c values indexing where each column block starts in *vbit*.

4.3 SpMV Kernel with ESB Format

The multiplication of a column block of ESB matrix is illustrated in Alg. 2. Due to the use of the bit array, every SIMD instruction in the inner loop, which processes one slice, has a write-mask. At the end of each inner iteration, the *popcnt* instruction (line 17) is used to count the number of 1's in *vbit*, which is equal to the number of nonzeros processed in this iteration. Since the rows of the matrix have been permuted, we use gather and scatter instructions to load and store y, using the offsets stored in *yorder*.

In practice, we also parallelize the SpMV operation across column blocks. Here, we use a temporary copy of y for each block and use a reduce operation across these temporary copies at the end of the computation.

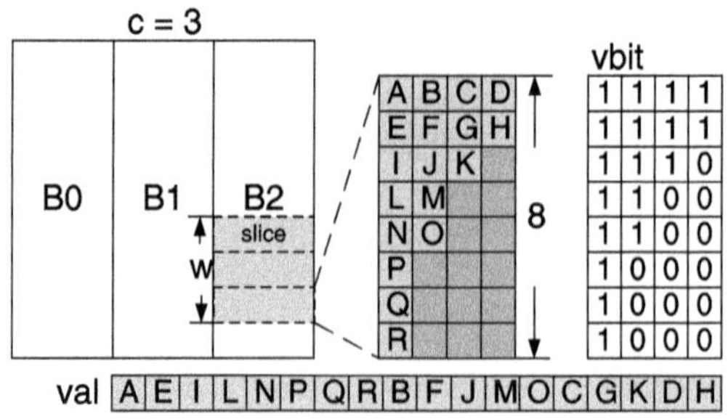

Figure 4: ELLPACK sparse block format. The sparse matrix is partitioned into c column blocks. Each column block is sorted by FWS with window size w and stored in SELLPACK format (slice height = 8) with a bit array.

The reconstruction of the dense arrays are implemented using load unpack instructions (lines 13 and 14), which are able to load contiguous elements from memory and write them sparsely into SIMD registers. The write-mask in the load unpack instruction is used to mark which positions of the SIMD register to write the loaded elements.

Algorithm 2: Multiply the i *th* column block of matrix in ESB format.

```
1  yr ← i × m;
2  startslice ← i × m/8;
3  endslice ← (i+1)m/8;
4  sliceidx ← startslice;
5  idx ← sliceptr [sliceidx];
6  while sliceidx < endslice do
7      k ← vbitptr [i];
8      end ← sliceptr [sliceidx+1];
       /* compute for a slice */
9      vec_offsets ← load (&yorder [yr]);
10     vec_y ← gather (vec_offsets, &y [0]);
11     while idx < end do
12         writemask ← vbit [k];
13         vec_idx ← loadunpack (&colidx [idx], writemask);
14         vec_vals ← loadunpack (&val [idx], writemask);
15         vec_x ← gather (vec_idx, &x [0], writemask);
16         vec_y ← fmadd (vec_vals, vec_x, vec_y, writemask);
17         idx ← idx+ popcnt (vbit [k]);
18         k ← k+1;
19     scatter (vec_y, vec_offsets, &y [0]);
20     yr ← yr+8;
21     sliceidx ← sliceidx+1;
```

Given the ESB kernel shown in Alg. 2, we can calculate η_{min} for the ESB format. From the ESB kernel assembly code, the basic SIMD sequence (lines 11-18) takes approximately 26 cycles. In ESB format, the working set for one nonzero includes one value and one column index, i. e., 12 bytes. Using Eq. 1, we have that the SIMD efficiency of any SpMV kernel using the ESB format needs to be larger than 68.3%.

4.4 Selecting c and w

To select the number of block columns c and the window height w, several values are tested for each matrix. Although c and w are not independent, we find that they are only weakly related and that it is better to select c before selecting w.

The choice of number of block columns c is dependent on the structure of the sparse matrix. Nishtala et al. [16] describes situations where cache blocking is beneficial, including the presence of very long rows. We found column blocking to be beneficial for three of our test matrices: *Rail4284*, *12month1* and *Spal_004*.

For matrices that favor cache blocking, the execution time of SpMV can be modeled as $T(c) = (12nnz + 16mc + M_x(c))/B$, where the first two terms in the numerator represent the memory traffic due to accessing the matrix and vector y respectively, and $M_x(c)$ is the memory traffic due to accessing vector x. Since M_x decreases as c increases and m is relatively small, this model suggests that the execution time of the SpMV kernel might first decrease as c decreases until a certain value, near where there is no more temporal locality of vector x to exploit. After that point, the execution time will increase since the memory traffic due to accessing vector y increases as c increases.

Fig. 5 shows the performance of the ESB kernel for the three matrices that favor cache blocking as c varies between 1 and 1024, which confirms the implication of our performance model. The figure also shows that the performance decreases slowly when c is larger than the optimal value. We thus use the heuristic that we can safely choose c as a power of 2.

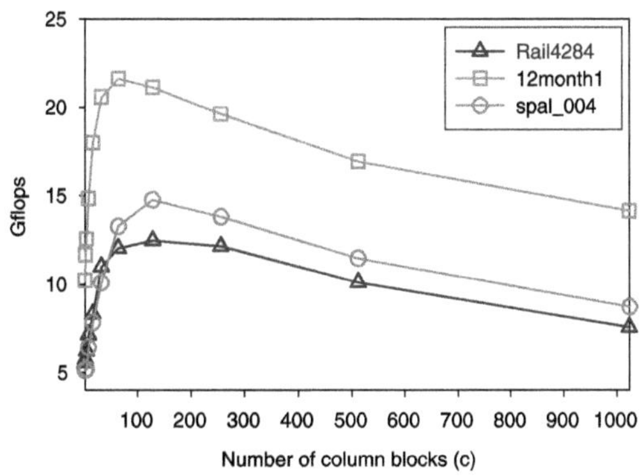

Figure 5: Performance of ESB kernel for *Rail4284 12month1*, and *Spal_004* as a function of the number of column blocks (c).

We select the window size w by gradually increasing it until the nonzero density of slices exceeds η_{min}. As discussed in Section 4.3, η_{min} of ESB format is 68.3%, however, we use 75% to be more conservative. The cost of search can be reduced by a matrix sampling scheme, proposed in [8] for choosing register block sizes. In the matrix sampling scheme, 1% of the slices are selected from the SELLPACK matrix to form a new matrix, and the new matrix is sorted to estimate the nonzero densities for various w.

5. LOAD BALANCERS FOR KNC

SpMV is parallelized across 240 threads on KNC, or 4 threads per core. To assign work to each thread, we consider three partitioning/load balancing schemes. The starting point for these schemes is a matrix in ESB format, where parameters such as c, w, and matrix ordering are considered fixed. We note that these balancers are general and may be applied to other KNC workloads.

5.1 Static Partitioning of Cache Misses

The performance of SpMV kernels highly depends on the amount of memory transfer and the number of cache misses. This leads to our first load balancer, called *static-miss*. Here, the sparse matrix is statically partitioned into row blocks that have equal numbers of L2 cache misses. This is accomplished approximately using a simple cache simulator which models key characteristics of the L2 cache of a single core of KNC: total capacity, line size and associativity.

The main drawback of *static-miss* is the high cost of cache simulation for each matrix of interest. In our implementation, the cost is greater than that of a single matrix-vector multiplication, which means that the application of *static-miss* is limited to cases where the SpMV kernel is required to execute a large number of times with the same matrix. Like other static partitioning methods, *static-miss* also does not capture dynamic runtime factors that affect performance, e. g., the number of cache misses is sometimes highly dependent on thread execution order.

5.2 Hybrid Dynamic Scheduler

A more sophisticated load balancing method for SpMV on KNC is to use dynamic schedulers, which are categorized into two types: work-sharing schedulers and work-stealing schedulers. However, both types have performance issues on KNC. For work sharing schedulers, the performance bottleneck is the contention for the public task queue. Due to the large number of cores, data contention on KNC is more expensive than on multi-core CPUs, especially when data is shared by many threads. On the other hand, work stealing schedulers on KNC suffer from the high cost of stealing tasks from remote threads. The stealing cost is proportional to the distance between the thief thread and the victim thread.

To address the performance issues of both work-sharing and work-stealing schedulers, we design a hybrid work-sharing/work-stealing scheduler, inspired by [18]. In the hybrid dynamic scheduler, the sparse matrix is first partitioned into P tasks with equal numbers of nonzeros. The tasks are then evenly distributed to N task queues, each of which is shared by a group of threads (each thread is assigned to a single queue). Within each thread group, the work-sharing scheduler is used to distribute tasks. Since each task queue is shared by a limited number of threads, the contention overhead is lowered. When a task queue is empty, the threads on the queue steal tasks from other queues. With this design, the number of stealing operations and the overhead of stealing are reduced.

The two parameters P and N need to be carefully selected to achieve high performance. P controls the maximum parallelism and also affects the temporal locality of memory accesses. With smaller tasks, the SpMV kernel will lose the temporal locality of accessing vector x. For our test matrices, P is chosen in the range of 1000-2000, based on the size of the sparse matrix. N is a tradeoff between the costs of work sharing and work stealing and is chosen to be 20 in our SpMV implementation, i. e., 12 threads (3 cores) share one task queue.

5.3 Adaptive Load Balancer

In many scientific applications, such as iterative linear equation solvers, the SpMV kernel is executed multiple times for the same matrix or matrix sparsity pattern. For these applications, it is possible to use performance data from earlier calls to SpMV to repartition the matrix to achieve better load balance.

This idea, which we call adaptive load balancing, was first proposed for SpMV by Lee and Eigenmann [12]. In their load balancer, the execution time of each thread is measured after each execution of SpMV. The normalized cost of each row of the sparse matrix is then approximated as the execution time of the thread to which the row is assigned, divided by the total number of rows assigned to that thread. For the next execution of SpMV, the sparse matrix is re-partitioned by evenly dividing costs of rows.

Although Lee and Eigenmann's method was originally designed for distributed memory systems, we adapted it to KNC with minor changes. To reduce the cost of re-partitioning, we used the 1D partitioning algorithm of Pinar and Aykanat [19]. Experiments show that the adaptive tuning converges in fewer than 10 executions.

6. EXPERIMENTAL RESULTS

6.1 Load Balancing Results

We first test the load balancing techniques discussed in Section 5 for parallelizing SpMV for matrices in ESB format. We compare the following load balancers:

- *static-nnz*: statically partition the matrix into blocks with approximately equal numbers of nonzeros;
- *static-miss*: statically partition the matrix into blocks with approximately equal numbers of cache misses;
- *work-sharing*: working-sharing dynamic scheduler;
- *work-stealing*: working-stealing dynamic scheduler;
- *hybrid-scheduler*: hybrid dynamic scheduler;
- *adaptive-balancer*: adaptive load balancer after 5 tuning executions.

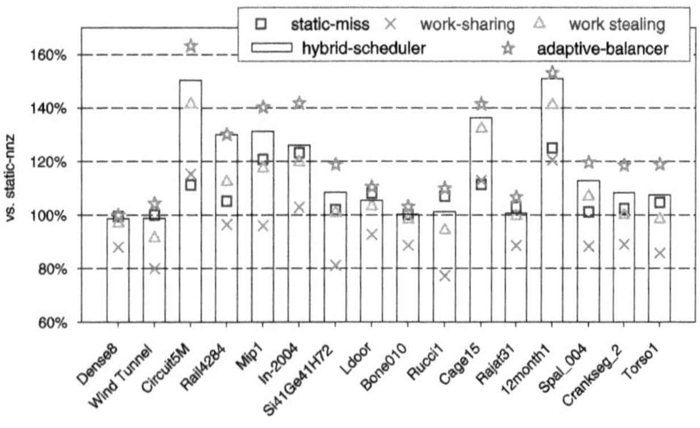

Figure 6: Normalized performance of SpMV using various load balancers.

Fig. 6 shows the results, which are normalized against those of *static-nnz*. As evident in the figure, *adaptive-balancer* gives the best SpMV performance, achieving on average 1.24x improvement over *static-nnz*. The *hybrid-scheduler* has best SpMV performance among all the dynamic schedulers, but is 5% worse than *adaptive-balancer*, likely due to scheduling overheads. Results for *hybrid-scheduler* are generally better than those for *work-stealing* and *work-sharing*. The *work-sharing* scheduler is worst for most matrices and only outperforms *static-nnz* and *static-miss* on the largest matrices, e. g., *Circuit5M* and *Cage15*, for which data contention overheads can be amortized.

The static partitioning methods have an advantage over dynamic schedulers when the matrices have regular sparsity patterns, such as even distributions of the number of nonzeros per row, as in *Wind Tunnel* and *Rajat31*. We found *static-miss* to give better performance than *static-nnz* for all the matrices, but its results are not uniformly good, likely because of the poor accuracy of our simple cache simulator for irregularly structured matrices.

6.2 ESB Results

SpMV performance results using ESB format are presented in Fig. 7. In these results, optimal values of w and c were selected using the method described in Section 4.4. The timings do not include time for selecting these parameters or for FWS. The hybrid dynamic scheduler was used for load balancing.

To quantify the effect of column blocking (CB), and the use of bit arrays and FWS, we also test SpMV kernels that incrementally implement these techniques. In the figure, green bars show SpMV performance using the SELLPACK format, which is our baseline. Yellow bars show the improvement by using column blocking only (applied to three matrices). Orange bars show the additional improvement by using bit arrays. Red bars show the performance using the full set of ESB optimizations.

We also use pink squares to show results using complete row sorting (no windows used for sorting). Finally, blue triangles are used to show the performance of the CSR kernel.

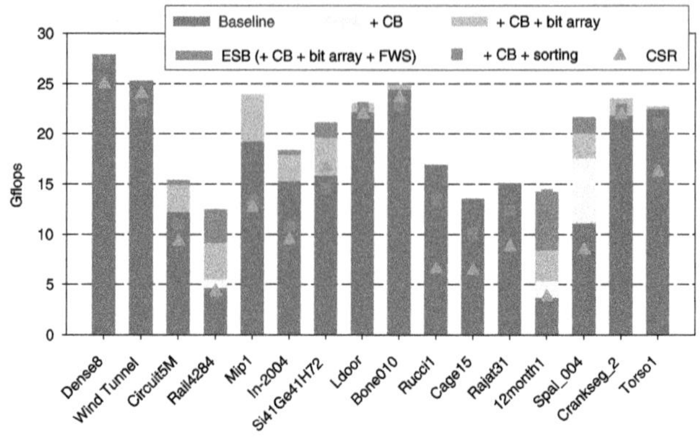

Figure 7: Performance of SpMV implementations using ESB format, showing increasing levels of optimizations of column blocking, bit array and finite-window sorting.

Although column blocking gives an improvement for the three matrices with very long rows, the improvement in two cases is very modest. A disadvantage of column blocking is that it can decrease the average nonzero density of the blocks and thus decrease SIMD efficiency.

The bit array technique improves performance in most cases, however, a small performance degradation ($< 3\%$) is also observed for some matrices, including *Dense8*, *Rucci1* and *Cage15*. This is expected for matrices with nonzero densities that are already large, since the bit array introduces additional overhead while there is no room to reduce bandwidth.

The figure also shows the significance of using FWS, which helps 6 matrices that have nonzero density lower than η_{min}. Due to its destruction of locality, complete sorting leads to poor results on KNC, with results that are poorer than the baseline for many matrices. This justifies the use of FWS.

The final ESB implementation outperforms the CSR implementation, as to be expected. On average, ESB is 1.85x faster than CSR. The greatest speedups come from the matrices with low SIMD efficiency, cache miss latency problems, and/or load imbalance.

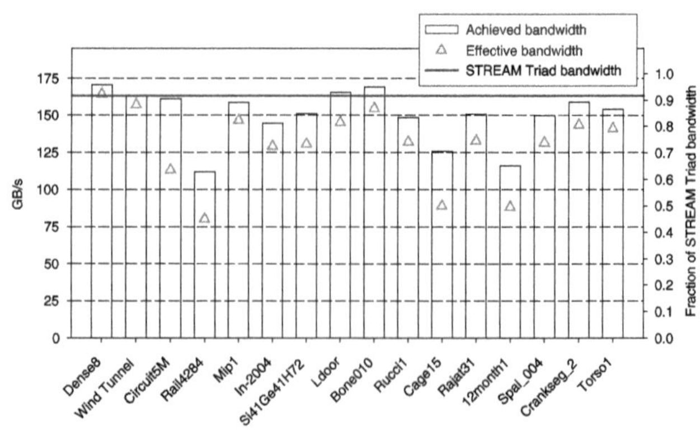

Figure 8: Achieved and effective bandwidth of SpMV implementation using ESB format.

Fig. 8 shows the achieved and the effective bandwidth of our ESB kernel. The achieved bandwidth was measured by Intel® VTune™. The effective bandwidth, which is used in prior work [26, 5], accounts only for the "effective" memory traffic of the kernel. For a sparse matrix with m rows, n columns and nnz nonzeros, the optimistic flop:byte ratio of SpMV in ESB format is $\lambda = 2\,nnz/(12\,nnz + 16\,m + 8\,n)$, which excludes redundant memory accesses to vectors x and y. Assuming SpMV on the matrix achieves P flops, the effective bandwidth is P/λ.

By comparing the achieved and the effective bandwidth with the STREAM bandwidth, we see how far the performance of our kernel is from the upper performance bound. On average, the achieved bandwidth and effective bandwidth are within 10% and 20% of the STREAM Triad bandwidth, respectively, indicating that the implementation is very efficient.

6.3 Performance Comparison

We now compare the performance of SpMV on KNC with SpMV performance on the following architectures:

- *NVIDIA K20X*: NVIDIA Tesla K20X (Kepler GPU), 6 GB GDDR5 memory, 1.31 Tflops peak double precision performance, 181 GB/s (ECC on) STREAM Triad bandwidth;
- *Dual SNB-EP*: 2.7 GHz dual-socket Intel® Xeon® Processor E5-2680 (Sandy Brige EP), 20 MB L2 cache, 32 GB DDR memory, 346 Gflops peak double precision performance, 76 GB/s STREAM Triad bandwidth.

For K20X, we used two SpMV codes: cuSPARSE v5.0[3] and CUSP v0.3 [2], which use a variety of matrix formats, CSR, COO, DIA, BCSR, ELLPACK, and ELL/HYB [1]. For each of the test matrices, we ran experiments with both codes using all the formats. For brevity, we only report the best of these results. For the dual SNB-EP system, we tested three SpMV codes: the CSR format implementation from Intel® MKL v11.0, the auto-tuning implementation from Williams et al. [26] and the Compressed Sparse Block (CSB) implementation (2011 release) from Buluç et al. [3]. Again, only the best performance of the three implementations is reported. For comparison purposes, ECC was turned on in all the platforms.

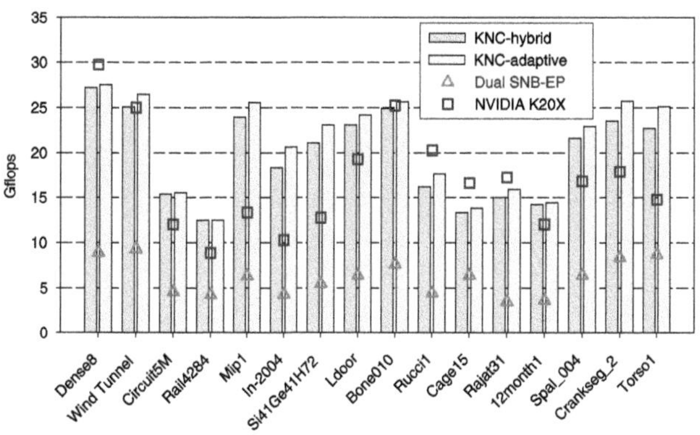

Figure 9: Performance comparison of SpMV implementations on KNC, SNB-EP and GPUs.

Fig. 9 shows the comparative results. KNC has a large advantage over dual SNB-EP; for most matrices, *KNC-adaptive* and *KNC-hybrid* are 3.52x and 3.36x faster, respectively, than SNB-EP, which is expected since KNC has significantly higher memory bandwidth. Compared to the K20X, although KNC has a lower STREAM bandwidth, *KNC-adaptive* is on average 1.32x faster than the best SpMV implementation on K20X. We believe that this mainly due to KNC having much larger caches than K20X, so accesses to vectors x and y are more likely to be directed to caches rather than memory. For the matrices with "regular" sparsity patterns, e. g., banded matrices, which are easily handled by small caches, KNC has little performance advantage over or is slower than K20X. For matrices that have complex sparsity patterns, KNC's advantage over K20X can be as high as 2x.

[3]https://developer.nvidia.com/cusparse

7. RELATED WORK

SpMV optimization has been extensively studied over decades on various architectures. Relevant for us is optimizations for CPUs and GPUs. For a comprehensive review, we refer to several survey papers [23, 8, 26, 7].

Blocking is widely used for optimizing SpMV on CPUs. Depending on the motivation, block methods can be divided into two major categories. In the first category, blocking improves the spatial and temporal locality of the SpMV kernel by exploiting data reuse at various levels in the memory hierarchy, including register [13, 8], cache [8, 16] and TLB [16]. In the second category, block structures are discovered in order to eliminate integer index overhead, thus reducing the bandwidth requirements [24, 20]. Besides blocking, other techniques have also been proposed to reduce the bandwidth requirements of SpMV. These techniques broadly include matrix reordering [17], value and index compression [25, 10], and exploiting symmetry [3].

Due to the increasing popularity of GPUs, in recent years numerous matrix formats and optimization techniques have been proposed to improve the performance of SpMV on GPUs. Among the matrix formats, ELLPACK and its variants have been shown to be most successful. The first ELLPACK-based format for GPUs was proposed by Bell and Garland [1], which mixed ELLPACK and COO formats. Monakov et al. [15] invented the Sliced ELLPACK format, in which slices of the matrix are packed in ELLPACK format separately, thus reducing zero padding. Vázquez et al. [22] used another approach to address zero-padding. Here, in ELLPACK-R, all the padding zeros are removed, and a separate array is used to store the length of each row. Kreutzer et al. [11] proposed the pJDS matrix format, which extended ELLPACK-R by row sorting. There are also blocked SpMV implementations on GPUs. Jee et al. [5] proposed the BELLPACK matrix format which partitions the matrix into small dense blocks and organizes the blocks in ELLPACK format. Monakov et al. [14] proposed a format also using small dense blocks, but augments it with ELLPACK format for nonzeros outside this structure.

8. CONCLUSIONS

This paper presented an efficient implementation of SpMV for the Intel® Xeon Phi™ Coprocessor. The implementation uses a specialized ELLPACK-based format that promotes high SIMD efficiency and data access locality. Along with careful load balancing, the implementation achieves close to optimal bandwidth utilization. The implementation also significantly outperforms an optimized implementation using the CSR format.

There has been much recent work on SpMV for GPUs, and high performance has been attained by exploiting the high memory bandwidth of GPUs. However, GPUs are not designed for irregularly structured computations, such as operations on sparse matrices with nonuniform numbers of nonzeros per row. For our test set, we find our SpMV implementation on KNC to perform better on average than the best implementations currently available on high-end GPUs. One general explanation is that KNC has much larger caches than GPUs, which helps reduce the cost of irregular accesses on vector x. Also, additional hardware support on KNC, such as load unpack, enables more delicate optimization techniques, e. g., the bit array technique used in this paper, than would be possible on GPUs without such support. Indeed, we expect that the many compression techniques for SpMV proposed in the literature (and independent of the ideas of this paper) can further reduce required bandwidth and improve the performance of our SpMV implementation, but these may be difficult to implement on GPUs.

The general performance issues raised in this paper for SpMV also apply to other workloads. Due to its large SIMD width, achieving high performance on KNC will require carefully designing algorithms to fully utilize SIMD operations, even for applications that are memory bandwidth bound. Careful attention to data locality and memory access patterns can help minimize the performance impact of high cache miss latencies. Our experience with SpMV also demonstrates the importance of a well-designed load balancing method.

9. ACKNOWLEDGMENTS

The authors would like to thank Aydin Buluç, Lenny Oliker and Samuel Williams for helpful discussions and for providing us with their SpMV implementations for performance comparisons.

10. REFERENCES

[1] N. Bell and M. Garland. Implementing sparse matrix-vector multiplication on throughput-oriented processors. In *Proc. ACM/IEEE Conf. Supercomputing*, SC '09, pp. 18. ACM, 2009.

[2] N. Bell and M. Garland. CUSP: Generic parallel algorithms for sparse matrix and graph computations, 2012. V0.3.0.

[3] A. Buluc, S. Williams, L. Oliker, and J. Demmel. Reduced-bandwidth multithreaded algorithms for sparse matrix-vector multiplication. In *Proc. 2011 IEEE Intl Parallel & Distributed Processing Symposium*, IPDPS 2011, pp. 721–733, Washington, DC, USA, 2011. IEEE.

[4] A. Buttari, V. Eijkhout, J. Langou, and S. Filippone. Performance optimization and modeling of blocked sparse kernels. *Intl J. High Perf. Comput. Appl.*, 21:467–484, 2007.

[5] J. Choi, A. Singh, and R. Vuduc. Model-driven autotuning of sparse matrix-vector multiply on GPUs. In *ACM SIGPLAN Notices*, volume 45, pp. 115–126. ACM, 2010.

[6] J. Davis and E. Chung. SpMV: A memory-bound application on the GPU stuck between a rock and a hard place. *Microsoft Technical Report*, 2012.

[7] G. Goumas, K. Kourtis, N. Anastopoulos, V. Karakasis, and N. Koziris. Performance evaluation of the sparse matrix-vector multiplication on modern architectures. *J. Supercomput.*, 50:36–77, 2009.

[8] E. Im, K. Yelick, and R. Vuduc. SPARSITY: Optimization framework for sparse matrix kernels. *Intl J. High Perf. Comput. Appl.*, 18:135–158, 2004.

[9] V. Karakasis, G. Goumas, and N. Koziris. A comparative study of blocking storage methods for sparse matrices on multicore architectures. In *Proc. 2009 Intl Conf. Comput. Sci. and Eng.*, CSE '09, pp. 247–256. IEEE, 2009.

[10] K. Kourtis, G. Goumas, and N. Koziris. Exploiting compression opportunities to improve SpMxV performance on shared memory systems. *ACM Trans. Architecture and Code Optimization*, 7:16, 2010.

[11] M. Kreutzer, G. Hager, G. Wellein, H. Fehske, A. Basermann, and A. R. Bishop. Sparse matrix-vector multiplication on GPGPU clusters: A new storage format and a scalable implementation. In *Proc. 2012 IEEE Intl Parallel and Distributed Processing Symposium Workshops*, IPDPS 2012, pp. 1696–1702, Washington, DC, USA, 2012. IEEE.

[12] S. Lee and R. Eigenmann. Adaptive runtime tuning of parallel sparse matrix-vector multiplication on distributed memory systems. In *Proc. 22nd Intl Conf. Supercomputing*, ICS '08, pp. 195–204. ACM, 2008.

[13] J. Mellor-Crummey and J. Garvin. Optimizing sparse matrix-vector product computations using unroll and jam. *Intl J. of High Perf. Comput. Appl.*, 18:225–236, 2004.

[14] A. Monakov and A. Avetisyan. Implementing blocked sparse matrix-vector multiplication on NVIDIA GPUs. In *Proc. 9th Intl Workshop Embedded Computer Systems: Architectures, Modeling, and Simulation*, SAMOS '09, pp. 289–297, Berlin, Heidelberg, 2009. Springer-Verlag.

[15] A. Monakov, A. Lokhmotov, and A. Avetisyan. Automatically tuning sparse matrix-vector multiplication for GPU architectures. In *Proc. 5th Intl Conf. High Perf. Embedded Architectures and Compilers*, HiPEAC'10, pp. 111–125, Berlin, Heidelberg, 2010. Springer-Verlag.

[16] R. Nishtala, R. W. Vuduc, J. W. Demmel, and K. A. Yelick. When cache blocking of sparse matrix vector multiply works and why. *Appl. Algebra Eng., Commun. Comput.*, 18:297–311, 2007.

[17] L. Oliker, X. Li, P. Husbands, and R. Biswas. Effects of ordering strategies and programming paradigms on sparse matrix computations. *SIAM Rev.*, 44:373–393, 2002.

[18] S. Olivier, A. Porterfield, K. Wheeler, and J. Prins. Scheduling task parallelism on multi-socket multicore systems. In *Proc. 1st Intl. Workshop Runtime and Operating Systems for Supercomputers*, ROSS '11, pp. 49–56. ACM, 2011.

[19] A. Pinar and C. Aykanat. Fast optimal load balancing algorithms for 1D partitioning. *J. Parallel Distrib. Comput.*, 64:974–996, 2004.

[20] A. Pinar and M. T. Heath. Improving performance of sparse matrix-vector multiplication. In *Proc. ACM/IEEE Conf. Supercomputing*, SC '99, New York, NY, USA, 1999. ACM.

[21] B. Su and K. Keutzer. clSpMV: A cross-platform OpenCL SpMV framework on GPUs. In *Proc. 26th Intl Conf. Supercomputing*, ICS '12, pp. 353–364. ACM, 2012.

[22] F. Vázquez, J. Fernández, and E. Garzón. A new approach for sparse matrix vector product on NVIDIA GPUs. *Concurr. Comput.: Pract. Exper.*, 23:815–826, 2011.

[23] R. W. Vuduc. *Automatic performance tuning of sparse matrix kernels*. PhD thesis, Univ. of California, Berkeley, 2003.

[24] R. W. Vuduc and H.-J. Moon. Fast sparse matrix-vector multiplication by exploiting variable block structure. In *Proc. High-Perf. Comput. and Commun. Conf.*, HPCC'05, pp. 807–816, Sorrento, Italy, 2005.

[25] J. Willcock and A. Lumsdaine. Accelerating sparse matrix computations via data compression. In *Proc. 20th Intl Conf. Supercomputing*, ICS '06, pp. 307–316. ACM, 2006.

[26] S. Williams, L. Oliker, R. Vuduc, J. Shalf, K. Yelick, and J. Demmel. Optimization of sparse matrix-vector multiplication on emerging multicore platforms. In *Proc. ACM/IEEE Conf. Supercomputing*, SC '07, pp. 38:1–38:12, New York, NY, USA, 2007. ACM.

[27] S. W. Williams. *Auto-tuning performance on multicore computers*. PhD thesis, Univ. of California, Berkeley, 2008.

Expressing Graph Algorithms Using Generalized Active Messages

Nicholas Edmonds
Indiana University
Bloomington, IN 47405
ngedmond@cs.indiana.edu

Jeremiah Willcock
Indiana University
Bloomington, IN 47405
jewillco@cs.indiana.edu

Andrew Lumsdaine
Indiana University
Bloomington, IN 47405
lums@cs.indiana.edu

ABSTRACT

Recently, graph computation has emerged as an important class of high-performance computing application whose characteristics differ markedly from those of traditional, compute-bound kernels. Libraries such as BLAS, LAPACK, and others have been successful in codifying best practices in numerical computing. The data-driven nature of graph applications necessitates a more complex application stack incorporating runtime optimization. In this paper, we present a method of phrasing graph algorithms as collections of asynchronous, concurrently executing, concise code fragments which may be invoked both locally and in remote address spaces. A runtime layer performs a number of dynamic optimizations, including message coalescing, message combining, and software routing. We identify a number of common patterns in these algorithms, and explore how this programming model can express those patterns. Algorithmic transformations are discussed which expose asynchrony that can be leveraged by the runtime to improve performance and reduce resource utilization. Practical implementations and performance results are provided for a number of representative algorithms.

Categories and Subject Descriptors

D.1.3 [**Programming Techniques**]: Concurrent Programming—*Parallel Programming*

General Terms

Performance, Design

1 Introduction

A growing and increasingly diverse group of scientific disciplines including bioinformatics, social network analysis, and data mining are beginning to utilize graph analytics at HPC scales. However, graph problems have a number of inherent characteristics that distinguish them from traditional scientific applications [29]. Graph computations are often completely *data-driven*: they are dictated by the vertex and edge structure of the graph rather than being expressed directly in code. Execution paths and data locations are therefore highly unpredictable. Moreover, the connectivity of many graphs is not determined by 3D space (as is the case for discretized partial differential equations), resulting in data dependencies and computations with *poor locality*. Finding high quality partitions in such situations is computationally impractical since no good separators may exist [18,27]. The resulting graph distributions have a high ratio of surface area to volume which can significantly limit scalability. Finally, graph algorithms are often based on exploring the structure of a graph rather than performing large numbers of computations on the graph data, which results in *fine-grained data accesses* and a *high ratio of data accesses to computation*. Latency costs (memory accesses as well as communication) can dominate such computations.

ICS'13, June 10–14, 2013, Eugene, Oregon, USA.

The standard parallelization approach for scientific applications follows the SPMD model which partitions the problem data among a number of processes and then uses a communicating sequential processes or bulk-synchronous-parallel [45] computation and communication pattern (typically with two-sided message passing) to effect the overall computation. Although this approach has been tremendously successful for scientific applications based on discretized partial differential equations, it is not well-suited for graph-based data-intensive applications [29]. To address these issues, we have developed an approach for portably expressing high-performance graph algorithms based on fine-grained generalized active messages, as provided by the Active Pebbles programming model [49].

As traditionally defined, an active message [46] is a message that is sent explicitly but not received explicitly: a previously registered handler is called automatically when an active message arrives. The Active Pebbles model adds to this the ability to send messages at granularities as small as single words, with the runtime system combining messages as appropriate for particular platforms; message handlers are also able to send new messages in unlimited ways, with termination detected automatically. The ability to send and process messages asynchronously enables a high degree of latency hiding and a large number of messages concurrently in flight, giving several performance benefits on general-purpose, distributed-memory platforms.

Formulating graph algorithms using active messages has the dual advantages of being both conceptually simple while not over-constraining implementations. To convert a sequential algorithm expressed in an iterative form using loops, the loop bodies become message bodies. Rather than the coarse-grained, implicit dependencies expressed by the ordering of loop iterations, the active message form of the algorithm expresses the minimal set of dependencies necessary for correctness by allowing message handlers to send other messages directly. This method of expressing dependencies allows the critical path of the application to be efficiently captured and executed without artificially extending it through coarse-grained programming constructs. Active messages allow the user to directly modify algorithm code in an understandable fashion (individual vertex and edge operations) rather than requiring the use of complicated, vendor-tuned primitives which operate at a coarser level.

With this approach, we are able to capture the fine-grained dependency structure of graph computations at runtime, exposing maximal parallelism. While this fine-grained expression may not be directly suited to certain hardware (e.g., due to message injection rate limits for network adapters), the active message model allows the runtime system to adapt the algorithms to the hardware using coalescing and other transformations. Deferring these decisions until runtime is especially appropriate for graph algorithms as the structure of the graph determines the computational structure of the algorithm and thus both are discovered dynamically.

Finally, the active message phrasing permits both shared- and distributed-memory parallelism, and is amenable to acceleration as well. Separating the expression of an algorithm (the code in the active messages) from the implementation (the messages themselves) enables performance portability across a variety of platforms without having to change the algorithm specification. A single algorithm specification may be executed using an active message library [6, 26, 49] in a distributed-memory environment, a threading library [34,47] possibly in combination with work-stealing [5] in a shared memory environment, and hardware-specific programming environments [1, 41] targeting various kinds of accelerators. Most importantly, arbitrary combinations of these hardware environments are also supported.

2 Related Work

This paper builds on previous work which described a programming and execution model that allows specification and implementation of data-driven applications to be separated [48]. Here we make the case for fine-grained active messages as a suitable programming abstraction for graph applications and discuss the algorithmic refinements and runtime optimization techniques necessary to make this phrasing efficient. Before we attempt to justify the use of a new abstraction and programming model for graph applications, it is first appropriate to examine existing abstractions and models, as well as past attempts to use active messages to implement graph algorithms. We refer readers to [49] for a discussion of related work on active messages.

2.1 Parallel Graph Libraries

A number of libraries targeted at parallel graph computation exist which utilize a variety of abstractions. The original version of the Parallel Boost Graph Library (Parallel BGL) [22] utilized a coarse-grained Bulk Synchronous Parallel [45] programming model and targeted only distributed-memory parallelism. Later extensions added some ad hoc forms of active messaging, though the performance of these approaches is limited by the underlying communication layer.

The Graph Algorithm and Pattern Discovery Toolbox (GAPDT, later renamed KDT) [21] provides both combinatorial and numerical tools to manipulate large graphs interactively. KDT runs in parallel over Star-P [38] and targets distributed memory parallelism. KDT focuses on algorithms though the underlying sparse matrix kernels are also exposed. Later versions of KDT use the Combinatorial BLAS [8] as the computational back-end. The Combinatorial BLAS also uses linear algebraic primitives to perform graph computation and incorporates two-dimensional data decompositions. We view linear algebraic kernels as complementary abstractions to our visitor-based approach, which could be joined in the future to allow users the flexibility of using both.

The MultiThreaded Graph Library (MTGL) [4] and Small-world Network Analysis and Partitioning (SNAP) [3] are shared-memory libraries for manipulating graphs and are thus limited to the resources available on a single symmetric multiprocessor. The MTGL uses loop-level parallelism and complicated dependency analysis to generate efficient code for the Cray XMT and, via virtualization, commodity SMPs. Experimental results indicate that out-of-core approaches are incapable of matching the performance of distributed-memory implementations [2] meaning that implementations capable of leveraging both shared and distributed memory parallelism are essential for graph computation at large scale.

2.2 Active Messages for Graph Algorithms

The Active Pebbles programming and execution models are based on the identification of a common set of techniques for expressing and executing data-driven problems [49]; graph algorithms are one of the specific motivating examples for that work. The implementations of graph algorithms presented here utilize AM++ [48], a library implementing the Active Pebbles model. Further details on Active Pebbles are given in Section 3.1.

STAPL is a generic parallel library for graph and other data structures and algorithms, built upon the ARMI active-message runtime system [43]. ARMI supports automatic message coalescing to coarsen message granularity for performance, but does not provide routing or message reductions natively. STAPL's parallel graph class pGraph is based on the sequential Boost Graph Library, and some of its algorithms use nested active messages to create distributed-memory parallelism, but details are not provided [42].

PGAS frameworks have also identified and are addressing limitations in their handling of graph algorithms. For example, Jose et al. introduced UPC Queues, a mechanism for faster producer-consumer communication in Unified Parallel C [24]. The goal of this work is to improve UPC's performance on the Graph 500 benchmark (breadth-first search).

The Chapel [9] language provides direct support for asynchronous active messages using the ***on ... do begin*** idiom [14], as well as native atomic blocks. This model inspired one of the intermediate languages described in Section 5, and (if combined with an appropriate execution model) would be a suitable abstraction for expressing graph algorithms using the approach described in this paper. The X10 language [10] has similar constructs using ***async*** and ***at*** keywords for sending active messages. That language has been used to create the ScaleGraph [13] graph library; their implementation techniques are not described.

3 Programming Model

Programming models which are well suited to traditional HPC applications depend heavily on the locality inherent in these applications, in particular, each node communicating with only a few local peers. Coarse-grained approaches based on the BSP "compute-communicate" model thus tend to yield scalable solutions on current system scales.

In contrast, graph applications possess no underlying natural locality which can be determined analytically. The locality information is **irregular**, and embedded directly in the data itself. This locality information describes a dependency graph for computations which is **non-local**, i.e., it does not have good separators [37]. To complicate matters further, graph problems tend to be **fine-grained**, i.e., they possess a large number of small objects. Performing efficient static coalescing of these objects into larger, coarser-grained objects is hampered by the irregularity of the problems. Rather than coarse-grained static (or compile-time) approaches, we apply the Active Pebbles programming and execution model, specifically designed for such fine-grained applications. This execution model performs transformations at runtime to efficiently map applications expressed in the programming model to the underlying machine in an architecture-aware fashion.

Message passing, an effective programming model for regular HPC applications, provides a clear separation of address spaces and makes all communication explicit. The Message Passing Interface (MPI) is the de facto standard for programming such systems [31]. However, graph applications need shared access to data structures which naturally cross address spaces. A number of choices exist for how to implement fine-grained, irregular remote memory access. The key requirement with regard to graph applications is that the remote memory updates performed by one process must be atomic with regard to those performed by other processes and must support "read-modify-write" operations (e.g., compare-and-swap, fetch-and-add, etc.). More importantly, only the process performing the updates has knowledge of which regions of memory are being updated and thus the process whose memory is the target of these updates cannot perform any sequencing or arbitration of the updates. Finally, some algorithms require dependent updates to multiple, non-contiguous locations in memory, which provides perhaps the greatest challenge to a programming model.

MPI-2 one-sided operations [31, ch. 11] and Partitioned Global Address Space (PGAS) models [33, 44] attempt to fill the gap left by two-sided MPI message passing by allowing transparent access to remote memory in an emulated global address space. However, mechanisms for concurrency control are limited to locks and critical sections; some models support weak predefined atomic operations (e.g., *MPI_Accumulate()*). Stronger atomic operations (e.g., compare and swap, fetch and add) and user-defined atomic operations are either not supported in current versions or do not perform well. Thus, we claim that these approaches do not provide the appropriate primitives for fine-grained graph applications. The designers of those approaches have also realized these limitations in the original models, leading to proposals such as UPC queues [24] and Global Futures [11] to add more sophisticated primitive operations (including active messages in some cases) to otherwise PGAS programming models. Additions to one-sided operations in MPI-3 [32, ch. 11] such as *MPI_Fetch_and_op()* and *MPI_Compare_and_swap()* may also rectify some of the shortcomings of the MPI one-sided communication model, though high performance implementations were unavailable when this work was conducted.

3.1 Background: Active Pebbles

Because of its specialization for the kinds of fine-grained applications that we consider, we use the Active Pebbles programming and execution model [49] as the underlying framework for our work. For completeness, we briefly summarize the model here. The Active Pebbles programming model takes traditional active messages [46] and generalizes them in a number of important ways, as well as providing an implementation designed to handle large numbers of tiny messages (both in data size and in computation) efficiently. The most important of the programming model generalizations is that Active Pebbles allows message handlers to directly send additional messages, to unbounded depth. In many cases this feature removes the need for application-level message buffering.

The primary abstractions in the Active Pebbles model are pebbles and targets. Pebbles are light-weight active messages that operate on targets (which can, transparently, be local or remote). Targets are created by binding together a data object with a message handler, through the use of a user-provided data distribution object. Pebbles are unordered (other than by termination detection), allowing flexibility in processing (such as threading or other forms of acceleration).

The termination detection features of Active Pebbles allow quiescence to be detected. In Active Pebbles, all messages must be sent within defined *epochs* (similar to the same concept in MPI-2 one-sided communication), and all messages globally are guaranteed to have been sent and handled—including those messages sent during handlers invoked by previous ones in the epoch—by the time the epoch completes. Active Pebbles provides runtime message coalescing to reduce network injection rate and increase bandwidth utilization, as well as software routing to reduce link and message buffer requirements in large networks. Finally, user-specified message reductions allow automatic message combining and duplicate message elimination, which is especially powerful in combination with routing and coalescing as will be seen in Section 5.

Active Pebbles allows graph applications to be expressed at their natural levels of granularity (e.g., individual vertex and edge operations) and then performs transformations at runtime to yield high performance. This programming model thus yields the expressiveness and programmability needed by a user-level library while providing the performance of hand-tuned code.

3.2 Message Configuration

Message information in the Active Pebbles model includes the data type to be sent, the C++ type of the message handler, and policies for coalescing, routing, and reductions. While the data type and message handler are algorithm-specific, other aspects are likely to be tied to hardware architecture and system configuration and possibly run-time information about the input data. Thus, we have extended Active Pebbles with a message configuration layer that separates the concerns of message semantics vs. configuration and run-time information.

The configuration layer allows algorithm users to create message configuration objects; each of these objects contains a desired coalescing approach, buffer size, and routing topology. The object also identifies whether the user would like message reductions to be used when applicable to a particular algorithm (and if so, which cache type and parameters to use). This configuration mechanism separates the specification of an algorithm's message semantics from the mapping of those semantics to a particular implementation. Thus optimizations can be applied to algorithm specifications by end users without modifying the algorithm specifications themselves. This mechanism allows algorithms to utilize optimization techniques that were unknown at the time the algorithm was developed, as long as the algorithm's implementation (and semantics) support that type of optimization. This retroactive optimization is key to supporting performance portability across current and future architectures without the need to reimplement algorithms.

4 Graph Algorithm Patterns

Identifying commonly used kernels or patterns has long been recognized as a useful method for enabling portability and high performance. A single common interface gives end users a target to program to, and system vendors a target to optimize for. Furthermore, a single widely-used implementation is more likely to be correct and efficient. The Basic Linear Algebra Subroutines (BLAS) [28] are perhaps the canonical example of such a library. Linear algebraic graph primitives have been proposed in [7]; we have observed higher-level patterns in visitor- or traversal-based algorithms as well. These patterns are representative of a significant fraction of existing graph algorithms (though by no means all of them). We examine how these patterns are implemented using Active Pebbles and possible implementations in other programming models.

4.1 Wavefront Expansion (Label-Setting)

Perhaps the simplest traversal-based pattern is the exploration of a graph from a single source vertex. As depth-first searches are inherently sequential [36], the most basic *parallelizable* search is breadth-first (BFS). The wavefront in this case represents the active vertices at each level in the search. This traversal pattern is *label-setting* in the sense that once a vertex is visited and a label (distance, predecessor, etc.) assigned it will not be revisited or have this label changed.

In order to achieve breadth-first exploration all vertices at distance i from the source vertex must be processed before any vertices at distance $i+1$. Messages in Active Pebbles are sent immediately with no ordering imposed between messages in the same epoch so this behavior requires one epoch per level, where level i consists of all vertices which have distance i from the source.

Alg. 1: Basic algorithm for breadth-first search.

In : Graph $\mathcal{G} = \langle V, E \rangle$, vertex s
Out : $\forall\, v \in V$: *distance*$[v]$ = distance of v from s

1 $Q \leftarrow nextQ \leftarrow$ empty queue;
2 $level \leftarrow 0$;
3 $distance[v] \leftarrow \infty, \forall v \in V$;
4 $distance[s] \leftarrow 0$;
5 enqueue $s \rightarrow Q$;
6 **while** Q not empty **do**
7     $level \leftarrow level + 1$;
8   **foreach** $v \in Q$ **do**
9   **foreach** neighbor w of v **do**
10   **if** $distance[w] = \infty$ **then**
11                 $distance[w] \leftarrow level$;
12   enqueue $w \rightarrow nextQ$;
13     $Q \leftarrow nextQ$;
14     $nextQ \leftarrow$ empty queue;

Algorithm 1 shows a breadth-first search implementation which uses two queues to force level-wise exploration. We have hidden the fact that in the distributed memory case each logical queue is actually composed of one local queue per process containing vertices from the set assigned to that process. Line 6 tests whether all local queues are non-empty, while line 8 iterates over the local queue on each process. To implement this algorithm using active messages (Algorithm 2), lines 10–12 become

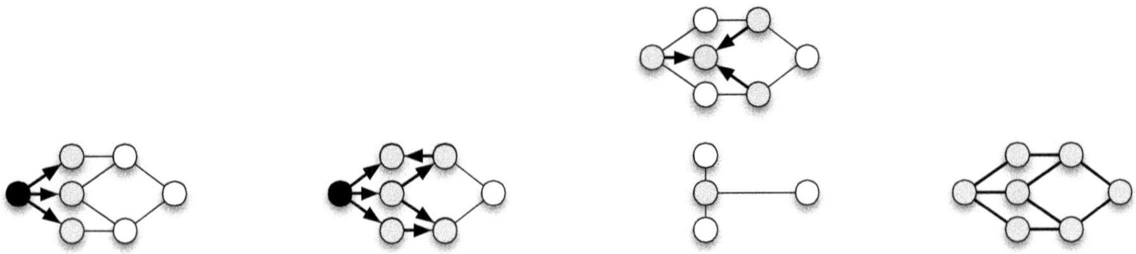

(a) Wavefront (b) Wavefront (wide) (c) Coarsening and Refinement (d) Iterative

Figure 1: Graph algorithm patterns.

Alg. 2: Parallel active message algorithm for BFS.

In : Graph $\mathcal{G} = \langle V, E \rangle$, vertex s,
$\forall v \in V$: *owner*$[v]$ = rank that owns v
Out : $\forall v \in V$: *distance*$[v]$ = distance of v from s
1 $Q \leftarrow nextQ \leftarrow$ empty queue;
2 $level \leftarrow 0$;
3 $distance[v] \leftarrow \infty, \forall v \in V$;
4 $distance[s] \leftarrow 0$;
5 enqueue $s \rightarrow Q$;
6 **message handler** explore(Vertex v)
7   **if** $distance[v] = \infty$ **then**
8         $distance[v] \leftarrow level$;
9   enqueue $v \rightarrow nextQ$;
10 **while** Q not empty **do**
11     $level \leftarrow level + 1$;
12   **active message epoch**
13   **parallel foreach** $v \in Q$ **do**
14   **parallel foreach** neighbor w of v **do**
15   **send** explore(w) **to** $owner(w)$;
16     $Q \leftarrow nextQ$;
17     $nextQ \leftarrow$ empty queue;

an active message that inserts w into the local queue at its target, removing the need for communication inside the distributed queue data structure itself. The messaging layer ensures that each *enqueue()* operation executes on the owning process of the vertex being enqueued. If we make the *enqueue()* method of Q thread-safe and add a critical section around lines 10–12, this implementation is also thread-safe and the **foreach** statements on lines 8 and 9 can be executed in parallel.

An implementation using MPI collectives would also use one epoch per iteration of the loop on line 6, but rather than communicating immediately on lines 10–12 it would buffer all remote *enqueue()* operations locally and send them at the conclusion of the loop using an *MPI_Alltoall()* operation (to communicate the number of operations) followed by an *MPI_Alltoallv()* operation to send the data. This approach fails to effectively overlap communication and computation in addition to being more complex than the active message formulation. Non-blocking collectives [23] and asynchronous point-to-point methods fail to alleviate this problem since we cannot begin the next BFS level until the previous one is complete.

Implementing a distributed queue of the sort described above using MPI-2 one-sided communications or the RDMA semantics provided by a number of PGAS languages is complicated by the absence of high-performance atomic operations such as compare and swap or fetch and add. In the absence of these operations, each process must allocate separate input buffers for each other remote process to write into. These buffers must be large enough to contain all remote updates and, if this cannot be guaranteed, logic must be provided to ensure all remote updates are received, possibly by using multiple epochs per level (with its attendant extra synchronization). At the conclusion of the BFS level, each process must apply the updates from all other processes and clear the input buffers. This approach either requires large amounts of additional memory to be allocated—to ensure that updates fit in the input buffers—or requires additional synchronization to perform multiple rounds of remote update exchanges per level.

4.2 Wavefront Expansion (Label-Correcting)

While breadth-first search is a simple and concise graph algorithm to use as an example, the strengths of the active message abstraction are more apparent in algorithms with more complex dependency structures. The label-correcting wavefront expansion pattern differs from the label-setting one in one important way. Instead of exploring vertices and edges once and labeling them, label-correcting wavefront algorithms may recompute and correct vertex and edge labels multiple times. Although this approach may be less work-efficient than a label-setting algorithm, it often exposes much more parallelism by allowing updates that are "usually independent" to proceed in parallel with exceptions repaired later.

Some label-correcting algorithms also use "thick" wavefronts: instead of only a single layer (i.e., frontier) of vertices being active at a time, vertices within a given "distance" (for an algorithm-specific definition of distance) are active. The thickness of the wavefront is controlled in an algorithm-specific manner, such as by using a parameter δ to define the thickness of the wavefront. Thicker wavefronts potentially expose more work at a given time and are thus more parallelizable, while thinner wavefronts are likely to be more work efficient. Figure 1(b) illustrates how a single level of the wavefront computation may contain paths of differing lengths in the graph, and thus computational dependencies within the wavefront. The canonical examples of label-correcting wavefront expansion are parallel single-source shortest path (SSSP) algorithms [12, 30].

Rather than each level of the wavefront containing a set of independent vertices with a common label as in the label-setting pattern, work is now grouped into sets of vertices with "tentative" labels in the range $[c\delta, (c+1)\delta)$ where c is the current level. Additionally, these vertices may now have dependencies between them (caused by "light" edges with weight less than δ, using the terminology from [30]). The fine-grained structure of these intra-level dependencies provides additional opportunities for parallelism, provided they can be captured efficiently. Using active messages, dependencies between vertices u, v, and w of the form $u \rightarrow v \rightarrow w$ can be handled directly by having vertex u send a message to vertex v which then performs the appropriate computation and sends a message to vertex w. Using MPI collectives, each stage in the dependency chain would require a separate *MPI_Alltoall()*/*MPI_Alltoallv()* pair leading to unnecessarily frequent synchronization and $\mathcal{O}(p \log p)$ overhead for each all-to-all communication amongst the p processors. As shown in the message diagrams in Figure 2, the BSP-style algorithm communicates in bursts at the end of a computation step (Figure 2(b)) while the active-message-based algorithm sends messages as coalescing buffers fill up, even if computation has not yet finished (Figure 2(b)). Modifying the BSP algorithm to communicate data early only partially solves this problem as messages must still be stored on the receiver until the conclusion of the epoch when they are processed. This approach more effectively hides the communication latency, but merely shifts the burden of additional memory utilization from the sender to the receiver.

4.3 Parallel Search

Both of the wavefront expansion patterns above use bounded descent (or lookahead) to maintain reasonable work efficiency. This limits the available parallelism by ensuring that only solutions reasonably close to the current optimal solution are explored. More work-efficient solutions synchronize more frequently, while infrequently-synchronizing approaches are less work-efficient but expose more parallelism. One pathological case of balancing work efficiency and parallelism is to discard the notion of work efficiency entirely. The parallel search pattern does this by phrasing the entire computation as a single epoch with unconstrained parallelism. This pattern is equivalent to the label-correcting wavefront pattern where $\delta = \infty$.

Reachability, computing the set of vertices reachable from one or more sources, is an example of a parallel search kernel that is straightforward to express using active messages. A traditional implementation using MPI collectives would most likely utilize the same structure as the breadth-first search example above. This would require a number of epochs equal to the distance of the farthest reachable vertex from the source. Using generalized active messages with message sends allowed inside message handlers, reachability can be performed in a single epoch, as shown in Algorithm 3.

Alg. 3: Reachability determination – Parallel Search pattern.

```
Input: Graph G = ⟨V, E⟩, vertex s
Output: ∀ v ∈ V: visited[v] = 1 iff v reachable from s
message handler explore(Vertex v)
    if visited[v] = 0 then
        visited[v] ← 1;
        parallel foreach neighbor w of v do
            send explore(w) to owner(w);
procedure main()
    active message epoch
        if owner[s] = this rank then
            run handler for explore(s);
```

4.4 Coarsening and Refinement

The coarsening and refinement pattern differs from search or wavefront patterns because rather than starting with a single source vertex and discovering additional parallelism, algorithms based on this pattern start with a logical work list containing a set of vertices or edges which can be processed in parallel. Vertices and edges are contracted to representative "supervertices" shrinking the work list until it is empty and the algorithm is complete. As the working set of the algorithm becomes smaller, parallelism is reduced and contention increases as each active supervertex represents a larger set of vertices and edges. Figure 1(c) shows an example of this process. The connected components algorithm due to Shiloach and Vishkin is one classic example of this pattern [39].

The Shiloach-Vishkin connected components algorithm, shown in Algorithm 4, consists of two phases. The first phase, *hooking* (lines 20–24), combines trees if there is an edge between them. The second phase, *shortcutting* (lines 25–31), contracts or flattens trees to a *root* or representative vertex. Component membership is tracked using a *parent* array in which $parent[u] = parent[v]$ iff u and v are in the same component. Hooking must be performed carefully to avoid cycles and requires the ability to scan all the adjacent vertices of each

Alg. 4: Connected components algorithm using active messages.

```
   Input: Graph G = ⟨V, E⟩, vertex s
   Output: ∀ v ∈ V: parent[v] = the component containing v
1  hooked ← doubled ← false;
2  message handler hook(Vertex pv, Vertex u)
3      pu ← parent[u];
4      if owner(pu) = this rank then
5          ppu ← parent[pu];
6          if pv < ppu then
7              hooked ← true;
8              parent[pu] ← pv;
9      else
10         send hook(pv, pu) to owner(pu);
11 message handler pointer-double(Vertex pv, Vertex v)
12     send pointer-double-reply(v, parent[v]) to owner(v);
13 message handler pointer-double-reply(Vertex v, Vertex ppv)
14     if ppv < parent[v] then
15         doubled ← true;
16         parent[v] ← ppv;
17 procedure main()
18     parent[v] ← v, ∀v ∈ V;
19     do
20         hooked ← false;
21         active message epoch
22             foreach v ∈ V do
23                 foreach neighbor u of v do
24                     send hook(parent[v], u) to owner(u);
25         do
26             doubled ← false;
27             active message epoch
28                 foreach v ∈ V do
29                     pv ← parent[v];
30                     send pointer-double(pv, v) to owner(pv);
31         while doubled on any node;
32     while hooked on any node;
```

component and access those vertices' *parent* values. In a BSP model, *MPI_Alltoall()/MPI_Alltoallv()* can be used to exchange *parent* values, but two stages of communication (and thus synchronization) may be required when u, v, and $parent[v]$ are all on different nodes. Shortcutting also requires two *MPI_Alltoall()/MPI_Alltoallv()* pairs to perform the operation $\{\forall v \in V : parent[v] \leftarrow parent[parent[v]]\}$ (one to send a request for the parent of each $parent[v]$ value, then a reply to that request).

The active message version of this algorithm avoids copying values in the *parent* array between processors and thus uses significantly less storage, in addition to requiring less synchronization. The multiple levels of messages can share a single epoch in the active message version, without extra synchronization between the stages. The outer loops in the code use reductions (sums) to determine globally whether parents were changed and whether any hooks occurred; this step is done using the end-of-epoch sum capability in Active Pebbles.

When hooking two vertices v and u connected by an edge $v \leftrightarrow u$, up to three processes may be involved: the owners of v, u, and $parent[v]$, since hooking requires sending $parent[v]$ to $owner(parent[u])$. The owner of v fills in the value of $parent[v]$ (line 29) and sends a message to $owner(u)$ to fill in the value of $parent[u]$ (line 3). The values of $parent[u]$ and $parent[v]$ must then be sent to $owner(parent[v])$ (line 10). Shortcuts are applied for local operations. For hooking to terminate, a monotonic ordering must be defined on vertices to ensure that only

(a) BSP

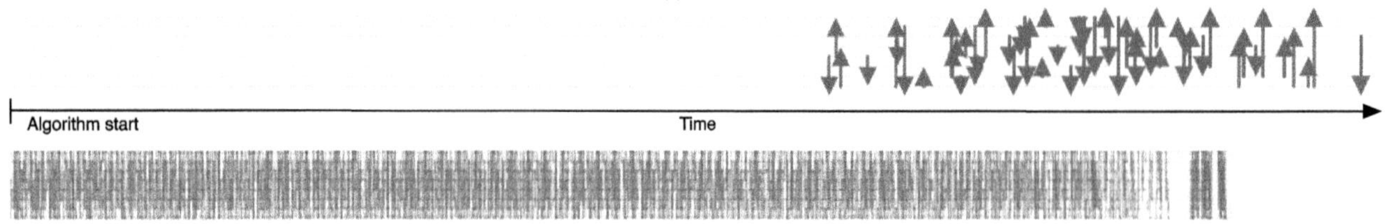

(b) Active Messages

Figure 2: Message trace of (a portion of) a breadth-first search algorithm in BSP and Active Message styles. Process ranks are represented on the Y axis. Each vertical arrow represents a message; arrow size is proportional to message size.

one update will ultimately succeed for each target vertex; it can also be used to eliminate redundant updates to the same parent. Though hooking can generate message chains of length 2, the messages can be interleaved arbitrarily and only a single epoch is required.

The shortcutting stage involves each process performing pointer-doubling of the form $\{\forall v \in V : parent[v] \leftarrow parent[parent[v]]\}$ using a two-stage process, all executed in one epoch. The owner of v first sends a request to perform $parent[v] \leftarrow parent[parent[v]]$ to the owner of $parent[v]$, giving it the value of v for the reply (line 30). The owner of $parent[v]$ then fills in $parent[parent[v]]$ and sends a message to perform the update back to the owner of v (line 12), which then processes it (line 16).

4.5 Iterative Methods

Iterative methods such as PageRank [35] or graph layout algorithms [20, 25] often iterate computations with the same structure over all the vertices and edges in the graph until a fixpoint is reached (i.e., no changes occur for a round of updates). These algorithms yield consistent parallelism as the work available remains constant (Figure 1(d)). Parallelization is straightforward using halo-zone communication with MPI or techniques similar to those described for coarsening and refinement algorithms above using active messages.

4.6 Combinations of These Patterns

What makes these algorithm patterns useful is that they occur repeatedly in higher-order algorithms. For example, the strongly connected components of a directed graph can be found by finding the intersection of a pair of breadth-first search trees [19]. Betweenness centrality can be parallelized using a label-correcting SSSP algorithm combined with a pair of topological-order traversals [16]. Optimizing the execution of these patterns, which may be used as kernels of more complex algorithms, is one important part of achieving high performance. Another important element in this goal is scheduling the kernels themselves so as to avoid coarse-grained synchronization between them. Projects in numerical computing [40] have demonstrated the effectiveness of scheduling applications consisting of multiple, dependent algorithm kernels in a fine-grained fashion in order to balance computations and ensure less time is wasted waiting for global synchronization. "Fusing" graph kernels at a much finer granularity offers similar benefits with regard to computational balance while also offering temporal locality (frequently absent in graph computations). When active messages are used to express graph algorithms, kernel scheduling is handled automatically by the runtime layer. Kernel fusion can be accomplished by combining the message dependencies of the individual kernels. This makes the active message formulation extremely powerful from an optimization standpoint. Furthermore, these optimizations may be applied dynamically at runtime as the structure of the input data, and thus the computation, is discovered.

5 Converting Algorithms to Active Messages

Explicit use of active messages is not always a familiar form for expressing parallel graph algorithms. However, more standard representations (e.g., with PRAM-like semantics) can be converted to active message form with a straightforward translation process, which we describe below. Possible future work would be to automate some or all of this translation process, likely based on programmer annotations of what data structures are distributed and how, and what operations must be atomic, as well as to generate efficient thread-safe code for **atomic** blocks (even for larger ones that do not correspond to processor atomics).

The conversion process has three steps:

1. Identify distributed data structures and their data distributions.
2. Annotate where each program statement should execute, and when control flow and data could be moved between nodes.
3. Lift active message handlers out of the code, replacing control flow movements with sends of active messages.

Listing 1: Pseudo-PRAM version of breadth-first search.

```
push(Q, s);
while (!empty(Q)) {
  parfor (v ∈ Q, w ∈ neighbors(v))
    atomic
      if (test_and_set(color[w]) == 0)
        push(nextQ, w);
  swap(Q, nextQ);
  clear(nextQ);
}
```

Identifying Distributed Data Structures The conversion process starts with a program format we refer to as *pseudo-PRAM*. In this form, sequential vs. parallel loops are explicit, as well as atomic blocks, while the system is assumed to support shared memory. An example of breadth-first search in this form is given in Listing 1. The first step in converting it to run on a distributed-memory computer is to identify the data distributions of the shared variables; in the example, those are *Q*, *nextQ*, *neighbors*, and *color*. The other variables are scalar local variables and thus are not distributed. This formulation assumes a partitioning of vertices amongst processes with structural adjacencies (*neighbors*) and properties (*color*) for a vertex stored on the process owning that vertex. The method for mapping vertices to processes is the *owner* map. Given this information, we can then assign statements and expressions to owning processes.

Conversion to Remote Spawns Each statement must be executed on a process that has ownership of all expressions used in that statement; satisfying this requirement may require moving data around between subexpressions in a larger expression. The example is simpler: the primitive expressions that have data distributions are *neighbors(v)* (which must be run on *owner(v)*), *color[w]*, and *push(nextQ, w)* (the latter two of which must be run on *owner(w)*). Lifting these constraints out to larger blocks of code, the entire ***atomic*** block must be executed on *owner(w)*, while the second loop in the ***parfor*** statement must be executed on *owner(v)*—that is guaranteed by the distribution of *Q*. In a system without distributed transactions, ***atomic*** blocks are unable to span multiple nodes, and thus the block must execute in a single process. Given information on its execution location, the ***atomic*** block must be wrapped in an ***async_spawn*** statement to move its execution

Listing 2: Remote-spawn version of breadth-first search.

```
push(Q, s);
while (!empty(Q)) {
  epoch
    parfor (v ∈ Q, w ∈ neighbors(v))
      async_spawn(owner(w))
        if (test_and_set(color[w]) == 0)
          push(nextQ, w);
  swap(Q, nextQ);
  clear(nextQ);
}
```

Listing 3: Explicit active message version of breadth-first search.

```
class update_handler {
  queue& nextQ; color_map& color;
  void handle(Vertex w) {
    if (test_and_set(color[w]) == 0)
      push(nextQ, w);
  }
};
register_message_type update_msg using
  type Vertex,
  handler update_handler(nextQ, color),
  owner_map owner;
push(Q, s);
while (!empty(Q)) {
  epoch
    parfor (v ∈ Q, w ∈ neighbors(v))
      send update_msg(w);
  swap(Q, nextQ);
  clear(nextQ);
}
```

to *owner(w)*. Additionally, an ***epoch*** block needs to be wrapped around the synchronization region in the code; here, that is the entire ***parfor*** loop. Those changes produce Listing 2.

Conversion to Explicit Active Messages Given an algorithm expressed using explicit ***async_spawn*** commands, conversion to a set of active message types is similar to closure conversion used to compile functional languages. For every body of an ***async_spawn***, going from inside to outside, identify its set of free variables. For the algorithm in Listing 2, this set contains *w*, *color*, and *nextQ*. Of these, *color* and *nextQ* are distributed data structures, and so references to them should be stored in the message handler; *w* is local and should be part of the active message data. Thus, the handler will be an object that contains references to the *nextQ* and *color* variables, and will accept active messages of type *Vertex* (the type of *w*). The destination of each message can be computed using the owner map *owner*. Conversion of ***async_spawn*** calls to active message sends produces the explicit active message version of breadth-first search in Listing 3. Further optimization can be enabled by declaratively specifying the semantics for message reductions.

6 Experimental Evaluation

We have applied the active message abstraction to the design the Parallel BGL "2.0" as a message-driven library of graph algorithms utilizing the Active Pebbles programming and execution model. The underlying communication infrastructure is provided by AM++, an implementation of the Active Pebbles model, tested using MPI as its underlying data-movement layer. We used Challenger, a 13.6 TF/s, 1 rack Blue Gene/P with 1024 compute nodes. Each node has 4 PowerPC 450 CPUs and 2 GiB of RAM. Our experiments used Version 1.0 Release 4.2 of the Blue Gene/P driver, IBM MPI, and `g++` 4.3.2 as the compiler (including as the back-end compiler for MPI).

6.1 Implementation Details

For our evaluation, we choose algorithms from each of the classes discussed in Section 4. As previously discussed, breadth-first search is an example of a label-setting wavefront algorithm (§ 4.1). For a label-correcting wavefront (§ 4.2), we chose the Δ-stepping single-source shortest paths algorithm [30]. The Shiloach-Vishkin connected components algorithm is an excellent example of a coarsening and refinement algorithm (§ 4.4). PageRank is a well-known iterative algorithm (§ 4.5) for ranking vertices in a graph. Where suitable, we have used the Graph 500 generator to generate synthetic graphs of suitable sizes for our weak-scaling experiments. The exception to this is the connected components experiments, for which Graph 500 graphs of the degree used in the other experiments would be likely to have a single large component and few other components beyond isolated vertices. Erdős-Rényi graphs have a more interesting component structure, especially around average degree 2 which is the hitting time of the giant component (e.g., the point at which the second largest component contains fewer than $\log n$ vertices with high probability, where n is the number of vertices in the graph). For this reason we have used Erdős-Rényi graphs of average degree 2 for our connected components experiments. All experiments use routing with a rook graph topology (an approximately-balanced rectangle of nodes where nodes in the same row and/or column are connected) to reduce the number of message buffers required for P processes from $\mathcal{O}(P)$ to $\mathcal{O}(\sqrt{P})$.

6.2 Results

The following experiments compare algorithms written in an active message (AM) style to the same algorithms written in a BSP [45] style. While AM graph algorithms have a number of advantages with regard to leveraging on-node parallelism, we compare only the single-threaded case in this work. To provide a fair comparison between the programming models rather than the efficiency of the underlying communication libraries, both the AM and BSP implementations use AM++. Previous work has demonstrated that AM++ has minimal latency and bandwidth overheads relative to the data transport layer it is implemented over (MPI in this case) [48]. Both the BSP and AM algorithms use the routing features of AM++, as well as message reduction (caching) in some cases. Note that in a traditional BSP implementation using MPI directly, adding routing or caching capabilities would greatly complicate the code. In the AM implementations, routing and caching are abstracted and encapsulated in the runtime. The primary distinction in the implementations is that while the active message algorithms overlap communication and computation aggressively and send messages from message handlers, the BSP algorithms defer communication (or at least the handling of communicated data) until the end of the epoch and handle dependent operations using algorithm-level queues to restrict each epoch to a single round of communication. It is likely that the BSP algorithms presented here perform *better* than versions which do not leverage the routing and message reduction features of AM++; however, disabling these features would increase memory consumption and make only small problems solvable using BSP algorithms.

Formulating graph algorithms using active messages allows increased overlap of communication and computation *provided algorithms expose sufficient asynchrony*. Active message graph algorithms also utilize less memory because once messages are executed they can be retired. BSP implementations may communicate data before the end of an epoch, but do not process that data and free the associated memory until the conclusion of the epoch. Our results demonstrate that AM algorithms reduce memory utilization enabling them to scale to larger numbers of nodes than similar algorithms implemented in a BSP style, which fail due to memory exhaustion. In the regions where both styles of algorithms execute successfully, AM algorithms are often more efficient due to their ability to more accurately capture the critical path of the application using fine-grained asynchronous operations. However, some graph algorithms have a coarse-grained structure that is well-suited to the BSP programming model. In these cases AM implementations are unable to outperform BSP implementations because insufficient asynchrony is available in the algorithm. For these algorithms we demonstrate that the overheads imposed by the AM implementations are limited, and represent a reasonable trade off for the benefits this model provides—reduced memory utilization, performance portability, and retroactive tuning of algorithm implementations without changing their specifications. In some cases, we describe algorithmic modifications which expose additional asynchrony and allow AM implementations to outperform their BSP counterparts.

The algorithms presented include a mixture of highly-synchronous algorithms (BFS and PageRank) well suited to BSP, and more asynchronous algorithms well suited to active messages (Δ-Stepping and several connected components variants). The core algorithm code is the same for the BSP versions and their AM counterparts. The desired level of granularity is achieved by specifying appropriate runtime parameters, not by modifying the algorithms themselves. In this fashion, fine-grained implementations can be converted to coarse-grained ones by the runtime system; however, the opposite conversion is non-trivial.

All of the runs have much better performance on a single node because of the lack of any messaging overheads and explicit checks for sends-to-self in AM++. Missing data values in the charts indicate that the algorithm failed to complete due to memory exhaustion.

6.2.1 Breadth-First Search

Breadth-first search (BFS) is a coarse-grained, BSP algorithm. Every vertex at level i must be processed before any vertex at level $i+1$ can be explored. This provides limited asynchrony for the AM implementation to leverage as shown in Figure 3. The runs annotated with "1M cache" use duplicate message elimination, implemented in this case with a 2^{20}-message cache per neighbor in the routing topology. With fewer than 32 nodes and no caching we see somewhat worse performance of the AM implementation vs. BSP. Enabling caching for both algorithms eliminates the overhead of the AM version for fewer than 32 nodes. The BSP implementations begin to fail due to memory exhaustion at 256 nodes but scale relatively well to 128 nodes. It is likely that memory exhaustion would occur much sooner due to increased communication buffer utilization were AM++ routing not in use here. The poor scaling performance beyond 32 nodes for the AM implementations is attributable to a number of factors. First, the static choice of coalescing factor (2^{10} messages) is well suited to small-scale execution but provides unreasonable overhead at larger scale. This demonstrates the need to dynamically vary the coalescing factor depending on the problem size. Second, we see that the scaling is worse for the AM implementation using message reductions than for the same algorithm without reductions. As the size of the graph increases, the fraction of data which is non-local increases proportionally. With a statically-sized message cache this means that the hit rate of the cache decreases. Making cache sizes dynamic, or even dynamically enabling/disabling caching, would allow maximal benefit to be derived from message reductions without introducing undesirable overheads. A suitably intelligent runtime would be capable of monitoring the system state and making these decisions appropriately without risking memory exhaustion. This algorithm demonstrates two important points:

1. Some algorithms lack sufficient asynchrony to benefit from AM implementations. However, features of the Active Pebbles model (e.g., message reductions) may still improve performance.
2. Because algorithm execution is dependent on the structure of the input graph, static runtime optimization parameters are suboptimal vs. varying parameters dynamically in response to system state.

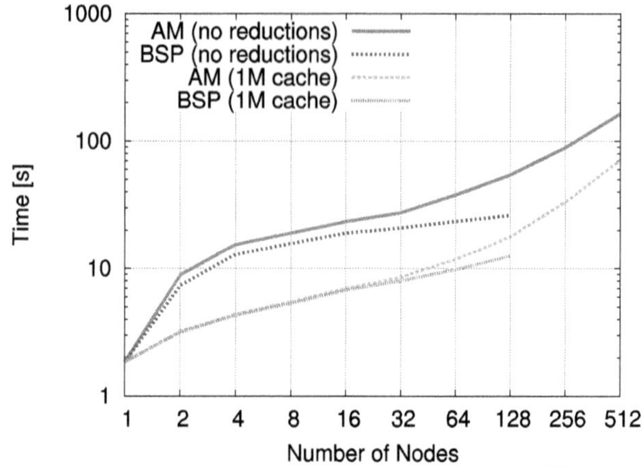

Figure 3: Breadth-first search weak scaling (Graph 500, 2^{19} vertices per node, average degree of 16, 2^{20}-message caches, average over 16 runs which are guaranteed to visit more than 100 vertices).

6.2.2 Δ-Stepping Shortest Paths

Figure 4 shows the performance of the active message and BSP implementations of Δ-stepping shortest paths. Δ-stepping allows all paths with weights in the range $(i\cdot\delta, (i+1)\cdot\delta]$ to be relaxed concurrently. This means that within a single step of the Δ-stepping algorithm there may be a path composed of multiple incident edges which need to be relaxed in sequence. The BSP implementation will require one epoch for each edge in the path to perform this relaxation due to the fact that the relaxation request for the first edge in the path is not processed until the conclusion of the epoch . This causes a second epoch to be initiated for the second edge in the path, and so on for each incident edge until the path distance is at least $(i+1)\cdot\delta$. The AM implementation requires only a single epoch to relax the entire path. The relaxation of the first edge sends a message to the target of that edge, which triggers relaxation of the second edge, and so on until the path length is at least $(i+1)\cdot\delta$. The termination detection feature of AM++ allows the runtime to wait until all dependent messages have been received before concluding the epoch.

The additional asynchrony in the Δ-stepping algorithm allows the AM implementations to outperform the BSP implementations in almost all cases. As with BFS, the BSP algorithms fail to complete due to memory exhaustion, in this case for more than 16 nodes. The fact that memory exhaustion occurs with fewer nodes than BFS is due to the fact that the Δ-stepping algorithm maintains an auxiliary data structure to order edge traversal which consumes significantly more memory than the BFS queue. In this implementation we do not remove a longer path to a vertex from this data structure when a shorter one is found because the AM algorithm supports multiple threads and this removal is difficult to perform in a manner that is both thread-safe and efficient. The increased memory requirements of the Δ-stepping algorithm require us to use a smaller graph and message reduction cache than in the BFS experiments.

As with BFS we see that message reductions improve performance at small scale but that the benefits decrease as the ratio of cache size to overall graph size shrinks. At larger node counts we see that the reduction caches are ineffectual but that because they are fast, direct-mapped caches their overhead does not adversely affect algorithm performance. The Δ-stepping algorithm also takes a δ parameter, the width of each bucket in vertex distances. The results shown use $\delta = 4$, which performed well across a range of input sizes. In addition to dynamically tuning the message coalescing factor and cache sizes to improve scalability, tuning δ would provide increased control over the amount of parallel work and asynchrony available vs. the likelihood that relaxing an edge contributed to the final solution of the algorithm (e.g., work efficiency). This trade off between work efficiency and parallelism is omnipresent in graph algorithms and careful control of it is the key to high performance.

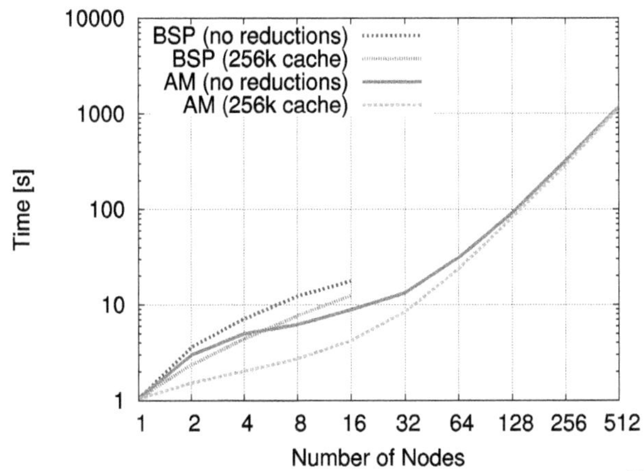

Figure 4: Δ-stepping shortest paths weak scaling (Graph 500, 2^{16} vertices per node, average degree 16, 2^{18}-element caches).

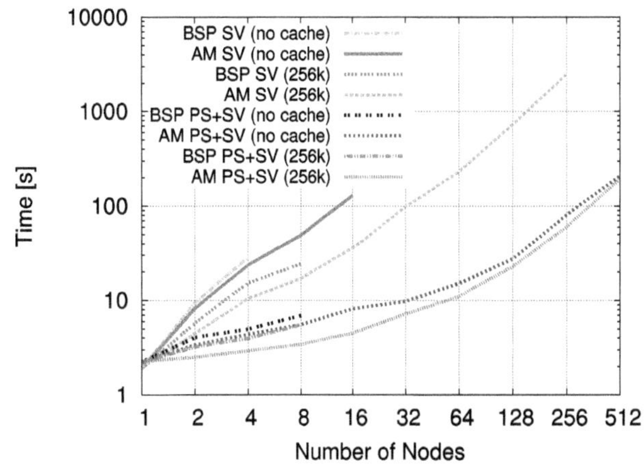

Figure 5: Shiloach-Vishkin connected components weak scaling (Erdős-Rényi, 2^{18} vertices/node, avg. degree 2, 2^{18}-element caches).[1]

6.2.3 *Shiloach-Vishkin Connected Components*

The Shiloach-Vishkin connected components algorithm requires a number of hooking and contraction steps proportional to the diameter of the largest component to complete. Because we know that it is likely that the graphs used have a giant component, we also implement an optimized algorithm which does a parallel exploration from the highest degree vertex (which is likely to be in the giant component), and then applies the Shiloach-Vishkin connected components algorithm to the undiscovered portion of the graph to label the remaining components. We call this variant "Parallel Search + Shiloach-Vishkin" (PS+SV).

Figure 5 demonstrates that initializing the SV algorithm with a parallel search to discover the giant component ("PS + SV") provides significant performance improvement for both AM and BSP, and improves the scaling of the AM implementation. This transformation is an example of an algorithmic refinement that exposes asynchrony which can be effectively utilized by AM implementations. Message reductions again provide performance improvements in both cases, which diminish as the graph grows. It is likely that dynamically tuning the coalescing factor would mitigate the poor scaling of the the AM "PS + SV" algorithm between 128 and 512 nodes and result in a scalable algorithm capable of executing on larger numbers of nodes.

The "PS + SV" algorithm demonstrates the ability of the AM implementation to more efficiently leverage the available asynchrony in an algorithm, as well as the ability to perform minor modifications to an algorithm to make it more suitable for AM. Figure 5 demonstrates that the AM implementation of the classical Shiloach-Vishkin ("SV") algorithm outperforms the BSP version because hooking and pointer-doubling operations that involve multiple communication stages can be performed in a single AM epoch, while the BSP implementation requires multiple epochs. As with BFS and Δ-stepping, the BSP algorithms fail due to memory exhaustion, this time between 4 and 8 nodes.

6.2.4 *PageRank*

The PageRank algorithm is a highly synchronous graph algorithm well suited to BSP execution. This algorithm is implemented using a variant of the Parallel BGL's distributed property map abstraction [15], a PGAS-like data movement layer. Neither implementation uses reductions in this case because they have yet to be integrated into the distributed property map. Figure 6 shows that once again the BSP form of the algorithm fails to complete at larger node counts (at least 16 in this case), while the AM implementation runs successfully up to 512 nodes. In the range where both execute successfully, the AM implementation has comparable performance to the BSP version.

[1]The missing data points for "AM SV" are due to the wall clock time limit expiring before the algorithm completed, not memory exhaustion. Challenger has a maximum time limit of 1 hour on all jobs.

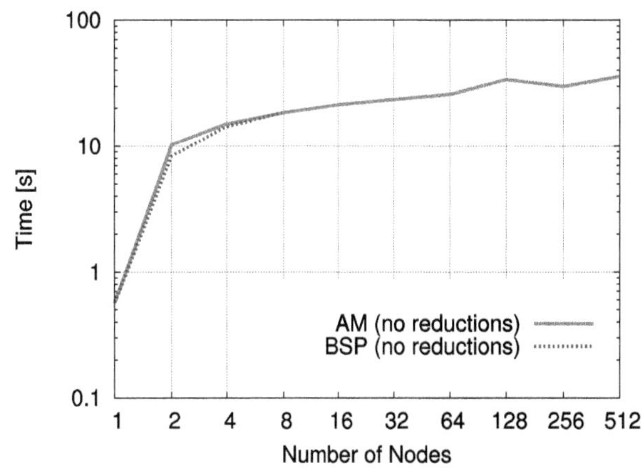

Figure 6: PageRank weak scaling (Graph 500, 2^{18} vertices per node, average degree 16, average of 20 iterations).

7 Conclusion

Phrasing graph algorithms as collections of asynchronous, concurrently executing, message-driven fragments of code allows for natural expression of algorithms, flexible implementations leveraging various forms of parallelism, and performance portability—all without modifying the algorithms themselves. Active messages are an effective abstraction for expressing graph applications because they allow the fine-grained dependency structure of the computations to be expressed directly in a form that can be observed dynamically at runtime as it is discovered. At this point a variety of optimizations are available (coalescing, reductions, etc.) that are difficult or impossible to apply effectively at compile time; if applied manually, they would greatly complicate the structure of the algorithm's implementation. This expression provides users a natural and flexible method to express applications in terms of individual operations on vertices and edges rather than in terms of artificially coarser operations. Furthermore, algorithms expressed in this form can be mapped to a many hardware platforms and parallelized using a variety of techniques (processes, threads, accelerators, and combinations thereof). By allowing algorithms to be expressed in a form that places minimal constraints on the implementation, the active message expression of algorithms can be implemented in the manner that is most efficient for a given execution context. Separating the specification of graph algorithms from the details of their execution using active messages yields flexible and expressive semantics and high performance.

One straightforward approach to improving performance would be to vary the parameters of the messaging framework dynamically at runtime in order to take advantage of the structure of the graph and algorithm workload as they are observed. The active message abstraction is extremely flexible with regard to its execution context which would make it straightforward to port to new architectures and accelerators including FPGAs and, given appropriate memory models, GPUs. The Active Pebbles model utilized here generalizes one-sided operations to user-defined handlers; applying the same technique to abstract transactions on the graph metadata to create a domain-specific language would enable similar optimization techniques to those utilized on the messaging portion of an application to be applied to the shared memory component.

8 Acknowledgements

This work was supported by NSF grant CCF-11118882. This research used resources of the Argonne Leadership Computing Facility at Argonne National Laboratory, which is supported by the Office of Science of the U.S. Department of Energy under contract DE-AC02-06CH11357. We would also like to thank Joseph Cottam for helpful visualizations, as well as the anonymous reviewers for their comments. A preliminary version of this work appeared as a poster [17].

9 REFERENCES

[1] *NVIDIA CUDA Programming Guide*, 2007.

[2] D. Ajwani, U. Meyer, and V. Osipov. Improved external memory BFS implementations. In *SIAM Meeting on Alg. Eng. and Exp.*, January 2007.

[3] D. A. Bader and K. Madduri. SNAP, Small-world Network Analysis and Partitioning: An open-source parallel graph framework for the exploration of large-scale networks. In *Intl. Par. and Dist. Proc. Symp.*, Apr. 2008.

[4] J. W. Berry, B. Hendrickson, S. Kahanz, and P. Konecny. Software and algorithms for graph queries on multithreaded architectures. In *Intl. Parallel and Distributed Processing Symposium*, March 2007.

[5] R. D. Blumofe, C. F. Joerg, B. C. Kuszmaul, et al. Cilk: an efficient multithreaded runtime system. *SIGPLAN Not.*, 30(8):207–216, 1995.

[6] D. Bonachea. GASNet specification, v1.1. Technical report, University of California at Berkeley, Berkeley, CA, USA, 2002.

[7] A. Buluç. *Linear algebraic primitives for parallel computing on large graphs*. PhD thesis, University of California, Santa Barbara, 2010.

[8] A. Buluç and J. R. Gilbert. The Combinatorial BLAS: Design, implementation, and applications. *J. HPC Applications*, 25(4), November 2011.

[9] D. Callahan, B. L. Chamberlain, and H. P. Zima. The Cascade high productivity language. In *Intl. Workshop on High-Level Parallel Programming Models and Supportive Environments*, pages 52–60, April 2004.

[10] P. Charles, C. Grothoff, V. A. Saraswat, et al. X10: An object-oriented approach to non-uniform cluster computing. In *Object Oriented Programming, Systems, Languages, and Applications*, 2005.

[11] D. Chavarria-Miranda, S. Krishnamoorthy, and A. Vishnu. Global Futures: A multithreaded execution model for Global Arrays-based applications. In *CCGRID*, pages 393–401, 2012.

[12] A. Crauser, K. Mehlhorn, U. Meyer, and P. Sanders. A parallelization of Dijkstra's shortest path algorithm. In *Mathematical Foundations of Computer Science*, volume 1450 of *LNCS*, pages 722–731. Springer, 1998.

[13] M. Dayarathna, C. Houngkaew, and T. Suzumura. Introducing ScaleGraph: an X10 library for billion scale graph analytics. In *X10 Workshop*, pages 6:1–6:9, New York, NY, USA, 2012. ACM.

[14] S. J. Deitz, S.-E. Choi, and D. Iten. Five powerful Chapel idioms, May 2010.

[15] N. Edmonds, D. Gregor, and A. Lumsdaine. Extensible PGAS semantics for C++. In *Conference on PGAS Programming Models*, Oct 2010.

[16] N. Edmonds, T. Hoefler, and A. Lumsdaine. A space-efficient parallel algorithm for computing betweenness centrality in distributed memory. In *Intl. Conference on High Performance Computing*, Goa, India, Dec. 2010.

[17] N. Edmonds, J. Willcock, and A. Lumsdaine. Expressing graph algorithms using generalized active messages. In *PPoPP*, Feb. 2013. Poster.

[18] P. Erdős, R. L. Graham, and E. Szemeredi. On sparse graphs with dense long paths. Technical Report CS-TR-75-504, Stanford University, 1975.

[19] L. Fleischer, B. Hendrickson, and A. Pinar. On identifying strongly connected components in parallel. In *Intl. Parallel and Distributed Processing Symposium*, volume 1800 of *LNCS*, pages 505–511. Springer, 2000.

[20] T. Fruchterman and E. Reingold. Graph drawing by force-directed placement. *Software–Practice and Experience*, 21(11):1129–1164, 1991.

[21] J. R. Gilbert, V. B. Shah, and S. Reinhardt. A unified framework for numerical and combinatorial computing. *Computing in Science & Engineering*, 10(2):20–25, 2008.

[22] D. Gregor and A. Lumsdaine. Lifting sequential graph algorithms for distributed-memory parallel computation. In *Object-oriented programming, systems, languages, and applications*, pages 423–437, October 2005.

[23] T. Hoefler, A. Lumsdaine, and W. Rehm. Implementation and performance analysis of non-blocking collective operations for MPI. In *Supercomputing*, Nov. 2007.

[24] J. Jose, S. Potluri, M. Luo, et al. UPC Queues for scalable graph traversals: Design and evaluation on InfiniBand clusters. In *Conference on PGAS Programming Models*, Oct. 2011.

[25] T. Kamada and S. Kawai. An algorithm for drawing general undirected graphs. *Information Processing Letters*, 31:7–15, 1989.

[26] S. Kumar, G. Dozsa, G. Almasi, et al. The Deep Computing Messaging Framework: Generalized scalable message passing on the Blue Gene/P supercomputer. In *Intl. Conference on Supercomputing*, pages 94–103, 2008.

[27] K. Lang. Fixing two weaknesses of the spectral method. In *Neural Information Processing Systems*, 2005.

[28] C. L. Lawson, R. J. Hanson, D. R. Kincaid, and F. T. Krogh. Basic Linear Algebra Subprograms for Fortran usage. *ACM Transactions on Mathematical Software*, 5(3):308–323, September 1979.

[29] A. Lumsdaine, D. Gregor, B. Hendrickson, and J. Berry. Challenges in parallel graph processing. *Parallel Proc. Letters*, 17(1):5–20, 2007.

[30] U. Meyer and P. Sanders. Δ-stepping: A parallelizable shortest path algorithm. *J. Algorithms*, 49(1):114–152, 2003.

[31] MPI Forum. MPI: A Message-Passing Interface Standard. v2.2, Sept. 2009.

[32] MPI Forum. MPI: A Message-Passing Interface Standard. v3.0, Sept. 2012.

[33] R. W. Numrich and J. Reid. Co-array Fortran for parallel programming. *SIGPLAN Fortran Forum*, 17(2):1–31, 1998.

[34] OpenMP Architecture Review Board. OpenMP application program interface. Specification, 2011.

[35] L. Page, S. Brin, R. Motwani, and T. Winograd. The PageRank citation ranking: Bringing order to the Web. Technical report, Stanford, November 1998.

[36] J. H. Reif. Depth-first search is inherently sequential. *Information Processing Letters*, 20(5):229–234, June 1985.

[37] A. L. Rosenberg and L. S. Heath. *Graph Separators, with Applications*. Kluwer Academic Publishers, Norwell, MA, USA, 2001.

[38] V. Shah and J. R. Gilbert. Sparse matrices in Matlab*P: Design and implementation. In *International Conference on High Performance Computing*, pages 144–155. Springer, 2004.

[39] Y. Shiloach and U. Vishkin. An $\mathcal{O}(log\ n)$ parallel connectivity algorithm. *Journal of Algorithms*, 3(1):57–67, 1982.

[40] F. Song, A. Yarkhan, and J. Dongarra. Dynamic task scheduling for linear algebra algorithms on distributed-memory multicore systems. In *Supercomputing*, Portland, OR, November 2009.

[41] J. E. Stone, D. Gohara, and G. Shi. OpenCL: A parallel programming standard for heterogeneous computing systems. *Computing in Science & Engineering*, 12(3):66–73, May 2010.

[42] G. Tanase, A. Buss, A. Fidel, et al. The STAPL parallel container framework. In *Principles and Practice of Parallel Programming*, pages 235–246, New York, NY, USA, 2011.

[43] N. Thomas, S. Saunders, T. Smith, G. Tanase, and L. Rauchwerger. ARMI: A high level communication library for STAPL. *Parallel Processing Letters*, 16(02):261–280, 2006.

[44] UPC Consortium. UPC Language Spec., v1.2. Technical report, Lawrence Berkeley National Laboratory, 2005. LBNL-59208.

[45] L. G. Valiant. A bridging model for parallel computation. *Communications of the ACM*, 33(8):103–111, 1990.

[46] T. von Eicken, D. E. Culler, S. C. Goldstein, and K. E. Schauser. Active Messages: A mechanism for integrated communication and computation. In *Intl. Symposium on Computer Architecture*, pages 256–266, 1992.

[47] K. Wheeler, R. C. Murphy, and D. Thain. Qthreads: An API for programming with millions of lightweight threads. In *Multithreaded Architectures and Applications*, 2008.

[48] J. Willcock, T. Hoefler, N. Edmonds, and A. Lumsdaine. AM++: A generalized active message framework. In *Par. Arch. and Comp. Tech.*, Sept. 2010.

[49] J. Willcock, T. Hoefler, N. Edmonds, and A. Lumsdaine. Active Pebbles: Parallel programming for data-driven applications. In *International Conference on Supercomputing*, Tucson, Arizona, May 2011.

HYKSORT: A New Variant of Hypercube Quicksort on Distributed Memory Architectures

Hari Sundar
The University of Texas at Austin, Austin, TX 78712
hsundar@gmail.com

Dhairya Malhotra
The University of Texas at Austin, Austin, TX 78712
dhairya.malhotra@gmail.com

George Biros
The University of Texas at Austin, Austin, TX 78712
gbiros@acm.org

ABSTRACT

In this paper, we present HYKSORT, an optimized comparison sort for distributed memory architectures that attains more than 2× improvement over bitonic sort and samplesort. The algorithm is based on the hypercube quicksort, but instead of a binary recursion, we perform a k-way recursion in which the pivots are selected accurately with an iterative parallel select algorithm. The single-node sort is performed using a vectorized and multithreaded merge sort. The advantages of HYKSORT are lower communication costs, better load balancing, and avoidance of $\mathcal{O}(p)$-collective communication primitives. We also present a staged-communication samplesort, which is more robust than the original samplesort for large core counts. We conduct an experimental study in which we compare hypercube sort, bitonic sort, the original samplesort, the staged samplesort, and HYKSORT. We report weak and strong scaling results and study the effect of the grain size. It turns out that no single algorithm performs best and a hybridization strategy is necessary. As a highlight of our study, on our largest experiment on 262,144 AMD cores of the CRAY XK7 "*Titan*" platform at the Oak Ridge National Laboratory we sorted 8 trillion 32-bit integer keys in 37 seconds achieving 0.9TB/s effective throughput.

Categories and Subject Descriptors

F.2.2 [**Analysis of Algorithms and Problem Complexity**]: Nonnumerical Algorithms and Problems—*Sorting and Searching*

Keywords

Sorting; Parallel Algorithms; shared-memory parallelism; distributed-memory parallelism; hypercube; quicksort; samplesort; bitonic sort

1. INTRODUCTION

The design and implementation of parallel algorithms for comparison-based sort is a well studied subject. Here we are concerned with the practical issue of scaling comparison sort algorithms to large core counts. Comparison sort is used in many data-intensive scientific computing and data analytics codes (e.g., [10, 17, 18]) and it is critical that we develop efficient sorting algorithms that can handle petabyte-sized datasets efficiently on existing and near-future architectures. To our knowledge, no parallel sort algorithm has been scaled to the core counts and problem sizes we are considering in this article.

Given an array A with N keys and an order (comparison) relation, we will like to sort the elements of A in ascending order. In a distributed memory machine with p tasks[1] every task is assigned an N/p-sized block of A. Upon completion, task i will have the i_{th} block of the sorted array. Designing and implementing an efficient sorting algorithm that can scale to thousands of cores is difficult since it requires irregular data access, communication, and load-balance.

The most popular algorithm used in actual parallel sort implementations is SAMPLESORT [2]: Given p tasks, we reshuffle the elements of A in p buckets so that keys in the i_{th} bucket are smaller or equal than keys in the $(i+1)_{th}$ bucket. Bucket i is assigned to task i and once we have reshuffled A, each task i can sort its keys locally. The challenge is to obtain good load-balancing so that every task i has roughly the same number of keys after reshuffling while minimizing communication costs.

SAMPLESORT reshuffles A by estimating the boundaries for each bucket using $p-1$ keys, which we call the "*splitters*". This can be done for example, by sampling a subset of keys in A, sorting them (say, by gathering these to the task 0 and using a sequential sort) and selecting the splitters from that set. Once these $p-1$ splitters have been selected, a global all-to-all data exchange redistributes the keys of every task to their correct bucket. An additional local sort is invoked to finalize the output array.

SAMPLESORT is well understood. However, its performance is quite sensitive to the selection of splitters, which can result in load imbalance. Most important, the all-to-all key redistribution scales linearly with the number of tasks and can congest the network. As a result SAMPLESORT may scale suboptimally, especially when the communication volume approaches the available hardware limits (Figure 1).

Contributions.

Our algorithm is based on well-known and well-tested algorithmic techniques. SAMPLESORT was proposed in [2]. We

[1]In the MPI context "*a task*" (or process) corresponds to an MPI rank, which may be a core, a socket, or a node.

ICS'13, June 10–14, 2013, Eugene, Oregon, USA.

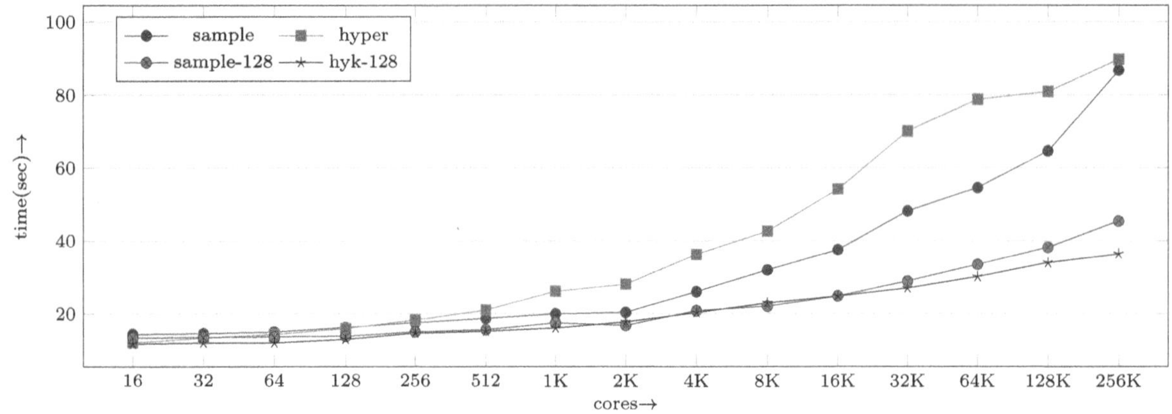

Figure 1: *As a highlight, we present a weak scalability study of our new* HykSort *algorithm against* SampleSort *(combined with bitonic sort to sort the splitters) and* HyperQuickSort *algorithms. We also compare with an improved k-way* SampleSort*. The grain size is 32M (32-bit) integers per core. For the largest run we sort 8.5 trillion integers (34TB) in 37 seconds on 262,144 cores, a throughput of nearly 0.9TB/sec on Titan. All runs were performed using* 2 MPI *tasks per node with* 8 OpenMP *threads per* MPI *task. We obtain* 2× *improvement over the standard* SampleSort *and* HyperQuickSort *algorithms and an 15% improvement over our modified samplesort algorithm.*

estimate our splitters using an approximate parallel selection algorithm first proposed in [16]. Our main contribution is the design of a load-balanced sort algorithm that does not involve any collective communications other than synchronization. In detail:

- **Method:** We present an algorithm that addresses the issues of splitter selection, load balancing, and bucket-reshuffling in samplesort. Our main contribution is the following simple idea: instead of splitting the array A in p buckets, we split it in $k < p$ buckets and then we recurse for every bucket. Indeed, if $k = 2$, our algorithm can be viewed as a distributed memory QuickSort (see Figure 2). At every recursion step, each task communicates only with another k tasks. (For $k = 2$ this resembles the hypercube QuickSort.) This communication is staged and at every stage we use only point-to-point exchanges. Finally, after every recursion step, we load balance so that every task has N/p keys in its working block at all stages of the algorithm.
- **Complexity analysis and implementation:** We analyze the overall scheme and provide complexity estimates. Our implementation combines MPI along with OpenMP. Also we have developed a vectorized multithreaded MergeSort, which we have used for the single socket sorting when we run experiments with one MPI task per socket. Furthermore instead of using a plain all-to-all collective with samplesort, we have implemented our own staged collective communication to avoid congestion.
- **Experimental evaluation:** We conduct an experimental study in which we compare the HykSort with different variants of SampleSort and QuickSort. As a highlight, we present results on up to 262,144 cores on Titan in which we sorted 8.8 trillion (arbitrarily distributed) integers (a 32TB dataset) in less than 37 seconds, achieving near 0.9TB/sec throughput.

Limitations.

Our implementation does not support heterogeneous architectures. Efficient sorting implementations exist and can

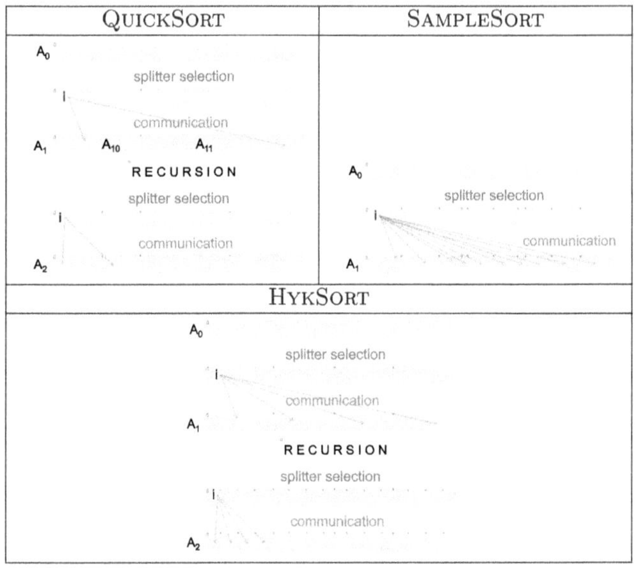

Figure 2: *Here we summarize the basic idea in the proposed method. Given the input array A_0, in* QuickSort *a pivot (splitter) is randomly selected to create two buckets: A_{10} contains all the keys that are strictly less than the pivot and A_{11} the remaining ones. (The first index indicates the recursion level and the second the bucket id.) A hypercube-like communication, here depicted just for MPI task i, can be used to collect the keys from A_0 to the correct bucket (see §3). Then we recurse on each bucket in A_1 to create A_2. The pivot selection and the data exchange can lead to load imbalance between buckets. In* SampleSort*, we use p buckets constructed using $p - 1$ splitters. There is no recursion, but the communication, typically done with an* `MPI_Alltoallv()` *can lead to network congestion (again, we just show communication for task i). In* HykSort*, we use a combination of recursion and multiple splitter selection to control communication costs and load balancing. It is a recursive algorithm in which at every step a small number of splitters is selected—not randomly but as accurately as possible—followed by a staged communication. The new algorithm has provably lower complexity, has predictable behavior, and avoids collective communication primitives.*

be coupled to our code, for example [11, 15]. Although we have tried to optimize our local sort, its performance is subpar to the implementation in [9], which (remarkably for the complexity of sorting) achieves near-memory bandwidth performance. In a nutshell, the efficiency of the local sorts can be significantly improved.

Organization of the paper.
In §2, we discuss the most relevant prior work. In §3, we present the overall methodology. Finally, in §4, we discuss weak and strong scaling results on two different architectures.

2. PRIOR WORK

As we mentioned in the introduction, HYKSORT is hybrid between a sample sort and a hypercube quick sort. The latter was originally proposed by Wagar [19] and several different algorithmic variants have been proposed since. In our discussion of prior work, we focus our attention to distributed memory algorithms that have been experimentally shown to scale to large core counts and large datasets.

- The SAMPLESORT [2] algorithm was one of the first instances of distributed sort that was adopted extensively in practice[2]. In [3] the authors compare, theoretically and experimentally, different sort algorithms and present results for sorting 132M 64-bit keys on a CM-2 machine. In these experiments SAMPLESORT performs well but the timings do not compare with current architectures.
- Parallel HISTOGRAMSORT [8, 17] is another variant of SAMPLESORT that estimates the splitters more effectively than the original method. The authors presented one of the largest distributed comparison sort runs (32K cores on BG/P) with 46% efficiency. The algorithm overlaps communication and computation in all stages. During the splitter estimation stage, the iterative estimation of the ranks of the splitters is combined with partial local sorting of the data, by using the splitter candidates as pivots for quicksort. Once the splitters are estimated, the communication of data is staged and overlapped with local merging. In [17] the best throughput was obtained on 16,384 cores of Jaguar XT4 at ORNL for 8M (64-bit) keys per core; the sort took 4.3 seconds achieving a throughput of 0.24TB/sec.
- CLOUDRAMSORT [9] is a recent paper demonstrating good scalability on 256 nodes with shared memory parallelism using pThreads and SIMD vectorization. The best results are for sorting 1TB of data (10byte key + 90byte record) in 4.6 secs achieving a throughput of 0.21 TB/sec. They use a variant of the HISTOGRAM SORT [8], where the samples are iteratively computed (in parallel) in order to ensure a minimum quality of load-balance across processes. They split the communication of the records into two parts by first communicating the keys followed by the values, during which the keys are merged.
- PSORT [4] is an efficient implementation of sample sort where the samples are determined using a parallel selection algorithm [16]. They report results for sorting 100 billion (32-bit) integers on 256 processes in under 4 minutes achieving 0.0017 TB/sec throughput.
- TRITONSORT [13] is the current record holder at the SortBenchmark [7]. It uses a hybrid TCP and `pthreads` implementation of histogram sort using efficient data structures (trie). As with other approaches, they do not sort the local samples initially, relying instead on random samples. The main challenge for scalability is the use of a single coordinator node that computes the global histogram and assigns segments to other nodes. This is the reason that the largest reported run is for 52 nodes. Still this group manages to sort 100TB input data (100-byte tuple, 10-byte key, 10 trillion keys) on 52 nodes achieving a throughput of 0.015TB/sec.
- Although not part of our code, for completeness, we report some representative efforts on accelerators. The performance of various sorting algorithms on GPUs [11] and the Intel Xeon Phi co-processor [15] has also been studied. The key findings from these studies are that radix sort is effective for short keys (less than 32bit) and that a k-way merge ($k = 32, 64, 128$) is more efficient than a 2-way merge on GPUs.

We focused on experimentally verified distributed memory sort algorithms with an emphasis in high performance computing. For more details on the theory of distributed sort see [1, 6].

[2]The idea of using splitters, first appeared in [14].

3. METHODOLOGY

Let us introduce notation for the remaining of the section in Table 1.

A	input array (distributed)
B	output array (ascending order, local block)
comm	MPI communicator
p	number of MPI tasks in *comm*
N	global number of keys in A
$n = N/p$	local number of keys in A
k	number of splitters ($k \neq p$)
s	the splitters
t_w	interconnect slowness (1/bandwidth)
t_s	interconnect latency
t_c	intranode memory slowness (1/ RAM bandwidth)
p_r	the task id (its MPI Rank)
A_r	array to be sorted (local block)
M_s^r	MPI message from s (send) task to r (recv) task
partner	indicates task id in point-to-point exchanges
Functions	
`Length`(B)	number elements in array B
`Rank`(s, B)	`Length`($\{B_i : B_i < s\}$)
`Sort`	local, non-MPI, sort
`BitonicSort`	parallel biotonic sort [6]
log	base-2 logarithm

Table 1: *Here we summarize the notation.* `Sort` *can be any sequential sort (in our experiments, when we have one thread for each MPI task, we use* `std::sort`*). Note the* `Rank`(s, B)*, is equal to the number of keys in B that are strictly smaller than s.*

We start our discussion presenting Wagar's [19] QUICKSORT on a hypercube, assuming that the input array has been locally sorted using a sequential sort. We select a pivot (or a single splitter) using the median of the root task, and proceed as in the sequential case by using the pivot to split the keys into two buckets and then recursing. If n and

Algorithm 3.1 HYPECUBEQUICKSORT

Input: A_r (locally sorted), n, N, *comm*; assume $p = 2^d$
Output: B_r (sorted)
if $p = 1$, $B_r \leftarrow A_r$, **return**
if $p_r = 0$, $m_0 \leftarrow$ `Median`(A)
`MPI_Bcast`$(m_0, 0)$
$A_L \leftarrow \{A_r[i] : A_r[i] < m_0\}$, $A_U \leftarrow \{A_r[i] : A_r[i] \geq m_0\}$
$partner \leftarrow (p_r + p/2) \mod p$
if $p_r < partner$
  $C \leftarrow$`MPI_Recv()`, `MPI_Send`(A_U), $A_r \leftarrow A_L$
else
  $C \leftarrow$`MPI_Recv()`, `MPI_Send`(A_L), $A_r \leftarrow A_U$
$A_r \leftarrow$ `Merge`(A_r, C) ▷ $\mathcal{O}(n)$
$comm' \leftarrow$ `MPI_Comm_split`$(comm)$ ▷ $\mathcal{O}(\log p)$
$n' \leftarrow$ `Length`(A_r)
$N' \leftarrow$ `MPI_Allreduce`$(n', comm')$ ▷ $\mathcal{O}(\log p)$
return `HypercubeQuickSort`$(A_r, n', N', comm')$

N remain balanced throughout the recursion, the expected complexity is

$$\mathcal{O}\left(t_c \frac{N}{p} \log \frac{N}{p} + t_s \log^2 p + (t_c + t_w) \frac{N}{p} \log p\right),$$

where the first term is the local post-processing sort, the second term is the latency of the collectives due to $\log p$ communication rounds and the last term corresponds to the merge and pairwise data exchange. However, this complexity estimate is highly inaccurate since it doesn't account for two sources of load imbalance. The first one is related to the imbalance between the global sizes of A_L and A_U since they will be unequal if median of A is not chosen as the pivot. Additionally, the pairwise exchanges will lead to imbalance of the number of global keys. As the number of cores increases, these imbalances get amplified. The algorithm therefore, although very simple to state, is not practical. The different approaches summarized in §2 summarize the efforts to address these issues.

One basic approach is to improve the partitioning is by generating not one pivot (or splitter) but $p - 1$ splitters. A further possible improvement is to select the splitters more accurately. These ideas motivate SAMPLESORT, described in Algorithm 3.2.

Algorithm 3.2 SAMPLESORT

Input: A_r (locally sorted), n, N, p
Output: Sorted array B_r ▷ $\mathcal{O}(n \log n)$
1: $s \leftarrow$ `SampleSplitters`(A) ▷ $\mathcal{O}(p\ (\log p)^2)$
2: $d_{i+1} \leftarrow$ `Rank`(s_i, B), $\forall i$ ▷ $\mathcal{O}(p \log n)$
3: $[d_0,\ d_p] \leftarrow [0,\ n]$
4: $M^i_{p_r} \leftarrow \{A_j |\ j \in d_i, ..., d_{i+1} - 1\}$, $\forall i$
5: $B_r \leftarrow$ `Alltoallv`(M_{p_r}) ▷ $\mathcal{O}(n \log p / \log k)$
6: `Sort`(B_r) ▷ $\mathcal{O}(n \log n)$
7: **return**

In *step 1*, `SampleSplitters` is a random sampling approach to choose the splitters and is outlined in Algorithm 3.3. We sample p keys per task that are sorted using a distributed BITONICSORT [6]. We select $p - 1$ splitters from the sorted distribution such that every task gets assigned an equal number of keys. In *step 2*, the rank refers to the global rank of the splitter and can be computed using binary search ($\mathcal{O}(p \log n)$) on every task followed by a reduction. In *step 4*, we compute the correct bucket of every key in MPI task i. Here $M^i_{p_r}$ are keys currently owned by task p_r that belong to bucket i and thus, need to be communicated to task i (from task p_r). By using p^2 samples, the expected load-imbalance is no larger than $2n$ [3]. *Step 5* is the all-to-all reshuffling. The standard MPI routine is very expensive (Figure 1). Instead, we're using our own staged all-to-all which we describe in the next section.

Algorithm 3.3 SAMPLESPLITTERS

Input: A (locally sorted), n, N, p
Output: $p - 1$ splitters s, worst imbalance: factor of 2
$r \leftarrow \{A_{i\,n/p} |\ i \in 0, ..., p - 1\}$
`BitonicSort` (r) ▷ $\mathcal{O}(p\ (\log p)^2)$
$s \leftarrow$ `All_Gather`(r_{p-1})
return $\{s_0, s_1, ..., s_{p-2}\}$

3.1 Alltoallv_kway

A major bottleneck in distributed implementations of SAMPLESORT and other similar sorting algorithms is the all-to-all communication using `MPI_Alltoallv`. For all MPI implementations that we have tried, `MPI_Alltoallv` does not scale well beyond 10^4 tasks. In our previous work [10] we used a hypercube scheme to avoid MPI all-to-all communication primitives (that work was in the context of N-body problems, not sorting). In that work we had demonstrated

Algorithm 3.4 SENDRECV_KWAY

Input: *comm*, p (w.l.g., assume $p = mk$) p_r of current task in *comm*, messages $\{M^j_i |\ i \in I_j\}$ destined for task $p_j, \forall j \in comm$.
Output: new communicator $comm'$, $p' = m = p/k$, messages $\{R^j_i |\ i \in \hat{I}_j\}$ destined for task $p'_j \in comm'\ \ \forall j$.
$R \leftarrow \emptyset$
$color \leftarrow \lfloor k\,p_r/p \rfloor$ ▷ for splitting *comm*
parallel for $i \in 1, ..., k - 1$ **do** ▷ asynchronous receive
  $p_{recv} \leftarrow m\,((color - i) \mod k) + (p_r \mod m)$
  $R \leftarrow R\ \cup$ `MPI_Irecv`$(p_{recv}, comm)$
end for
for $i \in 1, ..., k - 1$ **do** ▷ staged sends
  $p_{recv} \leftarrow m\,((color - i) \mod k) + (p_r \mod m)$
  $p_{send} \leftarrow m\,((color + i) \mod k) + (p_r \mod m)$
  `MPI_Issend`$(M^s|_{m\,i \leq s < m\,(i+1)}, p_{send}, comm)$
  `MPI_WaitRecv`(p_{recv})
end for
`MPI_WaitAll()`
$comm' \leftarrow$ `MPI_Comm_split`$(color, comm)$
return $[R, comm']$

scalability to $\mathcal{O}(10^5)$ cores. In every step of the hypercube communication pattern, each task sends and receives data from one other task and splits the problem into two smaller ones. The communication completes in $\log p$ steps, with $\mathcal{O}(N)$ data transfer in each step. Here we generalize this scheme to k-way splitting of the problem in each step (Algorithm 3.5). This reduces the number of steps by a factor of $\log k$ and the total data transfer from $\mathcal{O}(N \log p)$ to $\mathcal{O}(N \log p / \log k)$. Replacing the original `MPI_Alltoallv` in

SAMPLESORT with this implementation allowed us to improve its scalability as illustrated in Figure 1. In each stage

Algorithm 3.5 ALLTOALLV_KWAY

Input: *comm*, p (w.l.g., assume $p = k^l$), p_r of current task in *comm*, message $M^i_{p_r}$ destined for task p_i $\forall i$
Output: message $M^{p_r}_i$ received from task p_i $\forall i$
while $p > 1$ **do** $\triangleright$ iterations: $\mathcal{O}(\log p/\log k)$
  $[M, comm] \leftarrow$ `SendRecv_kway`$(\{M^j_i\}, comm)$
end while
return M

of the k-way communication, each task communicates with k other tasks. Sending all of these k messages asynchronously leads to network congestion. Therefore, we have used a staged communication scheme where we send a new message only upon receiving a message as described in [17]. In the extreme case of $k = p$, this method reduces to the scheme where every task communicates with every other task with $\mathcal{O}(p^2)$ total messages sent/received. This scheme worked well up to a few thousand tasks, but becomes costly for very large task counts.

Note that the load imbalance during an intermediate stage of the algorithm can be as large as a factor of $\sqrt{p}$. However, this level of load imbalance is not observed in random distributions. If a significant load imbalance is detected following a communication stage, we redistribute the data for those sub-problems.

3.2 Selecting Splitters using Parallel Select

As discussed, HYPERCUBEQUICKSORT, HISTOGRAMSORT, SAMPLE SORT and other splitter based sorting algorithms all rely on efficient determination of accurate splitters. For HYPERCUBEQUICKSORT, in each stage, a single splitter is determined, usually by choosing the median on any one task. However, this is not a reliable method and an error of ϵN in the rank of the splitter can lead to the final load on a task to be as large as $\mathcal{O}((1+\epsilon)^{\log p} n)$. In SAMPLESORT, a set of $p - 1$ splitters is generated by taking p evenly spaced samples in each locally sorted array.

In Algorithm 3.6, we use a technique also used in histogram sort. However, instead of computing $p - 1$ splitters, which becomes costly for large p, we only compute $k < p$ splitters: 1) Select βk samples from the entire data (across all tasks) and collect these on all tasks. 2) Sort samples and determine ranks locally using binary search. 3) Perform an `MPI_AllReduce` to determine the global ranks of the samples. 4) Select pairs of samples with ranks just greater and just smaller than the expected global rank for each of the k splitters. 5) Repeat steps $1 - 4$ by taking β samples in the narrowed range for each splitter and iterating till the range is within a tolerance value. The number of samples β must be such that the number of iterations needed is not very high and also the cost of each iteration is small. In our experiments, $\beta \in [20, 40]$ worked well.

3.3 HykSort

We improve upon the original HYPERCUBE QUICKSORT (Algorithm 3.1), by using Algorithm 3.6 to select splitters and by generalizing the 2-way splitting to a k-way splitting combined with Algorithm 3.5. We presort the local array and following data-exchanges, we locally merge the k

Algorithm 3.6 PARALLELSELECT

Input: A_r (locally sorted), n, N, $R[0, ..., k-1]$ (expected global ranks), N_ϵ global rank tolerance, $\beta \in [20, 40]$.
Output: global splitters $S \subset A$ with approximate global ranks $R[0, ..., k-1]$
$R^{start} \leftarrow [0, ..., 0]$ $\triangleright$ Start of range for sampling splitters
$R^{end} \leftarrow [n, ..., n]$ $\triangleright$ End of range for sampling splitters
$n_s \leftarrow [\beta/p, ..., \beta/p]$ $\triangleright$ #of local samples (each splitter)
$N_{err} \leftarrow N_\epsilon + 1$
while $N_{err} > N_\epsilon$ **do**
  $Q' \leftarrow A_r\left[\texttt{rand}\left(n_s, \left(R^{start}, R^{end}\right)\right)\right]$
  $Q \leftarrow$ `Sort(All_Gather(`$\hat{Q}'$`))` $\triangleright$ $\mathcal{O}(k \log p + k \log k)$
  $R^{loc} \leftarrow$ `Rank`(Q, A_r) $\triangleright$ $\mathcal{O}(k \log n)$
  $R^{glb} \leftarrow$ `All_Reduce`$\left(R^{loc}\right)$ $\triangleright$ $\mathcal{O}(k \log p)$
  $I[i] \leftarrow \text{argmin}_j |R^{glb}[j] - R[i]|$ $\forall i$
  $N_{err} \leftarrow \max\left|R^{glb} - R[I]\right|$
  $R^{start} \leftarrow R^{loc}[I-1]$
  $R^{end} \leftarrow R^{loc}[I+1]$
  $n_s \leftarrow \beta \frac{R^{end} - R^{start}}{R^{glb}[I+1] - R^{glb}[I-1]}$
end while
return $S \leftarrow Q[I]$

segments to maintain locally sorted arrays. Following [17], we overlap communication to receive the new keys with the merging of the keys with the local array. The overall algorithm is described in Algorithm 3.7.

3.3.1 SIMD Optimized Merge

For merging two sorted sequences we implemented a bitonic merge kernel using SIMD instructions as outlined in [5]. Specifically, we used SSE C intrinsics for integers and floats and AVX C intrinsics for the float and double data types.

Additional shuffle instructions are needed after the second level of the sorting network due to the nature of the data movement and lack of a general SSE shuffle operation which captures all possible permutations. The code for a 4-wide merging network using AVX instructions follows the same logic but extra complications arise due to the higher width which requires the use of instructions that permute in 128-bit chunks and those which permute across the 128-bit boundary, in addition to the shuffle instructions.

3.3.2 OpenMP Merge Sort

We add OpenMP parallelism by performing the local sorting using an OpenMP merge sort algorithm. We partition the array into equal parts and use `std::sort` to sort each part independently using OpenMP. Next, we merge the parts using the merge tree algorithm (Algorithm 3.7 lines: 16-20). Each merge is performed using an OpenMP parallel merge algorithm 3.8, which compute $p - 1$ splitters to split A and B, then merges each section independently to C.

3.4 Complexity analysis

In the previous section we discussed in detail the various algorithmic variants we have considered in our algorithm design. Here we summarize the complexity estimates assuming a hypercube topology.

- BITONICSORT requires no collectives and is very fast for small n (the grain size). The total time is local sort (making the array bitonic) plus exchange comparisons

Algorithm 3.7 HykSort

Input: A_r, *comm*, p (w.l.g., assume $p = mk$), p_r of current task in *comm*,

Output: globally sorted array B

$B \leftarrow$ `LocalSort`(A)
while $p > 1$ **do** ▷ Iters: $\mathcal{O}(\log p/\log k)$
  $N \leftarrow$ `MPI_AllReduce`$(|B|, comm)$
  $s \leftarrow$ `ParallelSelect` $(B, \{i N/k \mid i = 1, ..., k-1\})$
  $d_{i+1} \leftarrow$ `Rank`$(s_i, B), \ \forall i$
  $[d_0,\ d_k] \leftarrow [0,\ n]$
  $color \leftarrow \lfloor k\,p_r/p \rfloor$
  parallel for $i \in 0, ..., k-1$ **do**
    $p_{recv} \leftarrow m\,((color - i) \bmod k) + (p_r \bmod m)$
    $R_i \leftarrow$ `MPI_Irecv`$(p_{recv}, comm)$
  end for
  for $i \in 0, ..., k-1$ **do**
    $p_{recv} \leftarrow m\,((color - i) \bmod k) + (p_r \bmod m)$
    $p_{send} \leftarrow m\,((color + i) \bmod k) + (p_r \bmod m)$
    `MPI_Issend`$(B[d_i, ..., d_{i+1}-1], p_{send}, comm)$
    $j \leftarrow 2$
    while $i > 0$ *and* $i \bmod j = 0$ **do**
      $R_{i-j} \leftarrow$ `merge`$(R_{i-j}, R_{i-j/2})$
      $j \leftarrow 2j$
    end while
    `MPI_WaitRecv`(p_{recv})
  end for
  `MPI_WaitAll`$()$
  $B \leftarrow$ `merge`$(R_0, R_{k/2})$
  $comm \leftarrow$ `MPI_Comm_split`$(color, comm)$
  $p_r \leftarrow$ `MPI_Comm_rank`$(comm)$
end while
return B

Algorithm 3.8 OpenMP_Merge

Input: A, B sorted arrays to merge, p number of OpenMP threads, $\beta \sim 10$.

Output: C merged output.

$S \leftarrow A[0 : \frac{n_A}{\beta p} : n_A] \cup B[0 : \frac{n_B}{\beta p} : n_B]$
$R^A_{i+1} \leftarrow$ `Rank`$(S_i, A), \ \forall i$ ▷ in parallel
$R^B_{i+1} \leftarrow$ `Rank`$(S_i, B), \ \forall i$ ▷ in parallel
$R \leftarrow R^A + R^B$
$I_i \leftarrow \text{argmin}_j |R_j - i(n_A + n_B)/p|, \ \forall i = 1, .., p-1$
$d^A \leftarrow [0,\ R^A_I,\ n_A]$
$d^B \leftarrow [0,\ R^B_I,\ n_B]$
$d \leftarrow d^A + d^B$
parallel for $i \in 0, ..., p-1$ **do**
  $C_{d_i : d_{i+1}-1} \leftarrow$ `SIMD_Merge`$(A_{d^A_i : d^A_{i+1}-1}, B_{d^B_i : d^B_{i+1}-1})$
end for
return C

and point-to-point communication.

$$T_b = \left(t_c \frac{N}{p}\right) \log \frac{N}{p} + \left(t_s + t_w \frac{N}{p}\right) \log^2 p.$$

- The main costs for SampleSort is sorting splitters and collectives for data reshuffling. The latter can lead to load imbalance and network congestion represented by a constant c below.

$$T_s = t_c c \frac{N}{p} \log \frac{N}{p} + (t_s + t_w p) \log^2 p + t_w c \frac{N}{p}.$$

- ParallelSelect for determining k splitters, uses the `All_Gather()` and `All_Reduce()` communication collectives. The main computational cost is in determining the local ranks of the samples using binary search. The number of iterations η depend on the input distribution, the required tolerance $\epsilon = N_\epsilon/N$ and the parameter beta. The expected vaue of η varies as $-\log(\epsilon)/\log(\beta)$ and β must be chosen experimentally to minimize the running time T_{ps}:

$$T_{ps} = \eta\, t_c \beta k \log \frac{N}{p} + \eta(t_s + t_w \beta k) \log p.$$

- AlltoallV_kway uses only point-to-point communications with staged message sends and receives, minimizing network congestion. It has $\log p/\log k$ stages with $\mathcal{O}(N/p)$ data transfer and k messages for each task in every stage.

$$T_{a2a} = \left(t_s k + t_w \frac{N}{p}\right) \frac{\log p}{\log k}$$

- HykSort has the same communication pattern as AlltoallV_kway. In addition it relies on ParallelSelect to determine splitters. The main computational cost is in the initial local sort and merging k arrays during each iteration.

$$T_{Hk} = t_c \frac{N}{p} \log \frac{N}{p} + \left(t_c \frac{N}{p} + T_{ps}\right) \frac{\log p}{\log k} + T_{a2a}$$

Unlike SampleSort, the complexity of HykSort does not involve any $\mathcal{O}(p)$ terms. (Bitonic sort involves $\mathcal{O}(\log^2 p)$ terms but is quite slow when $N/p \gg 1$.)

4. EXPERIMENTAL STUDY

In this section we present results demonstrating the scalability and performance of k-way SampleSort and HykSort. We provide details regarding our implementation and the different datasets used for evaluation. Finally, we present weak and strong scalability experiments that demonstrate the performance of our scheme.

All experiments reported in this paper were performed on *Titan*, a Cray XK7 supercomputer at Oak Ridge National Laboratory (ORNL). Titan has a total of 18,688 nodes consisting of a single 16-core AMD Opteron 6200 series processor, for a total of 299,008 cores. Each node has with 32GB of memory. It is also equipped with a Gemini interconnect and 600 terabytes of memory across all nodes. (In addition, all of Titan's 18,688 compute nodes contain an NVIDIA Tesla K20 graphical processing unit, which we don't use currently). In our largest runs we use a total of 262,144 cores.

4.1 Implementation Details

All algorithms described in this work were implemented using C++ using OpenMP and MPI. In addition, SIMD acceleration (`SSE` and `AVX`) was employed to speed up the merge operation. SIMD acceleration was only employed for supported datatypes (`int`, `float` and `double`). The sequential sorting algorithm used in all parallel implementations was the C++ standard library sort (`std::sort`) which implements Introsort [12]. The PGI compiler (`v12.9`) was

Table 2: *Single-core performance, in seconds.*

data	size	Titan
int	128MB	4.81
int	2GB	88.35
treenode	128MB	3.01
treenode	2GB	56.68
100-byte	128MB	1.67
100-byte	2GB	39.62

Table 3: *Single-node performance on Titan. The column header specifies the number of MPI tasks and the number of OpenMP threads per task. In all instances, MPI performs better. See Figure 3 for results at higher node counts.*

	tasks : threads		
key type	16:1	2:8	1:16
int 128mb	0.51	0.61	0.63
int 2GB	9.09	10.65	10.96
treenode 128mb	0.39	0.76	1.13
treenode 2GB	6.4	12.78	18.61
100-byte 128mb	0.33	0.62	1.15
100-byte 2GB	5.54	10.52	15.79

used on Titan with the following optimization flags `-O3 -fastsse -mp`. Three different datatypes were used in our experiments; 32-bit integer keys (`4-byte`), a `56-byte`-key (`treenode`) used for representing octrees [18] and a `100-byte` structure commonly used in sort benchmarks [7]. The `100-byte` structure consists of a `10-byte` key and a `90-byte` payload. For the `int` and `treenode` keys, we generated datasets using uniform and Gaussian distributions.

4.2 Single-Node and MPI vs OpenMP Performance

In this section we report single-core performance on different datatypes, as a point of reference for the rest of the experiments. As previously mentioned, we use the C++ `std::sort` method as the sequential sort. We report the time to sort the different datatypes in Table 2.

We also consider single-node performance on Titan. Specifically, we make the choice between using pure MPI based parallelization and a MPI-OpenMP hybrid code. On both platforms, we test three configurations; pure MPI (16 MPI tasks), hybrid (2 MPI tasks, 8 OpenMP threads per task) and pure OpenMP (1 MPI task, 16 OpenMP threads). These results are summarized in Table 3. As can be seen, in all cases the pure MPI configuration is the most efficient. Although running a single MPI task per core is most efficient on a single node and at small node—and consequently small core—counts, the communication costs start to dominate at larger node counts. The difference between the two approaches is shown in Figure 3 for a grain size of 2GB per node using integer keys and the SampleSort algorithm. As can be seen, the communication costs are significantly lower by using the hybrid approach and using one MPI task per socket (i.e., two MPI tasks per node on Titan). For this reason, we used the hybrid approach for all scalability results reported in this paper.

4.3 Parallel Scalability

To study the parallel performance of our implementation, we performed strong (fixed-size) and weak (isogranular) scalability experiments. We report statistics for several stages of the algorithm. For every stage we report the maximum time for that stage across all MPI tasks. We evaluated the scalability of HykSort and the k-way SampleSort and compared them against the the classical SampleSort and Hypercube QuickSort. For the SampleSort algorithm we report the times for the following stages;

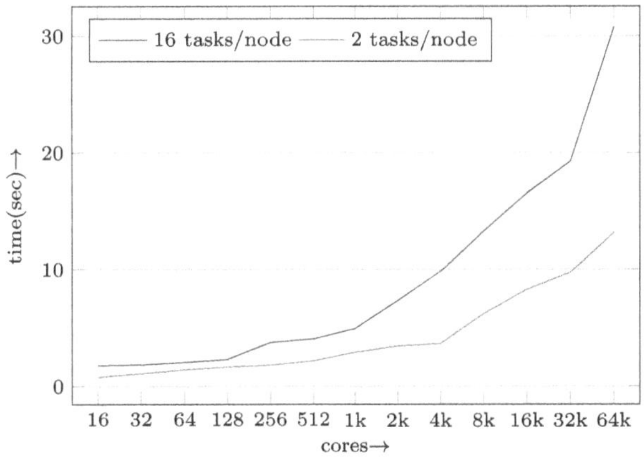

Figure 3: *Effect of number of MPI tasks per node on the* SampleSort *communication (`all2all`) stage on Titan. Both approaches use a 128-way `all2all`, which was the fastest for $8 \leq k \leq 256$. A grain size of 512M keys of type `int` (2GB) per node was used in both cases.*

- **sequential sort** the time spent in local sequential sorts,
- **splitters** the time spent in sampling, ranking, sorting and selecting the splitters, and
- **all2all** the time spent in the final exchange of data.

For HykSort, we report the times for the following stages;

- **sequential sort** the time spent in initial sequential sort,
- **splitters** the time spent in determining the k-splitters, cumulative over all stages, and
- **exchange-merge** the time spent in the overlapped k-way exchange and merging of sub-arrays.

Optimal k.

To select the best value of k, we performed several weak scaling studies. In these studies, we focussed on the `all2all` stage for SampleSort and the combined data exchange and merge for HykSort since these are the only stages that depend on k. The best performance for both approaches on Titan was obtained for $k = 128$ and is plotted in Figures 4 and 5 for values of $k = 64, 128$ and 256. It is important to note that the optimal k will depend on the network characteristics and will be specific to the cluster. In our experiments, we did not observe sensitivity to the datatype on the value of k.

Strong Scalability.

To assess the strong scalability of HykSort, especially at large core counts, we used a problem size of 1TB and increased the core count from 8K to 256K (a 32 fold increase) on Titan. For integer keys this reduced the number of keys per core from 32 million to one million. The strong scalability experiments were carried out for both HykSort as

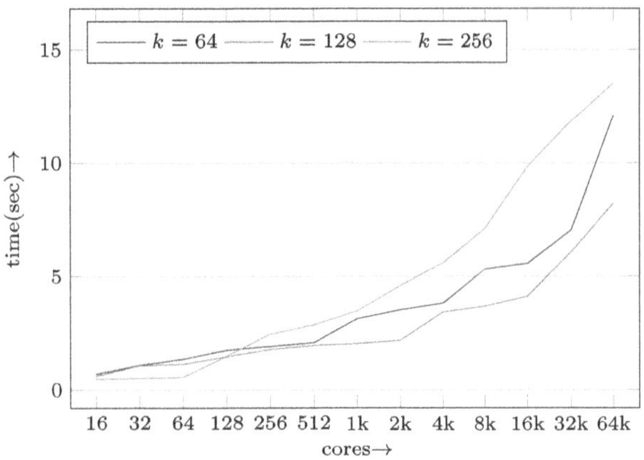

Figure 4: *Effect of different k values on the weak scalability of the* HykSort ***exchange data*** *stage on Titan. A grain size of 38M* **treenode** *keys (2GB) keys per node was used in all cases. The plots correspond to the communication part only. In addition, since we overlap communication with the merging stage, only the part where the task is waiting for data is measured.*

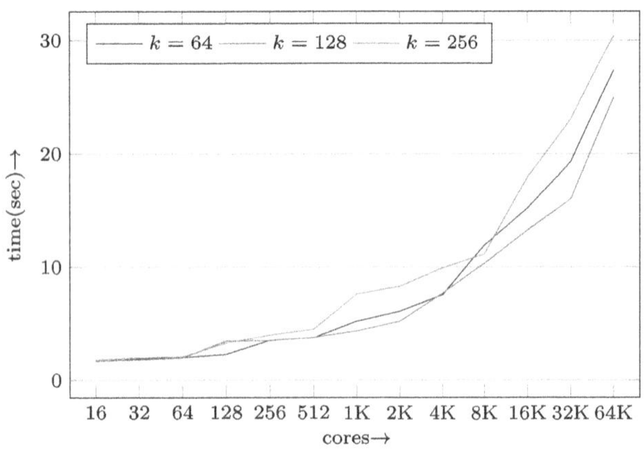

Figure 5: *Effect of different k on weak scalability of the* SampleSort *communication* (**all2all**) *stage on Titan. A grain size of 512M* **int** *(2GB) keys per node was used in all cases. The plots correspond to the communication part only.*

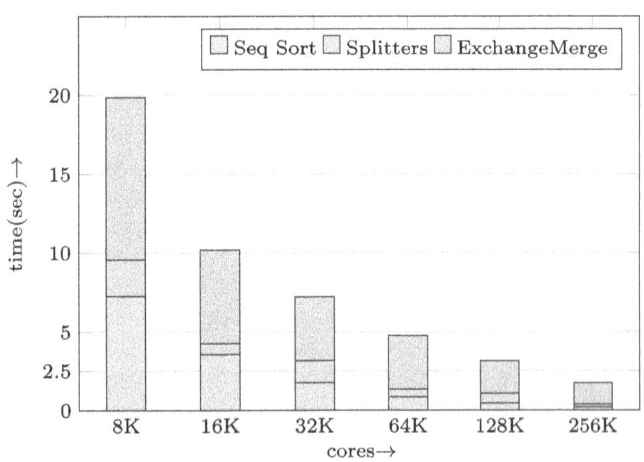

Figure 6: *Strong scalability using 128-way* HykSort *with integer datatype, with a fixed problem size of 1TB. All runs were performed using* 2 MPI *tasks per node with* 8 OpenMP *threads per* MPI *task. The 32 fold increase in core count reduces the number of keys from 32 million per core to just 1 million per core. We obtain a speedup of about* 12x *at 262,144 cores.*

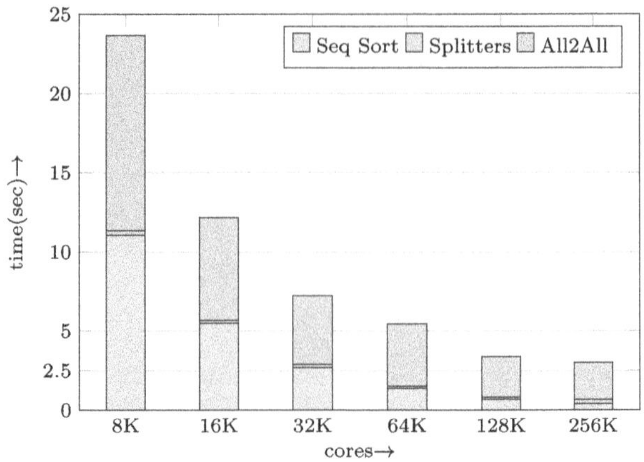

Figure 7: *Strong scalability using 128-way* SampleSort *with integer datatype, with a fixed problem size of 1TB. All runs were performed using* 2 MPI *tasks per node with* 8 OpenMP *threads per* MPI *task. The 32 fold increase in core count reduces the number of keys from 32 million per core to just 1 million per core. The scalability is lower than that obtained using* HykSort *for the same problem, with a speedup of about* 8x *at 256K cores. The sequential sort takes longer compared compared with* HykSort *because of the need to do two sequential sorts as opposed to just one for* HykSort.

well as the k-way SampleSort. These results are shown in Figure 6 and 7. For HykSort we obtain very good scalability all the way till 256K cores resulting in a 12x speedup. For SampleSort we obtain slightly lower speedup of 8x, as the cost of sorting splitters using BitonicSort increases at 256K cores.

Weak Scalability.

Weak scalability tests were performed using the integer and `100-byte` datatypes. For both cases, we choose a grain size of 128MB per core resulting in a total problem size of 34TB on 262,144 cores. This results in a total of 8.5 trillion integer keys and 350 billion 100-byte keys that need to be sorted. The results for the integer keys are reported in Figures 8 and 9. Using HykSort we are able to sort the 8.5 trillion keys in about 37 seconds for a throughput of approximately 0.9TB/s. The throughput using the 128-way SampleSort algorithm is slightly lower at 0.75TB/s. We see that the cost of sorting the splitters using BitonicSort starts to become significant at large core counts. The results for sorting the 100-byte keys are similar and are reported in Figures 10 and 11. With the larger datatype, the effects of load-imbalance are more pronounced and can be observed in the scalability of both HykSort and SampleSort. We are currently working on incorporating load balancing into these algorithms which should help maintain a high throughput with large datatypes at large core counts.

5. CONCLUSIONS

We have presented two new algorithms for distributed memory comparison sort. The first algorithm is a k-way all-to-all staged communication that can be used in the classical SampleSort sort algorithm to accelerate the data exchange by avoiding network congestion. The second algorithm, HykSort combines accurate splitter selection with a k-way recursion to minimize load imbalance and communica-

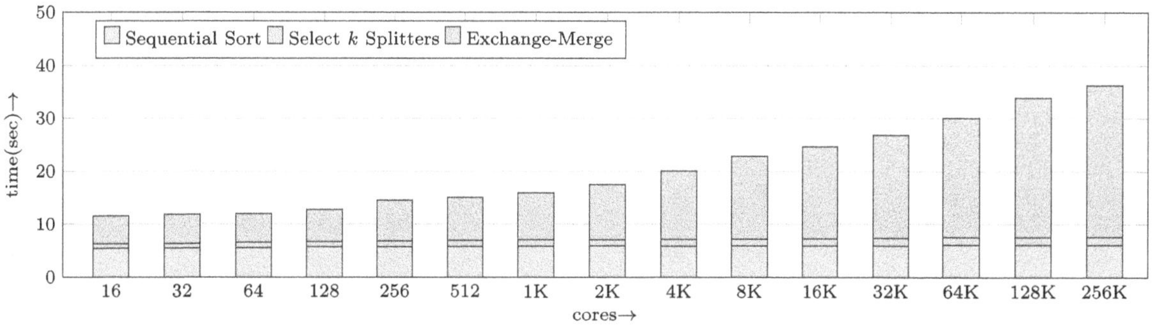

Figure 8: *Weak scaling for* 128*-way* HYKSORT *from 16 to 262,144 cores with a grain size of* 128MB *per core using the* INT *datatype. All runs were performed using* 2 MPI *tasks per node with* 8 OPENMP *threads per* MPI *task. A total of 8.5 trillion keys (*32TB*) were sorted in about 37 seconds, for a throughput of* 0.9TB/S. *Note that the problem size increases* 16,384X *during this experiment from* 2GB *to* 32TB.

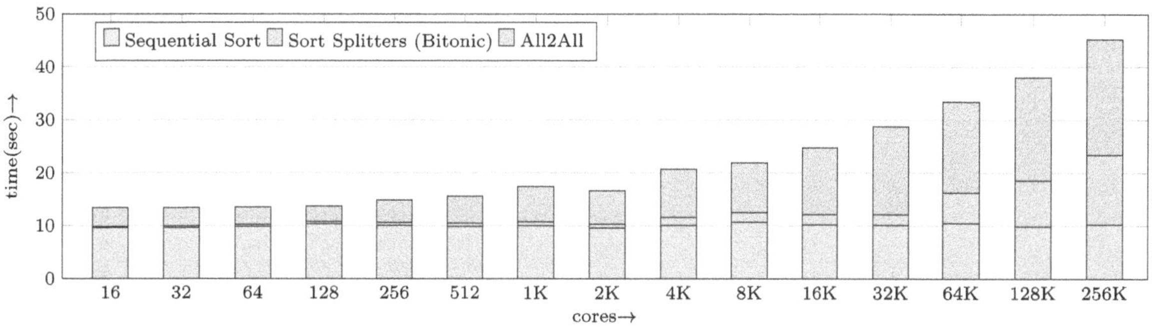

Figure 9: *Weak scaling for* 128*-way* SAMPLESORT *from 16 to 262,144 cores with a grain size of* 128MB *per core using the* INT *datatype. A total of 8.5 trillion keys (*32TB*) were sorted in about 45 seconds, for a throughput of* 0.75TB/S. *The lower throughput compared with* HYKSORT *is mainly due to the poor scalability of* BITONICSORT *at large core counts. The sequential sort takes longer compared compared with* HYKSORT *because of the need to do two sequential sorts as opposed to just one for* HYKSORT. *Note that the problem size increases* 16,384X *during this experiment from* 2GB *to* 32TB.

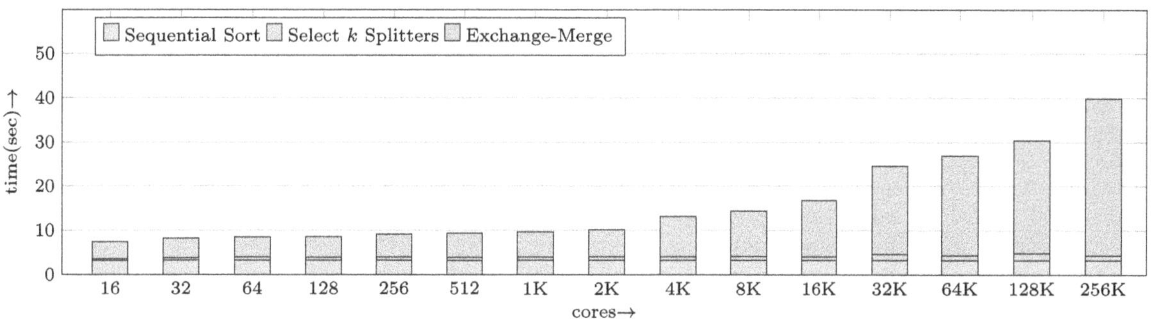

Figure 10: *Weak scaling for* 128*-way* HYKSORT *from 16 to 262,144 cores with a grain size of* 128MB *per core using the* 100-BYTE *datatype. A total of 351 billion keys (*32TB*) were sorted in about 40 seconds, for a throughput of* 0.85TB/S. *Note that the problem size increases* 16,384X *during this experiment from* 2GB *to* 32TB.

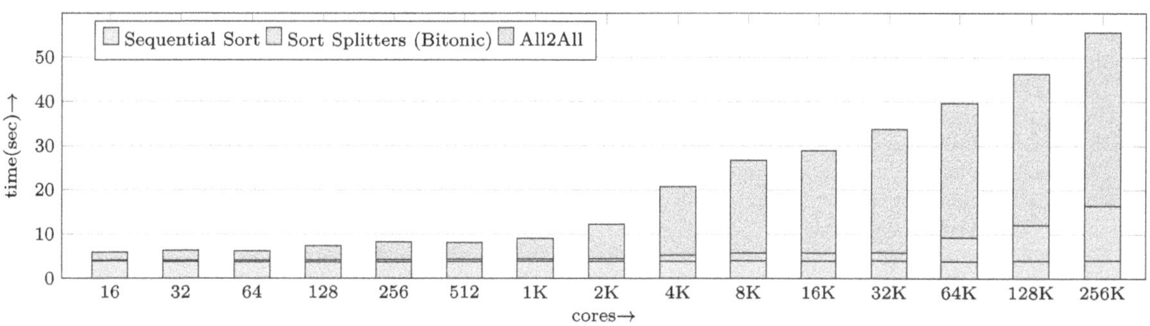

Figure 11: *Weak scaling for* 128*-way* SAMPLESORT *from 16 to 262,144 cores with a grain size of* 128MB *per core using the* 100-BYTE *datatype. A total of 351 billion keys (*32TB*) were sorted in about 55 seconds, for a throughput of* 0.63TB/S. *The lower throughput compared with* HYKSORT *is due to the poor scalability of* BITONICSORT *at large core counts as well as due to load-balance issues arising with the distribution of the* 100-BYTE *keys. Note that the problem size increases* 16,384X *during this experiment from* 2GB *to* 32TB.

tion. Our design avoids `MPI_Alltoall` and `MPI_Alltoallv` exchanges. The only remaining issue is the load imbalance introduced; not due to uneven bucket size, but due to variations in the local grain size due to the data exchanges. With large k and as the recursion progresses this is less of an issue but it is still present. The fix is easy: we need to add a load balancing step after every data exchange. This repartitioning can be done again without any all-to-all collectives. But even without repartitioning, our proposed design improves significantly over the state of the art by achieving 0.9TB/sec throughput for the `int` dataset. The source code for all algorithms described in this paper is available at `http://padas.ices.utexas.edu/`.

Moving forward, the main improvements in our implementation will be the inclusion of accelerators and algorithmic redesign to enable fault tolerance without excessive costs. Another possibility is that of tuning the code based on machine characteristics, number of MPI tasks, and the problem size. For example, for very small grain sizes bitonic sort is expected to perform very well. Also the k parameter can be selected by building a more accurate performance model.

Acknowledgment

This research was partially supported by AFOSR grant FA9550-12-10484; DOE grants DE-FG02-08ER2585 and DE-SC0009286; and NSF grants OCI-1047980, OCI-1029022 and OCI-0923710. Computing time on ORNL's Titan system was provided by an allocation from the Oak Ridge Leadership Computing Facility. We will also like to thank Dr. Judith Hill of ORNL for her assistance with porting our codes to Titan.

6. REFERENCES

[1] P. Berthomé, A. Ferreira, BM Maggs, S. Perennes, and CG Plaxton. Sorting-based selection algorithms for hypercubic networks. *Algorithmica*, 26(2):237–254, 2000.

[2] G.E. Blelloch, C.E. Leiserson, B.M. Maggs, C.G. Plaxton, S.J. Smith, and M. Zagha. A comparison of sorting algorithms for the connection machine CM-2. In *Proceedings of the third annual ACM symposium on Parallel algorithms and architectures*, pages 3–16. ACM, 1991.

[3] G.E. Blelloch, C.E. Leiserson, B.M. Maggs, C.G. Plaxton, S.J. Smith, and M. Zagha. An experimental analysis of parallel sorting algorithms. *Theory of Computing Systems*, 31(2):135–167, 1998.

[4] D.R. Cheng, V.B. Shah, J.R. Gilbert, and A. Edelman. A novel parallel sorting algorithm for contemporary architectures. *Int. J. Parallel Prog*, pages 1–12, 2007.

[5] Jatin Chhugani, Anthony D. Nguyen, Victor W. Lee, William Macy, Mostafa Hagog, Yen-Kuang Chen, Akram Baransi, Sanjeev Kumar, and Pradeep Dubey. Efficient implementation of sorting on multi-core simd cpu architecture. *Proc. VLDB Endow.*, 1(2):1313–1324, August 2008.

[6] A. Grama, A. Gupta, G. Karypis, and V. Kumar. *An Introduction to Parallel Computing: Design and Analysis of Algorithms*. Addison Wesley, second edition, 2003.

[7] Jim Gray. Sort benchmark home page. `http://sortbenchmark.org/`, April 2013.

[8] L.V. Kale and S. Krishnan. A comparison based parallel sorting algorithm. In *International Conference on Parallel Processing, 1993*, volume 3, pages 196–200. IEEE, 1993.

[9] C. Kim, J. Park, N. Satish, H. Lee, P. Dubey, and J. Chhugani. CloudRAMSort: fast and efficient large-scale distributed ram sort on shared-nothing cluster. In *Proceedings of the 2012 international conference on Management of Data*, pages 841–850. ACM, 2012.

[10] Ilya Lashuk, Aparna Chandramowlishwaran, Harper Langston, Tuan-Anh Nguyen, Rahul Sampath, Aashay Shringarpure, Richard Vuduc, Lexing Ying, Denis Zorin, and George Biros. A massively parallel adaptive fast multipole method on heterogeneous architectures. *Communications of the ACM*, 55(5):101–109, May 2012.

[11] N. Leischner, V. Osipov, and P. Sanders. GPU sample sort. In *Parallel & Distributed Processing (IPDPS), 2010 IEEE International Symposium on*, pages 1–10. IEEE, 2010.

[12] D.R. Musser. Introspective sorting and selection algorithms. *Software Practice and Experience*, 27(8):983–993, 1997.

[13] A. Rasmussen, G. Porter, M. Conley, H.V. Madhyastha, R.N. Mysore, A. Pucher, and A. Vahdat. Tritonsort: A balanced large-scale sorting system. In *USENIX NSDI*, volume 11, 2011.

[14] John H. Reif and Leslie G. Valiant. A logarithmic time sort for linear size networks. *Journal of the ACM*, 34(1):60–76, January 1987.

[15] N. Satish, C. Kim, J. Chhugani, A.D. Nguyen, V.W. Lee, D. Kim, and P. Dubey. Fast sort on CPUs, GPUs and intel MIC architectures. Technical report, Technical report, Intel, 2010.

[16] E.L.G. Saukas and SW Song. Efficient selection algorithms on distributed memory computers. In *SC98, IEEE/ACM Conference on Supercomputing, 1998*, pages 20–20. IEEE, 1998.

[17] E. Solomonik and L.V. Kale. Highly scalable parallel sorting. In *Parallel & Distributed Processing (IPDPS), 2010 IEEE International Symposium on*, pages 1–12. IEEE, 2010.

[18] Hari Sundar, Rahul S. Sampath, and George Biros. Bottom-up construction and 2:1 balance refinement of linear octrees in parallel. *SIAM Journal on Scientific Computing*, 30(5):2675–2708, 2008.

[19] BA Wagar. Hyperquicksort: A fast sorting algorithm for hypercubes. *Hypercube Multiprocessors*, 1987:292–299, 1987.

Diagnosis and Optimization of Application Prefetching Performance

Gabriel Marin
Innovative Computing Laboratory
University of Tennessee
gmarin@utk.edu

Collin McCurdy
Future Technologies
Oak Ridge National Laboratory
cmccurdy@ornl.gov

Jeffrey S. Vetter
Future Technologies
Oak Ridge National Laboratory
vetter@ornl.gov

ABSTRACT

Hardware prefetchers are effective at recognizing streaming memory access patterns and at moving data closer to the processing units to hide memory latency. However, hardware prefetchers can track only a limited number of data streams due to finite hardware resources. In this paper, we introduce the term *streaming concurrency* to characterize the number of parallel, logical data streams in an application. We present a simulation algorithm for understanding the streaming concurrency at any point in an application, and we show that this metric is a good predictor of the number of memory requests initiated by streaming prefetchers. Next, we try to understand the causes behind poor prefetching performance. We identified four prefetch unfriendly conditions and we show how to classify an application's memory references based on these conditions. We evaluated our analysis using the SPEC CPU2006 benchmark suite. We selected two benchmarks with unfavorable access patterns and transformed them to improve their prefetching effectiveness. Results show that making applications more prefetcher friendly can yield meaningful performance gains.

Categories and Subject Descriptors

D.2.8 [**Software Engineering**]: Metrics—*performance measures*

General Terms

Performance, Algorithms, Experimentation

Keywords

Stream prefetching, Performance modeling, Diagnosis

1. INTRODUCTION

The gap between CPU and memory speeds has constantly increased over the last few decades. Efforts have been made on both the hardware and software sides to improve system throughput by hiding part of the memory latency. One of the techniques most effective at hiding memory latency is to increase memory parallelism. Memory parallelism, or memory concurrency, can be increased by different means. One approach is to increase the number of processing cores connected to the memory system, another approach is to increase hardware threading concurrency through the use of simultaneous multithreading techniques, and finally, we can increase memory concurrency inside each thread.

Mandal et al. [11] empirically evaluate the level of memory parallelism per core, socket and node, needed to saturate the memory system of several current micro-architectures. Increasing memory parallelism beyond the capacity of the memory system does not bring direct performance benefits. However, increasing the level of memory concurrency inside each thread, ensures that an application runs efficiently in both low-threading and high-threading environments.

Data prefetching, that is, identifying data that will be needed in the near future and moving it closer to the processing units so that it is available when required by a running application, is an effective optimization both for increasing memory parallelism inside a thread and for overlapping memory latency with computation. Prefetchers based on Jouppi's stream buffers [8] are nowadays commonly found in modern micro-processors. These hardware structures recognize streaming memory access patterns and fetch the next elements of the streams in advance to hide memory latency. However, applications benefit differently from hardware prefetching, because they either do not traverse memory in a streaming pattern, or they exceed the resources provisioned for the hardware prefetchers.

In this paper, we describe techniques for modeling the streaming behavior of applications. We use these models to explain why applications benefit differently from hardware prefetching and to identify the causes behind poor prefetching performance. We use the SPEC CPU2006 benchmark suite [7] to evaluate our analysis. We selected two benchmarks with unfavorable access patterns, 436.CactusADM and 470.LBM, and changed them to improve their prefetching coverage. Our results show that tuning for the hardware prefetchers can yield meaningful performance benefits.

The rest of the paper is organized as follows. Section 2 provides a brief overview of related work. Section 3 presents background information on the AMD 10H hardware prefetchers. Section 4 describes a simulation algorithm for computing the *streaming concurrency* of applications, and evaluates its predictive power. Section 5 refines the simulation results using static analysis to identify the causes of poor prefetching performance. Section 6 presents the results of

ICS'13, June 10–14, 2013, Eugene, Oregon, USA.

our analysis applied to the SPEC CPU2006 benchmark suite and describes two tuning case studies. Section 7 summarizes the findings of this study and concludes the paper.

2. RELATED WORK

Prefetching comes in two main flavors, software prefetching and hardware prefetching. Both techniques have been extensively studied in the past. Literature on software prefetching focuses primarily on algorithms for understanding where compilers should automatically insert prefetch instructions [4, 15, 10]. Work regarding hardware prefetching tends to focus on new ideas for prefetching structures and implementations. The ideas are implemented in simulators and evaluated using benchmarks, or portions of benchmarks, meant to represent full applications [5, 17, 6].

Palacharla and Kessler [14] describe an algorithm for detecting streams as part of a stream buffer simulator. We improved on this algorithm and extended it to recognize streams with non-unit strides, and to compute the number of live data streams at any point in an application. We use streaming concurrency results in combination with static program analysis to understand which memory access patterns of an application are not effectively prefetched.

Williams et al. [19] have recognized the importance of writing code that is friendly to the hardware prefetchers. However, their optimizations are based on manual inspection of the code. We describe an analysis technique and tool implementation that abstractly understands streaming behavior in applications and provides insight into prefetch unfriendly memory access patterns. To our knowledge, this is the first description of such a tool.

3. BACKGROUND

The AMD 10H micro-architecture, represented by the Barcelona, Shanghai and Istanbul chips, has two streaming hardware prefetchers. The first prefetcher is associated with the data cache level and is replicated across all the cores of a microprocessor. We call it the DC prefetcher. The DC prefetcher monitors memory accesses that miss in the L1 cache. It tries to detect streaming data access patterns, and speculatively fetches the memory addresses predicted to be accessed in the near future. The second prefetcher is associated with the memory controller. Therefore, we call it the MC prefetcher. The MC prefetcher operates on the stream of memory addresses generated by misses in the last level of cache from all the cores connected to that memory controller. Because it operates on memory accesses that are filtered by the L3 cache, typically, it can discover a different set of data streams than the DC prefetcher, even when only a single core is active and generating addresses. The MC prefetcher fetches data into a separate prefetch buffer to avoid conflicts with the data loaded into the CPU caches.

Based on micro-benchmark testing, we found that the DC prefetcher recognizes streams with a maximum stride of one cache line, while the MC prefetcher understands streams with a stride of up to four cache lines. Both prefetchers recognize streams with either positive or negative strides. Hardware prefetching structures have limitations similar to other caching mechanisms. They keep track of streaming accesses that reference consecutive or nearby lines. However, successive accesses to nearby lines must exhibit a certain level of temporal locality, because the hardware structures

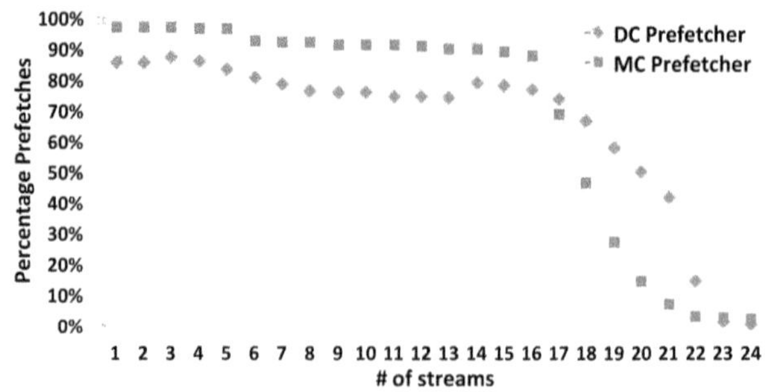

Figure 1: Prefetch requests as a function of stream count.

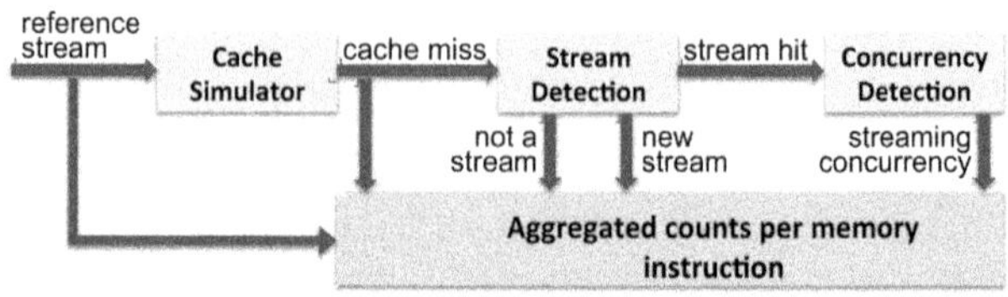

Figure 2: Diagram of the stream simulation tool.

used by the prefetchers have finite capacities. Again, we used micro-benchmarks to empirically understand the maximum number of data streams that can be handled by each AMD 10H hardware prefetcher.

We wrote a micro-benchmark that streams over a block of memory using a configurable number of concurrent streams. Figure 1 presents the fraction of memory requests that have been initiated by each of the hardware prefetchers as we varied the stream count. We measured these numbers using the hardware performance counters available on the AMD 10H architecture. The data in Figure 1 shows that the MC prefetcher is effective for up to 16 concurrent streams. This suggests the presence of a 16-entries hardware structure. The effectiveness of the DC prefetcher seems less stable. Overall, it stays relatively high up to a concurrency level of 16, and then decreases slowly up to a concurrency of 21 streams. However, its overall effectiveness is lower than that of the MC prefetcher for up to 16 streams.

4. STREAMING CONCURRENCY

Applications benefit from hardware prefetching in different degrees. To explain these differences, we developed a tool for identifying streaming behavior and for building a streaming concurrency model of an application. Our thesis is that the streaming concurrency model of an application can explain its observed prefetching performance.

We implemented a PIN [9] based tool to detect streaming behavior in optimized x86 binaries. Figure 2 shows the main components of our simulation tool. First, memory references are processed by a cache simulator, because the streaming hardware prefetchers on current micro-architectures are placed behind one or more levels of cache, with the cache acting as a filter on the address stream. Our cache simulator uses a true least recently used (LRU) replacement policy, but its capacity, block size and associativity are fully customizable otherwise. Accesses that miss in cache are further processed by a stream detection module, which is explained in the next section.

4.1 Stream Detection

Our stream detection algorithm is based on the stream buffer simulation algorithm described in [14]. We added extensions for detecting streaming behavior with non-unit strides. Because this algorithm is implemented in software, we could use a more general solution that does not require either knowing the PC of the instructions that perform memory accesses [1], or partitioning the address space and limiting stride detection within each partition [14].

Our stream detection algorithm uses two primary data structures, a *Stream Table* that stores information about streams already recognized, and a *History Buffer* that keeps track of memory locations recently accessed. The latter data structure is used to recognize new streams. A new stream is formed when two strided accesses, with the same stride, are detected. That is, the program must access locations i, $i+s$ and $i+2s$ to form a new stream with stride s, whose next access is expected to be at location $i+3s$.

The history table is a hybrid ring buffer / balanced search tree data structure. The ring buffer organization maintains a FIFO ordering of the entries. The balanced search tree organization is used to efficiently locate entries corresponding to nearby locations in memory for a history table that may be large in size. The history table entries are C structures with the following fields: *loc* - stores the memory location associated with an entry and is also the sorting key for the balanced search tree; *pstrides* and *nstrides* are two bit sets that keep track of positive and negative strides, respectively, of potential streams that include this memory location.

The stream table is also a hybrid data structure, organized both as a doubly linked list to maintain an LRU ordering between entries, and as a hash table to enable rapid detection of a stream hit. A stream table entry has the following fields: *next_loc* stores the next memory location expected to be accessed by a stream and is also the key used for hashing; *stride* stores the stride associated with a stream and is used to advance the stream on a stream hit; *prev* and *next* are pointers to other stream table entries, which are used to implement the doubly linked list view of the table.

Algorithm 1 shows the outline of the stream detection algorithm. On a memory access, we first check if the accessed memory location is predicted by any of the streams already stored in the *Stream Table*. If the location has been predicted by one of the streams, we call the access a *stream hit*. In this case, we only have to advance the stream, which consists of deleting its current entry from the hash table, updating the expected memory location field using the stride information, rehashing the entry based on the new value of the *next_loc* field, and updating the *next* and *prev* pointers to move the accessed stream into the most recently used (MRU) position. In addition, on a stream hit, we compute the instantaneous streaming concurrency value (see §4.2).

In case of a stream miss, we must check if the new memory access appears to be in a streaming pattern with other recently accessed locations stored in the history buffer (lines 10-31), allocate a new stream in the stream table if a stream is detected (lines 33-37), and finally, add a record of the newly accessed memory location to the history buffer (lines 38-44).

Algorithm 1 Stream detection algorithm.

```
 1: HistoryEntry histBuffer[H]
 2: Tree<HistoryEntry*> histTree
 3: function StreamDetect(mloc, sstride)
 4:     # mloc - accessed memory location
 5:     # sstride - stream stride (output parameter)
 6:     stream ← FindStream(mloc, sstride)
 7:     if stream ≠ 0 then
 8:         return AdvanceStream(stream)
 9:     else # stream miss, add to the history table
10:         uElem ← histTree.upper_bound(mloc + M)
11:         lElem ← histTree.lower_bound(mloc − M)
12:         pstrides ← 0
13:         nstrides ← 0
14:         min_stride ← MAX_INT
15:         min_elem ← 0
16:         for all lElem ≤ elem < uElem do
17:             s ← mloc − elem.loc
18:             if s > 0 then
19:                 pstrides.Set(s)
20:                 if elem.pstrides.IsSet(s) && s < abs(min_stride) then
21:                     min_stride ← s
22:                     min_elem ← elem
23:                 end if
24:             else if s < 0 then
25:                 nstrides.Set(−s)
26:                 if elem.nstrides.IsSet(−s) && −s < abs(min_stride) then
27:                     min_stride ← s
28:                     min_elem ← elem
29:                 end if
30:             end if
31:         end for
32:         status ← NO_STREAM
33:         if min_elem ≠ 0 then
34:             status ← NEW_STREAM
35:             sstride ← min_stride
36:             AllocateStream(mloc, sstride)
37:         end if
38:         if histBuffer.IsFull() then
39:             histTree.Erase(histBuffer[lastIdx])
40:             lastIdx ← (lastIdx + 1) mod H
41:         end if
42:         histBuffer[top] ← {mloc, pstrides, nstrides}
43:         histTree.Insert(histBuffer[top])
44:         top ← (top + 1) mod H
45:         return status
46:     end if
47: end function
```

4.2 Concurrency Detection

On a stream hit, we want to understand how many other data streams are active at the same time. We call this metric the *streaming concurrency* of an application. Previous stream buffer simulations matched an existing or proposed hardware implementation. They were using a predefined number of buffer streams, and were only interested in finding how many accesses have been stream hits (prefetchable) or stream misses. While we also use stream tables and history buffers of predetermined sizes during simulation, these sizes can be large, and have no relationship to any existing micro-architecture. We use simulation to build a model of an application's memory access patterns.

On each stream hit, we compute a streaming concurrency value for that memory access. We define the concurrency

Table 1: Simulation parameters.

Param	Description	DCsim	MCsim
C	Cache capacity (in KB)	64	6144
L	Cache line size (in bytes)	64	64
A	Cache associativity	2	48
M	Max stream stride(lines)	1	4
H	History buffer size	256	256
T	Stream table size	128	128

of a stream hit as the number of streams that have been advanced more recently than the previous hit on the current stream. This metric captures how many other streams are advancing concurrently with the current stream, which corresponds to the number of data arrays that are being streamed over by an application. This metric is also equivalent to computing the LRU stack distance [13, 2] for streams.

We compute the LRU stack distance using a balanced binary tree [3], which provides an $O(log(T))$ execution time per access, where T is the size of the tree. Our implementation, based on [12], uses a splay tree [16], and because we use a fixed size stream table during the simulation, the balanced tree size is upper bounded by the table size.

We aggregate application profiles at the memory instruction level. We process this profile information in a post-mortem step to compute different statistics at instruction, loop and routine level.

4.3 Simulation Results

We compare our histograms of streaming concurrency against hardware counter measurements of prefetching requests initiated by the two AMD 10H streaming hardware prefetchers. Our motivation for this work is to explain observed differences in prefetching performance and to identify opportunities for tuning in scientific applications. For this evaluation, we use the full SPEC CPU2006 benchmark suite because it provides a broad set of applications and it eliminates the temptation of cherry picking a small number of HPC applications that reflect better on our analysis.

We use the `train` input set instead of the `ref` input set for our evaluation because despite a careful implementation, simulating each memory access causes ≈60x execution slowdown. In addition, we believe that performance diagnosis based on performance modeling does not need to be done at scale to be useful. Our models capture features of an application, such as streaming behavior, that are true at different scales. Our tuning results in §6 include data for `ref` inputs.

The stream detection algorithm abstractly identifies the number of concurrent streams in an application. This measure is a machine independent application characteristic. However, on most micro-architectures, including the AMD 10H architecture, stream buffers are placed after one or more levels of cache. Caches act as filters on the stream of memory addresses. Therefore, we configured our simulation tool with an architecture dependent cache simulator in the first stage, as shown in Figure 2. We used a dual-socket AMD Istanbul based machine, with two 6-core processors running at 2.6GHz and 12GB of main memory for both our simulations and our hardware counter measurement results.

We performed two simulation runs, using the configurations shown in Table 1: 1) one simulation targeting the DC prefetcher uses a 64KB, 2-way set-associative cache in the first stage and detects streams with a stride of +/- one cache line; 2) a second simulation targeting the MC prefetcher detects streams with a stride of up to four cache lines, and accesses are filtered by a 6MB, 48-way set-associative cache.

Table 2: SPEC benchmark names.

Index	Name	Index	Name
400	perlbench	401	bzip2
403	gcc	410	bwaves
416	gamess	429	mcf
433	milc	434	zeusmp
435	gromacs	436	cactusADM
437	leslie3d	444	namd
445	gobmk	447	dealII
450	soplex	453	povray
454	calculix	456	hmmer
458	sjeng	459	GemsFDTD
462	libquantum	464	h264ref
465	tonto	470	lbm
471	omnetpp	473	astar
481	wrf	482	sphinx3
483	xalancbmk		

Figure 3a shows the streaming concurrency results side by side with the hardware counter measurements of prefetch requests initiated by the DC prefetcher, for all the benchmarks and all the `train` inputs. On the `x` axis we show the benchmark index followed by a colon and the name of the input file, as it was captured by our automated script. For some benchmarks, no input file could be detected, so that information is missing. For brevity, we did not include the benchmark names in the figure labels. Table 2 shows the benchmark names associated with each benchmark index.

For each benchmark, we show a stacked histogram of the streaming simulation results aggregated at the entire program level. The bin values are normalized by the number of cache misses observed for each benchmark. Only cache misses are processed by the stream detection simulation, and thus, the bins of the histograms stack up to 1. The bins labeled as `New` reflect the fraction of cache misses that resulted in new streams being created. The streaming concurrency values, measured only for stream hits, have been aggregated into 11 distinct bins, with increasingly coarser resolutions. Finally, the `Not` bins show the fraction of non-streaming accesses observed for each benchmark. The `DC_PF` metric, measured using hardware counters, shows the fraction of data accesses to the L2 cache initiated by the DC prefetcher.

The bins are color coded for easier inspection, and use different hash patterns to be legible in black and white. Thus, low streaming concurrency bins, 1 to 4 streams, use dot patterns and are colored in black. Medium concurrency bins, 5 to 16 streams, use diagonal hash lines and are colored in red. Finally, high concurrency bins, 17 streams and higher, use horizontal or vertical hash lines and are colored in blue. Non-streaming accesses are plotted with a grid hash, and are also colored in blue. We specifically decided to make these distinctions between the different concurrency levels.

When a new stream is detected, the hardware prefetcher will attempt to fetch the next location predicted to be part of the stream. Similarly, when a stream is advanced on a stream hit, the hardware prefetcher will fetch the next location predicted by the stream. Based on the prefetching effectiveness profile shown in Figure 1, we expect that most accesses with a streaming concurrency of up to 16 will hit

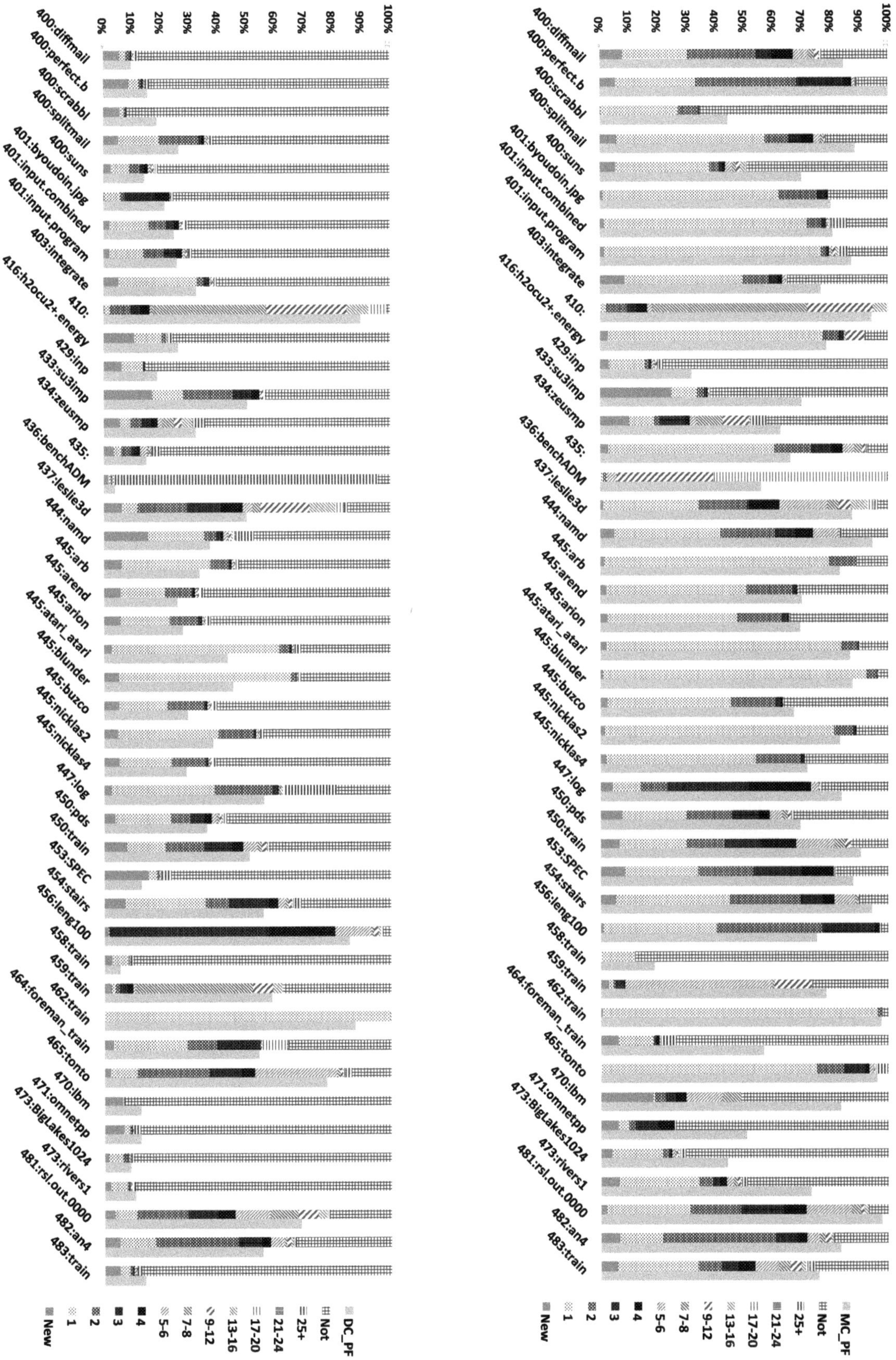

(a) DC prefetcher

(b) MC prefetcher

Figure 3: Streaming concurrency and prefetching measurements for the two AMD 10H hardware prefetchers.

in the hardware prefetcher's own hardware structures, and thus result in a new prefetch request to the L2 cache. The differences in color and filling patterns between streaming concurrencies below 16 and those of 17 and higher, make it easier to compare the simulation and measurement results.

We opted to present a graphical, qualitative comparison of these two metrics, because first, the streaming concurrency histograms include more information than a single quantitative prediction of prefetch requests computed by summing up the `New` bin and the bins with a concurrency of up to 16, and second, we want to show that the streaming concurrency metric provides a good explanation of prefetching effectiveness, even as we do not fully understand the precise implementation of the AMD 10H hardware prefetchers. As can be seen in Figure 1, the DC prefetcher is not 100% effective even when we generate clean streaming accesses at low concurrency levels, using a synthetic micro-benchmark.

Overall, we believe the results in Figure 3a explain well the measured prefetch counts. Across the entire suite, almost half of all DC cache misses are not streaming accesses. However, for most benchmarks, memory accesses that have streaming behavior are characterized by a low or medium concurrency level, which means that they can be effectively prefetched by the current hardware prefetchers. Only benchmark `436.cactusADM`, and to a lesser extent benchmarks `447.dealII` and `464.h264ref`, have a significant fraction of streaming accesses characterized by high concurrency. There are also three outliers for which the measured number of prefetch requests is lower than what we would expect based on the concurrency histograms: benchmark `437.leslie3d`, and inputs `atari_atari` and `blunder` of benchmark `445.gobmk`. We note that in these cases, the number of accesses to the L2 cache[1], measured with hardware performance counters, was 25% to 40% higher than the miss counts produced by our L1 cache simulator. Benchmark `gobmk` is known to have very poor branch predictability, which likely leads to many wrong-path loads, not visible to our PIN based simulation.

Often, prefetchers may initiate unnecessary prefetch requests, on one hand due to inaccurate predictions, but also due to superfluous requests at the end of streams when applications stop accessing data along those same patterns. The number of newly created streams computed by our simulation is a good indicator of how many superfluous requests are generated at the end of streams, because all the streams that are created will stop advancing eventually. The number of unnecessary prefetch requests generated at the end of streams depends also on how many lines are fetched in advance by each prefetcher. In the case of the DC prefetcher, this number seems to be small.

Similarly, Figure 3b compares the simulated streaming concurrency and the number of prefetch requests observed for the MC prefetcher. The `MC_PF` metric represents the fraction of memory requests initiated by the MC prefetcher, measured using hardware counters. Most of the discussion for the DC prefetcher applies to the MC prefetcher results as well. However, evaluating the behavior of the MC prefetcher is complicated by additional factors. Our simulation analyzes the stream of memory accesses generated by the application and filtered by a cache with the characteristics of the L3 cache on the target machine. However, in practice, the DC prefetcher will generate additional memory requests that may be filtered or not by the intervening levels of cache. Also, the three levels of cache of the AMD 10H architecture are not in an inclusive relationship. Simulating only the last cache level does not capture precisely the number of memory accesses that are processed by the MC stream buffers.

The results in Figure 3b show once again that the streaming concurrency metric explains well the measured MC prefetch counts. Benchmarks `433.milc` and `470.lbm` stand out with a high rate of stream creation. The high rate of stream creation results in a high number of superfluous prefetch requests at the end of the streams, which causes the measured prefetch counts to be higher than what we would expect. These results suggest that the MC prefetcher fetches multiple lines in advance, which is understandable considering the higher memory latency that it must hide.

5. PERFORMANCE INSIGHT

The simulation algorithm introduced in the previous section, abstractly identifies streaming behavior in applications. We performed simulations with a larger stream table size, to pinpoint cases when an application exhibits streaming behavior, but the number of streams exceeds the size of the hardware structures. However, even the data structures that we use in our simulations are finite in size, for performance reasons. Accesses with streaming concurrency levels higher than the size of the *Stream Table* are labeled instead as having non-streaming behavior. In this section, we refine the simulation results using static analysis. Besides improving the accuracy of the simulation results, we also want to identify opportunities for improving prefetching performance.

Our models assume that accesses that create new streams and streaming accesses with concurrency of up to 16 are prefetchable. We focus our attention on the other types of accesses. We base our analysis on the following observations:

1) Streaming accesses are strided accesses with a stride less than or equal to the maximum recognized stride, M. We generally think of streaming accesses as being generated by the loop immediately enclosing a memory instruction. However, consider the case of a two dimensional array laid out in row major order, as in C, and a two level loop nest where the inner loop iterates over the rows, and the outer loop iterates over the array's columns. Every iteration of the inner loop touches different rows, which are far apart in memory. Therefore, the inner loop does not create streaming accesses. However, on each iteration of the outer loop we access consecutive elements of each row. Thus, the outer loop advances a separate stream for each row of the array. We know that such an access pattern is sub-optimal due to long spatial reuse. However, it also creates a situation where, potentially, a very large number of streams are accessed in a round-robin fashion. We state that out of all the loops enclosing an instruction, the loop that produces the smallest access stride is the loop that creates streaming behavior.

2) Non-streaming accesses correspond either to non-strided memory instructions, also known as irregular accesses, or they correspond to strided accesses whose strides are larger than the maximum recognized stride.

Recall that our simulation tool uses PIN to understand streaming behavior in unmodified, optimized x86 binaries and that we collect streaming concurrency profiles at the instruction level. We use static analysis on the same application binaries to distinguish between the scenarios described above. We perform data flow analysis on a routine's control

[1]This is the denominator used for computing the DC_PF metric.

flow graph (CFG) to symbolically understand memory access patterns in applications. For each memory instruction, we build symbolic formulas that describe how the memory location accessed by that instruction changes from one iteration to the next of a particular loop. We compute one such formula for every loop level that encloses that instruction. These formulas describe the strides with which a memory instruction traverses over memory, with respect to each loop enclosing it. The data flow analysis also detects cases when the computed stride is not consistent across iterations, or when a memory access is indirect with respect to a loop. We classify these strides as *irregular*.

We use the derived stride formulas to further refine the simulation results for each memory instruction. We look at an instruction's stride formulas in order, from the innermost to the outermost loop, until we find an irregular stride, or until we exhaust all the loop levels. We want to find the smallest non-zero stride associated with an instruction and record the loop level that creates it. The smallest stride corresponds to the loop level that has the potential to stream over the associated source code data structure. We ignore strides that are equal to zero, because they correspond to loops whose index variables are not used to reference the source data structure. Repeated accesses to the same location do not create streaming behavior.

This first step of the analysis yields the following scenarios: 1) At least one loop creates a constant[2] non-zero stride. We record the loop that produces the smallest non-zero stride. 2) We find only symbolic strides that depend on run-time values. 3) We find an irregular stride before finding any non-zero stride. 4) We find no non-zero strides. Next, we look more closely at each of these scenarios.

1) If we find a smallest constant non-zero stride, S, we check if S is larger than the maximum recognized stride, M. If it is, then we classify all the non-streaming accesses produced by that instruction as being produced by an access pattern with a large stride. If $S \leq M$, this instruction has streaming behavior. If the simulation determined that this instruction produced any non-streaming accesses, it must be because the streaming concurrency level was higher than the size of the *Stream Table* data structure used in the simulation. We further check the position of the loop producing the smallest stride, S. If it is the loop immediately enclosing the instruction, we say that any non-streaming accesses are caused by a high inner concurrency level. Otherwise, we say that high outer concurrency causes non-streaming accesses.

2) If we find only symbolic strides, we can assume that the stride is too large to produce streaming behavior. However, for now, we classify such accesses as having a symbolic stride, to understand their rate of occurrence in real applications.

3) If the stride is irregular, we classify any non-streaming accesses as being caused by an irregular access pattern.

4) Finally, it may happen that we do not find any non-zero stride for a particular instruction, either because the memory instruction accesses a fixed location, or because the instruction is not enclosed in any loop. Our data flow analysis is performed only intra-procedurally at this time, and we found many instances, especially in `C++` code, where frequently executed routines did not contain any loops, but they accessed memory locations determined by the function input parameters. Currently, we cannot classify the non-streaming accesses produced by these instructions using static analysis. This is a limitation of our current implementation, not a limitation of the approach. Understanding if these accesses are strided or irregular requires at least partial inter-procedural analysis. For completeness, in Section 6, we classify such accesses as having no stride.

We use the above analysis to classify non-streaming memory accesses into four main categories: 1) accesses with irregular strides; 2) accesses with large strides, with the added sub-category of symbolic strides; 3) streaming accesses with high concurrency levels produced by an innermost loop; 4) streaming accesses with high concurrency levels produced by an outer loop. In addition, we also classify streaming accesses with a concurrency level higher than 16 into either category (3) or category (4), depending on which loop level produces the smallest stride.

[2]*constant* in this context means that the stride can be determined statically, it is not depended on run-time values.

6. EXPERIMENTAL RESULTS

We applied our post-mortem analysis to the SPEC CPU 2006 benchmark suite simulation results. Figure 4 presents the distribution of prefetch unfriendly accesses with respect to the DC prefetcher, for each of the benchmarks. As before, the labels on the `x` axis show the benchmark index and the name of the input file. Benchmark names are listed in Table 2. Most of the bin labels should be self explanatory. The bins labeled as `17+ Inner` and `17+ Outer` correspond to streaming accesses with high concurrency levels produced by the innermost loop or by an outer loop, respectively.

Figure 4 shows the fraction of non-prefetchable L1 cache misses for each of the categories described in Section 5. The stacked histograms do not sum up to 100% this time. The difference to 100% is represented by cache misses that were determined to be prefetcher friendly. Many benchmarks include a significant fraction of accesses for which our intra-procedural data flow analysis could not find an access stride.

If we focus on the accesses for which strides could be determined, we notice that many benchmarks have a large fraction of L1 cache misses that are produced by irregular or indirect accesses. This is not such a surprise when we look at the list of integer benchmarks included in the suite: `400.perlbench` is a perl interpreter, `401.bzip2` is a compression program, `403.gcc` is a C compiler, `429.mcf` implements a vehicle-depot scheduling algorithm, and `473.astar` implements a path finding algorithm for a computer game. Even among the floating point benchmarks we find a good fraction of irregular memory access patterns. Benchmark `435.gromacs` is a molecular dynamic code that uses a neighbor list method to compute interactions between nearby particles. While accesses to the neighbor list itself are strided, accesses to the actual particle data are indirect and irregular.

Somewhat surprisingly, only three benchmarks have any significant number of streaming accesses with high concurrency levels produces by an outer loop: `434.zeusmp` - a magnetohydrodynamics code, `447.dealII` - a partial differential equations solver, and `459.GemsFDTD` - a computational electromagnetic code. We think that such cases are not particularly interesting as targets for prefetching optimizations, because the access patterns that generate them are also characterized by long spatial reuse, and optimizing for data reuse should improve streaming behavior as well.

On the other hand, accesses with high concurrency levels produced by an inner loop are interesting for further analysis and optimization, because they capture situations

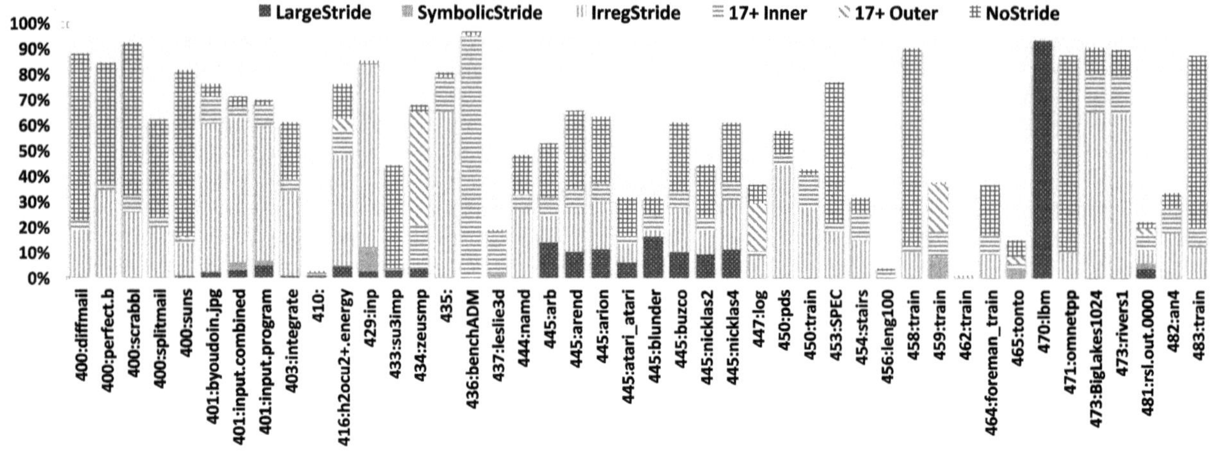

Figure 4: Distribution of prefetch unfriendly accesses with respect to the DC prefetcher.

where applications stream over many data arrays in an inner loop. All accesses are performed with a small stride and they should exhibit good spatial locality. However, streaming over too many arrays at the same time makes hardware prefetchers ineffective, which may significantly impact performance. Such cases can be improved either by data layout transformations such as fusing several arrays into one array, interleaving their elements, or by code transformations such as loop splitting, with each loop streaming over only some of the arrays. Each of these approaches can have negative side effects, so they should be applied on a case by case basis. Array fusion works best when the arrays that are fused are always accessed together. If we fuse arrays that are not always accessed by the same loops, we negatively impact spatial reuse and increase memory bandwidth use. Loop splitting should be applied when we do not create data reuse between the resulting loops, in other words, when the resulting loops access disjoint sets of arrays. We notice that benchmark `436.cactusADM` has a very large fraction of accesses with high inner concurrency levels. In Section 6.1 we attempt to improve its streaming behavior.

We also find several benchmarks that have a meaningful fraction of strided accesses where the stride is large. Benchmark `470.lbm` stands out, with a very high fraction of accesses characterized by a large stride. We want to take a closer look at this benchmark as well, because we do not know exactly what to expect. We observe that, in the case of the SPEC CPU benchmarks, only a small fraction of non-streamable accesses are associated with symbolic strides.

6.1 Tuning of benchmark 436.cactusADM

CactusADM is based on the open source Cactus problem solving environment, and on the computational kernel BenchADM. CactusADM solves the Einstein evolution equations, which describe how space-time curves in response to its matter content, using a set of ten coupled nonlinear partial differential equations [7]. Our analysis of the CactusADM results revealed that almost all of its `17+ Inner` accesses are produced by two loops in routine `Bench_StaggeredLeapfrog2`. This Fortran routine has 135 input arguments, and is called from within the Cactus framework. Around half of its input parameters are arrays, many of them three-dimensional arrays.

The Cactus framework auto generates a lot of the glue code that allocates and initializes data arrays, based on a custom input language. We could not determine how to modify the Cactus framework to do the layout transformations that we wanted. Instead, we wrote a custom wrapper code in C that allocates and initializes all the arrays expected by the Fortran routine, and then invokes the unmodified Fortran code, just as the Cactus code does. We call this version the CustomADM code.

Next, we created an optimized version of the code based on our analysis results. We fused 69 of the input arrays into 13 larger arrays, using their names[3] and their dimension sizes to guide our transformations. An additional six arrays locally declared in the Fortran routine were fused into a single array. We call this code the OptimizedADM version. We measured the performance of the three code versions, the original SPEC ADM code, the custom ADM code, and the optimized ADM code, using hardware performance counters.

Figure 5a shows the results for both the `train` and the `ref` inputs. The first four metrics shown in the figure are normalized to the performance of the Custom version. The number of L2 prefetch requests is shown as a percentage of the total number of L2 requests for each version of the code. Similarly, the number of memory prefetch requests is shown as a percentage of the total number of memory read requests for each code version. We first compare the SPEC and the custom versions of the code, to show that the custom version is a good substitute for the SPEC Cactus code. While the execution time of the custom version is 14% shorter than the original execution time because some of the Cactus specific code is not executed anymore, the measured metrics show that the memory behaviors of the two versions are similar.

We then compare the optimized and the custom versions. The fraction of L2 requests initiated by the DC hardware prefetcher increases dramatically, from about 2% to about 79% for the `train` input, and to 71% for the `ref` input. As a result, we see a similarly significant drop in the number of L1 misses for the optimized version. The fraction of memory requests initiated by the MC prefetcher also increases from 54% with the `train` input and 12% with the `ref` input, to about 100% for the optimized version. This increase in pre-

[3]Related arrays were named with a common prefix.

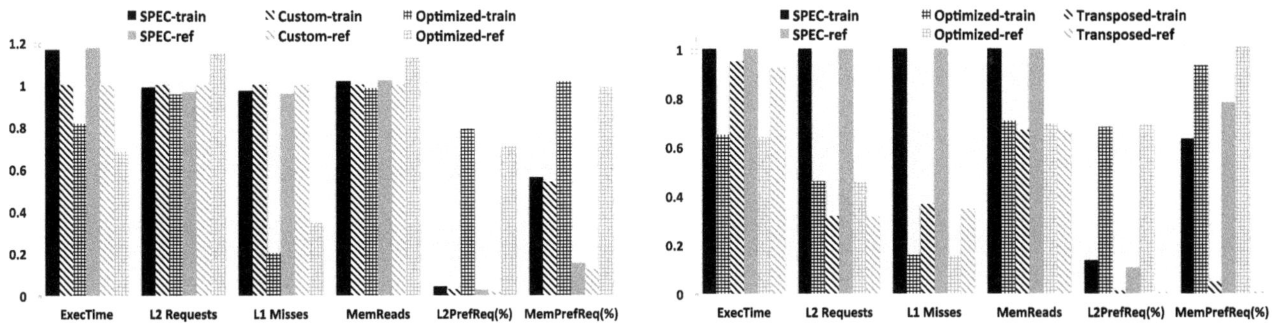

(a) 436.CactusADM results

(b) 470.LBM results

Figure 5: Tuning results for benchmarks CactusADM and LBM with the train and ref inputs.

fetching coverage yields a close to 19% and 32% reduction in execution time for the two inputs, or a 23% and 47% speed-up, respectively. The prefetch optimizations yield a larger speed-up for the `ref` input because the original code's MC prefetching performance was lower with the larger input. The `ref` input results show also an increase of 12-15% in memory and L2 traffic for the optimized version due to superfluous prefetch requests, mentioned in §4.3.

6.2 Tuning of benchmark 470.lbm

The SPEC LBM benchmark implements the Lattice Boltzmann Method to simulate incompressible fluids. We analyzed the results obtained for the LBM benchmark and we found that all the prefetch unfriendly accesses with a large stride were produced by routine `LBM_performStreamCollide`. The benchmark performs sweeps over a three-dimensional lattice, implemented as a one-dimensional array in the SPEC version of the code. The state of each lattice site is defined by a set of double precision floating-point numbers that represent the distribution functions with respect to the discrete directions of velocities [18]. Thus, the lattice data structure in the `470.lbm` benchmark is implemented as an array of records with 20 double precision floating point fields.

Routine `LBM_performStreamCollide` performs a 19-point Stencil 3D calculation using separate source and destination lattices. Only some of the fields of the destination lattice grid are updated for each of the sites. Each lattice element is a record with 20 double precision floating point values, thus, 160 bytes in size. Although all the lattice sites are traversed in sequential order, the type of sparse updating performed by the LBM code, results in accesses with strides larger than a cache line (64 bytes), and therefore, are not recognized as streaming accesses by the AMD 10H DC prefetcher.

To improve streaming behavior, we created an optimized version by splitting the array of records into three separate arrays of smaller sized records, each record's size being less than or equal to one cache line. Performance results for the `train` and `ref` inputs are summarized in Figure 5b. The first four metrics are normalized to the performance of the SPEC version. The number of L2 prefetch requests is shown as a percentage of the total number of L2 requests for each version of the code. Similarly, the number of memory prefetch requests is shown as a percentage of the total number of memory read requests for each code version. LBM's `ref` and `train` inputs differ mainly in the number of executed time steps. Thus, the performance profiles of the two inputs are very similar. The comments below apply to both.

We compare the SPEC and the Optimized versions of the code. The optimized version's execution time is 35% smaller than the SPEC LBM version, or in other words, it achieves a 54% speed-up. However, we immediately notice that the optimized version has much better data locality. The number of L2 requests and the number of memory reads dropped by 54% and 30%, respectively. We also observe a significant increase in the fraction of L2 requests that are initiated by the DC hardware prefetcher, on top of the overall reduction in L2 requests. Unfortunately, the transformation that improved prefetching effectiveness also improved data locality, and we cannot separate or evaluate their effects individually.

Instead, we created a new version of the code, where we split each state variable into its own array. The transformation consists of transposing the array of records into a record of arrays. Hence, we named this code the Transposed version. Naturally, this transformation produces the best data locality among all versions, as can be seen by looking at the counts of L2 requests and memory reads in Figure 5b. However, creating a separate array for each state variable increases the code's streaming concurrency beyond what the two AMD 10H hardware prefetchers can handle. As a result, this code version exhibits almost no DC or MC prefetches. We also notice that despite the incrementally improved data locality, the transposed version runs much slower, 46.5% slower than the optimized version.

7. CONCLUSIONS

Streaming hardware prefetchers can have an important beneficial effect on application performance, if applications traverse memory with the right access patterns. However, these hardware structures are largely hidden from users. Unlike cache memories for which a large number of analysis and tuning techniques have been proposed and studied, there has been little previous work that focused on application analysis techniques specifically targeted at identifying tuning opportunities for the hardware prefetchers.

In this paper, we introduced the metric *streaming concurrency* to characterize the number of parallel, logical data streams in applications. Our experiments show that the *streaming concurrency* metric explains well the number of prefetch requests initiated by the two AMD 10H hardware prefetchers for the SPEC CPU2006 benchmark suite. While not the focus of this paper, the *streaming concurrency* metric can also be used to guide the design of the hardware structures so that they handle well a particular workload.

We described an approach based on static analysis and simulation to understand if the memory access patterns of applications are amenable to hardware prefetching, and to identify opportunities for improving their prefetch friendliness. We identified four situations that make the streaming hardware prefetchers ineffective and we provided insight into the code transformations that are needed to increase the prefetching effectiveness in each of the four situations. We used this insight to tune the prefetching performance of two SPEC CPU2006 benchmarks. While some of the performance gains observed in Section 6 can be attributed to data locality improvements, our tuning results show that it is important to write prefetch friendly code whenever possible, to minimize unfulfilled performance.

We do not advocate prefetching optimizations at any cost, for example at the expense of data locality. A balanced approach is needed in most cases. Moreover, increasing data reuse and eliminating data movement between the different levels of the memory hierarchy altogether, can also improve the energy efficiency of an application. Our tuning results with the LBM benchmark show, however, that we should not pursue data reuse improvements exclusively, at the cost of prefetching effectiveness, because such an approach can negatively impact performance.

8. ACKNOWLEDGMENTS

This research is sponsored, in part, by the Office of Advanced Scientific Computing Research in the U.S. Department of Energy. The paper has been coauthored by Oak Ridge National Laboratory, which is managed by UT-Battelle, LLC under Contract #DE-AC05-00OR22725 to the U.S. Government. Accordingly, the U.S. Government retains a non-exclusive, royalty-free license to publish or reproduce the published form of this contribution, or allow others to do so, for U.S. Government purposes.

9. REFERENCES

[1] J.-L. Baer and T.-F. Chen. An effective on-chip preloading scheme to reduce data access penalty. In *Proceedings of the 1991 ACM/IEEE conference on Supercomputing*, Supercomputing '91, pages 176–186, New York, NY, USA, 1991. ACM.

[2] B. Bennett and V. Kruskal. LRU stack processing. *IBM Journal of Research and Development*, 19(4):353–357, July 1975.

[3] K. Beyls and E. H. D'Hollander. Reuse distance as a metric for cache behavior. In *Proceedings of the IASTED Conference on Parallel and Distributed Computing And Systems*, pages 617–662, 2001.

[4] D. Callahan, K. Kennedy, and A. Porterfield. Software prefetching. In *Proceedings of the fourth international conference on Architectural support for programming languages and operating systems*, ASPLOS-IV, pages 40–52, New York, NY, USA, 1991. ACM.

[5] T.-F. Chen and J.-L. Baer. A performance study of software and hardware data prefetching schemes. In *Proceedings of the 21st annual international symposium on Computer architecture*, ISCA '94, pages 223–232, Los Alamitos, CA, USA, 1994. IEEE Computer Society Press.

[6] E. Ebrahimi, C. J. Lee, O. Mutlu, and Y. N. Patt. Prefetch-aware shared resource management for multi-core systems. In *Proceedings of the 38th annual international symposium on Computer architecture*, ISCA '11, pages 141–152, New York, NY, USA, 2011.

[7] J. L. Henning. Spec cpu2006 benchmark descriptions. *SIGARCH Comp. Arch. News*, 34(4):1–17, Sept. 2006.

[8] N. P. Jouppi. Improving direct-mapped cache performance by the addition of a small fully-associative cache and prefetch buffers. In *Proceedings of the 17th annual international symposium on Computer Architecture*, ISCA '90, pages 364–373, New York, NY, USA, 1990. ACM.

[9] C.-K. Luk, R. Cohn, R. Muth, H. Patil, A. Klauser, G. Lowney, S. Wallace, V. J. Reddi, and K. Hazelwood. Pin: building customized program analysis tools with dynamic instrumentation. In *Proceedings of the 2005 ACM SIGPLAN conference on Programming language design and implementation*, PLDI '05, pages 190–200, New York, NY, USA, 2005.

[10] C.-K. Luk and T. C. Mowry. Automatic compiler-inserted prefetching for pointer-based applications. *IEEE Trans. Comput.*, 48(2):134–141, Feb. 1999.

[11] A. Mandal, R. Fowler, and A. Porterfield. Modeling memory concurrency for multi-socket multi-core systems. In *Performance Analysis of Systems Software (ISPASS), 2010 IEEE International Symposium on*, pages 66 –75, march 2010.

[12] G. Marin and J. Mellor-Crummey. Cross-architecture performance predictions for scientific applications using parameterized models. In *Proceedings of the Joint International Conference on Measurement and Modeling of Computer Systems*, pages 2–13. ACM Press, 2004.

[13] R. L. Mattson, J. Gecsei, D. R. Slutz, and I. L. Traiger. Evaluation techniques for storage hierarchies. *IBM Syst. J.*, 9(2):78–117, June 1970.

[14] S. Palacharla and R. E. Kessler. Evaluating stream buffers as a secondary cache replacement. In *Proceedings of the 21st annual international symposium on Computer architecture*, ISCA '94, pages 24–33, Los Alamitos, CA, USA, 1994.

[15] V. Santhanam, E. H. Gornish, and W.-C. Hsu. Data prefetching on the hp pa-8000. In *Proceedings of the 24th annual international symposium on Computer architecture*, ISCA '97, pages 264–273, New York, NY, USA, 1997. ACM.

[16] D. D. Sleator and R. E. Tarjan. Self-adjusting binary search trees. *J. ACM*, 32(3):652–686, July 1985.

[17] S. Srinath, O. Mutlu, H. Kim, and Y. N. Patt. Feedback directed prefetching: Improving the performance and bandwidth-efficiency of hardware prefetchers. In *Proceedings of the 2007 IEEE 13th International Symposium on High Performance Computer Architecture*, HPCA '07, pages 63–74, Washington, DC, USA, 2007. IEEE Computer Society.

[18] J. Wilke, T. Pohl, M. Kowarschik, and U. Rüde. Cache performance optimizations for parallel lattice boltzmann codes. In *Euro-Par*, pages 441–450, 2003.

[19] S. Williams, A. Waterman, and D. Patterson. Roofline: an insightful visual performance model for multicore architectures. *Commun. ACM*, 52(4):65–76, Apr. 2009.

Address-aware Fences

Changhui Lin
CSE Department
University of California,
Riverside CA 92521
linc@cs.ucr.edu

Vijay Nagarajan
School of Informatics
University of Edinburgh
United Kingdom
vijay.nagarajan@ed.ac.uk

Rajiv Gupta
CSE Department
University of California,
Riverside CA 92521
gupta@cs.ucr.edu

ABSTRACT

Many modern multicore architectures support shared memory for ease of programming and relaxed memory models to deliver high performance. With relaxed memory models, memory accesses can be reordered dynamically and seen by other processors. Therefore, fence instructions are provided to enforce the memory orderings that are critical to the correctness of a program. However, fence instructions are costly as they cause the processor to stall. Prior works have observed that most of the executions of fence instructions are unnecessary. In this paper we propose *address-aware fence*, a hardware solution for reducing the overhead of fence instructions without resorting to speculation. Address-aware fence only enforces memory orderings that are necessary to maintain the effect that the traditional fence strives to enforce. This is achieved by dynamically checking a condition for when an execution of a fence must take effect and delay the memory accesses following the fence. When a fence instruction is encountered, first, necessary memory addresses are collected to form a watchlist, and then, only the memory accesses to addresses that are contained in the watchlist are delayed. The memory accesses whose addresses are not contained in the watchlist are allowed to complete without waiting for the completion of pending memory accesses from before the fence. Our experiments conducted on a group of concurrent lock-free algorithms and SPLASH-2 benchmarks show that address-aware fence eliminates nearly all the overhead due to fences and achieves an average improvement of 12.2% on programs with traditional fences.

Categories and Subject Descriptors

C.1.2 [**Processor Architectures**]: Multiple Data Stream Architectures (Multiprocessors)—*Parallel processors*

General Terms

Design, Performance, Experimentation

ICS'13, June 10–14, 2013, Eugene, Oregon, USA.

Keywords

Memory models, Fence instructions, Microarchitecture

1. INTRODUCTION

Multiprocessors are becoming ubiquitous in all computing domains, from mobile devices to datacenter servers. They are able to deliver high performance via parallelism, and hence the importance of parallel programming continues to grow. To simplify programming for multiprocessors, shared memory is widely used as the primary system level programming abstraction. However, problems arise when accesses to shared memory are reordered. Hence, many memory consistency models have been proposed to constrain memory behaviors with respect to read and write operations originating from multiple processors [1]. Each of these models offers a trade-off between programming simplicity and high performance. To achieve high performance, many manufacturers (e.g., Intel, IBM, Sun, etc) typically choose to support relaxed/weak consistency models, such as total store order (TSO), relaxed memory order (RMO), release consistency (RC), etc [1]. With relaxed memory consistency models, memory accesses can be reordered dynamically and seen by other processors. To enforce the memory orderings that are critical to the correctness of programs, fence instructions are provided. A fence instruction guarantees that all memory accesses prior to it are completed before the memory accesses following it are performed. The stalling of the processor resulting from implementing this fence semantics is costly and often unnecessary [17, 20, 36].

The traditional fence instructions are processor-centric [36], i.e., a fence instruction only controls the ordering of memory accesses for the processor executing the fence while being unaware of memory accesses in other processors. However, when the reordering of memory accesses across a fence is not observed by other processors, it is safe to allow the reordering. Researchers have observed that most dynamic fence instances are unnecessary because the execution of the program already conforms to the effect that fences strive to enforce and therefore they have developed techniques for eliminating the performance degradation due to unnecessary execution instances of fence instructions. These techniques include both speculative techniques [3, 5, 14, 15, 37] and non-speculative techniques [17, 20, 36]. While the latter are more desirable because of their lower hardware complexity, they have two limitations: (a) they are only able to eliminate a subset of unnecessary fence instances; and (b) when a fence instance is necessary, no memory accesses are allowed

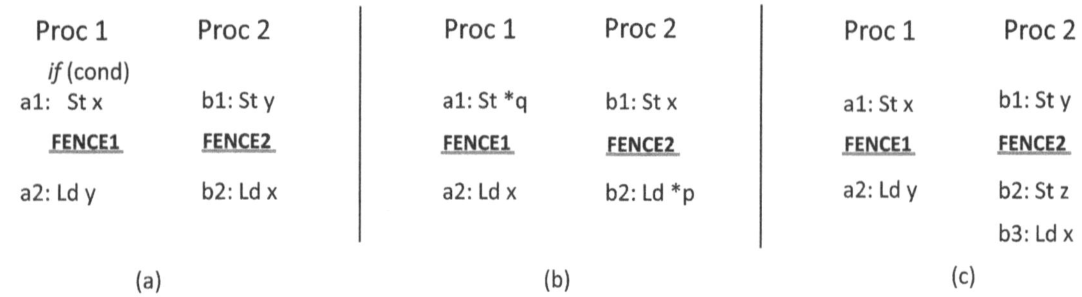

Figure 1: Unnecessary fence instances at runtime.

to be reordered across fence boundaries even though it may be safe to allow reordering of some of the memory accesses.

Fig. 1 shows several common scenarios which demonstrate the above limitations of existing techniques [17, 20, 36]. The example in Fig. 1(a) contains a conditional branch. Fence instructions are inserted to ensure that memory accesses to shared variables x and y are ordered properly. However, if at runtime the condition in Proc 1 evaluates to `false`, and hence $a1$ is not executed, then the shared variable x is not accessed concurrently by multiple processors. As a result, the fence instance is not necessary to effect the order of memory accesses of x and y. In Fig. 1(b), there are two pointers p and q pointing to some field of a shared object (e.g., a hash table [29]) respectively – since they may point to the same field, fence instructions are inserted. However, at runtime, if they point to different fields of the shared object, i.e., $a1$ and $b2$ do not access the same field concurrently, then the fence instances are not necessary. Finally, in Fig. 1(c), `FENCE2` orders both $b1 \rightarrow b2$ and $b1 \rightarrow b3$. However, if z is not accessed in any other processor concurrently, $b2$ need not be delayed and hence can be reordered across the fence. Thus, even though the instance of `FENCE2` is necessary, $b2$ need not be delayed. However, none of the existing techniques [17, 20, 36] can eliminate the above unnecessary fence instances.

We observe that with the knowledge of what is happening in other processors, we can eliminate the above restrictions and optimize the fence executions. In this paper, we propose a hardware solution *address-aware fence* to reduce the overhead due to fence instructions without resorting to speculation. Unlike a traditional fence which is processor-centric, an address-aware fence collects necessary information to decide whether it should effect the stalling of following memory accesses. In particular, an address-aware fence instance has an associated *watchlist*, which contains memory addresses that should not be accessed by the memory accesses following the fence. The completion of a memory access following the fence is allowed if its memory address is not contained in the watchlist, appearing as if the fence does not take effect. Otherwise, the memory access is delayed to ensure correctness. By doing so, unnecessary fence instances behave as a *nop* (i.e., they do not stall the processors) and the other fence instances selectively stall memory operations (i.e., stalling is minimized). Therefore this approach effectively reduces overhead of fences whenever possible.

The key contributions of this work are:

1. We propose a new fence mechanism, called *address-aware fence*. This is a hardware mechanism that eliminates stalling at unnecessary fence executions and reduces performance overhead due to fence instructions without resorting to speculation. The technique is implemented in the microarchitecture without instruction set support and is transparent to programmers.
2. We describe the architectural design of address-aware fence. The hardware support only amounts to less than 1KB added to a conventional multiprocessor core.
3. We conduct experiments with a group of concurrent lock-free algorithms and SPLASH-2 benchmarks. The results show that address-aware fence eliminates nearly all the overhead associated with the traditional fence and yields an average reduction of 12.2% in execution time.

The rest of the paper is organized as follows. Section 2 presents the background on fence instructions. Section 3 proposes address-aware fence. Section 4 describes the hardware design. The experimental results are presented in Section 5. We discuss related work in Section 6 and conclude in Section 7.

2. BACKGROUND

In this section, we begin with the introduction to fence instructions provided by modern architectures and their applications, and then briefly present some existing approaches to reducing fence overhead.

2.1 Fence Instructions

Fence instructions, or *fences* for short, are provided in modern processors as a mechanism to selectively constrain the default relaxed memory access orders [1, 11]. Fence instructions of commercial architectures have various names and semantics, enforcing different memory orderings. For example, in Intel IA-32, there are three types of fence instructions: *mfence*, *lfence*, and *sfence*. While *mfence* enforces all memory orderings, *lfence* only enforces orders between memory load instructions, and *sfence* only enforces orders between memory store instructions. Similarly, in SPARC V9, MEMBAR instruction can be customized to enforce different memory orderings; in PowerPC, there are *sync* and *lwsync*; and in Alpha model, there are memory barrier (MB) and write memory barrier (WMB). In the following discussion, we assume a traditional fence is a full fence, which guarantees that all memory operations prior to it have completed before its following memory operations can be performed.

(Applications of fences) For programs running on architectures that only support relaxed consistency models, it is important to enforce memory orderings that are critical to the correctness of the programs. This is because, under relaxed consistency models, the orders specified by the program are not guaranteed during execution. The correctness of the program may rely on some orders, which can be potentially reordered by the processor or memory systems without any protection. Hence, fence instructions have been used frequently to enforce such necessary memory orderings. In fact, many lock-free algorithms have to use fence instructions to ensure that the algorithms perform correctly under relaxed consistency models [4] (e.g., Dekker algorithm [9], lock-free dynamic memory allocation [26]). Fences are also used to implement synchronization operations [33]. In some memory models (e.g., TSO), fences are implied by atomic read-modify-write (RMW) instructions for acquire operations. In addition, sufficient fences can also guarantee sequential consistency (SC) for programs running in architectures only supporting relaxed consistency models [11, 19, 30, 22].

2.2 Reducing Fence Overhead

Although fence operations are cheaper than locks, excessive use of fences can still hurt performance. In commercial applications, frequent thread synchronizations result in significant ordering delays due to fence instructions [37]. However, it is possible to reduce the overhead, based on the observation that memory accesses across a fence can be reordered as long as they are not observed by other processors. Therefore, some techniques have been proposed to reduce the overhead of fence instructions.

Techniques	Applicability			
	Dekker-like	Lock-free algo.	Lock	Improving SC
CMO [36]	No	No	Yes	No
l-mfence [17]	Yes	No	No	No
C-Fence [20]	Yes*	Yes*	Yes*	Yes*
Address-aware fence	Yes	Yes	Yes	Yes*

Table 1: Comparison of existing approaches and our approach (*Compiler support required for inserting fences).

(Speculative Techniques) First, there is a group of techniques that can address the problem by speculation [3, 5, 14, 15, 37]. Memory accesses after a fence can be speculatively retired when there is any pending store before the fence. Before these speculatively retired memory accesses are committed, if a memory access in another processor conflicts with one of them, rollback is performed and instructions are then re-executed. However, the hardware complexity associated with aggressive speculation can hinder wide-spread adoption of these speculative techniques.

(Non-speculative Techniques) There are also three non-speculative techniques that are listed in Table 1. The table compares the applicability of these techniques in terms of the kind of applications they can handle. In [36], Praun *et al.* observed that memory ordering instructions used on acquire and release of a lock are often unnecessary. They proposed a combined HW/SW mechanism *conditional memory ordering* (CMO) to omit unnecessary memory ordering instructions. CMO only focuses on memory orderings associated with lock acquire and lock release, but cannot handle the other cases. Ladan-Mozes *et al.* [17] proposed *location-based memory fences* to reduce fence overhead. A new instruction (*l-mfence*) is introduced, but it is limited to Dekker-like algorithms. In our prior work [20], we proposed *conditional fence* (C-Fence) to enforce sequential consistency with the help of compiler inserting necessary fences. The compiler is also responsible for collecting the information of fence associates, which are conveyed to hardware to improve the performance of sequential consistency by only making associates be staggered enough. In addition, C-Fence is also able to handle other kinds of applications as long as fence associates can be provided by compiler. However, it is still not able to optimize the scenarios shown in Fig. 1.

Our non-speculative solution, address-aware fence, *presented in this paper is superior to the above non-speculative techniques in two respects. It is more effective as it is able to exploit all the optimization opportunities shown in Fig. 1. It is also broadly applicable as it can be applied in all situations in Table 1.*

3. ADDRESS-AWARE FENCE

In this section we propose the *address-aware fence* mechanism for reducing fence overhead. Our technique is implemented in the microarchitecture without introduction of any new instructions and is thus completely transparent to the programmer. Fence instructions are introduced, as usual, either by the compiler or by the programmer. Fence instructions in the executable are identified at runtime and processed by the hardware. Our technique handles all encountered fences without being aware of how they are used. Thus, our technique can naturally handles all cases listed in Table 1.

A fence instruction forces a strict ordering between memory accesses that precede it and those that follow it. A traditional fence enforces this by stalling the processor's execution till all memory accesses encountered before the fence have completed. However, the above approach is more restrictive than what is really required. The purpose of a fence is to prevent memory accesses from being reordered and *observed by other processors.* In other words, if the reordering is not observed by other processors, the reordering is allowed and hence stalling at the fence is not necessary. Let us call the order enforced by a fence as *fence order.* We can relax the execution of a fence such that the execution is correct – a fence execution is said to be *correct if the execution appears to maintain fence orders.* Obviously, the traditional fence execution is correct. However, it is inefficient due to unnecessary stalls.

The *address-aware fence* mechanism exploits the above observation to improve the efficiency of the fence execution mechanism. This section first presents a *sufficient condition* for a correct fence execution and then our solution *address-aware fence* that utilizes the condition.

3.1 The Condition for Enforcing Fence Orders

Fig. 2(a) shows two fences in two processors respectively. $A1, A2, B1$, and $B2$ represent blocks of instructions separated by fences. Furthermore, let us assume $a1$, $a2$, $b1$, and $b2$ are memory accesses in $A1$, $A2$, $B1$, and $B2$ respectively. Due to the fence, any memory access in $A1$ is ordered before any memory access in $A2$, represented by the solid line with arrow; and the same is the case for $B1$ and $B2$. Thus, the fence orders $a1 \rightarrow a2$ and $b1 \rightarrow b2$ are enforced by the fences. A correct fence execution should make these fence

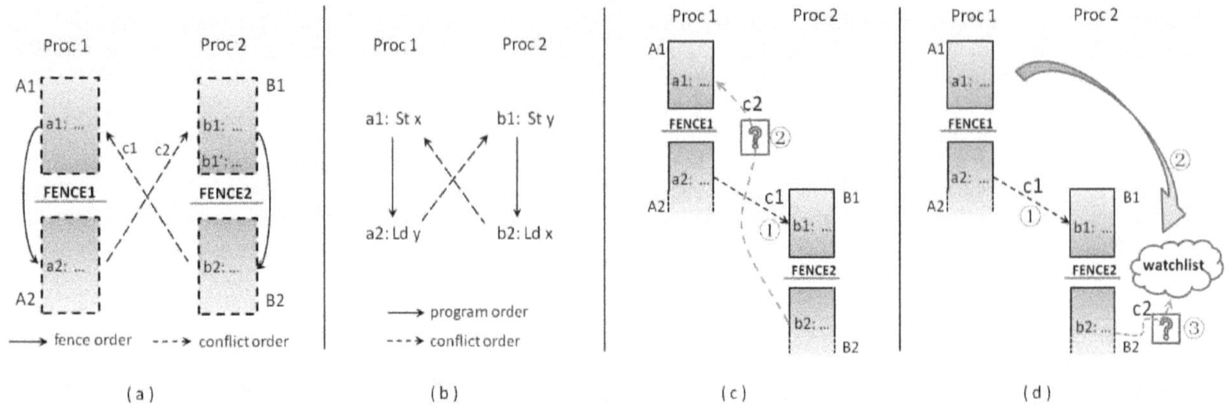

Figure 2: (a) Violation of fence order; (b) Violation of program order; (c) Cycle detection; (d) Our approach.

orders *appear* to be enforced. In [30], Shasha and Snir have shown the condition for enforcing program orders in context of sequential consistency (SC) enforcement. Extending that condition, we can have the condition for enforcing fence orders, as all fence orders is a subset of all program orders.

Recall that sequential consistency requires that all memory accesses *appear* to take place in the program order which is specified by the program, i.e., all program orders should be enforced. Shasha and Snir [30] have shown that an execution does not violate sequential consistency iff *program orders* (**P**) and *conflict orders* (**E**) do not form a cycle (i.e., no cycle in $\mathbf{P} \cup \mathbf{E}$). Here, a *conflict order* is an execution order of conflicting memory accesses [30]. Fig. 2(b) shows such a cycle $a1 \rightarrow a2 \rightarrow b1 \rightarrow b2 \rightarrow a1$, where $a1$ conflicts with $b2$ and $a2$ conflicts with $b1$. The execution sequence $a2 \rightarrow b1 \rightarrow b2 \rightarrow a1$ will violate sequential consistency, because no sequentially consistent execution can generate the same result, where both x and y read their old values before stores. In the case of fence orders in Fig. 2(a), we have to enforce all fence orders (**F**), analogous to program orders for SC in Fig. 2(b). In particular, all fence orders is a subset of all program orders ($\mathbf{F} \subseteq \mathbf{P}$). Accordingly, we can have the condition for enforcing fence orders – *fence orders are enforced iff fence orders and conflict orders do not form a cycle* (i.e., no cycle in $\mathbf{F} \cup \mathbf{E}$). This is because, without cycles, $\mathbf{F} \cup \mathbf{E}$ can be extended to a total order [7], which indicates all fence orders **F** are enforced. Therefore, in Fig. 2(a), to enforce fence orders, we have to prevent such cycles as $a1 \rightarrow a2 \rightarrow b1 \rightarrow b2 \rightarrow a1$, assuming $(a1, b2)$, $(b1, a2)$ are conflict relations. Note that, even if there is another memory access $b1'$ after $b1$ in $B1$, and $(a1, b1')$ and $(a2, b1)$ are conflict relations, there is no violation of fence orders involving $a1, a2, b1$, and $b1'$. This is because there is no fence order between $b1$ and $b1'$ and hence there is no cycle formed by fence orders and conflict orders.

3.2 Our Approach

Address-aware fence only orders memory operations involving certain memory addresses that must be ordered to maintain fence orders. In other words, even if there are stores from before the fence that are pending, the following memory operations can still complete if their addresses are not forbidden by the fence. This is why we name the fence as address-aware fence. An address-aware fence can decide whether it must stall memory operations according to their memory addresses. We make use of the condition described earlier to detect at runtime whether it is possible to form a cycle with fence orders and conflict orders. If no cycles can be formed, fences do not stall the memory operations following them; otherwise, fences will function so as to maintain fence orders.

In this section, we present the high-level algorithm of our approach; while in the next section we will describe the detailed hardware design. The key problem is how to detect possible cycles at runtime. During execution, fence orders are easily known, and hence we have to detect the conflict orders that can form a cycle along with the fence orders. Fig. 2(c) shows how cycles can be detected. In Proc 1, suppose all instructions in $A1$ have completed except some pending memory operations, and FENCE1 does not stall the following instructions in $A2$ initially. Hence, some memory operations are reordered across FENCE1 at runtime. At this point, in Proc 2, there is a memory operation in $B1$ which detects a conflicting memory operation in $A2$ (in the next section we will show how the detection is performed relying on cache coherence transactions). It forms a conflict order $c1$ from $A2$ to $B1$ as shown in the figure (①). This event triggers the following event: every memory operation after FENCE2 has to detect whether there is any pending memory operation prior to FENCE1 that conflicts with it, forming the conflict order $c2$ (②). Memory operations in $B2$ that do not conflict with pending memory operations in $A1$ can complete without being stalled by FENCE2 even when there is any pending memory operation in $B1$. However, if there does exist a potential conflict order $c2$ from $B2$ to $A1$, FENCE2 will delay the involved memory operation in $B2$ to break this potential conflict order. Moreover, if $c1$ does not exist, the detection of $c2$ is unnecessary, as no cycle will be formed without $c1$. Detecting $c2$ is only triggered when there is a possible $c1$.

The cycle detection discussed above does not consider how to relate $c1$ and $c2$. In particular, we should know where to check conflict, e.g., memory operations in $B2$ should check conflict with pending memory operations in $A1$. Furthermore, detecting $c2$ requires every memory operation in $B2$ to check conflict in $A1$ which is on a different processor and thus this is inefficient. Fig. 2(d) shows our approach to address this problem. If a conflict order $c1$ is detected (①), memory addresses of all pending memory operations before FENCE1 are collected to form a *watchlist*, which is associated with FENCE2 (②). Now, the memory operations after FENCE2 only need to check the local watchlist to detect conflict, i.e., to detect $c2$ (③). If the address of a memory operation is not contained in the watchlist, it indicates there is no conflict to form $c2$, which further indicates there is no cycle detected to violate fence orders. Hence, those memory operations whose addresses are not contained in the watchlist can still complete without being stalled by the fence even when there are pending memory operations from before the fence.

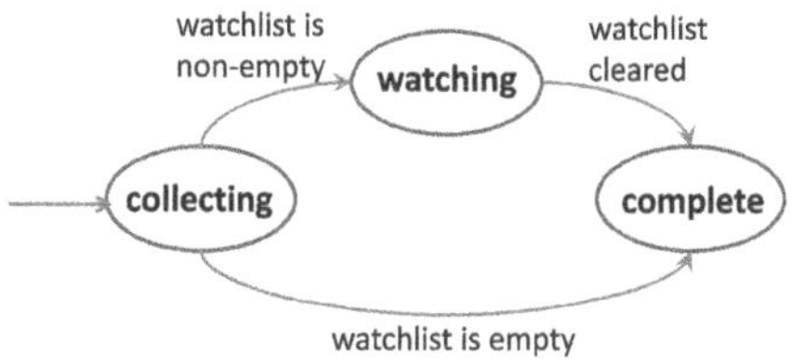

Figure 3: States of address-aware fence.

(Life cycle of a fence instance) The execution of a fence instruction proceeds according to the state transition graph in Fig. 3. There are three states: *collecting* state, *watching* state, and *complete* state. When the fence is issued it starts out being in *collecting* state where it waits for its watchlist. The memory operations following the fence cannot complete, as at this time the watchlist that is needed to detect cycles is not available. After the fence has collected all necessary addresses to form its watchlist, it switches to next state: the fence switches to *watching* state if the watchlist is non-empty; otherwise it switches directly to *complete* state. In *watching* state the memory operations following the fence must check the watchlist before completion. The watchlist is cleared when the corresponding pending memory operations have completed and the fence switches to *complete* state, where the fence has completed execution. If a fence directly switches from *collecting* to *complete* state, it causes no stalls; thus, it can be viewed as being dynamically eliminated.

4. HARDWARE DESIGN

In this section, we describe our hardware design for address-aware fence. The challenge is to detect and avoid cycles efficiently. In the following discussion, we present the detailed hardware design in context of a scalable CMP with distributed directory-based invalidation cache coherence protocol. Each processor has a local L1 cache, a bank of L2 cache, and a portion of directory. Each coherence transaction is kept in the directory until it receives the notification of the transaction completion. We assume each processor core to be a dynamically scheduled ILP processor with a reorder buffer (ROB). All instructions retire from ROB in program order. At the head of ROB, loads can retire when they complete, while stores can retire as soon as the value and destination address are available through store buffering technique [12], which allows stores to retire from the head of ROB even before they complete. We will see later that we use an augmented buffer which incorporates the function of store buffer, in which stores are allowed to complete out of order. The store buffering relaxes Store-Load and Store-Store orders, but the traditional fence requires the store buffer to be drained before executing following memory accesses.

Moreover, the processors also support in-window speculation [13], which guarantees Load-Load order by speculative load execution (a speculative load in ROB is squashed if its loaded data is invalidated or replaced before it retires). Besides, Load-Store order is naturally guaranteed by ROB. Therefore, memory operations cannot complete past a pending load, and hence the pending memory operations that can be bypassed can only be *pending stores.*

4.1 Operations on Address-aware Fence

Each processor functions as usual when there is no fence executing. However, when a fence is issued, the processor initiates the process of handling the fence using address-aware fence mechanism. The key operations are *collecting* and *clearing* watchlist for a fence, which are introduced in this section. After the watchlist has been collected, the fence can retire when it reaches the ROB head. If any load/store following the fence tries to *retire* while there are still pending stores from before the fence, the processor will check whether the address of the load/store is contained in the watchlist.

4.1.1 Collecting watchlist

When a fence is issued, the processor starts to collect watchlist for the fence, which is now in *collecting* state as shown in Fig. 3. As described in Section 3.2, a watchlist consists of the memory addresses of a set of pending memory operations that are all pending stores. It is important to obtain the set of pending stores quickly, as memory operations following the fence cannot retire until the watchlist is obtained. To do this, we utilize the directory, where we are able to find all pending stores being serviced by the directory. In the following discussion for simplicity we assume a centralized directory; however, later we describe the modifications needed for a distributed directory. When a fence is issued, the processor sends a request to the directory to fetch the addresses (block addresses) of all pending stores in other processors. The directory compresses the addresses into a watchlist using a bloom filter and sends it back to the requesting processor. Then the requesting processor records the replied watchlist locally for checking conflict. In this way, we conservatively assume there is a conflict order $c1$ (Fig. 2(d)①), and obtain the watchlist by fetching all pending stores (Fig. 2(d)②) from the directory.

The processor starts to collect the watchlist as soon as a fence is issued, because we would like to obtain the watchlist as early as possible, so that the fence does not stall the pipeline. However, the collected watchlist may become stale before it is used for checking conflict. Let us take Fig. 4(a) as an example for the following discussion. Suppose $a1$ is a store miss, and $a2$ completes past $a1$; then $b1$ completes after $a2$. If we do not take care of $b2$, the execution order $a2 \rightarrow b1 \rightarrow b2 \rightarrow a1$ will form a cycle and violate the fence order. In Fig. 4(b), let us assume `FENCE2` is issued at time $t1$, when no pending store is present in the directory (i.e., cache miss $a1$ has not reached the directory). So the watchlist obtained for `FENCE2` will be empty. If we use this empty watchlist, we cannot avoid the execution order $a2 \rightarrow b1 \rightarrow b2 \rightarrow a1$, as the empty watchlist will allow $b2$ to complete before $a1$. This is because the watchlist becomes stale and it does not contain x accessed by the pending store $a1$.

To address this problem, we observe that *the watchlist only needs to be updated when there is a cache miss before the fence.* To see why, let us recall cycle detection in Fig. 2(c). A cache miss in $B1$ would indicate that there is a potential conflict order like $c1$, so we need to avoid conflict order $c2$. The stale watchlist may not contain all pending stores in $A1$, as new pending stores may be generated after

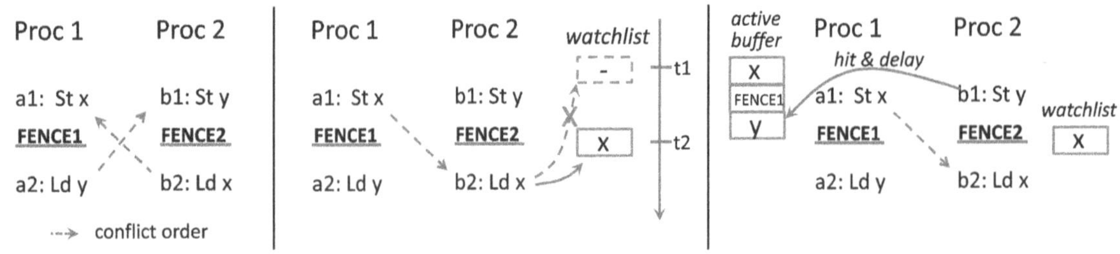

(a) potential fence violation (b) update watchlist (c) delay external transaction

Figure 4: Collecting and clearing watchlists.

the stale watchlist was obtained. Hence, we have to update the watchlist. On the other hand, a cache hit does not create a conflict order like $c1$, so there is no need to update the watchlist. Therefore, if there is any memory operation before the fence that is a cache miss (load/store miss) in the local cache, the cache miss transaction sent to the directory will also require the directory to reply with an updated watchlist. Note that, the fence can only retire after it has received the above reply from the directory. For the case in Fig. 4(b), if $a2$ completes past $a1$, $a1$ will be present in the directory if it has not completed. Thus, at time $t2$, $b1$ is found to be a miss, so the transaction sent to the directory will obtain an updated watchlist which includes x. Now the updated watchlist containing x will stall $b2$, enforcing the order $a1 \rightarrow b2$ and avoiding fence order violation.

(Unnecessary update) Although a cache miss may create the conflict order $c1$ as shown in Fig. 2(c), $c1$ does not really exist if the directory indicates the target block is not cached in other processors. In this case, the watchlist does not need to be updated. In particular, cache misses to local variables will fall into this case, which reduces much unnecessary traffic.

4.1.2 Clearing watchlist

A fence will be in *watching* state when it has retired, and memory operations after the fence have to check the watchlist to bypass it. But the fence cannot simply complete even when all pending stores before it have completed, because memory operations after the fence may still have to check the watchlist to avoid cycles. Let us consider the example in Fig. 4(b) again, where $a2$ completes past $a1$ and FENCE2 has obtained the watchlist containing x. But this watchlist cannot be cleared even when $b1$ has completed, as $b2$ still has to check the watchlist to avoid the cycle by ordering $a1 \rightarrow b2$. The watchlist can be cleared only when $a1$ has completed. That is, the watchlist can be cleared and hence the fence can complete *only when the pending stores whose addresses are contained in the watchlist have all completed.* If we make each complete store notify the processors which may contain its address, there will be complicated communication of tracking information between processors, complicating the hardware design.

To address this problem, we will delay $b1$ until $a1$ completes. Hence, we introduce a buffer for each processor, called *active buffer*. We consider a memory operation or a fence as *active* if (1) it has retired; and (2) the memory operation is a pending store or there is a pending store before the memory operation/fence. In other words, after retirement, a memory operation or a fence becomes inactive when there is no pending store before it. The *active buffer* records the addresses of all active memory operations, as well as active fences, in the order they are retired. Now, each external coherence transaction will also check the active buffer. If there is a conflict in the active buffer (i.e., the target memory address is found in the active buffer) and there is a fence prior to the conflicting entry, then this coherence transaction is delayed until the target address has been removed from the buffer (i.e., the corresponding memory operation is no longer active). Let us recall Fig. 2(d). By using active buffer, if there is a conflict order $c1$ from $A2$ to $B1$, the completion of $B1$ will indicate the completion of $A1$; otherwise, $B1$ cannot complete as coherence transactions sent to `Proc 1` will be delayed. Thus, the watchlist can be safely cleared as soon as $B1$ has completed, because it indicates all pending stores in $A1$ have completed. This simplifies the implementation for clearing watchlist, as the processor can decide when to clear watchlist based on the local information. Note that, to guarantee that any potential conflict is detected, the cache block whose address is in the active buffer is not allowed to be evicted from local cache.

We illustrate the algorithm in Fig. 4(c). Suppose $a1$ is a cache miss and $a2$ has completed past $a1$ (so $a1$ will be present in the directory if it has not completed). Now both $a1$ and $a2$ are active, so their addresses are recorded in the active buffer; and FENCE1 is recorded as well. In `Proc 2`, $b1$ is then executed, which will be a miss. It obtains the watchlist containing x from the directory and also sends a coherence transaction for y to `Proc 1`. Since y is in the active buffer and there is a fence prior to y, the transaction is delayed, and hence the watchlist is not cleared. If $b2$ tries to retire, it has to check the watchlist and hence it stalls. When $a1$ has completed, the active buffer will be empty, and the delayed coherence transaction for y from `Proc 2` can be satisfied. Thus, the completion of $b1$ indicates memory operations prior to FENCE1 have completed; otherwise, $a2$ is active and hence $b1$ cannot complete. Now the watchlist containing x can be safely cleared as soon as memory operations prior to FENCE2 have completed, without the risk of forming cycles.

(Deadlock freedom) In the above example, it seems possible that all four instructions $a1, a2, b1$, and $b2$ are active, and $b1$ is delayed by $a2$ and $a1$ is delayed by $b2$, which forms a deadlock. However, we show that it is not possible that all four instructions are active at the same time. Since $a1$ and $b1$ are misses (otherwise $a2 \rightarrow b1$ and $b2 \rightarrow a1$ do not exist), they are sent to the directory. Suppose $a1$ first reaches the directory. So the watchlist for FENCE2 will contain x accessed by $a1$. This watchlist stalls $b2$, which will not be able to retire and become active. Thus, the above scenario of deadlock is not possible.

4.1.3 Distributed directory

To make address-aware fence scalable, we now consider the implementation with a distributed directory. With a centralized directory, a cache miss transaction, that needs to update the watchlist, is sent to the directory and obtains all pending stores in other processors. However, when the directory is distributed, a cache miss transaction is only sent to its *home directory*, and only obtains the pending stores in that directory. Hence, the memory operations after the fence can use the watchlist for checking only if they are mapped to the same home directory where the watchlist is collected.

To accommodate distributed directory, we maintain a buffer called *watchlist buffer*, which has several entries recording watchlists collected from different home directories. Each entry in the buffer is also tagged with the ID of the tile where the home directory resides. When a cache miss brings back a watchlist, it is recorded in an entry of the buffer, tagged with the corresponding tile ID. Meanwhile, other entries are invalidated as they might contain stale watchlists. A memory operation trying to retire past the fence first checks whether there is a valid entry with the tile ID to which the memory access is mapped. If yes, the memory operation checks against the watchlist. Otherwise, it is forced to fetch the watchlist from its own home directory before it can check conflict for retirement. The fetched watchlist is also recorded, so that future memory operations mapped to the same home directory can check conflict locally. Thanks to spatial locality, most of the nearby memory accesses tend to be mapped to the same home directory, which allows most memory operations to check watchlists quickly and retire past fences. We use the distributed directory in our evaluation.

(Handling multiple fences) In the above discussion, we only consider one executing fence. However, it is also possible that multiple fences are executing in the pipeline. Since a watchlist has to be removed when the corresponding fence can complete, we have to know which watchlist is associated with which fence. To do this, each issued fence in the pipeline is associated with a unique tag, and the watchlist collected for the fence will also be associated with the same tag. When a fence completes, only the watchlists with the same tag as the fence are removed. Hence, the watchlists for uncompleted fences continue to remain recorded in the buffer. In particular, the watchlist for a fence can be replaced by the watchlist for a second fence if they are collected from the same home directory, because the latter is the updated watchlist from that directory.

4.2 Hardware Summary

Fig. 5 shows the overview of hardware support for address-aware fence. For simplicity, only main logic blocks related to our technique are presented. Each processor core is augmented with two new logic blocks to implement our technique: *active buffer* and *watchlist buffer* as discussed in the previous section. If a retired memory access or fence is active, it is added to the active buffer (①). Each external cache transaction has to check the active buffer, and is delayed if there is a hit (②). Each watchlist is recorded in the watchlist buffer when it is received from the directory (③). Each memory access has to check the watchlist buffer to see if it can retire (④). Although we leverage cache coherence to transfer metadata, the coherence protocol and its transactions are left unchanged. Next, we summarize the operations in the active buffer and watchlist buffer.

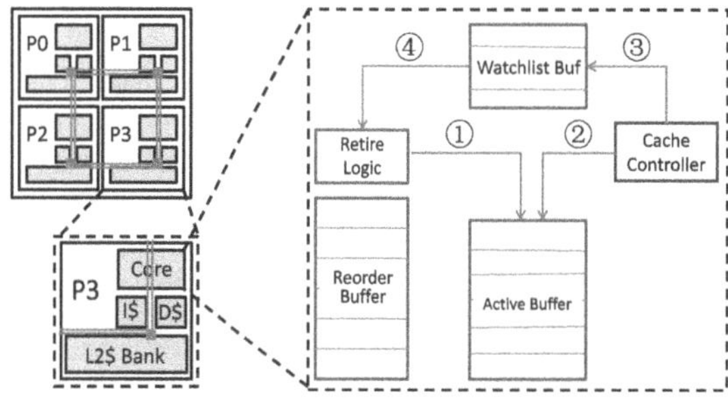

Figure 5: Overview of the architecture.

(Active buffer) The active buffer records the addresses of all active memory accesses and active fences. It also incorporates the function of store buffer. Each entry of the buffer consists of the following fields: *valid*, *type*, *done*, and *data*. Descriptions of fields are shown in Table 2. The *data* field depends on the type. For a store, it includes the destination memory address and a pointer to its data; for a load, it only includes the memory address; and for a fence, it includes a unique tag used to mark its watchlist.

Fields	Description
valid	whether it is a valid entry
type	load, store or fence
done	whether the operation has completed loads and fences are always complete
data	depending on the type

Table 2: Fields in active buffer.

The following are the operations for the active buffer. (1) *Add.* Active memory accesses and active fences are added to the active buffer in the order they retired. However, two consecutive loads or two consecutive stores can be merged if their destination addresses are mapped to the same cache block, reducing the size of active buffer. This is because the conflict detection is based on the block address. If the buffer is full, the retiring memory access or fence is delayed until there is an entry available. (2) *Delete.* If a memory access or fence is no longer active, it is removed. That is, at the head of active buffer, if a pending store has completed, entries until next pending store are invalidated. (3) *Conflict detection.* Each external coherence transaction has to detect conflict in the active buffer. If there is a conflict in the active buffer and there is an active fence prior to this conflicting entry, the transaction is delayed. It is important to make conflict detection efficient. We use a counting bloom filter to hash memory addresses in the active buffer. Conflict detection first checks the counting bloom filter before checking entries in the active buffer, which greatly reduces useless checks as conflicts are rare.

(Watchlist buffer) The watchlist buffer records all collected watchlists. Each watchlist is a bit vector which contains memory addresses compressed using bloom filter. This is to minimize the network bandwidth, because watchlists are exchanged along with cache transactions. Each entry consists of the following fields: *valid*, *fence tag*, *tile ID*, and *watchlist*. Descriptions of each field are shown in Table 3.

The following are the operations for the watchlist buffer. (1) *Add.* Each watchlist is recorded when it is replied from

Fields	Description
valid	whether it is a valid entry
fence tag	which fence is the watchlist for
tile ID	which directory the watchlist is collected
watchlist	bit vector of pending stores

Table 3: Fields in watchlist buffer.

the directory, with the corresponding fence tag and tile ID. (2) *Delete.* When all memory operations before a fence have completed, the entries with the same fence tag is invalidated. Moreover, when a cache miss before the fence brings back an updated watchlist, other entries are invalidated as they might contain stale watchlists. (3) *Retirement check.* Each retiring memory operation checks against the watchlist with the tile ID to which its memory address is mapped. If it does not find such watchlist, it is first forced to fetch the watchlist from its home directory. If the block address of the memory operation is not contained in the watchlist, it can retire even if there is a pending store prior to the fence. Otherwise, it indicates the retirement of the memory access may result in a violation of fence order, and hence it is delayed. It is worth noting that watchlist buffer will eventually become empty if the processor is stalled, which indicates that the forward progress is guaranteed.

5. EXPERIMENTAL EVALUATION

The goals of our evaluation are: (1) to understand why address-aware fence performs better; (2) to assess the performance of address-aware fence compared to traditional fence; and (3) to assess the space and traffic overhead.

(Simulation) We have developed a hardware simulation infrastructure using the Pin tool [24] that simulates a directory-based shared memory multiprocessor system. Each processor has a private 4-way 32KB L1 cache and all processors share a L2 cache (16-way 1MB/core). All L1 caches are kept coherent using a directory-based MESI protocol. All cores are connected via a mesh network, which has a link latency of 2 cycles and router latency of 3 cycles. Each instruction takes 1 cycle to execute, and it takes 2, 10, and 300 cycles to access the L1 cache, L2 cache, and main memory, respectively.

Benchmarks	Description
dekker	Dekker algorithm [9]
lamport	Lamport Queue [18]
msn	Non-blocking Queue [27]
wsq	Chase-Lev's Work Stealing Queue [6]
bst	Binary search tree
SPLASH-2	8 programs from SPLASH-2 [38]

Table 4: Benchmark description.

(Benchmarks) We evaluate our technique using benchmarks shown in Table 4. There are two groups, concurrent lock-free algorithms and SPLASH-2 benchmark programs. In the first group, concurrent lock-free algorithms are implemented using fences and atomic compare-and-swap (CAS) instructions. Dekker algorithm (*dekker*) [9] is a classic solution to mutual exclusion problems using only shared variables for communication. Lamport Queue (*lamport*) [18] is a single-producer and single-consumer queue. Non-blocking concurrent queue (*msn*) is a multiple-producer and multiple-consumer queue. Chase-Lev work-stealing queue (*wsq*) [6] is a lock-free work-stealing deque implemented with a growable cyclic array. *bst* is a concurrent search structure implemented using atomic CAS instructions. Since these lock-free data structures are not closed programs, we constructed harnesses to use them to assess the performance of address-aware fences. The second group of benchmarks are from SPLASH-2 [38]. In these benchmarks, fences are inserted to enforce sequential consistency. We identified the fence insertion points based on Shasha and Snir's delay set analysis, where we employed dynamic analysis to find conflicting accesses as in [10, 20]. We also use these benchmarks to compare address-aware fence and C-Fence [20].

5.1 Performance

In this section, we would like to understand how address-aware fences improve fence performance and evaluate the performance overhead induced by address-aware fences.

5.1.1 Effectiveness of address-aware fence

Benchmarks	#Fences	Address-aware fences		C-Fence
		#Check	#in W.L.	#Conf.
barnes	83M	47M	206	21M
fmm	5M	2M	223	1M
ocean	9M	15M	383	1M
radiosity	30M	5M	90	4M
raytrace	44M	34M	239	5M
volrend	39M	49M	436	3M
water-ns	9M	1M	79	656K
water-sp	7M	2M	88	395K
AVG.	28.8M	19.4M	218	4.9M

Table 5: Effectiveness of address-aware fence.

In this evaluation, we use SPLASH-2 benchmark programs where fences have been inserted for enforcing sequential consistency. All programs are run with 8 threads. Table 5 characterizes address-aware fences in terms of how often fences have to take effect. Column 2 in the table shows the number of dynamic fence instructions executed in each program. Although they only account for a small part of all instructions (~1%), they induce relatively larger execution time overhead, as shown later in Fig. 6. With address-aware fence, when there is any active fence, memory accesses have to check with watchlists before retirement. Column 3 shows the number of such memory accesses. Column 4 shows the number of memory accesses whose block addresses are found to be present in the watchlists. We can see that, compared with the number in Column 3, very few memory accesses are stalled by fences. In fact, the number of fences that need to stall (Column 3) is negligible compared with the total number of fences (Column 2). For example, *volrend* has the largest number of detected conflicts, but this is still very small compared the total number of fences – 436 *vs.* 39 Million. On average, only 218 memory accesses are found in watchlists; thus, avoiding nearly all fences from taking effect.

(Comparison with C-Fence) We also implemented and studied C-Fence mechanism [20], which is able to dynamically eliminate a fence as long as none of its associate fence (provided by compiler) is executing concurrently in other processors. We measured the number of fences which detect executing associates and have to stall. Numbers in Column 5 show that the number of fences that have to stall when C-Fence is used. On an average, around 15% of C-Fences have to stall. In contrast, address-aware fences require very few stalls (Column 4 *vs.* Column 5). This is because address-aware fence is able to exploit more optimization opportunities dynamically, e.g., scenarios in Fig. 1, which C-Fence is not able to optimize.

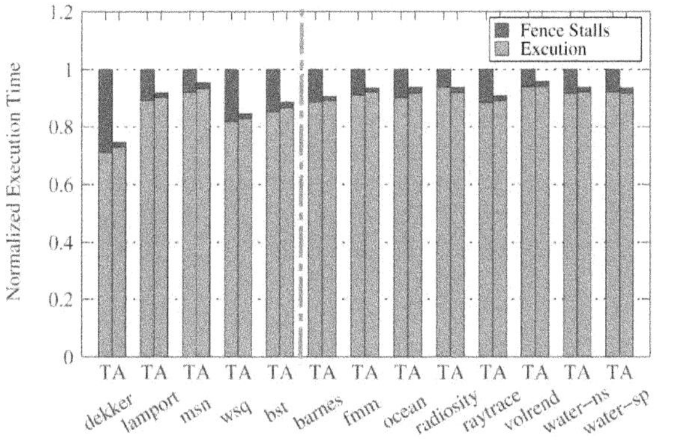

Figure 6: Execution time – T represents traditional fence and A represents address-aware fence.

5.1.2 Execution time

We measured the execution time of programs with traditional fences and address-aware fences, respectively. Fig. 6 shows the results, which are normalized to the execution time achieved using traditional fences. The execution time is broken down into two parts: the stall time due to fences (*Fence stalls*) and the rest of the execution time (*Execution*). For the first group (concurrent lock-free algorithms), with traditional fences, we can see that fence stalls account for 8%-29% of the total execution time. Actually, the fence overhead can be larger depending on the programs using them. Concurrent algorithms have to guarantee correct data accesses by multiple threads, and fences are used to guarantee this goal under relaxed consistency models. However, if data is not frequently accessed by multiple threads concurrently, address-aware fences are able to utilize this opportunity to reduce the fence overhead. In the second group (SPLASH-2 programs), fences are inserted to ensure sequential consistency. Similarly, they experience significant overhead due to fences (about 10% on average). However, since fences are inserted conservatively, many dynamic fence instances are unnecessary, some of which were illustrated in Fig. 1. With address-aware fence, only very few fences have to take effect and delay the memory accesses that follow them. On an average, address-aware fence improves the performance of all benchmark programs by 12.2%. More importantly, we can see that address-aware fence only induces negligible execution time overhead – a fence can retire as long as it has obtained its watchlist, which can be fetched from the directory efficiently. On the other hand, traditional fence has to stall the pipeline until all outstanding stores have completed, which takes a much longer time to access the memory or invalidate shared copies.

(Scalability) We vary the number of processors with 4, 8 and 16 processors and measure the execution time of benchmark programs from SPLASH-2. The results are shown in Fig. 7, where data are presented in the same way as in Fig. 6. Each benchmark program has execution time of traditional fence and address-aware fence with 4, 8 and 16 processors, respectively. We can see that, with different numbers of processors, the execution time overhead induced by

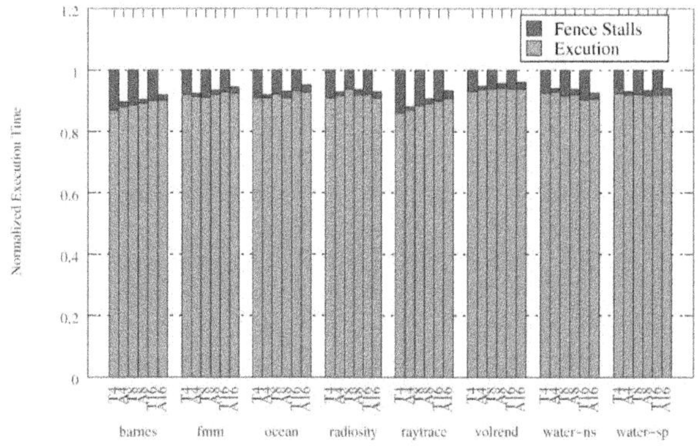

Figure 7: Scalability – Tn represents traditional fence with n processors and An represents address-aware fence with n processors.

address-aware fence is not affected significantly. Therefore, the implementation appears scalable. In fact, our implementation leverages directory-based cache coherence protocol, piggybacking required information on coherence transactions. Without introducing centralized structures, the implementation maintains the level of scalability delivered by the directory-based cache coherence.

5.2 Space and Traffic

Benchmarks	Active buffer		#Pend.	#Delay	Traffic
	%Emp.	%<64	stores	/1K inst.	%Inc.
barnes	77.9	98.7	2.2	0.0	13.0
fmm	85.5	99.4	2.8	0.0	18.6
ocean	59.6	84.1	8.7	0.0	9.7
radiosity	78.1	99.5	3.6	0.0	17.4
raytrace	82.5	98.9	2.3	0.0	22.1
volrend	75.2	98.7	4.5	0.0	13.9
water-ns	86.4	99.8	4.1	0.0	8.9
water-sp	89.0	99.9	5.2	0.0	12.5
AVG.	79.2	97.5	4.2	0.0	14.7

Table 6: Characterization of space and traffic.

To support address-aware fence, we introduced active buffer and watchlist buffer to record information and leveraged cache coherence to avoid fence order violation. Table 6 characterizes space and traffic induced by address-aware fence. We conducted the experiments using SPLASH-2 benchmark programs with 8 threads.

Recall that, active buffer stores addresses of active memory accesses and fences, and two consecutive loads or two consecutive stores are merged when they have the same block address. Column 2 shows that, on average, the active buffer is frequently empty – at the rate of 79.2%. When it is empty, memory accesses at the top of ROB can retire immediately, as there is no active fence prior to them. To size the active buffer, we tracked the number of active memory accesses during execution, and found that this number is less than 64 most of the time (97.5% on average as shown in Column 3). *ocean* has more than 64 active accesses most frequently (15.9%) among all programs, but the other benchmark programs almost never exceed 64 active accesses. Thus, we used 64 entries in our implementation. Besides, for watchlist buffer, we used the number of entries equal to the number of processors, with each entry recording the watchlist obtained from the corresponding processor.

A watchlist is obtained from the directory, consisting of the addresses of pending stores being serviced in the directory. Column 4 shows the average number of block addresses compressed in the directory when a processor requests for a watchlist. As we can see, the average number is 4.2, which is small. In our implementation, we compressed the addresses into a watchlist of 160 bits, which are enough to obtain very low false positive. Column 5 shows the number of external cache coherence transactions that are delayed due to its hit in the active buffer. We can see that all of them are 0.0 per 1K instructions. So it has little effect on the performance. Column 6 shows the traffic increase for each program. Address-aware fence induces additional traffic to transfer watchlists between processors and the directory, and this is the main source of the additional traffic. On an average, the traffic increases by 14.7%, which is modest.

(Hardware Cost Summary) In the highest performing configuration, address-aware fence only adds active buffer and watchlist buffer to each core. The active buffer has 64 entries, each of which has about 8 bytes; the watchlist buffer has 8 entries (for 8 processors), each of which has about 20 bytes. The above two buffers amount to a total of 672 bytes. We expect the extra power consumption of our technique to be small compared to the state-of-the-art aggressive speculative techniques, as the area overhead of our technique is small and it does not have to maintain speculative states or require rollback associated with misspeculations.

6. RELATED WORK

Our work is closely related to the techniques listed in Table 1, which are also aimed at reducing overhead of fence operations non-speculatively. In [36], Praun *et al.* proposed *conditional memory ordering* (CMO) based on the observation that memory ordering instructions used on acquire and release of a lock are often unnecessary. The goal of CMO is to optimize and reduce the cost of the acquire-release memory synchronization protocol using a purely runtime technique. However, it does not address the memory ordering situations using fences as shown in Fig. 1. Ladan-Mozes *et al.* [17] proposed *location-based memory fences* (`l-mfence`) to reduce fence overhead. It is a lightweight solution, but it is limited to the Dekker-like algorithms. Our prior work [20] proposed *conditional fence* (C-Fence) to enforce sequential consistency. Although it can greatly reduce dynamic fence instructions, it relies on compiler to provide fence associates information, and stalls due to fence associate conflict are still conservative as shown in our experiments. On the other hand, our work aims at reducing all kinds of memory ordering overhead induced by fences, and by looking at the addresses of memory operations across fences at runtime, we require much less fence stalls.

There has been work on optimizing lock implementations. Thin locks [2] and other refinements [16, 28] strive to reduce the overhead of locking in the context of Java. The basic idea is to allow a particular thread to reserve a lock, and hence acquisitions of the lock by the reserving thread can be performed efficiently. [35] proposed a fast biased lock, which simplifies and generalizes prior implementations of biased lock. The above work focuses on reducing the frequency of atomic RMW operations for implementing locks, while our work reduces the memory ordering overhead induced by fence instructions. Speculative lock elision [29] and lock elision with transactional memory [8, 34] both use speculative technique to dynamically eliminate lock operations. However, our technique does not simply focus on lock operations but also fences which are also used for lock implementation, and our technique does not require speculation.

Extensive research has been conducted on implementing sequential consistency (SC) efficiently. [11, 19, 30] rely on static analysis to minimize the number of fences which are required for enforcing SC, and [3, 5, 14, 15, 37, 21, 32] are various runtime solutions for implementing SC. Besides, in [23, 25, 31], researchers also argued that SC violation should be treated as exceptions. However, these techniques are designed to improve SC performance and provide programmers with a strengthened shared memory system, while our work is to reduce the cost of fence instructions. Although some of the above techniques can be adjusted to address the fence overhead [3, 5, 15, 37], they have to employ speculation. Memory accesses after a fence can be speculatively retired when there is any pending memory operation before the fence. However, the hardware complexity associated with aggressive speculation can hinder wide-spread adoption. [21, 32] are non-speculative SC implementations. End-to-End SC [32] proposes to identify thread-local and shared read-only data, and enforces SC by only ordering the accesses to remaining data. This approach is also useful for reducing the memory ordering overhead due to fences. But address-aware fence is more aggressive, as it further allows accesses to shared data to be reordered. In our prior work [21], we propose *conflict ordering* to enforce SC efficiently without speculation. However, address-aware fence only focuses on memory orderings enforced by fences which are present in the programs. The processor only initiates the process of handling fences when fences are encountered.

7. CONCLUSION

In this work, we propose a hardware solution *address-aware fence* to reduce the overhead due to fence instructions without speculation. Our technique is implemented in the microarchitecture without instruction set support and is transparent to programmers. Address-aware fences only enforce memory orderings that are necessary to maintain the effect that the traditional fences strive to enforce, while other fences are dynamically eliminated. Our experiments conducted on a group of concurrent lock-free algorithms and SPLASH-2 benchmarks show that address-aware fences eliminate nearly all the overhead associated with traditional fences and achieve an average performance improvement of 12.2% on all benchmark programs.

ACKNOWLEDGMENTS

We would like to thank all reviewers for their helpful comments and advice for improving this paper. This research work is supported by the National Science Foundation grant CCF-0963996 to the University of California, Riverside, and by the Centre for Numerical Algorithms and Intelligent Software, funded by EPSRC grant EP/G036136/1 and the Scottish Funding Council to the University of Edinburgh.

8. REFERENCES

[1] S. V. Adve and K. Gharachorloo. Shared memory consistency models: A tutorial. *IEEE Computer*, 29:66–76, 1995.

[2] D. F. Bacon, R. Konuru, C. Murthy, and M. Serrano. Thin locks: featherweight synchronization for Java. PLDI '98, pages 258–268.

[3] C. Blundell, M. M. Martin, and T. F. Wenisch. Invisifence: performance-transparent memory ordering in conventional multiprocessors. ISCA '09, pages 233–244.

[4] S. Burckhardt, R. Alur, and M. M. K. Martin. Checkfence: checking consistency of concurrent data types on relaxed memory models. PLDI '07, pages 12–21.

[5] L. Ceze, J. Tuck, P. Montesinos, and J. Torrellas. BulkSC: Bulk enforcement of sequential consistency. ISCA '07, pages 278–289.

[6] D. Chase and Y. Lev. Dynamic circular work-stealing deque. SPAA '05, pages 21–28.

[7] T. H. Cormen, C. E. Leiserson, R. L. Rivest, and C. Stein. *Introduction to Algorithms*, 2001.

[8] D. Dice, Y. Lev, M. Moir, and D. Nussbaum. Early experience with a commercial hardware transactional memory implementation. ASPLOS '09, pages 157–168.

[9] E. W. Dijkstra. Cooperating sequential processes. *The origin of concurrent programming: from semaphores to remote procedure calls*, pages 65–138, 2002.

[10] Y. Duan, X. Feng, L. Wang, C. Zhang, and P.-C. Yew. Detecting and eliminating potential violations of sequential consistency for concurrent C/C++ programs. CGO '09, pages 25–34.

[11] X. Fang, J. Lee, and S. P. Midkiff. Automatic fence insertion for shared memory multiprocessing. ICS '03, pages 285–294.

[12] K. Gharachorloo, A. Gupta, and J. Hennessy. Performance evaluation of memory consistency models for shared-memory multiprocessors. ASPLOS '91, pages 245–257.

[13] K. Gharachorloo, A. Gupta, and J. Hennessy. Two techniques to enhance the performance of memory consistency models. ISCA '91, pages 355–364.

[14] C. Gniady and B. Falsafi. Speculative sequential consistency with little custom storage. PACT '02, pages 179–188.

[15] C. Gniady, B. Falsafi, and T. N. Vijaykumar. Is SC + ILP = RC? ISCA '99, pages 162–171.

[16] K. Kawachiya, A. Koseki, and T. Onodera. Lock reservation: Java locks can mostly do without atomic operations. OOPSLA '02, pages 130–141.

[17] E. Ladan-Mozes, I.-T. A. Lee, and D. Vyukov. Location-based memory fences. SPAA '11, pages 75–84.

[18] L. Lamport. Specifying concurrent program modules. *ACM Trans. Program. Lang. Syst.*, 5(2):190–222, Apr. 1983.

[19] J. Lee and D. A. Padua. Hiding relaxed memory consistency with a compiler. *IEEE Trans. Comput.*, 50(8):824–833, 2001.

[20] C. Lin, V. Nagarajan, and R. Gupta. Efficient sequential consistency using conditional fences. PACT '10, pages 295–306.

[21] C. Lin, V. Nagarajan, R. Gupta, and B. Rajaram. Efficient sequential consistency via conflict ordering. ASPLOS '12, pages 273–286.

[22] F. Liu, N. Nedev, N. Prisadnikov, M. Vechev, and E. Yahav. Dynamic synthesis for relaxed memory models. PLDI '12, pages 429–440.

[23] B. Lucia, L. Ceze, K. Strauss, S. Qadeer, and H.-J. Boehm. Conflict exceptions: simplifying concurrent language semantics with precise hardware exceptions for data-races. ISCA '10, pages 210–221.

[24] C.-K. Luk, R. Cohn, R. Muth, H. Patil, A. Klauser, G. Lowney, S. Wallace, V. J. Reddi, and K. Hazelwood. Pin: building customized program analysis tools with dynamic instrumentation. PLDI '05, pages 190–200.

[25] D. Marino, A. Singh, T. Millstein, M. Musuvathi, and S. Narayanasamy. DRFx: a simple and efficient memory model for concurrent programming languages. PLDI '10, pages 351–362.

[26] M. M. Michael. Scalable lock-free dynamic memory allocation. PLDI '04, pages 35–46.

[27] M. M. Michael and M. L. Scott. Simple, fast, and practical non-blocking and blocking concurrent queue algorithms. PODC '96, pages 267–275.

[28] T. Ogasawara, H. Komatsu, and T. Nakatani. To-lock: Removing lock overhead using the owners' temporal locality. PACT '04, pages 255–266.

[29] R. Rajwar and J. R. Goodman. Speculative lock elision: enabling highly concurrent multithreaded execution. MICRO '01, pages 294–305.

[30] D. Shasha and M. Snir. Efficient and correct execution of parallel programs that share memory. *ACM Trans. Program. Lang. Syst.*, 10(2):282–312, 1988.

[31] A. Singh, D. Marino, S. Narayanasamy, T. Millstein, and M. Musuvathi. Efficient processor support for DRFx, a memory model with exceptions. ASPLOS '11, pages 53–66.

[32] A. Singh, S. Narayanasamy, D. Marino, T. Millstein, and M. Musuvathi. End-to-end sequential consistency. ISCA '12, pages 524–535.

[33] D. J. Sorin, M. D. Hill, and D. A. Wood. *A Primer on Memory Consistency and Cache Coherence*. Synthesis Lectures on Computer Architecture. Morgan & Claypool Publishers, 2011.

[34] T. Usui, R. Behrends, J. Evans, and Y. Smaragdakis. Adaptive locks: Combining transactions and locks for efficient concurrency. PACT '09, pages 3–14.

[35] N. Vasudevan, K. S. Namjoshi, and S. A. Edwards. Simple and fast biased locks. PACT '10, pages 65–74.

[36] C. von Praun, H. W. Cain, J.-D. Choi, and K. D. Ryu. Conditional memory ordering. ISCA '06, pages 41–52.

[37] T. F. Wenisch, A. Ailamaki, B. Falsafi, and A. Moshovos. Mechanisms for store-wait-free multiprocessors. ISCA '07, pages 266–277.

[38] S. C. Woo, M. Ohara, E. Torrie, J. P. Singh, and A. Gupta. The SPLASH-2 programs: characterization and methodological considerations. ISCA '95, pages 24–36.

Prefetching and Cache Management Using Task Lifetimes

Vassilis Papaefstathiou*
FORTH-ICS
Heraklion, Crete, Greece
papaef@ics.forth.gr

Manolis G.H. Katevenis*
FORTH-ICS
Heraklion, Crete, Greece
kateveni@ics.forth.gr

Dimitrios S. Nikolopoulos
Queen's University of Belfast
Belfast, United Kingdom
d.nikolopoulos@qub.ac.uk

Dionisios Pnevmatikatos†
FORTH-ICS
Heraklion, Crete, Greece
pnevmati@ics.forth.gr

ABSTRACT

Task-based dataflow programming models and runtimes emerge as promising candidates for programming multicore and manycore architectures. These programming models analyze dynamically task dependencies at runtime and schedule independent tasks concurrently to the processing elements. In such models, cache locality, which is critical for performance, becomes more challenging in the presence of fine-grain tasks, and in architectures with many simple cores.

This paper presents a combined hardware-software approach to improve cache locality and offer better performance is terms of execution time and energy in the memory system. We propose the explicit bulk prefetcher (EBP) and epoch-based cache management (ECM) to help runtimes prefetch task data and guide the replacement decisions in caches. The runtime software can use this hardware support to expose its internal knowledge about the tasks to the architecture and achieve more efficient task-based execution. Our combined scheme outperforms HW-only prefetchers and state-of-the-art replacement policies, improves performance by an average of 17%, generates on average 26% fewer L2 misses, and consumes on average 28% less energy in the components of the memory system.

Categories and Subject Descriptors

B.3.2 [**Design Styles**]: Cache memories; C.1.4 [**Parallel Architectures**]; D.1.3 [**Concurrent Programming**]

General Terms

Design, Measurement, Performance

*Also, with the Computer Science Department (CSD), University of Crete, Heraklion, Greece.
†Also, with the ECE Department, Technical University of Crete, Chania, Greece.

ICS'13, June 10–14, 2013, Eugene, Oregon, USA.

Keywords

Task-based Programming; Prefetching; Cache Management

1. INTRODUCTION

One common approach to parallel programming is to decompose a program into a set of tasks and distribute them among the processing elements. Many task-based programming models have been proposed in the literature [4, 9, 18] and promise to ease programming effort by abstracting out the elements of parallel programming that are traditionally considered hard and time consuming, such as scheduling, synchronization, and locality optimizations. This paper considers a class of emerging task-based dataflow programming models where the memory footprint of each task is declared by the programmer and the runtime software automatically detects task dependencies based on these footprints and schedules independent tasks concurrently [2, 6, 28, 33]. In this context, we focus on the memory behavior of fine-grain tasks and their impact on cache locality, which greatly affects performance. The use of fine-grain tasks can unleash large amounts of parallelism and has the potential to allow many-core computing resources to be utilized.

Each task has its own unique memory footprint and the associated data will eventually be transferred into the portion of the underlying memory hierarchy that is closest to the core that executes this task, i.e. L1 and/or L2 cache. Given that tasks are separate units of work, each with its own memory footprint, reuse of cache contents among tasks is a difficult problem that locality-aware schedulers are trying to alleviate [16]. However, task data reuse is not always possible, and depends on the distance between producer and consumer tasks, which is an intrinsic characteristic of each application. Moreover, several types of applications do not benefit from a single type of scheduler and their behavior may be incompatible with specific scheduling algorithms. Often times, applications benefit from load-balancing and work-stealing, which makes locality a conflicting goal; the most extreme case of locality scheduling dictates that all tasks execute sequentially in a single core.

The task-based dataflow programming models use the memory footprints of tasks to build dependency graphs (DAGs) and maintain significant amount of information that is used to dynamically drive runtime decisions. However, the underlying memory architecture is still agnostic of what runtimes are trying to achieve. Therefore, hardware decisions are based on rather simplistic assumptions. Our thesis is that the runtime software maintains important semantic knowledge regarding the execution sequence and memory footprints of tasks, which can be shared with the underlying hardware to achieve an effective hardware-software synergy.

To this end, we propose architectural support and runtime co-design to improve cache locality and optimize task-based execution. We introduce the *Explicit Bulk Prefetcher (EBP)*, a programmable prefetch engine that can be utilized by the runtime software to prefetch task data. EBP is reminiscent of an RDMA (remote direct memory access) engine, but it is designed for cache-based architectures, integrates with the local cache hierarchy of each core, and offers a low overhead memory-mapped interface that can be used at *user-level*. EBP enables runtime software to prefetch task data in bulk before each task executes and perform common optimizations such as double-buffering. This form of software-directed prefetching can overcome some of the challenging issues with hardware-only prefetchers such as *timeliness*, *accuracy*, and *access pattern prediction*.

Although prefetching has the potential to improve cache locality and hide memory latency, its effectiveness is affected by the ability of the cache to keep the prefetched data. When applying double-buffering optimizations, prefetching can pollute the cache and evict useful data. To address the latter issues and shortcomings, we propose *Epoch-based Cache Management (ECM)*, a mechanism that allows software to expose its knowledge of tasks to the cache hierarchy, assign cache resources to them, and isolate the effects of prefetching. ECM is based on the notion of *Epoch*, which is defined by software as the lifetime of a task, i.e. the time period during which a task executes. ECM offers a memory-mapped interface that allows software to advance epochs, i.e. signal the beginning of new tasks, and assign quotas to epochs, i.e. declare the space a task is allowed to allocate in the cache. All data accessed (or prefetched) by a task is associated with an epoch number in the cache. ECM guides the cache replacement policy, by allowing it to distinguish between data belonging to different tasks. The hardware cost of ECM is very small.

The contributions of this paper are the following:

- We propose the *Explicit Bulk Prefetcher (EBP)*, a programmable prefetch engine that allows software to accurately prefetch data ahead of time and improve cache locality in task-based programs.
- We introduce *Epoch-based Cache Management (ECM)*, a lightweight mechanism to guide cache replacement decisions, assign local cache resources to tasks, and isolate the effects of prefetching.
- We evaluate EBP and ECM using a task-based runtime and a set of benchmark applications. We demonstrate that EBP in conjunction with ECM outperforms HW-only prefetchers, improves performance by an average of 17%, generates on average 26% fewer L2 misses, and consumes on average 28% less energy in the components of the memory system.

The rest of this paper is organized as follows: Section 2 introduces the task-based dataflow programming model. Section 3 explains the proposed architectural support. Section 4 provides the experimental methodology. Section 5 presents our evaluation. Section 6 discusses related work. Finally, Section 7 offers our conclusions.

2. TASK DATAFLOW PROGRAMMING

The task-based dataflow programming models aim to simplify parallel programming by discovering task dependencies at runtime and dynamically extracting task parallelism. Such models require the programmer (or the compiler) to identify tasks (functions) that may run in parallel, annotate the memory footprint of their arguments (addresses), and declare the side-effect of each task argument in memory (read/write). Representative examples of such programming models include SmpSS/OmpSS [28, 29], BDDT [32], Legion [6], Serialization Sets [2] and other proposals that follow similar concepts and techniques [7, 10, 33].

The underlying runtime libraries use the memory footprints and the side-effects of each task argument to identify task dependencies and build dependency graphs as directed acyclic graphs (DAGs) at runtime. Independent tasks are immediately scheduled for execution on the available cores, while dependent tasks are kept in internal data structures and queues, waiting until all of their dependencies are satisfied. Tasks in this model may execute out-of-order using the scheduling techniques followed in processors, while respecting task dependencies in the same way that processors respect register dependencies, i.e. true dependencies (RAW), anti-dependencies (WAR) and output dependencies (WAW). Deterministic execution and the preservation of task dependencies are guaranteed by the order in which the main application thread issues tasks, similarly to the order that instructions are issued in a sequential program.

In this paper, we consider the programming model proposed in [28], which is based on *C pragmas* and follows syntax similar to the popular OpenMP task pragmas [4]. We use the same task constructs and multi-dimensional memory regions syntax as in [29]. The side-effects of task arguments may be declared as one of: *(i) input:* for read-only arguments, *(ii) output:* for write-only arguments, and *(iii) inout:* for arguments that are both read and written. A code example illustrating matrix multiplication with our task dataflow programming model is shown in Listing 1.

```
void matmul_block( double A[N][N],
                   double B[N][N],
                   double C[N][N] )
{
  for (int i=0 ; i < L ; i++)
    for (int j=0 ; j < L ; j++)
      for (int k=0 ; k < L ; k++)
        C[i][j] += A[i][k] + B[k][j];
}

double A[N][N], B[N][N], C[N][N];
...
for (int i=0 ; i < N ; i+=L)
  for (int j=0 ; j < N ; j+=L)
    for (int k=0 ; k < N ; k+=L)
      #pragma xss task input(A{0:L}{0:L}) \
                       input(B{0:L}{0:L}) \
                       inout(C{0:L}{0:L})
      matmul_block( &A[i][k],
                    &B[k][j],
                    &C[i][j] );

#pragma xss waitall
...
```

Listing 1: A matrix multiplication example using the task dataflow programming model

3. ARCHITECTURAL SUPPORT

Emerging task-based dataflow programming models require the memory footprint of each task to be declared. This requirement provides unique opportunities for optimizations in the memory system. The runtime system maintains important knowledge about the task execution sequence and task memory footprints, which can guide the resource allocation decisions of the underlying hardware.

To this end, we propose a set of hardware mechanisms which can improve task-based execution with low hardware and software overhead. We propose the *Explicit Bulk Prefetcher (EBP):* a hardware mechanism that allows the runtime to accurately prefetch task data (Section 3.1) and *Epoch-based Cache Management (ECM):* a hardware mechanism to guide the cache replacement decisions (Section 3.2).

3.1 Explicit Bulk Prefetcher

Task-based programming models with annotated memory footprints allow the runtime to know before-hand which data will be used by a task before that task executes. This observation offers the opportunity to prefetch task data in a timely fashion and improve cache locality. The *Explicit Bulk Prefetcher (EBP)* is a hardware unit that allows software to explicitly prefetch memory ranges that correspond to task arguments. Software can utilize EBP to prefetch data for the next task(s) waiting in the scheduling queue, effectively applying double- or multi- buffering, in order to minimize cache misses and improve task execution.

EBP is a programmable prefetch engine that offers a memory-mapped interface and accepts a set of commands at user-level. We design EBP as a per-core engine that operates on a private coherent L2 cache. We target L2 caches since their large capacity – when compared to L1 caches – makes them more suitable for bulk prefetching and because processor pipelines and critical paths are less susceptible to changes in the L2 cache. Moreover, we choose a memory-mapped interface instead of a register-mapped interface, in order to avoid ISA changes and make our design less intrusive. EBP is reminiscent of existing RDMA engines [3, 22].

The memory-mapped interface offered by EBP, is designed to allow memory ranges to be specified with virtual addresses, thus offering fast user-level access with low software overhead. In order to translate virtual addresses[1] and ensure protection, EBP requires access to the local TLBs; typically the 2nd level TLB. The use of virtual addresses provides EBP with the capability to prefetch across page boundaries, which is a common limiting factor in HW prefetchers. In addition, EBP can trigger page-table walking hardware early and minimize, or even hide, the effect of TLB misses.

The EBP engine supports *2D memory ranges* with a constant stride in order to minimize the number of required prefetch operations in common array patterns, such as blocking/tiling. The interface defines the following memory-mapped registers to initiate prefetch operations:

- *Address:* The starting virtual address for a prefetch.
- *Block Size:* The size (bytes) of each block.
- *Block Number:* The number of blocks to prefetch.
- *Block Stride:* A constant stride (measured in bytes) used for the calculation of the next block address.
- *Epoch:* This field is used by ECM as described later.

[1]We assume that the L2 cache is physically tagged.

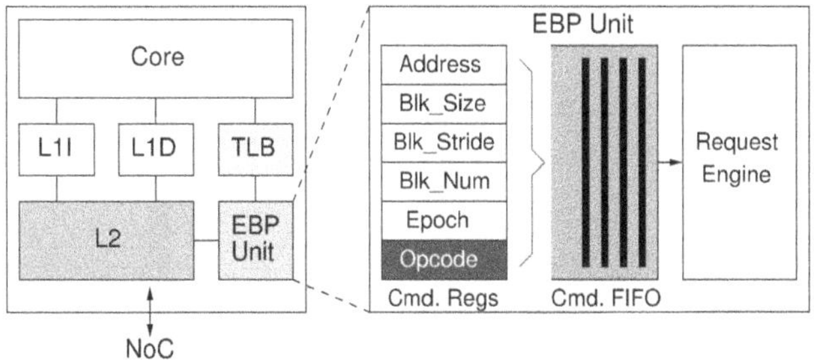

Figure 1: EBP Overview

- *Opcode:* This field marks whether this data will be used as Read-Only or Read-Write. Based on this value, the associated cache-lines are requested with the proper coherence permissions: *Shared* or *Exclusive*.

Upon writing the "Opcode" register, all command fields are atomically enqueued in a "Command FIFO" and each command is served in-order by the internal "Request Engine" (Figure 1). The "Request Engine" converts each memory range into multiple cache-line aligned requests, performs address translation, and probes the cache. If a cache-line is present in the cache with the appropriate coherence permissions, then the request is skipped. If the cache-line is not present, or present with "limited" permissions, then a new request is sent to the coherence directory to fetch or upgrade the cache-line. In case a cache set is full, an old cache-line is evicted to make space. The intermediate "Command FIFO" supports multiple outstanding prefetch operations (32 in our implementation). The "Request Engine" also supports multiple outstanding cache-line requests, the number of which is however limited by the number of miss status handling registers (MSHRs). We assume that up to 8 outstanding requests can be issued without occupying all MSHRs.

3.2 Epoch-based Cache Management

Current cache replacement policies base their decisions on the recent history of referenced cache-blocks and try to predict which blocks will be referenced in the near future. They typically assume that the most recent or the most referenced blocks should remain in the cache [21] and try to optimize this behavior. However, the behavior of task-based execution models is substantially different, since after the lifetime of a task, the reference history of many cache-blocks used by the completed task may be useless and can negatively affect performance.

The replacement decisions become even more challenging in the presence of prefetching [36], e.g. when utilizing EBP. The use of EBP has the potential to effectively hide memory latency when the software can initiate it ahead of time, before data is requested by a task, for example when the runtime software uses double-buffering. However, the effectiveness of EBP is also affected by the ability of the cache to keep the prefetched data. Prefetching is known to cause cache pollution, therefore double-buffering data for the next task may evict data needed by the current task. Likewise, the current task may evict data prefetched for the next task.

These inefficiencies offer an opportunity to improve performance by making the cache aware of the tasks' lifetimes and datasets. We propose *Epoch-based Cache Management*

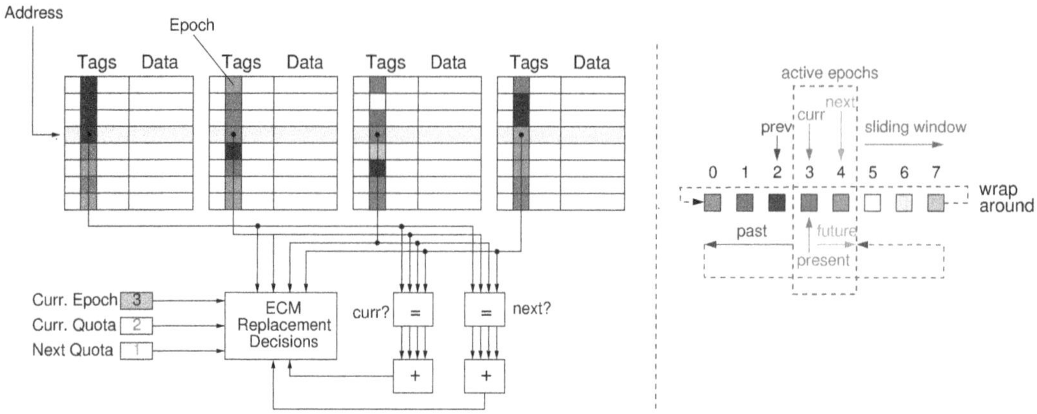

Figure 2: ECM Overview

(ECM), a hardware mechanism that allows software to expose the knowledge of tasks and their requirements to the cache hierarchy in order to improve replacement decisions and optimize cache locality.

ECM is based on the notion of *Epoch*, which is defined as the time period during which a task executes, which we refer to as the *task lifetime*. Epochs are tracked locally on each core, in the form of a memory-mapped register visible to the local cache. Every memory access that arrives from the processor, is augmented in hardware with the current epoch and marks the corresponding cache-line. The epoch number is kept in the tag of each cache-line and occupies a few bits, e.g. 3 bits to support 8 epochs. ECM only requires the software to advance the epoch register at the beginning of a new task. The epochs are free to wrap around without any special handling.

The epoch number is essentially an short identifier that allows the cache to distinguish between data that belong to different tasks while maintaining a short history, i.e. data accessed by the last 8 tasks. The replacement policy can use the epoch numbers contained in the tags of each set and the current epoch register, in order to quickly filter old data and decide which cache-lines to victimize when needed. This strategy effectively prioritizes data used by the current task. When all cache-lines in a set belong to the current epoch, the replacement policy operates as it would do without epochs and uses the reference state of cache-lines (e.g. LRU bits).

However, when the runtime employs double-buffering optimizations and uses EBP, the cache must also handle another active task context, i.e. the next task and its data. The cache has to ensure that data between these active task contexts do not interfere in a destructive manner. To address the latter issue, we introduce software-controlled *Quotas* for epochs and their corresponding tasks. ECM offers a set of memory-mapped quota registers that enables software to assign a portion of cache space for each "active" epoch. We consider active epochs to be the "current" and "next" epoch, which correspond to the current task and the first waiting task in the processor's task queue. Older epochs do not have quotas. The software assigns quotas, expressed in number of bytes for the active epochs, using the memory footprint of each task, in order reserve cache space for the task. We implement this scheme in private L2 caches.

The underlying hardware mechanism uses the quotas to construct flexible and lightweight partitions for each epoch. When a quota is assigned, the byte quantity is converted into equivalent number of ways, depending on the size and associativity of the cache. The scheme rounds up the quota to the closest multiple of equivalent cache ways and handles cases of over-booking; the sum of quotas cannot exceed the number of cache ways. ECM enforces the quotas in a best-effort manner and guarantees that each active epoch can allocate *at least* its assigned quota (ways) per set. However, an active epoch is allowed to allocate more than the assigned ways in a set, when another active epoch does not fully utilize its quota. Moreover, an active epoch is also free to use cache-lines that belong to old epochs.

The replacement policy counts the allocated ways for the active epochs in a per-set basis and based on the quotas, decides whether an epoch can allocate more space. When a cache set is fully utilized with cache-lines that belong to active epochs, the replacement policy selects a victim that belongs to the requesting epoch, by consulting only the reference state bits (e.g. LRU bits) that belong to this epoch. Cache-line allocation for an active epoch is not tied to specific cache ways but is instead dynamically selected. An overview of ECM is illustrated in Figure 2.

When EBP is used in conjunction with ECM, each prefetch request is augmented with the "Epoch" field of the prefetch command, to signify whether this request belongs to the current or the next epoch. In addition, EBP probes ECM to discover whether its quota has exceeded, i.e. the corresponding set is full with cache-lines that belong to active epochs. When a set is full, EBP throttles prefetching by skipping requests destined to this specific set, in order to avoid evicting cache-lines that were recently prefetched.

ECM can be easily implemented at low hardware cost, and in fact we have already implemented it along with EBP in an FPGA prototype [25]. Adding 3 epoch bits per tag in a 256KB 8-way set-associative L2 cache has a memory overhead of only 0.5%.

4. EXPERIMENTAL METHODOLOGY

4.1 Simulation Infrastructure

We use an execution-driven simulation framework that couples Pin [24] and GEMS [26] to model the memory hierarchy in detail. We use Garnet [1] for NoC modeling and Dramsim2 [31] for the off-chip DRAM memory controllers.

Master Core	out-of-order superscalar at 2 GHz, 4-wide, 128-entry ROB, 96-entry LD/ST queue,
Worker Cores	up to 64, in-order at 2 GHz
L1 Caches	32KB, 4-way, 64-byte block, 1 port, 1-cycle, LRU, split I/D
L2 Caches	private 256KB, 8-way, 64-byte block, 2-port, 8-cycles, NRU, 16 MSHRs, unified, coherent, inclusive
Coherence	MESI directory per memory controller, 4 virtual networks, 10-cycles, non-blocking
L2 Prefetcher	PC-based stride, 64 streams, degree of 4
NoC	2D Mesh at 2 GHz, 2 cores per node, 16-byte control packets, 80-byte data packets, 16-byte links, 1-cycle link, 5-stage routers, 4 virtual networks, 4 VCs per virtual network
DRAM	4 dual-channel memory controllers, 16GB DDR3 SDRAM, PC3-15400, 8 banks, FR-FCFS scheduling policy
EBP	32 commands, 8 outstanding requests
ECM	8 epochs using 3 bits per L2 tag

Table 1: Detailed architectural parameters for the simulated system.

Power estimation is for 32nm technology, uses Cacti 6.5 [17] for the caches and directories, Orion 2.0 [23] for the on-chip interconnect, and the infrastructure of Dramsim2 for the off-chip DRAM power. Our framework supports the x86 ISA and simulates user-level application and library code.

We model a tiled manycore architecture with directory-based cache coherence and distributed directories (per memory controller). Our design uses up to 64 in-order cores with a two-level private cache hierarchy, similar to the Intel Xeon-Phi Coprocessor [19]. We also add an out-of-order superscalar core for the role of the master processor that runs the main application thread and spawns tasks. Further details for simulation parameters appear in Table 1.

For the evaluation of our proposed architectural support we also implement a per-core PC-based stride prefetcher [5] that prefetches cache-lines into the L2 cache. We also model a state-of-the-art prefetch-aware replacement policy [36] for the purpose of comparison with ECM.

4.2 Runtime Software

We implement an in-house runtime system for the task-based dataflow programming model that supports the basic task spawning and waiting constructs as discussed in Section 2. It supports two-dimensional address ranges for declaring task footprints and uses a block-based approach with arbitrary granularity for dynamic dependence analysis [32]. Pragmas are converted into calls to the underlying runtime library using an in-house source-to-source compiler that is based on CIL [27].

The runtime, in its current form, can utilize an arbitrary number of worker threads but only a single master thread can spawn tasks. To issue tasks, the compiler generated code builds task descriptors containing: *(i)* the function pointer of each task, *(ii)* the base memory pointer for each argument, *(iii)* the dimensions of each argument, and *(iv)* the argument type describing the memory side-effects (input, output, inout). Upon task spawning, the runtime analyzes inter-task dependencies using internal metadata for the application memory and decides whether tasks are eligible for immediate execution. Ready (independent) tasks are scheduled to worker threads, while dependent tasks are kept in internal data structures until all their dependencies are satisfied. Eventually, all tasks become eligible for scheduling. The runtime fully supports out-of-order execution of tasks. The implementation utilizes private per-worker FIFO queues to schedule tasks and follows a *round-robin lowest occupancy first* scheduling policy to achieve load balancing in the presence of unbalanced tasks.

When the runtime executes on architectures that implement EBP and ECM, it utilizes our hardware support to optimize task-based execution. It prefetches task data in a double-buffered fashion using EBP and leverages ECM to manage the local cache resources. The runtime advances ECM epochs on task boundaries and assigns epoch quotas to tasks based on their memory footprint.

4.3 Benchmarks

We use six widely used benchmark applications, after converting them to the task-based dataflow programming model using *C pragmas*. Most of these benchmarks originate from the SmpSS distribution and are sketched in [29]. All benchmarks accept a block size as input parameter to allow controlling the memory footprint of tasks and, in effect, the task granularity. The benchmarks are the following:
Matrix Multiplication: An implementation of dense matrix multiplication using the BLAS [8] package. We run the benchmark with 1000 × 1000 double precision matrices.
Jacobi: The iterative 5-point stencil linear equation solver. We run Jacobi with 1000 × 1000 double precision matrices.
FFT: The 2D Fast Fourier Transform uses the FFTW [13] package for 1D FFT computations and performs transposition and twiddling in-place. We run FFT with 1M points.
Bitonic Sort: A comparison-based sorting kernel. The implementation uses Quicksort to create an initial bitonic sequence and then performs a logarithmic number of merge phases. We sort 1M long integers.
Cholesky: The Cholesky decomposition of a positive definite matrix into the product of a lower triangular matrix and its conjugate transpose. The implementation uses routines from the BLAS [8] package. We run Cholesky with a 1280 × 1280 double precision matrix.
Sparse LU: The LU factorization of a sparse matrix as the product of a lower triangular matrix and an upper triangular matrix. We run Sparse LU with a 1280 × 1280 double precision matrix.

5. EVALUATION

5.1 Performance Analysis

We evaluate the performance of our proposed architectural support (EBP and ECM) by comparing it to a baseline without and with HW-only prefetching. We run the benchmarks with block sizes that generate fine-grain tasks, each with a memory footprint size approximately equal the L1 cache size (32KB). Figure 3 shows percentage of performance improvement (execution time) over the baseline without prefetching for runs with up to 64 worker cores, for three configurations: *(i)* hardware L2 prefetcher (HWP), *(ii)* EBP, and *(iii)* EBP together with ECM. All measurements include the software runtime overhead. We also plot the speedup achieved by the baseline without prefetching, normalized to single core serial execution without runtime overhead (ignore pragmas), to show how each benchmark scales with the number or cores in our implementation.

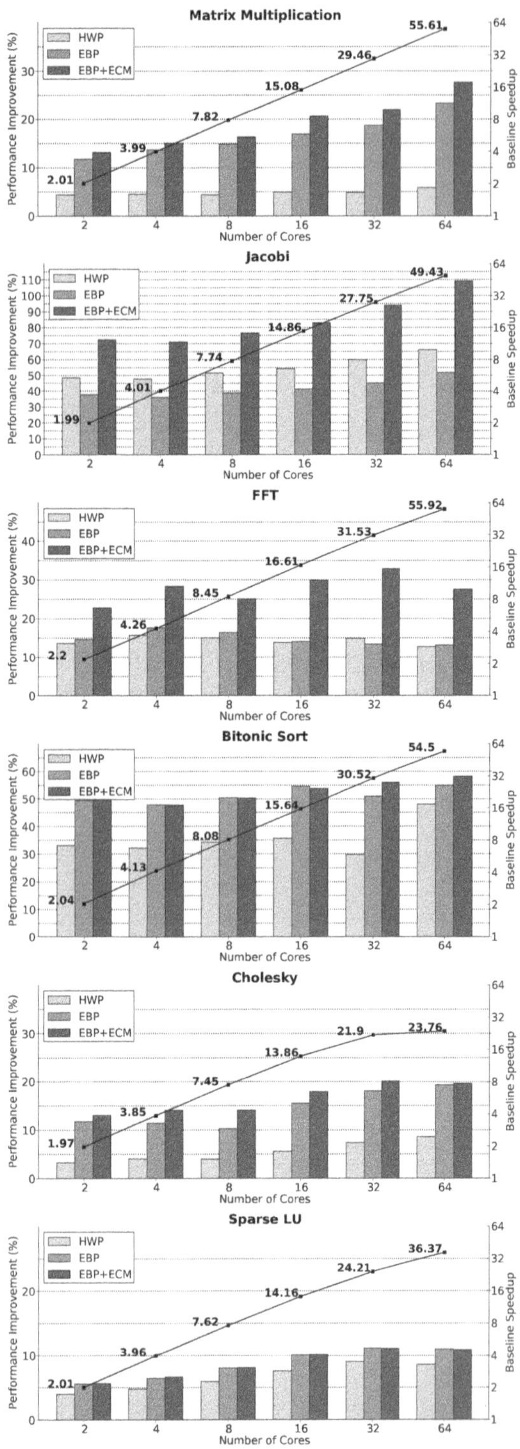

Figure 3: Performance improvement over the baseline without prefetching for each of the following configurations: (i) Hardware Prefetcher (HWP), (ii) Explicit Bulk Prefetcher (EBP), (iii) Explicit Bulk Prefetcher with Epoch-based Cache Management (EBP+ECM). The line shows the speedup of the baseline, normalized to the single core serial code execution time that ignores the task pragmas (no runtime overhead).

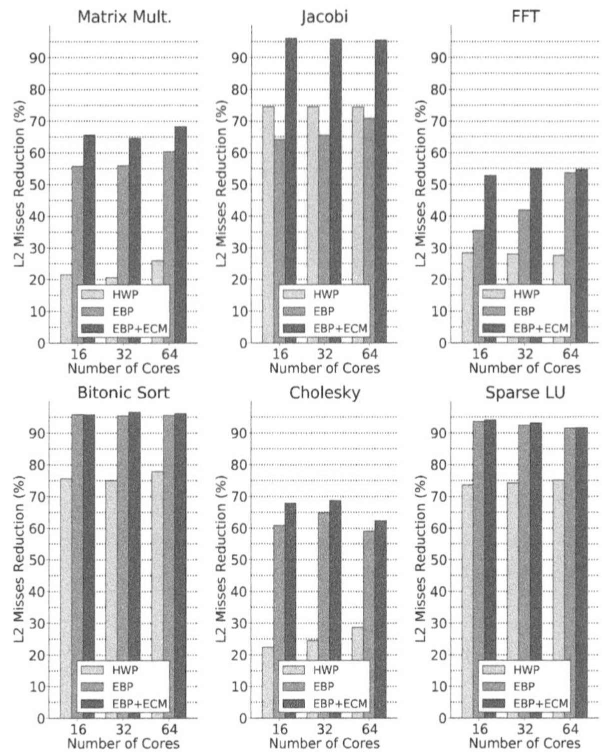

Figure 4: Reduction in the number of L2 misses over the baseline without prefetching when running with 16, 32, and 64 worker cores (higher is better).

We observe that the configuration with EBP in conjunction with ECM always outperforms HWP. For the benchmarks that scale almost linearly (Matrix multiplication, Jacobi, FFT, and Bitonic) the improvement over HWP for the higher core counts (>=16) ranges from 15% in FFT to 43% in Jacobi, which is the most memory intensive benchmark. Bitonic is 26% faster in 32 cores but appears 10% faster in 64 cores because the master thread saturates and cannot generate enough tasks for double-buffering. Matrix multiplication is consistently better by more than 16%. For benchmarks that do not scale linearly and are more compute intensive (Cholesky, Sparse LU) the improvement ranges from 3% in Sparse LU up to 11% in Cholesky. EBP alone (without ECM) is not always better than HWP. In Jacobi it performs worse than HWP by more than 13% and in FFT it achieves almost the same performance. In the rest of the benchmarks, EBP alone performs either worse than EBP+ECM (5% in Matrix multiplication) or achieves the same performance (Sparse LU). On average, for the 64-core setup, EBP+ECM is *17% faster* than the HW-only prefetcher and *13% faster* than EBP alone.

To gain more insight into the latter results, we study the impact of EBP and ECM in the number of L2 misses. Figure 4 presents the reduction in L2 misses over the baseline without prefetching for the three configurations and for setups with high cores counts (>=16). EBP with ECM significantly reduces the number of L2 misses, outperforms HWP, and achieves reduction of more than 90% on half of the benchmarks (Jacobi, Bitonic, Sparse LU). HWP performs relative well in a number of benchmarks (Jacobi, Bitonic,

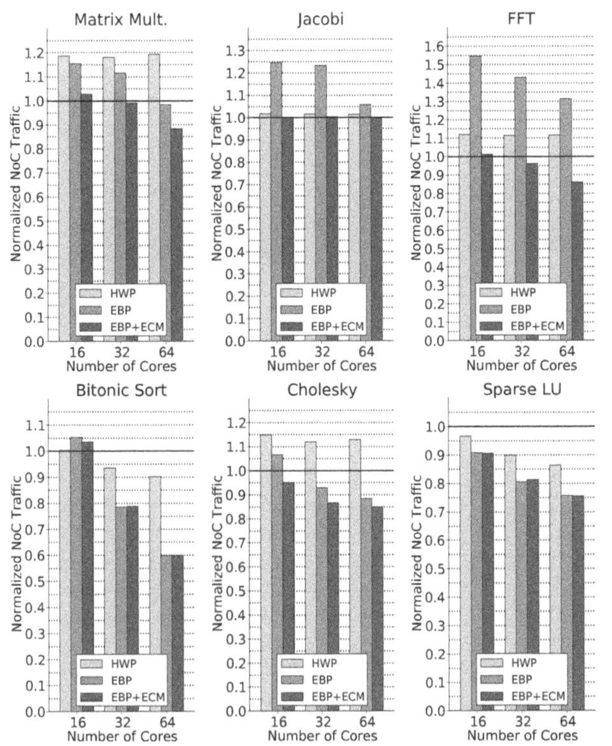

Figure 5: NoC traffic normalized to the baseline without prefetching when running with 16, 32, and 64 worker cores (lower is better).

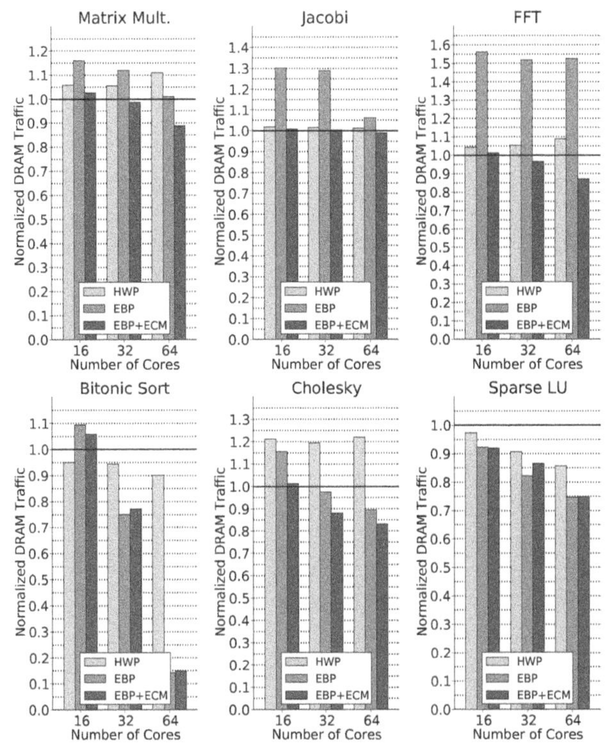

Figure 6: DRAM traffic normalized to the baseline without prefetching when running with 16, 32, and 64 worker cores (lower is better).

Sparse LU) and reduces the associated L2 misses by up to 75%, however, in the rest of the benchmarks it cannot identify the memory access patterns accurately and the reduction in L2 misses falls below 30%. On the other hand, EBP with ECM consistently provides more than 18% additional reduction in L2 misses over HWP. The additional reduction in L2 misses ranges from over 18% (Jacobi, FFT, Bitonic, Sparse LU) to 44% (Matrix multiplication, Cholesky). EBP alone cannot always perform better than HWP (e.g. Jacobi) and is less effective than EBP+ECM. When EBP prefetches data and requires L2 replacements, the replacement policy cannot distinguish between old task data, current task data and next task data, thus the victim selection is not optimal, causes interference, and reduces the effectiveness of prefetching. On average, for the 64-core setup, EBP+ECM reduces L2 misses by an *additional 26%* over the HW-only prefetcher and an *additional 7%* over EBP alone.

5.2 Memory Traffic Analysis

We study the implications of EBP and ECM on the memory system by measuring the on-chip and off-chip traffic. Given that the memory traffic is sensitive to task-scheduling, i.e. which task is executed on which core and in what order, we use a fixed off-line schedule that was captured when running the application on the baseline system. We replay the same schedule in the runtime for each of the three configurations. We present the results for on-chip network (NoC) traffic in Figure 5 and for off-chip memory (DRAM) traffic in Figure 6 for setups with high core counts (>=16). The traffic volumes are normalized to the traffic generated by the baseline without prefetching for each configuration.

The results indicate that EBP with ECM does not generate excessive traffic when compared to the baseline without prefetching. In some cases, EBP with ECM generates even less traffic than the baseline. On the contrary, HWP results in increased traffic on most benchmarks because of inaccuracy in its predictions and the associated cache pollution. The improved traffic behavior observed in the 64-core setups is partly attributed to the increased on-chip cache size when the number of cores increases; on high core counts a larger portion of the benchmarks' datasets fits on-chip[2]. In the presence of prefetching (either HWP or EBP), data from the producers' caches are transferred earlier to the consumers' caches (before they are evicted), thus saving traffic. However, the improved behavior of EBP+ECM is also because of the smarter cache management of the task datasets and the throttling technique employed (Section 3.2).

EBP+ECM generates less on-chip traffic on all benchmarks when compared to both HWP and EBP alone, Figure 5. On the other hand, EBP alone generates significantly more traffic in a number of benchmarks (Matrix multiplication, Jacobi, FFT) which can be up to 50% higher than the baseline (e.g. FFT on 16 cores). EBP alone prefetches the requested cache-lines blindly in the cache and incurs destructive interference between data belonging to the active task contexts (current and next). When EBP prefetches cache-lines that map to fully-occupied sets with data from active tasks, the replacement policy has to evict useful data, whereas ECM throttles prefetching for these sets by consult-

[2]We did not use larger datasets because of the prohibitive simulation times.

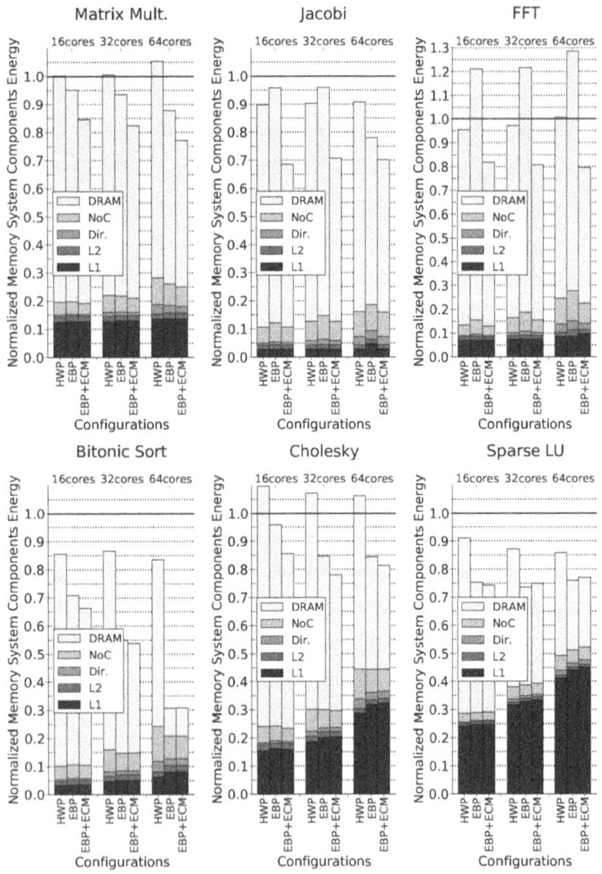

Figure 7: Dynamic energy consumption of the memory system's components. The energy is normalized to the baseline without prefetching when running with 16, 32, and 64 worker cores (lower is better).

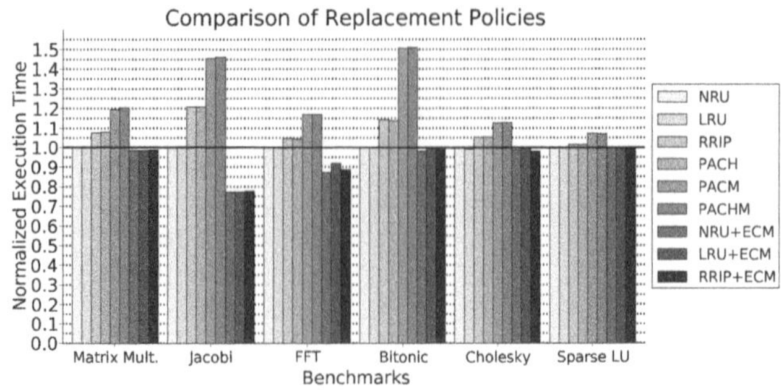

Figure 8: Comparison of replacement policies when EBP is utilized, running with 16 worker cores.

ing the epochs and their associated quotas. On average, for the 64-core setup, EBP+ECM generates *21% less* on-chip traffic than the HW-only prefetcher and *11% less* traffic than EBP alone.

The off-chip DRAM traffic shows a similar trend with on-chip traffic (Figure 6) and the pathological cases of EBP described earlier are again clearly shown. On average, for the 64-core setup, EBP+ECM generates *28% less* off-chip DRAM traffic than the HW-only prefetcher and *15% less* traffic than EBP alone.

Bitonic presents a noteworthy behavior on 64 cores, where EBP reduces off-chip traffic by more than 80% over the baseline. This behavior is explained by the nature of comparison-based sorting which leads to a coherence pattern where data come as shared (to compare) and then upgrade to exclusive (to swap). In Bitonic, the application has marked this data as *inout* and EBP fetches them directly in exclusive mode. This avoids writebacks when data is dirty in another cache and downgrades due to the reads required for comparisons, assuming a MESI cache coherence protocol.

5.3 Power Analysis

Following the methodology discussed in Section 5.2, we use the simulator infrastructure to measure the dynamic energy consumption[3] of the memory system components (L1, L2, Directory, DRAM) and the on-chip interconnect (NoC). We present our results using breakdowns in Figure 7. In almost all the benchmarks, the dynamic energy consumption is dominated by the off-chip DRAM, while the second major component is the L1 cache. The most important finding is the reduction of DRAM energy when prefetching is used (either HWP or EBP). This behavior is explained by the open-row management and the scheduling policy of the memory controller (FR-FCFS [30]). With prefetching, the memory controller has the potential to serve more requests from open rows and reduce the number of row activations and precharges, which contribute significantly to DRAM energy. With EBP, task data is requested in bulk and close in time, thus offering the memory controller more opportunities to exploit open row buffer locality. Moreover, the significant reduction in on-chip and DRAM traffic we observe when using EBP+ECM (Section 5.2) offers additional energy savings. On average, for the 64-core setup, EBP+ECM consumes *28% less* energy than the HW-only prefetcher and *11% less* energy than EBP alone.

5.4 Comparing Cache Replacement Policies

We explore a number of candidate replacement policies for use with EBP and present our findings for 16-cores in Figure 8. We examine the typical NRU and LRU replacement policies, RRIP [21], and the state-of-the-art prefetch-aware replacement policy called PACMan [36] in its three variants: PACH, PACM, PACHM[4]. Moreover, given that ECM is versatile and can be used in conjunction with many replacement policies, we also evaluate three variants with ECM: NRU+ECM, LRU+ECM, RRIP+ECM. We observe that when EBP is utilized, the PACMan variants perform worse than NRU and LRU, whereas the ECM variants can be up to 22% faster than LRU (Jacobi). In PACMan, the reference history that is accumulated during a task lifetime is useless for the next task and requires several misses before cache-lines with old task data become candidates for replacement. This behavior appears to have a negative effect on performance. On the other hand, the ECM epochs help to effectively filter "old" cache-lines and allow the data prefetched for the next task to be preserved in the cache.

[3]Note that we do not include static energy measurements which are influenced by execution time, thus our comparisons are conservative.

[4]For RRIP and PACMan we use 2-bit values and the version without set-dueling.

6. RELATED WORK

There is a vast amount of previous work on hardware prefetchers that try to predict memory access patterns and prefetch data without any software guidance such as [11, 12]. However, we propose a hardware-software approach for prefetching which is based on the fully-accurate knowledge about task memory footprints, known a-priori by the runtime software (before tasks start executing).

Guided region prefetching (GRP) [34] is a related scheme that augments load instructions with compiler generated hints to improve the accuracy of a hardware prefetcher. GRP requires sophisticated compiler analysis, the hints are not always accurate, and the prefetches are triggered by L2 misses during the execution of code. Our approach differs from GRP, since we use fully accurate memory footprints and the data are fetched early before task execution with the potential to hide all L2 misses.

Most pertinent to this work is Streamware [14] and the related architectural support [15] which target stream processing. They propose a software programmable Stream-Load-Store (SLS) hardware unit, that resembles EBP, and is used by the runtime software. However, they do not tackle the problem of cache pollution and interference due to prefetching, as we propose with the use of ECM. ARM's Preload Engine (PLE) [3], which is also similar to EBP, does not address cache pollution either.

"KILL" [20] and "Evict-me" [35] are two related schemes that try to improve cache replacement decisions and reduce pollution in the presence of prefetching. Both of them are based on sophisticated compiler analysis and instruction hints (using ISA modification) that are used in conjunction with the replacement policy. These approaches try to identify which data will not be used in the future and mark this data appropriately. In the task-based execution context, this approach could only be useful for the data of the current task, while there can be no information about the behavior of the next task, the data of which can be prefetched. In addition, when a task completes, such schemes would require massive marking (or eviction) of each task's dataset. The latter could be an erroneous behavior if some of the data is reused by the next task. ECM on the other hand, easily handles all these cases and only requires software to advance the local epoch. Moreover, the epoch quotas offer an additional criterion to throttle prefetching.

PACMan [36] is also a relevant prefetch-aware cache management scheme that builds on top of RRIP [21]. PACMan tries to reduce cache pollution and prefetch interference by handling demand and prefetch requests separately. To achieve this effect, PACMan modifies the cache insertion and hit promotion policies. Although this scheme might perform well for intra-task prefetching (when data for the current task is prefetched), it can not handle inter-task prefetching. ECM addresses prefetching across tasks and helps throttling prefetches to reduce traffic and pollution. We evaluated the performance of PACMan as a candidate cache replacement scheme for use with EBP in Section 5.4.

7. CONCLUSIONS

This paper presented a hardware-software approach to improve cache locality and optimize the execution of fine-grain tasks. We proposed the *Explicit Bulk Prefetcher (EBP)* and *Epoch-based Cache Management (ECM)* to allow runtime software to prefetch task data and guide replacement decisions in caches. Using EBP and ECM the runtime software can exploit its available information about task memory footprints and task lifetimes, and expose this information to the memory hierarchy with minimal software overhead. ECM assists the cache replacement policy to select victims and removes cache pollution and prefetch interference when EBP is used. We show that EBP in conjunction with ECM outperforms HW-only prefetchers, improves performance by an average of 17%, generates on average 26% fewer L2 misses, and consumes on average 28% less energy in the components of the memory system.

8. ACKNOWLEDGMENTS

We thankfully acknowledge the support of the European Commission under the 7th Framework Programs through the ENCORE (FP7-ICT-248647) and HiPEAC3 (FP7-ICT-287759) projects. This research is also supported by EPSRC through the GEMSCLAIM project (grant EP/K017594/1).

9. REFERENCES

[1] N. Agarwal, T. Krishna, L.-S. Peh, and N. K. Jha. Garnet: A detailed on-chip network model inside a full-system simulator. In *Proc. of IEEE Int. Symp. on Performance Analysis of Systems and Software*, ISPASS '09, pages 33–42, 2009.

[2] M. D. Allen, S. Sridharan, and G. S. Sohi. Serialization sets: a dynamic dependence-based parallel execution model. In *Proc. of the ACM Symp. on Principles and Practice of Parallel Programming*, PPoPP '09, pages 85–96, 2009.

[3] ARM Ltd. Cortex A9 Preload Engine. http://infocenter.arm.com/.

[4] E. Ayguadé, N. Copty, A. Duran, J. Hoeflinger, Y. Lin, F. Massaioli, X. Teruel, P. Unnikrishnan, and G. Zhang. The design of OpenMP tasks. *IEEE Trans. Parallel Distributed Systems*, 20(3):404–418, 2009.

[5] J.-L. Baer and T.-F. Chen. An effective on-chip preloading scheme to reduce data access penalty. In *Proc. of the ACM/IEEE Conf. on Supercomputing*, Supercomputing '91, pages 176–186, 1991.

[6] M. Bauer, S. Treichler, E. Slaughter, and A. Aiken. Legion: expressing locality and independence with logical regions. In *Proc. of the Int. Conf. on High Performance Computing, Networking, Storage and Analysis*, SC '12, pages 66–77, 2012.

[7] M. J. Best, S. Mottishaw, C. Mustard, M. Roth, A. Fedorova, and A. Brownsword. Synchronization via scheduling: techniques for efficiently managing shared state. In *Proc. of the ACM Conf. on Programming Language Design and Implementation*, PLDI '11, pages 640–652, 2011.

[8] L. S. Blackford et al. An Updated Set of Basic Linear Algebra Subprograms (BLAS). *ACM Transactions on Mathematical Software*, 28:135–151, 2001.

[9] R. D. Blumofe, C. F. Joerg, B. C. Kuszmaul, C. E. Leiserson, K. H. Randall, and Y. Zhou. Cilk: an efficient multithreaded runtime system. In *Proc. of the ACM Symp. on Principles and Practice of Parallel Programming*, PPOPP '95, pages 207–216, 1995.

[10] R. Bocchino et al. A type and effect system for deterministic parallel java. In *Proc. of the ACM Conf.*

on Object Oriented Programming Systems Languages and Applications, OOPSLA '09, pages 97–116, 2009.

[11] J. F. Cantin, M. H. Lipasti, and J. E. Smith. Stealth prefetching. In *Proc. of the Int. Conf. on Architectural support for programming languages and operating systems*, ASPLOS XII, pages 274–282, 2006.

[12] P. Diaz and M. Cintra. Stream chaining: exploiting multiple levels of correlation in data prefetching. In *Proc. of the Int. Symp. on Computer architecture*, ISCA '09, pages 81–92, 2009.

[13] M. Frigo and S. G. Johnson. The design and implementation of FFTW3. *Proc. of the IEEE*, 93(2):216–231, 2005.

[14] J. Gummaraju, J. Coburn, Y. Turner, and M. Rosenblum. Streamware: programming general-purpose multicore processors using streams. In *Proc. of the Int. Conf. on Architectural support for programming languages and operating systems*, ASPLOS XIII, pages 297–307, 2008.

[15] J. Gummaraju, M. Erez, J. Coburn, M. Rosenblum, and W. J. Dally. Architectural support for the stream execution model on general-purpose processors. In *Proc. of the Int. Conf. on Parallel Architecture and Compilation Techniques*, PACT '07, pages 3–12, 2007.

[16] Y. Guo, J. Zhao, V. Cave, and V. Sarkar. Slaw: a scalable locality-aware adaptive work-stealing scheduler for multi-core systems. In *Proc. of the ACM Symp. on Principles and Practice of Parallel Programming*, PPoPP '10, pages 341–342, 2010.

[17] HP Laboratories. Cacti 6.5: An integrated cache and memory access time, cycle time, area, leakage, and dynamic power model. http://www.hpl.hp.com/research/cacti/.

[18] Intel Corporation. Intel Threading Building Blocks (TBB). http://www.threadingbuildingblocks.org.

[19] Intel Corporation. The Intel Xeon Phi Coprocessor. http://www.intel.com/content/www/us/en/processors/xeon/xeon-phi-detail.html.

[20] P. Jain, S. Devadas, D. Engels, and L. Rudolph. Software-assisted cache replacement mechanisms for embedded systems. In *Proc. of the IEEE/ACM Int. Conf. on Computer-Aided Design*, ICCAD '01, pages 119–126, 2001.

[21] A. Jaleel, K. B. Theobald, S. C. Steely, Jr., and J. Emer. High performance cache replacement using re-reference interval prediction (RRIP). In *Proc. of the Int. Symp. on Computer Architecture*, ISCA '10, pages 60–71, 2010.

[22] J. A. Kahle et al. Introduction to the Cell Multiprocessor. *IBM Journal of Research and Develeopment*, 49(4/5):589–604, 2005.

[23] A. B. Kahng, B. Li, L.-S. Peh, and K. Samadi. Orion 2.0: A fast and accurate noc power and area model for early-stage design space exploration. In *Design, Automation & Test in Europe Conference*, DATE '09, pages 423–428, 2009.

[24] C.-K. Luk, R. Cohn, R. Muth, H. Patil, A. Klauser, G. Lowney, S. Wallace, V. J. Reddi, and K. Hazelwood. Pin: Building customized program analysis tools with dynamic instrumentation. In *Proc. of the ACM Conf. on Programming Language Design and Implementation*, PLDI '05, pages 190–200, 2005.

[25] S. Lyberis, G. Kalokerinos, M. Lygerakis, V. Papaefstathiou, D. Tsaliagkos, M. Katevenis, D. Pnevmatikatos, and D. Nikolopoulos. Formic: Cost-efficient and scalable prototyping of manycore architectures. In *Proc. of the IEEE Symp. on Field-Programmable Custom Computing Machines*, FCCM '12, pages 61–64, 2012.

[26] M. M. K. Martin, D. J. Sorin, B. M. Beckmann, M. R. Marty, M. Xu, A. R. Alameldeen, K. E. Moore, M. D. Hill, and D. A. Wood. Multifacet's general execution-driven multiprocessor simulator (GEMS) toolset. *SIGARCH Computer Architecture News*, 33(4):92–99, 2005.

[27] G. C. Necula, S. McPeak, S. P. Rahul, and W. Weimer. Cil: Intermediate language and tools for analysis and transformation of c programs. In *Proc. of the Int. Conf. on Compiler Construction*, CC '02, pages 213–228, 2002.

[28] J. Perez, R. Badia, and J. Labarta. A dependency-aware task-based programming environment for multi-core architectures. In *Proc. IEEE Conf. on Cluster Computing*, CLUSTER '08, pages 142 –151, 2008.

[29] J. M. Perez, R. M. Badia, and J. Labarta. Handling task dependencies under strided and aliased references. In *Proc. of the ACM Int. Conf. on Supercomputing*, ICS '10, pages 263–274, 2010.

[30] S. Rixner, W. J. Dally, U. J. Kapasi, P. Mattson, and J. D. Owens. Memory access scheduling. In *Proc. of the Int. Symp. on Computer architecture*, ISCA '00, pages 128–138, 2000.

[31] P. Rosenfeld, E. Cooper-Balis, and B. Jacob. Dramsim2: A cycle accurate memory system simulator. *Comp. Arch. Letters*, 10(1):16 –19, 2011.

[32] G. Tzenakis, A. Papatriantafyllou, J. Kesapides, P. Pratikakis, H. Vandierendonck, and D. S. Nikolopoulos. BDDT: block-level dynamic dependence analysis for deterministic task-based parallelism. In *Proc. of the ACM Symp. on Principles and Practice of Parallel Programming*, PPoPP '12, 2012.

[33] H. Vandierendonck, G. Tzenakis, and D. S. Nikolopoulos. A unified scheduler for recursive and task dataflow parallelism. In *Proc. of the Int. Conf. on Parallel Architectures and Compilation Techniques*, PACT '11, pages 1–11, 2011.

[34] Z. Wang, D. Burger, K. S. McKinley, S. K. Reinhardt, and C. C. Weems. Guided region prefetching: a cooperative hardware/software approach. In *Proc. of the Int. Symp. on Computer architecture*, ISCA '03, pages 388–398, 2003.

[35] Z. Wang, K. S. McKinley, A. L. Rosenberg, and C. C. Weems. Using the compiler to improve cache replacement decisions. In *Proc. of the Int. Conf. on Parallel Architectures and Compilation Techniques*, PACT '02, pages 199–208, 2002.

[36] C.-J. Wu, A. Jaleel, M. Martonosi, S. C. Steely, Jr., and J. Emer. PACMan: prefetch-aware cache management for high performance caching. In *Proc. of the IEEE/ACM Int. Symp. on Microarchitecture*, MICRO-44, pages 442–453, 2011.

The Role of Computer Designers in Reverse-Engineering the Brain

Keynote Talk

James E. Smith
770 Big Flat Road
Missoula, Montana 59804
jes@ece.wisc.edu

ABSTRACT

A truly grand challenge for science in general, and for computer architects and designers in particular, is to understand the mammalian brain's computing paradigm and then construct a computing device that embodies that paradigm. Although computer designers have a potential role to play in solving this grand challenge, it is up to us to define that role. From a computer designer's perspective, I will illustrate the current understanding of the brain's computational paradigm by describing several examples from experimental neuroscience. I will suggest an architecture hierarchy and discuss issues that arise when translating from the complex, asynchronous, electro- chemical device, which is the brain, to a synchronous digital device capable of performing computation in a similar manner. This translation presents many difficult challenges that will require science-inspired insight and discovery, added to the challenges of engineering a very large, unconventional digital system. But, as difficult as they may be, these challenges provide almost unlimited opportunities for forward-looking, risk-taking computer architects and designers.

Categories and Subject Descriptors

F.1.1 [**Theory of Computation**]: Computation by Abstract Devices – Self-modifying machines (e.g., neural networks)

Keywords

brain architecture; digital neurons; reverse-engineering

ICS'13, June 10–14, 2013, Eugene, Oregon, USA.
ACM 978-1-4503-2130-3/13/06.

Short Biography

James E. Smith is Professor Emeritus in the Department of Electrical and Computer Engineering at the University of Wisconsin-Madison. He received his PhD from the University of Illinois in 1976. He then joined the faculty of the University of Wisconsin-Madison, teaching and conducting research – first in fault-tolerant computing, then in computer architecture. He retired from the University of Wisconsin in 2007. He has been involved in a number of computer research and development projects both as a faculty member at Wisconsin and in industry (Control Data Corporation, Astronautics Corporation, Cray Research, Google, and Intel).

Prof. Smith made a number of significant contributions to the development of superscalar processors. These contributions include the basic mechanisms for dynamic branch prediction and implementing precise traps. He has also studied vector processor architectures and worked on the development of a number of microarchitecture paradigms: decoupled processors, clustered processors, and trace processors. He received the 1999 ACM/IEEE Eckert-Mauchly Award for these contributions.

More recently, Prof. Smith has focused on the virtual machine abstraction as a technique for providing high performance and power efficiency through co-design and tight coupling of virtual machine hardware and software. He is co-author, with Ravi Nair, of a book on Virtual Machines. Currently, he works at home along the Clark Fork near Missoula, Montana.

Holistic Run-time Parallelism Management for Time and Energy Efficiency

Srinath Sridharan Gagan Gupta Gurindar S. Sohi

Computer Sciences Department
University of Wisconsin-Madison
{sridhara, gagang, sohi}@cs.wisc.edu

ABSTRACT

The ubiquity of parallel machines will necessitate time- and energy-efficient parallel execution of a program in a wide range of hardware and software environments. Prevalent parallel execution models can fail to be efficient. Unable to account for dynamic changes in the execution environment, they may create non-optimum parallelism, leading to underutilization of, or contention for, resources. We propose ParallelismDial (PD), a model to dynamically, continuously and judiciously adapt a program's degree of parallelism to the prevailing dynamic execution conditions. PD uses a holistic metric to measure system efficiency. The metric is used to systematically optimize the program's execution.

We incorporated PD in two different parallel programming models: Intel TBB, an industry standard, and Prometheus, a recent research proposal. Two prototypes were implemented and evaluated on stock multicore machines. Dedicated and multiprogrammed environments were considered. Experimental results show that the prototypes outperform the state-of-the-art approaches, on an average, by 15% on time and 31% on energy efficiency, in the dedicated environment. In the multiprogrammed environment, the savings are to the tune of 19% and 21% in time and energy, respectively.

Categories and Subject Descriptors

D.1.3 [**Programming Techniques**]: Concurrent Programming - Parallel programming; D.3.4 [**Programming Languages**]: Processors - Run-time environments

General Terms

Design, Experimentation, Measurement, Performance

Keywords

Autotuning, parallel programming, performance portability, performance tuning, run-time optimization

1. INTRODUCTION

Trends in computing systems have put a spotlight on efficient execution of parallel programs [14]. Multicores are now standard in computing devices, ranging from mobile handsets to HPC servers. While time efficiency was traditionally the primary goal, energy efficiency is now equally significant. System designers have turned to parallel programs to achieve both objectives.

Multiple factors influence a parallel program's efficiency. In addition to the customary system artifacts (e.g., cache sizes), they include: (i) the parallelism exposed by the developer, and (ii) the interactions of the program's concurrent computations with each other and the host system. Too little parallelism can underutilize the system. Excess parallelism, on the other hand, can create contention for resources, such as processors, caches, main memory, bus, disk, other I/O, etc. Severe contention can lead to inefficient program execution, even worse than sequential execution. Hence performance optimization requires matching a program's parallelism to the execution environment.

Challenges to efficient execution in future systems will be further compounded by the dynamically changing operating conditions. Multiprogrammed platforms, executing a statically unknown mix of programs, will make continuously varying resources available to programs. Increasingly unreliable hardware will further exacerbate the variability [7].

In the past, efficiency was a concern for a select few parallel-program developers, but in the future it will be for many more. Until recently a small set of experts developed parallel programs for a very small set of machines. They tuned programs using intimate knowledge of the host, e.g., its microarchitecture. Often, they could assume the host was entirely available to them, and expect little or no interference from other programs. Going forward, we expect a multitude of developers to program commodity parallel systems, e.g., the vast array of cell phones, laptops, desktops, etc. We expect programs to be written without the detailed knowledge of the hardware, software, and operating conditions, e.g., resource demands of programs co-scheduled on an unknown system in a data center. Further, given the possibly large number of diverse target hosts, portability will be highly desired.

To achieve efficient program execution, it will be daunting for common programmers to account for the often complex and non-intuitive factors related to program behavior, operating conditions and system characteristics.

Therefore, we believe, optimizing performance of a parallel program on future systems will require automatic, dy-

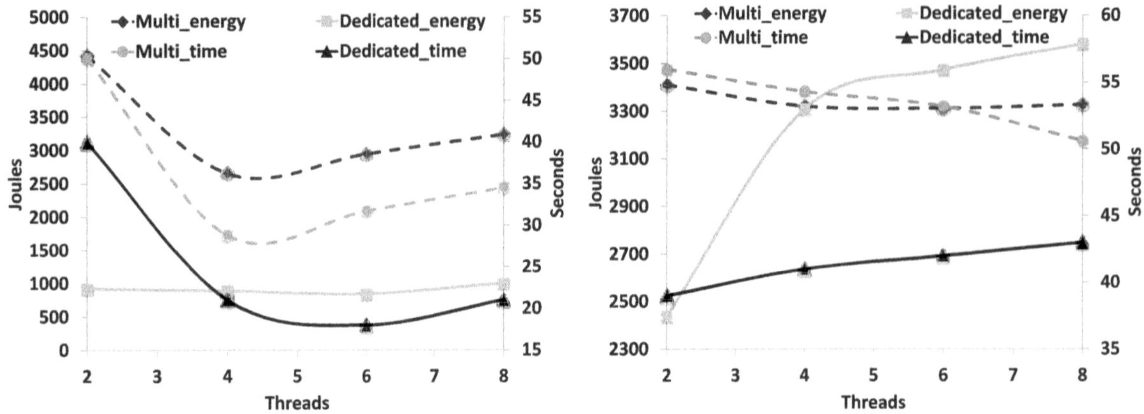

Figure 1: Execution time and energy trends of two programs, RE and Stream, in dedicated and multiprogrammed environments on a Core i7-2600 workstation.

namic and continuous harmonization of its parallelism with the execution environment, while being agnostic to the underlying platform. Both, under- and over-subscription to various resources will need to be avoided.

Prevalent approaches take a limited view of the efficiency issues programmers face. The traditional multithreaded models put the onus of efficient execution largely on programmers. Task-based programming models, e.g., Intel Thread Building Blocks (TBB) [42], ease some of the burden. They automate load-balancing of tasks to prevent resource underutilization. However, they do not address overutilization, nor account for co-scheduled programs. Although recent proposals take a broader view, some address contention in only a subset of resources [45], while others rely on offline profiling [9, 10, 26], and yet others may not optimize utilization of resources [39, 40] (§5).

We propose a model that takes a comprehensive and automated approach to efficient parallel program execution (§2). The model dynamically and continuously adapts a task-based program's demands to the currently available capacity of resources. It exploits inter-task dependence information to arbitrarily control the execution. The model defines a simple metric to measure the system's efficiency periodically. The metric effectively captures the changes in resource utilization, the operating environment, and the program's demands. Changes cause the model to search for the optimum operation point under the new conditions. We develop a hill climbing heuristic, based on the Tabu search [17], to locate the optimum point in the search space.

We applied the model to two different approaches to parallel programming: TBB, a well-established task execution model, and Prometheus, a sequentially-determinate model [3]. Two prototypes were developed (§3) and evaluated on two stock multicore machines (§4). Standard benchmarks were developed using both models and tested in a dedicated as well as a multiprogrammed environment. Experimental results show that the prototypes outperform a state-of-the-art proposal on an average by 15% on time and 31% on energy efficiency, in the dedicated environment. In the multiprogrammed environment, the savings are to the tune of 19% and 21% in time and energy, respectively.

2. THE ParallelismDial MODEL

2.1 Motivation

The key to efficient program execution lies in accounting for the execution environment's characteristics at run-time. A program's execution environment is defined by the program's behavior, resources provided by the system to the program, and the utilization of resources by all co-located programs in the system. Prevalent parallel programming models primarily focus on expressing parallelism and exposing it to the system. Although necessary, only exposing parallelism is inadequate for efficient execution. The dynamic execution environment also influences the program's efficiency.

Figure 1 shows how different aspects of an execution environment impact a program's efficiency. It plots the energy consumed by and the execution time of two benchmarks, *Stream* and *RE*, written using TBB, in a dedicated and an example multiprogrammed scenario, on an Intel Core i7 2600 workstation[1].

RE is a networking redundancy elimination application [4]. In the dedicated environment, at two threads the resources are underutilized (Figure 1(a)). Increasing the threads to up to six improves performance without consuming additional energy. Clearly, insufficient parallelism can lead to inefficiency.

Beyond six threads, RE's performance and energy degrade, slightly, in the dedicated environment, indicating resource contention. In the multiprogrammed environment, as more programs occupy the machine, the performance degrades beyond four threads. When the total number of threads exceeds the total number of hardware contexts, and the OS deschedules RE threads, including at times when they hold what is otherwise a very low-contention lock, the efficiency drops.

In contrast to RE, Stream exhibits an opposite trend (Figure 1(b)). Stream, designed to stress the memory bandwidth, has ample parallelism and is indicative of numerical vector kernels whose datasets are larger than the cache capacity [30]. Even a modest attempt at parallel execution in a dedicated environment results in excessive parallelism,

[1]Details of the applications, machine, and operating environments are presented in §4.

creating memory contention, and thus degrades execution time and energy. However, in the multiprogrammed environment, when it is contending with other programs for other resources (e.g., cache capacity or issue slots in the SMT processor), it naturally slows down, thereby slowing down the creation of parallelism and hence the memory contention. Thus, higher occupancy of the machine proves to be beneficial rather than detrimental in the case of Stream.

Other applications in different dynamic operation scenarios may oversubscribe other system resources. Examples include processing cores, caches, memory, I/O device (e.g., disk) operating system data structures (e.g. page tables), synchronization primitives, among others.

Contention arises because the existing programming models assume that resources (hardware and software) are *isolated*, *static* and *unlimited* (primarily due to the illusion provided by the OS). However, resources are *shared*, *dynamic* and *limited*. As seen above, oversubscribed resources may lead to artificial serialization, either causing, or easing contention. Thus, as programs and tasks execute, they can interact with each other and the system unpredictably. Furthermore, a program's own demands may vary, e.g., due to phase changes, and a system's resources may vary, e.g., due to hardware failures.

Therefore, to achieve efficient parallel execution, the challenge is to take a holistic, system-wide view, and to dynamically and continuously control the parallelism to match the instantaneous capacity of resources, without user-intervention.

2.2 The Model Architecture

We present ParallelismDial (PD), a model that optimizes a program's execution efficiency by dynamically and continuously adapting the program's parallelism to the execution environment.

To dynamically adapt a program's parallelism, PD: (i) assesses the efficiency of the system, (ii) detects contention, changes in the program, and changes in the available resources, (iii) responds to the changes by finding the optimum degree of parallelism (DoP) under the new conditions, and (iv) controls the execution to move to the desired DoP.

To adapt continuously, PD periodically repeats the above steps during a program's execution. Changes in successive measures of efficiency indicate changes in the execution environment. As we see below, responding to the changes requires arbitrary control of the execution.

To arbitrarily control a program's execution, we propose to use a task-based execution model that is also *dependence-aware*. We view a program to comprise appropriately-sized concurrent tasks. Tasks may be viewed as computations that compose a thread in a conventional multithreaded program. They are decoupled from the execution contexts (threads) and thus provide the flexibility needed to manage the program's execution, typically at task boundaries. The finer granularity of tasks permits distribution of tasks to contexts as soon as contexts become available, helping prevent resource underutilization. These aspects are also exploited by modern task-based models [13]. Further, as shown below, awareness of dependences between tasks permits the adaptability needed to prevent resource overutilization, while ensuring a program's forward progress.

PD consists of four main components: the *Spooler*, the *Regulator*, the *Scheduler* and the *Monitor*. It assumes an underlying system that provides a pool of worker threads, common in a modern OS, and a low-overhead means to measure an execution environment's characteristics, e.g., via performance counters provided by modern processors.

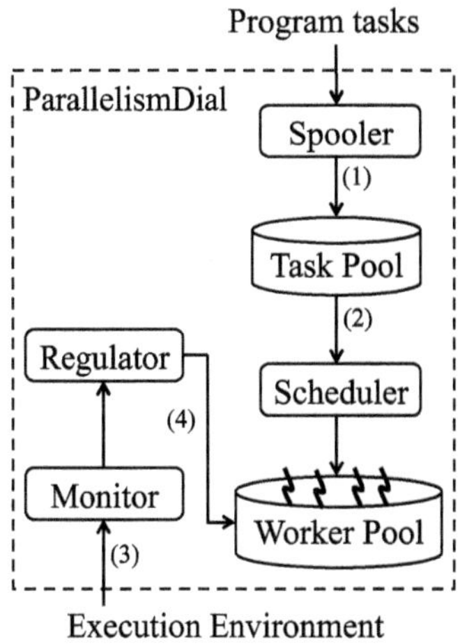

Figure 2: ParallelismDial model architecture.

Figure 2 summarizes the model's operations. The Spooler gathers the tasks exposed by the programmer and creates a task pool (1). The Scheduler assigns tasks from the task pool to threads, if available, from the worker pool (2). Once assigned, the threads execute the tasks. The Monitor periodically probes the system and measures the necessary parameters to compute the instantaneous efficiency of the program (3). The Regulator assesses the changes in the operating efficiency. It responds by continuously seeking the optimum point of operation by controlling the number of workers allotted to the program (4). The number of workers executing tasks directly corresponds to the maximum exposed parallelism of the program.

Each aspect of PD is further described below.

2.2.1 *Controlling the Execution of Programs*

Regulating parallelism requires the ability to arbitrarily block work from being performed when resources are oversubscribed, and introduce work into the execution environment when resources are undersubscribed. For example, in Figure 1(a), in the multiprogrammed environment, increasing the parallelism from four to six degrades RE's execution efficiency. In this case, it is ideal to execute no more than four threads. Doing so requires preventing additional work from being assigned to more threads. However, this can lead to unintended consequences in canonical parallel programs, especially in those with arbitrary dependence patterns.

Challenges in Independence-based Programs

Canonical parallel programs are *independence-based*; the programmer ensures independence amongst concurrently executing computations. Using appropriate synchronization primitives the programmer enforces an arbitrary order between the computations when they access shared data. However, in certain instances the enforced order is specific, e.g., to execute the consumer before a producer in a produce-consumer style program. Conventional parallel programming assumes that once introduced in the execution environment, work is guaranteed to receive resources. Not granting resources can violate this guarantee. Controlling the execution, without being aware of the programmer's intentions, e.g., blocking the producer, can hinder forward progress, or worse, deadlock the execution.

Consider the popular Pthreads implementation of Pbzip2 [16]. It reads data blocks serially from an input file, one at a time, compresses the blocks in parallel, and writes the results to an output file. The computations are organized into threads, as shown in Figure 3(a). Block-read operations are grouped into one thread, e.g., R0 to R3 in thread TH0. Compress operations are grouped across multiple *compress* threads (to achieve concurrency), e.g., C0 to C3 in threads TH1 and TH2. Block-write operations are grouped into one thread, e.g., W0 and W1 in thread TH3. The threads are expected to be co-scheduled.

When the program executes, say three processors, U0 to U2, are allotted to it. Threads TH0, TH1 and TH2 execute in epoch t0, (Figure 3(b))[2]. R0 and R1 in TH0 read blocks which are compressed by C0 and C1, respectively. Now, say, at the start of epoch t1, U0 is taken away from the program to regulte parallelism, and TH0 is blocked. TH1 and TH2 complete C0 and C1, and advance to execute C2 and C3. C2 and C3, in turn, wait for R2 and R3 in TH0 to read the blocks from the input file. However, if no more processors are available, TH0, which can make progress, remains blocked, stalling the program's progress, or even deadlocking it, while available resources are occupied by tasks that cannot make progress, defeating the very purpose of controlling the execution. Although the example is from a Pthreads program, a task-based implementation with a similar structure would be equally vulnerable.

Therefore, PD requires that either a program's concurrent tasks not enforce a specific order among themselves, or they are independent, or the dependence information is supplied to PD. Note that this condition does not preclude use of PD in independence-based programs. It is possible to write such programs without creating a specific order between tasks. For example, we rewrote Pbzip2, using TBB, without resorting to producer-consumer style parallelism. The program is divided into three non-overlapping phases: read, compress and write. Read and write phases are sequential. All tasks in the compress phase are independent. We show successful application of PD to both independence-based and dependence-aware program execution (§3). How PD uses dependence information to ensure forward progress is discussed next.

Dependence-aware Regulated Execution

The Spooler in the proposed model, accepts tasks exposed by the programmer, but admits only independent tasks into the task pool; dependent tasks, when identified, are suspended. Once their dependences have resolved, they are introduced into the task pool and become candidates for the Scheduler to assign to worker threads. (Two example implementations of the Spooler are presented in §3.)

The Regulator changes the DoP by changing the number of workers in the worker pool. The change is effected without pausing the program. It is straightforward to add idle or new workers to the pool. Workers are removed from the pool only after they complete their currently assigned tasks.

The Scheduler operates independently from the Regulator. Given a pool of workers, it assigns tasks from the task pool, if available, to a worker, as soon as the worker is free.

[2]For brevity, we do not show TH3 operations.

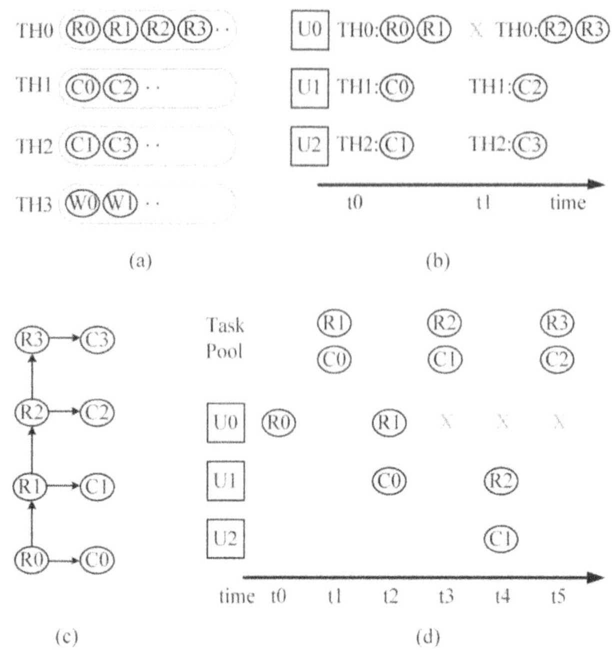

Figure 3: Comparison of independence-based and dependence-aware execution of Pbzip2

It also ensures that tasks eventually receive resources, either by way of a predefined or an aged-based priority. A decoupled Scheduler helps maximize resource utilization without waiting for the Regulator to optimize the DoP.

Now consider the same Pbzip2 example in our model. Figure 3(c) shows its computations formulated as tasks, R1, R2, C0 - C3, and the dependences between them[3]. Figure 3(d) shows the execution as per our model in finer time steps. At time t0, U0, U1 and U2 are alloted to the program. R0 executes. Since no other independent computations exist, the task pool is empty. When R0 completes in t1, dependences of R1 and C0 have resolved, and hence they are added to the task pool. The Scheduler assigns them to U0 and U1 in t2. In t2 the task pool is once again empty since R2 and C1 are suspended. R2 and C1 are added to the task pool once R1 completes in t3. In t3, say U0 is taken away. The Scheduler assigns R2 and C1 to U1 and U2 in t4. Note that unlike in Figure 3(b), C2 does not get scheduled unless R2 completes. Thus the model ensures dependent tasks do not occupy execution resources. The program can make forward progress as long as it is allotted at least one worker.

Recent research proposals also exploit task-dependence information, albeit for a different purpose, to execute parallel programs. SMPSs [38] and Gupta et al. [18] leverage this philosophy to discover distant parallelism. Prometheus [3] and DPJ [6] execute only independent tasks concurrently to achieve determinacy. We also note that TBB presents a "pipeline" abstraction that would capture the dependence information in the above Pbzip2 example, if used.

2.2.2 *Assessing Execution Efficiency*

To continuously regulate parallelism, the Regulator needs a metric to assess: (i) the instantaneous efficiency of the program for a given DoP, and (ii) changes in the execution

[3]Dependences not germane to the discussion are not shown.

environment without the involvement of any external entity such as the OS. We note that any change in the efficiency of the program or the execution environment ultimately manifests as a change in the total system energy expended and/or the program's instruction execution rate. Although changes in the system energy and the instruction rate may be used individually, we propose a simple, holistic, unified metric, *Joules Per Instruction (JPI)* that is affected by changes to both. As we demonstrate in our experiments (§ 4), JPI serves as an adequate metric.

In a program composed of N instructions, let JPI(P_1) be the system energy expended per instruction when parallelism P_1 is deployed. The total system energy expended to execute the entire program, TE(P_1) is

$$TE(P_1) = JPI(P_1) * N \tag{1}$$

If the parallelism is changed from P_1 to P_2, the total system energy expended, TE(P_2) is

$$TE(P_2) = JPI(P_2) * N \tag{2}$$

For the given program, to determine whether P_2 is more efficient than P_1, we define *Efficiency (Eff)* as follows:

$$Eff(P_1, P_2) = \frac{TE(P_2)}{TE(P_1)} = \frac{JPI(P_2)}{JPI(P_1)} \tag{3}$$

Eff(P_1,P_2) is a measure of relative JPI; a value less than 1 indicates P_2 is more efficient and is preferred over P_1, whereas a value greater than 1 indicates parallelism P_1 is preferred.

Equation (3) defines *Eff* for the entire program. In order to use *Eff* as an online metric, the Regulator computes *Eff* and adapts the parallelism at frequent intervals. Given two such intervals D_1 and D_2, and the respective parallelism points, P_1 and P_2, *Eff* is computed as follows.

$$Eff_{online}((P_1, D_1), (P_2, D_2)) = \frac{JPI(P_2, D_2))}{JPI(P_1, D_1)} \tag{4}$$

When P_1 is the same as P_2, Eff_{online} is expected to be around 1. Any other value would suggest a change in the execution environment indicating that the optimum parallelism point has shifted. We demonstrate how this observation is utilized, in the next subsection.

2.2.3 Optimizing Parallelism

Once the Regulator determines that the program efficiency can be improved, it employs a heuristic to optimize the DoP. The heuristic is based on the commonly used hill-climbing search algorithm. It locates the optimum DoP by systematically exploring the direction in the search space that yields higher efficiency.

Hill climbing algorithms are known to get "stuck" in a local optimum and fail to reach the global optimum. Hence the heuristic, developed using the guidelines due to Gendreau [15], incorporates *Tabu search* [17] to escape local optima. The Tabu search maintains a fixed-size *tabu_list* to log previously searched points along with their JPIs. The heuristic periodically "diversifies" the search from the current optimum by exploring unvisited points. Any time a point is searched, it is logged in the *tabu_list*. The oldest point in the list is evicted to make room for a new point, if needed. The heuristic, divided into five steps, is as follows:

Step 1: Establish Sequential Measure: Before beginning the search, the Regulator establishes a notion of *Sequential JPI* (JPI_{seq}) to ensure that the optimum point it finds is indeed profitable. Hence, whenever the program encounters new conditions, the Regulator alters the DoP to one (sequential) and executes the program for a pre-defined duration until the Monitor measures the baseline JPI_{seq}.

Step 2: Establish Initial Search Direction: Next, the Regulator establishes the search direction for the optimization process. It gathers JPIs corresponding to three DoPs, the mid-point, P_{mid}, of the predetermined maximum DoP (often, total hardware contexts in the system), and P_{mid} +/- 1. Tasks are executed for a pre-defined duration in each configuration. The better of the three points, P_{eff}, sets the search direction. The points are added to the *tabu_list* and the execution is switched to P_{eff}.

Step 3: Search for Optimum Parallelism: If P_{eff} is the same as P_{mid}, we already have the local optimum, else the Regulator linearly searches in the established direction [4]. It picks new unvisited points (not in the *tabu_list*) and executes tasks in each of these points for a pre-defined duration. Visited points are added to the *tabu_list* until a local optimum, P_{lopt}, is found. If JPI_{lopt} is not significantly better than JPI_{seq}, the Regulator starts over from step 1, otherwise it fixes the current configuration to P_{lopt}, and enters a "Sleep" mode.

Step 4: Sleep Mode: The Regulator continues to sleep until either: (i) the value of JPI_{lopt} changes by more than a pre-defined threshold, which may indicate phase change or introduction of another program in the system or change in the operating conditions, or (ii) the diversification threshold is reached. In case of (i), the Regulator clears the *tabu_list* and begins the search once again from step 1. In case of (ii), the Regulator saves the current JPI_{lopt} and moves to step 5.

Step 5: Diversification: The diversification threshold is a pre-defined interval after which the Regulator ensures that the execution is not trapped in a local optimum. The Regulator begins the search from the original mid-point in the direction opposite to the original, similar to step 3 (updating the *tabu_list* and avoiding already visited points), until a local optimum P_{lopt2} is reached. If JPI_{lopt2} is better than JPI_{lopt}, the configuration is switched to P_{lopt2}, else it is switched back to P_{lopt}. In either case, the Regulator enters the sleep mode and moves to step 4.

3. THE PROTOTYPES

We evaluated PD by applying it to independence-based and dependence-aware task-based parallel programming models. For the former we picked TBB due to its ubiquity and its rich programming APIs. For the latter we chose Prometheus, from among the different research proposals, for its TBB-like APIs. TBB details can be found in [42] and Prometheus details are described in [2,3]. Both models provide C++ runtime libraries. The runtimes provide the APIs to programmers, and employ state-of-the-art dynamic load balancing schedulers to avoid resource underutilization.

Two PD run-time library prototypes, one each for TBB and Prometheus, were developed. We incorporated the TBB and Prometheus runtimes into our prototypes to leverage

[4]In our experiments on 8- and 24-context machines, the search space is small enough to perform linear search. For larger search spaces, binary search may prove to be better.

their capabilities. Their runtime engines were modified and plugged into the PD runtime. The PD runtimes expose the respective APIs to programmers, and provide the efficiency mechanisms (common to both prototypes) described in §2. We describe the prototypes in this section and discuss their evaluation in §4.

Independence-based Prototype (PD_TBB)

Since TBB programs do not always convey dependence information, the Spooler in this prototype simply passes all dynamically discovered tasks into the task pool. For reasons described in §2, we ensured that the TBB-programs we developed did not explicitly enforce a specific order between their tasks.

Dependence-aware Prototype (PD_PM)

Prometheus exploits sequential program order and data objects accessed by tasks to automatically serialize dependent tasks while parallelizing the execution of independent tasks. It handles WAW dependences between tasks, but relies on the programmer to quiesce the parallel execution to prevent RAW and WAR hazards; the program may resume parallel execution once the hazards are avoided. Clearly this limits the degree of parallelism that the runtime can expose.

We enhanced the Prometheus runtime to also automatically handle RAW and WAR dependences, much like out-of-order superscalar processors. As the program executes, tasks stalled due to any dependence are skipped over in search of other dependence-free tasks, resources permitting. The Spooler in PD_PM uses the dependence information to only expose independent tasks to the task pool.

Given the above mechanisms in the two prototypes, to discover tasks in a program and expose them for execution, we now describe how they are efficiently executed.

3.1 Scheduling Execution

Both Prometheus and TBB use Pthreads as abstractions to create OS threads. Upon initialization, they create a fixed global pool of threads (by default, one per hardware context) and associate a worker with each thread. Each worker maintains a separate double ended queue (deque). Tasks are scheduled for execution by enqueuing them in the deques. Both TBB and Prometheus employ a Cilk-style work stealing algorithm to balance the load [13]. A worker seeks tasks first from its own deque, failing which it steals from someone else's deque. PD_TBB and PD_PM retain the schedulers from the respective runtimes, but replace the worker pool component with the PD worker pool design as described in §3.2.

3.2 Regulating Parallelism

To find the optimum operating point, the Regulator changes the DoP by controlling the size of the worker pool. Instead of a fixed pool of workers, it maintains two variable-sized disjoint pools: an *active pool* and a *suspended pool*. A worker can be associated either with the active pool or the suspended pool, but not both. Only the workers in the active pool are seen by the Scheduler. Workers in the suspended pool are put to sleep until the Regulator awakens and moves them to the active pool. The core algorithm for each worker remains the same as described in §3.1. An increase/decrease in the number of workers in the active pool results in an increase/decrease in the program's exposed DoP.

Table 1: Machine configurations

Machine Parameters	Xeon E5-2420	Core i7-2600
# Sockets	2	1
# Hardware Contexts	24	8
Clock Speed	1.9 GHz	3.4 GHz
Total Cache	15 MB	8 MB
Memory	32 GB	16 GB
Linux Kernel	2.6.32	2.6.32
Memory Controllers/Channels	1/2	2/6

Table 2: Benchmarks and input sizes

Benchmarks	Description	Input
Histogram [41]	Image analysis	1.4 GB bitmap file
Hash Join [11]	In-memory DB join	28 MB tables
Pbzip2 [16]	Compression	1.3 GB file
Reverse Index [41]	HTML Analysis	1.3 GB directory
Barneshut [24]	N-Body Simulation	100000 bodies
RE [4]	Packet dedup	1300000 packets
Stream [30]	Memory Streaming	915MB of data

3.3 Monitoring System Parameters

The Monitor is a system-specific component of the prototypes. It relies on information available from the system to measure *Eff* described in §2.2.2. At present, the monitor assumes an Intel SandyBridge-based microarchitecture which exports energy and performance counters. It can as easily work with other platforms with similar capabilities.

To measure processor energy, we use the RAPL (Running Average Power Limit) power management interface provided in the Intel SandyBridge microarchitecture [1]. To measure the number of instructions completed, we use the PAPI library APIs [32]. We do not count instructions that may cause potential side effects when determining the efficiency of the program. For example, we omit instructions used for synchronization, and OS mode instructions.

4. EVALUATION AND RESULTS

In this section, we describe our experimental setup, the hardware and the benchmarks used in our experiments, and the results obtained. Experiments were conducted on two 64-bit x86 machines, described in Table 1.

Table 2 lists the benchmarks and the input data sizes we selected from different benchmark suites to evaluate PD. The baseline parallel versions use the fast NPTL Pthreads library (which comes along with the 2.6.32 Linux kernel that both the platforms run) to parallelize their algorithms. We compiled all the benchmarks with GCC 4.4.3 using -O3 optimization and architecture flag (-march=core2).

We present results of PD for two different environments: dedicated, where a benchmark is the only program running on the machine (§4.1), and multiprogrammed, where other applications run simultaneously with the benchmarks (§4.2). We evaluated PD for performance and energy efficiency. We measured the execution time and energy of the entire program, including the overheads associated with any thread/task creation, rather than just the parallel regions. We used the RAPL interface to measure the total energy consumed. We fixed the measurement time interval for the Regulator at 100ms and the diversification threshold to 5s. PD sought a new DoP when JPI changed by more than 10%.

4.1 Dedicated Environment

To demonstrate the effectiveness of PD in a dedicated environment, we provide four points of comparison. The first

Table 3: Dedicated environment: Optimum DoP (execution time, energy consumed).

#	Benchmarks	i7-2600	E5-2420
1	Histogram	1 (*12s,93J*)	1 (*11s,102J*)
2	Hash Join	4 (*9.4s,353J*)	11 (*24s,898J*)
3	Pbzip2	8 (*36s,1608J*)	24 (*23s,999J*)
4	Reverse Index	4 (*31s,384J*)	10 (*38s,853J*)
5	Barneshut	8 (*26s,1163J*)	24 (*18s,919J*)
6	RE	5 (*15s,806J*)	13 (*32s,1401J*)
7	Stream	2 (*32s,562J*)	7 (*17s,821J*)

point is the Pthreads baseline. The second and third points are the Prometheus (PM) and TBB implementations. The fourth point of comparison is a recently proposed technique, Feedback Driven Threading (FDT) [45], which dynamically adjusts the number of threads for homogeneous loops and considers contention to only two types of resources, locks and memory bandwidth. The original version of FDT is implemented in OpenMP. We faithfully implemented FDT in the PM runtime to provide a fair comparison against PD. For PD, we present the results for the two prototypes: PD_PM and PD_TBB.

Figures 4 and 5 present the performance and energy results for all our benchmarks on both the platforms for the dedicated environment. Every data point in our results is an average of 10 runs and normalized to the Pthreads baseline (not shown). Table 3 shows the optimum DoP that PD reaches for each benchmark along with its execution time and energy consumed.

The results demonstrate the following: (i) in situations where there is resource contention, PD always results in time- and energy-efficient execution when compared to Pthreads, PM, TBB and FDT; (ii) PD is able to handle contention to different resources using a single holistic metric, unlike FDT, which can handle only synchronization and memory bandwidth issues; (iii) in situations where parallelism is not excessive and contention does not occur, PD is unlikely to be beneficial but does not incur overheads; and (iv) the optimum DoP depends on the benchmark and the underlying platform, and can range between one and the maximum number of hardware contexts. We organize the results into "contention" and "no contention" scenarios. We will refer to Figures 4 and 5 in the discussions to follow.

4.1.1 Contention Scenarios

Our benchmarks exhibit five different contention cases:

Contention in external software components

Histogram is a data parallel benchmark that carries out computations on a 1.4GB bitmap file. The benchmark invokes *mmap* which allocates memory in a region in the kernel space, marks the new region as allocated but defers updating the page table entries. Pages are loaded from the disk only when the application accesses them. When a new page is accessed, a page fault occurs and the kernel locks the entire region with a read lock. If multiple threads try to access different pages in parallel, concurrent page faults can occur, potentially creating contention for the lock [8]. The benchmark scales poorly and incurs degradation in both performance and energy for even a modest increase in the number of threads. As shown in Table 3, Histogram does not scale beyond one thread on either machine.

Histogram is an example of a very likely future scenario: a programmer can work hard to avoid contention, but has little or no control over external software components (e.g., libraries or the OS). By controlling the parallelism appropriately, PD is able to reduce the execution time and energy consumption by 20% and 68% on i7-2600, and 32% and 80% on E5-2420, respectively. FDT cannot detect this contention since it happens within the OS, and hence performs as poorly as Pthreads, PM and TBB.

Contention due to memory bandwidth

Stream mainly moves data from one region of the memory to another. Again, there is ample application-level parallelism, however, there is a significant demand for the memory (bus) bandwidth. i7-2600 has a single memory controller with two memory channels, while E5-2420 has two memory controllers with three channels each. Any parallelism beyond the total number of channels available on these platforms will result in contention leading to performance and energy degradation. Both PD and FDT are able to control the parallelism, alleviating the contention, thus preventing increase in memory latencies. This results in reducing the processor idle time, and thus more time- and energy-efficient execution. PD reduces the execution time and energy consumption by 12% and 64% on i7-2600, and 15% and 17% on E5-2420, respectively.

Contention due to disk bandwidth

Reverse Index is a benchmark whose parallel execution makes excessive demands for another resource, disk bandwidth. Each parallel computation in Reverse Index does the following: (i) open an HTML file, (ii) parse the file contents to identify links to other pages, (iii) extract the links and update a local data structure based upon some computation, and (iv) close the HTML file. In addition to significant disk activity, the benchmark performs CPU activity. Though there is abundant parallelism—each file can be processed independently—parallel accesses to the disk can be a source of contention.

As in the case of Histogram, Pthreads, PM, TBB and FDT have no mechanism in place to detect contention to disk bandwidth. On the other hand, PD's heuristic is able to detect and alleviate this contention by appropriately controlling parallelism. This demonstrates the effectiveness of the *Eff* metric that PD employs. PD is able to reduce the execution time and energy consumption by 0% and 65% on i7-2600 and 8% and 51% on E5-2420 respectively. Reductions in execution time are modest because the performance of this benchmark does not degrade significantly for higher thread counts *wrt* the best operating point. But not using unwanted processors (Table 3) significantly reduced energy consumption.

Contention due to cache capacity

In Hash Join there is potential for contention in a shared cache. The working set size of each thread is over 2MB. i7-2600 has a shared L3 cache capacity of 8 MB, whereas E5-2420 has L3 cache capacity of 15MB per socket and hence contention is likely if the working set size exceeds the respective capacities.

PD controls the parallelism to ensure that the working set does not exceed the available cache capacity, thereby reducing both energy consumption and execution time. FDT cannot detect contention to shared caches. While a more sophisticated technique like Thread Tailor [25] (TT) may detect contention to shared caches and control parallelism accord-

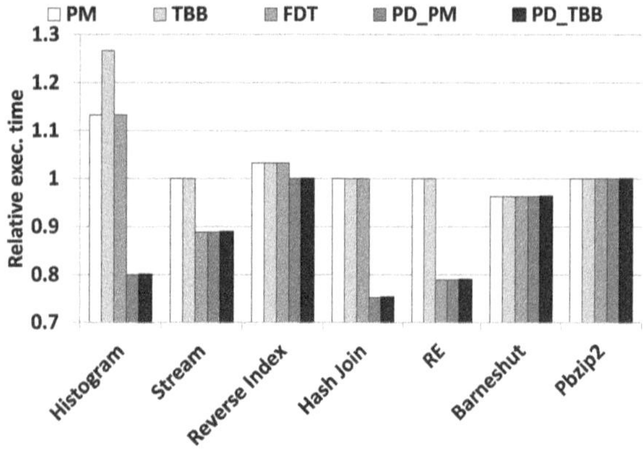

(a) Execution Time

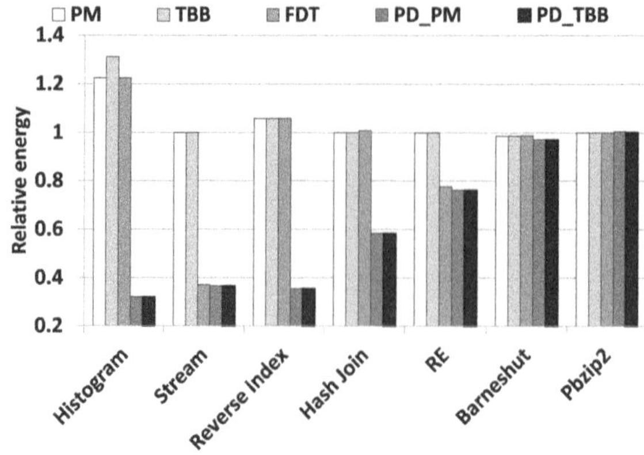

(b) Energy

Figure 4: Performance and energy comparison of PM, TBB, FDT and PD on i7-2600 relative to Pthreads.

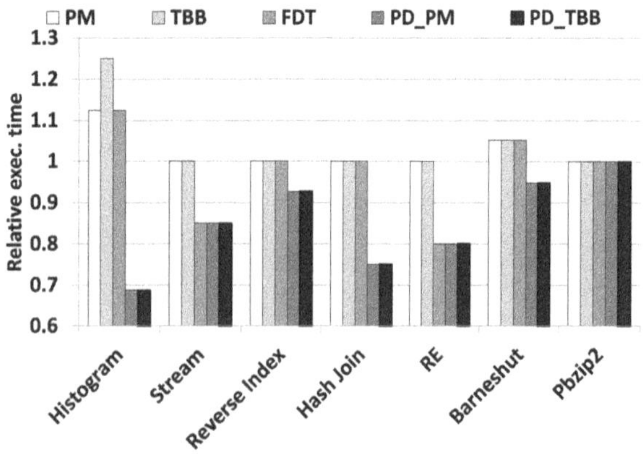

(a) Execution Time

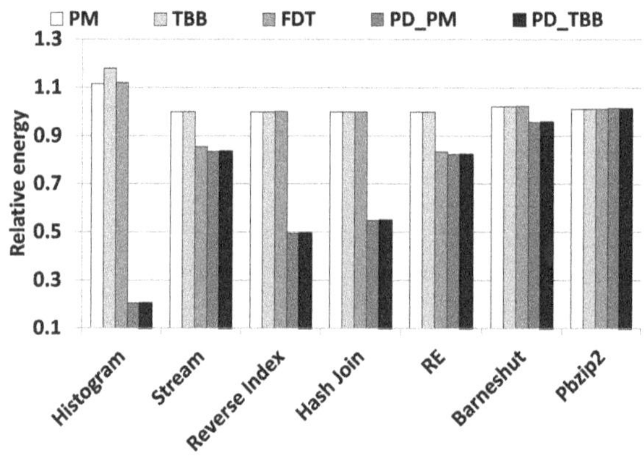

(b) Energy

Figure 5: Performance and energy comparison of PM, TBB, FDT and PD on E5-2420 relative to Pthreads.

ingly, TT cannot detect other types of contention, such as disk bandwidth and in external components, whereas PD's holistic approach easily can. PD reduces the execution time and energy consumption by 25% and 42% on i7-2600, and 25% and 46% on E5-2420, respectively.

Contention due to user-level locks

RE has abundant packet-level parallelism but uses a lock protected shared hash table that each concurrent packet must access. Only one packet (thread) can update the hash table at a given time. As the number of concurrent packets increases, updates to the hash table increase, which increases the contention to the critical section. The benchmark incurs degradation both in execution time and energy beyond a thread count of 5 and 13 on i7-2600 and E5-2420 respectively. Both PD and FDT avoid this degradation by accurately estimating the best number of threads, in turn reducing the execution time and energy up to 22% and 24% on i7-2600, and 20% and 18% on E5-2420, respectively.

4.1.2 No Contention Scenarios

We consider two benchmarks, Barneshut and Pbzip2, to illustrate no contention scenarios. Both have abundant parallelism and few contention concerns in common circumstances. PD neither incurs any degradation nor provides any savings. For PD_TBB, we wrote Pbzip2 such that we avoided the ordering issues described in §2.2.1.

4.2 Multiprogrammed Environment

We now consider the effectiveness of PD in a multiprogrammed environment. We consider two different scenarios. In the first, we launch our benchmark alongside other instances of non-adaptive, resource-intensive programs. In the second, we co-locate pairs of our benchmarks that have different resource constraints. We present data for Pthreads, PM, FDT and PD_PM (TBB and PD_TBB trends are similar to PM and PD_PM, respectively).

The results from these experiments demonstrate: (i) PD *continuously* adapts the parallel execution when the resources allocated to the program dynamically and continuously change due to the resource demands of other co-located programs; (ii) PD adapts the DoP to the instantaneous subscription of resources; and (iii) creating contention to one resource can indirectly alleviate contention to another resource, potentially improving a program's scalability.

4.2.1 Scenario 1

In this scenario, multiple instances of (non-adaptive) *mcf*, a highly cache- and memory-intensive single-threaded application, are executed simultaneously with our benchmarks.

Figure 6 shows PD adapting the DoP for Barneshut in re-

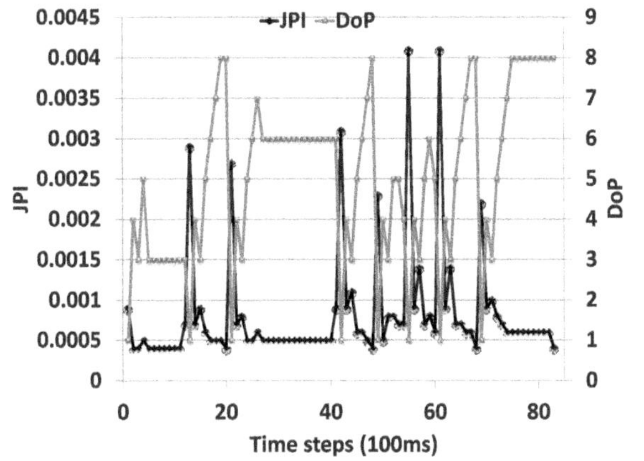

Figure 6: PD's continuous adaptation ability for Barneshut.

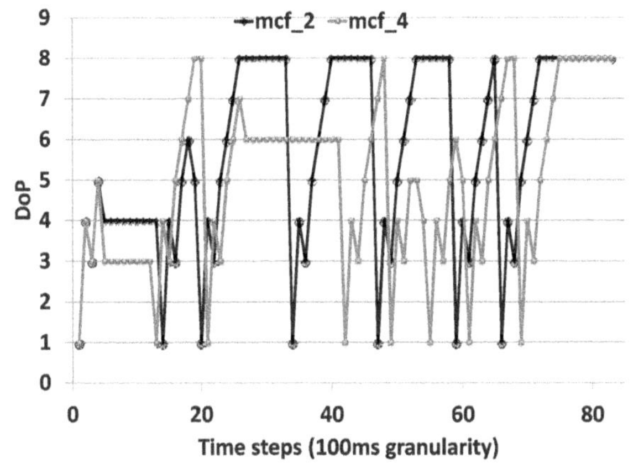

Figure 7: PD's heuristic under different degrees of contention for Barneshut.

sponse to the demands placed by four instances of *mcf*, on i7-2600. The X-axis shows time incremented in 100ms. There are two vertical axes: the primary axis shows the instantaneous JPI of the benchmark and the secondary axis shows the corresponding DoP predicted by PD. From *t=3* to *t=12*, Barneshut executes at a stable DoP of 3. A change in JPI, at *t=12*, indicates change in the resource demands of the co-scheduled *mcf* instances. At *t=13*, the PD runtime reacts by waking up from the sleep mode and restarting the search from sequential execution (§2.2.3) to find the new operating point. At *t=19*, PD arrives at the new optimum (DoP=8) after establishing the search direction and performing the necessary search, and re-enters the sleep mode. PD takes a similar course of action whenever JPI changes, e.g., at *t=41*, *t=68*, etc. Thus, PD continuously alters the parallelism to best suit the variations in the execution environment. Note that in Figure 6, there is no single best operating point for Barneshut unlike in the dedicated environment. Techniques that assume static operating conditions, e.g., FDT, are unable to handle this scenario. They identify the optimum degree of parallelism, typically once at the beginning of the program or at the inception of every user-defined phase, and fix that value for the rest of the program/phase. Techniques like Parcae [40] that propose to continuously adapt, employ search heuristics that can get stuck in local optima.

PD adapts a program's DoP to match the available capacity of resources. Figure 7 shows the DoP for Barneshut when co-scheduled with two (*mcf_2*) and four (*mcf_4*) instances of *mcf* on i7-2600. In general, two instances of *mcf* utilize fewer resources than four instances, and over time PD exposes higher DoP when Barneshut is co-scheduled with two rather than four instances of *mcf*.

Figure 8 shows the summary of execution time and the energy consumed by all the benchmarks normalized to Pthreads, when co-scheduled with four instances of *mcf* on i7-2600. PD outperforms its Pthreads, PM and FDT counterparts for all the benchmarks on average, 19% in time and 21% in energy. FDT measures a program's characteristics, when it begins, to establish the DoP. It can neither account for system-wide conditions nor run-time variations in the conditions. Hence it is inadequate in a multiprogrammed environment. Even for the two instances in which FDT performed as well as PD in the dedicated environment, Stream and RE, FDT fares poorly in the multiprogrammed environment since it makes the same decisions as it made in the dedicated environment.

Stream, in this environment, shows particularly interesting results as compared to the results shown in Figure 4 for the same platform, i7-2600. Unlike in the dedicated environment, in which it scales poorly due to memory bandwidth contention, Stream scaled up to the maximum number of hardware contexts in this environment (Figure 1(b)). This is because the contention created by *mcf* instances to cores and caches slowed down Stream's demand for resources, thus avoiding the memory contention in the first place. Note that FDT is unable to take advantage of this fact since it does not account for the co-located *mcf* instances in its metric. It picks the same DoP as in the dedicated environment and hence incurs significant degradation in both performance and energy consumption. This demonstrates the effectiveness of PD's holistic approach to controlling parallelism as opposed to taking a limited view of the execution environment.

4.2.2 Scenario 2

In the next scenario, we co-schedule selected pairs of our benchmarks on E5-2420. We compare the time and energy efficiency of PD with Pthreads and PM. Table 4 presents the results. The first main column shows the pairs of co-scheduled benchmarks. The next three main columns, one for each runtime, show the execution time of each benchmark and the total energy consumed by the pair. The last main column gives the stable DoP that PD reaches for each benchmark.

Pthreads and PM create as many threads as hardware contexts (24) to execute the benchmarks. As Table 3 shows, 24 contexts are already too many for most of them. Depending on their type, simultaneously executing Pthreads/PM benchmarks can make things worse. Note that PD ensures that only as many threads as the hardware contexts are created (Table 4, DoP column). We describe the other results using three types of benchmark pairs.

Contention-prone and contention-free

In this case, we co-schedule a benchmark prone to contention in the dedicated environment, e.g., Reverse Index and Hash Join, with one that is not, e.g., Barneshut. Row #1 and row #2 from Table 4 are examples of this case.

As shown in Table 3, Reverse Index and Hash Join do

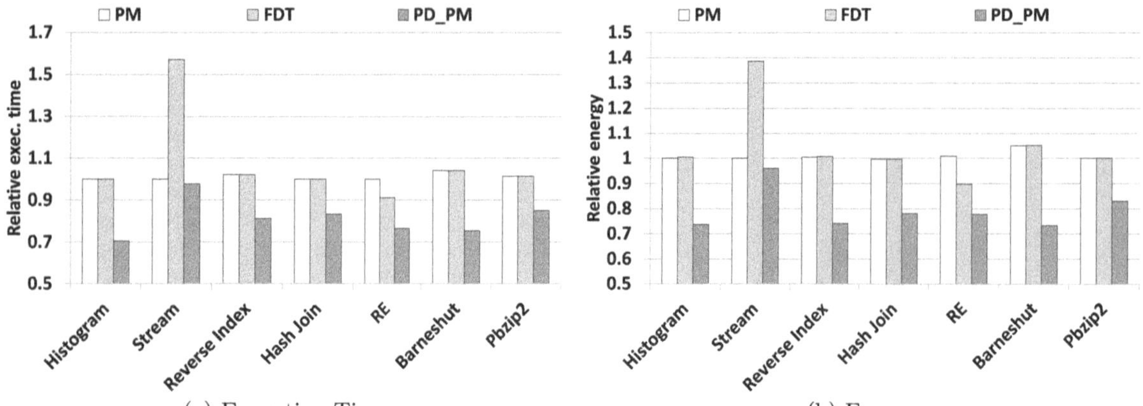

(a) Execution Time (b) Energy

Figure 8: Performance and energy comparison of PM, FDT and PD on i7-2600 relative to Pthreads, when scheduled with 4-instances of mcf.

not scale beyond 10 and 11 threads, respectively, when executed in isolation (row #4 and row #2 in Table 3). When their Pthreads and PM versions are co-scheduled with Barneshut, the contention created by Barneshut to cores and private caches further degrade their performance by a factor of 1.7x and 3x, respectively, as compared to the dedicated environment (not shown).

By using only the required number of contexts and returning the rest to the OS, PD versions of Reverse Index and Hash Join reduce contention not only to shared resources (disk and shared cache), but also to cores and private caches, reducing their execution times by 42% and 60% as compared to their Pthreads and PM counterparts. When compared to their dedicated versions (row #4 and row #2 in Table 3), PD limits the degradation in execution times of Reverse Index and Hash Join by 1.07x and 1.5x, respectively, as compared to 1.7x and 3x degradation incurred by Pthreads and PM.

PD is also able to reduce the execution time of Barneshut by more than a factor of 2 when compared to Pthreads and PM. Reducing the number of contexts to execute both Reverse Index and Hash Join allows Barneshut to take advantage of the free resources available to execute its computations in an uninterrupted fashion, thereby improving its performance.

Contention-prone and contention-prone

In the second case, both co-located benchmarks are prone to contention in the dedicated environment, e.g., Hash Join and Stream (row #3 and row #4 in Table 4).

When two instances of Hash Join (Pthreads/PM versions) are co-scheduled (Table 4, row #3), they create more contention to the shared L3 cache, degrading the performance (by a factor of 4 compared to the dedicated environment (not shown)), and energy consumption. PD alleviates this problem by dynamically decreasing the parallelism in each instance close to the best DoP (11). The execution time is almost comparable to the one in the dedicated environment (Table 3, row #2). The total energy reduces by a factor of 4 as compared to its Pthreads and PM counterparts.

The result for Hash Join co-scheduled with Stream (row #4, Table 4), reiterates the inference made in §4.2.1 for Stream. The interference caused by Hash Join slows down Stream's demand for memory bandwidth, thereby reducing the negative impact on performance for all its versions (Pthreads, PM and PD). However, the Pthreads/PM versions of Hash Join slowed down by a factor of 2 due to Stream's interference as compared to dedicated environment (not shown). PD improves the performance and energy of Hash Join by 20% and 27% respectively against its Pthreads/PM counterparts by reducing its DoP to 10 (Table 4, row #4, column DoP-B1).

Contention-free and contention-free

In the final case, both benchmarks were scalable, e.g., Barneshut and Pbzip2 (row #5, Table 4). PD has only marginal impact since neither suffers from contention. It simply divides the resources evenly amongst the benchmarks. For all the versions, the execution times are worse than the dedicated times since both benchmarks can benefit from higher number of resources which they are not provided in the multiprogrammed environment.

4.3 Summary

As above results show, PD provides the best time and energy efficiency in every case. Thus PD frees programmers to focus on composing functionally correct programs rather than optimizing/re-writing them for different execution environments. PD dynamically optimizes the program's parallel execution. Without PD, this is an arduous task.

5. RELATED WORK

Efficient parallel execution using hardware and software techniques is a much studied topic. We summarize the work here using broad categories.

OS scheduling techniques have been proposed to control parallelism in programs [5,29,31,44]. They mainly focus on controlling the resources allocated to a program. PD focuses on controlling the program's parallelism and the resources it occupies. It does not require OS support and can be applied at the user level. Lithe [37], a user level approach, controls the resources alloted to a heterogeneous mix of runtime systems, e.g., TBB alongside OpenMP. PD focuses within a runtime and can be deployed on top of Lithe.

Several recent proposals dynamically vary a program's degree of parallelism [9,10,25,26,39,40,45]. While [9,10,26] dynamically control parallelism, they require offline analysis and learning. It is unclear how their runtimes will adapt the program on a different machine with different character-

Table 4: Performance and energy comparison of Pthreads, PM and PD on E5-2420 when benchmarks with different resource constraints are co-scheduled. S(B*): B*'s execution time in seconds; J: Total energy consumed by B1 and B2 in joules; DoP: stable parallelism points for B1 and B2.

#	Benchmarks		Pthreads			PM			PD			DoP	
	B1	B2	S(B1) s	S(B2) s	J	S(B1) s	S(B2) s	J	S(B1) s	S(B2) s	J	B1	B2
1	Reverse Index	Barneshut	71	63	3245	73	68	3502	41	24	1552	9	15
2	Hash Join	Barneshut	97	68	3644	99	69	4764	38	21	1845	11	13
3	Hash Join	Hash Join	101	103	5404	102	104	5603	25	28	1352	13	11
4	Hash Join	Stream	46	19	2544	46	19	2565	37	19	1856	10	14
5	Barneshut	Pbzip2	25	36	1870	22	38	1889	23	38	1872	12	12

istics. Importantly, they cannot continuously and dynamically vary the degree of parallelism. Suleman's approach [45] employs a resource specific parallelism adaption mechanism which is not holistic. Thread Tailor [25] requires support from a static compiler tool chain to identify parallel interactions and is not purely dynamic. DoPE [39] and Parcae [40] are compiler-based approaches to controlling parallelism. Both pause a program's execution when altering its parallelism, potentially underutilizing resources. PD can be applied to existing programming models. It adapts the parallelism without pausing the execution. PD adapts to the dynamic changes and any contention in the system, whereas DoPE does not. Parcae's search for optimum DoP may stop at a local optima whereas PD searches for global optima.

Several papers have considered multiprogrammed environments. They have investigated a range of techniques, both architectural/microarchitectural and system software, to address contention in hardware resources such as on-chip caches [20, 21, 23, 33–36]. These proposals mostly partition the shared resources amongst the different programs, though recent work reduces the demand for a shared resource (and thus the resulting contention) by slowing down the execution speed of a program [12, 19]. PD simply views such scenarios as inefficiencies due to excessive parallelism and handles them without additional support.

Li and Martinez [27, 28] propose runtime heuristics for parallelism and DVFS control to find power/performance efficient execution points for specific soft performance/power targets. PD can achieve both time- and energy-efficient execution whereas their approaches can only achieve either time-efficiency or energy-efficiency, but not both. Unlike their approach, PD requires no soft targets to control parallelism; it begins executing from an unknown operating point to arrive at an optimized operating point.

PD may also be viewed as an example of autonomic computing, in which systems self-monitor and self-regulate to achieve desired objectives, without user-intervention [22]. PD's periodic monitoring and control of execution to improve efficiency is analogous to the MAPE cycle of autonomic systems and observer-controller paradigm of organic computing [43]. Invasive computing is another proposal whose one goal is to optimize parallel execution of programs [46]. It requires pervasive changes to all aspects of a system, whereas PD works with existing hardware and prevalent programming methods.

6. CONCLUSION

Parallel systems often consume more time and energy than necessary to execute parallel programs. This results from inefficient utilization of resources. Program behavior and unpredictable dynamic operating conditions can make performance-tuning complex and non-intuitive. As increasingly more programmers develop parallel programs that are portable to a diverse range of systems, an automated approach is necessary. We presented ParallelismDial, a model that automatically tunes a program's performance to the underlying system. It monitors the system efficiency, regulates the degree of exposed parallelism, and continuously navigates the execution to an optimum point of operation.

The model was applied to two different runtime systems: TBB and Prometheus. Programs were developed using both systems. ParallelismDial was used to tune their execution on two stock multicore workstations, in dedicated and multiprogrammed environments. Their efficiency improved on an average by 15% in execution time and 31% in energy in the dedicated environment and by 19% in time and 21% in energy in the multiprogrammed environment.

7. ACKNOWLEDGMENTS

This material is based upon work supported, in part, by the National Science Foundation under Grant CCF-0963737. Any opinions, findings, and conclusions or recommendations expressed in this material are those of the author(s) and do not necessarily reflect the views of the National Science Foundation.

8. REFERENCES

[1] Intel64 and IA-32 Architectures Software Developer's Manual Combined Volumes 3A and 3B: System Programming Guide, Parts 1 and 2. http://www.intel.com/Assets/PDF/manual/325384.pdf.

[2] M. D. Allen. *Data-Driven Decomposition of Sequential Programs for Determinate Parallel Execution.* PhD thesis, University of Wisconsin, Madison, 2010.

[3] M. D. Allen, S. Sridharan, and G. S. Sohi. Serialization sets: a dynamic dependence-based parallel execution model. In *PPoPP '09*, pages 85–96, New York, NY, USA, 2009.

[4] A. Anand, C. Muthukrishnan, A. Akella, and R. Ramjee. Redundancy in network traffic: findings and implications. SIGMETRICS '09, pages 37–48, New York, NY, USA, 2009.

[5] T. E. Anderson, B. N. Bershad, E. D. Lazowska, and H. M. Levy. Scheduler activations: effective kernel support for the user-level management of parallelism. In *Proceedings of the thirteenth ACM symposium on Operating systems principles*, SOSP '91, pages 95–109, New York, NY, USA, 1991. ACM.

[6] R. L. Bocchino, Jr., V. S. Adve, D. Dig, S. V. Adve, S. Heumann, R. Komuravelli, J. Overbey, P. Simmons, H. Sung, and M. Vakilian. A type and effect system for deterministic parallel java. OOPSLA '09, pages 97–116, New York, NY, USA, 2009.

[7] S. Borkar. Designing reliable systems from unreliable components: the challenges of transistor variability and degradation. *MICRO '05*, 25(6):10–16, 2005.

[8] S. Boyd-Wickizer, A. T. Clements, Y. Mao, A. Pesterev, M. F. Kaashoek, R. Morris, and N. Zeldovich. An analysis of linux scalability to many

cores. OSDI'10, pages 1–8, Berkeley, CA, USA, 2010. USENIX Association.

[9] M. Curtis-Maury, J. Dzierwa, C. D. Antonopoulos, and D. S. Nikolopoulos. Online power-performance adaptation of multithreaded programs using hardware event-based prediction. ICS '06, pages 157–166, New York, NY, USA, 2006.

[10] M. Curtis-Maury, A. Shah, F. Blagojevic, D. S. Nikolopoulos, B. R. de Supinski, and M. Schulz. Prediction models for multi-dimensional power-performance optimization on many cores. PACT '08, pages 250–259, New York, NY, USA, 2008.

[11] D. J. DeWitt, R. H. Katz, F. Olken, L. D. Shapiro, M. R. Stonebraker, and D. A. Wood. Implementation techniques for main memory database systems. SIGMOD '84, pages 1–8, New York, NY, USA, 1984.

[12] E. Ebrahimi, C. J. Lee, O. Mutlu, and Y. N. Patt. Fairness via source throttling: a configurable and high-performance fairness substrate for multi-core memory systems. In *ASPLOS '10*, pages 335–346, New York, NY, USA, 2010.

[13] M. Frigo, C. E. Leiserson, and K. H. Randall. The implementation of the Cilk-5 multithreaded language. In *PLDI '98*, pages 212–223, 1998.

[14] S. H. Fuller and E. Lynette I. Millett. *The Future of Computing Performance: Game Over or Next Level?* The National Academies Press, 2011.

[15] M. Gendreau. An Introduction to Tabu Search. In F. Glover and G. Kochenberger, editors, *Handbook of Metaheuristics*, chapter 2, pages 37–54. Kluwer Academic Publishers, 2003.

[16] J. Gilchrist. Parallel data compression with bzip2. In *ICPDCS '04*, pages 559–564, 2004.

[17] F. Glover and M. Laguna. *Tabu Search.* Kluwer Academic Publishers, Norwell, MA, USA, 1997.

[18] G. Gupta and G. S. Sohi. Dataflow execution of sequential imperative programs on multicore architectures. In *MICRO '11*, pages 59–70, New York, NY, USA, 2011.

[19] R. Illikkal, V. Chadha, A. Herdrich, R. Iyer, and D. Newell. PIRATE: QoS and performance management in CMP architectures. *SIGMETRICS Perform. Eval. Rev.*, 37:3–10, March 2010.

[20] R. Iyer. CQoS: a framework for enabling QoS in shared caches of CMP platforms. In *ICS '04*, pages 257–266, New York, NY, USA, 2004.

[21] R. Iyer, L. Zhao, F. Guo, R. Illikkal, S. Makineni, D. Newell, Y. Solihin, L. Hsu, and S. Reinhardt. Qos policies and architecture for cache/memory in cmp platforms. *SIGMETRICS Perform. Eval. Rev.*, 35(1):25–36, June 2007.

[22] J. O. Kephart and D. M. Chess. The vision of autonomic computing. *Computer*, 36(1):41–50, Jan. 2003.

[23] S. Kim, D. Chandra, and Y. Solihin. Fair cache sharing and partitioning in a chip multiprocessor architecture. In *PACT '04*, pages 111 – 122, 2004.

[24] M. Kulkarni, M. Burtscher, K. Pingali, and C. Cascaval. Lonestar: A suite of parallel irregular programs. In *ISPASS '09*, pages 65–76, April 2009.

[25] J. Lee, H. Wu, M. Ravichandran, and N. Clark. Thread tailor: dynamically weaving threads together for efficient, adaptive parallel applications. In *ISCA '10*, pages 270–279, New York, NY, USA, 2010.

[26] D. Li, B. de Supinski, M. Schulz, K. Cameron, and D. Nikolopoulos. Hybrid MPI/OpenMP power-aware computing. In *IPDPS '10*, pages 1 –12, April 2010.

[27] J. Li and J. Martinez. Power-performance implications of thread-level parallelism on chip multiprocessors. In *ISPASS '05*, pages 124 –134, March 2005.

[28] J. Li and J. Martinez. Dynamic power-performance adaptation of parallel computation on chip multiprocessors. In *HPCA '06*, pages 77 – 87, Feb. 2006.

[29] R. Liu, K. Klues, S. Bird, S. Hofmeyr, K. Asanović, and J. Kubiatowicz. Tessellation: space-time partitioning in a manycore client os. HotPar'09, pages 10–10, Berkeley, CA, USA, 2009.

[30] J. D. McCalpin. Memory bandwidth and machine balance in current high performance computers. *TCCA Newsletter*, pages 19–25, Dec. 1995.

[31] C. McCann, R. Vaswani, and J. Zahorjan. A dynamic processor allocation policy for multiprogrammed shared-memory multiprocessors. *ACM Trans. Comput. Syst.*, 11(2):146–178, May 1993.

[32] P. Mucci, S. Browne, C. Deane, and G. Ho. Papi: A portable interface to hardware performance counters. In *Proc. Dept. of Defense HPCMP Users Group Conference*, pages 7–10, 1999.

[33] O. Mutlu and T. Moscibroda. Stall-time fair memory access scheduling for chip multiprocessors. In *MICRO '07*, pages 146 –160, 2007.

[34] O. Mutlu and T. Moscibroda. Parallelism-aware batch scheduling: Enhancing both performance and fairness of shared dram systems. In *ISCA '08*, pages 63–74, 2008.

[35] K. J. Nesbit, N. Aggarwal, J. Laudon, and J. E. Smith. Fair queuing memory systems. In *MICRO '06*, pages 208–222, 2006.

[36] K. J. Nesbit, J. Laudon, and J. E. Smith. Virtual private caches. In *ISCA '07*, pages 57–68, New York, NY, USA, 2007.

[37] H. Pan, B. Hindman, and K. Asanović. Composing parallel software efficiently with lithe. In *PLDI '10*, pages 376–387, New York, NY, USA, 2010.

[38] J. Perez, R. Badia, and J. Labarta. A dependency-aware task-based programming environment for multi-core architectures. In *Cluster Computing, 2008 IEEE International Conference on*, pages 142 –151, 29 2008-oct. 1 2008.

[39] A. Raman, H. Kim, T. Oh, J. W. Lee, and D. I. August. Parallelism orchestration using DoPE: the degree of parallelism executive. In *PLDI '11*, pages 26–37, New York, NY, USA, 2011. ACM.

[40] A. Raman, A. Zaks, J. W. Lee, and D. I. August. Parcae: a system for flexible parallel execution. In *PLDI '12*, pages 133–144, New York, NY, USA, 2012.

[41] C. Ranger, R. Raghuraman, A. Penmetsa, G. Bradski, and C. Kozyrakis. Evaluating mapreduce for multi-core and multiprocessor systems. HPCA '07, pages 13–24, Washington, DC, USA, 2007.

[42] J. Reinders. *Intel Threading Building Blocks.* O'Reilly Media, Inc., 2007.

[43] U. Richter, M. Mnif, J. Branke, C. MÃijller-Schloer, and H. Schmeck. Towards a generic observer/controller architecture for organic computing. In C. Hochberger and R. Liskowsky, editors, *GI Jahrestagung (1)*, volume 93 of *LNI*, pages 112–119. GI, 2006.

[44] H. Sasaki, T. Tanimoto, K. Inoue, and H. Nakamura. Scalability-based manycore partitioning. In *PACT '12*, pages 107–116, New York, NY, USA, 2012.

[45] M. A. Suleman, M. K. Qureshi, and Y. N. Patt. Feedback-driven threading: power-efficient and high-performance execution of multithreaded workloads on CMPs. In *ASPLOS '08*, pages 277–286, 2008.

[46] J. Teich, J. Henkel, A. Herkersdorf, D. Schmitt-Landsiedel, W. Schroder-Preikschat, and G. Snelting. Invasive computing: An overview. In *Multiprocessor System-on-Chip*, pages 241–268. 2011.

G-Charm: An Adaptive Runtime System for Message-Driven Parallel Applications on Hybrid Systems

R.Vasudevan, Sathish Vadhiyar
SuperComputer Education and Research Centre
Indian Institute of Science
Bangalore, India
vasudevan@ssl.serc.iisc.in,
vss@serc.iisc.in

Laxmikant V. Kalé
Department of Computer Science
University of Illinois at Urbana-Champaign
Urbana, IL 61801, USA
kale@illinois.edu

ABSTRACT

The effective use of GPUs for accelerating applications depends on a number of factors including effective asynchronous use of heterogeneous resources, reducing memory transfer between CPU and GPU, increasing occupancy of GPU kernels, overlapping data transfers with computations, reducing GPU idling and kernel optimizations. Overcoming these challenges require considerable effort on the part of the application developers and most optimization strategies are often proposed and tuned specifically for individual applications. In this paper, we present *G-Charm*, a generic framework with an adaptive runtime system for efficient execution of message-driven parallel applications on hybrid systems. The framework is based on CHARM++, a message-driven programming environment and runtime for parallel applications. The techniques in our framework include dynamic scheduling of work on CPU and GPU cores, maximizing reuse of data present in GPU memory, data management in GPU memory, and combining multiple kernels. We have presented results using our framework on Tesla S1070 and Fermi C2070 systems using three classes of applications: a highly regular and parallel 2D Jacobi solver, a regular dense matrix Cholesky factorization representing linear algebra computations with dependencies among parallel computations and highly irregular molecular dynamics simulations. With our generic framework, we obtain 1.5 to 15 times improvement over previous GPU-based implementation of CHARM++. We also obtain about 14% improvement over an implementation of Cholesky factorization with a static work-distribution scheme.

Categories and Subject Descriptors

D.1.3 [**Programming Techniques**]: Concurrent Programming—*Parallel programming*
; D.3.4 [**Programming Languages**]: Processors—*Optimization, Run-time environments*

Keywords

GPU, CHARM++, Optimizations, Hybrid execution, Data management, Combining kernels

1. INTRODUCTION

GPU-based hybrid systems have become highly prevalent for high performance computing with about 62 systems in the Top500 [1] list, including the #1 Titan system of Oak Ridge National Laboratory, being powered using accelerator/co-processor technology. However, effective use of a GPU system for high performance requires overcoming several challenges including effective asynchronous use of heterogeneous resources, reducing memory transfers between CPU and GPU, increasing occupancy of GPU kernels, overlapping data transfers with computations, reducing GPU idling and kernel optimizations. Overcoming these challenges require considerable effort by the users. Many optimization strategies have been proposed and tuned for specific applications [14, 15, 6, 10, 5].

In this paper, we present *G-Charm*, a generic framework with an adaptive runtime system for efficient execution of message-driven parallel applications on hybrid systems. The framework is based on CHARM++ [7], a message-driven programming environment and runtime for parallel applications. CHARM++ is an object oriented parallel programming framework in which the application domain is partitioned among several migratable objects called *chares*, and the chares are distributed among allotted processors. By employing over-decomposition, dynamic load balancing using migration of chares, and asynchronous communications overlapped with computations, CHARM++ has been used to provide high performance for different scientific applications including NAMD [10], a molecular dynamics application, ChaNGa [5], a cosmological simulator and ParFUM [9], a framework for unstructured mesh applications. These principles are highly needed for executions on hybrid systems consisting of a number of heterogeneous CPU and GPU units.

Obtaining high performance for CHARM++ message-driven parallel applications on GPU systems is challenging. CHARM++ chares are usually small in size dealing with small subdomains to promote data locality and cache benefits, and to provide communication-computation overlap among chares. An existing GPU task library for CHARM++, *HybridAPI* [17], does not provide a way to automatically merge units of data across multiple chares into blocks that would provide good occupancy on the GPU. The user must perform this agglomeration manually [6], or expect poor occupancy if each chare issues its own kernels. Invocations of kernels by each chare also results in large number of kernel invocations. Also, in HybridAPI, it is the users' responsibility to specify when to allocate, copy, and delete GPU buffers, so as to reuse buffers over execution of multiple kernels. It is also the users' responsibility to schedule work on either GPU or CPU. This places significant burden on the programmer since the code for making scheduling decisions has to be written in addition to the main logic.

As an example, consider the case of a 2D Molecular dynamics (MD) simulations. In this application, two types of chare objects are used. The molecules or particles are distributed among a 2D array of chares called *patches*. Force calculations between particles present in a pair of patch chares is calculated by an element of a chare array called *compute object*. The particle coordinates change only at the end of an iteration. A patch needs to be transferred to GPU only once for an iteration, and can be used for force calculation with each of its neighbors. In HybridAPI, ensuring that the patch is transferred only once to the GPU, and merging the data for separate kernels to invoke a smaller number of kernels with better occupancy require significant programming effort by the user. Finally, in HybridAPI, the user has to decide if the force calculation for a compute object has to be done on either CPU or GPU.

Our G-Charm framework includes important set of techniques for achieving high performance on GPUs in a transparent and generic manner. G-Charm performs dynamic scheduling of work units to CPU or GPU based on the current loads and the estimated run time of the work units on CPU and GPU. Our framework also dynamically combines multiple kernels corresponding to the work units to reduce the number of kernel invocations. The G-Charm runtime system also minimizes CPU-GPU data movement by keeping track of the location of data of *GPU chares* in GPU device memory and avoiding redundant data transfers for work units. G-Charm also performs data management to maximize the reuse of most frequently used data in the GPU device memory. Our techniques are generic and require minimal overhead from the application programmers.

We have presented results using our framework on Tesla S1070 and Fermi C2070 systems using three classes of applications: a highly regular and parallel 2D Jacobi solver, a regular dense matrix Cholesky factorization representing linear algebra computations with dependencies among parallel computations and a highly irregular molecular dynamics simulation. We performed comparisons with the HybridAPI framework [17]. We also compared our adaptive executions of Cholesky factorization with MAGMA [14], an implementation of Cholesky factorization for GPUs that perform static distribution of work and data units to CPU and GPU cores. With our generic framework, we obtain 1.5 to 15 times improvement over HybridAPI and about 14% improvement over MAGMA.

Following are the primary contributions of our paper.

1. A novel runtime system for message-driven parallel applications on GPUs.
2. Strategies to automatically compose and dynamically schedule work to CPU and GPU units, and maintain load balance.
3. Novel techniques to manage GPU global memory automatically for minimizing CPU-GPU data transfers and maximizing the reuse of data in GPU memory.
4. Demonstration of improvements with our generic adaptive techniques over static strategies for three important classes of applications.

The rest of the paper is organized as follows. Section 2 gives background on CHARM++ and an existing GPU management framework in CHARM++ called HybridAPI upon which our runtime system has been implemented. Section 3 describes the different components of the G-Charm framework. In Section 4, the various optimization strategies applied by our framework have been discussed. Section 5 presents the experimental results for Jacobi, Cholesky and Molecular dynamics applications comparing G-Charm with existing methods. Section 6 presents related efforts. Finally, in Section 7, we conclude and present some future works.

2. BACKGROUND

CHARM++ is a message-driven object oriented parallel programming framework based on C++ [7]. A parallel application written using CHARM++ divides the data among an array of migratable objects called *chares*. The chares are mapped to physical processors, and can be migrated among processors by the CHARM++ runtime system to provide load balance. Typically, the number of chares are much larger than the number of physical processors, resulting in overdecomposition. The chares are associated with specialized methods called *entry* methods. Entry methods of a chare object can be invoked from chares present in same or other processors. Remote entry methods invoked by a chare are queued as messages in a message queue at the destination processor. An instance of CHARM++ runtime system runs on each processor. The runtime system dequeues a message and invokes the corresponding chare's entry method upon arrival of all inputs of the entry method from the other chares. Thus, while input data for a chare is communicated from a remote processor, a processor can perform computation on some other chare for which inputs have already arrived. This enables CHARM++ to effectively overlap communication with computations.

HybridAPI [17] is a GPU execution framework available in CHARM++. In this framework, application programmers create a work request structure specifying the data to be transferred between CPU and GPU before and after kernel invocation, the kernel to be invoked and a callback function provided by the user that will be invoked on the CPU once the work request is processed by the GPU. The HybridAPI runtime system performs the necessary data transfers based on the specifications in the work request structures. The runtime system also checks for the progress of GPU operations related to data transfers and kernel executions, and effectively overlaps kernel execution of one work request with output data transfer for the previous work request and input data transfer for the next work request. Figure 1 depicts the control flow of a HybridAPI based CHARM++ application. In the figure, the green, blue and black boxes denote operations that are performed by the application programs, HybridAPI and the CHARM++ runtime system, respectively.

3. G-CHARM ARCHITECTURE

As mentioned, using HybridAPI without manual agglomeration of kernels and data, and manual data management leads to a large number of kernels, large number of CPU-GPU data transfers, and low GPU occupancies. Our G-

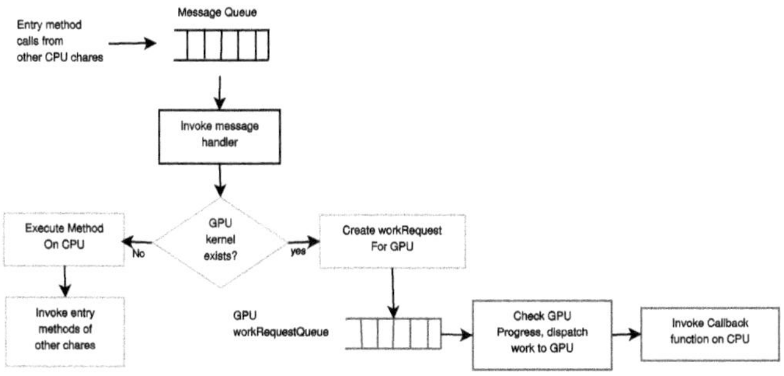

Figure 1: Charm++ Application Control Flow

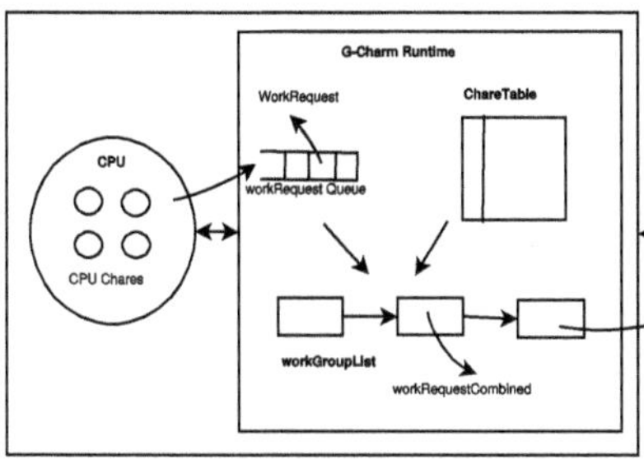

Figure 2: G-Charm architecture

Charm framework addresses these limitations. G-Charm is based on HybridAPI and consists of a runtime that performs various optimizations including minimizing data transfers, data management, dynamic scheduling and work agglomeration. The overall architecture is illustrated in Figure 2.

The application begins execution with the creation of chare objects. Each chare operates on a subset of data and executes its entry methods to update its own data on the arrival of input data from other chares and also to invoke entry methods of other chares. When a chare needs to invoke a kernel on the GPU, it creates a *workRequest* object and invokes a scheduler function in G-Charm runtime that performs dynamic scheduling of the workRequest to either CPU or GPU.

Otherwise, the workRequest is enqueued to GPU workRequestQueue. The queued workRequest object is processed by the G-Charm runtime. Specifically, the runtime checks the data region in the application domain represented by the workRequest data, and tries to avoid redundant data transfers to GPU by transferring only the data not already present in GPU. The G-Charm runtime then adds the workRequest to a node of a linked list called *workGroupList*, in which each node represents a set of workRequest objects that can be combined. G-Charm periodically combines workRequest objects from this list and creates objects of type *workRequestCombined*. The G-Charm runtime then schedules these objects for GPU execution. Thus the G-Charm runtime performs work agglomeration dynamically by combining kernels of multiple work requests for GPU execution. Once a workRequestCombined object finishes execution on the GPU, the runtime system transfers the output data back to the CPU and then invokes a callBack function on the CPU for each workRequest. The callBack functions enable the CPU chares to proceed with further computations by making use of the result computed on the GPU.

4. OPTIMIZATIONS

4.1 Dynamic Scheduling

G-Charm dynamically decides the allocation of a chare to either CPU or GPU for tasks for which kernel functions exist for both CPU and GPU. The workrequest object, after creation, is passed to the G-Charm runtime to check if it can be executed on the GPU. The decision is based on the estimated times of the corresponding task on CPU and GPU. The estimated time of a task in a time step is obtained as the average time taken by the task in the previous time steps.

The G-Charm runtime stores the average time taken by each kernel on GPU and CPU. Initially, the estimated time for each kernel on CPU and GPU is set to zero. The first workRequest for each kernel type is assigned to GPU and the second kernel is assigned to CPU to obtain the initial estimate for CPU and GPU execution time for each kernel. The estimation is for a single CPU or GPU kernel that is associated with a fixed amount of data (number of chares). For example, in a Jacobi application, a kernel corresponds to a certain rows of chares. When combining multiple GPU kernels (described in Section 4.4), the time for the combined kernel is scaled suitably based on the number of chares.

As mentioned in Section 3, the G-Charm runtime maintains a workGroupList where each node represents a set of workrequest objects that will be combined for execution on GPU. For the current workRequest for which the G-Charm runtime decides the allocation to CPU or GPU, the runtime compares the estimated CPU time of the current work request with the combined time of all the work requests in the workGroupList. The combined time is calculated by summing up the estimated GPU times of the workRequest objects in the list. If this combined time exceeds the estimated CPU time for the current work request, then the work request is assigned to CPU. Before execution of the current workrequest on the CPU, the *workRequestCombined* objects formed using the nodes in the workGroupList are scheduled for GPU execution using different CUDA streams. The control is then returned to the CPU chare to process the workRequest on the CPU. Thus, the G-Charm runtime attempts to maximize asynchronous execution of tasks on both GPU and CPU.

If the estimated time of the current work request is more than the combined estimated time, it is assigned to the GPU. In this case, it is added to the workRequestQueue and processed by the G-Charm runtime, which optimizes data transfers and adds it to the workGroupList for combined execution of multiple work requests on the GPU. The objective is to avoid GPU idling due to assigning a work request that can consume large amount of time on the CPU.

In the Molecular Dynamics (MD) example, G-Charm maintains the estimated average execution time of force computations between a pair of patches for CPU and GPU. These estimated times are updated after every execution on the corresponding unit, and are used for dynamic allocation to either CPU or GPU.

4.2 Memory Management

Each chare is associated with a region of data in the application domain. A chare maintains N_{buf} buffers, where N_{buf} is the total number of input and output data for the application. All the N_{buf} buffers of the application are divided among the chares. At a given instant, when the GPU work queue has a certain number of chares for scheduling to GPU, the G-Charm runtime allocates the maximum number of chare buffers that can fit into the GPU device memory. We divide the GPU device memory into two parts: a large *primary region* where memory management is performed, and a small scratch space where chare buffers for a workRequest are freed once the kernel of the workRequest completes. We use this scratch space when consecutive free memory cannot be found for a workRequest buffer in the primary region. For our work, we use 80% of the GPU device memory as the primary region and the rest as the scratch space.

For matrix applications, the G-Charm runtime divides GPU global memory into N_{buf} *buffer pools*. Each *buffer pool* is divided into *slots* of equal size. A *slot* is a placeholder for a chare buffer in GPU memory, and the size of the slot is equal to the size of the chare buffer. The size of a buffer pool i depends on the size of the primary region, *primarySize*, and the size of the chare buffer i, $sizeBuffer_i$, as shown in Equation 1.

$$bufPoolSize_i = Min(N_{chares} \times sizeBuffer_i, \frac{primarySize}{N_{buf}}) \quad (1)$$

where, N_{chares} is the total number of chares. In the equation, the first term denotes the case when all chare buffers of all chares can be accommodated in the primary region, and the second term denotes the case when the primary region is insufficient to accommodate all the chare buffers and is shared among the N_{buf} buffer pools. In the former case, each buffer pool will be divided into N_{chares} slots, while in the latter case, the number of slots will be less than N_{chares} and memory is managed using replacement and migration of chare buffers between CPU and GPU. The allocation of a large buffer pool for storing buffers from different chares for a given input or output array allows for dynamically combining multiple kernels of multiple chares into a single kernel for GPU execution, as discussed in Section 4.4 and also supports coalesced data access.

The G-Charm runtime keeps track of the mapping of chare buffers to slots in the device memory using a *chare table*. An entry in the table corresponding to a chare indicates the slots in the device memory that are occupied by each of the buffers in the chare. The runtime also periodically frees GPU memory, reclaiming the space used by chares that have not been used recently. Figure 3 illustrates the concepts of buffer pools, slots and chare table with $N_{buf} = 2$, $N_{chares} = 16$, and only 12 slots have been allocated in each buffer pool due to insufficient GPU memory. The figure indicates that the buffers in chares (0,0), (1,0), (1,2), (1,3), (2,0), (2,1) and (3,3) are currently in GPU memory occupying the respective slots in both the buffer pools.

4.3 Minimizing Data Transfers

In G-Charm, a workRequest object contains the indices of the chare buffers representing subregions in the application domain. Chares typically need data from other chares for their computations. When a workRequest for a chare is created, the G-Charm runtime uses the buffer indices of the workRequest to check if the buffers are already located in the GPU primary region due to the prior execution of kernels of other chares on the GPU (e.g., data generated from previous iterations). If located, the buffers are not copied to GPU, thus facilitating reuse of buffers and minimizing data transfers. In the MD example, if a buffer containing particle coordinates for a patch is present in GPU memory, it is reused by the workRequest objects corresponding to force calculations with the neighboring patches, thus avoiding redundant transfers.

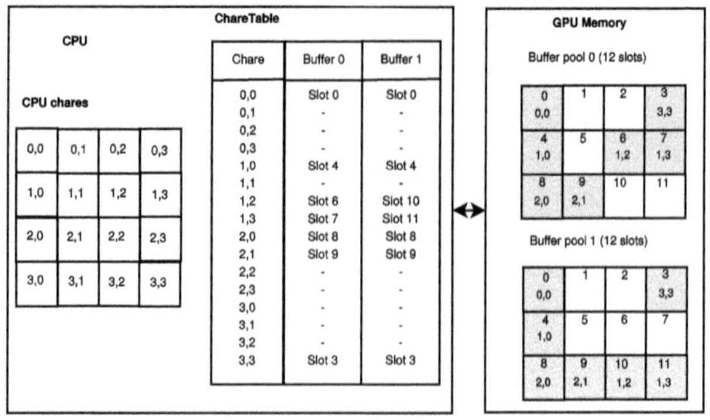

Figure 3: Chare table, Device Slots and GPU Buffer pools. In each slot in the buffer pools, the top entry corresponds to the slot number and the bottom entry denote the chare currently occupying the slot. Shaded slots are currently occupied.

If the buffers are not located in the GPU primary region, the G-Charm runtime finds the required number of free slots in the buffer pool. Chare buffers for a chare with chare index i are mapped to GPU slots using a simple hash function, $slot = i \ mod \ N_{slots}$, where N_{slots} is the number of slots in the buffer pools (12 in Figure 3). If a slot is already occupied, then the runtime scans all the slots in the buffer pool to check for a free slot, and assigns to a chare buffer. If a free slot is not found, memory from scratch space is assigned. Memory allocated from the scratch space is freed on completion of the workRequest.

The G-Charm runtime also uses LRU policy for buffer replacement in the GPU slots. Whenever the percentage of free slots becomes less than a threshold (in our work, 10%), the buffers corresponding to the least recently processed chares are reclaimed by the runtime, thus enabling the recently used chare buffers to stay in the GPU primary region for as long as possible. In addition to the strategies for reducing the amount of CPU-GPU data transfers by data reuse, G-Charm also reduces the data transfer latencies by combining workRequests of multiple chares into a single large kernel, and transferring contiguous data needed by the chares in a single step instead of multiple individual transfers. This is discussed further in the next section.

4.4 Combining Kernels

Combining multiple kernels of different chares into a single large kernel results in smaller number of kernel invocations, smaller CPU-GPU data transfer costs and larger GPU occupancy. Our G-Charm framework dynamically selects the workRequests objects of different chares for combining into a single kernel. In G-Charm, for each workRequest object, information is maintained about whether the kernel in the workRequest object reads from or writes to each chare buffer. This allows the G-Charm runtime to resolve dependencies among workRequests. workRequests for the same task that are independent can be potentially combined into a single kernel.

We refer to the chares with adjacent indices as *adjacent*

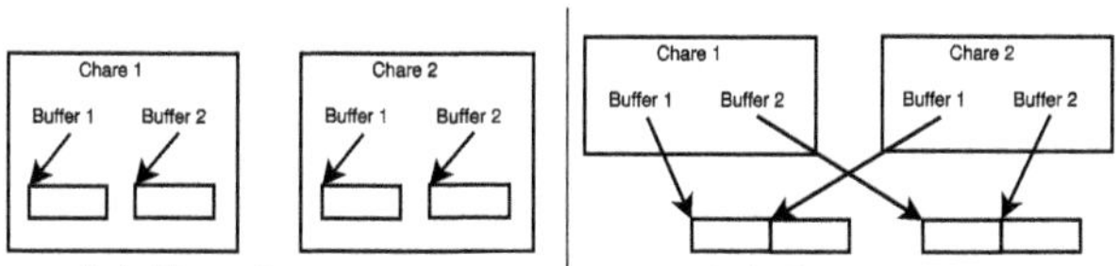

(a) Non Contiguous (b) Contiguous

Figure 4: Types of Memory Allocation

chares. In CHARM++ applications, adjacent chares are assigned adjacent regions in the application domain. The simple hash function described in the previous section allows allocation of the buffers of adjacent chares to adjacent slots or a continuous region in the GPU device memory irrespective of whether the buffers are stored contiguously in the CPU memory or not. This in turn enables combining multiple kernels of the different chares into a single kernel with single set of input data corresponding to large continuous regions in GPU memory instead of passing multiple sets of data corresponding to the buffers of the different chares located in different non-contiguous regions. Since G-Charm combines kernels only when the corresponding data regions are contiguous in GPU memory, the combined kernel operates on contiguous buffers.

The buffers for all the workRequest objects that are combined will have to be transferred to GPU memory before kernel invocation, if they are not already present in the GPU memory. If each buffer is transferred to GPU separately, though the number of kernels invoked decreases as a result of combining or agglomeration, the average number of memory transfers per kernel invocation increases. This results in GPU idling since the memory transfer time per kernel invocation is more than the kernel execution time. In order to reduce the memory transfer overhead, the buffers will have to be combined on the CPU before transferring to GPU.

G-Charm allows the chares to share memory allocated in the main chare in shared memory systems. In these systems, buffer i of individual chares can be either allocated within each chare at different locations in CPU memory as shown in Figure 4(a) or a single large buffer can be allocated in the main chare and then the individual chares can access their buffers using offsets into the contiguous region as shown in Figure 4(b). The latter approach is advantageous when combining multiple workRequests of different chares since the buffers needed by all the chares can be sent from a contiguous region in CPU memory using a single CPU-GPU data transfer, instead of multiple individual transfers. For example in Figure 4(b), instead of transferring Buffer 1 corresponding to Chare 1 and Chare 2 separately, a single buffer starting at address of Buffer 1 of Chare 1 and of size equal to the combined sizes of Buffer 1 in Chare 1 and Chare 2 can be transferred in a single step.

The G-Charm runtime maintains a workGroupList into which workRequest objects are added. Each node in the list contains a set of workRequest objects that do not have data access conflicts and can be executed concurrently. The workRequest objects of a node are eventually combined to form a single combinedWorkRequest and executed with a single kernel execution. The G-Charm runtime executes the workRequestObjects in the order maintained in the workGroupList. A workRequest, wr, is inserted into the workGroupList based on the following conditions.

1. If wr reads from buffer B, wr is inserted after the last node containing a workRequest that writes to this buffer. This is done to preserve Read After Write (RAW) data integrity constraint.
2. If wr writes to the buffer B, wr is inserted after the last node containing a workRequest that uses this buffer for read or write operations. This is done to preserve Write After Read(WAR) and Write After Write(WAW) data integrity constraints.
3. If there exists a node in the list that contains workRequests with same kernel as wr, then wr is added to the same node, otherwise a new node is inserted in the list and wr is added to it.

The G-Charm runtime periodically calls a *combine* routine to create *workRequestCombined* objects from the nodes of the workGroupList and enqueue them for GPU execution.

In the MD example, the workRequests for different compute objects do not have dependencies since the force calculations between different pairs of patches can be performed independently. Hence any set of workrequest objects can be combined into a large kernel that deals with multiple pairs of patches. However, in linear algebra operations like Cholesky decomposition, a column may be updated by several other columns, and the workrequests corresponding to these column updates have dependencies. In this case, the G-Charm runtime combines workrequest objects corresponding to a single column, since the updates of elements within a column can be performed independently.

4.5 Programming Interface

The GPU environment supported by G-Charm is CUDA. The application programmer writes a separate GPU CUDA kernel and CPU Charm++ function for each task, and these are compiled separately using *nvcc* compiler and *charmc* program, respectively, and then linked using *charmc* program. G-Charm provides some functions for use by applications to provide information to G-Charm runtime for memory management and dynamic scheduling. Each chare object in the chare array that owns a part of data has to initialize G-Charm runtime by invoking the *initGM* method with various information including chare array dimension, the number of chares along each dimension, the number of buffers in each chare (N_{buf}), if the application involves matrix operations, row and column dimensions of the submatrices assigned to each chare and whether chares share CPU memory. One instance of the G-Charm runtime runs per processor. Since each instance has to be initialized and the chares are distributed among all processors, each chare is required to call *initGM* method and only the first invocation on each processor actually initializes the G-Charm runtime. The initialization involves GPU memory allocation including allocation of buffer pools and slots, and initialization of the chare table.

The application also calls a *checkGPURun* function to decide whether a workRequest has to be run on CPU or GPU. If this function returns true, the G-Charm runtime adds the workrequest to workRequestQueue and invokes the GPU kernel specified in the workrequest. If the function returns false, the user program explicitly invokes the corresponding CPU function.

5. EXPERIMENTS AND RESULTS

We demonstrate the benefits of our G-Charm framework

with three classes of applications: a highly regular and parallel 2D Jacobi solver, a regular dense matrix Cholesky factorization representing linear algebra computations with dependencies among parallel computations and highly irregular molecular dynamics simulations. The experiments were run on a Tesla cluster with each node of the cluster containing 4 quad-core AMD Opteron 8378 cores and one Tesla S1070 GPU, and a Fermi cluster with each node containing one 4-core Intel Xeon W3550 processor and one Tesla C2070 GPU. The Tesla S1070 GPU system is composed of 4 GPUs with each GPU made up of 240 GPU cores. The Fermi C2070 GPU system is composed of a single GPU consisting of 448 GPU cores. All our experiments were performed on single GPU systems.

5.1 Jacobi application

This is a standard 2-D Jacobi Poisson's equation solver involving 5-point stencil computations. Optimizing such stencil computations on GPU systems is essential for high performance of large-scale multi-dimensional grid problems [4, 16]. In the CHARM++ Jacobi implementation, the 2-D grid is divided among a 2D array of chares. Each chare initializes its own data and in each iteration exchanges boundary information to its four neighboring chares, performs computations of local data and sends error values to the main chare. The main chare is responsible for computing the overall residual error for initializing the next iteration.

Figures 5(a) and 5(b) compare the performance using G-Charm with the performance using the other approaches, namely *CPUOnly* and *HybridAPI*, on both the Tesla and the Fermi systems. The CPUOnly approach denotes the execution using only a CPU core. We have included comparison to CPU only version, since an inefficient implementation on GPU can result in even slower performance than CPU only execution due to GPU overheads including kernel invocations and memory transfers. In the HybridAPI framework, each chare, after receiving the boundary data from the neighboring chares, creates a workRequest object and enqueues it into GPU workRequest queue for GPU computations of the local data. The G-Charm framework automatically performs asynchronous computations of parts of the 2-D domain on both the CPU and the GPU cores, manages the data, and combines multiple kernels. In order to isolate the advantages obtained using each of the three primary optimizations performed by G-Charm, we also show the results obtained by *G-Charm-combker-only*, involving only the optimization of combining kernels and reducing the number of kernel invocations, *G-Charm-(combker+datareuse)-only*, involving only the optimizations of combining kernels and data reuse, and *G-Charm*, also involving asynchronous CPU executions.

The average speedup of G-Charm over HybridAPI is about 10. The primary benefit with G-Charm is due to the combined kernel execution, as seen in the difference between *G-Charm-combker-only* and *HybridAPI* results. Combining kernels not only reduces the number of kernel invocations but also reduces the total number of data transfers due to concatenating and sending the large data needed for the combined kernel in a single step. The *G-Charm-combker-only* version gives a speedup of 2 in Tesla and 10 in Fermi System since data transfer rate between CPU and GPU is much larger in Fermi (144 GB/sec) compared to Tesla system (12.8 GB/sec). However, in the *G-Charm-combker-only* version, the same data can get transferred back and forth between the CPU and GPU across different iterations. As the matrix size becomes larger, the amount of data transfer increases. The *G-Charm-(combker+datareuse)-only* version, involving data reuse and management, gives an average benefit of about 5 times over the HybridAPI version in Tesla and about 16 times in Fermi systems. *G-Charm-(combker+datareuse)-only* gives best performance when the matrix completely fits in GPU as shown for sizes up to 15000×15000 in Tesla and 25000×25000 in Fermi. For matrix size of 40000×40000, the performance of *G-Charm-(combker+datareuse)-only* is the same as *G-Charm-combker-only*, i.e. without data reuse, since for this size, only one GPU chare could be accommodated in GPU at a time and the data corresponding to the chare has to be swapped out of the GPU memory to make way for another GPU chare execution. The optimization due to asynchronous CPU executions brings about 6% additional improvement in performance. Asynchronous CPU utilization has been employed only when a matrix cannot be fit completely in GPU memory.

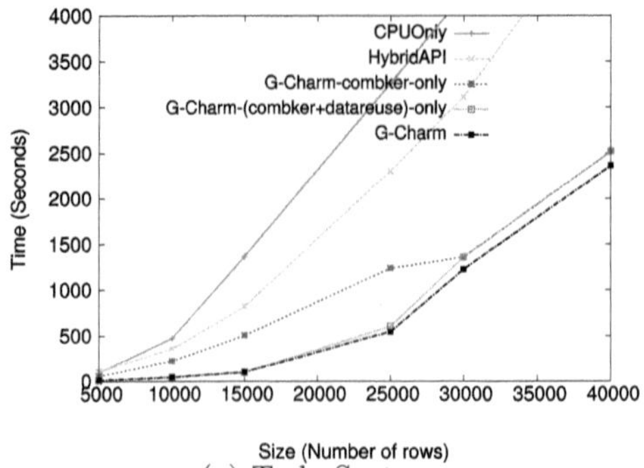

(a) Tesla System

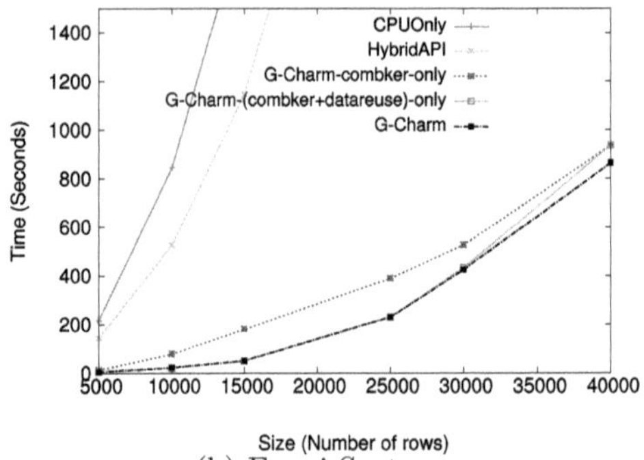

(b) Fermi System

Figure 5: Jacobi Execution Time

We also compare the G-Charm and the HybridAPI approaches in terms of the number of kernels invoked, the amount of data transferred, and the percentage of time CPU is utilized for useful computations during application execution. Figure 6 shows these results for the Fermi system. Similar results were obtained on the Tesla system. We find that G-Charm invokes about 30 times lesser number of kernels, and transfers about less than half the amount of data than the HybridAPI for matrix size 40000×40000 for which G-Charm has maximum number of migrations as well as maximum number of kernel invocations. We also find that

G-Charm, due to the optimization of asynchronous CPU executions, gives about 5% increased CPU utilization over HybridAPI. In our HybridAPI implementation, matrix update with neighbor values is performed on GPU and error calculation is performed on CPU. These error calculations constitute about 45% CPU utilization in the HybridAPI implementation. In G-Charm, asynchronous CPU utilization is employed only when matrices do not fit in GPU memory. Figure 6(c) shows the increase in CPU utilization for G-Charm as the matrix size increases.

The execution profiles of the different implementations on the Tesla system are illustrated in Figure 7. This figure shows the execution timeline for GPU and CPU for matrix size 25000 × 25000 for the first ten iterations for all implementations. The patterns are found to persist across all iterations. The CPU time shown in this figure corresponds to only performing useful computations. Figure 7(a) shows HybridAPI execution which involves large number of kernel invocations and memory transfers. The continuous CPU-GPU memory transfers for large number of small kernels in HybridAPI can be seen by the almost continuous green bar. Figure 7(b) illustrates the profile of *G-Charm-combker-only* in which the combination of kernels results in reduced number of CPU-GPU data transfers as shown by the vertical lines in the bars. The optimization related to data reuse is shown in Figure 7(c) in which the frequency of data transfers is smaller. This is illustrated by the larger gaps between the data transfers. Finally, Figure7(d) illustrates asynchronous CPU-GPU executions, in which the CPU is sufficiently utilized.

5.2 Cholesky Decomposition

Cholesky decomposition factorizes a real, symmetric, positive definite matrix $A = LL^T$, where L is a lower triangular matrix. Cholesky factorization primarily involves updates or multiplication (*cmod*), division (*cdiv*) and factorization steps. We have implemented a subcolumn Cholesky factorization using G-Charm in which the factorization step is performed on CPU, and the *cdiv* and *cmod* steps are performed on GPU.

We compare the G-Charm implementation of double precision Cholesky factorization with MAGMA [14], a highly tuned dense linear algebra library for GPUs. In G-Charm implementation, a main chare allocates memory for the entire input matrix and creates a set of chares, with each chare being responsible for factorization of a portion of the input matrix. Chares in a column perform the *cmod* operation using all the previous columns to update their submatrices. Once *cmod* is complete for the diagonal chare element of that column, it proceeds to the factorization step. After factorization, all the chares below the diagonal chare perform the *cdiv* operation. The application begins with *cmod* operation for the first column and ends with *cdiv* operation for the last column.

Figure 8 shows the results with G-Charm and MAGMA on Tesla and Fermi systems. We have tested for matrix sizes up to 40000 × 40000 in Tesla and 29760 × 29760 in Fermi system, the maximum sizes that can be accommodated in the CPU memory of these systems. The Tesla and Fermi systems can accommodate matrices of size up to 19840 × 19840 in the GPU device memory. We find that up to these matrix sizes, both MAGMA and G-Charm give similar results since for these smaller matrices, GPU data management functionality of G-Charm is not exercised, and MAGMA also performs careful data management and composition of large kernels. For larger matrix sizes, G-Charm performs up to 9% and 15% better than MAGMA for double and single precision computations, respectively. The higher performance is because G-Charm performs efficient GPU memory management, reduced number of kernel invocations, and reduced CPU-GPU data transfers by reuse of GPU data, while MAGMA performs large amount of CPU-GPU data migrations for these large matrix sizes.

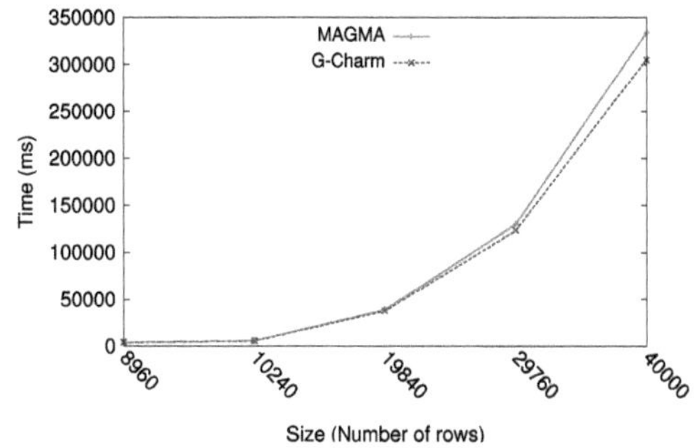

(a) Tesla System

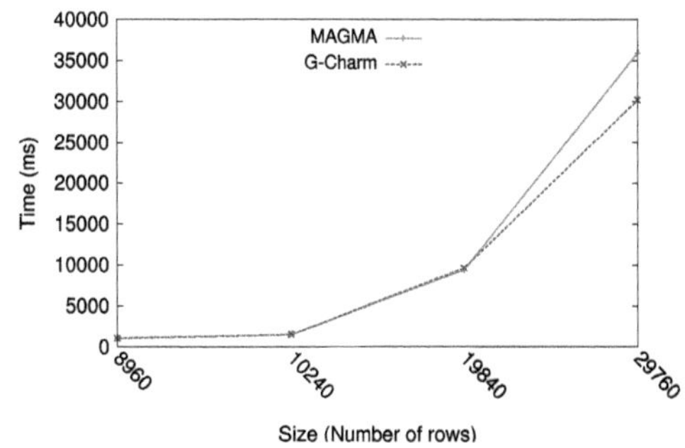

(b) Fermi System

Figure 8: Cholesky Decomposition Execution Time

We also performed comparisons with HybridAPI and StarPU [3] frameworks for Cholesky factorization. We obtained about 8x speedup with G-Charm over HybridAPI. Similar to G-Charm, StarPU [3] also performs dynamic scheduling of work to both CPU and GPU, and data management of GPU data. We found that StarPU gave very large execution times. For example, for matrix size of 29760 × 29760, the execution time with StarPU was 137 seconds on the Fermi system, while the execution times with G-Charm and MAGMA were 31.8 and 34.7 seconds respectively. The large execution times with StarPU is because StarPU invokes *cdiv* and *cmod* operations for each individual block of the matrix resulting in 11991 kernel invocations while G-Charm invokes a single kernel for contiguous chares resulting in only 1825 kernel invocations.

We also compared the G-Charm and the MAGMA approaches in terms of the number of kernels invoked, and the amount of data transferred. Figure 9 shows these results for the Fermi system. We find that G-Charm invokes about 2.5 times lesser number of kernels for matrix size 29760 × 29760, since it allocates adjacent chares in adjacent GPU slots and invokes a single kernel to process all chares that are con-

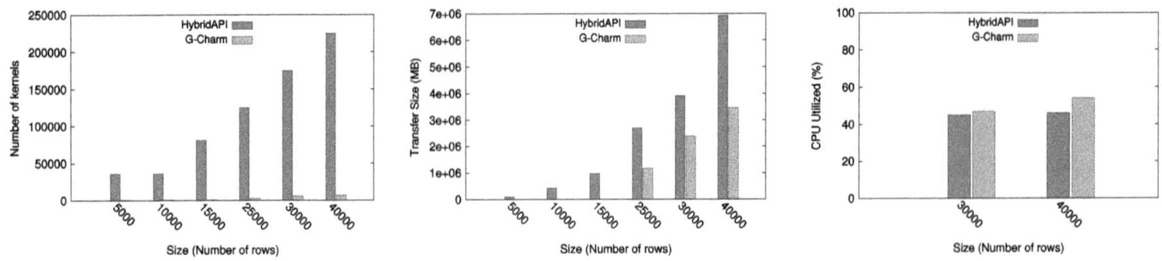

(a) Number of Kernel Invocations (b) Amount of CPU-GPU Data Transfer (c) CPU Utilization

Figure 6: Jacobi Execution Statistics on the Fermi System

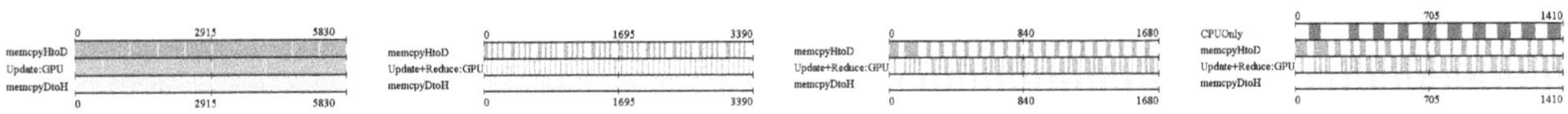

(a) HybridAPI (b) G-Charm-combker-only (c) G-Charm-(combker+datareuse)-only (d) G-Charm

Figure 7: Jacobi Execution Profile on the Tesla System

tiguous in GPU memory. For smaller matrices, we find that both MAGMA and G-Charm invokes similar number of kernels. G-Charm also transfers about 3 times lesser data than MAGMA due to dynamic data reuse and shared memory implementation when matrix size does not fit entirely in GPU memory. This efficient data management and reuse in our generic G-Charm framework results in improved performance of G-Charm (31810 milliseconds) over MAGMA (34740 milliseconds) for matrix size 29760 × 29760.

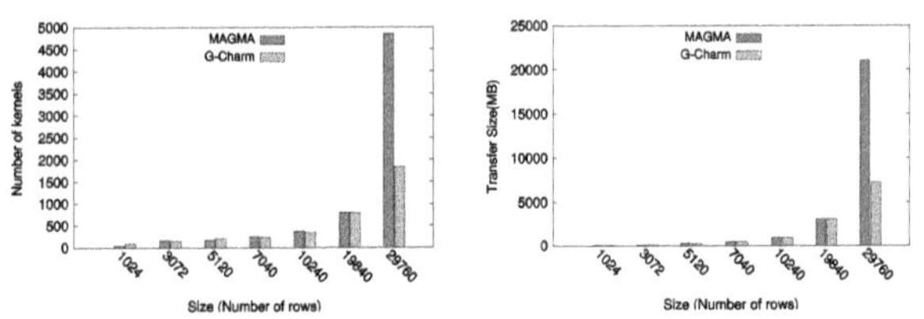

(a) Number of Kernel Invocations (b) Amount of CPU-GPU Data Transfer

Figure 9: Cholesky Decomposition Execution Statistics on the Fermi System

5.3 Molecular Dynamics

We have also conducted experiments on a non-matrix application, namely, molecular dynamics. Molecular dynamics is a highly irregular application for simulating the interactions between molecules over a period of time. We consider a two-dimensional molecular dynamics application in which the 2D space is partitioned into patches. Each patch owns the particles present in the region. In each timestep, force on each particle due to other particles within a cutoff distance is calculated and the position of the particles are updated. Particles migrate to neighboring patches according to new positions and the application proceeds to next timestep. This is repeated for a fixed number of timesteps.

In the CHARM++ implementation, a *compute object* calculates force between a pair of patches, as mentioned in Section 1. The entry method *interact* takes two vectors of particles belonging to two patches and updates force components of each particle. The widely-used NAMD [10, 12] molecular dynamics framework based on CHARM++ also adopts a similar parallelization scheme based on compute objects. The *interact* method has been implemented as a CUDA kernel for the HybridAPI and G-Charm implementations. The G-Charm framework automatically performs asynchronous computations of interaction calculations on both the CPU and the GPU cores.

Figure 10 compares the performance using G-Charm with the performance using the other approaches, namely *CPUOnly* and HybridAPI, on both the Tesla and the Fermi systems. The *CPUOnly* approach denotes the execution using only a CPU core. We find that the average performance improvement of G-Charm over the cpu-only version is about 33% and over HybridAPI is about 21%.

Figure 11 shows the number of kernels invoked, the amount of data transferred, and the percentage of time CPU is utilized during application execution, for the cpuOnly, HybridAPI and the G-Charm implementations on the Fermi system. We find that G-Charm invokes about 20% lesser number of kernels and transfers about 30% lesser data than HybridAPI. We also find that G-Charm gives 2.5 to 5 times increased CPU utilization over HybridAPI. Both in HybridAPI and in G-Charm, updating particle coordinates after each iteration and subsequent migration of particles were performed on CPU. These contribute to nearly 10% of CPU time for HybridAPI. In G-Charm, apart from these computations, force calculation for some compute objects are dynamically assigned to CPU for asynchronous execution, resulting in improved CPU utilization.

Figure 12 shows the profiling output of G-Charm and HybridAPI executions for 10 iterations on the Fermi system. We find that GPU remains idle for some time after every iteration during which CPU updates particle coordinates and migrates particles to other chares. This idle time can be reduced by providing kernel function for updating particle coordinates. We find that the primary reason for higher per-

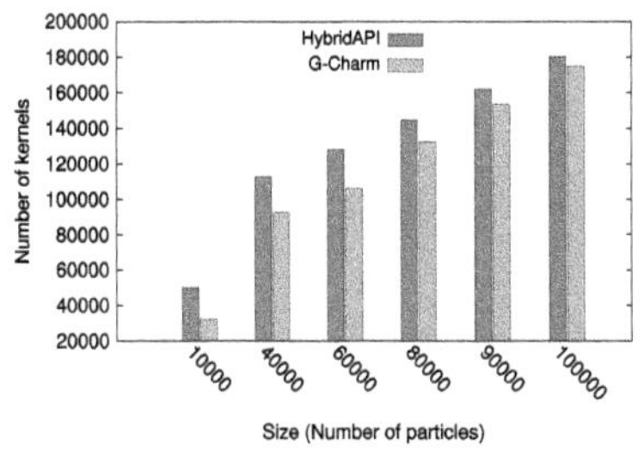

(a) Number of Kernel Invocations

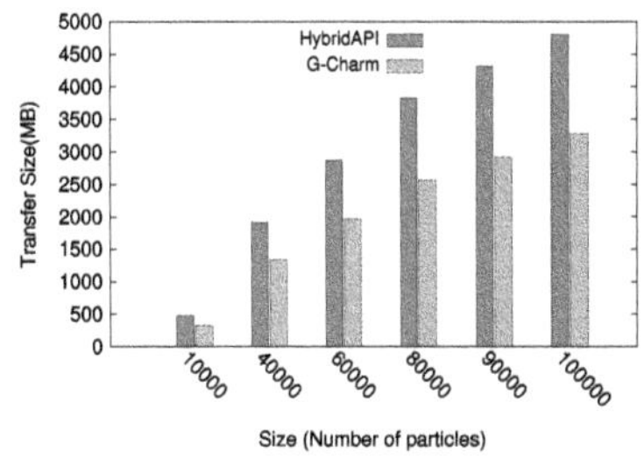

(b) Amount of CPU-GPU Data Transfer

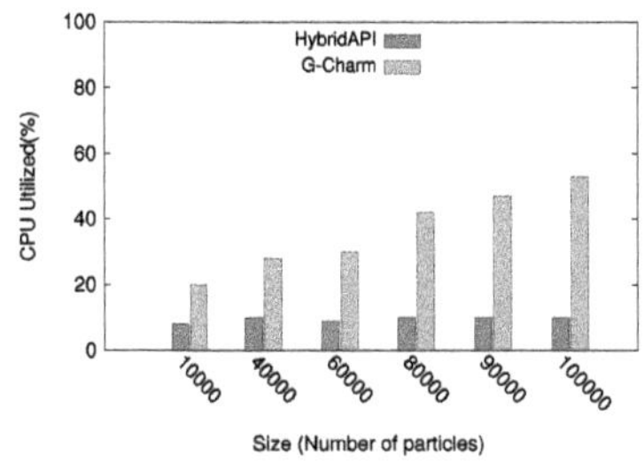

(c) CPU Utilization

Figure 11: Molecular Dynamics Execution Statistics on the Fermi System

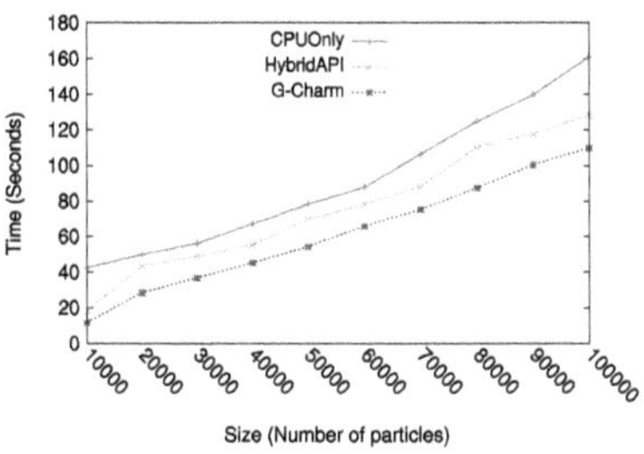

(a) Tesla System

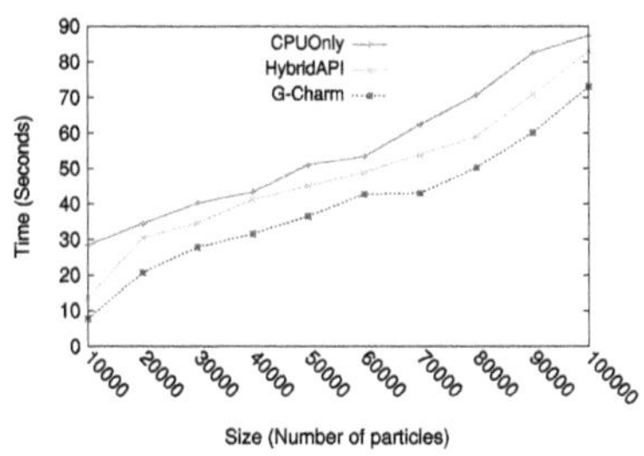

(b) Fermi System

Figure 10: Molecular Dynamics Execution Time

formance of G-Charm in molecular dynamics application is due to the efficient use of CPU for useful computations.

5.4 Discussion

In general, we find that combining kernels is beneficial not only in reduction of number of kernel invocations, but also in reducing the latencies of CPU-GPU data transfers. Data management and reuse of GPU data can provide significant benefits for large problem sizes in which the entire data cannot fit in the GPU memory. Finally, asynchronous CPU-GPU executions can provide added benefits, but the extent of the benefits is application-dependent and specifically depends on the CPU-GPU performance ratio obtained for the computations and the ability to estimate the performance to apportion the appropriate work to CPU.

Overall, we find higher gains of 10X and 8X in Jacobi and Cholesky applications, respectively, and smaller gains of about 21% in molecular dynamics application with G-Charm over HybridAPI implementation. The higher gains in Jacobi application is due to non dependency among chares in an iteration combined with very less CPU-GPU data transfers, and the higher gains in Cholesky factorization is due to more opportunities for efficient data management. The smaller gain in molecular dynamics application is because of non-shared memory implementation, memory copy overheads and less data reuse.

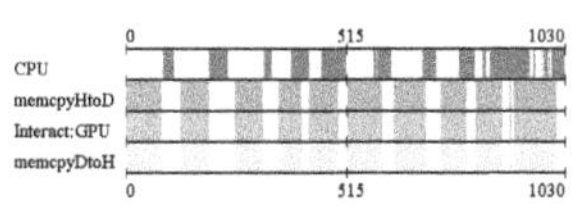

(a) HybridAPI

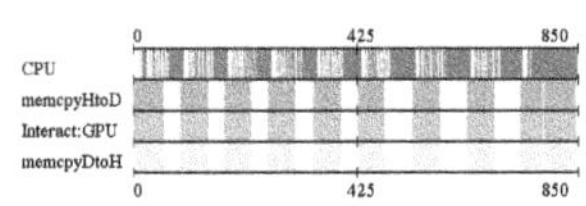

(b) G-Charm

Figure 12: Molecular Dynamics Execution Profile on the Fermi System

6. RELATED WORK

The AMM system [11] aims to reduce memory transfer between CPU and GPU automatically by avoiding transfer of non stale data between CPU and GPU, eager transfer of data to CPU and transfer of GPU only data to CPU by performing compiler analysis. Compiler analysis has limitations in identifying all non-stale data. Our framework, by relying on the user input, can reduce the amount of transfers of such data. Our framework also reduces the number of kernel invocations by agglomeration of kernels and the associated data. As shown in our results, combining multiple kernels provides clear performance benefits. The work by Ashwin Prasad et al. [13] maps a MATLAB basic block to either CPU or GPU at compile time using estimated run time of the block obtained through profiling. In our approach, work assignment to CPU and GPU is determined dynamically at runtime using information such as average times taken by CPU and GPU to process a kernel, and the number of messages waiting to be processed in CPU and GPU queues.

Some recent efforts have focused on efficient GPU computations of stencil computations [4, 16]. The work by Bandishti et al. [4] partitions the iteration space using hyperplanes for concurrent and load balanced executions. The work by Venkatasubramanian et al. [16] avoid synchronization delays at the end of the iterations using highly asynchronous computations. Our work is on providing a general framework based on asynchronous message-passing principles. Heterogeneous tiled algorithms implemented for Cholesky and QR factorizations [14] uses a static partitioning scheme to effectively utilize all CPU and GPU cores. In our work, the heterogeneous tile sizes are determining dynamically by agglomerating data and kernels. NAMD [10] is a widely used scalable molecular dynamics application that has GPU extensions [12] for calculating short range non bonded forces. However, this work does not attempt to reduce non-stale data and does not combine multiple kernels to reduce the number of kernel invocations.

Our runtime system is similar to StarPU [3] in which the application programmer creates CPU and GPU kernels and the runtime system decides whether to schedule a task to CPU or GPU. StarPU also automatically manages and moves data between CPU and GPU [2]. Our framework, in addition to data management, also automatically performs asynchronous CPU-GPU executions of non-dependent tasks and agglomeration of work.

Our work is closely related to the work by Kunzman [8] that has developed a unified programming model for abstracting different types of accelerators, with the runtime system performing various tasks such as load balancing, work agglomeration and data management . In this work, the user has to explicitly specify if a given data should be persistent in GPU memory across kernel invocations to avoid redundant data transfers, while in our work, such data management is performed automatically by the runtime system.

7. CONCLUSIONS AND FUTURE WORK

In this paper, we presented a framework called G-Charm for efficient execution of message-driven parallel applications on hybrid systems. G-Charm focuses on optimizing memory transfers to GPU by reusing data present in GPU memory, reducing the number of kernels by invoking a single kernel on the combined data of multiple chares and reducing CPU and GPU idle times by dynamic work distribution. By conducting experiments with three different applications belonging to three different categories, we found that the adaptive strategies in G-Charm provide a speedup of about 1.5 to 15 over a previous GPU-based implementation of CHARM++, and about 14% improvement over a highly tuned dense linear algebra routine. Currently, we have focused on effectively using single CPU and GPU for applications. In our future work, we plan to scale G-Charm to multi-GPU systems. We also plan to improve our programming abstractions, and explore more classes of large applications.

8. ACKNOWLEDGMENTS

This work is supported partly by DOE via DE-SC0001845, by NSF via the grant HECURA-0833188, and by CUDA Research Centre award from NVIDIA to SuperComputer Education and Research Centre, Indian Institute of Science.

9. REFERENCES

[1] Top500 supercomputer sites. `http://www.top500.org/lists/2012/11/`.

[2] E. Agullo, C. Augonnet, J. Dongarra, H. Ltaief, R. Namyst, S. Thibault, S. Tomov, and W. m. Hu. Faster, Cheaper, Better–a Hybridization Methodology to Develop Linear Algebra Software for GPUs. *GPU Computing Gems*, 2, 2010.

[3] C. Augonnet, S. Thibault, R. Namyst, and P. Wacrenier. StarPU: A Unified Platform for Task Scheduling on Heterogeneous Multicore Architectures. *Concurrency and Computation: Practice and Experience*, 23(2):187–198, 2011.

[4] V. Bandishti, I. Pananilath, and U. Bondhugula. Tiling Stencil Computations to Maximize Parallelism. In *In Proceedings of ACM/IEEE Supercomputing Conference (SC)*, 2012.

[5] P. Jetley, F. Gioachin, C. Mendes, L. Kalé, and T. Quinn. Massively Parallel Cosmological Simulations with ChaNGa. In *In Proceedings of IEEE International Symposium on Parallel and Distributed Processing (IPDPS)*, pages 1–12, 2008.

[6] P. Jetley, L. Wesolowski, F. G. L. Kalé, and T. Quinn. Scaling Hierarchical N-body Simulations on GPU Clusters. In *In Proceedings of ACM/IEEE Supercomputing Conference (SC)*, pages 1–11, 2010.

[7] L. Kalé and S. Krishnan. Charm++: Parallel Programming with Message-Driven Objects. *Parallel Programming using C++*, pages 175–213, 1996.

[8] D. Kunzman. *Runtime Support for Object-based Message-driven Parallel Applications on Heterogeneous Clusters*. PhD thesis, University of Illinois at Urbana-Champaign, 2012.

[9] O. Lawlor, S. Chakravorty, T. Wilmarth, N. Choudhury, I. Dooley, G. Zheng, and L. Kalé. ParFUM: A Parallel Framework for Unstructured Meshes for Scalable Dynamic Physics Applications. *Engineering with Computers*, 22(3):215–235, 2006.

[10] C. Mei, Y. Sun, G. Zheng, E. Bohm, L. Kalé, J. James, and C. Harrison. Enabling and Scaling Biomolecular Simulations of 100 Million Atoms on Petascale Machines with a Multicore-Optimized Message-Driven Runtime. In *In Proceedings of ACM/IEEE Supercomputing Conference (SC)*, 2011.

[11] S. Pai, R. Govindarajan, and M. Thazhuthaveetil. Fast and Efficient Automatic Memory Management for GPUs Using Compiler-Assisted Runtime Coherence Scheme. In *In the Proceedings of the 21st international conference on Parallel Architectures and Compilation Techniques (PACT)*, pages 33–42, 2012.

[12] J. Phillips, J. Stone, and K. Schulten. Adapting a Message-Driven Parallel Application to GPU-Accelerated Clusters. In *In the Proceedings of IEEE/ACM Supercomputing Conference (SC)*, pages 1–9, 2008.

[13] A. Prasad, J. Anantpur, and R. Govindarajan. Automatic Compilation of MATLAB Programs for Synergistic Execution on Heterogeneous Processors. In *In the Proceedings of the 32nd ACM SIGPLAN conference on Programming Language Design and Implementation (PLDI)*, pages 152–163, 2011.

[14] F. Song, S. Tomov, and J. Dongarra. Enabling and Scaling Matrix Computations on Heterogeneous Multi-core and Multi-GPU Systems. In *In the Proceedings of IEEE/ACM Supercomputing Conference (SC)*, pages 365–376, 2012.

[15] S. Tomov, J. Dongarra, and M. Baboulin. Towards Dense Linear Algebra for Hybrid GPU Accelerated Manycore Systems. *Parallel Computing*, 36(5):232–240, 2010.

[16] S. Venkatasubramanian and R. Vuduc. Tuned and Wildly Asynchronous Stencil Kernels for Hybrid CPU/GPU Systems. In *In Proceedings of the 23rd international Conference on Supercomputing (ICS)*, pages 244–255, 2009.

[17] L. Wesolowski. An Application Programming Interface for General Purpose Graphics Processing Units in an Asynchronous Runtime System. Master's thesis, University of Illinois at Urbana-Champaign, 2008.

Implementing OmpSs Support for Regions of Data in Architectures with Multiple Address Spaces

Javier Bueno
Barcelona Supercomputing Center
Universitat Politècnica de Catalunya
javier.bueno@bsc.es

Xavier Martorell
Barcelona Supercomputing Center
Universitat Politècnica de Catalunya
xavier.martorell@bsc.es

Rosa M. Badia
Barcelona Supercomputing Center
Artificial Intelligence Research Institute (IIIA)
Spanish National Research Council (CSIC)
rosa.m.badia@bsc.es

Eduard Ayguadé
Barcelona Supercomputing Center
Universitat Politècnica de Catalunya
eduard.ayguade@bsc.es

Jesús Labarta
Barcelona Supercomputing Center
Universitat Politècnica de Catalunya
jesus.labarta@bsc.es

ABSTRACT

The need for features for managing complex data accesses in modern programming models has increased due to the emerging hardware architectures. HPC hardware has moved towards clusters of accelerators and/or multicores, architectures with a complex memory hierarchy exposed to the programmer.

We present the implementation of data regions on the OmpSs programming model, a high-productivity annotation-based programming model derived from OpenMP. This enables the programmer to specify regions of strided and/or overlapped data used by the parallel tasks of the application. The data will be automatically managed by the underlying run-time environment, which could transparently apply optimization techniques to improve performance.

This approach based on a high-productivity programming model contrasts with more direct approaches like MPI, where the programmer has to explicitly deal with the data management. It is generally believed that these are capable of achieving the best possible performance, so we also compare the performance of several OmpSs applications against well-known counterparts MPI implementations obtaining comparable or better results.

Categories and Subject Descriptors

D.1.3 [**Programming Techniques**]: Concurrent programming—*Parallel programming*

Keywords

Cluster programming; Run-time environments; OpenMP; Non-contiguous memory access

1. INTRODUCTION

HPC systems have evolved to more complex systems over the last recent years. Clusters of multicores, with accelerators have become popular due to their price/performance ratio. However they severely impact the burden of application development, because of the presence of different address spaces and processor types.

When it comes to achieving a good performance, dealing with multiple address spaces becomes a critical task. Partitioning the application data and managing its movement across the different components may be a challenging task for the programmer, therefore programming models that provide mechanisms to automatically handle it are desired in order to boost productivity.

Programming models like MPI or more recently CUDA are the reference in terms of achieved performance but they are too explicit and developing with them can be a tedious and difficult task.

Because of this, many new programming models have emerged as an alternative to provide more simple approaches to develop parallel programs while also taking care of many decisions that otherwise would be left to the programmer.

OmpSs [12] is a programming model that follows this direction. The responsibility of the programmer is to identify the potential parallelism of the application using the concept of *tasks*, and specifying their data directionality. This information is used by the runtime to generate the corresponding data-dependence task graph. The decisions of how to execute the application are entirely left to the underlying run-time system. OmpSs has been successful in providing an easy way to program complex systems like clusters of GPUs[8].

However, the current OmpSs implementation had some limitations when it came to managing application data. Task data was limited to contiguous non-overlapping regions. While this was enough to implement many applications, some others required a more flexible mechanisms to be coded.

In this paper we present a mechanism to handle automatically regions of data that can be potentially overlapped among them. The mechanism has been implemented in Nanos++, the current OmpSs run-time environment, and it targets cluster environments, but it is generic enough to be used with other architectures that have different address spaces. We also evaluate the behavior of the system on a cluster environment and compare it against MPI, the reference programming model in this kind of systems.

The contributions presented in this paper are the following:

- The design and implementation of the data structures and mechanisms to manage the access to regions of data in OmpSs, and a simple optimization to improve the performance on a cluster environment.
- An evaluation of a set of benchmarks that take advantage of the proposed mechanisms and an evaluation of the effectiveness of the implemented optimization.
- The comparison of the results obtained from the OmpSs version of the applications and well-known high performance implementations using MPI.

The rest of the paper is organized as it follows. In Section 2 we introduce the details of the region support in the OmpSs programming model and how they can provide a productivity advantage to the programmer when paired with the proposed implementation. Section 3 summarizes the most important implementation details and the optimizations that these new changes. In Section 4 we evaluate the resulting OmpSs run-time environment with some applications that take advantage of the newly implemented mechanisms and also evaluate our optimizations and compare the system performance against well-known MPI versions of the same applications. Section 5 describes other projects that have similar contributions, and finally Section 6 summarizes the conclusions of this paper and the future directions that may arise from it.

2. REGIONS OF DATA IN OMPSS

In this paper we propose an implementation to enable the automatic management of the data regions offered by OmpSs on architectures with disjoint address spaces. The rest of this section offers a brief description of this OmpSs feature and how applications can take advantage of it.

2.1 OmpSs background

OmpSs[12] is a programming model that aims to be an efficient programming model for heterogeneous and multi-core architectures. It is derived from OpenMP 3.0 and offers asynchronous parallelism in the form of *tasks*. *Tasks* were introduced by OpenMP 3.0, as an effort to support a more generic way to express parallelism.

OmpSs differs of OpenMP in many aspects. It uses a different execution model and adds extra features and concepts around the parallel tasks.

One of these important additions is the concept of *data dependences* between tasks. A task can be annotated with data directionality clauses that specify the data used by it, and how it will be used (read-only, write-only, read-write). This information is used during the execution by the underlying OmpSs run-time to control the synchronization of the different instances of tasks by creating a dependence graph that will represent the proper order of execution. This mechanism provides a simple way to express the order in which tasks must be executed, without the need of adding explicit synchronization.

Another important feature is the *data usage* of the parallel tasks. This allows to specify which data will be accessed by the task. While this may be seen as the same concept as the data dependencies, it is not. This data usage specification is intended to be used when programming applications for architectures with disjoint address spaces, in order to specify which data must be actually transferred between them. This differs with the dependencies because this information is not used to determine the program order, it will only be used to generate the data movements between address spaces. While task data dependencies almost always match the data used by the task, having these two concepts separated is useful is many cases. This mechanism has allowed to offer support for heterogeneous architectures like clusters [7] and multi-GPU systems [8].

The clauses provided by OmpSs to support the *data usage* mechanism are the following:

copy_in(...) The data specified must be available in the address space where the task is finally executed, and this data will be read only.

copy_out(...) The data specified will be generated by the task in the address space where the task will be executed.

copy_inout(...) The data specified must be available in the address space where the task runs, in addition, this data will be be updated with new values.

copy_deps Use the directionality specification clauses (input/output/inout) also as if they were copy_[in/out/inout] clauses.

The copy clauses should contain the list of variables which represent the data that will be managed. Array variables contain an appropriate subscript to specify a region of the array. The array subscript syntax is extended from the standard C syntax to allow the declaration of the data regions. A subscript can have the following forms:

[] An empty expression is considered to take all the elements of the array as the data that is referenced.

[index] A single index is used to reference a single item of the array.

[start:end] *start* and *end* represent a range of the elements that are referenced. Both elements are included in the range.

[start;size] It specifies a range starting from index *start* and consisting of *size* number of elements.

As an example of how these expressions are used consider a two-dimensional square matrix declared as `Array[N][N]`. The expression `Array[0;N/2][]` references the first half rows of it. If we want to reference a set of the columns instead, the expression could be `Array[][N-10:N-1]` used to reference the last 10 columns of it. Examples of how are used can be seen in figures 1, 2, and 3.

2.2 Non-contiguous data regions on OmpSs

While these provide a lot of flexibility to the programmer, the current implementation of the *data-usage* was not fully compliant with the proposed OmpSs specification. The mechanism had serious limitations. Data specifications could only represent pieces of contiguous memory, and to guarantee a correct run-time behavior it was required that the different memory regions did not overlap between them. These limitations caused that some applications could not be implemented as efficient as it would have been desirable, but others could not even be implemented.

The dependence subsystem had also experienced the same problem, but Pérez et al. [18] proposed an implementation to manage regions for tracking dependencies between tasks. They implemented a new dependence tracking system that detected overlapping situations and thus offered much more control than the original. This proposal has some limitations, because it uses a very compact representation but only capable of containing precise information under certain circumstances. The base address of the data regions must be aligned to the size of the region, and the region size must be a power of two. If these conditions are not met, then dependencies are not precisely handled and the execution may be suboptimal, this, however, does not cause an incorrect execution in any case.

This paper presents an implementation of the *data-usage* mechanism with support for precise memory regions, allowing also overlapping between different regions. The proposed mechanism is implemented almost entirely by the OmpSs run-time library, with minimal compiler support. This means that the overlap analysis is computed with dynamic information. The compiler is only responsible of providing the information of the data layout to the run-time but it does not perform any kind of analysis even when the data is statically declared. The details of the implementation of it are described on section 3

2.3 Practical examples

Offering regions support is important because it increases the flexibility of the OmpSs programming model and allows more efficient and simple implementation of applications.

To demonstrate this, we can observe the differences between two different implementations of a simple matrix multiplication algorithm. Figure 1 contains the implementation without using the proposed data region support. In this implementation the arrays have been declared as a 3-dimensional arrays in order to have contiguous data blocks of `BS×BS` elements. Given this data layout, the references in the `input` and `inout` clauses refer to contiguous blocks of data (this requeriment is needed without the proposed mechanism). In comparison, figure 2 shows the code that takes advantage of the proposed feature. It has some clear benefits over the code in figure 1. First, the array declaration is simpler since forcing the layout to have contiguous blocks is no longer required. The references in the `input` and `inout` clauses now refer to data that is not contiguous in memory (a block of `BS×BS` elements is scattered since the array declaration has a leading dimension of `N` elements). In addition, multilevel parallelism can be used now to implement the matrix multiplication, since the programmer can reference complete rows and columns of the different arrays, which is needed to specify the top level tasks (lines 7-9, in the code of figure 2). While these examples show statically allocated objects, the proposed mechanism also works with dynamically allocated data.

```
double A[NBLOCKS][NBLOCKS][BS*BS];
double B[NBLOCKS][NBLOCKS][BS*BS];
double C[NBLOCKS][NBLOCKS][BS*BS];

//matmul main loop
for ( i=0; i < NBLOCKS; i++ )
   for ( j = 0; j < NBLOCKS; j++ )
      for ( k = 0; k < NBLOCKS; k++ )
         #pragma omp target device (smp) copy_deps
         #pragma omp task input(A[i][k], \
                                B[k][j]),\
                      inout(C[i][j])
         matmul_blk(A[i][k], B[k][j], C[i][j], BS);
```

Figure 1: DGEMM OmpSs implementation without regions support

Another example can be seen in figure 3, in this case it corresponds to a FFT1D implementation using a Cooley–Tukey algorithm, to allow the data to be distributed on a two dimensional array, which splits the main problem by performing a FFT1D on each row of this distribution. These sub-FFT1D computations can run on

```
1  double A[N][N], B[N][N], C[N][N];
2
3  //matmul main loop
4  for ( i=0; i < N; i += BS )
5     for ( j = 0; j < N; j += BS )
6        #pragma omp target device (smp) copy_deps
7        #pragma omp task input(A[i;BS][], \
8                               B[][j;BS]),\
9                     inout(C[i;BS][j;BS])
10       for ( k = 0; k < N; k += BS )
11          #pragma omp target device (smp) copy_deps
12          #pragma omp task input(A[i;BS][k;BS], \
13                                 B[k;BS][j;BS]),\
14                       inout(C[i;BS][j;BS])
15          matmul_blk(&A[i][k], &B[k][j], &C[i][j], BS, N);
```

Figure 2: DGEMM OmpSs implementation, with regions and multilevel parallelism

parallel, however, some extra transpositions are done to achieve the final result. The data region support provides an easy way to implement the transposition using tasks that work on different blocks of the matrix. In addition keeping a proper data layout is required by the `fft1d_row` call.

It also must be noted that these examples are capable of being executed on cluster environments, with many different configurations of nodes and accelerators. Being able of referencing data with this expressiveness is desirable because the run-time environment will be able to adapt the data distribution of the application according to the actual hardware configuration.

3. IMPLEMENTATION

The OmpSs environment is composed of two software components: the Mercurium C/C++ source-to-source compiler and the Nanos++ run-time library.

The changes needed to support the proposed mechanism affect both of them. However, the changes needed in the compiler were minimal since its only responsibility is to translate the OmpSs clauses into run-time calls, no specific region analysis is done by it. Thus the compiler changes are not discussed on this paper.

The Nanos++ architecture is well described in previous works [7], [8]. The rest of the section will discuss the relevant changes needed to handle the new features, all of them made with a cluster system as a reference architecture. However, the features described are generic enough to be usable with other architectures.

3.1 Representing regions

According to the OmpSs specification, regions are defined using a syntax similar to the one used to declare and access array types in the C programming language. A region is defined using a base object, what we will refer to as *program object*. This object will typically be an array with several dimensions. Array subscripts are used to specify which elements of each dimension are covered by the region. For each dimension, two integer values define the first element and the number of elements covered on that dimension. These values must always represent a range where all of its elements fall within the limits of the corresponding dimension. We will refer to these pair of values as *dimension-access*. Figure 4 shows a case where a *program object* `A` with two dimensions of size 4, has four regions registered. In this example, the *dimension-access* objects of region number 1 are `[2;2]` and `[0;2]` for dimension 1 and 0 respectively.

How to internally represent regions is a critical design decision. The run-time library will need to perform operations between many different regions. For example, the run-time library may need to

```
double (*A)[N][N];
size_t BS = getBlockSize();
A = malloc( N*N*sizeof(double) );

// first transpose
for ( i=0; i < N; i += BS )
   for ( j = 0; j < N; j += BS )
      #pragma omp target device (smp) copy_deps
      #pragma omp task inout(*A[i;BS][j;BS], \
                              *A[j;BS][i;BS])
      transpose_blk(A[i][j], A[j][i], BS, N);

// first row fft
for ( i=0; i < N; i += BS )
   #pragma omp target device (smp) copy_deps
   #pragma omp task inout(*A[i;BS][0;N])
   for ( j = i; j < i + BS; j++ )
      fft1d_row(A[j][0], N);

// transpose and twiddle
for ( i=0; i < N; i += BS )
   for ( j = 0; j < N; j += BS )
      #pragma omp target device (smp) copy_deps
      #pragma omp task inout(*A[i;BS][j;BS], \
                              *A[j;BS][i;BS])
      transpose_tw_blk(A[i][j], A[j][i], BS, N);

// second row fft
for ( i=0; i < N; i += BS )
   #pragma omp target device (smp) copy_deps
   #pragma omp task inout(*A[i;BS][0;N])
   for ( j = i; j < i + BS; j++ )
      fft1d_row(*A[j][0], N);

// last transpose
for ( i=0; i < N; i += BS )
   for ( j = 0; j < N; j += BS )
      #pragma omp target device (smp) copy_deps
      #pragma omp task inout(*A[i;BS][j;BS], \
                              *A[j;BS][i;BS])
      transpose_blk(A[i][j], A[j][i], BS, N);
```

Figure 3: FFT1D OmpSs implementation

check if two or more regions overlap with each other. In addition, these operations will be part of the critical path of the whole execution, therefore the representation must allow a fast implementation of these.

In order to achieve a simple design, we have set a few limitations to our system. These limitations are:

- Regions are associated always to a *program object*. Regions covering more than one object are not supported.
- All regions that refer to the same object must be consistent with each other, that means that all of them must provide the same number of dimensions of the given object and access valid elements of these dimensions.

These limitations have a very low impact to the programmer, since both describe situations that generally would be considered programming errors. In addition, the run-time can detect these cases and emit an error message to inform the user.

3.1.1 Region identification

Program objects are registered at run-time and are identified by their base address. Each region is associated to a single *program object*. A region is defined by a set of *dimension-access* objects, one for each dimension of its referred object. In order to have a simple way to identify regions an integer value, unique within its *program object* is assigned to each region. We will refer to this value as the *region identifier*.

The generation of the identifier is done using a dictionary implemented using a *trie* (or *digital tree*). Each node of the tree contains a value of each of the *dimension-access* values (first element and number of elements covered). With this, a region information is stored as the path from the leaf to the root of the tree. The leaf node contains the *region identifier*. An example of this can be seen in figure 4, labeled as Region Dictionary.

The *region identifier* provides a simple way to identify a region within an object, and it also is used to access the region meta-data, which is stored using an array of meta-data entries. The region meta-data contains the location information of the related data, that is, in which memory address spaces (GPUs, nodes) is stored.

3.1.2 Region overlaps

Regions may overlap. To detect which regions overlap with another region, we maintain an *intersection map*. An *intersection map* keeps, for each dimension, one mapping from *dimension-access* to a set of *region identifiers* that overlap along that dimension. Figure 4 shows the example of the *intersection map* created by the *program object* A, and its four regions.

To compute the set of regions that overlap with a given region, we must first obtain the sets of *region identifiers* using each *dimension-access* object of the region. The intersection of all obtained sets is the set of overlapping region identifiers.

Example: assuming the state described by figure 4, a new region, `A[0;2][2;2]`, is registered and the overlap detection process goes as follows. The first dimension, `[2;2]`, is used to access the *Dimension 0* map, which returns the set `{2,4}`. Then the second dimension, `[1;2]`, is used on the *Dimension 1* map and the result is `{1,2,3,4}`. The intersection of both result sets is `{2,4}`, meaning that regions 2 and 4 overlap with the new region.

3.1.3 Distributed region information

Region meta-data is generally accessed by the run-time when it starts the execution of a task since it requires to know where its needed data is located. Since the described design is a centralized one, it can suffer from contention problems when running with several threads at the same time, since all of them will try to access to the *intersection maps* if they access the same *program-objects*.

To mitigate this contention, we exploit the dependence subsystem of OmpSs. When a task depends on another one, it is likely that the regions that were accessed by the preceding task will be also accessed by the successor task. We transfer the regions metadata of a task to its successors hoping that they will be able to use it instead of having to request it to the centralized data structures.

3.1.4 Memoizing overlaps

A very common operation that the OmpSs run-time has to perform is to compute if two given regions overlap, and which is the resulting region of this overlap, if it exists. Because regions are always given unique identifiers we can apply memoization in order to perform the overlap check and store the result to avoid computing the same values in the future.

3.2 Region based memory management

The main subsystem of Nanos++ that had to be adapted was the memory management part. Moving from a management based on contiguous memory, to a one based on regions with potentially noncontiguous data caused important changes in the way Nanos++ allocates and transfers data among the different address spaces of the system.

The allocation of regions brings a few questions. When it comes to allocating strided regions of data, the actual allocated size will always be bigger than the used size by the application, because the shape of the data must remain the same. This can be a problem

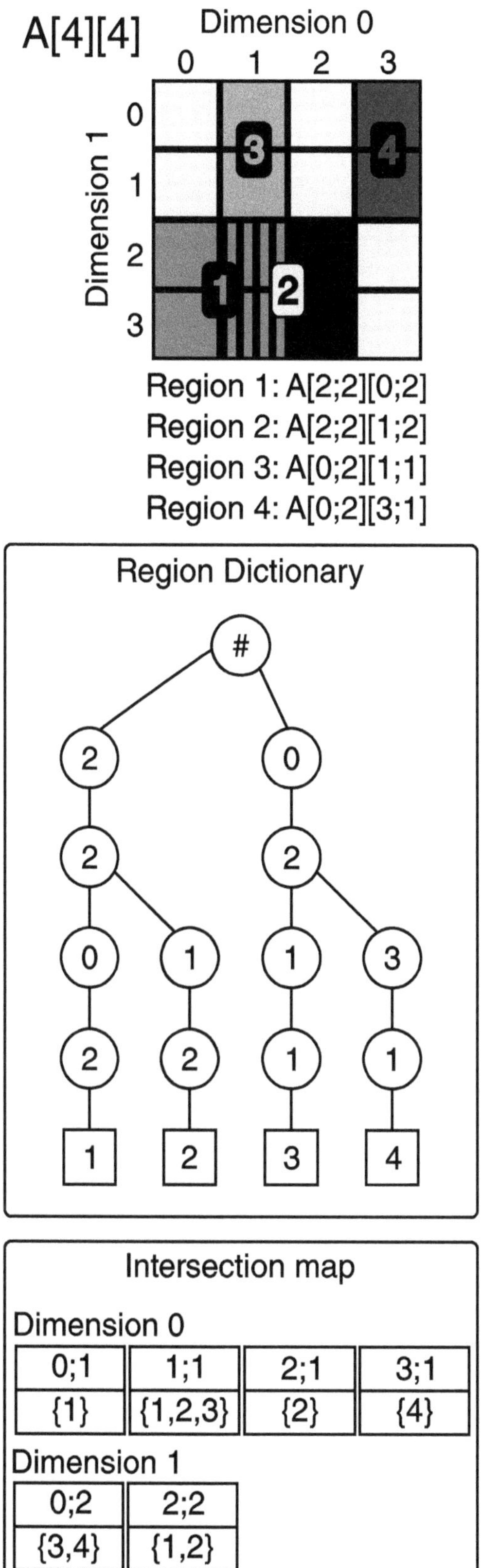

Figure 4: An array of 4x4 dimensions with 4 different regions and the data structures that hold the corresponding *region identifiers* and the *intersection map*

when we are working with accelerators with limited memory, but there is nothing that can be done from the run-time library to solve this, unless other techniques like data *reshaping* are implemented. For the case of this work targeting the cluster environment, this is not a problem because each node has plenty of memory available, and the decision here has been to allocate whole objects in remote nodes. This reduces the costs of allocating data on demand, which can potentially cause reallocations with severe performance penalties.

Data movement operations of strided data were originally implemented on a very naive way. For each region that had to be moved, a list of contiguous data chunks was generated, and then a movement operation was issued for each chunk. While this approach fulfills the requirements of correctness, its performance may vary depending on the architecture system that is the responsible for moving the data. Section 4 shows some measurements of this implementation on a cluster environment. The results for the cluster were not satisfactory so more effort was needed to improve them.

3.3 Optimizing for clusters

The main problem of the first implementation was the number of data movement operations that were generated for strided regions. In the cluster architecture these operations were translated to network messages. While sending a network message is an expensive operation by itself, some regions caused hundreds or thousands of these calls, which resulted in a poor application performance.

To overcome this problem, we implemented a simple mechanism to minimize the number of network messages that were needed to transfer regions of strided data. The idea is to use a temporal buffer where the strided data is placed contiguously prior to be sent through the network. Once the data arrives to its destination, the run-time library can reverse the operation and place it with its original shape.

An important implementation detail that had to be taken into account when we were implementing this mechanism is to control which thread is responsible for packing and unpacking the data. In Nanos++ there is a thread in each node which is responsible of monitoring the network for incoming messages, this is a requirement of the underlying communications library used (GASNet [6]). Delegating the task of unpacking the data to the thread which is actually selected to execute a parallel task was needed to keep a good network latency, if not, the communication thread could spend too much time dealing with this packing mechanism, stalling the execution of the whole application. In the case of data packing, the problem is more complex because it usually is the communication thread the one starting the transfers of data, so these tasks can not be delegated to another thread as easily as the unpacking. However, a mechanism was also implemented where idle threads could collaborate on sending data to remote nodes, with this the communication thread work load was lowered and more network efficiency was obtained.

As will be seen in Section 4, this technique greatly improved the performance of applications in the cluster environment, specially those that require an efficient usage of the network bandwidth.

While this technique is available for cluster environments, its implementation is generic enough to be applied on other architectures like GPUs. However, the effectiveness on other systems is yet to be evaluated.

4. EVALUATION

This section covers the evaluation performed to measure the performance of the OmpSs applications using the presented mechanism on a cluster of multicore processors.

4.1 Methodology and environment

To evaluate our environment we selected a set of OmpSs applications and measured their scalability with our run-time environment. These applications exploit the support for non-contiguous regions of data, and e also compare them against well known MPI implementations of the same applications.

The machine used to run the evaluation is a cluster with nodes consisting of two Intel® Xeon® E5649 @ 2.53GHz multicore processors with six cores each. Each node also has 24 GB of memory divided in two NUMA nodes. Each node has two Infiniband QDR network interface controllers connected to a non-blocking network.

All OmpSs benchmarks were compiled using the Mercurium C/C++ source-to-source compiler, using GCC 4.4.4 as a the final C compiler, and using -O3 optimization level. Benchmark kernels are compiled with the Intel® C Compiler (ICC) version 12.0.4, also with -O3 optimization level enabled, or invoked from the Intel® Math Kernel Library (MKL) version 10.3.4. The MPI distribution is provided by the hardware vendor, but it is derived from the Open MPI version 1.1.11.1.

For each one of the selected applications, we have performed tests with different configurations on the number of nodes and threads used on each node. We also show the impact of the optimization that has been discussed in section 3 in these applications. The metric measured for each application is the execution time.

4.2 Benchmarks

The applications selected have been a double precision matrix multiplication (DGEMM), the PTRANS benchmark and a one dimensional Fast Fourier Transform (FFT1D).

4.2.1 DGEMM

The DGEMM experiments have been done using a matrix size of 16384x16384. Two different OmpSs implementations have been tested. The first one is the more naive approach, it uses a single level of parallelism to perform the computation. The schema used corresponds to the code shown in figure 1, and it does not require the infrastructure implemented in this paper. The second one uses multilevel parallelism to improve locality and improve the distribution and creation of the computation tasks. The multilevel version required the support of the non-contiguous data regions implemented in this paper. The schema followed to implement this version can be seen in figure 2. We have compared both versions of OmpSs with the purpose of showing the performance benefits that can be achieved by using non-contiguous data regions. The parallelization is implemented by dividing the main algorithm in tasks that perform the matrix multiplication of blocks of 512x512 elements.

The MPI implementation used has been the ScaLAPACK [4] one provided by the Intel® Math Kernel Library (MKL). The OmpSs versions have also used the Intel® MKL.

4.2.2 PTRANS

The PTRANS benchmark measures the rate of transfer for larges arrays of data by implementing a parallel matrix transpose. It exercises the communications of the cluster heavily on a realistic problem where pairs of processors communicate with each other simultaneously. The arrays data used has also been two-dimensional arrays of 16384x16384 elements.

Following the same parallelization schema as the one used in the DGEMM experiments, the parallelization of the PTRANS is implemented using tasks that process sub-blocks 512x512 elements. We have tested the OmpSs version of this benchmark with two Nanos++ configurations, depending on whether the optimization technique of packing the strided data prior to send it over the network was enabled or not. This shows how effective this optimization can be on applications that stress the usage of the network.

The MPI implementation of this benchmark comes from the HPC Challenge Benchmark suite [15], [11].

4.2.3 FFT1D

The FFT1D application measures the floating point rate of execution of the double precision complex one-dimensional Discrete Fourier Transform (DFT). The OmpSs implementation uses the Cooley-Tukey algorithm to implement the one-dimensional DFT.

The data is distributed in a two-dimensional array of 16384×16384 complex double precision elements. The first step of the algorithm is to perform a in-place transposition of the data, after this, a FFT1D round is applied to each of the 16384 rows of the data. The next step is to transpose again the data and to apply a *twiddle* factor, to follow with a second round of FFT1D on each row. Finally, a last in-place transpose obtains the final result.

The parallelization of the transpose and the twiddle+transpose are also implemented using tasks that operate on sub-blocks of the matrix, the dimension of these blocks is also 512. The row-FFT1D processes are parallelized by creating tasks that process blocks of 512 rows of the main matrix, each of these tasks also create more parallel tasks to perform the final computation. This structure can be seen in figure 3. For this application, we have also evaluated the impact of the data-packing optimization implemented in Nanos++, to demonstrate its impact on a more complex application.

As for the selected MPI implementation, we have used the one provided by the HPC Challenge benchmark suite [15], [11], which is a FFT1D algorithm specifically tailored for MPI. We have also used the FFT1D kernel of this version in our OmpSs implementation.

4.3 Results

4.3.1 DGEMM

Figure 5 shows the performance obtained by the DGEMM benchmark. As stated in the previous section, we have implemented two versions of this benchmark, the one labeled "1L OmpSs" refers to the naive implementation (the schema used by corresponds to the source code shown in figure 1) which can be coded without the need of the work described in this paper. The second version, labeled "ML OmpSs" is the implementation using multilevel parallelism enabled by the data region specifications (same schema as the one shown in figure 2). The ScaLAPACK results are under the "MPI" label. Five charts are shown depending on the number of worker threads used by the run-time. Because the ScaLAPACK version is implemented using OpenMP, this could be controlled using the `OMP_NUM_THREADS` environment variable. In the last chart of the series, titled "Max threads per node", the OmpSs run-time environment uses only eleven threads as an extra thread is created to perform network polling and send control messages. However in the ScaLAPACK execution, twelve OpenMP threads are requested. The X axis represents the number of nodes used during the different executions, the Y axis shows the execution time in seconds. It must be noted that the Y axis scale is different for each of the charts. This has been done to be able to better appreciate the differences on the cases with a high number of threads per node.

The charts show how the version implemented using multilevel parallelism is capable of achieving the same scalability as the ScaLAPACK version, even being able to obtain a slightly better performance due to other available optimizations of Nanos++ [7], [8] (task pre-send, affinity scheduler) that increase the overlapping of communication and computation. The simple OmpSs version performs well with a low number of nodes, but it fails to scale properly with 16 or more nodes, this is caused by the fact that in this version, task creation is centralized on the master node, which creates a bottleneck when distributing the tasks among the rest of the threads of the cluster. This is why the problem is more noticeable with an increasing number of nodes and threads. The multilevel version is capable of delegating part of the task creation to the remote nodes, which reduces the overhead of task distribution from the master.

4.3.2 PTRANS

The PTRANS results are shown in Figure 6. The results are also organized in different charts depending on the number of threads per node used on each execution. In this case we have tested a single OmpSs implementation of the benchmark but we have run it with two Nanos++ configurations, the first without enabling the technique of packing the strided data prior to send it through the network, labeled as "NP OmpSs", and the second with this technique enabled, labeled as "OmpSs". The "MPI" label in these charts refers to the HPCC implementation of the benchmark. It must be noted that this benchmark is not implemented using OpenMP, so to enable the usage of more than one core per node, we executed it spawning the appropriate number of MPI tasks instead of threads. Again the X axis shows the number of nodes and the Y axis shows the measured execution time in seconds.

The results show how effective is the packing mechanism in this application. It greatly improves the performance of the OmpSs implementation in every situation and it actually makes OmpSs to be at the same level, or even better in some cases, than the HPCC version. The reasons for this are that the PTRANS performance relies on achieving a good network usage. Without the packing technique this is not possible because strided accesses are transformed in one network message per contiguous data, which leads to a very high number of messages. By packing the data the runtime library reduces this number of messages and communications are more efficient, and the execution time is significantly reduced. In some cases MPI can outperform OmpSs since task distribution is a cost that can not be avoided easily. In the PTRANS, all tasks are distributed from the master, in addition, the PTRANS tasks are not very computation intensive, which leaves few opportunities of overlapping communication and computation, exposing the distribution overhead. That is why the results of 32 nodes show a low scaling compared to the 16 node cases. Still, OmpSs performance is comparable to the one achieved by MPI. The cases where both OmpSs versions perform much better than MPI are explained because of the extra thread that the Nanos++ run-time library creates, since it helps when it comes to sending more messages and therefore, it can provide a better usage of network bandwidth, which is critical in this benchmark. This can make the comparison unfair from the resource point of view, however, the last case (the chart titled "Max threads") can be considered fair from this perspective, and it shows that the performance is almost on par.

4.3.3 FFT1D

Figure 7 shows the performance results of the FFT1D benchmark. Again the experiments are grouped by the number of threads used in each execution. X axis shows the number of nodes and Y axis the execution time in seconds of the experiments. As with the previous benchmark, we have executed the OmpSs version with the packing technique disabled and enabled to measure its impact on the FFT1D benchmark. The packing enabled data series is labeled with the "OmpSs" title, and the packing disabled is referred by the "NP OmpSs". The MPI version of the FFT1D benchmark provided by the HPC Challenge suite is implemented using MPI and OpenMP so in this case we can control the number of threads created on each node using the same way as in the DGEMM benchmark.

FFT1D is a demanding benchmark since combines some phases of high bandwidth requirements with phases of intense computation. Because of this, we see the same behavior of PTRANS when it comes to the effect of the packing optimization. Enabling the technique boosts performance in almost all cases and it is absolutely necessary to achieve a proper scalability with a large number of nodes and threads per node. In addition Nanos++ is capable of overlapping computation and communication, and this provides an extra performance edge over the MPI version on the majority of the cases. With 32 nodes the performance is almost identical, OmpSs losing the extra advantage because of the same problems of the PTRANS case, cost of task distribution with a large number of nodes and tasks with short execution time. It must be noted that the fact of having an extra thread can be the cause of performing better in some cases, specially with few threads per node, as it happened in the PTRANS benchmark. However OmpSs is capable to outperform the MPI version in the "Max threads per node" case, when the same resources are used in both versions. In this case, the asynchronous parallelism is capable of overlapping parts of the transposition with the execution of the row FFTs, which leads to a better overlapping of computation and communication.

The difference of performance on the 1 node cases between OmpSs and MPI can be explained because the former is actually a sequential algorithm which still while the latter is a SPMD program running on a single node.

5. RELATED WORK

MPI [16] has been the reference programming model when it comes to distributed memory systems. It is based on an API of explicit communication calls to transfer data among a set of processes running in the nodes of a distributed machine. MPI is not particularly friendly to the programmer, specially when he or she is not an expert in working with it, since it requires a conscious design of the application for this programming model. Despite this fact, it has been widely adopted by the scientific community, and there is already a high number of applications written with MPI.

It is worth noting that MPI has some features, similar to those that have been proposed in this paper, to handle strided movement of data through the network. This is provided in the form of a specific data type `MPI_TYPE_VECTOR`. However, the usage of them seems complex and we have not actually seen it used in the applications that we have worked with. This can be because of the way of dealing with data in MPI applications. The data layout is already explicitly distributed by the programmer, so he or she can adapt it to already be contiguous in memory, fact that reduces the need of such specific data type.

OpenMP is another programming model that focuses on being a high productivity environment by offering a simple way to parallelize sequential programs by using compiler annotations. The latest 3.0 version [17] offers asynchronous task based parallelism. While OpenMP only targets shared memory systems and it can not be compared directly to MPI, its ideas of annotating a sequential code to generate a parallel version have become very popular, and there are many other programming models for distributed environments that have adopted them.

Partitioned Global Address Space (PGAS) programming models are an example of this. They expose an abstracted shared address space to the programmer that simplifies its task. Data distribution and management is handled automatically by the compiler and the

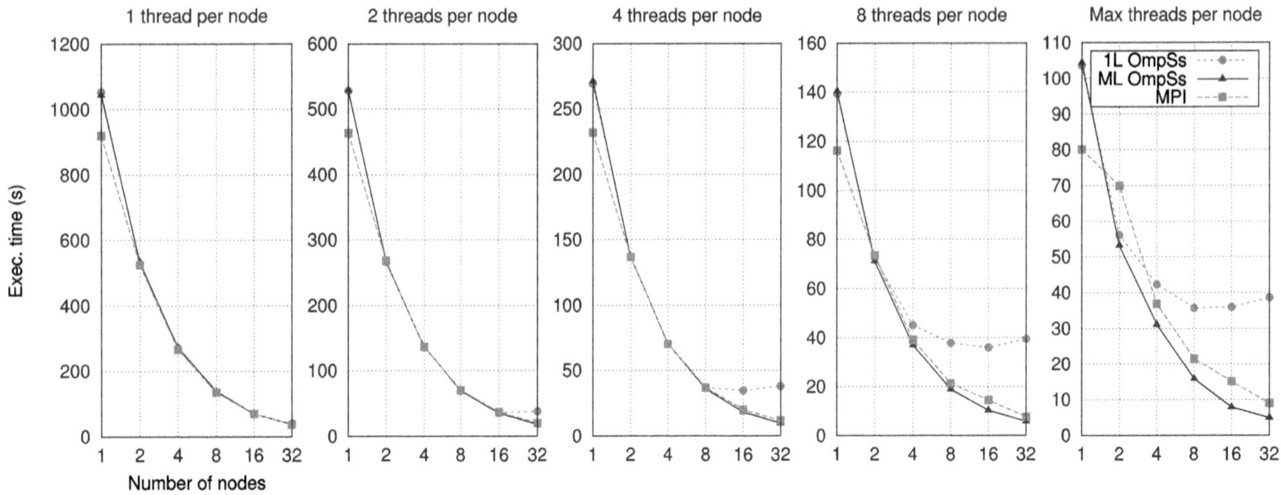

Figure 5: DGEMM performance comparison, OmpSs against MPI (different Y axis scale on each chart)

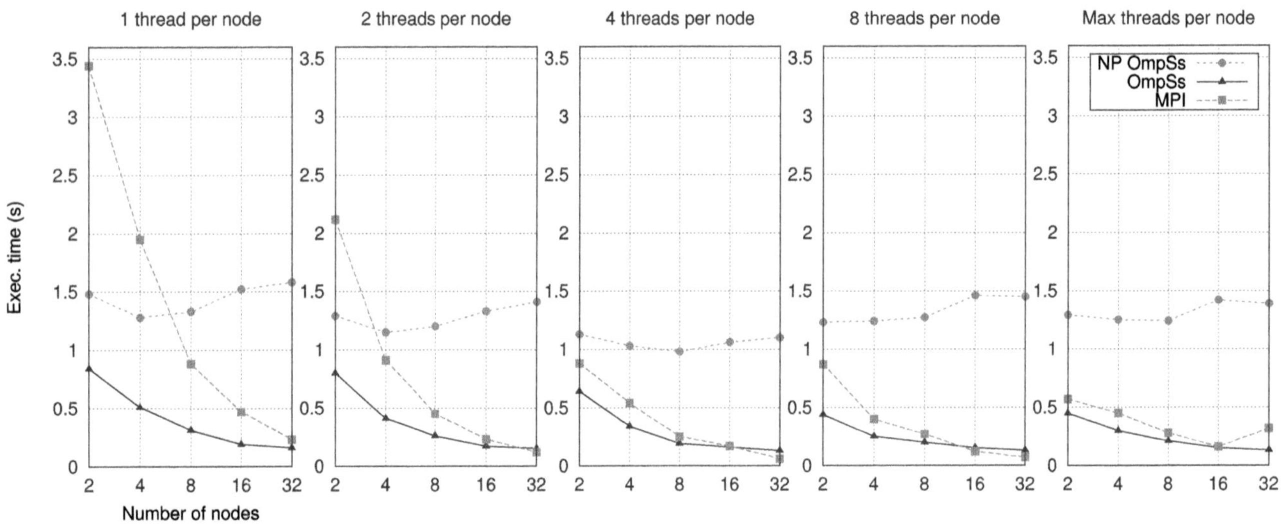

Figure 6: PTRANS performance comparison, OmpSs against MPI

run-time environment thanks to compiler annotations. Representative PGAS languages are UPC [1], and X10 [10]; and Chapel [9] and Titanium [20], which implement Asynchronous PGAS model, offering asynchronous parallelism.

UPC offers a series of statements to deal with loop parallelism, and also offers a more explicit operations for other more complex situations, however it does not offer support for strided data among them. [5] has proposed a set of extensions to add this kind of support to UPC. Chapel, X10 and Titanium, in contrast, offer the possibility of specifying array regions, but they use a representation based in Object-Orientation. Similarly to OmpSs, Chapel and X10 can also support accelerators like GPUs.

StarPU [2] is another programming model with similar goals as OmpSs. It provides an infrastructure to develop applications for architectures with accelerators using CUDA or OpenCL as base technology, although it does not support clusters directly, it offers some services to work together with MPI. StarPU There are also many programming models similar to OmpSs that target architectures with disjoint address spaces. StarPU has some features to partition the application data, however these come in the form of API calls, a more explicit mechanism when compared to OmpSs.

Sequoia [14] [13] is another interesting alternative focuses on the mapping of the application kernels onto the appropriate engines to exploit the memory hierarchy. Sequoia also supports some forms of irregular parallelism [3], using a form of tasks similar but more restricted than those defined by OpenMP 3.0. Sequoia also allows complex data specifications, but it is its compiler the responsible to generate the appropriate code to handle the data transfers, not the run-time environment. With this, the user has to specify the underlying hardware architecture at compile time.

Mint [19] is also a related project with a completely different approach. It implements a translator to transform stencil computations expressed in C, into CUDA code, to run on a GPU. While it targets GPU platform specifically, it is capable of generating op-

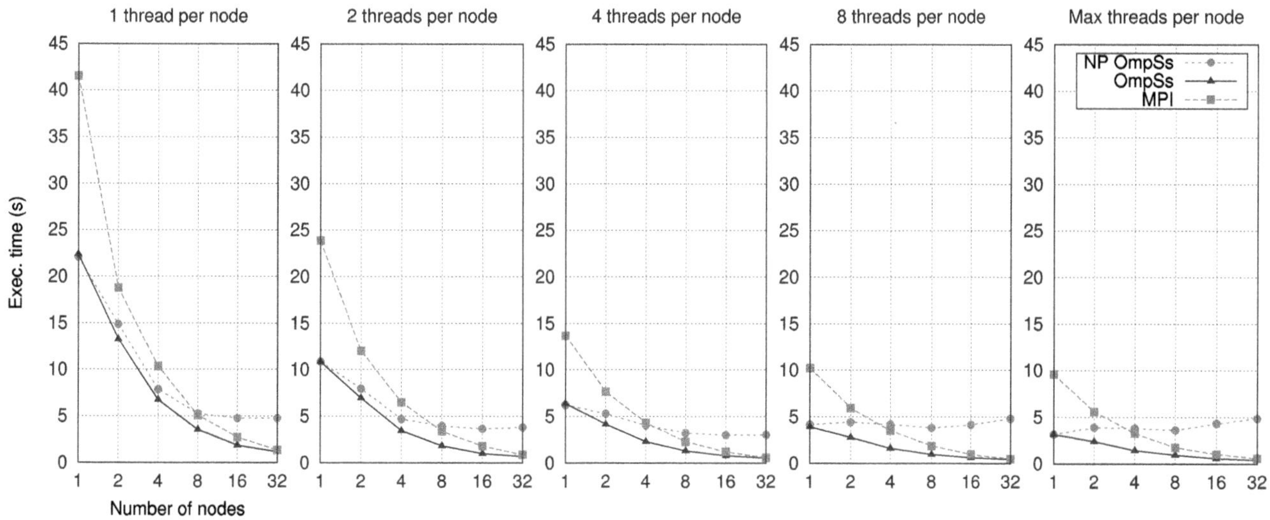

Figure 7: FFT1D performance comparison, OmpSs against MPI

timized code for accessing strided regions of data and move them from host memory to GPU memory. Such mechanism could be applied as well to a cluster environments.

6. CONCLUSIONS AND FUTURE WORK

In this paper we have presented the implementation of the support for managing regions of data in the OmpSs programming model on systems with disjoint address spaces. This allows the programmers to specify complex regions of data on their programs with a simple and flexible syntax, and the underlying run-time system will handle its movement among the memory of the different devices or nodes. We believe this feature is of high importance nowadays due to the increasing complexity of the HPC hardware, where machines with accelerators and/or distributed memory are ubiquitous. This makes desirable the automatic management of data that OmpSs provides.

Following the OmpSs philosophy, the programmer responsibility is just to specify which data will be used by each task, and the run-time system will provide the needed mechanisms to ensure the correct execution, regardless of the available hardware configuration. In addition the run-time environment may found optimization opportunities to be able to achieve the better possible performance.

The solution that we have implemented has allowed us to evaluate the effectiveness of having such mechanism implemented. Not only we have been able to implement more complex benchmarks but also we have made more efficient versions of others.

The evaluation has shown good performance results on a set of different benchmarks. We also have compared the performance of the OmpSs versions with the same applications but programmed using well-known implementations of MPI, and MPI+OpenMP. The results show that OmpSs can achieve a better performance in some cases and overall scalability is quite on par. It must be noted that this good performance would have been impossible if the optimization of packing strided data had not been implemented.

Still we would like to extend the evaluation presented. Stencil applications can be a good testing ground since they have complex access patterns. It is likely that new optimizations will be needed to efficiently handle these type of applications.

Additional research opportunities may arise from having the region support interact with other components of the run-time. The data conscious scheduling that Nanos++ uses (see [8]) could benefit from the more detailed information that the programmer provides. While the approach currently implemented may be effective enough, there may be applications that take advantage of more conscious decisions based on the data used. Tasks may be grouped by the regions that they access, which may help to optimize the communication operations.

In the case of cluster systems, managing the network bandwidth efficiently can boost the application performance. Using region information to optimize the usage of this resource can also be an interesting topic to explore.

Finally, some of the mechanisms presented in this work are generic enough to be able to be tested in other architectures. GPU environments may also be benefited from the region support, however the optimization techniques that these architectures allow can differ from the ones presented.

Acknowledgments

We thankfully acknowledge the support of the European Commission through the ENCORE project (FP7-248647), the TERAFLUX project (FP7-249013), the TEXT project (FP7-261580), and the HiPEAC-3 Network of Excellence (ICT FP7 NoE 287759), the support of the Spanish Ministry of Science and Technology (TIN2007-60625, TIN2012-34557, CSD2007-00050 and FPU program) and the Generalitat de Catalunya (2009-SGR-980).

7. REFERENCES

[1] UPC Language Specifications v1.2, May 2005.

[2] C. Augonnet, S. Thibault, and R. Namyst. StarPU: a Runtime System for Scheduling Tasks over Accelerator-Based Multicore Machines. Rapport de recherche RR-7240, INRIA, Mar. 2010.

[3] M. Bauer, J. Clark, E. Schkufza, and A. Aiken. Programming the memory hierarchy revisited: supporting irregular parallelism in sequoia. In *Proceedings of the 16th ACM symposium on Principles and practice of parallel programming*, PPoPP '11, pages 13–24, New York, NY, USA, 2011. ACM.

[4] L. S. Blackford, J. Choi, A. Cleary, E. D'Azevedo, J. Demmel, I. Dhillon, J. Dongarra, S. Hammarling, G. Henry, A. Petitet, K. Stanley, D. Walker, and R. C. Whaley. *ScaLAPACK Users' Guide*. Society for Industrial and Applied Mathematics, Philadelphia, PA, 1997.

[5] D. Bonachea. Proposal for extending the UPC memory copy library functions and supporting extensions to GASNet. Technical report, October 2004. LBNL-56495.

[6] D. Bonachea. GASNet Specification, v1.8 . Technical report, U.C. Berkeley, 2006.

[7] J. Bueno, L. Martinell, A. Duran, M. Farreras, X. Martorell, R. Badia, E. Ayguade, and J. Labarta. Productive cluster programming with OmpSs. *Euro-Par 2011 Parallel Processing*, pages 555–566, 2011.

[8] J. Bueno, J. Planas, A. Duran, R. Badia, X. Martorell, E. Ayguade, and J. Labarta. Productive Programming of GPU Clusters with OmpSs. In *Parallel & Distributed Processing Symposium (IPDPS), 2012 IEEE 26th International*, pages 557–568. IEEE, 2012.

[9] B. Chamberlain, D. Callahan, and H. Zima. Parallel programmability and the chapel language. *Int. J. High Perform. Comput. Appl.*, 21:291–312, August 2007.

[10] P. Charles, C. Grothoff, V. Saraswat, C. Donawa, A. Kielstra, K. Ebcioglu, C. von Praun, and V. Sarkar. X10: an object-oriented approach to non-uniform cluster computing. In *Proceedings of the 20th annual ACM SIGPLAN conference on Object-oriented programming, systems, languages, and applications*, OOPSLA '05, pages 519–538, New York, NY, USA, 2005. ACM.

[11] J. J. Dongarra, I. High, and P. C. Systems. Overview of the HPC Challenge Benchmark Suite.

[12] A. Duran, E. Ayguadé, R. M. Badia, J. Labarta, L. Martinell, X. Martorell, and J. Planas. OmpSs: A proposal for programming heterogeneous multi-core architectures, 2011-03-01 2011.

[13] K. Fatahalian, D. R. Horn, T. J. Knight, L. Leem, M. Houston, J. Y. Park, M. Erez, M. Ren, A. Aiken, W. J. Dally, and P. Hanrahan. Sequoia: programming the memory hierarchy. In *Proceedings of the 2006 ACM/IEEE conference on Supercomputing*, SC '06, New York, NY, USA, 2006.

[14] T. J. Knight, J. Y. Park, M. Ren, M. Houston, M. Erez, K. Fatahalian, A. Aiken, W. J. Dally, and P. Hanrahan. Compilation for explicitly managed memory hierarchies. In *Proceedings of the 2007 ACM SIGPLAN Symposium on Principles and Practice of Parallel Programming*, 2007.

[15] P. Luszczek, J. J. Dongarra, D. Koester, R. Rabenseifner, B. Lucas, J. Kepner, J. Mccalpin, D. Bailey, and D. Takahashi. Introduction to the HPC Challenge Benchmark Suite. Technical report, 2005.

[16] MPI Forum. MPI: A Message Passing Interface Standard. *Intl. Journal of Supercomputer Applications and High Performance Computing*, 8(3/4):159–416, 1994.

[17] OpenMP ARB. OpenMP Application Program Interface, v. 3.0, May 2008.

[18] J. M. Perez, R. M. Badia, and J. Labarta. Handling task dependencies under strided and aliased references. In *Proceedings of the 24th ACM International Conference on Supercomputing*, ICS '10, pages 263–274, New York, NY, USA, 2010. ACM.

[19] D. Unat, X. Cai, and S. B. Baden. Mint: Realizing cuda performance in 3d stencil methods with annotated c. In *Proceedings of the 25th ACM International Conference on Supercomputing*, ICS '11, pages 214–224. ACM, 2011.

[20] K. Yelick, L. Semenzato, G. Pike, C. Miyamoto, B. Liblit, A. Krishnamurthy, P. Hilfinger, S. Graham, D. Gay, P. Colella, and A. Aiken. Titanium: A high-performance java dialect. In *In ACM*, pages 10–11, 1998.

Automatically Adapting Programs for Mixed-Precision Floating-Point Computation

Michael O. Lam and
Jeffrey K. Hollingsworth
Dept. of Computer Science
University of Maryland
College Park, MD, USA
lam@cs.umd.edu, hollings@cs.umd.edu

Bronis R. de Supinski and
Matthew P. LeGendre
Center for Applied Scientific Computing
Lawrence Livermore National Laboratory
Livermore, CA, USA
bronis@llnl.gov, legendre1@llnl.gov

ABSTRACT

As scientific computation continues to scale, efficient use of floating-point arithmetic processors is critical. Lower precision allows streaming architectures to perform more operations per second and can reduce memory bandwidth pressure on all architectures. However, using a precision that is too low for a given algorithm and data set leads to inaccurate results. In this paper, we present a framework that uses binary instrumentation and modification to build mixed-precision configurations of existing binaries that were originally developed to use only double-precision. This framework allows developers to explore mixed-precision configurations without modifying their source code, and it enables automatic analysis of floating-point precision. We include a simple search algorithm to automate identification of code regions that can use lower precision. Our results for several benchmarks show that our framework incurs low overhead (less than 10X in most cases). In addition, we demonstrate that our tool can replicate manual conversions and suggest further optimization; in one case, we achieve a speedup of 2X.

Categories and Subject Descriptors

D.2.4 [**Software Engineering**]: Software/Program Verification

Keywords

binary instrumentation; floating-point; mixed precision

1. INTRODUCTION

"Floating-point" is a method of representing real numbers in a finite binary format. It stores a number in a fixed-width field with three segments: 1) a sign bit (b), 2) an exponent field (e), and 3) a significand (or mantissa) (s). The stored value is $(-1)^b \cdot s \cdot 2^e$. Floating-point was first used in computers in the early 1940's, and was standardized by IEEE in 1985, with the latest revision approved in 2008 [26]. The IEEE standard provides for different levels of precision by varying the field width, with the most common widths being 32 bits ("single" precision) and 64 bits ("double" precision). Figure 1 graphically represents these formats.

Double-precision arithmetic generally results in more accurate computations, but with several costs. The main cost is the higher memory bandwidth and storage requirement, which are twice that of single precision. Another cost is the reduced opportunity for parallelization, such as on the x86 architecture, where packed 128-bit XMM registers can only hold and operate on two double-precision numbers simultaneously compared to four numbers with single precision. Finally, some architectures even impose a higher cycle count (and thus also energy cost) for each arithmetic operation in double precision. In practice, it has been reported that single-precision calculations can be 2.5 times faster than corresponding double-precision calculations, because of the various factors described above [19].

As high-performance computing continues to scale, these concerns regarding precision, memory bandwidth, and energy usage will become increasingly important [15]. Thus, application developers have powerful incentives to use a lower precision wherever possible without compromising overall accuracy. Unfortunately, the numerical accuracy degradation of switching to single precision can be fatal in some cases, and many developers simply choose the "safe option" of sticking with double precision in all cases.

Many computational scientists are investigating another option: "mixed-precision" configurations. With these schemes, certain parts of the program use double-precision operations to preserve numerical accuracy while the rest of the program uses single-precision operations to increase speed and save memory bandwidth. Thus, the developer can still reap some of the benefits of single precision while maintaining the desired level of accuracy. However, building these mixed-precision configurations can be difficult. This task either requires extensive knowledge of numerical analysis and the problem domain or many trial-and-error experiments.

In this paper, we present a framework that uses automatic binary instrumentation and modification to build mixed-precision versions of existing binaries that were originally developed to use double precision only. Our framework allows developers to experiment with mixed-precision configurations easily, without modifying their source code. We also present a simple search algorithm to find a mixed-precision variation of the program automatically.

Our results for several benchmarks show that our frame-

ICS'13, June 10–14, 2013, Eugene, Oregon, USA.

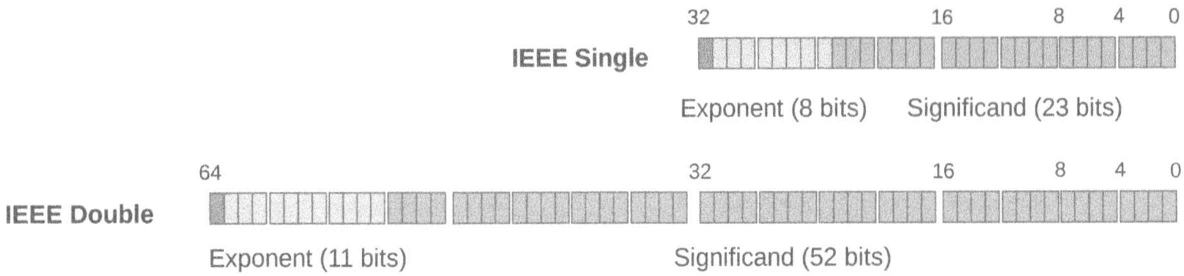

Figure 1: IEEE standard formats

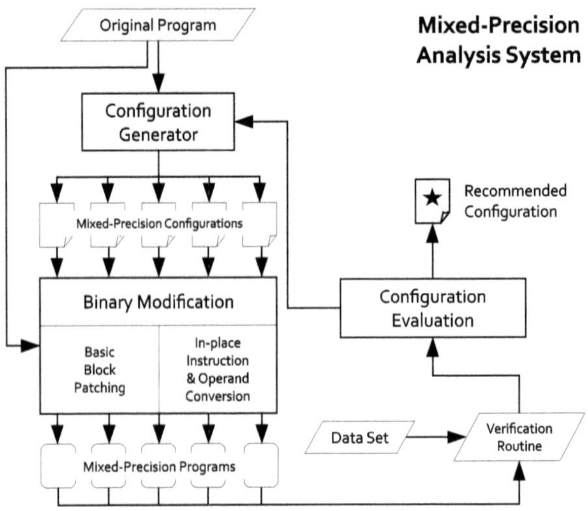

Figure 2: Mixed-precision analysis system overview

work is effective and incurs low overhead. In most cases, the overhead is less than 10X, which is several orders of magnitude lower that existing floating-point analysis tools. For several of these benchmarks, the tool found that over 20% of all floating-point operations could be replaced with their single-precision equivalents. We also tested the AMG microkernel and found that the entire kernel could be replaced with single-precision arithmetic, resulting in a speedup of nearly 2X. In addition, our tool was able to replicate a manual conversion of SuperLU from double precision to single precision, and we show that loosening the error bounds can increase the amount of the program that can be replaced with single precision arithmetic.

The rest of the paper is arranged as follows. First, we describe our approach and implementation in Section 2. Second, we relate our evaluation and results in Section 3. Finally, we briefly enumerate related work in Section 4.

2. OUR APPROACH

We introduce a comprehensive system for analyzing an application's precision requirements. Given a representative data set and a verification routine, this system builds multiple mixed-precision configurations of the application and evaluates them, choosing the one that promises the greatest benefit in terms of speedup and easing of memory bandwidth pressure. Figure 2 shows an overview of this system.

A key system component is our framework for automatic binary-level mixed-precision configuration of floating-point programs. Section 2.1 describes our format for storing floating-point configurations and our GUI editor for building and visualizing the resulting program. This framework is based on the Dyninst library [8] for binary code patching and uses XED from the Intel Pin library [37] for instruction parsing. Section 2.2 describes the current, simple search algorithm, which consists of a breadth-first search through the program structure to find the coarsest granularity at which each part of the program can be replaced by single precision while still passing a user-provided verification routine. We describe in Section 2.3 our novel technique that inserts single-precision operations to replace double-precision operations. Our technique modifies the 64 bits that hold the double-precision representation to simulate single precision, storing a flag in the extra bits to indicate the presence of a modified number. This approach does not fully realize the benefits of using single precision format but allows us to identify when single precision preserves sufficient accuracy. The source code can then be transformed to realize the full benefits for situations that we identify as safe. Finally, as we describe in Section 2.4, we use basic block patching to extract the original double-precision floating-point instructions and replace them with new code, contained in binary "snippets."

2.1 Configuration representations

Our "precision configurations" provide a method of communicating which parts of a program should be executed in single precision and which parts should be executed in double precision. A configuration is a series of mappings:

$$p \rightarrow \{single, double, ignore\}$$

The mappings involve all $p \in P_d$, where P_d is the set of all double-precision instructions in program P. Since there are natural parent-child containment aggregations in program structure (i.e., instructions are contained within basic blocks, which are contained within functions), the configuration allows decisions to be made about these aggregate structures, overriding any decisions about child members. The configuration controls the analysis engine as follows:

- If the mapping for p_i is *single*, then the opcode of p_i

```
    FUNC01: main()
      BBLK01
s       INSN01: 0x6f45ce "addsd %xmm1, %xmm0"
d       INSN02: 0x6f45d7 "mulsd %xmm2, %xmm1"
s       INSN03: 0x6f45da "subsd %xmm1, %xmm0"
d       INSN04: 0x6f45e8 "mulsd %xmm2, %xmm1"

    FUNC02: solve()
      BBLK02
s       INSN05: 0x6f7abe "addsd %xmm1, %xmm0"
s       INSN06: 0x6f7ac6 "addsd %xmm1, %xmm0"
s       INSN07: 0x6f7aca "addsd %xmm1, %xmm0"
d       INSN08: 0x6f7ad3 "mulsd %xmm1, %xmm2"
s       INSN09: 0x6f7ada "addsd %xmm1, %xmm0"
      BBLK03
d       INSN10: 0x6f7aee "mulsd %xmm1, %xmm2"
d       INSN11: 0x6f7af4 "subsd %xmm1, %xmm0"
d       INSN12: 0x6f7af9 "mulsd %xmm1, %xmm2"

s   FUNC03: split()
      BBLK04
s       INSN13: 0x6f8248 "subsd %xmm1, %xmm0"
d       INSN14: 0x6f824c "divsd %xmm2, %xmm1"
d       INSN15: 0x6f824f "divsd %xmm2, %xmm1"
```

Figure 3: Example replacement analysis configuration file

will be replaced with the corresponding single-precision opcode, the inputs will be cast to single precision before the operation, and the result will be stored as a replaced double-precision number with a flag.

- If the mapping for p_i is *double*, then the opcode of p_i will not be replaced, the inputs will be cast to double precision before the operation, and the result will be stored as a regular double-precision number.
- If the mapping for p_i is *ignore*, then instruction p_i will be ignored entirely, which is useful for flagging unusual constructs like random number generation routines.

We use a simple, human-readable exchange file format (Figure 3 shows an example) to store these configurations. The file is plain text and lists the program's functions, basic blocks, and instructions, using indentation to improve readability. The initial list of these structures is easily generated using a simple static analysis that traverses the program's control flow graph. The first column contains flags such as "d" (double precision), "s" (single precision), or "i" (ignore) that control the precision of the code structures during instrumentation. The format supports simple toggling of larger aggregate structures like functions. If an aggregate entry has a flag in the first column, it overrides any flags specified for its children; if the aggregate entry has no flag, each child requires a flag individually. Our automated search system automatically generates new configuration files, which we then pass to our instrumentation system.

In the example configuration of Figure 3, certain instructions from each function have been selected for replacement with single precision. In addition, the function `split()` has a single-precision replacement flag, overriding the individual flags of all instructions in that function.

We also built a GUI (shown in Figure 4) that displays a tree corresponding to the program structure, allowing a developer to adjust a configuration manually without having to edit a lengthy text file. The GUI also allows the developer to visualize the results of our automatic search to understand what part of the code can be changed to single precision. If debug information is available, the GUI can also present a view that shows the corresponding source code location for a particular instruction. This capability aids in the conversion of particular code regions to single precision.

2.2 Automatic breadth-first search

We developed a simple automatic search system that attempts to replace as much of the program as possible using a breadth-first search through the entire program's configuration space. There are 2^n total possible configurations to test, where n is the number of floating-point instructions in the program. Since evaluating each test configuration requires a full program run, exhaustively testing every configuration is not feasible. Our bread-first search strategy represents our initial attempt to exploit some structure in these configurations for a faster search. Improving the search strategy is an ongoing area of research.

Our search maintains a work queue of possible configurations, testing them one by one and adding to the final configuration any individual configurations that pass the application-defined verification process. This process is highly parallelizable, and the system can launch many independent tests if cores are available. The search first generates configurations for each module in the program. Each configuration replaces the entire corresponding module with single precision, leaving the rest of the program in double precision. If any of these module-level configurations fail to pass verification, the routine begins to descend recursively through the program structure, testing function-level configurations before continuing to basic blocks and finally individual instructions as necessary. The recursion terminates when any structure (module, function, or block) is replaced and passes verification, or when the search tests an individual instruction (which cannot be further subdivided). The search can also be configured to stop at basic blocks or functions, allowing for faster convergence with coarser results.

Our system includes two simple optimizations that enhance the search speed and help the search converge faster. The first optimization involves using a binary search to break up large functions and basic blocks into two equally-sized intermediate partitions, rather than adding them all immediately as individual configurations when the parent configuration fails. This reduces the amount of configurations that must be tested when there are a large number of replaceable sections sprinkled with a few non-replaceable sections. The second optimization prioritizes configurations based on an initial profiling run; the configurations that replace the most frequently executed instructions are tested first. This allows the search to rule out large replacements more quickly and to provide faster preliminary results to the user.

After performing a brute-force breadth-first search through the program's structure, our tool will have found the coarsest granularity at which each part of the program can successfully be replaced by single precision. The routine then assembles a "final" configuration by taking the union of all previously-found successful individual configurations. This configuration is also tested automatically, although it may not pass verification without further changes because the precision levels of various instructions are not independent. In other words, decreasing precision in one part of a program may impact the sensitivity of other portions. However, the final configuration serves as an interesting starting point for the developer to investigate since it represents a rough indicator of how much of the original program can be individually replaced by single precision while maintaining the original desired level of accuracy.

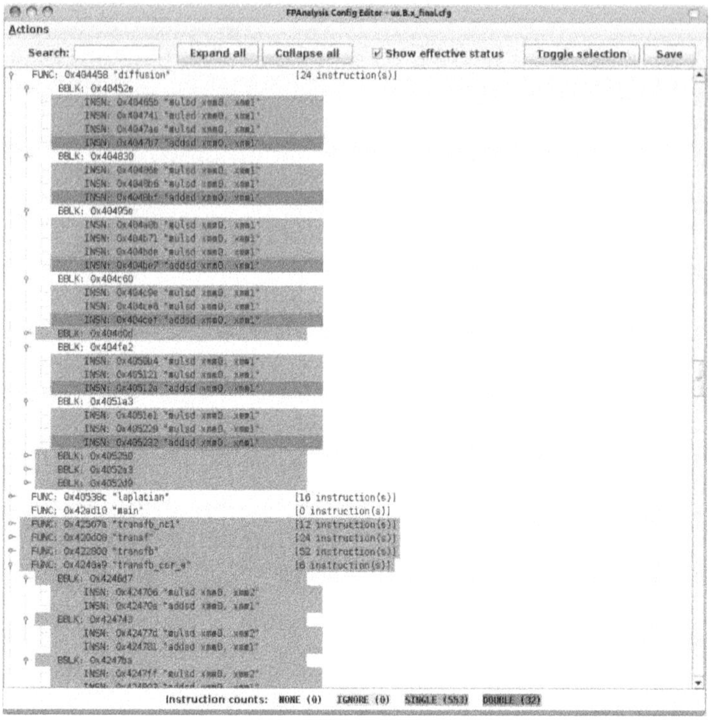

Figure 4: Graphical configuration editor, viewing a configuration for one of the NAS benchmarks

2.3 Binary modification

Our strategy for implementing mixed-precision configurations in existing binaries is to replace some double-precision instructions selectively with their single-precision equivalents, and to replace their double-precision operands with their single-precision equivalents in memory. Of course, after our system produces a final configuration, a programmer would then need to convert these operations to single precision in the original code. Recall that the purpose of our system is to identify regions of a program that can be computed in single precision, not to perform the code transformation in the original source language.

These narrowing conversions (double precision to single precision) allow our analysis to store the new (lower-precision) value in the same location as the old value. Thus, the 32 bits of the new single-precision value are stored in the lower 32 bits of the original 64-bit double-precision register or memory location. The remaining high 32 bits are set to a specific bit pattern (0x7FF4DEAD) [1] to indicate to the analysis that this value has been replaced. Figure 5 illustrates this process. This technique works for single values as well as "packed" floating-point values in 128-bit XMM registers.

To implement a replaced instruction, our framework can insert a streamlined "binary blob" snippet of machine code instructions. This snippet checks the operands (replacing them if necessary) and runs the original instruction in the desired precision. The desired precision is dictated for every floating-point instruction in the original program by a configuration file, described in Section 2.1. These new machine code instructions are generated by a simple mini-compiler, which implements routines for building flag tests and rewriting instruction opcodes in lower precisions. Figure 6 shows the template for these snippets in the case where we perform the instruction in single precision.

Since most of the snippet operations are integer instructions, the snippets impose a minimal overhead, and the downcast operation is performed only when the input has not already been replaced. In order to avoid hard-to-find synchronization bugs or writing to unwritable memory, the analysis copies any memory operands into a temporary register, and modifies the replaced instruction to use only register operands. In addition, once we replace any instruction with its single-precision equivalent, we must replace all floating-point instructions with our snippets, even the ones that are to be performed in double-precision. This change is necessary even if we do not replace a particular instruction with its single-precision equivalent, because we must add a check and possible upcast in case any of the incoming operands were replaced with single precision by an earlier operation. This requirement provides the benefit that anything that our analysis misses causes a crash, which is much easier to debug than mis-rounded operations.

2.4 Basic block patching

To modify the binary and insert our code snippets, we use Dyninst's CFG-patching API. This API allows us to split the original program's basic blocks at arbitrary points and rearrange the edges between blocks. To insert our code in the place of an instruction, we first split the basic block that contains the instruction into three blocks: 1) any instructions before the original instruction, 2) the original instruction,

[1] We choose this value for two reasons. The first four hex digits (0x7FF4) encode a NaN, ensuring that the program never silently propagates incorrect values. The second four hex digits (0xDEAD) form a common human-readable value that is easy to spot in a hex dump.

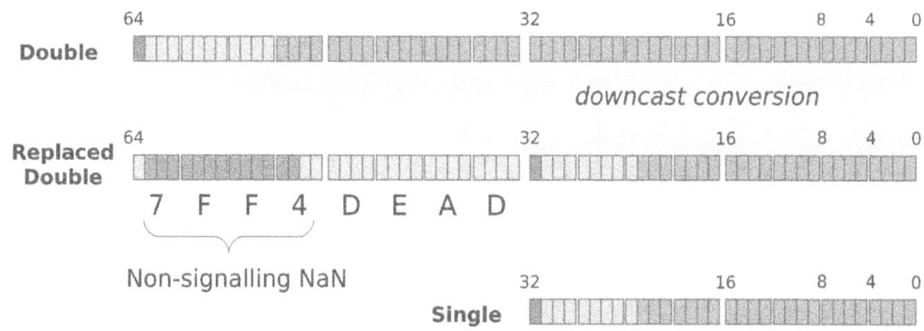

Figure 5: In-place downcast conversion and replacement

```
  push %rax
  push %rbx

  <for each input operand>
    <copy input into %rax>
    mov %rbx, 0xffffffff00000000
    and %rax, %rbx              # extract high word
    mov %rbx, 0x7ff4dead00000000
    test %rax, %rbx             # check for flag
    je next                     # skip if replaced
    <copy input into %rax>
    cvtsd2ss %rax, %rax         # down-cast value
    or %rax, %rbx               # set flag
    <copy %rax back into input>

next:
  <next operand>
  pop %rbx
  pop %rax
  <replaced operand>        # e.g. addsd => addss

  <fix flags in any packed outputs>
```

Figure 6: Single-precision replacement template

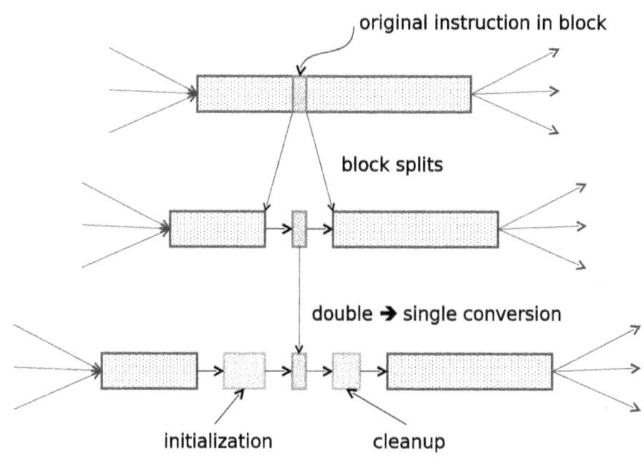

Figure 7: Basic block patching

and 3) any instructions after the original instruction. This allows us to insert our own code and re-arrange the edges from the surrounding parts of the original basic block to point to our new code instead of the original instruction. Figure 7 illustrates this process.

After performing the patching process, we use Dyninst's binary rewriter to create a new executable with the replaced code. The rewriter can also output modified shared libraries, allowing us to instrument and to modify functions in external dependencies. Thus, we can analyze third-party libraries even if the source code is not available.

2.5 Future optimizations

We have several avenues to improve our current system. First, we could reduce the runtime overhead by streamlining the machine code that is emitted, in order to produce more compact and efficient snippets. Second, we observe that in many cases the implementations of transcendental functions like sine, cosine, and logarithms contain lookup routines or bitwise manipulation for speed. Adding special handling for these functions improves performance and increases the fraction of the instructions in the original program that can be replaced with single precision. Third, static data flow analysis could improve overheads by detecting instructions that never encounter replaced double-precision numbers under a given configuration, and thus would not need to be replaced with a double-precision snippet. Finally, we could streamline the search algorithm to converge more quickly on the optimal configuration by adapting more conventional search heuristics rather than doing a simple breadth-first search.

3. RESULTS

In this section, we present results using our analysis technique. First, we show that the runtime overhead on several standard benchmarks is feasible for real workloads. Second, we show how our technique can inform developers about the floating-point behavior of their program and its sensitivity to roundoff error. Third, we show how our analysis can inform floating-point transformations for runtime speedup. Since most aspects of identifying mixed precision code regions amount to a single-node optimization, we confined our experiments to single nodes.

3.1 Correctness and runtime overheads

We first verified the correctness of our replacement on several NAS benchmarks [5] by manually converting the codes to use single precision and comparing the outputs to that of the instrumented version. The final results were identical, bit-for-bit, indicating that the instrumented versions were performing the exact same operations as the manually-converted versions of the original programs.

As a part of this verification, we developed a small script that attempted an automatic translation of Fortran source code to use single precision instead of double precision. How-

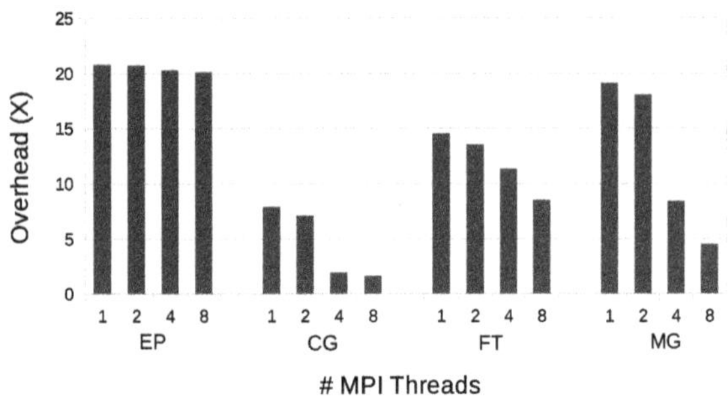

Figure 8: NAS MPI scaling results

Benchmark	Overhead
ep.A	3.4X
ep.C	5.5X
cg.A	3.4X
cg.C	4.5X
ft.A	4.2X
ft.C	7.0X
mg.A	5.8X
mg.C	14.7X

Figure 9: NAS benchmark overhead results

ever, we still had to tweak some files by hand, since some source files were generated by auto-configuration scripts. In some cases, while examining the results of the comparison, we found errors in our manual conversion, which needed to be corrected before the results matched. This process demonstrates that even by itself, the whole-program replacement routine is valuable as a complete automation of a error-prone manual (or semi-automated) process.

To examine the overhead of our tool, we looked at intra-node scaling by replacing all instructions with double-precision snippets. This transformation does not affect the semantics or results of the program, but shows how much overhead our inserted code causes in the base case in which it makes no conversions. Figure 8 shows the runtime overhead results from these experiments with Class A versions of the benchmarks. In general, the overall overhead decreases as the number of threads on a single core increases. Figure 9 shows specific runtime overheads from individual configurations for Class A and C inputs.

All benchmarks were MPI versions compiled by the Intel Fortran compiler with -O2 optimization enabled. Tests were performed on a distributed cluster, each node with twelve Intel Xeon 2.8GHz cores and 24 GB memory running 64-bit Linux. Each run used eight cores. The overhead was calculated as the ratio between the instrumented and original execution user CPU times as reported by the "time" command. In most cases, these overheads are under 20X, making this technique viable for test and trial runs on real data. In particular, these overheads are two orders of magnitude below those reported by the runtime cancellation detection tool [6] mentioned in the related work section, which range from 160X to over 1000X.

We also ran our automatic mixed-configuration search on these NAS benchmarks. For simplicity and speed of execution, we used the single-threaded versions of the benchmarks in this experiment. For each benchmark, we tested two input set sizes: class W and class A. All benchmarks were compiled by the Intel Fortran compiler with optimization enabled, and the tests were performed on the same cluster as the overhead experiments.

The benchmarks provided a wide range of replacement results. The percentages in Figure 10 indicate how sensitive the benchmark is to the precision level used. The columns contain the number of instructions that were candidates for replacement, the total number of configurations tested, the percentage of instructions replaced with single precision (measured statically), the percentage of instruction executions replaced (measured dynamically at runtime), and the verification result of the final composed configuration.

In nearly all cases, the system tested fewer configurations than there were candidates, showing that our techniques for pruning the search space are effective.[2] Some benchmarks (such as CG and FT) seem to be highly sensitive, since only a very low percentage of instruction executions can be replaced. Others seem to hold more promise for building a mixed-precision version. The ones that fail the final verification illustrate that using the simple union of all individually passing instructions does not automatically guarantee a passing configuration. This observation suggests that a second search phase may be useful, to determine the largest subset of individually-passing instruction replacements that may be composed to create a passing final configuration.

3.2 AMG Microkernel

To conduct an end-to-end test of our tool and a subsequent code modification by a programmer, we looked for a program that could run entirely in single precision, in order to simplify the manual conversion process. It was also necessary that the program include a verification routine that could be analyzed by our tool. The Algebraic Multi-Grid microkernel [1], which performs the critical sections of a multigrid solver, met our needs. For our experiments, we used 5,000 iterations on eight cores.

As expected, our system verified that the kernel could be replaced with single precision. The overhead of our analysis was only 1.2X for this benchmark, with all instructions replaced by single precision. We verified the results by manually converting the entire program to single precision and re-compiling. This conversion includes changing the verification routine to single precision, but in some circumstances this change is acceptable. In this instance, the adaptive nature of the multigrid method corrects for numerical inaccuracy by iterating to increasingly accurate results. For the microkernel, we observed a user CPU time decrease from 175.48s for the double-precision version to 95.25s for the single-precision version, a nearly 2X speedup.

3.3 SuperLU Linear Solver

To evaluate our tool further, we use a test program that is already implemented in both single- and double-precision versions, the SuperLU [14] general purpose linear solver. LU

[2]The one exception (SP) had many instructions in the final configuration that sequentially alternated between single and double precision, causing our search engine to spend an inordinate amount of time searching individual instructions rather than aggregated structures, leading to tests of more configurations than actual candidates.

Benchmark	Candidates	Configurations Tested	Instructions Replaced Static	Instructions Replaced Dynamic	Final Verification
bt.W	6,647	3,854	76.2%	85.7%	fail
bt.A	6,682	3,832	75.9%	81.6%	pass
cg.W	940	270	93.7%	6.4%	pass
cg.A	934	229	94.7%	5.3%	pass
ep.W	397	112	93.7%	30.7%	pass
ep.A	397	113	93.1%	23.9%	pass
ft.W	422	72	84.4%	0.3%	pass
ft.A	422	73	93.6%	0.2%	pass
lu.W	5,957	3,769	73.7%	65.5%	fail
lu.A	5,929	2,814	80.4%	69.4%	pass
mg.W	1,351	458	84.4%	28.0%	pass
mg.A	1,351	456	84.1%	24.4%	pass
sp.W	4,772	5,729	36.9%	45.8%	fail
sp.A	4,821	5,044	51.9%	43.0%	fail

Figure 10: NAS benchmark results, showing the benchmark name, number of candidates for replacement, number of configurations tested, percentage of instructions replaced with single precision (measured statically), percentage of instruction executions replaced (measured dynamically at runtime), and the verification result of the final composed configuration

Threshold	Instructions Replaced Static	Instructions Replaced Dynamic	Final Error
1.0e-03	99.1%	99.9%	1.59e-04
1.0e-04	94.1%	87.3%	4.42e-05
7.5e-05	91.3%	52.5%	4.40e-05
5.0e-05	87.9%	45.2%	3.00e-05
2.5e-05	80.3%	26.6%	1.69e-05
1.0e-05	75.4%	1.6%	7.15e-07
1.0e-06	72.6%	1.6%	4.77e-07

Figure 11: SuperLU linear solver memplus results

decomposition and linear solving comprise some of the most computationally expensive portions of larger scientific codes. The SuperLU library performs such operations, and it includes a single-core linear solver example program that can be compiled to use either single- or double-precision (but not mixed-precision). The program also reports an error metric that is useful in comparing the sensitivity of various mixed-precision configurations.

For these experiments we used the "memplus" memory circuit design data set from the Matrix Market [7], which contains nearly 18K rows. The linear solver for this data set runs for around three seconds on our machine, which allows us to test many configurations. The single-precision manually recompiled version achieves a 1.16X speedup over the double-precision version, which is equivalent to a 150 MFlops improvement. The reported error for the double-precision version of the solver is 2.16e-12, and the reported error for the single-precision version is 5.86e-04.

To run an automated search on the linear solver program, we wrote a driver script that ran the program and compared the reported error against a predefined threshold error bound. Using an error bound just above the error returned by the single-precision version, our search tool found that 99.1% of the double-precision solver's floating-point instructions could be replaced by single-precision. This equated to 99.9% of all runtime floating-point operations. That percentage matches the precision profile of the single-precision version of the program, and shows that our tool can find all replacements inserted manually by an expert.

Figure 11 shows the results of running our search tool using various error thresholds. The general trend is that when the error threshold is stricter, the search finds fewer static or dynamic instructions that can be replaced. For this application, the error of the final run (using the union of all passing configurations) tends to be much lower than the threshold used during the search. Thus, our tool can help identify the areas of a program that are sensitive to roundoff error.

4. RELATED WORK

4.1 Backwards & forwards error analysis

The analysis efforts regarding floating-point representation and its accompanying roundoff error initially focused on manual backward and forward error analysis. This field was active as early as 1959 [11], with Wilkinson's seminal work in the area being published in 1964 [44]. This research was continued by others throughout the following decades up to the present time [28, 33, 29, 31, 36] and recently summarized by Goldberg and Higham [21, 24].

Forward error analysis begins at the input and examines how errors are magnified by each operation. Backward error analysis is a complementary approach that starts with the computed answer and determines the exact floating-point input that would produce it. Both techniques provide an indication of how sensitive the computation is, and how incorrect the computed answer might be. Computations that are highly sensitive are called *ill-conditioned.*

Higham [24] describes examples of these analyses for a variety of different numerical analysis problems. Unfortunately, the results of these analyses are difficult for a programmer to understand or to apply without extensive training or error analysis background.

4.2 Interval & affine arithmetic

Researchers have attempted to model the behavior of a floating-point program using a technique called "interval arithmetic" [29, 30, 41], which represents every number x in a program using a range $\bar{x} = [x.lo, x.hi]$ instead of a fixed value. Arithmetic operations operate on these intervals, usually resulting in a wider interval in the result:

$$\bar{x} + \bar{y} = [x.lo + y.lo, x.hi + y.hi]$$

$$\bar{x} - \bar{y} = [x.lo - y.hi, x.hi - y.lo]$$

Unfortunately, regular interval arithmetic is not always useful due to the quick compounding of errors [2], and the difficulty of handling intervals containing zero [24]. In the worst case, division by zero will produce an invalid interval, or the interval will eventually expand to $(-\inf, +\inf)$, a result that is trivially correct but practically useless. Even in less extreme circumstances, however, the average-case error is rarely as bad as the worst-case, and so interval analysis by itself is usually of little value to programmers who are merely interested in the practical behavior.

Interval arithmetic was later improved by Andrade and others [2] with the concept of "affine arithmetic," replacing the ranges of interval arithmetic with a linear combination of error factors. In this scheme, a number x is represented as a first-degree polynomial $\hat{x}$:

$$\hat{x} = x_0 + x_1\epsilon_1 + x_2\epsilon_2 + \cdots + x_n\epsilon_n$$

Affine representation preserves information about error independence, and allows some errors to cancel out others. This sharing indicates that the error came from the same input and will cancel out in the sum. Thus, the bounds for the result are tighter than those that would be obtained in standard interval arithmetic.

More recently, Goubault and Martel and others [13, 16, 17, 22, 35, 38, 39] have built abstract semantics and static analyses using affine arithmetic. These techniques, like any static analysis, are *a priori* and give conservative error estimates. In addition, recent work by Martel and others [40] describes a system that can perform program transformations to increase accuracy. These transformations involve rearranging operations according to well-known rules of floating-point arithmetic, rather than by adjusting the precision.

Unfortunately, the fact that they are static analyses also means that they are not dataset-sensitive, and still give conservative estimates that may not be useful. In addition, they require some manual tuning by the programmer, particularly with regards to the extent that loops are unrolled: more unrolling produces better answers but requires more lengthy analyses. These techniques also only work for a subset of language features (often excluding HPC-specific interests like MPI communication), and are usually limited to C programs. Finally, these techniques merely make observations about error, and do not aid the programmer in building mixed-precision variants of their code.

4.3 Manual mixed-precision applications

More recently, many researchers [4, 9, 10, 25, 34, 42, 43] have demonstrated that mixed precision can achieve the same results as using purely double-precision arithmetic, while being much faster and memory-efficient. They usually present linear solvers (particularly sparse solvers) as examples, showing how the majority of operations can be performed in single precision. These solvers have been applied

1: $LU \leftarrow PA$
2: solve $Ly = Pb$
3: solve $Ux_0 = y$
4: **for** $k = 1, 2, ...$ **do**
5: $\quad r_k \leftarrow b - Ax_{k-1}$ (*)
6: $\quad$ solve $Ly = Pr_k$
7: $\quad$ solve $Uz_k = y$
8: $\quad x_k \leftarrow x_{k-1} + z_k$ (*)
9: $\quad$ **check for convergence**
10: **end for**

Figure 12: Mixed precision algorithm

to a wide range of problems, including fluid dynamics [3], lattice quantum chromodynamics [12], finite element methods [20], and Stokes flow problems [18]. Often, GPUs are cited as the target of these optimizations because of their streaming capabilities [3, 12, 19].

In the iterative algorithm shown in Figure 12, for example, only the steps marked with asterisks (lines 5 and 8) must be executed in double precision. The authors note that all $O(n^3)$ steps can be performed in single precision, while the double-precision steps are only $O(n^2)$. Thus, using mixed precision can yield significant performance and memory bandwidth savings. On the streaming Cell processor, for instance, the mixed-precision version performed up to eleven times faster than the original double-precision version. Even on non-streaming processors, they obtained a performance improvement between 50% and 80%.

Researchers in the field of computer graphics have also found that mixed-precision algorithms can improve performance [23]. By varying the number of bits used for graphics computations, they report speedups of up to 4X or 5X, with little or no apparent image degradation. They use fixed-point arithmetic, but the mixed-precision concepts are similar to floating-point. Unfortunately, these techniques do not automatically generalize to other domains because they involve very specialized vertex and lighting calculations.

In recent work, Jenkins and others [27] describe a novel scheme for reorganizing data structures by numerical significance. Their technique splits up a floating-point number into several chunks on byte boundaries. All pieces of corresponding significance are stored consecutively in memory for storage and I/O, and the original numbers are re-assembled only when needed for calculation. Thus, the developer can vary the precision of floating-point data during data movement by truncating the lower-precision blocks. In their experiments, they found that some applications can use as few as three bytes (24 bits) of floating-point data and retain an acceptable level of accuracy. This work focused on the I/O implications, however, and did not address the possibility of single-precision arithmetic. Their system also incurs overhead during data re-assembly.

4.4 Dynamic cancellation detection

In previous work, we developed a dynamic runtime analysis for detecting numerical cancellation [32], which is a loss of significant bits due to the subtraction of nearly identical numbers. Cancellation can be harmful if one of the numbers was subject to roundoff error from previous calculations. Our analysis can detect all cancellations above a given threshold, reporting aggregate results for each instruction as well as a sampling of detailed information about individual cancellations. These results can inform the developer about the floating-point behavior of their program. However, since cancellation does not necessarily always indicate that harmful roundoff error has occurred, the results can be difficult to interpret and to apply. Other authors have built on this work and developed more heavyweight techniques that quantify the "badness" of individual cancellations [6] in an attempt to be more helpful to the developer, but the overhead of their techniques make them prohibitively expensive for full-scale data sets. None of these efforts directly contribute towards mixed-precision computation.

5. CONCLUSION

We have shown that automated techniques can build mixed-precision configurations of existing binaries that use double-precision arithmetic, and that such techniques can be used to search an application automatically for portions that can be replaced with single-precision arithmetic. We have presented benchmark overhead results that show the technique's feasibility, and have described two experiments that demonstrated a speedup gained by a conversion guided by our analysis. In the future, we plan to optimize our implementation further by streamlining the inserted code to reduce overhead and by improving the search algorithm to converge more quickly. This work improves the ability of high-performance floating-point application developers to make informed decisions regarding the behavior of their code and the necessary precision levels for various parts of their programs.

Acknowledgments

We wish to acknowledge and thank Andrew R. Bernat at the University of Wisconsin, Madison for his contributions to the code patching library contained in Dyninst, as well as Osni Marques at the Laurence Berkeley National Laboratory for supporting our use of the SuperLU library. This work is supported in part by DOE grants DOEN.DESC0002351 and DOEN.DESC0002616.

This article has been authored by Lawrence Livermore National Security, LLC under Contract No. DE-AC52-07NA27344 with the U.S. Department of Energy. Accordingly, the United States Government retains and the publisher, by accepting the article for publication, acknowledges that the United States Government retains a non-exclusive, paid-up, irrevocable, world-wide license to publish or reproduce the published form of this article or allow others to do so, for United States Government purposes. (LLNL-CONF-635248).

6. REFERENCES

[1] ASC Sequoia Benchmark Codes. https://asc.llnl.gov/sequoia/benchmarks/. Accessed 21 September 2011.

[2] M. V. A. Andrade, J. a. L. D. Comba, and J. Stolfi. Affine Arithmetic, 1994.

[3] H. Anzt, B. Rocker, and V. Heuveline. Energy efficiency of mixed precision iterative refinement methods using hybrid hardware platforms. *Computer Science Research and Development*, 25(3-4):141–148, 2010.

[4] M. Baboulin, A. Buttari, J. Dongarra, J. Kurzak, J. Langou, J. Langou, P. Luszczek, and S. Tomov. Accelerating Scientific Computations with Mixed Precision Algorithms. *Computer Physics Communications*, 180(12):2526–2533, 2008.

[5] D. Bailey, T. Harris, W. Saphir, R. V. D. Wijngaart, A. Woo, and M. Yarrow. The NAS Parallel Benchmarks 2.0, 1995.

[6] F. Benz, S. Hack, and A. Hildebrandt. A Dynamic Program Analysis to find Floating-Point Accuracy Problems. In *ACM SIGPLAN Conference on Programming Language Design and Implementation*, 2012.

[7] R. F. Boisvert, R. Pozo, K. Remington, R. Barrett, and J. J. Dongarra. The Matrix Market: A web resource for test matrix collections. In R. F. Boisvert, editor, *Quality of Numerical Software, Assessment and Enhancement*, pages 125–137. Chapman & Hall, London, 1997.

[8] B. Buck and J. K. Hollingsworth. An API for runtime code patching. *The International Journal of High Performance Computing Applications*, 14:317–329, 2000.

[9] A. Buttari, J. Dongarra, J. Kurzak, J. Langou, P. Luszczek, and S. Tomov. Exploiting Mixed Precision Floating Point Hardware for Scientific Computation. In *High Performance Computing and Grids in Action*. IOS Press, 2008.

[10] A. Buttari, J. Dongarra, J. Kurzak, P. Luszczek, and S. Tomov. Using Mixed Precision for Sparse Matrix Computations to Enhance the Performance while Achieving 64-bit Accuracy. 2007.

[11] J. W. Carr. Error analysis in floating point arithmetic. *Communications of the ACM*, 2(5):10–16, May 1959.

[12] M. A. Clark, R. Babich, K. Barros, R. C. Brower, and C. Rebbi. Solving Lattice QCD systems of equations using mixed precision solvers on GPUs. *Computer Physics Communications*, 181(9):30, 2010.

[13] F. De Dinechin, C. Q. Lauter, and G. Melquiond. Assisted verification of elementary functions using Gappa. *Proceedings of the 2006 ACM symposium on Applied computing SAC 06*, page 1318, 2006.

[14] J. W. Demmel, S. C. Eisenstat, J. R. Gilbert, X. S. Li, and J. W. H. Liu. A Supernodal Approach to Sparse Partial Pivoting. *SIAM Journal on Matrix Analysis and Applications*, 20(3):720–755, 1999.

[15] J. Dongarra, P. Beckman, T. Moore, P. Aerts, G. Aloisio, J. C. Andre, D. Barkai, J. Y. Berthou, T. Boku, B. Braunschweig, F. Cappello, B. Chapman, A. Choudhary, S. Dosanjh, T. Dunning, S. Fiore, A. Geist, B. Gropp, R. Harrison, M. Hereld, M. Heroux, A. Hoisie, K. Hotta, Y. Ishikawa, F. Johnson, S. Kale, R. Kenway, D. Keyes, B. Kramer, J. Labarta, A. Lichnewsky, T. Lippert, B. Lucas, B. Maccabe, S. Matsuoka, P. Messina, P. Michielse, B. Mohr, M. S. Mueller, W. E. Nagel, H. Nakashima, M. E. Papka, D. Reed, M. Sato, E. Seidel, J. Shalf, D. Skinner, M. Snir, T. Sterling, R. Stevens, F. Streitz, B. Sugar, S. Sumimoto, W. Tang, J. Taylor, R. Thakur, A. Trefethen, M. Valero, A. Van Der Steen, J. Vetter, P. Williams, R. Wisniewski, and K. Yelick. The International Exascale Software Project roadmap. *International Journal of High Performance Computing Applications*, 25(1):3–60, 2011.

[16] S. P. Eric Goubault Matthieu Martel. Asserting the

Precision of Floating-Point Computations: A Simple Abstract Interpreter. *Programming Languages and Systems*, pages 287–306, 2002.
[17] C. F. Fang, R. A. Rutenbar, M. Püschel, and T. Chen. Toward efficient static analysis of finite-precision effects in DSP applications via affine arithmetic modeling. *Proceedings of the 40th conference on Design automation DAC 03*, page 496, 2003.
[18] M. Furuichi, D. a. May, and P. J. Tackley. Development of a Stokes flow solver robust to large viscosity jumps using a Schur complement approach with mixed precision arithmetic. *Journal of Computational Physics*, 230(24):8835–8851, Oct. 2011.
[19] D. Göddeke and R. Strzodka. Cyclic Reduction Tridiagonal Solvers on GPUs Applied to Mixed Precision Multigrid. *IEEE Transactions on Parallel and Distributed Systems*, 22(1):22–32, 2011.
[20] D. Göddeke, R. Strzodka, and S. Turek. Performance and accuracy of hardware-oriented native-, emulated- and mixed-precision solvers in FEM simulations. *International Journal of Parallel, Emergent and Distributed Systems*, 22(4):221–256, Aug. 2007.
[21] D. Goldberg. What every computer scientist should know about floating-point arithmetic. *ACM Computing Surveys*, 23(1):5–48, Mar. 1991.
[22] E. Goubault. Static Analyses of the Precision of Floating-Point Operations. *Static Analysis*, pages 234–259, 2001.
[23] X. Hao and A. Varshney. Variable-precision rendering. *Proceedings of the 2001 symposium on Interactive 3D graphics SI3D 01*, http:149–158, 2001.
[24] N. J. Higham. *Accuracy and Stability of Numerical Algorithms, Second Edition.* SIAM Philadelphia, 2002.
[25] J. D. Hogg and J. A. Scott. A fast and robust mixed-precision solver for the solution of sparse symmetric linear systems. *ACM Transactions on Mathematical Software*, 37(2):1–24, 2010.
[26] IEEE. *IEEE 754-2008, Standard for Floating-Point Arithmetic.* IEEE, New York, Aug. 2008.
[27] J. Jenkins, E. R. Schendel, S. Lakshminarasimhan, D. A. Boyuka II, T. Rogers, S. Ethier, R. Ross, S. Klasky, and N. F. Samatova. Byte-precision level of detail processing for variable precision analytics. In *Proceedings of the International Conference on High Performance Computing, Networking, Storage and Analysis*, SC '12, pages 48:1—-48:11, Los Alamitos, CA, USA, 2012. IEEE Computer Society Press.
[28] T. Kaneko and B. Liu. On Local Roundoff Errors in Floating-Point Arithmetic. *J. ACM*, 20(3):391–398, 1973.
[29] W. Kraemer. A Priori Worst Case Error Bounds for Floating-Point Computations. *IEEE transactions on computers*, 47(7):750–756, 1998.
[30] W. Krämer and A. Bantle. Automatic Forward Error Analysis for Floating Point Algorithms. *Reliable Computing*, 7(4):321–340, Aug. 2001.
[31] T. I. Laakso and L. B. Jackson. Bounds for floating-point roundoff noise. *IEEE transactions on circuits and systems*, 41(6):424–426, 1994.
[32] M. O. Lam, J. K. Hollingsworth, and G. W. Stewart. Dynamic Floating-Point Cancellation Detection. In *WHIST '11*, 2011.
[33] J. L. Larson, M. E. Pasternak, and J. A. Wisniewski. Algorithm 594: Software for Relative Error Analysis. *ACM Transactions on Mathematical Software*, 9(1):125–130, Mar. 1983.
[34] X. S. Li, M. C. Martin, B. J. Thompson, T. Tung, D. J. Yoo, J. W. Demmel, D. H. Bailey, G. Henry, Y. Hida, J. Iskandar, W. Kahan, S. Y. Kang, and A. Kapur. Design, implementation and testing of extended and mixed precision BLAS. *ACM Transactions on Mathematical Software*, 28(2):152–205, June 2002.
[35] M. D. Linderman, M. Ho, D. L. Dill, T. H. Meng, and G. P. Nolan. Towards program optimization through automated analysis of numerical precision. *Proceedings of the 8th annual IEEE ACM international symposium on Code generation and optimization CGO 10*, page 230, 2010.
[36] B. Liu and T. Kaneko. Error analysis of digital filters realized with floating-point arithmetic. *Proceedings of the IEEE*, 57(10):1735–1747, 1969.
[37] C.-K. Luk, R. Cohn, R. Muth, H. Patil, A. Klauser, G. Lowney, S. Wallace, V. J. Reddi, and K. Hazelwood. Pin: building customized program analysis tools with dynamic instrumentation. In *PLDI '05: Proceedings of the 2005 ACM SIGPLAN conference on Programming language design and implementation*, pages 190–200, New York, NY, USA, 2005. ACM.
[38] M. Martel. Propagation of Roundoff Errors in Finite Precision Computations: A Semantics Approach. *Programming Languages and Systems*, pages 159–186, 2002.
[39] M. Martel. Semantics-Based Transformation of Arithmetic Expressions. *Static Analysis*, pages 298–314, 2007.
[40] M. Martel. Program transformation for numerical precision. In *PEPM '09: Proceedings of the 2009 ACM SIGPLAN workshop on Partial evaluation and program manipulation*, pages 101–110, New York, NY, USA, Jan. 2009. ACM Press.
[41] P. L. Richman. Automatic error analysis for determining precision. *Communications of the ACM*, 15(9):813–820, Sept. 1972.
[42] Robert Strzodka and Dominik Goddeke. Mixed Precision Methods for Convergent Iterative Schemes. In *Proceedings of the 2006 Workshop on Edge Computing Using New Commodity Architectures, May 2006*, 2006.
[43] Robert Strzodka and Dominik Goddeke. Pipelined Mixed Precision Algorithms on FPGAs for Fast and Accurate PDE Solvers from Low Precision Components. *IEEE Proceedings on Field-Programmable Custom Computing*, 2006.
[44] J. H. Wilkinson. *Rounding Errors in Algebraic Processes.* Prentice-Hall, Inc., 1964.

CMP Off-chip Bandwidth Scheduling Guided by Instruction Criticality

Pablo Prieto
University of Cantabria
Santander, Spain
prietop@unican.es

Valentin Puente
University of Cantabria
Santander, Spain
vpuente@unican.es

Jose Angel Gregorio
University of Cantabria
Santander, Spain
monaster@unican.es

ABSTRACT

This paper explores the benefits of scheduling off-chip memory operations in a Chip Multiprocessor (CMP) according to their execution relevance. Assuming the scenario of having many out-of-order execution cores in the CMP, from the processor perspective, the importance of the instruction that triggers an access to off-chip memory may vary considerably. Consequently, it makes sense to consider this point of view at the memory controller level to reorder outgoing memory accesses. After exploring different processor-centric sorting criteria, we reach the conclusion that the most simple and useful metric for scheduling a memory operation is the position in the reorder buffer of the instruction that triggers the on-chip miss. We propose a simple memory controller scheduling policy that employs this information as its main parameter. This proposal significantly improves system responsiveness, both in terms of throughput and fairness. The idea is analyzed through full-system simulation, running a broad set of workloads with diverse memory behavior. When it is compared with other scheduling algorithms with similar complexity, throughput can be improved by an average of 10% and fairness enhanced by an average of 15% even in very adverse usage scenarios. Moreover, the idea supports the possibility of dynamically favoring throughput or fairness, according to the end-user requirements.

Categories and Subject Descriptors

B.3.2 [**Memory Structures**]: Design Styles – *primary memory, shared memory.* C.1.0 [**Processor Architectures**]: General.

General Terms

Algorithms, Management, Measurement, Performance, Design, Experimentation.

Keywords

Multi-core processor; Off-chip bandwidth wall; out-of-order; memory access scheduling.

1. INTRODUCTION

Moore's law seems to be keeping pace, without insurmountable roadblocks in sight, although further shrinking in feature size will finally be prevented by the laws of physics. In any case, other More-than-Moore technologies such as 3D stacking [4] will allow these problems to be circumvented. Since the mid-2000s, processor designers have had problems to translating device availability into ILP enhancement [26]. Therefore, chip multiprocessors (CMP) have flourished, today being pervasive in most computing fields. The virtuous cycle that in the pre-CMP era allowed performance enhancement to be transparently included in legacy software without any intervention of the final user has been broken. All computer science disciplines [1] are committed to facilitating the adjustment of all the elements of the computer stack to fully exploit the potentials of CMP systems and so guarantee that performance can keep up with device availability growth. Nevertheless, several problems could prevent that evolution. In this paper we will focus on one particularly interesting aspect, namely the off-chip bandwidth wall [3][29]. Packaging issues limit the number of pins available for a chip and clocking. Even under the assumption of a high-performance system, the actual ITRS roadmap [32] states that by 2020 the maximum number of pins will be fewer than 6000, which is less than double today's standard. According to the same report, the operation frequency will grow slightly. Combining both facts, the result is that the off-chip bandwidth available per million transistors will fall exponentially.

Architects and technologists will have to find imaginative solutions to help with this problem; otherwise it will be impossible to keep increasing the number of cores in a single chip. The solutions could be diverse and range from adding massive amounts of on-chip cache, to increasing pin bandwidth using photonics and ultra-dense wavelength multiplexing [25]. Even in these cases, off-chip bandwidth scarcity is foreseeable, and if we combine it with the fact that there will be a huge number of running threads in the CMP, not necessarily cooperating in the same task, it makes sense to pay special attention to how the bandwidth is used. In an extreme case, an intentionally or unintentionally misbehaving task could reduce the whole CMP performance. Therefore, bandwidth partitioning [18] will be paramount and this is where this paper is focused.

Although the work dealing with this problem is profuse, we have used a novel approach to deal with it. In particular we focus our interest on the processor side. Although there are CMPs based on simple cores, general purpose computing demands the utilization of cores capable of exploiting instruction level parallelism [12]. This will require, in one way or another, the use of cores with aggressive out-of-order execution [11]. This work analyzes how to effectively exploit the different nature of memory operations in this class of systems in order to optimize bandwidth utilization. We will explore and demonstrate the possible improvement in system behavior if memory operation scheduling is done taking into account the relevance of the instruction that triggers the operation. In particular we use the distance from such an instruction to the head of the Reorder Buffer (ROB). The proposed scheduling algorithm uses this distance when the

ICS'13, June 10–14, 2013, Eugene, Oregon, USA.

memory operation leaves the core and the off-chip miss-frequency behavior of each core to determine the sorting and aging criteria. The proposal (called DROB) outperforms similar scheduling algorithms both in terms of fairness and throughput. Additionally, the proposed idea has a noteworthy property of allowing the end-user to favor throughput or fairness according to the usage scenario simply by modifying a single parameter. Finally, we demonstrate that it is possible to use a simple mechanism to self-tune the memory controller in order to achieve the most balanced throughput-fairness behavior.

The paper is organized as follows: Section 2 presents the baseline organization for the memory controller and describes related work. Section 3 discusses how the processor viewpoint may be relevant as an ordering criterion and which metrics can be useful. Section 4 introduces a suitable implementation of a memory controller that can exploit this knowledge. Section 5 describes the methodology used to evaluate how effective our approach is. Section 6 reports the performance with different workloads and compares it with other similar scheduling approaches.

2. BASELINE ORGANIZATION AND RELATED WORK

Figure 1 shows the baseline system assumed. The system is composed of a set of N out-of-order execution cores, each one with one or more coherent private levels of cache, a shared write-back last level cache and M memory controllers, managing R ranks made up of B banks. When a memory access instruction, i.e. prefetch, fetch, store, load, atomic or requested block is not in the chip, depending on the memory interleaving, the corresponding memory controller should deal with the request applying the priority ordering used to each incoming request and issuing it to the corresponding DRAM bank. Outstanding accesses to the same memory block from the same core will coalesce in the MSHR of the Local cache level [16]. Outstanding memory requests from different cores will coalesce in the Last level cache MSHR. Write memory operations will be associated with write-back events in the last level cache when an on-chip miss evicts a dirty block.

The memory controller is responsible for applying the priority to the incoming memory transaction and enqueueing it, depending on the address translation, in the corresponding bank queue. From the bank queues, the memory access scheduler logic will chose one transaction and issue it to the appropriate bank. As a starting point, we will assume that this scheduler logic is FR-FCFS [28]. Although other more advanced policies, depending on the DRAM physical implementation, signaling interface, etc. could be used [9][10][22], in most cases this could be considered complementary to this work.

Our proposal, like many others, works at the arbiter level. We compose a policy that prioritizes the incoming memory transaction, based on different sorting criteria. The scheduling algorithm modifies the First-Come-First-Served policy of FR-FCFS, at each bank queue depending on the policy used. According to the priority determined by the arbiter we will insert the associated DRAM operations in the appropriate position of the corresponding queue and will leave the CMP in that order. Given that off-chip bandwidth limitation is a topic that it is attracting significant attention, there are many recent high quality works focused on memory scheduling [5][9][10][15][22][28]. In most of these works, the key point is to infer what the processor is doing in the memory controller and act accordingly with the scheduling decision, coordinating the decision across banks [15], [18]. In some cases the mechanism involved in this decision requires complex algorithms [14], [22] and/or modifications throughout the software stack or limits the flexibility of use of the CMP [21].

Intuitively, the underlying approach in many proposals [8], [20] is to limit the interference of bandwidth-demanding applications on bandwidth non-demanding ones. The objective is, with little performance penalty, to limit the bandwidth consumption of the former applications so as to significantly improve the latter. In a way our approach is similar to this, although it also takes into account the criticality of the instructions at scheduling time. For an out-of-order processor, the criticality of an instruction represents how large the performance penalty of delaying it can be.

3. MEMORY OPERATIONS FROM THE PROCESSOR PERSPECTIVE

There is a significant amount of work focused on managing off-chip bandwidth scarcity from the perspective of the DRAM itself. It makes sense to exploit the technological peculiarities of these systems while not precluding the combined utilization of other techniques focused on the opposite end of the problem: the processor. Although there are many works that introduce mechanisms to deduce the processor responsiveness [15][18][21]-[24] at the memory controller, we opt to directly look at what the processor is doing. Not all memory operations are equally important in an out-of-order execution core, therefore it seems pertinent to use their degree of relevance to carry out the

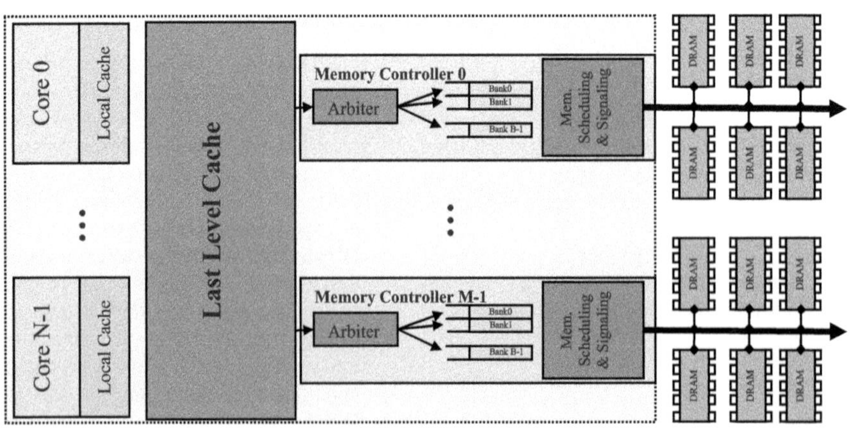

Figure 1. Baseline System

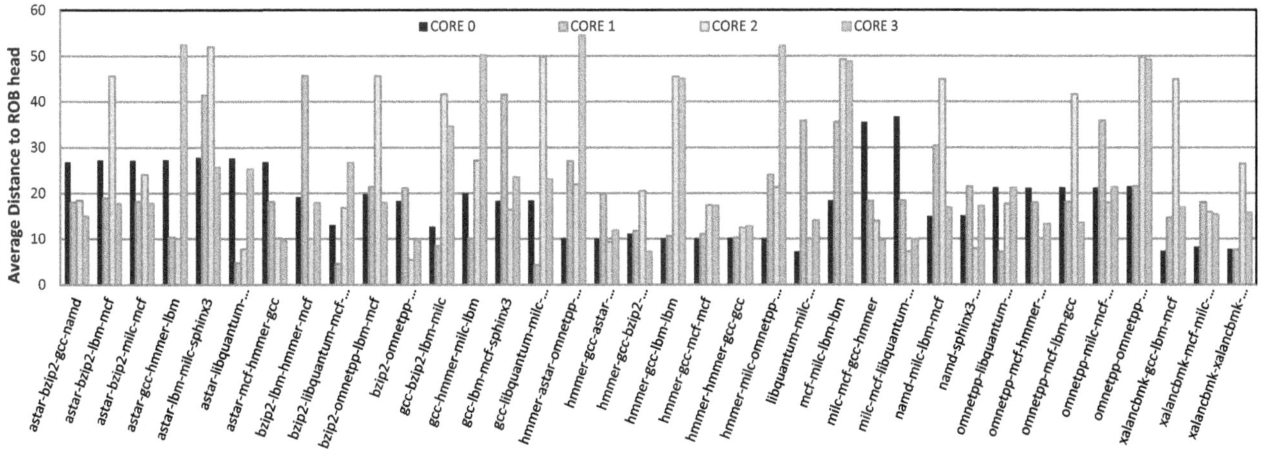

Figure 2 Average instruction distance to head of the Reorder Buffer when the triggered memory operation reaches the memory controller.

prioritization of the memory accesses. At a given time, in usual memory interleaving approaches, each memory controller may deal with memory operations coming from any of the cores in the system. These operations should be sorted and sent to the corresponding DRAM bank in order to be fulfilled. The sorting may have a non-negligible impact on performance, fairness and energy. We will explore the use of different criteria from the processor perspective. We will focus on operations that are in the critical path of the cores, i.e. memory reads. Note that memory write commands are always the result of replacements of dirty blocks in the on-chip cache. Like in systems such as Power5, write operations always have the lowest priority [13].

Although there are recent works, such as [31], focused on co-optimizing the replacement algorithm and the memory controller in order to minimize read-after-write waiting cycles, we do not consider this problem. This type of solutions can be complementary to the analysis carried out in this work. In our case memory write operations will be inserted with the lowest priority in the bank queue.

3.1 Optimize Retire Bandwidth

Retire bandwidth underutilization has a large effect on performance because it directly causes an IPC loss. The most common sources of retire underutilization are a slow operation blocked at the head of the ROB or frequent rollbacks due to miss-speculations. In current system configurations the most likely cause of a slow operation is an on-chip miss. Therefore, when a memory operation arrives at the memory controller, its criticality is higher when the distance to the head of the ROB is smaller. We carried out a simple experiment for thirty-six particular mixes of multiprogrammed workloads using SPEC2006 benchmarks (using the framework and system configuration described in Section 6.1). When an on-chip miss reaches the memory controller we determine the average number of instructions between the triggering instruction and the head of the ROB. As can be seen in Figure 2 the variability is large across all the running threads. For example in the *hmmer-gcc-lbm-lbm* case, memory operations from Core 0 (*hmmer*) and Core 1 (*gcc*)[1] seem to be much more critical than memory operations in other cores. If we can use that information judiciously to schedule memory operations, we can advance the resolution of more important memory operations by some cycles with little effect in other cores. In this example, at a given time, if we can somehow determine the situation in ROBs, it could be useful to favor *gcc* and *hmmer* memory operations over *lbm*. Note that these numbers are oversimplified because the variability is constant during the execution of the benchmark.

3.2 Optimize Fetch Bandwidth

An on-chip miss in the processor front-end, i.e. instruction fetch, has a critical impact on an out-of-order execution processor. In such situations, given that this operation is performed in order, the processor pipeline will stall. Although this type of misses is not very frequent in many applications, in others, such as commercial workloads, it might be quite probable. This behavior is due to the large code footprint of this type of applications [2]. Therefore, in a multiprogrammed environment, the number of memory operations triggered by a fetch from each core could be quite different depending on the characteristics of each thread. If the memory controller assigns the maximum priority to these operations, it could be possible to accelerate miss resolution and consequently unclog pipeline access faster. This would have a notable impact on performance not only when an unbalance in core fetches is observed but even for each core. Enabling some loads already enqueued in the bank queue from the same core to be overtaken would be beneficial, especially if these loads are far from the ROB head. In few applications, we have observed significant improvements in performance when accelerating fetches over other memory requests.

3.3 Degree of Speculation

When an on-chip miss reaches the memory controller, the triggering instruction/s can be speculatively issued. Let's denote the degree of speculation of an instruction as the number of operations issued without all the parameters being known, i.e. the number of unresolved branches, number of executed loads with ambiguous stores, etc. between it and the head of the ROB. Intuitively, not all instructions will be equally relevant from the point of view of the memory operation. If the triggering instruction of an on-chip cache miss has a higher degree of speculation than another triggering instruction of another pending memory operation at the memory controller, it could make sense to use this information somehow to order the priority of the requests to memory. Following a similar procedure to the one described previously, we show the number of unresolved branches

---

[1] We use the Solaris tool *processor_bind* to fix threads to cores.

for six different mixes of SPEC2006 applications. As we can see in Figure 3(a), for a 128-entry ROB, the average number of unresolved branches from application to application is quite similar, ranging from 1 to 3. This seems to indicate that this criterion might not be useful when ordering memory operations.

Nevertheless, this information is partial because the likelihood of being annulled is also dependent on the branch prediction accuracy. In particular, this could be very important if the thread executed by some cores has a higher chance of miss-speculation. For example, if we mix integer applications with floating point applications, the chances of miss-speculation are much higher in the former type of applications than in the latter due to branch prediction miss-speculations. To provide a better perspective, in Figure 3 (b) we show the probability of the instruction arriving at the memory controller being rolled-back. Where, M is the branch miss-prediction rate, and N the number of speculated branches, the probability of rolling back is calculated as:

$$P_{RB} = 1 - (1 - M)^N \quad (1)$$

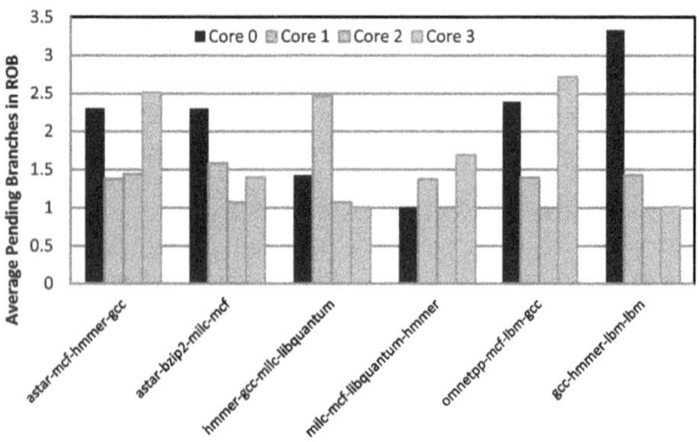

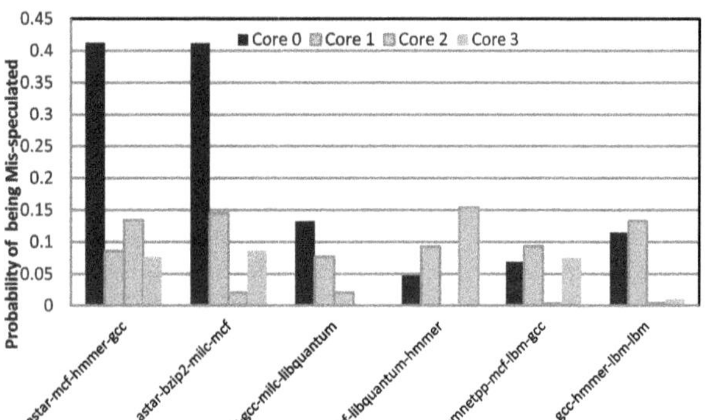

Figure 3 (a) Degree of speculation of triggering instructions at memory controller, (b) Probability of the triggering instruction being rolled-back later.

The result is that most of the benchmarks are fairly similar, the presence of some pathological behavior being noticeable only in *astar,* where almost half of memory accesses correspond to miss-speculated instructions. Therefore, this metric might not be so relevant as the previous one when sorting memory operations but it can be useful to discard pathological behavior such as *astar*'s. Anyway, the results obtained show that the complexity involved is not cost effective bearing in mind the performance benefits. Consequently this approach will not be considered in our ordering criteria.

Although other types of speculation can be considered, such as opportunistic load execution, with a simple dependency predictor, the number of miss-speculations is not relevant in comparison with branch-caused miss-speculation. Other speculative operations like "data value prediction" have not been analyzed.

3.4 Dependent instructions

3.4.1 Dependency Graph Depth

Looking backwards in the ROB could also provide hints about the relevance of the memory operation depending on the number of dependent instructions. Intuitively, a pending instruction with more dependent instructions waiting to be issued in the ROB should be considered more important than another one with fewer. The question that arises is whether on average it could be possible to observe a significant difference from core to core. We ran the same experiment again looking in the ROB for the number of dependent instructions (both direct and indirectly) on the output register of the instruction that generates the miss. Figure 4 shows how many dependent instructions are in the ROB when the triggering instruction of the memory operation reaches the memory controller. Any direct or indirect dependence of the instruction in the ROB is taken into account. As can be seen, in spite of having up to 128 in-flight instructions, the difference between each thread is not sufficient for clear discrimination. Moreover, in most cases there is a clear correlation between the distance of the triggering operation from the head of the ROB and the number of dependent instructions. Intuitively, if we assume a similar degree of usefulness for the block fetched from memory, then the shorter the distance from the head of the ROB, the longer the distance to the tail and consequently the more dependent instructions could be found. A classification in terms of this metric and distance to the head of the ROB, therefore, seems to be redundant and will not be used in the scheduling algorithm.

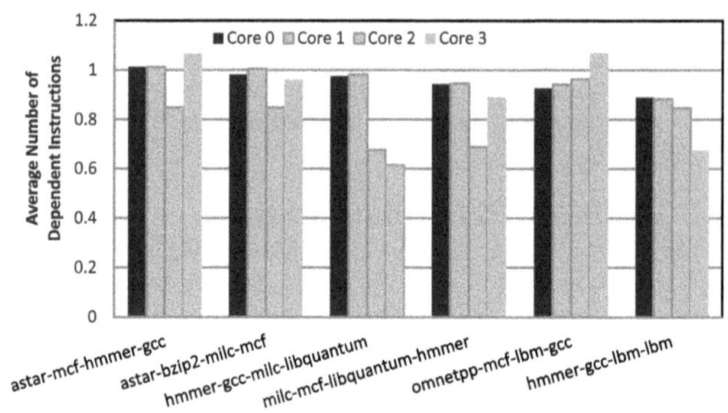

Figure 4. Average Number of dependent instructions at the ROB when the triggering operation reaches the memory controller.

3.4.2 Store Operations

In the previous analysis, the nature of each memory operation was not addressed. For the stores, technically the processor does not require the outcome of the execution of instructions to progress forward, i.e. there are no truly dependent instructions in the associated on-chip miss. Forwarding from the Store Queue or Write Buffer will provide the required value for any subsequent load to the same word. Therefore, at the memory controller, classification of memory operations according to the nature of the triggering instruction might be considered. Although it could make sense to prioritize the memory read when the instruction is a load [9], this decision should be carefully considered. Loads to a particular block can be overlapped with earlier stores misses, which will be pending in MSHR [16]. Under this situation, storing triggered memory operations will impact on performance. Next, we will show how frequently this situation could happen. We choose, as an example, nine applications of SPEC2006. Figure 5 shows the average number of coalescing loads in the MSHRs to the same memory block where a previous store has missed. The value is computed when the memory operation finalizes. The bars indicate the maximum and minimum number of coalescing loads-under-store miss observed when the application is executed concurrently in different mixes of applications. As we can see, from application to application there is a large disparity in the coalescent loads compared to stores. For *mcf* or *hmmer*, the average number of loads to the same block requested by a store is relatively large. In contrast, in other applications such as *lbm* the likelihood is negligible. The dissimilar spatial locality of each application determines this behavior. Moreover, when each application is running concurrently with three other applications, the variability is sometimes noticeable. Therefore, a careful analysis is necessary before delaying store operations at the memory controller, otherwise a large number of coalescing critical loads might be delayed. Nevertheless, this information is not easily accessible since, at scheduling time, even with idealized MSHR knowledge in memory controllers, most coalescing loads will still be pending. In practice, besides its complexity, this approach in most cases tends not to provide noticeable benefits. It is not unusual to observe substantial performance degradation, especially in applications such as *mcf* and *hmmer*.

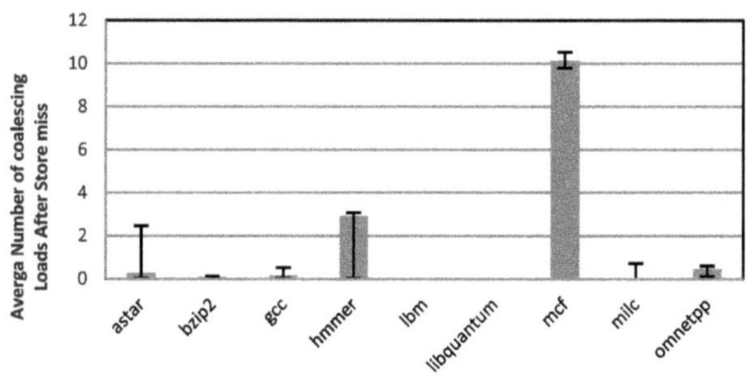

Figure 5. Average Number of coalescing Loads in the same cache block as a Store miss.

4. REALISTIC IMPLEMENTATION OF A CORE-CRITICALLY-BASED MEMORY SCHEDULER

The previous section discusses potential scheduling criteria assuming that the memory controller has full knowledge of the processor logic when the memory operation reaches it. This is unfeasible without impairing CMP scalability. Therefore, the information needed to reorder memory operations has to be generated when the triggering instruction leaves the core, i.e. it is executed if it is a load or committed if it is a store. We can embed the required information in requests and piggyback it in each successive on-cache miss until reaching the memory controller. However, when the memory operation reaches the controller, the processor status might have changed. We should readjust this information using local metrics.

4.1 Distance to ROB Head

As explained before, it is possible to send the distance of the instruction to the ROB head attached to the memory request it triggers, but this information arrives at the memory controller after a number of cycles and might have changed. It would be desirable to estimate its position in the ROB when the on-chip miss reaches the memory controller. Although achieving precision in the absolute value might be hard, a relative value to compare the criticality of the concurrent memory operations would be enough. In general, when a processor generates a memory request, the instruction that triggers it will reach the head of the Reorder Buffer approximately after the number of cycles given by:

$$NumCycles = \frac{DistToRoBHead}{IPC} = DistToRoBHead \cdot CPI \quad (2)$$

This information should be enough to order requests properly, but it is not easy to continuously provide it to the memory controller. Nevertheless, the memory controller has easy access to the on-chip misses in each core in the memory region that is mapped. From this metric, it is straightforward to derive the miss frequency, which is a good proxy for the CPI [18]. Although the correlation between CPI and miss frequency has been analyzed thoroughly in previous works, we simplify its practical use. We cannot obtain the absolute value for the CPIs of each core, but we can guess the relationship among them from the viewpoint of the ratio of their miss frequency at the memory controller. As it is a ratio, the result is no longer a measure of time, but a sort of corrected distance to the ROB head. As this parameter will only be used as a correction factor for the distance to the ROB head, this approximation is accurate enough to evaluate request criticality.

According to this and using (2), the corrected distance or priority level of a request *i*, with a distance of D_{ROB} to the ROB header at the time the operation leaves the core *p* for a CMP with *N* cores, when it arrives at the memory controller is calculated as:

$$\overline{PrioLevel_i} = D_{ROB} \cdot \frac{Miss\_freq_p}{\max\{Miss\_freq_0..Miss\_freq_N\}} \quad (3)$$

As the miss frequency is computed independently at each controller, no communication is required between the memory controllers. Miss frequency is calculated every 1M cycles, and to avoid momentary application singularities, miss frequency will be computed using the exponential moving average of each processor at the memory controller. Note that the priority level expressed in (3) is inverted, i.e. a memory request has higher priority when the normalized distance to the head of ROB is smaller.

4.2 Fetches and Writes

As previously discussed, prioritizing fetches over other memory requests might have impact on performance without noticeable cost, so we have implemented this feature. Fetches are considered high priority, and do not use the same formula as other memory reads. Instead, their priority level is automatically set to 0 (the maximum). On the other hand, we know memory writes corresponds to LLC write-backs and are not in the critical path. To keep the scheduling algorithm uniform, for such operations the priority level of the request is set to the size of the Reorder Buffer (the minimum priority).

4.3 Memory scheduling algorithm

Once a request reaches the memory controller, the operation will be inserted into the corresponding bank queue and then sorted according to the priority assigned using (3). When no previous high priority requests are pending in the queue, for example situation (a) depicted in Figure 6, a search for high priority requests is initiated. In the example, we represent the computed priority and the issuing processor in each entry of the queue. The algorithm uses an input parameter denoted *Threshold Distance*. If the priority is below this distance the request is tagged as high priority. If not, the request priority is recomputed decreasing the distance to the ROB header by the *Threshold Distance*, avoiding starvation issues for these requests. In the example presented in Figure 6, the Threshold distance used is 16. Therefore, in situation (b), only the first five requests will be tagged as high priority and the remaining requests are recomputed accordingly. Therefore, the sorting algorithm used is:

$$
\begin{aligned}
&For\ (i\ in\ requests)\\
&\quad if\ (PrioLevel_i < ThresholdDistance)\\
&\qquad\qquad \rightarrow Request\ i\ Become\ High\ Priority\\
&\quad else \rightarrow PrioLevel_i = PrioLevel_i - ThresholdDistance
\end{aligned}
$$

When all the high priority commands have left the queue, which corresponds to situation (c) in Figure 6, the search for new high priority requests is initiated. Note that since step (b) occurred, additional memory requests could have arrived at the memory controller, which correspond to the white boxes. After the application of the sorting, seven requests are tagged with high priority.

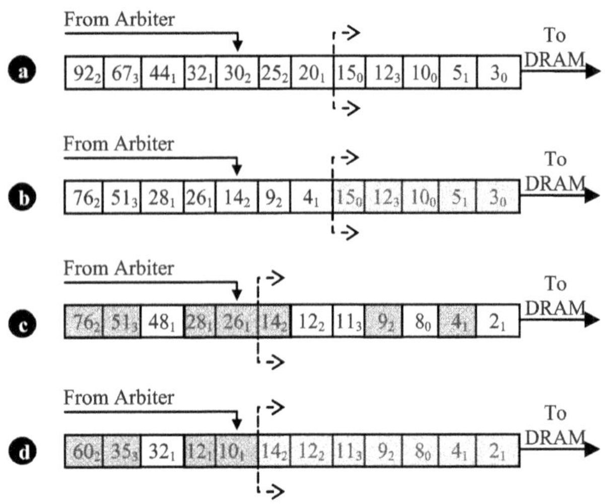

Figure 6 Memory scheduling Example.

In contrast to other batch-like scheduling algorithms, such as PAR-BS [24] the batch length and time between arbitrations is variable and no request for a processor can be tagged with high priority. In the first sorting in the example, no request from processor 2 has been tagged with high priority. Additionally, once the request is tagged for high priority, the processor *id* is no longer used in the scheduling of the memory operations. In PAR-BS the order of pending requests per processor is used to decide how the batch is sent to memory. This is equivalent to prioritizing the processor with lowest CPI for the current interval. In order to capture a global scope, ATLAS uses the exponential moving average of the pending request for each core to sort the batches. We combine the broad effect of the miss frequency and the local scope of the D_{ROB} of each request. Although miss frequency is useful as a proxy of the CPI, per request D_{ROB} is very useful to correct it with local effects.

The input parameter of *Threshold Distance*, as we will show later, could be used to adjust the system to favor fairness or global performance. This can be dynamically set in order to simultaneously optimize the two figures of merit.

5. EVALUATION METHODOLOGY

To perform the evaluation we use a modified version of the GEMS framework [19]. We use a DDR2/3 detailed memory controller provided by the latest GEMS version. It models bank busy time, memory bus occupancy and turnaround delays, and refresh. Our target machines run an unmodified SPARCv9 operating system and binaries. The operating system used by the target system is Solaris 10. We model hardware-assisted TLB fill and register window exceptions for all target machines. Multiple runs are used to achieve strict 95% confidence intervals (error bars are not visible in most cases). Benchmarks are fast-forwarded past their initialization phases, during which page tables, TLBs, predictors, and caches are warmed.

We will target our study towards aggressive core architecture, dimensioned with up to 128 in-flight instructions and 4-issue width. The main parameters of the architectural specification are summarized in Table 1. Note that the L3 characteristic is per core, therefore, in our system with four processors, there will be a total of 4MB. To interconnect all L3 banks, L1 caches and memory controllers, we will use an on-chip interconnection network based on [14]. L3 cache is shared and statically partitioned (S-NUCA) and interleaved using less significant address bits. L2 is exclusive with L1 and L3 is inclusive with private caches [17].

Table 1. Configuration per-core.

Core Parameters		Cache Hierarchy	
Issue/Retire Width	4/4	*L1 Instruction*	Private, 32KB, 4-way,2-cycle, Pipelined, 64B
Scheduler Size	Unified, Pointer Based[27], 128 entries	*L1 Data*	Private, 32KB, 4-way, 2-cycle, Pipelined, 64B
Functional Units	4 ALU/2 LD-ST, 2 FP, 2BR	*L2 Private Unified*	256KB, 8-way, 8-cycles, 64B, Exclusive With L1
Min. Latency Fetch-to-Dispatch	7 cycles	*L3 shared S-NUCA [8]*	2 Slices per core, each one: 512KB, 8-way, 8-cycles, 64B, Inclusive with Private caches
Branch Predictor	YAGS [6]16K PHT 8K Exception Table, 8KB BTB, 16-entry RAS	*Coherence Protocol*	In-cache MOESI Directory
Memory Scheduling	Unlimited Store-sets	*Interconnection Network*	4x4 Mesh
Dram System			
DRAM Controller	On-chip 1,6 GB/s peak DRAM bandwidth	*DRAM Parameters*	DDR2-200 8 banks tCL=15ns tRCD=15ns, tRP=15ns
DIMM Configuration	Single rank 8 RAM chips on a DIMM 64-bit wide channel		

Due to the computational effort of the current simulation infrastructure, we chose to use a reduced number of cores in our analysis. Therefore, to really provide insights about the relevance of this class of solutions, we should scale down the available off-chip bandwidth. The starting assumption [32] is that off-chip bandwidth will be scarce in the future. We think that scaling up the bandwidth availability for the small size of system we can simulate today will necessitate reduction of bandwidth availability if we want to understand the impact that this type of approaches will have in the long term [29] as the number of cores and application demands increase [7]. According to this reasoning, we assume a raw bandwidth of 1.6GB/s in a four-processor system, and eight memory banks.

In order to evaluate the effectiveness of the proposal, we will compare our approach with different static and dynamic design alternatives. In regard to the workloads, we will use multi-programmed workloads from SPEC 2006 [33].

6. PERFORMANCE RESULTS

In order to determine the benefits of our proposal, we will compare it with FR-FCFS [28], ATLAS[22] and PAR-BS[24]. We select this set of scheduling algorithms due to the similar complexity of the memory controller and level of intervention required at runtime. We have explored other scheduling algorithms based on bandwidth partitioning, such as [18], with discouraging results.

FR-FCFS, which will be considered as the baseline scheduler, has no tunable parameters. For PAR-BS, which successfully improves performance and fairness compared to FR-FCFS, after an exhaustive search, the optimal BatchCap used is 5. Therefore, in each scheduling up to 5 requests per processor will be chosen. ATLAS, a PAR-BS evolution which takes into account broader effects throughout the past, we use a HistoryWeight of 0.875 for the exponential moving average. In our proposal, which will be denoted as DROB, we use a HistoryWeight of 0.875 and Threshold Distance of 16.

We compare these scheduling algorithms' performance and fairness using three different metrics. As a performance metric we use the Harmonic Average of CPI, which is the inverse of the arithmetic average of IPC and represents the throughput as the number of instructions per cycle of the whole system. We also provide the commonly used Weighted Speedup of CPI which measures a balance of fairness and throughput. Finally, as a measure of fairness we use the maximum slowdown of IPC. All the metrics were chosen in order to guarantee the criteria of the lower, the better.

$$\begin{aligned} Weighted\ Speedup &= \sum_i \frac{CPI_i^{shared}}{CPI_i^{alone}} \\ Harmonic\ CPI &= \frac{N}{\sum_i 1/CPI_i} \\ Maximum\ Slowdown &= \max_i \frac{IPC_i^{alone}}{IPC_i^{shared}} \end{aligned} \qquad (4)$$

Both metrics are important, as our objective is to obtain the best system throughput and fairness, although there are some cases in which only pure throughput or fairness is needed. In section 6.4 we will discuss how our system can provide the best results in one of these metrics simply by varying a single parameter.

6.1 Workloads

We will use hybrid combinations of SPEC2006 workloads. We compiled each benchmark using gcc version 4.3.1 with –O3 optimizations. All workloads are executed with a reference input set. All threads are slept at the beginning of the region of interest and awakened at once, then running at least 500 million instructions. Each thread core has an affinity, using Solaris processor_bind facility, for a different core.

Since the number of combinations of applications can be really high, previously we characterized how memory demanding each considered benchmark is by obtaining the number of-chip misses for each thousand instructions executed (MPKI). From those results, we choose 12 applications shown in Table 2. Most of the missing applications (nine) have very low memory demands. Others (five) were not considered due to the simulation framework limitations.

Table 2 Applications

Memory-intensive			**Memory-non-intensive**		
Application	***MPKI***	***Avg. Dist. ROB Head***	***Application***	***MPKI***	***Avg. Dist. ROB Head***
Mcf	97.38	16.90	*Astar*	9.26	24.35
Libquantum	50.00	6.28	*Hmmer*	5.66	9.97
Lbm	43.52	44.95	*Bzip2*	3.98	19.76
Milc	27.90	33.41	*Gcc*	0.34	14.71
Sphinx3	24.94	21.48	*Namd*	0.19	15.05
Xalancbmk	22.95	7.36			
Omnetpp	21.63	20.21			

Seven of the selected applications are memory-intensive (a large number of misses per executed instruction) and five of them are non-memory-intensive (a small number of misses per executed instruction). Additionally, as can be appreciated in Table 2, there is no direct correlation between average distance to the ROB head and memory intensity. In some cases, such as Libquantum or Astar, there is a large discrepancy between the two values. In this case, the memory accesses tend to be clustered. In other cases, memory accesses are more homogenously distributed over time. Note that the numbers presented in this table were obtained in an isolated execution of each benchmark.

Using these categories, we created 40 workloads combining different numbers of applications, either memory intensive or not. Table 3 shows a summary of the workloads grouped by percentage of memory intensive applications in the workload. In each group, the number of times each benchmark is used in each workload is specified in brackets.

Table 3 Workloads evaluated

Mixture	*Combinations*	*Memory non-intensive benchmarks*	*Memory intensive benchmarks*
0%	3	Astar(2), bzip2(3), gcc(3), hmmer(3), namd(1)	
25%	5	Astar(4), bzip2(2), gcc(3), hmmer(4), namd(2)	Lbm(1), libquantum(1), mcf(1), omnetpp(1), xalancbmk(1)
50%	13	Astar(4), bzip2(6), gcc(7), hmmer(7), namd(2)	Lbm(6), libquantum(1), mcf(7), milc(6), omnetpp(3), xalancbmk(3)
75%	15	Astar(2), bzip2(4), gcc(4), hmmer(2), namd(3)	Lbm(7), libquantum(7), mcf(9), milc(7), omnetpp(4), sphinx3(8), xalancbmk(3)
100%	4		Lbm(5), mcf(2), milc(3), omnetpp(4), sphinx3(1), xalancbmk(1)

6.2 Throughput

We measure system throughput using two different metrics. Instruction throughput is the average number of instructions retired by all cores per cycle. As explained, we use the harmonic average of CPI to maintain the idea of the lower the better in all figures. We also use the commonly-employed weighted speedup [30] which sums the Cycles per Instruction (CPI) slowdown experienced by each benchmark compared to when it runs alone.

We present the performance of our proposal in comparison with counterpart scheduling algorithms (FR-FCFS, PARBS and ATLAS). Figure 7 shows the system throughput provided by each algorithm on the 40 representative workloads, grouped by their kind of mixture. Our proposal provides slightly better throughput results than the highest performance algorithm, ATLAS, outperforming FR-FCFS by 12.5% on average with a maximum of 37% in the hmmer-gcc-lbm-lbm workload, while ATLAS obtains an improvement of 11.9% on average and a maximum of 33%.

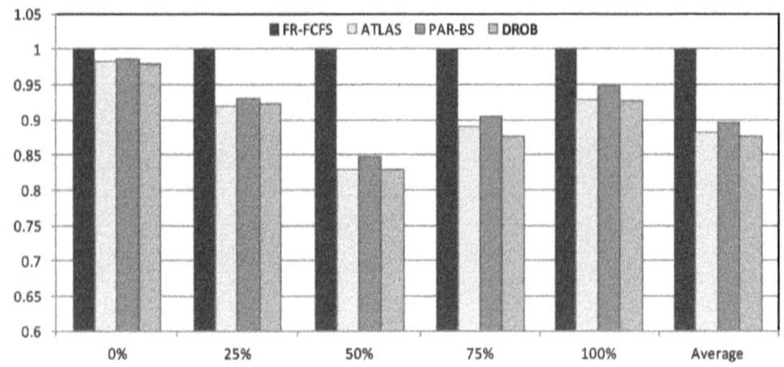

Figure 7. Harmonic Average of CPI normalized for FR-FCFS for different workload mixes.

As expected, the performance differences between the diverse scheduling algorithms, when all running applications are not memory intensive, are almost constant. In these cases, memory bandwidth is under-utilized and so there is little to no interference in sharing it. As the number of memory intensive applications is increased in the workload, the performance differences become significantly higher. When the pressure on the memory is very high (4 memory intensive applications) the benefits diminish slightly. Note that in this case, there is performance improvement because the applications, although intense in memory usage, have different MPKIs. In addition, these types of scheduling algorithms obtain their best results when running applications with substantial differences in their memory behavior. Considering just the workload sets where performance differences are most noticeable, ATLAS provides 16.4% higher instruction throughput than FR-FCFS, while PAR-BS increases it by 14.3% and our proposal outperforms FR-FCFS by approximately 17% on average.

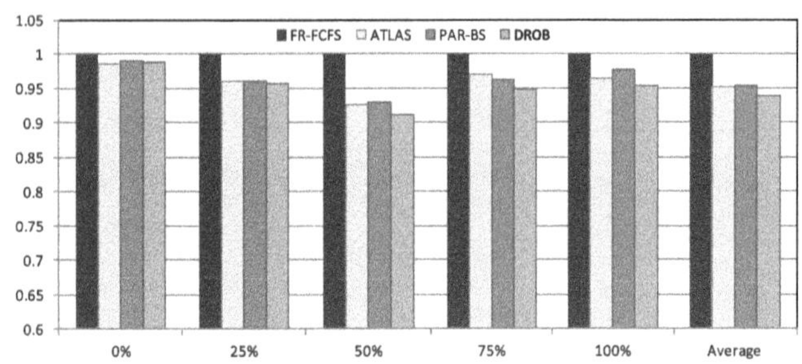

Figure 8. Weighted SpeedUp of CPI normalized for FR-FCFS for different workload mixes.

On the other hand, in Figure 8, when fairness is taken into account, ATLAS's weighted speedup results match those of PARBS, which outperforms FR-FCFS by 4.7%, while our proposal outperforms both of them by 1.6%. We can conclude that our proposal outperforms other throughput-oriented scheduling algorithms, while taking care of instruction criticality rather than just processor performance, obtaining better results in weighted CPI.

6.3 Fairness

We also report fairness using maximum slowdown [30]. This parameter measures the maximum slowdown of the applications running in each workload compared to their IPC running alone. Scheduling algorithms are likely to improve the performance of those high-IPC applications which suffer most when executed along with memory-intensive applications, and so they reduce the maximum slowdown. However, those algorithms which just deal with the IPC tend to penalize memory-intensive applications excessively, which could end up turning the tables and causing a decrease in fairness. As seen in Figure 9, our proposal obtains the best fairness results, taking into account instruction criticality, outperforming FR-FCFS by 10.6% on average and by up to 31%. It also outperforms PAR-BS and ATLAS by 6.1% and 7.6% on average respectively and by up to 20% at most. Although on average FR-FCFS is the worst in terms of fairness, as explained before, there are workloads where scheduling algorithms negatively affect fairness.

When all the applications in the workload stress the memory, both ATLAS and PAR-BS on average have slightly worse fairness than plain FR-FCFS (in the worst case this increases maximum slowdown by 32% and 40% respectively). Unsurprisingly, PAR-BS and ATLAS use on-chip misses only to arbitrate the memory access. When all the applications have a high miss frequency, they tend to over penalize more demanding applications, which negatively affects execution time. In contrast DROB uses instruction criticality to separate application behavior, which on average improves baseline fairness.

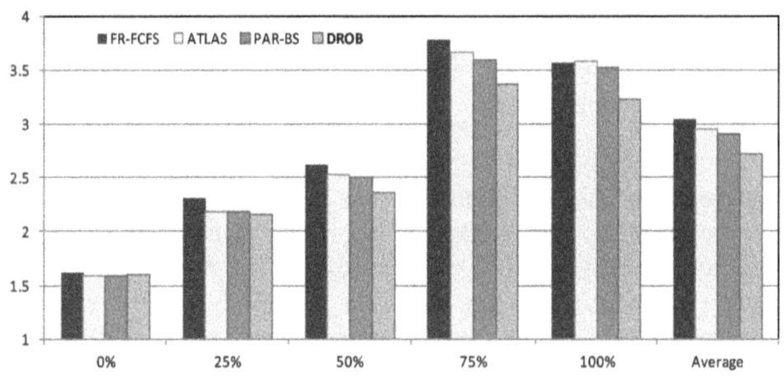

Figure 9. Maximum slowdown for each of the different scheduling algorithms normalized for FR-FCFS.

6.4 Statically Tunable Behavior

Throughout the previous discussion the fundamental parameter of the policy, i.e. *Threshold Distance* was fixed at a distance of 16 to the head of the ROB. Under these conditions, fairness and throughput balance is optimal, allowing DROB to outperform counterpart memory scheduling algorithms. Nevertheless, depending on the usage scenario, it could be more interesting to maximize throughput or fairness. Let us suppose a usage scenario where a CMP is running a set of virtual private servers (VPS) from different clients. In this situation, fairness is paramount. Nevertheless, in a usage scenario where all cores are running applications from the same user, maximizing throughput might be more interesting. A noteworthy property of our proposal is that by modifying *Threshold Distance*, we can maximize either metric.

As explained in section 4.3, the speed of the aging process can be modified considering a different "*Threshold Distance*". When we reduce the critical distance chosen, the aging process slows down because the queued requests would expect a higher number of jumps before becoming critical, meaning critical requests reaching the memory controller have less competition, thus improving performance. In contrast, when we increase the critical distance, the aging process accelerates causing critical requests that reach the controller to compete with a greater number of requests already queued, thus also reducing the average waiting time in the queue, which consequently improves fairness. Intuitively, reduced *Threshold Distance* tends to favor recent close-to-head requests whereas large Threshold Distance favors old waiting requests.

Figure 10 and Figure 11 show how throughput and fairness behave when *Threshold Distance* is modified. For the smallest value of this parameter, the highest throughput results are obtained, improving on FR-FCFS by 16% on average at most, 22% on average just considering the workloads where memory bandwidth is scarce. On the other hand, Figure 11 shows how we can improve fairness results simply by increasing the critical distance to the highest value, (half the ROB size), outperforming FR-FCFS by 12%. This throughput-fairness balance is consistent across all the workloads evaluated.

Other scheduling algorithms also have fixed parameters. For example PAR-BS limits the number of requests per core in the batch. If we change that parameter in the memory controller, as expected, there is no direct result in system metrics, which are quite inconsistent across the workload. In some cases one decision improves throughput and in other cases the same decision improves fairness. As we can see, the average variation of these changes is hardly noticeable. Therefore, in contrast to DROB, this parameterization is not useful for this purpose. Similar behavior would be observed with ATLAS.

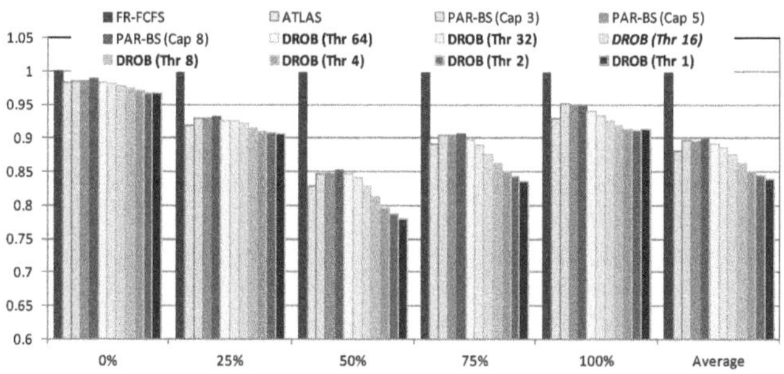

Figure 10. Harmonic Average of CPI of DROB varying the Threshold Distance (Thr) from 1 to half the ROB size (64) compared to other memory scheduling algorithms.

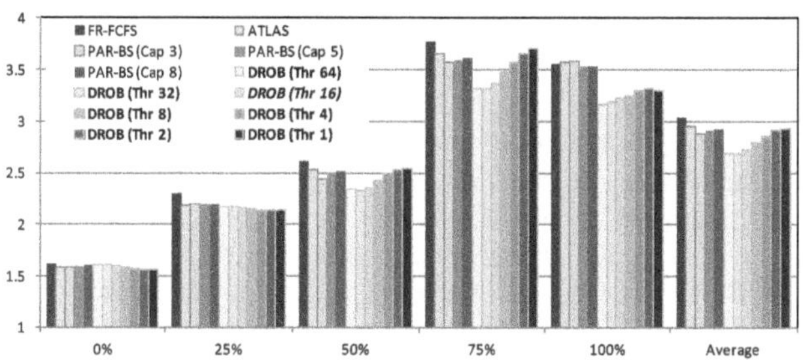

Figure 11. Maximum slowdown of DROB varying the Threshold Distance (Thr) from 1 to half the ROB size (64) compared to other memory scheduling algorithms.

6.5 Adaptive Behavior

According to the results in the previous section, it is possible to observe that, globally, the most balanced choice for Threshold Distance is 16. Nevertheless, when the applications' mixes change, we can observe better results with slightly different values. If we take into consideration that during the execution of the workload, application behavior will change, it might be interesting to allow the memory controller to self-adapt threshold distance in order to improve the throughput-fairness balance even more. In order to do so, we implement a simple approach that samples the tendency in the miss frequency of each core every million cycles. The change in this value could mean, that the application is entering in a high MPKI phase or that the last change in the Threshold Distance has improved CPI. To distinguish the two cases, we use the average distance to the ROB header. If there is no significant change between the two samples, we assume that MPKI is the same. We determine for all cores without variations in MPKI whether the last change in Threshold distance was positive (i.e. the average slope of the CPI is negative). If this is the case, the Threshold Distance is changed in the same direction. Otherwise the parameter is decreased. The changes are done gradually (in steps of one). If the average CPI change perceived is less than 5%, the Threshold distance is maintained. The throughput and fairness results are shown in Figure 12 and Figure 13 respectively. As can be seen, both throughput and fairness are slightly improved over the best static configuration.

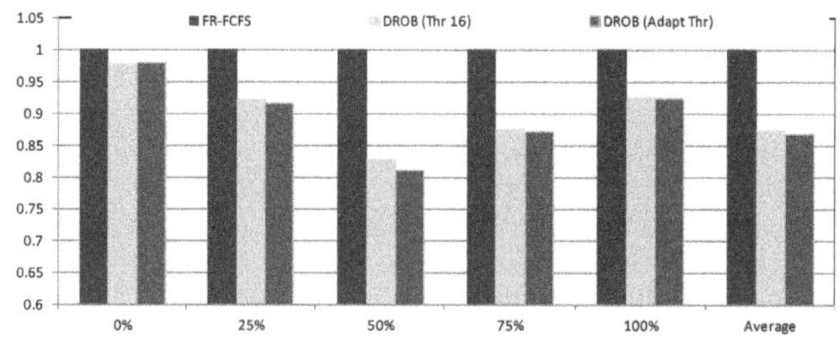

Figure 12. Harmonic Average of CPI for DROB with adaptive Threshold Distance.

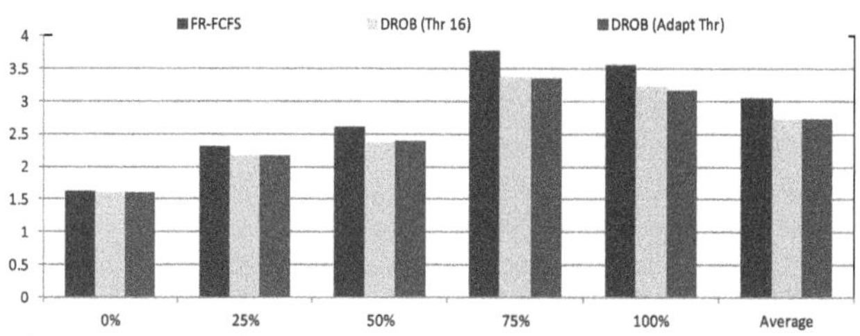

Figure 13. Maximum slowdown for DROB with adaptive Threshold Distance.

7. CONCLUDING REMARKS

We have presented DROB, a novel approach to the memory scheduling problem for chip multiprocessor systems. Previous memory scheduling algorithms are too complex or are focused on processor performance inference rather actual behavior. Our proposal obtains the information from the processor in a simple way, improving performance and fairness of the whole system.

Our evaluation using a wide variety of application mixtures shows that our proposal provides reasonable system throughput compared to previous memory scheduling algorithms, while obtaining significantly better fairness. In addition, our implementation is able to adapt in a simple manner to the needs of the system, obtaining even better results according to the usage scenario.

8. ACKNOLEDGEMENTS

The authors would like to thank Jose-Angel Herrero for his valuable assistance with computing environment HPC cluster Calderon within the datacenter 3Mares. This work has been supported by the MICCIN (Spain) under contract TIN2010-18159, MECD (Spain) under grant PRX12/00006, and by the HiPEAC European Network of Excellence.

9. REFERENCES

[1] Asanovic, K. et al. 2006. *Tech. Rep. UCB/EECS-2006-183.* Technical Report EECS Department, University of California, Berkeley.

[2] Barroso, L. A., Gharachorloo, K., and Bugnion, E. 1998 Memory system characterization of commercial workloads. In *Proc. of the 25th Annual Int. Symp. on Computer Architecture (ISCA 1998)*, 3–14.

[3] Burger, D. and Goodman, J. 1996. Memory bandwidth limitations of future microprocessors. In *Proc. of the 23rd Int. Symp. on Computer Architecture* (ISCA 1996), 78–89.

[4] Davis W., Wilson J., Mick S., and Xu J. 2005. Demystifying 3D ICs: The pros and cons of going vertical. *IEEE Design & Test of Computers (2005)*, 498–510.

[5] Ebrahimi E., Miftakhutdinov R., Fallin C., Lee C. J., Joao J. A., Mutlu O., and Patt Y. N. 2011. Parallel application memory scheduling. In *Proc. of the 44th IEEE/ACM Int. Symp. on Microarchitecture* (MICRO 2011), 362-373.

[6] Eden, A. N. and Mudge, T. 1998. The YAGS branch prediction scheme. In *Proc. of the 31st Annual ACM/IEEE Int. Symp. on Microarchitecture* (MICRO 1998), 69–77.

[7] Gustafson J. L. 1988. Reevaluating Amdahl's law. *Communications of the ACM*, vol. 31, no. 5 (May 1988), 532–533.

[8] Huh J., Kim C., Shafi H., Zhang L., Burger D., and Keckler S. W. 2007. A NUCA substrate for flexible CMP cache sharing. *IEEE Transactions on Parallel and Distributed Systems*, vol. 18, no. 8 (2007), 1028–1040.

[9] Ipek E., Mutlu O., Martínez J. F., and Caruana R. 2008. Self-Optimizing Memory Controllers: A Reinforcement Learning Approach. *In Proc. of the 35th Int. Symp. on Computer Architecture* (ISCA 2008), 39–50.

[10] Jacob B., Ng S., Wang D. 2007. *Memory Systems: Cache, DRAM, Disk.* Morgan Kaufmann Publishers Inc. 1st edition (Sep. 10th, 2007).

[11] Joao J., Suleman M., and Mutlu O. 2012. Bottleneck Identification and Scheduling in Multithreaded Applications. In *Proc. of the 17th Int. Conf. on ASPLOS* (2012), 223-234.

[12] Juurlink, B. H. H. and Meenderinck, C. H. 2012. Amdahl's law for predicting the future of multicores considered harmful. *ACM Computer Architecture News*, vol. 40, no. 2 (May 2012), 1-9

[13] Kalla R., Sinharoy B., and Tendler J. M. 2004. IBM power5 chip: a dual-core multithreaded processor. *IEEE Micro*, vol. 24, no. 2(Mar. 2004), 40-47.

[14] Kim J., Nicopoulos C., Park D., Das R,, Xie Y., Narayanan V., Yousif M. S., and Das C. R. 2007. A novel dimensionally-decomposed router for on-chip communication in 3D architectures. In *Proc. of the 34th Int. Symp. on Computer Architecture (ISCA* 2007), 138-149.

[15] Kim Y., Papamichael M., Mutlu O., and Harchol-Balter M. 2010. Thread Cluster Memory Scheduling: Exploiting Differences in Memory Access Behavior. *In Proc. of the 43rd IEEE/ACM Int. Symp. on Microarchitecture* (MICRO 2010), 65-76.

[16] Kroft D. 1998. Lockup-free instruction fetch/prefetch cache organization. In *25 years of the Int. Symp. on Computer Architecture (selected papers) ISCA* 1998, 195–201.

[17] Kurd, N., Douglas, J., Mosalikanti, P., and Kumar, R. 2008. Next generation Intel® micro-architecture (Nehalem) clocking architecture. In *IEEE Symposium on VLSI Circuits Digest of Technical Papers* (2008), 62–63.

[18] Liu, F., Jiang, X., and Solihin, Y. 2010. Understanding how off-chip memory bandwidth partitioning in Chip Multiprocessors affects system performance. In *Proc. of the 16th Int. Symp. on High-Performance Computer Architecture* (HPCA 2010), 1–12.

[19] Martin, M. M. K., Sorin, D. J., Beckmann, B. M., Marty, M. R., Xu, M., Alameldeen, A. R., Moore, K. R., Hill, M. D., and Wood, D. A. 2005. Multifacet's general execution-driven multiprocessor simulator (GEMS) toolset. *ACM Computer Architecture News*, vol. 33, no. 4 (2005), 99–107.

[20] Mukundan, J., and Martinez, J. F., 2012. MORSE: Multi-Objective Reconfigurable SElf-Optimizing Memory Scheduler. In *Proc. of the IEEE 18th Int. Symp. on High-Performance Computer Architecture* (HPCA 2012), 1-12.

[21] Muralidhara, S. P., Subramanian, L., Mutlu, O., Kandemir, M., and Moscibroda, T. 2011. Reducing Memory Interference in Multicore Systems via Application-Aware Memory Channel Partitioning. In *Proc. of the 44th IEEE/ACM Int. Symp. on Microarchitecture* (MICRO 2011), 374-385.

[22] Mutlu, O. and Harchol-Balter, M. 2010. ATLAS: A scalable and high-performance scheduling algorithm for multiple memory controllers. In *Proc. of the 16th Int. Symp. on High-Performance Computer Architecture* (HPCA 2010), 1–12.

[23] Mutlu, O. and Moscibroda, T. 2007. Stall-time fair memory access scheduling for chip multiprocessors. In *Proc. of the 40th IEEE/ACM Int. Symp. on Microarchitecture* (MICRO 2007), 146–160.

[24] Mutlu, O. and Moscibroda, T. 2008. Parallelism-Aware Batch Scheduling: Enhancing both Performance and Fairness of Shared DRAM Systems. *In Proc. of the Int. Symp. on Computer Architecture* (ISCA 2008), 63–74.

[25] Nitta, C., Farrens, M., and Akella, V. 2011. Addressing system-level trimming issues in on-chip nanophotonic networks. In *Proc. of the 17th Int. Symp. on High Perform. Computer Architecture* (HPCA 2011), 122–131.

[26] Olukotun, K. and Hammond, L. 2005. The future of microprocessors. *Queue - Multiprocessors*, vol. 3, no. 7 (Sep. 2005), 26-29

[27] Ramirez, M. A., Cristal, A., Veidenbaum, A. V., Villa, L., and Valero, M. 2005. A new pointer-based instruction queue design and its power-performance evaluation. In *Proc. of the Int. Conf. on Computer Design* (ICCD 2005), 647–653.

[28] Rixner, S., Dally, W. J., Kapasi, U. J., Mattson, P., and Owens, J. D. 2000. Memory access scheduling. In *Proc. of the 27th Int. Symp. on Computer architecture* (ISCA 2000), 128–138.

[29] Rogers, B. M., Krishna, A., Bell, G. B., Vu, K., Jiang, X., and Solihin, Y. 2009. Scaling the bandwidth wall. In *Proc. of the 36th Int. Symp. on Computer Architecture* (ISCA 2009), 371-382.

[30] Snavely, A. and Tullsen, D. M. 2000. Symbiotic Jobscheduling for a Simultaneous Multithreading Processor. In *Proc. of the 9th Int. Conf. on ASPLOS* (2000), 234-244.

[31] Stuecheli, J., Kaseridis, D., Daly, D., Hunter, H.C., and John, L. K. 2010. The virtual write queue: Coordinating DRAM and Last-level Cache Policies. In *Proc. of the 37th Int. Symp. On Computer Architecture* (ISCA 2010), 72-82.

[32] ITRS. 2011 Roadmap. [Online]. Available: http://www.itrs.net/links/2011itrs/home2011.htm.

[33] V. Standard Performance Evaluation Corporation, SPEC*, http://www.spec.org, Warrenton, SPEC 2006.

Massively Parallel Loading

Wolfgang Frings
Jülich Supercomputing Centre
Forschungszentrum Jülich
52425 Jülich, Germany
w.frings@fz-juelich.de

Dong H. Ahn
Lawrence Livermore
National Laboratory
Computation Directorate
Livermore, CA 94550
ahn1@llnl.gov

Matthew LeGendre
Lawrence Livermore
National Laboratory
Computation Directorate
Livermore, CA 94550
legendre1@llnl.gov

Todd Gamblin
Lawrence Livermore
National Laboratory
Computation Directorate
Livermore, CA 94550
tgamblin@llnl.gov

Bronis R. de Supinski
Lawrence Livermore
National Laboratory
Computation Directorate
Livermore, CA 94550
bronis@llnl.gov

Felix Wolf
German Research School for
Simulation Sciences
52062 Aachen, Germany
RWTH Aachen University
52056 Aachen, Germany
f.wolf@grs-sim.de

ABSTRACT

Dynamic linking has many advantages for managing large code bases, but dynamically linked applications have not typically scaled well on high performance computing systems. Splitting a monolithic executable into many dynamic shared object (DSO) files decreases compile time for large codes, reduces runtime memory requirements by allowing modules to be loaded and unloaded as needed, and allows common DSOs to be shared among many executables. However, launching an executable that depends on many DSOs causes a flood of file system operations at program start-up, when each process in the parallel application loads its dependencies. At large scales, this operation has an effect similar to a site-wide denial-of-service attack, as even large parallel file systems struggle to service so many simultaneous requests. In this paper, we present SPINDLE, a novel approach to parallel loading that coordinates simultaneous file system operations with a scalable network of cache server processes. Our approach is transparent to user applications. We extend the GNU loader, which is used in Linux as well as proprietary operating systems, to limit the number of simultaneous file system operations, quickly loading DSOs without thrashing the file system. Our experiments show that our prototype implementation has a low overhead and increases the scalability of Pynamic, a benchmark that stresses the dynamic loader, by a factor of 20.

Categories and Subject Descriptors

D.4.9 [**Software**]: Operating Systems—*Systems Programs and Utilities*

ICS'13, June 10–14, 2013, Eugene, Oregon, USA.

Keywords

HPC; Scalability; OS/runtime service

1. INTRODUCTION

Software complexity is increasing in high performance computing (HPC) applications, and dynamic linking and loading [13] offer advantages for managing this complexity. Dynamic libraries allow large applications to be modularized, or split into independently built packages. Modules can greatly reduce build time for developers, and each module can be loaded and unloaded dynamically at runtime as needed. This saves memory and frees developers from the burden of maintaining multiple pre-configured builds of large applications. Further, dynamic loading is used extensively by dynamic languages such as Python. High-level abstractions in these languages enable the rapid development of new plugins and packages, and they reduce software complexity for application programmers. These features are increasingly used to manage complexity in large, multi-physics simulation codes, which may have millions of lines of code and thousands of runtime-configurable parameters.

Despite these benefits, there are serious scalability problems with most modern loading mechanisms. Dynamic linking defers the process of locating object code and resolving its symbols until runtime. To load a library, most loaders first search a list of file system locations until the target library is found, then they load the library into memory. This mechanism does not differ significantly from the method used by the MULTICS [6] operating system that introduced dynamic linking in 1964. While it was suitable for a single-node machine, it breaks down in parallel. Jobs on today's largest machines [12] may have over a million concurrent processes, and concurrency is generally increasing. In practice, most processes load the same libraries they depend on simultaneously. Modern supercomputers typically lack node-local storage, and even large parallel file systems cannot quickly service millions or billions of small, simultaneous I/O requests. Loading an application initiates an I/O storm that manifests much like a denial-of-service attack. The file system, often shared site-wide, becomes unavailable, and dependent jobs sit idle until all requests are cleared.

The dynamic loader has remained much the same for over four decades, but it must change to reach extreme scale. To load object code on systems with potentially billions of processors, the loading service itself must be made parallel, and it must efficiently coordinate trillions of concurrent load requests. In this paper, we take advantage of the inherent parallelism of large-scale loading. In most cases, object code is read-only, and the same code is requested simultaneously by many processes. Parallel loading is very similar to a broadcast. We have developed Scalable Parallel Input Network for Dynamic Loading Environments (SPINDLE), a novel solution that extends the dynamic loader to route load operations through a network of scalable file-cache servers. Only a small set of designated daemons communicate directly with the file system, and SPINDLE proactively distributes and caches DSOs.

This paper makes the following contributions:

- Detailed analysis of real-world impact of scalability problems with today's dynamic loader;
- Novel techniques to transparently coordinate dynamic loaders through an existing interface;
- An architectural blueprint for a global parallel loading service;
- A portable implementation of this architecture including integration with portable software infrastructure.

We have applied SPINDLE to Pynamic, a parallel benchmark that stresses dynamic loading performance. Using SPINDLE, Pynamic can run on 20 times as many processes without overloading the file system. Further, the performance overhead of our scheme is constant with respect to the number of processes. Overall, our evaluation suggests that our approach to dynamic loading offers a viable path to massively scalable loading on extreme-scale systems.

The remainder of the paper is organized as follows. Section 2 motivates our work and reviews the state-of-the-art techniques. Section 3 then describes the software architecture and key elements of SPINDLE. Section 4 details our experimental evaluations, and Section 5 summarizes our findings and discusses future work.

2. SCALING CHALLENGES

The dynamic loader, also called the dynamic linker, is responsible for locating object code and making it available within a process's address space. These actions make the object code's subroutines callable by the main program. Dynamic linking and loading first appeared in the MULTICS [6] operating system (OS) in 1964, as a way to share common code between processes. For this reason, dynamically linked libraries are also often called *shared libraries*, and any object files that can be linked and loaded by the dynamic loader are called *dynamic shared objects* (DSOs). Most HPC systems including Linux clusters, IBM Blue Gene, and Cray machines use the dynamic loader implementation from GNU's libc, which is based on standards detailed in the System V Application Binary Interface (ABI) [1].

The dynamic loader is implemented as a DSO that is loaded by the OS during process start-up. The OS gives control to the loader, which then loads the main executable's dependent libraries and transfers control to the executable's entry point. The executable may re-invoke routines in the dynamic loader to resolve symbols or to load new DSOs during runtime (via routines such as `dlopen`). The tasks of finding and loading object code involve many file system operations, and the simultaneous execution of many such operations is not scalable. Loading massively parallel applications thus has the potential to overwhelm a site-wide shared file system, which can disrupt other applications running across the entire computing facility.

2.1 Scaling Challenges with the KULL Code

KULL [15] is a large multi-physics application developed at LLNL. When it was first run on Dawn, an IBM Blue Gene/P system, its start-up exposed serious scaling challenges and significantly disrupted the entire computing center. The KULL executable was dynamically linked to about one thousand shared libraries, most of them staged in an NFS file system to ease maintenance. Loading these libraries during program start-up scaled *extremely* poorly. The time from job launch to the initial invocation of KULL's `main` function, for instance, took about one hour at 2,048 MPI processes and *ten* hours at 16,384 processes. Further, during start-up, the NFS server was overwhelmed with load requests from KULL, and other users and jobs were unable to connect to the NFS while KULL start-up continued.

Our initial analysis revealed that the large-scale parallel loading created an enormous I/O storm that far exceeded the file server's capability. In particular, the dynamic loader (`ld.so`) was making massive numbers of unnecessary open calls at scale. On 16,384 MPI processes, we instrumented the loader and determined that it issued 300 million `open` calls to the NFS server. As a first attempt to address the problem, we staged the application executable and its library dependencies on Lustre [17], a parallel file system mounted on this machine. When we saw no improvement, we commenced a more detailed analysis.

2.2 Non-Scalable Loader Algorithm

The dynamic loader performs two types of file system operations: queries to locate a DSO and reads to load its contents into memory. Locating a DSO is necessary because an executable does not specify its dependent libraries with full path information, but instead provides the *names* of the libraries it needs loaded. To load a particular library, the dynamic loader searches for files with its name in system locations (e.g., `/lib`), directories named in the executable (rpaths), or directories named in environment variables such as `LD_LIBRARY_PATH`. The GNU implementation tests for existence by appending the name to each directory and calling `open` on the resulting path.

Search paths are a form of late binding that supports a flexible user environment. By simply modifying the search path, users can run the same executable with an updated or improved version of a library without recompiling. The concept has remained largely unchanged since MULTICS. However, this algorithm requires a large number of file system operations, which are not a problem for a sequential program with a dedicated file system. A parallel application with P processes, L library dependencies, and D directories in its search path will perform $O(PDL)$ file system operations simply to locate shared libraries; this accounted for the bulk of the 300 million `open` calls in our KULL example.

Once a library has been located, the dynamic loader maps

it into memory. Each library contains a table of program headers that describe what parts of the library on disk should be mapped into memory. Typically, its code and data are mapped into memory while its debug and linking information are not. Unfortunately, the loading protocol is similarly unscalable. The GNU loader uses `open` and `read` system calls to access the program headers, then `mmap` system calls to load the bulk of the library into memory. A parallel application with the GNU loader will thus perform $O(PL)$ load operations during its start-up.

Nearly all major runtime environments in use today use these algorithms to locate and to load executable code. Languages like Python and Java use search paths to find and to load modules. Major OSs such as Mac OS X and Windows also use search paths in their dynamic loaders. When run in parallel, these approaches produce $O(PDL)$ search operations and $O(PL)$ load operations, and this will thrash the file systems in the scaling limit of P.

2.3 State-of-the-Art Approaches to Loading

We are not the first to address the problem of scalable parallel loading. In this section, we discuss existing solutions to put our work in context. The approaches discussed here can be broken down into two categories: those that attempt to improve I/O and storage technologies so that the existing, unscalable loading algorithm will perform faster, and those that attempt to modify the loader.

2.3.1 Parallel File Systems

Staging object code in parallel file systems [9, 17] so that the loader can access it more effectively seems like a simple solution to our problem. Modern parallel file systems are clusters themselves that combine multiple disks spread across their nodes into a logical unit. While access to a single disk does not scale well, parallel access to the array of disks scales to the number of nodes in the cluster. Thus, parallel file systems like Lustre [17] significantly improve data-parallel access to large data-set files that are striped across the array of disks. Unfortunately, parallel loading does not exhibit this access pattern.

Parallel loading exhibits no data parallelism, as each process accesses the same, small files. Worse, for library search, parallelism is needed for large numbers of *metadata* operations, and parallel file systems typically have far fewer metadata servers than data servers. As a result, our analysis shows that while they offer a performance advantage over NFS when used with a traditional loader, they do not address the fundamental scaling problem in the loader. Coordinating I/O in parallel among the loaders themselves can easily outperform both Lustre and NFS.

2.3.2 Caching and Staging Solutions

Many large-scale systems, such as IBM's Blue Gene machines and more recent Cray XT machines, have dedicated I/O nodes that sit closer to the compute nodes than the parallel file system. A common approach to loading on these architectures stages object code on these nodes and mounts the staging area on the compute nodes. This approach has been used at Argonne National Laboratory (ANL) to accelerate the loading of Python applications on the Intrepid Blue Gene/P machine. It is effective in speeding up the loading process, but it is not transparent to users.

First, it requires application developers to stage their application in a custom I/O node image, which can be tedious when there are large numbers of libraries. Second, users often cannot easily determine which libraries an application needs to load. Most end-users of Python, for example, are not familiar with its standard libraries or with those that have DSOs which need to be staged. Third, in some cases the library search path is not known until runtime, so it is impossible to stage *all* loads that the application performs.

Cray uses DVS [10, 11], a proprietary I/O forwarding service, to make this process more transparent. DVS dedicates an NFS server to compute nodes on which it attempts to aggressively populate a hierarchy of caches along the I/O forwarding path. However, this approach requires users to stage all application-shared libraries to the dedicated NFS server, which can be tedious — similar to ANL's approach. Further, they do not exploit the full available parallelism of read-only dynamic load routines. Caching directly in the loader is a more direct, coordinated and scalable approach.

2.3.3 A Peer-to-Peer Solution

Dosanjh, et al. propose a peer-to-peer (P2P) architecture for distributing shared libraries across a network [7]. The approach is similar in spirit to our own, in that it caches loaded libraries in a RAM disk and aims to satisfy most load requests within the HPC network to reduce file system load. The approach has the potential for high-bandwidth file distribution, as it is based on the BitTorrent protocol. The authors share our vision of a high-availability parallel loading service; their architecture integrates a loading daemon with the OS. It is difficult to draw a fair comparison with this work, because it is still in early design stages.

As proposed, the P2P approach does not address two key problems that SPINDLE addresses. First, the authors' design requires users to specify all library dependencies in a job description so that they can be seeded to the compute nodes for P2P sharing. This requires, as do the techniques in Sections 2.3.1 and 2.3.2, that users know all library dependencies of their application and specify them in advance. SPINDLE optimizes the case where dependencies are known in advance, but it is still efficient when dependencies are not known until runtime. Second, the proposed approach does not address the metadata storm resulting from large-scale application start-up. The authors mention that initial seeder processes must handle the first set of requests for libraries as well as a large number of `stat()` calls issued by the dynamic loader. However, they do not discuss a coordinated I/O strategy that would allow these seeders to satisfy millions of requests quickly for each job launch. The authors mention distributed hashing techniques in the paper, which are promising for scalable P2P loading. We have addressed these problems in SPINDLE with a low-latency tree-based architecture, and by using the rtld-audit interface to modify the loader's behavior. Our approach does not require OS daemons and runs entirely in user space.

2.3.4 Solutions that Modify the Loader

The `collfs` library [4] developed jointly by ANL and the King Abdullah University of Science and Technology (KAUST) provides a scalable dynamic loading service for Python applications. `collfs` allows one process to load libraries that it broadcasts synchronously to the full system. This solution customizes the GNU loader and the Python runtime to use MPI collectives to load libraries. This approach is effective and can drastically speed up many Python programs, but the implementation changes the semantics of loading by requiring that it be synchronous. When used this way, some Python programs will require modification so that all loads are performed at the same time, otherwise programs may deadlock.

Our solution handles asynchronous loads of different libraries as well as synchronous loads of the same DSO. `collfs` is a good example of how coordinated I/O can speed up loading, but its synchronous semantics and application-specific nature limit its use. It also has technical limitations for system-wide use: it requires a modified version of `glibc`, which makes it very difficult to install. In contrast, SPINDLE uses the rtld-audit interface, which allows us to intercept GNU loader actions without requiring direct modifications to the loader itself. `collfs` also relies on the MPI library, which is not always available at runtime. Our solution works with any programming model for large-scale systems.

2.4 Loading as a Parallel Service

Parallel loading is an example of a case in which a sequential solution applied by each of P processes does not yield good parallel performance. Our key observation is that most processes request the *same* objects from the file system, or at least objects that have also been loaded by nearby processes. Rather than accessing the remote file system each time a file is needed, we should exploit the likelihood that a neighbor has already requested the file. Thus, we can coordinate I/O to distribute files much more efficiently and, thus, reduce the stress on the limited file system resources.

Alternative techniques such as DVS (discussed above) attempt to increase the level of I/O coordination transparently at the file system level while keeping loader behavior fixed. These techniques have the advantage of maintaining existing abstractions, such as POSIX I/O, which are familiar to users of UNIX-like OSs and which make sense in a sequential environment. However, the strict semantics of such abstractions can limit their scalability in a parallel environment. As an example, POSIX file I/O semantics disallow caching of failed `open` calls, forcing every library search query to go all the way to the file system. Further, traditional file I/O abstractions are oblivious to the *type* of data being transferred, which precludes many parallel optimizations.

We raise the abstraction to the level of the loader, which allows the loader to perform its own coordinated I/O. Thus, we can exploit knowledge about the files in parallel use. Object code is nearly always read-only and further ample parallelism exists in parallel loading. The performance advantages of exploiting both of these characteristics are too great to be ignored in a parallel environment. For this reason, we recommend that the loader architecture be changed for parallel machines. SPINDLE represents a significant step towards such a truly massively parallel loading service architecture.

3. THE SPINDLE APPROACH

Parallel applications that follow the SPMD model, which is the standard in modern HPC, issue duplicate load requests across a potentially large number of processes. On large-scale systems, even applications that employ the MPMD model tend to divide processes into SPMD groups. Thus, most load requests occur at program start-up and are concentrated in a very short interval to a common set of files, which causes the type of file-access storm that we described previously. However, we can also exploit this temporal locality to solve the problem. SPINDLE intercepts requests for libraries made by the dynamic loader, and it services them with a combination of scalable parallel broadcasts and a local file-system cache. The cache provides efficient local access, and broadcast operations allow each requested object to be loaded from the file system only once, then propagated scalably to the nodes that need it. This removes the $O(P)$ scaling bottleneck that we discussed in Section 2.2.

In addition to temporal locality, parallel loading exhibits spatial locality. With high probability, each process loads the same sequence of libraries at start-up, because link dependencies are embedded in the executable and libraries. While we do not *require* this strong locality of reference for efficient loading, our SPINDLE implementation can exploit it.

The SPINDLE broadcast operation can be initiated in two different ways. With the *push* model, we assume that when SPINDLE receives the first request for a particular library, other processes are likely making the same request. With *push*, SPINDLE immediately broadcasts each library to all processes when it is first requested. In contrast, the *pull* model sends libraries to nodes only as they request them. The *push* model is more efficient for SPMD applications where each process needs the same DSOs. However, it can waste memory in MPMD applications by pushing libraries onto processes that do not require them. The *pull* model, which we are still developing and testing, will be more appropriate in MPMD applications.

Figure 1 shows SPINDLE's architecture for coordinating the loading procedure among different processes of a parallel application. It maintains a collection of load servers (daemons) alongside the application processes, which cache replicas of DSOs in local RAM disks. A client adapter dynamically linked into each application process redirects all load requests to a nearby load server. In this way, we keep the client adapter as lightweight as possible. To combine load requests for the same object issued by different application processes, and to facilitate efficient broadcasts, the servers are attached to a network that connects them to each other and to the underlying file system.

3.1 Overall Architecture

As mentioned, application processes usually load most of their required libraries during start-up. However, MPI and other runtime communication systems are typically unavailable during this time. That makes it difficult to coordinate loading in parallel. This restriction leads to our first design decision: SPINDLE establishes its own independent communication network, implemented as an overlay network on top of the existing one. The load servers are designed to communicate with an arbitrary number of application processes and other load servers at the same time. This provides the flexibility needed to build customized overlay network topologies that optimally match the underlying hardware communication structure and also the capabilities of the file systems. While Figure 1 shows a tree topology with one root server connected to the file system, SPINDLE can configure more efficient topologies such as a forest of trees whereby multiple roots connect to a more capable file system. Further, the daemon concept keeps our design open to an integration with other system services, thus forming the precursor of a more general parallel loading service architecture.

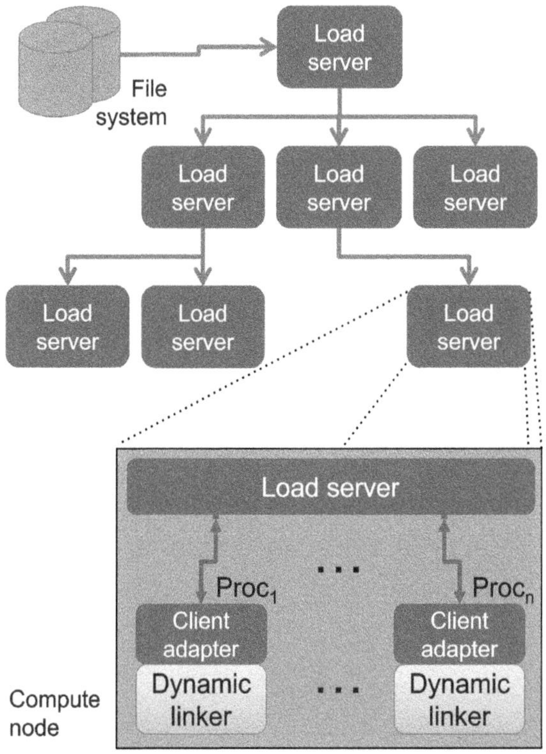

Figure 1: Overall architecture of SPINDLE

Finally, the application client adapter has to reroute all file-system requests such as searching for libraries or loading the library code to the SPINDLE servers. To avoid implementing our own dynamic loader, we decided to use the rtld-audit auditing API of the GNU loader for this purpose. This interface allows user code to intercept load requests and modify the dynamic loader's behavior. Our design allows us to run all components of SPINDLE in user space without having to modify the runtime system. Below, we explain the components of SPINDLE including the client, the server, the overlay network, and the motivation behind their design.

3.2 Client Adapter

The client adapter hooks into the dynamic loader, intercepts load requests and file searches, and redirects them to a nearby load server. To implement the interception, we use the rtld-audit [16] interface provided by the GNU dynamic loader. The interface allows us to register callbacks that are invoked when the dynamic loader performs certain operations. One of these callbacks triggers before the loader tests a directory for the existence of a library. This callback can optionally return an alternate location that the loader should look in. Our implementation of this function reroutes load requests to the SPINDLE load server, which obtains the DSO and returns its location in the local RAM disk. Our callback then returns this location to the loader for access from the faster local storage.

The rtld-audit interface was originally intended to help debug the dynamic loader, thus enabling it has several implications when used for our purpose. First, the callbacks for rtld-audit are supplied in a DSO, which is specified via the `LD_AUDIT` environment variable, and loaded into a special library namespace. While this namespace protects the rtld-audit library by disallowing other application libraries from seeing its symbols, the strong isolation also restricts its access to functionalities in other libraries, with an exception for libc. This restriction prevents the client adapter from using the TCP/IP stack, which resides in additional dynamic libraries. Instead, our adapters use UNIX-named pipes to communicate with their load servers, which can be managed directly using libc. Because named pipes do not allow inter-node communication, our design currently runs at least one load server on each node.

Second, enabling rtld-audit puts the dynamic loader into debug mode and has a performance impact on the application. Under normal execution mode, the first time an inter-library call-site is invoked, the dynamic loader will look up its target function and cache it in the global offset table (GOT). Subsequent invocations of the call-site will use the GOT entry and skip the lookup. This binding has performance advantages, in particular when this call-site is executed multiple times. With rtld-audit enabled, however, the loader will not finalize the binding by filling in the GOT, which allows rtld-audit callbacks to be delivered upon every inter-library call. This can impose an additional performance overhead, which we address by having the client adapter take over the responsibility of filling in the GOT for the dynamic loader.

Third, the rtld-audit interface does not provide any mechanism for intercepting loading of the executable or rtld-audit library. However, loading the executable through SPINDLE is particularly important because executables can contain a large percent of application code and cause significant load on shared file systems. SPINDLE solves this using LaunchMON [2], a scalable tools infrastructure component for launching parallel applications and tools across a wide range of HPC platforms. The user gives SPINDLE the command that launches the parallel application. SPINDLE then modifies it to launch a small statically-linked bootstrapper executable first and transfers control to LaunchMON. Next, LaunchMON starts this bootstrapper alongside the load server on each node. Finally, the bootstrapper works with the load server to move the executable and rtld-audit library into the RAM disk and then `exec`'s the application.

In addition to DSOs, SPINDLE can accelerate the parallel reading of Python modules. Interpreted languages like Python load not only DSOs, but also the script and byte-code files required by external modules. These can often be more numerous than shared libraries. When the Python interpreter `opens` such a file, our client adapter intercepts the attempt using another rtld-audit callback function, which is called when an entry in the procedure linkage table (PLT) is resolved. We route these files through the same caching mechanism: they are stored on the local RAM disk and the `open` call is rerouted to their new location.

3.3 Load Server

To handle DSO search and load requests for clients, the load server plays three roles: it manages local replicas, interacts with other load servers through an overlay network, and accesses the file system if designated as a reader. Locally, the server stores copies of DSOs and metadata on search directories and libraries. The files are stored in a RAM disk, and the server maintains the metadata in a hash table.

3.3.1 Operation

File existence tests contribute to a significant part of the shared file system load, and the SPINDLE server caches the contents of directories to optimize these operations. When the dynamic loader tests a file path for existence, the operation is rerouted to the load server. The server looks up the corresponding directory in its metadata table. If it exists, the table provides information on all files in the directory and the existence of a file can be verified locally. Otherwise, the load server triggers a designated-reader protocol, whereby a server responsible for the directory reads it via file-system operations and broadcasts the results to the rest of the servers. Similarly for file data, one server reads the file from the file system and distributes it to the remaining servers, which store it on their local RAM disks.

In terms of data management, we use *replication* schemes, where all objects are proactively replicated across servers, as opposed to *distribution* schemes where data distributed among the servers reactively services requests. Although replication requires more memory, we have made this design choice because it offers a significant performance advantage over the alternative. The load requests typically occur in the same order in a short interval, and thus our replication-based *push* model can better exploit such strong locality of reference. For example, the replicated metadata allow the bulk of search operations to be satisfied locally without relying on frequent server-to-server communication. Library files themselves will also be locally available, shortly after one server reads the file from the file system, ready to service other identical requests anticipated shortly.

Figure 2 shows the implementation details as to how the load server quickly replicates file data as well as metadata. Figure 2(a) illustrates the metadata handling: on a search request, a server either parses the directory by itself or forwards the search request to another nearby server in the overlay network. Figure 2(b) shows the file data: one reads the file from the file system, stores it on its local RAM disk, and distributes it to the remaining servers. These are enough to trigger our designated reader scheme.

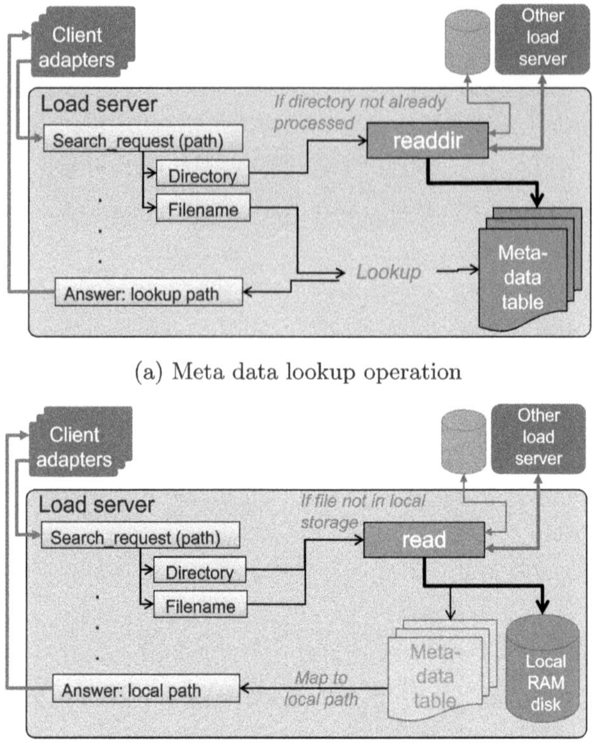

(a) Meta data lookup operation

(b) File read operation

Figure 2: Load requests handling in load server

3.3.2 Memory Overhead

While SPINDLE improves the performance and scalability of shared library loading, it does this at the expense of using extra memory on each node. The amount used is approximately equal to the total amount of code in libraries and the executable minus the amount of code in the application's working set. In other words, SPINDLE makes an application use memory as if every code page were in its working set.

During normal execution, Linux loads code pages into physical memory only when they are first touched. Under SPINDLE, all code is stored in a RAM disk and kept in physical memory for the entire execution of an application. The RAM disk is not a direct duplication of code pages—Linux is smart enough to use the same physical memory to back both the RAM disk and the application's virtual memory pages. The bulk of SPINDLE's memory overhead thus comes from placing code pages into the RAM disk that would not have been touched or loaded without SPINDLE.

While code preloading incurs extra memory overhead, it has advantages for extreme-scale environments. Loading pages from disk as-needed during execution is a well-known source of undesirable OS noise. Thus, high-end systems like IBM Blue Gene intentionally preload pages into memory and avoid this noise [8].

As an optimization, SPINDLE does not load the entire library file into RAM disk. Each DSO specifies parts of itself that should be loaded into memory via a table of *program headers*. Typically, a DSO will specify that its code and data should be mapped into memory, while debug information and the symbol table are left on disk. The load server reads these program headers and caches only the parts of a library that are needed at runtime. Essentially, SPINDLE strips libraries before transmitting them. This does make using a debugger on a SPINDLE application difficult, and we have future plans to hide these effects by pointing debuggers back to the original library files.

Memory used by libraries loaded by SPINDLE is treated differently in low-memory situations. Since the memory pages that store libraries are backed by a RAM disk, they cannot be paged out when the system runs low on memory. If those pages were backed by a shared file system, they could be dropped and reloaded as needed. This means an application using SPINDLE may run out of memory if it uses paging without SPINDLE.

3.4 Overlay Network

To funnel requests to the file system and to broadcast DSOs back to the application, SPINDLE load servers have to rely on a communication infrastructure. In the absence of an application runtime communication system like MPI, at start-up we have to create our own overlay network on top of the system network infrastructure.

For this, we use COBO [5], the Collective Bootstrapper,

a scalable implementation of the PMGR collective protocol that is used as an MPI job start-up mechanism. Unlike the original PMGR protocol, which connects all clients to one master client, COBO uses a scalable tree topology. COBO is part of the LaunchMON software infrastructure, which allows tool servers to be co-located with a parallel job. As discussed before, SPINDLE integrates LaunchMON to start the load servers along with the application processes.

The overlay network is initialized during application start-up. Given a list of hosts as input, COBO establishes the overlay network by distributing connection information from the root down to the leaf nodes. Given that the servers—in contrast to the clients—are not part of the parallel application and are not restricted to libc functions, we can use TCP/IP sockets for inter-server communications. COBO provides collective communication operations, which we use to distribute libraries from the root server to all others.

In the following, we present two network topologies: a single tree as our base configuration and a forest to exploit the bandwidth of parallel file systems. We also discuss bulk preloading, an optimization that anticipates load requests even earlier based on static analysis of the executable.

3.4.1 Single Tree

To connect n nodes, COBO creates a binomial tree of degree d ($n < 2^d$). According to the properties of such a tree, messages broadcast from the root will arrive at each node after not more than d hops. Thus, tree depth and walk distance vary no more than logarithmically with the number of load servers.

3.4.2 Forest

For larger configurations, we also offer the option of a forest consisting of multiple trees. In this way, we can take advantage of parallel file systems, reading file data from a moderate number of root nodes concurrently. Assuming that these root nodes read their data in parallel, the propagation of data inside individual trees is also accelerated. For example, when using d trees, the size of individual trees will be reduced by a factor of 2 in comparison to a single tree and the maximum distance will reduced to $d-1$ hops. In the current implementation, the forest is built by dividing the host list into different partitions and deploying a separate overlay network for each of these partitions.

3.4.3 Bulk Preloading

SPINDLE normally loads a library if at least one of the processes requests it at runtime. A complementary approach is to predict the demand in advance and stage all required libraries in advance. SPINDLE statically analyzes the executable and extracts its library dependencies. With these, it can initialize the caches of the load servers without waiting for runtime load requests. The subsequent requests for the preloaded files are fulfilled immediately. Bulk preloading does not have to cover every possible library. Libraries accessed dynamically, such as those loaded via `dlopen`, can still be loaded through SPINDLE's push mechanism. In the future other hints, such as suggestions from the user, could be used to increase the number of preloaded DSOs.

SPINDLE provides bulk preloading through the LaunchMON front-end client. LaunchMON replaces the normal start-up command such as `mpiexec` and starts the parallel application along with the tool servers. Since the front-end client is also part of the overlay network, it enables direct communication with our load servers. This allows us to proactively push a collection of libraries to the load servers before the application requests them. On HPC systems where the runtime environment differs between front- and back-end nodes, the paths of preloaded library have to be changed to the back-end location. For this, we use FGFS [3], a scalable utility to obtain global file properties.

3.5 Caching Algorithms

Our design is flexible enough to support a variety of algorithms for request handling, caching, and information forwarding. In its most general form, search and read requests are injected into the server network by a client. The server forwards the request to another server that is designated as responsible for the desired file. An internal mapping function decides which server this is. The server returned by this function then performs the actual file operation on behalf of the client and broadcasts the file data to all remaining servers. Changing the mapping function is one way of configuring SPINDLE's behavior.

In the current implementation, the network topology is a tree or a forest. This constrains the communication scheme to a top-down distribution of information from the root node to other nodes. (Figure 1). The mapping function in this case is quite simple: the root server is responsible for all library files. Viewed from the perspective of the file system, the load a parallel application generates is equal to the load of a single process times the number of trees in the forest, which is a configurable number and usually small. Our initial implementation assumes that all processes request the same libraries in the same order, which is not uncommon for SPMD codes. In this case, a load server does not have to forward an incoming request up the tree. Since the root server will receive all possible requests from its local client, an arbitrary server just has to wait until the root server pushes the desired libraries in its direction. This policy reflects a proactive top-down distribution of cache data, but can cause problems if different processes load different libraries. This assumption eased our initial implementation and provided convenient optimizations, but it is not fundamental to the SPINDLE approach.

In the future, we plan to provide more sophisticated file-distribution schemes. Using point-to-point communication between servers, a function we already added to COBO, can provide an on-demand distribution scheme where each server can actively inject search requests into the network and maintain full authority over the contents of its local cache. This will allow us to combine the *pull* model with the *push* model. Further optimizations include the automatic reduction of data exchanged among load servers. For example, we could check whether a requested library is a system library. System libraries may reside in a node-local file system, where caching is not needed. Finally, we plan to improve server efficiency through multithreading to allow local and network operations to be performed concurrently.

4. EVALUATION

The main purpose of SPINDLE is to reduce the start-up time for parallel applications that extensively use DSOs. To verify this and also to show the scalability of our approach, we tested SPINDLE with a synthetic benchmark named Pynamic on the Sierra Linux cluster installed at LLNL. In the

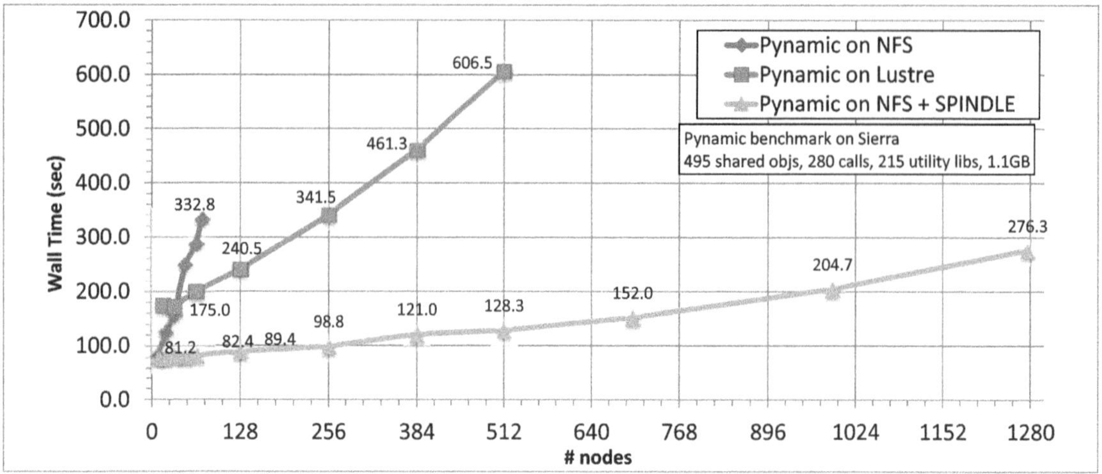

(a) NFS and Lustre file systems vs. NFS under SPINDLE

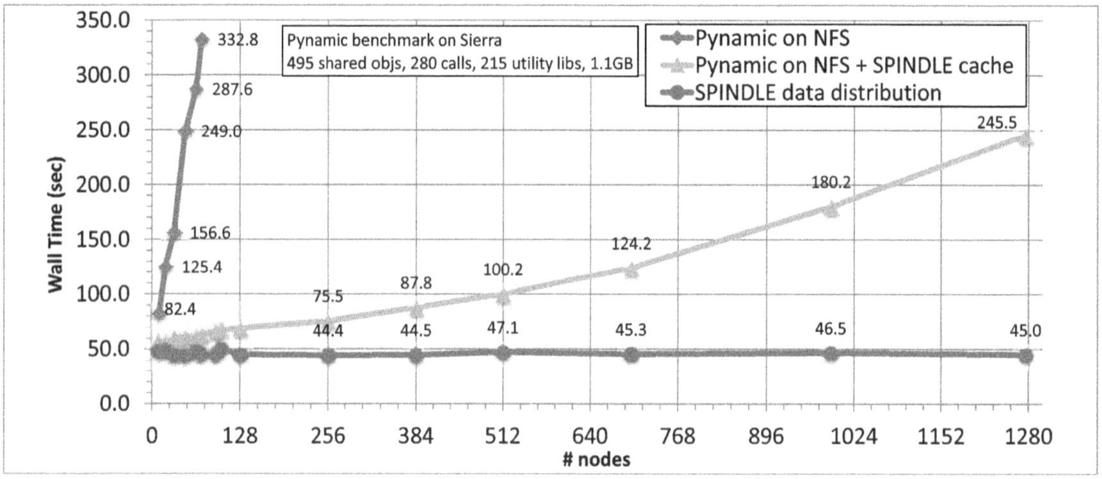

(b) Using bulk preloading

Figure 3: Pynamic benchmark run on LLNL Linux cluster Sierra

following, we will introduce the Pynamic benchmark, show the results of Pynamic running without and with SPINDLE support for the Sierra system up to 1,276 nodes, and discuss the memory footprint of SPINDLE.

4.1 Pynamic Benchmark

Pynamic is a benchmark that supports configurable emulation of dynamic loading in Python-based applications on massively parallel systems. This pyMPI-based [14] benchmark allows users to configure and generate arbitrary numbers of Python dynamic modules and utility libraries of a arbitrary sizes. It uses a code generator to create these DSOs, which are then used by a dummy application to closely model the behavior of Python-based multi-physics applications. Pynamic outputs three performance metrics that capture three phases of real-world dynamic loading and linking: start-up time for the initial library loading; module-import time for symbol resolution; and visit time for execution. Because dynamic loaders typically provide options that can shift these overheads from one phase to another, the sum of the three metrics is the overall figure of merit.

4.2 Results on Sierra

We ran our tests on the Sierra Linux cluster at LLNL, which is equipped with 1,856 compute nodes. The nodes have a 2-socket Intel Xeon EP X5660 CPU (2.8 GHz) with 12 cores and 24 GB of RAM. Nodes are connected by a Qlogic Infiniband QDR interconnect. We used two systems: NFS and Lustre. On Sierra, NFS is used for the home file system and Lustre is used for scratch data space. In all of these tests, we configured Pynamic to load 495 shared objects, a total of 1.1 GB of library files.

For our first test, we ran Pynamic without SPINDLE and loaded libraries from NFS. As shown in Figure 3(a) the overall runtime increased rapidly. We stopped this measurement at a small scale (< 100 nodes) to prevent an I/O storm that would affect other users on the system. The run-time increased exponentially, which can be explained by the poor parallel support of NFS.

As described in Section 2.3.1, a parallel file system is better suited to the types of file operations used in Pynamic. Therefore, we ran the same test on Sierra with the library files staged on Lustre. Figure 3(a) shows more linear growth in the runtime under Lustre, and we ran the test up to 512 nodes, 6,144 processes. The linear scaling of these runs shows significant improvement compared to prior experiences with Lustre (which had suggested that NFS might perform better than Lustre). A likely cause was the relatively recent enabling of read caches on the Lustre servers. We would expect further improvements if Lustre were better configured for the type of I/O access pattern associated with Pynamic (small files and high metadata rate), though this is not the typical file access pattern for HPC file systems (large files and data parallelism). Our measurements show that Lustre could be a partial solution to the loading problem, but only up to a moderate number of processes. The Lustre performance was already starting to degrade at these scale, and would likely have suffered more at larger scales.

In our third test case, we ran Pynamic with SPINDLE, with libraries hosted on NFS. As shown in Figure 3(a), SPINDLE allows us to run Pynamic at the largest allocation size on Sierra, with 15,312 processes distributed over 1,276 compute nodes. SPINDLE reduced the overall Pynamic runtime to 276 seconds. This is faster than the NFS test with 64 nodes and the Lustre test with 256 nodes.

Though SPINDLE allowed us to run Pynamic at a significantly larger scale, we still saw unexpected growth in the total runtime, from 81 seconds at a small scale to 276 seconds at higher scales. Pynamic's built-in timings did not help us to distinguish whether this time increase was due to poor scaling in SPINDLE or whether it was part of Pynamic's reliance on PyMPI (which was known to have scalability issues). To get a better understanding of this effect, we designed a further benchmark run where the library load process was separated from the benchmark execution. We enabled the bulk-preloading feature of SPINDLE (see Section 3.4.3) where the front-end process reads the list of prerequisite libraries and populates the load server caches before Pynamic starts.

This allowed us to measure the timing for SPINDLE data distribution, but removed from the Pynamic overhead. Figure 3(b) shows the results. Bulk-preloading takes constant time (though in theory it should be logarithmic at large enough scales). The larger SPINDLE scale tests were performed with multiple COBO trees (see Section 3.4.2), which limited the depth of each individual tree and the time to broadcast data. The largest test was done with four trees, each with depth eight. Given that the total Pynamic runtime continued to grow, even with all files pre-staged to the RAM disk, we concluded that this growth came from Pynamic's communication rather than library I/O. We will work with the Pynamic developers to eliminate these scaling problems in a new version of the benchmark.

Given the flat scaling of the data distribution phase, we expect that SPINDLE will continue performing well on future systems and it represents a viable path towards dynamic loading at exascale.

4.3 Memory Usage

As discussed in Section 3.3.2, the SPINDLE memory overhead is dependent on the percent of code pages that an application normally maps into memory. SPINDLE causes the application to use memory as if 100% of its code pages were always resident. We measured this overhead on a single node of Sierra using Pynamic, configured to load 495 libraries, which produced an application with 488 MB of loadable code. We modified this version of Pynamic to touch a certain percent of its memory pages artificially, loading them into its working set. This allowed us to compare SPINDLE memory overheads for different working set sizes. The amount of memory used was measured by running Pynamic, touching the pages and then checking how much remaining memory could be allocated before the system began paging out to make room for the new allocations.

Figure 4 illustrates two aspects of our memory overhead. First, it shows that the memory overhead is predominately a factor of the application's working set size. In the worst cases, where the application only has a small working set, SPINDLE has loaded many unneeded pages into memory via the RAM disk and produced overheads approximately equal to the application's size. In the best cases, where the application needed most of its code, the RAM disk shares most of its physical memory with the process and the amount of memory available does not change significantly. Second, Figure 4 shows that the memory overhead of the client and server is relatively small. The data point at 100% represents the case where the RAM disk memory is completely shared with the virtual memory of the process. The remaining overhead of 15.2 MB is approximately equal to the memory used by the client and the server.

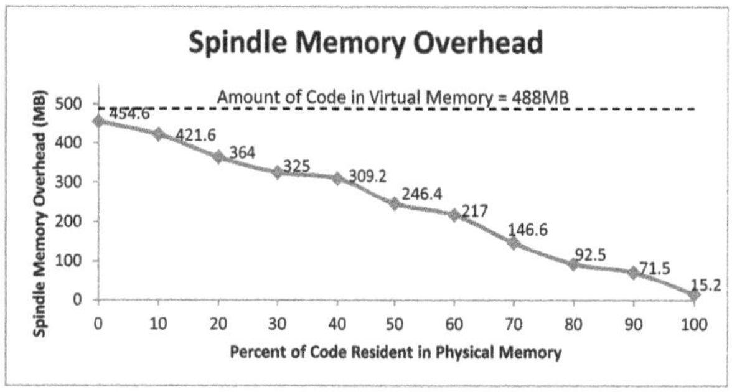

Figure 4: SPINDLE memory overhead

5. CONCLUSION

Dynamic linking and loading have gained broad acceptance in HPC due to their advantages for managing growing application complexity. However, the mechanisms used to load shared objects today do not scale to the level required by the largest supercomputers. The tasks of locating and loading a dynamic shared object involve many file system operations, and when a large number of processes load many DSOs simultaneously, the resulting I/O storm can cripple even the largest parallel file systems. This manifests much like a denial-of-service-attack and can disrupt an entire computing facility. SPINDLE addresses these critical challenges by extending the dynamic loader to coordinate its file system operations with an overlay network of file-cache servers. It is transparent to applications and does not require users to make changes to their applications or workflow. Our Pynamic experiments show that SPINDLE is highly scalable with limited memory and performance overhead.

SPINDLE is already capable of addressing scalability challenges in our production environments with no apparent scalability limit in sight. Thus, what lies ahead of us are mostly engineering efforts to port, optimize, and customize our solution to a broader range of high-end systems including IBM Blue Gene machines with millions of cores. Already, SPINDLE is well positioned for these efforts, as it is an integrated, portable code base. Perhaps more importantly, this basic architecture and our future work will pave the way for a massively parallel OS/runtime loading service for future exascale machines.

6. ACKNOWLEDGMENTS

This article has been authored by Lawrence Livermore National Security, LLC under Contract No. DE-AC52-07NA27344 with the U.S. Department of Energy. Accordingly, the United States Government retains and the publisher, by accepting the article for publication, acknowledges that the United States Government retains a non-exclusive, paid-up, irrevocable, world-wide license to publish or reproduce the published form of this article or allow others to do so, for United States Government purposes. (LLNL-CONF-610893). Part of the compute time used in our experiments was provided by the Jülich Supercomputing Centre.

7. REFERENCES

[1] System V application binary interface. http://refspecs.linuxbase.org/elf/gabi41.pdf.

[2] D. H. Ahn, D. C. Arnold, B. R. D. Supinski, G. L. Lee, B. P. Miller, and M. Schulz. Overcoming scalability challenges for tool daemon launching. In *Proceedings of the 37th International Conference on Parallel Processing (ICPP '08)*, pages 578–585, 2008.

[3] D. H. Ahn, M. J. Brim, B. R. de Supinski, T. Gamblin, G. L. Lee, M. P. LeGendre, B. P. Miller, A. Moody, and M. Schulz. Efficient and scalable retrieval techniques for global file properties. In *The International Parallel and Distributed Processing Symposium*, Boston, MA, 2013.

[4] J. Brown, W. Scullin, and A. Ahmadia. Solving the import problem: Scalable dynamic loading network file systems. Talk at SciPy conference, Austin, Texas, July 2012. http://pyvideo.org/video/1201/solving-the-import-problem-scalable-dynamic-load.

[5] PMGR collective. http://sourceforge.net/projects/pmgrcollective/ (visited April 2013).

[6] R. C. Daley and J. B. Dennis. Virtual memory, processes, and sharing in MULTICS. *Commun. ACM*, 11(5):306–312, May 1968.

[7] M. G. F. Dosanjh, P. G. Bridges, S. M. Kelly, and J. H. Laros III. A peer-to-peer architecture for supporting dynamic shared libraries in large-scale systems. In *Fifth International Workshop on Parallel Programming Models and Systems Software for High-End Computing (P2S2)*, 2012.

[8] M. Giampapa, T. Gooding, T. Inglett, and R. Wisniewski. Experiences with a lightweight supercomputer kernel: Lessons learned from Blue Gene's CNK. In *High Performance Computing, Networking, Storage and Analysis (SC), 2010 International Conference for*, pages 1 –10, Nov. 2010.

[9] IBM. General Parallel File System. `http://www-03.ibm.com/systems/software/gpfs/` (visited April 2013).

[10] G. Johansen and B. Mauzy. Cray XT programming environment's implementation of dynamic shared libraries. In *Cray User Group*, Atlanta, Georgia, May 2009.

[11] S. M. Kelly, R. Klundt, and J. H. Laros III. Shared libraries on a capability class computer. In *Cray User Group*, Fairbanks, Alaska, May 2011.

[12] Lawrence Livermore National Laboratory. Advanced simulation and computing Sequoia. `https://asc.llnl.gov/computing_resources/sequoia/` (visited April 2013).

[13] J. R. Levine. *Linkers and Loaders*. October 1999.

[14] P. Miller. Parallel, Distributed Scripting with Python. In *Proceedings of the 3rd Linux Clusters Institute International Conference on Linux Cluster: The HPC Revolution*, Chatham, MA, USA, 2002. *IEEE* Computer Society Press, Los Alamitos, CA.

[15] J. A. Rathkopf, D. S. Miller, J. M. Owen, L. M. Stuart, M. R. Zika, P. G. Eltgroth, N. K. Madsen, K. P. McCandless, P. F. Nowak, M. K. Nemanic, N. A. Gentile, N. D. Keen, and T. S. Palmer. KULL: LLNL's ASCI Inertial Confinement Fusion Simulation Code. *Physor 2000, ANS Topical Meeting on Advances in Reactor Physics and Mathematics and Computation into the Next Millennium*, May 2000.

[16] rtld-audit man page. http://man7.org/linux/man-pages/man7/rtld-audit.7.html (visited April 2013).

[17] W. Yu, R. Noronha, S. Liang, and D. K. Panda. Benefits of High Speed Interconnects to Cluster File Systems: A Case Study with Lustre. In *The International Parallel and Distributed Processing Symposium*, Rhodes Island, Greece, 2006.

MIC-RO: Enabling Efficient Remote Offload on Heterogeneous Many Integrated Core (MIC) Clusters with InfiniBand *

Khaled Hamidouche, Sreeram Potluri, Hari Subramoni, Krishna Kandalla and Dhabaleswar K. Panda

Department of Computer Science and Engineering
The Ohio State University
Columbus, OH, USA 43210
{hamidouc, potluri, subramon, kandalla, panda}@cse.ohio-state.edu

ABSTRACT

Xeon Phi, the latest Many Integrated Core (MIC) co-processor from Intel, packs up to 1 TFLOP of double precision performance in a single chip while providing x86 compatibility and supporting popular programming models like MPI and OpenMP. One of the easiest way to take advantage of the MIC is to use compiler directives to offload appropriate compute tasks of an application. However, with the Xeon Phi being an expensive resource, it is believed that production systems will be designed in a heterogeneous manner with only a subset of compute nodes comprising the MIC co-processor. Moreover, not all applications will be able to take advantage of the complete compute power offered by a Xeon Phi. In such scenarios, the existing state-of-the-art frameworks which require applications to be scheduled on compute nodes that have the MIC co-processor, lead to inefficient utilization of the computing power offered by the MIC. In order to address this limitation, it is critical to design an efficient framework to facilitate applications to offload compute tasks on remote MICs. In this paper, we take on this challenge and design *MIC-RO* - a novel framework to enable efficient remote offload on heterogeneous MIC clusters. To the best of our knowledge, this is the first design that enables application scientists to offload computation to remote MICs. Our experimental results show that, using MIC-RO, applications are able to offload computation to remote MICs with no overhead compared to offloading on local MICs. Moreover, MIC-RO outperforms the default Intel compiler based offload techniques by up to a factor of two for multiple benchmarks and application kernels.

Categories and Subject Descriptors

D.1.3 [**Programming Techniques**]: Concurrent Programming—*Parallel Programming*

Keywords

Heterogeneous Clusters, MIC, Remote offload, InfiniBand

*This research is supported in part by National Science Foundation grants #OCI-0926691, #OCI-1148371 and #CCF-1213084.

ICS'13, June 10–14, 2013, Eugene, Oregon, USA.

1. INTRODUCTION AND MOTIVATION

The emergence of accelerators such as NVIDIA GPUs and co-processors such as Intel Many Integrated Cores (MICs) is changing the landscape of supercomputing. The unprecedented computational power per watt they offer is making them an increasingly indispensable component in modern system architectures. This is evident in the recent Nov'12 TOP500 list [22] with a total of 62 systems using either accelerator or co-processor technology. Networking technologies, such as InfiniBand [2] have also rapidly evolved over the years to offer low latency and high bandwidth communication to address the increasing communication requirements of current generation peta-scale applications. Message Passing Interface (MPI) [4] continues to be one of the most popular parallel programming model across scientific domains.

Intel's Xeon Phi co-processor [3], based on the Many Integrated Core (MIC) architecture, packs up to 1 TFLOP of double precision performance in one chip. It runs a version of the Linux operation system and provides x86 compatibility. Xeon Phi offers the flexibility for application developers to use it like a many-core node, in "native" mode or as an accelerator, in "offload" mode. In "offload" mode compute intensive regions of an application can be offloaded onto the co-processor, using compiler directives [1]. Several real-world scientific applications have already been successfully ported to take advantage of the MIC in this manner [18, 16]. Figure 1(a) depicts the current state-of-the-art offload techniques offered by Intel compilers. They allow application processes to offload computation to MICs that are connected directly to the compute node on which they are running (Local Offload - LO). A process can use a MIC exclusively or share it with other processes running on the same node.

The Intel Xeon Phi co-processor is an expensive computing resource and it is likely that supercomputing systems will be designed in a heterogeneous manner in which only a subset of the compute nodes will comprise of the co-processor. In such scenarios, the existing state-of-the-art frameworks which require applications to be scheduled on compute nodes that have the MIC co-processor, lead to inefficient utilization of the computing power offered by the MIC. For such heterogeneous systems, there is a critical need for run-time frameworks that allow applications to offload computation to remote MICs (Remote Offload - RO). Such framework needs to allow applications to utilize a single remote MIC (Remote Offload Single - ROS) or multiple remote MICs (Remote Offload Multiple - ROM) based on its compute requirements. These scenarios are depicted in Figures 1(b)

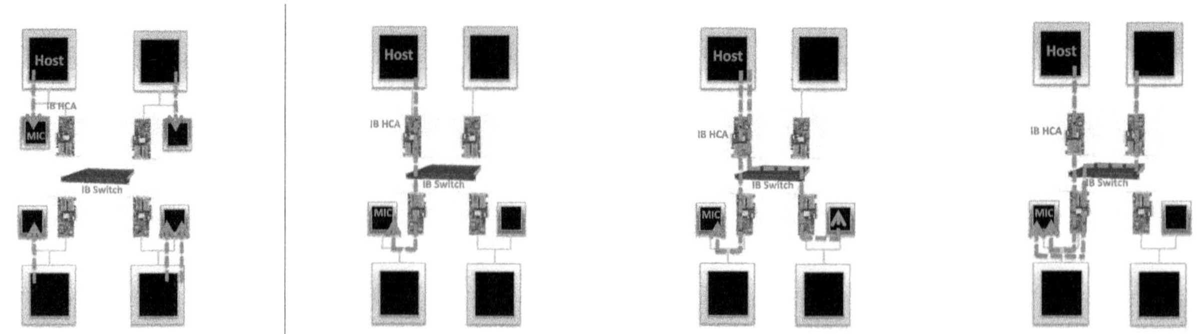

(a) **Current:** Local Offload (LO)

(b) **Proposed:** Remote Offload Single (ROS)

(c) **Proposed:** Remote Offload Multiple (ROM)

(d) **Proposed:** Remote Offload Sharing (ROSh)

Figure 1: Comparison of capabilities of current and proposed framework

and 1(c) respectively. However, as seen above, the MIC is a very powerful computing resource and not all applications will be able to take advantage of the complete compute power offered by it in an *exclusive* manner. Such applications will require the run-time framework to allow multiple jobs to *share* one or more common remote MICs (Remote Offload Sharing - ROSh) as envisioned in Figure 1(d). The run-time framework for such a heterogeneous system must also facilitate the data movement operations associated with offloading with the least possible overheads. This leads us to the following broad challenges: *(1) Can we design a framework to efficiently offload compute tasks onto remote Intel Many Core (MIC) co-processors? and (2) Can we demonstrate the potential benefits of such a framework with various micro-benchmarks and application benchmarks?*

1.1 Problem Statement

Designing an efficient framework supporting remote offload for MIC presents several new opportunities and challenges when compared to other frameworks [6, 21, 7, 17] that allow parallel jobs to leverage remote accelerators, such as GPUs. The proposed framework needs to automatically extract code segments to be offloaded to the MICs from the application. This is unlike offloading to GPUs, where the compute kernels are required to be provided in separate files. The framework also has to automatically detect and handle the data movement between the hosts and MIC (local or remote). In the case of GPUs, the data movement is explicitly expressed by the user through specific APIs. The framework will also have to address the problems associated with launching the extracted code components on the remote MIC. In the context of GPUs, this is relatively simpler, as it entails a call to the user-kernels by the daemons running on the remote nodes comprising of GPUs. Furthermore, such a framework needs to be designed in a highly efficient manner in order to minimize the overheads associated with remote offload to allow applications to effectively leverage the compute power offered by the remote MIC devices. To summarize, the following critical challenges need to be addressed to achieve offload on remote MIC co-processors:

1. Can code components to be offloaded on remote MIC co-processors be extracted in an efficient and transparent manner?
2. Is it possible to automatically detect and handle data movement operations between hosts and remote MIC?
3. Will modern high performance networks such as InfiniBand be used to reduce the overhead of such data movement?
4. Can the extracted code be launched on the remote MIC with low overheads?

1.2 Contributions

In this paper, we take on the above challenges and propose *MIC-RO*, an efficient framework to enable remote offload on heterogeneous MIC clusters. We make the following important contributions:

1. Provide a transparent and effective way to identify and extract compute regions annotated for offload using PIPS based source to source transformation
2. Enable efficient launch of offloaded computation to local or remote MIC using Dynamic Process Management feature of MPI
3. Provide flexibility for applications to use a single MIC or multiple MICs in a shared or an exclusive manner
4. Design efficient data movement between offload computation and the rest of the application using InfiniBand features
5. Enable efficient sharing of MIC resources through integration with scheduler and launcher

Our experimental evaluations indicate that MIC-RO outperforms the default Intel compiler based offload techniques by up to a factor of two, and delivers similar performance with offload on either a local MIC or a remote MIC. We have evaluated our framework with two application benchmarks: HOMB [13] and Jacobi Method [12]. For HOMB, the proposed design delivers up to a factor of two improvement for small matrix sizes and up to 25% improvement for large matrix sizes. With Jacobi, our framework improves the performance by up to *50%*, when compared to the default framework.

2. BACKGROUND

2.1 Intel MIC Architecture

Current generation Xeon Phi (SE10P) is equipped with 61 processor cores interconnected by a high performance bidirectional ring. Each core is an in-order, dual-issue core which supports fetch and decode instructions from four hardware threads. There are eight memory controllers which can deliver a theoretical bandwidth of up to 352 GB/s. Additionally, MIC offers the following modes [8]: 1) Offload mode, 2) Co-processor-only mode and 3) Symmetric mode.

In offload mode, all the MPI processes execute either on the host or on the MIC with the other being used as an accelerator. In the co-processor-only mode, all MPI processes are contained within the MIC and in the symmetric mode MPI processes can execute either on the host or the MIC. In the symmetric mode, the MPI job needs to be run in the Multiple Program Multiple Data (MPMD) mode. This is because all binaries which run on the MIC must be cross-compiled on the host for compatibility with MIC architecture. In this paper we focus on the offload mode, which is the easiest way for applications to take advantage of the MIC. This is the common mode on current-generation MIC.

2.2 Intel MIC Offload using LEO

Intel Language Extension Offload (LEO) is a standard for offloading compute to a MIC. It is a directive based extension to C/C++ and Fortran languages. The user marks the compute intensive phases of the code using *# pragma offload* directives. The corresponding data as well as the direction can be specified using *in/out/inout/nocopy* directives and the *length* clause to indicate the data size to be copied.

2.3 InfiniBand Network

The InfiniBand Architecture [2] (IBA) defines a switched network fabric for interconnecting compute and I/O nodes. It is a high-speed, general purpose I/O interconnect that is widely used by scientific computing centers world-wide. The TOP-500 [22] rankings (Nov 2012) reveal that more than 44% of the computing systems use InfiniBand as their primary interconnect.

2.4 Message Passing Interface MPI

Message Passing Interface (MPI) [4] has been the de-facto programming model for developing parallel applications over the past two decades. MPI provides various classes of communication operations: point-to-point, one-sided and collective. In this work, we use the MVAPICH2 software library. MVAPICH2 [5] is a high-performance MPI implementation for multi-core clusters with InfiniBand, 10Gigabit Ethernet/iWARP and the emerging RDMA over Converged Enhanced Ethernet (RoCE) interconnects.

Dynamic Process Management in MVAPICH2: Dynamic process management (DPM) is an MPI-2 feature that allows an MPI process to create new process groups and manage communication with such groups. The dynamic creation of processes allows application writers to develop multiscale applications or master/worker based programs. MVAPICH2 supports a high performance implementation of DPM that allows for very high spawn rates [11].

2.5 PIPS Compiler

PIPS is a source-to-source parallelizer that uses interprocedural techniques for program analysis [15]. PIPS currently supports transformations for the C and FORTRAN programming languages. PIPS is based on linear algebra techniques for analysis (dependence testing), as well as for code generation (loop interchange or tiling).

3. THE MIC-RO FRAMEWORK AND DESIGN CONSIDERATIONS

The Intel compiler framework only allows applications to offload computation to a MIC attached to the node it is running on. This limits the flexibility and utilization of MICs in heterogeneous clusters. MIC-RO alleviates this by enabling Remote Offload (RO) with the flexibility for an application to use single or multiple MICs and to use a MIC exclusively or in a shared mode.

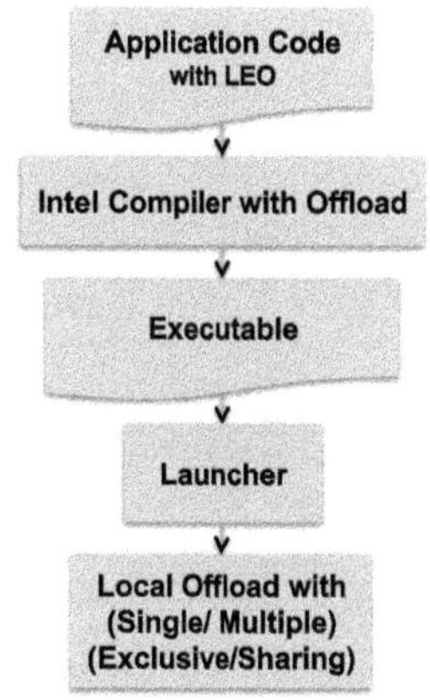

Figure 2: Existing Intel compiler framework

Figure 2 presents the steps involved in preparing an application for local offload using the existing Intel compiler framework. The executable generated by compiling a LEO annotated code, when run on a node with a MIC, automatically offloads the annotated part of computation to the MIC. When a MIC is not available, the computation is run on the host.

MIC-RO takes advantage of source code analysis and transformation techniques coupled with the Dynamic Process Management (DPM) feature offered in MPI to enable computation offload to a MIC independent of its location (local or remote). Given an application annotated with LEO programs, MIC-RO detects and extracts the offloaded part of computation as an independent function and compiles it as a separate executable, in a way transparent to the user. This provides the flexibility to run the computation to be offloaded on a local or a remote MIC, using DPM. MIC-RO takes care of efficiently exchanging any data between the offloaded computation and the rest of the application. As depicted in Figure 3, MIC-RO works in conjunction with the scheduler and launcher to enable efficient launch of kernels and sharing of MICs available on a cluster. We present the compile-time and run-time techniques involved in more detail in the following sections.

3.1 Compile Time Challenges in Enabling Efficient Remote Offload

To simplify the task of extending MIC-RO to other accelerators and offload primitives, we separate the compile-time component into three modules: Offload Code Extractor, Data Dependency Analyzer and Source Code Generator. We use the sample matrix-vector multiplication code shown in Figure 5 to explain the various steps involved in MIC-RO.

3.1.1 Offload Code Extractor (OCE)

One of the key challenges in offloading to a MIC is to identify the code that is annotated with LEO pragmas and its data dependencies with the rest of the application. We take advantage of PIPS, a source-to-source compilation framework, to address this. Major components of the MIC-RO framework and associated steps are illustrated in Figure 4. As the first step of OCE, we make an "Outliner Pass" over the application code and mark the parts annotated with offload pragmas, into separate functions. We refer to each function as a "hotspot". This code in the original application is replaced by a call to the function. PIPS converts the data required by this portion of the code into parameters of the function. To minimize the number of parameters and hence the data movement, we first perform a privatization of all scalars and local variables. A good example would be any loop iterator variables. When there are multiple offload regions marked in an application, a separate hotspot function is created for each region. The "C pretty-printer Pass" prints each of the hotspots into a separate file.

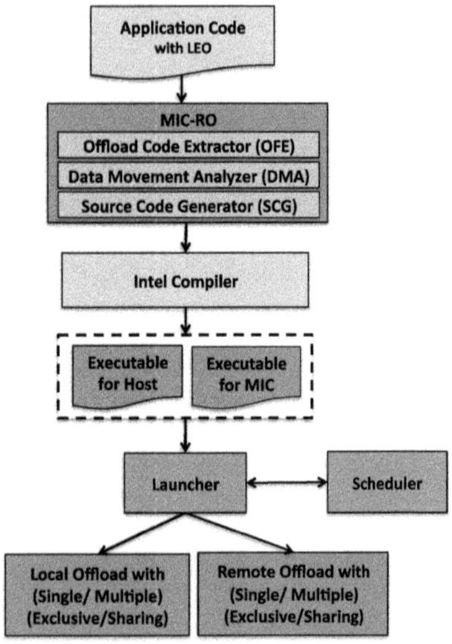

Figure 3: The proposed MIC-RO framework

We then perform an IN/OUT analysis on parameters to each of the hotspots. It extracts information regarding the direction (IN and/or OUT) as well as the size of each parameter using the Def/Use and Read/Write analysis offered by the PIPS framework. The output of this pass for the example code is shown in Figure 6. IN/OUT analysis cannot automatically identify data represented by dynamically allocated variables. In the example, we see that variables A and X are identified as IN variables and their bounds are identified. However, the pass does not recognize variable Y which is allocated on the heap. This information has to be provided by the developer as part of the LEO pragmas to ensure efficient data movement. This is a requirement even in the case of Intel compiler based offload. This information is parsed in the following "Data Movement Analyzer" step.

When the offload pragma is in a loop, which is common in iterative applications, the DPM launch is carried out only once during the first iteration of the loop. We introduce a new pass in the PIPS compiler to detect these cases and extract the loop information. The remote program receives these information from the application and manages execution of the hotspot accordingly.

3.1.2 *Data Movement Analyzer (DMA)*

The DMA module is responsible for identifying data that needs to be exchanged between each of the hotspots and the rest of the application. DMA parses the IN/OUT information generated in the previous step. It then parses the LEO pragmas from the application code to extract the address, size and direction of movement of dynamically allocated data. This information about the buffers is stored as 3-tuple of the following format (pointer, size, direction). The size can be a variable that is initialized at runtime. A challenging case is when different portions (overlapping or non-overlapping) of the same buffer are exchanged at different points of the execution. One such example is a parallel iterative solver where the complete input data has to be moved from the host to the MIC in the first iteration and only the boundary information has to be exchanged in each iteration thereof. Generally, the data movement in the first iteration can be represented as an outer pragma to the loop while the later can be represented inside the loop. DMA has to analyze these pragmas and ensure that the data in the later information is copied to the appropriate region of the buffer allocated in the first iteration. When a new (pointer, size, direction) 3-tuple is added, a backward lookup is performed to consider any overlapping regions. The sets generated during this step are used to generate the communication calls in the next step. The output of DMA for the sample program is shown in Figure 7.

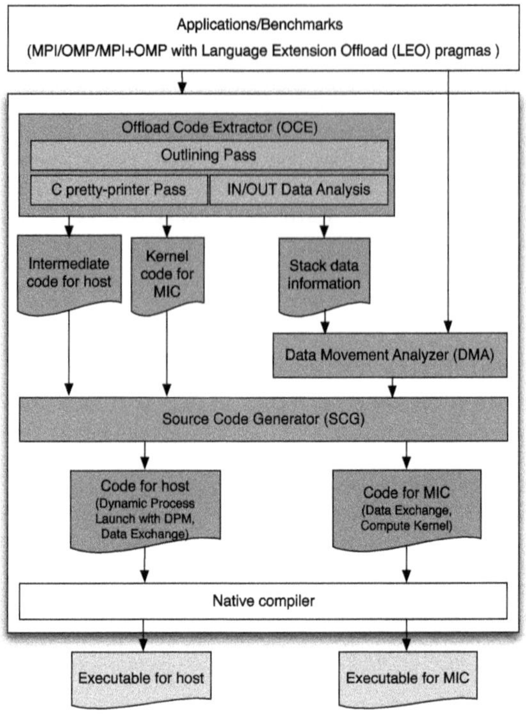

Figure 4: Components of the MIC-RO framework

3.1.3 *Source Code Generator (SCG)*

The last step is to generate the code for launching the hotspot on a MIC and for data movement between the host and the MIC. We take advantage of the Dynamic Process Management (DPM) feature available in MPI to launch and manage the hotspot on a MIC, local or remote. We use MPI Send/Recv to exchange data between the application process and the hotspot process on the MIC. Using MPI provides a highly portable and simple abstraction compared to directly using low level system and network calls. DPM also prevents need for an agent/proxy to be running on the MIC to handle launch of kernels.

SCG creates a wrapper program that runs on the MIC and contains data initialization calls, communication calls

```
int main()
{
    int A[10][10], X[10];
    int *Y;
    int, i,j;
    MPI_Init()

    Y=(int*) malloc(10*sizeof(int));
    ......
        #pragma offload target (mic:0) \
      in(Y: length(10)) out(Y:length(10))
   {
    #pragma omp parallel for
      for(i=0;i<10;i++)
       for(j=0;j<10;j++)
          Y[i]+=A[i][j]*X[j];
    }

    print(Y);
    MPI_Finalize();
}
```

Figure 5: Sample application code

```
// <A[PHI1][PHI2]-IN-EXACT-{0<=PHI1, PHI1<=9,\
         0<=PHI2, PHI2<=9}>
// <X[PHI1]-IN-EXACT-{0<=PHI1, PHI1<=9}>
```

Figure 6: Stack data information generated in IN/OUT analysis

```
Name =A, type= int, IN=1, OUT=0, NOCOPY=0,
    Size=10*10, start=0, offset=100, static=1
Name =X, type= int, IN=1, OUT=0, NOCOPY=0,
    Size=10, start=0, offset=10, static=1
Name =Y, type= int*, IN=1, OUT=1, NOCOPY=0,
    Size=10, start=0, offset=10, static=0
```

Figure 7: Buffer information generated in data movement analyzer

```
 1 int main()
 2 {
 3     int A[10][10], X[10];
 4     int, i,j;
 5          MPI_Comm intercomm;
 6     MPI_Init()
 7     Y=(int*) malloc(10*sizeof(int));
 8     ......
 9     MPI_Comm_spawn(remote, 1,..,&intercomm);
10
11     MPI_Send(A,10*10,.....,intercom);
12     MPI_Send(X,10,.....,intercom);
13     MPI_Send(Y,10,.....,intercom);
14     // Wait for result
15     MPI_Recv(Y,10,.....intercomm,..);
16
17     print(Y);
18     MPI_Finalize();
19 }
```

Figure 8: Sample code for host generated by MIC-RO

and a call to the hotspot function. We call this the "offload program". The call to the hotspot function in the application code is now replaced with a call to MPI_Comm_spawn with the parameters required to launch the wrapper program on a MIC (Line 9 in Figure 8). However, MPI_Comm_spawn is a collective call that has to be called from all the processes in a communicator and only the root launches the new process. This causes an issue as different processes in the application have a compute kernel to offload. We work around this by creating a communicator for each process. The DPM launch is carried out over this communicator.

As part of the "offload program", SCG generates code to declare and allocate any buffers required to hold incoming data used by the hotspot or results generated by it (Lines 15 – 17 in Figure 9). All the information about statically declared variables and variables whose sizes are determined at compile-time is readily available in the table created by the DMA. For buffers whose size is determined at runtime, the size information has to be exchanged between the application code and the offload program before they can be allocated. SCG generates MPI_Send/MPI_Recv calls to exchange the size information followed by memory allocation calls in the offload program. Corresponding MPI_Send/MPI_Recv calls are added in the application program. Similar to the DPM launch, buffers are allocated only during the first iteration in the case of kernels that are iteratively called in the application code. Finally, SCG generates MPI_Send/MPI_Recv calls to send IN data from application program to the offload program and to return any OUT data from the offload program to the application. Lines 11 – 15 of Figure 8 show the communication calls generated for the host program and Lines 18 – 23 of Figure 9 show the communication calls generated for the offloaded program.

```
 1 void hotspot(int A[10][10], int X[10], int *Y)
 2 {
 3     int i,j;
 4     #pragma omp parallel for
 5     for(i=0;i<10;i++)
 6         for(j=0;j<10;j++)
 7              Y[i]+=A[i][j]*X[j];
 8 }
 9
10 int main()
11 {
12     MPI_Init()
13     MPI_getParent( intercomm....);
14
15     int A[10][10], X[10];
16     int *Y;
17     Y=malloc(10*sizeof(int));
18     MPI_Recv(A,10*10,.....,intercom,..);
19     MPI_Recv(X,10,.....,intercom..);
20     MPI_Recv(Y,10,.....,intercom..);
21     // Call the Kernel
22     hotspot(A,X,Y);
23     MPI_Send(Y,10,.....intercomm);
24
25     MPI_Finalize();
26 }
```

Figure 9: Sample code for MIC generated by MIC-RO

3.2 Run Time Challenges in Enabling Efficient Remote Offloading

It is critical that the overhead of launching and executing the offload program on a MIC is kept minimal for application to benefit from MIC-RO. The XeonPhi's are IP addressable and our use of DPM to launch the offload program directly on the remote MIC removes the need for any intervention from the host to which the MIC is directly connected. Through DPM we also avoid the need for a management proxy to be running on the MIC to which compute is offloaded. This avoids any waste in resources which is an issue in the existing remote offload solutions available for GPU clusters. As mentioned in Section 3.1.3. we minimize the launch overhead in iterative applications by doing the DPM launch only during the first iteration. The offload program internally takes care of the iterative execution of the kernel.

It is also important that we minimize the overheads incurred in moving data between the application and the offload program. We use the MVAPICH2 MPI library, which provides an InfiniBand channel for communication between host and MIC. This reduces the overhead of data movement in offload to a local MIC, compared to Intel Compiler based offload. Since the same communication channel is used independent of whether the MIC is local to a node or is connected to a remote node, we do not see any additional data movement cost for remote offload, compared to local offload. Data movement is further optimized by taking advantage of the information in the LEO pragmas provided by the user.

3.3 Compatibility with Third-Party Libraries

Scientific applications and simulations commonly rely on third-party libraries, math kernels and solvers. Such libraries typically perform both compute intensive, as well as MPI communication operations. In order to improve the performance of scientific applications, these third-party libraries need to be designed to offload their compute intensive tasks to either local or remote MIC co-processors. We would like to note that MIC-RO can be leveraged to realize this objective. MIC-RO requires that the third-party libraries be compiled and installed using our compile-time solutions (Section 3.1) to generate the appropriate hotspots. Since MIC-RO handles dynamically allocated data, the hotspot information can be directly re-used during the execution of any application that relies on such third-party libraries.

4. SYSTEM-LEVEL COORDINATION FOR UTILIZING MICS IN SHARING AND MULTIPLE MODE

An effective co-ordination between our framework and various HPC system services is essential to enable end users of modern HPC systems to seamlessly share MICs with other users as well as to scale their applications on multiple MIC units on different compute nodes. In this section we discuss how our framework enables such integration with minimal changes to the various HPC system services.

4.1 Scheduler Integration

Most HPC systems use some form of a job scheduler [23, 20, 9, 14] to launch user jobs. While queuing up jobs with the scheduler, each user will have to give at least the following details to the scheduler: 1) how many nodes they want and 2) how many cores they want on each node. Depending on these and other factors, the scheduler would then allocate a set of resources to the user to run their job. On modern heterogeneous MIC based systems that support sharing and remote use of MICs, the scheduler will already have support for users to request the number of MICs as well as the number of cores on each MIC they want. In the coming sections we describe how our framework can utilize this information to effectively share a MIC or utilize multiple MICs to accelerate an application.

Allowing Application to use Multiple MICs (ROM): As depicted in Figure 1(c), the user can request for multiple MIC units to accelerate their application. In such a scenario, the scheduler (as described above) will provide a list of MICs on which the user can launch their jobs as part of the hostlist. Depending on the number of MICs allocated, our framework will split up the computation equally among each MIC. The DPM module within our framework (described in Section 3.2) will use the information regarding the MICs to launch the split up compute kernels on each MIC.

Sharing a MIC between Applications (ROSh): In this scenario (depicted in Figure 1(d)), the user will request for only a few compute cores within a MIC. For such a request, we envision that the scheduler will allocate a host core and the requested number of cores on any MIC on the system and launch the job on the reserved host core. In such a scenario (apart from the challenge of launching processes on the MIC addressed above), ensuring the user application respects the job schedulers allocation on the MIC will be a challenge. Addressing this challenge requires tight coordination between our framework as well as the scheduler. On launching the job, the scheduler will set the environment variable *OMP_NUM_THREADS* to the number of cores the user requested on the MIC. Our framework is co-designed so that it always relies on this environment variable to identify the number threads it can launch on the MIC. Also we use the process-to-core binding features provided in MVAPICH2 to ensure different applications do not compete for the same cores. Furthermore, MIC-RO can be integrated with the memory limit per CPU features of existing schedulers like Slurm to efficiently share MIC's memory between job. Thus through a careful co-design of our framework with the scheduler, we can allow end users of modern heterogeneous HPC systems to seamlessly share a MIC or utilize multiple MICs to accelerate their applications.

5. PERFORMANCE RESULTS

In this section, we describe our experimental setup and evaluate our designs presented in Section 3. To evaluate the performance of MIC-RO, we use different microbenchmarks and application kernels. These codes exhibit different computation and data movement characteristics. Execution time indicated in the various graphs includes the time taken to launch the compute kernels on the MICs. We report our results based on the average statistics of 10 runs. Note that the standard deviation value of 10 runs is less than 3%.

5.1 Experimental Setup

We use the Stampede supercomputing system at TACC [10] for our experiments. Each Stampede node is a dual socket node containing Intel Sandy Bridge (E5-2680) dual octa-core processors, running at 2.70GHz, with 32GB of memory, a SE10P (B0-KNC) co-processor, a Mellanox IB FDR MT4099 HCA and PCIe Gen3. The host processors are running CentOS release 6.3 (Final), with kernel version 2.6.32-279.el6.x86_64. The KNC runs MPSS 4346-16 (Gold). Additional details of the KNC architecture are provided in Section 2.1. We used an experimental version of MVAPICH2 for our designs and experiments. The Intel compiler version is composer_xe_2013.1.117.

5.2 Micro-benchmark Level Performance

In the following sections, we demonstrate the benefits observed with various microbenchmarks by using MIC-RO to offload computation to local and remote MICs. We use matrix-matrix and matrix-vector multiplication benchmarks for initial evaluation of our framework. The two benchmarks vary in the ratio of computation and communication. The Matrix-Matrix multiplication kernel takes three matrices as input and this data has to be moved from the host to the MIC before computation can be offloaded. It returns one matrix as the output which is the data that has to be moved back from the MIC to the host. Matrix-Vector Multiplication kernel on the other hand takes one matrix and two vectors as the input. It returns one vector as the output.

Matrix-Matrix Multiplication Benchmark: Figure 10(a) and 10(b) compare the performance of the matrix-matrix multiplication benchmark for small and large matrices, respectively. We observe that the proposed framework is able to offload computation to a remote MIC with no additional overhead, when compared to offloading compute onto a local MIC. Indeed, the overhead for a host to remote MIC transfer compared to a host to local MIC transfer (IB loop back) is only an extra hop over the switch and this is negligible within the IB network. Moreover, as seen in Figure 10(a), for small matrices, the proposed design is able to outperform the default compiler based offload scheme (that offloads computation to local MIC) up to a factor of two irrespective of the physical location of the target MIC (local or remote). For larger matrices, as depicted in Figure 10(b), the proposed approach is able to deliver similar or slightly better performance when compared to the default compiler based offload scheme irrespective of the physical location of the target MIC (local or remote).

Further analysis of these results indicate that, for small matrices, the benefits of the proposed scheme arise from improvements in both computation time and the data movement overheads between the host and the MIC. In Figure 10(c), we compare the fraction of the overall execution time being spent in computation and data movement phases for the default compiler based offload technique and the proposed design. For this experiment, we consider offloading the compute only to the local MIC. We pick two representative sizes for small (32) and large (8K) matrices to show the trends. For brevity, we do not include the graphs comparing the split up of overall execution time for offloading computation to remote MIC. Analysis of the compute phase of default compiler based offload technique shows that it has a small overhead for executing OpenMP codes. For small matrices, this overhead has a significant impact on the overall execution time, given that the compute time is small. However, as the computation time increases, this overhead becomes negligible and does not impact the overall execution time. We are still investigating this overhead.

The improvements in the data movement phase of the benchmark is due to the use of high performance network interconnects such as InfiniBand for data transfer between host and MIC. As we can see from Figure 10(c), for small message sizes, this contributes significantly to the overall performance improvements. However, the improvement is reduced for larger matrices. This is primarily due to the limited IB bandwidth available for communication between MIC and Host in the Sandy Bridge architecture.

Matrix-Vector Multiplication Benchmark: Figures 11(a) and 11(b) compare the performance of the matrix-vector multiplication benchmark for small and large matrix sizes respectively. As we can see from the graphs, the proposed design is able to offload computation to a remote MIC with no additional overhead when compared to offloading it on a local MIC. Moreover, the proposed design is able to outperform the default compiler based offload scheme by up to a factor of two for all matrix sizes irrespective of the physical location of the target MIC (local or remote).

Figure 11(c) compares the portion of overall execution time spent in computation and data movement phases for the default compiler based offload scheme and the proposed design with offloading computation to local MIC. We pick two representative sizes for small (32) and large (16K) matrices to show the trends. We do not show the graphs showing the split up of overall execution time for offloading computation to remote MIC due to their repetitive nature. As we can see, for small messages, the benefits of the proposed design come from improvements in both computation time and time for data movement between host and MIC as we explained in the previous section. However, unlike the matrix-matrix multiplication benchmark, the matrix-vector multiplication benchmark only transfers a vector from the MIC back to the host. Consequently, the communication bottleneck that we faced for large matrix sizes in the matrix-matrix multiplication benchmark (described above) does not impact performance. As a result, we are able to extract the complete benefits of InfiniBand based communication for large matrix-vector multiplication operations for both local and remote MICs.

5.3 Performance of Application Benchmarks

In the following sections, we demonstrate the benefits observed with various application level benchmarks by using MIC-RO to offload computation to local and remote MICs. We use HOMB and a Jacobi application kernel for our evaluations. HOMB [13], a benchmark based on a parallel iterative Laplace solver aimed at comparing the performance of MPI, OpenMP, and hybrid codes. We have extended this to offload the solver code to MIC using LEO pragmas. HOMB, unlike the earlier two benchmarks, transfers the same amount of data from host to the MIC and from the MIC to the host. The size of the data varies based on the size of the matrix involved. The Jacobi application kernel is an implementation of the Jacobi method for solving a system of linear equations. It is an iterative application with a nearest neighbor boundary exchange at the end of each iteration. It involves a large amount of data (data grids) exchange from the host to the MIC during start-up and a periodic exchange of smaller amount of data (data grid boundaries) between the host and the MIC in each iteration.

HOMB: Figures 12(a) and 12(b) depict the performance of HOMB benchmark for small and large matrix sizes respectively. We can see that the proposed design is able to offload computation to a remote MIC with no additional overhead when compared to offloading it on a local MIC. Moreover, the proposed design is able to outperform the

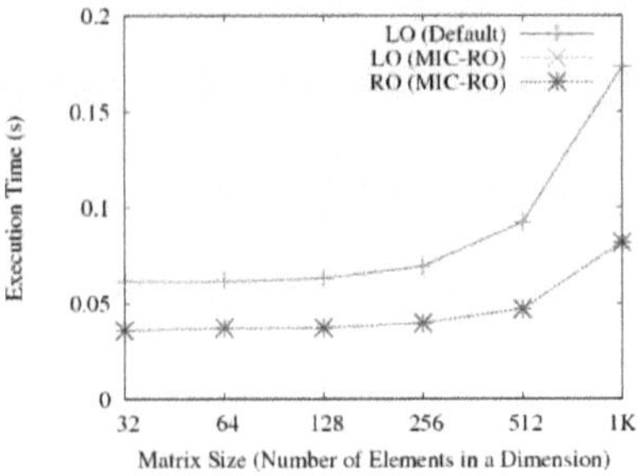

(a) Small matrix sizes

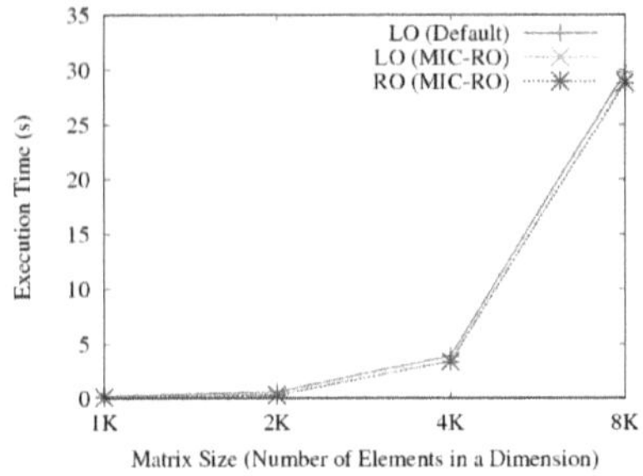

(b) Large matrix sizes

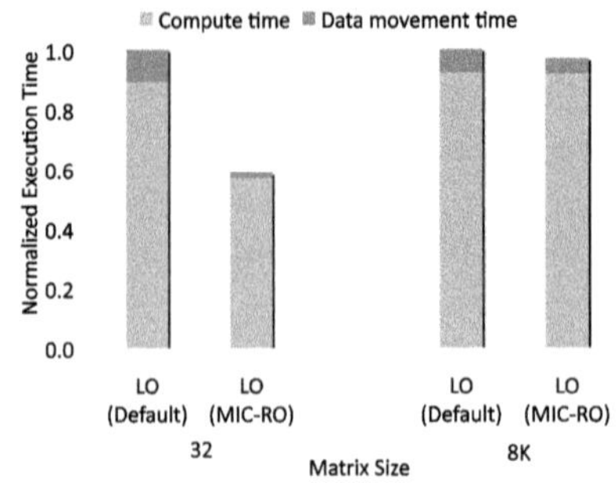

(c) Split-up of computation and data movement

Figure 10: Performance of Matrix-Matrix multiplication benchmark

default compiler based offload scheme for all matrix sizes irrespective of the physical location of the target MIC (local or remote). The proposed design is able to outperform the default compiler based offload techniques by a factor of two for small matrix sizes and up to 25% for large matrix sizes. As with the matrix-vector multiplication benchmark in the previous section, the benefits for small matrix sizes come from improvements in both computation and communication while the improvements for large matrix sizes comes from improvements in communication time through the usage of high performance InfiniBand interconnect.

Jacobi Application Kernel: Figures 13(a) and 13(b) depict the performance of the Jacobi application kernel for small and large matrix sizes respectively. We observe that the proposed design is not only able to offload computation to a remote MIC with no additional overhead when compared to offloading it on a local MIC, it is also able to outperform the default compiler based offload scheme by up to *50%* for all matrix sizes irrespective of the physical location of the target MIC (local or remote). As for the matrix-vector multiplication benchmark in the previous section, the benefits for small matrix sizes come from improvements in both computation and communication while the improvements for large matrix sizes comes from improvements in communication time through the usage of high performance InfiniBand interconnect.

5.4 Performance of Microbenchmarks in Sharing (ROSh) and Multiple (ROM) Mode

In this section we analyze the performance MIC-RO is able to deliver to applications running on shared MICs and those applications that want to scale their performance by utilizing the compute power offered by multiple MICs as described in Section 4. We used the matrix-matrix multiplication benchmark described in Section 5.2 for these experiments. The size of the matrix used was 2,048 x 2,048 doubles and 8,192 x 8,192 doubles, respectively.

Figure 14(a) depicts the performance MIC-RO is able to deliver to applications that want to share the compute power offered by the modern MIC architecture. In this experiment each application is launched on a different node with all of them sharing the same MIC. Each application uses eight OpenMP threads for execution on the MIC. As we can see, there is no impact due to sharing on performance of other processes using the same MIC. This is a very encouraging trend for users of heterogeneous HPC systems that do not have MICs deployed on every compute node. Figure 14(b) depicts the performance benefits an application gains by utilizing multiple remote MICs through MIC-RO (ROM) mode. This experiment was run with varying number of MICs (1 to 32). Each MIC is connected to a different node. For experiments up to 16 MICs, the processes were launched from a single node (consisting of 16 cores). For experiments with 32 MICs, the processes were launched from two nodes (a total of 32 cores). As we can see, the performance scales linearly as we increase the number of MICs.

6. RELATED WORK

Sharing remote accelerator hardware resources, specifically GPUs has received considerable attention, recently. This technique potentially allows applications to utilize both local and remote GPUs in a transparent manner and can potentially reduce system costs and ease of system administration by allowing multiple parallel jobs to concurrently share the accelerators. The rCUDA middleware [6] allows CUDA-compatible GPUs to be available to all compute nodes in a cluster. However, the rCUDA framework requires application developers to modify their GPU programs to use the rCUDA API. Further, this work requires all CUDA kernels to be separated into different files so that they can be easily transferred to the remote GPUs for execution.

Similarly, VOCL [21], is a framework to virtualize the OpenCL programming model to expose GPU devices as decoupled virtual resources that can be transparently managed. Both frameworks are based on the same client-server design where server daemons are started on the remote hosts that consist of GPUs. However, unlike rCUDA, VOCL uses MPI for the communication. The MOSIX-VCL framework supports transparent utilization of cluster-based GPUs based on the MOSIX platform [7]. It provides the same API as the OpenCL programming model, but supports the utilization of all GPUs within a system. Similarly, vCUDA [17], is another framework to allow high performance computing applications in virtual machines to share the same local GPU. It provides a virtual GPU view to each application running on the same node, though multiple applications actually share a single physical GPU.

While the challenges of enabling remote offload for GPUs have been explored, to the best of our knowledge, the current state-of-the-art does not allow parallel applications to offload compute intensive phases on to remote MICs. When compared to solutions proposed for GPUs, there are many additional non-trivial challenges that MIC-RO addresses. MIC-RO extracts code segments to be offloaded to the MICs from the application. This is unlike offloading to GPUs, where the compute kernels are required to be provided in

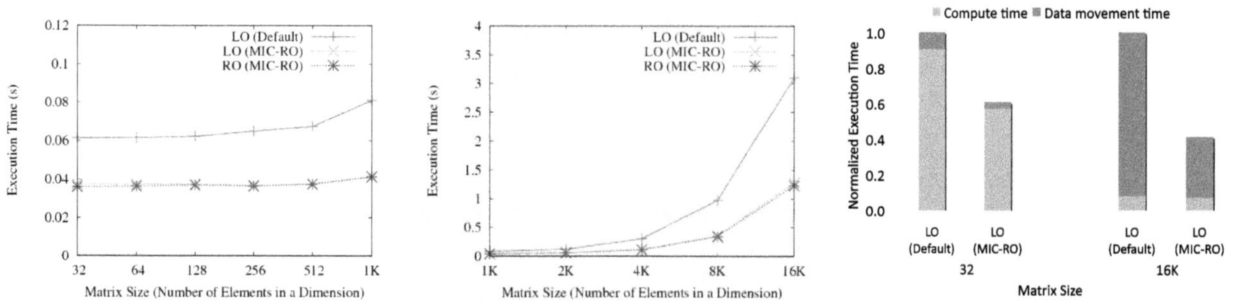

(a) Small matrix sizes (b) Large matrix sizes (c) Split-up of computation and data movement

Figure 11: Performance of Matrix-Vector multiplication benchmark

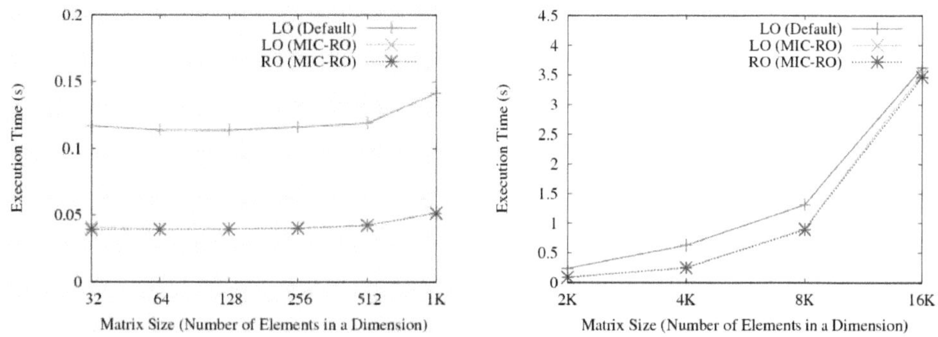

(a) Small matrix sizes (b) Large matrix sizes

Figure 12: Performance of HOMB

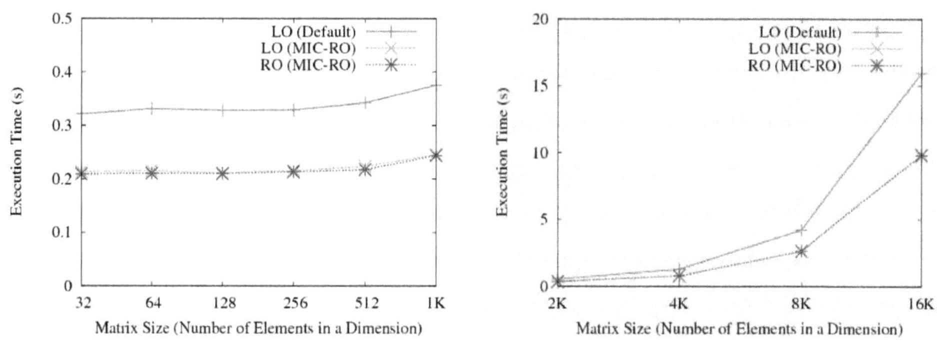

(a) Small matrix sizes (b) Large matrix sizes

Figure 13: Performance of Jacobi application kernel

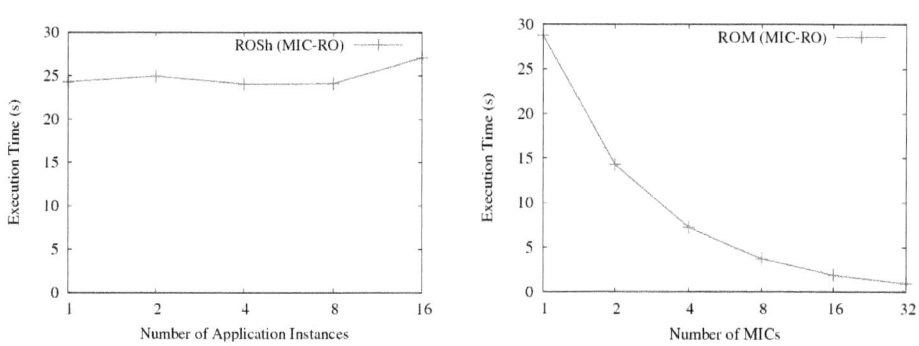

(a) Multiple matrix-matrix microbenchmarks sharing one MIC (b) One matrix-matrix microbenchmark using varying number of MICs

Figure 14: Performance of matrix-matrix microbenchmarks in sharing and multiple mode

separate files. MIC-RO also automatically detects and handles the data movement between the hosts and MIC (local or remote). In the case of GPUs, the data movement is explicitly expressed by the user through specific APIs.

The Apricot [19] tool is a source-to-source framework, that inserts automatically the Language Extensions for Offload (LEO) pragmas to existing OpenMP codes. Apricot is intended to assist programmers in porting existing multi-core applications and writing new ones to take advantage of the MIC co-processor by generating the LEO. We believe that their work is complementary to ours and can be used as a first step to generate the input file of our framework.

7. CONCLUSION AND FUTURE WORK

In this work, we present a framework that allows an application running on a compute node to efficiently offload its computation to a MIC independent of its location: connected directly to the node or to a remote node. It identifies standard Intel LEO pragmas and enables remote offload in a way transparent to the user. It takes advantage of the DPM feature offered by MPI for launching the offload code and the InfiniBand interconnect for data movement. The proposed design outperforms the default Intel compiler based offload techniques by up to a factor of two with both Matrix-Matrix and Matrix-Vector multiplication benchmarks. It delivers similar performance with offload on either a local MIC or a remote MIC. We have evaluated our framework with two application benchmarks: HOMB and Jacobi Method. For HOMB, the proposed design delivers up to a factor of two improvement for small matrix sizes and up to 25% improvement for large matrix sizes. With Jacobi, our framework improves the performance by up to *50%*, when compared to the default Intel compiler based framework. For both the application benchmarks, our framework delivers the same performance with offload on either a local MIC or a remote MIC. Our framework enables efficient use of MIC resources available on a cluster. Our experiments show that multiple processes can efficiently share a MIC and one application running on a node can take advantage of multiple MICs distributed across the cluster, without any additional overhead. As part of future work, we plan to evaluate our framework on larger-scale applications. We envision also to extend our framework to heterogeneous GPU clusters with the emerging OpenACC programming model.

8. REFERENCES

[1] Heterogeneous Offload model for Intel MIC. http://software.intel.com/sites/default/files/article/326701/heterogeneous-programming-model.pdf.

[2] InfiniBand Trade Association. http://www.infinibandta.org.

[3] Intel MIC Architecture. http://www.intel.com/content/www/us/en/processors/xeon/xeon-phi-detail.html.

[4] Message Passing Interface Forum. http://www.mpi-forum.org/.

[5] MVAPICH2: MPI over InfiniBand, 10GigE/iWARP and RoCE. http://mvapich.cse.ohio-state.edu/.

[6] rCUDA: Remote CUDA. http://www.rcuda.net/.

[7] Virtual OpenCL (VCL). http://www.mosix.org/txt_vcl.html.

[8] XEON-PHI Software Developer's Guide. http://www.intel.com/content/dam/www/public/us/en/documents/product-briefs/xeon-phi-software-developers-guide.pdf.

[9] Adaptive Computing. http://www.adaptivecomputing.com/resources/docs/maui/3.2environment.php.

[10] Texas Advanced Computing Center. Stampede cluster. http://www.tacc.utexas.edu/stampede.

[11] T. Gangadharappa, M. Koop, and D.K. Panda. Designing and Evaluating MPI-2 Dynamic Process Management Support for InfiniBand. *2012 41st International Conference on Parallel Processing Workshops*, 0:89–96, 2009.

[12] J. Götze. On the Parallel Implementation of Jacobi and Kogbetliantz Algorithms. *SIAM Journal on Scientific Computing*, 15(6):1331–1348, 1994.

[13] HOMB. http://sourceforge.net/projects/homb/.

[14] IBM Platform Computing. LoadLeveler Job Scheduler for Linux. http://www-03.ibm.com/systems/technicalcomputing/platformcomputing/products/lsf/index.html.

[15] F. Irigoin, P. Jouvelot, and R. Triolet. Semantical interprocedural parallelization: an overview of the PIPS project. In *Proceedings of the 5th international conference on Supercomputing*, ICS '91, pages 244–251, New York, NY, USA, 1991. ACM.

[16] K. W. Schulz, R. Ulerich, N. Malaya, P. T. Bauman, R. Stogner and C. Simmons. Early Experiences Porting Scientific Applications to the Many Integrated Core (MIC) Platform. In *TACC-Intel Highly Parallel Computing Symposium*, April 2012.

[17] L. Shi, H. Chen, J. Sun and K. Li. vCUDA: GPU-Accelerated High-Performance Computing in Virtual Machines. *Computers, IEEE Transactions on*, 61(6):804–816, 2012.

[18] L. Meadows. Experiments with WRF on Intel Many Integrated Core (Intel MIC) Architecture. In *Proceedings of the 8th international conference on OpenMP in a Heterogeneous World*, IWOMP'12, pages 130–139, Berlin, Heidelberg, 2012. Springer-Verlag.

[19] N. Ravi, Y. Yang, T. Bao, and S. Chakradhar. Apricot: An Optimizing Compiler and Productivity Tool for x86-Compatible Many-Core Coprocessors. In *Proceedings of the 26th ACM international conference on Supercomputing*, pages 47–58. ACM, 2012.

[20] PBS Works. http://www.pbsworks.com/Product.aspx?id=1.

[21] S. Xiao, P. Balaji, Q. Zhu, R. Thakur, S. Coghlan, H. Lin, G. Wen, J. Hong and W. Feng. VOCL: An Optimized Environment for Transparent Virtualization of Graphics Processing Units. *Proc. of Innovative Parallel Computing*, 2012.

[22] Top500. Top500 Supercomputing systems. http://www.top500.org/, Nov 2012.

[23] Andy B. Yoo, Morris A. Jette, and Mark Grondona. SLURM: Simple Linux Utility for Resource Management. In Dror G. Feitelson, Larry Rudolph, and Uwe Schwiegelshohn, editors, *JSSPP*, volume 2862 of *Lecture Notes in Computer Science*, pages 44–60. Springer, 2003.

Efficient Scheduling of Recursive Control Flow on GPUs

Xin Huo
Department of Computer Science and Engineering
The Ohio State University
huox@cse.ohio-state.edu

Sriram Krishnamoorthy
High Performance Computing Group
Pacific Northwest National Laboratory
sriram@pnnl.gov

Gagan Agrawal
Department of Computer Science and Engineering
The Ohio State University
agrawal@cse.ohio-state.edu

ABSTRACT

Graphics processing units (GPUs) have rapidly emerged as a very significant player in high performance computing. Single instruction multiple thread (SIMT) pipelines are typically used in GPUs to exploit parallelism and maximize performance. Although support for unstructured control flow has been included in GPUs, efficiently managing thread divergence for arbitrary parallel programs remains a critical challenge. In this paper, we focus on the problem of supporting recursion in modern GPUs. We design and comparatively evaluate various algorithms to manage thread divergence encountered in recursive programs. The results improve upon traditional post-dominator based reconvergence mechanisms designed to handle thread divergence due to control flow within a procedure.

Categories and Subject Descriptors

B.2.2 [**Arithmetic and Logical Structures**]: Performance Analysis and Design Aids—*Simulation*; C.1.2 [**Processor Architectures**]: Multiple Data Stream Architectures (Multiprocessors)—*Single-instruction-stream, multiple-data-stream processors (SIMD)*

General Terms

Performance

Keywords

GPU; SIMD; Recursion; Reconvergence Methods

1. INTRODUCTION

Modern architectures are trying to utilize the increasing density of transistors by increasing the number of processing cores, and using parallelism to improve application performance. One popular approach has been the use of Single Instruction Multiple Data (SIMD) designs, since they simplify control logic and allow resources to be used towards supporting a larger number of cores. SIMD instruction sets have been available in popular processors in the form of SSE (supported in Intel processors 1999 onwards) and, more recently, in the form of AVX instructions. SSE instructions have been used to speedup a variety of applications, including graphics [15], signal processing [10], and scientific and engineering applications [13, 25].

In recent years, the use of SIMD parallelism has become more widespread due to graphics processing units (GPUs) and other accelerators. Modern GPUs have emerged as the means for achieving extreme-scale, cost-efficient, and power-efficient high performance computing within the last few years. Some of the fastest machines in the world today involve GPUs. Specifically, in the top 500 supercomputers list released in November 2012 [26], a total of 62 systems use accelerators or co-processors. The current number 1 and 8 fastest supercomputers, i.e., Titan and Tianhe-1A, both use NVIDIA GPUs.

The use of SIMD parallelism, including in GPUs, has been limited for applications that involve complex control flow, since these applications either have limited data parallelism, or the control flow makes it harder to exploit data parallelism. One such class of applications, which have almost never been successfully mapped to SIMD instruction sets, comprises the applications programmed with recursion. The class of algorithms that are popularly or conveniently expressed using recursion is extremely large. For example, if one considers the thirteen *dwarfs* or patterns in the Berkeley view of parallel processing [8], several or all of the applications corresponding to each of the following eight dwarfs—spectral methods, N-body problems, combinatorial logic, graph traversal, dynamic programming, backtrack and branch-and-bound, graphical models, and finite state machines—are likely to be programmed using recursion. Thus, as speed of a single core does not improve and additional transistor density is at least partially targeted towards SIMD parallelism, speeding up this large class of recursive applications is a major challenge.

This paper focuses on the problem of obtaining high performance from recursive applications on modern GPU architectures through better hardware-level thread scheduling. To motivate this problem, consider the following background. GPUs did not even support recursive applications for a considerable amount of time. In the case of NVIDIA GPUs, support for recursion has been available only from CUDA SDK 3.1 and computing capability 2.0. AMD GPUs do not yet support recursion. The existing programming models for GPUs, such as CUDA, OpenCL, and DirectX, all employ the Single Instruction Multiple Threads (SIMT) paradigm. In this paradigm, though programmers can write code assuming independent execution of threads, the actual execution is in SIMD fashion to match the SIMD architecture. Particularly, a modern GPU comprises a set of streaming multiprocessors (SMs), within which a batch of the threads, referred to as warp in CUDA or wavefront in OpenCL, is executed in a lock-step manner. If there is divergence between the threads in the same warp, the threads executing different branches have to be scheduled serially. The result is that while

ICS'13, June 10–14, 2013, Eugene, Oregon, USA.

very regular applications, such as dense matrix or structured grid computations and graphics applications, use the GPU architecture extremely well, applications with a high degree of branch divergence achieve limited speedups. Thus, even if the GPU allows execution of the recursive applications, the control flow involved with recursive function calls and the resulting thread divergence is likely to limit performance.

To help improve the state-of-the-art, we study the behavior of various thread scheduling strategies in the context of recursive control flow. We first show that using immediate post-dominator based reconvergence, a variation of which is used in current NVIDIA GPUs, to schedule threads executing recursive computations in a warp results in poor performance. We then consider the notion of dynamic reconvergence, where threads can re-converge either before or after the traditional immediate post-dominator. We introduce two dynamic reconvergence implementations and their variations, namely the greedy method, greedy return-first method, the majority method, and the majority threshold method.

We implement the various dynamic reconvergence methods using GPGPU-sim, a cycle level GPU performance simulator [2]. Through extensive evaluation, we show that our dynamic reconvergence mechanisms obtain significant performance improvement on a set of six recursion benchmarks, which have different characteristics. The majority method achieved speedups from 1.05 to 6.00 for Fibonacci, Bio-coefficient, NQueens, Graph Coloring, Tak function, and Mandelbrot benchmarks over the immediate post-dominator reconvergence method.

2. BACKGROUND

This section introduces SIMD architectures, particularly GPU devices, discusses scheduling of recursive applications on such systems, and finally, details the performance achieved on current GPUs.

2.1 Modern GPU Architectures and Thread Divergence

The processing component of a typical modern GPU consists of streaming multiprocessors (SMs). Each streaming multiprocessor, in turn, contains a set of SIMD cores that perform in-order processing of instructions. To achieve high performance, a large number of threads, typically a few tens of thousands, are launched. These threads execute the same operation on different sets of data. A block of threads are mapped to and executed on a streaming multiprocessor. Furthermore, threads within a block are divided into multiple groups, termed warps (wavefronts in OpenCL). Threads within a warp are co-scheduled on a streaming multiprocessor with all threads executing the same instruction in a lock-step manner. If threads in the same warp need to execute different instructions, they have to be executed serially, i.e., at any time, only threads executing the same instruction can proceed while other threads stall. An instruction is said to be divergent if it can lead to different threads executing different instructions. Conditional branches are common examples of divergent instructions.

The serialization of divergent instructions is a basic limitation in supporting threads in SIMD architectures, and cannot be overcome with software and hardware scheduling schemes. However, scheduling strategies can maximize opportunities to make progress on all threads by exploiting the structure of the program. These strategies can be further aided by hardware and/or software. For example, one can identify reconvergence points through compiler analyses, and execute one group of divergent threads serially until they reach the reconvergence point, before stalling this group and executing the other group of divergent threads. To illustrate, in Figure 1, threads diverge when executing conditions *cond1* and

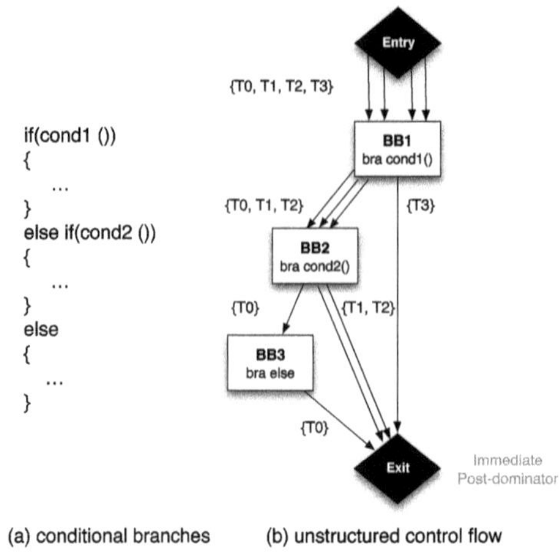

Figure 1: An example of unstructured control flow and its immediate post-dominator

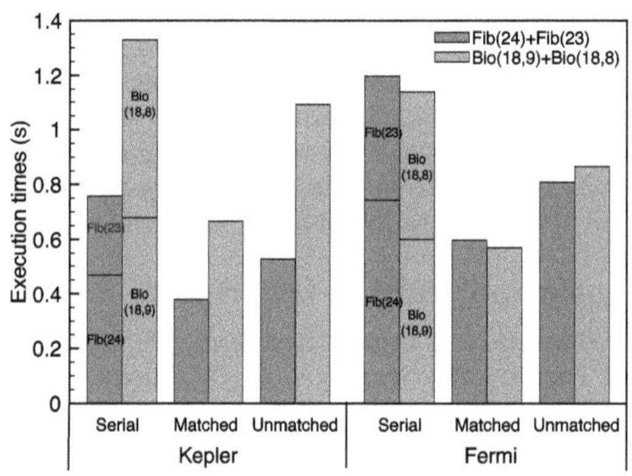

Figure 2: Performance of Fibonacci and Binomial Coefficients benchmarks on Kepler (Tesla K20M) and Fermi (Tesla C2050) architectures: 20 Fib(24)+Fib(23) and 20 Bio(18,9)+Bio(18,8) invocations on one thread, two threads in matched pattern, and two threads in unmatched pattern

cond2, and converge after executing the conditional statements. This scheme, referred to as immediate post-dominator based reconvergence and described in detail in Section 3, has been shown to be beneficial in handling control-flow divergence within a procedure [6, 12].

2.2 Performance of Recursive Control Flow on GPUs

While control flow resulting from branches has been extensively studied in the literature, recursion has only been preliminarily investigated (a detailed description of related work is covered in Section 7). While traditional data-parallel applications are implemented in an iterative manner or using a combination of outer recursion and inner data-parallelism, not all applications can be expressed in this fashion. We focus on the scheduling of threads within a warp, with each thread executing a recursive function. While the flow of control can vary widely among the threads executing such recursive functions, tasks performing similar operations still expose significant optimization opportunities.

As mentioned earlier, AMD GPUs do not support recursive control flow. To understand the performance of recursive programs on modern NVIDIA GPUs, we conduct the following experiment using two benchmarks—Fibonacci and Binomial coefficients. On Fibonacci, we compute the 24th (Fib(24)) and 23rd (Fib(23)) Fibonacci numbers, each 20 times, in three different ways—using a single thread, using two threads in a *matched* pattern, and using two threads in an *unmatched* pattern. When using two threads, each thread executes half the work as in the serial case, depicting a strong scaling scenario. In the matched pattern, work is assigned to the two threads in the same order, alternating between Fib(24) and Fib(23). For example, when the first thread computes Fib(24), the second thread also computes Fib(24). In the unmatched pattern, the tasks are assigned to the two threads in different orders. The first thread alternates between Fib(24) and Fib(23) starting with Fib(24), while the second thread does the same computation starting with Fib(23). We conduct the same experiment in computing the binomial coefficients ${}^{18}C_9$ and ${}^{18}C_8$, for terms x^9 and x^8, respectively, in the expansion of $(1+x)^{18}$.

Figure 2 shows the results of the experiment on Tesla K20M and C2050 GPUs, which are based on the Kepler and Fermi architectures, respectively. We observe that execution on two threads using the matched pattern achieves perfect speedup compared to execution on one thread. However, unmatched pattern shows significant performance degradation on both Kepler and Fermi GPUs. For example, on Kepler, we only gained 1.4 and 1.2 speedup on Fibonacci and Binomial coefficient benchmarks, respectively, in the unmatched pattern, demonstrating that divergence introduces significant overheads. In fact, this execution time is greater than the time to compute only the more expensive of the two terms, Fib(24) or ${}^{18}C_9$ in the two benchmarks, on a single thread. This establishes that there are a significant number of wasted cycles with the current scheduling method.

We also observe that the two GPUs exhibit similar behavior, indicating that the newer Kepler architecture faces similar challenges as Fermi in thread scheduling under intra-warp thread divergence due to recursion. Note that launching a kernel using dynamic parallelism in Kepler GPUs [23] blocks the executing kernel until the invoked kernel completes, and does not address the problems related to intra-warp scheduling or thread divergence we tackle in this paper.

3. STATIC IMMEDIATE POST-DOMINATOR RECONVERGENCE

In a control flow graph, a post-dominator of a given node is a node through which all paths (across different branches) from the given node must pass through. The immediate post-dominator is the post-dominator that is not dominated by any other post-dominators. Figure 1 shows an example code with conditional branches and the corresponding control flow graph. Four threads, T0 to T3, diverge in different branches. First, all the threads start from the *Entry* node. Then, T1 and T2 go through basic blocks {BB1, BB2}, while T0 and T3 go through {BB1, BB2, BB3} and {BB1}, respectively. In the end, all threads converge at the *Exit* node. Thus, in this example, the *Exit* node is the immediate post-dominator.

One possible scheduling scheme for SIMT execution is static immediate post-dominator reconvergence. The compiler analyzes the code to determine the immediate post-dominator of the divergent branch as the reconvergence point. Returning to the example in Figure 1, while scheduling the threads within a warp, this scheme will use the *Exit* node as the reconvergence point.

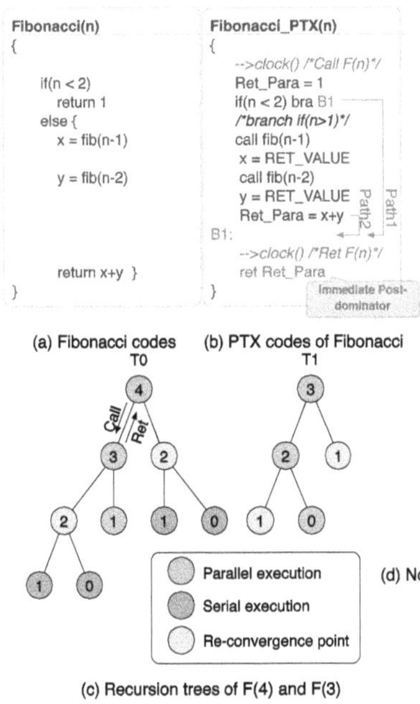

Clock Time	T0 F(4)	T1 F(3)
0	Call F(4)	Call F(3)
863	Call F(3)	Call F(2)
1597	Call F(2)	Call F(1)
2365	Call F(1)	Stall
3007	Ret F(1)	Stall
3947	Call F(0)	Stall
4535	Ret F(0)	Stall
5124	Ret F(2)	Ret F(1)
6381	Call F(1)	Call F(0)
7044	Ret F(1)	Ret F(0)
7692	Ret F(3)	Ret F(2)
8961	Call F(2)	Call F(1)
9733	Call F(1)	Stall
10319	Ret F(1)	Stall
10989	Call F(0)	Stall
11575	Ret F(0)	Stall
12164	Ret F(2)	Ret F(1)
12812	Ret F(4)	Ret F(3)

(d) Nominalized clock time on each step

Figure 3: Timing the steps on two threads computing the fourth and third Fibonacci numbers. F() in (c) and (d) denotes the Fibonacci function.

3.1 Reconvergence in NVIDIA (Kepler) GPUs

For establishing a baseline, we wanted to determine the reconvergence mechanism used in the NVIDIA Kepler GPUs. Because this information is not publicly documented, we determine the reconvergence method by studying the generated code, and by instrumenting and monitoring its execution. The compiled PTX code of the Fibonacci function is simplified and shown in Figure 3 (b). Compared to the original Fibonacci code (Figure 3 (a)), the compiler simplified the conditional branch control, and unified the two return instructions in each branch to a single one, which is then moved to the end of the function. Because the address labeled by *B1* points to the first instruction after convergence of the two paths (*Path1* and *Path2*), instruction *ret Ret_Para* is the immediate post-dominator of the two paths.

Inside the Fibonacci function, we insert two *clock* function invocations to identify the clock cycle at which specific execution points are reached. One, representing *Call F(n)*, is inserted at the beginning of the function, and the other, representing *Ret F(n)*, is inserted just before the return instruction, which is the immediate post-dominator. We then schedule two threads, denoted by T0 and T1 in Figure 3, to compute the fourth and third Fibonacci numbers ($F(4)$ and $F(3)$), respectively. Figures 3(c) and 3(d) show their recursion trees and the gathered clock time. In Figure 3(c), we show which nodes of the recursion trees are executed in parallel or serial, and the reconvergence, using different shades. From Figure 3(d), we can see that when divergence happens after cycle 1597, thread T1 is stalled, while thread T0 executes the next recursion level (leftmost nodes 1 and 0 shown in Figure 3(c)). On cycle 5124, threads T0 and T1 reconverge on *Ret F(2)* and *Ret F(1)*.

Based on this experiment, coupled with similar other experiments, we infer that static immediate post-dominator reconvergence mechanism is used in NVIDIA Kepler GPUs in the case of thread divergence due to recursive function calls.

3.2 Frontier-Based Early Reconvergence

In an unstructured control flow, there is a chance that the same basic block may appear on different branch paths. Based on this observation, the frontier-based reconvergence method [6] improves up on immediate post-dominator reconvergence by supporting two kinds of reconvergence points. In addition to the immediate post-dominator, any thread can join the currently active threads in execution, if it needs to execute the same basic block as the active threads (e.g., basic block BB3 in Figure 4 (b)).

In this approach, a compiler analysis is conducted to do a topological sort on all the basic blocks between the divergent branch and its immediate post-dominator. Then, early reconvergence checks are inserted at the appropriate points in the code. The key of this approach is to schedule the basic blocks in a valid scheduling order—topological sort of the control flow graph—to ensure that each basic block is executed exactly once.

Thus, compared to immediate post-dominator reconvergence, the frontier method can eliminate code expansion due to branch divergence in unstructured control flow. However, the question is whether it can be applied to recursive control flow.

3.3 Limitations for Recursive Functions

First, let us see immediate post-dominator reconvergence. While it has been shown to be effective in handling unstructured control flow within a function, immediate post-dominator reconvergence has limitations when it comes to recursive applications. Figures 4(a) and 4(b) show a modified recursive Fibonacci example and its control flow graph. In this example, a boolean value *ret* is introduced in our Fibonacci function. The function returns when $ret = TRUE$ and $n = 1 \| n = 2$. Otherwise, the *else* branch involves recursive function invocations with arguments $n-1$ and $n-2$. Once a thread goes through the *else* branch, the recursion level is increased by one, and the two function calls are produced with the control flow graph for the new recursion level.

At each recursion level, we can see that the *Exit* node at each recursion level is the immediate post-dominator at that level. When two threads diverge at a particular recursion level, the returning thread waits for the thread that enters into the deeper recursion level to return, so as to reconverge on the *Exit* node at the same level. We next explain this point through a detailed example.

Figure 4(c) shows the execution steps of two threads using the immediate post-dominator reconvergence method. Thread T0 computes the third Fibonacci number, while thread T1 computes the second. Both threads begin executing identical instructions, but begin to diverge at step 7. Thread T0 chooses the function call branch, while thread T1 chooses the other branch so as to return to the invoking function. Because the *Exit* node is the immediate post-dominator, thread T1 cannot return until T0 returns to the same recursion level and also reaches the *Exit* node. Consequently T1 stalls for the next 11 steps, waiting for T0 to finish its recursive function execution.

This is in addition to the stalls that occur within each function call due to conditional execution. For example, when the input values in T0 and T1 are 1 and 0, respectively, T0 chooses the path {Entry, cond1, cond3, Exit}, while T1 goes through {Entry, cond1, cond2, cond3, Exit}. That results in three additional stalls starting at step 22 in Figure 4(c). Assuming the execution of one instruction costs one cycle, in this example, the instructions per clock (IPC) of the immediate post-dominator method is only 1.42 for 2 threads. Moreover, the thread with the lesser amount of work—T1 in this case—cannot being executing its next task early.

For frontier-based early reconvergence, it can eliminate the repeat execution of the same basic block in different divergent paths. For example, in Figure 4(d), we show the execution steps using frontier-based early reconvergence method. Unlike with the immediate post-dominator method, threads T0 and T1 can reconverge early on step 23 in *cond3*, because both threads execute code block *cond3* in their own branches. However, this approach only works for unstructured control flow. Moreover, the static immediate post-dominator is still kept in this method, incurring the disadvantages discussed above for static immediate post-dominator method. This is the reason why thread T1 still waits for thread T0 to return to the same recursion level, with the associated stall of 11 steps observed in Figure 4 (d).

To summarize, when scheduling using static reconvergence-based methods—immediate post-dominator and frontier methods—threads with shorter branches stall for threads with longer branches. If the execution time of the i-th branch of a recursive application on the t-th thread is T_{it}, the total execution time of N threads on a recursive task with M branches is given by $T_{task} = \sum_i^M max_t^N(T_{it})$. Moreover, if there are multiple recursive tasks to be executed by each thread, the threads with the smaller tasks cannot continue to subsequent tasks before the threads with the larger tasks finish. Consequently, if there are N threads, each of which has P recursive tasks to execute, and the execution time of the t-th thread on the i-th task is T_{it}, the total execution time $\sum_i^P T_{task}$ is equal or greater than the sum of the maximum execution time to execute each task, $\sum_i^P max_t^N(T_{it})$.

4. DYNAMIC RECONVERGENCE AND SCHEDULING

In this section, we consider the design of dynamic reconvergence mechanisms. Unlike static reconvergence mechanisms, dynamic reconvergence does not rely on a static (fixed and compiler determined) reconvergence point.

4.1 Dynamic Greedy Reconvergence

Dynamic greedy reconvergence method removes the reconvergence on the static immediate post-dominator. But sharing the same intuition of frontier-based reconvergence, we greedily reconverge the threads with the same program counter (PC). In this approach, we define a *convergence group*, which refers to the group of threads that are at the same PC address as the currently active threads. In particular, although the instructions at different recursion levels can be viewed as belonging to different basic blocks, they might still execute at the same PC address. So different from frontier-based reconvergence, reconvergence with the convergence group on the same PC address can be applied across different recursion levels. Different from immediate post-dominator reconvergence, before reaching an immediate post-dominator point, we keep looking up whether there are inactive threads in convergence group, and greedily reconverge them as soon as possible. Moreover, due to the avoidance of the immediate post-dominator and reconvergence on the same PC address, static (compile-time) knowledge is not needed in our greedy reconvergence method.

Figure 4(e) shows the execution steps with our dynamic greedy reconvergence method. We can see that although threads T0 and T1 diverge at step 7, they reach the same PC address (*if cond3*) in four more steps. Thus although the two threads are in different recursion levels, they can reconverge based on the same convergence group. The threads can then execute the next few instructions without divergence. Compared to the execution steps of immediate post-dominator method, the total number of execution steps is decreased by 12% and 31% for threads T0 and T1, respectively. Thus, greedy reconvergence can not only overlap the common ba-

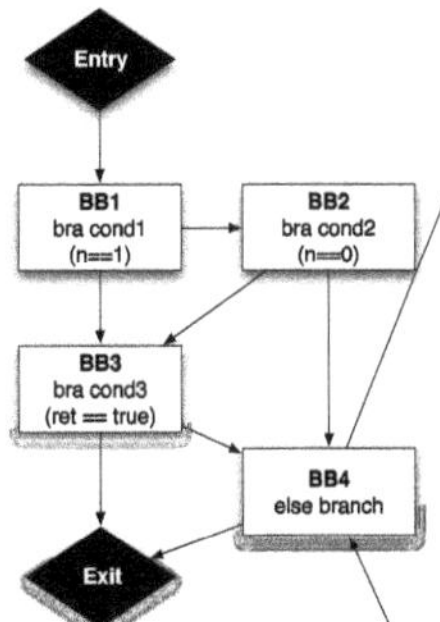


```
Fib(n, ret)
{
  if((n == 1 || n == 0)
    && ret == TRUE)
  {
    return 1;
  }
  else
  {
    x = Fib(n-1, ret);
    y = Fib(n-2, ret);
    return x+y;
  }
}
```

(a) Fibonacci recursive application

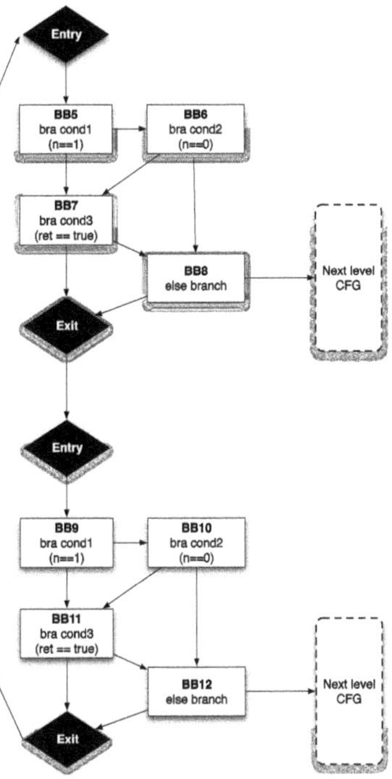

(b) Fibonacci control flow

	T0 Fib(3)	T1 Fib(2)
Step 1	Entry (3)	Entry (2)
Step 2	if cond1	if cond1
Step 3	if cond2	if cond2
Step 4	else branch	else branch
Step 5	Entry (2)	Entry (1)
Step 6	if cond1	if cond1
Step 7	if cond2	Stall
Step 8	else branch	Stall
Step 9	Entry (1)	Stall
Step 10	if cond1	Stall
Step 11	if cond3	Stall
Step 12	Exit (1)	Stall
Step 13	Entry (0)	Stall
Step 14	if cond1	Stall
Step 15	if cond2	Stall
Step 16	if cond3	Stall
Step 17	Exit (0)	Stall
Step 18	Stall	if cond3
Step 19	Exit (2)	Exit (1)
Step 20	Entry (1)	Entry (0)
Step 21	if cond1	if cond1
Step 22	if cond3	Stall
Step 23	Stall	if cond2
Step 24	Stall	if cond3
Step 25	Exit (1)	Exit (0)
Step 26	Exit (3)	Exit (2)
Step 27	Done	Done

(c) Execution steps for immediate post-dominator mechanism

	T0 Fib(3)	T1 Fib(2)
Step 1	Entry (3)	Entry (2)
Step 2	if cond1	if cond1
Step 3	if cond2	if cond2
Step 4	else branch	else branch
Step 5	Entry (2)	Entry (1)
Step 6	if cond1	if cond1
Step 7	if cond2	Stall
Step 8	else branch	Stall
Step 9	Entry (1)	Stall
Step 10	if cond1	Stall
Step 11	if cond3	Stall
Step 12	Exit (1)	Stall
Step 13	Entry (0)	Stall
Step 14	if cond1	Stall
Step 15	if cond2	Stall
Step 16	if cond3	Stall
Step 17	Exit (0)	Stall
Step 18	Stall	if cond3
Step 19	Exit (2)	Exit (1)
Step 20	Entry (1)	Entry (0)
Step 21	if cond1	if cond1
Step 22	Stall	if cond2
Step 23	if cond3	if cond3
Step 24	Exit (1)	Exit (0)
Step 25	Exit (2)	Exit (2)
Step 26	Done	Done
Step 27	Done	Done

(d) Execution steps for frontier-based early reconvergence mechanism

	T0 Fib(3)	T1 Fib(2)
Step 1	Entry (3)	Entry (2)
Step 2	if cond1	if cond1
Step 3	if cond2	if cond2
Step 4	else branch	else branch
Step 5	Entry (2)	Entry (1)
Step 6	if cond1	if cond1
Step 7	if cond2	Stall
Step 8	else branch	Stall
Step 9	Entry (1)	Stall
Step 10	if cond1	Stall
Step 11	if cond3	if cond3
Step 12	Exit (1)	Exit (1)
Step 13	Entry (0)	Entry (0)
Step 14	if cond1	if cond1
Step 15	if cond2	if cond2
Step 16	if cond3	if cond3
Step 17	Exit (0)	Exit (0)
Step 18	Exit (2)	Exit(2)
Step 19	Entry (1)	Done
Step 20	if cond1	Done
Step 21	if cond3	Done
Step 22	Exit (1)	Done
Step 23	Exit (3)	Done
Step 24	Done	Done
Step 25	Done	Done
Step 26	Done	Done
Step 29	Done	Done

(e) Execution steps for dynamic greedy reconvergence mechanism

Figure 4: Recursive Fibonacci code, its control flow graph, and execution steps to compute the 3rd and 2nd Fibonacci numbers on two threads under various scheduling mechanisms

sic blocks in different branches, but also let the threads in shorter branches return sooner to have an opportunity to execute subsequent tasks.

4.1.1 Dynamic Greedy-return Mechanism

The motivation for this scheme is as follows. For our greedy method, the threads with the same PC are encouraged to reconverge as soon as possible. However, when divergence occurs, the threads are arranged in the stack depending on their thread ID. In our implementation, which will be elaborated in next section, we iterate over the threads in the reverse order of their ID, so the threads with the smaller ID have a larger chance to be put on top of the stack. While a different order can be used as well, the key point is that the order in which the threads are traversed is fixed. This could lead to additional stalls. For example, if the tasks with longer branches are in threads that are put on top of the stack, they will be popped and executed first. Other threads, potentially working on tasks with shorter branches, will have to wait longer to get their next tasks.

We address this problem by collecting additional control-flow information during compilation. Specifically, we define a branch (if-then-else) as *recursive*, if a recursive function call or a return statement is reachable from any of the instructions starting from the branch to its immediate post-dominator in the control flow graph. Based on this notion, we insert the threads with a return statement to the top of the stack, when divergence occurs on a recursive branch. The resulting scheme is referred to as the *dynamic greedy-return mechanism.* When divergence occurs, greedy-return method utilizes the compile-time information to check for threads in the return branch. These threads are placed on the top of the stack and are processed with higher priority in the following execution. Note that this variation might not be universally beneficial, because preferentially executing a small number of the threads in return branches can decrease the instructions executed per clock cycle (IPC).

4.2 Dynamic Majority-based Scheduling

In the dynamic greedy scheme, each time an instruction is scheduled, the active threads are a subset of the threads at the top of the stack. However, if the threads in the top active group are a minority of all the threads in the warp, we exploit less parallelism, and IPC could be negatively impacted. Note that because we are using a dynamic scheme, finishing a larger number of threads sooner could very well imply that other work may be available to be scheduled together with the threads that are currently a minority. For example, if the tasks in threads T0 to T3 are [A, C], [B, A], [B, A], and [B, A] respectively, on the static or greedy mechanism, it will require 4 steps to finish, as [T0: A, T1-3:B, T0:C, T1-3:A]. However, in the majority mechanism, it only requires 3 steps, as [T1-3:B, T0-3:A, T0:C]. We can see that the minority group, which only includes T0 on the first step, has the chance to be changed to the majority group, which includes T0 to T3.

Based on this observation, we introduce the dynamic majority-based mechanism. In this method, before issuing an instruction, all threads are activated. Then, a selector is used to find the majority group of threads with the same PC address. The PC address and

Number of SM	15
Number of SP / SM	32
Number of Registers / Core	32768
Shared Memory / Core	48KB
L1 Cache	16KB, 128B line, 4-way assoc
L2 Unified Cache	768KB, 256B line, 8-way assoc
Number of Memory Channels	6
Core Clock	700MHZ
Interconnect Clock	1400MHZ
DRAM Clock	1848MHZ
DRAM Scheduler Queue Size	6
Memory Controller	out of order (FR-FCFS)
Memory Channel Bandwidth	8 Bytes/Cycle

Table 1: GPGPU-sim Configuration

active mask of this majority group are put on the top of the stack to be issued.

Though a key advantage of this scheme is the ability to improve the number of instructions executed per clock cycle, it has additional benefits. Because all threads are active before scheduling, there is no need to record the PC for the threads that are inactive. Thus, compared to the greedy reconvergence in which the stack size increases with increasing number of the branches, only one entry is required for the stack in the dynamic majority method. In addition, this method can be easily implemented in hardware. Moreover, simple stack operations introduce less cost on instruction issuing compared to the greedy and immediate post-dominator methods.

4.2.1 Dynamic Majority-threshold Scheduling

In the dynamic majority-based scheme described above, there is a possibility of starvation for the threads in the minority group. This is overcome through a variant we now describe, referred to as *majority-threshold* scheduling. To prevent starvation while keeping IPC high, we introduce two thresholds. The threads in the minority group will be scheduled only when their waiting time is greater than a predefined value *TS*. At the same time, threads in the minority group cannot be scheduled if the current number of threads in the majority group is greater than another parameter, *TP*.

In our implementation of the majority-threshold method, *TP* is set to $Max(available\_thread/8, min\_value)$, in which *available_thread* refers to the number of the threads that are still alive (not waiting for warp termination). So if there are 32 available threads, *TP* is 4. Only when the current number of threads in majority group is not greater than 4, the starved threads in minority group are considered for scheduling. With decrease in the number of the available threads, *TP* also decreases. However, when the number of available threads is too small, *TP* is set to a minimum value. Thus, when the number of the threads in majority group is high, the original dynamic majority-based scheme is employed in order to achieve high IPC. However, when high IPC cannot be achieved, the scheduling strategy is altered to prevent starvation.

To summarize, the dynamic reconvergence mechanisms we have presented not only provide more flexible reconvergence, especially allowing threads at different recursion levels to reconverge, but also support different scheduling options, allowing us to increase IPC and prevent starvation. In next section, we discuss the implementation of greedy, greedy-return, majority, and majority-threshold schemes.

5. IMPLEMENTATION

GPGPU-sim [2] is a cycle-level GPU performance simulator for general purpose computation on GPUs. In our work, we have implemented the various reconvergence mechanisms on the latest version of GPGPU-sim (3.1.1), which has the capability to model GPU micro-architectures that are similar to NVIDIA GeForce 8x, 9x, and the Fermi series. We chose GPGPU-sim for our work because it has been widely used in GPU research [2, 11, 29], and has been shown to have a high simulation accuracy (gaining correlations of 98.3% and 97.3% versus GT200 and the Fermi hardware, respectively), on the RODINIA benchmark suite with scaled down problem sizes [14].

Our modified GPGPU-sim is configured to model a GPU similar to the NVIDIA's GTX480, which is based on the Fermi architecture. The major configuration parameters of GPGPU-sim are shown in Table 1.

5.1 Distinguishing Branch Types

Because our methods target recursive applications, it is important to distinguish control flow related to recursion from other types of control flow. We classify all the branches into *recursive* branches—branches that include a recursive function call or a return statement—and all other (*general*) branches. When divergence occurs due to a recursive branch, threads may revisit the same PC, though some threads might reach it having followed a different control flow path. Thus, the dynamic reconvergence mechanisms, which allow reconvergence to occur before, on, or after the immediate post-dominator, can provide higher parallelism. However, for a *general branch*, there is typically no benefit in allowing threads to stay divergent after the immediate post-dominator.

The detection of branch types is carried out at compile-time. During compilation, for each branch instruction, we scan the instructions from the branch target, leading up to the immediate post-dominator, to determine if there is any recursive function call or a return statement. If so, we classify this branch instruction as a recursive branch. At runtime, we switch between static and dynamic reconvergence, for general and recursive branches, respectively.

5.2 Implementation of the New Schemes

In implementing the dynamic mechanisms discussed in the last section, we build on prior work by Fung et al. [12], who provided a stack-based implementation of the immediate post-dominator reconvergence method. To implement our own reconvergence mechanisms, we modified the structure of the SIMT stack, which is used to store the next instruction PC for a warp. Specifically, for each of our proposed schemes, we provided a new implementation of the *SIMT stack updating* procedure, which is used to generate the next scheduled instruction for a warp.

5.2.1 Implementation of Dynamic Greedy Mechanism

There are two important data objects in the modified structure of the SIMT stack—the *PC slot*, which is used to store the address of the instructions to be scheduled, and the *active mask*, which is used to track which threads are active at the corresponding PC. The active mask is implemented as a bitset, with one bit per thread and active threads represented by 1.

Algorithm 1 shows the method for updating the SIMT stack with the dynamic greedy and greedy-return reconvergence methods. If the input parameter *ret_first* is TRUE, the algorithm switches to the greedy-return scheme. The critical part of Algorithm 1 is the *while* loop, where a new pair of PC and its corresponding active mask is added into the SIMT stack. When divergence occurs, all target PCs and their corresponding active masks are added into the SIMT stack. Similar to the original stack update implementation, each time, before updating the stack, we read the last active mask as *top_active_mask*. Subsequent operations only impact the threads that are active in *top_active_mask*. This step by itself is not suffi-

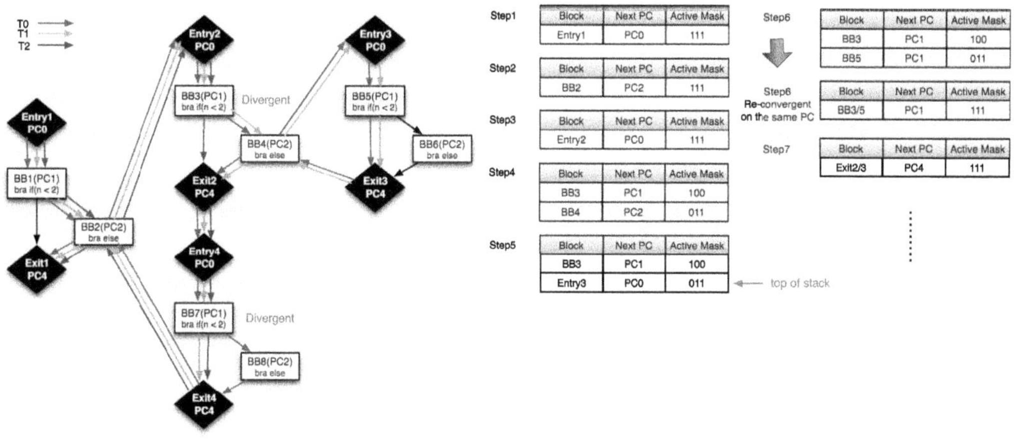

(a) Fibonacci control flow graph

(b) Stack-based implementation

Figure 5: Fibonacci control flow graph with three threads and stack-based implementation of dynamic greedy reconvergence method

Algorithm 1: stack::update_greedy(stack_t &m_stack, addr_t &next_pc, bool ret_first)

```
top_active_mask = m_stack.back().m_active_mask;
top_pc = m_stack.back().m_pc;
/*Add the pair of PC and active mask to stack*/
while top_active_mask.any() do
    mask_t tmp_active_mask = NULL_PC;
    address_type tmp_next_pc;
    tmp_active_mask.reset();
    /*Find out the active threads with the same
      PC*/
    for i = warp_size - 1 -> 0 do
        if thread_done.test(i) then
            top_active_mask.reset(i);
        else if tmp_next_pc = NULL_PC then
            tmp_next_pc = next_pc[i];
            tmp_active_mask.set(i);
            top_active_mask.reset(i);
        else if tmp_next_pc = next_pc[i] then
            tmp_active_mask.set(i);
            top_active_mask.reset(i);
    /*Add new pc and active mask into
      simt_stack*/
    m_stack.back().m_pc = tmp_next_pc;
    m_stack.back().m_active_mask = tmp_active_mask;
    m_stack.push_back(simt_stack_entry());
m_stack.pop_back();
/*Merge entries for the threads in the same
  convergence group*/
for i = m_stack.size() - 2 -> 0 do
    if m_stack[i].m_pc = m_stack.back().m_pc then
        merge(m_stack, i, size-1);
/*Prefer to execute the branch with RET first*/
if ret_first = TRUE then
    if warp_diverged = TRUE and branch_type =
    RECURSIVE_BRANCH then
        for i = m_stack.size() - 1 -> 0 do
            if checkRet(m_stack[i].m_pc) = TRUE then
                move_top(m_stack, i);
                break;
```

cient, as inactive threads that have the same next PC as the PC on top of the stack, cannot be scheduled. Therefore, after the *while* loop, we scan the SIMT stack and activate the threads having the same PC as the top PC address by merging the different entries of the stack.

To further elaborate the runtime procedures, Figure 5 shows an example. In this example, three threads execute Fibonacci, shown in Figure 5(a). The corresponding SIMT stack operations are shown in Figure 5(b). Here, we give the information about the block number, the next PC address, and the active mask showing the threads that will be scheduled next. From steps 1 to 3, there is no divergence. Thus, only one entry is kept in the stack, and the active mask is 111. However, in the step 4, there is divergence: the next PC of thread T2 is PC1, whereas for threads T0 and T1, it is PC2. We insert the PC and the corresponding active mask of all the different branches into the stack. In our implementation, we always put the PC with the smaller thread ID on the top of the stack. In this example, PC2 and its corresponding active mask are put on the top of the stack, and threads T0 and T1 will be scheduled in the next step. Because the threads on top of the stack have higher priority, in steps 4 and 5, threads T0 and T1 are executed, but T2 is stalled. Then, in step 6, the next PC for threads T0 and T1 is PC1, which is the same as the next PC for thread T2. Thus, threads T0, T1, and T2 can reconverge with our dynamic greedy method. The two entries with the same PC in the stack are also merged, and the active mask is updated back to 111.

From Algorithm 1, we can see that in the *for* loop, the active threads are added to the SIMT stack in the reverse order of their thread ID, so the threads with the smaller ID have a larger chance of being inserted at the top of stack and scheduled first. As discussed earlier, this can lead to a performance loss, and the greedy-return mechanism was designed to address this. Thus, in the algorithm of the dynamic greedy mechanism with return-first priority, which is activated by setting *ret_first* parameter as TRUE, we use compile-time information to give higher priority to instructions in the return branch. Because only a *recursive branch* can have a return statement, we check the type of the branch before taking actions for return-first priority. On divergence, we scan the SIMT stack, and move the PC in the path that includes the return instruction, to the top of the stack.

5.2.2 *Implementation of the Dynamic Majority-based Mechanisms*

The implementation of the dynamic majority-based mechanism

Algorithm 2: stack::update_majority(stack_t &m_stack, addr_t &next_pc, bool if_threshold)

```
top_active_mask = m_stack.back().m_active_mask;
top_pc = m_stack.back().m_pc;
/*Active all the threads*/
top_active_mask.set();
mask_t tmp_active_mask = NULL_PC;
address_type tmp_next_pc;
tmp_active_mask.reset();
/*Find out the majority thread group and
  corresponding PC*/
tmp_next_pc = majority_PC(top_active_mask, next_pc);
tmp_active_mask = majority_mask(top_active_mask, next_pc);
if if_threshold = TRUE then
    /*Generate threshold TP*/
    int available_threads;
    for i = 0 → m_warp_size do
        if !thread_done.test(i) then
            available_threads++;
    int TP = max(available_threads/8, 2);
    /*Parallel level is smaller than TP, change
      model to prevent starvation*/
    if tmp_active_mask.count() < TP then
        for tid = 0 → m_warp_size do
            /*check whether the thread is stalled
              more than TS*/
            if m_stack.back().stall[tid] >= TS then
                tmp_next_pc = next_pc[tid];
                tmp_active_mask.reset();
                m_stack.back().stall[tid]=0;
                /*Find out the active threads with
                  the same PC*/
                for i = 0 → m_warp_size − 1 do
                    if top_active_mask.test(i) then
                        if thread_done.test(i) then
                            top_active_mask.reset(i);
                        else if tmp_next_pc = next_pc[i] then
                            tmp_active_mask.set(i);
                            top_active_mask.reset(i);
/*Add new pc and active mask into simt_stack*/
m_stack.back().m_pc = tmp_next_pc;
m_stack.back().m_active_mask = tmp_active_mask;
```

is shown in Algorithm 2. Unlike the dynamic greedy method, all threads are activated at the beginning for computing the majority group. Two functions—*maj_pc* and *maj_mask*—are used to find out the majority group of the threads and their corresponding PC. Last, only majority PC, together with its active mask, is added into the SIMT stack. Finding the majority group of threads can be implemented by a selector in hardware.

If *if_threshold* is set to TRUE in Algorithm 2, the implementation switches to the majority-threshold scheme. The threshold model uses two thresholds, TP and TS. TS is a threshold provided by the user, fixed at runtime. TP, on the other hand, is typically a fraction of the number of available threads, and its value can vary at runtime as explained earlier in Section 4.2.1. If the number of active threads is greater than TP, the scheduling is identical to the original majority version. Otherwise, we utilize the information about the stalling step, number of steps a thread is stalled, on each thread (counted at runtime), to compare with TS. When iterating over threads in the same warp, we check the stalling step of each thread. If a thread's stalling step is greater than threshold TS, the PC associated with this thread is inserted into the top of SIMT stack. At this time, the number of stalling steps of the thread is reinitialized to 0.

There is a key difference between the implementation of this scheme and those of the dynamic greedy method and the static methods. Specifically, there is always only one entry—the majority group of the PC and the active mask—in the SIMT stack. So, even if there is divergence, only one branch is required to be in the stack. Consequently, the implementation of the majority dynamic method requires less space and fewer operations on the stack.

6. EXPERIMENT EVALUATION

We evaluated the various reconvergence mechanisms using our implementation in GPGPU-sim. Because recursive applications have not received attention in the context of GPUs, standard benchmark suites currently do not include many recursive benchmarks. For our study, we implemented six recursive algorithms commonly described in popular textbooks. **Fibonacci** computes the n-th Fibonacci number by recursively computing the $(n-1)$-th and $(n-2)$-th Fibonacci numbers. **Binomial Coefficient** [18] is used to compute the coefficient of the x^k term in the polynomial expansion of the binomial power $(1+x)^n$. **Tak Function** [17] is a recursive function, where the results from the first three branches in Tak are inputs of its fourth branch. **NQueens** searches for all valid arrangement of queens on an $N \times N$ chess board so that no two queens attack each other using a simple backtracking algorithm. We consider $N = 6$. **Graph Coloring** [16] colors the nodes of a graph, with a given number of colors, such that no two adjacent nodes share the same color. Similar to NQueens, a backtracking algorithm is employed, but the search is terminated when one solution is found. We use a graph with 32 nodes, 64 edges, and 3 colors. **Mandelbrot** [9] computes a visualization of the Mandelbrot set. Unlike other recursive benchmarks considered, only one branch is generated on each recursive step. If the coordinate of a node is in the maximum radius or if the search depth is smaller than a threshold, a new coordinate is computed from the original one and checked recursively. In our experiment, the maximum radius and the search threshold are 2.0 and 25, respectively. Among these six benchmarks, Fibonacci and NQueens are also part of the BOTS benchmark suite [7]. The tasks used in the evaluation can be produced from recursive expansion of corresponding benchmarks from a recursive formulation, e.g., using OpenMP Tasks on GPU [1] or CUDA async-finish extensions [5].

6.1 Evaluation Goals

Our experiments were conducted with the following goals: 1) evaluating the performance of the reconvergence mechanisms with increasing *divergence degree*, 2) examining the scalability of the various scheduling schemes with increasing warp size (from 4 to 32), 3) understanding the variation in the performance of our methods on the recursions with different characteristics, noting that the six recursive benchmarks used in our experiments can be classified into four categories—recursion with a small number of branches (Fibonacci and Binomial Coefficient), recursion with a large number of branches (NQueens and Graph Coloring), recursion with dependency (Tak function), and recursion with only one branch (Mandelbrot), and 4) evaluating SIMD utilization by studying the distribution of number of active threads over the execution.

6.2 Performance of Methods with Increasing Divergence

In this section, we compare the performance of the five scheduling mechanisms—immediate post-dominator, greedy, greedy-return, majority, and majority-threshold—while varying the degree of di-

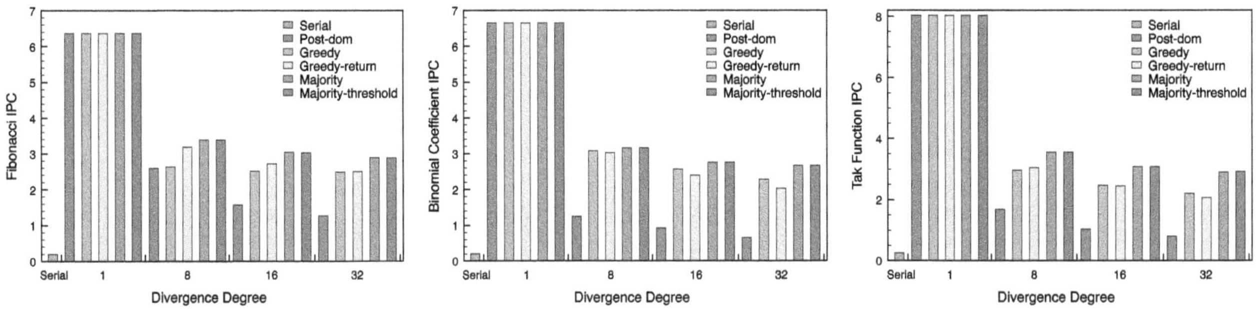

Figure 7: IPC of Post-dom (Immediate post-dominator), Greedy, Greedy-return, Majority, and Majority-threshold methods with 1, 8, 16, and 32 divergence degree in Fibonacci, Binomial Coefficients, and Tak benchmarks (32 threads in a warp)

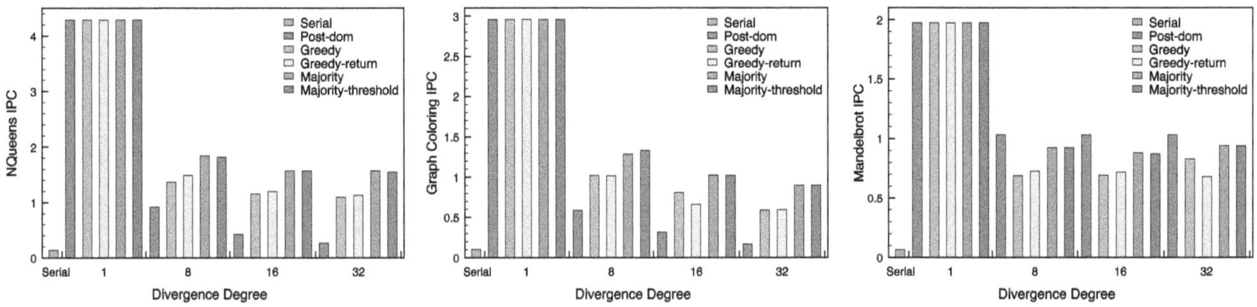

Figure 8: IPC of Post-dom (Immediate post-dominator), Greedy, Greedy-return, Majority, and Majority-threshold methods with 1, 8, 16, and 32 divergence degree in NQueens, Graph Coloring, and Mandelbrot benchmarks (32 threads in a warp)

vergence between the threads. By changing the order of elements in the datasets assigned to each thread, we can control the divergence between threads. The first version, *0-offset*, is created by assigning the same set of N tasks in the same order to each thread. In this case, we expect all threads to execute the same instructions at any given time, thus exhibiting no divergence and a perfect speedup. Next, *1-offset* version is created by doing a rotation on the order of the tasks in each set. Specifically, the i-th thread begins execution starting with the i-th task. Thus, all threads will obtain a different task in the beginning, representing the case with the largest divergence. Between the *0-offset* and *1-offset* cases, we also create two other cases by rotating the order of the tasks left by multiples of 2 and 4. The resulting *2-offset* and *4-offset* cases exhibit some divergence across threads, but also contain some threads doing identical work. Figure 6 shows an example of task rotation with 0, 1, 2, and 4 offsets on 8 threads for Fibonacci.

Based on the number of distinct tasks in each case, we define the divergence degree as 1, 8, 16, and 32 for *0-offset*, *4-offset*, *2-offset*, and *1-offset* on 32 threads, respectively. Figures 7 and 8 show the instruction per clock cycle (IPC) for the different methods on the six recursive benchmarks with 32 threads per warp. The baseline shown in the figures is the IPC on one thread for the corresponding benchmark. As expected, all methods achieve nearly perfect speedup of 32 for all benchmarks when the divergence degree is 1. With increasing divergence degree the performance of all the methods decreases. However, the majority method achieves the best performance on all benchmarks. For Fibonacci, when increasing the divergence degree to 8, 16, and 32, the performance of the immediate post-dominator method decreases by factors of 2.45, 4.04, and 5.02, respectively, However, the performance of the majority method only decreases by factors of 1.87, 2.09, and 2.21, respectively. The performance of the greedy method also decreases slower than the immediate post-dominator method, but faster than the majority method. A similar trend is observed for other benchmarks, though the trends are somewhat different for Mandelbrot, which we will elaborate in the next subsection.

6.3 Scalability with Respect to Warp Width

In this section, we discuss the scalability of the different scheduling schemes with respect to change in warp size. For this experiment, the tasks with different problem sizes and/or control flow structures are generated and assigned to each thread in a random fashion. However, the total amount of work assigned to all threads is the same. Moreover, with increasing number of threads in a warp, the workload for each thread is decreased to study strong scaling.

In Figures 9 and 10, we show the IPC for the different schemes while warp width is increased from 4 threads to 32 threads. The baseline used in reporting the results is the IPC when we execute just one thread. When warp width is 4, the IPC achieved from all the methods is very similar. However, with increasing warp width, for all the benchmarks, the scalability of the majority and the majority-threshold methods improve as compared to immediate post-dominator, greedy, and greedy-return methods. The immediate post-dominator method has the worst performance on all benchmarks, except Mandelbrot. In Fibonacci, when increasing the warp width to 4, 8, 16, and 32, the IPC of the majority method is 2.36, 4.16, 6.84, and 10.83 times higher than the IPC with the baseline. Moreover, the relative improvement (majority method over the im-

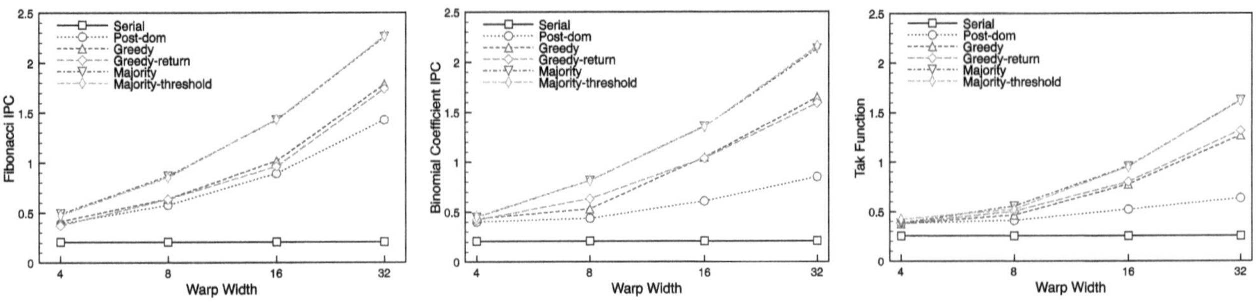

Figure 9: IPC of Post-dom (Immediate post-dominator), Greedy, Greedy-return, Majority, and Majority-threshold methods while increasing the number of threads in a warp in Fibonacci, Binomial Coefficient, and Tak benchmarks

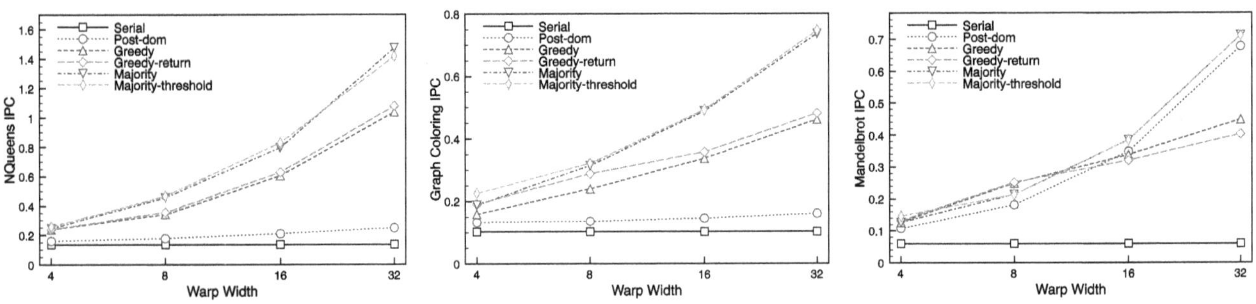

Figure 10: IPC of Post-dom (Immediate post-dominator), Greedy, Greedy-return, Majority, and Majority-threshold methods while increasing the number of threads in a warp in N-Queens, Graph Coloring, and Mandelbrot benchmarks

mediate post-dominator method) also increases from 1.25 to 1.58 with increase in warp width.

The performance trends do vary depending on the benchmark. For benchmarks with a small number of branches, such as Fibonacci and Binomial Coefficients (both of which have only two branches at each recursion level), increasing warp width resulted in better performance with all methods. With 32 threads, immediate post-dominator, greedy, and majority methods obtain speedups factors 6.8, 8.5, and 10.8, respectively, on Fibonacci, and speedup factors 4.0, 7.8, and 10.2, respectively, on Binomial Coefficients. Trends are different for the benchmarks with a large number of branches, such as NQueens and Graph Coloring. While increasing the warp width from 4 to 32, the immediate post-dominator method only gains 1.5x and 1.2x speedups on these benchmarks. This is because with larger number of branches, there is a greater chance that longer branches can block the return of the shorter branches. As majority and greedy methods support the early return of shorter branches, increasing the warp width from 4 to 32 yields 5.75x and 5.03x speedup. For the benchmarks with dependencies on different recursion levels, such as the Tak Function, the control flow is more complex than Fibonacci or Binomial Coefficient. The scalability of the immediate post-dominator method is still much worse than that of majority and greedy methods.

Finally, we explain the observed trends with Mandelbrot. In this benchmark, there is only one branch in each recursion level, and all branches have the same control flow and the same longest branch length (25 with the problem size considered). Thus, in the worse case, the immediate post-dominator method requires execution time equal to the sum of the execution times on the 25 recursion levels. When the warp width is less than 16, it is more likely that we see such a worst case (longest branch length) execution time. In this case, the immediate post-dominator method is slower than the majority and the greedy methods. However, with increasing warp width, more tasks with the same longest branch length are likely to be grouped together. Thus, the immediate post-dominator method turns out to be faster than the greedy method, as the benefit of dynamic reconvergence is small. The majority scheme can still achieve a small improvement compared to the immediate post-dominator method.

To further understand the reasons underlying the performance of the different schemes, we did an additional analysis. In Figure 11, we show the distribution of the active threads on the six benchmarks for a warp width 16 threads. Each bar in the figure corresponds to the execution of one benchmark with one scheme, and different shades within a block show the percentage of execution time during which a specific number of threads were active. For example, *w1* represents the percentage of time when there is only 1 active thread, whereas *w16* represents the percentage of the time when all 16 threads are active.

We can see that for most benchmarks, *w1* takes the largest percentage of the execution time with immediate post-dominator, greedy, and greedy-return methods. In NQueens and Graph Coloring, with the use of the immediate post-dominator method, 79% and 95% of the time there is only one active thread. With the greedy method, w1 is reduced to 37% and 50%, respectively, for these 2 benchmarks. The majority method can further decrease w1 to 4% and 13%. In the majority method, the largest percentage of the execution time is for w8, showing the benefits of scheduling based on the majority group. Thus, although the greedy method has all 16 threads active for a larger fraction of time than the majority scheme,

0-Offset Rotation									2-Offset Rotation								
Threads	Tasks								Threads	Tasks							
Thread-0	10	8	6	9	7	5	2	4	Thread-0	10	8	6	9	7	5	2	4
Thread-1	10	8	6	9	7	5	2	4	Thread-1	6	9	7	5	2	4	10	8
Thread-2	10	8	6	9	7	5	2	4	Thread-2	7	5	2	4	10	8	6	9
Thread-3	10	8	6	9	7	5	2	4	Thread-3	2	4	10	8	6	9	7	5
Thread-4	10	8	6	9	7	5	2	4	Thread-4	10	8	6	9	7	5	2	4
Thread-5	10	8	6	9	7	5	2	4	Thread-5	6	9	7	5	2	4	10	8
Thread-6	10	8	6	9	7	5	2	4	Thread-6	7	5	2	4	10	8	6	9
Thread-7	10	8	6	9	7	5	2	4	Thread-7	2	4	10	8	6	9	7	5
1-Offset Rotation									4-Offset Rotation								
Threads	Tasks								Threads	Tasks							
Thread-0	10	8	6	9	7	5	2	4	Thread-0	10	8	6	9	7	5	2	4
Thread-1	8	6	9	7	5	2	4	10	Thread-1	7	5	2	4	10	8	6	9
Thread-2	6	9	7	5	2	4	10	8	Thread-2	10	8	6	9	7	5	2	4
Thread-3	9	7	5	2	4	10	8	6	Thread-3	7	5	2	4	10	8	6	9
Thread-4	7	5	2	4	10	8	6	9	Thread-4	10	8	6	9	7	5	2	4
Thread-5	5	2	4	10	8	6	9	7	Thread-5	7	5	2	4	10	8	6	9
Thread-6	2	4	10	8	6	9	7	5	Thread-6	10	8	6	9	7	5	2	4
Thread-7	4	10	8	6	9	7	5	2	Thread-7	7	5	2	4	10	8	6	9

Figure 6: An example of task rotation with 0, 1, 2, and 4 offsets on 8 threads

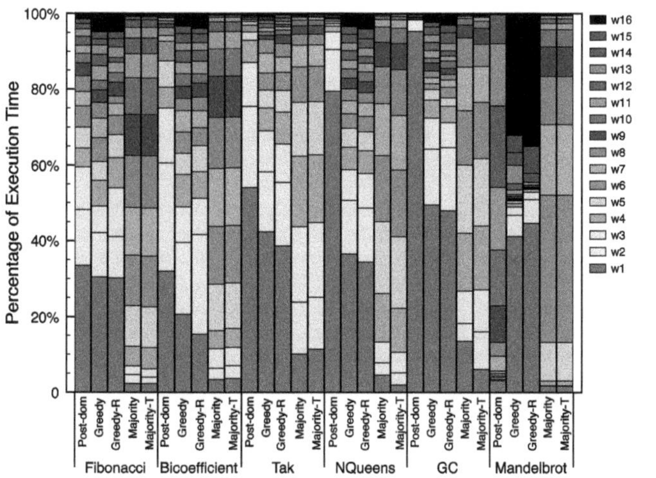

Figure 11: Distribution of scheduled warp sizes for a warp width of 16

the average number of threads that are active at any given time is higher for the majority scheme. Thus, the majority scheme gives better overall performance.

By comparing greedy and greedy-return methods, Figures 7 and 8 show that when the divergence degree is low, such as with a divergence degree of 8, the greedy-return method can usually provide better performance. However, with increase in divergence degree, the greedy-return method may introduce additional overheads by excessively scheduling the threads in the return branch. Similarly, from Figures 9 and 10, we can see that when warp width is small, say 4 or 8, better performance is obtained by the greedy-return method. This is because an execution with small warp width also incurs a smaller degree of divergence. By comparing the majority and majority-threshold methods, we can see that their performance is very similar in both divergence and scalability experiments. This is due to the fact that starvation occurs very rarely in our benchmarks. Moreover, if we are focusing on the starving threads, IPC may also decrease because the starving threads are often not be in the majority group. However, from Figure 11, we do see that both greedy-return and majority-threshold methods often have smaller w1, as compared to greedy and the majority methods, respectively.

7. RELATED WORK

Since SIMD architectures have emerged, supporting control flow on them has been a topic of much interest. The ILLIAC IV system [3] used a single predicate register, together with a vector masked instruction, to support unnested *if-then-else* branches and *while* loops. CHAP [19], a SIMD graphics processor, introduced a runflag stack and explicit *if-else-endif* and *do-while* instructions to handle structured control flow. It also supported nested branch statements by introducing push and pop operations on the stack. However, these techniques cannot be easily applied to unstructured control flow or recursive applications.

Specifically on GPUs, the threads in the same warp are executed in the SIMD manner. The popular branch control method on GPUs involves allowing the threads that have taken the same branch to execute, while all other threads stall. To implement this method, Lorie and Strong [20] proposed a method using mask bits and special instructions such as *else* and *join*. Woop et al. [27] demonstrated a hardware stack and mask to implement this method. Fung et al. [12] presented an implementation of the immediate post-dominator reconvergence method, in which arbitrary control flow can be supported by pushing all the branches into the stack and popping the reconvergence instruction. However, it may still involve significant serialization in the presence of unstructured control flow. The thread frontier method [6] provides an approach to early reconvergence.

Besides intra-warp thread scheduling in the presence of divergence, the focus of the above schemes as well as our work, another direction pursued involves optimizing the mapping of threads in a block to warps to reduce divergence. Dynamic warp formation [12] increases warp utilization by creating a new warp comprising the threads that have taken the same branch. Thread block compaction [11] optimizes intra-warp utilization by using a block-width stack instead of a warp-width stack. Warp subdivision [21] creates warp-splits, which are simply extra schedulable entities, to interleave their execution. Two-level warp scheduling [22] combines threads from large warps to improve utilization of SIMD processors. Simultaneous branch and warp interleaving [4] and dual-path execution model [24] are similar concepts, though they differ in hardware implementation and the level of compiler support needed. All these methods change the warp structure using hardware support and can complement our approaches to handle recursion.

The work discussed above mainly focused on structured or unstructured control flow in the same function. Recursion, where divergence arises because of new function calls or returns is not a major target for the above work. Some other studies have considered supporting recursion on SIMD architectures. Abdou [30] developed an approach to translate recursive serial codes to SIMD target codes. Such automatic transformation continues to be a non-trivial challenge for general recursive applications and inputs. Ke et al. [28] proposed a method to implement recursion by simulating a call stack. Compared to the built-in recursion support in GPUs, using a stack to simulate recursion in software can be inefficient.

In summary, there have been no systematic studies on hardware thread scheduling for recursive applications on SIMD architectures.

8. CONCLUSIONS

GPUs and other SIMD architectures have emerged as a major player in high performance computing, but recursive applications either cannot be mapped to such hardware or do not perform well. This is due to branch divergence and the fact that current reconvergence schemes are not optimized for recursive applications. This paper has thoroughly studied the branch reconvergence issue for recursive applications. We first analyzed and identified the limitations of existing (static) methods—the immediate post-dominator and frontier methods—for recursive control flow. We then introduced novel (dynamic) schemes, including the dynamic greedy and majority-based methods, which allow more flexible reconvergence of threads either before or after the immediate post-dominator, as well as allowing simultaneous execution of the same instruction from threads that have different recursive call depths.

The main observations from our detailed evaluation using six recursive benchmarks are as follows. First, our dynamic reconvergence mechanisms outperform the immediate post-dominator scheme, with average speedups over the latter method of 1.66, 1.65, 2.23, and 2.24, with greedy, greedy-return, majority, and majority-threshold schemes, respectively. Second, the dynamic majority mechanism, which focuses on improving instructions per clock, achieves the best scalability both with increasing divergence among the threads and increasing warp sizes. Finally, across 6 applications, the arithmetic mean of the speedups using the majority scheme (with 32 threads in a warp) is 9.2, over serial execution, establishing that recursive applications can benefit from GPUs and similar accelerators.

9. REFERENCES

[1] E. Ayguadé, R. M. Badia, P. Bellens, D. Cabrera, A. Duran, R. Ferrer, M. González, F. D. Igual, D. Jiménez-González, and J. Labarta. Extending openmp to survive the heterogeneous multi-core era. *International Journal of Parallel Programming*, 38(5-6):440–459, 2010.

[2] A. Bakhoda, G. L. Yuan, W. W. L. Fung, H. Wong, and T. M. Aamodt. Analyzing CUDA workloads using a detailed GPU simulator. In *IEEE International Symposium on Performance Analysis of Systems and Software (ISPASS '09)*, pages 163–174, 2009.

[3] W. J. Bouknight, S. A. Denenberg, D. E. McIntyre, J. M. Randall, A. H. Sameh, and D. L. Slotnick. The Illiac IV system. *Proc. of IEEE*, 60(4):369–388, 1972.

[4] N. Brunie, S. Collange, and G. F. Diamos. Simultaneous branch and warp interweaving for sustained GPU performance. In *International Symposium on Computer Architecture (ISCA '12)*, pages 49–60, 2012.

[5] S. Chatterjee, M. Grossman, A. S. Sbîrlea, and V. Sarkar. Dynamic task parallelism with a gpu work-stealing runtime system. In *International Workshop on Languages and Compilers for Parallel Computing (LCPC'11)*, pages 203–217, 2011.

[6] G. Diamos, B. Ashbaugh, S. Maiyuran, A. Kerr, H. Wu, and S. Yalamanchili. SIMD re-convergence at thread frontiers. In *IEEE/ACM International Symposium on Microarchitecture (MICRO '11)*, pages 477–488, 2011.

[7] A. Duran, X. Teruel, R. Ferrer, X. Martorell, and E. Ayguade. Barcelona OpenMP tasks suite: A set of benchmarks targeting the exploitation of task parallelism in OpenMP. In *International Conference on Parallel Processing (ICPP '09)*, pages 124–131, 2009.

[8] Dwarf mine. `http://view.eecs.berkeley.edu/wiki/Dwarf\_Mine`.

[9] J. Ewing and G. Schober. The area of the mandelbrot set. *Numerische Mathematik*, 61(1):59–72, 1992.

[10] F. Franchetti and M. Puschel. A SIMD vectorizing compiler for digital signal processing algorithms. In *International Parallel and Distributed Processing Symposium (IPDPS '02)*, pages 20–26, 2002.

[11] W. W. L. Fung and T. M. Aamodt. Thread block compaction for efficient SIMT control flow. In *IEEE International Symposium on High Performance Computer Architecture (HPCA '11)*, pages 25–36, 2011.

[12] W. W. L. Fung, I. Sham, G. Yuan, and T. M. Aamodt. Dynamic warp formation and scheduling for efficient GPU control flow. In *IEEE/ACM International Symposium on Microarchitecture (MICRO '07)*, pages 407–420, 2007.

[13] C. Garcia, R. Lario, M. Prieto, L. Pinuel, and F. Tirado. Vectorization of multigrid codes using SIMD ISA extensions. In *International Parallel and Distributed Processing Symposium (IPDPS '03)*, pages 8–pp, 2003.

[14] GPGPU-Sim 3.x manual. `http://gpgpu-sim.org/manual/index.php5/GPGPU-Sim_3.x_Manual#Introduction`.

[15] N. Ide, M. Hirano, Y. Endo, S. Yoshioka, H. Murakami, A. Kunimatsu, T. Sato, T. Kamei, T. Okada, and M. Suzuoki. 2.44-GFLOPS 300-MHz floating-point vector-processing unit for high-performance 3D graphics computing. *IEEE Journal of Solid-State Circuits*, 35(7):1025 –1033, Jul 2000.

[16] W. Klotz. Graph coloring algorithms. *Mathematics Report*, pages 1–9, 2002.

[17] D. E. Knuth. Textbook examples of recursion. *Artificial Intelligence and Mathematical Theory of Computation: Papers in Honor of John McCarthy, Academic Press, San Diego, CA*, pages 207–229, 1991.

[18] D. E. Knuth. *The art of computer programming, volume 1: (3rd ed.) fundamental algorithms*. Addison Wesley Longman Publishing Co., Inc., 1997.

[19] A. Levinthal and T. Porter. Chap—a SIMD graphics processor. In *Conference on Computer Graphics and Interactive Techniques (SIGGRAPH '84)*, pages 77–82, 1984.

[20] R. A. Lorie and H. R. Strong Jr. Method for conditional branch execution in simd vector processors, Mar. 6 1984. US Patent 4,435,758.

[21] J. Meng, D. Tarjan, and K. Skadron. Dynamic warp subdivision for integrated branch and memory divergence tolerance. In *International Symposium on Computer architecture (ISCA '10)*, pages 235–246, 2010.

[22] V. Narasiman, M. Shebanow, C. J. Lee, R. Miftakhutdinov, O. Mutlu, and Y. N. Patt. Improving gpu performance via large warps and two-level warp scheduling. In *IEEE/ACM International Symposium on Microarchitecture (MICRO '11)*, pages 308–317, 2011.

[23] NVIDIA. Cuda dynamic parallelism programming guide. August 2012.

[24] M. Rhu and M. Erez. The dual-path execution model for efficient GPU control flow. In *IEEE International Symposium on High Performance Computer Architecture (HPCA '13)*, 2013.

[25] T. Rognes and E. Seeberg. Six-fold speed-up of smith–waterman sequence database searches using parallel processing on common microprocessors. *Bioinformatics*, 16(8):699–706, 2000.

[26] Top 500 supercomputers. `http://www.top500.org/lists/2012/11/`.

[27] S. Woop, J. Schmittler, and P. Slusallek. RPU: a programmable ray processing unit for realtime ray tracing. In *ACM SIGGRAPH 2005 Papers*, SIGGRAPH '05, pages 434–444, 2005.

[28] K. Yang, B. He, Q. Luo, P. V. Sander, and J. Shi. Stack-based parallel recursion on graphics processors. In *ACM SIGPLAN symposium on Principles and practice of parallel programming*, PPoPP '09, pages 299–300, 2009.

[29] Y. Yang, P. Xiang, M. Mantor, and H. Zhou. CPU-assisted GPGPU on fused CPU-GPU architectures. In *IEEE International Symposium on High Performance Computer Architecture (HPCA '12)*, pages 1–12. IEEE, 2012.

[30] A. Youssef. Translation of serial recursive codes to parallel SIMD codes. In *IFIP WG10.3 Working Conference on Parallel Architectures and Compilation Techniques*, pages 254–263, 1995.

SemCache: Semantics-aware Caching for Efficient GPU Offloading

Nabeel AlSaber and Milind Kulkarni
School of Electrical and Computer Engineering
Purdue University
West Lafayette, IN, USA
{nalsaber, milind}@purdue.edu

ABSTRACT

Recently, GPU libraries have made it easy to improve application performance by offloading computation to the GPU. However, using such libraries introduces the complexity of manually handling explicit data movements between GPU and CPU memory spaces. Unfortunately, when using these libraries with complex applications, it is very difficult to optimize CPU-GPU communication between multiple kernel invocations to avoid redundant communication.

In this paper, we introduce SemCache, a semantics-aware GPU cache that automatically manages CPU-GPU communication and dynamically optimizes communication by eliminating redundant transfers using caching. Its key feature is the use of library semantics to determine the appropriate caching granularity for a given offloaded library (*e.g.*, matrices in BLAS). We applied SemCache to BLAS libraries to provide a GPU drop-in replacement library which handles communications and optimizations automatically. Our caching technique is efficient; it only tracks matrices instead of tracking every memory access at fine granularity. Experimental results show that our system can dramatically reduce redundant communication for real-world computational science application and deliver significant performance improvements, beating GPU-based implementations like CULA [9] and CUBLAS [18].

Categories and Subject Descriptors

D.1.3 [**Programming Techniques**]: Concurrent Programming—*Parallel Programming*; D.4.2 [**Operating Systems**]: Storage Management—*Distributed Memories*

Keywords

GPU offloading; GPGPU; Communication optimization

1. INTRODUCTION

With the rise of general purpose GPU (GPGPU) programming, programmers have increasingly turned to the GPU as a cheap (both in cost and in energy) means of boosting the performance of their application. Recent years have shown that GPU implementations of linear algebra kernels [9, 18, 21, 23], graph algorithms [15], stencil codes [5], among others, can vastly outperform CPU implementations. However, while these results hold for individual kernels, it is still unclear how best to leverage GPUs to improve the performance of applications.

Consider how a developer of a large-scale computational science application might attempt to use GPU resources. One option would be to try and run the entire application on the GPU (in a sense, taking the same approach as kernel developers, but applying it to the entire program). Clearly, such a tactic is impractical. Not only are GPU programming models (*e.g.*, CUDA [17]) somewhat cumbersome, but not all portions of an application are well-suited to running on a GPU; while computation-heavy portions of an application (*e.g.*, loops performing linear algebra operations) may perform well, more control-heavy portions that do not have much parallelism may instead run *slower* on the GPU than on the CPU. Hence, our programmer may invest significant time in porting an application to the GPU only to find her efforts wasted as GPU performance fails to meet expectations.

Instead of porting the entire application to the GPU, the programmer might instead adopt a *heterogeneous* approach: portions of the application well-suited to GPU execution will be offloaded, while the remainder of the application will be run on the CPU. The programmer may attempt to use systems designed to facilitate such heterogeneous scheduling [14, 19], but these approaches require changes to the programming model, and work only for specific domains, necessitating significant porting work. Alternately, the programmer may offload portions of their code to the GPU, targeting specifically those kernels that are well-suited to GPU execution. Note, however, that a major cost in offloading computations to the GPU is *data movement overhead*: getting data to and from the GPU requires transferring data over a (relatively) slow PCIe bus, and hence data movement consumes a significant portion of the overall time required to perform operations on the GPU. While some data movement is unavoidable, when targeting an application that performs many offloadable operations, *much of this data movement is redundant.*

Consider the simple case of a series of matrix multiply operations, as shown in Figure 1. Each matrix multiply requires that the source matrices be on the GPU and the result matrix be transferred back to the CPU. However, the naïve

ICS'13, June 10–14, 2013, Eugene, Oregon, USA.
Copyright 2013 ACM 978-1-4503-2130-3/13/06 ...$15.00.

```
GEMM(A, B, C); //C = A * B
...
GEMM(B, C, D); //D = B * C
...
GEMM(C, D, E); //E = C * D
```

Figure 1: Simple example with repeated matrix multiplication

approach of transferring the sources to the GPU and the results back on every operation results in redundant communication. Some source matrices (*e.g.*, B) are transferred to the GPU twice, while other matrices (*e.g.*, C in the second operation) are transferred to the GPU even though they were computed on the GPU originally. A better approach is to transfer B just once, and use it for both operations, while consuming C directly from the GPU for the second operation.

There exist libraries of GPU kernels (*e.g.*, CULA Standard Interface) that attempt to ease the process of offloading computation to the GPU by automatically handling data movement and execution on the GPU. Because these libraries target specific operations (*e.g.*, linear algebra), using them is often as simple as replacing operations in an application with equivalent GPU versions; in fact, because computational applications are often already implemented with libraries such as BLAS [4] and LAPACK [2], CULA implementations of those operations can be used with essentially no modifications to program code and no need for GPU expertise. Unfortunately, such drop-in replacement libraries come with drawbacks. The libraries do not consider the composition of library calls, instead implementing each offloaded operation as a self-contained unit. As a result, the libraries do not consider the possibility of redundant data movement across operations (in other words, they adopt the naïve communication approach described above). *Because each operation is offloaded in isolation, the composition of operations may not be implemented efficiently.*

To correctly minimize data movement and avoid redundancy when offloading computation to the GPU, the composition of offloaded operations must be considered. While lower-level libraries (such as CUBLAS, CULA's "device interface," or MAGMA [23]) give the programmer precise control over data movement (so that, *e.g.*, he can avoid transferring matrix B to the GPU twice in the previous example), it is often difficult to reason about which data movement might be redundant and which might be necessary. This is especially true in large, modular applications, where operations might be quite distant from one another both in the code and during execution, and where a single piece of static code may exhibit data redundancy based entirely on when and where the code is invoked during execution (consider a method called from several places in an application that performs several linear algebra operations on matrices passed in as parameters). In such a scenario, any attempt to statically determine whether communication is necessary is doomed to failure; *simply providing low-level control of data movement is not enough to allow eliminating redundant communication.*

What is needed is an *automatic* approach to managing data movement between GPU and CPU that can *dynamically* determine whether data movement is necessary and hence provide drop-in replacements for computational libraries. Such an approach will allow programmers to achieve efficient communication for heterogeneous computing without adopting a new programming model.

1.1 Semantics-aware GPU Caching

In this paper, we propose a *semantics-aware GPU cache* to reduce redundant communication between the CPU and the GPU. At a high level, our software caching approach treats the CPU and GPU memory spaces as two caches, and uses an MSI (modified/shared/invalid) protocol to maintain coherence between them. When a method is called to execute on the GPU, the cache state of the data used by the method is inspected, and data is transferred to the GPU only if it does not already reside there. When data is modified on the CPU, the cache is used to invalidate any corresponding data on the GPU.

This type of software caching has been proposed before for other architectures, such as distributed shared memory systems [1, 7, 10, 16] and accelerator-based systems like the Cell [8, 12]. The key drawback of these prior approaches is that the granularity of caching is fixed (*e.g.*, OS pages for DSM approaches, or fixed line sizes for accelerators), and did not take into account program behavior. As a result, the cache granularity might be too big, resulting in excessive data movement, or too small, resulting in too many cache lookups and more data transfers and hence higher overhead. In contrast, our system adopts a semantics-aware approach: the granularity of our caching is determined by the semantics of the libraries being offloaded to the GPU. For example, when applying our approach to the BLAS library, rather than caching at the granularity of pages, our cache will track data at the granularity of the arrays in the application. Hence the granularity of the cache is dependent not only on the libraries in a program but also on the specific way those libraries are used in an application. By matching our cache granularity to the libraries, we can more efficiently use the space on the GPU (by caching only data that is needed for computations) and reduce caching overheads (by performing fewer cache lookups per library call). We also show how the same caching principles can leverage additional library semantics to not only save data movement, but also eliminate redundant computations.

Crucially, the cache we develop is *generic*: the system itself is not tied to any particular library. Instead, all of the semantic information is provided in the library implementation, allowing the same caching system to be reused for different libraries, in each case providing tuned cache implementations that use the correct granularity for a given library.

1.2 Contributions

This paper makes the following contributions:

- The design and implementation of SemCache, a generic GPU cache that automatically manages CPU-GPU communication and dynamically optimizes communication. It is augmented with semantic information to provide *tuned, library-specific caching.*

- A generalization of this caching solution (akin to memoization) that creates *semantic links* between data on the CPU and GPU, allowing SemCache to automatically eliminate redundant computation and translate between different layouts.

- An annotated GPU BLAS library that provides a *drop in replacement* for existing BLAS libraries that, in conjunction with SemCache, delivers optimized communication between the CPU and GPU.

- Experimental results showing, both for microbenchmarks and a large, real-world computational science application, that SemCache can dramatically reduce redundant communication, and deliver significant performance improvements, beating not only CPU implementations but also GPU-based implementations using existing, tuned libraries.

2. RELATED WORK

There are multiple libraries that optimizes the performance of Linear Algebra Kernels on GPUs. CUBLAS [18] is an implementation of BLAS [4] (Basic Linear Algebra Subprograms) on top of the NVIDIA's CUDA driver that allows access to the computational resources of NVIDIA GPUs. MAGMA [23] and CULA [9] have implemented hybrid GPU accelerated linear algebra routines (LAPACK and BLAS libraries). CULA provides a standard interface that needs no GPU knowledge in addition to the advanced interface. These approaches all focus on individual kernels; across kernels, data management must be handled by the programmer.

SuperMatrix [22] and StarSs [3] have a runtime system to solve dense linear systems on platforms with multiple hardware accelerators. Both systems use software-caching schemes to reduce data transfer cost within a single kernel. Fogue *et al.* ported the PLAPACK library to GPU-accelerated clusters [6]. They require that CPUs compute the diagonal block factorizations while GPUs compute all the remaining operations. They also store all data for a single kernel in GPU memories to reduce communication. Our caching approach is different from these libraries since we optimize communication across kernels (at the application level).

Other programming models are designed to facilitate heterogeneous scheduling. Intel's Merge [13] is a programming model for heterogeneous multi-core systems. Qilin is a generic programming system that can automatically map computations to GPUs and CPUs through off-line trainings [14]. MDR [19] is a performance model-driven runtime for heterogeneous parallel platforms. Such systems try to optimize CPU-GPU communication across the entire program. However, to use them, the programmer must rewrite their application using the specified programming model. In contrast, we are targeting existing large-scale applications, with the goal of optimizing communication without significant programmer effort.

Prior work implemented automatic data management and communication optimization systems for GPUs [7, 10, 11]. Jablin et al. have developed a fully automatic CPU-GPU communication management system (CGCM) [11]. CGCM manages data using a combined run-time and compile-time system without programmer annotations. CGCM requires static analysis (type-inference and alias analysis) because it manages data and optimizes communication at compile-time. The imprecision of static analysis limits CGCM's applicability and performance. In contrast, SemCache uses a more sophisticated run-time system that keeps tracks of data validity status and hence can better optimize communication with less overhead than a static compiler analysis.

DyManD [10] and GMAC [7] attempt to manage communication between the GPU and CPU automatically by adopting distributed shared memory (DSM) techniques [1, 16]. The two systems use the operating system's page-protection mechanism to detect when data needs to be transferred. While these techniques are fully automated, they suffer from two primary limitations compared to SemCache's approach. First, to effectively use page-based systems, the layout of data must be changed to align data with page boundaries, avoid false sharing, etc., which precludes using such systems with existing custom allocators. Second, as DSM systems, GMAC and DyManD require direct mappings between the CPU and GPU memory spaces. As a result, the amount of data shared between the CPU and GPU is limited to the GPU memory size; in fact, the largest inputs that we used in our case study (Section 7.2) cannot be handled by existing systems. Furthermore, this direct mapping precludes more complex *semantic* mappings between the CPU and the GPU, such as transforming row-major layout to column-major layout, or SemCache's computation caching (Section 5).

3. OFFLOADING LIBRARIES TO GPUS

Over the past few years, graphics processing units (GPUs) have become attractive platforms for computing. The programmable vector units on GPUs offer the potential for massive, energy efficient parallelism. There are two downsides, to GPU computing, though. First, to achieve their energy efficiency, GPU cores are very simple, and only provide performance benefits when executing carefully parallelized code. Hence, attempting to port general code to GPUs is a tedious task, and often results in ineffective code. Instead, it is more effective to execute only those portions of an application that are amenable to GPU-style parallelism, such as linear algebra code, on the GPU, leaving the remainder of the application code on the CPU. Because writing efficient implementations on a GPU is difficult even for algorithms well-suited to parallel execution, there has been a proliferation of libraries that provide GPU implementations of common linear algebra kernels (often providing the BLAS interface [4]), easing the task of offloading these operations to the GPU.

The second downside to using GPUs for general purpose computing is that most GPUs use separate memory from the CPU. In other words, the GPU uses a separate address space from the CPU, and hence the two processing units cannot readily share data. Instead, data must be explicitly transferred between the CPU and the GPU. This limitation is especially problematic when only portions of a computation are offloaded to the GPU: because both the CPU and the GPU perform operations on the same data, the data must be transferred back and forth as necessary. Worse, transferring data between CPU and GPU is *slow*, especially in comparison to the speed of each processing unit's own memory. Performing data transfers are often a significant cost of GPU computation, and there have been several approaches that have attempted to avoid even offloading computation when data transfer costs exceed the benefit of GPU computation [14, 19, 24].

The necessity for explicit data movement between GPU and CPU makes providing modular libraries that provide GPU kernels more difficult. Consider the example code in Figure 1. As discussed in the introduction, there are several

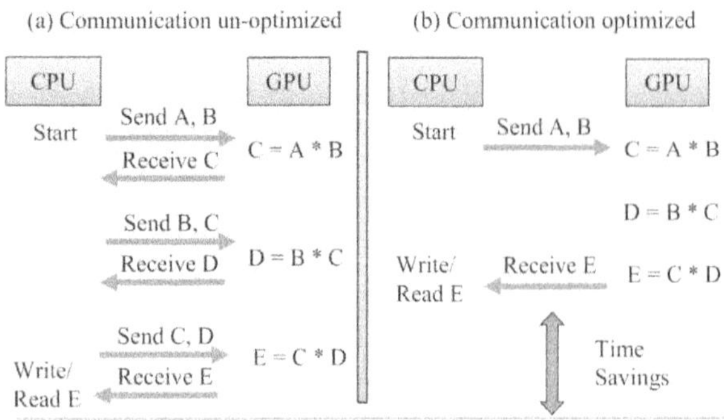

Figure 2: Communication comparison for optimized and un-optimized communication

distinct linear algebra operations performed in this example, each of which would be performed by a different library call. In the interests of modularity and encapsulation, some libraries handle communication between the CPU and GPU "under-the-hood" like CULA standard interface. While this makes using the library easier, it results in redundant communication. The library calls are implemented to execute in isolation, and as self-contained units, they assume that the data resides on the CPU. When invoking a method, a library call must (i) allocate space for the arguments and result on the GPU; (ii) transfer the arguments from the CPU to the GPU; (iii) perform the computation on the GPU; and (iv) transfer the result back to the CPU. As a result, even if multiple library calls could make use of the same data, new space is allocated and the data is transferred for each call. Hence, as we see in Figure 2(a), at each call two matrices are transferred to the GPU and one is transferred back, for a total of 9 matrix transfers.

Clearly, full encapsulation introduces too many performance problems. Instead, other library approaches, such as CUBLAS [18], give the programmer control over data allocation and movement. Hence, as in Figure 2(b), the programmer can explicitly transfer `A` and `B` to the GPU, allocate space for the results matrices in GPU memory (assuming matrices fit in the GPU memory), and operate only in GPU memory until the final result, `E`, is transferred back to the CPU. This results in the minimal amount of communication, 3 matrix transfers. Unfortunately, forcing a programmer to explicitly manage data requires the programmer to reason about the composition of GPU operations. This is a global task that may be impractical for large codes.

In fact, for highly modular codes, it may not be possible to manually manage data movement. Consider, for example, if the three matrix-multiply calls of our example occurred during different invocations of the same larger method within an application. In other words, the three matrix multiplies occurred from library calls from the same line of code, just with different arguments. Clearly, there is no way to introduce data transfer operations statically to such code to correctly transfer the matrices only when necessary. Whether or not data needs to be transferred to the GPU is a purely *run-time* property, based on what other library methods have been called, and what arguments are being passed to a particular library invocation.

The following section describes SemCache, our approach to tracking exactly this dynamic information in a manner that can be readily encapsulated into easy-to-use libraries for offloading GPU computations.

4. SemCache

This section introduces SemCache, a variable-granularity, *Semantics-aware Cache* that can be used to efficiently and easily manage sharing and transferring data between the disjoint CPU and GPU address spaces.

4.1 High Level Overview

A software cache between CPU and GPU, at a high level, is simple and intuitive. One variant, using a MSI (*m*odified, *s*hared, *i*nvalid) protocol might operate as follows: a given piece of memory (*e.g.*, a contiguous block of memory, a page, etc.) is tracked by a run-time system. The run-time tracks whether the contents of the piece of memory are currently valid on both devices (shared), valid only on the GPU (modified on the GPU, invalid on the CPU) or valid only on the CPU (invalid on the GPU, modified on the CPU). Whenever memory is read on a particular device, the cache can be consulted to determine whether the local memory has valid data; if not, communication between GPU and CPU is necessary, and the cache state is changed to shared. When a piece of memory is written on a device, the local cache state is changed to modified, and the state for the other device is changed to invalid.

Such an implementation has been used in numerous previous projects targeting different architectures, from distributed shared memory systems (*e.g.*, [1, 16]) to software caches between Cell processing units (*e.g.*, [8, 12]). The downside to prior implementations is that the granularity at which memory was tracked was constant (*e.g.*, an entire OS page, or a fixed-size block of contiguous memory). However, a fixed granularity may not be appropriate for a given application. If the granularity of the cache is too large (the blocks being tracked are too big), excessive communication will happen, both from transferring unnecessary data and from performing too many invalidations due to false sharing. If the granularity of the cache is too small, more cache lookups will be necessary for a given set of operations, and communication will be broken up into more transfers, resulting in more overhead. Unfortunately, it is difficult to tell for a given application, what the appropriate cache granularity should be, and different applications may require different granularities.

The key insight of SemCache is that when using libraries to offload computation to GPUs, *the correct granularity for a cache can be inferred*. In particular, the appropriate granularity for the cache should be the data structures operated on during offloaded library calls. Moreover, the library's semantics *directly capture what the relevant data structures are*. As a result, by tying SemCache's granularity to a library's semantics, we can track data at exactly the right granularity for a given application.

For example, when SemCache is used in conjunction with a linear algebra library, the data structures being operated on are matrices; as a result, SemCache will track data at the granularity of the matrices used in a particular application. In contrast, if SemCache is used in conjunction with a graph library, the data structures being operated on might be adjacency lists. SemCache will correctly track data at the granularity of entire adjacency lists representing the graphs being operated on.

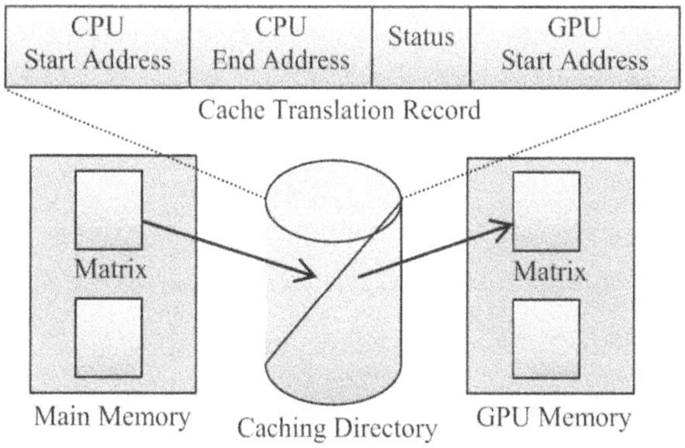

Figure 3: Structures of the Caching Directory

SemCache is composed of multiple, interlocking components: (a) a variable-granularity cache structure and interfaces for performing cache lookups, triggering data transfers, and performing invalidations; (b) a strategy for setting the granularity of the cache based on library behavior; and (c) instrumentation and protocols for tracking and maintaining the correct cache state for memory. The following subsections describe these components.

4.2 Cache Design and Structure

The basic design of SemCache is shown in Figure 3. There is a single data structure, consisting of a set of *translation records* that tracks the status of the various data structures used in a program. Note that even though data may reside on either the CPU or the GPU, it is the CPU that is in charge of maintaining the cache data, and of performing all lookups and invalidations. This is due to the basic approach used for GPGPU computation. Operations are dispatched to the GPU by transferring data (if necessary) to the GPU and invoking a single kernel method. Once the kernel method completes, control transfers back to the CPU and any necessary data is transferred back. In other words, the CPU alone is responsible for controlling execution and for transferring data between the two memory spaces. As a result, SemCache consists of a single set of translation records maintained by the CPU.

The primary data structure of SemCache is the set of translation records that maintain a mapping between CPU data and the corresponding data on the GPU, as well as the current location of the data. In a sense, SemCache serves as a translation lookaside buffer (TLB), except that its entries point to variable-length regions of memory rather than fixed-size pages. The cache entries are hence indexed by both a start address (cpu_s) and an end address (cpu_e) *of the data's location on the CPU*. Each entry also contains a status field (*status*) to keep track of the data's status. These statuses can be one of C, for valid only on the CPU, G, for valid only on the GPU, or S, for valid at both locations. Finally, the translation record contains the putative location of the same data on the GPU (gpu_s)[1].

SemCache's interface provides a number of operations. A memory range $[s, e)$ refers to start and end addresses for a memory range on the CPU.

[1]This location is putative because it is only valid if the status of the range is S or G; if the status is C, the next time the data is sent to the GPU, new space will be allocated for the data

lookup(s, e) Retrieves the translation record associated with memory range $[s, e)$. If the memory range is not currently tracked, create a new entry for the range, and set the status to C.

transferToGPU(entry) Assumes that the status of the entry is S or C. Transfers the contents of memory range $[cpu_s, cpu_e)$ on the CPU to the GPU, allocating new space on the GPU. Sets the GPU start address appropriately. Sets the status of the entry to S.

transferToCPU(entry) Assumes that the status of the entry is S or G. Transfers the contents of memory range $[gpu_s, gpu_s + (cpu_e - cpu_s))$ from the GPU back to the CPU. Sets the status of the entry to S.

invalidateOnGPU(entry) Sets the status of entry to C.

invalidateOnCPU(entry) Sets the status of entry to G.

SemCache maintains the invariant that the ranges tracked by its translation records are disjoint. If a range being looked up is a *subset* of some tracked memory range, then lookup returns the entry associated with the larger memory range. If a range being looked up spans multiple tracked ranges, SemCache*merges all the matching translation records* and creates a new record that tracks a range that spans all of the merged records.

To perform lookups and merges efficiently, SemCache maintains the entries sorted by start address. To look up the range $[s, e)$, SemCache searches for the entry with the largest start address less than or equal to s. If the end address of the found entry is less than or equal to s, SemCache creates a new entry for the range. If the end address of the found entry is greater than or equal to e, it returns the entry. If the end address of the found entry is greater than s and less than e, SemCache iterates through the subsequent entries until it finds all the entries that overlap with the current range. It then merges the ranges together, performing appropriate data movement operations so that the eventual state of the new entry is C.

Managing available GPU memory. The amount of data sent to the GPU might be too large to fit the available GPU memory. In such a situation, to allocate new data in the GPU memory, cached data must to be freed. To determine which address ranges should be freed, SemCache keeps track of the number of hits for each tracked range in the cache, and, when necessary, removes infrequently used ranges from the GPU. The simple strategy we adopted produced the minimal "miss rate" for our test applications. Note that depending on the application other polices such as least-recently-used may result in better handling of capacity misses. Multiple replacement polices can be easily integrated with SemCache and the programmer can have the option to choose between them.

4.3 Determining Granularity

SemCache by itself is simply a variable-granularity cache that supports a few methods to transfer data between the CPU and GPU. The key to SemCache's utility is that the granularity of the cache is determined by the semantics of the GPU libraries being used in a program. In particular, we note that the address ranges tracked by the cache are determined during cache lookup: if a particular range has

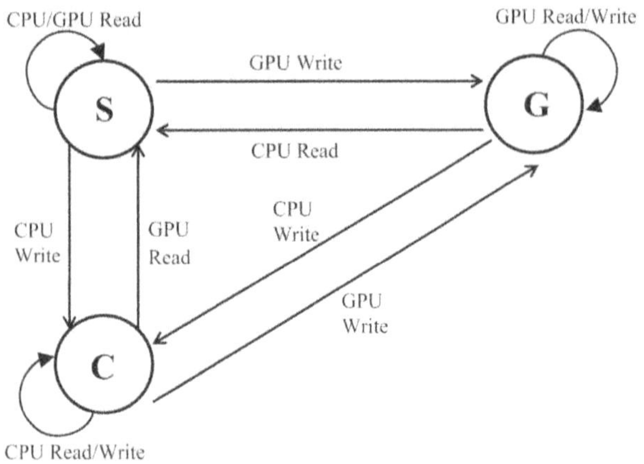

Figure 4: Write-back protocol (States: GPU/CPU/Shared)

not been seen before, a new entry for that range is created. Hence, if a library call takes as input matrices `A` and `B` and produces as output a matrix `C`, the three matrices can be individually tracked by performing lookups on their address ranges. For example, if `A` were an $n \times n$ matrix (of floats), invoking `lookup(A, A + 4 * n * n)` would cause SemCache to start tracking matrix A, and whether it existed on the GPU or not. Note that the current implementation of SemCache only tracks contiguous memory ranges; data structures that are not contiguous ranges have to be tracked with multiple entries.

4.4 SemCache Instrumentation and Protocols

The interfaces of SemCache can be used to implement a basic protocol to manage data movement between the CPU and GPU. The protocol tracks reads and writes on both devices, and transfers data when necessary. Figure 4 shows the basic protocol, which behaves similarly to an MSI coherence protocol. Data that is computed on the GPU remains on the GPU until the CPU needs to read it. Similarly, data computed on the CPU remains on the CPU until the GPU needs it. If either the CPU or GPU writes a piece of data, that data is invalidated on the other device. Adopting the terminology of Quintana-Orti *et al.*, we call this a *write-back* protocol [21]. Figure 5 shows the operations performed on the various devices to implement this protocol. Note that these methods return the translation record, as invoking methods on the GPU may require knowing the addresses where the necessary data is stored. Section 6 discusses how a library writer can use these interface methods to manage data movement for a particular library.

While `writeGPU` and `readGPU` are used before and after invocations of library calls offloaded to the GPU, in the worst case, every read and write on the CPU must be guarded by `writeCPU` and `readCPU` (as in software caching approaches for accelerators like the Cell). Section 4.5 discusses two approaches to inserting these guards.

We introduce a further protocol simplification. Because reads on the CPU are much more prevalent than writes, and because most results computed by the GPU are eventually needed on the CPU, we eagerly transfer any data *written* by the GPU during a library operation back to the CPU. This affects how library operations that modify data are handled. In the write-back protocol, `writeGPU` is invoked to invalidate the data on the CPU. In the write-through protocol, `writeGPU` is never invoked, but instead `readCPU` is immediately called to transfer the data back to the CPU. Section 6 gives a concrete example of how the implementation of a library changes based on the protocol.

```
//execute after writing CPU address range [s,e)
TranslationRecord writeCPU(s, e) {
  entry = lookup(s, e);
  invalidateOnGPU(entry);
  return entry;
}

//execute before reading CPU address range [s,e)
TranslationRecord readCPU(s, e) {
  entry = lookup(s, e);
  if (entry.status == G) //CPU data not current
    transferToCPU(entry)
  return entry;
}

//called after a GPU method that writes [s, e)
TranslationRecord writeGPU(s, e) {
  entry = lookup(s, e);
  invalidateOnCPU(entry);
  return entry;
}

//called before a GPU method that reads [s, e)
TranslationRecord readGPU(s, e) {
  entry = lookup(s, e);
  if (entry.status == C) //GPU data not current
    transferToGPU(entry);
  return entry;
}
```

Figure 5: Operations to implement write-back protocol

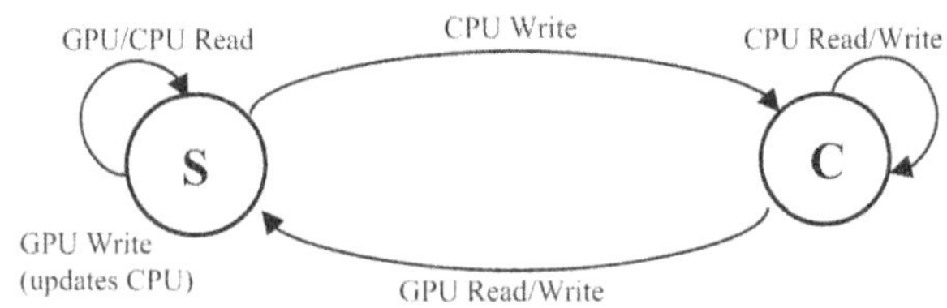

Figure 6: Write-through protocol (States: CPU/Shared)

In the write-through protocol, data is never in the G state; it can only be in C or S. The simplified protocol is shown in Figure 6. Because data is eagerly written back to the CPU, we again adopt previous terminology and call this a *write-through* protocol [21]. Note that because data is never in the G state, we no longer need to instrument CPU reads, reducing instrumentation overheads.

4.5 Instrumenting CPU Reads and Writes

SemCache provides two approaches to inserting instrumentation to implement the write-back and write-through protocols: statically-inserted instrumentation (either by the programmer or the compiler), and dynamic instrumentation using the operating system's page-protection facilities.

4.5.1 *Statically-inserted Instrumentation*

Conservatively, the programmer or compiler must guard every read or write on the CPU with appropriate instrumentation. In practice, because data movement between the CPU and GPU can only occur when GPU libraries are invoked, simple analyses can reduce this instrumentation overhead. For example, any data that will never be sent to the GPU (*i.e.*, can never be passed to a method call executed on the GPU) does not need to be instrumented. Furthermore, reads or writes to array locations that occur in loops can be guarded by a single call, with the parameters determined by array analyses that determine what portions of an array are accessed in a loop. These analyses, of which many exist, are beyond the scope of this paper; we assume that such an analysis has already been performed, allowing array accesses to be efficiently guarded.

The run-time nature of SemCache tolerates instrumentation imprecision. In particular, looking up address ranges that are not shared with the GPU does not introduce extra communication, nor does invalidating the same range more than once; these operations merely introduce extra caching overhead. Conservatively invalidating an address region is also safe: while this unnecessary invalidation causes unnecessary communication, it does not affect the correctness of the program.

Note also that although we instrument particular reads and writes, as well as particular GPU operations, to perform our caching, the cache lookups, etc., are based on address ranges. As a result, program behaviors such as aliasing do not present correctness problems; the caching is performed based on the underlying memory, not the specific name given to that memory.

Even after removing unnecessary instrumentation through the above analyses, and avoiding the instrumentation of reads on the CPU with the write-through protocol, invoking `writeCPU` before every write to data that may reside on the GPU still introduces unnecessary instrumentation. For example, on a write to data that has already been invalidated on the GPU, it is redundant to look up the data and "re-invalidate" it. Developing an analysis to remove redundant instrumentation is a subject for future work.

4.5.2 *Page-protection-based Instrumentation*

Rather than using statically-inserted instrumentation of CPU reads and writes to drive its protocols, SemCache can also use the operating system's virtual memory system to detect when `readCPU` and `writeCPU` should be invoked. For each data structure that SemCache tracks on the CPU, SemCache sets page protection flags for all the pages the data structure spans. The page protection flags are set according to the state of the data structure. If the structure is in G state, its pages are set to `PROT_NONE`; if the structure is in S state, its pages are set to `PROT_READ`; and if the structure is in C state, the pages are set to `PROT_READ | PROT_WRITE`. If a CPU access triggers a page fault, SemCache invokes `readCPU` or `writeCPU` as appropriate to change the data structure's state in the cache and perform any necessary communication. The structure's page protection flags are then reset to correspond to its new cache state.

Note that although *detection* of accesses that require communication occurs at the page granularity, *communication* does not: if a structure needs to be communicated from the GPU to the CPU, SemCache transfers the entire structure, and changes the status of all of the associated pages on the CPU. This preserves SemCache's variable-granularity advantages.

The advantage of page-based invalidations over statically-inserted invalidations is that these invalidations are handled fully automatically; no additional instrumentation or compiler analysis is required. However, there are disadvantages as well: to work correctly with page-protection operations, and to avoid false sharing issues, page-based invalidations require that a program's memory layout must be changed to ensure that all data structures that may be communicated to the GPU are page-aligned and padded out to page boundaries.

We note that this page-based strategy is similar to that used by DyManD [10]. However, unlike DyManD, SemCache still tracks data structures and maintains mappings between the CPU and GPU according to semantic information, rather than requiring direct memory mapping between the CPU and GPU. In addition to allowing programs whose working sets exceed GPU memory, SemCache's approach allows for *semantic links* to be formed between data on the CPU and data on the GPU, as the next section explains.

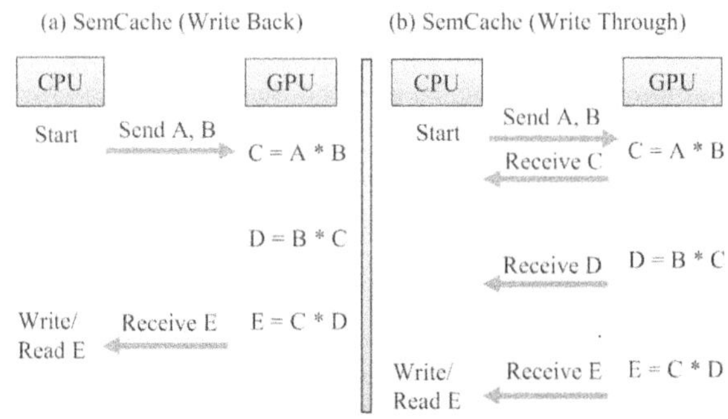

Figure 7: SemCache communication model

4.6 SemCache in Practice

Figure 7 shows the data movement performed by our system on the simple example of Figure 1 using the two different protocols. We note that when using the write-back protocol (Figure 7(a)), SemCache performs the minimum required data movement (*cf.* Figure 2(b)). At the first invocation of matrix-multiply, `A` and `B` are transferred to the GPU, and SemCache tracks them in S state. When `C` is computed, it is tracked in G state. Because both `B` and `C` are current on the GPU, later invocations of matrix multiply need not perform any more data transfer. Finally, `E` will be transferred back to the CPU once that matrix is read by other portions of the program. In the write-through protocol (Figure 7(b)), the amount of communication from the CPU to the GPU is minimal. However, because GPU results are eagerly communicated back to the CPU, we see that some extra communication is performed from the GPU to the CPU.

Crucially, because all of the necessary instrumentation is either automatically inserted or encapsulated in a GPU library (see Section 6), programmers can simply use SemCache-enhanced GPU libraries as drop-in replacements for their existing libraries.

5. SEMANTIC MAPPING WITH SemCache

This section discusses how the basic principles of SemCache can be extended and generalized to achieve additional savings. In particular, we describe how ancillary structures can be added to SemCache to allow it to "cache" the results of arbitrary functional computations, essentially allowing SemCache to serve as a memoizing service for GPU computations. This facility can be used for many purposes, from avoiding expensive recomputations (*e.g.*, storing only the factorized forms of matrices on the GPU) to performing data layout transformations (*e.g.*, mapping row-major data structures on the CPU to column-major layouts on the GPU). In essence, instead of directly mapping between CPU and GPU data, SemCache can create a *semantic link* between data on the CPU and a transformed version of that data on the GPU.

To see how SemCache can create these semantic links, we note that memoization effectively maps a particular input of a function to its pre-computed output. That is, for a function $f : X \to Y$, a memoized input x is used to look up its previously-computed output y, rather than evaluating $f(x)$. If we consider x as data residing on the CPU, and y as data residing on the GPU, then we can abstract SemCache's default behavior as simply the memoization of the identity function $f(x) = x$. For a given input (*i.e.*, data on the CPU), SemCache provides the previously-computed (*i.e.*, previously-communicated) output (*i.e.*. data on the GPU). In other words, SemCache is indexed by inputs on the CPU and provides a map to the results of the identity function stored on the GPU.

We can see that there is no need for SemCache's operation to be restricted to memoizing the identity function on to the GPU. The results of other functions can be memoized as well. Consider performing matrix factorization (*e.g.*, LU factorization) as an intermediate step in equation solve (GESV), the factorization is not saved. Such factorizations on the GPU are time consuming, so repeatedly factorizing a matrix can be wasteful. Instead, we can use an extended version of SemCache to cache the *results* of the factorization on the GPU, instead of just the inputs to the factorization operation.

Figure 8 shows how SemCache is extended. The same address ranges tracked by the baseline cache are used to index into a computation cache, which stores the GPU location of the *results* of a particular computation. Since this data is computation-specific, each type of computation to be memoized will need separate lookup tables. Note that the computation structures need not separately track the status of the data. If the data in the main cache is ever invalidated on the GPU (*i.e.*, its status is changed to C), the corresponding entries in any computation caches are simply removed.

To attempt to skip performing a GPU computation on an address range $[s, e)$, SemCache takes the following steps. First, the range is found in the main cache. If the status of the range is S or G, the lookup is repeated in the computation cache, and, if a result is found, the GPU computation can be elided. If the status of the range is C, or there is no entry in the computation cache, the GPU computation is performed, the status of the range is set to S, and the computation cache is updated.

We note that the particular set of lookups, and particular data stored, is based on the semantics of the computation being cached. Using SemCache to create semantic links hence requires adding instrumentation to GPU libraries to perform the necessary lookups, etc. Nevertheless, this instrumentation can be completely encapsulated in a library, and its effects need not be visible to the programmer, preserving the library as a drop-in replacement.

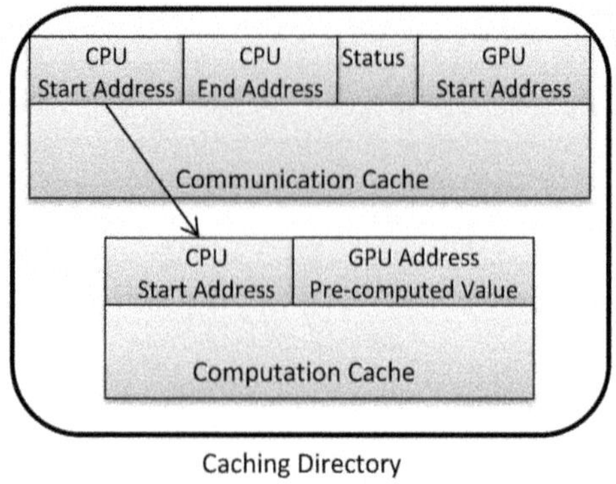

Figure 8: Caching Directory Components

```
cudaMalloc(A) //Allocate space on device mem.
cudaMalloc(B) //Allocate space on device mem.
cudaMalloc(C) //Allocate space on device mem.

cublasSetMatrix(A) //Move matrix A to device
cublasSetMatrix(B) //Move matrix B to device
cublasSetMatrix(C) //Move matrix C to device

cublasDgemm(TRANSA,TRANSB,M,N,K,ALPHA,
  A,LDA,B,LDB,BETA,C,LDC)

cublasGetMatrix(C) //Get matrix C from device
```

Figure 9: Matrix multiply using CUBLAS code

6. IMPLEMENTATION

To demonstrate how SemCache can be used to improve the performance of GPU computation libraries, we use it to produce a drop-in replacement for BLAS. This allows programmers to replace BLAS calls in their code with calls to our library, automatically offloading computation to the GPU and handling memory management transparently. The GPU kernels of our library are based on the corresponding CUBLAS implementations. Our library supports either the write-back protocol or the write-through protocol, controlled by a compile-time flag. If instrumentation-based invalidation is used, then CPU reads and writes must be instrumented as described in Section 4.4. If page-based invalidations are used instead, no instrumentation need be inserted, but `malloc` calls must be modified to page-align allocations and pad to page boundaries to avoid false sharing, as described in Section 4.5.2.

Figure 9 shows the sequence of calls that would be required to use CUBLAS to perform matrix multiply, with all communication explicitly managed by the programmer. In contrast, Figure 10 shows the interface for the SemCache-enhanced version of matrix multiply.

Figure 11 shows how matrix multiply is implemented. Under the hood, we still invoke the CUBLAS matrix multiply method. However, all communication is managed by SemCache, and is only performed when necessary. When SemCache is called, the caching directory is searched for each matrix using the start and end address in the main memory. The start address is the pointer address and the end address is calculated using the matrix size. The cache keeps a record

```
SemCacheDemm(TRANSA,TRANSB,M,N,K,ALPHA,
     A,LDA,B,LDB,BETA,C,LDC)
```

Figure 10: SemCache library interface

```
SemCacheDemm(TRANSA,TRANSB,M,N,K,ALPHA,
    A,LDA,B,LDB,BETA,C,LDC)
{
  //A stored on CPU in memory range [A, A+(M*K*8))
  //A will be read by GPU, its state will be "S"
  entryA = readGPU(A, A + (M*K*8));

  //B stored on CPU in memory range [B, B+(K*N*8))
  //B will be read by GPU, its state will be "S"
  entryB = readGPU(B, B + (K*N*8))

  //C stored on CPU in memory range [C, C+(M*N*8))
  //C will be read by GPU, its state will be "S"
  entryC = readGPU(C, C + (M*N*8))

  cublasDgemm(TRANSA,TRANSB,M,N,K,ALPHA,
      entryA.gpu_s,LDA,
      entryB.gpu_s,LDB,BETA,
      entryC.gpu_s,LDC)

  //C was written by cublasDgemm
#ifdef WRITEBACK
  //If we're using write-back, writeGPU must be
      called to invalidate, C state will be "G"
  writeGPU(C, C + (M*N*8))
#else
  //If we're using write-through, we eagerly
    communicate to the CPU, C state will be "S"
  readCPU(C, C + (M*N*8))
#endif
}
```

Figure 11: Implementation of SemCache matrix multiply (DGEMM)

of the start and end address in the main memory for each matrix accessed using our library. If the matrix does not exist, it is transferred to the GPU and cached. A new record is created for it in the cache. If the matrix is found in the cache and it is in S state, then it is a hit and there is no need to transfer the matrix to the GPU. The matrix address in the GPU memory is taken from the translation record. This address is used to access the matrix using CUBLAS. If the matrix is not valid on the GPU (it is in C state), it is transferred to the GPU and the record in the cache is updated. After all of the matrices are transferred or located in the GPU memory, the CUBLAS call is executed. Then the result is transferred back to the main memory.

CUBLAS does not provide an implementation of general equation solve (GESV), instead only providing triangular solves for factorized matrices. While there exist several efficient GPU implementations of LU factorization [23, 25], our implementation instead implements equation solve in two steps: we compute the LU factorization on the CPU, then perform the equation solve on the GPU using CUBLAS's triangular-solve routines. We then use SemCache's computation caching capability to avoid performing the factorization whenever possible. This implementation was chosen to demonstrate SemCache's generalized memoization ability.

7. EXPERIMENTAL EVALUATION

Experiments were run on a server with 24 AMD Opteron 6164 HE Processors (1.7 GHz, 512 KB L2 cache), 32 GB memory, running 64-bit Fedora Linux, and NVIDIA Tesla C2070 card (6 GB memory) with a peak memory bandwidth of 144 GB/s. Three libraries were used: CUBLAS version 4.0, CULA Dense R15 and MAGMA version 1.2. Each test was run 3 times, distributed over a wide range of time, on an unloaded machine and the median time selected.

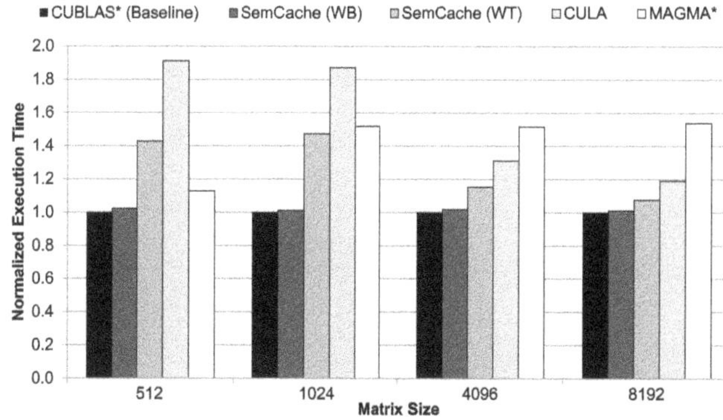

Figure 12: Test case normalized execution time *(Communication in CUBLAS and MAGMA is hand optimized)

We evaluated our library in two ways. First, we used a test case based on a series of matrix multiplications (as in Figure 1). The simplicity of the test case allowed us to perform several comparisons with other libraries, as well as test the two SemCache protocols. Nevertheless, the primary target for our work is large-scale computational applications where hand-tuning is infeasible. To study SemCache's effectiveness in this setting, we used our modified BLAS libraries (see Section 6) on a large-scale, real-world computational mechanics application, which uses finite element methods and domain decomposition to solve a structural dynamics problem.

As described in Section 4.4, SemCache can perform invalidations either with statically-inserted instrumentation at CPU reads and writes, or using a page-protection-based mechanism. We found empirically that the two approaches perform equivalently; in the experiments presented here, we use instrumentation to perform invalidations.

7.1 Test Case Performance Evaluation

Figure 12 shows the total execution time for the test case. The results are collected using CUBLAS, CULA Standard Interface (which automatically manages communication between the CPU and GPU), MAGMA and SemCache using both write-back and write-through policies. Communication in CUBLAS and MAGMA are hand tuned. The total execution time is normalized to CUBLAS execution time. The best performance is achieved by hand tuning the memory transfers using CUBLAS. CULA performance was slowed down due to the repeated unnecessary transfers. SemCache write-back performance matches the optimal communication performance using CUBLAS, but is slightly slower due to caching overhead. SemCache write-through performance is the next closest to the optimal communication performance. The slowdown is due to the eager copying back of the result to the CPU after each multiplication. MAGMA's performance varies based on the matrix size (as it uses different kernels tuned to different matrix sizes), but overall uses slower implementations than CUBLAS.

Communication savings. Figure 13 breaks down the communication performed for a medium-sized squared matrix (N=4096), distinguishing between data sent and data received. We collected data for CUBLAS, MAGMA, SemCache write-back, SemCache write-through and CULA. Hand-tuned communication for CUBLAS and MAGMA minimize the memory transfers. SemCache write-back performs exactly as much communication as hand-tuned libraries. It

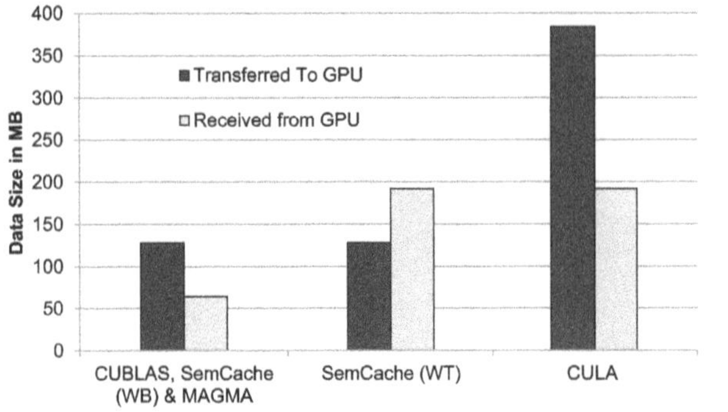

Figure 13: Test case communication results (N=4096)

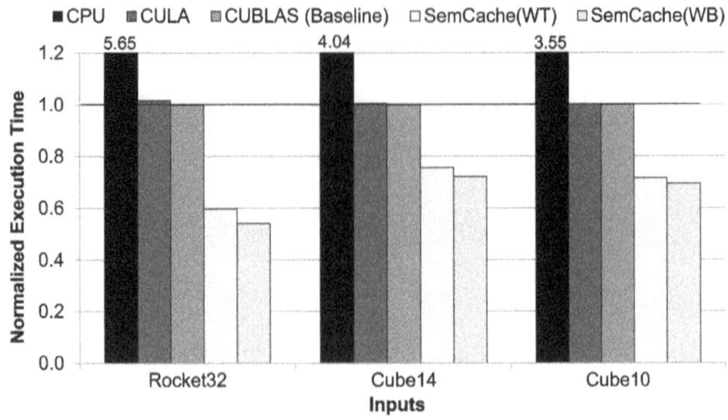

Figure 14: Testing application normalized execution time

performs the minimum amount of data transfers, as the data is already cached on the GPU and is only sent back when needed. In SemCache write-through, the data sent to the GPU is minimized. However, data is always copied back, introducing redundant communication. CULA shows the most overhead since matrices are sent to the GPU for every calculation. The results are also sent back to main memory after each calculation, introducing extra communication.

7.2 Computational Mechanics Case Study

We next tested SemCache's performance in a real-world setting. We studied a large computational mechanics application. In this application domain decomposition is used for the simulation of structural dynamics problems. Domain decomposition methods solve a boundary value problem by splitting it into smaller boundary value problems on subdomains and iterating to coordinate the solution between adjacent subdomains. Then the Newmark-beta method of numerical integration is used to solve differential equations. The application we use solves the subdomains recursively. This method was introduced by [20]. Typical structural dynamics problem include simulation of the effect of cracks in structures, or buildings under stress.

Most of the application's execution is spent performing linear algebra routines. Three main double-precision linear algebra subroutines are used: matrix multiplications (DGEMM) and scalar multiplication/vector addition (DXPY) to couple and update the subdomains results and equation solve (DGESV) to solve the system of equations at each node. Because these operations make up a large fraction of the application's computation, they are attractive targets for offloading. However, optimizing communication in this application is essentially impossible. The application has tens of thousands lines of code, and the relationship between various linear algebra operations is difficult to reason about due to recursive calls and multiple abstraction layers.

We evaluated five versions of this application. A serial CPU version that performed no offloading, a CUBLAS version with hand-inserted unoptimized communication (communication can't be optimized manually due to program abstraction), a CULA version that simply replaces all CPU BLAS calls with CULA BLAS calls, a version using our SemCache write-through library, and another version using our SemCache write-back library.

The SemCache versions of the application exploit computation caching in two ways. First, as described in Section 6, our implementation of equation solve leverages SemCache's computation-saving capabilities to memoize the results of matrix factorization. Second, the baseline CPU version of the application uses row-major storage for its matrices, while CUBLAS assumes column-major storage. SemCache thus creates a semantic link between the two representations, avoiding performing the transformation unless the data changes[2].

We used three inputs with different characteristics, ranging across various sizes: Rocket32, which has 7262 nodes and takes 246 seconds to run on the CPU; Cube14, which has 3375 nodes and takes 130 seconds to run on the CPU; and Cube10, which has 1331 nodes and takes 10 seconds to run on the CPU.

Execution time. Figure 14 shows the total execution time for the five variants of the application, across the three inputs. Run time is normalized to the CUBLAS variant. All inputs gained from three to six times speedups when running on the GPU over the CPU version. CULA and CUBLAS performance was very similar. CULA uses CUBLAS as an underlying library with a few additional optimizations. Both approaches incur the cost of extra communication. Using SemCache with write-through policy, the performance improved (30% to 40%) over the GPU CUBLAS baseline version due to the communication savings from caching. SemCache with write-back gained an additional 4–10% over write-through, as data was only transferred back to the CPU when needed. The inputs speedup ranges are different based on the structure of input and domain decomposition. Inputs whose subdomains have larger shared interfaces generate more matrices that will be repeatedly reused. As a result, caching yields more benefits.

Communication savings. Table 1 shows the amount of data transferred to the GPU. The SemCache results show the optimal communication for the application since all of the calculations were computed on the GPU and the hit rate was 100%. Using SemCache, more than 80% of the unoptimized communication is reduced. Both write-through and write-back policies reduced the size of the data sent to the GPU. Write-back policy reduced the size of the data received from the GPU. These savings are a result of eliminating redundant transfers since the data in the testing application is shared between different subdomains. The same matrices will be reused multiple times for different subdomains.

[2]Because the row-major/column-major transformation is only necessary due to an implementation detail of the original application, we factor out the transformation time for the non-SemCache versions in all our results.

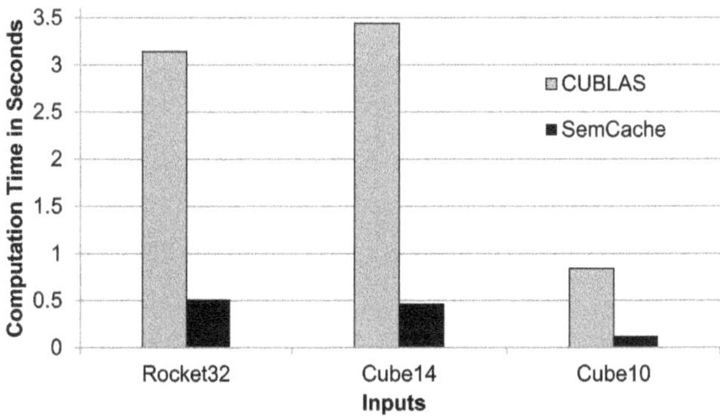

Figure 15: Computation time for factorization

Input/Library	CUBLAS		SemCache	
	Sent	Received	Sent	Received
Rocket32	23.70	5.58	2.02	2.45
Cube14	10.67	1.53	1.01	0.63
Cube10	3.01	0.33	0.29	0.13

Table 1: Size of transferred data using CUBLAS versus SemCache (in GB)

Computation caching. We evaluated the savings of performing computation saving for LU factorization. Figure 15 shows the LU factorization time on the CPU for out testing application. Using SemCache, repeated computations are eliminated since the factorized matrices are already cached. Fewer factorizations are needed, which reduces the total computation time by more than 80% .

Caching overhead. Table 2 shows the data transfer time to GPU for different inputs. The results show that the caching overhead is very low (less than 4% of SemCache total runtime). The overhead comes mainly from searching and updating the cache directory. The transfer time using our library including the caching overhead is significantly less than the transfer time for CUBLAS without caching. We note, however, that our low caching overhead is due to SemCache's variable granularity, which requires fewer invalidations and fewer lookups.

Instrumentation statistics. For our testing application, more than 10,000 lines of code and around 45 BLAS and LAPACK calls are used. No writeCPU invalidations were needed because the all of the calculations were computed on the GPU. For the write back protocol, reads were instrumented using readCPU API. Seven API calls were needed.

Table 3 shows how many times matrix multiply (GEMM), equation solve (GESV), scalar multiplication and vector addition (XPY), copy (COPY), lookup and invalidation operations were executed. The lookup matches exactly the number of matrices sent to the GPU (3 per GEMM, 2 per GESV, XPY and COPY).

Comparison with fixed-granularity approaches. One of the primary advantages of SemCache over distributed-shared memory systems is its ability to track data and perform communication with variable granularity, rather than using a fixed granularity. To quantify this benefit, we modified the page-protection version of SemCache (Section 4.5.2) to perform communication in page-sized chunks, rather than tracking entire data structures[3]. Figure 16 compares the

Input/Library	CUBLAS	SemCache	
	Transfer	Transfer	Caching Over.
Rocket32	11.09	0.86	0.38
Cube14	5.27	0.47	0.05
Cube10	1.32	0.12	0.023

Table 2: Data transfer time from CPU to GPU for CUBLAS versus SemCache with overhead (in seconds)

Input/Op.	GEMM	GESV	XPY	COPY	Lookup
Rocket32	6720	1209	3520	480	30578
Cube14	944	233	688	104	4882
Cube10	470	131	394	62	2584

Table 3: Operations count at runtime

CUBLAS baseline with this DSM-like approach as well as SemCache's variable-granularity approach on our case study[4]. Clearly, fixed-granularity tracking does not perform as well as SemCache.

Interestingly, the total amount of data communicated is the same for both the fixed-granularity and variable-granularity versions. The performance difference arises because fixed-granularity tracking breaks that communication into more discrete communication operations, incurring additional overhead. Clearly, taking advantage of semantic information to perform variable-granularity tracking and communication yields a notable performance benefit.

8. CONCLUSIONS

The proliferation of libraries of GPU kernels has made it easy to improve application performance by offloading computation to the GPU. However, using such libraries still introduces the complexity of managing explicit data movement. Unfortunately, when using these libraries with complex applications with multiple levels of abstraction, it is very difficult to reason about how multiple kernel invocations interact with one another, and hence avoid redundant communication. In this paper, we introduced SemCache, a semantics-driven caching technique that can tune its granularity based on the semantics of the GPU libraries in an application. SemCache can automatically detect and avoid redundant communication. We evaluated SemCache on a large, real-world application and showed that our approach can deliver significant performance improvements over state-of-the-art GPU libraries.

There are many promising avenues of future work. SemCache's computation-caching mechanism already supports mapping a data layout on the CPU to a different layout on the GPU. This facility can be extended to allow SemCache to track non-contiguous data structures, for example mapping a set of locations on the GPU to a single, contiguous, packed location on the GPU. We also plan to extend SemCache to support kernels distributed/offloaded across multiple GPUs and to automatically manage and optimize communication between the CPU main memory and several GPUs not only for a single kernel but for the entire application.

[3]This variant is not strictly correct, as without transferring data at matrix granularity, the semantic mapping between row-major and column-major representations cannot be maintained. Nevertheless, this variant lets us explore the penalty of page-granularity caching.

[4]Due to limitations of the page-based approach, large inputs (such as Rocket32) cannot be run.

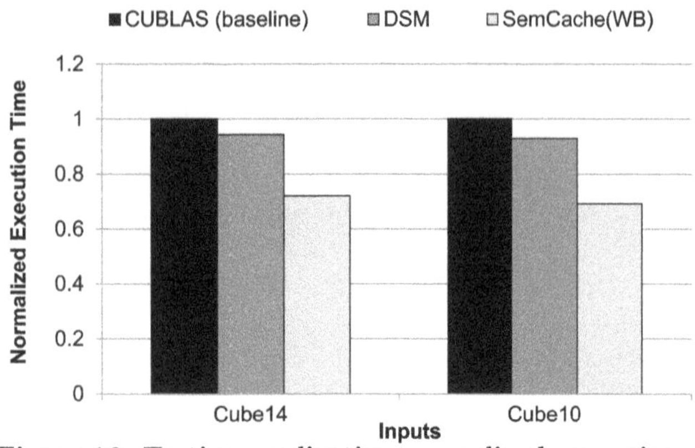

Figure 16: Testing application normalized execution time for CUBLAS, SemCache write-back and DSM

9. ACKNOWLEDGMENTS

We would like to thank Hasan Jamal, Chenyang Liu and Arun Prakash for the computational mechanics application code we used in our case study and for their support and feedback during this work. We would also like to thank the anonymous reviewers for their feedback and suggestions. This research is supported by the Department of Energy under contract DE-FC02-12ER26104. The GPU hardware we used was provided by an equipment grant from Nvidia.

References

[1] C. Amza, A. L. Cox, H. Dwarkadas, P. Keleher, H. Lu, R. Rajamony, W. Yu, and W. Zwaenepoel. TreadMarks: Shared memory computing on networks of workstations. *IEEE Computer*, 29:18–28, 1996.

[2] E. Anderson, Z. Bai, C. Bischof, S. Blackford, J. Demmel, J. Dongarra, J. Du Croz, A. Greenbaum, S. Hammarling, A. McKenney, and D. Sorensen. *LAPACK users' guide*. Society for Industrial and Applied Mathematics, Philadelphia, PA, third edition, 1999.

[3] E. Ayguadé, R. M. Badia, F. D. Igual, J. Labarta, R. Mayo, and E. S. Quintana-Ortí. An extension of the StarSs programming model for platforms with multiple GPUs. In *Proceedings of the 15th International Euro-Par Conference on Parallel Processing*, Euro-Par '09, pages 851–862, 2009.

[4] BLAS. Basic linear algebra subprograms. `http://www.netlib.org/blas/`.

[5] K. Datta, M. Murphy, V. Volkov, S. Williams, J. Carter, L. Oliker, D. Patterson, J. Shalf, and K. Yelick. Stencil computation optimization and auto-tuning on state-of-the-art multicore architectures. In *Proceedings of the 2008 ACM/IEEE conference on Supercomputing*, SC '08, pages 4:1–4:12, 2008.

[6] M. Fogue, F. D. Igual, E. S. Quintana-Ortí, and R. A. van de Geijn. Retargeting PLAPACK to clusters with hardware accelerators. In *HPCS*, pages 444–451, 2010.

[7] I. Gelado, J. E. Stone, J. Cabezas, S. Patel, N. Navarro, and W.-m. W. Hwu. An asymmetric distributed shared memory model for heterogeneous parallel systems. In *Proceedings of the fifteenth edition of ASPLOS on Architectural support for programming languages and operating systems*, ASPLOS XV, pages 347–358, 2010.

[8] M. Gonzàlez, N. Vujic, X. Martorell, E. Ayguadé, A. E. Eichenberger, T. Chen, Z. Sura, T. Zhang, K. O'Brien, and K. O'Brien. Hybrid access-specific software cache techniques for the Cell BE architecture. In *Proceedings of the 17th international conference on Parallel architectures and compilation techniques*, PACT '08, pages 292–302, 2008.

[9] J. R. Humphrey, D. K. Price, K. E. Spagnoli, A. L. Paolini, and E. J. Kelmelis. CULA: hybrid GPU accelerated linear algebra routines. *SPIE Defense and Security Symposium (DSS)*, pages 770502–770502-7, 2010.

[10] T. B. Jablin, J. A. Jablin, P. Prabhu, F. Liu, and D. I. August. Dynamically managed data for CPU-GPU architectures. In *Proceedings of the Tenth International Symposium on Code Generation and Optimization*, CGO '12, pages 165–174, 2012.

[11] T. B. Jablin, P. Prabhu, J. A. Jablin, N. P. Johnson, S. R. Beard, and D. I. August. Automatic CPU-GPU communication management and optimization. *SIGPLAN Not.*, 47(6):142–151, June 2011.

[12] J. A. Kahle, M. N. Day, H. P. Hofstee, C. R. Johns, T. R. Maeurer, and D. Shippy. Introduction to the Cell multiprocessor. *IBM Journal of Research and Development*, 49(4.5):589 –604, july 2005.

[13] M. D. Linderman, J. D. Collins, H. Wang, and T. H. Meng. Merge: a programming model for heterogeneous multi-core systems. *SIGPLAN Not.*, 43(3):287–296, Mar. 2008.

[14] C.-K. Luk, S. Hong, and H. Kim. Qilin: exploiting parallelism on heterogeneous multiprocessors with adaptive mapping. In *Proceedings of the 42nd Annual IEEE/ACM International Symposium on Microarchitecture*, MICRO 42, pages 45–55, 2009.

[15] D. Merrill, M. Garland, and A. Grimshaw. Scalable GPU graph traversal. *SIGPLAN Not.*, 47(8):117–128, Feb. 2012.

[16] B. Nitzberg and V. Lo. Distributed shared memory: a survey of issues and algorithms. *Computer*, 24(8):52 –60, aug. 1991.

[17] NVIDIA. CUDA. `http://www.nvidia.com/object/cuda_home_new.html`.

[18] NVIDIA. CUDA toolkit 4.0 CUBLAS library. `http://docs.nvidia.com/cuda/cublas/index.html`.

[19] J. A. Pienaar, A. Raghunathan, and S. Chakradhar. MDR: performance model driven runtime for heterogeneous parallel platforms. In *Proceedings of the international conference on Supercomputing*, ICS '11, pages 225–234, 2011.

[20] A. Prakash and K. D. Hjelmstad. A FETI-based multi-time-step coupling method for Newmark schemes in structural dynamics. *International Journal for Numerical Methods in Engineering*, 61(13):2183–2204, 2004.

[21] G. Quintana-Ortí, F. D. Igual, E. S. Quintana-Ortí, and R. A. van de Geijn. Solving dense linear systems on platforms with multiple hardware accelerators. *SIGPLAN Not.*, 44(4):121–130, Feb. 2009.

[22] G. Quintana-Ortí, F. D. Igual, E. S. Quintana-Ortí, and R. A. van de Geijn. Solving dense linear systems on platforms with multiple hardware accelerators. In *Proceedings of the 14th ACM SIGPLAN symposium on Principles and practice of parallel programming*, PPoPP '09, pages 121–130, 2009.

[23] P. D. S. Tomov, R. Nath and J. Dongarra. MAGMA version 0.2 users' guide. `http://icl.eecs.utk.edu/magma/`, 2009.

[24] C.-Y. Shei, P. Ratnalikar, and A. Chauhan. Automating GPU computing in MATLAB. In *Proceedings of the international conference on Supercomputing*, ICS '11, pages 245–254, 2011.

[25] V. Volkov and J. W. Demmel. Benchmarking GPUs to tune dense linear algebra. In *Proceedings of the 2008 ACM/IEEE conference on Supercomputing*, SC '08, pages 31:1–31:11, 2008.

Exploiting Uniform Vector Instructions for GPGPU Performance, Energy Efficiency, and Opportunistic Reliability Enhancement

Ping Xiang, Yi Yang*, Mike Mantor#, Norm Rubin#, Lisa R. Hsu#, Huiyang Zhou

Dept. of Electrical and Computer Engineering
North Carolina State University
Raleigh, NC, USA
{pxiang, hzhou}@ncsu.edu

*Dept. of Computing Systems Architecture
NEC Laboratories America
Princeton, NJ, USA
yyang@nec-labs.com

#Graphics Products Group
AMD Inc.
Orlando, FL, USA
Michael.Mantor, Norman.Rubin, Lisa.Hsu}@amd.com

Abstract

State-of-art graphics processing units (GPUs) employ the single-instruction multiple-data (SIMD) style execution to achieve both high computational throughput and energy efficiency. As previous works have shown, there exists significant computational redundancy in SIMD execution, where different execution lanes operate on the same operand values. Such value locality is referred to as uniform vectors. In this paper, we first show that besides redundancy within a uniform vector, different vectors can also have the identical values. Then, we propose detailed architecture designs to exploit both types of redundancy. For redundancy within a uniform vector, we propose to either extend the vector register file with token bits or add a separate small scalar register file to eliminate redundant computations as well as redundant data storage. For redundancy across different uniform vectors, we adopt instruction reuse, proposed originally for CPU architectures, to detect and eliminate redundancy. The elimination of redundant computations and data storage leads to both significant energy savings and performance improvement. Furthermore, we propose to leverage such redundancy to protect arithmetic-logic units (ALUs) and register files against hardware errors. Our detailed evaluation shows that our proposed design has low hardware overhead and achieves performance gains, up to 23.9% and 12.0% on average, along with energy savings, up to 24.8% and 12.6% on average, as well as a 21.1% and 14.1% protection coverage for ALUs and register files, respectively.

Categories and Subject Descriptors

C.1.4 [**Processor Architectures**]: Parallel Architectures

General Terms

Performance, Design, Experimentation

Keywords

GPGPU, Redundancy

1. INTRODUCTION

State-of-art GPUs manage, schedule, and execute parallel threads in groups. While each individual thread has its own register state, a group of threads, called a warp/wavefront, share a single program counter (PC) as well as the instruction fetch, decode, and processing logic. When executing an instruction, different threads in a warp operate upon different data, which are typically specified using their thread identifiers (ids). To hide instruction execution latencies, especially off-chip memory accesses, GPUs are designed to host a high number of warps so that when one warp is stalled, another warp can issue instructions so as to keep the arithmetic/logic units (ALUs) busy. As a result, throughput-oriented GPUs can spend most energy budget and die area on computational logic rather than sophisticated instruction processing logic as in latency-oriented central processing units (CPUs). The combined single-instruction multiple-data (SIMD) style execution and warp-level parallelism, also referred to as single-instruction multiple-thread (SIMT) processing, is the key for GPU's high energy efficiency and computational throughput. In this paper, we propose a novel approach to further improve the performance, energy efficiency and reliability of GPU computing.

Our approach is built upon the following observations on SIMT processing. During SIMD execution, different threads in the same warp are supposed to operate upon different data. However, certain program structures in the kernel code, such as loops, and some intermediate computations, including loading data from the same address, calculating configuration numbers, or initializing registers with constant values, result in identical computations among the threads in a warp. In such cases, different threads in a warp have the same source values and therefore produce the same output. This value locality was referred to as uniform vectors [5]. In this paper, we observe that such computational redundancy does not only exist among the threads within a warp, but also happens at the warp level. In other words, different warps may have identical input and output values. Therefore, we refer to them as *intra-warp* and *inter-warp uniform vector* instructions, respectively.

We propose detailed architecture designs to detect and remove redundancy resulting from intra- and inter-warp uniform vector instructions to achieve both performance gains and energy savings, and to leverage such redundancy for reliability enhancement. For intra-warp uniform vector instructions, we present two designs. The first one adds a token bit to each vector register to detect and track intra-warp redundancy. For an instruction, when all of its source operands have this token bit set and there is no control divergence, this instruction is recognized as an intra-warp uniform vector instruction. In this case, only one thread in the warp will carry out the computation, store the result in its destination scalar register, and set the token bit associated with the destination vector register. Additional multiplexers (MUXes) are introduced to reuse the existing broadcast logic to feed the register value to other threads, when it is used in subsequent instructions as a source operand. In our second design, we propose to add a separate small scalar register file (SRF) to eliminate redundant values in the vector register file (VRF). For uniform vector accesses, this approach replaces VRF reads and writes with SRF operations, thereby lowering the power consumption. Furthermore, the SRF simplifies the design for the corner case when a uniform vector register is used as both a source and the destination operand. A register renaming table and a freelist are introduced to manage the SRF. Note that although register renaming apparently adds the complexity of instruction processing, it is done at the warp level, therefore the overhead is amortized by the high number of threads (e.g., 32) in a warp.

To detect and eliminate inter-warp redundancy, we leverage the idea of instruction reuse [19] and propose a warp-level instruction reuse buffer (IRB). When an instruction hits in the IRB, it skips execution and directly writes back the results stored in the IRB into the destination register. To reduce the complexity of the warp-level IRB, we choose to allow only the instructions, which are detected as intra-warp uniform, to access it. This eliminates the need for the IRB to store and compare the input values of all the threads in a warp.

We model our proposed designs in a cycle-accurate GPGPU architecture simulator and our experimental results show that our proposed deigns achieve significant energy savings, up to 25.3% and 12.7% on average, along with performance gains of up to 23.9% and 12.0% on average.

Since GPUs are getting more and more popular in general-purpose computations, there is a growing concern on reliability [8][18]. We propose to leverage both intra- and inter-warp uniform vector instructions for opportunistic reliability enhancement. For intra-warp uniform vector instructions, we simply use two threads to carry out the computations and store the two results to provide the necessary redundancy. For inter-warp uniform vector instructions, we choose to protect the warp-level IRB with parity bits. Our results show that our approach achieves 21.1% and 14.1% reliability coverage for ALUs and register files, respectively, with no performance penalty and only 0.29% dynamic energy overhead (or 0.14% in total energy) compared to our proposed designs that completely eliminate the redundancy from uniform vector instructions.

The rest of the paper is organized as follows. Section 2 presents the background and quantifies how often intra- and inter-warp uniform vector instructions exist in typical GPGPU workloads. Section 3 describes in detail our architectural designs. The experimental methodology and results are discussed in Section 4 and Section 5, respectively. Related work is addressed in Section 6. Section 7 concludes the paper.

2. BACKGROUND AND MOTIVATION

Modern GPUs employ the SIMT programming model. A GPU program, commonly referred to as a kernel, follows the single-program multiple-data (SPMD) model. A kernel specifies the workloads of all threads and differentiates them using thread ids. The threads are organized into a two-level hierarchy. The kernel is launched to a GPU as a grid of threads, which contains multiple thread blocks/workgroups. Each thread block/workgroup in turn contains multiple warps/wavefronts. A warp/wavefront is a group of threads that are executed in the SIMD manner by sharing the PC.

In GPU hardware, a high number of cores are also organized in a hierarchy. Each GPU has multiple Streaming Multiprocessors (SMs) or Compute Units (CUs). Each SM/CU in turn has multiple streaming processors (SPs)/processing elements (PEs). The resources in each SM/CU include a vector register file, the shared memory, and L1 caches. The threads in the same thread block/workgroup will be executed on the same SM/CU so as to support synchronization and data exchange among the threads in the same thread block/workgroup. One SM can host one or more thread blocks depending on the resource requirement of each thread block.

In the SIMT model, each thread has its own register state. As a result, each thread needs to carry out computations even they are essentially scalar operations. For example, in the code shown in Figure 1 , we can see that the loop control '(int i = 0; i < width; i++)' on line 3 is independent on the thread id. As all the threads in a warp are executed in lock steps, the corresponding instructions to the loop control will have identical input and output values for all the threads in the warp. Such value locality among the threads in a warp has also been observed in [5] and is referred to as uniform vectors given the similarity between a warp in SIMT architecture and a vector in vector processors. In this paper, we adopt this term to indicate that an operand is the same for all the threads in a warp. For an instruction, if all of its source operands, including the current active mask, are uniform vectors, it is called a uniform vector instruction.

```
1. __global__ void foo (float *A, float *B, float *C, int width) {
2.   int idx = (blockIdx.x*blockDim.x+threadIdx.x);
3.   for (int i = 0; i < width; i++) {
4.     a = A[i+idx*width];
5.     if(B[idx] > 0)
6.       b = C[i];
7.     else
8.       b = 0;
9.   }...}
```

Figure 1. A code example to illustrate both intra- and inter-warp uniform vector instructions.

The code in Figure 1 also shows that besides the identical computation (or redundancy) among the threads within a warp, there exist identical computations among different warps. For example, the computation on line 2 'blockIdx.x*blockDim.x' only depends on thread block ids. All the warps in the same thread block will perform the same computation. In addition, the loop control on line 3 may also result in redundancy across different warps as long as one warp reaches the same loop iteration before another leaves it. Due to the commonly used round-robin warp scheduling policy [11], the warps in a thread block usually make similar progress. As a result, these warps tend to carry out identical loop iterator update and bound check operations. To differentiate identical computations within a warp and across multiple warps, we refine the definition of uniform vector instructions and refer to them as intra-warp uniform vector instructions and inter-warp uniform vector instructions.

In the current GPU architectures, both intra- and inter-warp uniform vector instructions result in redundant computations as well as redundant register file reads and writes since the exactly same computation is repeated for many threads in the same warp or different warps. As a warp/wavefront contains 32/64 threads in NVIDIA/AMD GPUs, one intra-warp uniform vector will lead to 31/63 redundant computations. To address this issue, a scalar unit is added to each CU in AMD's latest Graphics Core Next (GCN) architecture [1] and it relies on the compiler to identify the uniform vector instructions and to encode them as scalar instructions to be executed in the scalar unit. The scalar unit in AMD's GCN architecture has a scalar register file, which can forward scalar register values to the SPs/PEs when they are used as source operands for vector instructions, and a scalar ALU to perform scalar computations.

Although the GCN architecture reduces redundant operations, several limitations remain. First, the scalar instructions are generated using the compiler and there are fundamental limitations of static analysis by the compiler. For example, the if-statement 'if (B[idx]>0)' on line 5 in Figure 1 may result in control divergence among the threads in a warp, i.e., some threads satisfy the condition while others do not. Therefore, the compiler cannot classify the operations 'b = C[i]' on line 6 and 'b = 0' on line 8 as scalar operations although they do not have data dependence on the thread id. In other words, the control dependency on thread id makes the static analysis very challenging. Second, the scalar unit incurs additional hardware cost and the dedicated scalar instructions are not compatible with previous GPUs with the same vector instruction set architecture (ISA). Third, the AMD GCN cannot handle inter-warp uniform vectors since the scalar instructions are embedded in the same instruction stream as vector operations, which are executed separately for each warp.

Before discussing our proposed solution, we quantify how often uniform vector instructions present in typical GPGPU workloads. We profile a set of applications using GPGPUSim [2] with the detailed methodology presented in Section 4. Our results are shown in Figure 2. In this experiment, for each vector instruction that is not control divergent, we consider that there are 32 scalar operations, one for each thread due to the warp size of 32. For each intra-warp uniform instruction, we consider that there are 31 redundant operations. For each inter-warp uniform vector instruction being detected, we consider that there are 32 redundant operations when we focus only on inter-warp uniform vector instructions. When we target at both types of uniform vector instructions, for each inter-warp uniform vector instruction being detected, we consider that there is 1 redundant operation since 31 of them are already counted as intra-warp redundant ones. Then, we normalize the numbers of redundant operations to the total number of dynamic scalar instructions and report the ratios in Figure 2. The reason why we do not use the number of vector instructions is due to the presence of control divergence. In such a case, the number of scalar instructions captures the application's computational needs more accurately than the number of vector instructions. Note that in our redundant instruction statistics, we do not include branch instructions as the PC is already updated at a per-warp basis in SIMT architectures. Memory instructions are not considered as redundant operations either as we assume the memory coalescing logic and miss status handling registers (MSHRs) already detect/merge redundant memory requests.

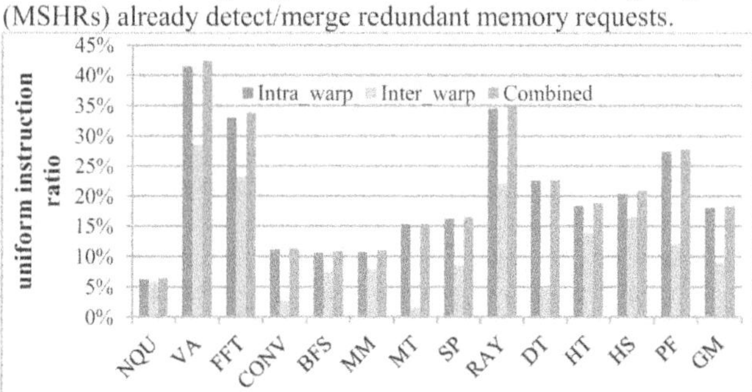

Figure 2 Percentage of redundant operations resulting from intra-and inter-warp uniform vector instructions.

As we can see from Figure 2, among the 13 applications under our study, there exist significant redundant operations. The contribution from intra-warp uniform vector instructions can be as high as 41.5% and 18.1% on average using the geometric mean (GM). The inter-warp uniform vector instructions also result in up to 28.5% and an average of 8.9% redundant operations. When both types are combined, up to 42.4% and an average of 18.4% of all scalar operations are redundant. Although the difference between intra-warp and combined intra- and inter-warp results is apparently small, it does not mean that the contribution from inter-warp uniform vector instruction would be low. The reason is that we only count 1 redundant scalar operation for each inter-warp uniform vector instruction as discussed above. As shown in Section 5, eliminating redundancy from inter-warp uniform vector instructions can lead to significant performance gains and energy savings even after we already leverage intra-warp uniform vector instructions.

3. ARCHITECTURE DESIGN

The significant amount of uniform vector instructions presents an interesting opportunity for optimizing SIMT architectures. First, eliminating redundant computations and register file accesses can reduce dynamic power consumption. Second, when the number of SPs in an SM is smaller than the warp size, converting an intra-warp uniform vector instruction to a scalar operation can improve the instruction issue rate so as to improve the performance. Considering a warp size of 32 and a SIMD width of 8 (i.e., 8 SPs per SM), it takes 4 cycles to issue a regular vector instruction. As discussed in Section 3.1.1, by converting a uniform vector instruction into a scalar one, we can increase the instruction issue rate to 1 instruction per cycle as only one SP is needed to carry out the computation. Third, the execution of any inter-warp uniform vector instruction can be skipped after it is detected, resulting in performance enhancement due to the reduced execution latency. Fourth, redundant computations and data storage can also be leveraged for hardware error detection to opportunistically improve the reliability. In this section, we present our proposed architecture design to achieve these goals. Figure 3 shows the baseline architecture of an SM for our discussion.

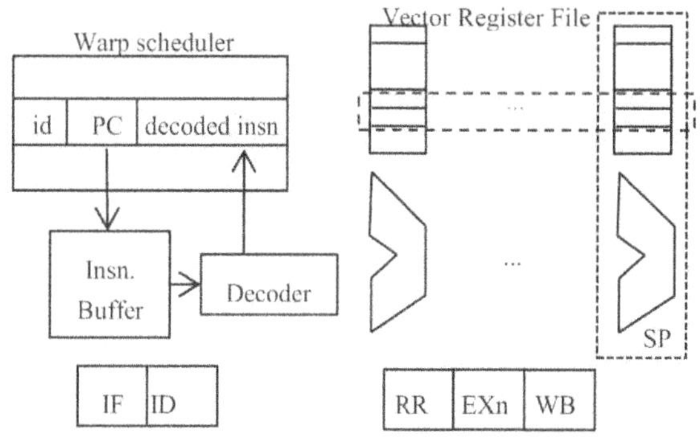

Figure 3. The baseline architecture of an SM. The number of EX stage depends on the instruction latency.

As shown in Figure 3, there is a warp scheduler in an SM and it issues instructions from the 'ready' warps, meaning that they have all the source operands ready for their current instructions. During the register read (RR) stage, the multi-lane vector register file (VRF) is accessed to provide the source operands for each thread in the warp. The aggregated registers from all the threads in a warp can be viewed as a vector register. For example, for an instruction 'ADD r1, r2, r3', the register r1 for all the threads in warp can be viewed as a vector register VR1, which contains 32 scalar registers. Here, we use the notation 'VR1.i' to denote the scalar register r1 of the ith thread in a warp. Depending on the number of

SPs (denoted as 'NumSP') in an SM, which are used for executing instructions from a warp, the warp scheduler issues one instruction to the SPs every 'warpsize/NumSP' cycles. In NVIDIA GTX285 GPUs, NumSP is 8, and in GTX480 (aka Fermi architecture), NumSP is 16 as each warp occupies 16 SP lanes. Typically, the threads in a warp are assigned to the SPs in a round-robin manner. In other words, if NumSP is 8, the first SP (i.e., SP0) executes the instruction for thread 0, 8, 16, 24; the second SP executes thread 1, 9, 17, 25; etc. Also, the VRF lane in each SP provides the corresponding register operands. For example, with 8 SPs in an SM, the VRF lane in SP0 provides VR1.0, VR1.8, VR1.16, and VR1.24. The warp id in the warp scheduler is used to map the same architectural registers in different warps into different physical vector registers.

3.1. Exploiting Intra-Warp Uniform Vector Instructions

To detect intra-warp uniform vectors, we start with the instruction decode (ID) stage in the GPU pipeline. During the ID stage, an instruction's source operands are checked to see whether they are uniform vectors. If an operand is an immediate or a special register used for thread id independent information such as thread block dimensions, it is detected as a uniform vector. An instruction is detected as a uniform vector instruction if all its source operands are uniform and the current active mask is all 1's, indicating that the instruction is not under a control divergent path. In this case, the destination register will be a uniform vector. Next, we propose two architectural designs to implement the propagation of uniform vectors. The two designs differ in where to store uniform vectors. One reuses the VRF and extends it with token bits. The other introduces a small scalar register file (SRF) to replace VRF accesses with SRF accesses.

3.1.1. Token-based design

In this design, we add a token file, which contains 1 token bit for each vector register. A token bit is set in two scenarios: (1) when a uniform vector instruction is detected and is updating its destination vector register, and (2) when the value to be written back is from the broadcast path even the instruction is not yet detected as uniform. The broadcast path, which is used for accessing the same address in either shared memory or global memory, ensures that all the threads in the warp will have the same value. A token bit is reset when the corresponding vector register is redefined by a regular (i.e., non-uniform) vector instruction.

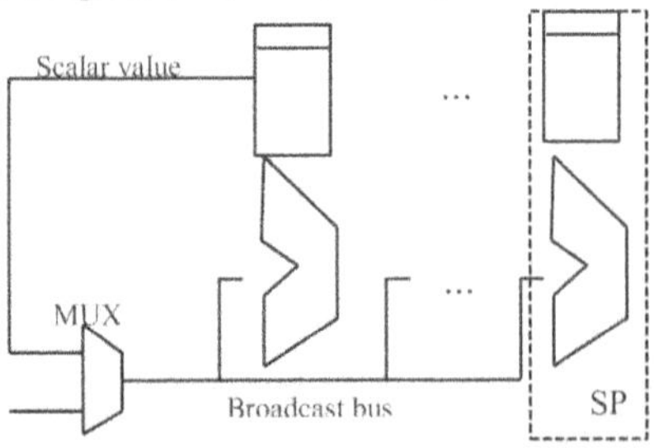

Figure 4. Reusing the existing broadcast logic to feed the scalar value to multiple SPs.

The token file will be accessed during the ID stage to determine whether an instruction is a uniform vector one. If so, once this instruction is issued, it does not need to update all the 32 scalar registers in the destination vector register. Instead, updating one of them is sufficient. As this vector register can be used as a source operand of a non-uniform vector instruction, we add a MUX to reuse the existing broadcast bus, as shown in Figure 4, to provide the data. This way, an intra-warp uniform vector instruction is essentially converted to a scalar one. Compared to a regular vector instruction, it saves (warpsize − 1) computations as well as the associated read and write accesses to the VRF lanes.

Another important advantage of converting a uniform vector instruction into a scalar one is the opportunity to improve instruction issue rate. As our uniform vector instruction detection happens in the ID stage, the warp scheduler can increase the issue rate from one per 'warpsize/NumSP' cycle to one every cycle for uniform vector instructions. In other words, after a uniform vector instruction, which is converted to a scalar one, is issued, the warp scheduler can issue another ready instruction in the next cycle.

Although the token-based design is relatively straightforward, there are several corner cases that need to be carefully considered. First, when a uniform vector register is used as both a source and the destination register, such as in the case of 'VR1 = VR1 + VR2' where the token bit of VR1 is set but the token bit of VR2 is not. Depending on the number of SPs in an SM, the source scalar value may be overwritten before its due time. For example, assuming 8 SPs in an SM, threads 0-7 in the warp will execute the instruction before other threads. If the scalar value of the uniform vector VR1 is stored in VR1.0 (i.e., the register for the first thread in the warp), this value (VR1.0) may be updated with 'VR1.0+VR2.0' before it is used for the remaining threads, e.g., thread 31 'VR1.31 = VR1.0+VR2.31'. To resolve this issue, we propose to store the scalar value of a uniform vector VRx in VRx.N, where N is determined as 'N = warp size − NumSP'. In the case of NumSP being 8, VR1.24 is used to store the scalar value of the uniform vector register VR1. This ensure that there is no write-after-read data hazard for instructions like 'Add VR1, VR1, VR2' as thread 24 is among the last patch of threads to be executed in a warp. When there are as many SPs as the warp size, all the threads in a warp will be executed at the same time, this hazard disappears naturally and the formula can still be used to specify VRx.0 to be used for the scalar value. Note that for the instruction 'Add VR1, VR1, #2' with the token bit set for VR1, there is no hazard since this instruction will be detected as a uniform vector instruction. The token bit will remain set and only the ALU in SP0 will be used to carry out the computation (VR1.24 = VR1.24 + #2).

Second, control divergence complicates the processing of uniform vectors. Consider the case with the instruction 'VR1 = VR1 + 2' with the token bit of VR1 set and the active mask indicates that only threads 24-31 are to be executed in a warp. Although our intra-warp uniform vector instruction detection logic will detect it as a non-uniform vector instruction due to the condition on the active mask, there still is a correctness issue. The reason is that the scalar value VR1.24 will be overwritten with 'VR1.24+2' and for threads 0 to 23, the register VR1's value would be corrupted. To resolve this problem, we propose the following copy-on-write solution. When the warp scheduler finds that the current instruction is under a control divergent path by checking the active mask and the instruction has its destination register being the same as one of its source uniform vector operands, the warp scheduler inserts a copy instruction, which explicitly copies the scalar value of the uniform vector to all of its scalar registers. This way, all the threads have their private copy of the register and the correctness is ensured. As we show in Section 5.1, this copy-on-write happens fairly infrequently, resulting in negligible performance overhead.

3.1.2. Scalar register file based design

In this design, we introduce a separate scalar register file (SRF) to store the scalar value of uniform vectors. The intra-warp vector instruction detection logic is the same as the token-based design described in Section 3.1.1. The advantage of the SRF-based design over the token-based design is that for uniform vectors, it replaces the vector register file (VRF) accesses with SRF accesses. In state-of-art GPUs, an SM typically has a very large vector register file (e.g., 64/128 kB in GTX285/GTX480 GPUs, corresponding to 16k/32k scalar registers or 512/1024 vector registers). Each access incurs nontrivial energy consumption. Using a small scalar register file reduces the energy consumption at a small area overhead.

To manage the SRF, we add a freelist and a renaming map table to dynamically allocate and free the scalar registers in the SRF. In the ID stage, the renaming map table is accessed to see whether its source vector register operands are remapped to scalar registers. For a detected uniform vector instruction, its destination vector register will be renamed by obtaining a scalar register from the freelist and updating the renaming map table accordingly. Decoded and renamed instructions will be kept in the warp scheduler waiting to be issued to the SPs. During instruction execution, the renamed register operands specify whether the SRF or the VRF is to be accessed. For an intra-warp uniform vector instruction, both its source and destination registers will be from the SRF. In this case, the ALU of the first SP is reused to carry out the computation. The register renaming logic may affect the timing of the ID stage and lead to an additional register renaming stage. Such a new pipeline stage at the frontend will not increase pipeline hazards, thereby having very limited performance impact as confirmed in our experiments.

The SRF is also connected to the existing broadcast path to handle the case when a scalar register is needed for a regular vector instruction. For a regular vector instruction, its destination vector register number will be used to check the renaming map table at the ID stage. If this vector register is currently being mapped to a scalar register, the mapping information will be cleared and the scalar register is pushed back to the freelist.

Our SRF-based design simplifies the processing of the corner case where the destination and a source operand share the same register, like in the case of 'VR1 = VR1 + VR2' where VR1 is currently mapped to a scalar register, e.g., SR4, but VR2 is not. With the renaming process, the instruction becomes 'VR1 = SR4 + VR2'. During execution, the value of SR4 is broadcasted to all the SPs from the SRF. Since SR4 will not be overwritten during the execution, the correctness is ensured.

For the corner case of control divergence, we resort to the same copy-on-write solution as in our token-based design when the destination operand shares the same register with a source operand, which is currently mapped to a scalar register. In other words, for the instruction 'VR1 = VR1 + 2' under a control divergent path with VR1 being currently mapped a scalar register SR5, the warp scheduler will insert a copy instruction 'VR1 = SR5', before issuing the instruction 'VR1 = VR1 + 2'.

Note that our renaming process is based on physical vector register numbers. For the same architectural register, different warps map them to different physical vector registers based on their warp ids. Therefore, there is no conflict among the warps when the same registers are used.

Compared to the token-based design, the disadvantage of the SRF-based design is that due to the SRF's limited size, when all the scalar registers are used up, we cannot convert newly detected intra-warp uniform vector instructions to scalar ones until a scalar register is freed to the freelist. We study this structural hazard effect in Section 5.3.

3.2. Exploiting Inter-Warp Uniform Vector Instructions

As shown in Section 2, different warps may perform the same computations. To exploit such inter-warp uniform vector instructions, we propose to leverage the idea of instruction reuse [19], which was proposed to reduce repeating computations in CPU architecture. In each SM, we add an instruction reuse buffer (IRB), which is a cache structure with the partial PC as the tag. Each entry in the data store includes opcode, three source operand values and one destination operand value. Here, we focus on instruction reuse only for intra-warp uniform vector instructions. Otherwise, for an arbitrary vector instruction, we have to compare the source operands for all 32 threads with those stored in the IRB, which would incur too much overhead. Partial PCs are used as tags to reduce the power consumption of fully associative searches. To avoid possible aliases due to partial PC match, we include the opcode field in the data store since identical inputs and opcode ensure the same outputs. Therefore, a hit in IRB means that both the partial PC and opcode match.

The IRB is accessed during the Register Read (RR) stage. If there is a hit in the IRB, the source operand values from the IRB will be compared with those read from either the first lane of the VRF, when our token-based design is used, or the SRF, when our SRF-based design is used. If all the source operands match, the execution stage will be skipped and the destination operand value from the IRB will be used to update either the first lane of the VRF or the SRF. If the source operand values do not match, the instruction will be executed in the first SP and the result will be used to update the corresponding IRB entry. If the PC misses in the IRB, the least-recently-used (LRU) replacement policy is used to find a victim entry in the IRB.

3.3. Leveraging Uniform Vector Instructions for Reliability Enhancement

As discussed in Section 1, reliability is an important issue for general purpose computation on GPUs (GPGPU). Both intra- and inter-warp uniform vector instructions can be leveraged for hardware error detection. For intra-warp uniform vector instructions, we choose to use two vector lanes (or two SPs) to carry out the computation and compare them before updating the register file. Furthermore, we also store two copies of a scalar value to protect the VRF against errors. In our token-based design, the two copies can be stored in the first two lanes of the VRF. For our SRF-based design, one copy is stored in the SRF and the other is stored in the first lane of the VRF. Adding parity bits to each 32-bit scalar value is another option to detect errors in either the VRF or the SRF. Redundant data storage, however, adds error correction capability when used together with the parity protection: when two copies differ, the parity bit detects which one is uncorrupted.

For inter-warp uniform vector instructions, we propose to protect the IRB with parity bits so as to protect the ALUs in an indirect manner. In this scheme, we add 1 parity bit for each IRB entry. For an instruction with uniform vector operands, if its PC hits in the IRB and an error is detected in the IRB entry using the parity bit, the instruction will be executed and the IRB will be updated accordingly. When there is no error detected in IRB, the ALU computation is skipped. This way, the ALUs become less vulnerable to errors as they are being used less often to carry out computations.

Since redundant computations or parity bit checks are performed in parallel with original computations, there is no performance impact. The additional energy spent on redundant computations is analyzed in Section 5.4.

4. EXPERIMENTAL METHODOLOGY

We modified GPGPUsim V3.0.1 [2] to model our proposed schemes to exploit intra- and inter-warp uniform vector instructions. Our baseline GPU configuration, modeled based on NVIDIA GTX285 GPUs, is shown in Table 1. The default SIMD width (or NumSP) is 8 and we vary this parameter in Section 5.3. In our experiments, we use an 8-entry IRB for inter-warp uniform vector instructions. Each IRB entry contains a 10-bit partial PC as the tag, three 32-bit source values, one 32-bit destination value, a 3-bit LRU field, and an 8-bit opcode field. In total, the hardware overhead of an instruction reuse buffer is 8*(10 + 3*32 + 32 + 3 + 8) = 1192 bits. For our SRF-based design, a SRF of 128 scalar registers (= 128*32 = 4096 bits) and a renaming table of 512 entries (512*7=3584 bits) are used. Compared to other resources shown in Table 1, such hardware overhead is quite limited. We examine the impact of these parameters in Section 5.3.

Table 1. The baseline GPU configuration.

Shader core frequency	1.3GHz
Number of SMs	30
Warp size	32
SIMD width(i.e., NumSP)	8 /16
Max. num. of thread blocks/threads per SM	8 thread blocks/1024 threads
Register file	64KB
Shared memory	16 KB
L1 cache	8-way set assoc. 64B cache block (48KB in total)
L2 Cache	8-way set assoc. 64B (256kb per MEM channel)
Number of MEM channels	16
GDDR Memory	8 banks, 800Mhz, total bandwidth: 200GB/S, TCL = 10, TRP = 10, TRCD = 12

Table 2. Area and energy consumption of the proposed components

	Area (mm^2)	Static Power (W)	Energy per access/operation (J)
VRF	2.44	0.09	2.46/5.82 E -12
SRF	0.005	0.001	1.76/1.62 E -13

To analyze power/energy consumption, we instrumented the GPGPUsim to collect the statistics including vector register file accesses, ALU operations, different types of memory accesses, the number of IRB accesses and the number of SRF accesses. We then modified McPAT [14] using the similar approach to GPUWattch [13] to compute the area overhead and energy/power consumption. The resulting area and the energy per access of the VRF and the SRF using the 40nm technology are shown in Table 2. The energy consumption for different ALU operations is extracted from GPUWattch.

We select 13 benchmarks from Nvidia CUDA SDK [17], the Rodinia benchmark suite [3] and GPGPUsim to cover a wide range of application domains. The inputs to the benchmarks, the total number of scalar instructions as well as the baseline performance measured with instructions per cycle (IPC) are shown in Table 3.

Table 3. The benchmarks used for evaluation.

Benchmarks	Inputs	Total inst.	IPC
N-Queen solver (NQU) [2]	32	0.78M	89.3
Vector add (VA) [17]	(512, 512)	5.5M	207.5
Fast Fourier Trans. (FFT) [17]	(128, 128)	14M	164.1
Convolution (CONV) [17]	(512, 512)	157M	220.2
Breadth first search (BFS) [2]	4096	11M	12.2
Matrix Multiply (MM) [17]	(128,80)	2M	135.2
MersenneTwister (MT) [17]	48000000	1478M	122.9
ScalarProduct (SP) [17]	524288	28M	177.1
Ray Tracing (RAY) [2]	(512, 512)	123M	193.6
dxtc (DT) [17]	1024	573M	215.6
HeartWall(HT) [3]	(512,1)	4M	169.8
HotSpot (HS) [3]	(512, 2, 2)	103M	182.3
PathFinder(PF) [3]	100000	582M	209.0

5. EXPERIMENTAL RESULTS

5.1. Performance Impact from Eliminating Uniform Vector Instructions

In the first experiment, we examine the performance impact of eliminating both intra- and inter-warp uniform instructions. As we propose two designs for intra-warp uniform instructions, we present the results in Figures 5 and 6, for the token-based design and the SRF-based design, respectively. In either figure, we also report the cases when only intra-warp uniform vector instructions are exploited (labeled 'Intra'), when only inter-warp uniform vector instructions are exploited (labeled 'Inter), and when both are exploited ('labeled 'Combined'). When exploiting only inter-warp uniform vector instructions, either the token-based design or the SRF-based design is still used for detecting intra-warp uniform vector instructions. However, if such an intra-warp uniform vector instruction does not hit in the IRB, it is not converted to scalar operations so as to isolate the performance impacts.

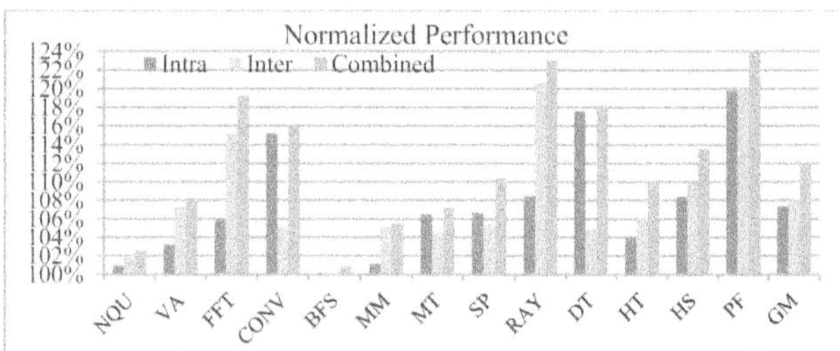

Figure 5. Performance gains from eliminating uniform vector instructions. The *token-based design* is used to handle intra-warp uniform vector instructions.

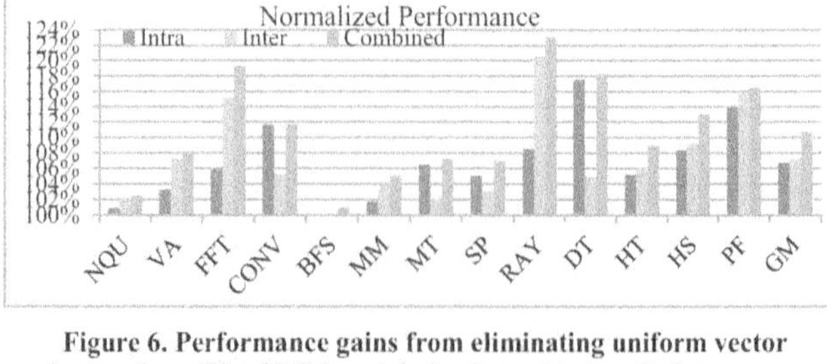

Figure 6. Performance gains from eliminating uniform vector instructions. The *SRF-based design* is used to handle intra-warp uniform vector instructions.

We first examine the performance impact from exploiting intra-warp uniform vector instructions. As discussed in Section 3.1, converting an intra-warp uniform vector instruction to a scalar one can improve the instruction issue rate to one scalar instruction every cycle. In our baseline GPU model, the warp scheduler in an SM has an issue rate of one vector instruction every 4 cycles. Therefore, for an application with sufficient thread-level parallelism (TLP), eliminating more intra-warp uniform vector instructions can result in more independent instructions being issued more promptly, thereby achieving higher performance. This is the case for the benchmarks CONV, MT, SP, DT, HS, and PF. On the other hand, when the performance of a workload is limited by the off-chip memory access bandwidth, as for the benchmarks, VA, FFT, BFS and HT, the performance gains are limited although VA and FFT have a high amount of redundant operations due to intra-warp uniform vector instructions, as shown in Figure 2. For the benchmark, RAY, many of its intra-warp uniform vector instructions are long latency ones. Converting them to scalar ones will not reduce such latency and their dependent instructions are still stalled. Therefore, its performance gain (8.6%), although not trivial, is not proportional to its high ratio of redundant operations (34.5%) shown in Figure 2. The benchmarks, NQU and MM have a relatively small ratio of intra-warp uniform vector instructions. Consequently, their performance gains are also small.

Between the token-based and the SRF-based designs, most benchmarks show similar performance gains from eliminating intra-warp uniform vector instructions, except a few like CONV, SP, and PF. The reason is that the detected intra-warp uniform instructions in these benchmarks define many different vector registers. Therefore, there is a high pressure on the SRF. Once the SRF is used up, subsequently detected intra-warp uniform vector instructions are not utilized. In Section 5.3, we show that these benchmarks require a 256-entry SRF to achieve similar performance to the token-based design. On average using GM, leveraging intra-warp uniform vector instructions using the token-based design and the SRF-based design achieves 7.4% and 6.7% performance improvement, respectively.

For inter-warp uniform vector instructions, our proposed IRB can reduce the execution latency as well as improve the instruction issue rate, as discussed in Section 3.2. Among the benchmarks, FFT, RAY, HS and PF, show impressive performance gains as they have significant amount of inter-warp uniform vector instructions and most of them are long latency ones. In general, the performance gains closely follow the ratio of the inter-warp uniform vector instructions, shown in Figure 2. The only exception is VA. Although VA has a high inter-warp uniform vector instruction ratio of 28.5%, the performance gain from skipping them is 7.3%. The reason is that most of these instructions are short latency ALU operations such as SHL (shift left) and AND, while the overall performance for VA is dominated by memory bandwidth. As discussed in Section 3.2, the IRB is only accessed when an instruction has been detected as an intra-warp uniform vector instruction. Therefore, different designs to detect intra-warp uniform vector instructions also have an impact on IRB effectiveness. As the token-based design captures more intra-warp uniform vector instructions, there are more hits in the IRB, thereby performing better than the SRF-based design. On average, exploiting only inter-warp uniform vector instruction achieves the performance gains of 8.1% and 7.2%, using the token-based design and the SRF-based design, respectively.

When eliminating both intra- and inter-warp uniform vector instructions, the performance gains are typically smaller than the sum of those by exploiting the two separately. The reason is that IRB exploits part of the intra-warp uniform vector instructions. Overall, as shown in Figures 5 and 6, our proposed token based and SRF-based designs improve the performance by up to 23.9% (PF), and 12.0% and 10.7% on average, respectively. Note that for benchmarks CONV, DT and PF, the resulting performance actually exceeds the theoretical maximum IPC (240 = 8 SP per SM * 30 SMs). The reason is that our scheme only takes 1 cycle to 'execute' an inter-warp uniform vector instruction for 32 threads, thereby having an IPC of 32. Similarly, for an intra-warp uniform vector instruction, it takes one cycle to issue rather than 4 cycles, which also essentially increases the IPC from 8 to 32 for this cycle.

As discussed in Section 3, in the case of a uniform vector register re-define under a control divergent path, we resort to our proposed copy-on-write solution. This leads to one extra copy instruction to be issued and executed. Next, we examine how often such cases happen. In Figure 7, we report the ratio of the overall number of copy instructions inserted over the overall number of dynamic vector instructions. From the figure, we can see that many benchmarks have no such cases. The benchmark FFT has the highest ratio of 0.044% and the average is 0.010%. Therefore, there is no noticeable impact from these extra copy instructions.

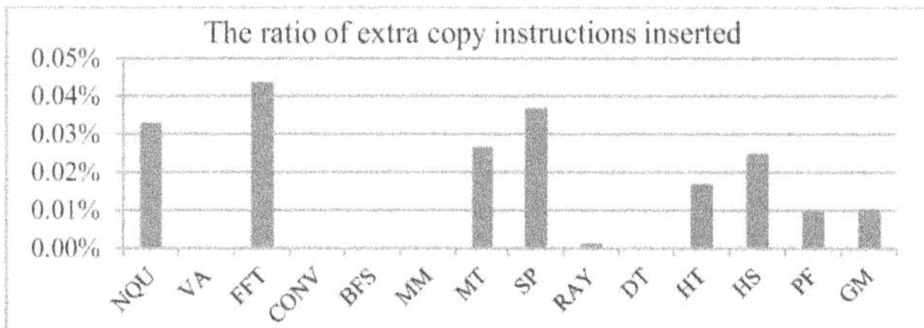

Figure 7. The ratio of extra copy instructions introduced over the overall number of dynamic vector instructions.

5.2 Energy Savings from Eliminating Uniform Vector Instructions

Our proposed schemes achieve energy savings in three ways: (a) reducing execution time results in static energy savings, (b) converting an intra-warp uniform vector instruction to a scalar one eliminates (warpsize – 1) redundant computations as well as associated register file accesses, and (c) eliminating an inter-warp uniform vector instruction eliminate 1 computation. We first look into the dynamic energy consumption and show the normalized results over the baseline GPU in Figure 8 for both the token-based design ('labeled 'token') and the SRF-based design (labeled 'SRF').

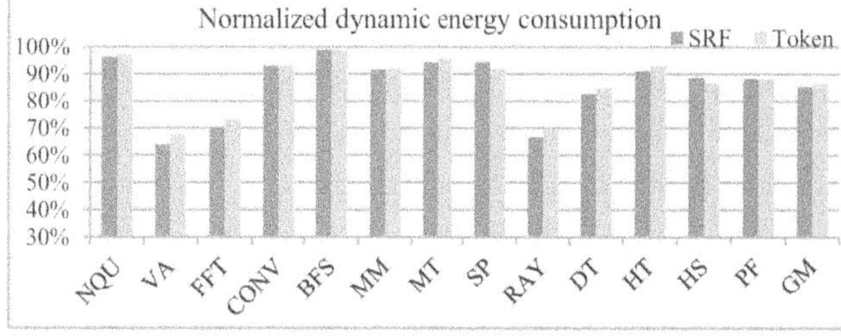

Figure 8. Dynamic energy consumption of our approaches normalized over the baseline GPU.

From Figure 8, we can see that eliminating both intra- and inter-warp redundant operations results in an average of 14.7% and

13.6% dynamic energy reduction using the SRF-based design and the token-based design, respectively. The SRF-based design saves more dynamic energy than the token based design. The reason is that the SRF-based design replaces VRF accesses with SRF accesses. Among the benchmarks, the benchmark, VA, has the highest dynamic energy reduction (36.0%) due to its high ratio (42.4%) of redundant operations shown in Figure 2.

The structures that we introduced for our approaches, including the 8-entry IRB and the 128-entry SRB, are quite small, less than 0.01% based on the area estimation using McPAT, compared to existing the 8 ALUs, the VRF, and caches in an SM. Therefore, the static energy savings follows very closely with the execution time reduction or performance gains. As a result, we only show the total energy consumption for our two designs in Figures 9 and 10. Similar to our performance results, we also report the normalized energy consumption for the case when only the intra-warp uniform vector instructions are exploited (labeled 'Intra'), and when only the inter-warp uniform vector instructions are exploited (labeled 'Inter'), and when both types of uniform vector instructions are exploited (labeled 'Combined').

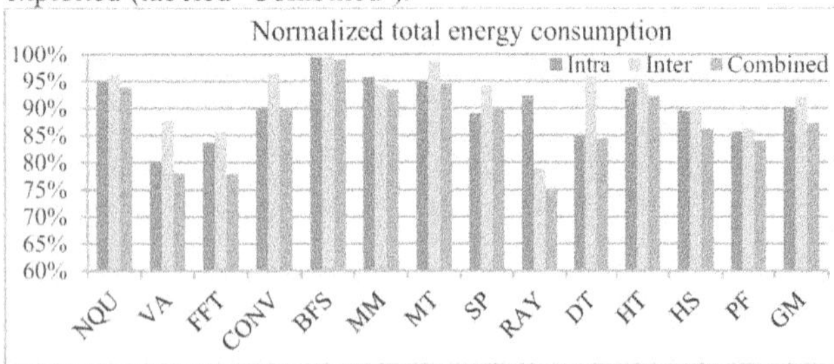

Figure 9. Normalized total energy consumption when using the *token-based design* to handle intra-warp uniform vector instructions.

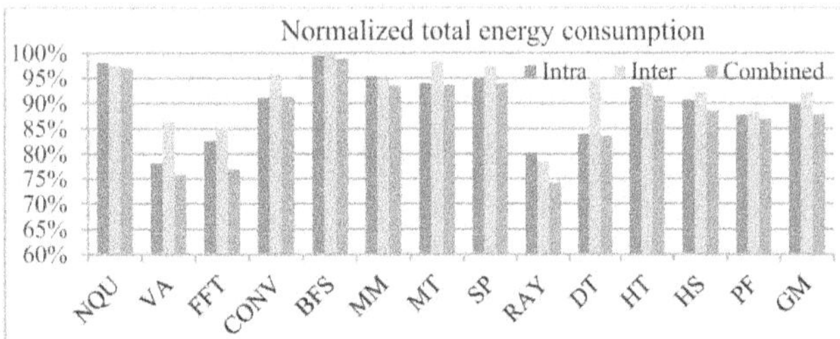

Figure 10. Normalized total energy consumption when using the *SRF-based design* to handle intra-warp uniform vector instructions.

From Figures 9 and 10, we can see that the intra-warp uniform vector instruction removal reduces the total energy consumption by 9.8% and 10.3% on average, for the token-based design and the SRF-based design, respectively. Eliminating inter-warp uniform vector instructions reduces the total energy consumption by 8.0% and 7.6%, for the two designs, respectively. When both intra- and inter-warp uniform vector instructions are exploited, the token design shows slightly higher energy saving (12.7%) than the SRF design (12.2%).

5.3. Design Space Exploration

In our first experiment, we analyze the impact of the SRF size in the SRF-based design. We vary the SRF from 16to 256 registers. The results in Figure 11 show that for many of the applications including NQU, VA, FFT, BFS, MM, MT, RAY and DT, a SRF with 64 entries captures most of the uniform vector instructions. For remaining workloads, including CONV, HT, HS SP, and PF, the performance improves as we increase the number of entries. A 256-entry SRF performs almost the same as the unlimited one, which is equivalent to our token-based design.

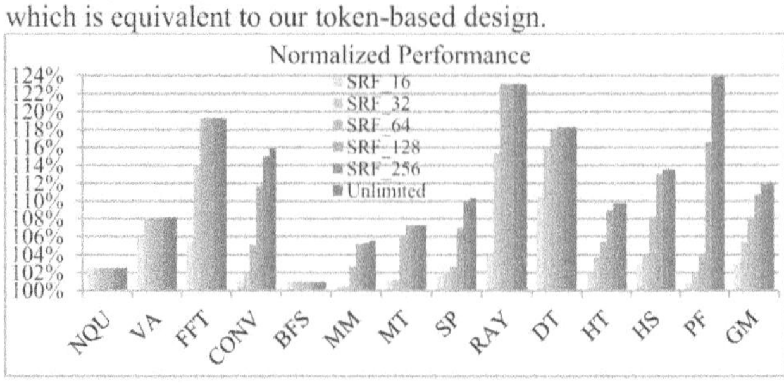

Figure 11. The performance impact of the SRF size.

In our second experiment, we analyze the performance impact of IRB. We vary the IRB size from 2 to 16 and the results in Figure 12 show that the average performance gains of the token-based design are 10.8%, 11.5%, 12.0% and 12.3% for the IRB size of 2, 4, 8 and 16, respectively. Therefore, we choose the reuse buffer size as 8 as the cost effective solution. The key reason why small IRBs (even with 2 entries) work well is that different warps make similar progress under the round-robin scheduling policy. After one inter-warp uniform vector instruction is detected from a leading warp and stored in the IRB, it will be quickly used by other warps. It is seldom the case that the warps have such different execution speeds that different warps detect and use a highly different set of inter-warp uniform vector instructions.

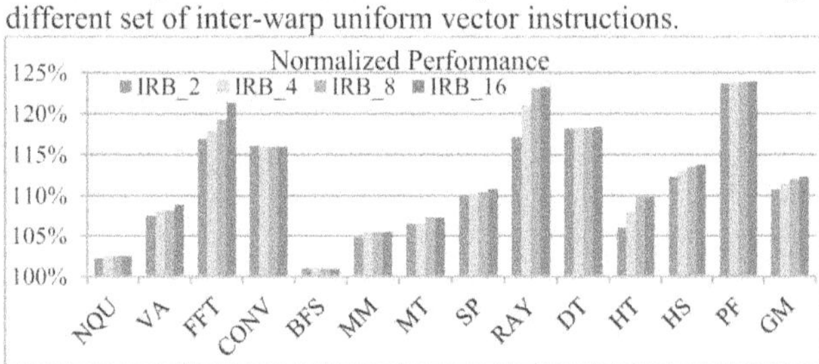

Figure 12. The performance impact of the IRB size.

In our third experiment, we investigate the impact of SIMD width (i.e., NumSP) on the effectiveness of our proposed approaches. In order to keep the same ALU-to-MEM bandwidth ratio when we increase NumSP from 8 to 16 (i.e., there are 16 SPs in each SM), we reduce the number of SMs from 30 to 15. The performance gains from eliminating only intra-warp uniform vector instructions (labeled 'Intra'), from eliminating only inter-warp uniform vector instructions (labeled 'Inter'), and eliminating both types of uniform vector instructions (labeled 'Combined') using the token-based design are shown in Figure 13. Here, the performance improvement is over the GPU with 15 SMs and 16 SPs per SM.

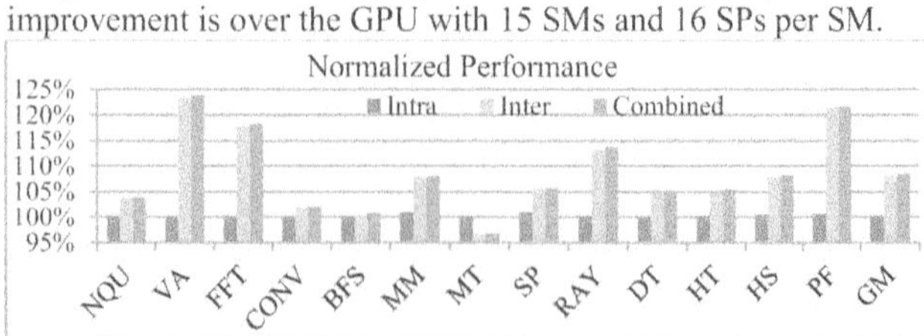

Figure 13. The performance improvement from eliminating uniform vector instructions on a GPU with 15 SMs and 16 SPs per SM.

From Figure 13, we can see that when NumSP is increased to 16, the performance gains from eliminating intra-warp uniform vector instructions become marginal. There are two reasons for this impact. First, with NumSP increased from 8 to 16, the baseline instruction issue rate is improved from one instruction every four cycles into one instruction every two cycles. Although converting an intra-warp uniform vector instruction into a scalar one can improve the issue rate to one instruction every cycle, the room for improvement is reduced. Second, as each SM has more SPs, it requires more concurrent threads to run on each SM to fully utilize the increased number of SPs. Therefore, the insufficient TLP becomes the performance bottleneck rather than the instruction issue rate. On the other hand, with increased NumSP, we are able to achieve higher performance benefits from exploiting inter-warp uniform vector instructions for most benchmarks. The reason is that with more SPs, each SM requires more concurrent threads to hide execution latencies. For example, considering an instruction with 4 cycle latency, with 8 SPs per SM, the execution latency can be completely hidden when there is just 1 warp running on the SM. With 16 SPs per SM, in comparison, it requires 2 warps to hide the 4 cycle execution latency. With our IRB approach, if an instruction hits in the IRB, its execution can be skipped and the latency is reduced to 1 cycle. Therefore, it lowers the requirement on TLP and becomes more beneficial. One interesting anomaly is the benchmark MT, for which exploiting inter-warp uniform vector instructions leads to a 3.1% performance degradation. We looked into this benchmark and discovered that the performance loss is due to longer memory access latency resulting from decreased DRAM row access locality [12]. The DRAM row access locality means the average number of row accesses after a row is activated. The reason for such reduced row access locality is due to the fact that with our IRB approach, some warps, if their instructions hit in the IRB, make faster progress than others. Combined with the round-robin scheduling policy, the memory access sequence from different warps is altered, leading to such an anomaly.

Overall, when NumSP is 16, an average of 0.3%, 8.2%, and 8.5% performance improvement is achieved from eliminating only intra-warp uniform vector instruction, from eliminating only inter-warp uniform vector instruction, and from eliminating both types of uniform vector instructions, respectively.

We also study the energy savings when NumSP is increased to 16. Our results show that dynamic energy savings are not affected when NumSP is increased. It is expected as changing NumSP does not affect the amount of the redundant operations from uniform vector instructions. Static energy savings, in contrast, are directly proportional to execution time reduction. On average, with NumSP as 16, our token-based approach show an 13.6% reduction in dynamic energy, an 7.8% reduction in static energy, and a 10.0% reduction in total energy.

5.4. Leveraging Uniform Vector Instructions for Reliability Enhancement

In this experiment, we study the effectiveness of the opportunistic reliability improvement approach discussed in Section 3.3. Figure 14 shows how often the ALUs can be protected against hardware errors during execution. The reliability coverage is computed as the average ratio of (number of scalar ALU operations that are protected using redundancy from uniform vector instructions / overall number of scalar ALU operations). In Figure 14, we present the results for both the token-based design and the SRF-based design. Redundancy from both intra- and inter-warp uniform instructions is exploited in either design.

From Figure 14, we can see that either design is able to protect a significant amount of ALU operations, up to 42.9% (VA) and an average of 19.5% or 21.1%. The token-based design has higher coverage for CONV, SP, and PF, for the same reason as discussed in Section 5.2 that these applications require a SRF with more than 128 scalar registers. Therefore, it has higher coverage on average.

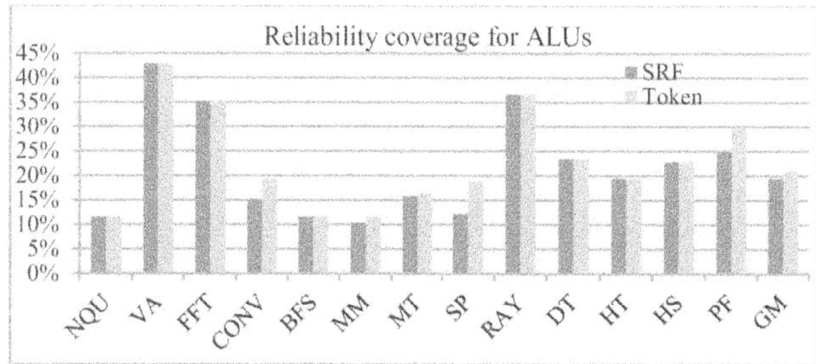

Figure 14. Reliability coverage of ALUs by leveraging the redundancy in uniform vector instructions.

We also study the reliability coverage for the data stored in the VRFs. The coverage is computed as follows. In each cycle, we identify the live vector registers, meaning that they will be used later on as source operands, in a VRF and determine how many live vector registers are protected using the redundancy provided from detected uniform vector instructions (i.e., identical copies of the same data). The average ratio of two accumulated numbers, i.e., the total number of protected live vector register / the total number of live registers, across multiple SMs throughout the execution time, is the reported coverage shown in Figure 15.

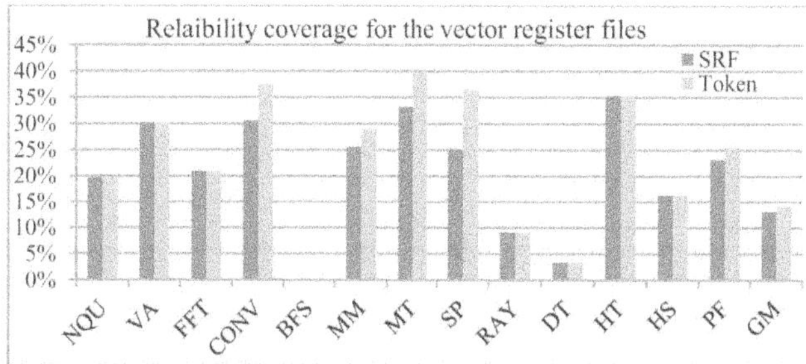

Figure 15. Reliability coverage of vector register files by leveraging the redundancy in uniform vector instructions.

From Figure 15, we can see that the token-based design can protect up to 40.0% and 14.1% on average of the live registers in VRFs. For the benchmark BFS, although there exists a non-trivial amount of uniform vector instructions as shown in Figure 2, its reliability coverage for the VRFs is minimal (0.1%). The reason is that most of the uniform vector instructions in BFS define and redefine a very limited set of the vector registers. The small number of protected vector register combined with short live time result in such a low coverage. For the benchmarks MM and MT, the protected vector registers have relatively long live time. Therefore, their reliability coverage for VRFs is higher than it for ALUs shown in Figure 14. In contrast, for the benchmark VA, although it has very high ALU coverage, the coverage for VRFs is lower due to the short live time of the protected vector registers. The SRF-based design has lower VRF reliability coverage than the token-based design for the same reason as discussed above for ALU reliability.

As discussed in Section 3.3, the redundancy checks have no performance overhead. Therefore, we focus on the dynamic energy consumption impact from such redundant computations and storage. The results are shown in Figure 16 for both the token based and the SRF-based designs compared to the same approaches without redundancy checks.

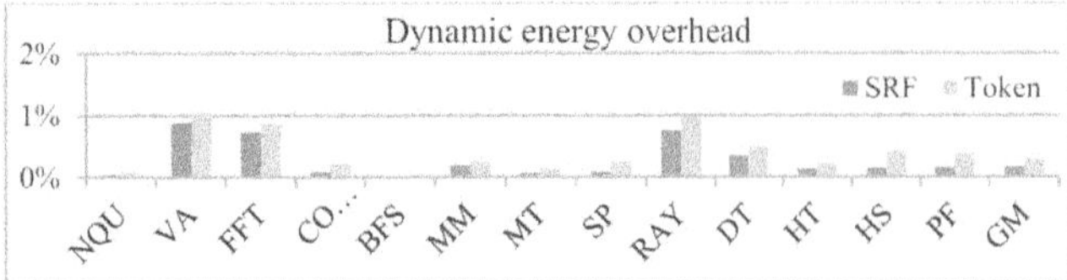

Figure 16. The overhead for redundancy checks in dynamic energy consumption.

From Figure 16, we can see that either the token-based design or the SRF-based design can offer reliability coverage for ALUs and VRFs at very little overhead on dynamic energy consumption with an average of 0.29% and 0.17%, respectively. Such results can be expected as we only add one additional scalar ALU computation to protect a vector ALU instruction and one VRF lane access to store the redundant data. In other words, with the warp size as 32, converting an intra-warp uniform vector instruction to a scalar operation (i.e., without redundancy checks) saves 31 scalar computations while converting an intra-warp uniform vector instruction to two scalar operations (i.e., one for redundancy checking) saves 30 scalar computations. The difference is very small. When total energy is considered, the overhead of the token-based design and the SRF-based design is 0.14% and 0.08%, respectively.

Overall, with our proposed approaches to exploit both intra- and inter-warp uniform vector instructions, we can achieve 12.0% performance gains, 12.6% energy savings, along with 21.1% reliability coverage for ALUs and 14.1% reliability coverage for VRFs.

6. RELATED WORK

It has been observed that there are identical computations across multiple threads in both CPUs [15] and GPUs [5][9]. In [5], such scalar behavior in GPU workloads is referred to as uniform vectors. Compiler analysis approaches have been proposed in [4][6][7][16] to identify uniform vectors. A hardware approach, similar to our token-based design, is also presented in [5] to detect intra-warp uniform vector instructions. Compared to [5], the novelty of this work includes (1) we introduce inter-warp uniform vector instructions and exploit them with instruction reuse; (2) we show that converting an intra-warp uniform vector instruction to a scalar one can improve the instruction issue rate so as to improve performance; (3) we propose a new SRF-based design to exploit intra-warp uniform vector instructions; (4) we propose to leverage the redundancy from uniform vector instructions to improve hardware reliability; and (5) we present a detailed performance, energy, as well as reliability analysis. As shown in Section 5.3, with high SIMD widths, the performance benefits from intra-warp uniform vector instructions become very limited while inter-warp uniform vector instructions provide more performance gains. Compared to compiler approaches for uniform vector identification (i.e., scalarization), our proposed hardware approach is more effective to detect intra-warp uniform vector instructions from potentially control divergent code as discussed in Section 2. On the other hand, our proposed approach to leverage inter-warp uniform vector instructions can work with either compiler- or hardware-based intra-warp uniform vector detection.

Instruction reuse is exploited in [10] for opportunistic soft error detection in CPUs. In this work, we adopt the instruction reuse idea to improve performance and reliability as well as reduce energy consumption for GPUs.

7. CONCLUSIONS

In this paper, we show that in many GPU applications, besides (intra-warp) uniform vector instructions observed in previous work, there exists a significant amount of inter-warp uniform vector instructions. We propose detailed architectural designs to exploit both types of uniform vector instructions. For a detected intra-warp uniform vector instruction, we convert it into a scalar operation and propose different ways to store the scalar register data. For inter-warp uniform vector instructions, we leverage instruction reuse to skip computations so as to reduce instruction execution latency as well as energy consumption. We also exploit the redundancy in uniform vector instructions to provide opportunistic reliability enhancement.

Our experiments show that the proposed approaches can achieve an average of 12.0% performance gains and 12.7% energy savings at very little hardware cost. Also, we show that with a little less energy savings (12.6%) and the same performance gains (12.0%), we can protect 21.1%ALU operations and 14.1%live vector registers.

8. ACKNOWLEDGEMENTS

We thank the anonymous reviewers for their insightful comments to improve our paper. This work is supported by an NSF project 1216569, an NSF CAREER award CCF-0968667, a grant from the DARPA PERFECT program, and a gift fund from AMD Inc.

9. REFERENCES

[1] AMD Accelerated Parallel Processing OpenCL Programming Guide 2.1, May 2012

[2] A. Bakhoda, et al., Analyzing CUDA workloads using a detailed GPU simulator. IPASS 2009.

[3] S. Che, et al., Rodinia: a benchmark suite for heterogeneous computing, IISWC 2009.

[4] Z. Chen, et al., Characterizing Scalar Opportunities in GPGPU Applications, ISPSS, 2013

[5] S. Collange, et al., Dynamic detection of uniform and affine vectors in GPGPU computations, Euro-Par, 2009

[6] S. Collange. Identifying scalar behavior in CUDA kernels. *Technical report hal-00555134*, 2011.

[7] B. Coutinho, et al., Divergence analysis and optimizations, PACT 2011.

[8] M. Dimitrov, et al., Understanding software approaches for GPGPU reliability, GPGPU-2, 2009

[9] S. Gilani, N. Kim, M. Schulte: Power-efficient computing for compute-intensive GPGPU applications. PACT 2012.

[10] M. Gomaa and T. Vijaykumar, "Opportunistic Transient-Fault Detection", ISCA-32, 2005.

[11] N. B. Lakshminarayana and H. Kim, Effect of Instruction Fetch and Memory Scheduling on GPU Performance, Workshop on Language, Compiler, and Architecture Support for GPGPU, 2010.

[12] C. J. Lee, et al. Prefetch-aware DRAM controllers. MICRO-41, 2008.

[13] J. Leng, et al., GPUWattch: Enabling Energy Optimizations in GPGPUs, ISCA, 2013

[14] S. Li at al., McPAT: an integrated power, area and timing modeling framework for multicore and manycore architectures, MICRO 2009.

[15] G. Long, et al., Minimal Multi-Threading: Finding and Removing Redundant Instructions in Multi-Threaded Processors. MICRO, 2010.

[16] Y. Lee, et al. Convergence and Scalarization for Data-Parallel Architectures. CGO 2013.

[17] NVIDIA GPU Computing SDK 3.1.

[18] J. Sheaffer, et al. A Hardware Redundancy and Recovery Mechanism for Reliable Scientific Computation on Graphics Processors. Graphics Hardware 2007.

[19] A. Sodani and G. S. Sohi. Dynamic Instruction Reuse. ISCA 1997.

Scaling Large-Data Computations on Multi-GPU Accelerators

Amit Sabne
Purdue University
asabne@purdue.edu

Putt Sakdhnagool
Purdue University
psakdhna@purdue.edu

Rudolf Eigenmann
Purdue University
eigenman@purdue.edu

ABSTRACT

Modern supercomputers rely on accelerators to speed up highly parallel workloads. Intricate programming models, limited device memory sizes and overheads of data transfers between CPU and accelerator memories are among the open challenges that restrict the widespread use of accelerators. First, this paper proposes a mechanism and an implementation to automatically pipeline the CPU-GPU memory channel so as to overlap the GPU computation with the memory copies, alleviating the data transfer overhead. Second, in doing so, the paper presents a technique called *Computation Splitting, COSP*, that caters to arbitrary device memory sizes and automatically manages to run out-of-card OpenMP-like applications on GPUs. Third, a novel adaptive runtime tuning mechanism is proposed to automatically select the pipeline stage size so as to gain the best possible performance. The mechanism adapts to the underlying hardware in the starting phase of a program and chooses the pipeline stage size. The techniques are implemented in a system that is able to translate an input OpenMP program to multiple GPUs attached to the same host CPU. Experimentation on a set of nine benchmarks shows that, on average, the pipelining scheme improves the performance by 1.49x, while limiting the runtime tuning overhead to 3% of the execution time.

Categories and Subject Descriptors: D.3.4 [*Programming Languages*] : Processors – Compilers

Keywords: GPU, Large-Data, OpenMP, Tuning, Out-of-card Computations, Pipelining

1. INTRODUCTION

Accelerators have become the forerunners of high-performance computing. Many supercomputers now use GPU devices as accelerators. Among many open issues are those related to programming models and program optimization. The present paper addresses these issues.

First, even though accelerators can be used as independent computational devices, they commonly serve as co-processors. Eligible computation is offloaded from the CPU - either explicitly by the programmer, or implicitly by the system software/hardware. Offloading involves data transfer from the CPU to the accelerator, which causes significant overhead – up to 95% of the program execution time, in our experiments. The primary contribution of this paper is an automatic pipelining generation technique that reduces this overhead. To do so, the pipelining technique overlaps data transfer with computation. It creates opportunities for such overlap by transforming the computation into multiple chunks and transferring the data for chunk '$(i+1)$' while executing chunk 'i'. Our technique contrasts with those that reduce data transfer overhead by eliminating redundant memory transfers [1, 2] and by advancing or delaying the data copy operations [3].

Second, the pipelining technique builds on an enabling technique that deals with another important issue in accelerators: The accelerator's memory space is limited; computation that fits in the CPU's memory may exceed the accelerator's capacity. The simple-most form of the technique splits computation into blocks that fit in memory. The same technique can be a key enabler for optimizations that tend to increase memory demand. Examples of such optimizations are data privatization, prefetch, and our pipelining technique. The difficulty in designing the technique is to model the increase in memory demand and determine the maximum chunk size that fits in the device memory. While most common accelerator benchmarks use data sizes that fit in memory, researchers have recognized the issue of limited memory sizes as well. For example, Liang [4] et al. discuss an example of an out-of-card FFT computation; a set of map-reduce based systems [5, 6] need to handle large data sizes that can exceed the GPU memory size. With the evolution of big-data systems, we expect the computing focus to move to large datasets. Our technique is the first to automatically tailor computation to the available memory space while considering optimizations that increase memory demand. The ability of splitting the computation also provides an opportunity to perform multi-device mapping of the program. Multiple GPUs attached to a single computation node are becoming an architectural reality. Several techniques have been proposed [7, 8] to port custom applications to multi-GPUs. Our framework automates this process.

The third issue addressed in this paper is the programmability of accelerators. An important issue is the design of a suitable high-level programming model, with one of the key

ICS'13, June 10–14, 2013, Eugene, Oregon, USA.

questions being what architectural details need to be exposed to the programmer. Among many proposed models [9, 10, 2, 11, 12, 13], recently, the idea of using OpenMP extended with directives for accelerators, has gotten traction. We will integrate and evaluate our techniques in one of the most advanced compilers that has been pursuing this idea, OpenMPC [2]. In doing so, we introduce a novel component that addresses a fundamental problem in high-level programming environments for accelerators: The architectural complexity of the CPU-Accelerator systems exacerbates the difficulty of advanced compilers in making optimization decisions that need runtime information. These architectural intricacies are detrimental to the portability of the code. An optimally tuned program on one platform may perform poorly on another. The most advanced compilers make use of *offline tuning* techniques to obtain the optimal choices of system-specific parameters. By contrast, we describe an adaptive runtime tuning mechanism that learns about the architectural details in the initial phase of the program in a short time and determines the most suitable pipeline stage size to attain best performance.

In this paper, we make the following specific contributions:

- We design and implement an automatic pipelining technique that reduces CPU-accelerator data transfer overhead by overlapping the data transfers with computation. We will demonstrate the efficacy of this technique by displaying the performance benefits achieved on a set of benchmarks, including kernels and applications. On average, pipelining achieves a speed-up of 1.49x over the baseline OpenMPC codes.
- We design and implement an automatic computation splitting technique, *COSP*, that fits large computations into the accelerator's device memory. In doing so, it considers program transformations that increase memory demand, including our pipelining technique. We will show that large, out-of-card data sizes that can not be otherwise handled by OpenMPC/CUDA can be successfully run.
- We describe a low-overhead (less than 3% execution time) adaptive runtime tuning method that chooses a good split size for a problem and the underlying hardware so as to approach the best pipelining performance.
- We describe a system containing our novel techniques that automatically translates an input OpenMP code into a multi-device CUDA code that can employ multiple GPUs attached to the same host node. We evaluate the performance of benchmarks executed on multi-GPU systems.

The remainder of the paper is organized as follows : Section 2 provides background information about GPGPU programming and OpenMPC. Section 3 analyzes the benefits of *COSP* and describes implementation details. Section 4 explains how pipelining and multi-GPU code generation are enabled by *COSP* and provides compiler design details for both. Section 5 describes the proposed adaptive runtime tuning system. Finally, Section 6 evaluates our system on a set of benchmarks from the StreamIt benchmark suite, CUDA SDK and Rodinia benchmarks.

2. PRELIMINARIES

This section describes the GPU system architecture and the CUDA programming model. We also describe the OpenMPC compiler system that translates an input OpenMP program into CUDA code.

2.1 GPUs and CUDA

Typically, one or more GPUs are connected to a Host CPU via a PCIe bus. The CPU can offload computation kernels onto the GPU(s). Since the CPU and the GPU have different memories, input data must be copied from the CPU to the GPU before the start of a kernel. This operation is called *copy-in*. Similarly, copying the outputs of a kernel from the GPU to the CPU is termed *copy-out*. CPU-GPU data transfers are initiated and governed by the CPU.

GPUs are SIMD units with a large number of processors. NVIDIA GPUs have termed these processors *Streaming Multiprocessors* or *SMs*, each being an SIMD processor. CUDA [9] is a multi-threaded, SIMD programming model. The threads on the GPU device are divided into *ThreadBlocks*. Each *ThreadBlock* consists of a set of threads, each executing the same code. When the CPU launches a kernel, it prescribes the number of threads in a *ThreadBlock* along with the number of *ThreadBlocks* to launch. The set of *ThreadBlocks* launched by a kernel is called a *grid*.

CUDA has a complicated memory hierarchy. Each thread has its own local memory and a set of registers. Local memory contains a stack which is primarily used to spill the registers. A *ThreadBlock* has its on-chip local storage in the form of *shared memory*. The off-chip global memory is accessible to all threads in the grid. Further, on-chip *constant* and *texture* memories can act as read-only buffers.

Various factors impact the performance of a GPU kernel: coalesced memory accesses, register and shared memory usage, number of threads in a *ThreadBlock*, shared memory bank conflicts etc., making it difficult to predict the GPU performance [14, 15, 16]. To obtain good performance results, tuning is essential for GPU programs.

2.2 OpenMPC

OpenMPC [2] is a programming framework that synthesizes CUDA programs from OpenMP codes. The framework includes an extended OpenMP programming interface, a source-to-source translator [17], and an automatic compiler-assisted tuning system. The programming interface extends OpenMP with a new set of directives and environment variables for controlling CUDA specific parameters and optimizations. OpenMPC applies various code transformations and CUDA extensions to the input OpenMP code.

We chose OpenMPC as the underlying compiler for our system implementation because of the following reasons : (a) OpenMP-like programming models are becoming popular, especially with the advent of OpenACC [13]. The OpenMP standard itself is in the process of being extended to support accelerator devices [18]. OpenMPC is a research framework pursuing the same idea. (b) OpenMPC automatically performs many safe and beneficial code transformations so as to coalesce memory accesses and map data to different kinds of memories available on the GPU. OpenMPC also implements sophisticated CPU-GPU live variable analysis to remove or hoist the redundant memory transfers. (c) Considering the complexity of the CUDA programming model, its not always possible for a compiler to find the performance optimal CUDA parameters. OpenMPC provides OpenMP extensions for the programmer that can be

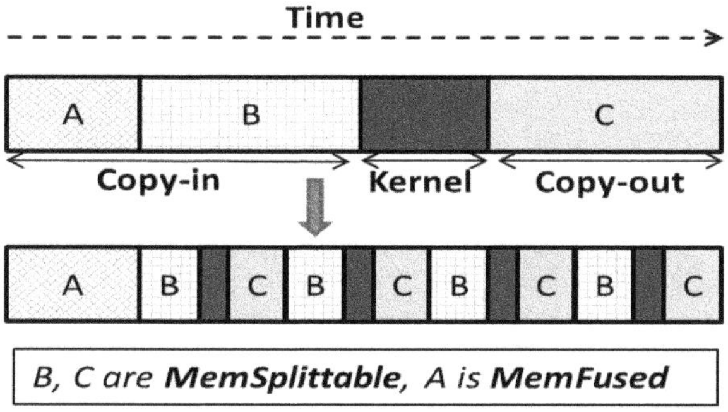

Figure 1: *COSP* - *MemSplittable* data can be split since only a part of them is required per chunk of computation, *MemFused* is the part of the data accessed by every chunk.

used to set the CUDA related parameters. (d) The OpenMPC translator is realized on top of the Cetus [19] compiler, which provides an efficient implementation infrastructure.

3. COSP - AN ENABLER TECHNIQUE

COSP, or *Computation Splitting*, divides a given problem into smaller, homogeneous subproblems. It acts as an enabler technique to other optimizations. In this section, we describe the nature of *COSP* and the optimizations it enables. While doing so, we establish an analytical upper bound on the size of a problem that can be run on an accelerator with limited memory. We provide a lower bound on the number of splits that the problem must undergo in order to fit in the device memory. We also describe the implementation of *COSP*.

3.1 Catering to Arbitrary Device Memory Sizes

COSP reduces the runtime device memory requirement of a problem; every subproblem requires less memory than the overall computation. We now analyze the factors that impact the device memory requirement. The total device memory requirement of a kernel depends upon the following:

- *COSP* converts a large problem into smaller subproblems. An example of such operation is shown in Fig. 1. In this example, data A, B, and C are a part of OpenMP *'shared'* data objects i.e. all threads work on a single copy of the data. In the original computation, data A and B are copied-in. The kernel uses these elements to generate data C, which is copied out of the device memory. The kernel, even after splitting, requires all data A for generating even a part of data C; we call A *MemFused* type of data. On the other hand, data B and C can be split, and each subproblem only requires a part of these elements. We call B and C *MemSplittable* data. If the splitting is perfect, amongst $numSplits$ subproblems, the original runtime device memory space for the shared data goes down from ($MemSplittable + MemFused$) to ($MemSplittable/numSplits + MemFused$). However, a subproblem may also use the data of another (mostly neighboring) subproblem. We model this extra data requirement overhead by *SplitOverlap*.
- Every OpenMP *Private* data element in the input OpenMP program has to be allocated per thread in the computation. If the size of the private element is small (e.g. scalars), the element is generally stored in the device register. However, if the size of the private element is large (e.g. for arrays), the element needs to be placed in the local memory of the thread. Therefore, if P is the size of all such elements together and $NumThreads$ is the number of total threads, the device memory requirement is $P \times NumThreads$. Further, if the problem is split amongst $numSplits$ subproblems, the device memory requirement for the private data would be $P \times NumThreads/numSplits$.
- Memory prefetching is an important technique in accelerator programming. Device memory prefetching advances the copy-in operation for the ready data so as to overlap the copying time with the CPU computation. Similarly, for the data that is not immediately required by the CPU, the copy-out can be delayed while overlapping the copy-out time with the CPU computation. Both these optimizations require device memory to hold the buffered data. We denote this size as $PrefBuffer$.

To ensure that the device memory, $DevMem$, can fit all of the above components, the following constraint must be met:

$$DevMem \geq \left(P \times \frac{NumThreads}{numSplits} + PrefBuffer + MemFused + \frac{MemSplittable}{numSplits} + SplitOverlap\right)$$

$$\Rightarrow numSplits \geq \left\lceil \frac{(MemSplittable + P \times NumThreads)}{(DevMem - PrefBuffer - MemFused - SplitOverlap)} \right\rceil \quad (1)$$

Equation 1 provides a lower bound on the number of splits required on the input problem to make it fit in the device memory. Equation 1 also indicates that the benefits of *COSP* are multi-faceted. *COSP* can enable an accelerator program to run successfully even when the OpenMP *private* elements push the device memory requirements beyond available. *COSP* can also partition the computation into appropriate subproblems so as to enable prefetching in the device memory.

3.2 COSP Through a Code Example

Section 3.1 provided a discussion on the lower bound of the number of splits required by the computation so as to make it fit in the device memory. We now describe a mechanism to achieve *COSP* through a compiler transformation. If all the parameters in Eq.1 are known, the compiler can choose the number of splits required to make the computation fit in the device memory. As we would show later in Section 4, *COSP* creates an opportunity for pipelining the subproblems. The number of subproblems required to obtain efficient pipelining can be less than the upper bound provided by Eq.1. Our compiler therefore abstracts out the number of splits as a variable.

OpenMP programs usually encapsulate parallelism using large *for* loops. We introduce the *COSP* mechanism through an example of *Scalar Product* code, as shown in Listing 1. This program generates scalar products for a set of vectors. The split version of the code generated by our compiler is shown in Listing 2. The input *parallel for* loop is split into many small loops. The upper bound for the inner *for* loop is set to be *SplitSize.* SplitSize is left as a parameter that can be set by the user or the automated tuning system. The inner loop body represents a subproblem of the initial large problem. We hereafter refer to the inner loop as a ***Split*** and the outer loop as ***Split Loop***.

Listing 1: Input Scalar Product OpenMP Code

```
#pragma omp parallel for shared(D, E, F)
private(vec, pos, sum)
for(vec = 0; vec < NUM_VECTORS; vec++) {
  sum = 0;
  for(pos = 0; pos < NUM_ELEMENTS; pos++) {
    sum += D[NUM_ELEMENTS * vec + pos ] *
     E[NUM_ELEMENTS * vec + pos];
  }
  F[vec] = (float)sum;
}
```

Listing 2: Split Parallel Region for Scalar Product

```
for (split=0; split < NUM_VECTORS/SplitSize; split = split+1) {
  #pragma omp parallel for shared(D, E, F)
  private(vec, pos, sum) shared(split, SplitSize)
  for (vec = 0; vec < SplitSize; vec++ ) {
    sum=0;
    for (pos = 0; pos < NUM_ELEMENTS; pos++ ) {
      sum+=(D[(pos + (NUM_ELEMENTS *
      (vec + split*SplitSize)))]*
      E[(pos + (NUM_ELEMENTS * (vec + split*SplitSize))]);
    }
    F[(vec + split*SplitSize)] = (float)sum;
  }
}
```

For the *Scalar Product* program, the total number of splits created is equal to *NUM_VECTORS/SplitSize*. This number needs to be larger than the *numSplits* calculated by Eq. 1 in Section 3.1 so as to meet the device memory size constraint. The number of splits in the problem is controlled by the SplitSize. Further, SplitSize governs the data size required by the kernel as well as the number of GPU threads synthesized by the OpenMPC system. Note that the *COSP* version in Listing 2 does not explicitly formulate the data partitions per Split. We defer the data partitioning analysis till the next section.

COSP can lead to extra data copy overheads in cases where the computation splitting is not perfect. As an example, consider stencil programs where computing each output requires an array element along with its neighbors. In such cases, *COSP* would require to account for the storage of boundary elements of each split, increasing the amount of overall data copied from the CPU to the GPU.

Since the subproblems provided by *COSP* are devoid of data dependences, they can be run in parallel. *COSP* can therefore generate opportunities for pipelining the slow host-device memory channel in an accelerator-based system. It also offers an easy- to-distribute program structure to the compiler system, which can then map subproblems to different devices.

4. PIPELINING

Pipelining, in general, is a throughput-enhancing technique that overlaps the execution phases of one computation with another so as to make the best use of the available computational resources. We introduce an example of pipelining in Fig. 2. After performing *COSP*, one Split's kernel execution is overlapped with the next Split's memory copies; i.e. while the first subproblem kernel is working on the already copied-in data B, the copy-in for the next subproblem kernel's data B is taking place. It is important to note that to achieve successful pipelining, there should be two buffers present for each *MemSplittable* data so as to obtain the necessary prefetching.

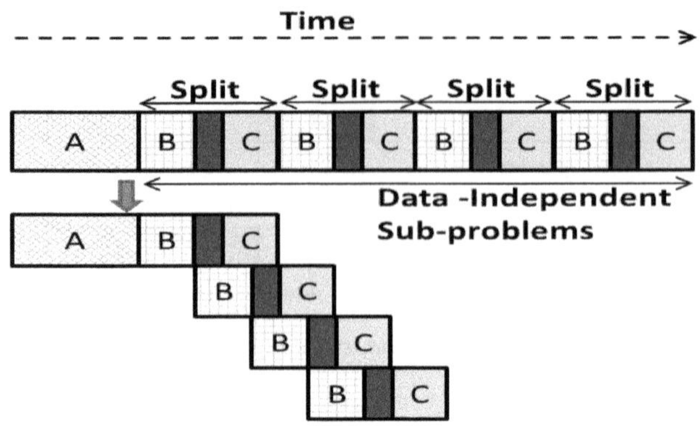

Figure 2: Pipelining Opportunity Generated by *COSP* : Individual Splits are independent; they can be pipelined

In the case at hand, the three resources that we propose to pipeline include the CPU-GPU channel, GPU-CPU channel (if different than the first) and the GPU computational units. This section focuses on the pipelining code generation of the compute-split code. It also explains the strategy to perform multi-device code mapping and implementation mechanisms adopted by our compiler.

4.1 Achievable Speedup from Pipelining

Maximum attainable speedup from pipelining is restricted by the number of pipelining stages. In the proposed scheme, there are three pipeline stages : (i) Memory channel between the CPU and the GPU (ii) Memory channel between the GPU and the CPU (iii) GPU Computation cores. Hence, the pipelining speedup can be at most three. Most new GPUs support overlaps between the computation and transfers. Some advanced GPUs, such as Tesla M2090, also support overlaps in the memory copy operations in different directions, since they have different channels for copying in each direction. For GPUs without dedicated copy engines, the speedup would be restricted by two.

$$Speedup = \frac{t_{compute} + t_{MemFused} + t_{co} + t_{ci}}{t_{MemFused} + max(t_{compute}, t_{co}, t_{ci})} \quad (2)$$

where
$t_{compute}$ = Time spent in kernel computation
$t_{MemFused}$ = Time spent in transferring MemFused data
t_{ci} = Time spent for copy-in of MemSplittable data
t_{co} = Time spent for copy-out of MemSplittable data

Equation 2 provides an upper bound on the pipelining speedup, assuming the *COSP* overhead is zero. It also assumes the presence of different memory copy channels for copy-in and copy-out operations.

All outputs of a parallel program fall under the *MemSplittable* category unless they are reductions. Although *COSP* can always 'split' the outputs of a program, it may not be always able to do so for its inputs, if the inputs fall under the *MemFused* category. The worst case scenario would be a program wherein computation of a single output element requires input data of type *MemFused* that has a size larger than the device memory. In such a case, algorithmic change in the program structure is the only alternative.

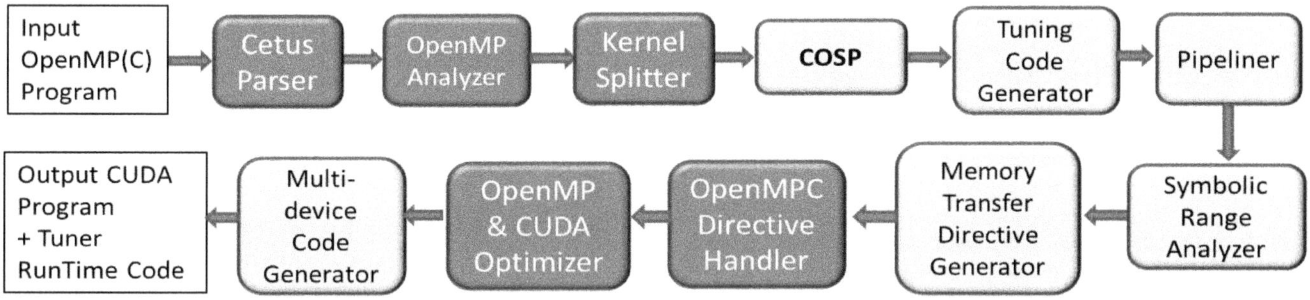

Figure 3: Overall System Flow : Darker boxes indicate the base OpenMPC passes.

4.2 Compiler Organization

Figure 3 shows the structure of our compiler. It builds on OpenMPC, representing the program using Cetus IR [19]. After parsing the source code, OpenMPC system-internal decision making is performed to identify the kernels to be offloaded to the GPU. *COSP* is performed next on the kernel regions recognized by the OpenMP analyzer. For each eligible kernel region, tuning code is generated. The pipelining pass is applied next. Pipelining is optional in the sense that a user could simply generate only the compute-split code. Communication generation for each pipeline chunk is handled by the advanced symbolic range analysis [20] stage, which encodes its results as OpenMPC memory transfer pragmas. Once the OpenMPC directive handler and CUDA optimizer have finished their work on the IR, the multi-device code generation pass maps the pipelines to their respective devices. For the correct functioning of the multi-device code generation pass, the pipelining pass is made multi-device aware, in the sense that it keeps a map of the pipelines to devices, which is utilized later on by the multi-device code generation pass.

4.3 Generating Pipelined Code

At the heart of realizing the pipelining is the ability of the CPU to execute memory copy and kernel operations on the device asynchronously. The underlying CUDA model provides a mechanism called *'CUDA streams'* that realizes this asynchronous operation. A *'cudaStream'* [9] represents an instruction stream of computation on the host CPU that queues the launches of device commands i.e. kernel launches and memory transfers. All operations on a given *cudaStream* are launched sequentially, however, different *cudaStreams* can run independently of each other. Our pipelining implementation describes the strategy using *cudaStreams*.

The pipelining stage unrolls the Split Loop in Listing 2 twice. Listing 3 displays the intermediate code generated by our compiler. The unrolling factor of two corresponds to the two data buffers required; one for the currently executing Split and another for prefetching the inputs of the next Split. Each unrolled Split is transformed into a separate kernel and the required memory buffers are allocated for each kernel by the base OpenMPC system. Unrolling the Split Loop eases the software pipelining implementation.

Bounds for the data required by each Split need to be precisely calculated to avoid transferring more than necessary data (lines 8-13 in Algo. 1). We develop an aggregate data sections analysis using the advanced symbolic range analysis techniques offered in Cetus. This algorithm determines the starting locations and data lengths per Split required for all aggregate data elements.

Listing 3: Intermediate Representation for Pipelining the Compute Split Parallel Region

```
for (split=0; split<NUM_VECTORS/SplitSize; split=split+2) {
  //Determine starting points and ranges required per Split
  E_c2gstart_stream_0=((split*NUM_ELEMENTS)*SplitSize);
  E_c2grange_stream_0=(NUM_ELEMENTS*SplitSize);
  F_g2cstart_stream_0=(split*SplitSize);
  F_g2crange_stream_0=SplitSize;
  D_c2gstart_stream_0=((split*NUM_ELEMENTS)*SplitSize);
  D_c2grange_stream_0=(NUM_ELEMENTS*SplitSize);
  E_c2gstart_stream_1=((NUM_ELEMENTS*SplitSize)+
  ((split*NUM_ELEMENTS)*SplitSize));
  E_c2grange_stream_1=(NUM_ELEMENTS*SplitSize);
  F_g2cstart_stream_1=(SplitSize+
  (split*SplitSize));
  F_g2crange_stream_1=SplitSize;
  D_c2gstart_stream_1=((NUM_ELEMENTS*SplitSize)+
  ((split*NUM_ELEMENTS)*SplitSize));
  D_c2grange_stream_1=(NUM_ELEMENTS*SplitSize);

  //Code to be launched by cudaStream 0
  #pragma omp parallel for  private(pos, sum, vec) shared \
  (NUM_ELEMENTS, NUM_VECTORS, split, SplitSize, D, E, F)
  #pragma cuda gpurun \
  g2cmemtr(F[F_g2cstart_stream_0: F_g2crange_stream_0]) \
  c2gmemtr(D[D_c2gstart_stream_0: D_c2grange_stream_0]) \
  c2gmemtr(E[E_c2gstart_stream_0: E_c2grange_stream_0])
  #pragma cuda gpurun noc2gmemtr(F) \
  nog2cmemtr(NUM_ELEMENTS, NUM_VECTORS, D, E)
  for (vec=0; vec<SplitSize; vec ++ ) {
    sum=0;
    for (pos=0; pos<NUM_ELEMENTS; pos ++ ) {
      sum+=(D[(pos+(NUM_ELEMENTS*
      (vec + split*SplitSize)))]*
      E[(pos+(NUM_ELEMENTS*(vec + split*SplitSize)))]);
    }
    F[(vec + split*SplitSize)]=((float)sum);
  }

  //Code to be launched by cudaStream 1
  #pragma omp parallel for  private(pos, sum, vec) shared \
  (NUM_ELEMENTS, NUM_VECTORS, split, SplitSize, D, E, F)
  #pragma cuda gpurun \
  g2cmemtr(F[F_g2cstart_stream_1: F_g2crange_stream_1]) \
  c2gmemtr(D[D_c2gstart_stream_1: D_c2grange_stream_1]) \
  c2gmemtr(E[E_c2gstart_stream_1: E_c2grange_stream_1])
  #pragma cuda gpurun noc2gmemtr(F) \
  nog2cmemtr(NUM_ELEMENTS, NUM_VECTORS, D, E)
  for (vec=0; vec<SplitSize; vec ++ ) {
    sum=0;
    for (pos=0; pos<NUM_ELEMENTS; pos ++ ) {
      sum+=(D[(pos+(NUM_ELEMENTS*
      (vec + (split+1)*SplitSize)))]*
      E[(pos+(NUM_ELEMENTS*(vec + (split+1)*SplitSize)))]);
    }
    F[(vec + (split+1)*SplitSize)]=((float)sum);
  }
}
```

It also categorizes the data into *MemSplittable* and *MemFused* categories. The algorithm determines the range of access for each usage of the given variable. It then performs a union operation on the individual ranges to get the comprehensive access range as well as the starting address of the data. Both these expressions are symbolic in nature and are parameterized by *SplitSize* and *Split* (Lines 3-17 in Listing 3).

The starting address and length for data copy are specified to the OpenMPC system using *c2gmemtr* and *g2cmemtr pragmas* that govern the generation of CPU-to-GPU and GPU-to-CPU communication, respectively. (Lines 23-25 and 42-44 in Listing 3). For *MemFused* data elements, for every Split, entire aggregate datatype transfer is required. In such cases, transfers for these data elements are hoisted outside the Split Loop.

Algorithm 1 Pipelined Code Generation from Compute Split Program

Input: Compute Split Loop '*Region*'
Output: Pipelined *CUDA* code

```
Unroll Region by a factor of 2;
Create cudaStreams stream0, stream1;
StreamMap = new Map(cudaStream, Split);
StreamMap.insert(stream0, first Split in Region);
StreamMap.insert(stream1, second Split in Region);
For each split ∈ Region do
//Static code contains only two Splits
    For each sharedVar ∈ split do
    //sharedVar is OpenMP shared type
        range = rangeAnalysis(sharedVar , split);
        if (range contains SplitSize) then
            start = getStartingPoint(range);
            insertCopyPragmas(sharedVar, start, range);
        else
        //this is a MemFused Variable, hoist memory
        //transfers out of the Split Loop
            insertCopyPragmas(sharedVar, Region);
        end if
    end for
end for
cudaCode = translate(Region, StreamMap);
//Format CUDA code to achieve desired
//queueing using streams
reOrganize(cudaCode, stream0, stream1);
```

Since GPUs have at most one data copy engine in the CPU-to-GPU or GPU-to-CPU direction, it is necessary to schedule the operations on this channel wisely in order to avoid bottlenecks on the data copy engines. Correct scheduling is necessary to assure maximum overlapping benefits as well. The first Split in the unrolled Split Loop is assigned to *cudaStream 0*. That is, the kernel launches and memory transfers for this Split are handled by *cudaStream 0*. Similarly, the second Split is attached to *cudaStream 1*. In this manner, unrolling of the Split loop helps in (a) Creating private buffers on the device per *cudaStream* and (b) Providing an easy kernel- *cudaStream* mapping. Memory copy requests in a given direction from both *cudaStreams* get serialized. Hence, the corresponding queueing strategy performs copy-in from *cudaStream 0* for Split 1, then issues the kernel from *cudaStream 0* for Split 1 and simultaneously performs copy-in via *cudaStream 1* for Split 2. Next, the system launches the kernel from *cudaStream 1* and subsequently issues copy-out from *cudaStream 0* and *cudaStream 1* respectively. Listing 3 shows that alternate Splits go on different *cudaStreams*.

Our system maintains a mapping between a Split and its corresponding *cudaStream*. After the CUDA code is generated by OpenMPC, the compiler reorganizes the memory transfer and kernel launches so as to realize the queuing strategy. We portray the complete pipelining code generation algorithm in Algorithm 1.

4.4 Multi-GPU Code Generation

As seen in the previous section, to implement pipelining, two *cudaStreams* are required for a single GPU. For multi-device code generation, our system extends this strategy and assigns two *cudaStreams* per device, the overall number of *cudaStreams* used being twice the number of devices. In other words, the Split Loop is unrolled twice per device.

The next important stage in multi-device code generation is to perform work partitioning amongst devices. We use block-cyclic partitioning wherein two contiguous Splits are attached to the same device, since these Splits are more likely to access data elements in the vicinity of each other; this method improves spatial locality while performing CPU-GPU transfers.

Further, data elements that need to be present completely inside the device memory even for a single Split computation (*MemFused* elements) need to be made 'private' per device, and the memory copies for such elements need to be hoisted out of the Split Loop. An example with the overall multi-device code generation strategy for two devices is shown in Fig. 4. Note that the dependences are caused due to the queueing on the memory copy channels.

5. ADAPTIVE RUNTIME TUNING SYSTEM

SplitSize is the number of iterations of the parallel loop in a given Split. SplitSize can therefore be thought of as the size of the pipeline stage. Each iteration of the Split is mapped to a GPU thread by OpenMPC. Hence, the choice of SplitSize determines the number of *ThreadBlocks* issued per Split, governing both the time required for computation and CPU-GPU communication. In this section, we describe how the choice of SplitSize impacts the pipelining performance. We then propose a heuristic tuning algorithm that selects the most suitable SplitSize.

5.1 Performance Variation with SplitSize

Equation 1 gave the maximum SplitSize that fits in the device memory. The SplitSize that yields the best performance results is usually less than this upper bound. Fig. 5 shows such execution time variation with different SplitSizes for two benchmarks. Experiments were run on Tesla M2090, which has separate memory copy engines in CPU-to-GPU and GPU-to-CPU directions. *Vector Add* is a memory copy-intensive application, whereas *Filterbank* is a compute-intensive one. *Vector Add* results were generated for problem size (iteration space) of 2^{27}; for *Filterbank*, the problem size was 2^{24}. Fig. 5 shows that the performance becomes better with increasing SplitSize for *Vector Add*, while better results can be achieved at lower SplitSize values for *Filterbank*. The choice of SplitSize is therefore important to achieve good performance, but selecting the correct SplitSize is not straightforward for the programmer. To build an intuition for choosing the SplitSize, we begin by analyzing the performance results on both memory copy-intensive and compute-intensive programs. The former spend most

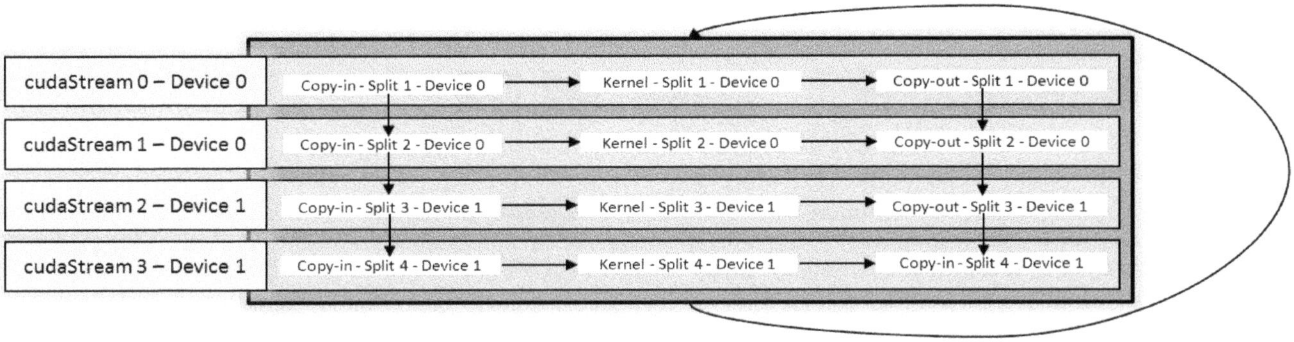

Figure 4: System Strategy to generate and run programs on Multiple Devices - In this case, the number is 2. Straight arrows depict dependences, the curved arrow represents Split loop

of their execution time on CPU-GPU transfers. The latter spend most of their execution time running the GPU kernels.

Fig 6 shows examples of the different behaviors of compute-intensive and memory copy-intensive programs. *Monte Carlo* is compute-intensive, while *Black Scholes* is memory copy-intensive. SplitSizes are chosen such that the number of *ThreadBlocks* launched by each SplitSize is a multiple of the number of SMs, *SMCount*, of the GPU. Note that the memory copy times show linear increase at smaller SplitSizes as compared to the kernel execution times. Since the pipelining benefits are higher when the pipelining stages are of equal size, relative increase in kernel execution time as compared to the memory copy time leads to better performance. Once the kernel execution starts to grow linearly with SplitSize, there is no more opportunity for higher benefits. This explains the performance variation with SplitSizes for *Vector Add* and *Black Scholes* benchmarks. Both these benchmarks have the highly memory copy-intensive *Type 1* overlapping pattern as shown in Fig. 7.

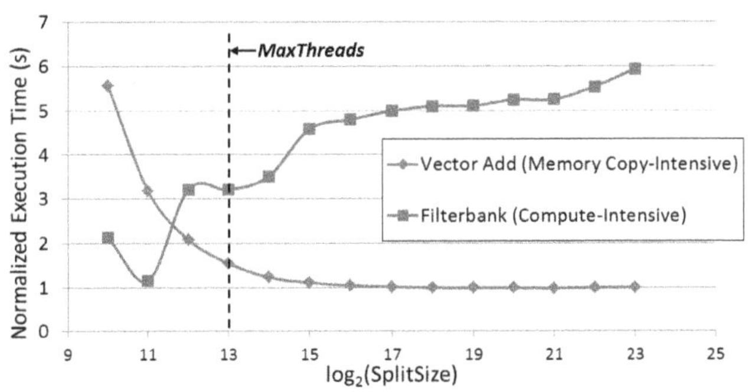

Figure 5: Performance Variation with SplitSize : Performance is higher for smaller SplitSizes for compute-intensive benchmarks, while for memory copy-intensive ones, performance is higher for larger SplitSizes. *MaxThreads* is the maximum number of threads that can co-exist on the GPU.

Compute-intensive programs like *Filterbank, Monte Carlo,* show the second type of overlap displayed in Fig. 7. In both these codes, the kernel execution time is larger than the sum of copy-in and copy-out times. A quick look at Fig. 7 shows that when the kernels are executing, the memory channel(s) are unused. One way to increase the kernel and memory copy overlap would be to run more *cudaStreams* so that the kernel time between the overlap of t_K^1 and t_K^2 (Fig. 7) can be further overlapped by memory transfers. Another alternative is to reduce the SplitSize and allow concurrent kernel execution, supported by the newer GPUs. Kernel-kernel

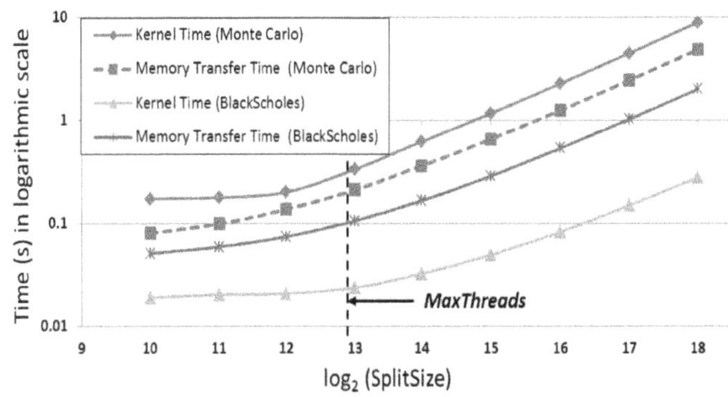

Figure 6: Kernel execution and Memory copy times per Split for different SplitSizes. Monte Carlo is compute-intensive; Black Scholes is memory copy-intensive. Experiments were run on Tesla M2090.

overlaps can easily occur in compute-intensive benchmarks. Due to the limited knowledge in GPU *ThreadBlock* scheduling mechanisms in the presence of multiple kernels, kernel-kernel overlap performance is difficult to predict or model and the performance tuning would need explicit runs with different SplitSizes. However, increasing the SplitSize to be larger than the maximum number of threads that can coexist on a GPU (*MaxThreads*) would only lead to queueing up of *ThreadBlocks* in the launching process. Hence, the SplitSize search space of interest in case of compute-intensive benchmarks is fairly small i.e. $SplitSize \leq MaxThreads$.

5.2 Adaptive Runtime Tuning Algorithm

With the aforementioned observations, we have developed a heuristic adaptive runtime tuning algorithm (Algorithm 2) for finding the SplitSize that would yield the best performance. First, the algorithm determines if the kernel is highly memory copy-intensive *(Type 1)* or highly compute-intensive *(Type 2)* or neither *(Type 3)* by running a pilot run with SplitSize equal to the $MaxThreads$.

Note that running just one Split (RUN_ONE_SPLIT, line 20 of Algo. 2) of the Split Loop is sufficient for the algorithm to determine the type of the kernel. The algorithm then generates a unique set of SplitSizes, named *CSet* or *configuration set*, depending upon the type of the program. Each SplitSize is chosen such that the number of *ThreadBlocks* contained in it is a multiple of *SMCount*, so as to evenly distribute the *ThreadBlocks* on *SM*s. The *CSet* generation is handled by the GENERATE_CONFIGS function (line 17 of Algo. 2). The largest SplitSize generated by the GENERATE_CONFIGS function is bounded by the device memory

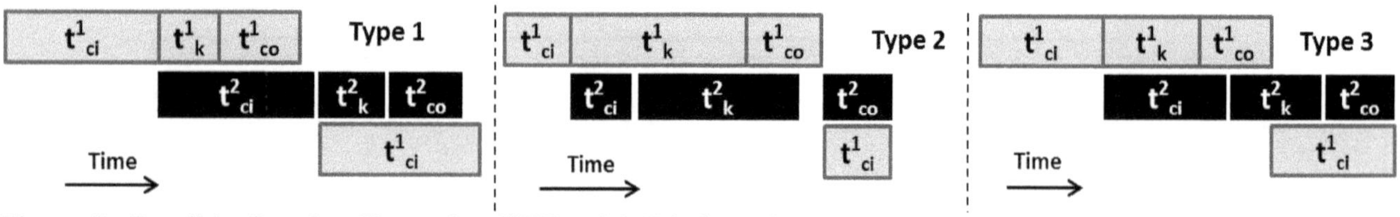

Figure 7: Possible Overlap Types for GPUs with Distinct Copy-in and Copy-out Engines : t_{ci} is the copy-in time, t_{co} is the copy-out time and t_k is the kernel execution time. Number in the superscript represents the *cudaStream*. Type 1 is the highly memory copy-intensive type with $t_{ci} > t_{co} + t_k$. Note that t_{ci} and t_{co} are interchangeable. Type 2 is highly compute-intensive, with $t_k > t_{ci} + t_{co}$. Type 3 is neither ($t_{ci} > t_k > t_{co}$ & $t_k + t_{co} > t_{ci}$). Note that shown is one of the many cases of different program patterns that can fit in *Type 3*.

capacity. It is worthwhile to note that the algorithm is agnostic of the number of threads per *ThreadBlock*.

Algorithm 2 Heuristic SplitSize Tuning Algorithm

Input: T is the *Number of Threads per ThreadBlock*
Input: $SMCount$ is the *Number of SMs*
Input: B is the maximum *ThreadBlocks* per *SM*
Output: Best SplitSize configuration

1: ———
2: //t_{ci} is copy-in time, t_k is kernel execution //time, t_{co} is copy-out time //t_o is the overlapped time : $t_o = $ //$min[max((t_{ci} + t_k), t_{co}), max((t_{co} + t_k), t_{ci})]$ //timer is an array of structures storing //quadruplet t_{ci}, t_{co}, t_k, t_o //$Normalizer(i) = MaxThreads/CSet(i)$
3: ———
4: **function** TUNER
5: $MaxThreads \leftarrow T \times SMCount \times B$
6: *Type* ← Nil
7: $(t_{ci}, t_k, t_{co}, t_o) \leftarrow RUN\_ONE\_SPLIT(MaxThreads)$;
8: **if** $(t_{ci} + t_{co} \leq t_k)$ **then**
9: *Type* ← 2;
10: **else if** $(t_{ci} + t_k \leq t_{co} \vee t_{co} + t_k \leq t_{ci})$ **then**
11: *Type* ← 1;
12: **else**
13: *Type* ← 3;
14: **end if**
15: //GENERATE_CONFIGS creates a sorted set of //SplitSize configurations
16: $CSet \leftarrow GENERATE\_CONFIGS(Type)$;
17: $min \leftarrow 1$;
18: **for** $i = 1 \rightarrow length(CSet)$ **do**
19: $timer[i] = RUN\_ONE\_SPLIT(CSet[i])$;
20: **if** $(Type = 1)$ **then**
21: **if** $(i > 1)$ **then**
22: $diff \leftarrow ((timer[i].t_k \times Normalizer(i)) - (timer[i-1].t_k \times Normalizer(i-1))$;
23: **if** $(|diff| \approx 0)$ **then return** $CSet[i-1]$;
24: **end if**
25: **end if**
26: **else if** $(timer[min].t_o \times Normalizer(min) < timer[i].t_o \times Normalizer(i))$ **then**
27: $min = i$;
28: **end if**
29: **end for**
30: **if** $(Type = 1)$ **then** **return** $CSet[i-1]$;
31: **else** **return** $CSet[min]$;
32: **end if**
33: **end function**
34:
35: **function** RUN_ONE_SPLIT(SplitSize)
36: Run one *Split* from the *Split loop*
37: Return corresponding t_{co}, t_{ci}, t_k, t_o
38: **end function**
39: ———

*This algorithm assumes bidirectional copy channels.

For *Type 1* programs, generated *CSet* contains SplitSizes $\geq MaxThreads$ in an increasing order. As explained earlier, a linear increase in the kernel execution time indicates the highest performance for memory copy-intensive programs. The algorithm therefore runs one Split per SplitSize in the *CSet* until the kernel time starts to grow linearly. Linear growth is established by comparing the kernel execution time of the previous SplitSize in the *CSet* (Line 23, in Algo. 2). This results in the selection of smallest SplitSize that would generate high performance while maintaining low device memory requirements.

For *Type 2* programs, algorithm generates the *CSet* with SplitSizes that are $\leq MaxThreads$. For each SplitSize, the runtimes for a single Split are noted, and the SplitSize with the best normalized overlapped time (Line 2, Algo. 2), t_o, is selected as the candidate.

Type 3 programs are neither highly compute-intensive nor memory copy-intensive. In such cases, the algorithm generates all possible SplitSizes (bounded by the device memory size) and runs one Split for each of them. The SplitSize with the best normalized overlapped time, t_o, is selected. *Type 3* denotes the worst case for the algorithm, since it requires a traversal in a larger space. However, most of the programs that we tried fell into either *Type 1* or *Type 2*.

Since the algorithm needs to run only a single Split to learn about the characteristics of a given SplitSize, the runtime overhead incurred is low.

5.3 Compiler Support for Tuning

The adaptive runtime tuning algorithm is automated in the compiler. The compiler automatically generates a tuning function for each kernel region. The tuning function contains an outlined copy of the parallel region, which is used to realize RUN_ONE_SPLIT function. This outlining is performed at the OpenMP level. Since the tuning function involves execution of some extra Splits, the original data may get modified. Outlining prevents this potentially harmful behavior to the kernel data during the tuning execution, as it forces the data elements in the tuning function to be allocated separately. Timer calls are inserted in this outlined copy to gather t_k, t_{ci} and t_{co}. Certain parts of the algorithm are inserted in this function, while others, such as GENERATE_CONFIGS, are implemented in a run-time library. The compiler automatically inserts the necessary calls to the runtime library functions. The tuning function is invoked only during the first call to the kernel; subsequent kernel calls use the SplitSize value that was generated during the first run.

Notice that the tuning system may not represent the best SplitSize if the control flow of the parallel region is divergent. However, if the parallel region is invoked only once, the first invoke runs the tuner which indeed finds the correct SplitSize.

6. EVALUATION

This section evaluates the performance of the presented computation splitting, pipelining and multi-device code generation regimes. We study seven kernels and two applications. *DCT, FFT* and *Filterbank* are traditional streaming benchmarks from the StreamIt benchmark suite [21]. These are compute-intensive applications. Other kernels, such as *Scalar Product*, *Black Scholes* and *Vector Add*, are from the CUDA SDK [22] and are mostly memory copy-intensive. *Monte Carlo*, also from CUDA SDK, is compute-intensive. *SRAD* and *CFD* are two applications from the Rodinia benchmark suite [23] and both are memory copy-intensive. To explore out-of-card situations, the benchmarks were run with larger datasets than provided in the benchmark suites. The baseline, non-pipelined translation from OpenMPC is used as the comparison point.

We used an NVIDIA Tesla M2090 GPU for our experiments. The device has 16 Streaming Multiprocessors (SMs) and remarkably large 6GB of DRAM. The GPU is connected via an x16 PCIe link to a host system consisting of an AMD Opteron Processor 6282 with 16 cores, running at 2.6 GHz. The host system has 64GB RAM. Up to 4 GPUs were connected to the host using the same PCIe bus.

We evaluate the contributions of our system in the following manner : (a) We demonstrate the ability of our system to handle large out-of-card data sizes by performing *COSP*. We compare the scalability of our approach against hand-written CUDA and baseline OpenMPC programs. (b) We evaluate the efficacy of our tuning method by comparing its performance to a naive compiler-only strategy. We also measure the overheads incurred by the tuning system. (c) To evaluate the benefits of pipelining and multi-GPU code generation, we compare the results obtained by these techniques over baseline OpenMPC.

6.1 System Scalability

COSP allows large, out-of-card data sizes to run on GPUs with limited device memories. Table 1 shows the system scalability of the *COSP* approach for three different representative benchmarks and also compares the results with hand-written CUDA and baseline OpenMPC codes. We calculate the maximum achieveable speedup from pipelining and compare it with the achieved speedup. To generate these results, we used hand-written CUDA codes from the CUDA SDK. Asynchronous transfers between the CPU and GPU require the corresponding memory to be allocated in 'pinned' pages i.e. the OS pages that can not be swapped out of the host memory. This can be achieved using the CUDA *cudaHostAlloc* API call. Since OS pages allocated in this fashion improve the overall application performance, the hand-written and base OpenMPC-generated CUDA codes were modified, allocating the host memories using *cudaHostAlloc*, to produce consistent comparison results with the CUDA versions generated by our system.

The scalability problems faced by the hand-written CUDA programs and the base OpenMPC-produced programs can be clearly seen from Table 1, since whenever the data size goes out-of-card, both these codes fail. For hand-written CUDA programs, as seen for the *Monte Carlo* benchmark, the number of *ThreadBlocks*, or the grid size, launched by the code crosses the CUDA-imposed limit of 65536 in a single dimension and the code starts failing even when the memory space requirement is sufficiently small to fit in the device. This is a severe programmability issue, as the programmer must consider all possible input sizes and manage the grid formation accordingly. A high-level programming model, such as OpenMPC, can easily tackle this issue by launching two dimensional grids if one dimension exceeds the limit. Hand-written CUDA codes underperform the baseline OpenMPC-generated codes as the input sizes grow large for the *Black Scholes* and *Monte Carlo* benchmarks. In the *Black Scholes* hand-written CUDA code, the launched grid size is constant and is better suited for small data sizes. In the *Monte Carlo* hand-written CUDA code, a part of the parallel loop is left out from the kernel and is instead run on the CPU. Our system translates this entire loop for GPU execution. Further, the *constant* memory allocation in the hand-written *Monte Carlo* CUDA code is proportional to the data size, and *constant* memory can run out of space if the problem size increases. High-level programming models can alleviate these programmability issues, ensuring the scalability of programs for arbitrary data sizes.

Performance benefits of our pipelining scheme can be seen in Table 1. This table also dispays the effectiveness of our implementation by comparing the ideal speedup that can be achieved from pipelining against the one obtained by our system. Except for the smallest data sizes, pipelining speedup numbers closely follow the ideal speedups for the *Monte Carlo* and *Scalar Product* programs. The differences between the ideal and achieved speedups are mainly due to the underperformance of the bidirectional transfer overlaps on the PCI Express (PCIe). This effect becomes a performance limiter for programs like *Black Scholes*, which have large bidirectional data transfers. For the small dataset of *Monte Carlo*, the optimal SplitSize suggested by our tuning system was 8192, being just one fourth of the input iteration space, thereby lowering the obtained pipelining benefits. Similar is the case for *Black Scholes*. Constant speedups for any large data size demonstrate the scalability of our approach.

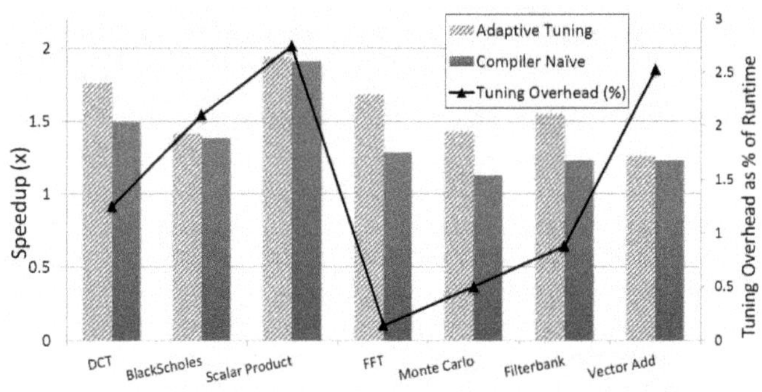

Figure 8: Performance of Adaptive Runtime Tuning System : Speedups are with respect to the OpenMPC non-pipelined baseline. Higher performance of the tuned program versions over a naive pipelining approach emphasize the necessity of tuning.

6.2 Tuning System Performance

To measure the performance benefits gained from tuning the pipelined system, we compare the speedups achieved by our adaptive tuning method over the baseline OpenMPC codes against a *naive* compiler-driven splitting strat-

Benchmark	DataSize (Iteration Space)	CUDA Time (s)	OpenMPC Base Time (s)	%Copy-in Time(s)	%Copy-out Time(s)	%Kernel Time(s)	OpenMPC Pipelined Time (s)	Speedup Ideal	Speedup Achieved
Scalar Product	1024 x 1024	0.633	0.88807	52.19789	0.22676	47.57535	0.46297	1.91579	1.91822
	1024 x1024 x2	1.267	1.7723				0.91496		1.93703
	1024 x1024 x4	----	----				1.73067		
Monte Carlo	1024 x32	0.00537	0.00454	21.55109	13.71958	64.72933	0.0037	1.54489	1.22733
	1024 x1024 x32	***	1.79902				1.24699		1.44268
	1024 x1024 x64	***	3.5924				2.51465		1.42859
	1024 x1024 x128	----	----				5.02565		
Black Scholes	1024 x16	0.00105	0.00158	46.64777	41.9736	11.37863	0.00164	2.14373	0.96344
	1024 x1024 x128	1.8598	1.22591				0.87698		1.39786
	1024 x1024 x256	----	2.457				1.73985		1.41219
	1024 x1024 x384	----	----				2.60183		

Table 1: Scalability of the *COSP* and Pipelining Mechanism : We compare the execution times of hand-written CUDA, baseline OpenMPC and compute split, pipelined OpenMPC programs. The ideal speedup is calculated using Eq. 2. In the table, '*' represent failure of the code due to larger-than-allowed grid sizes used. '—' represent code failure due to out-of-memory data size errors. Scalability of our approach can be gauged as arbitrarily large problems with out-of-card data sizes can be run and the speedup achieved for any large data size remains almost constant.**

egy. We found 1024 splits to be a good number that generated performance improvements and chose it as the "naive" reference point.

Fig. 8 displays the effectiveness of the adaptive runtime tuning system over this naive strategy. The superior performance of the tuned codes over the naive strategy indicates the importance of tuning; a static estimate of the number of splits can not provide the best performance. Further, a number of splits that yields good results for a given program may be suboptimal for another program. We also measure the overheads incurred by the adaptive runtime tuning system in terms of the percentage runtime spent in tuning. Because the tuning system runs only a single Split of the Split Loop per tuning configuration, the runtime overhead is low. The maximum overhead, measured as the percentage runtime of the total execution time, is less than 3%. Note that the tuning overhead decreases as the computation size grows.

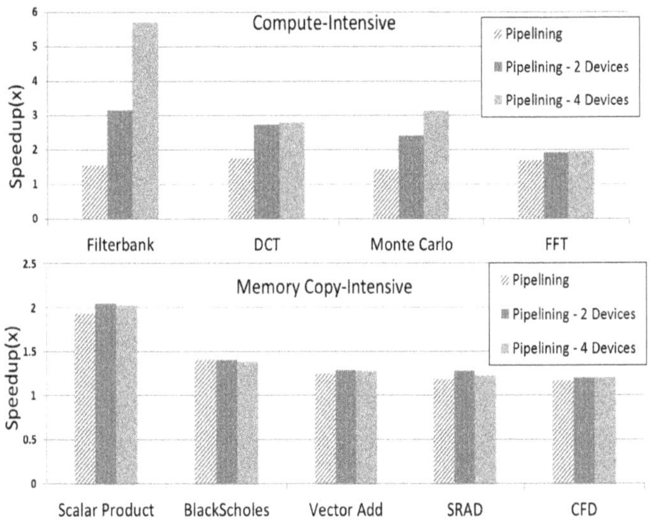

Figure 9: Speedup over the Baseline OpenMPC Generated Codes (without pipelining) : Compute-intensive applications show good scalability with multiple GPUs. Memory copy-intensive programs scale poorly with multiple GPUs since PCIe bus forms a bottleneck.

6.3 Overall Performance Comparison

We now present comprehensive results over all benchmarks showing the effects of pipelining on 1, 2 and 4 GPUs in Fig. 9. Since the maximum speedup over the baseline system that can be achieved with pipelining is limited by three in our setup, the theoritical maximum speedup that can be achieved by pipelining, implemented on four GPUs, can be at most twelve.

Benchmarks like *DCT, FFT, Scalar Product, Monte Carlo, Filterbank* show large performance benefits since they have balanced computation and memory transfer contents, translating into equally sized pipeline stages. *SRAD, CFD and Vector Add* have a low computation-to-communication ratio and therefore show lesser overall speedups. Highly compute-intensive benchmarks like *Filterbank, Monte Carlo* show excellent scalability when multiple devices are used.

Secondly, not all benchmarks show large performance benefits when run with multiple GPUs; the reason being the bottleneck formed on the PCIe bus while transferring the data.

7. RELATED WORK

An alternative to deal with problems of arbitrarily large data sizes can be to write the basic program flow in terms of a stream graph. Each kernel can then be made to have a granularity of a single iteration of the stream graph. Two recent systems propose mechanisms to convert streaming programs written in StreamIt [24] language into GPU codes. The first system, Sponge [25], suggests mechanisms to optimize the stream graph. It then splits the graph into multiple kernels. Huynh et al. propose another system [26] that takes a different approach and places an entire iteration of a stream graph on a single Streaming Multiprocessor (SM). This mechanism can face scalability issues due to the restriction of running just one iteration on an SM. Since each filter in a StreamIt graph consists of its own inputs and outputs, global memory accesses can be overwhelming. Both these systems therefore propose mechanisms to prefetch data into the GPU shared memory and optimize the shared memory usage. However, the behavior of these systems is undefined if the data size required is larger than the GPU memory. Secondly, the applicability of the stream programming model to large applications is still an open challenge. Further work by Huynh et al. [27] performs multi-level partitioning of the stream graph to overcome the scalability challenges in [26]. In this work, a mechanism to port StreamIt programs to multi-GPUs on the same system has also been proposed. This system heterogeneously executes kernels on several GPUs, owing to the outcome of the multi-level partitioning performed on the StreamIt graph. By contrast, our system partitions the work homogeneously amongst GPUs and yields the best possible pipelining code with the help of a fast tuning system.

A naive CUDA-provided solution to deal with out-of-card data sizes is to make use of *Zero Copy* memory. The *Zero Copy* memory mechanism allocates the corresponding buffers in the host memory instead of the device memory. The pointers to the buffers on the CPU and the GPU are mapped to each other. GPU reads the memory objects directly from the host during the kernel execution. Therefore, if the kernel has significant amount of reuse, the overheads of copying from the CPU memory would degrade the performance.

Pipelining benefits have been previously explored for GPUs to hide the global memory access latencies by generating a software pipeline that copies data into shared memory [28, 29, 26, 25]. Aji et al. propose an approach [30] that deals with a network of nodes containing GPUs, aiming to overlap the communication between nodes with computations. Our work complements these techniques since our goal is to efficiently pipeline the CPU-GPU bus.

GPU performance tuning has been a research challenge; many approaches try to model and tune the GPU performance. While many proposed tuning systems are specific to the problem domains (3D Stencil [31], N-body simulations [32], 3-D FFT [33], SpMV [34]) , Ryoo et al. [15] propose generic performance metrics that help pre-select some potential parameter configurations to choose from. A distinguishing factor of our work is the tuning objective: In contrast to approaches that try to optimize the size of the *ThreadBlock*, our work attempts to optimize the grid size i.e. the number of *ThreadBlocks*. OpenMPC's inherent tuning system performs compiler-driven optimization option pruning to generate a set of parameter configurations. However, both the OpenMPC tuning system and the space pruning proposed by Ryoo et al. are run offline and require multiple complete runs of the entire programs to choose the best configuration.

Partitioning the application so as to make use of multiple GPUs attached to the same host CPU is an emerging research challenge. While some approaches target specific applications, e.g. Matrix multiply [7], fluid simulations [8], Kim et al. [35] provide an OpenCL based approach that provides a single device image of a multi-GPU system to the application developer. However, the scalability of this approach is bound by the total GPU memory sizes.

By contrast, ours is the first work that automatically deals with out-of-card data sizes and generates pipelined, multi-GPU code for generic applications, starting with a high-level program representation.

8. CONCLUSION

We have described a novel pipelining optimization that is able to scale large-data computations on multi-GPU accelerators. To this end, the technique splits a computation so it fits in the available memory resources and overlaps data transfer with computation. The execution can take advantage of multiple GPU devices. We have demonstrated that the technique can successfully execute out-of-card datasets that would fail without our optimization. For programs and datasets whose baseline versions succeed, our technique improves performance by 1.49x, on average, owing to the computation-communication overlap. We have implemented our optimization in one of the most advanced compilation platforms for GPGPUs: OpenMPC. This system converts OpenMP programs to CUDA, performing several advanced transformations. OpenMPC provided a state-of-the-art baseline for our measurements; it also allowed us to demonstrate our technique in the context of an important current language trend, which is the extension of OpenMP with accelerator directives.

9. ACKNOWLEDGMENTS

This work was supported, in part, by the National Science Foundation under grants No. CNS-0720471, 0707931-CNS, 0833115-CCF, and 0916817-CCF.

10. REFERENCES

[1] Thomas B. Jablin, Prakash Prabhu, James A. Jablin, Nick P. Johnson, Stephen R. Beard, and David I. August. "Automatic CPU-GPU communication management and optimization". *SIGPLAN Not.*, 47(6):142–151, June 2011.

[2] Seyong Lee and Rudolf Eigenmann. "OpenMPC: Extended OpenMP Programming and Tuning for GPUs". In *Proceedings of the 2010 ACM/IEEE International Conference for High Performance Computing, Networking, Storage and Analysis*, SC '10, pages 1–11. IEEE Computer Society, 2010.

[3] Mehdi Amini, Fabien Coelho, Francois Irigoin, and Ronan Keryell. "Static Compilation Analysis for Host-Accelerator Communication Optimization". In *24th Int. Workshop on Languages and Compilers for Parallel Computing (LCPC)*, sep 2011. Also Technical Report MINES ParisTech A/476/CRI.

[4] Liang Gu, Jakob Siegel, and Xiaoming Li. "Using GPUs to compute large out-of-card FFTs". In *Proceedings of the international conference on Supercomputing*, ICS '11, pages 255–264. ACM, 2011.

[5] Bingsheng He, Wenbin Fang, Qiong Luo, Naga K. Govindaraju, and Tuyong Wang. "Mars: a MapReduce framework on graphics processors". In *Proceedings of the 17th international conference on Parallel architectures and compilation techniques*, PACT '08, pages 260–269. ACM, 2008.

[6] J.A. Stuart and J.D. Owens. "Multi-GPU MapReduce on GPU Clusters". In *Parallel Distributed Processing Symposium (IPDPS), 2011 IEEE International*, pages 1068 –1079, may 2011.

[7] Fengguang Song, Stanimire Tomov, and Jack Dongarra. "Enabling and scaling matrix computations on heterogeneous multi-core and multi-GPU systems". In *Proceedings of the 26th ACM international conference on Supercomputing*, ICS '12, pages 365–376. ACM, 2012.

[8] Fengquan Zhang, Lei Hu, Jiawen Wu, and Xukun Shen. "A SPH-based method for interactive fluids simulation on the

multi-GPU". In *Proceedings of the 10th International Conference on Virtual Reality Continuum and Its Applications in Industry*, VRCAI '11, pages 423–426. ACM, 2011.

[9] NVIDIA Corporation. *NVIDIA CUDA Compute Unified Device Architecture Programming Guide.* NVIDIA Corporation, 2011.

[10] T.D. Han and T.S. Abdelrahman. "hiCUDA: High-Level GPGPU Programming". *Parallel and Distributed Systems, IEEE Transactions on*, 22(1):78 -90, jan. 2011.

[11] Sain zee Ueng, Melvin Lathara, Sara S. Baghsorkhi, and Wen mei W. Hwu. "CUDA-Lite: Reducing GPU programming complexity". In *In: LCPCâĂŹ08. Volume 5335 of LNCS*, pages 1–15. Springer, 2008.

[12] Y. Yan, M. Grossman, and V. Sarkar. "JCUDA: A Programmer-Friendly Interface for Accelerating Java Programs with CUDA". *Euro-Par 2009 Parallel Processing*, page 887âĂŞ899, 2009.

[13] OpenACC. `http://www.openacc-standard.org/`, November 2011.

[14] Sunpyo Hong and Hyesoon Kim. "An analytical model for a GPU architecture with memory-level and thread-level parallelism awareness". In *Proceedings of the 36th annual international symposium on Computer architecture*, ISCA '09, pages 152–163. ACM, 2009.

[15] Shane Ryoo, Christopher I. Rodrigues, Sam S. Stone, Sara S. Baghsorkhi, Sain-Zee Ueng, John A. Stratton, and Wen-mei W. Hwu. "Program optimization space pruning for a multithreaded gpu". In *Proceedings of the 6th annual IEEE/ACM international symposium on Code generation and optimization*, CGO '08, pages 195–204. ACM, 2008.

[16] NVIDIA Corporation. *CUDA C Best Practices Guide*, May 2011.

[17] Seyong Lee, Seung-Jai Min, and Rudolf Eigenmann. "OpenMP to GPGPU: a compiler framework for automatic translation and optimization". *SIGPLAN Not.*, 44(4):101–110, February 2009.

[18] OpenMP. Improvement to support Accelerators `http://openmp.org/wp/2012/03/openmp-is-being-improved-for-accelerators-multicore-and-embedded-systems/`, 2012.

[19] Hansang Bae, Dheya Mustafa, Jae-Woo Lee, Aurangzeb, Hao Lin, Chirag Dave, Rudolf Eigenmann, and Samuel Midkiff. "The Cetus Source-to-Source Compiler Infrastructure: Overview and Evaluation". *International Journal of Parallel Programming*, pages 1–15, 2012. 10.1007/s10766-012-0211-z.

[20] Hansang Bae and Rudolf Eigenmann. "Interprocedural symbolic range propagation for optimizing compilers". In *Proceedings of the 18th international conference on Languages and Compilers for Parallel Computing*, LCPC'05, pages 413–424. Springer-Verlag, 2006.

[21] StreamIt Benchmarks [Online]. Available: `http://groups.csail.mit.edu/cag/streamit/shtml/benchmarks.shtml`.

[22] NVIDIA. GPU Computing SDK [Online] `https://developer.nvidia.com/gpu-computing-sdk`.

[23] Shuai Che, Michael Boyer, Jiayuan Meng, David Tarjan, Jeremy W. Sheaffer, Sang-Ha Lee, and Kevin Skadron. "Rodinia: A benchmark suite for heterogeneous computing". In *Proceedings of the 2009 IEEE International Symposium on Workload Characterization (IISWC)*, IISWC '09, pages 44–54. IEEE Computer Society, 2009.

[24] William Thies, Michal Karczmarek, and Saman P. Amarasinghe. "StreamIt: A Language for Streaming Applications". In *Proceedings of the 11th International Conference on Compiler Construction*, CC '02, pages 179–196. Springer-Verlag, 2002.

[25] Amir H. Hormati, Mehrzad Samadi, Mark Woh, Trevor Mudge, and Scott Mahlke. "Sponge: portable stream programming on graphics engines". In *Proceedings of the sixteenth international conference on Architectural support for programming languages and operating systems*, ASPLOS '11, pages 381–392. ACM, 2011.

[26] A. Hagiescu, Huynh Phung Huynh, Weng-Fai Wong, and R.S.M. Goh. "Automated Architecture-Aware Mapping of Streaming Applications Onto GPUs". In *Parallel Distributed Processing Symposium (IPDPS), 2011 IEEE International*, pages 467 -478, may 2011.

[27] Huynh Phung Huynh, Andrei Hagiescu, Weng-Fai Wong, and Rick Siow Mong Goh. "Scalable framework for mapping streaming applications onto multi-GPU systems". In *Proceedings of the 17th ACM SIGPLAN symposium on Principles and Practice of Parallel Programming*, PPoPP '12, pages 1–10. ACM, 2012.

[28] M. Bauer, H. Cook, and B. Khailany. "CudaDMA: Optimizing GPU memory bandwidth via warp specialization". In *High Performance Computing, Networking, Storage and Analysis (SC), 2011 International Conference for*, pages 1 -11, nov. 2011.

[29] Abhishek Udupa, R. Govindarajan, and Matthew J. Thazhuthaveetil. "Software Pipelined Execution of Stream Programs on GPUs". In *Proceedings of the 7th annual IEEE/ACM International Symposium on Code Generation and Optimization*, CGO '09, pages 200–209. IEEE Computer Society, 2009.

[30] A.M. Aji, J. Dinan, D. Buntinas, P. Balaji, Wu chun Feng, K.R. Bisset, and R. Thakur. "MPI-ACC: An Integrated and Extensible Approach to Data Movement in Accelerator-based Systems". In *High Performance Computing and Communication 2012 IEEE 9th International Conference on Embedded Software and Systems (HPCC-ICESS), 2012 IEEE 14th International Conference on*, pages 647 -654, june 2012.

[31] Yongpeng Zhang and Frank Mueller. "Auto-generation and auto-tuning of 3D stencil codes on GPU clusters". In *Proceedings of the Tenth International Symposium on Code Generation and Optimization*, CGO '12, pages 155–164. ACM, 2012.

[32] Pritish Jetley, Lukasz Wesolowski, Filippo Gioachin, Laxmikant V. Kalé, and Thomas R. Quinn. "Scaling Hierarchical N-body Simulations on GPU Clusters". In *Proceedings of the 2010 ACM/IEEE International Conference for High Performance Computing, Networking, Storage and Analysis*, SC '10, pages 1–11. IEEE Computer Society, 2010.

[33] Akira Nukada and Satoshi Matsuoka. "Auto-tuning 3-D FFT library for CUDA GPUs". In *Proceedings of the Conference on High Performance Computing Networking, Storage and Analysis*, SC '09, pages 30:1–30:10. ACM, 2009.

[34] Jee W. Choi, Amik Singh, and Richard W. Vuduc. "Model-driven autotuning of sparse matrix-vector multiply on GPUs". In *Proceedings of the 15th ACM SIGPLAN Symposium on Principles and Practice of Parallel Programming*, PPoPP '10, pages 115–126. ACM, 2010.

[35] Jungwon Kim, Honggyu Kim, Joo Hwan Lee, and Jaejin Lee. "Achieving a single compute device image in OpenCL for multiple GPUs". In *Proceedings of the 16th ACM symposium on Principles and practice of parallel programming*, PPoPP '11, pages 277–288. ACM, 2011.

Hybrid Approach for Data-flow Analysis of MPI Programs

Sriram Aananthakrishnan
University of Utah
sriram@cs.utah.edu

Greg Bronevetsky
Lawrence Livermore National Laboratory
greg@bronevetsky.com

Ganesh Gopalakrishnan
University of Utah
ganesh@cs.utah.edu

ABSTRACT

With the increasing cost of developing robust HPC software, precise data-flow analysis for MPI programs – the mainstay of HPC programming – are essential. The knowledge of communication is essential for precise data-flow analysis and the difficulty of statically determining it makes the conventional techniques insufficient. Hybrid methods combining static and dynamic techniques are needed and in this work we demonstrate one such approach in building the parallel control-flow graph which can then be used to leverage the precision of data-flow analyses for MPI programs.

Categories and Subject Descriptors

D.3.4 [**Programming Languages**]: Processors—*compilers*; F.3.2 [**Logics and Meaning of Programs**]: Semantics of Programming Languages—*Program analysis*

Keywords

Data-flow analysis; MPI; parallel control-flow graph

1. INTRODUCTION

Sequential data-flow analyses are insufficient to analyze MPI applications that are, by nature, concurrent. Existing data-flow techniques for MPI [1] [2] suffer from imprecision as they over approximate the communication behavior. The framework based on [3]is communication sensitive, however to determine a send-receive match statically, it employs a complex matching algorithm that requires non-standard inferences such as function composition on its abstractions. To address the matching problem, for a MPI program with N processes, we create N instances of the control-flow graph (CFG) and connect a send with its receive by concretely executing the respective MPI operations. The matchings are then handled by the MPI runtime.

The edges that a connect a send with its receive are called communication edges, i.e pairs (s, r) where s is a node of CFG_i with send semantics and r is a node of CFG_j with receive semantics. The parallel control-flow graph CFG^N consists of N replicated sequential CFG with such communication edges. The CFG^N construction requires composition of multiple analyses, which is the main focus of our work.

ICS'13, June 10–14, 2013, Eugene, Oregon, USA.
ACM 978-1-4503-2130-3/13/06.

2. HYBRID ANALYSIS

Our key insight is that in majority of MPI applications the communication is determined by the values of pid (rank) and size of the MPI communicator. We treat these variables as concrete values instead of symbolic abstractions, enabling us identify the value of the target expressions in a send/receive function. We associate an analysis instance (also a MPI process) for each process of the MPI application. Each instance is a composition of following analyses (i) slicing (ii) constant propagation and folding, (iii) unreachable code elimination (iv) communication invariance (v) dynamic send-receive matching.

The control-flow graph is sliced to contain only statements affecting the communication. Constant propagation and folding allow us to determine the values of target expressions such as $rank\%size - 1$ in MPI functions as each analysis instance gets its copy of rank, size. Unreachable code elimination prunes the path not reachable by an analysis instance. Communication invariance determines that the communication is not input dependent and does not involve ambiguous paths, where execution is dependent on input or the message. The dynamic send-receive matching on reaching the control-flow node of a MPI function concretely executes it. It sends information about the MPI function and the corresponding receiver interprets this information to build the communication edges. Our approach employs hybrid method to build the CFG^N for MPI programs. Data-flow analyses to improve precision can exchange state information along the communication edges using MPI.

The framework in this paper is being implemented based on [4] and is integrated with the ROSE[5] compiler framework. Preliminary evaluations are in progress.

3. REFERENCES

[1] Strout. M, Kreaseck. B, Hovland. P D., *Data-Flow Analysis for MPI Programs*, ICPP '06

[2] Shires. D, Pollock. L,Sprenkle. S, *Program Flow Graph Construction For Static Analysis of MPI Programs*, PDPTA 1999

[3] Bronevetsky. G, *Communication-Sensitive Static data-flow for Parallel Message Passing Applications*, CGO '09

[4] Bronevetsky. G, Burke. M, Aananthakrishnan. S, Zhao. J, Sarkar. V, *Compositional data-flow via Abstract Transition Systems*, (TR)

[5] Quinlan. D, *ROSE Compiler*,http://www.rosecompiler.org

Improving Performance of All-to-All Communication Through Loop Scheduling in PGAS Environments

Michail Alvanos[∓]
Programming Models
Barcelona Supercomputing Center
malvanos@bsc.es

Gabriel Tanase
IBM TJ Watson Research Center
Yorktown Heights, NY, US
igtanase@us.ibm.com

Montse Farreras
Dep. of Computer Architecture
Universitat Politècnica de Catalunya
mfarrera@ac.upc.edu

Ettore Tiotto
Static Compilation Technology
IBM Toronto Laboratory
etiotto@ca.ibm.com

José Nelson Amaral
Dep. of Computing Science
University of Alberta
jamaral@ualberta.ca

Xavier Martorell
Dep. of Computer Architecture
Universitat Politècnica de Catalunya
xavim@ac.upc.edu

Categories and Subject Descriptors

C.4 [**Performance of Systems**]; D.3.4 [**Compilers**]; D.1.3 [**Parallel programming**]; D.3.2 [**Concurrent, distributed, and parallel languages**]

Keywords

Unified Parallel C, Partitioned Global Address Space, One-Sided Communication, Performance Evaluation

1. LOOP SCHEDULING

The Unified Parallel C language promises a simple programming model for applications that can run on distributed-shared memory systems. One of the inherited limitations of UPC language is the transparency provided to the programmer. The core idea of this optimization is to schedule memory accesses distinct so that each thread accesses distinct the same shared data. We use the XLUPC compiler framework [1] for the experimental prototype. First, the compiler collects loops that are normalized, they do not have any loop carried dependencies, and they contain shared references. The compiler categorizes the loops in two categories:

- Loops with coarse-grain UPC transfer calls and whose upper bound is the number of UPC threads. In this case, the compiler creates a lookup table that contains the UPC threads randomly shuffled.
- Loops that contain fine-grain communication. In this case, the compiler skews the iterations in such a way that each UPC thread starts executing from a different point in the shared array. To calculate the new induction variable of the loop we use the following equation:

$$NEW\_IV = (IV + MYTHREAD \times Block)\%UB;$$

Where $Block = \frac{SIZE\_OF\_ARRAY}{THREADS}$ and UB is the upper bound of the loop.

Finally, the compiler replaces the induction variable occurrences inside the loop body with the new value.

2. EVALUATION

The evaluation uses a Power 775 machine. Figure 1 shows the performance with different versions of a **microbenchmark**. Figure 2 presents the results for two applications: **bucketsort** and **NPB FT**.

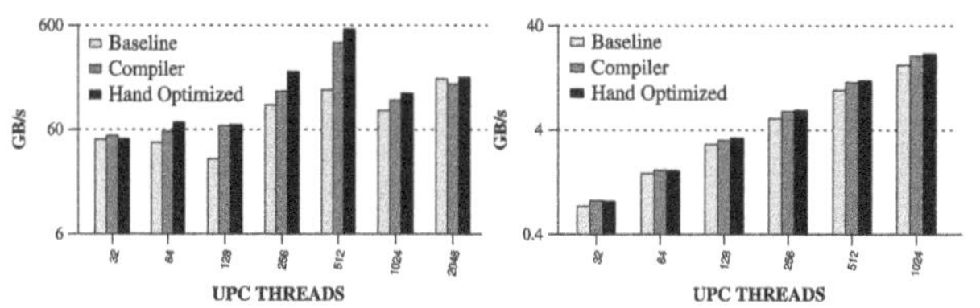

Figure 1: Performance numbers for upc_memput (left) and fine-grained get (right).

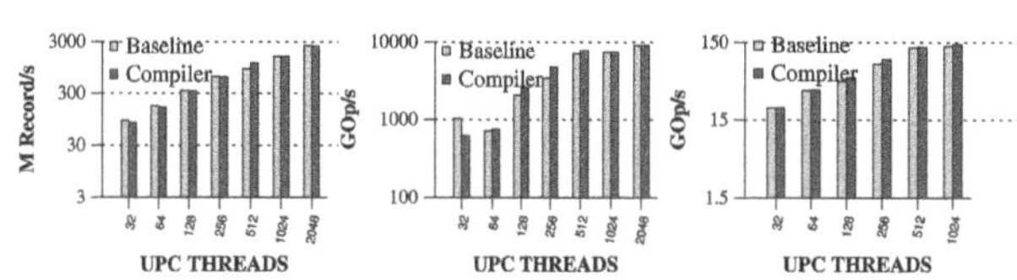

(a) (b) (c)

Figure 2: Performance for bucketsort (a), bucketsort with communication only (b), and FT (c).

3. REFERENCES

[1] G. Tanase, G. Almási, E. Tiotto, M. Alvanos, A. Ly, and B. Daltonn. Performance Analysis of the IBM XL UPC on the PERCS Architecture. Technical report, 2013. RC25360.

[∓]Also, with IBM Canada CAS Research, Markham, Ontario, Canada

We would like to acknowledge the support from the IBM CAS (2012-069), the Spanish Ministry of Science and Innovation (TIN2012-34557), the DARPA (HR0011-07-9-0002), DOE (DE-AC02-05CH11231), and the NSERC CRD program of Canada.

ICS'13, June 10–14, 2013, Eugene, Oregon, USA.
ACM 978-1-4503-2130-3/13/06.

CUPL : A Compile-time Uncoalesced Memory Access Pattern Locator for CUDA

Madhur Amilkanthwar, Shankar Balachandran
Dept. of Computer Science and Engineering
Indian Institute of Technology, Madras
{madhur, shankar}@cse.iitm.ac.in

ABSTRACT

Coalesced memory access patterns in CUDA yields high performance but achieving such patterns in an application can be tedious. We propose a tool, CUPL, which locates uncoalesced access patterns (UCAP) in a given kernel at compile-time. CUPL does static analysis of a given kernel using polyhedral model and reports warnings if the input kernel exhibits UCAP. CUPL has two-fold use 1) It can help the programmer to locate regions of the code to optimize 2) It can help a compiler to locate an opportunity to perform efficient data layout transformations. Initial experiments show that CUPL reports warnings at appropriate places in kernels from Rodinia benchmark and NVIDIA SDK suites.

Categories and Subject Descriptors

D.3.4 [**Programming Languages**]: Compilers

Keywords

Polyhedral tool, GPU, access pattern, static analysis

1. MOTIVATION AND DESIGN

Optimizing UCAP in CUDA programming is a tedious task and it may require series of execute-optimize passes to obtain high performance. We design a polyhedral model based tool, CUPL, which can locate UCAP at compile-time. CUPL is divided into two phases. Input to CUPL is an annotated valid CUDA kernel and the corresponding kernel launch configuration. In its first phase, CUPL extracts a polyhedral model representation from a given CUDA kernel. In its second phase, it uses Algorithm 1 to get the distance between accesses to memory locations accessed by consecutive threads. Given a kernel and an array A that it accesses, Algorithm 1 starts by lifting zero dimensional set S_j to an infinite space with extra dimensions (lines 7–9). Further, to get a set of memory locations accessed by an access relation, the set S_j is intersected with range set of access relation variables (line 10). To get just the set accessed by a thread, Algorithm 1 further intersects S_j with plane P such that

$$P : \left(x\vec{0}\right)\left(\vec{t}\,E\,\vec{b}\,\vec{i}\right)^T = y$$

$$\vec{b} = \begin{pmatrix} blockIdx.x \\ blockIdx.y \end{pmatrix};\ \vec{t} = \begin{pmatrix} threadIdx.x \\ threadIdx.y \\ threadIdx.z \end{pmatrix}$$

where $\vec{i}$ is a vector of loop iterators surrounding an access relation under consideration. $\{S_j \cap P_{x=1,y=k}\}$ represents a set of memory locations accessed by the thread k in a warp

1 Let A be an array accessed in the kernel
2 B $\leftarrow$ Get bounds on CUDA specific variables
3 R $\leftarrow$ {get all access relations}
4 **foreach** *relation r in R* **do**
5   Add bound B to domain of r
6   **foreach** *i ension j o A* **do**
7         $S_j \leftarrow \phi$; $E \leftarrow$ Get access expression
8   Add the expression E to S_j;
9   Add bounds from B to S_j; Space(S_j) $\leftarrow \infty$
10         $S_j \leftarrow S_j \cap$ {Range(r)};
11         $S_{1j} \leftarrow S_j \cap P_{(x=1,y=0)}$; $S_{2j} \leftarrow S_j \cap P_{(x=1,y=1)}$;
12   Project out all set variables but E from S_{1j} and S_{2j}; $D \leftarrow$ `min`(S_{2j}) - `min`(S_{1j})
        // Assumming D is same for any two contiguous threads
13   if $D > 1$ print "UCAP in array A: dimension j"
14   **end**
15 **end**
16

Algorithm 1: Locating UCAP in a kernel accessing an array A

(line 11). Projecting out all the set variables except E gives the range of memory locations accessed by thread k (line 12). If the difference, in the lowest address accessed is greater than 1, a warning is issued. By calling Algorithm 1 once for each array, we can get all the UCAPs present in the kernel. The first and second phases of CUPL are implemented using PET[3] and ISL[2] library respectively. Please note that Algorithm 1 assumes few PET specifics which are not explained for the sake of brevity.

2. EXPERIMENTATION

We have tested correctness of CUPL on kernels from Rodinia[1] benchmark suite and NVIDIA SDK samples. Warnings were reported for `kmeans` and `streamcluster` benchmarks in Rodinia benchmark suite and `box_filter`, `histogram` and `transpose` kernels in NVIDIA SDK Samples.

3. CONCLUSIONS AND FUTURE WORK

We propose a polyhedral model based tool, CUPL, to locate UCAP at compile-time for CUDA. It handles few cases of UCAP. We are working on automatic data layout transformation with CUPL as a preprocessor.

4. REFERENCES

1 S. he et al. *A Characterization of the Rodinia Benchmark Suite with Comparison to Contemporary CMP Workloads.* In *IISWC* pa es 1–11 2010.
2 S. Verdoolae e. `isl` *An Integer Set Library for the Polyhedral Model.* In *ICMS* pa es 299–302 2010.
3 S. Verdoolae e and G. obias. *Polyhedral Extraction Tool.* In *In Second Int. Workshop on Polyhedral Compilation Techniques (IMPACT 2012)* Jan. 2012.

ICS'13, June 10–14, 2013, Eugene, Oregon, USA.
ACM 978-1-4503-2130-3/13/06.

Imbalance Optimization in Scientific Workflows

Weiwei Chen
Information Science Institute
University of Southern California
Marina del Rey, CA, U.S.A.
wchen@isi.edu

Ewa Deelman
Information Science Institute
University of Southern California
Marina del Rey, CA, U.S.A.
deelman@isi.edu

Rizos Sakellariou
School of Computer Science
University of Manchester
Manchester, U.K.
rizos@cs.man.ac.uk

ABSTRACT
Scientific workflows are a means of defining and orchestrating large, complex, multi-stage computations that perform data analysis and/or simulation. Task clustering is a runtime optimization technique that merges multiple short workflow tasks into a single job such that the job execution overhead is reduced and the overall runtime performance of the workflow is significantly improved. However, current task clustering strategies fail to consider the imbalance problem of both task runtime and task dependency. In our work, we first investigate the different causes of runtime imbalance and dependency imbalance. We then introduce a series of metrics based on our prior work to measure the severity of runtime and dependency imbalance respectively. Finally, we study a wide range of real scientific workflows to generalize the relationship between these metrics and balancing methods.

Categories and Subject Descriptors
D.1.3 [**Concurrent Programming**]: Distributed Programming;

Keywords
Scientific workflow, data locality, overhead, balance

1. SUMMARY
In recent years, with the emergence of the fourth paradigm for science discovery, scientific workflows received a lot of attention among many science disciplines. Although the majority of the tasks within these workflow applications are often relatively small (from a few seconds to a few minutes in runtime), in aggregate, they represent a significant amount of computation and data. When executing these applications on a multi-system parallel environment, such as the Grid or the Cloud, significant system overheads may exist [2]. In order to minimize the impact of such overheads, task clustering [1] has been developed to merge small tasks into larger jobs so that the number of computational activities is reduced and their computational granularity is increased thereby reducing the (mostly scheduling related) system overheads. There are several challenges that are not yet addressed.

The first challenge is the imbalance measurement. Tasks may have diverse task runtimes and merging tasks into jobs that have diverse runtimes increases the difficulty of load balancing; this may lead to *runtime imbalance*. At the same time, merging non-dependent tasks that share no intermediate data between them seems safe at the first sight. However, any subsequent tasks that rely on the output data that their parent tasks produce may suffer a data locality problem since data may be distributed poorly and the data transfer time is increased; this may lead to *dependency imbalance*. None of the existing work has provided a solution to evaluate the severity of the two types of imbalance together. The first contribution we make is the classification of imbalance into two categories, runtime imbalance and dependency imbalance, and the specification of measurement metrics to evaluate their respective severity.

Existing workflow task clustering strategies have ignored or underestimated the imbalance problem a workflow may suffer. In [1][3], task clustering strategies use structural information of the workflows to develop algorithms to iterate through the nodes, for example, horizontal clustering that merges tasks at the same level of the workflow. However, such strategies typically ignore runtime information that may significantly influence overall runtime performance. As our second contribution, we first introduce the basic runtime-based clustering method and then two other balancing methods that can address the dependency imbalance problem. A trace-based simulation is performed on a series of widely used scientific workflows. In our experiments, we randomly selected 20% of workflow tasks and increased their runtime from 0% to 100% to simulate various runtime variations. For a selected astronomy application, we observed a speedup of up to 1.45 compared to a no clustering executions.

However, what makes this problem even more challenging is that the solutions are usually conflicting. For example, balancing runtime may aggravate the dependency imbalance problem, and vice versa. Dependency imbalance usually means that task clustering at one horizontal level forces the tasks at the next level (or even the next few levels) to have severe data locality problems. At the same time, runtime balancing methods are only concerned with the current level in a workflow. Thereby the third challenge is to provide a quantitative measurement of workflow characteristics as a criterion to select and balance these solutions. To achieve this goal, we studied a wide range of scientific workflows to establish a relationship between imbalance metrics and the balancing methods.

2. REFERENCES
[1] Singh, G. et al. Workflow task clustering for best effort systems with Pegasus. *Mardi Gras Conference '08* (2008).

[2] Chen, W. and Deelman E. Workflow Overhead Analysis and Optimizations. The 6th Workshop on Workflows in Support of Large-Scale Science, Nov 2011, 11-20

[3] Chen, W. and Deelman, E. Integration of Workflow Partitioning and Resource Provisioning, *CCGrid 2012, Doctoral Symposium*, Ottawa, Canada, May 2012

ICS'13, June 10–14, 2013, Eugene, Oregon, USA.
ACM 978-1-4503-2130-3/13/06.

FASTER Run-time Reconfiguration Management

Cătălin Bogdan Ciobanu
Chalmers University of Technology, Sweden
catalin@chalmers.se

Dionisios N. Pnevmatikatos
Foundation for Research and Technology - Hellas, Greece
pnevmati@ics.forth.gr

Kyprianos D. Papadimitriou
Foundation for Research and Technology - Hellas, Greece
kpapadim@ics.forth.gr

Georgi N. Gaydadjiev
Chalmers University of Technology, Sweden
georgig@chalmers.se

ABSTRACT

The FASTER project Run-Time System Manager offloads programmers from low-level operations by performing task placement, scheduling, and dynamic FPGA reconfiguration. It also manages device fragmentation, configuration caching, pre-fetching and reuse, bitstream compression, and optimizes the system thermal and power footprints. We propose a micro-reconfiguration aware, configuration content agnostic ISA interface and a technology independent Task Configuration Microcode format targeting Maxeler Data Flow computers and Xilinx XUPV5 platforms. We achieve improved resource utilization with negligible performance overhead. Up to 4Gbps for DMA transfers, and up to 3Gbps for FPGA reconfiguration on Xilinx Virtex-5/6 devices is achieved.

Categories and Subject Descriptors

D.3.4 [**Programming Languages**]: Processors—*Run-time Environments*; D.4.1 [**Operating Systems**]: Process Management—*Scheduling*; C.1.3 [**Processor Architectures**]: Other Architecture Styles—*Adaptable Architectures, Dataflow Architectures, Heterogeneous (Hybrid) Systems*

Keywords

FPGA; Run-time System Manager; Partial Reconfiguration

In recent years, processor clock frequencies stagnated due to power and thermal constraints. The additional transistors provided by new technology generations are transformed into supplementary processors or application-specific functional units. Custom accelerators boost performance with low power consumption by specializing the hardware for the workload. By using reconfigurable logic, new hardware units can be dynamically instantiated on-demand. Such hardware adaptability is often preferable to software in performance critical domains, e.g., High Performance Computing (HPC). The design and verification of run-time reconfigurable systems, however, is a time consuming and difficult process.

The Facilitating Analysis and Synthesis Technologies for Effective Reconfiguration (FASTER) project [1] aims to provide a complete methodology allowing easy implementation and verification of systems constituting multiple accelerators in reconfigurable hardware, primarily focusing on partial dynamic reconfiguration, from initial design to dynamic runtime management. It benefits both from region-based reconfiguration, i.e. dynamic alteration of large portions of the device with precompiled circuits, and micro-reconfiguration, which reconfigures small parts of the device with circuits specialized at runtime based on the input parameter values.

The FASTER Run-Time System Manager (RTSM) software library offloads programmers from low-level scheduling and resource management decisions on partially reconfigurable FPGA-based systems. The RTSM handles task placement and scheduling, converts technology independent representations into FPGA-specific commands, and communicate with the FPGA configuration port. Additional RTSM functionality includes tasks relocation, configuration caching, pre-fetching and reuse, and bitstream compression. In addition, it manages power and energy consumption and monitors temperature for hotspot management and task migration. The RTSM architectural interface consists of the configuration agnostic Instruction Set Architecture (ISA) extension and the technology independent bitstream format. Our customized Molen ISA extension offers support for micro-reconfiguration and for two-level nested reconfiguration.

At design time, the configuration data and the task specific information (e.g., expected execution time and a region-/micro-reconfiguration flag) are encapsulated in a configuration agnostic Task Configuration Microcode block (TCM). The FASTER tool-chain compilation phase provides the baseline schedule and relevant task information such as the size of the reconfigurable areas and the estimated reconfiguration times. The RTSM updates selected parameters at run-time, e.g., the current status of the reconfigurable area (e.g., *empty, being reconfigured*) and of the tasks (e.g., *ready for execution, running*), and profiles the task execution times.

We target Maxeler Technologies systems for HPC and Xilinx University Program (XUP) Virtex-5 boards connected via PCIe for the desktop domain. Maxeler provides large Xilinx Virtex-6 Data Flow Engines, each featuring up to 48GB of dedicated high-speed DRAM. The results show that RTSM can improve resource utilization and can be implemented with minimal overhead on overall system performance. Currently, our custom RTSM software running on the host GPP controls both execution and reconfiguration, by loading the bitstreams from the host memory on demand. Our RTSM has shown very good system-level performance with initial measurements reaching DMA transfers of up to 4Gbps and FPGA reconfiguration speeds of up to 3Gbps.

Acknowledgments

This work was supported by the European Commission in the context of FP7 FASTER project (#287804).

1. REFERENCES

[1] The FASTER Project. URL `www.fp7-faster.eu/`.

ICS'13, June 10–14, 2013, Eugene, Oregon, USA.
ACM 978-1-4503-2130-3/13/06.

MAD7: a Memory Architecture Simulator Targeted at Design Space Exploration

Hadrien A. Clarke[†‡], Antoine Trouvé[†] and Kazuaki J. Murakami[†‡]
[†] Institute of Systems, Information Technologies and Nanotechnologies (Fukuoka, Japan)
[‡] Kyushu University (Fukuoka, Japan)
clarke@isit.or.jp, trouve@isit.or.jp, murakami@ait.kyushu-u.ac.jp

ABSTRACT

We introduce MAD7, a tool that rapidly simulates many-core memory architectures at a functional level. MAD7 focuses on tracking access patterns and data spatial localities rather than enforcing any precise on-chip arbitration protocols. Although not cycle accurate by nature, it provides useful insights when comparing different memory architectures under real-world workloads. Potential cache access and on-chip network usage bottlenecks can be easily spotted visually thanks to figures generated by our tool. MAD7 simulations are multi-threaded and are typically up to two orders of magnitude faster than those of a fully cycle accurate simulator.

Categories and Subject Descriptors

B.8.2 [**Performance and Reliability**]: Performance Analysis and Design Aids; C.4 [**Performance of Systems**]: Measurement Techniques

Keywords

Simulation; Memory Architecture; Visualization

1. MOTIVATION

Processors have seen their numbers of core increase steadily while the bandwidth between the chip and the main shared memory has not improved by much, thereby exacerbating the "memory wall." Not so much can be done off-chip to address this issue partly due to the limited number of pins available on chip packages. Alternatively, processor architects have been creating more complex on-chip memory architectures to reduce accesses to the main memory.

For mono-core processors, design options for on-chip memory architectures are relatively limited. Architects can decide on the number of cache levels and the features of these caches such as capacities, line sizes, associativities as well as replacement and allocation policies. With many-core processors, however, the number of caches is multiplied and caches can be shared among higher-level elements in the memory hierarchy. Moreover these caches can be interconnected by network topologies more complex than a simple bus to avoid memory contentions. Using cycle-accurate simulators to explore this rather large memory architecture design space could prove time consuming. Yet, fast simulations are desirable to refine designs according to simulation results.

Our tool MAD7 was created with these aspects of the design process in mind. It relaxes the coherency precision constraint at the benefit of simulation speed allowing for multi-threading schemes. MAD7 relies on an almost-coherent approach instead of simulating fully coherent memories. As it is trace-driven, it is fed through piping with memory access traces without actually saving them to avoid large trace logs. MAD7 captures cache accesses and on-chip network usage and produces relative performance assessments in terms of access cost.

2. OVERVIEW OF MAD7

MAD7's simulation flow is as follows. At start-up, MAD7 takes as an input a memory architecture description specified by the user. This includes the number of guest cores, cache features, the policies and the interconnect topology which is a set of point-to-point connections, crossbars, buses and/or rings. The relative cost associated with the usage of each node and interconnect in the simulated architecture must also be stipulated.

At runtime, memory access traces are read through a pipe. In our framework, these traces are obtained through instrumented binaries with each host thread representing a guest core. Traces could also stem from other sources as long as the binary trace format is respected. Furthermore, traces need not be saved but can nonetheless be directed to several instances of MAD7 in order to simulate several memory architectures simultaneously – provided the number of cores in all designs is the same. Incoming traces are packed into frames representing chunks of time. MAD7 simulates on a frame basis. Once a frame is collected, each trace in it is dispatched to its corresponding guest core reservation station. Then, all cores issue their memory requests simultaneously. At the end of each frame, statistics are either recorded separately or accumulated. Collectable statistics include average access costs for each core, miss rates for each cache, as well as network usage. Once the simulation is over, results can be visualized through figures generated by our tool.

Although still work-in-progress, preliminary results obtained with MAD7 demonstrated simulation speedups of over an order of magnitude when compared to gem5. In MAD7's current implementation, policies and routes are statically predefined at the beginning of the simulation. In upcoming versions, the user will be able to specify some algorithm for the architecture to adapt to different workloads. Also, some power consumption estimation will be performed.

ICS'13, June 10–14, 2013, Eugene, Oregon, USA.
ACM 978-1-4503-2130-3/13/06.

A Decomposition Method With Minimal Communication Volume for Parallelization of Multi-dimensional FFTs

Truong Vinh Truong Duy
Japan Advanced Institute of Science and Technology & The University of Tokyo
1-1 Asahidai, Nomi, Ishikawa 923-1292, Japan
duytvt@{jaist.ac.jp,issp.u-tokyo.ac.jp}

Taisuke Ozaki
Research Center for Simulation Science, Japan Advanced Institute of Science and Technology
1-1 Asahidai, Nomi, Ishikawa 923-1292, Japan
t-ozaki@jaist.ac.jp

ABSTRACT

We present a decomposition method for the parallelization of multi-dimensional FFTs with two distinguishing features: adaptive decomposition and transpose order awareness for achieving minimal communication volume. Based on a row-wise decomposition that translates the multi-dimensional data into one-dimensional data for equally allocating to the processes, our method can adaptively decompose the data in the lowest possible dimensions to reduce communication volume in the first place, differently from previous works that have pre-defined dimensions of decomposition. Also, this decomposition offers plenty of orders in data transpose, and different transpose orders result in different volumes of communication. By analyzing all the possible cases, we find out the best transpose orders with minimal communication volumes for 3-D, 4-D, and 5-D FFTs.

Categories and Subject Descriptors

G.1.0 [**Mathematics of Computing**]: General—*Parallel algorithms; Numerical algorithms*

Keywords

Fast Fourier transform, multi-dimensional FFTs, domain decomposition for FFTs, parallel FFTs, domain decomposition

1. DOMAIN DECOMPOSITION METHOD

In our method, the FFT data is decomposed based on a row-wise basis that maps the M-D data into 1-D data, and translates the corresponding coordinates from multi-dimensions into one-dimension for equally dividing and allocating the resultant 1-D data to the processes. Therefore, the method decomposes in one dimension if the number of processes is less than or equal to the size of one dimension, in two dimensions if the number of processes is greater than the size of one dimension and less than or equal to the size of two dimensions, and so on up to M-dimensions. Figure 1(a) illustrates the decomposition for 3-D FFTs.

The decomposition results in $(M-1)!^M$ data transpose orders with different volumes of communication for M-D FFTs. Figure 1(b) exemplifies the operation of our method with transpose-order awareness, where a large amount of data can be reused from *cab* to *cba*. By computationally analyzing all the cases, we find the representative best communication efficient orders: $abc \rightarrow cab \rightarrow cba$, $abcd \rightarrow abdc \rightarrow dcba \rightarrow dcab$, and $abcde \rightarrow abced \rightarrow abedc \rightarrow cedba \rightarrow cedab$, for 3-D, 4-D, and 5-D FFTs, respectively.

Figures 1(c) and 1(d) show that our method outperforms other methods with performance gap of up to several orders of magnitude. Actually, this method with the 2-D decomposition has been employed in our density functional theory code called OpenMX for solving 3-D FFTs [2].

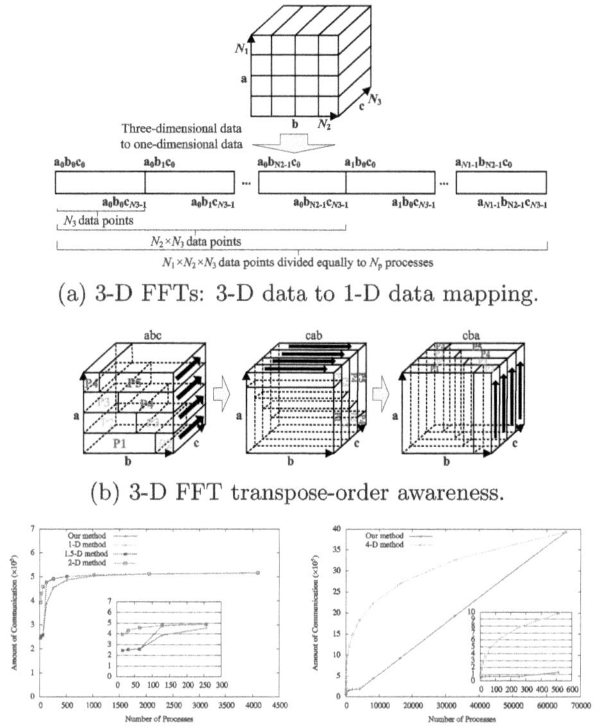

(a) 3-D FFTs: 3-D data to 1-D data mapping.

(b) 3-D FFT transpose-order awareness.

(c) 3-D FFT comparison. (d) 4-D FFT comparison.

Figure 1: Domain decomposition method.

2. REFERENCES

[1] T. V. T. Duy and T. Ozaki. A decomposition method with minimum communication amount for parallelization of multi-dimensional FFTs. *ArXiv e-prints*, Feb. 2013.

[2] OpenMX. Open source package for Material eXplorer. http://www.openmx-square.org/, retrieved 2013-04-19.

ICS'13, June 10–14, 2013, Eugene, Oregon, USA.
ACM 978-1-4503-2130-3/13/06.

A Massively Parallel Domain Decomposition Method for Large-Scale DFT Electronic Structure Calculations

Truong Vinh Truong Duy
Japan Advanced Institute of Science and Technology & The University of Tokyo
1-1 Asahidai, 923-1292, Japan
duytvt@{jaist.ac.jp,issp.u-tokyo.ac.jp}

Taisuke Ozaki
Research Center for Simulation Science, Japan Advanced Institute of Science and Technology
1-1 Asahidai, Nomi, Ishikawa 923-1292, Japan
t-ozaki@jaist.ac.jp

ABSTRACT

We present a massively parallel domain decomposition method for atoms and grids to enable large-scale density functional theory (DFT) electronic structure calculations. In the atom decomposition, we develop a modified recursive bisection method based on the moment of inertia tensor for reordering the atoms from 3D to 1D along a principal axis so that atoms that are close in real space are also close on the axis to ensure data locality. The atoms are then divided into sub-domains depending on their projections onto the principal axis in a balanced way among the processes. In the grid decomposition, we define four data structures to make data locality consistent with that of the clustered atoms, and propose a 2D decomposition method for solving the Poisson equation using the 3D FFT with communication volume minimized. Benchmark results show that the parallel efficiency at 131,072 cores is 67.7% compared to the baseline of 16,384 cores on the K computer.

Categories and Subject Descriptors

G.1.0 [**Mathematics of Computing**]: General—*Parallel algorithms; Numerical algorithms*

Keywords

First principles calculations, domain decomposition, modified recursive bisection, moment of inertia tensor

1. DOMAIN DECOMPOSITION METHOD

We develop a modified recursive bisection method to decompose a system with any number of processes and atoms. It involves constructing a binary tree, and each tree node has a number representing the number of processes treating the domain under that node (Fig. 1(a)). To ensure data locality, the moment of inertia tensor is applied to find a principal axis for each domain so that the atoms that are close in real space are also close on the principal axis. Then, the atoms in the domain are reordered from 3D to 1D by projecting them onto the principal axis, and are divided into two sub-domains depending on their projections in a balanced way among the processes to fit the structure of the binary tree (Fig. 1(b)). The decomposition is performed recursively until there are as many sub-domains as processes.

ICS'13, June 10–14, 2013, Eugene, Oregon, USA.
ACM 978-1-4503-2130-3/13/06.

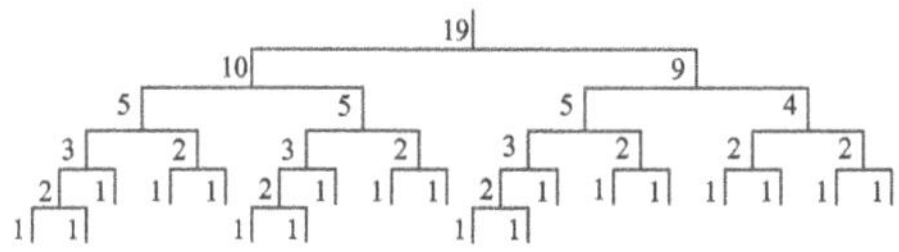

(a) Modified recursive bisection method.

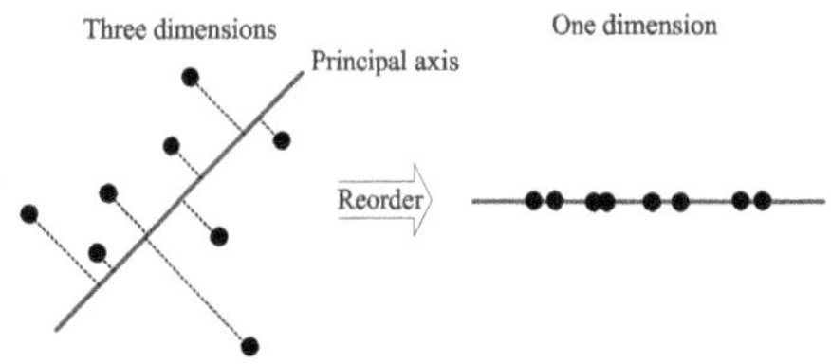

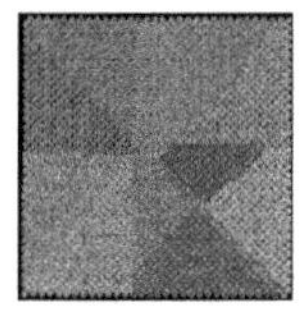

(b) Atom reordering by a principal axis. (c) Top view.

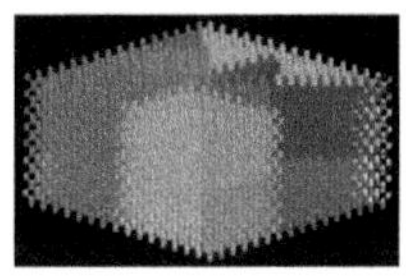

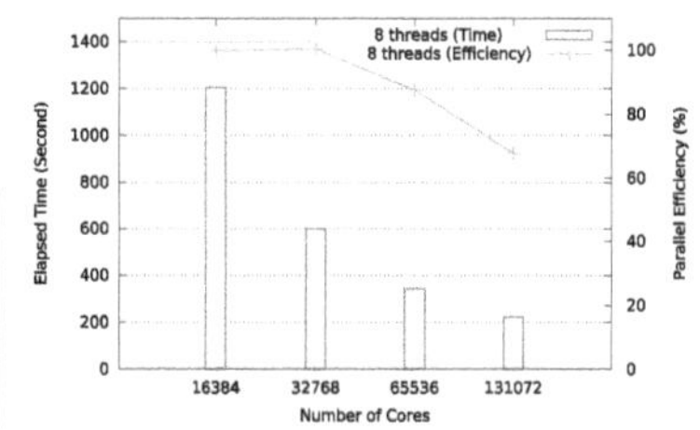

(d) Side view. (e) Strong scaling on the K computer with 131,072 diamond atoms.

Figure 1: Domain decomposition method.

We then define four data structures for the partitioning of grids that are carefully constructed to make data locality consistent with that of the clustered atoms for minimizing communications. We also propose a communication-efficient 2D decomposition method for parallelizing the 3D FFT, where the distribution of grid points is carried out in a 2D grid defined by the first two dimensions [1].

We perform benchmark calculations with our DFT code called OpenMX [2]. Figures 1(c) and 1(d) demonstrate the atom decomposition with 16,384 diamond atoms and 19 processes, and Fig. 1(e) shows the strong scaling result.

2. REFERENCES

[1] T. V. T. Duy and T. Ozaki. A three-dimensional domain decomposition method for large-scale DFT electronic structure calculations. *ArXiv e-prints*, 2012.

[2] OpenMX. Open source package for Material eXplorer. http://www.openmx-square.org/, retrieved 2013-04-19.

Multi-Layered Unstructured Mesh Generation

Panagiotis Foteinos
Department of Computer Science
College of William and Mary
Old Dominion University
pfot@cs.wm.edu

Daming Feng
Department of Computer Science
Old Dominion University
dfeng@cs.odu.edu

Andrey Chernikov
Department of Computer Science
Old Dominion University
achernik@cs.odu.edu

Nikos Chrisochoides
Department of Computer Science
Old Dominion University
nikos@cs.odu.edu

ABSTRACT

Finite Element Mesh Generation is a critical component for many (bio-)engineering and science applications. In this project we will develop a novel framework for guaranteed quality mesh generation for 3D and 4D Finite Element (FE) analysis, able to scale to thousands of cores.

Categories and Subject Descriptors

J.6 [**Computer Applications**]: COMPUTER-AIDED ENGINEERING

General Terms

Algorithms, Performance

Keywords

Delaunay refinement, scalability, quality, fidelity, multi-layer

Introduction

In our past work, we developed a 3D tightly-coupled parallel Image to Mesh conversion method (PI2M) [4] able to scale for up to 100 cores (i.e., 10^2 concurrency).

With carefully designed application-specific layers that we introduced in [3] for 2D, and extend them in 3D in this poster, we expect to boost the scalability of PI2M to thousands of cores. The **Data Decomposition** layer [2] will exploit data locality and the **Domain Decomposition** layer [1, 5] will avoid intensive communication and by using over-decomposition of the object, we could reach the thousands of core concurrency.

Data and Domain Decomposition

The Data Decomposition technique layer will group the poor elements into zones, such that zones separated by a well defined distance can be refined without synchronization and communication, thus, improving data locality. See Figure 1a. This technique offers an efficiency of 69% on 10 cores. Therefore, by combining PI2M with this technique, we expect to reach a $10^2 \times 6.9 = 690$ concurrency in a rack with 10 nodes.

cores	6	10	12
speedup	4.9	6.9	7.8

(a)

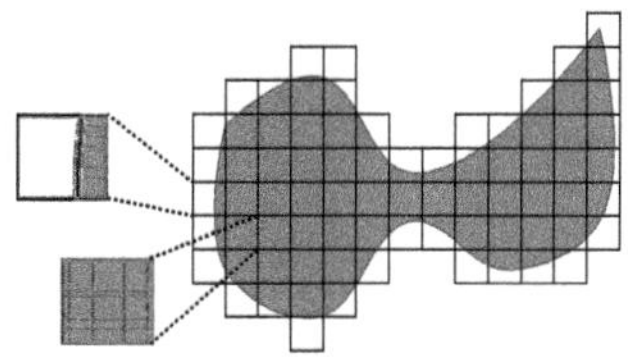

(b)

Figure 1: (a) Data decomposition. (b) The red area denotes the object $\mathcal{O}$ to be meshed and the blue curve the surface $\partial\mathcal{O}$. The part of the subdomains that lie inside the object can be treated as additional surface (see the blue parts in the zoomed domains.)

The Domain decomposition technique we propose (see Figure 1b) will further constrict the areas that multiple threads work on, and thus, decrease communication overhead and add more concurrency. Partial or completely decoupled techniques need to guarantee that the refinement of an element inside a domain will not necessitate the insertion or the removal of a point outside that domain. This can be achieved by treating the boundary of the domains (see the blue part of the boundary of the two zoomed subdomains in Figure 1b) as part of the surface $\partial\mathcal{O}$ to be recovered.

References

[1] A. Chernikov and N. Chrisochoides. Algorithm 872: Parallel 2d constrained delaunay mesh generation. *ACM Transactions on Mathematical Software*, 2008.

[2] A. Chernikov and N. Chrisochoides. Three-dimensional delaunay refinement for multi-core processors. In *ACM International Conference on Supercomputing*, 2008.

[3] N. Chrisochoides, A. Chernikov, A. Fedorov, A. Kot, L. Linardakis, and P. Foteinos. Towards exascale parallel delaunay mesh generation. In *International Meshing Roundtable*, 2009.

[4] P. Foteinos and N. Chrisochoides. High quality real-time image-to-mesh conversion for finite element simulations. In *27th ACM International Conference on Supercomputing (ICS'13)*, June 2013. to appear.

[5] L. Linardakis and N. Chrisochoides. Graded delaunay decoupling method for parallel guaranteed quality planar mesh generation. *SIAM Journal on Scientific Computing*, 30(4):1875–1891, March 2008.

ICS'13, June 10–14, 2013, Eugene, Oregon, USA.
ACM 978-1-4503-2130-3/13/06.

Network-on-Chip for a Partially Reconfigurable FPGA System

Justin A. Hogan
ECE Department
Montana State University
Bozeman, Montana 59717
justin.hogan@msu.montana.edu

Raymond J. Weber
ECE Department
Montana State University
Bozeman, Montana 59717
raymond.weber@msu.montana.edu

Brock J. Lameres
ECE Department
Montana State University
Bozeman, Montana 59717
lameres@ece.montana.edu

Todd Kaiser
ECE Department
Montana State University
Bozeman, Montana 59717
tjkaiser@ece.montana.edu

ABSTRACT

A custom FPGA-based, 1U CubeSat form-factor reconfigurable computing development platform has been designed and built for the purpose of implementing and testing multicore and multiprocessor systems. The platform was designed to leverage the active partial reconfiguration and configuration readback capabilities of the Xilinx Virtex-6 device. This enables myriad research opportunities in parallel processing, high-performance reconfigurable computing, and multicore/multiprocessor system design. An example application features a nine-processor radiation tolerant computer system which motivates further research into network-on-chip solutions for reducing multicore system routing complexity.

Categories and Subject Descriptors

C.4 [**Performance of Systems**]: Fault tolerance;
J.2 [**Physical Sciences and Engineering**]: Aerospace

Keywords

Reconfigurable computing, FPGA, fault tolerant, network-on-chip, partial reconfiguration, readback

1. INTRODUCTION

The presented system is a highly flexible, FPGA-based, general-purpose reconfigurable computing platform designed to enable research in numerous areas related to computer architecture. Some of the research areas of interest include high-performance computing, parallel processing, reconfigurable computing, multicore and multiprocessor system design, fault-tolerant architecture design, and interconnect on multicore or multiprocessor systems. A current multiprocessor research system demonstrates the need for a network-on-chip (NoC) to alleviate the complexity of inter-tile routing. This system is a radiation tolerant reconfigurable computer designed and implemented on the research hardware. It features nine Microblaze processors implemented as partially reconfigurable tiles.

ICS'13, June 10–14, 2013, Eugene, Oregon, USA.
ACM 978-1-4503-2130-3/13/06.

2. TECHNIQUE AND RESULTS

The FPGA board features two Xilinx FPGAs. A Virtex-6 is the primary FPGA used for research designs. A Spartan-6 serves as a control and interface device between the Virtex-6 and the user. The board leverages the active partial reconfiguration, readback, and configuration scrubbing capabilities of the Virtex-6 through direct access to the device's configuration port. In a multicore system, active partial reconfiguration enables instantiation of computational resources, such as hardware accelerators, input/output interface cores, or microprocessors, on an as-needed basis at runtime without system interruption. A specific research problem of interest is the reduction of resource utilization by the interconnect among computational tiles in a multicore or multiprocessor FPGA system due to the complexity of the interconnect increasing with the number of cores A dedicated bus architecture is a fast, but inefficient implementation as each connection requires a unique set of wires. In an FPGA, this means that logic resources that could otherwise be used by logic cores are consumed by routing. This research seeks to leverage work done in network-on-chip (NoC) studies and apply it to dynamically allocated multicore FPGA computer architectures.

3. CONCLUSION

A custom FPGA-based research platform is presented. A research system implemented on this platform demonstrates the need for a NoC. The example system is a radiation tolerant reconfigurable computer designed and implemented on the research hardware. It features nine Microblaze processors implemented as partially reconfigurable tiles. Complexity in the inter-tile routing reduces the amount of logic resources available for computational use. A shared network layer is proposed as a way to alleviate the routing complexity and enhance the flexibility of the multi-tile system.

Exploiting Data Parallelism in the yConvex Hypergraph Algorithm for Image Representation using GPGPUs

Saurabh Jha
VIT University, Chennai, India
saurabh.jha2010@vit.ac.in

Tejaswi Agarwal
VIT University, Chennai, India
tejaswi.agarwal2010@vit.ac.in

B. Rajesh Kanna
VIT University, Chennai, India
rajeshkanna.b@vit.ac.in

ABSTRACT

To define and identify a region-of-interest (ROI) in a digital image, the shape descriptor of the ROI has to be described in terms of its boundary characteristics. To address the generic issues of contour tracking, the yConvex Hypergraph (yCHG) model was proposed by Kanna et al [1]. In this work, we propose a parallel approach to implement the yCHG model by exploiting massively parallel cores of NVIDIA's Compute Unified Device Architecture (CUDA). We perform our experiments on the MODIS satellite image database by NASA, and based on our analysis we observe that the performance of the serial implementation is better on smaller images, but once the threshold is achieved in terms of image resolution, the parallel implementation outperforms its sequential counterpart by 2 to 10 times (2x-10x). We also conclude that an increase in the number of hyperedges in the ROI of a given size does not impact the performance of the overall algorithm.

Categories and Subject Descriptors

I.3 [**Computer Graphics**]: Hardware Architecture –*Graphics Processor, Parallel Processing*

Keywords

Parallel Processing, GPGPU, Image Analysis

1. INTRODUCTION

Contour tracking in digital images faces generic issues which are illustrated in [1, 2, 3]. It becomes essential to solve contour tracking challenges in multiply-connected regions and regions bounded by non-Jordan curves. To overcome these challenges, Kanna et al. [1] proposed the yCHG model which is used to track the contour deterministically. Our results with the sequential implementation of the yCHG show that:

a. The runtime of the yCHG algorithm increases linearly for images up to a resolution of 2000x2000 but a significant change in runtime is observed for images with a higher resolution.

b. The runtime remains constant for images with varying number of hyperedges.

2. PROPOSED METHOD

To remove the data dependencies in the existing algorithm, we divide the algorithm into two steps. The first function computes the number of cut-vertices of an image in parallel by dividing the image into a number of column vectors and each column is scheduled on a separate thread on the GPU. Each thread computes the number of cut-vertices and stores the result in an array. In the second step of the algorithm, each CUDA thread checks the number of cut-vertices in the preceding column vector of the input image. If a change is observed in the number of cut-vertices, it indicates there has been a change in the number of yConvex hyperedges for that particular column vector.

ICS'13, June 10–14, 2013, Eugene, Oregon, USA.
ACM 978-1-4503-2130-3/13/06

3. RESULTS

In order to keep constant hyperedges, we take an image of a resolution of 21000x21000 and vary the resolution. Our results are graphically plotted in Figure 1. It shows performance of the proposed parallel algorithm as compared to the existing serial implementation. Our CPU implementation consists of a 2-core Intel i5 480M having a clock speed of 2660 MHz. The GPU we used is a 16 core NVIDIA GeForce 310M having a clock speed of 1468 MHz. We understand that while newer hardware (such as cards based on the recent FERMI architecture) would undoubtedly be faster, we want to show what is possible with only limited hardware investment.

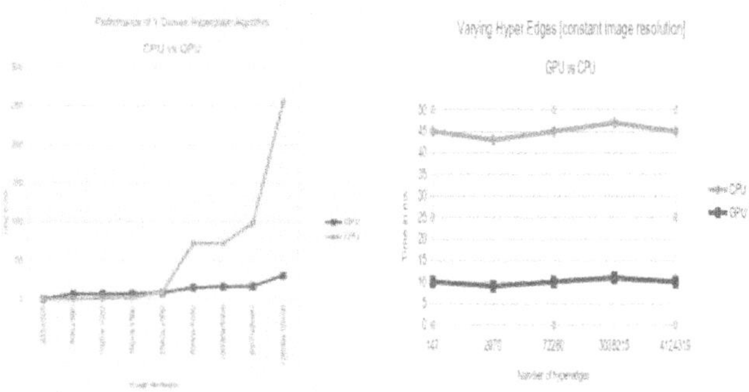

Figure 1. Results with varying resolution and hyperedges

To vary the number of hyperedges, we consider different images keeping the same resolution. We observe that the time taken is constant, with the number of hyperedges varying from 147 to 4124319. This was expected as our algorithm is dependent directly on the resolution of the input image irrespective of other factors. Our implementation results show that with an increase in the image resolution the parallel implementation improves the performance by 2X-10X, opening up a host of potential new applications that require real time image processing.

4. REFERENCES

[1] B. Rajesh Kanna, C. Aravindan, and K. Kannan, Development of yConvex hypergraph model for contour-based image analysis, in Proceedings of the 2nd IEEE International Conference Computer Communication and Informatics (ICCCI-2012), 2, 1-5, 2012

[2] B. Rajesh Kanna, C. Aravindan, and K. Kannan, A contour-based scheme for representing arbitrary shapes in digital images, in Proceedings of ACM International Conference and Workshop on Emerging Trends in Computer applications, 1, 535-540, 2011

[3] B. Rajesh Kanna, C. Aravindan, and K. Kannan, Image-based area estimation of any connected region using y-convex region decomposition, AEU -International Journal of Electronics and communications, 66 (2):172- 183, 2012

[4] Hall, Dorothy K., George A. Riggs, and Vincent V. Salomonson. 2006, updated daily. MODIS/Terra Snow Cover Daily L3 Global 500m Grid V005 [November 2000-October 2001]

The ARMv8 Simulator

Tao Jiang[1,2], Lele Zhang[1,2], Rui Hou[1], Yi Zhang[1,2], Qianlong Zhang[1], Lin Chai[1,2], Jing Han[1,2], Wuxiang Zhang[1], Cong Wang[1,2], Lixin Zhang[1]

Institute of Computing Technology, Chinese Academy of Sciences[1]
University of Chinese Academy of Sciences, Beijing, China[2]
{ jiangtao, zhanglele, hourui, zhangyi, zhangqianlong, chailin, hanjing, zhangwuxiang, wangcong, zhanglixin } @ict.ac.cn

ABSTRACT

In this work, we implement an ARMv8 function and performance simulator based on gem5 infrastructure, which is the first open source ARMv8 simulator. All the ARMv8 A64 instructions other than SIMD are implemented using gem5 ISA description language. The ARMv8 simulator supports multiple CPU models, multiple memory systems, and McPAT power model.

Categories and Subject Descriptors

C.4 [**Computer Systems Organization**]: Performance of System; B.8.2 [**Hardware**]: Performance and Reliability - *performance analysis and design aids*

Keywords

ARMv8; Simulator.

1. INTRODUCTION

ARMv8 architecture combines high performance with power efficiency, with the target markets like high-performance smartphones, tablet computers as well as energy-efficient data center server. The first ARMv8 commercial products are due in 2014. To the best of our knowledge, it is the first open source ARMv8 performance simulator. Based on the platform, people can conduct applications developments, architectural optimizations and ISA evaluations before ARMv8 chip is available.

Table 1. ARMv8 simulator features

Features	Support details
CPU Modes	Atomic Simple, Timing Simple, In-Order, O3
TLP	Multi-core and SMT
Memory	Ruby and Classic
System mode	SE mode
Power model	McPAT [2]
ISA	All the instructions other than SIMD

2. IMPLIMENTATION

We have analyzed existing *ARMv8 Instruction Set Overview* [3] and source code of ARMv8 gcc compiler [4] to figure out semantics and format of each instruction. The gem5 [1] ISA description language is used to define all the instructions, including control flow instructions, load/store instructions, data processing instructions, integer multiply/divide instructions and scalar floating-point instructions.

We design the system call interface by referring to the ARMv8 Linux kernel and glibc source code for developing the SE model in ARMv8 simulator. In addition, for the purpose of making this simulator run correctly, we develop the executable file initializing module, amend the interface of Ruby, modify the pipeline interface, correct the checkpoint module and amend SMT module. After the above efforts, the supported features of ARMv8 simulator are shown in Table 1.

ICS'13, June 10–14, 2013, Eugene, Oregon, USA.
ACM 978-1-4503-2130-3/13/06.

3. EVALUATION

In order to validate the simulator and evaluate the performance, we run some typical benchmarks on ARMv8 simulator, including SPEC CPU2006, Fhourstones, Dhrystone and stream. We also compare the simulation results with ARMv8 Foundation Model [5] to verify our simulator. The partial results are shown in Figure 1.

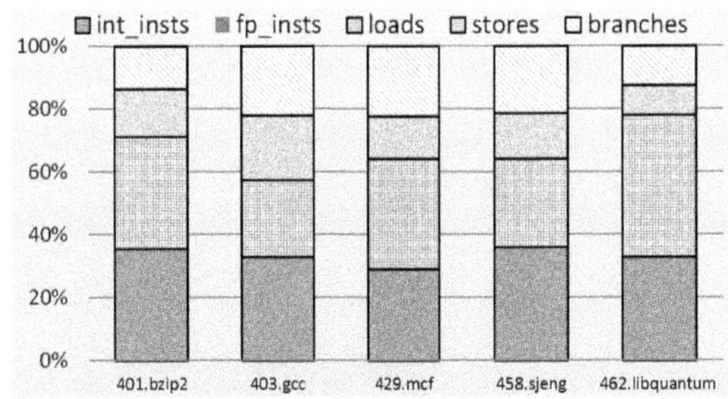

Figure 1. Instruction mix

4. ACKNOWLEDGMENTS

We are grateful to the anonymous reviewers. This work was supported by the Strategic Priority Research Program of the Chinese Academy of Sciences under grant No.XDA06010401, National Science Foundation of China under grant No. 61100010 and No. 61202057.

5. REFERENCES

[1] N. Binkert, B. Beckmann, G. Black, S. K. Reinhardt, A. Saidi, A. Basu, J. Hestness, D. R. Hower, T. Krishna, S. Sardashti, R. Sen, K. Sewell, M. Shoaib, N. Vaish, M. D. Hill, and D. A. Wood, "The gem5 simulator", SIGARCH Comput. Archit. News, vol 39, no 2, pp 1–7, 2011.

[2] Li, S., Ahn, J. H., Strong, R. D., Brockman, J. B., Tullsen, D. M., and Jouppi, N. P. McPAT: an integrated power, area, and timing modeling framework for multicore and manycore architectures. In Proceedings of International Symposium on Microarchitecture, pp. 469-480, 2009.

[3] ARMv8 Instruction Set Overview, *http://infocenter.arm.co-m/help/index.jsp?topic=/com.arm.doc.genc010197a/index.html*

[4] Linaro Toolchain for ARMv8, *https://launchpad.net/linaro-toolchain-binaries/+milestone/2013.02*

[5] ARMv8 Foundation Model, *http://www.arm.com/zh/product-s/tools/models/fastmodels/foundation-model.php*

Imogen: A Parallel 3D Fluid and MHD Code for GPUs

Erik Keever
Institute of Theoretical Science
5203 University of Oregon
450 Willamette Hall
Eugene, Oregon, 97403-5203
ekeever1@uoregon.edu
Advisor: James N. Imamura

James N. Imamura
Institute of Theoretical Science
5203 University of Oregon
450 Willamette Hall
Eugene, Oregon, 97403-5203
imamura@uoregon.edu

We present Imogen, a fully parallel code for simulating either the Euler or Ideal MHD equations, in two or three dimensions, on GPUs and GPU clusters. Fluid dynamic codes have historically been written entirely in either Fortran or C/C++. Imogen combines the power of GPU acceleration and compiled CUDA solver modules under the hood with the ease of development, ease of use, and ease of modification characteristic of interpreted languages as everything but the core numeric routines is written in Matlab.

Our basic goal of writing a highly parallel and fast fluid simulation code driven by Matlab which is GPU accelerated and fully parallel has been largely achieved at this time. We have tested simulations with up to 350 million cells using as many as 50 GPUs on the University of Oregon's ACISS supercomputer, and see no technical reason we could not use many more. Depending on the complexity of the physics used, a single C2070 device can handle as many as 25 million computation cells and still achieve simulation rates as high as a few seconds per timestep. Even though the code runs in an interpreted environment, we have found that interpretation overhead is quite small. Tests simulations with a resolution of 8^3 found roughly 80ms per complete iteration of overhead on a test workstation, which would be no more than a few percent of the time used by a large simulation.

We use a standard fluid scheme neatly summarized in [1] and the exactly $\nabla \cdot \mathbf{B}$ preserving magnetic update algorithm of [2]. Fluid and MHD problems are tested against Imogen and we find that its convergence is second order in both space and time. Because Imogen is a relatively new code, implementation and testing of support for extended physics is a continuous and ongoing process. The use of operator splitting means that new non-ideal effects can be implemented and tested without amending the fluid code.

The structures which kernels follow depending on the specifics of the finite differencing they will be undertaking is examined for patterns. Common errors encountered in the development process are explored.

In addition, work in progress on the application of Imogen to research into two astrophysical phenomenon, accretion shocks and the protostellar disks, is briefly presented. The linear instability of MHD shock waves for many/most possible parameters is established, and while there has been nonlinear work [3] it appears to largely be assumed that the distortion will keep growing and completely destroy the shock front in the nonlinear regime; We have observed severe distortion but have not seen a breakup. We also present early experiments in applying Imogen to differentially rotating disks.

Categories and Subject Descriptors

J.2 [**Computer Applications: Physical Sciences And Engineering**]: Physics

General Terms

Performance, Algorithms

Keywords

GPU acceleration, interpreted languages, Matlab, CFD, MHD

1. ACKNOWLEDGMENTS

Authors wish to acknowledge the work of Dr. Scott Ernst in the creation of the original Imogen as his PhD thesis project, Craig Rasmussen for the creation of the Parallel Gateway library, and Bonnie Dominguez in poster layout and design.

This research was supported by a Major Research Instrumentation grant from the National Science Foundation, Office of Cyber Infrastructure, "MRI-R2: Acquisition of an Applied Computational Instrument for Scientific Synthesis (ACISS)," Grant #: OCI-0960354.

2. REFERENCES

[1] H. Trac, U. L. Pen. A primer on Eulerian Computational Fluid Dynamics for Astrophysics. *Publications of the Astronomical Society of the Pacific, 115* 805, 303-321

[2] U. L. Pen, P. Arras, S. Wong. A Free, Fast, Simple, and Efficient Total Variation Diminishing Magnetohydrodynamic Code. *Astrophysical Journal Supplement Series, 149* 2, 447-455

[3] J. M. Stone, M. Edelman. The Corrugation Instability in Slow Magnetosonic Waves. *Astrophysical Journal, 454* 182

ICS'13 June 10–14, 2013, Eugene, Oregon, USA.
ACM 978-1-4503-2130-3/13/06.

SMIO: I/O Similarity Aware Virtual Machine Management in Virtual Desktop Environments

Min Li†, Sushil Mantri†, Pin Zhou‡, Ali R. Butt†
† Dept. of Computer Science, Virginia Tech; ‡ IBM Almaden Research Center
{limin,sushil,butta}@cs.vt.edu, pinzhou@us.ibm.com

ABSTRACT

Virtual desktop environments (VDEs) typically employ shared storage with the goal to benefit from the I/O optimizations therein. However, the Virtual Machine (VM) management that enables VDEs is typically agnostic of VM I/O characteristics. Thus, the opportunities for I/O reduction techniques, e.g., deduplication, which improve storage scalability and efficiency are constrained. We present SMIO, a VM management system that detects VM I/O similarities, and places the VMs such that the effectiveness of I/O reduction techniques is enhanced—as much as 4.9× compared to the standard approach.

Categories and Subject Descriptors

C.2.4 [**Computer-Communication Networks**]: Distributed Systems — *distributed applications*
General Terms: Algorithms, Performance, Evaluation.
Keywords: virtual machine placement and migration

1. INTRODUCTION

Virtual desktop environments (VDEs) are becoming popular due to their lower cost, high performance and scalability. Shared storage is a key component of VDEs, and I/O optimizations are considered crucial to sustaining high scalability. In this context, researchers have observed large amounts of duplicate IOPS across VDEs. This is because the Virtual Machine (VM) images are usually created using the same golden image and deploy a similar set of applications such as anti-virus software. A number of I/O reduction techniques such as dedup-box, Atlantis ILIO, Capo [FAST'11], and Seacache [MASCOTS'12], have been proposed to identify and remove such duplicated I/O load from the shared storage system to improve efficiency. The effectiveness of these techniques depends on the amount of duplicated data accessed by the VMs running on a physical host. The goal of this work is to avoid sub-optimal VM placement and co-locate similar VMs on the same hosts, which increases similar accesses on the hosts, consequently creating higher opportunity for I/O reduction.

2. DESIGN

We propose SMIO, a VM placement technique that considers I/O similarity among VMs to improve the efficiency of I/O reduction techniques by locating VMs with similar I/Os on the same physical host.

Figure 1 shows the architecture of SMIO. SMIO: (1) detects I/O similarity among different VMs; (2) utilizes hierarchical clustering to produce a new I/O-similarity-aware VM placement scheme periodically; and (3) migrates the VMs when benefits of similar VM consolidation outweigh migration cost. We employ sampling instead of continuous I/O monitoring to control the network and I/O overhead and ensure scalability to thousands of VMs. We also adopt a hybrid hierarchical clustering technique, where computation of cost-benefit analysis of VM migration is offloaded to the individual physical hosts on which the VMs are running, and the results from the hosts are combined at a centralized manager to determine global VM migration scheme.

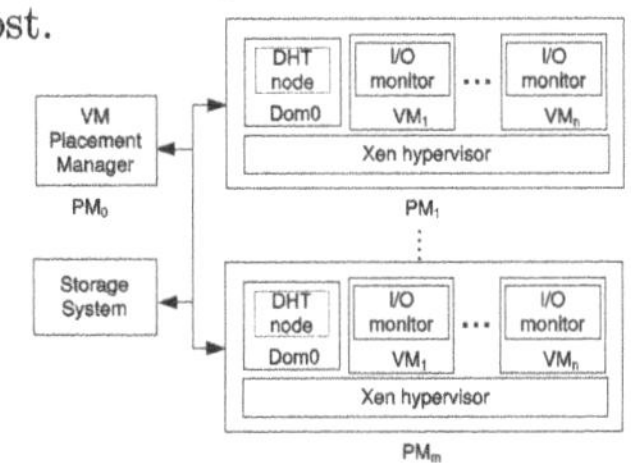

Figure 1: SMIO architecture.

3. EVALUATION

We evaluated the effectiveness of SMIO through trace driven simulations. Figure 2 shows that SMIO effectively detects similarities between different set of VMs and reduces the I/O bandwidth consumption by as much as 4.9× for read path and 2.1% for write path compared to state-of-the-art FFD [VEE'09] that manages VMs without considering I/O similarities.

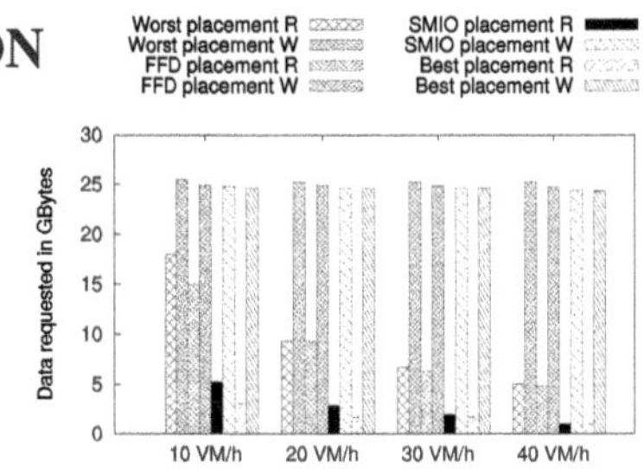

Figure 2: I/O bandwidth consumption under training center trace.

4. CONCLUSION

By incorporating I/O similarity information in VM management decision, SMIO is able to improve the effectiveness of I/O reduction techniques. Moreover, SMIO paves the way for designing innovative holistic I/O optimizations, which further improves scalability and storage efficiency.

Acknowledgment: This work is supported in part by the NSF under Grants CCF-0746832, CNS-1016793, and CNS-1016408.

ICS'13, June 10–14, 2013, Eugene, Oregon, USA.
ACM 978-1-4503-2130-3/13/06.

Inspector/Executor Load Balancing Algorithms for Block-Sparse Tensor Contractions

David Ozog, Sameer Shende, Allen Malony
Dept. of Computer and Information Science
University of Oregon
Eugene, Oregon 97403
{ozog, sameer, malony}@uoregon.edu

Jeff R. Hammond, James Dinan, Pavan Balaji
Mathematics and Computer Science Division
Argonne National Laboratory
Lemont, Illinois
{jhammond, dinan, balaji}@anl.gov

ABSTRACT

Developing effective yet scalable load-balancing methods for irregular computations is critical to the successful application of simulations in a variety of disciplines at petascale and beyond. This poster explores a set of static and dynamic scheduling algorithms for block-sparse tensor contractions within the NWChem computational chemistry code for different degrees of sparsity (and therefore load imbalance). In this particular application, a relatively large amount of task information can be obtained at minimal cost, which enables the use of static partitioning techniques that take the entire task list as input. However, fully static partitioning is incapable of dealing with dynamic variation of task costs, such as from transient network contention or operating system noise, so we also consider hybrid schemes that utilize dynamic scheduling within subgroups. These two schemes, which have not been previously implemented in NWChem or its proxies (i.e. quantum chemistry mini-apps) are compared to the original centralized dynamic load-balancing algorithm as well as improved centralized scheme. In all cases, we separate the scheduling of tasks from the execution of tasks into an inspector phase and an executor phase. The impact of these methods upon the application is substantial on a large InfiniBand cluster: execution time is reduced by as much as 50% at scale. The technique is applicable to any scientific application requiring load balance where performance models or estimations of kernel execution times are available.

ICS'13, June 10–14, 2013, Eugene, Oregon, USA.
ACM 978-1-4503-2130-3/13/06.

Categories and Subject Descriptors

J.2 [**Computer Applications**]: Physical Sciences and Engineering

General Terms

Algorithms, Performance

Keywords

Dynamic Load Balancing, Static Paritioning, Tensor Contractions, Quantum Chemistry, Global Arrays

Improving Performance of OpenSHMEM Reference Library by portable PE Mapping Technique

Swaroop Pophale
University of Houston
Texas, 77204
spophale@cs.uh.edu

Tony Curtis
University of Houston
Texas, 77204
tonyc@cs.uh.edu

Barbara Chapman
University of Houston
Texas, 77204
chapman@cs.uh.edu

ABSTRACT

Reducing data communication cost is a critical performance consideration and the need is more acute when using libraries like the OpenSHMEM Reference library which has to sacrifice some performance optimizations for portability. Being a Partitioned Global Address Space library the OpenSHMEM reference library provides more control over data placement, yet, some communication intensive applications would benefit from the libraries prior knowledge of its communication pattern. In this poster we discuss a low cost portable methodology to provide PE re-numbering to facilitate maximum on-node communication. We validate our method using the well-documented 2D heat transfer application.

Categories and Subject Descriptors

D.2.2 [**Design Tools and Techniques**]: Software libraries

Keywords

Communication optimizations, PGAS, OpenSHMEM

1. INTRODUCTION

OpenSHMEM is a Partitioned Global Address Space library that provides overlap between communication and computation by providing an API for explicit one-sided communication for parallel SPMD applications. Since the computation-communication ratio for different applications is different, a per application analysis of the communication pattern is essential to determine the placement of the PEs across a target architecture. From that profiling information of the application and the topology of the underlying hardware better processor mappings can be obtained. The OpenSHMEM reference library can use this information and provide a low cost process re-naming scheme that will, in turn reduce communication over the network.

2. BACKGROUND, MOTIVATION

Topology mapping is a popular field of research and there are many contributions out there with respect to the optimal process placement. Most of these studies involve specific hardware platforms [1], and/or are limited to the distributed message passing paradigm [2, 3]. For example, several vendor distributed MPI implementations use graph theory algorithms to formulate a near optimum placement of resources. But these solutions are implementation specific. To meet the portable needs of our OpenSHMEM library implementation we have devised our own methodology which can be extended to all other PGAS libraries and language extensions. Moreover since it relies on the communication pattern within the application and the relative communication volume between processes the preliminary run used to collect the required profiling information need not be a production run (since the pattern of communication does not change with change in the amount of data to be processed). As long as the ratio of the individual point-to-point communication is the same the mapping will be optimum for all future runs using the same number of processes.

ICS'13, June 10–14, 2013, Eugene, Oregon, USA.
ACM 978-1-4503-2130-3/13/06.

3. METHODOLOGY

The hardware information is collected prior to execution of the application using the portable **hwloc** [4] package. We use the portable TAU profiling tool [5] to collect the information pertaining to the OpenSHMEM communication events within the application. We compute the communication density matrix by considering the total volume of data exchanged between the PEs. We then place the results of our analysis in the working directory. When the OpenSHMEM library is initialized and the PE numbers are assigned based on the analysis discussed above. This enables optimum placement of PEs.

4. RESULTS

We first adapt the parallel MPI implementation of 2D heat conduction finite difference over a regular domain to use the OpenSHMEM API for computation and communication.

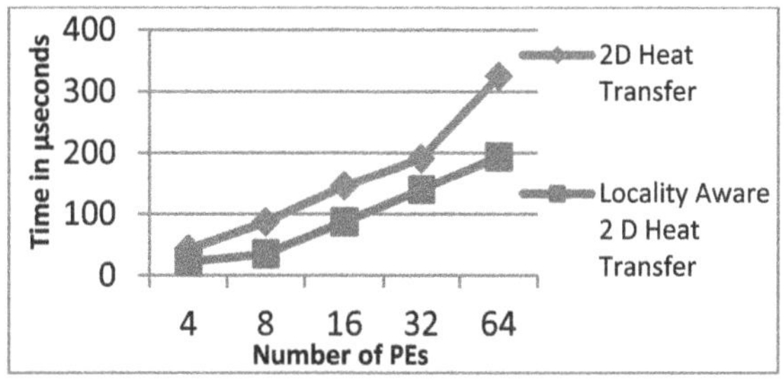

5. ACKNOWLEDGEMENTS

This work is supported by the United States Department of Defense & used resources of the Extreme Scale Systems Center at Oak Ridge National Laboratory.

6. REFERENCES

1. H. Yu, I.-H. Chung, and J. Moreira. Topology mapping for Blue Gene/L supercomputer. In SC'06, page 116, New York, NY, USA, 2006. ACM.
2. J. L. Träff. Implementing the MPI process topology mechanism. In SC'02, pages 1–14, 2002.
3. T. Hoefler et al. The Scalable Process Topology Interface of MPI 2.2. CCPE, 23(4):293–310, Aug. 2010.
4. Broquedis, F., Clet-Ortega, J., Moreaud et al. hwloc: A Generic Framework for Managing Hardware Affinities in HPC Applications. PDP 2010. February 2010.
5. S. S. Shende and A. D. Malony. "The TAU parallel performance system," Int. J. High Perform. Comput. Appl., vol. 20, no. 2, pp. 287–311, May 2006.

Using Platform-independent Data Locality Analysis to Predict Cache Performance on Abstract Hardware Platforms

Sonish Shrestha
University of Texas at El Paso
500 West University Avenue
El Paso, TX 79968
+1 915 747-5892
sshrestha2@miners.utep.edu

ABSTRACT

The context of the research is a co-design project that has the goals of designing hardware systems to match application requirements and mapping applications to the hardware efficiently. To determine application requirements, we characterize the application using platform-independent locality metrics. Next we use locality data to predict cache performance of sequential versions of the application codes for various cache configurations. After using an analytical model to select a candidate set of cache configurations, we use architectural simulation to refine the selection for the target multicore systems.

Categories and Subject Descriptors

C.4 [**Computer Systems Organization**]: Performance of Systems – *measurement techniques, modeling techniques*

Keywords

Hardware-software co-design, cache modeling

In our poster, we briefly describe the overall context of the CoDAASH hardware-software co-design project, which has the goals of designing hardware to match the requirements of computational chemistry and physics algorithms important to the materials science problems of interest. We then describe our specific contribution, which is to design the optimal cache configuration for a given algorithm.

Our first step is to evaluate tools for obtaining platform-independent locality metrics and to validate the results. We are evaluating the PMaC locality measurement tool from SDSC and the MACPO data access analysis tool from TACC. We also use the PAPI hardware counter library to sanity check results returned by these tools. The PMaC locality measurement tool instruments the application using PEBIL in order to measure reuse distances and strides for data accesses. It computes reuse distances per basic block rather than by data structure, but we are working with SDSC on refining the tool to obtain per data structure metrics. The MACPO data access analysis tool reports reuse distance per non-scalar variable and also reports the strides with which these data structures are accessed. PAPI gives the information of different events related to cache memory like cache hits, cache misses etc.

ICS'13, June 10–14, 2013, Eugene, Oregon, USA.
ACM 978-1-4503-2130-3/13/06.

To validate the results reported by each tool, we wrote simple matrix and blocked matrix multiplication benchmark codes for which we know the expected reuse distances and strides. After manipulating the results to compensate for the different ways in which the tools work, we found discrepancies between expected and actual results that are currently being fixed by the tool developers.

Our second step is to use locality data to predict cache performance of sequential versions of the applications for various cache configurations. The application code that we are using initially is the LULESH benchmark, which serves as a proxy for full shock physics applications CTH and ALEGRA. We can use a straightforward analytical model to predict cache misses for a fully associative cache, and we can use a probabilistic model to predict cache misses for a set-associative cache.

Our applications will need to need to run in parallel mode to scale to realistic problem sizes. Predicting cache behavior for a thread-parallel program running on a multicore system is much more complicated, and our predictions will be only approximate. To accurately evaluate and select optimal cache configurations without building the actual hardware, we make use of architectural simulators. Simulators we are evaluating include MacSim, SST, gem5, as well as GPGPU simulators.

Other participants in the CoDAASH project are designing the abstract hardware platforms that are to be co-designed along with the application software to be optimized for these platforms. The initial abstract platform to be evaluated is a multicore cluster with attached GPUs. We will focus on selecting the cache configuration of the multicore system that best matches the data access patterns of the application. We will first use an analytical model based on the platform-independent locality metrics described above to select a candidate set of cache configurations. We will then use architectural simulation to refine our selection.

In the poster, we report the results of our evaluations of locality measurement tools and architectural simulators. We also describe initial results from our characterization of the LULESH benchmark and predictions of its cache performance for various cache configurations. The novel contribution of our work is using platform-independent data access analysis for systematic hardware-software co-design and co-optimization for a given class of applications, rather than just for performance optimization for existing architectures.

Towards Shared Memory Consistency Models for GPUs

Tyler Sorensen
University of Utah
Salt Lake City, UT
t.sorensen@utah.edu

Ganesh Gopalakrishnan
University of Utah
Salt Lake City, UT
ganesh@cs.utah.edu

Vinod Grover
NVIDIA
Santa Clara, CA
vgrover@nvidia.com

ABSTRACT

With the widespread use of graphical processing units (GPUs), it is important to ensure that programmers have a clear understanding of their shared memory consistency model, i.e. what values can be read when issued concurrently with writes. Compared to CPUs, GPUs present different shared memory behavior, and we know of no published formal consistency model for them. To fill this void, we establish a formal state transition model of GPU loads, stores, and fences in the language Murphi [2], and check properties – captured in litmus tests that pertain to ordering and visibility properties – over executions using the Murphi model checker.

Categories and Subject Descriptors

C.1.2 [**Computer Systems Organization**]: Processor Architectures—*Multiple Data Stream Architectures (Multiprocessors)*; D.2.4 [**Software Engineering**]: Software/Program Verification—*model checking, reliability*

General Terms

Verification, Reliability

Keywords

GPU; Shared Memory Consistency; Memory Fences

1. MOTIVATION

We study GPU shared memory consistency with a focus on memory fences. Well-synchronized code can hide weak memory model issues from the programmer [4, p.64-65]; however, synchronization operations can be very expensive. Cutting-edge algorithms bypass these expensive operations to obtain significant speedup, at the cost of exposing the memory model [3], which must be understood for correct implementation. If developers write unsynchronized code assuming certain instruction orderings or memory visibilities which are not in line with the shared memory consistency model, then code can be buggy. We have found instances of such assumptions in real world code.

Memory fences can enforce different visibility semantics, including static (ordering within a thread) or dynamic (transitive visibility across threads) properties. Fences can also be cumulative which requires ensuring the visibility of values observed (but not written) by a given thread [1]. The current CUDA documentation only has scanty detail on these semantics.

ICS'13, June 10–14, 2013, Eugene, Oregon, USA.
ACM 978-1-4503-2130-3/13/06.

2. CONTRIBUTIONS

This work presents a variety of litmus tests i.e. short executions which are allowed, disallowed or guaranteed, that we believe illustrate the behavior of our subset of instructions. We provide tests that investigate classical properties such as coherence and write atomicity [4, p.11,69] as well as tests that take into account the unique memory and concurrency systems of GPUs. For example, different fences enforce different visibilities for inter and intra block threads. The results of the tests were determined by feedback from industry experts, the limited documentation available, and properties desired in modern multi-core systems. Some behaviors e.g. write atomicity, remain unresolved.

Using the results of the litmus tests, we developed an operational shared memory consistency model using intuitive data structures and simple operations. At a high level, each thread has: an instruction queue for each address, a view of global and shared memory and a set of unissued loads. Instructions are issued nondeterministically from instruction queues. Memory locations have flags and are shared between threads based on these flags.

Finally, we implemented our model in the Murphi [2] modeling language and validated our litmus tests through model checking. We provide our model at: `http://www.cs.utah.edu/~tylers/CUMM` along with instructions how to investigate custom tests which can aid developers.

Our GPU shared memory consistency model is currently being reviewed by industry experts and is expected to grow and change based on feedback. We have shown real world motivation for a GPU memory model and provided a reasonable model based on related work and industry feedback.

3. REFERENCES

[1] J. Alglave, L. Maranget, S. Sarkar, and P. Sewell. *Fences in weak memory models,* CAV 2010. Springer-Verlag.

[2] D. Dill. *The Murphi verification system,* CAV 1996. Springer.

[3] N. M. Lê, A. Pop, A. Cohen, and F. Zappa Nardelli. *Correct and efficient work-stealing for weak memory models,* PPoPP 2013. ACM.

[4] D. J. Sorin, M. D. Hill, and D. A. Wood. *A Primer on Memory Consistency and Cache Coherence,* 2011. Morgan & Claypool Publishers.

Exploiting Reuse Information to Reduce Refresh Energy in On-Chip eDRAM Caches

Alejandro Valero, Julio Sahuquillo, Salvador Petit, and José Duato
Department of Computer Engineering
Universitat Politècnica de València
Valencia, Spain
alvabre@gap.upv.es, {jsahuqui, spetit, jduato}@disca.upv.es

ABSTRACT

This work introduces a novel refresh mechanism that leverages reuse information to decide which blocks should be refreshed in an energy-aware eDRAM last-level cache. Experimental results show that, compared to a conventional eDRAM cache, the energy-aware approach achieves refresh energy savings up to 71%, while the reduction on the overall dynamic energy is by 65% with negligible performance losses.

Categories and Subject Descriptors

B.3.2 [**Design Styles**]: Cache memories

Keywords

MRU-Tour; on-chip caches; selective refresh

1. PROPOSED APPROACH

Refresh operations in on-chip eDRAM caches incur in a significant fraction of the total dynamic energy consumed by these memories. Prior works have addressed this energy overhead by reducing the impact of inter-cell variability on refresh energy [3].

Unlike these proposals, this work pursues to minimize the number of refresh operations by applying selective refresh in an *energy-aware* eDRAM last-level (L2) cache. The proposal aims to avoid refreshing *useless* lines in order to save energy and prevent performance losses. The devised refresh policy exploits reuse information to decide whether a cache block should be refreshed. To this end, the proposal works on the MRU-Tour (MRUT) concept [2], which is referred to as the number of times that a block enters in the MRU position of the LRU stack. Based on the observation that most blocks in L2 caches exhibit a single MRUT at the time they are evicted, the refresh mechanism does not periodically refresh the target block if it has only one MRUT.

To save energy, the proposed energy-aware cache only accesses in a first stage the tag array and a predicted cache bank in the data array. If the requested block is not stored in the predicted bank, then the target bank is accessed in a second stage. This mechanism always predicts the same physical bank, and MRU blocks are stored in that bank by performing data movements between ways similar to as done in [1]. Each bank implements two cache ways.

2. EXPERIMENTAL RESULTS

The proposed cache has been modeled with SimpleScalar and CACTI to obtain performance and energy consumption, respectively, for SPEC benchmarks.

ICS'13, June 10–14, 2013, Eugene, Oregon, USA.
ACM 978-1-4503-2130-3/13/06.

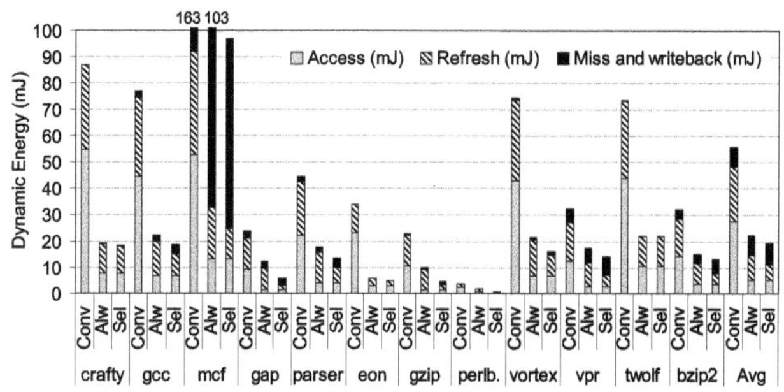

Figure 1: Dynamic energy consumption (in mJ).

Figure 1 plots the dynamic energy of a 2MB-16way L2 cache organization classified into *Access*, *Refresh*, and *Miss and write-back* energy. The latter covers the expenses of accessing to a 2GB DRAM main memory. The energy consumption of the data movements between ways has been taken into account in the *Access* category. Label *Conv* refers to a conventional eDRAM cache that accesses in parallel all the tags and all the banks and uses a conventional refresh policy. *Alw* and *Sel* refer to the conventional and selective policies, respectively, both applied in the energy-aware scheme.

Compared to *Conv*, both *Access* and *Refresh* energy are largely reduced by the energy-aware scheme mainly because it accesses first just the MRU bank. As observed, *Sel* reduces the refresh consumption with respect to *Alw*, and it compensates the increase in the *Miss and writeback* energy caused by requests to non-refreshed blocks. Overall, the refresh savings of *Sel* are on average by 71% with respect to *Conv*. This percentage is by 65% when the whole energy is considered. These benefits come with minimal performance degradation (by 1.3% on average) with respect to *Conv*.

3. ACKNOWLEDGMENTS

This work was supported by the Spanish Ministerio de Economía y Competitividad (MINECO) and Plan E funds, under Grants TIN-2009-14475-C04-01 and TIN2012-38341-C04-01.

4. REFERENCES

[1] J. Lira et al. Implementing a hybrid SRAM/eDRAM NUCA architecture. In *Proc. 18th Int'l Conf. High Perform. Comput.*, pages 1–10, 2011.

[2] A. Valero et al. Combining Recency of Information with Selective Random and a Victim Cache in Last-Level Caches. *ACM Trans. Arch. Code Opt.*, 9(3):16:1–16:20, 2012.

[3] C. Wilkerson et al. Reducing Cache Power with Low-Cost, Multi-bit Error-Correcting Codes. In *Proc. 37th Int'l Symp. Comput. Arch.*, pages 83–93, 2010.

V-OpenCL: A Method to Use Remote GPGPU

Cong Wang, Tao Jiang, Rui Hou
{wangcong,jiangtao,hourui}@ict.ac.cn
Institute of Computing Technology, Chinese Academy of Sciences

ABSTRACT

GPGPU can boost the performance significantly for many compute intensive tasks. However, in datacenter scenarios, not all the applications need GPGPU. Thus, it is not necessary to equip GPGPU in each node considering its high price and infrequent usage demands. By leveraging high bandwidth of emerging interconnects like 100Gb Ethernet, PCI Express or RapidIO etc., it is reasonable to figure out a mechanism to allow nodes to share the remote GPGPUs. In this work, we proposed V-OpenCL, which supports transparently using of remote GPGPU in data center.

Categories and Subject Descriptors

C.0 [**Computer Systems Organization**]: System architectures

Keywords

Remote GPGPU, Datacenter, High Bandwidth Interconnect, Virtualization

1. INTRODUCTION

Increasingly diversified applications in data center request more mechanism to share special resources. For example, GPGPU is precious computing resource but may not be used effectively when equipped for all nodes in datacenter. In a partially GPGPU equipped datacenter, applications running on nodes without GPGPU need an effective method to access GPGPUs of other nodes. Thus it is valuable to find a cost-effective way to enable efficient resource sharing. This poster focuses on GPGPU sharing with low-price method and the final goal is to allow nodes to transparently use GPGPUs of other nodes in datacenter.

2. Basic design of sharing GPGPU

We build a prototype system using PCIe switch to reduce costs and provide flexible mechanism to share GPGPUs[1]. To share a GPGPU through the PCIe interface, the equipped node must first expose a memory region to other nodes to hold GPGPU execution binary, data and some flags for synchronization. When Node A wants to use GPGPU in Node B, it first negotiates with Node B to get the ownership of the corresponding memory region of Node B. Then it copies the program and data to the remote memory using DMA writes and notifies Node B by changing flags. When ready, Node B copies the data to the memory of GPGPU and loads program for the GPGPU to process the data. After execution, the results will be copied from GPGPU memory to the exposed memory region and then to node A by DMA through PCIe.

3. Performance evaluation

Four computing intensive workloads from the NVIDIA GPU Computing SDK[2] are chosen for evaluation. Using GPU remotely (RGPU) is almost as effective as using GPU locally for Matrix Multiply and Optical flow. For separate convolution and fast Walsh transform, the data transfer time dominates the execution time, leading to significant performance loss for RGPU, but using RGPU is still much better than using local CPU.

4. V-OpenCL: Sharing GPGPUs in a Better Way

We propose V-OpenCL for the ease of GPGPU sharing in this section. Further work is to support transparent sharing of RGPU. We intend to virtualize the OpenCL[3] (OCL) APIs by redirecting the API calls from GPGPU unequipped nodes to GPGPU equipped nodes. Then a virtualized OCL framework is seen on GPGPU unequipped nodes, we call it V-OpenCL. As shown in figure 1, we re-implement the OCL APIs with an interposer library which is responsible to get available GPU(s) from GPGPU manager and redirect API Calls to RGPU(s). API Calls are first packed with the function name, parameters, data and OCL context ID, and then sent through high speed interconnection. On GPGPU equipped node, there is a buffer to hold incoming API call packets. GPGPU provider daemon picks packets from the buffer, unpacks them and sends them to the corresponding context or creates new context for it by calling the real OCL APIs. Local applications on GPGPU equipped nodes can also work by directly interact with real OCL APIs. The results of remote API calls are sent back to the node where they come from in the same way through the interconnection.

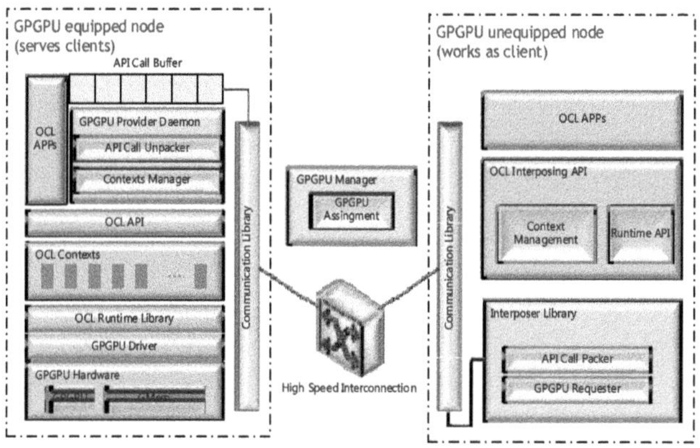

Figure1. V-OpenCL GPGPU sharing system

5. Acknowledgements

This work was supported by the Strategic Priority Research Program of the Chinese Academy of Sciences under grant No.XDA06010401, and National Science Foundation of China under grant No.61100010. And we wish to thank the anonymous reviewers for their hard work.

References

[1] Hou, R. et al. Cost Effective Data Center Servers. *Proceedings of the 19th IEEE International Symposium on High Performance Computer Architecture* 179–187.

[2] NVIDIA GPU Computing SDK. https://developer.nvidia.com/gpu-computing-sdk

[3] OpenCL - The open standard for parallel programming of heterogeneous systems. http://www.khronos.org/opencl/

ICS'13, June 10–14, 2013, Eugene, Oregon, USA.
ACM 978-1-4503-2130-3/13/06.

Power Efficiency in a Partially Reconfigurable Multiprocessor System

Raymond J. Weber
ECE Department
Montana State University
Bozeman, Montana 59717
raymond.weber@msu.montana.edu

Justin A. Hogan
ECE Department
Montana State University
Bozeman, Montana 59717
justin.hogan@msu.montana.edu

Brock J. Lameres
ECE Department
Montana State University
Bozeman, Montana 59717
lameres@ece.montana.edu

Todd Kaiser
ECE Department
Montana State University
Bozeman, Montana 59717
tjkaiser@ece.montana.edu

ABSTRACT

This paper describes the benchmarking of an FPGA-based computing system that uses partially reconfigurable tiles for real-time allocation of hardware resources. This system was developed for use in the aerospace industry in order to provide redundancy for fault mitigation and real-time hardware reallocation to reduce mass associated with separate functional systems. In this paper, we present the results of performance studies on our Xilinx Virtex-6 platform using the Dhrystone, LINPACK and NAS-Kernel benchmarks. We further present the impact on power consumption as processors and hardware accelerators are brought online to increase performance.

Categories and Subject Descriptors

C.4 [**Performance of Systems**]: Performance attributes; J.2 [**Physical Sciences and Engineering**]: Aerospace

Keywords

FPGA, Partial Reconfiguration, Benchmarking

1. INTRODUCTION

In partially reconfigurable computation most of the research attention has been focused on the performance and logic space improvements that are yielded by using the technique with less attention paid to the power enhancements for low power systems. In this research we have implemented a nine-tile partially reconfigurable system consisting of microprocessors and hardware accelerator tiles andmeasured power consumption versus the benchmarking performance.

2. TECHNIQUE AND RESULTS

For our system design, we seek to maximize system performance while minimizing power to favor system implementation in space based applications. We have implemented Whetstone, Dhrystone and LINPACK benchmarks to measure performance on single microprocessor tiles and single microprocessor + hardware accelerator systems. We have determined that NAS benchmarking kernels fit well with our multiprocessor system and have chosen to implement the EP kernel in this system.

We use a Microblaze microprocessor on the Spartan-6 FPGA for system control. This Microblaze is tasked with programming, monitoring, and activating/deactivating tiles on the Virtex-6 FPGA as well as communicating with a user PC. This arrangement leaves the Virtex-6 free to be used entirely by computational tiles. The lower power of the Spartan-6 makes it the ideal fabric to be constantly running from the overall power consumption standpoint.

We are able to dynamically activate and deactivate tiles on the Virtex-6 chip while monitoring the power consumption. Tracking power consumption versus benchmarking scores achieved by the system allows us to view the effects that hardware accelerators have, not only on performance, but also on the amount of power consumed by the system. This will allow for us to develop higher efficiency systems and identify trade-offs between additional generic microprocessors and specialized hardware accelerators.

We are running multiple benchmarking routines to evaluate the different applications of the chip. Testing integer, single precision and double precision floats, as well as matrix manipulations, extends the generality of this study making it useful for both PR and static FPGA designs. This enables evaluation on the trade-offs between hardware and software solutions with respect to the power requirements of the system.

3. CONCLUSION

The testing with the benchmarking tools to date has shown that our system is capable of running the benchmarking tools, and the monitoring capabilities of our hardware are able to record the power consumption changes in real-time as additional tiles are programmed and activated.

ICS'13, June 10–14, 2013, Eugene, Oregon, USA.
ACM 978-1-4503-2130-3/13/06.

Author Index

www.ingramcontent.com/pod-product-compliance
Ingram Content Group UK Ltd.
Pitfield, Milton Keynes, MK11 3LW, UK
UKHW051415290926
15471UKWH00009B/1608

9 781450 321303